The Language of the Constitution

The Language of the

Stuart B. Flexner
Editor-in-Chief

Douglas M. Arnold
Managing Editor

Christopher Collier
Consulting Editor

Dominick Egan
Assistant Editor

Constitution

A Sourcebook and Guide to the Ideas, Terms, and Vocabulary Used by the Framers of the United States Constitution

THURSTON GREENE

Foreword by WARREN E. BURGER

GREENWOOD PRESS
New York • Westport, Connecticut • London

Library of Congress Cataloging-in-Publication Data

Greene, Thurston.
The language of the Constitution : a sourcebook and guide to the ideas, terms, and vocabulary used by the framers of the United States Constitution / Thurston Greene ; foreword by Warren E. Burger.
p. cm.
Includes bibliographical references and index.
ISBN 0–313–28202–1 (alk. paper)
1. United States—Constitutional law—Language—Sources.
2. United States—Constitutional law—Terms and phrases—Sources.
I. Title.
KF4548.5.G74 1991
342.73′02′014—dc20
[347.3022014] 91–29197

British Library Cataloguing in Publication Data is available.

Library of Congress Catalog Card Number: 91–29197
ISBN: 0–313–28202–1

First published in 1991

Greenwood Press, 88 Post Road West, Westport, CT 06881
An imprint of Greenwood Publishing Group, Inc.

Printed in the United States of America

The paper used in this book complies with the Permanent Paper Standard issued by the National Information Standards Organization (Z39.48–1984).

10 9 8 7 6 5 4 3 2 1

Copyright Acknowledgments

The following publishers have generously granted permission to reproduce documentary materials from their works:

Carol Publishing Group: Extracts from Philip S. Foner, ed., *The Complete Writings of Thomas Paine*, Vol. 1. New York: Citadel Press, 1945.

The Electronic Text Corporation: For use of WordCruncher Text Retrieval Software and an electronic database entitled "The Constitution Papers" (1987).

Harvard University Press: Extracts from Alexander Hamilton, James Madison, and John Jay, *The Federalist*, ed. Benjamin F. Wright. Cambridge, Mass.: Harvard University Press, 1961. Extracts from Robert J. Taylor, et al., eds., *The Papers of John Adams*, Vol. 4. Cambridge, Mass.: Harvard University Press, 1979.

The MacMillan Company: Extracts from George B. Adams and H. Morse Stephens, eds., *Select Documents of English Constitutional History*. New York: MacMillan, 1927.

State Historical Society of Wisconsin: Extracts from Merrill Jensen, John P. Kaminski, Gaspare J. Saladino, et al., eds., *The Documentary History of the Ratification of the Constitution*, published by the State Historical Society of Wisconsin, Madison, Wisc.; Vol. 2, 1976; Vol. 8, 1988; Vol. 16, 1986.

University of Pennsylvania Press: Extracts from Richard S. Dunn, Mary Maples Dunn, et al., eds., *The Papers of William Penn*, Vol. 3. Philadelphia: University of Pennsylvania Press, 1986.

Yale University Press: Extracts from Max Farrand, ed., *The Records of the Federal Convention of 1787*, Vol. 3. New Haven: Yale University Press, 1911. Extracts from William B. Willcox, et al., eds., *The Papers of Benjamin Franklin*, Vol. 22. New Haven: Yale University Press, 1982.

This work is dedicated to three pragmatic philosophers whose lives overlapped, covering a critical 130 year period of world history:

James Madison, who as chief architect of the Constitution imbued its structure with the recorded experience of history and thereby assured its durability;

George Washington, who as Commander-in-Chief led the American colonies to victory on the battlefield, later presided over the Constitutional Convention as Chairman, and finally as President dedicated eight years of his life to nurturing the newly created nation toward its maturity; and

Benjamin Franklin, who saw the fruition of his life-long plans for an American union when the final vote was taken to promulgate the Constitution.

"THEY BUILDED BETTER THAN THEY KNEW."

CONTENTS

FOREWORD

Respect for the printed word is an essential ingredient of the impartial and effective delivery of justice. Courts are regularly called upon to interpret the meaning of words, as used by legislatures, executives, other judges, or private parties. To understand fully the meaning of those words, we must have some knowledge of the context from which meanings and usages arise—what was meant by the writer and understood by the reader.

This unique work applies modern computer technology to assist our understanding of the words of the United States Constitution, and what the key words and phrases in that document meant in the context of the legal and political discourse of the eighteenth century. It reminds us that the meaning of some words in our language has undergone change since the Framers' time—a time when "to demean" meant primarily "to conduct (oneself)," not "to disparage."

But if much has changed, much has also remained the same. Now, as then, this nation is dedicated to preserving the rights of the people through the rule of law. The printed word makes the law and the reasoning behind the law available to everyone. This book helps to provide the keys to unlock the Constitution and its reasoning; it will be a tool for the enlightenment of students everywhere.

Warren E. Burger
Chairman, Commission on the Bicentennial
of the United States Constitution
Chief Justice of the United States, 1969–1986

PREFACE

The constitution is more than the law of our land. It is the supreme law, and the Supreme Court is its ultimate arbiter. It was composed in late eighteenth-century English. The language was that of its period; definitions could hardly have been based upon dictionaries of the 1990s. To find out what the law is today, we need to know how the words of the law were understood by the people who used them then.

People constantly use old words to convey new meaning, thus putting the old meaning in jeopardy. Take, for example, the word "parameter," which has undergone a painful metamorphosis during the past thirty years. At one time a well-recognized term in higher mathematics, the 1987 *Random House Dictionary* added a new meaning: "Usually, parameters, limits or boundaries: guidelines; the basic parameters of our foreign policy." The lexicographer's entry reads: "Some object strongly to the use of PARAMETER in these newer senses. Nevertheless, the criticized uses are now well established both in well educated speech and in edited writings." This is an enormous change since the 1962 edition, when one of the more succinct meanings was "one of the independent variables in a set of parametric equations."

If such a change can happen to a word in one generation, how long will it take to catch up with Humpty Dumpty's immortal declaration, "When I use a word, it means what I intend it to mean—neither more nor less"? Perhaps, in answer, as long as it took "*auto*biography" to mean a book one has paid someone *else* to write about one's *own* life? As time keeps passing and the words of the Constitution take on new meanings, the more important will the revelations of this sourcebook become.

Our work is a compilation. It is confined to the original Constitution and the Bill of Rights in order to determine what the founding generation understood the document to mean. It is in the nature of a concordance: an alphabetical index to contemporaneous and antecedent sources expanded to such an extent that a lexicographer could use them to create a dictionary, without going further afield.

Because words have different meanings in different contexts, we have provided long enough passages to enable the reader to grasp how the word was used wherever it appears in the Constitution, with possibly different meanings in different places. For readers whose curiosity is not satisfied, but whetted, we provide citations to publications readily available in the larger libraries.

In these years of bicentennial commemoration, there has been a deluge of literature by scholars already renowned in the constitutional sphere, and by equally well qualified ones who are new to it. This has been stimulated in large part by the encouragement of Justice Warren E. Burger's Commission on the Bicentennial of the United States Constitution. Without that encouragement it is highly doubtful that this sourcebook would have been produced.

Why still another work on the Constitution? To fill a gap. It is strictly factual. There is no commentary, no speculation, no theorizing, no argumentation. Not a word that was written after the constitutional cake was baked. It is not in itself "scholarly," but a new tool for scholars to use.

This is a "how to" book: How to read the Constitution through the eyes of those who enacted it—the fifty-five delegates to the Philadelphia Convention and those who sat in the state ratifying conventions—and how to connect the document to the long chain of political history of which it is the golden link.

James Bryce observed:

> The American Constitution is no exception to the rule that everything which has to win the obedience and respect of men must have its roots deep in the past, and the more slowly each institution has grown, so much the more enduring it is likely to prove. (*The American Commonwealth*. New York: The MacMillan Co., 1931, Vol. I, p. 28).

Our laws run back into the beginning of recorded time. This work goes only as far back as 1215; we hope in a later edition to carry it back another twenty-seven centuries to the Law of Moses. Modern computer technology and the methodology described in the introduction, which follows, have only recently made this kind of production possible.

Twenty years before ratification of the Constitution, the preface of the 1769 edition of the *Encyclopedia Britannica* opened by saying: "Utility ought to be the principal intention of every publication. Wherever this intention does not plainly appear, neither the books nor their authors have the smallest claim to the approbation of mankind." By adherence to that intention, we aim to earn such approbation.

This book is a tool for the curious, for all those who realize how much more there is for them to know. It is a chart for the constitutional traveller who wants to get from point A to point B. Like a traveller reading a map, the first question is, "Where do I start from?" This sourcebook says, "You start here," by linking words and phrases in the Constitution to exact, verifiable quotations from recognized documents and writings in circulation between May 25, 1787, when the delegates convened at Philadelphia, and December 15, 1791, when ratification of the Bill of Rights was completed. The better positioned we are to furnish our own minds with reflections from the minds of our ancestors, the better will we be able to read and understand the document they so painfully hammered out on the sturdy anvil of patriotic resolve to furnish us with so hardy a foundation for our heritage.

James Madison's manuscript notes of the debates in the Constitutional Convention were not in the public domain during the ratification process. He purposely sequestered them. They did not emerge as public documents until 1840 after the Congress purchased them from his widow for $30,000 thereby revealing their character as proprietary papers. They were not in the public domain either in Philadelphia or during the ratification debates. For that reason we have omitted them as source material, however useful they have been as windows opening upon Madison's mind.

To the extent this work fails in fulfilling its limited mission, we hope to receive useful suggestions for additions and improvements, and welcome such from users resigned to accepting this effort as the best available today, but hopeful that more may be done in the next edition. This is a pioneer effort and its creators hope it will be received with appreciation for what it is, mercy for what it is not, and encouragement for what it may become. For those who feel they already know all they need to know about the Constitution, consulting these pages would misdirect their time away from projects more rewarding to their limited purposes. But it should prove important to those whose curiosity leads them to look at the Constitution in a new light. Why? Because time, money, and human skill are finite resources, and the effort required to uncover even one of the eighty-five entries we have catalogued would be out of proportion for any but the rare one who can afford to be prodigal of time and money. Without the methodology described in the introduction, and the machinery required to use it, it would take days beyond number to assemble even a fraction of the information embraced between these covers.

Why select "the curious" as the needful group? Because of the belief that it is largely through curiosity that the sum of total human knowledge is expanded: the chief limitation on that expansion is the availability of the tools needed to multiply, exponentially, the restrictions on human capacity. As telescopes have improved since Galileo's best effort, so has our knowledge of the solar system. With publication of this work, we can fathom the past in width and in depth as never before.

This is not just one more book on the Constitution, but a wholly different one about its antecedents. Necessarily, it can be nothing but objective. It is a painstaking compilation of documents and quotations from authenticated original sources available to the framers, the Congress, and the ratifiers. Readers of these documents, quotations, and the works cited can now, for the first time, find out how those words were used and understood at the time they became law, because we all know that new meanings are given to old words until they can in extreme cases come to mean the opposite of what they formerly meant. Examples abound: A "qualified" statement used to mean one that is modified or limited or restricted in some way, such as a ''qualified endorsement.'' Today (as used in federal tax legislation), ''qualified'' means an act (such as a waiver) that is unqualified in any way. ''This'' used to mean (as in frontier dialect) ''this-here'' and ''that'' used to mean ''that-there.'' Today they have been reversed. A ''gifted'' child used to be one born with a certain talent; today ''gifted'' has replaced ''given'' as the past participle of the verb ''to give,'' and we speak of property that has been ''gifted.'' Employees used to be ''discharged''; now they are ''terminated'' meaning, it must be supposed, that their employment is terminated. In federal statutory language, we now ''gross up'' (instead of ''mark up'') the value ascribed to certain assets, and we ''grandfather'' (now a verb, not a noun) preexisting conditions in order to avoid retroactivity of laws. Judges now ''recuse'' themselves instead of ''excusing'' themselves, though originally ''to recuse'' meant to challenge. ''Terrific'' has come to mean ''splendid,'' while only a short while ago it meant something that struck terror, like a stroke of lightening. ''Awful'' is no longer an adjective meaning inspire with wonder; it is merely an intensive adverb. Modern dictionaries are replete with definitions marked ''obsolete,'' and those marked ''colloq.'' a while ago now appear shorn of that degrading adjective, and at last accepted in respectable linguistic society. The use of quotation marks to indicate the author's disavowal of a word's use has been largely abandoned and the misused work thus invested with legitimacy until ''liberated'' means ''conquered.''

After 290 years of common usage as a standard bible, the King James version of 1611 was retranslated and the American version substituted in 1901. The preface to the Revised Standard version observed that many words had changed their meaning and had become misleading. Over 300 of them in 1901 were used in the King James version in a sense substantially different from that which they conveyed in 1611. Biblical translations can be rewritten through the appointment of a commission to do so. Our Constitution can be brought down to date only by amendment. That is a cumbersome process. Substituting new words to fit old definitions is not necessary. It is easier to learn how the old words were understood in the beginning, as we do with Latin or Greek. Publication of this volume promises to serve well into the indefinite future, if not forever, making the amendment process unnecessary.

We have not ''concorded'' the Reconstruction Amendments of the 1860s. Those amendments were written in a time of widely disseminated dictionary publication. For elucidation, all you need to do is to go to the Webster-Merriam dictionary of 1864 because those amendments were written in dictionary language. In the years between 1787 and 1791 no such American dictionaries existed; the best was Samuel Johnson's, but that was English. American definitional art did not blossom until first publication of Noah Webster's *Dictionary of the American Language,* financed in part by our first Chief Justice, John Jay, and published in 1828. So for the Constitution and Bill of Rights, we must go to the raw material lexicographers use—the original writings of the time, known to those who promulgated the Constitution and those who ratified it.

There must be a need for such a work as this or else the Bicentennial Commission would not have encouraged it and no publisher would have risked publishing it. But why is the author unknown and with no more academic credentials than a well-worn B.A. from Williams College and a much used Harvard LL.B.? Because, I suppose, there was a gap to be filled, and someone had to fill it. Could he circulate the likely learned periodicals for help? And how to describe a project that starts out aiming to become a simple concordance, next expects to become a sort of ex post facto dictionary as of September 17, 1787, and finally, as the data starts to roll out of the computer, takes on a life of its own, like a monarch butterfly from its chrysalis, to become a full-fledged sourcebook! No, the answer was not to do the work and recruit a well known surrogate to lend it his name, but to go the do-it-yourself route, assemble some fellow-travellers along the ideological fairway, locate the best dynamo to energize the editorial department, make suitable commitment of time and purse, and keep on pressing forward, praying for the best. The resultant publication has been gratifying far beyond the author-compiler's hopes at the project's inception three years ago, as it seemed to grow into maturity and greater usefulness. By way of apology for stepping in "where angels fear to tread," some comfort comes from the lines by William A. Neilson, in his Preface to Merriam Webster's *Second International Dictionary* (1934) when he said: "For the conception of the educated man as a finished product is being substituted the intellectually curious person." On that ground I must rest my case, for more than a persevering kind of curiosity I cannot claim.

Thurston Greene

ACKNOWLEDGMENTS

I would like to thank the following persons and organizations for their help in producing this book: Hon. Warren E. Burger, Chairman, and Herbert M. Atherton, Deputy Staff Director, of the Commission on the Bicentennial of the United States Constitution, for their help and encouragement during all stages of the work; R/TSI Typesetting Company of Hamden, Connecticut, for optical character scanning of a number of texts used in the database; Dr. John P. Kaminski for providing us with electronic texts for Volumes VIII and XVI of The *Documentary History of the Ratification of the Constitution*; Robert A. Hendrickson, founder of the Hamiltonian Institute, for his wholehearted support; and Mark Sexton for his expertise in publishing. Special thanks are due two staff members: to Stuart B. Flexner, for his basic architectural approach to the formulation and structure of the work until his untimely death in 1990, and to Douglas M. Arnold, the scholarly wheelhorse of the project throughout, who, with the help of his wife, Margo, met every project deadline despite a number of other demands on his time.

Important encouragement was also provided by Hon. Herbert Brownell, Attorney General of the United States for eight years; James Capua, president of a Canada-oriented charitable organization; Mary Hyde Eccles, writer, book collector, and founder of The Johnsonians; Boris Feinman, founder of U.S. Constitutional "Convention II;" Hon. Stanley H. Fuld, retired chief judge, New York Court of Appeals; Edmund Fuller, scholar and long-time dean of American book reviewers; Thomas H. Henriksen, senior fellow of the Hoover Institute; Amb. William Macomber, U.S. diplomat; Professor John H. McElroy, University of Arizona; Helen and Hamilton Meserve, publishers of Taconic Press; General John W. Nicholson, U.S.A. (Ret.); Stephen Parks, Beinecke Library, Yale University; Charles E. Pierce, director of the Pierpont Morgan Library; Dr. James T. Sabin, Executive Vice President of Greenwood Publishing Group, Inc.; Professor Richard B. Sewall, Yale University; Hon. John A. Speziale, retired chief judge, Supreme Court of Connecticut; Samuel G. Walker, publisher; and

Justice Antonin Scalia of the U.S. Supreme Court. Thanks are also due to my wife, Marta, who sacrificed much while her husband was bushwhacking his way through the friendly but unfamiliar world of publishing, and to my secretary, Linda S. Turgeon, who gave this project a deservedly high office priority, kept me on schedule, and saw that I avoided a sea of errors that would have been altogether too easy to drown in.

Thurston Greene

INTRODUCTION

Electronic data processing was essential to all aspects of this work. The basic software used was WordCruncher for text retrieval and WordPerfect for word processing.

The Database

The first stage of the work was construction of an electronic database of representative historical sources. During the planning stage, we drew up a list of the basic reading sources of the generation of the American Founding Fathers. These included English and American fundamental laws and constitutions, political tracts and pamphlets, classical and modern literary works, essays, sermons, newspaper columns, and articles. We soon discovered that only a limited part of this vast amount of material is available in electronic form for the purpose of computerized searching. We determined that it would be unjustifiably expensive and time-consuming to develop a database involving all of these sources. However, since much of this material is repetitious and since a sample would suffice to show the common usage of words and phrases, we decided to use only the essential, most representative sources. Colonial charters and early state constitutions (to 1791) provided fundamental legal background for the American Founders, while the 1787–1791 debates over ratification set the context for general public understanding of the Constitution and the Bill of Rights. Consequently, we gave highest priority to those sources.

The second stage involved purchase of available electronic files, including key American constitutional documents and pamphlets from the Electronic Text Corporation of Orem, Utah, and two volumes of *The Documentary History of the Ratification of the Constitution* from the project's offices at the University of Wisconsin at Madison.

Stage three began when we found that electronic versions of other essential texts (including English and American charters and fundamental laws to 1791 and additional 1787–1788 political pamphlets) were not available for purchase or barter. We consequently arranged to have these scanned optically by R/TSI Typesetting Company of Hamden, Connecticut, from *The Federal and State Constitutions, Colonial Charters, and Other Organic Laws*... (Francis N. Thorpe, ed., 1909–1911) and *Pamphlets on the Constitution of the United States* (Paul L. Ford, ed., Brooklyn, N.Y., 1888). Finally, we added to the database a variety of supplementary texts from other recognized sources listed in the bibliography.

The Search for Words and Phrases

Our search for words and phrases was not exhaustive. The sourcebook, in the interest of maximum usefulness to its readers, focuses on words and phrases from the Constitution and Bill of Rights that have been the subject of continuing interest—and differing interpretation—since the era of the Founding Fathers. We omitted many non-controversial words and phrases from the work. In determining which words and phrases to include, we relied on our own legal and historical knowledge. Those seeking a simple internal concordance to the words of the Constitution itself can consult Charles W. Stearns, ed., *A Concordance to the Constitution of the United States of America* (1872), which we have included as an appendix.

The central principle in conducting the electronic search of the database was to retrieve all or major parts of paragraphs that contained the key words and phrases or close variants thereof. The following are two examples: (1) In the case of "Arms" we defined the search to encompass every paragraph containing the word "arms" that also included modifying words having to do with the people's use of arms or their right or obligation to bear them; (2) in the case of "Regulate Commerce" we searched for all paragraphs that contained variants on the word "commerce" (including "commercial" and "trade," since the Founders often used the latter word in the place of "commerce"), together with the word "regulate" or its variants. Normally, searches went no farther afield. In instances involving more than a simple search for a single word and its plural, we have explained the precise mode of search in a brief note at the beginning of the list.

In the case of about a dozen words and phrases (such as "citizen" and "people") the number of occurrences in the database was so large that to include them all would have been redundant, repetitious, and wasteful of labor and printed space. In these cases, we confined the search to: (1) a complete search of those fundamental laws and documents in the database which applied to the colonies and states as a whole; and (2) a random sample of the remaining material. On the rare occasions when such sampling was necessary, we have included a note at the beginning of the list.

We have omitted from the search occurrences of the key words or phrases that are direct quotations from the Constitution or the Bill of Rights unmodified by any illuminating language by the author.

Organization of the Sourcebook

1. The word and phrase lists are arranged in alphabetical order.

2. Extracts from the database appear chronologically under each key word or phrase. This chronological arrangement is not designed to pinpoint the first historical occurrence of each word or phrase (since the database is a sample only), but it will show how understanding of the words and phrases developed over the course of time.

3. At the end of each extract we have provided an abbreviated citation to an accessible version of the full text for the convenience of scholars who wish to see the complete source from which the extract is taken or to verify the accuracy of the quotation.

Editorial Principles and Practices

1. All material has been proofread twice.

2. The key word or phrase is printed in italics. Original italics in the source material are omitted in the interest of allowing the user more easily to focus on the key words and phrases.

3. We have reproduced enough of the text to assure that the user will fully understand the context of the word or phrase.

4. We have used suspension points to indicate any material omitted. In almost every case, such editorial excisions represent tangential material that either precedes or follows the section reproduced. On only the rarest of occasions have we deleted words from within the section itself, and such occasions almost always involve unrelated phrases or repetitious listings of proper names and the like.

5. We follow the original spelling and punctuation in the source material. This leads to some variation due to the nature of the sources: seventeenth- and eighteenth-century spelling and punctuation are often erratic and inconsistent by modern standards and follow no consistent usage or rules, since there were none. We have expanded obscure abbreviations when necessary.

6. On occasion, we have added brief editorial notes in brackets to provide special information, or to clarify obscure or unclear spelling or phraseology.

7. We have provided identifications of pseudonymous authors of newspaper articles in cases where they are conclusively known or in which scholars have made reasonable conjectures about their identity; in all other cases, there is no evidence that allows such identification.

8. The introductory line for each excerpt consists of author (if appropriate), title, and date. On occasion, we have provided additional information when it is of use in understanding the nature of the source. We have also, when appropriate, given specific references to sections within the source.

Readers are invited to write the publisher with any suggestions that might improve the utility of any subsequent edition.

Douglas M. Arnold

BIBLIOGRAPHY AND SHORT TITLE LIST

The electronic database used to construct this book consisted of the following major parts: (1) A collection of sources (called "The Constitution Papers") related to English and American constitutional history vended by the Electronic Text Corporation of Orem, Utah; (2) the complete text of all American colonial charters and fundamental laws through 1791 taken from Francis N. Thorpe, ed., *The Federal and State Constitutions, Colonial Charters, and Other Organic Laws . . .*; (3) two volumes from *The Documentary History of the Ratification of the Constitution*: Volume 8, which covers the ratification controversy in Virginia from September 1787 to March 1788, and Volume 16, which covers the national arena in February and March 1788; and (4) a volume, edited by Paul Ford, reproducing a number of major pamphlets from the years 1787–1788. We have used other sources for a small number of supplementary documents.

The following list provides short titles of readily available sources in which the reader can find full texts of the documents from which our excerpts have been taken. Excerpts from the three fundamental documents of the American Founding Era (the Declaration of Independence, Articles of Confederation, and Federal Constitution) are given without specific page citations to a source because they are available in a variety of modern reprints; we provide exact references for all other documents.

Annals *Page Number*

Joseph Gales, comp., *Debates and Proceedings in the Congress of the United States,* Volume 1 (Washington, D.C.: Gales and Seaton, 1834).

CVA8 *Page Number*

Code of Virginia 1950 . . . , Volume 8 (1986 Replacement Volume; Charlottesville, Va.: The Michie Co., 1986).

CWTP1 *Page Number*

Philip S. Foner, ed., *The Complete Writings of Thomas Paine,* Volume 1 (New York: Citadel Press, 1945).

DHRC *Volume Number Page Number*
Merrill Jensen, John P. Kaminski, Gaspare J. Saladino, et al., eds., *The Documentary History of the Ratification of the Constitution* (Madison, Wis.: State Historical Society of Wisconsin, 1976-present).

Farrand3 *Page Number*
Max Farrand, ed., *The Records of the Federal Convention of 1787*, Volume 3 (New Haven: Yale University Press, 1911).

Fed. *Page Number*
Alexander Hamilton, James Madison, and John Jay, *The Federalist*, ed. Benjamin F. Wright (Cambridge, Mass.: Harvard University Press, 1961).

Ford *Page Number*
Paul L. Ford, ed., *Pamphlets on the Constitution* (Brooklyn, N.Y., 1888).

PBF22 *Page Number*
William B. Willcox, et al., eds., *The Papers of Benjamin Franklin*, Volume 22 (New Haven: Yale University Press, 1982).

PJA4 *Page Number*
Robert J. Taylor, et al., eds., *The Papers of John Adams,* Volume 4 (Cambridge, Mass.: Harvard University Press, 1979).

PWP3 *Page Number*
Richard S. Dunn, Mary Maples Dunn, et al., eds., *The Papers of William Penn,* Volume 3 (Philadelphia: University of Pennsylvania Press, 1986).

SDECH *Page Number*
George B. Adams and H. Morse Stephens, eds., *Select Documents of English Constitutional History* (New York: The MacMillan Co., 1927).

Thorpe *Page Number*
Francis Newton Thorpe, ed., *The Federal and State Constitutions, Colonial Charters, and Other Organic Laws* . . . 7 vols. (House Document No. 357, U.S. Government Printing Office: Washington, D.C., 1909–1911). Page numbers are continuous throughout the seven volumes.

The Language of the Constitution

ACCUSATION, ACCUSATIONS

(Judicial)

United States Constitution, Bill of Rights, December 15, 1791:

[Article VI:] In all criminal prosecutions, the accused shall enjoy the right to a speedy and public trial, by an impartial jury of the State and district wherein the crime shall have been committed, which district shall have been previously ascertained by law, and to be informed of *the nature and cause of the accusation;* to be confronted with the witnesses against him; to have compulsory process for obtaining witnesses in his favor, and to have the Assistance of Counsel for his defence.

* * * * *

Fundamental Constitutions of East New Jersey, 1683:

[Article 8:] The choosing the great and publick officers, as Secretary, Register, Treasurer, Surveyor General, Marshal, and after death of turning out of those now first to be nominated, shall be in the Governor and Common Council; as also of all sheriffs, judges and justices of the peace. But upon any malversation or *accusation,* they shall be liable to the examination and censure of the great Council, and if condemn'd by them, the Governor and Common Council must name others in their places. [Thorpe 2578]

First Continental Congress, Declaration and Resolves, October 14, 1774:

And it has lately been resolved in Parliament, that by force of a statute made in the thirty-fifth year of the reign of king Henry the Eighth, colonists may be transported to England, and tried there upon *accusations* for treasons and misprisions, or concealments of treasons committed in the colonies; and by a late statute, such trials have been directed in cases therein mentioned. [JCC1 65]

Virginia Bill of Rights, June 12, 1776:

[Section 5:] That in all-capital or criminal prosecutions, a man hath a right to demand the cause and nature of his *accusation,* to be confronted with the accusers and witnesses, to call for evidence in his favor, and to a speedy trial by an impartial jury of his vicinage, without whose unanimous consent he cannot be found guilty; nor can he be compelled to give evidence against himself; that no man be deprived of his liberty except by the law of the land, or the judgment of his peers. [Thorpe 3813]

Pennsylvania Constitution, September 28, 1776:

[Declaration of Rights, Article 9:] That in all prosecutions for criminal offences, a man hath a right to be heard by himself and his council, to demand *the cause and nature of his accusation,* to be confronted with the witnesses, to call for evidence in his favour, and a speedy public trial, by an impartial jury of the country, without the unanimous consent of which jury he cannot be found guilty; nor can he be compelled to give evidence against himself; nor can any man be justly deprived of his liberty except by the laws of the land, or the judgment of his peers. [Thorpe 3083]

Maryland Constitution, November 11, 1776:

[Declaration of Rights, Article 19:] That, in all criminal prosecutions, every man hath a right to be informed of the *accusation* against him; to have a copy of the indictment or charge in due time (if required) to prepare for his defence; to be allowed counsel; to be confronted with the witnesses against him; to have process for his witnesses; to examine the witnesses, for and against him, on oath; and to a speedy trial by an impartial jury, without whose unanimous consent he ought not be found guilty. [Thorpe 1688]

North Carolina Constitution, December 18, 1776:

[Declaration of Rights, Article 7:] That, in all criminal prosecutions, every man has a right to be informed of the *accusation* against him, and to confront the accusers and witnesses with other testimony, and shall not be compelled to give evidence against himself. [Thorpe 2787]

Vermont Constitution, July 8, 1777:

[Declaration of Rights, Article 10:] That, in all prosecutions for criminal offences, a man hath a right to be heard, by himself and his counsel—to demand *the cause and nature of his accusation*—to be confronted with the witnesses—to call for evidence in his favor, and a speedy public trial, by an impartial jury of the country; without the unanimous consent of which jury, he cannot be found guilty; nor can he be compelled to give evidence against himself; nor can any man be justly deprived of his liberty, except by the laws of the land or the judgment of his peers. [Thorpe 3741]

Massachusetts Constitution, March 2, 1780:

[Declaration of Rights, Article 21:] The freedom of deliberation, speech, and debate, in either house of the legislature, is so essential to the rights of the people, that it cannot be the foundation of any *accusation* or prosecution, action or complaint, in any other court or place whatsoever. [Thorpe 1892]

Vermont Constitution, July 4, 1786:

[Declaration of Rights, Article 11:] That in all prosecutions for criminal offences, a man hath a right to be heard by himself and his counsel—to demand *the cause and nature of his accusation*—to be confronted with the witnesses—to call for evidence in his favour, and a speedy public trial by an impartial jury of the country, without the unanimous consent of which jury he cannot be found guilty—nor can he be compelled to give evidence against himself—nor can any man be justly deprived of his liberty, except by the laws of the land, or the judgment of his peers. [Thorpe 3753]

[Declaration of Rights, Article 16:] The freedom of deliberation, speech, and debate, in the legislature, is so essential to the rights of the people, that it can not be the foundation of any *accusation* or prosecution, action or complaint, in any other court or place whatsoever. [Thorpe 3753]

William Pierce to St. George Tucker, September 28, 1787, published in the *Gazette of the State of Georgia,* March 20, 1788:

As to trial by jury in criminal cases, it is right, it is just, perhaps it is indispensable,—the life of a citizen ought not to depend on the fiat of a single person. Prejudice, resentment, and partiality, are among the weaknesses of human nature, and are apt to pervert the judgment of the greatest and best of men. The solemnity of the trial by jury is suited to the nature of criminal cases, because, before a man is brought to answer the indictment, the fact or truth of every *accusation* is inquired into by the Grand Jury, composed of his fellow citizens, and the same truth or fact afterwards (should the Grand Jury find the *accusation* well founded) is to be confirmed by the unanimous suffrage of twelve good men, "superior to all suspicion." I do not think there can be a greater guard to the liberties of a people than such a mode of trial on the affairs of life and death. . . . [DHRC16 445]

Alexander Hamilton, *The Federalist*, No. 6, November 14, 1787:

The celebrated Pericles, in compliance with the resentment of a prostitute, at the expense of much of the blood and treasure of his countrymen, attacked, vanquished, and destroyed the city of the Samnians. The same man, stimulated by private pique against the Megarensians, another nation of Greece, or to avoid a prosecution with which he was threatened as an accomplice in a supposed theft of the statuary of Phidias, or to get rid of the *accusations* prepared to be brought against him for dissipating the funds of the state in the purchase of popularity, or from a combination of all these causes, was the primitive author of that famous and fatal war, distinguished in the Grecian annals by the name of the Peloponnesian war . . . [Fed. 109]

Dissent of the Pennsylvania Convention's Minority, December 18, 1787:

That in all capital and criminal prosecutions, a man has a right to demand *the cause and nature of his accusation,* as well in the federal courts as in those of the several States; to be heard by himself and his counsel; to be confronted with the accusers and witnesses; to call for evidence in his favor, and a speedy trial by an impartial jury of his vicinage, without whose unanimous consent he cannot be found guilty, nor can he be compelled to give evidence against himself; and, that no man be deprived of his liberty, except by the law of the land or the judgment of his peers. [DHRC2 623]

Alexander C. Hanson, *Remarks on the Proposed Plan of a Federal Government*, c. January 31, 1788:

The institution of the trial by jury has been sanctified by the experience of ages. It has been recognised by the constitution of every state in the union. It is deemed the birthright of Americans; and it is imagined, that liberty cannot subsist without it. The proposed plan expressly adopts it, for the decision of all criminal *accusations,* except impeachment; and is silent with respect to the determination of facts in civil causes. [Ford 240–41]

"The Impartial Examiner," No. 1, March 5, 1788:

. . . Hence it is evident that the most flagrant acts of oppression may be inflicted; yet, still there will be no apparent object injured: there will be no unconstitutional infringement. For instance, if Congress should pass a law that persons charged with capital crimes shall not have a right to demand *the cause or nature of the accusation,* shall not be confronted with the accusers or witnesses, or call for evidence in their own favor; and a question should arise respecting their authority therein,—can it be said that they have exceeded the limits of their jurisdiction, when that has no limits; when no provision has been made for such a right?—When no responsibility on the part of Congress has been required by the constitution? . . . [DHRC8 462]

James Iredell, "Marcus," No. 3, March 5, 1788:

[1] . . . It is a consideration also of some moment, that there is scarcely any *accusation* more apt to excite popular prejudice than the charge of treason. There is perhaps no country in the world where justice is in general more impartially administered than in England; yet let any man read some of the trials for treason in that country even since the Revolution, he will see sometimes a fury influencing the Judges, as well as the Jury, that is extremely disgraceful. . . .

[DHRC16 323]

[2] . . . If a President should pardon an accomplice, that accomplice then would be an unexceptionable witness. Before, he would be a witness with a rope about his own neck, struggling to get clear of it at all events. Would any men of understanding, or at least ought they to credit an *accusation* from a person under such circumstances? [DHRC16 324]

Alexander Hamilton, *The Federalist*, No. 65, March 7, 1788:

Could the Supreme Court have been relied upon as answering this description [*i.e.*, as a court for impeachments]? It is much to be doubted, whether the members of that tribunal would at all times be endowed with so eminent a portion of fortitude, as would be called for in the execution of so difficult a task; and it is still more to be doubted, whether they would possess the degree of credit and authority, which might, on certain occasions, be indispensable towards reconciling the people to a decision that should happen to clash with an *accusation* brought by their immediate representatives. A deficiency in the first, would be fatal to the accused∞ the last, dangerous to the public tranquillity. The hazard, in both these respects, could only be avoided, if at all, by rendering that tribunal more numerous than would consist with a reasonable attention to economy. . . .

[Fed. 427–28]

Alexander Hamilton, *The Federalist*, No. 66, March 8, 1788:

A fourth objection to the Senate, in the capacity of a court of impeachments, is derived from its union with the Executive in the power of making treaties. This, it has been said, would constitute the senators their own judges, in every case of a corrupt or perfidious execution of that trust. After having combined with the Executive in betraying the interests of the nation in a ruinous treaty, what prospect, it is asked, would there be of their being made to suffer the punishment they would deserve, when they were themselves to decide upon the *accusation* brought against them for the treachery of which they have been guilty?

[Fed. 434–35]

Alexander Hamilton, *The Federalist*, No. 84, May 28, 1788:

. . . The observations of the judicious Blackstone, in reference to the latter, are well worthy of recital: "To bereave a man of life, (says he,) or by violence to confiscate his estate, without *accusation* or trial, would be so gross and notorious an act of despotism, as must at once convey the alarm of tyranny throughout the whole nation; but confinement of the person, by secretly hurrying him to jail, where his sufferings are unknown or forgotten, is a less public, a less striking, and therefore a more dangerous engine of arbitrary government.'' And as a remedy for this fatal evil he is everywhere peculiarly emphatical in his encomiums on the habeas corpus act, which in one place he calls ''the BULWARK of the British Constitution.'' [Fed. 533]

Pennsylania Constitution, September 2, 1790:

[Article IX, Section 9:] That in all criminal prosecutions the accused hath a right to be heard by himself and his counsel, to demand *the nature and cause of the accusation* against him, to meet the witnesses face to face, to have compulsory process for obtaining witnesses in his favor, and, in prosecutions by indictment or information, a speedy public trial, by an impartial jury of the vicinage; that he cannot be compelled to give evidence against himself, nor can he be deprived of his life, liberty, or property, unless by the judgment of his peers or the law of the land. [Thorpe 3100]

ADVICE AND CONSENT

United States Constitution, September 17, 1787:

[Article II, Section 2:] He [the President] shall have Power, by and with the *Advice and Consent* of the Senate, to make Treaties, provided two thirds of the Senators present concur; and he shall nominate, and by and with the *Advice and Consent* of the Senate, shall appoint Ambassadors, other public Ministers and Consuls, Judges of the supreme Court, and all other Officers of the United States, whose Appointments are not herein otherwise provided for, and which shall be established by Law: but the Congress may by Law vest the Appointment of such inferior Officers, as they think proper, in the President alone, in the Courts of Law, or in the Heads of Departments.

* * * * *

Council of New England, Grant of New Hampshire, November 7, 1629:

That they ye sd president & Councill shall at all times hereafter upon reasonable request at ye only proper cost and charges in ye Law of ye sd Capt. John Mason his heires & assigness doe make performe suffer execute & willingly *consent* unto any farther, act or acts conveyance or conveyances assurance or assurances wtsoever for yt good & perfect investing assureing conveying & sure making of all ye aforsd porc'ons of lands Islands Rivers & all & singular their appurten'ces to ye sd Capt John Mason his heires & Assignees as by him his heires & assignees or by his their or any of their Counceill learned in ye law shalbe devised *advised* or required. . . . [Thorpe 2435–36]

The New England Confederation, May 19, 1643:

[Article 12:] Lastly, this perpetual Confederation, and the several articles and agreements thereof being read and seriously considered, both by the General Court for the Massachusetts, and by the Commissioners for Plymouth, Connecticut, and New Haven, were fully allowed and confirmed by three of the forenamed Confederates, namely, the Massachusetts, Connecticut, and New Haven; only the Commissioners for Plymouth having no commission to conclude, desired respite until they might *advise* with their General Court; whereupon it was agreed and concluded by the said Court of the Massachusetts, and the Commissioners for the other two Confederates, that, if Plymouth *consent,* then the whole treaty as it stands in these present articles is, and shall continue, firm and stable without alteration . . . [Thorpe 81]

Carolina Proprietors, Declaration and Proposals, August 25, 1663:

We shall, as far as our charter permits us, empower the major part of the freeholders, or their deputies or assembly-men, to be by them chosen out of themselves, viz: two out of every tribe, division, or parish, in such manner as shall be agreed on, to make their own laws, by and with the *advise and consent* of the Governor and council, so as they be not repugnant to the laws of England, but, as near as may be, agreeing with them in all civil affairs, with submission to a superintendency of a general council, to be chosen out of every government of the province, in manner as shall be agreed on for the common defence of the whole . . . [Thorpe 2754–55]

New Jersey Proprietors, Concession and Agreement, February 10, 1664:

[1] Imprimus. We do *consent* and agree, that the Governor of the said Province hath power, by the *advice* of his Council, to depute one in his place and authority, in case of death or removal, to continue until our further order, unless we have commissionated one before. [Thorpe 2535]

[2] Item. That he [the governor] hath likewise power to make choice of and to take to him six councellors at least, or twelve at most, or any even number between six and twelve, with whose *advice and consent,* or with at least three of the six, or four of a greater number (all being summon'd) he is to govern according to the limitations and instructions following, during our pleasure. [Thorpe 2535]

[3] . . . The Governor with the *advice* of his Council, unless some present danger will not permit him, to *advise* to muster and train all forces within the said Province, to prosecute war, pursue an enemy, suppress all rebellions, and mutinies, as well by sea as land; and to exercise the whole militia, as fully as we by the grant from his Royal Highness can impower them to do: Provided, that they appoint no military forces but what are freeholders in the said Province, unless the General Assembly shall *consent.* [Thorpe 2540]

Carolina Proprietors, Concessions and Agreements, 1665:

[1] Imprts. Wee doe *consent* and agree that the Governor of each County hath power by the *advise* of his Councill to depute one in his place and Authority in case of death or removall to continue untill our further order unless wee have commissionated one before. [Thorpe 2756]

[2] That he [the governor] hath likewayes power to choyce of and to take to him six Councillors at least or twelve at moast or any even Number between six and twelve with whose *advise and consent* or with at least three of the six or fower of a greater Number all being summoned he is to govern according to the Lymitacons and Instructions following during our pleasure . . . [Thorpe 2756]

[3] Item to place officers and soldiers for the safety strenkt and defence of the Forts Castles Cittyes &c according ye number appointed by the Genll Assembly to nominate place and commissionate all military officers under ye dignity of ye Leut: Genll whoe is commissionated by us, over the sevll trayned bands and Companys constituted by ye Genll Assembly as Collonels Capts: &c and theire comissions to revoake at pleasure, ye Leut: Gen: with the *advise* of his Councill unless some present danger will soe permit him to *advize* to muster and trayne all ye soldiers wthin the said County of Countyes to presecute warr persue an Enemy suppress rebelions and mewtinies as well by sea as Land and to exercise the whole Millitia as fully as by our Letters pattents from the kinge wee can impower him or them to doe Provided yt they appoint noe Military officers but wt are freeholders in the sd Countyes unless ye Genll Assembly shall *consent*. [Thorpe 2760]

Pennsylvania Frame of Government, 1683:

[Article 12:] That the Governor, or his Deputy, shall always preside in the provincial Council, and that he shall, at no time, therein perform any public act of state whatsoever, that shall, or may, relate unto the justice, trade, treasury, or safety of the province and territories as aforesaid, but by and with the *advice and consent* of the provincial Council thereof. [Thorpe 3066]

James II, Commission to Sir Edmund Andros for the Dominion of New England, April 7, 1688:

[1] And Wee do hereby give and grant unto you full power and authority, by and with the *advise and consent* of our said Councill or the major part of them, to make constitute and ordain lawes statutes and ordinances for the public peace welfare and good governmt of our said territory . . . [Thorpe 1864]

[2] And Wee do by these presents give and grant unto you full power and authority by and with the *advise and consent* of our said Councill, or the major part of them, to impose assess and raise and levy rates and taxes as you shall

find necessary for the support of the government within our territory and dominion of New England . . . [Thorpe 1864]

[3] And for the better supporting the charge of the governmt of our said Territory and Dominion, our will and pleasure is and wee do by these presents authorize and impower you the sd Sr Admund Andros and our Councill, to continue such taxes and impositions as are now laid and imposed upon the Inhabitants thereof; and to levy and distribute or cause the same to be levyed and distributed to those ends in the best and most equall manner, untill you shall by & with the *advise and consent* of our Councill agree on and settle such other taxes as shall be sufficient for the support of our government there, which are to be applied to that use and no other. [Thorpe 1864–65]

[4] And our further will and pleasure is, that all publick money raised or to be raised or appointed for the support of the government within our said territory and dominion be issued out by warrant or order from you by & with the *advise and consent* of our Councill as aforesaid. [Thorpe 1865]

And Wee do further hereby give and grant unto you full power and authority with the *advise and consent* of our said Councill to erect constitute and establish such and so many Courts of Judicature and public Justice within our said Territory and Dominion as you and they shall think fitt and necessary for the determining of all causes as well Criminall as Civill according to law and equity . . . [Thorpe 1865]

[5] And Wee do likewise give and grant unto you full power and authority by and with the *advice and Consent* of our said Councill to agree with the planters and inhabitants of our said Territory and Dominion concerning such lands, tenements & hereditaments as now are or hereafter shall be in our power to dispose of, and them to grant unto any person or persons for such terms and under such moderat Quit Rents, Services and acknowledgements to be thereupon reserved unto us as shall be appointed by us. . . . [Thorpe 1868]

[6] As likewise to order and appoint within our said Territory such and so many ports harbors, bayes havens and other places for the convenience and security of shipping, and for the better loading and unloading of goods and merchandize as by you with the *advice and consent* of our Councill shall be thought fitt and necessary; and in them or any of them to erect nominat and appoint Custom houses ware houses and officers relating thereto; and them to alter change, place, or displace from time to time, as with the *advice* aforesaid shal be thought fitt. [Thorpe 1868–69]

English Bill of Rights, December 16, 1689:

All which Their Majesties are contented and pleased shall be declared, enacted and established by authority of this present parliament and shall stand, remain and be the law of this realm for ever; and the same are by Their said Majesties by and with the *advice and consent* of the lords spiritual and temporal and commons in parliament assembled, and by the authority of the same, declared, enacted and established accordingly. [SDECH 468–469]

William and Mary, Charter of Massachusetts Bay, October 7, 1691:

[1] And Wee doe further Grant and Ordeyne that it shall and may be lawfull for the said Governour with the *advice and consent* of the Councill or Assistants from time to time to nominate and appoint Judges Commissioners of Oyer and Terminer Sheriffs Provosts Marshalls Justices of the Peace and other Officers to Our Councill and Courts of Justice belonging . . . [Thorpe 1879]

[2] . . . And alsoe to impose Fines mulcts Imprisonments and other Punishments And to impose and leavy proportionable and reasonable Assessments Rates and Taxes upon the Estates and Persons of all and every the Proprietors and Inhabitants of our said Province or Territory to be Issued and disposed of by Warrant under the hand of the Governor of our said Province for the time being with the *advice and Consent* of the Councill for Our service in the necessary defence and support of our Government of our said Province or Territory and the Protection and Preservation of the Inhabitants there according to such Acts as are or shall be in force within our said Province . . . [Thorpe 1882]

[3] . . . Provided alwayes and Wee doe by these presents for Us Our Heires and Successors Grant Establish and Ordeyne That the said Governour shall not at any time hereafter by vertue of any power hereby granted or hereafter to be granted to him Transport any of the Inhabitants of Our said Province or Territory or oblige them to march out of the Limitts of the same without their Free and voluntary consent or the Consent of the Great and Generall Court or Assembly or Our said Province or Territory nor grant Comissions for exerciseing the Law Martiall upon any the Inhabitants of Our said Province or Territory without the *Advice and Consent* of the Councill or Assistants of the same . . .
[Thorpe 1883]

Pennsylvania Frame of Government, November 7, 1696:

[1] . . . he, the said Proprietary and Governor, at the request of the freemen of the said three counties, by their deputies, in Assembly met, with the representatives of the freemen of the said province at Chester, alias Upland, on the sixth day of the tenth month, 1682, did (with the *advice and consent* of the Members of the said Assembly) enact, that the said three counties should be annexed to the province of Pennsylvania, as the proper territories thereof . . .
[Thorpe 3070]

[2] Now, forasmuch as the former frame of government, modelled by act of settlement, and charter of liberties, is not deemed, in all respects, suitably accommodated to our present circumstances, therefore it is unanimously desired that it may be enacted, And be it enacted by the Governor aforesaid, with the *advice and consent* of the representatives of the freemen of the said province

and territories in Assembly met, and by the authority of the same, that thus government shall, from time to the, consist of the Governor, or his Deputy, or Deputies, and the freemen of the said province, and territories thereof, in form of a Council and Assembly . . . [Thorpe 3071]

[3] And be it further enacted by the authority aforesaid, That the Governor, or his Deputy, shall always preside in the Council, and that he shall, at no time, perform any public act of state whatsoever, that shall, or may relate unto the justice, treasury or trade of the province and territories, but by and with the *advice and consent* of the Council thereof, or major part of them that shall be present. [Thorpe 3071–72]

South Carolina Constitution, March 26, 1776:

[Article 24:] That in case of vacancy in any of the offices above directed to be filled by the general assembly and legislative council, the president and commander-in-chief, with the *advice and consent* of the privy council, may appoint others in their stead, until there shall be an election by the general assembly and legislative council to fill their vacancies respectively. [Thorpe 3246]

[Article 25:] That the president and commander-in-chief, with the *advice and consent* of the privy council, may appoint during pleasure, until otherwise directed by resolution of the general assembly and legislative council, all other necessary officers, except such as are by law directed to be otherwise chosen. [Thorpe 3247]

John Adams, *Thoughts on Government*, April 1776:

Judges, Justices, and all other officers, civil and military, should be nominated and appointed by the Governor, with the *advice and consent* of Council, unless you choose to have a government more popular; if you do, all officers, civil and military, may be chosen by joint ballot of both houses, or, in order to preserve the independence and importance of each House, by ballot of one House, concurred in by the other. Sheriffs should be chosen by the freeholders of counties—so should Registers of Deeds and Clerks of Counties. [PJA4 90]

United States Continental Congress, Draft Articles of Confederation, July 12, 1776:

[Article 13:] No Colony or Colonies shall engage in any War without the previous *Consent* of the United States assembled, unless such Colony or Colonies be actually invaded by Enemies, or shall have received certain *Advice* of a Resolution being formed by some Nations of Indians to invade such Colony or Colonies, and the Danger is so imminent, as not to admit of a Delay, till the other Colonies can be consulted . . . [DHRC1 81]

Delaware Constitution, September 10, 1776:

[Article 9:] The president, with the *advice and consent* of the privy council, may embody the militia, and act as captain-general and commander-in-chief of them, and the other military force of this State, under the laws of the same.

[Thorpe 564]

Maryland Constitution, November 11, 1776:

[Form of Government, Article 33:] That the governor, by and with the *advice and consent* of the council, may embody the militia; and, when embodied, shall alone have the direction thereof; and shall also have the direction of all the regular land and sea forces, under the laws of this state, (but he shall not command in person, unless *advised* thereto by the council, and then only so long as they shall approve thereof;) and may alone exercise all other the executive powers of government, where the concurrence of the council is not required . . .

[Thorpe 1696]

[*Ibid.,* Article 48:] That the governor for the time being, with the *advice and consent* of the council, may appoint the chancellor, and all judges and justices, the attorney-general, naval officers, officers in the regular land and sea service, officers of the militia, registers of the land office, surveyors, and all other civil officers of government, (assessors, constables, and overseers of the roads, only excepted,) and may also suspend or remove any civil officer, who has not a commission during good behavior . . . [Thorpe 1699]

New York Constitution, April 20, 1777:

[Article 23:] That all officers, other than those who, by this constitution, are directed to be otherwise appointed shall be appointed in the manner following, to wit: The assembly shall, once in every year, openly nominate and appoint one of the senators from each great district, which senators shall form a council for the appointment of the said officers, of which the governor for the time being, or the lieutenant-governor, or the president of the senate, when they shall respectively administer the government, shall be president and have a casting voice, but no other vote; and with the *advice and consent* of the said council, shall appoint all the said officers . . . [Thorpe 2633–34]

[Article 36:] . . . And further, that all such of the officers described in the said charters respectively as, by the terms of the said charters, were to be appointed by the governor of the colony of New York, with or without the *advice and consent* of the council of the said King, in the said colony, shall henceforth be appointed by the council established by this constitution for the appointment of officers in this State, until otherwise directed by the legislature.

[Thorpe 2636]

United States Articles of Confederation, November 15, 1777:

[Article VI:] No state shall engage in any war without the *consent* of the united states in congress assembled, unless such state be actually invaded by enemies, or shall have received certain *advice* of a resolution being formed by some nation of Indians to invade such state, and the danger is so imminent as not to admit of a delay, till the united states in congress assembled can be consulted . . .

South Carolina Constitution, March 19, 1778:

[Article 12:] That each parish and district throughout this State shall on the last Monday in November next and the day following, and on the same days of every succeeding year thereafter, elect by ballot one member of the senate . . . to meet on the first Monday in January then next, at the seat of government, unless the casualties of war or contagious disorders should render it unsafe to meet there, in which case the governor and commander-in-chief for the time being may, by proclamation, with the *advice and consent* of the privy council, appoint a more secure and convenient place of meeting . . . [Thorpe 3250]

[Article 13:] That on the last Monday in November next and the day following, and on the same days of every second year thereafter, members of the house of representatives shall be chosen, to meet on the first Monday in January then next, at the seat of government, unless the casualties of war or contagious disorders should render it unsafe to meet there, in which case the governor and commander-in-chief for the time being may, by proclamation, with the *advice and consent* of the privy council, appoint a more secure and convenient place of meeting, and to continue for two years from the said last Monday in November. . . . [Thorpe 3251–52]

[Article 17:] That neither the senate nor house of representatives shall have power to adjourn themselves for any longer time than three days, without the mutual consent of both. The governor and commander-in-chief shall have no power to adjourn, prorogue, or dissolve them, but may, if necessary, by and with the *advice and consent* of the privy council convene them before the time to which they shall stand adjourned. . . . [Thorpe 3252–53]

[Article 31:] That in case of vacancy in any of the offices above directed to be filled by the senate and house of representatives, the governor and commander-in-chief, with the *advice and consent* of the privy council, may appoint others in their stead, until there shall be an election by the senate and house of representatives to fill those vacancies respectively. [Thorpe 3255]

[Article 32:] That the governor and commander-in-chief, with the *advice and consent* of the privy council, may appoint during pleasure, until otherwise directed by law, all other necessary officers, except such as are now by law directed to be otherwise chosen. [Thorpe 3255]

[Article 35:] That the governor and commander-in-chief for the time being, by and with the *advice and consent* of the privy council, may lay embargoes or prohibit the exportation of any commodity, for any time not exceeding thirty days, in the recess of the general assembly. [Thorpe 3255]

Massachusetts Constitution, March 2, 1780:

[Frame of Government, Chapter I:1:4:] And further, full power and authority are hereby given and granted to the said general court . . . to impose and levy, reasonable duties and excises, upon any produce, goods, wares, merchandise, and commodities, whatsoever, brought into, produced, manufactured, or being within the same; to be issued and disposed of by warrant, under the hand of the governor of this Commonwealth for the time being, with the *advice and consent* of the council, for the public service, in the necessary defence and support of the government of the said Commonwealth, and the protection and preservation of the subjects thereof, according to such acts as are or shall be in force within the same. [Thorpe 1894–95]

[*Ibid.,* Chapter II:1:9:] All judicial officers, the attorney-general, the solicitor general, all sheriffs, coroners, and registers of probate, shall be nominated and appointed by the governor, by and with the *advice and consent* of the council; and every such nomination shall be made by the governor, and made at least seven days prior to such appointment. [Thorpe 1902]

[*Ibid.,* Chapter II:1:11:] No moneys shall be issued out of the treasury of this Commonwealth, and disposed of (except such sums as may be appropriated for the redemption of bills of credit or treasurer's notes, or for the payment of interest arising thereon) but by warrant under the hand of the governor for the time being, with the *advice and consent* of the council, for the necessary defence and support of the Commonwealth; and for the protection and preservation of the inhabitants thereof, agreeably to the acts and resolves of the general court.
[Thorpe 1902–03]

New Hampshire Constitution, June 2, 1784:

[Form of Government:] . . . [General Court has power] to impose and levy proportional and reasonable assessments, rates and taxes, upon all the inhabitants of, and residents within the said state; and upon all estates within the same; to be issued and disposed of by warrant under the hand of the president of this state for the time being, with the *advice and consent* of the council, for the public service, in the necessary defence and support of the government of this state, and the protection and preservation of the subjects thereof, according to such acts as are, or shall be in force within the same. [Thorpe 2458–59]

James Madison, *The Federalist,* No. 18, December 7, 1787:

The cities composing this league [the Greek Achaean League] retained their municipal jurisdiction, appointed their own officers, and enjoyed a perfect equality. The senate, in which they were represented, had the sole and exclusive right of peace and war; of sending and receiving ambassadors; of entering into treaties and alliances; of appointing a chief magistrate or praetor, as he was called, who commanded their armies, and who, with the *advice and consent* of ten of the senators, not only administered the government in the recess of the senate, but had a great share in its deliberations, when assembled. . . . [Fed. 173–74]

"Tamony," January 9, 1788:

Had the Constitution said, the president can do no wrong, nor shall he be re-elected—corruption in the man, might be guarded against by that rotation, which inculcates the idea of certain dissolution, and a council answerable to the people for *consenting to, or advising* measures, would cautiously give their sanction to a ruler whose official shield, must inevitably revert to dust. [DHRC8 288]

James Iredell, "Marcus," February 27, 1788:

. . . By the first, I presume, is meant in regard to the making of laws; because the usual introductory expressions in most acts of Parliament, viz. "By the King's Most Excellent Majesty, by and with the *advice and consent* of the Lords Spiritual and Temporal, and Commons, &c." shew, that in a constitutional sense, they are deemed the King's laws, after a ratification in Parliament. . . . [DHRC16 244]

John Jay, *The Federalist*, No. 64, March 5, 1788:

[1] . . . The convention have done well, therefore, in so disposing of the power of making treaties, that although the President must, in forming them, act by the *advice and consent* of the Senate, yet he will be able to manage the business of intelligence in such a manner as prudence may suggest. [Fed. 422]

[2] . . . Those matters which in negotiations usually require the most secrecy and the most despatch, are those preparatory and auxiliary measures which are not otherwise important in a national view, than as they tend to facilitate the attainment of the objects of the negotiation. For these, the President will find no difficulty to provide; and should any circumstance occur which requires the *advice and consent* of the Senate, he may at any time convene them. Thus we see that the Constitution provides that our negotiations for treaties shall have every advantage which can be derived from talents, information, integrity, and deliberate investigations, on the one hand, and from secrecy and despatch on the other. [Fed. 423]

Political Club of Danville, Kentucky, Debates on the Constitution, March 8, 1788:

Every bill which shall have passed the House of Representatives and the Senate (money Bills excepted) before it becomes a law, shall be presented to the President of the United States; and by him laid before the Executive Counsel and Judges of the supreme Court for their opinion on the same; to be by him with the *advice and consent* of the Counsel & Judges signed when it shall become a Law, or returned with their objections to that house in which it shall have originated . . . [DHRC8 412–13]

Alexander Hamilton, *The Federalist*, No. 66, March 8, 1788:

It will be the office of the President to nominate, and, with the *advice and consent* of the Senate, to appoint. There will, of course, be no exertion of choice on the part of the Senate. They may defeat one choice of the Executive, and oblige him to make another; but they cannot themselves choose—they can only ratify or reject the choice of the President. They might even entertain a preference to some other person, at the very moment they were assenting to the one proposed, because there might be no positive ground of opposition to him; and they could not be sure, if they withheld their assent, that the subsequent nomination would fall upon their own favorite, or upon any other person in their estimation more meritorious than the one rejected. . . . [Fed. 434]

Alexander Hamilton, *The Federalist*, No. 67, March 11, 1788:

The second clause of the second section of the second article empowers the President of the United States "to nominate, and by and with the *advice and consent* of the Senate, to appoint ambassadors, other public ministers and consuls, judges of the Supreme Court, and all other officers of United States whose appointments are not in the Constitution otherwise provided for, and which shall be established by law." Immediately after this clause follows another in these words: "The President shall have power to fill up all vacancies that may happen during the recess of the Senate, by granting commissions which shall expire at the end of their next session." It is from this last provision that the pretended power of the President to fill vacancies in the Senate has been deduced. A slight attention to the clauses, and to the obvious meaning of the terms, will satisfy us that the deduction is not even colorable. [Fed. 438]

Alexander Hamilton, *The Federalist*, No. 69, March 14, 1788:

[1] The President is to have power, with the *advice and consent* of the Senate, to make treaties, provided two thirds of the senators present concur. The king of Great Britain is the sole and absolute representative of the nation in all foreign transactions . . . In this respect, therefore, there is no comparison between the intended power of the President and the actual power of the British sovereign. The one can perform alone what the other can do only with the concurrence of a branch of the legislature. It must be admitted, that, in this instance, the power of the federal Executive would exceed that of any State Executive. But this

arises naturally from the sovereign power which relates to treaties. If the Confederacy were to be dissolved, it would become a question whether the Executives of the several States were not solely invested with that delicate and important prerogative. [Fed. 447–48]

[2] The President is to nominate, and, with the *advice and consent* of the Senate, to appoint ambassadors and other public ministers, judges of the Supreme Court, and in general all officers of the United States established by law, and whose appointments are not otherwise provided for by the Constitution. The king of Great Britain is emphatically and truly styled the fountain of honor. He not only appoints to all offices, but can create offices. He can confer titles of nobility at pleasure; and has the disposal of an immense number of church preferments. There is evidently a great inferiority in the power of the President, in this particular, to that of the British king; nor is it equal to that of the governor of New York . . . [Fed. 448–49]

Alexander Hamilton, *The Federalist*, No. 75, March 26, 1788:

The President is to have power, "by and with the *advice and consent* of the Senate, to make treaties, provided two thirds of the senators present concur."

Though this provision has been assailed, on different grounds, with no small degree of vehemence, I scruple not to declare my firm persuasion, that it is one of the best digested and most unexceptionable parts of the plan. One ground of objection is the trite topic of the intermixture of powers: some contending that the President ought alone to possess the power of making treaties; others, that it ought to have been exclusively deposited in the Senate. Another source of objection is derived from the small number of persons by whom a treaty may be made. Of those who espouse this objection, a part are of opinion that the House of Representatives ought to have been associated in the business, while another part seem to think that nothing more was necessary than to have substituted two thirds of all the members of the Senate, to two thirds of the members present. . . . [Fed. 475–76]

Alexander Hamilton, *The Federalist*, No. 76, April 1, 1788:

The President is "to nominate, and, by and with the *advice and consent* of the Senate, to appoint ambassadors, to her public ministers and consuls, judges of the Supreme Court, and all other officers of the United States whose appointments are not otherwise provided for in the Constitution. But the Congress may by law vest the appointment of such inferior officers as they think proper, in the President alone, or in the course of law, in the heads of departments. The President shall have power to fill up all vacancies which may happen during the recess of the Senate, by granting commissions which shall expire at the end of their next session."

It has been observed in a former paper, that "the true test of a good government is its aptitude and tendency to produce a good administration." If the justness of this observation be admitted, the mode of appointing the officers of the United States contained in the foregoing clauses, must, when examined, be allowed to be entitled to particular commendation. . . . [Fed. 480–81]

United States Congress, Act for the Government of the Northwest Territory, August 7, 1789:

. . . and the President shall nominate, and, by and with the *advice and consent* of the Senate shall appoint, all officers which, by the said ordinance, were to have been appointed by the United States in Congress assembled, and all officers so appointed shall be commissioned by him; and in all cases where the United States in Congress assembled might, by the said ordinance, revoke any commission, or remove from any office, the President is hereby declared to have the same powers of revocation and removal. [Thorpe 964]

United States Congress, Act for the Government of the Territory South of the Ohio River, May 26, 1790:

And be it further enacted, That the salaries of the officers, which the President of the United States shall nominate, and with the *advice and consent* of the Senate appoint, by virtue of this act, shall be the same as those, by law established, of similar officers in the government northwest of the river Ohio . . .
[Thorpe 3413]

AID AND COMFORT

United States Constitution, September 17, 1787:

[Article III, Section 3:] Treason against the United States, shall consist only in levying War against them, or in adhering to their Enemies, giving them *Aid and Comfort*. No Person shall be convicted of Treason unless on the Testimony of two Witnesses to the same overt Act, or on Confession in open Court.

* * * * *

Luther Martin, "Genuine Information," February 1, 1788:

By the third section of this article it is declared that treason against the United States, shall consist in levying war against them, or in adhering to their enemies giving them *aid or comfort*.

By the principles of the American revolution, arbitrary power may and ought to be resisted even by arms if necessary—The time may come when it shall be the duty of a State, in order to preserve itself from the oppression of the general government, to have recourse to the sword—In which case the proposed form of government declares that the State and every of its citizens who act under its authority are guilty of a direct act of treason . . . [DHRC16 10–11]

Alexander Hamilton, *The Federalist*, No. 69, March 14, 1788:

The better to judge of this matter, it will be necessary to recollect, that, by the proposed Constitution, the offence of treason is limited "to levying war upon the United States, and adhering to their enemies, giving them *aid and comfort*"; and that by the laws of New York it is confined within similar bounds. [Fed. 447]

Alexander Hamilton, *The Federalist*, No. 84, May 28, 1788:

[Proposed U.S. Constitution contains a number of provisions securing essential rights, including:] Section 3, of the same article—"Treason against the United

States shall consist only in levying war against them, or in adhering to their enemies, giving them *aid and comfort*. No person shall be convicted of treason, unless on the testimony of two witnesses to the same overt act, or on confession in open court.'' And clause 3, of the same section—''The Congress shall have power to declare the punishment of treason; but no attainder of treason shall work corruption of blood, or forfeiture, except during the life of the person attainted.''

It may well be a question, whether these are not, upon the whole, of equal importance with any which are to be found in the constitution of this State. . . .

[Fed. 532–533]

ARMS

[Note: The excerpts on this list have been selected with reference to the use of the word ''arms'' and its variants in conjunction with the words ''bear'' and ''keep'' from the United States Bill of Rights. Also selected from the database are passages which contain references to the people's use of arms (''take up arms,'' etc.), including references to arming the militia.]

United States Constitution, September 17, 1787:

[Article I, Section 8:] [Congress shall have power] To provide for organizing, *arming,* and disciplining, the Militia, and for governing such Part of them as may be employed in the service of the United States, reserving to the States respectively, the Appointment of the Officers, and the Authority of training the Militia according to the discipline prescribed by Congress. . . .

United States Constitution, Bill of Rights, December 15, 1791:

[Article II:] A well regulated Militia, being necessary to the security of a free State, the right of the people *to keep and bear Arms,* shall not be infringed.

* * * * *

Carolina Proprietors, Declaration and Proposals, August 25, 1663:

[Article 7:] We will grant to every present undertaker for his own head, one hundred acres of land, to him and his heires forever, to be held in free and common soccage; and for every man-servant that he shall bring or sent thither, that is fit to *bear arms,* armed with a good firelock musket, performed bore, twelve bullets to the pound, and with twenty pounds of powder and twenty pounds of bullets, fifty acres of land . . . [Thorpe 2755]

Fundamental Constitutions of Carolina, March 1, 1669:

[Article 116:] All inhabitants and freemen of Carolina above seventeen years of age, and under sixty, shall be bound to *bear arms* and serve as soldiers, whenever the grand council shall find it necessary. [Thorpe 2786]

Charles II, Commission Constituting a President and Council for New Hampshire, September 18, 1680:

. . . Our further will & pleasure is, and hereby we do authorize, require & com'and said Pres: & Councell for the time being, in Our name & under the seal by Us appointed to be used, to issue forth and give Com'issions from time to time, to such psen & persons, whom they shall judge shall be best qualified for regulation & discipline of ye militia of Our said Province; & for ye arraying and mustering ye Inhabitants thereof; & instructing them how to *bear and use their arms;* & that care be taken, that such good discipline shall be observed, as by ye said Councell shall be prscribed . . . [Thorpe 2448]

Fundamental Constitutions of East New Jersey, 1683:

[Article 7:] . . . And that amongst the present Proprietors there are several that declare, that they have no freedom to defend themselves with *arms,* and others who judge it their duty to defend themselves, wives and children, with *arms;* it is therefore agreed and consented to, and they the said Proprietors do by these presents agree and consent, that they will not in this case force each other against their respective judgments and consciences; in order whereunto it is Resolved, that on the one side, no man that declares he cannot for conscience sake *bear arms,* whether Proprietor or planter, shall be at any time put upon so doing in his own person, nor yet upon sending any to serve in his stead. And on the other side, those who do judge it their duty to *bear arms* for the publick defence, shall have their liberty to do in a legal way. In pursuance thereof, there shall be a fourth committee erected, consisting of six proprietors, or their proxies, and three of the freemen, that are to set in the other three committees, which shall be such as to understand it their duty to *use arms* for the publick defence; which committee shall provide for the publick defence without and peace within, against all enemies whatsoever; and shall therefore be stiled the committee for the preservation of the publick peace . . . [Thorpe 2576–77]

[*Ibid.:*] . . . all further deliberations about it, as the raising of men, giving of commissions both by sea and land, making Governors of forts, and providing money necessary for maintaining the same, shall belong only to those members of the great Council who judge themselves in duty bound to make *use of arms* for the defence of them and theirs. Provided, that they shall not conclude any thing but by the consent of at least five parts out of six of their number; and that none of the Proprietors and other inhabitants may be forced to contribute any money for the *use of arms,* to which for conscience sake they have not freedom, that which is necessary for the publick defence, shall be borne by such as judge themselves in duty bound to *use arms.* Provided that the other, that for conscience sake do oppose the *bearing of arms,* shall on the other hand bear so much other charges, as may make up that portion in the general charge of the Province. And as the refusing to subscribe such acts concerning the use and exercise of *arms* abovesaid, in the Governor and Secretary, if scrupulous in conscience so to do, shall not be esteemed in them an omission or neglect of duty, so the wanting thereof shall not make such acts invalid, they being in lieu thereof, subscribed by the major part of the six Proprietors of the committees for the preservation of the publick peace. [Thorpe 2577–78]

English Bill of Rights, December 16, 1689:

[1] By causing several good subjects being Protestants to be disarmed at the same time when Papists were both *armed* and employed contrary to law. [SDECH 463]

[2] That the subjects which are Protestants may *have arms* for their defence suitable to their conditions and as allowed by law. [SDECH 465]

Thomas Paine, *Common Sense*, January 9, 1776:

[1] The object contended for, ought always to bear some just proportion to the expense. The removal of North, or the whole detestable junto, is a matter unworthy the millions we have expended. A temporary stoppage of trade, was an inconvenience, which would have sufficiently balanced the repeal of all the acts complained of, had such repeals been obtained; but if the whole continent must *take up arms,* if every man must be a soldier, it is scarcely worth our while to fight against a contemptible ministry only. . . . [CWTP1 24]

[2] 'Tis not in numbers but in unity, that our great strength lies; yet our present numbers are sufficient to repel the force of all the world. The continent has at this time the largest body of *armed* and disciplined men of any power under heaven: and is just arrived at that pitch of strength, in which no single colony is able to support itself, and the whole, when united, is able to do any thing. . . . [CWTP1 31]

[3] While we profess ourselves the subjects of Britain, we must, in the eye of foreign nations, be considered as Rebels. The precedent is somewhat dangerous to their peace, for men to be in *arms* under the name of subjects; we on the spot, can solve the paradox: but to unite resistance and subjection, requires an idea much too refined for common understanding. [CWTP1 39]

[4] Besides, the *taking up arms,* merely to enforce the repeal of a pecuniary law, seems as unwarrantable by the divine law, and as repugnant to human feelings, as the *taking up arms* to enforce obedience thereto. The object, on

either side, doth not justify the ways and means; for the lives of men are too valuable to be cast away on such trifles. It is the violence which is done and threatened to our persons; the destruction of our property by an *armed* force; the invasion of our country by fire and sword, which conscientiously qualifies the use of *arms;* and the instant in which such mode of defence became necessary, all subjection to Britain ought to have ceased; and the independence of America should have been considered as dating its era from, and published by, the first musket that was fired against her. . . . [CWTP1 45]

[Address to the Quakers:] O ye partial ministers of your own acknowledged principles. If the *bearing arms* be sinful, the first going to war must be more so, by all the difference between wilful attack and unavoidable defence. Wherefore, if ye really preach from conscience, and mean not to make a political hobby-horse of your religion, convince the world thereof, by proclaiming your doctrine to our enemies, for they likewise *bear ARMS*. Give us proof of your sincerity by publishing it at St. James's, to the commanders in chief at Boston, to the Admirals and Captains who are practically ravaging our coasts, and to all the murdering miscreants who are acting in authority under HIM whom ye profess to serve. . . .

[*Ibid.:*] Alas! it seems by the particular tendency of some part of your testimony, and other parts of your conduct, as if all sin was reduced to, and comprehended in the act of *bearing arms,* and that by the people only. Ye appear to us, to have mistaken party for conscience, because the general tenor of your actions wants uniformity: And it is exceedingly difficult to us to give credit to many of your pretended scruples; because we see them made by the same men, who, in the very instant that they are exclaiming against the mammon of this world, are nevertheless, hunting after it with a step as steady as Time, and an appetite as keen as Death.

South Carolina Constitution, March 26, 1776:

[Preamble:] . . . And whereas large fleets and armies having been sent to America in order to enforce the execution of those laws, and to compel an absolute and implicit submission to the will of a corrupt and despotic administration, and in consequence thereof, hostilities having been commenced in the Massachusetts Bay, by the troops under command of General Gage, whereby a number of peaceable, helpless, and unarmed people were wantonly robbed and murdered, and there being just reason to apprehend that like hostilities would be committed in all the other colonies. The colonists were therefore driven to the necessity of *taking up arms,* to repel force by force, and to defend themselves and their properties against lawless invasions and depredations. . . . [Thorpe 3342]

John Adams, *Thoughts on Government,* April 1776:

A MILITIA LAW requiring all men, or with very few exceptions, besides cases of conscience, to be *provided with arms* and ammunition, to be trained at certain seasons, and requiring counties, towns, or other small districts to be provided with public stocks of ammunition and entrenching utensils, and with some settled plans for transporting provisions after the militia, when marched to defend their country against sudden invasions . . . is always a wise institution . . . [PJA4 91]

Virginia Bill of Rights, June 12, 1776:

[Article 13:] That a well regulated militia, composed of the body of the people, trained to *arms,* is the proper, natural, and safe defence of a free state; that standing armies, in time of peace, should be avoided, as dangerous to liberty; and that, in all cases, the military should be under strict subordination to, and governed by, the civil power. [Thorpe 3814]

United States Declaration of Independence, July 4, 1776:

He [*i.e.*, the King] has constrained our fellow Citizens taken Captive on the high Seas to *bear Arms* against their Country, to become the executioners of their friends and Brethren, or to fall themselves by their Hands.

Pennsylvania Constitution, September 28, 1776:

[Declaration of Rights, Article 8:] That every member of society hath a right to be protected in the employment of life, liberty and property, and therefore is bound to contribute his proportion towards the expence of that protection, and yield his personal service when necessary, or an equivalent thereto: But no part of a man's property can be justly taken from him or applied to public uses, without his own consent, or that of his legal representatives: Nor can any man who is conscientiously scrupulous of *bearing arms*, be justly compelled thereto, if he will pay such equivalent, nor are the people bound by any laws, but such as they have in like manner assented to, for their common good.

[Thorpe 3083]

[*Ibid.,* Article 13:] That the people have a right to *bear arms* for the defence of themselves and the state; and as standing armies in the time of peace are dangerous to liberty, they ought not to be kept up; And that the military should be kept under strict subordination to, and governed by, the civil power. [Thorpe 3083]

North Carolina Constitution, December 18, 1776:

[Declaration of Rights, Article 17:] That the people have a right to *bear arms,* for the defence of the state; and as standing armies, in time of peace, are dangerous to liberty, they ought not to be kept up; and that the military should be kept under strict subordination to, and governed by, the civil power.

[Thorpe 2788]

Georgia Constitution, February 5, 1777:

[Article 35:] Every county in this State that has, or hereafter may have, two hundred and fifty men, and upwards, liable to *bear arms,* shall be formed into a battalion; and when they become too numerous for one battalion, they shall be formed into more, by bill of the legislature; and those counties that have a less number than two hundred and fifty shall be formed into independent companies. [Thorpe 782]

New York Constitution, April 20, 1777:

[Article 40:] . . . this convention [of New York State] therefore, in the name and by the authority of the good people of this State, doth ordain, determine, and declare that the militia of this State, at all times hereafter, as well in peace as in war, shall be armed and disciplined, and in readiness for service. That all such of the inhabitants of this State being of the people called Quakers as, from scruples of conscience, may be averse to the *bearing of arms,* be therefrom excused by the legislature; and do pay to the State such sums of money in lieu of their personal service, as the same may, in the judgement of the legislature, be worth. . . . [Thorpe 2637]

Vermont Constitution, July 8, 1777:

[Declaration of Rights, Article 9:] . . . nor can any man who is conscientiously scrupulous of *bearing arms,* be justly compelled thereto, if he will pay such equivalent; nor are the people bound by any law, but such as they have, in like manner, assented to, for their common good. [Thorpe 3740–41]

[*Ibid.,* Article 15]: That the people have a right to *bear arms* for the defence of themselves and the State; and, as standing armies, in the time of peace, are dangerous to liberty, they ought not to be kept up; and that the military should be kept under strict subordination to, and governed by, the civil power. [Thorpe 3741]

United States Articles of Confederation, November 15, 1777:

[Article 6:] . . . but every state shall always keep up a well regulated and disciplined militia, sufficiently *armed* and accoutered, and shall provide and constantly have ready for use, in public stores, a due number of field pieces and tents, and a proper quantity of *arms,* ammunition and camp equipage.

[Article 9:] The united states in congress assembled shall have authority . . . to build and equip a navy—to agree upon the number of land forces, and to make requisitions from each state for its quota, in proportion to the number of white inhabitants in such state; which requisition shall be binding, and thereupon the legislature of each state shall appoint the regimental officers, raise the men and clothe, *arm* and equip them in a soldier like manner, at the expense of the united states, and the officers and men so clothed, *armed* and equipped shall march to the place appointed, and within the time agreed on by the united states in congress assembled. But if the united states in congress assembled shall, on consideration of circumstances judge proper that any state should not raise men, or should raise a smaller number than its quota, and that any other state should raise a greater number of men than the quota thereof, such extra number shall be raised, officered, clothed, *armed* and equipped in the same manner as the quota of such state, unless the legislature of such state shall judge that such extra number cannot be safely spared out of the same, in which case they shall raise officer, clothe, *arm* and equip as many of such extra number as they judge can be safely spared. And the officers and men so clothed, *armed* and equipped, shall march to the place appointed, and within the time agreed on by the united states in congress assembled.

Massachusetts Constitution, March 2, 1780:

[Declaration of Rights, Article 17:] The people have a right to *keep and to bear arms* for the common defence. And as, in time of peace, armies are dangerous to liberty, they ought not to be maintained without the consent of the legislature; and the military power shall always be held in an exact subordination to the civil authority, and be governed by it. [Thorpe 1892]

New Hampshire Constitution, June 2, 1784:

[Bill of Rights, Article 13:] No person who is conscientiously scrupulous about the lawfulness of *bearing arms,* shall be compelled thereto, provided he will pay an equivalent. [Thorpe 2455]

Vermont Constitution, July 4, 1786:

[Declaration of Rights, Article 10:] . . . nor can any man, who is conscientiously scrupulous of *bearing arms,* be justly compelled thereto, if he will pay such equivalent; nor the people bound by any law, but such as they have in like manner assented to, for their common good. . . . [Thorpe 3753]

[*Ibid.,* Article 18:] That the people have a right to *bear arms*, for the defence of themselves and the State: and as standing armies, in the time of peace, are dangerous to liberty, they ought not to be kept up; and that the military should be kept under strict subordination to, and governed by the civil power. [Thorpe 3753–54]

Richard Henry Lee [?], "The Federal Farmer," No. 3, October 10, 1787:

. . . It is true, the yeomanry of the country possess the lands, the weight of property, *possess arms,* and are too strong a body of men to be openly offended—

and, therefore, it is urged, they will take care of themselves, that men who shall govern will not dare pay any disrespect to their opinions. It is easily perceived, that if they have not their proper negative upon passing laws in congress, or on the passage of laws relative to taxes and armies, they may in twenty or thirty years be by means imperceptible to them, totally deprived of that boasted weight and strength: This may be done in a great measure by congress, if disposed to do it, by modelling the militia. Should one fifth or one eighth part of the men capable of *bearing arms,* be made a select militia, as has been proposed, and those the young and ardent part of the community, possessed of but little or no property, and all the others put upon a plan that will render them of no importance, the former will answer all the purposes of an army, while the latter will be defenseless. . . . [Ford 305]

Dissent of the Pennsylvania Convention's Minority, December 18, 1787:

[1] That the people have a right to *bear arms* for the defence of themselves and their own state or the United States, or for the purpose of killing game; and no law shall be passed for disarming the people or any of them unless for crimes committed, or real danger of public injury from individuals; and as standing armies in the time of peace are dangerous to liberty, they ought not to be kept up; and that the military shall be kept under strict subordination to, and be governed by the civil powers. [DHRC2 623–24]

[2] That the power of organizing, *arming* and disciplining the militia (the manner of disciplining the militia to be prescribed by Congress), remain with the individual States, and that Congress shall not have authority to call or march any of the militia out of their own state, without the consent of such state, and for such length of time only as such state shall agree. [DHRC2 624]

[3] . . . the rights of conscience may be violated, as there is no exemption of those persons who are conscientiously scrupulous of *bearing arms*. These compose a respectable proportion of the community in the state. . . . [DHRC2 638]

Alexander Hamilton, *The Federalist*, No. 28, December 26, 1787:

. . . In a single state, if the persons intrusted with supreme power become usurpers, the different parcels, subdivisions, or districts of which it consists, having no distinct government in each, can take no regular measures for defence. The citizens must rush tumultuously to *arms,* without concert, without system, without resource, except in their courage and despair. . . . [Fed. 224]

Alexander Hamilton, *The Federalist*, No. 29, January 9, 1788:

[1] . . . This desirable uniformity can only be accomplished by confiding the regulation of the militia to the direction of the national authority. It is, therefore,

with the most evident propriety, that the plan of the convention proposes to empower the Union, "to provide for organizing, *arming,* and disciplining the militia . . . [Fed. 226–27]

[2] . . . To oblige the great body of the yeomanry, and of the other classes of citizens, to be *under arms* for the purpose of going through military exercises and evolutions, as often as might be necessary to acquire the degree of perfection which would entitle them to the character of a well-regulated militia, would be a real grievance to the people, and a serious public inconvenience and loss. It would form an annual deduction from the productive labor of the country, to an amount which, calculating upon the present numbers of the people, would not fall far short of the whole expense of the civil establishments of all the States. To attempt a thing which would abridge the mass of labor and industry to so considerable an extent would be unwise; and the experiment, if made, could not succeed, because if would not long be endured. Little more can reasonably be aimed at, with respect to the people at large, than to have them properly *armed* and equipped; and in order to see that this be not neglected, it will be necessary to assemble them once or twice in the course of a year. [Fed. 228]

[3] . . . but if circumstances should at any time oblige the government to form an army of any magnitude that army can never be formidable to the liberties of the people while there is a large body of citizens, little, if at all, inferior to them in discipline and the *use of arms,* who stand ready to defend their own rights and those of their fellow-citizens. This appears to me the only substitute that can be devised for a standing army, and the best possible security against it, if it should exist. [Fed. 229]

James Madison, *The Federalist*, No. 46, January 29, 1788:

[1] . . . Let a regular army, fully equal to the resources of the country, be formed; and let it be entirely at the devotion of the federal government; still it would not be going too far to say, that the State governments, with the people on their side, would be able to repel the danger. The highest number to which, according to the best computation, a standing army can be carried in any country, does not exceed one hundreth part of the whole number of souls; or one twenty-fifth part of the number able to *bear arms.* This proportion would not yield, in the United States, an army of more than twenty-five or thirty thousand men. To these would be opposed a militia amounting to near half a million of citizens with *arms* in their hands, officered by men chosen from among themselves, fighting for their common liberties, and united and conducted by governments possessing their affections and confidence. It may well be doubted, whether a militia thus circumstanced could ever be conquered by such a proportion of regular troops. . . . [Fed. 334]

[2] . . . Besides the advantage of being *armed,* which the Americans possess over the people of almost every other nation, the existence of subordinate govern-

ments, to which the people are attached, and by which the militia officers are appointed, forms a barrier against the enterprises of ambition, more insurmountable than any which a simple government of any form can admit of. . . . Notwithstanding the military establishments in the several kingdoms of Europe, which are carried as far as the public resources will bear, the governments are afraid to trust the people with *arms*. And it is not certain, that with this aid alone they would not be able to shake off their yokes. . . . [Fed. 335]

Alexander White, "To the Citizens of Virginia," February 22, 1788:

. . . There are other things so clearly out of the power of Congress, that the bare recital of them is sufficient, I mean the "rights of conscience, or religious liberty—the rights of *bearing arms* for defence, or for killing game—the liberty of fowling, hunting and fishing—the right of altering the laws of descents and distribution of the effects of deceased persons and titles of lands and goods, and the regulation of contracts in the individual States." These things seem to have been inserted among their [*i.e.*, the Pennsylvania convention's minority's] objections, merely to induce the ignorant to believe that Congress would have a power over such objects and to infer from their being refused a place in the Constitution, their intention to exercise that power to the oppression of the people. . . . [DHRC8 404]

Pennsylvania Constitution, September 2, 1790:

[Article VI, Section 2:] The freemen of this commonwealth shall be *armed* and disciplined for its defence. Those who conscientiously scruple to *bear arms* shall not be compelled to do so, but shall pay an equivalent for personal service. The militia officers shall be appointed in such manner and for such time as shall be directed by law. [Thorpe 3099]

[Article IX, Section 21:] That the right of citizens to *bear arms,* in defence of themselves and the State, shall not be questioned. [Thorpe 3101]

ART, ARTS

United States Constitution, September 17, 1787:

[Article I, Section 8:] [Congress shall have power] To promote the Progress of Science and *useful Arts,* by securing for limited Times to Authors and Inventors the exclusive Right to their respective Writings and Discoveries . . .

* * * * *

Pennsylvania Frame of Government, April 25, 1682:

. . . Thirdly, [there shall be established] a committee of trade and treasury, who shall regulate all trade and commerce, according to law, encourage manufacture and county growth, and defray the public charge of the Province. And, Fourthly, a committee of manners, education, and *arts,* that all wicked and scandalous living may be prevented, and that youth may be successively trained up in virtue and useful knowledge and *arts* . . . [Thorpe 3057]

Fundamental Constitutions of East New Jersey, 1683:

[Article 5:] . . . which common Council will thus consist of six and thirty, whereof they [there?] shall be three committees; twelve for the public policy, and to look to manners, education and *arts;* twelve for trade and management of the publick Treasury; and twelve for plantations and regulating of all things, as well as deciding all controversies relating to them . . . [Thorpe 2576]

George II, Charter of Georgia, June 9, 1732:

. . . and we do, by these presents, nominate, constitute, and appoint our right trusty and well-beloved John Lord Viscount Percival, our trusty and beloved Edward Digby, George Carpenter, James Oglethorpe, George Heathcote, Thomas Laroche, James Vernon, William Beletha, esqrs., and Stephen Hales,

Master of *Arts,* to be the common council of the said corporation, to continue in the said office during their good behavior. . . . [Thorpe 768]

Thomas Paine, *Common Sense*, January 9, 1776:

[1] I draw my idea of the form of government from a principle in nature which no *art* can overturn, viz. that the more simple any thing is, the less liable it is to be disordered, and the easier repaired when disordered; and with this maxim in view, I offer a few remarks on the so much boasted constitution of England. . . . [CWTP1 6]

[2] 'Tis repugnant to reason, to the universal order of things, to all examples from former ages, to suppose that this continent can longer remain subject to any external power. The most sanguine in Britain doth not think so. The utmost stretch of human wisdom cannot, at this time, compass a plan, short of separation, which can promise the continent even a year's security. Reconciliation is now a fallacious dream. Nature hath deserted the connection, and *art* cannot supply her place. For, as Milton wisely expresses, "never can true reconcilement grow where wounds of deadly hate have pierced so deep." [CWTP1 23]

Pennsylvania Constitution, September 28, 1776:

[Preamble:] We, the representatives of the freemen of Pennsylvania, in general convention met, for the express purposes of framing such a government, confessing the goodness of the great Governor of the universe (who alone knows to what degree of earthly happiness mankind may attain, by perfecting the *arts* of government) in permitting the people of this State, by common consent and without violence, deliberately to form for themselves such just rules as they shall think best, for governing their future society . . . [Thorpe 3082]

Vermont Constitution, July 8, 1777:

[Preamble:] We the representatives of the freemen of Vermont, in General Convention met, for the express purpose of forming such a government,—confessing the goodness of the Great Governor of the universe, (who alone, knows to what degree of earthly happiness, mankind may attain, by perfecting the *arts* of government) in permitting the people of this State, by common consent, and without violence, deliberately to form for themselves, such just rules as they shall think best for governing their future society . . . [Thorpe 3739]

Massachusetts Constitution, March 2, 1780:

[Frame of Goverment, Chapter V:2:1:] Whereas our wise and pious ancestors, so early as the year one thousand six hundred and thirty-six, laid the foundation of Harvard College, in which university many persons of great eminence have, by the blessing of God, been initiated in those *arts* and sciences which qualified them for public employments, both in church and state; and whereas the encouragement of *arts* and sciences, and all good literature, tends to the honor of God, the advantage of the Christian religion, and the great benefit of this and the other United States of America,—it is declared, that the PRESIDENT AND FELLOWS OF HARVARD COLLEGE, in their corporate capacity, and their successors in that capacity, their officers and servants, shall have, hold, use, exercise, and enjoy, all the powers, authorities, rights, liberties, privileges, immunities, and franchises, which they now have, or are entitled to have, hold, use, exercise, and enjoy . . . [Thorpe 1906]

[Frame of Government, Chapter V:2:] Wisdom and knowledge, as well as virtue, diffused generally among the body of the people, being necessary for the preservation of their rights and liberties; and as these depend on spreading the opportunities and advantages of education in the various parts of the country, and among the different orders of the people, it shall be the duty of legislatures and magistrates, in all future periods of this common-wealth, to cherish the interests of literature and the sciences, and all seminaries of them; especially the university at Cambridge, public schools and grammar schools in the towns; to encourage private societies and public institutions, rewards and immunities, for the promotion of agriculture, *arts,* sciences, commerce, trades, manufactures, and a natural history of the country; to countenance and inculcate the principles of humanity and general benevolence, public and private charity, industry and frugality, honesty and punctuality in their dealings; sincerity, good humor, and all social affections, and generous sentiments, among the people.
[Thorpe 1907–08]

New Hampshire Constitution, July 2, 1784:

[Frame of Government:] . . . it shall be the duty of the legislators and the magistrates, in all future periods of this government to cherish the interest of literature and the sciences and all seminaries and public schools, to encourage private and public institutions, rewards and immunities for the promotion of agriculture, *arts,* sciences, commerce, trades manufactures and natural history of the country . . . [Thorpe 2467]

Vermont Constitution, July 4, 1786:

[Preamble:] We the Representatives of the freemen of Vermont, in General Convention met, for the express purpose of forming such a government—confessing the goodness of the great Governor of the universe (who alone knows to what degree of earthly happiness mankind may attain by perfecting the *arts* of government) in permitting the people of this State, by common consent, and without violence, deliberately to form for themselves such just rules as they shall think best, for governing their future society . . . [Thorpe 3751]

Noah Webster, *An Examination into the Leading Principles of the Federal Constitution*, October 17, 1787:

. . . The house of representatives may be composed of new and unexperienced members—strangers to the forms of proceeding, and the science of legislation. But either positive institutions, or customs, which may supply their place, fill the senate with men venerable for age and respectability, experienced in the ways of men, and in the *art* of governing, and who are not liable to the bias of passions that govern the young. . . . [Ford 32]

John Jay, *The Federalist*, No. 2, October 31, 1787:

These and similar considerations then induced the people to rely greatly on the judgment and integrity of the Congress; and they took their advice, notwithstanding the various *arts* and endeavors used to deter them from it. [Fed. 96]

John Jay, *The Federalist*, No. 5, November 10, 1787:

The history of Great Britain is the one with which we are in general the best acquainted, and it gives us many useful lessons. We may profit by their experience without paying the price which it cost them. Although it seems obvious to common sense that the people of such an island should be but one nation, yet we find that they were for ages divided into three, and that those three were almost constantly embroiled in quarrels and wars with one another. Notwithstanding their true interest with respect to the continental nations was really the same, yet by the *arts* and policy and practices of those nations, their mutual jealousies were perpetually kept inflamed, and for a long series of years they were far more inconvenient and troublesome than they were useful and assisting to each other. [Fed. 105]

Alexander Hamilton, *The Federalist*, No. 6, November 14, 1787:

The three last numbers of this paper have been dedicated to an enumeration of the dangers to which we should be exposed, in a state of disunion, from the arms and *arts* of foreign nations. I shall now proceed to delineate dangers of a different and, perhaps, still more alarming kind—those which will in all probability flow from dissensions between the States themselves, and from domestic factions and convulsions. . . . [Fed 108]

Alexander Hamilton, *The Federalist*, No. 8, November 20, 1787:

[1] . . . The disciplined armies always kept on foot on the continent of Europe, though they bear a malignant aspect to liberty and economy, have, notwithstanding, been productive of the signal advantage of rendering sudden conquests impracticable, and of preventing that rapid desolation which used to mark the

progress of war prior to their introduction. The *art* of fortification has contributed to the same ends. The nations of Europe are encircled with chains of fortified places, which mutually obstruct invasion. . . . [Fed. 119–20]

[2] . . . The industrious habits of the people of the present day, absorbed in the pursuits of gain, and devoted to the improvements of agriculture and commerce, are incompatible with the condition of a nation of soldiers, which was the true condition of the people of those republics. The means of revenue, which have been so greatly multiplied by the increase of gold and silver and of the *arts* of industry, and the science of finance, which is the offspring of modern times, concurring with the habits of nations, have produced an entire revolution in the system of war, and have rendered disciplined armies, distinct from the body of the citizens, the inseparable companions of frequent hostility. [Fed. 121–22]

James Madison, *The Federalist*, No. 10, November 22, 1787:

In the next place, as each representative will be chosen by a greater number of citizens in the large than in the small republic, it will be more difficult for unworthy candidates to practice with success the vicious *arts* by which elections are too often carried; and the suffrages of the people being more free, will be more likely to center in men who possess the most attractive merit and the most diffusive and established characters. [Fed. 134]

Alexander Hamilton, *The Federalist*, No. 11, November 24, 1787:

Under a vigorous national government, the natural strength and resources of the country, directed to a common interest, would baffle all the combinations of European jealousy to restrain our growth. This situation would even take away the motive to such combinations, by inducing an impracticability of success. An active commerce, an extensive navigation, and a flourishing marine would then be the offspring of moral and physical necessity. We might defy the little *arts* of the little politicians to control or vary the irresistible and unchangeable course of nature. [Fed. 139]

James Madison, *The Federalist*, No. 14, November 30, 1787:

Let it be remarked, in the third place, that the intercourse throughout the Union will be facilitated by new improvements. Roads will everywhere be shortened, and kept in better order; accommodations for travellers will be multiplied and meliorated; an interior navigation on our eastern side will be opened throughout, or nearly throughout, the whole extent of the thirteen States. The communication between the Western and Atlantic districts, and between different parts of each, will be rendered more and more easy by those numerous canals with which the beneficence of nature has intersected our country, and which *art* finds it so little difficult to connect and complete. [Fed. 153]

"A True Friend," December 6, 1787:

. . . But, as notwithstanding their [the framers of the Constitution] extensive knowledge and their pure intentions, they are not exempted from the common lot of human frailty, and as it is possible, that they may have erred in some parts of that great *art,* so difficult to be attained, of governing without enslaving; as the extent of our country, our situation, our manners and national character cannot be pertinently compared to any thing, which has hitherto existed on earth, we should not, consequently, model ourselves servilely on any system of government, which has yet appeared, or pin our faith on any political writer whatsoever, be his reputation what it may. . . . [DHRC8 219]

James Madison, *The Federalist*, No. 18, December 7, 1787:

[1] . . . Philip [of Macedon] gladly seized the opportunity of executing the designs he had long planned against the liberties of Greece. By his intrigues and bribes he won over to his interests the popular leaders of several cities; by their influence and votes, gained admission into the Amphictyonic council; and by his *arts* and his arms, made himself master of the confederacy. [Fed. 173]

[2] One important fact seems to be witnessed by all the historians who take notice of Achaean affairs. It is, that as well after the renovation of the league by Aratus, as before its dissolution by the *arts* of Macedon, there was infinitely more of moderation and justice in the administration of its government, and less of violence and sedition in the people, than were to be found in any of the cities exercising singly all the prerogatives of sovereignty. . . . [Fed.174]

[3] Whilst the Amphictyonic confederacy remained, that of the Achaeans, which comprehended the less important cities only, made little figure on the theatre of Greece. When the former became a victim to Macedon, the latter was spared by the policy of Philip and Alexander. Under the successors of these princes, however, a different policy prevailed. The *arts* of division were practiced among the Achaeans. Each city was seduced into a separate interest; the union was dissolved. . . . [Fed. 175]

[4] . . . By these *arts* this union, the last hope of Greece, the last hope of ancient liberty, was torn into pieces; and such imbecility and distraction introduced, that the arms of Rome found little difficulty in completing the ruin which their *arts* had commenced. The Achaeans were cut to pieces, and Achaia loaded with chains, under which it is groaning at this hour. [Fed. 176]

Alexander Hamilton, *The Federalist*, No. 21, December 12, 1787:

The wealth of nations depends upon an infinite variety of causes. Situation, soil, climate, the nature of the productions, the nature of the government, the genius of the citizens, the degree of information they possess, the state of commerce, of *arts,* of industry,—these circumstances and many more, too complex, minute, or adventitious to admit of a particular specification, occasion differences hardly conceivable in the relative opulence and riches of different countries. . . .

[Fed. 189]

Dissent of the Pennsylvania Convention's Minority, December 18, 1787:

The representation is unsafe because in the exercise of such great powers and trusts, it is so exposed to corruption and undue influence, by the gift of the numerous places of honor and emolument, at the disposal of the executive; by the *arts* and address of the great and designing; and by direct bribery.

[DHRC2 632]

Alexander Hamilton, *The Federalist*, No. 24, December 19, 1787:

. . . The improvements in the *art* of navigation have, as to the facility of communication, rendered distant nations, in a great measure, neighbors. Britain and Spain are among the principal maritime powers of Europe. A future concert of views between these nations ought not to be regarded as improbable. . . .

[Fed. 207]

Alexander Hamilton, *The Federalist*, No. 35, January 5, 1788:

[1] . . . Those discerning citizens [the mechanics and manufacturers] are well aware that the mechanic and manufacturing *arts* furnish the materials of mercantile enterprise and industry. Many of them, indeed, are immediately connected with the operations of commerce. They know that the merchant is their natural patron and friend; and they are aware, that however great the confidence they may justly feel in their own good sense, their interests can be more effectually promoted by the merchant than by themselves. . . . [Fed. 256]

[2] . . . Will not the merchant understand and be disposed to cultivate, as far as may be proper, the interests of the mechanic and manufacturing *arts,* to which his commerce is so nearly allied? Will not the man of the learned profession, who will feel a neutrality to the rivalships between the different branches of industry, be likely to prove an impartial arbiter between them, ready to promote either, so far as it shall appear to him conducive to the general interests of the society? [Fed. 257–58]

Alexander Hamilton, *The Federalist*, No. 36, January 8, 1788:

. . . It is notorious that there are often as great rivalships between different branches of the mechanic or manufacturing *arts* as there are between any of the departments of labor and industry, so that, unless the representative body were to be far more numerous than would be consistent with any idea of regularity or wisdom in its deliberations, it is impossible that what seems to be the spirit of the objection we have been considering should ever be realized in practice. . . . [Fed. 259]

Alexander Hamilton, *The Federalist*, No. 29, January 9, 1788:

. . . Do the persons who rave at this rate imagine that their *art* or their eloquence can impose any conceits or absurdities upon the people of America for infallible truths? [Fed. 230]

James Madison, *The Federalist*, No. 43, January 23, 1788:

A power "to promote the progress of science and *useful arts*, by securing, for a limited time, to authors and inventors, the exclusive right to their respective writings and discoveries."

The utility of this power will scarcely be questioned. The copyright of authors has been solemnly adjudged, in Great Britain, to be a right of common law. The right to useful inventions seems with equal reason to belong to the inventors. The public good fully coincides in both cases with the claims of individuals. The States cannot separately make effectual provision for either of the cases, and most of them have anticipated the decision of this point, by laws passed at the instance of Congress. [Fed. 309]

"Valerius," January 23, 1788:

[1] Have you, sir [Richard Henry Lee], weighed the consequences of committing your name, accompanied with such misrepresentations, to the free discussion, and merited censures of an insulted people? Are you aware of the injury which you do your favorite cause? Do you think that the people are to be deceived by such low *arts?* . . . [DHRC8 318]

[2] . . . As long as I am capable of exercising that rational intellect which the good being has been pleased to impart to me, I shall consider it as my duty to stand forth and endeavour to undeceive the people, when the vilest *arts* are made use of to mislead and delude them. [DHRC8 319]

Letter from Maryland, January 29, 1788, published in Philadelphia *Independent Gazetteer*, February 8, 1788:

It is plain to see, that those who have had the *art* to blindfold them [the people], will have the constitutional legal privilege of judging for them forever after, with respect to life, liberty and property: These being trifling matters not worthy the people's consideration, and of course, not fit to be entrusted to them, who neither know their value, nor use. . . . [DHRC16 88]

James Madison, *The Federalist*, No. 47, January 30, 1788:

The British Constitution was to Montesquieu what Homer has been to the didactic writers on epic poetry. As the latter have considered the work of the immortal bard as the perfect model from which the principles and rules of the epic *art* were to be drawn, and by which all similar works were to be judged, so this great political critic appears to have viewed the Constitution of England as the standard, or to use his own expression, as the mirror of political liberty . . .
[Fed. 337]

Alexander C. Hanson, *Remarks on the Proposed Plan of a Federal Government*, c. January 31, 1788:

[1] The house of representatives is to be the immediate choice of the people, and one man is to represent 30,000 souls. In an affair of so much importance, and in districts containing so many suffrages, it is not to be supposed, that a worthless character will succeed by those *arts,* which have, sometimes, prevailed in county elections. It is to be expected, that, in general, the people will choose men of talents and character. . . . [Ford 225]

[2] . . . The election of a president is not carried on in a single assembly, where the several *arts* of corruption may be essayed. He is elected by persons chosen on the same day, in thirteen different assemblies, in thirteen different states. . . .
[Ford 233]

[3] . . . Two or three federal republics might possibly retain their independence. But they would be in the same situation, with respect to each other, as France, England, and Spain, scarcely ever free from war; practicing the *arts* of dissimulation and intrigue; in vain striving to impose, by endless negotiation; and, after all, relying only on the immense naval and land forces, which they continually maintain. . . . [Ford 249]

[4] . . . Are not the regulations of property, the regulations of the penal law, the protection of the weak, the promotion of *useful arts,* the whole internal government of their respective republics; are not these the main objects of every wise and honest legislature? Are not these things still in their power; and, whilst free from invasion or injuries abroad, are not these almost the only things, in which sovereignty is exercised? [Ford 252]

Samuel Bryan, "Centinel," No. 14, February 5, 1788:

. . . His [Luther Martin's] public spirit has drawn upon him the rage of the conspirators, for daring to remove the veil of secrecy, and announcing to the public the meditated, gilded mischief: all their powers are exerting for his destruction; the mint of calumny is assiduously engaged in coining scandal to blacken his character, and thereby to invalidate his testimony; but this illustrious patriot will rise superior to all their low *arts,* and be the better confirmed in the good opinion and esteem of his fellow-citizens, upon whose gratitude he has an additional claim by standing forth their champion at a crisis when most men would have shrunk from such a duty. . . . [DHRC16 32]

Spencer Roane, "A Plain Dealer," February 13, 1788:

. . . And it can be no impeachment of the talents of any man who has not served a regular apprenticeship to politics, to say, that his opinions on an intricate political question are erroneous: For if, as the celebrated Dr. Blackstone observes, "in every *art*, occupation, or science, commercial or mechanical, some method of instruction or apprenticeship is held necessary, how much more requisite will such apprenticeship be found to be, in the science of government, the noblest and most difficult of any! [DHRC8 366]

Samuel Bryan, "Centinel," No. 15, February 22, 1788:

. . . The conspirators, well aware of their advantage, have seized the favorable moment, and by the most unparalleled *arts* of deception, have obtained the sanction of the conventions of several states to the most tyrannic system of government ever projected. [DHRC16 190]

John Hancock, Speech to the Massachusetts Legislature, February 27, 1788:

. . . I hope and pray, that the gratitude of their [the people's] Hearts may be expressed by a proper use of those inestimable blessings,—by the greatest exertions of Patriotism,—by forming and supporting Institutions for cultivating the human Understanding, and for the greatest Progress of the *Arts* and Sciences,—by establishing Laws for the support of Piety, Religion and Morality, as well as for punishing Vice and Wickedness,—and by exibiting in the great Theatre of the World, those social, public and private Virtues, which give more Dignity to a People, possessing their own Sovereignty, than Crowns and Diadems afford to Sovereign Princes. . . . [DHRC16 226]

Alexander White, "To the Citizens of Virginia," February 29, 1788:

. . . It is said the representation is unsafe because it is so exposed to corruption and undue influence, by the gift of the numerous places of honor and emolument at the disposal of the executive, by the *arts* and address of the great and designing, and by direct bribery? The members of Congress can hold no office during the time they remain members, nor can they enjoy any office which shall be created, or the emoluments of which shall be increased during the time for which they were elected.—Name to me the country in which the members of the legislature or the executive council are so far removed from influence—and before you consent to give each state a controul over the purse and sword, be well informed whether the Grecian confederacy was ruined by the practice of *art,* address, and bribery in the council of Amphyctions, or in the assemblies of the people of the different states? And whether it will not be easier to corrupt a few leading men, in some one of 13 assemblies than a majority of Congress? . . .

[DHRC8 439–40]

Mercy Otis Warren, *Observations on the New Constitution*, February 1788:

[1] . . . behold the insiduous *arts,* and the strenuous efforts of the partisans of arbitrary power, by their vague definitions of the best established truths, endeavoring to envelope the mind in darkness the concomitant of slavery, and to lock the strong chains of domestic despotism on a country, which by the most glorious and successful struggles is but newly emancipated from the sceptre of foreign dominion. . . . [DHRC16 277]

[2] . . . while a supple multitude are paying a blind and idolatrous homage to the opinions of those who by the most precipitate steps are treading down their dear bought privileges; and who are endeavouring by all the *arts* of insinuation, and influence, to betray the people of the United States, into an acceptance of a most complicated system of government . . . [DHRC16 277]

[3] . . . and there are few who do not unite in the general wish for the restoration of public faith, the revival of commerce, *arts,* agriculture, and industry, under a lenient, peaceable and energetick government . . . [DHRC16 278]

[4] . . . But if the authors of the present visionary project [the Constitution], can by the *arts* of deception, precipitation and address, obtain a majority of suffrages in the conventions of the states to try the hazardous experiment, they may then make the same inglorious boast with this insidious politician, who may perhaps be their model, that "the union of the colonies was pretty well broken, and that he hoped never to see it renewed." [DHRC16 282]

[5] . . . [Quoting Luther Martin:] "The great *art* of governing is to lay aside all prejudices and attachments to particular opinions, classes or individual characters; to consult the spirit of the people; to give way to it; and in so doing, to give it a turn capable of inspiring those sentiments, which may induce them to relish a change, which an alteration of circumstances may hereafter make necessary." [DHRC16 286]

[6] . . . And while the statesman is plodding [plotting] for power, and the courtier practising the *arts* of dissimulation without check—while the rapacious are growing rich by oppression, and fortune throwing her gifts into the lap of fools, let the sublimer characters, the philosophic lovers of freedom who have wept over her exit, retire to the calm shades of contemplation, there they may look down with pity on the inconsistency of human nature, the revolutions of states, the rise of kingdoms, and the fall of empires. [DHRC16 289]

William Ward [?], "Republicus," March 1, 1788:

. . . [The Africans were] Ignorant, and comparatively innocent, till we taught them the diabolical *arts* of destruction, captivity, and death; and provided them with the infernal means of carrying them into practice; and all this to furnish ourselves with slaves, at the guilty expence oftimes, of the blood of, ten times the number of those thus enslaved, who lost their lives in the gallant, the virtuous defence of themselves, and families. . . . [DHRC8 450]

Philadelphia *Independent Gazetteer*, March 7, 1788:

The system of deception practised by its [the Constiution's] advocates, is pretty generally found out by the people; their *arts* of making each place on the continent believe that every other part but their own was in favor of it, will serve them no longer. Their runners and story carriers will no longer be attended to. [DHRC16 342]

Jonathan Williams, Jr., "The Fabrick of Freedom," March 8, 1788:

[1] May Science and her handmaid *Art*,
To this new world belong!
And infant muses joy impart
In strains of sportive song!—
Apollo see! with glory drest,
Appears refulgent in the west. [DHRC16 361]

[2] America is thus become.
A seat to freedom dear,
Where virtuous strangers find a home,
And no oppression fear.
These rising States shall be renown'd,
By Plenty, *Art*, and Science crown'd. [DHRC16 361]

Alexander Hamilton, *The Federalist*, No. 66, March 8, 1788:

So far as might concern the misbehavior of the Executive in perverting the instructions or contravening the views of the Senate, we need not be apprehensive of the want of a disposition in that body to punish the abuse of their confidence, or to vindicate their own authority. We may thus far count upon their pride, if not upon their virtue. And so far even as might concern the corruption of leading members, by whose *arts* and influence the majority may have been inveigled into measures odious to the community, if the proofs of that corruption should be satisfactory, the usual propensity of human nature will warrant us in concluding that there would be commonly no defect of inclination in the body to divert the public resentment from themselves by a ready sacrifice of the authors of their mismanagement and disgrace. [Fed. 436]

Alexander Hamilton, *The Federalist*, No. 67, March 11, 1788:

I have taken the pains to select this instance of misrepresentation, and to place it in a clear and strong light, as an unequivocal proof of the unwarrantable *arts* which are practiced to prevent a fair and impartial judgment of the real merits of the Constitution submitted to the consideration of the people. . . .
[Fed. 440]

Alexander Hamilton, *The Federalist*, No. 68, March 12, 1788:

The process of election affords a moral certainty, that the office of President will never fall to the lot of any man who is not in an eminent degree endowed with the requisite qualifications. Talents for low intrigue, and the little *arts* of popularity, may alone suffice to elevate a man to the first honors in a single State; but it will require other talents, and a different kind of merit, to establish him in the esteem and confidence of the whole Union, or of so considerable a portion of it as would be necessary to make him a successful candidate for the distinguished office of President of the United States. It will not be too strong to say, that there will be a constant probability of seeing the station filled by characters preeminent for ability and virtue. . . . [Fed. 442–43]

George Nicholas [?], "The State Soldier," No. 3, March 12, 1788:

To a man thus zealous, the want of authority to pass ex post facto laws may be a great objection to the new constitution indeed, as they might be rendered highly useful to, and a great improvement on, the *art* of speculation. But in all other cases they have ever been considered a great curse, since they can only be productive of a halter to the innocent and ignorant. [DHRC8 488]

James Iredell, "Marcus," No. 4, March 12, 1788:

One of the powers given to Congress is, "To promote the progress of science and *useful arts,* by securing for limited times to authors and inventors, the exclusive right to their respective writings and discoveries." I am convinced Mr. [George] Mason did not mean to refer to this clause. He is a gentleman of too much taste and knowledge himself to wish to have our government established upon such principles of barbarism as to be able to afford no encouragement to genius. [DHRC16 386]

"An Impartial Citizen," No. 6, March 13, 1788:

. . . in almost every country in the world;—in almost every age; the best schemes, the most politic and equitable measures, have been impeded or destroyed by the violent exertions, and unwarrantable opposition of such pretended patriots, but real enemies of their country. Carthage fell by such *arts* and intrigues. . . .
[DHRC8 502]

Alexander Hamilton, *The Federalist,* No. 69, March 14, 1788:

. . . The king of Great Britain, on his part, has an absolute negative upon the acts of the two houses of Parliament. The disuse of that power for a considerable time past does not affect the reality of its existence; and is to be ascribed wholly to the crown's having found the means of substituting influence to authority, or the *art* of gaining a majority in one or the other of the two houses, to the necessity of exerting a prerogative which could seldom be exerted without hazarding some degree of national agitation. . . . [Fed. 445]

Alexander Hamilton, *The Federalist,* No. 71, March 18, 1788:

. . . The republican principle demands that the deliberate sense of the community should govern the conduct of those to whom they intrust the management of their affairs; but it does not require an unqualified complaisance to every sudden breeze of passion, or to every transient impulse which the people may receive from the *arts* of men, who flatter their prejudices to betray their interests. . . . [Fed. 459]

"Brutus," No. 15, March 20, 1788:

. . . In the mean time all the *art* and address of those who wish for the change will be employed to make converts to their opinion. The people will be told, that their state officers, and state legislatures are a burden and expence without affording any solid advantage, for that all the laws passed by them, might be equally well made by the general legislature. . . . [DHRC16 434]

Archibald Maclaine, "Publicola," March 20, 1788:

. . . But were it [the Constitution] completely adapted to our present situation, so as to be unexceptionable to all, time would render it defective—Improvements in commerce and manufactures, in *arts* and sciences; an increase in population, and an alteration in manners, would render amendments to the new constitution necessary—nothing in this world can be permanent . . . [DHRC16 438]

Luther Martin, "To the Citizens of Maryland," No. 2, March 21, 1788:

In the recognition which the Landholder [Oliver Ellsworth] professes to make "of what occurred to my advantage," he equally deals in the *arts* of misrepresentation, as while he was "only the record of the bad," and I am equally obliged, from a regard to truth, to disclaim his pretended approbation as his avowed censure. [DHRC16 452]

Oliver Ellsworth, "The Landholder," No. 13, March 24, 1788:

[1] . . . The present state of America will limit the greatest part of its inhabitants to agriculture; for as the *art* of tilling the earth is easily acquired, the price of land low, and the produce immediately necessary for life, greater encouragement to this is offered here than in any country on earth. . . . [DHRC16 473]

[2] The Nail Manufacture might be another source of wealth to the northern states. Why should we twice transport our own iron, and pay other nations for labour which our boys might perform as well. The *art* of nail making is easily acquired. Three thousand men and boys in Connecticut, might spend our long and idle winters in this business, without detriment to their agricultural service. . . . [DHRC16 474]

"George Bryan," March 26, 1788:

. . . As the Convention of Massachusetts was finishing, a vessel is made to arrive at a port 15 miles off, with account that N. Carolina had adopted, tho' that Convention sits not before July. Again, as the Convention of New-Hampshire was near finishing, this falshood is newly published at Newport in Rhode-Island, and another vessel pretended, to seduce another adoption. These are but a specimen of these *arts* and inventions. But a lying tongue is but for a moment. . . . [DHRC16 488]

Luther Martin, "To the Citizens of Maryland," No. 3, March 28, 1788:

. . . But if the *arts* and influence of ambitious and interested men, even in their present situation, while more on a level with yourselves, and unarmed with any extraordinary powers, should procure you to adopt this system, dangerous as it is admitted to be to your rights, I will appeal to the understanding of every one of you, who will, on this occasion, give his reason fair-play, whether there is not every cause to believe they will, should this government be adopted, with that additional power, consequence and influence it will give them, most easily prevent the necessary alterations which might be wished for, the purpose of which would be directly opposite to their views, and defeat every attempt to procure them. . . . [DHRC16 501]

Melancton Smith, *An Address to the People of the State of New York*, April 1788:

[1] On this head, all the powers of rhetoric, and *arts* of description, are employed to paint the condition of this country, in the most hideous and frightful colors. . . . [Ford 94]

[2] . . . The farmer cultivates his land, and reaps the fruit which the bounty of heaven bestows on his honest toil. The mechanic is exercised in his *art*, and

receives the reward of his labour. The merchant drives his commerce, and none can deprive him of the gain he honestly acquires; all classes and callings of men amongst us are protected in their various pursuits, and secured by the laws in the possession and enjoyment of the property obtained in those pursuits. . . .
[Ford 94]

[3] . . . We are amused with the fair prospects that are to open, when this government is put into operation—Agriculture is to flourish, and our fields to yield an hundred fold—Commerce is to expand her wings, and bear our productions to all the ports in the world—Money is to pour into our country through every channel—*Arts* and manufactures are to rear their heads, and every mechanic find full employ . . . [Ford 106–107]

Alexander Hamilton, *The Federalist*, No. 78, May 28, 1788:

This independence of the judges is equally requisite to guard the Constitution and the rights of individuals from the effects of those ill humors, which the *arts* of designing men, or the influence of particular conjunctures, sometimes disseminate among the people themselves, and which, though they speedily give place to better information, and more deliberate reflection, have a tendency, in the meantime, to occasion dangerous innovations in the government, and serious oppressions of the minor party in the community. [Fed. 494]

Alexander Hamilton, *The Federalist*, No. 79, May 28, 1788:

The want of a provision for removing the judges on account of inability has been a subject of complaint. But all considerate men will be sensible that such a provision would either not be practiced upon or would be more liable to abuse than calculated to answer any good purpose. The mensuration of the faculties of the mind has, I believe, no place in the catalogue of known *arts*. An attempt to fix the boundary between the regions of ability and inability, would much oftener give scope to personal and party attachments and enmities than advance the interest of justice or the public good. . . . [Fed. 498]

John Dickinson, "Fabius," No. 5, 1788:

The great Bacon, in enumerating the *art* by which Caesar enslaved his country, says—"His first artifice was to break the strength of the senate . . .
[Ford 190n]

John Dickinson, "Fabius," No. 6, 1788:

Yet, what were the consequences to Scotland of that dreaded union with England? The cultivation of her virtues and the correction of her errors—The emancipation of one class of her citizens from the yoke of her superiors—A relief of other classes from the injuries and insults of the great—Improvements in agriculture, science, *arts,* trade, and manufactures—The profits of industry and ingenuity enjoyed under the protection of laws—peace and security at home, and encrease of respectability abroad. . . . [Ford 198–99]

John Dickinson, "Fabius," No. 8, 1788:

They [the American states] will be civil and military stations, conveniently planted throughout the empire, with lively and regular communications. A stroke, a touch upon any part, will be immediately felt by the whole. Rome famed for imperial *arts,* had a glimpse of this great truth; and endeavoured, as well as her hard-hearted policy would permit, to realize it in her colonies. . . . [Ford 208]

John Dickinson, "Fabius," No. 9, 1788:

These gentlemen will acknowledge, that Britain has sustained many internal convulsions, and many foreign wars, with a gradual advancement in freedom, power, and prosperity. They will acknowledge, that no nation has existed that ever so perfectly united those distant extremes, private security of life, liberty, and property, with exertion of public force—so advantageously combined the various powers of militia, troops, and fleets—or so happily blended together arms, *arts,* science, commerce, and agriculture. . . . [Ford 211]

Pennsylvania Constitution, September 2, 1790:

[Article VII, Section 2:] The *arts* and sciences shall be promoted in one or more seminaries of learning. [Thorpe 3099]

ASSEMBLE, RIGHT OF THE PEOPLE PEACEABLY TO

[Note: This list focuses on the people assembling outside of the framework of the established government; a full list of words related to ''assemble'' or ''assembly'' would draw in a large number of references to constituted legislative assemblies and conventions. It does, however, include some references to the people assembled in order to constitute government or to directly administer it themselves, and all references to the people assembled in the militia.]

United States Constitution, Bill of Rights, December 15, 1791:

[Article I:] Congress shall make no law respecting an establishment of religion, or prohibiting the free exercise thereof; or abridging the freedom of speech, or of the press; or the *right of the people peaceably to assemble,* and to petition the Government for a redress of grievances.

* * * * *

English Petition of Right, June 7, 1628:

Yet nevertheless, of late divers commissions directed to sundry Commissioners in several counties, with instructions, have issued; by means whereof *your people have been in divers places assembled,* and required to lend certain sums of money unto your Majesty, and many of them upon their refusal so to do, have had an oath administered unto them, not warrantable by the laws or statutes of this realm, and have been constrained to become bound and make appearance and give attendance before your Privy Council and in other places, and others of them have been therefore imprisoned, confined, and sundry other ways molested and disquieted . . . [SDECH 340]

Fundamental Agreement of New Haven Colony, June 4, 1639:

The 4th day of the 4th month, called June, 1639, all the free planters *assembled together in a general meeting,* to consult about settling civil government, according to God, and the nomination of persons that might be found, by consent of all, fittest in all respects for the foundation work of a church, which was intended to be gathered in Quinipiack. . . . [Thorpe 523]

Charles II, Charter of Connecticut, April 23, 1662:

And We do further for Us, Our Heirs and Successors, give and grant unto the said Governor and Company, and their Successors, by these Presents, That it shall and may be lawful to, and for the Chief Commanders, Governors and Officers of the said Companv for the Time being, who shall be resident in the Parts of New-England hereafter mentioned, and others inhabiting there, by their Leave, Admittance, Appointment, or Direction, from Time to Time, and at all Times hereafter, for their special Defence and Safety, to *Assemble,* Martial-Array, and put in warlike Posture *the Inhabitants* of the said Colony, and to Commissionate, Impower, and Authorize such Person or Persons as they shall think fit, to lead and conduct the said Inhabitants, and to encounter, expulse, repel and resist by Force of Arms, as well by Sea as by Land . . .

[Thorpe 534]

Charles II, Charter of Rhode Island, July 8, 1663:

. . . and that itt shall and may bee lawfull to and for all and every such Commander, governour and military officer, that shall bee soe as aforesayd, or by the Governour, or, in his absence, the Deputy-Governour, and six of the sayd Assistants, and majour parte of the freemen of the sayd Company present att any Generall Assemblies, nominated, apoynted and constituted accordinge to the tenor of his and theire respective commissions and directions, to *assemble,* exercise in arms, martiall array, and putt in warlyke posture, the *inhabitants* of the sayd collonie, for theire speciall defence and safety . . . [Thorpe 3218]

William and Mary, Charter of Massachusetts Bay, October 7, 1691:

And Wee doe by these presents for us Our Heires and Successors Grant Establish and Ordaine that the Governor of our said Province or Territory for the time being shall have full Power by himselfe or by any Cheif Comander or other Officer or Officers to be appointed by him from time to time to traine instruct Exercise and Governe the Militia there and for the speciall Defence and Safety of Our said Province or Territory to *assemble* in Martiall Array and put in Warlike posture *the Inhabitants* of Our said Province or Territory . . . [Thorpe 1884]

George II, Charter of Georgia, June 9, 1732:

. . . And we do by these presents for us, our heirs and successors, will, grant and ordain, that the said corporation and their successors, shall have full power for and during and until the full end and term of twenty-one years, to commence from the date of these our letters patent, by any commander or other officer or officers, by them for that purpose from time to time appointed, to train and instruct, exercise and govern a militia, for the special defence and safety of our said colony, to *assemble* in martial array, *the inhabitants* of the said colony, and to lead and conduct them . . . [Thorpe 776]

First Continental Congress, Declaration and Resolves, October 14, 1774:

[1] And whereas, *Assemblies have been frequently dissolved*, contrary to the *rights of the people*, when they attempted to deliberate on grievances; and their dutiful, humble, loyal, & reasonable petitions to the crown for redress, have been repeatedly treated with contempt, by his majesty's ministers of state . . . [JCC1 66]

[2] That they [the colonies] have a *right peaceably to assemble*, consider of their grievances, and petition the King; and that all prosecutions, prohibitory proclamations, and commitments for the same, are illegal. [JCC1 70]

Thomas Paine, *Common Sense*, January 9, 1776:

. . . The property of no man is secure in the present unbraced system of things. The mind of the multitude is left at random, and feeling no fixed object before them, they pursue such as fancy or opinion starts. Nothing is criminal; there is no such thing as treason; wherefore, every one thinks himself at liberty to act as he pleases. The Tories dared not to have *assembled* offensively, had they known that their lives, by that act, were forfeited to the laws of the state. . . . [CWTP1 43–44]

Pennsylvania Constitution, September 28, 1776:

[Declaration of Rights, Article 16:] That the *people have a right to assemble together*, to consult for their common good, to instruct their representatives, and to apply to the legislature for redress of grievances, by address, petition, or remonstrance. [Thorpe 3084]

North Carolina Constitution, December 18, 1776:

[Declaration of Rights, Article 18:] That the *people have a right to assemble together*, to consult for the common good, to instruct their representatives, and to apply to the legislature for redress of grievances. [Thorpe 2788]

Vermont Constitution, July 8, 1777:

[Declaration of Rights, Article 18:] That the *people have a right to assemble together*, to consult for their common good—to instruct their representatives, and to apply to the legislature for redress of grievances, by address, petition or remonstrance. [Thorpe 3741–42]

Massachusetts Constitution, March 2, 1780:

[Bill of Rights, Article 19:] The *people have a right, in an orderly and peaceable manner, to assemble* to consult upon the common good: give instructions to their representatives, and to request of the legislative body, by the way of addresses, petitions, or remonstrances, redress of the wrongs done them, and of the grievances they suffer. [Thorpe 1892]

[Frame of Government, Chapter II:1:7:] The governor of this Commonwealth for the time being, will be the commander-in-chief of the army and navy, and of all the military forces of the state, by seas and land; and shall have full power by himself, or by any commander, or other officer from time to time, to train, instruct, exercise and govern the militia and navy; and for the special defence and safety of the Commonwealth, to *assemble* in martial array, and put in warlike posture, the *inhabitants* thereof . . . [Thorpe 1901]

New Hampshire Constitution, June 2, 1784:

[Bill of Rights, Article 32:] The *people have a right in an orderly and peaceable manner, to assemble* and consult upon the common good, give instructions to their representatives; and to request of the legislative body, by way of petition or remonstrance, redress of the wrongs done them, and of the grievances they suffer. [Thorpe 2457]

[Form of Government:] The president of this state for the time being, shall be commander in chief of the army and navy, and all the military forces of the state, by sea and land; and shall have full power by himself, or by any chief commander, or other officer, or officers, from time to time, to train, instruct, exercise and govern the militia and navy; and for the special defence and safety of this state to *assemble* in martial array, and put in warlike posture, the *inhabitants* thereof . . . [Thorpe 2463–64]

Vermont Constitution, July 4, 1786:

[Declaration of Rights, Article 22:] That the *people have a right to assemble together,* to consult for their common good—to instruct their representatives, and to apply to the Legislature for redress of grievances, by address, petition or remonstrance. [Thorpe 3754]

Richard Henry Lee [?], "The Federal Farmer," No. 2, October 9, 1787:

The essential parts of a free and good government are a full and equal representation of the people in the legislature, and the jury trial of the vicinage in the administration of justice—a full and equal representation, is that which possesses the same interests, feelings, opinions, and views the *people* themselves would were they all *assembled*—a fair representation, therefore, should be so regulated, that every order of men in the community, according to the common course of elections, can have a share in it . . . [Ford 288]

Richard Henry Lee, Proposed Amendments to the Constitution, October 16, 1787:

. . . That *the right of the people to assemble peaceably,* for the purpose of petitioning the legislature, shall not be prevented . . . [DHRC8 65]

Noah Webster, *An Examination of the Leading Principles of the Federal Constitution*, October 17, 1787:

I cannot help remarking the singular jealousy of the constitution of Pennsylvania, which requires that a bill shall be published for the consideration of the people, before it is enacted into a law, except in extraordinary cases. This annihilates the legislature, and reduces it to an advisory body. It almost wholly supersedes the uses of representation, the most excellent improvement in modern governments. Besides the absurdity of constituting a legislature, without supreme power, such a system will keep the state perpetually embroiled. It carries the spirit of discussion into all quarters, without the means of reconciling the opinions of *men, who are not assembled* to hear each others' arguments. . . .

[Ford 34–35n]

James Madison, *The Federalist*, No. 10, November 22, 1787:

From this view of the subject it may be concluded that a pure democracy, by which I mean a society consisting of a small number of *citizens,* who *assemble* and administer the government in person, can admit of no cure for the mischiefs of faction. A common passion or interest will, in almost every case, be felt by a majority of the whole; a communication and concert result from the form of government itself; and there is nothing to check the inducements to sacrifice the weaker party or an obnoxious individual. [Fed. 133]

James Madison, *The Federalist*, No. 14, November 30, 1787:

[1] The error which limits republican government to a narrow district has been unfolded and refuted in preceding papers. I remark here only that it seems to owe its rise and prevalence chiefly to the confounding of a republic with a democracy, applying to the former reasonings drawn from the nature of the latter. The true distinction between these forms was also adverted to on a former occasion. It is, that in a democracy, the *people* meet and exercise the government in person; in a republic, they *assemble* and administer it by their representatives

and agents. A democracy, consequently, will be confined to a small spot. A republic may be extended over a large region. [Fed. 150]

[2] As the natural limit of democracy is that distance from the central point which will just permit the most remote *citizens to assemble* as often as their public functions demand, and will include no greater number than can join in those functions; so the natural limit of a republic is that distance from the center which will barely allow the representatives to meet as often as may be necessary for the administration of public affairs. . . . [Fed. 151]

Dissent of the Pennsylvania Convention's Minority, December 18, 1787:

[1] In the city of Philadelphia and some of the eastern counties the junto that took the lead in the business [*i.e.*, the ratification of the U.S. Constitution] agreed to vote for none but such as would solemnly promise to adopt the system in toto, without exercising their judgment. In many of the counties the people did not attend the elections as they had not an opportunity of judging of the plan. Others did not consider themselves bound by the call of *a set of men who assembled* at the State-house in Philadelphia and assumed the name of the legislature of Pennsylvania. . . . [DHRC2 622]

[2] The legislature of a free country should be so formed as to have a competent knowledge of its constitutents, and enjoy their confidence. To produce these essential requisites, the representation ought to be fair, equal and sufficiently numerous to possess the same interests, feelings, opinions and views, which the *people* themselves would possess were they all *assembled* . . . [DHRC2 631]

Alexander Hamilton, *The Federalist*, No. 29, January 9, 1788:

[On the militia]: . . . Little more can reasonably be aimed at, with respect to the *people at large,* than to have them properly armed and equipped; and in order to see that this be not neglected, it will be necessary to *assemble* them once or twice in the course of a year. [Fed. 229]

Alexander Hamilton, *The Federalist*, No. 58, February 20, 1788:

. . . In the ancient republics, where the whole body of the *people assembled* in person, a single orator, or an artful statesman, was generally seen to rule with as complete a sway as if a sceptre had been placed in his single hand. On the same principle, the more multitudinous a representative *assembly* may be rendered, the more it will partake of the infirmities incident to collective meetings of the people. Ignorance will be the dupe of cunning, and passion the slave of sophistry and declamation. . . . [Fed. 392]

"The New Litany," February 21, 1788:

Good Lord deliver us.

From intestine war; from the *assemblies* of such clubs as are gathered to oppose the new constitution; and from the rage of those who burn with choler, as knowing their consequence will be lessened by the adoption thereof . . . [DHRC16 178]

Philadelphia *Federal Gazette*, March 8, 1788:

[A report from Virginia]: "We had great rejoicings here yesterday, by the federal men, on account of the ratification of the new constitution, by the state of Massachusetts. The *citizens assembled* at the Union tavern, about twelve o'clock, and hoisted up a flag on the top of the house, and kept it up till about 11 o'clock at night, when each repaired to his habitation pretty mellow with Madeira: a number of cannon were fired on this occasion . . . " [DHRC8 475]

"George Bryan," March 26, 1788:

. . . By the last accounts from Harrisburg, *large numbers were assembled,* from York and Dauphin, as well as Cumberland, to set the prisoners at large. This gives much uneasiness to the Conspirators here. . . . [DHRC16 489]

John Dickinson, "Fabius," No. 8, 1788:

In the democracies of antiquity, *the people assembled together* and governed personally. This mode was incompatible with greatness of number and dispersion of habitation. [Ford 206]

Pennsylvania Constitution, September 2, 1790:

[Article IX, Section 20:] That the *citizens have a right, in a peaceable manner, to assemble together* for their common good, and to apply to those invested with the powers of government for redress of grievances, or other proper purposes, by petition, address, or remonstrance. [Thorpe 3101]

BAIL

United States Constitution, Bill of Rights, December 15, 1791:

[Article VIII:] Excessive bail shall not be required, nor excessive fines imposed, nor cruel and unusual punishments inflicted.

* * * * *

English Bill of Rights, December 16, 1689:

[1] And *excessive bail* hath been required of persons committed in criminal cases, to elude the benefit of the laws made for the liberty of the subjects. [SDECH 463]

[2] That *excessive bail* ought not to be required nor excessive fines imposed nor cruel and unusual punishment inflicted. [SDECH 465]

Virginia Bill of Rights, June 12, 1776:

[Section 9:] That *excessive bail* ought not to be required, nor excessive fines imposed, nor cruel and unusual punishments inflicted. [Thorpe 3813]

Delaware Constitution, September 10, 1776:

[Article 12:] . . . The president and privy council shall appoint the secretary, the attorney-general, registers for the probate of wills and granting letters of administration, registers in chancery, clerks of the courts of common pleas and orphans' courts, and clerks of the peace, who shall be commissioned as aforesaid, and remain in office during five years, if they behave themselves well; during which time the said registers in chancery and clerks shall not be justices of either of the said courts of which they are officers, but they shall have authority to sign all writs by them issued, and take recognizances of *bail*. . . . [Thorpe 564–65]

Pennsylvania Constitution, September 28, 1776:

[Declaration of Rights, Section 29:] Excessive bail shall not be exacted for bailable offences: And all fines shall be moderate. [Thorpe 3089]

Maryland Constitution, November 11, 1776:

[Declaration of Rights, Article 22:] That *excessive bail* ought not to be required, nor excessive fines imposed, nor cruel or unusual punishments inflicted, by the courts of law. [Thorpe 1688]

North Carolina Constitution, December 18, 1776:

[Declaration of Rights, Article 10:] That *excessive bail* should not be required, nor excessive fines imposed, nor cruel or unusual punishments inflicted. [Thorpe 2788]

Georgia Constitution, February 5, 1777:

[Article 59:] Excessive fines shall not be levied, nor *excessive bail* demanded. [Thorpe 785]

Vermont Constitution, July 8, 1777:

[Frame of Government, Section 26:] Excessive bail shall not be exacted for bailable offences: and all fines shall be moderate. [Thorpe 3746]

Massachusetts Constitution, March 2, 1780:

[Declaration of Rights, Article 26:] No magistrate or court of law shall demand *excessive bail* or sureties, impose excessive fines, or inflict cruel or unusual punishments. [Thorpe 1892]

[Frame of Government, Chapter I:3:10:] And no member of the house of representatives shall be arrested, or held to *bail* on mean [mesne] process, during his going unto, returning from, or his attending the general assembly. [Thorpe 1899]

New Hampshire Constitution, June 2, 1784:

[Bill of Rights, Article 33:] No magistrate or court of law shall demand *excessive bail* or sureties, impose excessive fines, or inflict cruel or unusual punishments. [Thorpe 2457]

[Frame of Government:] No member of the house of representatives or senate, shall be arrested or held to *bail* on mean [mesne] process, during his going to, returning from, or attendance upon the court. [Thorpe 2462]

Vermont Constitution, July 4, 1786:

[Frame of Government, Section 30:] . . . And all prisoners, unless in execution, or committed for capital offences, when the proof is evident or presumption great, shall be bailable by sufficient sureties: nor shall *excessive bail* be exacted for bailable offences. [Thorpe 2759]

Richard Henry Lee, Proposed Amendments to the Constitution, October 16, 1787:

. . . That the right administration of justice should be secured by the independency of the judges; That *excessive bail*, excessive fines, or cruel and unusual punishments, should not be demanded or inflicted . . . [DHRC8 65]

Dissent of the Pennsylvania Convention's Minority, December 18, 1787:

That *excessive bail* ought not to be required, nor excessive fines imposed, nor cruel nor unusual punishments inflicted. [DHRC2 623]

Alexander White, "To the Citizens of Virginia," February 29, 1788:

. . . The writ of habeas corpus gives a decided superiority to the State courts in all cases where personal liberty is concerned, by refering to their judgment, the legality of all imprisonments, incident to which is the right of determining the amount of *bail* to be required, where the commitment is judged lawful . . . [DHRC8 442]

"The Impartial Examiner," No. 1, March 5, 1788:

. . . can it be said that they have exceeded the limits of their jurisdiction, when that has no limits; when no provision has been made for such a right?—When no responsibility on the part of Congress has been required by the constitution? The same observation may be made on any arbitrary or capricious imprisonments contrary to the law of the land. The same may be made, if *excessive bail* should be required; if excessive fines should be imposed; if cruel and unusual punishments should be inflicted; if the liberty of the press should be restrained; in a word—if laws should be made totally derogatory to the whole catalogue of rights, which are now secure under your present form of government. [DHRC8 462]

"George Bryan," March 26, 1788:

. . . Nothing being done however, in this way, about 26th of February the sheriff was set to work. Eight or nine refusing to give *bail,* they were imprisoned. By

the last accounts from Harrisburg, large numbers were assembled, from York and Dauphin, as well as Cumberland, to set the prisoners at large . . .
[DHRC16 489]

United States Congress, Judiciary Act of September 24, 1789:

[Section 33:] . . . That for any crime or offence against the United States, the offender may, by any justice or judge of the United States, or by any justice of the peace, or other magistrate of any of the United States where he may be found agreeably to the usual mode or process against offenders in such state, and at the expense of the United States, be arrested, and imprisoned or *bailed,* as the case may be, for trial before such court of the United States as by this act has cognizance of the offence. . . . [USSL1 91]

[*Ibid.:*] . . . And if a person committed by a justice of the supreme or a judge of a district court for an offence not punishable with death, shall afterwards procure *bail,* and there be no judge of the United States in the district to take the same, if may be taken by any judge of the supreme or superior court of law of such state. [USSL1 91–92]

South Carolina Constitution, June 30, 1790:

[Article 9, Section 4:] Excessive bail shall not be required, nor excessive fines imposed, nor cruel punishments inflicted. [Thorpe 3264]

Pennsylvania Constitution, September 2, 1790:

[Article 9, Section 13:] That *excessive bail* shall not be required, nor excessive fines imposed, nor cruel punishments inflicted. [Thorpe 3101]

BILL, BILLS

(Legislative)

United States Constitution, September 17, 1787:

[Article I, Section 7:] All *Bills* for raising Revenue shall originate in the House of Representatives; but the Senate may propose or concur with Amendments as on other *Bills*.

[Article I, Section 7:] Every *Bill* which shall have passed the House of Representatives and the Senate, shall, before it become a Law, be presented to the President of the United States; If he approve he shall sign it, but if not he shall return it, with his Objections to that House in which it shall have originated, who shall enter the Objections at large on their Journal, and proceed to reconsider it. If after such Reconsideration two thirds of that House shall agree to pass the *Bill,* it shall be sent, together with the Objections, to the other House, by which it shall likewise be reconsidered, and if approved by two thirds of that House, it shall become a Law. But in all such Cases the Votes of both Houses shall be determined by yeas and Nays, and the Names of the Persons voting for and against the *Bill* shall be entered on the Journal of each House respectively. If any *Bill* shall not be returned by the President within ten Days (Sundays excepted) after it shall have been presented to him, the Same shall be a Law, in like Manner as if he had signed it, unless the Congress by their Adjournment prevent its Return, in which Case it shall not be a Law.

[Article I, Section 7:] Every Order, Resolution, or Vote to which the Concurrence of the Senate and House of Representatives may be necessary (except on a question of Adjournment) shall be presented to the President of the United States; and before the Same shall take Effect, shall be approved by him, or being disapproved by him, shall be repassed by two thirds of the Senate and House of Representatives, according to the Rules and Limitations prescribed in the Case of a *Bill*.

[Article I, Section 9:] No *Bill* of Attainder or ex post facto Law shall be passed.

[Article I, Section 10:] No State shall enter into any Treaty, Alliance, or Confederation; grant Letters of Marque and Reprisal; coin Money; emit *Bills* of Credit; make any Thing but gold and silver Coin a Tender in Payment of Debts; pass any *Bill* of Attainder, ex post facto Law, or Law impairing the Obligation of Contracts, or grant any Title of Nobility.

* * * * *

The New England Confederation, May 19, 1643:

[Article 10:] That in extraordinary occasions, when meetings are summoned by three magistrates of any Jurisdiction, or two as in the fifth article, if any of the Commissioners come not, due warning being given or sent, it is agreed that four of the Commissioners shall have power to direct a war which cannot be delayed, and to send for due proportions of men out of each Jurisdiction, as well as six might do if all met; but not less than six shall determine the justice of the war, or allow the demands or *bills* of charges, or cause any levies to be made for the same. [Thorpe 81]

Pennsylvania Frame of Government, April 25, 1682:

[Article 5:] That the provincial Council, in all cases and matters of moment, as their arguing upon *bills* to be passed into laws, erecting courts of justice, giving judgment upon criminals impeached, and choice of officers, in such manner as is hereinafter mentioned, not less than two-thirds of the whole provincial Council shall make a quorum, and that the consent and approbation of two-thirds of such quorum shall be had in all such cases and matters of moment . . .

[Thorpe 3056]

[Article 7:] That the Governor and provincial Council shall prepare and propose to the General Assembly, hereafter mentioned, all *bills,* which they shall, at any time, think fit to be passed in to laws, within the said province; which *bills* shall be published and affixed to the most noted places, in the inhabited parts thereof, thirty days before the meeting of the General Assembly, in order to the passing them into laws or rejecting of them as the General Assembly shall see meet.

[Thorpe 3056]

[Article 14:] And, to the end that all laws prepared by the Governor and provincial Council aforesaid, may yet have the more full concurrence of the freemen of the province, it is declared, granted and confirmed, that, at the time and place or places, for the choice of a provincial Council, as aforesaid, the said freemen shall yearly chuse Members to serve in a General Assembly, as their representatives, not exceeding two hundred persons, who shall yearly meet on the twentieth day of the second month, which shall be in the year one thousand six hundred eighty and three following, in the capital town, or city, of the said province, where, during eight days, the several Members may freely confer with one another; and, if any of them see meet, with a committee of the provincial

Council (consisting of three out of each of the four committees aforesaid, being twelve in all) which shall be, at that time, purposely appointed to receive from any of them proposals, for the alterations or amendment of any of the said proposed and promulgated *bills:* and on the ninth day from their so meeting, the said General Assembly, after reading over the proposed *bills* by the Clerk of the provincial Council, and the occasions and motives for them being opened by the Governor or his Deputy, shall give their affirmative or negative, which to them seemeth best, in such manner as hereinafter is expressed. . . .

[Thorpe 3057]

[Article 19:] That the General Assembly shall continue so long as may be needful to impeach criminals, fit to be there impeached, to pass *bills* into laws, that they shall think fit to pass into laws, and till such time as the Governor and provincial Council shall declare that they have nothing further to propose unto them, for their assent and approbation . . . [Thorpe 3058]

[Article 20:] That all the elections of members, or representatives of the people, to serve in provincial Council and General Assembly, and all questions to be determined by both, or either of them, that relate to passing of *bills* into laws, to the choice of officers, to impeachments by the General Assembly, and judgment of criminals upon such impeachment by the provincial Council, and to all other cases by them respectively judged of importance, shall be resolved and determined by the ballot . . . [Thorpe 3059]

Pennsylvania Frame of Government, Laws Agreed Upon in England, May 5, 1682:

[Article 20:] And, to prevent frauds and vexatious suits within the said province, that all charters, gifts, grants and conveyances of and (except leases for a year or under) and all *bills,* bonds, and specialties above five months, and not under three months, made in the said province, shall be enrolled, or registered in the public enrolment office of the said province, within the space of two months next after the making thereof, else to be void in law . . . [Thorpe 3061]

[Article 21:] That all defacers or corrupters of charters, gifts, grants, bonds, *bills,* wills, contracts, and conveyances, or that shall deface or falsify any enrolment, registry or record, within this province, shall make double satisfaction for the same; half whereof shall go to the party wronged, and they shall be dismissed of all places of trust, and be publicly disgraced as false men.

[Thorpe 3061]

Pennsylvania Frame of Government, April 2, 1683:

[Article 4:] That the provincial Council in all cases and matters of moment, as their arguing [agreeing] upon *bills* to be passed into laws, or proceedings about erecting of courts of justice, sitting in judgment upon criminals impeached, and choice of officers, in such manner as is herein after expressed, not less than two-thirds of the whole shall make a quorum; and that the consent and approbation of two-thirds of that quorum shall be had in all such cases, or matters, of moment. . . . [Thorpe 3065]

[Article 5:] That the Governor and provincial Council shall have the power of preparing and proposing to the Assembly, hereafter mentioned, all *bills,* which they shall see needful, and that shall, at any time, be past into laws, within the said province and territories thereof, which *bills* shall be published and affixed to the most noted places, in every county of this province and territories thereof, twenty days before the meeting of the Assembly, in order to passing them into laws. [Thorpe 3065]

[Article 13:] And to the end that all *bills* prepared and agreed by the Governor and provincial Council, as aforesaid, may yet have the more full concurrence of the freemen of the province and territories thereof, it is declared, granted and confirmed, that, at the time and place in every country for the choice of one person to serve in provincial Council, as aforesaid, the respective Members thereof, at their said meeting, shall yearly chuse out of themselves six persons of most note, for virtue, wisdom and ability, to serve in Assembly, as their representatives, who shall yearly meet on the tenth day of the third month, in the capital town or city of the said province, unless the Governor and provincial Council shall think fit to appoint another place to meet in, where, during eight days, the several Members may confer freely with one another; and if any of them see meet, with a committee of the provincial Council, which shall be, at that time, purposely appointed, to receive from any of them proposals for the alterations, or amendments, of any of the said proposed and promulgated *bills;* and on the ninth day from their so meeting, the said Assembly, after their reading over the proposed *bills,* by the Clerk of the provincial Council, and the occasions and motives for them being opened by the Governor or his Deputy, shall, upon the question by him put, give their affirmative or negative, which to them seemeth best, in such manner as is hereafter expressed: but not less than two-thirds shall make a quorum in the passing of all *bills* into laws, and choice of such officers as are by them to be chosen. [Thorpe 3066]

[Article 17:] That the Assembly shall continue so long as may be needful to impeach criminals, fit to be there impeached, to pass such *bills* into laws as are proposed to them, which they shall think fit to pass into laws, and till such time as the Governor and provincial Council shall declare, that they have nothing further to propose unto them, for their assent and approbation, and that declaration shall be a dismiss to the assembly, for that time . . . [Thorpe 3067]

[Article 18:] That all the elections of members, of representatives of the people to serve in provincial Council and Assembly, and all questions to be determined by both or either of them, that relate to choice of officers, and all other personal matters, shall be resolved or determined by the ballot, and all things relating to the preparing and passing of *bills* into laws, shall be openly declared and resolved by the vote. [Thorpe 3067]

Fundamental Constitutions of East New Jersey, 1683:

[Article 4:] It shall be the priviledge of every member of the great Council, to propose any *bill* in order to a law, which being admitted to be debated, shall be determined by the vote, wherein two parts of three shall only conclude; but of this twelve of the Proprietors, or their proxies, must be assenting; which shall also be requisite after the number of freemen are double . . . [Thorpe 2575]

[Article 14:] In all civil and ordinary actions, the Proprietors shall be judged after the same manner, and lyable to the same censure with any other; but in all cases that are capital, or may inferr for forfeiture of their trust or Proprietorship, they shall be adjudged by a jury of twelve of the Proprietors, or their proxies, or such as has share in a propriety not under one twentieth part; the *bill* being first found relevant against them by a grand jury of twelve Proprietors and twelve free men to be chosen by the ballot, as in article nineteen. [Thorpe 2579]

English Bill of Rights, December 16, 1689:

[Article 12:] And be it further declared and enacted by the authority aforesaid, That from and after this present session of parliament no dispensation by non obstante of or to any statute or any part thereof shall be allowed, but that the same shall be held void and of no effect, except a dispensation be allowed of in such statute, and except in such cases as shall be specially provided for by one or more *bill or bills* to be passed during this present session of Parliament. [SDECH 469]

Pennsylvania Frame of Government, November 7, 1696:

[1] And be it further enacted by the authority aforesaid, That the Council, in all cases and matters of moment, as about erecting courts of justice, sitting in judgment upon persons impeached, and upon *bills* and other matters, that may be, from time to time, presented by the Assembly, not less than two-thirds shall make a quorum; and that the consent and approbation of the majority of that quorum shall be had in all such cases and matters of moment . . .
[Thorpe 3074]

[2] And be it further enacted by the authority aforesaid, That the representatives of the freemen, when met in Assembly, shall have power to prepare and propose to the Governor and Council all such *bills* as they or the major part of them, shall, at any time, see needful to be passed into laws, within the said province and territories. [Thorpe 3075]

[3] Provided always, That nothing herein contained shall debar the Governor and Council from recommending to the Assembly all such *bills* as they shall think fit to be passed into laws; and that the Council and Assembly may, upon occasion, confer together in committees, when desired; all which proposed and prepared *bills,* or such of them, as the Governor, with the advice of the Council,

shall, in open Assembly, declare his assent unto, shall be the laws of this province and territories thereof . . . [Thorpe 3075]

[4] And be it further enacted by the authority aforesaid, That the Assembly, shall sit upon their own adjournments, and committees, and continue, in order to prepare and propose *bills,* redress grievances, and impeach criminals, or such persons as they shall think fit to be there impeached, until the Governor and Council, for the time being, shall dismiss them . . . [Thorpe 3075]

William Penn, Charter of Privileges for Pennsylvania, October 28, 1701:

. . . Which Assembly shall have Power to chuse a Speaker and other their Officers; and shall be Judges of the Qualifications and Elections of their own Members; sit upon their own Adjournments; appoint Committees; prepare *Bills* in order to pass into Laws; impeach Criminals, and redress Grievances; and shall have all other Powers and Privileges of an Assembly, according to the Rights of the free-born Subjects of England, and as is usual in any of the King's Plantations in America. [Thorpe 3078]

William Penn, Charter of Delaware, October 28, 1701:

[Article 2:] . . . Which Assembly shall have Power to chuse a Speaker and other their Officers; and shall be Judges of the Qualifications and Elections of their own Members; sit upon their own Adjournments; appoint Committees; prepare *Bills* in order to pass into Laws; impeach Criminals, and redress Grievances; and shall have all other powers and Privileges of an Assembly, according to the Rights of the free-born Subjects of England, and as is usual in any of the King's Plantations in America. [Thorpe 559]

New Hampshire Constitution, January 5, 1776:

That all *bills,* resolves, or votes for raising, levying and collecting money originate in the house of Representatives. [Thorpe 2452]

Thomas Paine, *Common Sense*, January 9, 1776:

[1] But as the same constitution which gives the Commons a power to check the king by withholding the supplies, gives afterwards the king a power to check the Commons, by empowering him to reject their other *bills;* it again supposes that the king is wiser than those whom it has already supposed to be wiser than him. A mere absurdity! [CWTP1 7]

[2] . . . The king's negative here is ten times more dangerous and fatal than it can be in England; for there he will scarcely refuse his consent to a *bill* for putting England into as strong a state of defence as possible, and in America he would never suffer such a *bill* to be passed. [CWTP1 26]

South Carolina Constitution, March 26, 1776:

[Article 7:] That the legislative authority be vested in the president and commander-in-chief, the general assembly and legislative council. All *money-bills* for the support of government shall originate in the general assembly, and shall not be altered or amended by the legislative council, but may be rejected by them. All other *bills* and ordinances may take rise in the general assembly or legislative council, and may be altered, amended, or rejected by either. *Bills* having passed the general assembly and legislative council may be assented to or rejected by the president and commander-in-chief. Having received his assent, they shall have all the force and validity of an act of general assembly of this colony. . . . [Thorpe 3244]

[Article 8:] That the general assembly and legislative council may adjourn themselves respectively, and the president and commander-in-chief shall have no power to adjourn, prorogue, or dissolve them, but may, if necessary, call them before the time to which they shall stand adjourned. And where a *bill* has been rejected, it may, on a meeting after adjournment of not less than three days of the general assembly and legislative council, be brought in again.
[Thorpe 3244]

New Jersey Constitution, July 2, 1776:

[Article 5:] That the Assembly, when met, shall have power to choose a Speaker, and other their officers; to be judges of the qualifications and elections of their own members; sit upon their own adjournments; prepare *bills,* to be passed into laws; and to empower their Speaker to convene them, whenever any extraordinary occurrence shall render it necessary. [Thorpe 2595–96]

[Article 6:] That the Council shall also have power to prepare *bills* to pass into laws, and have other like powers as the Assembly, and in all respects be a free and independent branch of the Legislature of this Colony; save only, that they shall not prepare or alter any *money bill*—which shall be the privilege of the Assembly; that the Council shall, from time to time, be convened by the Governor or Vice-President, but must be convened, at all times, when the Assembly sits; for which purpose the Speaker of the House of Assembly shall always, immediately after an adjournment, give notice to the Governor, or Vice-President, of the time and place to which the House is adjourned. [Thorpe 2596]

Delaware Constitution, September 10, 1776:

[Article 6:] All *money-bills* for the support of government shall originate in the house of assembly, and may be altered, amended, or rejected by the legislative council. All other *bills* and ordinances may take rise in the house of assembly or legislative council, and may be altered, amended, or rejected by either.
[Thorpe 563]

Pennsylvania Constitution, September 28, 1776

[Frame of Government, Section 9:] The members of the house of representatives shall be chosen annually by ballot, by the freemen of the commonwealth, on the second Tuesday in October forever, (except this present year,) and shall meet on the fourth Monday of the same month, and shall be stiled, The general assembly of the representatives of the freemen of Pennsylvania, and shall have power to choose their speaker, the treasurer of the state, and their other officers; sit on their own adjournments; prepare *bills* and enact them into laws . . .
[Thorpe 3084–85]

[*Ibid.*, Section 10:] I — do swear (or affirm) that as a member of this assembly, I will not propose or assent to any *bill,* vote, or resolution, which shall appear to me injurious to the people; nor do or consent to any act or thing whatever, that shall have a tendency to lessen or abridge their rights and privileges, as declared in the constitution of this state; but will in all things conduct myself as a faithful honest representative and guardian of the people, according to the best of my judgment and abilities. [Thorpe 3085]

[*Ibid.*, Section 15:] To the end that laws before they are enacted may be more maturely considered, and the inconvenience of hasty determinations as much as possible prevented, all *bills* of public nature shall be printed for the consideration of the people, before they are read in general assembly the last time for debate and amendment; and, except on occasions of sudden necessity, shall not be passed into laws until the next session of assembly; and for the more perfect satisfaction of the public, the reasons and motives for making such laws shall be fully and clearly expressed in the preambles. [Thorpe 3086]

[*Ibid.*, Section 16:] The stile of the laws of this commonwealth shall be, "Be it enacted, and it is hereby enacted by the representatives of the freemen of the commonwealth of Pennsylvania in general assembly met, and by the authority of the same." And the general assembly shall affix their seal to every *bill,* as soon as it is enacted into a law, which seal shall be kept by the assembly, and shall be called, The seal of the laws of Pennsylvania, and shall not be used for any other purpose. [Thorpe 3086]

Maryland Constitution, November 11, 1776:

[Form of Government, Article 10:] That the house of delegates may originate all *money bills,* propose *bills* to the senate, or receive those offered by that body, and assent, dissent, or propose amendments; that they may inquire, on the oath of witnesses, into all complaints, grievances, and offenses, as the grand inquest of this state, and may commit any person, for any crime, to the public jail, there to remain till he be discharged by due course of law. . . . [Thorpe 1692]

[*Ibid.*, Article 11:] That the senate may be at full and perfect liberty to exercise their judgment in passing laws- and that they may not be compelled by the house of delegates, either to reject a *money bill,* which the emergency of affairs may require, or to assent to some other act of legislation, in their conscience and judgment injurious to the public welfare—the house of delegates shall not, on any occasion, or under any pretence, annex to, or blend with, a *money bill,* any matter, clause, or thing not immediately relating to, and necessary for the imposing, assessing, levying, or applying the taxes or supplies to be raised for the support of government, or the current expenses of the state; and to prevent altercation about such *bills,* it is declared, that no *bill* imposing duties or customs for the mere regulation of commerce, or inflicting fines for the reformation of morals, or to enforce the execution of the laws, by which an incidental revenue may arise, shall be accounted a *money bill;* but every *bill* assessing, levying, or applying taxes or supplies for the support of government or the current expenses of the state, or appropriating money in the treasury, shall be deemed a *money bill.* [Thorpe 1692–93]

[*Ibid.,* Article 22:] That the senate may originate any other, except *money bills* to which their assent or dissent only shall be given: and may receive any other *bills* from the house of delegates, and assent, dissent, or propose amendments. [Thorpe 1694–95]

[*Ibid.,* Article 59:] That this Form of Government, and the Declaration of Rights, and no part thereof, shall be altered, changed, or abolished, unless a *bill* so to alter change or abolish the same shall pass the General Assembly, and be published at least three months before a new election, and shall be confirmed by the General Assembly, after a new election of Delegates, in the first session after such new election . . . [Thorpe 1701]

[*Ibid.,* Article 60:] That every *bill* passed by the General Assembly, when engrossed, shall be presented by the Speaker of the House of Delegates, in the Senate, to the Governor for the time being, who shall sign the same, and thereto affix the Great Seal, in the presence of the members of both Houses . . . [Thorpe 1701]

North Carolina Constitution, December 18, 1776:

[Form of Government, Article 10:] That the Senate and House of Commons, when met, shall each have power to choose a speaker, and other their officers; be judges of the qualifications and elections of their members; sit upon their own adjournments from day to day; and prepare *bills,* to be passed into laws. The two Houses shall direct writs of election for supplying intermediate vacancies; and shall also jointly, by ballot, adjourn themselves to any future day and place. [Thorpe 2790–91]

[*Ibid.,* Article 11:] That all *bills* shall be read three times in each House, before they pass into laws, and be signed by the Speakers of both Houses. [Thorpe 2791]

Georgia Constitution, February 5, 1777:

[Article 35:] Every county in this State that has, or hereafter may have, two hundred and fifty men, and upwards, liable to bear arms, shall be formed into a battalion; and when they become too numerous for one battalion, they shall be formed into more, by *bill* of the legislature; and those counties that have a less number than two hundred and fifty shall be formed into independent companies. [Thorpe 782]

[Article 45:] No grand jury shall consist of less than eighteen, and twelve may find a *bill*. [Thorpe 784]

New York Constitution, April 20, 1777:

[Article 3:] And whereas laws inconsistent with the spirit of this constitution, or with the public good, may be hastily and unadvisedly passed: Be it ordained, that the governor for the time being, the chancellor, and the judges of the supreme court, or any two of them, together with the governor, shall be, and hereby are, constituted a council to revise all *bills* about to be passed into laws by the legislature; and for that purpose shall assemble themselves from time to time, when the legislature shall be convened; for which, nevertheless, they shall not receive any salary or consideration, under any pretence whatever. And that all *bills* which have passed the senate and assembly shall, before they become laws, be presented to the said council for their revisal and consideration; and if, upon such revision and consideration, it should appear improper to the said council, or a majority of them, that the said *bill* should become a law of this State, that they return the same, together with their objections thereto in writing, to the senate or house of assembly (in which soever the same shall have originated) who shall enter the objection sent down by the council at large in their minutes, and proceed to reconsider the said *bill*. But if, after such reconsideration, two-thirds of the said senate or house of assembly shall, notwithstanding the said objections, agree to pass the same, it shall, together with the objections, be sent to the other branch of the legislature, where it shall also be reconsidered, and, if approved by two-thirds of the members present, shall be a law.

And in order to prevent any unnecessary delays, be it further ordained, that if any *bill* shall not be returned by the council within ten days after it shall have been presented, the same shall be a law, unless the legislature shall, by their adjournment, render a return of the said *bill* within ten days impracticable; in which case the *bill* shall be returned on the first day of the meeting of the legislature after the expiration of the said ten days. [Thorpe 2628–29]

Vermont Constitution, July 8, 1777:

[Frame of Government, Section 8:] The members of the House of Representatives, shall be chosen annually . . . and shall have power to choose their Speaker,

Secretary of the State, their Clerk, and other necessary officers of the house—sit on their own adjournments—prepare *bills* and enact them into laws . . . [Thorpe 3742]

[*Ibid.*, Section 9:] I ——— do solemnly swear, by the ever living God, (or, I do solemnly affirm in the presence of Almighty God) that as a member of this assembly, I will not propose or assent to any *bill*, vote, or resolution, which shall appear to me injurious to the people . . . [Thorpe 3743]

[*Ibid.*, Section 14:] To the end that laws, before they are enacted, may be more maturely considered, and the inconveniency of hasty determination as much as possible prevented, all *bills* of public nature, shall be first laid before the Governor and Council, for their perusal and proposals of amendment, and shall be printed for the consideration of the people, before they are read in General Assembly, for the last time of debate and amendment . . . [Thorpe 3744]

South Carolina Constitution, March 19, 1778:

[Article 16:] That all *money bills* for the support of government shall originate in the house of representatives, and shall not be altered or amended by the senate, but may be rejected by them, and that no money be drawn out of the public treasury but by the legislative authority of the State. All other *bills* and ordinances may take rise in the senate or house of representatives, and be altered, amended, or rejected by either. . . . [Thorpe 3252]

[Article 17:] . . . And where a *bill* hath been rejected by either house, it shall not be brought in again that session, without leave of the house, and a notice of six days being previously given. [Thorpe 3253]

Massachusetts Constitution, March 2, 1780:

[Frame of Government, Chapter I:1:2:] No *bill* or resolve of the senate or house of representatives shall become a law, and have force as such, until it shall have been laid before the governor for his revisal; and if he, upon such revision, approve thereof, he shall signify his approbation by signing the same. But if he have any objection to the passing of such *bill* or resolve, he shall return the same, together with his objections thereto, in writing, to the senate or house of representatives, in whichsoever the same shall have originated; who shall enter the objections sent down by the governor, at large, on their records, and proceed to reconsider the said *bill* or resolve. But if after such reconsideration, two-thirds of the said senate or house of representatives, shall, notwithstanding the said objections, agree to pass the same, it shall, together with the objections, be sent to the other branch of the legislature, where it shall also be reconsidered, and if approved by two-thirds of the members present, shall have the force of law: but in all such cases, the votes of both houses shall be determined by yeas and

nays; and the names of the persons voting for, or against, the said *bill* or resolve, shall be entered upon the public records of the commonwealth.
[Thorpe 1893–94]

[*Ibid.*, Chapter I:1:2:] And in order to prevent unnecessary delays, if any *bill* or resolve shall not be returned by the governor within five days after it shall have been presented, the same shall have the force of a law. [Thorpe 1894]

[*Ibid.*, Chapter I:3:7:] All *money bills* shall originate in the house of representatives; but the senate may propose or concur with amendments, as on other *bills*. [Thorpe 1899]

New Hampshire Constitution, June 2, 1784:

[Form of Government:] All *money bills* shall originate in the house of representatives, but the senate may propose or concur with amendments as on other *bills*. [Thorpe 2462]

Vermont Constitution, July 4, 1786:

[Frame of Government, Section 9:] The representatives, so chosen, (a majority of whom shall constitute a quorum for transacting any other business than raising a State tax, for which two thirds of the members elected shall be present) shall meet on the second Thursday of the succeeding October and shall be styled, The General Assembly of the State of Vermont: they shall have power to choose their Speaker, Secretary of the State, their Clerk and other necessary officers of the house—-sit on their own adjournments—prepare, *bills*, and enact them into laws—judge of the elections and qualifications of their own members . . .
[Thorpe 3755]

[*Ibid.*, Section 12:] You — do solemnly swear, (or affirm) that, as a member of this Assembly, you will not propose or assent to any *bill*, vote or resolution, which shall appear to you injurious to the people . . . [Thorpe 3757]

Charles Pinckney's Plan of Union, May 29, 1787:

[Article 10:] Each State retains its Rights not expressly delegated—But no *Bill* of the Legislature of any State shall become a Law till it shall have been laid before S[enate] and H[ouse of] D[elegates] in C[ongress] assembled and received their Approbation. [DHRC1 246]

United States Confederation Congress, The Northwest Ordinance, July 13, 1787:

. . . And the governor, legislative council, and house of representatives shall have authority to make laws in all cases for the good government of the district, not repugnant to the principles and articles in this ordinance established and declared.

And all *bills,* having passed by a majority in the house, and by a majority in the council, shall be referred to the governor for his assent; but no *bill,* or legislative act whatever, shall be of any force without his assent. The governor shall have power to convene, prorogue, and dissolve the general assembly when, in his opinion, it shall be expedient. [Thorpe 960]

Tench Coxe, *An Examination of the Constitution for the United States of America*, No. 1, September 26, 1787:

. . . They [the members of the House of Representatives] are not to be restrained from the firm and plain language, which becomes the independent representatives of freedom, for there is to be a perfect liberty of speech. Without their consent, no monies can be obtained, no armies raised, no navies provided. They, alone, can originate *bills* for drawing forth the revenues of the union, and they will have a negative upon every legislative act of the other house.—So far, in short, as the sphere of foederal jurisdiction extends, they will be controulable only by the people, and, in contentions with the other branch, so far as they shall be right, they must ever finally prevail. [Ford 144–45]

Richard Henry Lee [?], "The Federal Farmer," No. 4, October 12, 1787:

. . . It is here wisely stipulated, that the federal legislature shall never pass a *bill of attainder,* or expost facto law; that no tax shall be laid on articles exported, &c. The establishing of one right implies the necessity of establishing another and similar one. [Ford 314]

Noah Webster, *An Examination into the Leading Principles of the Federal Constitution*, October 17, 1787:

[1] I cannot help remarking the singular jealousy of the constitution of Pennsylvania, which requires that a *bill* shall be published for the consideration of the people, before it is enacted into a law, except in extraordinary cases. This annihilates the legislature, and reduces it to an advisory body. It almost wholly supersedes the uses of representation, the most excellent improvement in modern governments. . . . [Ford 34n]

[2] Every *bill* that passes a majority of both houses of Congress, must be sent to the president for his approbation; but it must be returned in ten days, whether approved by him or not; and the concurrence of two thirds of both houses passes the *bill* into a law, notwithstanding any objections of the president. The constitution therefore gives the supreme executive a check but no negative, upon the sense of Congress. [Ford 45]

Tench Coxe, *An Examination of the Constitution for the United States of America*, No. 4, October 21, 1787:

. . . The old foederal constitution contained many of the same things, which from error or disingenousness are urged against the new ones. Neither of them have a *bill of rights,* nor does either notice the liberty of the press, because they are already provided for by the state constitutions; and relating only to personal rights, they could not be mentioned in a contract among foreign states.

[Ford 148]

Virginia House of Representatives, Proceedings, December 4, 1787:

Mr. Henry presented according to order, a *bill* Concerning the convention to be held in June next, and the same was received and read the first time, and ordered to [be] read a second time.

On a motion made, a *bill* Concerning the convention to be held in June next, was read the second time, and ordered to be committed to a committee of the whole House on Friday next. [DHRC8 186]

"Americanus," No. 1, December 5, 1787:

What are then the mighty powers which he [the President] possesses distinct and separate from the senate? He shall have a negative upon all *bills*. But, if two thirds of each house, upon reconsideration, should agree to the *bill,* it shall become a law, and the president's negative will be no impediment . . .

[DHRC8 203]

Tobias Lear, "Brutus," December 6, 1787:

The 7th section of the first article in the proposed constitution says, "All *bills* for raising revenue shall originate in the House of Representatives; but the Senate may propose or concur with amendments as on other *bills*." This is putting a power into the hands of the Senate with more safety than can generally be done—it is giving them the power of doing good, almost without the possibility of doing harm; for it would be folly to suppose that the House of Representatives, or any other body of men, could form a *bill* so completely perfect in all its parts as to admit of no amendment. A *revenue bill* will now have a double chance of attaining to perfection. The House of Representatives will discuss, form and send it up—the Senate will have it in their power to deliberate, debate upon it, and propose amendments, if necessary; but they can go no further, the House of Representatives must concur with their amendments or they have no effect; and this will for ever prevent any pernicious consequences which might result from this part of their power. Indeed I do not conceive that the rights or liberties of the people would have been injured, even if the Senate had been empowered to originate *money-bills,* for our abhorrence of that measure arises wholly, I imagine, from assimulating a Senate to the House of Lords in Great Britain, whereas they are essentially different . . . [DHRC8 214]

Alexander Hamilton, *The Federalist*, No. 22, December 14, 1787:

[1] . . . It is not, therefore, to be wondered at that Mr. Jenkinson, in ushering into the House of Commons a *bill* for regulating the temporary intercourse between the two countries, should preface its introduction by a declaration that similar provisions in former *bills* had been found to answer every purpose to the commerce of Great Britain, and that it would be prudent to persist in the plan until it should appear whether the American government was likely or not to acquire greater consistency. [Ford 191]

"Americanus," No. 2, December 19, 1787:

. . . In all the American governments this native truth "that taxation and representation are inseparable"—has been religiously observed, and perhaps in no one is it more exactly ascertained, than in the Foederal Constitution. The house of representatives, which has the exclusive right of originating *bills of taxation,* is composed of members elected directly by the people in the most exact proportion. The object of this representation is the common defence and general welfare of the United States. The concomitant right of taxation extends no farther. . . . [DHRC8 248]

"An Impartial Citizen," January 10, 1788:

. . . The Executive has not any real share in the Legislation; no absolute negative on the laws, but a power of preventing the passing a law by a bare majority; of pointing out to both Houses the impolicy of their decision, and forcing them to review their *bills,* which cannot after such reconsideration pass, but by the concurrence of two thirds of both Houses; in which case the names of the persons voting for and against are to be entered at large on the journals: A measure highly judicious and politic, tending powerfully to aid the imbecillity of human sagacity, and to exclude entirely the very shadow of corruption: A measure which I may safely venture to affirm, to be the best incident that any government can possibly have, in regulating the connexion that the Executive power ought to have with the Legislature: An infinite advantage over the so much extolled constitution of England, where the Executive can put an absolute negative on the best law, and prevent the Legislative from proceeding on the most necessary and urgent occasion. . . . [DHRC8 295]

"Valerius," January 23, 1788:

. . . The senate has the power of originating all *bills,* except revenue *bills,* in common with the house of representatives, and no *bill* can pass into a law without the approbation of two thirds of both houses. From this exclusion of the senate with respect to *money bills,* it is plain, that this body does not possess such extensive legislative power, as the house of representatives. The president can originate no *bill* of any denomination, and his negative, which, by the bye, is his only legislative power, is of no avail, provided two thirds of both houses concur in the *bill*. Hence, it is clear, that the president does not even possess such extensive legislative power as the house of representatives, and the president as the senate, how can it, justly, be made to appear, that the president and senate have two thirds of the legislative power? [DHRC8 316]

Alexander White [?], "An Independent Freeholder," January 25, 1788:

. . . Why should not the senate have the power of altering *money bills?* Would such an idea have ever existed had not something in the British policy given rise to it? True it is, the British House of Lords are not permitted to amend *money bills*. The Peers of Great Britain are a great hereditary body, possessing immense wealth, composing one branch of the legislature, their honors derived from the crown, and their numbers increased at the will of the Prince, it was therefore necessary that the House of Commons, in order to support their influence, and keep the balance even, should exercise the sole right of taxation. But our senators are not created by a Prince, their honors do not descend to their posterity, they can have no interest distinct from that of the people at large, nor will they enjoy wealth sufficient to enable them to give an undue bias to government. . . . [DHRC8 326]

James Madison, *The Federalist*, No. 44, January 25, 1788:

Bills of attainder, ex post facto laws, and laws impairing the obligation of contracts, are contrary to the first principles of the social compact, and to every principle of sound legislation. The two former are expressly prohibited by the declarations prefixed to some of the State constitutions, and all of them are prohibited by the spirit and scope of these fundamental charters. Our own experience has taught us, nevertheless, that additional fences against these dangers ought not to be omitted. Very properly, therefore, have the convention added this constitutional bulwark in favor of personal security and private rights . . . [Fed. 319]

"Civis Rusticus," January 30, 1788:

[1] The senate have the power of altering all *money bills,* and of originating appropriations of money and the salaries of the officers of their own appointment, in conjunction with the president of the United States; although they are not the representatives of the people, or amenable to them. These, with their other great

power (viz. their power in the appointment of ambassadors and other public officers, in making treaties, and in trying all impeachments) their influence upon and connection with the supreme executive from these causes, their duration of office, and their being a constant existing body almost continually sitting, joined with their being one complete branch of the legislature, will destroy any balance in the government, and enable them to accomplish what usurpations they please upon the rights and liberties of the people. [Thorpe 322]

[2] "The senate have the power of altering *money bills;*" and why not? because the Lords in England, an hereditary aristocracy, have not, of late years, been permitted by the commons to exercise this power, shall the senate, a rotatory body, chosen by the representatives of the people, be deprived of this essential right of legislation? . . . [Thorpe 335]

Alexander C. Hanson, *Remarks on the Proposed Plan of a Federal Government*, c. January 31, 1788:

. . . What then are the powers an individual state will lose? She will no longer be able to deny congress that, which congress, at this moment, has a right to demand. She will have no power to enter into a treaty, alliance, or confederation. She shall, in time of war, grant no letters of marque and reprisal. She shall coin no money, emit no bills of credit, nor make any thing but gold and silver a tender in payment of debts. She shall pass no *bill of attainder,* or ex post facto law, or law impairing the obligation of a contract. . . . [Ford 251]

James Madison, *The Federalist*, No. 48, February 1, 1788:

A great number of laws had been passed, violating, without any apparent necessity, the rule requiring that all *bills* of a public nature shall be previously printed for the consideration of the people; although this is one of the precautions chiefly relied on by the constitution against improper acts of the legislature. [Fed. 346]

William Ward [?], "Republicus," February 16, 1788:

[1] . . . But it may be said that a second house or senate, being generally fewer in number, do, by their separation acquire an influence which would have been lost, had the whole been incorporated in one house. I answer, perhaps it might not have been lost; it would no doubt sometimes so happen, that they, in conjunction with the minority in the other house would be able to set aside some *bills,* which for want of their assistance there, [would] have passed, this would have been a shorter, and easier way; and attended besides, with much less expence of time and excepting in some such instances, all such influence ought to be lost: for in no instance ought the minority to govern the majority. . . . [DHRC8 379]

[2] . . . But the grand argument of all, is that by being separate they [the two houses] have a power of checking some *bills* which would otherwise pass into laws and might be detrimental to society. [DHRC8 380]

[3] Had not this argument been produced on the other side, I should certainly have produced it in favour of one house: however I ask is a minority in one house, properly entitled to over rule a majority in the other? Are they not as likely to check a good *bill* as a bad one? and has it not in fact often happened? Is it not as probable that the second house would lay some of their checks on a good *bill* which perhaps they had little considered as that the first, should pass a bad one, where it had originated and been thoroughly canvassed? But let us turn the argument over and take a view of the other side of it. The inconsistencies that attend the idea of two houses are innumerable. Take one, supposing them both our representatives (tho' it will be hard to prove them so) it makes their constituents to say in many instances by their representatives in one house, "this shall be a law, by their representatives in the other with respect to the same *bill;* "This shall not be a law". It impowers one body of men to enact statutes; and another to forbid their being carried into execution. It resembles a man putting forth his right hand to do some important business and then stretching forth his left hand to prevent it; but supposing them not our representatives at all, they have no business there, and all their mighty power of checking, is a mere farce. [DHRC8 380]

James Madison, *The Federalist*, No. 58, February 20, 1788:

[1] Notwithstanding the equal authority which will subsist between the two houses on all legislative subjects, except the originating of *money bills,* it cannot be doubted that the House, composed of the greater number of members, when supported by the more powerful States, and speaking the known and determined sense of a majority of the people, will have no small advantage in a question depending on the comparative firmness of the two houses. [Fed. 390]

[2] . . . Those who represent the dignity of their country in the eyes of other nations, will be particularly sensible to every prospect of public danger, or of dishonorable stagnation in public affairs. To those causes we are to ascribe the continual triumph of the British House of Commons over the other branches of the government, whenever the engine of a *money bill* has been employed. An absolute inflexibility on the side of the latter, although it could not have failed to involve every department of the state in the general confusion, has neither been apprehended nor experienced. . . . [Fed. 391]

James Iredell, "Marcus," No. 1, February 20, 1788:

[1] . . . [The King of England] . . . has the creation of as many Peers as he pleases, is not restricted from bestowing places on the members of both Houses of

Parliament, and has a direct negative on all *bills,* besides the power of dissolving the Parliament at his pleasure. [DHRC16 166]

[2] . . . The House of Representatives, as immediately representing the people, are to originate all *money bills.* This I think extremely right, and it is certainly a very capital acquisition to the popular Representative. But what harm can arise from the Senate, who are nearly a popular Representative also, proposing amendments when those amendments must be concurred with by the original proposers? . . . [DHRC16 166–67]

"James Bowdoin," February 27, 1788:

. . . And that these laws and the treaties of the little senate should be the supreme law of the land, over the constitutions and laws of the several states. These would have been quite sufficient for us; with them alone we could chain down all America; we might have given up the rest to the winds: the controul over the elections; the command of the militia; the power of the senate to alter *money bills;* the powers of president to pardon criminals, to command in person the armies, navies, and militia, &c. and his long appointment, his right of being re-elected; omission of declarations in favor of liberty of conscience, and twenty others, which have been of great hurt to us, might have been left out. . . .
[DHRC16 240]

William Ward [?], "Republicus," March 1, 1788:

. . . An extraordinary refinement this [the mode of presidential election in the Constitution], on the plain simple business of election; and of which the grand convention have certainly the honour of being the first inventors; and that for an officer too, of so much importance as a president; invested with legislative and executive powers—who is to be commander in chief of the army, navy, militia, &c. grant reprieves and pardons, have a temporary negative on all *bills* and resolves, convene and adjourn both houses of congress, be supreme conservator of laws, commission all officers, make treaties, &c. &c. . . .
[DHRC8 448]

Alexander Hamilton, *The Federalist*, No. 66, March 8, 1788:

But independent of this most active and operative principle, to secure the equilibrium of the national House of Representatives, the plan of the convention has provided in its favor several important counterpoises to the additional authorities to be conferred upon the Senate. The exclusive privilege of originating *money bills* will belong to the House of Representatives. . . . [Fed. 433]

Alexander Hamilton, *The Federalist*, No. 69, March 14, 1788:

[1] The President of the United States is to have power to return a *bill,* which shall have passed the two branches of the legislature, for reconsideration; and

the *bill* so returned is to become a law, if, upon that reconsideration, it be approved by two thirds of both houses. The king of Great Britain, on his part, has an absolute negative upon the acts of the two houses of Parliament. . . .
[Fed. 445]

[2] A writer in a Pennsylvania paper, under the signature of TAMONY, has asserted that the king of Great Britain owes his prerogative as commander-in-chief to an annual mutiny *bill*. The truth is, on the contrary, that his prerogative, in this respect, is immemorial . . . [Fed. 446n]

Alexander Hamilton, *The Federalist*, No. 71, March 18, 1788:

This was the case with respect to Mr. Fox's India *bill*, which was carried in the House of Commons, and rejected in the House of Lords, to the entire satisfaction, as it is said, of the people. [Fed. 462n]

Alexander Hamilton, *The Federalist*, No. 73, March 21, 1788:

The first thing that offers itself to our observation, is the qualified negative of the President upon the acts or resolutions of the two houses of the legislature; or, in other words, his power of returning all *bills* with objections, to have the effect of preventing their becoming laws, unless they should afterwards be ratified by two thirds of each of the component members of the legislative body.
[Fed. 468]

Alexander Hamilton, *The Federalist*, No. 78, May 28, 1788:

The complete independence of the courts of justice is peculiarly essential in a limited Constitution. By a limited Constitution, I understand one which contains certain specified exceptions to the legislative authority; such, for instance, as that it shall pass no *bills of attainder*, no ex post facto laws, and the like. . . .
[Fed. 491]

John Dickinson, "Fabius," No. 2, 1788:

. . . These representatives will also command the public purse, as all *bills* for raising revenue, must originate in their house. [Ford 171]

Georgia Constitution, May 6, 1789:

[Article II, Section 10:] He [the Governor] shall have the revision of all *bills* passed by both houses, before the same shall become laws; but two-thirds of both houses may pass a law, notwithstanding his dissent, and, if any *bill* should not be returned by the governor within five days after it hath been presented to him, the same shall be a law, unless the general assembly, by their adjournment, shall prevent its return. [Thorpe 788]

South Carolina Constitution, June 3, 1790:

[Article I, Section 15:] *Bills* for raising a revenue shall originate in the house of representatives, but may be altered, amended, or rejected by the senate. All other *bills* may originate in either house, and may be amended, altered, or rejected by the other. [Thorpe 3260]

[Article I, Section 16:] No *bill* or ordinance shall have the force of law, until it shall have been read three times, and on three several days, in each house, has had the great seal affixed to it, and has been signed in the senate-house, by the president of the senate and speaker of the house of representatives. [Thorpe 3260–61]

[Article I, Section 20:] No *bill* or ordinance which shall have been rejected by either house shall be brought in again during the sitting, without leave of the house, and notice of six days being previously given. [Thorpe 3261]

[Article IX, Section 2:] No freemen of this State shall be taken, or imprisoned, or disseized of his freehold, liberties, or privileges, or outlawed or exiled, or in any manner destroyed, or deprived of his life, liberty or property, but by the judgment of his peers, or by the law of the land; nor shall any *bill of attainder,* ex post facto law, or law impairing the obligation of contracts, ever be passed by the legislature of this State. [Thorpe 3264]

[Article XI:] No part of this constitution shall be altered, unless a *bill* to alter the same shall have been read three times in the house of representatives, and three times in the senate, and agreed to by two-thirds of both branches of the whole representation; neither shall any alteration take place until the *bill* so agreed to be published three months previous to a new election for members to the house of representatives; and if the alteration proposed by the legislature shall be agreed to in their first session, by two-thirds of the whole representation in both branches of the legislature, after the same shall have been read three times, or three several days, in each house, then, and not otherwise, the same shall become a part of the constitution. [Thorpe 3265]

Pennsylvania Constitution, September 2, 1790:

[Article I, Section 20:] All *bills* for raising revenue shall originate in the house of representatives; but the senate may propose amendments, as in other *bills*. [Thorpe 3094]

[Article I, Section 22:] Every *bill,* which shall have passed both houses, shall be presented to the governor. If he approve, he shall sign it; but if shall not approve, he shall return it, with his objections, to the house in which it shall have originated, who shall enter the objections at large upon their journals, and proceed to reconsider it. If after such reconsideration two-thirds of that house shall agree to pass the *bill,* it shall be sent, with the objections, to the other house, by which likewise it shall be reconsidered; and if approved by two-thirds of that house it shall be a law. But in such cases the votes of both houses shall be determined by yeas and nays, and the names of the persons voting for or against the *bill* shall be entered on the journals of each house respectively. If any *bill* shall not be returned by the governor within ten days (Sundays excepted) after it shall have been presented to him, it shall be a law in like manner as if he had signed it, unless the general assembly, by their adjournment, prevent its return; in which case it shall be a law, unless sent back within three days after their next meeting. [Thorpe 3094–95]

[Article I, Section 23:] Every order, resolution, or vote to which the concurrence of both houses may be necessary (except on a question of adjournment) shall be presented to the governor, and, before it shall take effect, be approved by him, or, being disapproved, shall be repassed by two-thirds of both houses, according to the rules and limitations prescribed in case of a *bill*.
[Thorpe 3095]

BILL OF RIGHTS

Virginia Bill of Rights, June 12, 1776:

BILL OF RIGHTS

A declaration of rights made by the representatives of the good people of Virginia, assembled in full and free convention; which rights do pertain to them, and their posterity, as the basis and foundation of government.

[Thorpe 3812–13]

New Hampshire Constitution, June 2, 1784:

Part I.—The *Bill of Rights*

[Article I:] All men are born equally free and independent; therefore, all government of right originates from the people, is founded in consent, and instituted for the general good. [Thorpe 2453]

[Form of Government:] All the laws which have heretofore been adopted, used and approved, in the province, colony, or state of New Hampshire, and usually practiced on in the courts of law, shall remain and be in full force, until altered and repealed by the legislature; such parts thereof only excepted, as are repugnant to the rights and liberties contained in this constitution: Provided that nothing herein contained, when compared with the twenty-third article in the *bill of rights,* shall be construed to affect the laws already made respecting the persons or estates of absentees. [Thorpe 2469]

[*Ibid.*:] The Returns from the several towns being examined; and it appearing that the foregoing *Bill of Rights* and Form of Government, were approved of by the people; the same are hereby agreed on and established by the Delegates of the People, declared to be the Civil Constitution for the State of New-Hampshire, to take place on the first Wednesday of June, 1784 . . . [Thorpe 2470]

William Pierce to St. George Tucker, September 28, 1787, published in *Gazette of the State of Georgia*, March 20, 1780:

[1] Many objections have been already started to the Constitution because it was not founded on a *Bill of Rights;* but I ask how such a thing could have been effected; I believe it would have been difficult in the extreme to have brought the different states to agree in what probably would have been proposed as the very first principle, and that is, "that all men are born equally free and independent." Would a Virginian have accepted it in this form? Would he not have modified some of the expressions in such a manner as to have injured the strong sense of them, if not to have buried them altogether in ambiguity and uncertainty? [DHRC16 443]

[2] In my judgment, when there are restraints on power to prevent its invading the positive rights of a people, there is no necessity for any such thing as a *Bill of Rights*. I conceive civil liberty is sufficiently guarded when personal security, personal liberty, and private property, are made the peculiar care of government. Now the defined powers of each department of the government, and the restraints that naturally follow, will be sufficient to prevent the invasion of either of those rights. Where then can be the necessity for a *Bill of Rights?* It is with diffidence I start this question; I confess I cannot help doubting the negative quality which it conveys, as some of the greatest men I ever knew have objected to the government for no other reason but because it was not bottomed with a *Bill of Rights;* men whose experience and wisdom are sufficient to give authority and support to almost any opinion they may choose to advance. [DHRC16 443–44]

[3] . . . The absolute rights of Englishmen are founded in nature and reason, and are coeval with the English Constitution itself. They were always understood and insisted on by them as well without as with a *Bill of Rights*. This same spirit was breathed into the Americans, and they still retain it, nor will they, I flatter myself, ever resign it to any power, however plausible it may seem. The *Bill of Rights* was not introduced into England until the Revolution of 1688, (upwards of 600 years after the Conquest) when the Lords and Commons presented it to the Prince and Princess of Orange. And afterwards the same rights were asserted in the Act of Settlement at the commencement of the present century, when the Crown was limited to the House of Hanover. It was deemed necessary to introduce such an instrument to satisfy the public mind in England, not as a bottom to the Constitution, but as a prop to it; and hereafter, if the same necessity should exist in America, it may be done by an act of the Legislature here, so that the Constitution not being founded on a *Bill of Rights* I conceive will not deprive it at any future time of being propt by one, should it become necessary. [DHRC16 444]

James Wilson, Speech on the Federal Constitution, October 6, 1787:

. . . Hence, it is evident, that in the former case, everything which is not reserved, is given: but in the latter, the reverse of the proposition prevails, and every thing which is not given, is reserved. This distinction being recognized, will furnish an answer to those who think the omission of a *bill of rights,* a defect in the proposed constitution: for it would have been superfluous and absurd, to have stipulated with a foederal body of our own creation, that we should enjoy those privileges, of which we are not divested either by the intention or the act that has brought that body into existence. . . . [Ford 156]

Richard Henry Lee [?], "The Federal Farmer," No. 2, October 9, 1787:

But I do not pay much regard to the reasons given for not bottoming the new constitution on a better *bill of rights*. I still believe a complete federal *bill of rights* to be very practicable. . . . [Ford 291]

Richard Henry Lee [?], "The Federal Farmer," No. 4, October 12, 1787:

[1] . . . The state legislatures are obliged to take notice of the *bills of rights* of their respective states. The *bills of rights,* and the state constitutions, are fundamental compacts only between those who govern, and the people of the same state. [Ford 313]

[2] . . . In fact, the 9th and 10th Sections in Art. 1, in the proposed constitution, are no more nor less, than a partial *bill of rights;* they establish certain principles as part of the compact upon which the federal legislators and officers can never infringe. It is here wisely stipulated, that the federal legislature shall never pass a bill of attainder, or expost facto law; that no tax shall be laid on articles exported, &c. The establishing of one right implies the necessity of establishing another and similar one. [Ford 314]

[3] On the whole, the position appears to me to be undeniable, that this *bill of rights* ought to be carried farther, and some other principles established, as a part of this fundamental compact between the people of the United States and their federal rulers. [Ford 315]

Richard Henry Lee [?], "The Federal Farmer," No. 5, October 15, 1787:

Under these impressions, and keeping in view the improper and unadvisable lodgment of powers in the general government, organized as it at present is, touching internal taxes, armies and militia, the elections of its own members, causes between citizens of different states, &c. and the want of a more perfect *bill of rights,* &c. I drop the subject for the present, and when I shall have leisure to revise and correct my ideas respecting it, and to collect into points the opinions of those who wish to make the system more secure and safe, perhaps I may proceed to point out particularly for your consideration, the amendments which ought to be ingrafted into this system, not only in conformity to my own, but the deliberate opinions of others . . . [Ford 324–25]

Richard Henry Lee, Proposed Amendments to the Constitution, October 16, 1787:

It having been found from universal experience, that the most express declarations and reservations are necessary to protect the just rights and liberty of mankind from the silent, powerful and ever active conspiracy of those who govern; and it appearing to be the sense of the good people of America, by the various *bills or declarations of rights* whereon the government of the greater number of states are founded. That such precautions are necessary to restrain and regulate the exercise of the great powers given to rulers. In conformity with these principles, and from respect for the public sentiment on this subject, it is submitted,—That the new constitution proposed for the government of the United States be bottomed upon a declaration or *bill of rights,* clearly and precisely stating the principles upon which this social compact is founded, to wit: That the rights of conscience in matters of religion ought not to be violated—That the freedom of the press shall be secured—That the trial by jury in criminal and civil cases, and the modes prescribed by the common law for the safety of life in criminal prosecutions, shall be held sacred—That standing armies in times of peace are dangerous to liberty, and ought not to be permitted, unless assented to by two-thirds of the members composing each house of the legislature under the new constitution—That the elections should be free and frequent; That the right administration of justice should be secured by the independency of the judges; That excessive bail, excessive fines, or cruel and unusual judges; That excessive bail, excessive fines, or cruel and unusual punishments, should not be demanded or inflicted; That the right of the people to assemble peaceably, for the purpose of petitioning the legislature, shall not be prevented; that the citizens shall not be exposed to unreasonable searches, seizure of their persons, houses, papers or property . . . [DHRC8 65]

Noah Webster, *An Examination into the Leading Principles of the Federal Constitution*, October 17, 1787:

It is alledged that the liberty of the press is not guaranteed by the new constitution. But this objection is wholly unfounded. The liberty of the press does not come within the jurisdiction of federal government. It is firmly established in all the states either by law, or positive declarations in *bills of right;* and not being mentioned in the federal constitution, is not—and cannot be abridged by Congress, it stands on the basis of the respective state-constitutions. . . . [Ford 48]

Tobias Lear, "Brutus," December 6, 1787:

[1] "There is no *bill of rights.*" As the principles contained in a *bill of rights* have ever been considered as the foundation of civil liberty, this, at the head of a long string of objections to a government, certainly makes a very formidable appearance, and would of itself be sufficient to condemn the whole system, if it could not be clearly shewn that it was not only unnecessary, but would even have been absurd to have introduced it in the proposed constitution.

[DHRC8 212]

[2] . . . that part of natural liberty which is given up at the behest of society is fully and completely denied, and whatever is not there expressly granted remains to the people.—Upon this last mentioned principle the proposed constitution was formed; it would therefore have been not only absurd but even dangerous to have inserted a *bill of rights;* because, if, in the enumeration of rights and privileges to be reserved, any had been omitted or forgotten, and the people, at a future period, should assume those so omitted, the rulers might with propriety dispute their right to exercise them, as they were not specified in the *bill of rights;*—and, on the other hand, the people would deny the authority of the rulers to deprive them of the exercise of those rights because they were not expressly given up by them. Thus a *bill of rights,* in the proposed constitution, instead of securing to the people those rights and privileges which God and nature has rendered unalienable, might have been productive of disputes, contentions, and, perhaps, ultimately of ruin to them. This is the light in which the matter was viewed in the convention, and it was there fully discussed. . . .

[DHRC8 212–13]

Dissent of the Pennsylvania Convention's Minority, December 18, 1787:

The first consideration that this review suggests is the omission of a *BILL OF RIGHTS* ascertaining and fundamentally establishing those unalienable and personal rights of men, without the full, free and secure enjoyment of which there can be no liberty, and over which it is not necessary for a good government to have the control—the principal of which are the rights of conscience, personal liberty by the clear and unequivocal establishment of the writ of habeas corpus, jury trial in criminal and civil cases, by an impartial jury of the vicinage or county, with the common law proceedings for the safety of the accused in criminal prosecutions; and the liberty of the press, that scourge of tyrants, and the grand bulwark of every other liberty and privilege. The stipulations heretofore made in favor of them in the state constitutions, are entirely superseded by this Constitution. [DHRC2 630–31]

Alexander Hamilton, *The Federalist*, No. 24, December 19, 1787:

This statement of the matter is taken from the printed collection of State constitutions. Pennsylvania and North Carolina are the two which contain the interdiction in these words: ''As standing armies in time of peace are dangerous to liberty, THEY OUGHT NOT to be kept up.'' This is, in truth, rather a CAUTION than a PROHIBITION. New Hampshire, Massachusetts, Delaware, and Maryland have, in each of their *bills of rights,* a clause to this effect: ''Standing armies are dangerous to liberty, and ought not to be raised or kept up WITHOUT THE CONSENT OF THE LEGISLATURE''; which is a formal admission of authority of the Legislature. New York has no *bills of rights,* and her constitution says not a word about the matter. No *bills of rights* appear annexed to the constitutions of the other States, except the foregoing, and their constitutions are equally silent. I am told, however, that one or two States have *bills of rights* which do not appear in this collection; but that those also recognize the right of the legislative authority in this respect. [Fed. 205n]

Alexander Hamilton, *The Federalist*, No. 25, December 21, 1787:

All violent policy, as it is contrary to the natural and experienced course of human affairs, defeats itself. Pennsylvania, at this instant, affords an example of the truth of this remark. The *Bill of Rights* of that State declares that standing armies are dangerous to liberty, and ought not to be kept up in time of peace. Pennsylvania, nevertheless, in a time of profound peace, from the existence of partial disorders in one or two of her counties, has resolved to raise a body of troops; and in all probability will keep them up as long as there is any appearance of danger to the public peace. [Fed. 212]

Alexander Hamilton, *The Federalist*, No. 26, December 22, 1787:

. . . Even in some of the States, where this error was not adopted, we find unnecessary declarations that standing armies ought not be kept up, in time of peace, WITHOUT THE CONSENT OF THE LEGISLATURE. I call them unnecessary, because the reason which had introduced a similar provision into the English *Bill of Rights* is not applicable to any of the State constitutions. The power of raising armies at all, under those constitutions, can by no construction be deemed to reside anywhere else, than in the legislatures themselves; and it was superfluous, if not absurd, to declare that a matter should not be done without the consent of a body, which alone had the power of doing it . . .

[Fed. 215]

James Madison, *The Federalist*, No. 38, January 12, 1788:

[1] . . . A third does not object to the government over individuals, or to the extent proposed, but to the want of a *bill of rights.* A fourth concurs in the absolute necessity of a *bill of rights,* but contends that it ought to be declaratory, not of the personal rights of individuals, but of the rights reserved to the States in their political capacity. A fifth is of opinion that a *bill of rights* of any sort

would be superfluous and misplaced, and that the plan would be unexceptionable but for the fatal power of regulating the times and places of election. . . .

[Fed. 275]

[2] . . . Is a *bill of rights* essential to liberty? The Confederation has no *bill of rights*. . . . [Fed. 278]

George Nicholas [?], "The State Soldier," No. 1, January 16, 1788:

[1] . . . The want of a *bill of rights,* a charter for the press, and a thousand other things which are now discovered, have been heretofore unnoticed although they existed then in as great a degree as they now do. Whenever any alterations have been made in any of these lesser faults, they have universally been for the better. . . . [DHRC8 305–6]

[2] . . . And thus too respecting a *bill of rights,* and the liberty of the press, it may also be said, the objection has been diminished by the new plan: For what security had we on this head before but that which was in our state constitutions? And of what is the republican form of government which Congress is now to guarantee to each state to consist? Certainly of any thing each state shall think proper that does not take from Congress what this constitution absolutely claims. . . . [DHRC8 306]

Alexander White [?], "An Independent Freeholder, January 18, 1788:

. . . A *Bill of Rights* has a pleasing sound, and in some instances has been deemed necessary, but on occasions very different from the present. When by the abdication of James IId. there was a suspension of Regal Government in England, the two houses of Parliament, accompanied the solemn tender of the Crown, which they made to William and Mary, with a *Bill of Rights,* stating certain acts, which the King, who has the executive powers of government, and is one branch of the legislature, should not do, without the consent of the other two branches the Lords and Commons; but it never entered into the minds of the people of England to declare a *Bill of Rights* restrictive of the powers of the whole legislative body, tho' they have the choice of one branch only, the other two holding their seats by hereditary right, and one of them claiming by divine. At the American Revolution there was not only an end to the power of the crown, but a total dissolution of government; the people were reduced to a state of nature, under these circumstances several of the states conceived it necessary, previous to granting legislative powers, to declare that certain rights were inherent in the people, and to reserve those rights out of the grant. But is America in the situation Great Britain was in at the time of the revolution in that country, or in which she herself was at the time of the revolution in this? Nothing can be more remote; here is neither a total nor partial dissolution of Government; our social compacts and all our ancient rights remain entire, except such as are expressly granted to Congress. And this affords an answer to many objections, such as that religious liberty, the Freedom of the Press, the right of Petitioning the Legislature, &c. &c. &c. are not secured; no power over these matters being granted to Congress, she never can interpose to destroy them. Much more safely may we rest the Constitution on this ground than on a *bill of rights,* in that case all powers would be considered as granted which were not expressly reserved, it would not only be incongruous but dangerous, and might tend to sap the foundation of the whole structure. . . . [DHRC8 310–11]

"Civis Rusticus," January 30, 1788:

There are only five states in the union that have *declarations of rights*—the proposed government is thoroughly popular—the house of representatives are immediately chosen by the people, the senate mediately by their representatives in Assembly, and the president by electors, in such manner as the legislature of the state may direct—at the end of four years, he may, and will be removed from his situation, unless he discharge the duties of it, to the approbation of the people, and to the glory and advantage of America. A government thus constituted stands in need of no *bill of rights;* the liberties of the people never can be lost, until they are lost to themselves, in a vicious disregard of their dearest interests, a sottish indolence, a wild licentiousness, a dissoluteness of morals, and a contempt of all virtue. [DHRC8 335]

[2] "No declaration of the liberty of the press." Our [Virginia's] *Bill of Rights* declares, and it is not repealed, that the freedom of the press is one of the great bulwarks of the liberty of the people, and never can be restrained, but by despotic power. The people of England have no other security for the liberty of the press, than we have—Their own spirit, and an act of parliament—their act of parliament may be repealed—our *Bill of Rights* may be repealed. Of that no man has any fear, of this no man need have, while this spirit is in the people . . .
[DHRC8 337]

Alexander C. Hanson, *Remarks on the Proposed Plan of a Federal Government*, c. January 31, 1788:

[1] . . . This objection applies with equal force to each particular power, defined by the constitution; and, if there were a *bill of rights,* congress might be said to be the judge of that also. They may reflect however, that every judge in the union, whether of federal or state appointment, (and some persons would say every jury) will have a right to reject any act, handed to him as a law, which he may conceive repugnant to the constitution. [Ford 234]

[2] I proceed to attack the whole body of anti-federalists in their strong hold. The proposed constitution contains no *bill of rights.* [Ford 241]

[3] This doctrine is so obvious and plain, that I am amazed any good man should deplore the omission of a *bill of rights.* [Ford 242]

[4] It is, however, the idea of another most respectable character, that, as a *bill of rights* could do no harm, and might quiet the minds of many good people, the convention would have done well to indulge them. With all due deference, I apprehend, that a *bill of rights* might not be this innocent quieting instrument. Had the convention entered on the work, they must have comprehended within it everything, which the citizens of the United States claim as a natural or a civil right. An omission of a single article would have caused more discontent, than is either felt or pretended, on the present occasion. A multitude of articles might be the source of infinite controversy, by clashing with the powers intended to be given. To be full and certain, a *bill of rights* might have cost the convention more time, than was expended on their other work. The very appearance of it might raise more clamour than its omission,—I mean from those who study pretexts for condemning the whole fabric of the constitution.—"What! (might they say) did these exalted spirits imagine, that the natural rights of mankind depend on their gracious concession. If indeed they possessed that tyrannic sway, which, the kings of England had once usurped, we might humbly thank them for their magna charta, defective as it is. As that is not the case, we will not suffer it to be understood, that their new-fangled federal head shall domineer with the powers not excepted by their precious *bill of rights*. . . . [Ford 243]

[5] The restraints laid on the state legislatures will tend to secure domestic tranquility, more than all the *bills, or declarations, of rights,* which human policy could devise. It is very justly asserted, that the plan contains an avowal of many rights. It provides that no man, shall suffer by ex post facto laws or bills of attainder. It declares, that gold and silver only shall be a tender for specie debts; and that no law shall impair the obligation of a contract. [Ford 243]

Tench Coxe, "A Freeman," No. 3, February 6, 1788:

Those three gentlemen who with-held their names from the act of the foederal convention could not have apprehended the annihilation of the state governments, while that house was sitting, or they would, under the influence of such a fear, certainly have pressed for a *bill of rights*. It appears they did not think one so necessary, as to concert a single motion to obtain it: A conclusive proof, in my mind, that they saw no symptoms of a design to consolidate in the framers of the plan, and that they had no apprehensions of the kind themselves.

[DHRC16 50]

"An Old Whig," No. 8, February 6, 1788:

[1] First then, the general expectation seems to be that our future rulers will rectify all that is amiss. If a *bill of rights* is wanting, they will frame a *bill of rights*. If too much power is vested in them, they will not abuse it; nay, they will divest themselves of it. . . . [DHRC16 53]

[2] . . . Judges, unincumbered by juries, have been ever found much better friends to government than to the people. Such judges will always be more desireable than juries to a self-created senate, upon the same principle that a large standing army, and the entire command of the militia and of the purse, is ever desireable to those who wish to enslave the people, and upon the same principle that a *bill of rights* is their aversion. [DHRC16 55]

Benjamin Workman [?], "Philadelphiensis," No. 9, February 6, 1788:

. . . When government thinks proper, under the pretence of writing a libel, &c. it may imprison, inflict the most cruel and unusual punishment, seize property, carry on prosecutions, &c. and the unfortunate citizen has no magna charta, no *bill of rights,* to protect him; nay, the prosecution may be carried on in such a manner that even a jury will not be allowed him. Where is that base slave who would not appeal to the ultima ratio, before he submits to this government? . . .

[DHRC16 59]

"A Citizen of the United States," February 13, 1788:

. . . In the middle states the clamor of opposition has been from the want of a *bill of rights*—Besides these, the commercial states object to parting with their commercial revenues . . . [DHRC16 115]

"The Impartial Examiner," No. 1, February 20, 1788:

[1] . . . It is true, "the United States shall guarantee to every state in this union a republican form of government:" yet they do not guarantee to the different states their present forms of government, or the *bill of rights* thereto annexed, or any of them; and the expressions are too vague, too indefinite to create such a compact by implication. . . . [DHRC8 393]

[2] It has been held in a northern state by a zealous advocate for this constitution that there is no necessity for "a *bill of rights*" in the foederal government; although at the same time he acknowledges such necessity to have existed when the constitutions of the separate governments were established. . . .

[DHRC8 393]

James Iredell, "Marcus," No. 1, February 20, 1788:

It appears to me a very just remark of Mr. Wilson in his celebrated speech, that a *Bill of Rights* would have been dangerous, as implying that without such a reservation the Congress would have authority in the cases enumerated, so that if any had been omitted (and who would undertake to recite all the state and individual rights not relinquished by the new Constitution?) they might have been considered at the mercy of the general Legislature. [DHRC16 168]

"The Landholder," No. 10, February 29, 1788:

Since the publication of the Constitution, every topic of vulgar declamation has been employed to persuade the people, that it will destroy the trial by jury, and is defective for being without a *bill of rights*. You, Sir [Luther Martin], had more candour in the Convention than we can allow to those declaimers out of it; there you never signified by any motion or expression whatever, that it stood in need of a *bill of rights,* or in anywise endangered the trial by jury. In these respects the Constitution met your entire approbation: for had you believed it defective in these essentials, you ought to have mentioned it in Convention, or had you thought it wanted further guards, it was your indispensable duty to have proposed them. . . . [DHRC16 267–68]

Alexander White, "To the Citizens of Virginia," February 29, 1788:

Friends and Countrymen, It is objected that there is no *Bill of Rights*—a clear understanding of that matter will obviate many objections. A *Bill of Rights* is only necessary, where the rights of different men or orders of men are uncertain, and is rather calculated to inform than to restrain. Paper chains are too feeble to bind the hands of tyranny or ambition. In England the king claimed supreme power, as inseperably annexed to the kingly office, the people claimed privileges, these different claims occasioned many contests, until they were defined by a *Bill of Rights* presented to William and Mary at their accession. But no doubt can arise in the American governments, the fundamental maxim of which is, that sovereignty is vested in the people, a position so plain and simple that the meanest capacity can comprehend it, and so well established both in theory and practice, that no man will deny it. Consequently should Congress attempt to exercise any powers which are not expressly delegated to them, their acts would be considered as void, and disregarded. In America it is the governors not the governed that must produce their *Bills of Right:* unless they can shew the charters under which they act, the people will not yield obedience. [DHRC8 438]

Mercy Otis Warren, *Observations on the New Constitution*, February 1788:

There is no provision by a *bill of rights* to guard against the dangerous encroachments of power in too many instances to be named: but I cannot pass over in silence the insecurity in which we are left with regard to warrants unsupported by evidence . . . [DHRC16 281]

"The Impartial Examiner," No.1, March 5, 1788

. . . For a system, which is to supersede the present different governments of the states, by ordaining that "laws made in pursuance thereof shall be supreme, and shall bind the judges in every state, any thing in the constitution or laws of any state to the contrary notwithstanding,'' must be alarming indeed! What cannot this omnipotence of power effect? How will your [Virginia's] *bill of rights* avail you any thing? By this authority the Congress can make laws, which shall bind all, repugnant to your present constitution—repugnant to every article of your rights; for they are a part of your constitution,—they are the basis of it. So that if you pass this new constitution, you will have a naked plan of government unlimited in its jurisdiction, which not only expunges your *bill of rights* by rendering ineffectual, all the state governments . . . [DHRC8 462]

James Iredell, "Marcus," No. 4, March 12, 1788:

[1] . . . It may be observed in the first place, that a declaration against ''cruel and unusual punishments,'' formed part of an article in the *Bill of Rights* at the Revolution in England, in 1688. The prerogative of the Crown having been grossly abused in some preceding reigns, it was thought proper to notice every grievance they had endured, and those declarations went to an abuse of power in the crown only, but were never intended to limit the authority of Parliament. Many of these articles of the *Bill of Rights* in England, without a due attention to the difference of the cases, were eagerly adopted when our Constitutions were formed, the minds of men then being so warmed with their exertions in the cause of liberty, as to lean too much perhaps towards a jealousy of power to repose a proper confidence in their own government. . . . [DHRC16 381]

[2] . . . The two last of the Stuarts having kept up a considerable body of standing forces in time of peace, for the clear and almost avowed purpose of subduing the liberties of the people, it was made an article of the *Bill of Rights* at the Revolution, ''That the raising or keeping a standing army within the kingdom in time of peace, unless it be with the consent of Parliament, is against law;'' but no attempt was made, or I dare say, ever thought of, to restrain the Parliament from the exercise of that right. . . . [DHRC16 384]

[3] . . . It has been observed by the Foederalist that Pennsylvania and North-Carolina appear to be the only States in the union, which have attempted any restraint of the Legislative authority in this particular, and that their restraint appears rather in the light of a caution than a prohibition; but, that notwithstanding that, Pennsylvania had been obliged to raise forces in the very face of that article of her *Bill of Rights*. That great writer, from the remoteness of his situation, did not know that North-Carolina had equally violated her *Bill of Rights* in a similar manner. . . . [DHRC16 385]

George Nicholas [?], "The State Soldier," No. 4, March 19, 1788

And in doing this, I have been unavoidably led to answer some of the individual objections to the constitution themselves—among these are the want of a *bill of rights,* the equality in the senate, and the liberty of the press—all of which I shall avoid recapitulating at this time, with an intention of confining myself wholly to those objections which I have not heretofore entered fully into. [DHRC8 509–10]

Luther Martin, "To the Citizens of Maryland," No. 2, March 21, 1788:

[1] . . . if such treaties or laws were inconsistent with our constitution and *bill of rights,* the judiciaries of this state would be bound to reject the first and abide by the last; since in the form I introduced the clause, notwithstanding treaties and the laws of the general government were intended to be superior to the laws of our state government, where they should be opposed to each other, yet that they were not proposed, nor meant to be superior to our constitution and *bill of rights. . . .* [DHRC16 453]

[2] . . . These consist, as he tells us, in giving my entire approbation to the system, as to those parts which are said to endanger a trial by jury, and as to its want of a *bill of rights,* and in having too much candour there to signify that I thought it deficient in either of these respects . . . [DHRC16 454]

[3] With respect to a *bill of rights*—Had the government been formed upon principles truly federal, as I wished it, legislating over and acting upon the states only in their collective or political capacity, and not on individuals, there would have been no need of a *bill of rights,* as far as related to the rights of individuals, but only as to the rights of states . . . [DHRC16 455]

[4] . . . The more the system advanced, the more was I impressed with the necessity of not merely attempting to secure a few rights, but of digesting and forming a complete *bill of rights,* including those of states and of individuals, which should be assented to, and prefixed to the constitution, to serve as a barrier between the general government and the respective states and their citizens; because the more the system advanced, the more clearly it appeared to me that the framers of it did not consider that either states or men had any rights at all, or that they meant to secure the enjoyment of any to either the one or the other; accordingly, I devoted a part of my time to the actually preparing and draughting such a *bill of rights,* and had it in readiness before I left the Convention, to have laid it before a committee.—I conversed with several members on the subject; they agreed with me on the propriety of the measure, but, at the same time, expressed their sentiments that it would be impossible to procure its adoption if attempted.—A very few days before I left the Convention, I shewed to an honourable member sitting by me, a proposition, which I then had in my hand, couched in the following words, "Resolved, that a committee be appointed to prepare and report a *bill of rights,* to be prefixed to the proposed constitution," and I then would instantly have moved for the appointment of a committee for that purpose, if he would have agreed to second the motion, to do which he hesitated, not as I understood from any objection to the measure, but from a conviction in his own mind, that the motion would be in vain. [DHRC16 456]

[5] Thus, my fellow-citizens, you see that so far from having no objections to the system on this account, while I was at Convention, I not only then thought a *bill of rights* necessary, but I took some pains to have the subject brought forward, which would have been done, had it not been for the difficulties I have stated . . . [DHRC16 456]

Luther Martin, "To the Citizens of Maryland," No. 3, March 28, 1788:

. . . or what state is there that would have been averse to a *bill of rights,* or that would have wished for the destruction of jury trial in a great variety of cases, and in a particular manner in every case, without exception, where the government itself is interested? . . . [DHRC16 501]

John Jay, *An Address to the People of the State of New York*, c. April 15, 1788:

. . . Complaints are also made that the proposed constitution is not accompanied by a *bill of rights;* and yet they who would make these complaints, know and are content that no *bill of rights* accompanied the Constitution of this State. In days and countries, where Monarchs and their subjects were frequently disputing about prerogative and privileges, the latter often found it necessary, as it were to run out the line between them, and oblige the former to admit by solemn acts, called *bills of rights,* that certain enumerated rights belonged to the people, and were not comprehended in the royal prerogative. But thank God we have no such disputes—we have no Monarchs to contend with, or demand admission from—the proposed Government is to be the government of the people—all its officers are to be their officers, and to exercise no rights but such as the people commit to them. . . . [Ford 76–77]

Melancton Smith, *An Address to the People of the State of New York*, c. April 1788:

The author manifests levity in referring to the constitution of this state, to shew that it was useless to stipulate for the liberty of the press, or to insert a *bill of rights* in the constitution. With regard to the first, it is perhaps an imperfection in our constitution that the liberty of the press is not expressly reserved; but still there was not equal necessity of making this reservation in our State as in the general Constitution, for the common and statute law of England, and the laws of the colony are established, in which this privilege is fully defined and secured. It is true, a *bill of rights* is not prefixed to our constitution, as it is in that of some of the states; but still this author knows, that many essential rights are reserved in the body of it . . . [Ford 114]

Alexander Hamilton, *The Federalist*, No. 84, May 28, 1788:

[1] The most considerable of the remaining objections is that the plan of the convention contains no *bill of rights*. Among other answers given to this, it has been upon different occasions remarked that the constitutions of several of the States are in a similar predicament. I add that New York is of the number. And yet the opposers of the new system, in this State, who profess an unlimited admiration for its constitution, are among the most intemperate partisans of a *bill of rights*. To justify their zeal in this matter, they allege two things: one is that, though the constitution of New York has no *bill of rights* prefixed to it, yet it contains, in the body of it, various provisions in favor of particular privileges and rights, which, in substance, amount to the same thing; the other is, that the Constitution adopts, in their full extent, the common and statute law of Great Britain, by which many other rights, not expressed in it, are equally secured. [Fed. 532]

[2] It has been several times truly remarked that *bills of rights* are, in their origin, stipulations between kings and their subjects, abridgements of prerogative in favor of privilege, reservations of rights not surrendered to the prince. Such was MAGNA CHARTA, obtained by the barons, sword in hand, from King John. Such were the subsequent confirmations of that charter by succeeding princes. Such was the Petition of Right assented to by Charles I., in the beginning of his reign. Such, also, was the Declaration of Right presented by the Lords and Commons to the Prince of Orange in 1688, and afterwards thrown into the form of an act of parliament called the *Bill of Rights*. It is evident, therefore, that, according to their primitive signification, they have no application to constitutions, professedly founded upon the power of the people, and executed by their immediate representatives and servants. Here, in strictness, the people surrender nothing; and as they retain every thing they have no need of particular reservations. "WE, THE PEOPLE of the United States, to secure the blessings of liberty to ourselves and our posterity, do ordain and establish this Constitution for the United States of America." Here is a better recognition of popular rights, than volumes of those aphorisms which make the principal figure in several of our State *bills of rights,* and which would sound much better in a treatise of ethics than in a constitution of government. [Fed. 534]

[3] I go further, and affirm that *bills of rights,* in the sense and to the extent in which they are contended for, are not only unnecessary in the proposed Constitution, but would even be dangerous. They would contain various exceptions to powers not granted; and, on this very account, would afford a colorable pretext to claim more than were granted. . . . This may serve as a specimen of the numerous handles which would be given to the doctrine of constructive powers, by the indulgence of an injudicious zeal for *bills of rights*. [Fed. 535]

[4] There remains but one other view of this matter to conclude the point. The truth is, after all the declamations we have heard, that the Constitution is itself,

in every rational sense, and to every useful purpose, A *BILL OF RIGHTS*. The several *bills of rights* in Great Britain form its Constitution, and conversely the constitution of each State is its *bill of rights*. And the proposed Constitution, if adopted, will be the *bill of rights* of the Union. Is it one object of a *bill of rights* to declare and specify the political privileges of the citizens in the structure and administration of the government? This is done in the most ample and precise manner in the plan of the convention; comprehending various precautions for the public security, which are not to be found in any of the State constitutions. Is another object of a *bill of rights* to define certain immunities and modes of proceeding, which are relative to personal and private concerns? This we have seen has also been attended to, in a variety of cases, in the same plan. Adverting therefore to the substantial meaning of a *bill of rights,* it is absurd to allege that it is not to be found in the work of the convention. It may be said that it does not go far enough, though it will not be easy to make this appear; but it can with no propriety be contended that there is no such thing. . . . [Fed. 536]

Alexander Hamilton, *The Federalist*, No. 85, May 28, 1788:

It is remarkable, that the resemblance of the plan of the convention to the act which organizes the government of this State holds, not less with regard to many of the supposed defects, than to the real excellences of the former. Among the pretended defects are the re-eligibility of the Executive, the want of a council, the omission of a formal *bill of rights,* the omission of a provision respecting the liberty of the press. . . . [Fed. 541]

John Dickinson, "Fabius," No. 3, 1788:

. . . As some persons seem to think, a *bill of rights* is the best security of rights, the sovereignties of the several states have this best security by the proposed constitution, and more than this best security, for they are not barely declared to be rights, but are taken into it as component parts for their perpetual preservation—by themselves. . . . [Ford 179]

John Dickinson, "Fabius," No. 4, 1788:

Trial by jury and the dependence of taxation upon representation, those corner stones of liberty, were not obtained by a *bill of rights,* or any other records, and have not been and cannot be preserved by them. They and all other rights must be preserved, by soundness of sense and honesty of heart. Compared with these, what are a *bill of rights,* or any characters drawn upon paper or parchment, those frail remembrances? . . . [Ford 186]

BILLS OF CREDIT

(Bills of Exchange)

United States Constitution, September 17, 1787:

[Article I, Section 10:] No State shall enter into any Treaty, Alliance, or Confederation; grant Letters of Marque and Reprisal; coin Money; emit *Bills of Credit;* make any Thing but gold and silver Coin a Tender in Payment of Debts; pass any Bill of Attainder, ex post facto Law, or Law impairing the Obligation of Contracts, or grant any Title of Nobility.

* * * * *

United States Continental Congress, Draft Articles of Confederation, July 12, 1776:

[Article 18:] The United States assembled shall have Authority for the Defence and Welfare of the United Colonies and every of them, to agree upon and fix the necessary Sums and Expences—To emit *Bills,* or to borrow Money on the Credit of the United Colonies—To raise Naval Forces . . . [DHRC1 83]

[*Ibid.:*] . . . The United States assembled shall never engage the United Colonies in a War, nor grant Letters of Marque and Reprisal in Time of Peace, nor enter into Treaties or Alliances, nor coin Money nor regulate the Value thereof, nor agree upon nor fix the Sums and Expences necessary for the Defence and Welfare of the United Colonies, or any of them, nor emit *Bills,* nor borrow Money on the *Credit* of the United Colonies, nor raise Naval Forces, nor agree upon the Number of Land Forces to be raised, unless the Delegates of nine Colonies freely assent to the same . . . [DHRC1 84]

United States Articles of Confederation, November 15, 1777:

[Article IX:] [Congress shall have power] to ascertain the necessary sums of Money to be raised for the service of the united states, and to appropriate and apply the same for defraying the public expences—to borrow money, or emit *bills on the credit* of the united states, transmitting every half year to the respective states an account of the sums of money so borrowed or emitted . . .

[*Ibid.*:] The united states in congress assembled shall never engage in a war, nor grant letters of marque and reprisal in time of peace, nor enter into any treaties or alliances, nor coin money, nor regulate the value thereof, nor ascertain the sums and expenses necessary for the defence and welfare of the united states, or any of them, nor emit *bills,* nor borrow money on the *credit* of the united states, nor appropriate money, nor agree upon the number of vessels of war, to be built or purchased, or the number of land or sea forces to be raised, nor appoint a commander in chief of the army or navy, unless nine states assent to the same . . .

[Article XII:] All *bills of credit* emitted, monies borrowed and debts contracted by, or under the authority of congress, before the assembling of the united states, in pursuance of the present confederation, shall be deemed and considered as a charge against the united states, for payment and satisfaction whereof the said united states, and the public faith are hereby solemnly pledged.

Massachusetts Constitution, March 2, 1780:

[Frame of Government, Chapter II:1:11:] No moneys shall be issued out of the treasury of this common wealth, and disposed of (except such sums as may be appropriated for the redemption of *bills of credit* or treasurer's notes, or for the payment of interest arising thereon) but by warrant under the hand of the governor for the time being, with the advice and consent of the council, for the necessary defence and support of the commonwealth; and for the protection and preservation of the inhabitants thereof, agreeably to the acts and resolves of the general court. [Thorpe 1902–1903]

New Hampshire Constitution, June 2, 1784:

[Form of Government:] No monies shall be issued out of the treasury of this state, and disposed of (except such sums as may be appropriated for the redemption of *bills of credit* or treasurers' notes, or for the payment of interest arising there on) but by warrant under the hand of the president for the time being, by and with the advice and consent of the council, for the necessary support and defence of this state, and for the necessary protection and preservation of the inhabitants thereof, agreeably to the acts and resolves of the general court. [Thorpe 2465]

James Madiscn, *The Federalist*, No. 38, January 12, 1788:

. . . But waiving illustrations of this sort, is it not manifest that most of the capital objections urged against the new system lie with tenfold weight against the

existing Confederation? Is an indefinite power to raise money dangerous in the hands of the federal government? The present Congress can make requisitions to any amount they please, and the States are constitutionally bound to furnish them; they can emit *bills of credit* as long as they will pay for the paper; they can borrow, both abroad and at home, as long as a shilling will be lent. . . .
[Fed. 277–78]

James Madison, *The Federalist*, No. 44, January 25, 1788:

The extension of the prohibition to *bills of credit* must give pleasure to every citizen, in proportion to his love of justice and his knowledge of the true springs of public prosperity. The loss which America has sustained since the peace, from the pestilent effects of paper money on the necessary confidence between man and man, on the necessary confidence in the public councils, on the industry and morals of the people, and on the character of republican government, constitutes an enormous debt against the States chargeable with this unadvised measure, which must long remain unsatisfied . . . [Fed. 318]

Alexander C. Hanson, *Remarks on the Proposed Plan of a Federal Government*, c. January 31, 1788:

[1] . . . Too long have we sustained evils, resulting from injudicious emissions of paper, and from the operation of tender laws. To *bills of credit* as they are now falsely called, may we impute the entire loss of confidence between men. Hence it is, that specie has, in a great degree, ceased its proper office, and been confined to speculations, baneful to the public, and enriching a few enterprising sharp-sighted men, at the expence not only of the ignorant, slothful, and needy, but of their country's best benefactors. Hence chiefly are the bankruptcies throughout America, and the disreputable ruinous state of our commerce. Hence is it principally, that America hath lost its credit abroad, and American faith become a proverb. The convention plainly saw, that nothing short of a renunciation of the right to emit *bills of credit* could produce that grand consummation of policy, the RESTORATION OF PUBLIC AND PRIVATE FAITH.
[Ford 243]

[2] Were it possible for the nations abroad to suppose Great Britain would emit *bills* on the terms whereon they have issued in America, how soon would the wide arch of that mighty empire tumble into ruins? In no other country in the universe has prevailed the idea of supplying, by promissory notes, the want of coin, for commerce and taxes. . . . [Ford 243]

[3] . . . What then are the powers an individual state will lose? She will no longer be able to deny congress that, which congress, at this moment, has a right to demand. She will have no power to enter into a treaty, alliance, or confederation. She shall, in time of war, grant no letters of marque and reprisal. She shall coin no money, emit no *bills of credit,* nor make any thing but gold and silver a

tender in payment of debts. She shall pass no bill of attainder, or ex post facto law, or law impairing the obligation of a contract. . . . [Ford 251]

David Ramsay, "Civis," February 4, 1788:

. . . be on your guard against the misrepresentations of men who are involved in debt; such may wish to see the constitution rejected, because of the following clause "no state shall emit *bills of credit,* make any thing but gold and silver coin, a tender in payment of debts, pass any expost facto law, or law impairing the obligation of contracts." This will doubtless bear hard on debtors who wish to defraud their creditors, but it will be of real service to the honest part of the community. . . . [DHRC16 26]

"Brutus," No. 14, March 6, 1788:

. . . For it has provided, "that no state shall emit *bills of credit,* or make any thing but gold and silver coin a tender in payment of debts." It has also declared, that "no state shall pass any law impairing the obligation of contracts."—These prohibitions give the most perfect security against those attacks upon property which I am sorry to say some of the states have but too wantonly made, by passing laws sanctioning fraud in the debtor against his creditor. . . .
[DHRC16 330]

United States Congress, Judiciary Act of September 24, 1789:

[Section 11:] . . . And no civil suit shall be brought before either of said [circuit] courts against an inhabitant of the United States, by any original process in any other district than that whereof he is an inhabitant, or in which he shall be found at the time of serving the writ, nor shall any district or circuit court have cognizance of any suit to recover the contents of any promissory note or other chose in action in favor of an assignee, unless a suit might have been prosecuted in such court to recover the said contents if no assignment had been made, except in cases of foreign *bills of exchange*. . . . [USSL1 79]

BREACH OF THE PEACE

United States Constitution, September 17, 1787:

[Article I, Section 6:] The Senators and Representatives shall receive a Compensation for their Services, to be ascertained by Law, and paid out of the Treasury of the United States. They shall in all Cases, except Treason, Felony and *Breach of the Peace,* be privileged from Arrest during their Attendance at the Session of their respective Houses, and in going to and returning from the same; and for any Speech or Debate in either House, they shall not be questioned in any other Place.

* * * * *

Georgia Constitution, February 5, 1777:

[Article 39:] All matters of *breach of the peace,* felony, murder, and treason against the State to be tried in the county where the same was committed. All matters of dispute, both civil and criminal, in any county where there is not a sufficient number of inhabitants to form a court, shall be tried in the next adjacent county where a court is held. [Thorpe 783]

United States Articles of Confederation, November 15, 1777:

[Article V:] Freedom of speech and debate in Congress shall not be impeached or questioned in any Court, or place out of Congress, and the members of congress shall be protected in their persons from arrests and imprisonments, during the time of their going to and from, and attendance on congress, except for treason, felony, or *breach of the peace.*

"Brutus," No. 12, February 7, 1788:

[1] . . . Another end declared is to insure domestic tranquility. This comprehends a provision against all private *breaches of the peace,* as well as against

all public commotions or general insurrections; and to attain the object of this clause fully, the government must exercise the power of passing laws on these subjects, as well as of appointing magistrates with authority to execute them. And the courts will adopt these ideas in their expositions. . . . [DHRC16 75]

"Brutus," No. 12, February 14, 1788:

But supposing that the party, who alledges that he is a citizen of another state, has recourse to fiction in bringing in his suit, it is well known, that the courts have high authority to plead, to justify them in suffering actions to be brought before them by such fictions. In my last number I stated, that the court of exchequer tried all causes in virtue of such a fiction. The court of king's bench, in England, extended their jurisdiction in the same way. Originally, this court held pleas, in civil cases, only of trespasses and other injuries alledged to be committed vi et armis. They might likewise, says Blackstone, upon the division of the aula regia, have originally held pleas of any other civil action whatsoever (except in real actions which are now very seldom in use) provided the defendant was an officer of the court, or in the custody of the marshall or prison-keeper of this court, for *breach of the peace,* &c. In process of time, by a fiction, this court began to hold pleas of any personal action whatsoever . . .

[DHRC16 121]

Georgia Constitution, May 6, 1789:

[Article I, Section 14:] No senator or representative shall be liable to be arrested during his attendance on the general assembly, or for a reasonable time in going thereto or returning home, except it be for treason, felony, or *breach of the peace;* nor shall any member be liable to answer for anything spoken in debate in either house, in any court or place elsewhere. [Thorpe 786]

South Carolina Constitution, June 3, 1790:

[Article I, Section 14:] The members of both houses shall be protected in their persons and estates, during their attendance on, going to, and returning from, the legislature, and ten days previous to their sitting, and ten days after the adjournment of the legislature. But these privileges shall not be extended so as to protect any member who shall be charged with treason, felony, or *breach of the peace.* [Thorpe 3260]

Pennsylvania Constitution, September 2, 1790:

[Article I, Section 17:] The senators and representatives shall receive a compensation for their services, to be ascertained by law, and paid out of the treasury of the commonwealth. They shall, in all cases, except treason, felony, and *breach or surety of the peace,* be privileged from arrest during their attendance at the session of the respective houses, and in going to and returning from the same: And for any speech or debate in either house they shall not be questioned in any other place. [Thorpe 3094]

[Article III, Section 3:] Electors shall, in all cases except treason, felony, and *breach or surety of the peace,* be privileged from arrest during their attendance on elections, and in going to and returning from them. [Thorpe 3096]

BRIBERY

United States Constitution, September 17, 1787:

[Article II, Section 4:] The President, Vice President and all civil Officers of the United States, shall be removed from Office on Impeachment for, and Conviction of, Treason, *Bribery,* or other high Crimes and Misdemeanors.

* * * * *

Pennsylvania Frame of Government, Laws Agreed Upon in England, May 5, 1682:

[Article 17:] That all *briberies* and extortion whatsoever shall be severely punished. [Thorpe 3061]

Fundamental Constitutions of East New Jersey, 1683:

. . . and all elections must be free and voluntary, but where any *bribe* or indirect means can be proved to have been used, both the giver and acquirer shall forfeit their priviledge of electing and being elected forever . . . [Thorpe 2575]

Thomas Paine, *Common Sense,* January 9, 1776:

. . . And he will take the tenth of your seed, and of your vineyards, and give them to his officers and to his servants (by which we see that *bribery,* corruption, and favouritism are the standing vices of kings) and he will take the tenth of your men servants, and your maid servants, and your goodliest young men and your asses, and put them to his work . . . [CWTP1 12]

Maryland Constitution, November 11, 1776:

[Form of Government, Article 54:] That if any person shall give any *bribe,* present, or reward, or any promise, or any security for the payment or delivery of any money, or any other thing, to obtain or procure a vote to be Governor, Senator, Delegate to Congress or Assembly, member of the Council, or Judge, or to be appointed to any of the said offices, or to any office of profit or trust, now created or hereafter to be created in this State—the person giving, and the person receiving the same (on conviction in a court of law) shall be forever disqualified to hold any office of trust or profit in this State. [Thorpe 1700]

Georgia Constitution, February 5, 1777:

[Article 15:] . . . "I, A B, do solemnly swear that I will bear true allegiance to the State of Georgia, and will truly perform the trusts reposed in me; and that I will execute the same to the best of my knowledge, for the benefit of this State, and the support of the constitution thereof, and that I have obtained my election without fraud or *bribe* whatever; so help me God." [Thorpe 780]

Massachusetts Constitution, March 2, 1780:

[Frame of Government, Chapter VI:2:] And no person shall ever be admitted to hold a seat in the legislature, or any office of trust or importance under the government of this commonwealth, who shall, in the due course of law, have been convicted of *bribery* or corruption in obtaining an election or appointment. [Thorpe 1910]

New Hampshire Constitution, June 2, 1784:

[Form of Government:] No person shall ever be admitted to hold a seat in the legislature, or any office of trust or importance under this government, who in the due course of law, has been convicted of *bribery* or corruption, in obtaining an election or appointment. [Thorpe 2470]

Virginia Statute of Religious Liberty, January 16, 1786:

. . . that therefore the proscribing of any citizen as unworthy the public confidence by laying upon him an incapacity of being called to offices of trust and emolument, unless he profess or renounce this or that religious opinion, is depriving him injuriously of those privileges and advantages to which, in common with his fellow-citizens, he has a natural right; that it tends only to corrupt the principles of that religion it is meant to encourage, by *bribing* with a monopoly of worldly honors and emoluments, those who will externally profess and conform to it . . . [CVA8 690]

Richard Henry Lee [?], *The Federal Farmer*, No. 3, October 10, 1787:

. . . The power of making any law will be in the president, eight senators, and seventeen representatives, relative to the important objects enumerated in the constitution. Where there is a small representation a sufficient number to carry any measure, may, with ease, be influenced by *bribes,* offices and civilities; they easily form private juntoes, and out-door meetings, agree on measures, and carry them by silent votes. [Ford 300]

Noah Webster, *An Examination into the Leading Principles of the Federal Constitution*, October 17, 1787:

[1] In ancient Rome, the king was elective, and so were the consuls, who were the executive officers in the republic. But they were elected by the body of the people, in their public assemblies; and this circumstance paved the way for such excessive *bribery* and corruption as are wholly unknown in modern times. The president of the United States is also elective; but by a few men—chosen by the several legislatures—under their inspection—separated at a vast distance—and holding no office under the United States. Such a mode of election almost precludes the possibility of corruption. . . . [Ford 35]

[2] In the decline of the [Roman] republic, *bribery* or military force obtained this office for persons who had not attained this age—Augustus was chosen at the age of twenty; or rather obtained it with his sword. [Ford 36n]

[3] . . . Were it possible, as it is in small states, it would be an improvement in the doctrine of representation, to give every freeman the right of voting for every member of the legislature, and the privilege of choosing the men in any part of the state. This would totally exclude *bribery* and undue influence; for no man can *bribe* a state; and it would almost annihilate partial views in legislation. But in large states it may be impracticable. [Ford 41n]

James Madison, *The Federalist*, No. 18, December 7, 1787:

. . . The latter [The Thebans], being the weaker party, invited the assistance of Philip of Macedon, who had secretly fostered the contest. Philip gladly seized the opportunity of executing the designs he had long planned against the liberties of Greece. By his intrigues and *bribes* he won over to his interests the popular leaders of several cities; by their influence and votes, gained admission into the Amphictyonic council; and by his arts and his arms, made himself master of the confederacy. [Fed. 173]

Alexander Hamilton, *The Federalist* No. 22, December 14, 1787:

Suppose, for instance, we were engaged in a war, in conjunction with one foreign nation, against another. Suppose the necessity of our situation demanded peace, and the interest or ambition of our ally led him to seek the prosecution of war, with views that might justify us in making separate terms. In such a state of things, this ally of ours would evidently find it much easier, by his *bribes* and intrigues, to tie up the hands of government from making peace, where two thirds of all the votes were requisite to that object, than where a simple majority would suffice. In the first case, he would have to corrupt a smaller number; in the last, a greater number. . . . [Fed. 195–96]

Dissent of the Pennsylvania Convention's Minority, December 18, 1787:

[1] The legislature of a free country should be so formed as to have a competent knowledge of its constituents, and enjoy their confidence. To produce these essential requisites, the representation ought to be fair, equal and sufficiently numerous to possess the same interests, feelings, opinions and views which the people themselves would possess, were they all assembled; and so numerous as to prevent *bribery* and undue influence, and so responsible to the people, by frequent and fair elections, as to prevent their neglecting or sacrificing the views and interests of their constituents to their own pursuits. [DHRC2 631]

[2] The representation is unsafe because in the exercise of such great powers and trusts, it is so exposed to corruption and undue influence, by the gift of the numerous places of honor and emolument, at the disposal of the executive; by the arts and address of the great and designing, and by direct *bribery*. [DHRC2 632]

[3] And this great power may be exercised by the president and ten senators (being two-thirds of fourteen, which is a quorum of that body). What an inducement would this offer to the ministers of foreign powers to compass by *bribery* such concessions as could not otherwise be obtained . . . [DHRC2 634]

Alexander C. Hanson, *Remarks on the Proposed Plan of a Federal Government*, c. January 31, 1788:

. . . From the mode of his election, it is impossible he [the President] can intrigue to advantage; and, from the nature of other things, he will never succeed by *bribery* and corruption. Like any other individual, he is liable to punishment. Finally, at the expiration of his office, he returns into the mass of the people. [Ford 226]

James Madison, *The Federalist*, No. 57, February 19, 1788:

Is it supported by reason? This cannot be said, without maintaining that five or six thousand citizens are less capable of choosing a fit representative, or more liable to be corrupted by an unfit one, than five or six hundred. Reason, on the contrary, assures us, that as in so great a number a fit representative would be most likely to be found, so the choice would be less likely to be diverted from him by the intrigues of the ambitious or the *bribes* of the rich. [Fed. 386]

Benjamin Workman [?], "Philadelphiensis," No. 10, February 20, 1788:

. . . In that state, through the influence of the tyrants of Boston, very little information has reached the people; the press, generally speaking, was devoted to the well-born and their tools; yet out of near 400 members, of which that convention consisted, only a majority of 19 could be procured, notwithstanding every possible method of overawing, threatening and *bribing* was practised. [DHRC16 159–60]

Samuel Bryan, "Centinel," No. 16, February 26, 1788:

. . . Besides, should Congress be disposed to violate the fundamental articles of the constitution for the sake of public justice, they would be prevented in so doing by their oaths, but even if this should not prove an obstacle, if it can be supposed that any set of men would perjure themselves for the public good, and combat an host of enemies on such terms, still it would be of no avail, as there is a further barrier interposed between the public and these defaulters, namely, the supreme court of the union, whose province it would be to determine the constitutionality of any law that may be controverted; and supposing no *bribery* or corrupt influence practised on the bench of judges, it would be their sworn duty to refuse their sanction to laws made in the face and contrary to the letter and spirit of the constitution, as any law to compel the settlement of accounts and payment of monies depending and due under the old confederation would be. . . . [DHRC16 219–20]

Alexander White, "To the Citizens of Virginia," February 29, 1788

. . . It is said the representation is unsafe because it is so exposed to corruption and undue influence, by the gift of the numerous places of honor and emolument at the disposal of the executive, by the arts and address of the great and designing, and by direct *bribery?* The members of Congress can hold no office during the time they remain members, nor can they enjoy any office which shall be created, or the emoluments of which shall be increased during the time for which they were elected.—Name to me the country in which the members of the legislature or the executive council are so far removed from influence—and before you consent to give each state a controul over the purse and sword, be well informed whether the Grecian confederacy was ruined by the practice of art, address, and *bribery* in the council of Amphyctions, or in the assemblies of the people of the different states? And whether it will not be easier to corrupt a few leading men, in some one of 13 assemblies than a majority of Congress? The assembly of Pennsylvania would be a cheap purchase if what the dissentients say is true, "that a majority of them were lately under the influence of the city members," who I presume never *bribed* higher than a good dinner. [DHRC8 439–40]

Mercy Otis Warren, *Observations on the New Constitution*, February 1788:

There is no provision for a rotation, nor any thing to prevent the perpetuity of office in the some hands for life; which by a little well timed *bribery,* will probably be done, to the exclusion of men of the best abilities from their share in the offices of government.—By this neglect we lose the advantages of that check to the overbearing insolence of office, which by rendering him ineligible at certain periods, keeps the mind of man in equilibrio, and teaches him the feelings of the governed, and better qualifies him to govern in his turn.

[DHRC16 280–81]

William Ward [?], "Republicus," March 1, 1788:

. . . An extraordinary refinement this [the electoral college], on the plain simple business of election; and of which the grand convention have certainly the honour of being the first inventors; and that for an officer too, of so much importance as a president; invested with legislative and executive powers—who is to be commander in chief of the army, navy, militia, &c. grant reprieves and pardons, have a temporary negative on all bills and resolves, convene and adjourn both houses of congress, be supreme conservator of laws, commission all officers, make treaties, &c. &c. and who is to continue four years, and is only removable on conviction of treason or *bribery* and triable only by the senate, who are to be his own council whose interest in every instance runs paralel with his own: and who are neither the officers of the people nor accountable to them. . . .

[DHRC8 448]

"The Impartial Examiner," No. 1, March 5, 1788:

. . . The altar of liberty is no longer watched with such attentive assiduity;—a new train of passions succeeds to the empire of the mind;—different objects of desire take place;—and, if the nation happens to enjoy a series of prosperity, voluptuousness, excessive fondness for riches, and luxury gain admission and establish themselves—these produce venality and corruption of every kind, which open a fatal avenue to *bribery*. Hence it follows, that in the midst of this general contageon a few men—or one—more powerful than all others, industriously endeavor to obtain all authority; and by means of great wealth—or embezzling the public money,—perhaps totally subvert the government, and erect a system of aristocratical or monarchic tyranny in its room. . . . [DHRC8 465]

Alexander Hamilton, *The Federalist*, No. 69, March 14, 1788:

The President of the United States would be liable to be impeached, tried, and, upon conviction of treason, *bribery,* or other high crimes or misdemeanors, removed from office; and would afterwards be liable to prosecution and punishment in the ordinary course of law. The person of the king of Great Britain is sacred and inviolable . . . [Fed. 444–45]

"Brutus," No. 15, March 20, 1788:

The only clause in the constitution which provides for the removal of the judges from offices, is that which declares, that "the president, vice-president, and all civil officers of the United States, shall be removed from office, on impeachment for, and conviction of treason, *bribery,* or other high crimes and misdemeanors." By this paragraph, civil officers, in which the judges are included, are removable only for crimes. Treason and *bribery* are named, and the rest are included under the general terms of high crimes and misdemeanors.—Errors in judgement, or want of capacity to discharge the duties of the office, can never be supposed to be included in these words, high crimes and misdemeanors. . . .

[DHRC16 433]

Samuel Bryan, "Centinel," No. 17, March 24, 1788:

Could it have been supposed seven years ago, that, before the wounds received in the late conflict for liberty were scarcely healed, a post master-general and his deputies would have had the daring presumption to convert an establishment intended to promote and secure the public welfare into an engine of despotism, by suppressing all those newspapers that contain the essays of patriotism and real intelligence, and propagating instead thereof falsehoods and delusion? Such a supposition at that time, would have been treated as chimerical; but how must our indignation rise when we find this flagitious practice is persevered in, after being publicly detected! Must not the *bribe* from the conspirators be very great to compensate the post master-general and his deputies, for the loss of character and infamy consequent upon such conduct, and for the danger they incur of being impeached and turned out of office? [DHRC16 476–77]

Georgia Constitution, May 6, 1789:

[Article I, Section 15:] The members of the senate and house of representatives shall take the following oath or affirmation: "I, A B, do solemnly swear (or affirm, as the case may be) that I have not obtained my election by *bribery,* or other unlawful means; and that I will give my vote on all questions that may come before me, as a senator, (or representative,) in such manner as, in my judgment, will best promote the good of this State; and that I will bear true faith and allegiance to the same, and to the utmost of my power observe, support, and defend the constitution thereof." [Thorpe 787]

CAPITATION

United States Constitution, September 17, 1787:

[Article I, Section 9:] No *Capitation,* or other direct, Tax shall be laid, unless in Proportion to the Census or Enumeration herein before directed to be taken.

* * * * *

Dissent of the Pennsylvania Convention's Minority, December 18, 1787:

The power of direct taxation applies to every individual, as Congress, under this government, is expressly vested with the authority of laying a *capitation or poll tax* upon every person to any amount. This is a tax that, however oppressive in its nature, and unequal in its operation, is certain as to its produce and simple in its collection; it cannot be evaded like the objects of imposts or excise, and will be paid, because all that a man hath will he give for his head. This tax is so congenial to the nature of despotism, that it has ever been a favorite under such governments. Some of those who were in the late general convention from this state have labored to introduce a poll tax among us. [DHRC2 635–36]

Alexander C. Hanson, *Remarks on the Proposed Plan of Federal Government*, c. January 31, 1788:

To the five per cent impost most of the states have more than once given their assent. This is the only tax which congress wishes immediately to impose. Of the imposition of assessment, *capitation,* or direct taxes of any kind, the congress entertains no idea at present; and although it be proper for the federal head to possess this power in reserve, nothing but some unforeseen disaster will ever drive them to such ineligible expedients. . . . [Ford 253]

Samuel Bryan, "Centinel," No. 14, February 5, 1788:

[Quoting Luther Martin] . . . By the power to lay and collect taxes, they may proceed to direct taxation on every individual either by a *capitation tax* on their heads, or an assessment on their property. By this part of the section, therefore, the government has a power to lay what duties they please on goods imported—to lay what duties they please afterwards on whatever we use or consume—to impose stamp duties to what amount they please, and in whatever cases they please—afterwards to impose on the people direct taxes, by *capitation tax,* or by assessment, to what amount they choose, and thus to sluice them at every vein as long as they have a drop of blood, without any controul, limitation or restraint—while all the officers for collecting these taxes, stamp duties, imposts and excises, are to be appointed by the general government, under its direction, not accountable to the states . . . [DHRC16 33]

CITIZEN, CITIZENS

[Note: This is a sample list, including all occurrences from constitutions and fundamental laws and one occurrence out of eight from the other sources.]

United States Constitution, September 17, 1787:

[Article I, Section 2:] No Person shall be a Representative who shall not have attained to the Age of twenty five Years, and been seven Years a *Citizen* of the United States, and who shall not, when elected, be an Inhabitant of that State in which he shall be chosen.

[Article I, Section 3:] No Person shall be a Senator who shall not have attained to the Age of thirty Years, and been nine Years a *Citizens* of the United States, and who shall not, when elected, be an Inhabitant of that State for which he shall be chosen.

[Article II, Section 1:] No Person except a natural born *Citizen,* or a *Citizen* of the United States, at the time of the Adoption of this Constitution, shall be eligible to the Office of President; neither shall any Person be eligible to that Office who shall not have attained to the Age of thirty five Years, and been fourteen Years a Resident within the United States.

[Article III, Section 2:] The judicial Power shall extend . . . to Controversies between two or more States;—between a State and *Citizens* of another State;—between *Citizens* of different States,—between *Citizens* of the same State claiming Lands under Grants of different States, and between a State, or the *Citizens* thereof, and foreign States, *Citizens* or Subjects.

[Article IV, Section 2:] The *Citizens* of each State shall be entitled to all Privileges and Immunities of *Citizens* in the several States.

* * * * *

Henry VII, Letters Patent to John Cabot, March 5, 1496:

Be it knowen that we have given and granted, and by these presents do give and grant for us and our heires, to our welbeloved John Cabot *citizen* of Venice, to Lewis, Sebastian, and Santius, sonnes of the sayd John, and to the heires of them, and every of them, and their deputies, full and free authority, leave, and power to saile to all parts, countreys, and seas of the East, of the West, and of the North, under our banners and ensignes . . . [Thorpe 46]

Charles I, Patent to Sir Robert Heath, October 30, 1629:

Furthermore least the way to Honours & Dignityes may seem to be shutt & altogether barr'd up to men honestly borne, & are willing to undertake this present expedition & are desirous in soe remote and far distant a Region to deserve well of us & of our kingdomes in peace & warre for that doe for ourselves our heires & successors give full & free power to the foresayd Sr. Robert Heath Knight his heires & assignes to confere favours graces & honours upon those well deserveing *citizens* that inhabit within the foresayd province & the same with whatever Titles & dignityes (provided they be not the same as are now used in England) to adorne at his pleasure . . . [Thorpe 74]

Council of New England, Grant of New Hampshire, April 18, 1635:

This Indenture made ye Eighteenth day of Aprill in ye Eleaventh yeare of ye raigne of our Soveraigne Lord Charles by ye Grace of God King of England Scottland france & Ireland Defender of the faith &c Between ye Councill established at Plymouth in ye County of Devon for ye planting ruleing ordering & governing of New England in America of one part & John Wollaston *cittizen* & Gold-Smith of London of ye other part wittnesseth yt . . . [Thorpe 2437]

John Wollaston, Grant of New Hampshire, June 11, 1635:

This Indenture Made the 11th day of June in the 11th yeare of ye Raigne of our Soveraign Lord Charles by the grace of God King of England Scotland france & Ireland Defender of ye faith &ca. Between John Wolaston *Citizen* & Goldsmith of London of the one part and Capt John Mason Esqr. of the, other part Witnesseth that whereas ye Councill of New England by their Indenture under their Com'on Seale bearing date the 18th day of Aprill last past before the Date hereof made between ye Said Councill by Name of ye Councill Established at Plymouth in ye County of Devon for ye planting ordering ruling & Governing of New England in America of one part & ye Said John Wollaston by the name of John Wollaston *Citizen* & Goldsmith of London of the other part . . . [Thorpe 2439]

Duke of York, Grant of West New Jersey, August 24, 1680:

This Indenture made the sixth day of August, Anno Domini, 1680 and in the two and thirtieth year of the reign of King Charles the Second, over England, &c. between his Royal Highness, James Duke of York, and Albany, Earl of Ulster, &c. and brother to our Sovereign Lord the King of the one part; Edward

Byllynge of Westminster, the county of Middlesex, gentleman: William Penn, late of Rickmansworth, in the county of Hertford, and now of Warminghurst, in the county Sussex, Esq; Gawen Lawry, of London, merchant; Nicholas Lucas, of Hertford, in the said county of Hertford maulster, John Eldridge, of St. Pauls Shadwell, in the County of Middlesex, tanner, and Edmond Warner, *citizen* of London, of the other part. . . . [Thorpe 2560]

Duke of York, Confirmation of Deed to the New Jersey Proprietors, March 14, 1682:

. . . Thomas Cooper, *citizen* and merchant taylor, of London; Gawn Lawry, of London, merchant; Edward Billinge, of the city of Westminster, in the county of Middlesex, gentleman; James Braine, of London, merchant; William Gibson, *citizen* and haberdasher, of London; John Maywood, *citizen* and skinner, of London; Hugh Hartshorn, *citizen* and skinner, of London; Clement Plumstead, *citizen* and draper, of London . . . [Thorpe 2567]

Thomas Paine, *Common Sense,* January 9, 1776:

. . . Let the names of Whig and Tory be extinct; and let none other be heard among us, than those of a good *citizen,* an open and resolute friend; and a virtuous supporter of the RIGHTS of MANKIND and of the FREE AND INDEPENDENT STATES OF AMERICA. [CWTP1 46]

United States Declaration of Independence, July 4, 1776:

He [the King] has constrained our fellow *Citizens* taken Captive on the high Seas to bear Arms against their Country, to become the executioners of their friends and Brethren, or to fall themselves by their Hands.

Pennsylvania Constitution, September 28, 1776:

[Declaration of Rights, Article 2:] . . . Nor can any man, who acknowledges the being of a God, be justly deprived or abridged of any civil right as a *citizen,* on account of his religious sentiments or peculiar mode of religious worship . . . [Thorpe 3082]

North Carolina Constitution, December 18, 1776:

[Form of Government, Article 40:] That every foreigner, who comes to settle in this State, having first taken an oath of allegiance to the same, may purchase, or, by other means, acquire, hold, and transfer land or other real estate; and after one year's residence, shall be deemed a free *citizen.* [Thorpe 2793–94]

Georgia Constitution, February 5, 1777:

[Article 11:] . . . nor shall any person who holds any title of nobility be entitled to a vote, or be capable of serving as a representative, or hold any post of honor, profit, or trust in this State, whilst such person claims his title of nobility; but if the person shall give up such distinction, in the manner as may be directed by any future legislation, then, and in such case, he shall be entitled to a vote, and represent, as before directed, and enjoy all the other benefits of a free citizen. [Thorpe 780]

Vermont Constitution, July 8, 1777:

[Declaration of Rights, Article 3:] . . . nor can any man who professes the protestant religion, be justly deprived or abridged of any civil right, as a *citizen,* on account of his religious sentiment, or peculiar mode of religious worship, and that no authority can, or ought to be vested in, or assumed by, any power whatsoever, that shall, in any case, interfere with, or in any manner controul, the rights of conscience, in the free exercise of religious worship . . .
[Thorpe 3740]

United States Articles of Confederation, November 15, 1777:

[Article IV:] The better to secure and perpetuate mutual friendship and intercourse among the people of the different states in this union, the free inhabitants of each of these states, paupers, vagabonds and fugitives from Justice excepted, shall be entitled to all privileges and immunities of free *citizens* in the several states; and the people of each state shall have free ingress and regress to and from any other state, and shall enjoy therein all the privileges of trade and commerce, subject to the same duties, impositions and restrictions as the inhabitants thereof respectively, provided that such restriction shall not extend so far as to prevent the removal of property imported into any state, to any other state of which the Owner is an inhabitant; provided also that no imposition, duties or restriction shall be laid by any state, on the property of the united states, or either of them.

Massachusetts Constitution, March 2, 1780:

[Preamble:] The body politic is formed by a voluntary association of individuals: it is a social compact, by which the whole people covenants with each *citizen,* and each *citizen* with the whole people, that all shall be governed by certain laws for the common good. It is the duty of the people, therefore in framing a constitution of government, to provide for an equitable mode of making laws, as well as for an impartial interpretation and a faithful execution of them; that every man may, at all times, find his security in them. [Thorpe 1899]

[Declaration of Rights, Article 13:] In criminal prosecutions, the verification of facts, in the vicinity where they happen, is one of the greatest securities of the life, liberty, and property of the *citizen*. [Thorpe 1891]

[*Ibid.*, Article 29:] It is essential to the preservation of the rights of every individual, his life, liberty, property, and character, that there be an impartial interpretation of the laws, and administration of justice. It is the right of every *citizen* to be tried by judges as free, impartial, and independent as the lot of humanity will admit. It is, therefore, not only the best policy, but for the security of the rights of the people, and of every *citizen,* that the judges of the supreme judicial court should hold their offices as long as they behave themselves well; and that they should have honorable salaries ascertained and established by standing laws. [Thorpe 1893]

[Frame of Government, Chapter I:3:2:] And in order to provide for a representation of the *citizens* of this commonwealth, founded upon the principle of equality, every corporate town containing one hundred and fifty ratable polls may elect one representative . . . [Thorpe 1898]

[*Ibid.*, Chapter II:4:1:] . . . And, that the *citizens* of this commonwealth may be assured, from time to time, that the moneys remaining in the public treasury, upon the settlement and liquidation of the public accounts, are their property, no man shall be eligible as treasurer and receiver-general more than five years successively. [Thorpe 1905]

Virginia Assembly, Act of Cession of Western Territories, December 20, 1783:

. . . That the French and Canadian inhabitants, and other settlers of the Kaskaskies, Saint Vincents, and the neighboring villages, who have professed themselves *citizens* of Virginia, shall have their possessions and titles confirmed to them, and be protected in the enjoyment of their rights and liberties. . . .
[Thorpe 956]

New Hampshire Constitution, June 2, 1784:

[Bill of Rights, Article 17:] In criminal prosecutions, the trial of facts in the vicinity where they happen, is so essential to the security of the life, liberty and estate of the *citizen,* that no crime or offence ought to be tried in any other county than that in which it is committed.. [Thorpe 2455]

Ibid., Article 35:] It is essential to the preservation of the rights of every individual, his life, liberty, property and character, that there be an impartial interpretation of the laws, and administration of justice. It is the right of every *citizen* to be tried by judges as impartial as the lot of humanity will admit. It is therefore not only the best policy, but for the security of the rights of the people, that the judges of the supreme (or superior) judicial court should hold their offices so long as they behave well; and that they should have honorable salaries, ascertained and established by standing laws. Thorpe 2457]

Virginia Statute of Religious Liberty, January 16, 1786:

. . . that therefore the proscribing any *citizen* as unworthy the public confidence by laying upon him an incapacity of being called to offices of trust and emolument, unless he profess or renounce this or that religious opinion, is depriving him injuriously of those privileges and advantages to which, in common with his *fellow-citizens,* he has a natural right; that it tends only to corrupt the principles of that religion it is meant to encourage, by bribing, with a monopoly of worldly honors and emoluments, those who will externally profess and conform to it . . . [CVA8 690]

Vermont Constitution, July 4, 1786:

[Declaration of Rights, Article 3:] . . . nor can any man be justly deprived or abridged of any civil right as a *citizen,* on account of his religious sentiments, or peculiar mode of religious worship . . . [Thorpe 3752]

The Virginia Plan of Union, May 29, 1787:

[Article 9:] . . . that the jurisdiction of the inferior tribunals shall be to hear & determine in the first instance, and of the supreme tribunal to hear and determine in the dernier resort, all piracies & felonies on the high seas, captures from an enemy; cases in which foreigners or *citizens* of other States applying to such jurisdictions may be interested, or which respect the collection of the National revenue . . . [DHRC1 244–45]

The New Jersey Plan of Union, June 15, 1787:

[Article 3:] Res[olve]d that whenever requisitions shall be necessary, instead of the rule for making requisitions mentioned in the articles of Confederation, the United States in Cong[res]s be authorized to make such requisitions in proportion to the whole number of white & other free *citizens* & inhabitants of every age sex and condition including those bound to servitude for a term of years and three fifths of all other persons not comprehended in the foregoing description, except Indians not paying taxes . . . [DHRC1 251]

[Article 6:] Resolved that all Acts of the U. States in Cong[res]s made by virtue & in pursuance of the powers hereby & by the articles of Confederation vested in them, and all Treaties made & ratified under the authority of the U. States shall be the supreme law of the respective States so far forth as those Acts or Treaties shall relate to the said States or their *Citizens,* and that the Judiciary of the several States shall be bound thereby in their decisions, any thing in the respective laws of the Individual States to the contrary notwithstanding . . . [DHRC1 252]

[Article 9:] Res[olve]d that a *Citizen* of one State committing an offence in another State of the Union, shall be deemed guilty of the same offence as if it had been committed by a *Citizen* of the State in which the offence was committed. [DHRC1 253]

Alexander Hamilton's Plan of Union, June 18, 1787:

[1] The supreme judicial authority of the United States to be vested in twelve Judges, to hold their offices during good behaviour with adequate and permanent salaries. This Court to have original jurisdiction in all causes of capture and an appellate jurisdiction (from the Courts of the several states) in all causes in which the revenues of the general government or the *citizens* of foreign nations are concerned. [DHRC1 254]

[2] The Legislature of the United States to have power to institute Courts in each State for the determination of all causes of capture and of all matters relating to their revenues, or in which the *Citizens* of foreign nations are concerned. [DHRC1 254]

United States Confederation Congress, The Northwest Ordinance, July 13, 1787:

[1] . . . and personal property may be transferred by delivery, saving, however, to the French and Canadian inhabitants, and other settlers of the Kaskaskies, Saint Vincents, and the neighboring villages, who have heretofore professed themselves *citizens* of Virginia, their laws and customs now in force among them, relative to the descent and conveyance of property. [Thorpe 958]

[2] . . . Provided, That no person be eligible or qualified to act as a representative, unless he shall have been a *citizen* of one of the United States three years, and be a resident in the district, or unless he shall have resided in the district three years; and, in either case, shall likewise hold in his own right, in fee-simple, two hundred acres of land within the same: Provided also, That a freehold in fifty acres of land in the district, having been a *citizen* of one of the States, and being resident in the district, or the like freehold and two years' residence in the district, shall be necessary to qualify a man as an elector of a representative. [Thorpe 959]

[3] [Article 4:] . . . The navigable waters leading into the Mississippi and Saint Lawrence, and the carrying places between the same, shall be common highways, and forever free, as well to the inhabitants of the said territory as to the *citizens* of the United States, and those of any other States that may be admitted into the confederacy, without any tax, impost, or duty therefor. [Thorpe 961–62]

Tench Coxe, *An Examination of the Constitution for the United States of America*, No. 1, September 26, 1787:

It is impossible for an honest and feeling mind, of any nation or country whatever, to be insensible to the present circumstances of America. Were I an East Indian, or a Turk, I should consider this singular situation of a part of my fellow creatures as the most curious and interesting. Intimately connected with the country, as a *citizen* of the union, I confess it entirely engrosses my mind and feelings.
[Ford 135]

Berkeley, Virginia, County Meeting, September 28, 1787:

That it is the opinion of the meeting, that every friend to America ought, and will contribute all in his power, to establish and support the federal government proposed by the late Convention, as it appears sufficient and well adopted to secure peace, liberty and safety to the *citizens* of the United States.
[DHRC8 22]

Edmund Randolph, Letter on the Federal Constitution, October 10, 1787:

My opinion always was, and still is, that every *citizen* of America, let the crisis be what it may, ought to have a full opportunity to propose through his representatives any amendment, which in his apprehension tends to the public welfare . . . [DHRC8 271]

Richard Henry Lee [?], "The Federal Farmer," No. 3, October 10, 1787:

[1] There are some powers proposed to be lodged in the general government in the judicial department, I think very unnecessarily, I mean powers respecting questions arising upon the internal laws of the respective states. It is proper the federal judiciary should have powers co-extensive with the federal legislature—that is, the power of deciding finally on the laws of the union. By Art. 3, Sec. 2. the powers of the federal judiciary are extended (among other things) to all cases between a state and *citizens* of another state—between *citizens* of different states—between a state or the *citizens* thereof, and foreign states, *citizens* or subjects. Actions in all these cases, except against a state government, are now brought and finally determined in the law courts of the states respectively and as there are no words to exclude these courts of their jurisdiction in these cases, they will have concurrent jurisdiction with the inferior federal courts in them; and, therefore, if the new constitution be adopted without any amendment in this respect, all those numerous actions, now brought in the state courts between our *citizens* and foreigners, between *citizens* of different states, by state governments against foreigners, and by state governments against *citizens* of other

states, may also be brought in the federal courts; and an appeal will lay in them from the state courts or federal inferior courts to the supreme judicial court of the union. In almost all these cases, either party may have the trial by jury in the state courts; except paper money and tender laws, which are wisely guarded against in the proposed constitution; justice may be obtained in these courts on reasonable terms; they must be more competent to proper decisions on the laws of their respective states, than the federal states can possibly be. I do not, in any point of view, see the need of opening a new jurisdiction in these causes—of opening a new scene of expensive law suits, of suffering foreigners, and *citizens* of different states, to drag each other many hundred miles into the federal courts. It is true, those courts may be so organized by a wise and prudent legislature, as to make the obtaining of justice in them tolerably easy; they may in general be organized on the common law principles of the country: But this benefit is by no means secured by the constitution. The trial by jury is secured only in those few criminal cases, to which the federal laws will extend—as crimes committed on the seas, against the laws of nations, treason and counterfeiting the federal securities and coin: But even in these cases, the jury trial of the vicinage is not secured—particularly in the large states, a *citizen* may be tried for a crime committed in the state, and yet tried in some states 500 miles from the place where it was committed . . . [Ford 306–8]

[2] This court is to have appellate jurisdiction in all the other cases before mentioned: Many sensible men suppose that cases before mentioned respect, as well the criminal cases as the civil ones mentioned antecedently in the constitution, if so an appeal is allowed in criminal cases—contrary to the usual sense of law. How far it may be proper to admit a foreigner or the *citizen* of another state to bring actions against state governments, which have failed in performing so many promises made during the war is doubtful: How far it may be proper so to humble a state, as to oblige it to answer to an individual in a court of law, is worthy of consideration; the states are now subject to no such actions; and this new jurisdiction will subject the states, and many defendants to actions, and processes, which were not in the contemplation of the parties, when the contract was made; all engagements existing between *citizens* of different states, *citizens* and foreigners, states and foreigners; and states and *citizens* of other states were made the parties contemplating the remedies then existing on the laws of the states—and the new remedy proposed to be given in the federal courts, can be founded on no principle whatever. [Ford 309]

Noah Webster, *An Examination of the Leading Principles of the Federal Constitution*, October 17, 1787:

In ancient Rome none but the free *citizens* had the right of a suffrage in the comitia or legislative assemblies. But in Sylla's time the Italian cities demanded the rights of the Roman *citizens;* alledging that they furnished two-thirds of the armies, in all their wars, and yet were despised as foreigners. . . . [Ford 43n]

"Cato Uticensis," October 17, 1787:

. . . Did it ever enter the mind of any one of you, that you could live to see the day, that any other government, but the General Assembly of Virginia, should have power of direct taxation in this state? How few of you ever expected to see excise laws, the instruments of tyranny, in force in your country? But, who could imagine, that any man but a Virginian, were they found to be necessary, would ever have a voice towards enacting them? That any tribunal, but the Courts of Virginia, would be allowed to take cognizance of disputes between her *citizens* and their tax-gatherers and their excisemen? And that, if it should ever be found necessary to curse this land with these hateful excisemen, any one, but a fellow *citizen,* should be intrusted with that office? [DHRC8 73]

Tench Coxe, *An Examination of the Constitution for the United States of America*, No. 4, October 21, 1787:

. . . Trials for lands lying in any state between persons residing in such state, for bonds, notes, book debts, contracts, trespasses, assumptions, and all other matters between two or more *citizens* of any state, will be held in the state courts by juries, as now. In these case the foederal courts cannot interfere. But when a dispute arises between the *citizens* of any state about lands lying out of the bounds thereof, or when a trial is to be had between the *citizens* of any state and those of another, or the government of another, the private *citizen* will not be obliged to go into a court constituted by the state, with which, or with the *citizens* of which, his dispute is. He can appeal to a disinterested foederal court. This is surely a great advantage, and promises a fair trial, and an impartial judgment. The trial by jury is not excluded in these foederal courts. In all criminal cases, where the property, liberty or life of the *citizen* is at stake, he has the benefit of a jury. . . . [Ford 149]

Virginia House of Representatives, October 25, 1787:

Resolved, That it is the opinion of this committee, That every *citizen* being a freeholder in this commonwealth ought to be eligible to a seat in the Convention, and that the people therefore ought not to be restrained in their choice of Delegates by any of those legal or constitutional restrictions which confine them in their choice of members to the Legislature. [DHRC8 116]

Pelatiah Webster, *The Weakness of Brutus Exposed*, November 4, 1787:

There can be no doubt that each State will receive from the union great support and protection against the invasions and inroads of foreign enemies, as well as against riots and insurrections of their own *citizens;* and of consequence, the course of their internal administration will be secured by this means against any interruption or embarrassment from either of these causes. [Ford 128]

Alexander Hamilton, *The Federalist*, No. 7, November 17, 1787:

. . . There are even dissimilar views among the States as to the general principle of discharging the public debt. Some of them, either less impressed with the importance of national credit, or because their *citizens* have little, if any, immediate interest in the question, feel an indifference, if not a repugnance, to the payment of the domestic debt at any rate. These would be inclined to magnify the difficulties of a distribution. Others of them, a numerous body of whose *citizens* are creditors to the public beyond the proportion of the State in the total amount of the national debt, would be strenuous for some equitable and effective provision. The procrastinations of the former would excite the resentments of the latter. The settlement of a rule would, in the meantime, be postponed by real differences of opinion and affected delays. The *citizens* of the States interested would clamor; foreign powers would urge for the satisfaction of their just demands, and the peace of the States would be hazarded to the double contingency of external invasion and internal contention. [Fed. 117]

James Madison, *The Federalist*, No. 10, November 22, 1787:

The two great points of difference between a democracy and a republic are: first, the delegation of the government, in the latter, to a small number of *citizens* elected by the rest; secondly, the greater number of *citizens,* and greater sphere of country, over which the latter may be extended. [Fed. 133–34]

Tobias Lear, "Brutus," November 22, 1787:

. . . Let the constitution proposed by the late Convention be dispassionately considered and fully canvassed.—Let no *citizen* of the United States of America, who is capable of discussing the important subject, retire from the field . . .
[DHRC8 174]

Alexander Hamilton, *The Federalist*, No. 15, December 1, 1787:

. . . Except as to the rule of apportionment, the United States [under the Confederation] has an indefinite discretion to make requisitions for men and money; but they have no authority to raise either, by regulations extending to the individual *citizens* of America. The consequence of this is, that though in theory their resolutions concerning those objects are laws, constitutionally binding on the members of the Union, yet in practice they are mere recommendations which the States observe or disregard at their option. [Fed. 158]

Oliver Ellsworth, "The Landholder," No. 6, December 10, 1787:

I intreat you, my fellow *citizens,* to read and examine the new constitution with candor; examine it for yourselves, you are most of you as learned as the objector, and certainly as able to judge of its virtues or vices as he is. . . .
[DHRC8 230]

Alexander Hamilton, *The Federalist*, No. 22, December 14, 1787:

. . . Though the genius of the people of this country might never permit this description to be strictly applicable to us, yet we may reasonably expect, from the gradual conflicts of State regulations, that the *citizens* of each would at length come to be considered and treated by the others in no better light than that of foreigners and aliens. [Fed. 192]

Dissent of the Pennsylvania Convention's Minority, December 18, 1787:

. . . The minority attempted to prevent this by agreeing to vote for some of the leading members, who they knew had influence enough to be appointed at any rate, in hopes of carrying with them some respectable *citizens* of Philadelphia, in whose principles and integrity they could have more confidence; but even in this they were disappointed, except in one member: the eighth member was added at a subsequent session of the assembly. [DHRC2 619–20]

Robert Yates and John Lansing, Objections to the Constitution, December 21, 1787:

Exclusive of our objections originating from the want of power, we entertained an opinion that a general government, however guarded by declarations of rights, or cautionary provisions, must unavoidably, in a short time, be productive of the destruction of the civil liberty of such *citizens* who could be effectually coerced by it . . . [Farrand3 246]

Alexander Hamilton, *The Federalist*, No. 28, December 26, 1787:

The obstacles to usurpation and the facilities of resistance increase with the increased extent of the state, provided the *citizens* understand their rights and are disposed to defend them. . . . [Fed. 225]

Alexander Hamilton, *The Federalist*, No. 35, January 5, 1788:

There is no part of the administration of government that requires extensive information and a thorough knowledge of the principles of political economy so much as the business of taxation. The man who understands those principles best will be least likely to resort to oppressive expedients, or to sacrifice any particular class of *citizens* to the procurement of revenue. . . . [Fed. 258]

James Madison, *The Federalist*, No. 40, January 18, 1788:

. . . The forbearance can only have proceeded from an irresistible conviction of the absurdity of subjecting the fate of twelve States to the perverseness or corruption of a thirteenth; from the example of inflexible opposition given by a majority of one sixtieth of the people of America to a measure approved and called for by the voice of twelve States, comprising fifty-nine sixtieths of the people—an example still fresh in the memory and indignation of every *citizen* who has felt for the wounded honor and prosperity of his country. . . .

[Fed. 290]

Alexander White [?], "An Independent Freeholder," January 18, 1788:

. . . If a prince would do this or [CHECK THIS] his subjects what may we expect from our fellow *citizens,* when invested with power by the voice of their country; and when they and their posterity are to feel the consequence of all their acts? When you add to this, that the jurisdiction of the federal courts will not extend to disputes relating to property, real or personal, to contracts or personal injuries between *citizens,* which in general are the subjects of litigation; the apprehension of oppression from those courts must appear groundless. . . . [DHRC8 312]

James Madison, *The Federalist*, No. 42, January 22, 1788:

The dissimilarity in the rules of naturalization has long been remarked as a fault in our system, and as laying a foundation for intricate and delicate questions. In the fourth article of the Confederation, it is declared "that the free inhabitants of each of these States, paupers, vagabonds, and fugitives from justice excepted, shall be entitled to all privileges and immunities of free *citizens* in the several States; and the people of each State shall, in every other, enjoy all the privileges of trade and commerce," etc. There is a confusion of language here, which is remarkable. Why the terms free inhabitants are used in one part of the article, free *citizens* in another, and people in another; or what was meant by superadding to "all privileges and immunities of free *citizens;*" "all the privileges of trade and commerce," cannot easily be determined. It seems to be a construction scarcely avoidable, however, that those who come under the denomination of free inhabitants of a State, although not *citizens* of such State, are entitled, in every other State, to all the privileges of free *citizens* of the latter; that is, to greater privileges than they may be entitled to in their own State: so that it may be in the power of a particular State, or rather every State is laid under a necessity, not only to confer the rights of *citizenship* in other States upon any whom it may admit to such rights within itself, but upon any whom it may allow to become inhabitants within its jurisdiction. But were an exposition of the term "inhabitants" to be admitted which would confine the stipulated privileges to *citizens* alone, the difficulty is diminished only, not removed. The very improper power would still be retained by each State, of naturalizing aliens in every other State. In one State, residence for a short term confirms all the rights of *citizenship:* in another, qualifications of greater importance are required. An alien, therefore legally incapacitated for certain rights in the latter, may, by previous residence only in the former, elude his incapacity; and thus the law of one State be preposterously rendered paramount to the law of another, within the jurisdiction of the other. We owe it to mere casualty, that very serious embarrassments on this subject have been hitherto escaped. By the laws of several States, certain descriptions of aliens, who had rendered themselves obnoxious, were laid under interdicts inconsistent not only with the rights of *citizenship* but with the privilege of residence. What would have been the consequence, if such persons, by residence or otherwise, had acquired the character of *citizens* under the laws of another State, and then asserted their rights as such, both to residence and *citizenship,* within the State proscribing them? Whatever the legal consequences might have been, other consequences would probably have resulted, of too serious a nature not to be provided against. . . . [Fed. 307–8]

James Madison, *The Federalist*, No. 46, January 29, 1788:

. . . Let us not insult the free and gallant *citizens* of America with the suspicion, that they would be less able to defend the rights of which they would be in actual possession, than the debased subjects of arbitrary power would be to rescue theirs from the hands of their oppressors. . . . [Fed. 335]

Alexander C. Hanson, *Remarks on the Proposed Plan of a Federal Government*, c. January 31, 1788:

[1] Before this appointment can be entailed, and before even the term can be enlarged, the constitution must be changed, by consent of the people. By what method, then, shall the president effect this alteration? Every *citizen* in the union will be a censor on his conduct. . . . [Ford 233]

[2] When the compact confers the aforesaid general power, making nevertheless some special reservations and exceptions, then is the *citizen* protected further, so far as these reservations and exceptions shall extend. [Ford 241–42]

Luther Martin, "Genuine Information," No. 10, February 1, 1788:

[1] . . . To the courts of the general government are also confined all cases in law or equity, arising under the proposed constitution, and treaties made under the authority of the United States—all cases affecting ambassadors, other public

ministers and consuls—all cases of admiralty and maritime jurisdiction—all controversies to which the United States are a party—all controversies between two or more States—between a State and *citizens* of another State—between *citizens* of the same State claiming lands under grants of different States, and between a State or the *citizens* thereof, and foreign States, *citizens,* or subjects.—Whether therefore, any laws or regulations of the Congress, or any acts of its president or other officers are contrary to, or not warranted by the constitution, rests only with the judges, who are appointed by Congress to determine; by whose determinations every State must be bound.—Should any question arise between a foreign consul and any of the *citizens* of the United States, however remote from the seat of empire, it is to be heard before the judiciary of the general government, and in the first instance to be heard in the supreme court, however inconvenient to the parties, and however trifling the subject of dispute. [DHRC16 8]

[2] Thus, Sir, in consequence of this appellate jurisdiction and its extension to facts as well as to law, every arbitrary act of the general government, and every oppression of all those variety of officers appointed under its authority for the collection of taxes, duties, impost, excise, and other purposes, must be submitted to by the individual, or must be opposed with little prospect of success and almost a certain prospect of ruin, at least in those cases where the middle and common class of *citizens* are interested—Since to avoid that oppression, or to obtain redress, the application must be made to one of the courts of the United States—by good fortune should this application be in the first instance attended with success, and should damages be recovered equivalent to the injury sustained, an appeal lies to the supreme court, in which case the *citizen* must at once give up his cause, or he must attend to it at the distance of perhaps more than a thousand miles from the place of his residence . . . [DHRC16 10]

David Ramsay, "Civis," February 4, 1788:

. . . Without money, without a navy, or the means of even supporting an army of our own *citizens* in the field, we lie at the mercy of every invader; our sea port towns may be laid under contribution, and our country ravaged.

[DHRC16 26]

Tench Coxe, "A Freeman," No. 3, February 6, 1788:

The construction of the senate affords an absolute certainty, that the states will not lose their present share of separate powers. No state is to lose its voice therein without its own consent. Governor [Edmund] Randolph justly observes, that the force of the constitution of any state can only be lessened by the absolute grant of its own *citizens*. Whatever therefore is now possessed will remain, unless transferred by new grants. . . . [DHRC16 50]

Massachusetts Convention, Proposed Amendments to the Constitution, February 6, 1788:

[Article 7:] The supreme judicial federal court shall have no jurisdiction of causes between *citizens* of different states, unless the matter in dispute, whether it concerns the reality or personality, be of the value of three thousand dollars, at the least: Nor shall the federal judicial powers extend to any actions between *citizens* of different states where the matter in dispute, whether it concerns the reality or personality, is not of the value of fifteen hundred dollars, at the least. [DHRC16 69]

James Madison, *The Federalist*, No. 55, February 13, 1788:

. . . The charges exhibited against it [the House of Representatives] are, first, that so small a number of representatives will be an unsafe depositary of the public interests; secondly, that they will not possess a proper knowledge of the local circumstances of their numerous constituents; thirdly, that they will be taken from that class of *citizens* which will sympathize least with the feelings of the mass of the people, and be most likely to aim at a permanent elevation of the few on the depression of the many . . . [Fed. 374]

Spencer Roane, "A Plain Dealer," February 13, 1788:

. . . I doubt not you will publish the following observation in your useful paper.—To know the head which dictated them can be of no use to the public, and will add no weight to the publication; being written by an obscure *citizen,* but anxiously wishing for the prosperity of this country. . . . [DHRC8 363]

"Brutus," No. 12, February 14, 1788:

[1] I presume there will be no difficulty in accomplishing this. Nothing more is necessary than to set forth, in the process, that the party who brings the suit is a *citizen* of a different state from the one against whom the suit is brought, & there can be little doubt but that the court will take cognizance of the matter, & if they do, who is to restrain them? . . . [DHRC16 121]

[2] . . . Moreover, the constitution expressly declares, that "the *citizens* of each state shall be entitled to all the privileges and immunities of *citizens* in the several states." It will therefore be no fiction, for a *citizen* of one state to set forth, in a suit, that he is a *citizen* of another; for he that is entitled to all the privileges and immunities of a country, is a *citizen* of that country. And in truth, the *citizen* of one state will, under this constitution, be a *citizen* of every state.
[DHRC16 121]

James Madison, *The Federalist*, No. 58, February 20, 1788:

There is a peculiarity in the federal Constitution which insures a watchful attention in a majority both of the people and of their representatives to a constitutional augmentation of the latter. The peculiarity lies in this, that one branch of the legislature is a representation of *citizens,* the other of the States: in the former, consequently, the larger States will have most weight; in the latter, the advantage will be in favor of the smaller States. . . . [Fed. 389]

"The Impartial Examiner," No. 1, February 20, 1788:

Permit me now, my country men, to make a few observations on the proposed Foederal Constitution. In this attempt the subject, as it is arduous and difficult, naturally impresses the modest mind with diffidence: yet being of the last importance, as involving in it the highest interest, that freemen can have—all that is dear and valuable to the *citizens* of these United States; a consciousness of the strong claim, which this subject has, to a free and general discussion, has prevailed over that discouraging idea so far as to produce the present address to you. . . . [DHRC8 391]

Benjamin Workman [?], "Philadelphiensis," No. 10, February 20, 1788:

The allegiance of freemen to government will ever be a consequence of protection; the Congress of America withdrew their allegiance from the king of Great-Britain when he changed his protection into acts of cruelty; and on the same account the *citizens* of these United States will not chearfully bear allegiance to the new government; which, instead of protecting them in their sacred rights and privileges, will be a system of tyranny and oppression. . . .

[DHRC16 160]

"Brutus," No. 13, February 21, 1788:

. . . For if the *citizen* of one state, possessed of a written obligation, given in pursuance of a solemn act of the legislature, acknowledging a debt due to the bearer, and promising to pay it, cannot recover in the supreme court, I can conceive of no case in which they can recover. . . . [DHRC16 174–74]

"A Real Patriot," February 26, 1788:

I sincerely congratulate the *citizens* of America upon the fair prospect which now presents itself to their view; and promises a long reign of virtue, happiness, and glory, as the result of a constitution which is the real vox populi so often ardently desired by mankind, in vain, and now, for the first time, discovered by the patriotic sages of America. [DHRC16 119]

Circular Letter to the Fayette, Kentucky, County Court, February 29, 1788:

. . . The power Over the Militia, may leave us in a defenceless State and subject us to the ravages of the Merciless Savages; And Upon Our Separation being established, a Number of our *Citizens* will be draged by the power of the Foedral Court Six or eight hundred Miles to contest their Legal Claims. [DHRC8 435]

Mercy Otis Warren, *Observations on the New Constitution,* February 1788:

. . . but mankind must think for themselves, and to many very judicious and discerning characters, the whole constitution with very few exceptions appears a perversion of the rights of particular states, and of private *citizens*. . . . [DHRC16 281]

John Jay, *The Federalist,* No. 64, March 5, 1788:

As the select assemblies for choosing the President, as well as the State legislatures who appoint the senators, will in general be composed of the most enlightened and respectable *citizens,* there is reason to presume that their attention and their votes will be directed to those men only who have become the most distinguished by their abilities and virtue, and in whom the people perceive just grounds for confidence. . . . [Fed. 421]

"A Federal Republican," March 5, 1788:

. . . But if a Continental Collector, in the execution of his office, should invade your freedom (according to this new government, which has expressly declared itself paramount to all State laws and Constitutions) the State of which you are a *citizen,* will have no authority to afford you relief. A Continental Court may, indeed, be established in the State, and it may be urged that you will find a remedy here, but, my fellow *citizens,* let me ask, what protection this will afford you against the insults or rapacity of a Continental officer, when he will have it in his power to appeal to the seat of Congress perhaps at several hundred miles distance . . . [DHRC8 459]

Benjamin Workman [?], "Philadelphiensis," No. 11, March 8, 1788:

. . . As our holy religion expressly enjoins it as a duty, not to return evil for evil, but to overcome evil with good; consequently our resentment against these ungrateful men should be moderated christian charity: Yet as freemen and *citizens,* determined to hand down to posterity sacred liberty unimpaired, we are solemnly bound, at the hazard of our fortunes and lives, to oppose this base attempt [*i.e.,* the Constitution] of theirs to enslave our country.[DHRC16 363]

James Iredell, "Marcus," No. 4, March 12, 1788:

. . . Is it not the aim of every wise country to be as much the carriers of their own produce as can be? And would not this be the means in our own of producing a new source of activity among the people, giving to our own fellow *citizens* what otherwise must be given to strangers, and laying the foundation of an independent trade among ourselves, and of gradually raising a navy in America, which, however distant the prospect, ought certainly not to be out of our sight. . . . [DHRC16 380]

"An Impartial Citizen," No. 6, March 13, 1788:

. . . The only way then whereby Congress can oppress us in any considerable degree, will be by raising money and an army, unnecessarily, and by ordering the militia to be embodied and marched to destroy their fellow *citizens*. The publication of the applications of the public revenue, and the notoriety of the situation of public affairs, most clearly will prevent the former. . . .
[DHRC8 500]

Archibald Maclaine, "Publicola," March 20, 1788:

. . . It is well known to every one who has looked into the new constitution, with any degree of attention, that the federal courts can have nothing to do with suits between *citizens* of the same state, unless where they claim lands under grants of different states. This [is] a power reserved by the confederation, and it is necessary for the purpose of giving each party a fair and impartial trial, before Judges who may be supposed indifferent to both states—The *citizen* of this state will have the benefit of this regulation, when he claims land in another state, either under a grant of that state, or his own. . . . [DHRC16 439–40]

Luther Martin, "To the *Citizens* of Maryland," No. 2, March 21, 1788:

. . . It [*i.e.*, the Federal Constitution] was afterwards altered and amended (if it can be called an amendment) to the form in which it stands in the system now published, and, as inferior continental, and not state, courts are originally to decide on those questions, it is now worse than useless; for being so altered as to render the treaties and laws made under the general government superior to our [*i.e.*, Maryland's] constitution, if the system is adopted, it will amount to a total and unconditional surrender to that government, by the *citizens* of this state, of every right and privilege secured to them by our constitution . . .
[DHRC16 453]

Luther Martin, "To the *Citizens* of Maryland," No. 3, March 28, 1788:

There is, my *fellow-citizens*, scarcely an individual of common understanding, I believe, in this State, who is any ways acquainted with the proposed constitution, who doth not allow it to be, in many instances, extremely censurable, and that a variety of alterations and amendments are essentially requisite, to render it consistent with a reasonable security for the liberty of the respective states, and their *citizens*. [DHRC16 499]

John Jay, *An Address to the People of the State of New York*, c. April 15, 1788:

. . . Reflect that the present plan [the Constitution] comes recommended to you by men and fellow *citizens* who have given you the highest proofs that men can give, of their justice, their love for liberty and their country of their prudence, of their application, and of their talents. . . . [Ford 85]

Alexander Hamilton, *The Federalist*, No. 80, May 28, 1788:

The power of determining causes between two States, between one State and the *citizens* of another, and between the *citizens* of different States,is perhaps not less essential to the peace of the Union than that which has been just examined. . . . [Fed. 501]

Alexander Hamilton, *The Federalist*, No. 84, May 28, 1788:

. . . Is it one object of a bill of rights to declare and specify the political privileges of the *citizens* in the structure and administration of the government? This is done in the most ample and precise manner in the plan of the convention; comprehending various precautions for the public security, which are not to be found in any of the State constitutions. . . . [Fed. 536]

John Dickinson, "Fabius," No. 5, 1788:

The protection herein mentioned, refers to cases between *citizens* and *citizens*, or states and states: But there is also a protection to be afforded to all the *citizens*, or states, against foreigners. . . . [Ford 188]

George Washington, First Inaugural Address, April 30, 1789:

Fellow-*Citizens* of the Senate and of the House of Representatives: . . . On the other hand, the magnitude and difficulty of the trust to which the voice of my country called me, being sufficient to awaken in the wisest and most experienced of her *citizens* a distrustful scrutiny into his qualifications, could not but overwhelm with despondence one who, inheriting inferior endowments from nature, and unpracticed in the duties of civil administration, ought to be peculiarly conscious of his own deficiencies. In this conflict of emotions, all I dare aver is, that it has been my faithful study to collect my duty from a just appreciation of every circumstance by which it might be affected. All I dare hope is that if, in executing this task, I have been too much swayed by a grateful remembrance of former instances, or by an affectionate sensibility to this transcendent proof of the confidence of my *fellow-citizens,* and have thence too little consulted my incapacity as well as disinclination for the weighty and untried cares before me, my error will be palliated by the motives which misled me, and its consequences be judged by my country with some share of the partiality in which they originated. [Annals 27]

Georgia Constitution, May 6, 1789:

[Article I, Section 3:] No person shall be a member of the senate who shall not have attained to the age of twenty-eight years, and who shall not have been nine years an inhabitant of the United States, and three years a *citizen* of this State . . . [Thorpe 786]

[Article I, Section 7:] No person shall be a member of the house of representatives who shall not have attained to the age of twenty-one years, and have been seven years a *citizen* of the United States, and two years an inhabitant of this State . . . [Thorpe 786]

[Article II, Section 3:] No person shall be eligible to the office of governor who shall not have been a *citizen* of the United States twelve years, and an inhabitant of this State six years, and who hath not attained to the age of thirty years, and who does not possess five hundred acres of land, in his own right, within this State, and other species of property to the amount of one thousand pounds sterling. [Thorpe 787]

[Article IV, Section 1:] The electors of the members of both branches of the general assembly shall be *citizens* and inhabitants of this State, and shall have attained to the age of twenty-one years, and have paid tax for the year preceding the election, and shall have resided six months within the county. [Thorpe 789]

United States Congress, Judiciary Act of September 24, 1789:

[Section 11:] . . . That the circuit courts shall have original cognizance, concurrent with the courts of the several States, of all suits of a civil nature at common law or in equity, where the matter in dispute exceeds, exclusive of costs, the sum or value of five hundred dollars; and the United States are plaintiffs or petitioners; or an alien is a party, or the suit is between a *citizen* of the State where the suit is brought and a *citizen* of another State. . . . [USSL1 78–79]

[Section 12:] . . . That if a suit be commenced in any state court against an alien, or by a *citizen* of the state in which the suit is brought against a citizen of another state, and the matter in dispute exceeds the aforesaid sum of value of five hundred dollars, exclusive of costs, to be made to appear to the satisfaction of the court . . . [USSL1 79]

[Section 13:] . . . That the Supreme Court shall have exclusive jurisdiction of all controversies of a civil nature, where a state is a party, except between a state and its *citizens;* and except also between a state and *citizens* of other states, or aliens, in which latter case it shall have original but not exclusive jurisdiction. And shall have exclusively all such jurisdiction of suits or proceedings against ambassadors, or other public ministers, or their domestics, or domestic servants, as a court of law can have or exercise consistently with the law of nations; and original, but not exclusive jurisdiction of all suits brought by ambassadors, or other public ministers, or in which a consul or vice consul shall be a party. And the trial of issues in fact in the Supreme Court in all actions at law against *citizens* of the United States, shall be by jury. . . . [USSL1 80–81]

[Section 29:] . . . and the jurors shall have the same qualifications as are requisite for jurors by the laws of the State of which they are *citizens,* to serve in the highest courts of law of such State . . . [USSL1 88]

South Carolina Constitution, June 3, 1790:

[Article I, Section 2:] The house of representatives shall be composed of members chosen by ballot every second year, by the *citizens* of this State, qualified as in this constitution provided. [Thorpe 3258]

[Article I, Section 4:] Every free white man, of the age of twenty-one years, being a *citizen* of this State, and having resided therein two years previous to the day of election, and who hath a freehold of fifty acres of land or a town lot, of which he hath been legally seized and possessed at least six months before such election, or, not having such freehold or town lot, hath been a resident in the election district in which he offers to give his vote six months before the said election, and hath paid a tax the preceding year of three shillings sterling towards the support of this government, shall have a right to vote for a member or members to serve in either branch of the legislature for the election district in which he holds such property or is so resident. [Thorpe 3258–59]

[Article I, Section 5:] The returning officer, or any other person present entitled to vote, may require any person who shall offer his vote at an election to produce a certificate of his *citizenship* and a receipt from the tax collector of his having paid a tax entitling him to vote, or to swear or affirm that he is duly qualified to vote, agreeably to this constitution. [Thorpe 3259]

[Article I, Section 6:] No person shall be eligible to a seat in the house of representatives unless he is a free white man, of the age of twenty-one years, and hath been a *citizen* and resident in this State three years previous to his election. . . . [Thorpe 3259]

[Article I, Section 7:] The senate shall be composed of members to be chosen for four years, in the following proportions, by the *citizens* of this State qualified to elect members to the house of representatives, at the same time, and in the same manner, and at the same places where they shall vote for representatives . . . [Thorpe 3259]

[Article I, Section 8:] No person shall be eligible to a seat in the senate unless he is a free white man, of the age of thirty years, and hath been a *citizen* and resident in this State five years previous to his election. . . . [Thorpe 3259]

Article II, Section 2:] No person shall be eligible to the office of governor unless he hath attained the age of thirty years, and hath resided within this State and been a *citizen* thereof ten years, and unless he be seized and possessed of a settled estate within the same, in his own right, of the value of fifteen hundred pounds sterling, clear of debt. [Thorpe 3262]

Pennsylvania Constitution, September 2, 1790:

Article I, Section 2:] The representatives shall be chosen, annually, by the *citizens* of the city of Philadelphia, and of each county respectively, on the second Tuesday of October. [Thorpe 3092]

[Article I, Section 3:] No person shall be a representative, who shall not have attained the age of twenty-one years, and have been a *citizen* and inhabitant of the State three years next preceding his election, and the last year thereof an inhabitant of the city or county in which he shall be chosen . . . [Thorpe 3092]

[Article I, Section 5:] The senators shall be chosen for four years by the *citizens* of Philadelphia, and of the several counties, at the same time, in the same manner, and at the same places where they shall vote for representatives. [Thorpe 3093]

[Article I, Section 8:] No person shall be a senator, who shall not have attained the age of twenty-five years, and have been a *citizen* and inhabitant of the State four years next before his election, and the last year thereof an inhabitant of the district for which he shall be chosen, unless be shall have been absent on the public business of the United States, or of this State. [Thorpe 3093]

[Article II, Section 2:] The governor shall be chosen on the second Tuesday of October, by the *citizens* of the commonwealth, at the places where they shall respectively vote for representatives. . . . [Thorpe 3095]

[Article II, Section 4:] He [the Governor] shall be, at least, thirty years of age, and have been a *citizen* and inhabitant of this State seven years next before his election; unless he shall have been absent on the public business of the United States, or of this State. [Thorpe 3095]

[Article II, Section 8:] He [the Governor] shall appoint all officers, whose offices are established by this constitution, or shall be established by law, and whose appointments are not herein otherwise provided for; but no person shall be appointed to an office within any county who shall not have been a *citizen* and inhabitant therein one year next before his appointment, if the county shall have been so long erected . . . [Thorpe 3095]

[Article III, Section 1:] In elections by the *citizens*, every freeman of the age of twenty-one years, having resided in the State two years next before the election, and within that time paid a State or county tax, which shall have been assessed at least six months before the election, shall enjoy the rights of an elector . . . [Thorpe 3096]

[Article VI, Section 1:] Sheriffs and coroners shall, at the times and places of election of representatives, be chosen by the *citizens* of each county; two persons shall be chosen for each office, one of whom, for each respectively, shall be appointed by the governor. . . . [Thorpe 3098]

[Article IX, Section 7:] . . . The free communication of thoughts and opinions is one of the invaluable rights of man; and every *citizen* may freely speak, write, and print on any subject, being responsible for the abuse of that liberty. . . . [Thorpe 3100]

[Article IX, Section 20:] That the *citizens* have a right, in a peaceable manner, to assemble together for their common good, and to apply to those invested with the powers of government for redress of grievances, or other proper purposes, by petition, address, or remonstrance. [Thorpe 3101]

[Article IX, Section 21:] That the right of *citizens* to bear arms, in defence of themselves and the State, shall not be questioned. [Thorpe 3101]

COMMERCE, REGULATE

(Regulation, Regulations, Regulating; Commercial; Trade)

United States Constitution, September 17, 1787:

[Article I, Section 8:] To *regulate Commerce* with foreign Nations, and among the several States, and with the Indian Tribes;

[Article I, Section 9:] No Preference shall be given by any *Regulation of Commerce* or Revenue to the Ports of one State over those of another: nor shall Vessels bound to, or from, one State, be obliged to enter, clear, or pay Duties in another.

* * * * *

Charter of the Dutch West India Company, June 3, 1621:

[Article 38:] And if it happens (which we by no means expect) that any person will, in any manner, hurt or hinder the navigation, business, *trade,* or traffic of this Company, contrary to the common right and the contents of the aforesaid treaties, leagues, and covenants, they shall defend it against them, and *regulate* it by the instructions we have given concerning it. [Thorpe 65]

Pennsylvania Frame of Government, April 25, 1682:

[Article 13:] That, for the better management of the powers and trust aforesaid, the provincial Council shall, from time to time, divide itself into four distinct and proper committees, for the more easy administration of the affairs of the Province, which divides the seventy-two into four eighteens, every one of which eighteens shall consist of six out of each of the three orders, or yearly elections, each of which shall have a distinct portion of business, as followeth: . . . Thirdly, a committee of *trade* and treasury, who shall regulate all *trade and commerce,* according to law, encourage manufacture and county growth, and defray the public charge of the Province. . . . [Thorpe 3056–57]

The Albany Plan of Union, July 10, 1754:

That they [*i.e.*, the Grand Council] make such laws as they judge necessary for *regulating all Indian trade*. [Thorpe 84]

First Continental Congress, Declaration and Resolves, October 14, 1774:

. . . But, from the necessity of the case, and a regard to the mutual interest of both countries, we cheerfully consent to the operation of such acts of the British parliament, as are bona fide restrained to the *regulation of our external commerce*, for the purpose of securing the *commercial* advantages of the whole empire to the mother country, and the *commercial* benefits of its respective members; excluding every idea of taxation, internal or external, for raising a revenue on the subjects in America without their consent. [JCC1 68–69]

United States Continental Congress, Draft Articles of Confederation, July 12, 1776:

[Article 18:] The United States assembled shall have the sole and exclusive Right and Power of . . . *Regulating the Trade*, and managing all Affairs with the Indians . . . [DHRC1 82]

Maryland Constitution, November 11, 1776:

[Form of Government, Article 11:] . . . it is declared, that no bill imposing duties or customs for the mere *regulation of commerce,* or inflicting fines for the reformation of morals, or to enforce the execution of the laws, by which an incidental revenue may arise, shall be accounted a money bill; but every bill assessing, levying, or applying taxes or supplies for the support of government or the current expenses of the state, or appropriating money in the treasury, shall be deemed a money bill. [Thorpe 1693]

United States Articles of Confederation, November 15, 1777:

[Article 9:] The united states in congress assembled shall also have the sole and exclusive right and power of regulating the alloy and value of coin struck by their own authority, or by that of the respective states—fixing the standard of weights and measures throughout the united states.—*regulating the trade* and managing all affairs with the Indians, not members of any of the states, provided that the legislative right of any state within its own limits be not infringed or violated . . .

Report of the Annapolis Convention, September 14, 1786:

[1] . . . they found, that the States of New York, Pennsylvania and Virginia had, in substance, and nearly in the same terms, authorised their respective Commissioners "to meet such commissioners as were, or might be, appointed by the other States in the Union, at such time and place, as should be agreed upon by the said Commissioners to take into consideration the *trade and Commerce* of the United States, to consider how far an uniform system in their *commercial intercourse and regulations* might be necessary to their common interest and permanent harmony, and to report to the several States, such an Act, relative to this great object, as when unanimously ratified by them would enable the United States in Congress assembled effectually to provide for the same."

[DHRC1 182–83]

[2] That the State of New Jersey had enlarged the object of their Appointment, empowering their Commissioners, "to consider how far an uniform system in their *commercial regulations* and other important matters, might be necessary to the common interest and permanent harmony of the several States," and to report such an Act on the subject, as when ratified by them "would enable the United States in Congress-Assembled, effectually to provide for the exigencies of the Union." [DHRC1 183]

[3] In this persuasion, Your Commissioners submit an opinion, that the Idea of extending the powers of their Deputies, to other objects, than those of *Commerce* which has been adopted by the State of New Jersey, was an improvement on the original plan, and will deserve to be incorporated into that of a future Convention, they are the more naturally led to this conclusion, as in the course of their reflections on the subject, they have been induced to think, that the power of *regulating trade* is of such comprehensive extent, and will enter so far into the general System of the foederal government, that to give it efficacy, and to obviate questions and doubts concerning its precise nature and limits may require a correspondent adjustment of other parts of the Foederal System.

[DHRC1 183–84]

Charles Pinckney's Plan of Union, May 29, 1787:

[Article 12:] The [Senate and House of Delegates] in C[ongress] ass[embled] shall have the exclusive Power of *regulating Trade* and levying Imposts . . .

[DHRC1 246]

The New Jersey Plan of Union, June 15, 1787:

[1] Resd. that in addition to the powers vested in the U. States in Congress, by the present existing articles of Confederation, they be authorized . . . to pass Acts for the *regulation of trade & commerce* as well with foreign nations as with each other: provided that all punishments, fines, forfeitures and penalties to be

incurred for contravening such acts rules and regulations shall be adjudged by the Common law Judiciarys of the State in which any offence contrary to the true intent & meaning of such Acts rules & regulations shall have been committed or perpetrated, with liberty of commencing in the first instance all suits & prosecutions for that purpose in the superior common law Judiciary in such State, subject nevertheless, for the correction of all errors, both in law & fact in rendering Judgment, to an appeal to the Judiciary of the U. States.

[DHRC1 251]

[2] . . . that the Judiciary so established shall have authority to hear & determine in the first instance on all impeachments of federal officers, & by way of appeal in the dernier resort in all cases touching the rights of Ambassadors, in all cases of captures from an enemy, in all cases of piracies & felonies on the high Seas, in all cases in which foreigners may be interested, in the construction of any treaty or treaties, or which may arise on any of the Acts for *regulation of trade*, or the collection of the federal Revenue . . . [DHRC1 251]

James Wilson, Speech on the Federal Constitution, October 6, 1787:

. . . For instance, the liberty of the press, which has been a copious subject of declamation and opposition, what controul can proceed from the foederal government, to shackle or destroy that sacred palladium of national freedom? If, indeed, a power similar to that which has been granted for the *regulation of commerce*, had been granted to regulate literary publications, it would have been as necessary to stipulate that the liberty of the press should be preserved inviolate, as that the impost should be general in its operation. . . . [Ford 156]

George Mason, Objections to the Constitution, October 7, 1787:

By requiring only a Majority to make all *Commercial* & Navigation Laws, the five Southern States (whose Produce & Circumstances are totally different from that of the eight Northern & Eastern States) will be ruined; for such rigid & premature *Regulations* may be made as will enable the Merchants of the Northern & Eastern States not only to demand an exorbitant Freight, but to monopolize the Purchase of the Commodities at their own Price, for many Years: to the great Injury of the landed Interest, & Impoverishment of the People . . .

[DHRC8 45]

Richard Henry Lee [?], "The Federal Farmer," No. 1, October 8, 1787:

[1] The first principal question that occurs, is, Whether, considering our situation, we ought to precipitate the adoption of the proposed constitution? If we remain cool and temperate, we are in no immediate danger of any commotions; we are in a state of perfect peace, and in no danger of invasions; the state governments

are in the full exercise of their powers; and our governments answer all present exigencies, except the *regulation of trade*,securing credit, in some cases, and providing for the interest, in some instances, of the public debts . . .

[Ford 280–81]

[2] . . . We find, therefore, members of congress urging alterations in the federal system almost as soon as it was adopted. It was early proposed to vest congress with powers to levy an impost, to *regulate trade,* &c. but such was known to be the caution of the states in parting with power, that the vestment even of these, was proposed to be under several checks and limitations. . . . [Ford 283]

[3] . . . A general convention for mere *commercial* purposes was moved for—the authors of this measure saw that the people's attention was turned solely to the amendment of the federal system; and that, had the idea of a total change been started, probably no state would have appointed members to the convention. The idea of destroying, ultimately, the state government, and forming one consolidated system, could not have been admitted—a convention, therefore, merely for vesting in congress power to *regulate trade* was proposed. This was pleasing to the *commercial* towns; and the landed people had little or no concern about it. September, 1786, a few men from the middle states met at Annapolis, and hastily proposed a convention to be held in May, 1787, for the purpose, generally, of amending the confederation . . . [Ford 284]

Richard Henry Lee [?], "The Federal Farmer," No. 3, October 10, 1787:

In the second place it is necessary, therefore, to examine the extent, and the probable operations of some of those extensive powers proposed to be vested in this government. These powers, legislative, executive, and judicial, respect internal as well as external objects. Those respecting external objects, as all foreign concerns, *commerce,* impost, all causes arising on the seas, peace and war, and Indian affairs, can be lodged no where else, with any propriety, but in this government. Many powers that respect internal objects ought clearly to be lodged in it; as those to *regulate trade* between the states, weights and measures, the coin or current monies, post offices, naturalization, &c. These powers may be exercised without essentially effecting the internal police of the respective states . . . [Ford 300–301]

Edmund Randolph, Letter on the Federal Constitution, October 10, 1787:

[1] In the prosecution of this enquiry, we shall find the general prosperity to decline under a system thus unnerved. No sooner is the merchant prepared for foreign ports, with the treasures which this new world kindly offers to his acceptance, than it is announced to him, that they are shut against American shipping, or opened under oppressive *regulations.* He urges congress to a

counter-policy, and is answered only by a condolence on the general misfortune. He is immediately struck with the conviction, that until exclusion shall be opposed to exclusion, and restriction to restriction, the American flag will be disgraced. For who can conceive, that thirteen legislatures, viewing *commerce under different regulations,* and fancying themselves discharged from every obligation to concede the smallest of their *commercial* advantages for the benefit of the whole, will be wrought into a concert of action and defiance of every prejudice? . . . [DHRC8 265]

[2] . . . Against each of [these ways to coerce the states into obedience] there are separate unconquerable objections. A blockade is not equally applicable to all the States, they being differently circumstanced in *commerce* and in ports; nay an excommunication from the privilege of the union would be vain, because every *regulation or prohibition* may be easily eluded under the rights of American citizenship, or of foreign nations. . . . [DHRC8 266]

Richard Henry Lee [?], "The Federal Farmer," No. 5, October 13, 1787:

While the radical defects in the proposed system [*i.e.,* the Constitution] are not so soon discovered, some temptations to each state, and to many classes of men to adopt it, are very visible. It uses the democratic language of several of the state constitutions, particularly that of Massachusetts; the eastern states will receive advantages so far as the *regulation of trade,* by a bare majority, is committed to it . . . [Ford 319]

Richard Henry Lee, Proposed Amendments to the Constitution, October 16, 1787:

. . . That the constitution be so amended as to increase the number of votes necessary to determine questions in cases where a bare majority may be seduced by strong motives of interest to injure and oppress the minority of the community, as in *commercial regulations,* where advantage may be taken of circumstances to ordain rigid and premature laws, that will in effect amount to monopolies, to the great impoverishment of those states whose peculiar situation expose[s] them to such injuries. [DHRC8 66]

"Cato Uticensis," October 17, 1787:

It has been the language, since the peace, of the most virtuous and discerning men in America, that the powers vested in Congress were inadequate to the procuring of the benefits, that should result from the union: . . . it could make treaties of *commerce,* but could not enforce the observance of them, and it was felt, that we were suffering from the restrictions of foreign nations, who seeing the want of energy in our Foederal Constitution, and the unlikelihood of co-operation in thirteen separate Legislatures, had shackled our *commerce,* without any dread of recrimination on our part: To obviate these grievances, it was, I believe, the general opinion, that new powers should be vested in Congress, to enable it, in the amplest manner, to *regulate the commerce,* to lay and collect duties on the imports, of the United States. . . . [DHRC8 72]

Noah Webster, *An Examination into the Leading Principles of the Federal Constitution*, October 17, 1787:

. . . Without powers lodged somewhere in a single body, fully competent to lay and collect equal taxes and duties—to adjust controversies between different states—to silence contending interests—to suppress insurrections—to *regulate commerce*—to treat with foreign nations, our confederation is a cobweb—liable to be blown asunder by every blast of faction that is raised in the remotest corner of the United States. [Ford 61–62]

John Jay, *The Federalist*, No. 4, November 7, 1787:

But whatever may be our situation, whether firmly united under one national government, or split into a number of confederacies, certain it is, that foreign nations will know and view it exactly as it is; and they will act towards us accordingly. If they see that our national government is efficient and well administered, our *trade prudently regulated,* our militia properly organized and disciplined, our resources and finances discreetly managed, our credit re-established, our people free, contented, and united, they will be much more disposed to cultivate our friendship than provoke our resentment. . . .

[Fed. 104]

Pelatiah Webster, *The Weakness of Brutus Exposed*, November 4, 1787:

'Tis vain, 'tis childish, 'tis contentious to object to a constitution thus framed and guarded, on pretence that the commonwealth may suffer by a bad administration of it; or to withhold the necessary powers of government, from the supreme rulers of it, least they should abuse or misapply those powers. This is an objection which will operate with equal force against every institution that can be made in this world, whether of policy, religion, *commerce,* or any other human concern, which can require *regulations:* for 'tis not possible to form any institution however necessary, wise and good, whose uses may not be lessened or destroyed by bad management. [Ford 125]

Hugh Williamson, Speech at Edenton, North Carolina, November 8, 1787:

[1] . . . The other objections that have been made to the new plan of Government, are: That it absorbs the powers of the several States: That the national Judiciary

is too extensive: That a standing army is permitted: That Congress is allowed to *regulate trade:* That the several States are prevented from taxing exports, for their own benefit. [DHRC16 202–203]

[2] . . . It has been objected in some of the Southern States, that the Congress, by a majority of votes, is to have the power to *regulate trade*. It is universally admitted that Congress ought to have this power, else our *commerce,* which is nearly ruined, can never be restored; but some gentlemen think that the concurrence of two thirds of the votes in Congress should have been required. By the sundry *regulations of commerce,* it will be in the power of Government not only to collect a vast revenue for the general benefit of the nation, but to secure the carrying trade in the hands of citizens in preference to strangers. . . . [DHRC16 204–205]

[3] . . . Does one of the States attempt to raise a little money by imposts or other *commercial regulations*.—A neighboring State immediately alters her laws and defeats the revenue, by throwing the trade into a different channel. Instead of supporting or assisting, we are uniformly taking the advantage of one another. Such an assemblage of people are not a nation. . . . [DHRC16 206]

John Jay, *The Federalist*, No. 5, November 10, 1787:

When did the independent states, into which Britain and Spain were formerly divided, combine in such alliance, or unite their forces against a foreign enemy? The proposed confederacies will be distinct nations. Each of them would have its *commerce with foreigners to regulate* by distinct treaties; and as their productions and commodities are different and proper for different markets, so would those treaties be essentially different. Different *commercial* concerns must create different interests, and of course different degrees of political attachment to and connection with different foreign nations. . . . [Fed. 107]

"A True Friend," November 14, 1787:

We have seen how much our predilection, prejudices and customs, have favored the skill and endeavors of the British to keep us under their subjection; let us now examine what use we have made of our liberty as sovereign states. Far from having a fixed and combined plan of *commerce* for the thirteen states, analogous to that of the nations, with whom we are or wish to be connected, and conforming our *regulations,* to their exemptions, privileges and prohibitions, so as to maintain an equal balance of the advantages which they offer us, and keep for themselves our several legislative powers, have passed acts to cross and oppose one another reciprocally! . . . [DHRC8 161–62]

Alexander Hamilton, *The Federalist*, No. 7, November 17, 1787:

[1] . . . The spirit of enterprise, which characterizes the *commercial* part of America, has left no occasion of displaying itself unimproved. It is not at all probable

that this unbridled spirit would pay much respect to those *regulations of trade* by which particular States might endeavor to secure exclusive benefits to their own citizens. The infractions of these *regulations,* on one side, the efforts to prevent and repel them, on the other, would naturally lead to outrages, and these to reprisals and wars. [Fed. 116]

[2] The opportunities which some States would have of rendering others tributary to them by *commercial regulations* would be impatiently submitted to by the tributary States. The relative situation of New York, Connecticut, and New Jersey, would afford an example of this kind. . . . [Fed. 116]

Alexander Hamilton, *The Federalist*, No. 11, November 24, 1787:

If we continue united, we may counteract a policy so unfriendly to our prosperity in a variety of ways. By *prohibitory regulations,* extending, at the same time, throughout the States, we may oblige foreign countries to bid against each other, for the privileges of our markets. This assertion will not appear chimerical to those who are able to appreciate the importance of the markets of three millions of people—increasing in rapid progression, for the most part exclusively addicted to agriculture, and likely from local circumstances to remain so—to any manufacturing nation; and the immense difference there would be to the *trade* and navigation of such a nation, between a direct communication in its own ships, and an indirect conveyance of its products and returns, to and from America, in the ships of another country. [Fed. 137]

Alexander Hamilton, *The Federalist*, No. 12, November 27, 1787:

The relative situation of these States; the number of rivers with which they are intersected, and of bays that wash their shores; the facility for communication in every direction; the affinity of language and manners; the familiar habits of intercourse;—all these are circumstances that would conspire to render an illicit *trade* between them a matter of little difficulty, and would insure frequent evasions of the *commercial regulations* of each other. . . . [Fed. 144–45]

Oliver Ellsworth, "The Landholder," No. 6, December 10, 1787:

. . . To make the objections the more plausible, they are called The Objections of the Hon. George Mason, &c.—They may possibly be his, but be assured they were not those made in convention, and being directly against what he there supported in one instance, ought to caution you against giving any credit to the rest; his violent opposition to the powers given congress to *regulate trade,* was an open decided preference of all the world to you. A man governed by such narrow views and local prejudices, can never be trusted . . . [DHRC8 230]

Alexander Hamilton, *The Federalist*, No. 22, December 14, 1787:

[1] The want of a power to *regulate commerce* is by all parties allowed to be of the number. The utility of such a power has been anticipated under the first head of our inquiries; and for this reason, as well as from the universal conviction entertained upon the subject, little need be added in this place. It is indeed evident, on the most superficial view, that there is no object, either as it respects the interest of *trade* or finance, that more strongly demands a federal superintendence. The want of it has already operated as a bar to the formation of beneficial treaties with foreign powers, and has given occasions of dissatisfaction between the States. . . . It is not, therefore, to be wondered at that Mr. Jenkinson, in ushering into the House of Commons a bill for *regulating the temporary intercourse* between the two countries, should preface its introduction by a declaration that similar provisions in former bills had been found to answer every purpose to the *commerce* of Great Britain, and that it would be prudent to persist in the plan until it should appear whether the American government was likely or not to acquire greater consistency. [Fed. 191]

[2] The interfering and unneighborly *regulations* of some States, contrary to the true spirit of the Union, have, in different instances, given just cause of umbrage and complaint to others, and it is to be feared that examples of this nature, if not restrained by a national control, would be multiplied and extended till they became not less serious sources of animosity and discord than injurious impediments to the intercourse between the different parts of the Confederacy. [Quoting an encyclopedia article:] "The *commerce* of the German empire is in continual trammels from the multiplicity of the duties which the several princes and states exact upon the merchandises passing through their territories, by means of which the fine streams and navigable rivers with which Germany is so happily watered are rendered almost useless." Though the genius of the people of this country might never permit this description to be strictly applicable to us, yet we may reasonably expect, from the gradual conflicts of State *regulations*, that the citizens of each would at length come to be considered and treated by the others in no better light than that of foreigners and aliens. [Fed. 192]

Alexander Hamilton, *The Federalist*, No. 23, December 18, 1787:

[1] The principal purposes to be answered by union are these—the common defence of the members; the preservation of the public peace, as well against internal convulsions as external attacks; the *regulation of commerce* with other nations and between the States; the superintendence of our intercourse, political and *commercial*, with foreign countries. [Fed. 199]

[2] . . . The government of the Union must be empowered to pass all laws, and to make all *regulations* which have relation to them. The same must be the case in respect to *commerce*, and to every other matter to which its jurisdiction is permitted to extend. [Fed. 201]

Dissent of the Pennsylvania Convention's Minority, December 18, 1787:

. . . It was found that our national character was sinking in the opinion of foreign nations. The Congress could make treaties of *commerce,* but could not enforce the observance of them. We were suffering from the restrictions of foreign nations, who had shackled our *commerce* while we were unable to retaliate, and all now agreed that it would be advantageous to the union to enlarge the powers of Congress; that they should be enabled in the amplest manner to *regulate commerce* and to lay and collect duties on the imports throughout the United States. . . . [DHRC2 619]

Robert Yates and John Lansing, Report to Governor of New York, December 21, 1787:

Reasoning in this manner, we were of opinion that the leading feature of every amendment ought to be the preservation of the individual states in their uncontrolled constitutional rights, and that, in reserving these, a mode might have been devised of granting to the Confederacy, the moneys arising from a general system of revenue, the power of *regulating commerce* and enforcing the observance of foreign treaties, and other necessary matters of less moment.

Alexander Hamilton, *The Federalist*, No. 36, January 8, 1788:

. . . The quantity of taxes to be paid by the community must be the same in either case; with this advantage, if the provision is to be made by the Union—that the capital resource of *commercial imposts,* which is the most convenient branch of revenue, can be prudently improved to a much greater extent under federal than under State *regulation,* and of course will render it less necessary to recur to more inconvenient methods . . . [Fed. 263–64]

James Madison, *The Federalist*, No. 40, January 18, 1788:

. . . But pretermitting these instances, was it not an acknowledged object of the convention and the universal expectation of the people, that the *regulation of trade* should be submitted to the general government in such a form as would render it an immediate source of general revenue? . . . [Fed. 289]

James Madison, *The Federalist*, No. 42, January 22, 1788:

[1] The second class of powers, lodged in the general government, consist of those which *regulate the intercourse with foreign nations,* to wit: to make treaties; to send and receive ambassadors, other public ministers, and consuls; to define and punish piracies and felonies committed on the high seas, and offences against the law of nations; to *regulate foreign commerce,* including a power to prohibit,

after the year 1808, the importation of slaves, and to lay an intermediate duty of ten dollars per head, as a discouragement to such importations. [Fed. 302]

[2] The *regulation of foreign commerce,* having fallen within several views which have been taken of this subject, has been too fully discussed to need additional proofs here of its being properly submitted to the federal administration. [Fed. 304]

[3] . . . I shall confine myself to a cursory review of the remaining powers comprehended under this third description, to wit: to *regulate commerce* among the several States and the Indian tribes . . . [Fed. 305]

[4] The defect of power in the existing Confederacy to *regulate the commerce* between its several members, is in the number of those which have been clearly pointed out by experience. To the proofs and remarks which former papers have brought into view on this subject, it may be added that without this supplemental provision, the great and essential power of *regulating foreign commerce* would have been incomplete and ineffectual. A very material object of this power was the relief of the States which import and export through other States, from the improper contributions levied on them by the latter. Were these at liberty to *regulate the trade* between State and State, it must be foreseen that ways would be found out to load the articles of import and export, during the passage through their jurisdiction, with duties which would fall on the makers of the latter and the consumers of the former. . . . [Fed. 305]

[5] The *regulation of commerce* with the Indian tribes is very properly unfettered from two limitations in the articles of Confederation, which render the provision obscure and contradictory. The power is then restrained to Indians, not members of any of the States, and is not to violate or infringe the legislative right of any State within its own limits. What description of Indians are to be deemed members of a State, is not yet settled, and has been a question of frequent perplexity and contention in the federal councils. And how the *trade* with Indians, though not members of a State, yet residing within its legislative jurisdiction, can be *regulated* by an external authority, without so far intruding on the internal rights of legislation, is absolutely incomprehensible. . . . [Fed. 306]

[6] The power of establishing uniform laws of bankruptcy is so intimately connected with the *regulation of commerce,* and will prevent so many frauds where the parties or their property may lie or be removed into different States, that the expediency of its seems not likely to be drawn into question. [Fed. 308]

James Madison, *The Federalist*, No. 44, January 25, 1788:

The restraint on the power of the States over imports and exports is enforced by all the arguments which prove the necessity of submitting the *regulation of trade* to the federal councils. It is needless, therefore, to remark further on this head, than that the manner in which the restraint is qualified seems well calculated at once to secure to the States a reasonable discretion in providing for the conveniency of their imports and exports, and to the United States a reasonable check against the abuse of this discretion. . . . [Fed. 320]

Alexander White [?], "An Independent Freeholder," January 25, 1788

. . . Colonel M——n [*i.e.*, George Mason] applies his objection to *commercial regulations* only, and assigns this reason, "that the produce and circumstances of the five southern states are totally different from that of the eight northern and eastern," and thence infers rigid and unjust regulations may be made. When gentlemen deviate so far from the real state of facts to support their arguments, those arguments can have little weight. . . . [DHRC8 326]

James Madison, *The Federalist*, No. 45, January 26, 1788:

If the new Constitution be examined with accuracy and candor, it will be found that the change which it proposes consists much less in the addition of NEW POWERS to the Union, than in the invigoration of its ORIGINAL POWERS. The *regulations of commerce,* it is true, is a new power; but that seems to be an addition which few oppose, and from which no apprehensions are entertained. . . . [Fed. 329]

"Civis Rusticus," January 30, 1788:

By requiring only a majority to make all *commercial* and navigation laws, the five southern states (whose produce and circumstances are totally different from that of the eight northern and eastern states) will be ruined; for such rigid and premature *regulations* may be made, as will enable the merchants of the northern and eastern states not only to demand an exorbitant freight, but to monopolise on the purchase of the commodities at their own price, for many years, to the great injury of the landed interest, and impoverishment of the people: And the danger is the greater, as the gain on one side will be in proportion to the loss on the other: Whereas requiring two thirds of the members present in both houses would have produced mutual moderation, promoted the general interest, and removed an insuperable objection to the adoption of the government.

[DHRC8 333–34]

James Madison, *The Federalist*, No. 53, February 9, 1788:

[1] . . . . Yet some knowledge of the affairs, and even of the laws, of all the States, ought to be possessed by the members from each of the States. How can *foreign trade be properly regulated* by uniform laws, without some acquaintance with the *commerce,* the ports, the usages, and the regulations of the different States? How can the *trade* between the different States be duly *regulated* without some knowledge of their relative situations in these and other respects. . . .

[Fed. 367]

[2] A branch of knowledge which belongs to the acquirements of a federal representative, and which has not been mentioned, is that of foreign affairs. In *regulating our own commerce,* he ought to be not only acquainted with the treaties between the United States and other nations, but also with the *commercial* policy and laws of other nations. [Fed. 368]

"A Citizen of the United States," February 13, 1788:

. . . Mr. R. H. Lee and other gentlemen of the southern states object that *commercial regulations* will be under the undue controul of the eastern states—the inhabitants of the latter complain of the unequal burthen of an impost, of which the southern states must pay but very little from the nature of their population—In the middle states the clamor of opposition has been from the want of a bill of rights . . . [DHRC16 115]

James Madison, *The Federalist*, No. 56, February 16, 1788:

[1] A proper *regulation of commerce* requires much information, as has been elsewhere remarked; but as far as this information relates to the laws and local situation of each individual State, a very few representatives would be very sufficient vehicles of it to the federal councils. [Fed. 380]

[2] Taxation will consist, in a great measure, of duties which will be involved in the *regulation of commerce*. So far the preceding remark is applicable to this object. As far as it may consist of internal collections, a more diffusive knowledge of the circumstances of the State may be necessary. But will not this also be possessed in sufficient degree by a very few intelligent men, diffusively elected within the State? . . . [Fed. 380]

James Madison, *The Federalist*, No. 62, February 27, 1788:

Another effect of public instability is the unreasonable advantage it gives to the sagacious, the enterprising, and the moneyed few over the industrious and uninformed mass of the people. Every new *regulation concerning commerce* or revenue, or in any manner affecting the value of the different species of property, presents a new harvest to those who watch the change, and can trace its consequences; a harvest, reared not by themselves, but by the toils and cares of the great body of their fellow-citizens. . . . [Fed. 412]

Circular Letter to the Fayette, Kentucky, County Court, February 29, 1788:

[1] There are many Objections thrown Out against it which are of a general Nature and affect the interests of the States at large, but there are Others of a

local Nature which in Our Opinion Strike immediately at the happiness & greatness of the Western Country. These local Objections arise by the Vesting in Congress the power To *regulate commerce* with foreign Nations.

[DHRC8 435]

[2] By the power to *regulate commerce,* we loose the Navigation of the Mississippi; population will cease, and Our lands become of little Value. . . .

[DHRC8 435]

Mercy Otis Warren, *Observations on the New Constitution,* February 1788:

Connecticut has pushed it [*i.e.*, the Constitution] through with the precipitation of her neighbour, with few dissentient voices;—but more from irritation and resentment to a sister State, perhaps partiality to herself in her *commercial regulations,* than from a comprehensive view of the system, as a regard to the welfare of all. . . . [DHRC16 287]

John Jay, *The Federalist,* No. 64, March 5, 1788:

There are a few who will not admit that the affairs of *trade* and navigation should be *regulated* by a system cautiously formed and steadily pursued; and that both our treaties and our laws should correspond with and be made to promote it. It is of much consequence that this correspondence and conformity be carefully maintained; and they who assent to the truth of this position will see and confess that it is well provided for by making concurrence of the Senate necessary both to treaties and to laws. [Fed. 422]

"A Federal Republican," March 5, 1788:

. . . It was then perceived that the articles of Confederation were inadequate to the purposes of the union; and it was particularly suggested as necessary to vest in Congress the further power of exclusively *regulating the commerce* of the United States, as well to enable us, by a system more uniform, to counteract the policy of foreign nations, as for other important reasons. . . .

[DHRC8 458]

"The Impartial Examiner," No. 1, March 5, 1788:

. . . Is it not possible to strengthen the hands of Congress so far as to enable them to comply with all the exigencies of the union—to *regulate the great commercial concerns* of the continent,—to superintend all affairs, which relate to the United States in their aggregate capacity, without devolving upon that body the supreme powers of government in all its branches? . . . [DHRC8 463]

James Iredell, "Marcus," No. 4, March 12, 1788:

. . . I should suppose it arose from a jealousy of the Eastern States, very well known to be often expressed by some gentlemen of Virginia. They fear, that a majority of the States may establish *regulations of commerce* which will give great advantage to the carrying trade of America, and be a means of encouraging New England vessels rather than old England.—Be it so.—No *regulations* can give such advantage to New England vessels, which will not be enjoyed by all other American vessels, and many States can build as well as New England, tho' not at present perhaps in equal proportion. . . . [DHRC16 380]

Luther Martin, "To the Citizens of Maryland," No. 3, March 28, 1788:

The principal question in which the state interests had any material effect, were those which related to representation, and the number in each branch of the legislature, whose concurrence should be necessary for passing navigation acts, or making *commercial regulations*.—But what state is there in the union whose interest would prompt it to give the general government the extensive and unlimited powers it possesses in the executive legislature and judicial departments, together with the powers over the militia, and the liberty of establishing a standing army without any restriction? . . . [DHRC16 500]

John Jay, *An Address to the People of the State of New York*, c. April 15, 1788:

[1] Prior to the revolution we had little occasion to inquire or know much about national affairs, for although they existed and were managed, yet they were managed for us, but not by us. Intent on our domestic concerns, our internal legislative business, our agriculture, and our buying and selling, we were seldom anxious about what passed or was doing in foreign Courts. As we had nothing to do with that department of policy, so the affairs of it were not detailed to us, and we took as little pains to inform ourselves, as others did to inform us of them. War, and peace, alliances, and treaties, and *commerce,* and navigation, were conducted and *regulated* without our advice or controul. . . . [Ford 72]

[2] By the Confederation as it now stands, the direction of general and national affairs is committed to a single body of men, viz. the Congress. They may make war, but are not empowered to raise men or money to carry it on. They may make peace, but without power to see the terms of it observed.—They may form alliances, but without ability to comply with the stipulations on their part—They may enter into treaties of *commerce,* but without power to enforce them at home or abroad—They may borrow money, but without having the means of repayment—They may partly *regulate commerce,* but without authority to execute their ordinances . . . [Ford 72]

[3] Let those who are sanguine in their expectations of a better plan from a new Convention, also reflect on the delays and risque to which it would expose us. Let them consider whether we ought, by continuing much longer in our present humiliated condition, to give other nations further time to perfect their restrictive systems of *commerce,* to reconcile their own people to them, and to fence and guard and strengthen them by all those *regulations* and contrivances in which a jealous policy is ever fruitful. . . . [Ford 83]

Melancton Smith, *An Address to the People of the State of New York,* c. April 1788:

Far be it from me to object to granting the general government the power of *regulating trade,* and of laying imposts and duties for that purpose, as well as for raising a revenue: But it is as far from me to flatter people with hopes of benefits to be derived from such a change in our government which can never be realized. Some advantages may accrue from vesting in one general government, the right to *regulate commerce,* but it is a vain delusion to expect anything like what is promised. The truth is, this country buys more than it sells: It imports more than it exports. There are too many merchants in proportion to the farmers and manufacturers. Until these defects are remedied, no government can relieve us. . . . [Ford 107]

John Dickinson, "Fabius," No. 6, 1788:

[Quoting Lord Belhaven in Parliament:] "When I consider this treaty as it hath been explained, and spoke to, before us these three weeks by past; I see the English constitution remaining firm, the same two houses of Parliament, the same taxes, the same customs, the same excises, the same *trading companies,* the same municipal laws and courts of judicature; and all ours either subject to *regulations* or annihilations, only we are to have the honor to pay their old debts, and to have some few persons present for witnesses, to the validity of the deed, when they are pleased to contract more." [Ford 198]

COMPACT, COMPACTS

United States Constitution, September 17, 1787:

[Article I, Section 10:] No State shall, without the Consent of Congress, lay any Duty of Tonnage, keep Troops, or Ships of War in time of Peace, enter into any Agreement or *Compact* with another State, or with a foreign Power, or engage in War, unless actually invaded, or in such imminent Danger as will not admit of delay.

* * * * *

Fundamental Constitutions of Carolina, March 1, 1669:

[Article 97:] But since the natives of that place, who will be concerned in our plantation, are utterly strangers to Christianity, whose idolatry, ignorance, or mistake gives us no right to expel or use them ill; and those who remove from other parts to plant there will unavoidably be of different opinions concerning matters of religion, the liberty whereof they will expect to have allowed them, and it will not be reasonable for us, on this account, to keep them out, that civil peace may be maintained amidst diversity of opinions, and our agreement and *compact* with all men may be duly and faithfully observed; the violation whereof, upon what pretence soever, cannot be without great offence to Almighty God, and great scandal to the true religion which we profess . . . [Thorpe 2783–84]

First Continental Congress, Declaration and Resolves, October 14, 1774:

That the inhabitants of the English Colonies in North America, by the immutable laws of nature, the principles of the English constitution, and the several charters or *compacts*, have the following Rights: [JCC1 67]

Thomas Paine, *Common Sense*, January 10, 1776:

[1] Secondly, as no man at first could possess any other public honors than were bestowed upon him, so the givers of those honors could have no power to give away the right of posterity, and though they might say "We choose you for our head," they could not without manifest injustice to their children, say "that your children and your children's children shall reign over ours for ever." Because such an unwise, unjust, unnatural *compact* might (perhaps) in the next succession put them under the government of a rogue or a fool. Most wise men, in their private sentiments, have ever treated hereditary right with contempt . . . [CWTP1 13]

[2] . . . The last cord now is broken, the people of England are presenting addresses against us. There are injuries which nature cannot forgive; she would cease to be nature if she did. As well can the lover forgive the ravisher of his mistress, as the continent forgive the murders of Britain. The Almighty hath implanted in us these inextinguishable feelings for good and wise purposes. They are the guardians of his image in our hearts. They distinguish us from the herd of common animals. The social *compact* would dissolve, and justice be extirpated from the earth, or have only a casual existence were we callous to the touches of affection. . . . [CWTP1 30]

Virginia Bill of Rights, June 12, 1776:

[Section 1:] That all men are by nature equally free and independent, and have certain inherent rights, of which, when they enter into a state of society, they cannot, by any *compact*, deprive or divest their posterity; namely, the enjoyment of life and liberty, with the means of acquiring and possessing property, and pursuing and obtaining happiness and safety. [Thorpe 3813]

New Jersey Constitution, July 2, 1776:

Whereas all the constitutional authority ever possessed by the kings of Great Britain over these colonies, or their other dominions, was, by *compact*, derived from the people, and held of them, for the common interest of the whole society; allegiance and protection are, in the nature of things, reciprocal ties, each equally depending upon the other, and liable to be dissolved bv the others being refused or withdrawn. . . . [Thorpe 2594]

Maryland Constitution, November 11, 1776:

[Declaration of Rights, Article 1:] That all government of right originates from the people, is founded in *compact* only, and instituted solely for the good of the whole. [Thorpe 1686]

Massachusetts Constitution, March 2, 1780:

[Preamble:] The body politic is formed by a voluntary association of individuals: it is a social *compact,* by which the whole people covenants with each citizen, and each citizen with the whole people, that all shall be governed by certain laws for the common good. It is the duty of the people, therefore in framing a constitution of government, to provide for an equitable mode of making laws, as well as for an impartial interpretation and a faithful execution of them; that every man may, at all times, find his security in them. [Thorpe 1889]

[*Ibid.:*] We, therefore, the people of Massachusetts, acknowledging with grateful hearts, the goodness of the great Legislator of the universe, in affording us, in the course of His providence, an opportunity, deliberately and peaceably, without fraud, violence, or surprise, of entering into an original, explicit, and solemn *compact* with each other; and of forming a new constitution of civil government, for ourselves and posterity; and devoutly imploring His direction in so interesting a design, do agree upon, ordain, and establish, the following Declaration of Rights, and Frame of Government, as the CONSTITUTION OF THE COMMONWEALTH OF MASSACHUSETTS. [Thorpe 1889]

United States Confederation Congress, Ordinance for the Government of the West, April 23, 1784:

That the preceding articles shall be formed into a charter of *compact;* shall be duly executed by the president of the United States in Congress assembled, under his hand, and the seal of the United States; shall be promulgated; and shall stand as fundamental constitutions between the thirteen original states, and each of the several states now newly described, unalterable from and after the sale of any part of the territory of such state, pursuant to this resolve, but by the joint consent of the United States in Congress assembled, and of the particular state within which such alteration is proposed to be made. [DHRC1 153]

United States Confederation Congress, The Northwest Ordinance, July 13, 1787:

It is hereby Ordained and declared, by the authority aforesaid, That the following articles shall be considered as Articles of *compact* between the original States and the people and states in the said territory, and forever remain unalterable, unless by common consent, to wit: [DHRC1 172]

James Wilson, Speech on the Federal Constitution, October 6, 1787:

. . . With respect, likewise, to the particular district of ten miles, which is to be the seat of government, it will undoubtedly be proper to observe this salutary precaution, as there the legislative power will be vested in the president, senate,

and house of representatives of the United States. But this could not be an object with the convention: for it must naturally depend upon a future *compact;* to which the citizens immediately interested, will, and ought to be parties . . .
[Ford 156]

Richard Henry Lee [?], "The Federal Farmer," No. 1, October 8, 1787:

In the first place, I shall premise, that the plan proposed [the Constitution[is a plan of accommodation—and that it is in this way only, and by giving up a part of our opinions, that we can ever expect to obtain a government founded in freedom and *compact*. This circumstance candid men will always keep in view, in the discussion of this subject. [Ford 285–86]

Richard Henry Lee [?], "The Federal Farmer," No. 2, October 9, 1787:

[1] There are certain unalienable and fundamental rights, which in forming the social *compact,* ought to be explicitly ascertained and fixed—a free and enlightened people, in forming this *compact,* will not resign all their rights to those who govern, and they will fix limits to their legislators and rulers, which will soon be plainly seen by those who are governed, as well as by those who govern: and the latter will know they cannot be passed unperceived by the former, and without giving a general alarm—These rights should be made the basis of every constitution . . . [Ford 290]

[2] . . . However, it is now said that the states differ so essentially in these respects, and even in the important article of the trial by jury, that when assembled in convention, they can agree to no words by which to establish that trial, or by which to ascertain and establish many other of these rights, as fundamental articles in the social *compact*. If so, we proceed to consolidate the states on no solid basis whatever. [Ford 291]

Richard Henry Lee [?], "The Federal Farmer," No. 3, October 10, 1787:

. . . The branches of the legislature are essential parts of the fundamental *compact,* and ought to be so fixed by the people, that the legislature cannot alter itself by modifying the elections of its own members. This, by a part of Art. 1, Sect. 4, the general legislature may do, it may evidently so regulate elections as to secure the choice of any particular description of men. . . . [Ford 295]

Richard Henry Lee [?], "The Federal Farmer," No. 4, October 12, 1787:

[1] . . . The state legislatures are obliged to take notice of the bills of rights of their respective states. The bills of rights, and the state constitutions, are fun-

damental *compacts* only between those who govern, and the people of the same state. [Ford 313]

[2] In the year 1788 the people of the United States made a federal constitution, which is a fundamental *compact* between them and their federal rulers; these rulers, in the nature of things, cannot be bound to take notice of any other *compact*. It would be absurd for them, in making laws, to look over thirteen, fifteen, or twenty state constitutions, to see what rights are established as fundamental, and must not be infringed upon, in making laws in the society. It is true, they would be bound to do it if the people, in their federal *compact*, should refer to the state constitutions, recognize all parts not inconsistent with the federal constitution, and direct their federal rulers to take notice of them accordingly; but this is not the case, as the plan stands proposed at present . . . [Ford 313–14]

[3] . . . As to expost facto laws, the convention has done the same in one case, and gone further in another. It is a part of the *compact* between the people of each state and their rulers, that no expost facto laws shall be made. But the convention, by Art. 1, Sect. 10, have put a sanction upon this part even of the state *compacts*. In fact, the 9th and 10th Sections in Art. 1, in the proposed constitution, are no more nor less, than a partial bill of rights; they establish certain principles as part of the *compact* upon which the federal legislators and officers can never infringe. It is here wisely stipulated, that the federal legislature shall never pass a bill of attainder, or expost facto law . . . [Ford 314]

[4] On the whole, the position appears to me to be undeniable, that this bill of rights ought to be carried farther, and some other principles established, as a part of this fundamental *compact* between the people of the United States and their federal rulers. [Ford 315]

[5] It is true, we are not disposed to differ much, at present, about religion; but when we are making a constitution, it is to be hoped, for ages and millions yet unborn, why not establish the free exercise of religion, as a part of the national *compact*. There are other essential rights, which we have justly understood to be the rights of freemen . . . [Ford 315]

[6] I confess I do not see in what cases the congress can, with any pretence of right, make a law to suppress the freedom of the press; though I am not clear, that congress is restrained from laying any duties whatever on printing, and from laying duties particularly heavy on certain pieces printed, and perhaps congress may require large bonds for the payment of these duties. Should the printer say, the freedom of the press was secured by the constitution of the state in which he lived, congress might, and perhaps, with great propriety, answer, that the federal constitution is the only *compact* existing between them and the people; in this *compact* the people have named no others, and therefore congress, in exercising the powers assigned them, and in making laws to carry them into execution, are restrained by nothing beside the federal constitution, any more than a state legislature is restrained by a *compact* between the magistrates and

people of a county, city, or town of which the people, in forming the state constitution, have taken no notice. [Ford 316–17]

Richard Henry Lee [?], "The Federal Farmer," No. 5, October 15, 1787:

. . . as a citizen of the country, I wish to see these objects secured, and licentious, assuming, and overbearing men restrained; if the constitution or social *compact* be vague and unguarded, then we depend wholly upon the prudence, wisdom and moderation of those who manage the affairs of government; or on what, probably, is equally uncertain and precarious, the success of the people oppressed by the abuse of government, in receiving it from the hands of those who abuse it, and placing it in the hands of those who will use it well. [Ford 324]

Richard Henry Lee, Proposed Amendments to the Constitution, October 16, 1787:

. . . it is submitted,—That the new constitution proposed for the government of the United States be bottomed upon a declaration or bill of rights, clearly and precisely stating the principles upon which this social *compact* is founded, to wit: That the rights of conscience in matters of religion ought not to be violated—That the freedom of the press shall be secured . . . [DHRC8 65]

Noah Webster, *An Examination of the Leading Principles of the Federal Constitution*, October 17, 1787:

. . . If in any instance the powers necessary for protecting the general interest, interfere with the constitutional rights of an individual state, such state has assumed powers that are inconsistent with the safety of the United States, and which ought instantly to be resigned. Considering the states as individuals, on equal terms, entering into a social *compact,* no state has a right to any power which may prejudice its neighbors. If therefore the federal constitution has collected into the federal legislature no more power than is necessary for the common defence and interest, it should be recognized by the states, however particular clauses may supersede the exercise of certain powers by the individual states. [Ford 46]

Tench Coxe, *An Examination of the Constitution for the United States of America*, No. 4, October 21, 1787:

. . . This power given to the foederal legislature is no more than what is possessed by the governments of all the states. The constitution of Pennsylvania permits two thirds of such cities and counties, as shall elect representatives, to exercise all the powers of the General Assembly, "as fully and amply as if the whole were present," should any part of the state neglect or refuse to perform their duty in this particular. In short, it is a power necessary to preserve the social *compact* of each state and the confederation of the United States. [Ford 152]

Frederick, Virginia, County Meeting, October 22, 1787:

. . . but we need not now recur to the histories of other nations for proof of these positions; peace was no sooner restored, than the federal government relaxed; the wisest and most necessary recommendations of Congress, as well as their most solemn *compacts*, have been either totally disregarded, or partially complied with: hence hath ensued a breach of faith, both with respect to foreign nations and our own citizens . . . [DHRC8 92]

John Jay, *The Federalist*, No. 2, October 31, 1787:

. . . To all general purposes we have uniformly been one people; each individual citizen everywhere enjoying the same national rights, privileges, and protection. As a nation we have made peace and war; as a nation we have vanquished our common enemies; as a nation we have formed alliances, and made treaties, and entered into various *compacts* and conventions with foreign states. [Fed. 94]

Pelatiah Webster, *The Weakness of Brutus Exposed*, November 4, 1787:

. . . It appears very evident to me, that the Constitution gives an establishment, support, and protection to the internal and separate police of each State, under the superintendency of the federal powers, which it could not possibly enjoy in an independent state. Under the confederation each State derives strength, firmness and permanency from its *compact* with the other States. Like a stave in a cask well bound with hoops, it stands firmer, is not so easily shaken, bent, or broken, as it would be were it set up by itself alone, without any connection with its neighbours. [Ford 128]

John Jay, *The Federalist*, No. 4, November 7, 1787:

It is too true, however disgraceful it may be to human nature, that nations in general will make war whenever they have a prospect of getting any thing by it; nay, absolute monarchs will often make war when their nations are to get nothing by it, but for purposes and objects merely personal, such as a thirst for military glory, revenge for personal affronts, ambition, or private *compacts* to aggrandize or support their particular families or partisans. . . . [Fed. 101]

Alexander Hamilton, *The Federalist*, No. 7, November 17, 1787:

. . . It is well known that they [the states] have heretofore had serious and animated discussion concerning the rights to the lands which were ungranted at the time of the Revolution, and which usually went under the name of crown lands. The States within the limits of whose colonial governments they were comprised have claimed them as their property, the others have contended that the rights of the crown in this article devolved upon the Union; especially as to all that part of the Western territory which, either by actual possession, or through the submission of the Indian proprietors, was subjected to the jurisdiction of the king of Great Britain, till it was relinquished in the treaty of peace. This, it has been said, was at all events an acquisition to the Confederacy by *compact* with a foreign power. It has been the prudent policy of Congress to appease this controversy, by prevailing upon the States to make cessions to the United States for the benefit of the whole. . . . [Fed. 114]

Alexander Hamilton, *The Federalist*, No. 15, December 1, 1787:

[1] . . . Are we entitled by nature and *compact* to a free participation in the navigation of the Mississippi? Spain excludes us from it. Is public credit an indispensable resource in time of public danger? We seem to have abandoned its cause as desperate and irretrievable. . . . [Fed. 156]

[2] There is nothing absurd or impracticable in the idea of a league or alliance between independent nations for certain defined purposes precisely stated in a treaty regulating all the details of time, place, circumstance, and quantity; leaving nothing to future discretion; and depending for its execution on the good faith of the parties. *Compacts* of this kind exist among all civilized nations, subject to the usual vicissitudes of peace and war, of observance and non-observance, as the interests or passions of the contracting powers dictate. In the early part of the present century there was an epidemical rage in Europe for this species of *compacts,* from which the politicians of the times fondly hoped for benefits which were never realized. With a view to establishing the equilibrium of power and the peace of that part of the world, all the resources of negotiations were exhausted, and triple and quadruple alliances were formed; but they were scarcely formed before they were broken, giving an instructive but afflicting lesson to mankind, how little dependence is to be placed on treaties which have no other sanction than the obligations of good faith, and which oppose general considerations of peace and justice to the impulse of any immediate interest or passion. [Fed. 158–59]

James Madison, *The Federalist*, No. 19, December 8, 1787:

The diet [of the German empire] possesses the general power of legislating for the empire; of making war and peace; contracting alliances; assessing quotas of troops and money; constructing fortresses; regulating coin; admitting new members; and subjecting disobedient members to the ban of the empire, by which the party is degraded from his sovereign rights and his possessions forfeited. The members of the confederacy are expressly restricted from entering into *compacts* prejudicial to the empire; from imposing tolls and duties on their mutual intercourse, without the consent of the emperor and diet . . . [Fed. 177–78]

Alexander Hamilton, *The Federalist*, No. 21, December 12, 1787:

The next most palpable defect of the subsisting Confederation is the total want of a SANCTION to its laws. The United States,as now composed, have no powers to exact obedience, or punish disobedience to the resolutions, either by pecuniary mulcts, by a suspension of divestiture of privileges, or by any other constitutional mode. There is no express delegation of authority to them to use force against delinquent members; and if such a right should be ascribed to the federal head, as resulting from the nature of the social *compact* between the States, it must be by inference and construction, in the face of that part of the second article, by which it is declared, "that each State shall retain every power, jurisdiction, and right, not expressly delegated to the United States in Congress assembled." . . . [Fed. 186]

Alexander Hamilton, *The Federalist*, No. 22, December 14, 1787:

It has not a little contributed to the infirmities of the existing federal system, that it never had a ratification by the PEOPLE. Resting on no better foundation than the consent of the several legislatures, it has been exposed to frequent and intricate questions concerning the validity of its powers, and has, in some instances, given birth to the enormous doctrine of a right of legislative repeal. Owing its ratification to the law of a State, it has been contended that the same authority might repeal the law by which it was ratified. However gross a heresy it may be to maintain that a party to a *compact* has a right to revoke that *compact,* the doctrine itself has had respectable advocates. The possibility of a question of this nature proves the necessity of laying the foundations of our national government deeper than in the mere sanction of delegated authority. . . .
[Fed. 198–99]

Dissent of the Pennsylvania Convention's Minority, December 18, 1787:

In short, consolidation pervades the whole constitution. It begins with an annunciation that such was the intention. The main pillars of the fabric correspond with it, and the concluding paragraph is a confirmation of it. The preamble begins with the words, "We the people of the United States," which is the style of a *compact* between individuals entering into a state of society, and not that of a confederation of states. The other features of consolidation, we have before noticed. [DHRC2 680]

Alexander Hamilton, *The Federalist*, No. 24, December 19, 1787:

[1] . . . It would probably occur to him that he would be likely to find the precautions he was in search of in the primitive *compact* between the States. Here, at length, he would expect to meet with a solution of the enigma. No doubt, he would observe to himself, the existing Confederation must contain the most explicit provisions against military establishments in time of peace; and a departure from this model, in a favorite point, has occasioned the discontent which appears to influence these political champions. [Fed. 205]

[2] . . . The improvements in the art of navigation have, as to the facility of communication, rendered distant nations, in a great measure, neighbors. Britain and Spain are among the principal maritime powers of Europe. A future concert of views between these nations ought not to be regarded as improbable. The increasing remoteness of consanguinity is every day diminishing the force of the family *compact* between France and Spain. And politicians have ever with great reason considered the ties of blood as feeble and precarious links of political connection. . . . [Fed. 207]

Alexander Hamilton, *The Federalist*, No. 30, December 28, 1787:

The present Confederation, feeble as it is, intended to repose in the United States an unlimited power of providing for the pecuniary wants of the Union. But proceeding upon an erroneous principle, it has been done in such a manner as entirely to have frustrated the intention. Congress, by the articles [of Confederation] which composed that *compact* (as has already been stated), are authorized to ascertain and call for any sums of money necessary, in their judgment, to the service of the United States; and their requisitions, if conformable to the rule of apportionment, are in every constitutional sense obligatory upon the States. . . . [Fed. 232–33]

James Madison, *The Federalist*, No. 39, January 16, 1788:

. . . It is true that in controversies relating to the boundary between the two jurisdictions, the tribunal which is ultimately to decide, is to be established under the general government. But this does not change the principle of the case. The decision is to be impartially made, according to the rules of the Constitution; and all the usual and most effectual precautions are taken to secure this impartiality. Some such tribunal is clearly essential to prevent an appeal to the sword and a dissolution of the *compact;* and that it ought to be established under the general rather than under the local governments, or, to speak more properly, that it could be safely established under the first alone, is a position not likely to be combated. [Fed. 285]

Alexander White [?], "An Independent Freeholder," January 18, 1788:

. . . But is America in the situation Great Britain was in at the time of the revolution in that country, or in which she herself was at the time of the revolution in this? Nothing can be more remote; here is neither a total nor partial dissolution of Government; our social *compacts* and all our ancient rights remain entire, except such as are expressly granted to Congress. And this affords an answer to many objections, such as that religious liberty, the Freedom of the Press, the right of Petitioning the Legislature, &c. &c. &c. are not secured; no power over these matters being granted to Congress, she never can interpose to destroy them. . . . [DHRC8 311]

James Madison, *The Federalist*, No. 43, January 23, 1788:

[1] . . . The extent of this federal district [*i.e.*, the seat of national government under the Constitution] is sufficiently circumscribed to satisfy every jealousy of an opposite nature. And as it is to be appropriated to this use with the consent of the State ceding it; as the State will no doubt provide in the *compact* for the rights and the consent of the citizens inhabiting it; as the inhabitants will find sufficient inducements of interest to become willing parties to the cession . . . [Fed. 310]

[2] In a confederacy founded on republican principles, and composed of republican members, the superintending government ought clearly to possess authority to defend the system against aristocratic or monarchical innovations. The more intimate the nature of such a union may be, the greater interest have the members in the political institutions of each other; and the greater right to insist that the forms of government under which the *compact* was entered into should be substantially maintained. But a right implies a remedy; and where else could the remedy be deposited, than where it is deposited by the Constitution? . . . [Fed.311–12]

[3] Two questions of a very delicate nature present themselves on this occasion: 1. On what principle the Confederation, which stands in the solemn form of a *compact* among the States, can be superseded without the unanimous consent of the parties to it? 2. What relation is to subsist between the nine or more States ratifying the Constitution, and the remaining few who do not become parties to it? [Fed. 316]

[4] . . . Perhaps, also, an answer may be found without searching beyond the principles of the *compact* itself. It has been heretofore noted among the defects of the Confederation, that in many of the States it had received no higher sanction than a mere legislative ratification. The principle of reciprocality seems to require that its obligation on the other States should be reduced to the same standard. A *compact* between independent sovereigns, founded on ordinary acts of legislative authority, can pretend to no higher validity than a league or treaty between

the parties. It is an established doctrine on the subject of treaties, that all the articles are mutually conditions of each other; that a breach of any one article is a breach of the whole treaty; and that a breach, committed by either of the parties, absolves the others, and authorizes them, if they please, to pronounce the *compact* violated and void. Should it unhappily be necessary to appeal to these delicate truths for a justification for dispensing with the consent of particular States to a dissolution of the federal pact, will not the complaining parties find it a difficult task to answer the MULTIPLIED and IMPORTANT infractions with which they may be confronted? . . . [Fed. 316]

James Madison, *The Federalist*, No. 44, January 25, 1788:

Bills of attainder, ex-post-facto laws, and laws impairing the obligation of contracts, are contrary to the first principles of the social *compact,* and to every principle of sound legislation. The two former are expressly prohibited by the declarations prefixed to some of the State constitutions, and all of them are prohibited by the spirit and scope of these fundamental charters. . . .

[Fed. 319]

Alexander C. Hanson, *Remarks on the Proposed Plan of a Federal Government*, c. January 31, 1788:

[1] How then was I, some months after, disgusted at the repetition, of the arguments respecting the inequality of representatives in the first branch. We were told, that the minority in convention reasoned on first principles, that, as all men, in a state of nature, are equal with respect to rights, so also are equal all separate and distinct states;—that, when individuals form a free government, they must all have equal suffrage, either in framing laws by themselves, or in choosing representatives, although one man be ten times stronger, richer, or wiser than another; so also, when several states unite, for common convenience, they must meet on terms of perfect equality, although one be ten times more wealthy, expensive and populous than another;—that, under our present *compact,* the states are equal, and that no injury has resulted from the equality.

[Ford 223]

[2] The convention has been censured for an excess of its authority. But with no other power was it invested, than is possessed by every free citizen of the states. Its office was to advise, and no further has it proceeded. Had it been even invested with full powers to amend the present *compact,* their proposed plan would not have exceeded their trust. . . . [Ford 224]

[3] Consider again the nature and intent of a federal republic. It consists of an assemblage of distinct states, each completely organized for the protection of its own citizens, and the whole consolidated, by express *compact,* under one head, for the general welfare and common defence. [Ford 241]

[4] Should the *compact* authorize the sovereign, or head to do all things it may think necessary and proper, then there is no limitation to its authority; and the liberty of each citizen in the union has no other security, than the sound policy, good faith, virtue, and perhaps proper interests, of the head. [Ford 241]

[5] When the *compact* confers the aforesaid general power, making nevertheless some special reservations and exceptions, then is the citizen protected further, so far as these reservations and exceptions shall extend. [Ford 241–42]

[6] But, when the *compact* ascertains and defines the power delegated to the federal head, then cannot this government, without manifest usurpation, exert any power not expressly, or by necessary implication, conferred by the *compact*. [Ford 242]

[7] . . . She [*i.e.*, Maryland under the Constitution] shall not, without consent of congress, lay any duty on imports or exports, except what may be necessary for executing her inspection laws. She shall not, without consent of congress, lay any duty on tonnage, keep troops or ships of war, in time of peace; enter into any agreement, or *compact*, with another state, or with a foreign power; or engage in war, unless actually invaded, or in such imminent danger, as will not admit of delay. [Ford 251]

[8] The examples of a genuine aristocracy are rare. They were founded in times of profound ignorance, and when the mass of property was in the hands of a few, whilst the rest pined in want and wretchedness. One European aristocratic government, if such it can be called, has grown out of the original defective form, the offspring of necessity, and commenced amidst the horrors of a civil war. Although the people of that country fought, and intended, to be free, their *compact* of government never was complete; they did not attend to the principle of rotation, and checks; and a genuine representation did never there prevail. [Ford 256]

Massachusetts Convention, Ratification of the Federal Constitution, February 6, 1788:

The convention having impartially discussed, and fully considered, the constitution for the United States of America, reported to Congress, by the convention of delegates from the United States, of America, and submitted to us, by a resolution of the General Court of the said commonwealth, passed the twenty fifth day of October last past; and acknowledging with grateful hearts the goodness of the Supreme Ruler of the universe, in affording the people of the United States, in the course of his Providence, an opportunity, deliberately and peaceably, without fraud or surprise, of entering into an explicit and solemn *compact* with each other, by assenting to and ratifying a new constitution, in order to form a more perfect union, establish justice, insure domestick tranquillity, provide for the common defence, promote the general welfare, and secure the blessings of liberty to themselves, and their posterity—DO, in the name and in behalf of the people of the commonwealth of Massachusetts, ASSENT to and RATIFY the said constitution, for the United States of America.

[DHRC16 67–68]

"Brutus," No. 12, February 7, 1788:

. . . If it be further considered, that this constitution, if it is ratified, will not be a *compact* entered into by states, in their corporate capacities, but an agreement of the people of the United States, as one great body politic, no doubt can remain, but that the great end of the constitution, if it is to be collected from the preamble, in which its end is declared, is to constitute a government which is to extend to every case for which any government is instituted, whether external or internal. . . . [DHRC16 74]

Luther Martin, "Genuine Information," No. 12, February 8, 1788:

[1] . . . That in forming our original federal government every member of that government, that is each State, expressly consented to it;—that it is a part of the *compact* made and entered into in the most solemn manner, that there should be no dissolution or alteration of that federal government without the consent of every State, the members of, and parties to the original *compact;* that therefore no alteration could be made by the consent of a part of the States, or by the consent of the inhabitants of a part of the States, which could either release the States so consenting from the obligation they are under to the other States, or which could in any manner become obligatory upon those States that should not ratify such alterations.—Satisfied of the truth of these positions, and not holding ourselves at liberty to violate the *compact,* which this State had solemnly entered into with the others, by altering it in a different manner from that which by the same *compact* is provided and stipulated, a number of the members and among those the delegation of this State opposed the ratification of this system in any other manner than by the unanimous consent and agreement of all the States.

[DHRC16 89–90]

[2] . . . I, Sir, opposed it also upon a more extensive ground—as being directly contrary to the mode of altering our federal government established in our original *compact,* and as such being a direct violation of the mutual faith plighted by the States to each other, I gave it my negative. [DHRC16 90]

Spencer Roane, "A Plain Dealer," February 13, 1788:

. . . A Constitution ought to be like Caesar's wife, not only good; but unsuspected, since it is the highest *compact* which men are capable of forming, and involves the dearest rights of life, liberty and property. . . . [DHRC8 366]

William Ward [?], "Republicus," February 16, 1788:

[1] . . . but as universal observation assures us, that mankind are more generally actuated by their passions and appetites, than by their reason; something is necessary to restrain, controul, or at least to counteract those passions: hence the necessity of civil government; and on that necessity it originates: the lust of power, or of property, would stimulate the strong, or the artful, to seize the persons, or properties of the weak, or the simple, and appropriate them to their own use, in contempt of the sacred law of nature. Hence mankind found it necessary to enter into solemn *compacts* of mutual defence, and security, and in those *compacts,* to establish certain rules, founded upon, or at least agreeable to, the universal reason of mankind, (the common law of nature) to which they should all be equally subject . . . [DHRC8 376–77]

[2] . . . I said above that civil government originates in necessity: I now add it originates with the people under that necessity. They form the *compact,* they prescribe the rules and they also enact them or delegate others to do it for them; who are indiscriminately, and in the proper sense of the word their servants and accountable to them and to them only how they execute those trusts . . . [DHRC8 377]

[3] . . . This I think an observation of some consequence; all this power they are justly authorized to exercise and that in their own joint and equal right: for if at the time of entring into such *compact,* a compleat equality in point of right subsists; it ever ought to subsist as there can be no legitimate superior, or even co ordinate power, to destroy or diminish that equality. . . . [DHRC8 377]

"The Impartial Examiner," No. 1, February 20, 1788:

[1] In pursuing this address I beg leave to premise that the only true point of distinction between arbitrary and free governments seems to be, that in the former the governors are invested with powers of acting according to their own wills, without any other limits than what they themselves may understand to be necessary for the general good; whereas in the latter they are intrusted with no such unlimited authority, but are restrained in their operations to conform to certain fundamental principles, the preservation whereof is expressly stipulated for in the civil *compact:* and whatever is not so stipulated for is virtually and impliedly given up. . . . [DHRC8 389]

[2] . . . Men, therefore, agree to enter into society, that by the united force of many the rights of each individual may be protected and secured. These are in all just governments laid down as a foundation to the civil *compact,* which contains a covenant between each with all, that they shall enter into one society to be governed by the same powers; establishes for that purpose the frame of government; and consequently creates a Convention between every member . . . [DHRC8 389]

[3] . . . It is true, "the United States shall guarantee to every state in this union a republican form of government:" yet they do not guarantee to the different states their present forms of government, or the bill of rights thereto annexed, or any of them; and the expressions are too vague, too indefinite to create such a *compact* by implication. It is possible that a "republican form" of government may be built upon as absolute principles of despotism as any oriental monarchy ever yet possessed. . . . [DHRC8 393]

Samuel Bryan, "Centinel," No. 16, February 26, 1788:

. . . However if this matter admitted of any doubt, it would be removed by the following consideration, viz. that the new constitution is founded upon a dissolution of the present articles of confederation and is an original *compact* between those states, or rather those individuals who accede to it; consequently all contracts, debts and engagements in favor or against the United States, under the old government, are cancelled unless they are provided for in the new constitution. . . . [DHRC16 219]

Mercy Otis Warren, *Observations on the New Constitution*, February 1788:

. . . While several very worthy characters, too timid for their situation, magnified the hopeless alternative, between the dissolution of the bands of all government, and receiving the proffered system in toto, after long endeavouring to reconcile it to their consciences, swallowed the indigestible panacea, and in a kind of sudden desperation lent their signature to the dereliction of the honorable station they held in the Union, and have broken over the solemn *compact,* by which they were bound to support their own excellent constitution till the period of revision. . . . [DHRC16 286]

Letter from a New York Quaker, March 3, 1788, published in *Poughkeepsie Country Journal*, March 18, 1788:

I know it may be said, that treaties with foreign powers may be contracted, and *compacts* made with the few antifederal States (if any such) to secure to this State its soil and its rights: However contradictory to cool reason this hypothesis may be, I will for a moment suppose it practicable; and what a scene of carnage and devastation rises to view! . . . [DHRC16 410]

"A Federal Republican," March 5, 1788:

. . . Should the Sheriff, or State [tax] Collector in any manner aggrieve you either in person or property, these sacred rights are amply secured by the most solemn *compact:* Beside, the arm of government is always at hand to shield you from his injustice and oppression. But if a Continental Collector, in the execution of his office, should invade your freedom (according to this new government, which has expressly declared itself paramount to all State laws and Constitutions) the State of which you are a citizen, will have no authority to afford you relief. . . . [DHRC8 459]

Alexander Hamilton, *The Federalist*, No. 69, March 14, 1788:

. . . Every jurist of that kingdom [Great Britain], and every other man acquainted with its Constitution, knows, as an established fact, that the prerogative of making treaties exists in the crown in its utmost plentitude; and that the *compacts* entered into by the royal authority have the most complete legal validity and perfection, independent of any other sanction. . . . [Fed. 448]

"Brutus," No. 15, March 20, 1788:

. . . A constitution is a *compact* of a people with their rulers; if the rulers break the *compact,* the people have a right and ought to remove them and do themselves justice; but in order to enable them to do this with the greater facility, those whom the people chuse at stated periods, should have the power in the last resort to determine the sense of the *compact;* if they determine contrary to the understanding of the people, an appeal will lie to the people at the period when the rulers are to be elected, and they will have it in their power to remedy the evil; but when this power is lodged in the hands of men independent of the people, and of their representatives, and who are not, constitutionally, accountable for their opinions, no way is left to controul them but with a high hand and an outstretched arm. [DHRC16 435]

Luther Martin, "To the Citizens of Maryland," No. 1, March 21, 1788:

[1] . . . for being so altered as to render the treaties and laws made under the general government superior to our constitution, if the system is adopted, it will amount to a total and unconditional surrender to that government, by the citizens of this state, of every right and privilege secured to them by our constitution, and an express *compact* and stipulation with the general government, that it may, at its discretion, make laws in direct violation of those rights . . .
[DHRC16 453]

[2] . . . It was my opinion, that to agree upon a ratification of the constitution by any less number than the whole thirteen states, is so directly repugnant to our present articles of confederation, and the mode therein prescribed for their alteration, and such a violation of the *compact* which the states, in the most solemn manner, have entered into with each other, that those who could advocate a contrary proposition, ought never to be confided in and entrusted in public life . . . [DHRC16 454]

Melancton Smith, *An Address to the People of the State of New York*, c. April 1788:

[1] Government is a *compact* entered into by mankind, in a state of society, for the promotion of their happiness. In forming this *compact,* common sense dictates, that no articles should be admitted that tend to defeat the end of its institution. If any such are proposed, they should be rejected. When the *compact* is once formed and put into operation, it is too late for individuals to object. The deed is executed—the conveyance is made—and the power of reassuming the right is gone, without the consent of the parties. . . . [Ford 92]

[2] . . . And is a *compact* for the government of ourselves and our posterity of less moment than contracts between individuals? certainly not. But to this reasoning, which at first view would appear to admit of no reply, a variety of objections are made, and a number of reasons urged for adopting the system, and afterwards proposing amendments. . . . [Ford 93]

[3] . . . There can be no reason to apprehend, that the other states will make war with us for not receiving the constitution proposed, until it is amended, but from one of the following causes: either that they will have just cause to do it, or that they have a disposition to do it. We will examine each of these:—That they will have no just cause to quarrel with us for not acceding, is evident, because we are under no obligation to do it, arising from any existing *compact* or previous stipulation. The confederation is the only *compact* now existing between the states: By the terms of it, it cannot be changed without the consent of every one of the parties to it. Nothing therefore can be more unreasonable than for part of the states to claim of the others, as matter of right, an accession to a system to which they have material objections. No war can therefore arise from this principle, but on the contrary, it is to be presumed, it will operate strongly the opposite way.—The states will reason on the subject in the following manner: On this momentous question, every state has an indubitable right to judge for itself: This is secured to it by solemn *compact,* and if any of our sister states disagree with us upon the question, we ought to attend to their objections, and accommodate ourselves as far as possible to the amendments they propose. [Ford 96–97]

[4] . . . But the idea of one or more states attacking another, for insisting upon alterations upon the system, before it is adopted, is more extravagant still; it is contradicting every principle of liberty which has been entertained by the states, violating the most solemn *compact,* and taking from the state the right of deliberation. . . . [Ford 97]

[5] . . . Can it then be presumed, that a country divided among themselves, upon a question where even the advocates for it, admit the system they contend for needs amendments, would make war upon a sister state, who only insist that that should be done before they receive it, which it is granted ought to be done after, and where it is confessed no obligation lies upon them by *compact* to do

it. Can it, I say, be imagined, that in such a case, they would make war on a sister state? The idea is preposterous and chimerical. [Ford 98]

Alexander Hamilton, *The Federalist*, No. 85, May 28, 1788:

[1] . . . The result of the deliberations of all collective bodies must necessarily be a compound, as well of the errors and prejudices, as of the good sense and wisdom, of the individuals of whom they are composed. The *compacts* which are to embrace thirteen distinct States in a common bond of amity and union, must as necessarily be a compromise of as many dissimilar interests and inclinations. How can perfection spring from such materials? [Fed. 544]

[2] . . . Every Constitution for the United States must inevitably consist of a great variety of particulars, in which thirteen independent States are to be accommodated in their interests or opinions of interest. We may of course expect to see, in any body of men charged with its original formation, very different combinations of the parts upon different points. Many of those who form a majority on one question, may become the minority on a second, and an association dissimilar to either may constitute the majority on a third. Hence the necessity of moulding and arranging all the particulars which are to compose the whole, in such a manner as to satisfy all the parties to the *compact;* and hence, also, an immense multiplication of difficulties and casualties in obtaining the collective assent to a final act. . . . [Fed. 545]

CONTRACT, CONTRACTS

(Contracted, Contracting)

United States Constitution, September 17, 1787:

[Article I, Section 10:] No State shall enter into any Treaty, Alliance, or Confederation; grant Letters of Marque and Reprisal; coin Money; emit Bills of Credit; make any Thing but gold and silver Coin a Tender in Payment of Debts; pass any Bill of Attainder, ex post facto Law, or Law impairing the Obligation of *Contracts,* or grant any Title of Nobility.

[Article VI:] All Debts *contracted* and Engagements entered into, before the Adoption of this Constitution, shall be as valid against the United States under this Constitution, as under the Confederation.

* * * * *

Magna Carta, June 15, 1215:

Heirs shall be married without disparity, so nevertheless that before the marriage be *contracted,* it shall be announced to the relatives by blood of the heir himself. [SDECH 43]

James I, Third Charter of Virginia, 1611–1612:

And furthermore, whereas We have been certified, That divers lewd and ill disposed Persons, both Sailors, Soldiers, Artificers, Husbandmen, Labourers and others, having received Wages, Apparel and other Entertainment, from the said [Virginia] Company, or having *contracted* and agreed with the said Company to go, or to serve, or to be employed in the said Plantation of the said first Colony in Virginia, have afterwards either withdrawn, hid, or concealed themselves, or have refused to go thither, after they have been so entertained and agreed withal . . . [Thorpe 3807]

James I, The Charter of New England, November 3, 1620:

And to the End that now lewd or ill-disposed Persons, Saylors Soldiers, Artificers, Labourers, Husbandmen, or others, which shall receive Wages, Apparel, or other Entertainment from the said Councill [of New England], or *contract* and agree with the said Councill to goe, and to serve, and to be imployed, in the said Plantation, in the Collony in New-England, do afterwards withdraw, hide, and conceale themselves, or refuse to go thither, after they have been so entertained and agreed withall . . . [Thorpe 1838]

Charter of the Dutch West India Company, June 3, 1621:

[Article 2:] That, moreover, the aforesaid Company may, in our name and authority, within the limits herein before prescribed, make *contracts,* engagements and alliances within the limits herein before prescribed, make *contracts,* engagements and alliances with the princes and natives of the countries comprehended therein, and also build any forts and fortifications there, to appoint and discharge Governors, people for war, and officers of justice, and other public officers, for the preservation of the places, keeping good order, police and justice, and in like manner for the promoting of trade; and again, others in their place to put, as they from the situation of their affairs shall see fit: Moreover, they must advance the peopling of those fruitful and unsettled parts, and do all that the service of those countries, and the profit and increase of trade shall require: and the Company shall successively communicate and transmit to us such *contracts* and alliances as they shall have made with the aforesaid princes and nations; and likewise the situation of the fortresses, fortifications, and settlements by them taken. [Thorpe 60]

Fundamental Constitutions of Carolina, March 1, 1669:

[Article 38:] The chief justice's court, consisting of one of the proprietors and his six councillors, who shall be called justices of the bench, shall judge all appeals in cases both civil and criminal, except all such cases as shall be under the jurisdiction and cognizance of any other of the proprietor's courts, which shall be tried in those courts respectively. The government and regulation of registries of writings and *contracts* shall belong to the jurisdiction of this court. The twelve assistants of this court shall be called masters. [Thorpe 2777]

[Article 81:] There shall be a registry in every precinct, wherein shall be enrolled all deeds, leases, judgments, mortgages, and other conveyances, which may concern any of the lands within the said precinct; and all such conveyances not so entered and registered shall not be of force against any person or party to the said *contract* or conveyance. [Thorpe 2782]

[Article 87:] No marriage shall be lawful, whatever *contract* and ceremony they have used, till both the parties mutually own it before the register of the place where they were married, and he register it, with the names of the father and mother of each party. [Thorpe 2782]

Charles II, Commission Establishing a President and Council for New Hampshire, September 18, 1680:

. . . And We do by these prts, for Us Our heirs & successors, constitute, establish, declare & appoint Our said Pres. & Councell & their successors for ye time being, to be a constant & setled Court of record, for ye administrac'on of Justice to all Our subjects inhabiting within ye limits aforesaid, in all causes, as well criminal as civill; & yt ye Pres: & any 5 of the Councell for ye time being shall have full power & authority, to hold plea in all causes from time to time, as well in pleas of ye Crown, as in matters relating to ye conservation of ye peace, & punishment of offenders, as in civill suits & actions between partie & partie; or between Us & any of Our subjects there; whether ye same do concern ye realty, & relate to a right of freehold & inheritance, or whether ye same do concern ye personalty, & relate to some matter of debt, *contract,* damage, or other personal injury; & also in all mixt actions, wch may concern both realty & personalty and therein after due & orderly proceeding, & deliberate hearing on both sides, to give Judgmt, to award execuc'on, as well in criminall as in civill causes as aforesaid . . . [Thorpe 2447]

Pennsylvania Frame of Government, Laws Agreed Upon in England, May 5, 1682:

[Article 21:] That all defacers or corrupters of charters, gifts, grants, bonds, bills, wills, *contracts,* and conveyances, or that shall deface or falsify any enrolment, registry or record, within this province, shall make double satisfaction for the same; half whereof shall go to the party wronged, and they shall be dismissed of all places of trust, and be publicly disgraced as false men. [Thorpe 3061]

James II, Commission to Sir Edmund Andros for the Dominion of New England, April 7, 1688:

[1] And wee do by these presents ordain constitute and appoint you or the Commander in Cheif for the time being, and the Councill of our said territory & dominion for the time being, to be a constant and setled Court of Record for ye administration of justice to all our subjects inhabiting within our said Territory and Dominion, in all causes as well civill as Criminall with full power and authority to hold pleas in all cases, from time to time, as well in Pleas of the Crown and in all matters relateing to the conservation of the peace and punishment of offenders, as in Civill causes and actions between party and party, or between us and any of our subjects there, whether the

same do concerne the realty and relate to any right of freehold & inheritance or whether the same do concerne the personalty and relate to matter of debt *contract* damage or other personall injury; and also in all mixt actions which may concern both realty and personalty . . . [Thorpe 1865]

[2] And forasmuch as pursuant to the lawes & customes of our Colony of the Massachusetts Bay and of our other Colonies and Provinces aforementioned, divers marriages have been made and performed by the Magstrats of our said territory; Our royall will and pleasure is hereby to confirm al the said marriages and to direct that they be held good and valid in the same manner to all intents and purposes whatsoever as if they had been made and *contracted* according to the lawes established within our kingdom of England. [Thorpe 1869]

George II, Charter of Georgia, June 9, 1732:

. . . therefore we do will, ordain and establish, that the said common council for the time being, of the said corporation, being assembled for that purpose, or the major part of them, shall from time to time, and at all times hereafter, have full power and authority to dispose of, extend and apply all the monies and effects belonging to the said corporation, in such manner and ways and by such expenses as they shall think best to conduce to the carrying on and effecting the good purposes herein mentioned and intended; and also shall have full power in the name and on account of the said corporation, and with and under their common seal, to enter under any covenants or *contracts,* for carrying on and effecting the purposes aforesaid. . . . [Thorpe 772]

Benjamin Franklin, Proposed Articles of Confederation, c. July 21, 1775:

[Article 11:] A perpetual Alliance offensive and defensive, is to be entered into as soon as may be with the Six Nations; their Limits to be ascertain'd and secur'd to them; their Land not to be encroach'd on; nor any private or Colony Purchases made of them hereafter to be held good; nor any *Contract* for Lands to be made but between the Great Council of the Indians at Onondaga and the General Congress. . . . [PBF22 124]

Thomas Paine, *Common Sense*, January 9, 1776:

[1] Debts we have none; and whatever we may *contract* on this account will serve as a glorious memento of our virtue. Can we but leave posterity with a settled form of government, an independent constitution of its own, the purchase at any price will be cheap. . . . [CWTP1 31]

[2] The debt we may *contract* doth not deserve our regard if the work be but accomplished. No nation ought to be without a debt. A national debt is a national bond; and when it bears no interest, is in no case a grievance. . . .
[CWTP1 32]

[3] . . . The intimacy which is *contracted* in infancy, and the friendship which is formed in misfortune, are of all others the most lasting and unalterable. Our present union is marked with both these characters: we are young, and we have been distressed; but our concord hath withstood our troubles, and fixes a memorable era for posterity to glory in. [CWTP1 36]

[4] Should affairs be patched up with Britain, and she to remain the governing and sovereign power of America, (which as matters are now circumstanced, is giving up the point entirely) we shall deprive ourselves of the very means of sinking the debt we have, or may *contract*. The value of the back lands which some of the provinces are clandestinely deprived of, by the unjust extension of the limits of Canada, valued only at five pounds sterling per hundred acres, amount to upwards of twenty-five millions, Pennsylvania currency; and the quit-rents at one penny sterling per acre, to two millions yearly. [CWTP1 42–43]

[5] . . . To be on the footing of 1763, it is not sufficient, that the laws only be put on the same state, but, that our circumstances likewise be put on the same state; our burnt and destroyed towns repaired or built up, our private losses made good, our public debts (*contracted* for defence) discharged; otherwise, we shall be millions worse than we were at that enviable period. Such a request, had it been complied with a year ago, would have won the heart and soul of the Continent but now it is too late. "The Rubicon is passed." [CWTP1 44–45]

United States Declaration of Independence, July 4, 1776:

We, therefore, the Representatives of the united States of America, in General Congress, Assembled, appealing to the Supreme Judge of the world for the rectitude of our intentions, do, in the Name, and by Authority of the good People of these Colonies, solemnly publish and declare, That these United Colonies are, and of Right ought to be Free and Independent States; that they are Absolved from all Allegiance to the British Crown, and that all political connection between them and the State of Great Britain, is and ought to be totally dissolved; and that as Free and Independent States, they have full Power to levy War, conclude Peace, *contract* Alliances, establish Commerce, and to do all other Acts and Things which Independent States may of right do. . . .

United States Continental Congress, Draft Articles of Confederation, July 12, 1776:

[Article 14:] . . . No Purchases of Lands, hereafter to be made of the Indians by the Colonies or private Persons before the limits of the Colonies are ascertained, to be valid: All Purchases of Land not included within those Limits, where ascertained, to be made by *Contracts* between the United States assembled, or by Persons for that Purpose authorized by them, and the great Councils of the Indians, for the general Benefit of all the United Colonies. [DHRC1 81]

Delaware Constitution, September 10, 1776

[Article 18:] The justices of the supreme court and courts of common pleas, the members of the privy council, the secretary, the trustees of the loan office, and clerks of the court of common pleas, during their continuance in office, and all persons concerned in any army or navy *contracts,* shall be ineligible to either house of assembly; and any member of either house accepting of any other of the offices hereinbefore mentioned (excepting the office of a justice of the peace) shall have his seat thereby vacated, and a new election shall be ordered.

[Thorpe 565–66]

Maryland Constitution, November 11, 1776:

[Declaration of Rights, Article 33:] . . . nor ought any person to be compelled to frequent or maintain, or contribute, unless on *contract,* to maintain any particular place of worship, or any particular ministry; yet the Legislature may, in their discretion, lay a general and equal tax, for the support of the Christian religion . . . [Thorpe 1689]

North Carolina Constitution, December 18, 1776:

[Form of Government, Article 27:] That no officer in the regular army or navy in the service and pay of the United States, of this or any other State, nor any *contractor* or agent for supplying such army or navy with clothing or provisions, shall have a seat either in the Senate, House of Commons, or Council of State, or be eligible thereto: and any member of the Senate, House of Commons, or Council of State, being appointed to and accepting of such office, shall thereby vacate his seat. [Thorpe 2792]

New York Constitution, April 20, 1777:

[Article 37:] And whereas it is of great importance to the safety of this State that peace and amity with the Indians within the same be at all times supported and maintained; and whereas the frauds too often practised towards the said Indians, in *contracts* made for their lands, have, in divers instances, been productive of dangerous discontents and animosities: Be it ordained, that no purchases or *contracts* for the sale of lands, made since the fourteenth day of October, in the year of our Lord one thousand seven hundred and seventy-five, or which may hereafter be made with or of the said Indians, within the limits of this State, shall be binding on the said Indians, or deemed valid, unless made under the authority and with the consent of the legislature of this State. [Thorpe 2636]

United States Articles of Confederation, November 15, 1777:

[Article XII:] All bills of credit emitted, monies borrowed and debts *contracted* by, or under the authority of congress, before the assembling of the united states, in pursuance of the present confederation, shall be deemed and considered as a charge against the united states, for payment and satisfaction whereof the said united states, and the public faith are hereby solemnly pledged.

Massachusetts Constitution, March 2, 1780:

[Declaration of Rights, Article 3:] Provided notwithstanding, that the several towns, parishes, precincts, and other bodies politic, or religious societies, shall, at all times, have the exclusive right of electing their public teachers, and of *contracting* with them for their support and maintenance. [Thorpe 1890]

United States Confederation Congress, Ordinance for the Government of the West, April 23, 1784:

That they [the new States] shall be subject to pay a part of the federal debts, *contracted* or to be *contracted;* to be apportioned on them by Congress, according to the same common rule and measure by which apportionments thereof shall be made on the other states. [DHRC1 152]

New Hampshire Constitution, June 2, 1784:

[Bill of Rights, Article 6:] Provided notwithstanding, That the several towns, parishes, bodies-corporate, or religious societies, shall at all times have the exclusive right of electing their own public teachers, and of *contracting* with them for their support and maintenance. And no portion of any one particular religious sect or denomination, shall ever be compelled to pay towards the support of the teacher or teachers of another persuasion, sect or denomination. [Thorpe 2454]

[*Ibid.*:] And nothing herein shall be understood to affect any former *contracts* made for the support of the ministry; but all such contracts shall remain, and be in the same state as if this constitution had not been made. [Thorpe 2454]

United States Congress, The Northwest Ordinance, July 13, 1787:

[Article 2:] . . . And, in the just preservation of rights and property, it is understood and declared, that no law ought ever to be made or have force in the said territory, that shall, in any manner whatever, interfere with or affect private *contracts,* or engagements, bona fide, and without fraud previously formed. [Thorpe 961]

[Article 4:] . . . The inhabitants and settlers in the said territory shall be subject to pay a part of the Federal debts, *contracted,* or to be *contracted,* and a proportional part of the expenses of government to be apportioned on them by Congress, according to the same common rule and measure by which apportionments thereof shall be made on the other States . . . [Thorpe 961]

James Wilson, Speech on the Federal Constitution, October 6, 1787:

The power of direct taxation has likewise been treated as an improper delegation to the foederal government; but when we consider it as the duty of that body to provide for the national safety, to support the dignity of the union, and to discharge the debts *contracted* upon the collective faith of the states, for their common benefit, it must be acknowledged that those, upon whom such important obligations are imposed, ought, in justice and in policy, to possess every means requisite for a faithful performance of their trust. [Ford 160]

Richard Henry Lee [?], "The Federal Farmer," No. 3, October 10, 1787:

. . . How far it may be proper so to humble a state, as to oblige it to answer to an individual in a court of law, is worthy of consideration; the states are now subject to no such actions; and this new jurisdiction will subject the states, and many defendants to actions, and processes, which were not in the contemplation of the parties, when the *contract* was made; all engagements existing between citizens of different states, citizens and foreigners, states and foreigners; and states and citizens of other states were made the parties contemplating the remedies then existing on the laws of the states—and the new remedy proposed to be given in the federal courts, can be founded on no principle whatever.

[Ford 309]

Edmund Randolph, Letter on the Federal Constitution, October 10, 1787:

It follows, too, that, as the general government will be responsible to foreign nations, it ought to be able to annul any offensive measure, or inforce any public right. Perhaps among the topics on which they may be aggrieved or complain, the commercial intercourse, and the manner,in which *contracts* are discharged, may constitute the principal articles of clamor. [DHRC8 266]

Tench Coxe, *An Examination of the Constitution for the United States of America*, No. 4, October 21, 1787:

. . . Trials for lands lying in any state between persons residing in such state, for bonds, notes, book debts, *contracts,* trespasses, assumptions, and all other matters between two or more citizens of any state, will be held in the state courts by juries, as now. In these case the foederal courts cannot interfere.

[Ford 149]

Alexander Hamilton, *The Federalist*, No. 7, November 17, 1787:

Laws in violation of private *contracts,* as they amount to aggressions on the rights of those States whose citizens are injured by them, may be considered as another probable source of hostility. We are not authorized to expect that a more liberal or more equitable spirit would preside over the legislations of the individual States hereafter, if unrestrained by any additional checks, than we have heretofore seen in too many instances disgracing their several codes. . . .

[Ford 118]

Alexander Hamilton, *The Federalist*, No. 15, December 1, 1787:

[1] . . . Do we owe debts to foreigners and to our own citizens *contracted* in a time of imminent peril for the preservation of our political existence? These remain without any proper or satisfactory provision for their discharge.

[Ford 156]

[2] There is nothing absurd or impracticable in the idea of a league or alliance between independent nations for certain defined purposes precisely stated in a treaty regulating all the details of time, place, circumstance, and quantity; leaving nothing to future discretion; and depending for its execution on the good faith of the parties. Compacts of this kind exist among all civilized nations, subject to the usual vicissitudes of peace and war, of observance and non-observance, as the interests or passions of the *contracting* powers dictate. . . . [Ford 158]

"Americanus," No. 1, December 5, 1787:

[1] . . . It was found, that a want of energy prevailed in our national Assembly, and that jealousies pervaded our local legislatures; that the pressing requisitions of Congress were treated with haughty contempt; that the continental treasury was exhausted and government unable to discharge the necessary debts, which were *contracted* during the war, and for the punctual payment of which, the credit of the United States was solemnly pledged. It was found, that the national character was rapidly depreciating in the opinion of foreign nations . . .

[DHRC8 201]

[2] Can a government exist without a strong executive power? Can the national character be preserved without the punctual performance of our *contracts?* Can the union exist without an adequate foederal head? . . . [DHRC8 204]

James Madison, *The Federalist*, No. 19, December 8, 1787:

The diet possesses the general power of legislating for the [German] empire; of making war and peace; *contracting* alliances; assessing quotas of troops and money; constructing fortresses; regulating coin; admitting new members; and subjecting disobedient members to the ban of the empire, by which the party is degraded from his sovereign rights and his possessions forfeited. . . .

[Ford 177]

Dissent of the Pennsylvania Convention's Minority, December 18, 1787:

. . . and that the United States in Congress assembled shall not have power to enact laws, which shall alter the laws of descents and distribution of the effects of deceased persons, the titles of lands or goods, or the regulation of *contracts* in the individual States. [DHRC2 625]

Alexander Hamilton, *The Federalist*, No. 30, December 28, 1787:

[1] . . . But these are not the only objects to which the jurisdiction of the Union, in respect to revenue, must necessarily be empowered to extend. It must embrace a provision for the support of the national civil list; for the payment of the national debts *contracted,* or that may be *contracted;* and, in general, for all those matters which will call for disbursements out of the national treasury. The conclusion is that there must be interwoven, in the frame of the government, a general power of taxation, in one shape or another. [Fed. 232]

[2] The power of creating new funds upon new objects of taxation, by its own authority, would enable the national government to borrow as far as its necessities might require. Foreigners, as well as the citizens of America, could then reasonably repose confidence in its engagements; but to depend upon a government that must itself depend upon thirteen other governments for the means of fulfilling its *contracts,* when once its situation is clearly understood, would require a degree of credulity not often to be met with in the pecuniary transactions of mankind, and little reconcilable with the usual sharp-sightedness of avarice.

[Fed. 236]

Alexander Hamilton, *The Federalist*, No. 34, January 4, 1788:

[1] In the kingdom of Great Britain, where all the ostentatious apparatus of monarchy is to be provided for, not above a fifteenth part of the annual income of the nation is appropriated to the class of expenses last mentioned; the other fourteen fifteenths are absorbed in the payment of the interest of debts *contracted* for carrying on the wars in which that country has been engaged, and in the maintenance of fleets and armies. . . . [Fed. 251]

[2] But let us advert to the large debt which we have ourselves *contracted* in a single war, and let us only calculate on a common share of the events which disturb the peace of nations, and we shall instantly perceive, without the aid of

any elaborate illustration, that there must always be an immense disproportion between the objects of federal and state expenditures. . . . [Fed. 251–2]

George Nicholas [?], "The State Soldier," No. 1, January 16, 1788:

. . . The credit of the UNION, like that of an individual, was only to be kept up by a prospect of being at some time or another able to pay the debts it had necessarily *contracted*—and that prospect could no way begin but by the establishment of some fund whereon the CONTINENT could draw with certainty. . . . [DHRC8 305]

Alexander White [?], "The Independent Freeholder," January 18, 1788:

. . . When you add to this, that the jurisdiction of the federal courts will not extend to disputes relating to property, real or personal, to *contracts* or personal injuries between citizens, which in general are the subjects of litigation; the apprehension of oppression from those courts must appear groundless. . . . [DHRC8 312]

James Madison, *The Federalist*, No. 44, January 25, 1788:

Bills of attainder, ex post facto laws, and laws impairing the obligation of *contracts,* are contrary to the first principles of the social compact, and to every principle of sound legislation. The two former are expressly prohibited by the declarations prefixed to some of the State constitutions, and all of them are prohibited by the spirit and scope of these fundamental charters. Our own experience has taught us, nevertheless, that additional fences against these dangers ought not to be omitted. . . . [Fed. 319]

Alexander C. Hanson, *Remarks on the Proposed Plan of a Federal Government*, c. January 31, 1788:

[1] The restraints laid on the state legislatures will tend to secure domestic tranquility, more than all the bills, or declarations, of rights, which human policy could devise. It is very justly asserted, that the plan contains an avowal of many rights. It provides that no man, shall suffer by ex post facto laws or bills of attainder. It declares, that gold and silver only shall be a tender for specie debts; and that no law shall impair the obligation of a *contract*. [Ford 243]

[2] . . . and they talk of gratitude to paper money, as if it were a sensible benefactor, entitled to the highest rank and distinction; and as if, to abandon it, would be a deadly sin. But when everything demonstrates the season to be past; when the credit of America, in all places, depends on the security she shall give to *contracts,* it would be madness in the states to be tenacious of their right. So long as Europe shall believe we regard not justice, gratitude and honour, so long

will America labour under the disadvantages of an individual, who attempts to make good his way through the world with a blasted reputation. . . .
[Ford 244]

[3] . . . What then are the powers an individual state will lose? She will no longer be able to deny congress that, which congress, at this moment, has a right to demand. She will have no power to enter into a treaty, alliance, or confederation. She shall, in time of war, grant no letters of marque and reprisal. She shall coin no money, emit no bills of credit, nor make any thing but gold and silver a tender in payment of debts. She shall pass no bill of attainder, or ex post facto law, or law impairing the obligation of a *contract*. She shall grant no title of nobility. . . . [Ford 251]

David Ramsay, "Civis," February 4, 1788:

[1] When you authorised Congress to borrow money, and to *contract* debts, for carrying on the late war, you could not intend to abridge them of the means of paying their engagements, made on your account. You may observe that their future power is confined to provide common defence and general welfare of the United States. If they apply money to any other purposes, they exceed their powers. The people of the United States who pay, are to be judges how far their money is properly applied. . . . [DHRC16 22]

[2] . . . Content that what regards all the states should be managed by that body which represents all of them; be on your guard against the misrepresentations of men who are involved in debt; such may wish to see the constitution rejected, because of the following clause, "no state shall emit bills of credit, make any thing but gold and silver coin, a tender in payment of debts, pass any ex post facto law, or law impairing the obligation of *contracts*." This will doubtless bear hard on debtors who wish to defraud their creditors, but it will be real service to the honest part of the community. . . . [DHRC16 26]

Samuel Bryan, "Centinel," No. 14, February 5, 1788:

. . . By the power of imposing stamp duties the Congress will have a right to declare that no wills, deeds, or other instruments of writing, shall be good and valid, without being stamped—that without being reduced to writing and being stamped, no bargain, sale, transfer of property, or *contract* of any kind or nature whatsoever shall be binding; and also that no exemplifications of records, depositions, or probates of any kind shall be received in evidence, unless they have the same solemnity—They may likewise oblige all proceedings of a judicial nature to be stamped to give them effect—those stamp duties may be imposed to any amount they please, and under the pretence of securing the collection of these duties, and to prevent the laws which imposed them from being evaded, the Congress may bring the decision of all questions relating to the conveyance, disposition and rights of property and every question relating to *contracts* between man and man into the courts of the general government. . . . [DHRC16 32–3]

"The Impartial Examiner," No. 1, February 20, 1788:

[1] . . . There can be no other just origin of civil power, but some such mutual *contract* of all the people: and although their great object in forming society is an intention to secure their natural rights; yet the relations arising from this political union create certain duties and obligations to the state, which require a sacrifice of some portion of those rights and of that exuberance of liberty, which obtains in a state of nature. . . . [DHRC8 389–90]

[2] . . . It has been before observed that the only just origin of civil power is a *contract* entered into by all the people for that purpose.—If this position be true (and, I dare presume, it is not controverted, at least in this country) right reason will always suggest the expediency of adhering to the essential requisites in forming that *contract* upon true principles. . . . [DHRC8 390]

"An Old Planter," February 20, 1788:

Let us look around amongst the other states, would any wise or virtuous representation ever have proposed, far less issued (in a time of full peace and tranquility) paper money as a legal tender? Would there have been in any of the states opposition to laws for the furtherance of justice, the sole end and object of all government? Would there ever have been such an insult offered to the probity and understanding of men; as to suggest with impunity, the breach of public *contracts,* and the defrauding of the public creditors? Where such things are heard without censure, we may safely pronounce the governments defective . . . [DHRC8 396]

"Brutus," No. 13, February 21, 1788:

[1] The states are now subject to no such actions. All *contracts* entered into by individuals with states, were made upon the faith and credit of the states, and the individuals never had in contemplation any compulsory mode of obliging the government to fulfil its engagements. [DHRC16 173]

[2] The situation of the states will be deplorable. By this system, they will surrender to the general government, all the means of raising money, and at the same time, will subject themselves to suits at law, for the recovery of the debts they have *contracted* in effecting the revolution. [DHRC16 173]

Samuel Bryan, "Centinel," No. 16, February 26, 1788:

. . . However if this matter admitted of any doubt, it would be removed by the following consideration, viz. that the new constitution is founded upon a dissolution of the present articles of confederation and is an original compact between those states, or rather those individuals who accede to it; consequently all *contracts,* debts and engagements in favor or against the United States, under the old government, are cancelled unless they are provided for in the new constitution. The framers of this constitution appear to have been aware of such consequence by stipulating in article 6th, that all debts *contracted,* and engagements entered into before the adoption of this constitution shall be valid against the United States under the new constitution, but there is no provision that the debts, &c. due to the United States, shall be valid or recoverable. This is a striking omission, and must have been designed, as debts of the latter description would naturally occur and claim equal attention with the former. This article implied, cancels all debts due to the United States prior to the establishment of the new constitution. . . . [DHRC16 219]

"James Bowdoin," February 27, 1788:

I have lately received a letter from Mr. J—— A—— [John Adams], our A——d-r at London, he is pleased with my compliment on his volume, it was, I told him of much service to us. He has endeavoured through Bobby's credit, to contract for the necessaries we wrote for; but he found it would not do: He then pledged the faith of the United States to fulfil the *contracts* he has made. He has also entered into other treaties for the other articles, which I shall be more particular about, by a safer opportunity. [DHRC16 239]

"The Landholder," No. 10, February 29, 1788:

[Quoting "Massachusetts Centinel":] "That Mr. [Elbridge] Gerry, by giving his dissent to the proposed Constitution, could have no motives for preserving an office—for he holds none under the United States, or any of them; that he has not, as has been asserted, exchanged Continental for State Securities, and if he had, it would have been for his interest to have supported the new system, because thereby the States are restrained from impairing the obligation of *contracts,* and by a transfer of such securities, they may be recovered in the new federal court . . . [DHRC16 270]

John Jay, *The Federalist*, No. 64, March 5, 1788:

[1] . . . They who make laws may, without doubt, amend or repeal them; and it will not be disputed that they who make treaties may alter or cancel them; but still let us not forget that treaties are made, not by only one of the *contracting* parties, but by both; and consequently, that as the consent of both was essential to their formation at first, so must it ever afterwards be to alter or cancel them. The proposed Constitution, therefore, has not in the least extended the obligation of treaties. They are just as binding, and just as far beyond the lawful reach of

legislative acts now, as they will be at any future period, or under any form of government. [Fed. 424]

[2] As to corruption, the case is not supposable. He must either have been very unfortunate in his intercourse with the world, or possess a heart very susceptible of such impressions, who can think it probable that the President and two thirds of the Senate will ever be capable of such unworthy conduct. The idea is too gross and too invidious to be entertained. But in such a case, if it should ever happen, the treaty so obtained from us would, like all other fraudulent *contracts,* be null and void by the law of nations. [Fed. 425]

"Brutus," No. 14, March 6, 1788:

. . . It has also declared, that "no state shall pass any law impairing the obligation of *contracts.*"—These prohibitions give the most perfect security against those attacks upon property which I am sorry to say some of the states have but too wantonly made, by passing laws sanctioning fraud in the debtor against his creditor. . . . [DHRC16 330]

Letter from a New York Quaker, published in *Poughkeepsie County Journal*, March 18, 1788:

I know it may be said, that treaties with foreign powers may be *contracted,* and compacts made with the few antifederal States (if any such) to secure to this State its soil and its rights: However contradictory to cool reason this hypothesis may be, I will for a moment suppose it practicable; and what a scene of carnage and devastation rises to view! . . . [DHRC16 410]

Archibald Maclaine, "Publicola," March 20, 1788:

We have among us some characters who have uniformly opposed giving Congress any additional powers—what idea such persons have of a government, which by its constitution is empowered to make treaties, *contract* debts and to demand monies from the several states, without being able to raise a single shilling, or inforce obedience to any one of its acts, they would do well to inform us. . . . [DHRC16 436]

Alexander Hamilton, *The Federalist*, No. 75, March 26, 1788:

. . . The power of making treaties is, plainly, neither the one nor the other. It relates neither to the execution of the subsisting laws, not to the enaction of new ones; and still less to an exertion of the common strength. Its objects are *CONTRACTS* with foreign nations, which have the force of law, but derive it from the obligations of good faith. They are not rules prescribed by the sovereign to the subject, but agreements between sovereign and sovereign. The power in question seems therefore to form a distinct department, and to belong, properly, neither to the legislative nor to the executive. The qualities elsewhere detailed as indispensable in the management of foreign negotiations, point out the Executive as the most fit agent in those transactions; while the vast importance of the trust, and the operation of treaties as laws, plead strongly for the participation of the whole or a portion of the legislative body in the office of making them. [Fed. 476–77]

Archibald Maclaine, "Publicola," March 27, 1788:

. . . If it should appear hereafter, that any one who uses these arguments against adopting the new constitution, should be found to be deeply indebted to British subjects, what shall we think of his patriotism? We shall be apt to conclude that private interest is at the bottom of his objections. But if we should be told that such a one acquired the most valuable part of his property, by *contracting* debts with British subjects, and that the same property remains at this day entire, and even considerably improved (the loss of a tame deer excepted) shall we not be convinced that his resentment against our late enemies is excited by the love of wealth, to the attainment of which he sacrifices the national faith. . . . [DHRC16 494]

John Jay, *An Address to the People of the State of New York*, c. April 15, 1788:

. . . Nay, does not experience also tell us, that it is as difficult to pay as to borrow? That even our houses and lands cannot command money—that law suits and usurious *contracts* abound—that our farms sell on executions for less than half their value, and that distress in various forms, and in various ways, is approaching fast to the doors of our best citizens. [Ford 73–74]

Melancton Smith, *An Address to the People of the State of New York*, c. April 1788:

[1] But it is contended, adopt it first, and then amend it. I ask, why not amend, and then adopt it? Most certainly the latter mode of proceeding is more consistent with our ideas of prudence in the ordinary concerns of life. If men were about entering into a *contract* respecting their private concerns, it would be highly absurd in them to sign and seal an instrument containing stipulations which are contrary to their interests and wishes, under the expectation, that the parties, after its execution, would agree to make alterations agreeable to their desire.—They would insist upon the exceptionable clauses being altered before they would ratify the *contract*. And is a compact for the government of ourselves and our posterity of less moment than *contracts* between individuals? Certainly not. . . . [Ford 93]

[2] It is true, many individuals labour under embarrassments, but these are to be imputed to the unavoidable circumstances of things, rather than to any defect

in our governments. We have just emerged from a long and expensive war. During its existence few people were in a situation to increase their fortunes, but many to diminish them. Debts *contracted* before the war were left unpaid while it existed, and these were left a burden too heavy to be borne at the commencement of peace. . . . [Ford 95]

Alexander Hamilton, *The Federalist*, No. 80, May 28, 1788:

. . . It is the peculiar province, for instance, of a court of equity to relieve against what are called hard bargains: these are *contracts* in which, though there may have been no direct fraud or deceit, sufficient to invalidate them in a court of law, yet there may have been some undue and unconscionable advantage taken of the necessities or misfortunes of one of the parties, which a court of equity would not tolerate. In such cases, where foreigners were concerned on either side, it would be impossible for the federal judicatories to do justice without an equitable as well as a legal jurisdiction. . . . [Fed. 504]

Alexander Hamilton, *The Federalist*, No. 81, May 28, 1788:

. . . A recurrence to the principles there established will satisfy us, that there is no color to pretend that the State governments would, by the adoption of that plan, be divested of the privilege of paying their own debts in their own way, free from every constraint but that which flows from the obligations of good faith. The *contracts* between a nation and individuals are only binding on the conscience of the sovereign, and have no pretensions to a compulsive force. They confer no right of action, independent of the sovereign will. To what purpose would it be to authorize suits against States for the debts they owe? How could recoveries be enforced? It is evident, it could not be done without waging war against the *contracting* State; and to ascribe to the federal courts, by mere implication, and in destruction of a preexisting right of the State governments, a power which would involve such a consequence, would be altogether forced and unwarrantable. [Fed. 511–12]

John Dickinson, "*Fabius*," No. 6, 1788:

[Quoting Lord Belhaven in Parliament:] "When I consider this treaty as it hath been explained, and spoke to, before us these three weeks by past; I see the English constitution remaining firm, the same two houses of Parliament, the same taxes, the same customs, the same excises, the same trading companies, the same municipal laws and courts of judicature; and all ours either subject to regulations or annihilations, only we are to have the honor to pay their old debts, and to have some few persons present for witnesses, to the validity of the deed, when they are pleased to *contract* more." [Ford 198]

South Carolina Constitution, June 3, 1790:

[Article I, Section 21:] No person shall be eligible to a seat in the legislature whilst he holds any office of profit or trust under this State, the United States, or either of them, or under any other power, except officers in the militia, army or navy of this State, justices of the peace or justices of the county courts, while they receive no salaries; nor shall any *contractor* of the army or navy of this State, the United States, or either of them, or the agents of such *contractor,* be eligible to a seat in either house. And if any member shall accept or exercise any of the said disqualifying offices, he shall vacate his seat. [Thorpe 3261]

[Article IX, Section 2:] No freemen of this State shall be taken, or imprisoned, or disseized of his freehold, liberties, or privileges, or outlawed or exiled, or in any manner destroyed, or deprived of his life, liberty or property, but by the judgment of his peers, or by the law of the land; nor shall any bill of attainder, ex post facto law, or law impairing the obligation of *contracts,* ever be passed by the legislature of this State. [Thorpe 3264]

Pennsylvania Constitution, September 2, 1790:

[Article IX, Section 17:] That no ex post facto law, nor any law impairing *contracts,* shall be made. [Thorpe 3101]

[Schedule, Section 1:] That all laws of this commonwealth, in force at the time of making the said alterations and amendments in the said constitution, and not inconsistent therewith, and all rights, actions, prosecutions, claims, and *contracts,* as well of individuals as of bodies-corporate, shall continue as if the said alterations and amendments had not been made. [Thorpe 3102]

CRIME, CAPITAL

(Criminal; Case, Prosecution, Offence, etc.)

United States Constitution, Bill of Rights, December 15, 1791:

[Article V:] No person shall be held to answer for a *capital, or otherwise infamous crime,* unless on a presentment or indictment of a Grand Jury, except in cases arising in the land or naval forces, or in the Militia, when in actual service in time of War or public danger; nor shall any person be subject for the same offense to be twice put in jeopardy of life or limb; nor shall be compelled in any criminal case to be a witness against himself, nor be deprived of life, liberty, or property, without due process of law; nor shall private property be taken for public use, without just compensation.

* * * * *

Elizabeth I, Letters Patent to Sir Humphrey Gilbert, June 11, 1578:

. . . wee for us, our heires and successours are likewise pleased and contented, and by these presents doe give and graunt to the sayd sir Humfrey and his heires and assignes for ever, that he and they, and every or any of them, shall and may, from time to time, for ever hereafter within the sayd mentioned remote lands and countreys, and in the way by the Seas thither, and from thence, have full and meere power and authoritie to correct, punish, pardon, governe and rule by their, and every or any of their good discretions and policies, as well in *causes capitall or criminall,* as civill, both marine and other, all such our subjects and others, as shall from time to time hereafter adventure themselves in the sayd journeys or voyages habitative or possessive, or that shall at any time hereafter inhabite any such lands countreys or territories as aforesayd . . . [Thorpe 51]

Elizabeth I, Charter to Sir Walter Raleigh, March 25, 1584:

. . . we for us, our heires and successors, are likewise pleased and contented, and by these presents do give and graunt to the said Walter Ralegh, his heires and assignes for ever, that hee and they, and every or any of them, shall and may from time to time for ever hereafter, within the said mentioned remote landes and Countreis in the way by the seas thither, and from thence, have full and meere power and authoritie to correct, punish, pardon, governe, and rule by their and every or any of their good discretions and pollicies, as well in *causes capital, or criminall,* as civil, both marine and other, all such our subjects as shall from time to time adventure themselves in the said journies or voyages, or that shall at any time hereafter inhabite any such landes, countreis, or territories as aforesaide . . . [Thorpe 55]

James I, Second Charter of Virginia, May 23, 1609:

. . . We for Us, our Heirs, and Successors are likewise pleased and contented, and by these Presents do Give and Grant unto the said Treasurer and Company, and their Successors, and to such Governors, Officers, and Ministers, as shall be by our said Council constituted and appointed according to the Natures and Limits of their Offices and Places respectively, that they shall and may from Time to Time, for ever hereafter, within the said Precincts of Virginia, or in the way by Seas thither and from thence, have full and absolute Power and Authority to correct, punish, pardon, govern, and rule all such the Subjects of Us, our Heires, and Successors as shall from Time to Time adventure themselves in any Voyage thither, or that shall at any Time hereafter, inhabit in the Precincts and Territories of the said Colony as aforesaid, according to such Orders, Ordinances, Constitutions, Directions, and Instructions, as by our said Council as aforesaid, shall be established; And in Defect thereof in case of Necessity, according to the good Discretions of the said Governor and Officers respectively, as well in *Cases capital and criminal,* as civil, both Marine and other . . . Statutes, Ordinances and Proceedings as near as conveniently may be, be agreeable to the Laws, Statutes, Government, and Policy of this our Realm of England.

[Thorpe 3800–01]

James I, The Charter of New England, November 3, 1620:

. . . Wee, for Us, our Heires and Successors, are likewise pleased and contented, and by these Presents do give and grant unto the said Council [of New England] and their Successors, and to such Governors, Officers, and Ministers, as shall be by the said Councill constituted and appointed according to the natures and Limitts of their Offices and Places respectively, that they shall and may, from time to time for ever heerafter, within the said Precincts of New-England, or in the Way by the Seas thither, and from thence have full and absolute Power and Authority to correct, punish, pardon, governe, and rule all such the Subjects of Us, our Heires and Successors, as shall from time to time adventure themselves in any Voyage thither, or that shall att any Time heerafter inhabit in the Precincts or Territories of the said Collony as aforesaid, according to such Laws, Orders,

Ordinances, Directions, and Instructions as by the said Councill aforesaid shall be established; and in Defect thereof, in Cases of Necessity, according to the good Discretions of the said Governors and Officers respectively, as well in *Cases capitall and criminall,* as civill, both marine and others, so allways as the said Statutes, Ordinances, and Proceedings, as near as conveniently may be, agreeable to the Laws, Statutes, Government and Policie of this our Realme of England. . . . [Thorpe 1833]

Council of New England, Grant of New Hampshire, April 18, 1635:

. . . Sd Councill & their successors wth ye power of Judicature in all *causes & matters wtsoever as well criminall capitall & civill* ariseing or wch may hereafter arise wthin ye limits bounds & percincts aforesaid to be exercised & exccuted according to ye laws of England as near as can be by ye sd Capt John Mason his heires & assignes or his or their Deputies Lieutenants Judges Stewards or officers thereunto by him or them assigned deputed or appointed . . .
[Thorpe 2442]

Government of New Haven Colony, October 27, 1643

All the magistrates for the whole juridsiction shall meete twice a yeare att Newhaven, namely, the Munday immediately before the sitting of the two fixed Generall Courts hereafter mentioned, to keep a Court called the Court of Magistrates, for the tryall of *weighty and capitall cases,* whether civill or criminall, above those lymitted to the ordinary judges in the perticular plantations, and to receive and try all appeales brought unto them from the aforesaid Plantation Courts, and to call all the inhabitants, whether free burgesses, free planters, or others, to account for the breach of any lawes established, and for other misdeameanours, and to censure them according to the quallity of the offence . . .
[Thorpe 527]

Charles II, Grant of the Province of Maine to the Duke of York, March 12, 1664:

. . . wee do further of our speciall grace certaine knowledge and meere mocon [motion] for us our heires and successors give and grant unto our said dearest brother James Duke of Yorke his heires deputyes agents commissioners and assignes by these presents full and absolute power and authority to correct punish pardon governe and rule all such the subjects of us our heires and successors who may from time to time adventure themselves into any of the parts or places aforesaid or that shall or doe at any time hereafter inhabite within the same according to such lawes orders ordinances direccons and instruments as by our said dearest brother or his assignes shall be established and in defect thereof in cases of necessity according to the good direccons of his deputyes commissioners officers or assignes respectively as well in all *causes and matters capitall and criminall* as civill both marine and others soe always as the said statutes ordinances and proceedings be not contrary to but as neare as conveniently may be agreeable to the lawes statutes and government of this our realme of England . . . [Thorpe 1638]

Charles II, Grant of the Province of Maine to the Duke of York, June 29, 1674:

. . . wee do further, of our speciall grace certaine knowledge and meer motion for Us Our heirs and successors give and graunt unto our said Dearest brother James Duke of Yorke his heirs Deputyes Agents commissioners and assignes by these presents full and absolute power and authority to correct punish pardon govern and rule all such the subjects of us our heirs and successors or any other person or persons as shall from time to time adventure themselves into any of the parts or places aforesaid or that shall or do at any time hereafter inhabit within the same according to such Lawes orders ordinances directions and instructions as by our said dearest brother or his assignes shall bee established and in defect thereof in cases of necessity according to the good discretions of his Deputyes Commissioners Office or Agents respectively as well in all *cases and matters capitall and criminall* as Civill Marine and Others so alwayes as the said Statutes ordinances and proceedings bee not contrary to but as neare as may bee agreeable to the Lawes Statutes and Government of this our realm of England . . . [Thorpe 1641–42]

New Jersey Proprietors, Deed of Revision, July 1, 1676:

. . . in and by which said Letters Patent his said Majesty did likewise give and grant unto his said dearest brother James Duke of York, his heirs, deputies, agents commissioners and assigns, full and absolute power and authority for the correcting, punishing, pardoning, governing and ruling such of the subjects of his said Majesty, of his heirs and successors, as shall at any time adventure themselves into the said port and places, or inhabit there, according to such laws, orders, ordinances, directions and instructions, as by his said Majesty's said dearest brother, or his assigns, shall be established; and in defect thereof, in case of necessity, according to the good discretions of his deputies, commissioners, officers or assigns respectively, as well in *all causes and matters capital and criminal,* as civil, both marinc and others, in such manner, and under such restrictions as is therein specified . . . [Thorpe 2552–53]

Pennsylvania Frame of Government, Laws Agreed Upon in England, May 5, 1682:

[Article 11:] That all prisoners shall be bailable by sufficient sureties, unless for *capital offences,* where the proof is evident, or the presumption great. [Thorpe 3061]

[Article 25:] That the estates of *capital offenders,* as traitors and murderers, shall go, one-third to the next of kin to the sufferer, and the remainder to the next of kin to the criminal. [Thorpe 3062]

Fundamental Constitutions of East New Jersey, 1683:

[Article 10:] Forasmuch as by the Patent, the power of pardoning in *capital offences,* is vested in the four and twenty Proprietors; it is hereby declared, that the said power of pardoning shall never be made use of but by the consent of eighteen of the Proprietors, or their proxies: Nevertheless, it shall be in the power of the Governor, in conjunction with four Proprietors, who for the time are judges of the Court of Appeals, to reprieve any person after the day of execution appointed, for some time, not exceeding a month. [Thorpe 2578]

[Article 14:] In all civil and ordinary actions, the Proprietors shall be judged after the same manner, and lyable to the same censure with any other; but in all *cases that are capital,* or may inferr for forfeiture of their trust or Proprietorship, they shall be adjudged by a jury of twelve of the Proprietors, or their proxies, or such as has share in a propriety not under one twentieth part; the bill being first found relevant against them by a grand jury of twelve Proprietors and twelve free men to be chosen by the ballot, as in article nineteen. [Thorpe 2579]

[Article 22:] . . . And whoever forfeits his estate to the government by commtting treason against the Crown of England, or in this Province, or by any other *capital crime,* the nearest of kin may redeem it within two months after the criminals death, by paying to the public treasury not above one hundred pounds, and not under five pounds sterling, which proportion the common Council shall determine, according to the value of the criminals estate, and to the nature of the offence . . . [Thorpe 2581]

James II, Commission to Sir Edmund Andros for the Dominion of New England, April 7, 1688:

And Wee do hereby give and graunt unto you full power where you shall see cause and shall judge and offender or offenders in *capitall and criminall matters,* or for any fines or forfeitures due unto us, fit objects of our mercy, to pardon such offenders and to remit such fines & forfeitures, treason and wilfull murder only excepted, in which case you shall likewise have power upon extraordinary occasions to grant reprieves to the offenders therein untill and to the intent our pleasure may be further known. [Thorpe 1866]

William and Mary, Charter of Massachusetts Bay, October 7, 1691:

And wee doe of our further Grace certaine knowledge and meer mocon [motion] Grant Establish and Ordaine for Us our heires and Successors that the great and Generall Court or Assembly of our said Province or Territory for the time being Convened as aforesaid shall for ever have full Power and Authority to Erect and Constitute Judicatories and Courts of Record or other Courts to be held in the name of Us Our heires and successors for the Hearing Trying and Determining of ail manner of *Crimes* Offences Pleas Processes Plaints Accons [actions] Matters Causes and things whatsoever ariseing or happening within Our said Province or Territory or between persons Inhabiting or resideing there whether the same be Criminall or Civill and whether the said *Crimes be Capitall or not Capitall* and whether the said Pleas be Reall personall or mixt and for the awarding and makeing out of Execution thereupon . . . [Thorpe 1881]

New Jersey Proprietors, Surrender of Rights, April 15, 1702:

. . . And by the same Letters Patents the late King Charles the Second, for himself, his heirs and successors, did give and grant to the said James Duke of York, his heirs, deputies, agents, commissioners and assigns, full and absolute power and authority to correct, punish, pardon, govern and rule all such subjects of the said King his heirs and successors, as should from time to time adventure themselves into the parts and places aforesaid, or that should at any time then after inhabit within the same, according to such laws, orders, ordinances, directions and instructions as by the said Duke of York, or his assigns, should be established; and in defect thereof, in case of necessity, according to the good directions of his deputies, commissioners, officers or assigns respectively, as well in *all causes and matters as well capital and criminal* as civil, both marine and others, so always as the said statutes, ordinances and proceedings were not contrary, but as near as might be agreeable to the laws and statutes and government of the realm of England . . . [Thorpe 2586]

George II, Charter of Georgia, June 9, 1732:

. . . And we do, of our further grace, certain knowledge and mere motion, grant, establish and ordain, for us, our heirs and successors, that the said corporation and their successors, shall have full power and authority, for and during the term of twenty-one years, to commence from the date of these our letters patent, to erect and constitute judicatories and courts of record, or other courts, to be held in the name of us, our heirs and successors for the hearing and determining of all manner of *crimes,* offences, pleas, processes, plaints, actions, causes and things whatsoever, arising or happening, within the said province of Georgia, or between persons of Georgia; whether the same be criminal or civil, and whether the said *crimes be capital or not capital,* and whether the said pleas be real, personal or mixed; and for awarding and making out executions thereupon . . . [Thorpe 774]

South Carolina Constitution, March 26, 1776:

[Preamble:] . . . persons are liable to be sent to and tried in Great Britain for an *offence created and made capital* by one of those statutes, though committed in the colonies . . . [Thorpe 3241]

Virginia Bill of Rights, June 12, 1776:

[Section 8:] That in all *capital or criminal prosecutions* a man hath a right to demand the cause and nature of his accusation, to be confronted with the accusers and witnesses, to call for evidence in his favor, and to a speedy trial by an impartial jury of twelve men of his vicinage without whose unanimous consent he cannot be found guilty; nor can he be compelled to give evidence against himself; that no man be deprived of his liberty, except by the law of the land or the judgment of his peers. [Thorpe 3813]

Pennsylvania Constitution, September 28, 1776:

[Frame of Government, Section 28:] The person of a debtor, where there is not a strong presumption of fraud, shall not be continued in prison, after delivering up, bona fide, all his estate real and personal, for the use of his creditors, in such manner as shall be hereafter regulated by law. All prisoners shall be bailable by sufficient sureties, unless for *capital offences,* when the proof is evident, or presumption great. [Thorpe 3089]

[*Ibid.,* Section 39:] To deter more effectually from the commission of crimes, by continued visible punishments of long duration, and to make sanguinary punishments less necessary; houses ought to be provided for punishing by hard labour, those who shall be convicted of *crimes not capital;* wherein the criminals shall be imployed for the benefit of the public, or for reparation of injuries done to private persons . . . [Thorpe 3090]

Maryland Constitution, November 11, 1776:

[Declaration of Rights, Article 36:] . . . And further, on such affirmation, warrants to search for stolen goods, or for the apprehension or commitment of offenders, ought to be granted, or security for the peace awarded, and Quakers, Dunkers or Menonists ought also, on their solemn affirmation as aforesaid, to be admitted as witnesses, in all *criminal cases not capital.* [Thorpe 1690]

North Carolina Constitution, December 18, 1776:

[Form of Government, Article 39:] That the person of a debtor, where there is not a strong presumption of fraud, shall not be continued in prison, after delivering up, bona fide, all his estate real and personal, for the use of his creditors, in such manner as shall be hereafter regulated by law. All prisoners shall be bailable by sufficient sureties, unless for *capital offences,* when the proof is evident, or the presumption great. [Thorpe 2793]

Vermont Constitution, July 8, 1777:

[Frame of Government, Section 25:] The person of a debtor, where there is not a strong presumption of fraud, shall not be continued in prison, after delivering up, bona fide, all his estate, real and personal, for the use of his creditors, in such manner as shall be hereafter regulated by law. All prisoners shall be bailable by sufficient securities, unless for *capital offences,* when the proof is evident or presumption great. [Thorpe 3746]

[*Ibid.,* Section 35:] To deter more effectually from the commission of *crimes,* by continued visible punishment of long duration, and to make sanguinary punishments less necessary; houses ought to be provided for punishing, by hard labor, those who shall be convicted of *crimes not capital;* wherein the criminal shall be employed for the benefit of the public, or for reparation of injuries done to private persons . . . [Thorpe 3747]

Massachusetts Constitution, March 2, 1780:

[Declaration of Rights, Article 12:] And the legislature shall not make any law that shall subject any person to a *capital or infamous punishment,* excepting for the government of the army and navy, without trial by jury. [Thorpe 1891]

[Frame of Government, Chapter I:1:3:] The general court shall forever have full power authority to erect and constitute judicatories and courts of record, or other courts, to be held in the name of the commonwealth, for the hearing, trying, and determining of all manner of *crimes,* offences, pleas, processes, plaints, actions, matters, causes, and things, whatsoever, arising or happening within the commonwealth, or between or concerning persons inhabiting, or residing, or brought within the same: whether the same be criminal or civil, or whether the said *crimes be capital or not capital,* and whether the said pleas be real, personal, or mixed; and for the awarding and making out of execution thereupon. . . . [Thorpe 1894]

New Hampshire Constitution, June 2, 1784:

[Bill of Rights, Article 16:] No subject shall be liable to be tried, after an acquittal, for the same crime or offence.—Nor shall the legislature make any law that shall subject any person to a *capital punishment,* excepting for the government of the army and navy, and the militia in actual service, without trial by jury. [Thorpe 2455]

[Form of Government:] The general court shall forever have full power and authority to erect and constitute judicatories and courts of record, or other courts, to be holden in the name of the state, for the hearing, trying, and determining all manner of *crimes,* offences, pleas, processes, plaints, actions, causes, matters and things whatsoever, arising, or happening within this state, or between or concerning persons inhabiting or residing, or brought within the same, whether the same be criminal or civil, or whether the *crimes be capital or not capital,* and whether the said pleas be real, personal, or mixed; and for the awarding and issuing execution thereon. . . . [Thorpe 2458]

Vermont Constitution, July 4, 1786:

[Frame of Government, Article 30:] The person of a debtor, where there is not strong presumption of fraud, shall not be continued in prison after delivering up and assigning over, bona fide, all his estate, real and personal, in possession, reversion, or remainder, for the use of his creditors, in such manner as shall be hereafter regulated by law. And all prisoners, unless in execution, or committed for *capital offences,* when the proof is evident or presumption great, shall be bailable by sufficient sureties: nor shall excessive bail be exacted for bailable offences. [Thorpe 3759]

[*Ibid.*, Article 34:] To deter more effectually from the commission of *crimes,* by continued visible punishment, of long duration, and to make sanguinary punishment less necessary, means ought to be provided for punishing by hard labour, those who shall be convicted of *crimes not capital,* whereby the criminal shall be employed for the benefit of the public, or for reparation of injuries done to private persons . . . [Thorpe 3760]

United States Confederation Congress, The Northwest Ordinance, July 13, 1787:

[Article 2:] The inhabitants of the said territory shall always be entitled to the benefits of the writs of habeas corpus, and of the trial by jury; of a proportionate representation of the people in the legislature, and of judicial proceedings according to the course of the common law. All persons shall be bailable, unless for *capital offences,* where the proof shall be evident, or the presumption great. . . . [Thorpe 960–61]

Dissent of the Pennsylvania Convention's Minority, December 18, 1787:

That in all *capital and criminal prosecutions,* a man has a right to demand the cause and nature of his accusation, as well in the federal courts as in those of the several States; to be heard by himself and his counsel; to be confronted with the accusers and witnesses; to call for evidence in his favor, and a speedy trial by an impartial jury of his vicinage, without whose unanimous consent he cannot be found guilty, nor can he be compelled to give evidence against himself; and that no man be deprived of his liberty, except by the law of the land or the judgment of his peers. [DHRC2 623]

Alexander White, "To the Citizens of Virginia," February 29, 1788:

. . . Now the House of Lords in England have not only the power of trying impeachments, in which they may proceed to judgment of death, and of all *capital crimes* committed by their own members; but appeals ly from all other courts of law and equity to them in the last resort. The Lord Chancellor is speaker of the house, and the judges of the common law courts may be and sometimes are members. The Lord Chancellor holds his office during pleasure, and when Montesque wrote the judges commissions expired with the life of the king who granted them. The American Senate is to have no judicial power except in impeachments . . . [DHRC8 441]

"The Impartial Examiner," No. 1, March 5, 1788:

. . . For instance, if Congress should pass a law that persons charged with *capital crimes* shall not have a right to demand the cause or nature of the accusation, shall not be confronted with the accusers or witnesses, or call for evidence in their own favor; and a question should arise respecting their authority therein,—can it be said that they have exceeded the limits of their jurisdiction, when that has no limits; when no provision has been made for such a right?—When no responsibility on the part of Congress has been required by the constitution? . . . [DHRC8 462]

Pennsylvania Constitution, September 2, 1790:

[Article V, Section 5:] The judges of the court of common pleas in each county shall, by virtue of their offices, be justices of over and terminer and general jail-delivery, for the trial of *capital and other offenders* therein . . . [Thorpe 3097]

[Article IX, Section 14:] That all prisoners shall be bailable by sufficient sureties, unless for *capital offences,* when the proof is evident or presumption great; and the privilege of the writ of habeas corpus shall not be suspended, unless when, in cases of rebellion or invasion, the public safety may require it. [Thorpe 3101]

CRIMES (HIGH) AND MISDEMEANORS

United States Constitution, September 17, 1787:

[Article II, Section 4:] The President, Vice President and all civil Officers of the United States, shall be removed from Office on Impeachment for, and Conviction of, Treason, Bribery, or other *high Crimes and Misdemeanors*.

* * * * *

Government of New Haven Colony, October 27, 1643:

All the magistrates for the whole juridsiction shall meete twice a yeare att Newhaven, namely, the Munday immediately before the sitting of the two fixed Generall Courts hereafter mentioned, to keep a Court called the Court of Magistrates, for the tryall of weighty and capitall cases, whether civill or *criminall,* above those lymitted to the ordinary judges in the perticular plantations, and to receive and try all appeales brought unto them from the aforesaid Plantation Courts, and to call all the inhabitants, whether free burgesses, free planters, or others, to account for the breach of any lawes established, and for other *misdeameanours,* and to censure them according to the quallity of the offence, in which meetings of magistrates, less then fower shall nott be accounted a Court . . . [Thorpe 527]

James II, Commission to Sir Edmund Andros for the Dominion of New England, April 7, 1688:

. . . In which case our will and pleasure is that the Captain or Commander so by you suspended shall during his suspension and commitmt be succeeded in his said office, by such commission or Warrant Officer of our said ship appointed by our self or our High Admirall for the time being, as by the known practice and discipline of our Navy doth and ought next to succeed him, as in case of death sickness or other ordinary disability hapning to the Commander of any of our ships & not otherwise; you standing also accountable to us for the truth & importance of the *crimes and misdemeanours* for which you shall so proceed to the suspending of such our said Captain or Commander. Provided also that all disorders and *misdemeanors* committed on shore by any Captain Commander, Lieutent, Master, or other officer seaman soldier or person whatsoever belonging to any of our ships of warr or other vessel acting by immediate commission or warrent from our self under the Great Seal of our Admiralty or from our High Admll from England for the time being may be tryed & punished according to the lawes of the place where any such disorders offences and *misdemeanors* shall be so committed on shore, notwithstanding such offender be in our actuall service and borne in our pay on board any such our shipps of warr or other vessels acting by immediate Commission or warrant from our self or our High Admirall as aforesaid . . . [Thorpe 1868]

Maryland Constitution, November 11, 1776:

[Form of Government, Article 10:] That the house of delegates may originate all money bills, propose bills to the senate, or receive those offered by that body, and assent, dissent, or propose amendments; that they may inquire, on the oath of witnesses, into all complaints, grievances, and offenses, as the grand inquest of this state, and may commit any person, for any *crime*, to the public jail, there to remain till he be discharged by due course of law. They may expel any member for a *great misdemeanor*, but not a second time for the same cause. . . . [Thorpe 1692]

New York Constitution, April 20, 1777:

[Article 34:] And it is further ordained, That in every trial on impeachment, or indictment for *crimes or misdemeanors*, the party impeached or indicted shall be allowed counsel, as in civil actions. [Thorpe 2635]

Alexander Hamilton, *The Federalist*, No. 69, March 14, 1788:

The President of the United States would be liable to be impeached, tried, and, upon conviction of treason, bribery, or other *high crimes or misdemeanors*, removed from office; and would afterwards be liable to prosecution and punishment in the ordinary course of law. The person of the king of Great Britain is sacred and inviolable; there is no constitutional tribunal to which he is amenable; no punishment to which he can be subjected without involving the crisis of a national revolution. In this delicate and important circumstance of personal responsibility, the President of confederated America would stand upon no better ground than a governor of New York, and upon worse ground than the governors of Maryland and Delaware. [Fed. 444–45]

"Brutus," No. 15, March 20, 1788:

The only clause in the constitution which provides for the removal of the judges from offices, is that which declares, that "the president, vice-president, and all civil officers of the United States, shall be removed from office, on impeachment for, and conviction of treason, bribery, or other *high crimes and misdemeanors.*" By this paragraph, civil officers, in which the judges are included, are removable only for *crimes*. Treason and bribery are named, and the rest are included under the general terms of *high crimes and misdemeanors.*—Errors in judgement, or want of capacity to discharge the duties of the office, can never be supposed to be included in these words, *high crimes and misdemeanors*. A man may mistake a case in giving judgment, or manifest that he is incompetent to the discharge of the duties of a judge, and yet give no evidence of corruption or want of integrity. To support the charge, it will be necessary to give in evidence some facts that will shew, that the judges commited the error from wicked and corrupt motives. [DHRC16 433]

Pennsylvania Constitution, September 2, 1790:

[Article IX, Section 10:] That no person shall, for any indictable offence, be proceeded against *criminally* by information, except in cases arising in the land or naval forces, or in the militia, when in actual service in time of war or public danger, or, by leave of the court, for oppression and *misdemeanor* in office. No person shall, for the same offence, be twice put in jeopardy of life or limb; nor shall any man's property be taken or applied to public use without the consent of his representatives, and without just compensation being made.

[Thorpe 3100–01]

DANGER, PUBLIC

United States Constitution, Bill of Rights, December 15, 1791:

[Article V:] No person shall be held to answer for a capital, or otherwise infamous crime, unless on a presentment or indictment of a Grand Jury, except in cases arising in the land or naval forces, or in the Militia, when in actual service in time of War or *public danger;* nor shall any person be subject for the same offence to be twice put in jeopardy of life or limb; nor shall be compelled in any criminal case to be a witness against himself, nor be deprived of life, liberty, or property, without due process of law; nor shall private property be taken for public use, without just compensation.

* * * * *

Alexander Hamilton, *The Federalist*, No. 15, December 1, 1787:

. . . Are we entitled by nature and compact to a free participation in the navigation of the Mississippi? Spain excludes us from it. Is public credit an indispensable resource in time of *public danger?* We seem to have abandoned its cause as desperate and irretrievable. Is commerce of importance to national wealth? Ours is at the lowest point of declension. Is respectability in the eyes of foreign powers a safeguard against foreign encroachments? The imbecility of our government even forbids them to treat with us. . . . [Fed. 156]

Dissent of the Pennsylvania Convention's Minority, December 18, 1787:

That the people have a right to bear arms for the defence of themselves and their own state, or the United States, or for the purpose of killing game; and no law shall be passed for disarming the people or any of them unless for crimes committed, or real *danger of public injury* from individuals; and as standing armies in the time of peace are dangerous to liberty, they ought not to be kept up; and that the military shall be kept under strict subordination to and be governed by the civil powers. [DHRC2 623–24]

Alexander Hamilton, *The Federalist*, No. 25, December 21, 1787:

. . . Pennsylvania, nevertheless, in a time of profound peace, from the existence of partial disorders in one or two of her counties, has resolved to raise a body of troops; and in all probability will keep them up as long as there is any appearance of *danger to the public peace*. The conduct of Massachusetts affords a lesson on the same subject, though on different ground. . . . [Fed. 212]

Alexander Hamilton, *The Federalist*, No. 30, December 28, 1787:

Let us attend to what would be the effects of this situation in the very first war in which we should happen to be engaged. We will presume, for argument's sake, that the revenue arising from the impost duties answers the purposes of a provision for the public debt and of a peace establishment for the Union. Thus circumstanced, a war breaks out. What would be the probable conduct of the government in such an emergency? Taught by experience that proper dependence could not be placed on the success of requisitions, unable by its own authority to lay hold of fresh resources, and urged by considerations of *national danger,* would it not be driven to the expedient of diverting the funds already appropriated from their proper objects to the defence of the State? . . . [Fed. 235]

James Madison, *The Federalist*, No. 58, February 20, 1788:

. . . in all cases the smaller the number, and the more permanent and conspicuous the station, of men in power, the stronger must be the interest which they will individually feel in whatever concerns the government. Those who represent the dignity of their country in the eyes of other nations, will be particularly sensible to every prospect of *public danger,* or of dishonorable stagnation in public affairs. To those causes we are to ascribe the continual triumph of the British House of Commons over the other branches of the government, whenever the engine of a money bill has been employed. . . . [Fed. 391]

John Dickinson, "Fabius," No. 4, 1788:

Constitutional properties are only, as has been observed at the beginning of this letter, parts in the organization of the contributed rights. As long as those parts preserve the orders assigned to them respectively by the constitution, they may so far be said to be balanced: but, when one part, without being sufficiently checked by the rest, abuses its power to the manifest *danger of public happiness,* or when the several parts abuse their respective powers so as to involve the commonwealth in the like peril, the people must restore things to that order, from which their functionaries have departed. . . . [Ford 183n]

Pennsylvania Constitution, September 2, 1790:

[Article IX, Section 10:] That no person shall, for any indictable offence, be proceeded against criminally by information, except in cases arising in the land or naval forces, or in the militia, when in actual service in time of war or *public danger,* or, by leave of the court, for oppression and misdemeanor in office. No person shall, for the same offence, be twice put in jeopardy of life or limb; nor shall any man's property be taken or applied to public use without the consent of his representatives, and without just compensation being made.

[Thorpe 3100–01]

DEFENCE, DEFENSE (COMMON)

United States Constitution, September 17, 1787:

[Preamble:] WE THE PEOPLE of the United States, in Order to form a more perfect Union, establish Justice, insure domestic Tranquility, provide for the *common defence,* promote the general Welfare, and secure the Blessings of Liberty to ourselves and our Posterity, do ordain and establish this Constitution for the United States of America.

[Article I, Section 8:] The Congress shall have Power To lay and collect Taxes, Duties, Imposts and Excises, to pay the Debts and provide for the *common Defence* and general Welfare of the United States; but all Duties, Imposts and Excises shall be uniform throughout the United States . . .

* * * * *

Carolina Proprietors, Declaration and Proposals, August 25, 1663:

We shall, as far as our charter permits us, empower the major part of the freeholders, or their deputies or assembly-men, to be by them chosen out of themselves, viz: two out of every tribe, division, or parish, in such manner as shall be agreed on, to make their own laws, by and with the advise and consent of the Governor and council, so as they be not repugnant to the laws of England, but, as near as may be, agreeing with them in all civil affairs, with submission to a superintendency of a general council, to be chosen out of every government of the province, in manner as shall be agreed on for the *common defence* of the whole; which laws shall, within one year after publication, be presented to us to receive our ratification, and to be in force until said ratification be desired and by us certified; but if once ratified, to continue until repealed by the same power, or by time expired. [Thorpe 2754–55]

Benjamin Franklin, Proposed Articles of Confederation, c. July 21, 1775:

[Article 2:] The said United Colonies hereby severally enter into a firm League of Friendship with each other, binding on themselves and their Posterity, for their *common Defence* against their Enemies, for the Security of their Liberties and Propertys, the Safety of their Persons and Families, and their mutual and general welfare. [PBF22 122]

United States Continental Congress, Draft Articles of Confederation, July 12, 1776:

[Article 2:] The said Colonies united themselves so as never to be divided by an Act whatever, and hereby severally enter into a firm League of Friendship with each other, for their *common Defence,* the Security of their Liberties, and their mutual and general Welfare, binding the said Colonies to assist one another against all Force offered to or attacks made upon them or any of them, on Account of Religion, Sovereignty, Trade, or any other Pretence whatever. [DHRC1 79]

[Article 10:] When Troops are raised in any of the Colonies for the *common Defence,* the Commission Officers proper for the Troops raised in each Colony, except the General Officers, shall be appointed by the Legislature of each Colony respectively, or in such manner as shall by them be directed. [DHRC1 80]

[Article 11:] All Charges of Wars and all other Expences that shall be incurred for the *common Defence,* or general Welfare, and allowed by the United States assembled, shall be defrayed out of a common Treasury, which shall be supplied by the several Colonies in Proportion to the Number of Inhabitants of every Age, Sex and Quality, except Indians not paying Taxes, in each Colony, a true Account of which, distinguishing the white Inhabitants, shall be triennially taken and transmitted to the Assembly of the United States . . . [DHRC1 80]

United States Articles of Confederation, November 15, 1777:

[Article III:] The said states hereby severally enter into a firm league of friendship with each other, for their common *defence,* the security of their Liberties, and their mutual and general welfare, binding themselves to assist each other, against all force offered to, or attacks made upon them, or any of them, on account of religion, sovereignty, trade, or any other pretence whatever.

[Article VII:] When land-forces are raised by any state for the *common defence,* all officers of or under the rank of colonel, shall be appointed by the legislature of each state respectively by whom such forces shall be raised, or in such manner as such state shall direct, and all vacancies shall be filled up by the state which first made the appointment.

[Article VIII:] All charges of war, and all other expenses that shall be incurred for the *common defence* or general welfare, and allowed by the united states in congress assembled, shall be defrayed out of a common treasury, which shall be supplied by the several states, in proportion to the value of all land within each state, granted to or surveyed for any Person, as such land and the buildings and improvements thereon shall be estimated according to such mode as the united states in congress assembled, shall from time to time direct and appoint. . . .

Massachusetts Constitution, March 2, 1780:

[Declaration of Rights, Article 17:] The people have a right to keep and to bear arms for the *common defence*. And as, in time of peace, armies are dangerous to liberty, they ought not to be maintained without the consent of the legislature; and the military power shall always be held in an exact subordination to the civil authority, and be governed by it. [Thorpe 1892]

The Virginia Plan of Union, May 29, 1787:

[Article 1:] Resolved that the articles of Confederation ought to be so corrected & enlarged as to accomplish the objects proposed by their institution; namely "*common defence,* security of liberty and general welfare." [DHRC1 243]

Richard Henry Lee [?], " The Federal Farmer," No. 4, October 12, 1787:

Third, there appears to me to be not only a premature deposit of some important powers in the general government—but many of those deposited there are undefined, and may be used to good or bad purposes as honest or designing men shall prevail. By Art. 1, Sec. 2, representatives and direct taxes shall be apportioned among the several states, &c.—same art. sect. 8, the congress shall have powers to lay and collect taxes, duties, &c. for the *common defence* and general welfare, but all duties, imposts and excises, shall be uniform throughout the United States . . . [Ford 310]

Noah Webster, *An Examination into the Leading Principles of the Federal Constitution*, October 17, 1787:

[1] . . . Considering the states as individuals, on equal terms, entering into a social compact, no state has a right to any power which may prejudice its neighbors. If therefore the federal constitution has collected into the federal legislature no more power than is necessary for the *common defence* and interest, it should be recognized by the states, however Particular clauses may supersede the exercise of certain powers by the individual states. [Ford 46]

[2] It is insinuated that the constitution gives Congress the power of levying internal taxes at pleasure. This insinuation seems founded on the eighth section of the first article, which declares, that "Congress shall have power to lay and collect taxes, duties, imposts and excises, to pay the debts and provide for the *common defence* and general welfare of the United States." [Ford 48]

[3] But the idea that Congress can levy taxes at pleasure is false, and the suggestion wholly unsupported. The preamble to the constitution is declaratory of the purposes of our union, and the assumption of any powers not necessary to establish justice, insure domestic tranquility, provide for the *common defence,* promote the general welfare, and to secure the blessings of liberty to ourselves and our Posterity, will be unconstitutional, and endanger the existence of Congress. Besides,in the very clause which gives the power of levying duties and taxes,the purposes to which the money shall be appropriated are specified, viz. to pay the debts and provide for the *common defence* and general welfare of the United States. For these purposes money must be collected, and the power of collection must be lodged, sooner or later, in a federal head; or the *common defence* and general welfare must be neglected. [Ford 50]

[4] . . . for no powers are vested in Congress but what are included under the general expressions, of providing for the *common defence* and general welfare of the United States. Any powers not promotive of these purposes, will be unconstitutional;—consequently any appropriations of money to any other purpose will expose the Congress to the resentment of the states, and the members to impeachment and loss of their seats. [Ford 50–51n]

[5] The states in their separate capacity, cannot provide for the *common defence;* nay in case of a civil war, a state cannot secure its own existence. The only question therefore is, whether it is necessary to unite, and provide for our *common defence* and general welfare. For this question being once decided in the affirmative, leaves no room to controvert the propriety of constituting a power over the whole United States, adequate to these general purposes. [Ford 50–51]

"Cato Uticensis," October 17, 1787:

In the hour of distress, in the moment of confusion and perilous danger, after separately declaring themselves sovereign and independent, the Thirteen States of America associated together in a Foederal league, for their *common defence,* an affair of such magnitude, formed under the influence of such unfavorable circumstances, could not fail of receiving a tinge from them; consequently, when the war, that link, which supplied each defect was over, the yawnings and the chasms of the building began to give evident marks of the hastiness of the workmen . . . [DHRC8 71]

Alexander Hamilton, *The Federalist*, No. 16, December 4, 1787:

It remains to inquire how far so odious an engine of government, in its application to us, would even be capable of answering its end. If there should not be a large army constantly at the disposal of the national government it would either not be able to employ force at all, or, when this could be done, it would amount to a war between parts of the Confederacy concerning the infractions of a league, in which the strongest combination would be most likely to prevail, whether it consisted of those who supported or of those who resisted the general authority. It would rarely happen that the delinquency to be redressed would be confined to a single member, and if there were more than one who had neglected their duty, similarity of situation would induce them to unite for *common defence*. . . . [Fed. 163]

Alexander Hamilton, *The Federalist*, No. 23, December 18, 1787:

[1] The principal purposes to be answered by union are these—the *common defence* of the members; the preservation of the public peace, as well against internal convulsions as external attacks; the regulation of commerce with other nations and between the States; the superintendence of our intercourse, political and commercial, with foreign countries. [Fed. 199]

[2] The authorities essential to the *common defence* are these: to raise armies; to build and equip fleets; to prescribe rules for the government of both; to direct their operations; to provide for their support. These powers ought to exist without limitation, because it is impossible to foresee or define the extent and variety of national exigencies, or the correspondent extent and variety of the means which may be necessary to satisfy them. The circumstances that endanger the safety of nations are infinite, and for this reason no constitutional shackles can wisely be imposed on the power to which the care of it is committed. This power ought to be co-extensive with all the possible combinations of such circumstances; and ought to be under the direction of the same councils which are appointed to preside over the *common defence*. [Fed. 199–200]

[3] Whether there ought to be a federal government intrusted with the care of the *common defence* is a question in the first instance, open for discussion; but the moment it is decided in the affirmative, it will follow that that government ought to be clothed with all the powers requisite to complete execution of its trust. And unless it can be shown that the circumstances which may affect the public safety are reducible within certain determinate limits, unless the contrary of this position can be fairly and rationally disputed, it must be admitted, as a necessary consequence, that there can be no limitation of that authority which is to provide for the *defence and protection of the community,* in any matter essential to its efficacy—that is, in any matter essential to the formation, direction, or support of the NATIONAL FORCES. [Fed. 200]

[4] Defective as the present Confederation has been proved to be, this principle appears to have been fully recognized by the framers of it, though they have not made proper or adequate provision for its exercise. Congress have an unlimited discretion to make requisitions of men and money; to govern the army and navy;

to direct their operations. As their requisitions are made constitutionally binding upon the States, who are in fact under the most solemn obligations to furnish the supplies required of them, the intention evidently was that the United States should command whatever resources where by them judged requisite to the "*common defence* and general welfare." It was presumed that a sense of their true interests, and a regard to the dictates of good faith, would be found sufficient pledges for the punctual performance of the duty of the members to the federal head. [Fed. 200–01]

[5] Who [is] so likely to make suitable provisions for the *public defence* as that body to which the guardianship of the public safety is confided; which, as the center of information, will best understand the extent and urgency of the dangers that threaten; as the representative of the WHOLE, will feel itself most deeply interested in the preservation of every part; which, from the responsibility implied in the duty assigned to it, will be most sensibly impressed with the necessity of proper exertions; and which, by the extension of its authority throughout the States, can alone establish uniformity and concert in the plans and measures by which the *common safety* is to be secured? Is there not a manifest inconsistency in devolving upon the federal government the care of the *general defence,* and leaving in the State governments the effective powers by which it is to be provided for? Is not a want of co-operation the infallible consequence of such a system? . . . [Fed. 202]

"Americanus," No. 2, December 19, 1787:

. . . The house of representatives, which has the exclusive right of originating bills of taxation, is composed of members elected directly by the people in the most exact proportion. The object of this representation is the *common defence* and general welfare of the United States. The concomitant right of taxation extends no farther. It is the express language of the constitution, that all monies, arising from the taxes imposed by Congress shall be appropriated to the support of the foederal government, the *common defence* of the United States, and the regular discharge of the national debts. The interests of the representatives are so intermixed with that of the people, that they cannot, without a partiality too flagrant to be endured, impose a tax in which they will not take a share themselves: nor can they scarcely adopt an advantageous regulation, in which their own interests will not participate of the advantage. [DHRC8 248]

Alexander Hamilton, *The Federalist*, No. 25, December 21, 1787:

It may perhaps be urged that the objects enumerated in the preceding number ought to be provided for by the State governments, under the direction of the Union. But this would be, in reality, an inversion of the primary principle of our political association, as it would in practice transfer the care of the *common defence* from the federal head to the individual members: a project oppressive to some States, dangerous to all, and baneful to the Confederacy. [Fed. 208]

Alexander Hamilton, *The Federalist*, No. 26, December 22, 1787:

. . . Few persons will be so visionary as seriously to contend that military forces ought not to be raised to quell a rebellion or resist an invasion; and if the *defence of the community* under such circumstances should make it necessary to have an army so numerous as to hazard its liberty, this is one of those calamities for which there is neither preventative nor cure. It cannot be provided against by any possible form of government; it might even result from a simple league offensive and defensive, if it should ever be necessary for the confederates or allies to form an army for *common defence*. [Fed. 218]

Alexander Hamilton, *The Federalist*, No. 29, January 9, 1788:

The power of regulating the militia, and of commanding its services in times of insurrection and invasion are natural incidents to the duties of superintending the *common defence,* and of watching over the internal peace of the Confederacy. [Fed. 226]

James Madison, *The Federalist*, No. 41, January 19, 1788:

[1] Some, who have not denied the necessity of the power of taxation, have grounded a very fierce attack against the Constitution, on the language in which it is defined. It has been urged and echoed, that the power "to lay and collect taxes, duties, imposts, and excises, to pay the debts, and provide for the *common defence* and general welfare of the United States," amounts to an unlimited commission to exercise every power which may be alleged to be necessary for the *common defence* or general welfare. No stronger proof could be given of the distress under which these writers labor for objections, than their stooping to such a misconstruction. [Fed. 300]

[2] The objection here is the more extraordinary, as it appears that the language used by the convention is a copy from the articles of Confederation. The objects of the Union among the States, as described in article third, are, "their *common defence,* security of their liberties, and mutual and general welfare." The terms of article eighth are still more identical: "All charges of war and all other expenses that shall be incurred for the *common defence* or general welfare, and allowed by the United States in Congress, shall be defrayed out of a common treasury," etc. A similar language again occurs in article ninth. Construe either of these articles by the rules which would justify the construction put on the new Constitution, and they vest in the existing Congress a power to legislate in all cases whatsoever. But what would have been thought of that assembly, if, attaching themselves to these general expressions, and disregarding the specifications

which ascertain and limit their import, they had exercised an unlimited power of providing for the *common defence* and general welfare? I appeal to the objectors themselves, whether they would in that case have employed the same reasoning in justification of Congress as they now make use of against the convention. How difficult it is for error to escape its own condemnation!

[Fed. 301–302]

"Valerius," January 23, 1788:

The reflection you [Richard Henry Lee] have thrown upon the house of representatives, savours strongly of an exasperated spirit; you stile it "a mere shred or rag of representation." But, the description is as false, as the language is vulgar. What! shall a body of the choicest sons of America, elected by the unbought, unbiassed voices of a whole nation, entrusted with sovereign powers, and whose important charge is the *common defence* and general welfare of thirteen confederated states, shall this body be stiled "the mere shred and rag of representation." For shame! sir, for shame! . . . [DHRC8 318]

James Madison, *The Federalist*, No. 45, January 26, 1788:

. . . The powers relating to war and peace, armies and fleets, treaties and finance, with the other more considerable powers, are all vested in the existing Congress by the articles of Confederation. The proposed change does not enlarge these powers; it only substitutes a more effectual mode of administering them. The change relating to taxation may be regarded as the most important; and yet the present Congress have as complete authority to REQUIRE of the States indefinite supplies of money for the *common defence* and general welfare, as the future Congress will have to require them of individual citizens; and the latter will be no more bound than the States themselves have been, to pay the quotas respectively taxed on them. . . . [Fed. 329]

Alexander C. Hanson, *Remarks on the Proposed Plan of a Federal Government*, c. January 31, 1788:

Consider again the nature and intent of a federal republic. It consists of an assemblage of distinct states, each completely organized for the protection of its own citizens, and the whole consolidated, by express compact, under one head, for the general welfare and *common defence*. [Ford 241]

David Ramsay, "Civis," February 4, 1788:

[1] . . . If then we are to be an united people, and the obvious ground of union must be, that all continental concerns should be managed by Congress—let us by those principles examine the new constitution. Look over the 8th section, which enumerates the powers of Congress, and point out one that is not essential

on the before recited principles of union. The first is a power to lay and collect taxes, duties, imposts, and excises, to pay the debts, and provide for the *common defence* and general welfare of the United States. [DHRC16 22]

[2] When you authorised Congress to borrow money, and to contract debts, for carrying on the late war, you could not intend to abridge them of the means of paying their engagements, made on your account. You may observe that their future power is confined to provide *common defence* and general welfare of the United States. If they apply money to any other purposes, they exceed their powers. The people of the United States who pay, are to be judges how far their money is properly applied. . . . [DHRC16 22]

[3] . . . Take another instance—the Congress are authorized to provide and maintain a navy.—Our sea-coast, in its whole extent needs the protection thereof; but if this was to be done by the states, they who build ships, would be more secure than they who do not. Again, if the local legislatures might build ships of war at pleasure, the Eastern would have a manifest superiority over the Southern states. Observe, how much better this business is referred to the regulations of Congress. A common navy, paid out of the common treasury, and to be disposed of by the united voice of a majority for the *common defence* of the weaker as well as of the stronger states, is promised, and will result from the federal constitution. Suffer not yourselves to be imposed on by declamation. Ask the man who objects to the powers of Congress two questions, is it not necessary that the supposed dangerous power should be lodged somewhere? And secondly, where can it be lodged, consistently with the general good, so well as in the general government? Decide for yourselves on these obvious principles of union. [DHRC16 23]

Massachusetts Convention, Ratification of the Constitution, February 6, 1788:

The convention having impartially discussed, and fully considered, the constitution for the United States of America, reported to Congress, by the convention of delegates from the United States, of America, and submitted to us, by a resolution of the General Court of the said commonwealth, passed the twenty fifth day of October last past; and acknowledging with grateful hearts the goodness of the Supreme Ruler of the universe, in affording the people of the United States, in the course of his Providence, an opportunity, deliberately and peaceably, without fraud or surprise, of entering into an explicit and solemn compact with each other, by assenting to and ratifying a new constitution, in order to form a more perfect union, establish justice, insure domestick tranquillity, provide for the *common defence,* promote the general welfare, and secure the blessings of liberty to themselves, and their posterity—DO, in the name and in behalf of the people of the commonwealth of Massachusetts, ASSENT to and RATIFY the said constitution, for the United States of America.

[DHRC16 67–68]

"Brutus," No. 12, February 7, 1788:

To discover the spirit of the constitution, it is of the first importance to attend to the principal ends and designs it has in view. These are expressed in the preamble, in the following words, viz. "We, the people of the United States, in order to form a more perfect union, establish justice, insure domestic tranquility, provide for the *common defence,* promote the general welfare, and secure the blessings of liberty to ourselves and our posterity, do ordain and establish this constitution," &c. If the end of the government is to be learned from these words, which are clearly designed to declare it, it is obvious it has in view every object which is embraced by any government. The preservation of internal peace—the due administration of justice—and to provide for the defence of the community, seems to include all the objects of government; but if they do not, they are certainly comprehended in the words, "to provide for the general welfare." . . . [DHRC16 74]

"An Impartial Citizen," No. 6, March 13, 1788:

. . . To compel any State by dint of arms to pay her quota, would be the utmost degree of political madness; it would generate the most implacable hatred of the citizens of some States to the rest: It seems also impracticable to effect it. Yet the public credit ought to be supported, and the *common defence* and general welfare provided for. How could this have been done, but by recurring to the same process whereby money is levied by the different State Governments? But even this will be seldom practised, or not to a great extent, as the impost will be very productive. . . . [DHRC8 499]

Alexander Hamilton, *The Federalist*, No. 75, March 26, 1788:

. . . The essence of the legislative authority is to enact laws, or, in other words, to prescribe rules for the regulation of the society; while the execution of the laws, and the employment of the common strength, either for this purpose or for the *common defence,* seem to comprise all the functions of the executive magistrate. The power of making treaties is, plainly, neither the one nor the other. It relates neither to the execution of the subsisting laws, nor to the enaction of new ones; and still less to an exertion of the common strength. Its objects are CONTRACTS with foreign nations, which have the force of law, but derive it from the obligations of good faith. . . . [Fed. 476]

DISORDERLY BEHAVIOR

United States Constitution, September 17, 1787:

[Article I, Section 5:] Each House may determine the Rules of its Proceedings, punish its Members for *disorderly Behaviour,* and, with the Concurrence of two thirds, expel a Member.

* * * * *

Maryland Constitution, November 11, 1776:

[Form of Government, Article 12:] That the house of delegates may punish, by imprisonment, any person who shall be guilty of a contempt, in their view, By any *disorderly or riotous behavior,* or by threats to, or abuse of their members, or by any obstruction to their proceedings. . . . [Thorpe 1693]

Massachusetts Constitution, March 2, 1780:

[Frame of Government, Chapter I:3:10:] The house of representatives shall be the judge of the returns, elections, and qualifications of its own members, as pointed out in the constitution; shall choose their own speaker; appoint their own officers, and settle the rules and others of proceeding in their own house. They shall have authority to punish by imprisonment, every person not a member, who shall be guilty of disrespect to the house, by any *disorderly, or contemptuous behavior* in its presence . . . [Thorpe 1899]

New Hampshire Constitution, June 2, 1784:

[Form of Government:] The house of representatives shall choose their own speaker, appoint their own officers, and settle the rules of proceedings in their own house. They shall have authority to punish by imprisonment, every person who shall be guilty of disrespect to the house in its presence, by any *disorderly or contemptuous behaviour,* or by threatening, or ill treating any of its members . . . [Thorpe 2462]

Georgia Constitution, May 6, 1789:

[Article I, Section 13:] Each house shall be judges of the elections, returns, and qualifications of its own members, with powers to expel or punish for *disorderly behavior.* [Thorpe 786]

South Carolina Constitution, June 3, 1790:

[Article I, Section 12:] Each house shall choose by ballot its own officers, determine its rules of proceeding, punish its members for *disorderly behavior,* and (with the concurrence of two-thirds) expel a member, but not a second time for the same cause. [Thorpe 3260]

[Article I, Section 13:] Each house may punish, by imprisonment, during sitting, any person not a member, who shall be guilty of disrespect to the house, by any *disorderly or contemptuous behavior* in its presence, or who, during the time of its sitting, shall threaten harm to the body or estate of any member, for anything said or done in either house, or who shall assault any of them therefor, or who shall assault or arrest any witness, or other person, ordered to attend the house, in his going to or returning there from, or who shall rescue any person arrested by order of the house. [Thorpe 3260]

Pennsylvania Constitution, September 2, 1790:

[Article I, Section 13:] Each house may determine the rules of its proceedings, punish its members for *disorderly behavior,* and, with the concurrence of two-thirds, expel a member, but not a second time for the same cause; and shall have all other powers necessary for a branch of the legislature of a free State. [Thorpe 3094]

DUE PROCESS OF LAW

United States Constitution, Bill of Rights, December 15, 1791:

[Article V:] No person shall be held to answer for a capital, or otherwise infamous crime, unless on a presentment or indictment of a Grand Jury, except in cases arising in the land or naval forces, or in the Militia, when in actual service in time of War or public danger; nor shall any person be subject for the same offence to be twice put in jeopardy of life or limb; nor shall be compelled in any criminal case to be a witness against himself, nor be deprived of life, liberty, or property, without *due process of law;* nor shall private property be taken for public use, without just compensation.

* * * * *

English Petition of Right, June 7, 1628:

[Article 4:] And in the eight and twentieth year of the reign of King Edward the Third, it was declared and enacted by authority of Parliament, that no man of what estate or condition that he be, should be put out of his land, or tenements, nor taken, nor imprisoned, nor disinherited, nor put to death without being brought to answer by *due process of law.* [SDECH 340]

EMOLUMENT, EMOLUMENTS

United States Constitution, September 17, 1787:

[Article I, Section 6:] No Senator or Representative shall, during the Time for which he was elected, be appointed to any civil Office under the Authority of the United States, which shall have been created, or the *Emoluments* whereof shall have been increased during such time; and no Person holding any Office under the United States, shall be a Member of either house during his Continuance in Office.

[Article I, Section 9:] No Title of Nobility shall be granted by the United States: And no Person holding any Office of Profit or Trust under them, shall, without the Consent of the Congress, accept of any present, *Emolument,* Office, or Title, of any kind whatever, from any King, Prince, or foreign State.

[Article II, Section 1:] The President shall, at stated Times, receive for his Services, a Compensation, which shall neither be encreased nor diminished during the Period for which he shall have been elected, and he shall not receive within that Period any other *Emolument* from the United States, or any of them.

* * * * *

James II, Second Charter of Virginia, May 23, 1609:

And finally our Will and Pleasure is, and we do further hereby for Us, our Heirs, and Successors, Grant and Agree, to and with the said Treasurer and Company, and their Successors, that all and singular Person and Persons, which shall at any Time or Times hereafter adventure any Sum or Sums of Money, in and towards the said Plantation of the said Colony in Virginia, and shall be admitted by the said Council and Company, as Adventurers of the said Colony in Form aforesaid, and shall be enrolled in the Book or Records of the Adventurers of the said Company, shall and may be accounted, accepted, taken, held, and reputed Adventurers of the said Colony, and shall, and may enjoy all and singular Grants, Privileges, Liberties, Benefits, Profits, Commodities and Immunities,

Advantages and *Emoluments* whatsoever, as fully, largely, amply, and absolutely, as if they and every of them, had been precisely, plainly, singularly, and distinctly named and inserted in these our Letters-patents. [Thorpe 3801–02]

Council of New England, Charter of Plymouth Colony, January 13, 1629:

. . . And now seeinge that by the speciall providence of God, and their extraordinary care and industry they have increased their plantacon to neere three hundred people, and are uppon all occasions able to relieve any new planters or others his Ma[jes]t[y]s subjects whoe may fall uppon that coaste; have given graunted bargained sould enfeoffed allotted assigned and sett over and by these presents doe cleerly and absolutely give graunt bargaine sell alien enfeoffe allott assigne and confirme unto the said William Bradford, his heires associatts and assignes all that part of New-Englande in America aforesaid and tracte and tractes of lande . . . [details of boundaries] . . . and all lands rivers waters havens creeks ports fishings fowlings and all hereditaments proffitts comodities and *emoluments* whatsoever situate lyinge and beinge or ariseinge within or betweene the said limitts and grounds or any of them. . . . [Thorpe 1842–43]

South Carolina Constitution, March 26, 1776:

[Article 10:] That if a member of the general assembly or of the legislative council shall accept any place of *emolument* or any commission except in the militia, he shall vacate his seat, and there shall thereupon be a new election, but he shall not be disqualified from serving upon being reelected.

[Thorpe 3244]

Virginia Bill of Rights, June 12, 1776:

[Section 4:] That no man, or set of men, are entitled to exclusive or separate *emoluments* or privileges from the community, but in consideration of public services; which, not being descendible, neither ought the offices of magistrate, legislator, or judge to be hereditary. [Thorpe 3813]

United States Continental Congress, Draft Articles of Confederation, July 12, 1776:

[Article 4:] No Colony or Colonies, without the Consent of the United States assembled, shall send any Embassy to or receive any Embassy from, or enter into any Treaty, Convention or Conference with the King or Kingdom of Great-Britain, or any foreign Prince or State; nor shall any Colony or Colonies, nor any Servant or Servants of the United States, or of any Colony or Colonies, accept of any Present, *Emolument,* Office, or title of any Kind whatever, from the King or Kingdom of Great-Britain, or any foreign Prince or State; nor shall the United States assembled, or any Colony grant any Title of Nobility. [DHRC1 79]

[Article 18:] No Person holding any Office under the United States, for which he, or another for his Benefit, receives any Salary, Fees, or *Emolument* of any Kind, shall be capable of being a Delegate. [DHRC1 84]

Pennsylvania Constitution, September 28, 1776:

[Declaration of Rights, Article 5:] That government is, or ought to be, instituted for the common benefit, protection and security of the people, nation or community; and not for the particular *emolument* or advantage of any single man, family or set of men, who are a part Only of that community; And that the community hath an indubitable, unalienable and indefeasible right to reform, alter, or abolish government in such manner as shall be by that community judged most conducive to the public weal. [Thorpe 3082–83]

North Carolina Constitution, December 18, 1776:

[Declaration of Rights, Article 3:] That no man, or set of men, are entitled to exclusive or separate *emoluments* or privileges from the community, but in consideration of public services. [Thorpe 2787]

[*Ibid.*, Article 22:] That no hereditary *emoluments*, privileges, or honors ought to be granted or conferred in this state. [Thorpe 2788]

Vermont Constitution, July 8, 1777:

[Declaration of Rights, Article 6:] That government is, or ought to be, instituted for the common benefit, protection, and security of the people, nation or community; and not for the particular *emolument* or advantage of any single man, family or set of men, who are a part only of that community; and that the community hath an indubitable, unalienable and indefeasible right to reform, alter, or abolish, government, in such manner as shall be, by that community, judged most conducive to the public weal. [Thorpe 3740]

United States Articles of Confederation, November 15, 1777:

[Article V:] No state shall be represented in Congress by less than two, nor by more than seven Members; and no person shall be capable of being a delegate for more than three years in any term of six years; nor shall any person, being a delegate, be capable of holding any office under the united states, for which he, or another for his benefit receives any salary, fees or *emolument* of any kind.

[Article VI:] No state without the Consent of the united states in congress assembled, shall send any embassy to, or receive any embassy from, or enter into any conference, agreement, or alliance or treaty with any King prince or state; nor shall any person holding any office of profit or trust under the united states, or any of them, accept of any present, *emolument,* office or title of any kind whatever from any king, prince or foreign state; nor shall the united states in congress assembled, or any of them, grant any title of nobility.

South Carolina Constitution, March 19, 1778:

[Article 20:] That if any member of the senate or house of representatives shall accept any place of *emolument,* or any commission, (except in the militia or commission of the peace, and except as is excepted in the tenth article,) he shall vacate his seat, and there shall thereupon be a new election; but he shall not be disqualified from serving upon being reelected, unless he is appointed secretary of the State, a commissioner of the treasury, an officer of the customs, register of mesne conveyances, a clerk of either of the courts of justice, sheriff, powder-reviewer, clerk of the senate, house of representatives, or privy council, surveyor-general, or commissary of military stores, which officers are hereby declared disqualified from being members either of the senate or house of representatives. [Thorpe 3253]

New Hampshire Constitution, June 2, 1784:

[Bill of Rights, Article 10:] Government being instituted for the common benefit, protection, and security of the whole community, and not for the private interest or *emolument* of any one man, family or class of men; therefore, whenever the ends of government are perverted, and public liberty manifestly endangered, and all other means of redress are ineffectual, the people may, and of right ought, to reform the old, or establish a new government. The doctrine of non-resistance against arbitrary power, and oppression, is absurd, slavish, and destructive of the good and happiness of mankind. [Thorpe 2455]

[Form of Government:] No person shall be capable of being a delegate to Congress, for more than three years in any term of six years; nor shall any person being a delegate, be capable of holding any office under the United States, for which he, or any other for his benefit, receives any salary, or *emolument* of any kind. [Thorpe 2467]

Virginia Statute of Religious Liberty, January 16, 1786:

. . . that therefore the proscribing any citizen as unworthy the public confidence by laying upon him an incapacity of being called to offices of trust and *emolument,* unless he profess or renounce this or that religious opinion, is depriving him injuriously of those privileges and advantages to which in common with his fellow citizens, he has a natural right; that it tends only to corrupt the principles of that religion it is meant to encourage, by bribing, with a monopoly of worldly honors and *emoluments,* those who will externally profess and conform to it . . . [CVA8 690]

Tench Coxe, *An Examination of the Constitution for the United States of America*, No. 2, September 28, 1787:

They [the Senators] can hold no other office civil or military under the United States, nor can they join in making provision for themselves, either by creating new places, or encreasing the *emoluments* of old ones. As their sons are not to succeed them, they will not be induced to aim at an increase or perpetuity of their powers, at the expence of the liberties of the people, of which those sons will be a part. . . . [Ford 140–41]

Tench Coxe, *An Examination of the Constitution for the United States*, No. 3, September 29, 1787:

. . . The vote of each representative can be always known, as well as the proceedings of the house, that so the people may be acquainted with the conduct of those in whom they repose so important a trust. As was observed of the Senators, they cannot make new offices for themselves, nor increase, for their own benefit, the *emoluments* of old ones, by which the people will be exempted from needless additions to the public expences, on such sordid and mercenary principles . . . [Ford 144]

James Wilson, Speech on the Federal Constitution, October 6, 1787:

. . . All the officers of government, and all the appointments for the administration of justice and the collection of the public revenue, which are transferred from the individual to the aggregate sovereignty of the states, will necessarily turn the stream of influence and *emolument* into a new channel. Every person, therefore, who either enjoys, or expects to enjoy a place of profit under the present establishment, will object to the proposed innovation? not, in truth, because it is injurious to the liberties of his country, but because it effects his schemes of wealth and consequence. . . . [Ford 161]

Richard Henry Lee [?], "The Federal Farmer," No. 3, October 10, 1787:

. . . The members of the legislature are not excluded from being elected to any military offices, or any civil offices, except those created, or the *emoluments* of which shall bc increased by themselves: two-thirds of the members present, of either house, may expel a member at pleasure. . . . [Ford 298]

Tench Coxe, *An Examination of the Constitution for the United States of America*, No. 4, October 21, 1787:

The influence which foreign powers may attempt to exercise in our affairs was foreseen, and a wholesome provision has been made against it; for no person holding an office under the United States is permitted to enjoy any foreign honours, powers or *emoluments*. [Ford 150]

Alexander Hamilton, *The Federalist*, No. 1, October 27, 1787:

Among the most formidable of the obstacles which the new Constitution will have to encounter may readily be distinguished the obvious interest of a certain class of men in every State to resist all changes which may hazard a diminution of the power, *emolument,* and consequence of the offices they hold under the State establishments . . . [Fed. 89]

Dissent of the Pennsylvania Convention's Minority, December 18, 1787:

The representation is unsafe because in the exercise of such great powers and trusts, it is so exposed to corruption and undue influence, by the gift of the numerous places of honor and *emolument,* at the disposal of the executive; by the arts and address of the great and designing; and by direct bribery.
[DHRC2 632]

Alexander Hamilton, *The Federalist*, No. 36, January 8, 1788:

As to any argument derived from a supposed system of influence, it is a sufficient answer to say that it ought not to be presumed; but the supposition is susceptible of a more precise answer. If such a spirit should infest the councils of the Union, the most certain road to the accomplishment of its aim would be to employ the State officers as much as possible, and to attach them to the Union by an accumulation of their *emoluments*. This would serve to turn the tide of State influence into the channels of the national government, instead of making federal influence flow in an opposite and adverse current. But all suppositions of this kind are invidious, and ought to be banished from the consideration of the great question before the people. . . . [Fed. 263]

"An Impartial Citizen," January 10, 1788:

. . . The President in many important cases, must have the concurrence of the Senate, wherein his sole decision might be dangerous. The compensation for his services cannot be augmented, nor can he receive any other *emolument* from the United States, or any of them, during the period for which he shall have been elected: Nor can he appropriate the public money to any use, but what is expressly provided by law; which, together with the minutely complex mode of election (from which arises the strong improbability of his being re-elected) so cautiously guards and limits his quadrennial power, as to leave him dignity enough for the execution of his office, without the possibility of making a bad use of it,—and this security is still heightened by his responsibility to impeachment. . . . [DHRC8 295]

James Madison, *The Federalist*, No. 46, January 29, 1788:

Many considerations, besides those suggested on a former occasion, seem to place it beyond doubt that the first and most natural attachment of the people will be to the governments of their respective States. Into the administration of these a greater number of individuals will expect to rise. From the gift of these a greater number of offices and *emoluments* will flow. By the superintending care of these, all the most domestic and personal interests of the people will be regulated and provided for. . . . [Fed. 330]

John Williams to ———, January 29, 1788, published in Albany *Federal Herald*, February 25, 1788:

. . . If the new constitution is adopted, Congress hath all the impost and excise; this latter may be laid heavy on taverns and spirits, so that the *emoluments* from taverns, which are now converted to the use of the poor, must go to Congress; and what is yet worse, all the duties arising from any duties or excise, are to be appropriated to the use of Congress. [DHRC16 200]

Luther Martin, "Genuine Information," No. 11, February 5, 1788:

Let it not be forgotten at the same time, that a great part of the territory of these large and extensive States, which they now hold in possession, and over which they now claim and exercise jurisdiction, were crown lands, unlocated and unsettled when the American revolution took place—Lands which were acquired by the common blood and treasure, and which ought to have been the common stock, and for the common benefit of the Union.—Let it be remembered that the State of Maryland was so deeply sensible of the injustice that these lands should be held by particular States for their own *emolument,* even at a time when no superiority of authority or power was annexed to extensive territory, that in the midst of the late war and all the dangers which threatened us, it withheld for a long time its assent to the articles of confederation for that reason, and when it ratified those articles it entered a solemn protest against what it considered so flagrant injustice . . . [DHRC16 42]

James Madison, *The Federalist*, No. 51, February 6, 1788:

It is equally evident, that the members of each department should be as little dependent as possible on those of the others, for the *emoluments* annexed to their offices. Were the executive magistrate, or the judges, not independent of the legislature in this particular, their independence in every other would be merely nominal. [Fed. 356]

George Nicholas [?], "The State Soldier," February 6, 1788:

The present foederal constitution, though under the name of a UNION, wanted every proper, strong, and well-tried string at its formation (if I may so express myself) to produce a perfect unison—the want of authority and independence rendered it too feeble an instrument to produce the wished for effects. When on the contrary had the general government of the continent been set at a proper distance above those of the states, the objections now started might never been known perhaps. The representative instead of contending for the particular interest of his own state, would then have had something of higher dignity in view—Congress being considered the only head of the continent, to ornament which so as to make a figure among the other nations of the world, would [have] been his only object—since from that source alone would spring the only political reputation worth adding to his name. And all preferments of the highest honor and *emolument* coming from the continent at large, it would thence have been immediately his interest to consult the dignity of the whole, and not the contracted, and too often illiberal interest of a part. [DHRC8 347]

Tench Coxe, "A Freeman," No. 3, February 6, 1788:

. . . The state legislatures too being the immediate representatives and guardians of their respective constituents, and being the powerful creators of the senators, it cannot be apprehended, either that they will give away their own powers, or that they will chuse men who are unfriendly to them; nor is it at all probable that a senator would hazard the displeasure of the people, or the vengeance of so potent a body as a state legislature, by sacrificing their interests or powers. Rather may it be expected, that his interest and connexions in the state will too partially attach him to it, to the injury of national objects; or that he may neglect general concerns, from a desire to please a legislature or a people, who will be to him the source of honors, *emolument* and power. [DHRC16 50]

Luther Martin, "Genuine Information," No. 12, February 8, 1788:

. . . But, Sir, it would be well to remember, that this system is not calculated to diminish the number or the value of offices—on the contrary, if adopted, it will be productive of an enormous increase in their number—many of them will be also of great honour and *emolument*. Whether, Sir, in this variety of appointments and in the scramble for them, I might not have as good a prospect to advantage myself as many others is not for me to say—but this, Sir, I can say with truth, that so far was I from being influenced in my conduct by interest, or the consideration of office, that I would cheerfully resign the appointment I now hold—I would bind myself never to accept another either under the general government or that of my own State . . . [DHRC16 93]

James Madison, *The Federalist*, No. 55, February 13, 1788:

[1] Is the danger apprehended from the other branches of the federal government? But where are the means to be found by the President, or the Senate, or both? Their *emoluments* of office, it is to be presumed, will not, and without a previous corruption of the House of Representatives cannot, more than suffice for very different purposes; their private fortunes, as they must all be American citizens, cannot possibly be sources of danger. [Fed. 378]

[2] . . . But, fortunately, the Constitution has provided a still further safeguard. The members of the Congress are rendered ineligible to any civil offices that may be created, or of which the *emoluments* may be increased, during the term of their election. No offices therefore can be dealt out to the existing members but such as may become vacant by ordinary casualties: and to suppose that these would be sufficient to purchase the guardians of the people, selected by the people themselves, is to renounce every rule by which events ought to be calculated, and to substitute an indiscriminate and unbounded jealousy, with which all reasoning must be vain. . . . [Fed. 378]

Alexander Hamilton, *The Federalist*, No. 59, February 22, 1788:

. . . The scheme of separate confederacies, which will always multiply the chances of ambition, will be a never failing bait to all such influential characters in the State administrations as are capable of preferring their own *emolument* and advancement to the public weal. With so effectual a weapon in their hands as the exclusive power of regulating elections for the national government, a combination of a few such men, in a few of the most considerable States, where the temptation will always be the strongest, might accomplish the destruction of the Union, by seizing the opportunity of some casual dissatisfaction among the people (and which perhaps they may themselves have excited), to discontinue the choice of members for the federal House of Representatives . . . [Fed. 397]

Alexander White, "To the Citizens of Virginia," February 29, 1788:

. . . It is said the representation is unsafe because it is so exposed to corruption and undue influence, by the gift of the numerous places of honor and *emolument* at the disposal of the executive, by the arts and address of the great and designing, and by direct bribery? The members of Congress can hold no office during the time they remain members, nor can they enjoy any office which shall be created, or the *emoluments* of which shall be increased during the time for which they

were elected.—Name to me the country in which the members of the legislature or the executive council are so far removed from influence . . .
[DHRC8 439–40]

Alexander Hamilton, *The Federalist*, No. 65, March 7, 1788:

. . . The punishment which may be the consequence of conviction upon impeachment, is not to terminate the chastisement of the offender. After having been sentenced to a perpetual ostracism from the esteem and confidence, and honors and *emoluments* of his country, he will still be liable to prosecution and punishment in the ordinary course of law. Would it be proper that the persons who had disposed of his fame, and his most valuable rights as a citizen, in one trial, should, in another trial, for the same offence, be also the disposers of his life and his fortune? . . . [Fed. 428]

Benjamin Workman [?], "Philadelphienis," No. 11, March 8, 1788:

If on the broad basis of equity and justice, crimes and punishments have their proper proportion: What punishment then, on the scale of moderation, could counterpoise, or atone, for a crime so aggravated as that charged to the majority of the members of the late federal convention? I assert roundly, that another assembly of men never met in this, or any other country, possessing so fully the confidence of so many freemen: and to their shame be it said, they abused this confidence; their own private interest, private *emolument,* and hopes of dominion, overcame every consideration of duty, honor, and gratitude.
[DHRC16 363]

"An Impartial Citizen," No. 6, March 13, 1788:

. . . Senators are to be thirty years of age, must have been nine years citizens of the United States, must be inhabitants of the States for which they are elected, can enjoy no other office or place and can receive no present or *emolument* from a foreign State or Prince. Representatives are to be twenty-five years of age, must have been seven years citizens of the United States, and be inhabitants of the States for which they are chosen; and are restricted as to offices, presents, and *emoluments,* in the same manner that Senators are. By these means, their judgment will be matured, their characters known, their interest in, and attachment to their community ascertained and established; their integrity guarded, and their independence secured. Such characters will not be very ready to make open and great usurpations on the rights of the people. . . . [DHRC8 497]

Alexander Hamilton, *The Federalist*, No. 72, March 19, 1788:

Another ill effect of the exclusion would be the temptation to sordid views, to peculation, and, in some instances, to usurpation. An avaricious man, who might happen to fill the office, looking forward to a time when he must at all events yield up the *emoluments* he enjoyed, would feel a propensity, not easy to be resisted by such a man, to make the best use of the opportunity he enjoyed while it lasted, and might not scruple to have recourse to the most corrupt expedients to make the harvest as abundant as it was transitory; though the same man, probably, with a different prospect before him, might content himself with the regular perquisites of his situation, and might even be unwilling to risk the consequences of an abuse of his opportunities. . . . [Fed. 464]

Alexander Hamilton, *The Federalist*, No. 73, March 21, 1788:

[1] The third ingredient towards constituting the vigor of the executive authority, is an adequate provision for its support. It is evident that, without proper attention to this article, the separation of the executive from the legislative department would be merely nominal and nugatory. The legislature, with a discretionary power over the salary and *emoluments* of the Chief Magistrate, could render him as obsequious to their will as they might think proper to make him. . . . [Fed. 467]

[2] . . . It is there provided that "The President of the United States shall, at stated times, receive for his services a compensation which shall neither be increased nor diminished during the period for which he shall have been elected; and he shall not receive within that period any other *emolument* from the United States, or any of them." It is impossible to imagine any provision which would have been more eligible than this. The legislature, on the appointment of a President, is once for all to declare what shall be the compensation for his services during the time for which he shall have been elected. This done, they will have no power to alter it, either by increase or diminution, till a new period of service by a new election commences. They can neither weaken his fortitude by operating on his necessities, nor corrupt his integrity by appealing to his avarice. Neither the Union, nor any of its members, will be at liberty to give, nor will he be at liberty to receive, any other *emolument* than that which may have been determined by the first act. He can, of course, have no pecuniary inducement to renounce or desert the independence intended for him by the Constitution. [Fed. 468]

Alexander Hamilton, *The Federalist*, No. 76, April 1, 1788:

. . . The Constitution has provided some important guards against the danger of executive influence upon the legislative body: it declares that "No senator or representative shall, during the time for which he was elected, be appointed to any civil office under the United States, which shall have been created, or the *emoluments* whereof shall have been increased, during such time; and no person, holding any office under the United States, shall be a member of either house during his continuance in office." [Fed. 484]

Alexander Hamilton, *The Federalist*, No. 77, April 2, 1788:

. . . The power of influencing a person, in the sense in which it is here used, must imply a power of conferring a benefit upon him. How could the Senate confer a benefit upon the President by the manner of employing their right of negative upon his nominations? If it be said they might sometimes gratify him by an acquiescence in a favorite choice, when public motives might dictate a different conduct, I answer, that the instances in which the President could be personally interested in the result, would be too few to admit of his being materially affected by the compliances of the Senate. The POWER which can originate the disposition of honors and *emoluments,* is more likely to attract than to be attracted by the POWER which can merely obstruct their course. If by influencing the President be meant restraining him, this is precisely what must have been intended. And it has been shown that the restraint would be salutary, at the same time that it would not be such as to destroy a single advantage to be looked for from the uncontrolled agency of that Magistrate. . . .

[Fed. 485–86]

Melancton Smith, *An Address to the People of the State of New York,* c. April 1788:

. . . When the government is once organized, and all the offices under it filled, the inducements which our great men will have to support it, will be much stronger than they are now to urge its reception. Many of them will then hold places of great honour and *emolument,* and others will then be candidates for such places. It is much harder to relinquish honours or *emoluments,* which we have in possession, than to abandon the pursuit of them, while the attainment is held in a state of uncertainty. . . . [Ford 91–91]

George Washington, First Inaugural Address, April 30, 1789:

. . . When I was first honored with a call into the service of my country, then on the eve of an arduous struggle for its liberties, the light in which I contemplated my duty required that I should renounce every pecuniary compensation. From this resolution I have in no instance departed. And being still under the impressions which produced it, I must decline as inapplicable to myself any share in the personal *emoluments* which may be indispensably included in a permanent provision for the executive department, and must accordingly pray that the pecuniary estimates for the station in which I am placed may during my continuance in it, be limited to such actual expenditures as the public good may be thought to require. [Annals 29]

United States House of Representatives, Address to George Washington, May 5, 1789:

In forming the pecuniary provisions for the Executive Department we shall not lose sight of a wish resulting from motives which give it a peculiar claim to our regard. Your resolution, in a moment critical to the liberties of your country, to renounce all personal *emolument,* was among the many presages of your patriotic services which have been amply fulfilled; and your scrupulous adherence now to the law then imposed on yourself can not fail to demonstrate the purity, whilst it increases the luster of a character which has so many titles to admiration. [Annals 258]

Georgia Constitution, May 6, 1789:

[Article II, Section 5:] The governor shall, at stated times, receive for his service a compensation which shall neither be increased nor diminished during the period for which he shall be elected; neither shall he receive, within that period, any other *emolument* from the United States, or any of them, or from any foreign power. . . . [Thorpe 787–88]

United States Congress, Act for the Government of the Territory South of the Ohio River, May 26, 1790:

[Section 2:] And be it further enacted, That the salaries of the officers, which the President of the United States shall nominate, and with the advice and consent of the Senate appoint, by virtue of this act, shall be the same as those, by law established, of similar officers in the government northwest of the river Ohio, And the powers, duties, and *emoluments* of a superintendent of Indian affairs for the southern department shall be united with those of the governor. [Thorpe 3413]

Pennsylvania Constitution, September 2, 1790:

[Article I, Section 18:] No senator or representative shall, during the time for which he shall have been elected, be appointed to any civil office under this commonwealth, which shall have been created, or the *emoluments* of which shall have been increased, during such time; and no member of Congress, or other person holding any office (except of attorney at law and in the militia) under the United States, or this commonwealth, shall be a member of either house during his continuance in Congress, or in office. [Thorpe 3094]

EXCISE, EXCISES

United States Constitution, September 17, 1787:

[Article I, Section 8:] The Congress shall have Power To lay and collect Taxes, Duties, Imposts and *Excises,* to pay the Debts and provide for the common Defence and general Welfare of the United States; but all Duties, Imposts and *Excises* shall be uniform throughout the United States . . .

* * * * *

Charter of the Dutch West India Company, June 3, 1621:

[Article 35:] That all the goods of this Company which shall be sold by weight shall be sold by one weight, to wit, that of Amsterdam; and that all such goods shall be put on board ship, or in store without paying any *excise,* import or weigh-money: provided, that they being sold, shall not be delivered in any other way than by weight; and provided that the impost and weigh-money shall be paid as often as they are alienated, in the same manner as other goods subject to weigh-money. [Thorpe 65]

Pennsylvania Constitution, September 28, 1776:

[Frame of Government, Article 19:] The treasurer of the state, trustees of the loan office, naval officers, collectors of customs or *excise,* judge of the admiralty, attornies general, sheriffs, and prothonotaries, shall not be capable of a seat in the general assembly, executive council, or continental congress.

[Thorpe 3087]

Massachusetts Constitution, March 2, 1780:

[Chapter I:1:4:] And further, full power and authority are hereby given and granted to the said general court, from time to time, to make, ordain, and establish, all manner of wholesome and reasonable orders, laws, statutes, and ordinances, directions and instructions, either with penalties or without . . . and to impose and levy proportional and reasonable assessments, rates, and taxes, upon all the inhabitants of, and persons resident, and estates lying, within the said commonwealth; and also to impose and levy reasonable duties and *excises* upon any produce goods, wares, merchandise, and commodities, whatsoever, brought into, produced, manufactured, or being within the same; to be issued and disposed of by warrant, under the hand of the governor of this commonwealth for the time being, with the advice and consent of the council, for the public service, in the necessary defence and support of the government of the said commonwealth, and the protection and preservation of the subjects thereof, according to such acts as are or shall be in force within the same.

[Thorpe 1894–95]

Richard Henry Lee [?], "The Federal Farmer," No. 3, October 10, 1787:

A power to lay and collect taxes at discretion, is, in itself, of very great importance. By means of taxes, the government may command the whole or any part of the subject's property. Taxes may be of various kinds; but there is a strong distinction between external and internal taxes. External taxes are import duties, which are laid on imported goods; they may usually be collected in a few seaport towns, and of a few individuals, though ultimately paid by the consumer; a few officers can collect them, and they can be carried no higher than trade will bear, or smuggling permit—that in the very nature of commerce, bounds are set to them. But internal taxes, as poll and land taxes, *excises,* duties on all written instruments, &c. may fix themselves on every person and species of property in the community; they may be carried to any lengths, and in proportion as they are extended, numerous officers must be employed to assess them, and to enforce the collection of them. . . . [Ford 301]

"Cato Uticensis," October 17, 1787:

[1] In Art. 1, Sect. 8. of the proposed Foederal Constitution; it is said, "Congress shall have power to lay and collect taxes, duties, imposts and *excises.*"—Are you then, Virginians, about to abandon your country to the depredations of *excisemen,* and the pressure of *excise* laws? Did it ever enter the mind of any one of you, that you could live to see the day, that any other government, but the General Assembly of Virginia, should have power of direct taxation in this state? How few of you ever expected to see *excise* laws, the instruments of tyranny, in force in your country? But, who could imagine, that any man but a Virginian, were they found to be necessary, would ever have a voice towards enacting them? That any tribunal, but the Courts of Virginia, would be allowed to take cognizance of disputes between her citizens and their tax-gatherers and their *excisemen?* And that, if it should ever be found necessary to curse this

land with these hateful *excisemen,* any one, but a fellow citizen, should be intrusted with that office? [DHRC8 73]

[2] For my part, I cannot discover the necessity there was of allowing Congress to subject us to *excise* laws, unless, that considering the extensiveness of the single republic into which this Constitution would collect all the others, and the well known difficulty of governing large republics with harmony and ease, it was thought expedient to bit our mouths with massive curbs, to break us, bridled with *excise* laws, and managed by *excisemen,* into an uniform, sober pace, and thus, gradually, tame the troublesome mettle of the freeman. . . . [DHRC8 73]

Richard Henry Lee [?], "The Federal Farmer," No. 4, October 12, 1787:

. . . By Art. 1, Sec. 2, representatives and direct taxes shall be apportioned among the several states, &c.—same art. sect. 8, the congress shall have powers to lay and collect taxes, duties, &c. for the common defence and general welfare, but all duties, imposts and *excises,* shall be uniform throughout the United States: By the first recited clause, direct taxes shall be apportioned on the states. This seems to favour the idea suggested by some sensible men and writers that congress, as to direct taxes, will only have power to make requisitions; but the latter clause, power to lay and collect taxes, &c. seems clearly to favour the contrary opinion, and, in my mind, the true one, the congress shall have power to tax immediately individuals, without the intervention of the state legislatures . . . [Ford 310]

Noah Webster, *An Examination into the Leading Principles of the Federal Constitution*, October 17, 1787:

[1] It is insinuated that the constitution gives Congress the power of levying internal taxes at pleasure. This insinuation seems founded on the eighth section of the first article, which declares, that "Congress shall have power to lay and collect taxes, duties, imposts and *excises,* to pay the debts and provide for the common defence and general welfare of the United States." [Ford 48]

[2] That Congress should have power to collect duties, imposts and *excises,* in order to render them uniform throughout the United States will hardly be controverted. The whole objection is to the right of levying internal taxes. [Ford 48–49]

[3] The clause may at first appear ambiguous. It may be uncertain whether we should read and understand it thus—"The Congress shall have power to lay and collect taxes, duties, imposts and *excises* in order to pay the debts," &c. or whether the meaning is—"The Congress shall have power to lay and collect taxes, duties, imposts and *excises,* and shall have power to pay the debts" &c. On considering the construction of the clause, and comparing it with the preamble, the last sense seems to be improbable and absurd. . . . [Ford 50n]

***Virginia Independent Chronicle*, October 31, 1787:**

[1] The futility of this assertion, that, "the trial by jury is abolished in civil cases," is detected by him [James Wilson], "taking the advantage of his professional experience," and from this we learn, that it is not yet abolished, but that it may, if Congress think fit; but he undoubtedly knows, that juries are found inconvenient in *excise* business. He says, that the vesting of a power in Congress to keep up a standing army in time of peace is no new prerogative, because it is exercised at present on the banks of the Ohio: But this subtle reasoner did not consider, that it is now a time of war on the banks of the Ohio. [DHRC8 138]

[2] But why shall we be so wayward as to be alarmed at Congress's having the power of internal taxation and of laying on *excise* duties, do not we hear how he says: "I will venture to predict, that the great revenue of the United States must and always will be raised by impost, for being less obnoxious and more productive, the interests of the government will be best promoted by the accommodation of the people." . . . [DHRC8 139]

Hugh Williamson, Speech at Edenton, North Carolina, November 8, 1787:

. . . If *excises* are laid on wine, spirits, or other luxuries, they must be uniform throughout the States. By a careful management of imposts and *excises,* the national expences may be discharged without any other species of tax; but if a poll-tax, or land-tax shall ever become necessary, the weight must press equally on every part of the Union. . . . [DHRC16 207]

Alexander Hamilton, *The Federalist*, No. 12, November 27, 1787:

[1] . . . In so opulent a nation as that of Britain, where direct taxes from superior wealth must be much more tolerable, and, from the vigor of the government, much more practicable, than in America, far the greatest part of the national revenue is derived from taxes of the indirect kind, from imposts, and from *excises*. Duties on imported articles form a large branch of this latter description. [Fed. 144]

[2] In America, it is evident that we must a long time depend for the means of revenue chiefly on such duties. In most parts of it, *excises* must be confined within a narrow compass. The genius of the people will ill brook the inquisitive and peremptory spirit of *excise* laws . . . [Fed. 144]

[3] . . . A nation cannot long exist without revenues. Destitute of this essential support, it must resign its independence, and sink into the degraded condition of a province. This is an extremity to which no government will of choice accede. Revenue, therefore, must be had at all events. In this country, if the principal part be not drawn from commerce, it must fall with oppressive weight upon land. It has been already intimated that *excises,* in their true signification, are

too little in unison with the feelings of the people, to admit of great use being made of that mode of taxation; nor, indeed, in the States where almost the sole employment is agriculture, are the objects proper for *excise* sufficiently numerous to permit very ample collections in that way . . . [Fed. 146–47]

Virginia Independent Chronicle, November 28, 1787:

[1] Great apprehensions are entertained from the general establishment of an *excise* law. It is considered as too dangerous an instrument to be put into the hands of Congress. But these apprehensions, Sir, are absurd. They originate from trifles, light as air: They exist only in idea. *Excise* laws are no more violations of the rights of the people than any other laws, and they may be as safely executed. In Pennsylvania *excise* laws have long prevailed. It was the original mode of taxation, practised by as virtuous a legislature as ever was delegated, to raise money for the support of government. To execute it, no standing army was thought necessary. No man's house was broke open. The rights and properties of the people were not outraged. On the contrary, it was submitted to without murmurring, executed without violence; and I challenge any man to mention a single instance in which any individual was injured in that state by the operation of an *excise* law for near one hundred years. Why, then, may we not intrust Congress with the power of establishing *excise* laws and regulating the operation of them? Why may not *excise* laws be executed with the same safety and same convenience by officers appointed by Congress, as it has been in the state of Pennsylvania by officers appointed by its legislature? In the framing of the law, is it not to be presumed, that Congress will as cautiously preserve the property of the people from the depredation of *excise* officers, as the legislature of Pennsylvania has preserved the property of its subjects, from the depredations of its *excise* officers? Will not Congress constitute the aggregate body of the people? . . . [DHRC8 178–79]

[2] . . . You, then, Sir, will acquit me of every sinister design, when I solemnly declare to you with my hand upon my heart, that, in my humble opinion no danger ought to be apprehended or will issue from the establishment and operation of a general *excise* law. [DHRC8 179]

Alexander Hamilton, _The Federalist_, No. 21, December 12, 1787:

There is no method of steering clear of this inconvenience, but by authorizing the national government to raise its own revenues in its own way. Imposts, *excises,* and, in general, all duties upon articles of consumption, may be compared to a fluid, which will, in time, find its level with the means of paying them. The amount to be contributed by each citizen will in a degree be at his own option, and can be regulated by an attention to his resources. The rich may be extravagant, the poor can be frugal; and private oppression may always be avoided by a judicious selection of objects proper for such impositions. If inequalities should arise in some States from duties on particular objects, these will, in all probability, be counterbalanced by proportional inequalities in other States, from the duties on other objects. . . . [Fed. 189–91]

Dissent of the Pennsylvania Convention's Minority, December 18, 1787:

[1] The powers of Congress under the new constitution are complete and unlimited over the purse and the sword, and are perfectly independent of, and supreme over, the state governments; whose intervention in these great points is entirely destroyed. By virtue of their power of taxation, Congress may command the whole or any part of the property of the people. They may impose what imposts upon commerce; they may impose what land taxes, poll taxes, *excises,* duties on all written instruments and duties on every other article that they may judge proper; in short, every species of taxation, whether of an external or internal nature, is comprised in section the eighth of article the first . . . [DHRC2 627]

[2] As there is no one article of taxation reserved to the state governments, the Congress may monopolize every source of revenue, and thus indirectly demolish the state governments, for without funds they could not exist. The taxes, duties, and *excises* imposed by Congress may be so high as to render it impracticable to levy further sums on the same articles; but whether this should be the case or not, if the state governments should presume to impose taxes, duties, or *excises* on the same articles with Congress, the latter may abrogate and repeal the laws whereby they are imposed, upon the allegation that they interfere with the due collection of their taxes, duties or *excises,* by virtue of the following clause, part of section 8th, Article 1st . . . [DHRC2 627]

[3] The power of direct taxation applies to every individual, as Congress, under this government, is expressly vested with the authority of laying a capitation or poll tax upon every person to any amount. This is a tax that, however oppressive in its nature, and unequal in its operation, is certain as to its produce and simple in its collection; it cannot be evaded like the objects of imposts or *excise,* and will be paid, because all that a man hath will he give for his head. This tax is so congenial to the nature of despotism, that it has ever been a favorite under such governments. Some of those who were in the late general convention from this State, have labored to introduce a poll tax among us. [DHRC2 635–36]

Alexander Hamilton, *The Federalist*, No. 32, January 2, 1788:

. . . These three cases of exclusive jurisdiction in the federal government may be exemplified by the following instances . . . The first clause of the same section empowers Congress "to lay and collect taxes, duties, imposts and *excises*"; and the second clause of the tenth section of the same article declares that "no State shall, without the consent of Congress, lay any imposts or duties on imports or exports, except for the purpose of executing its inspection laws." Hence would result an exclusive power in the Union to lay duties on imports and exports, with the particular exception mentioned; but this power is abridged by another clause, which declares that no tax or duty shall be laid on articles exported from any State; in consequence of which qualification, it now only extends to the duties on imports. . . . [Fed. 241–42]

Alexander Hamilton, *The Federalist*, No. 35, January 5, 1788:

. . . The States which can go farthest towards the supply of their own wants, by their own manufactures, will not, according to their numbers or wealth, consume so great a proportion of imported articles as those States which are not in the same favorable situation. They would not, therefore, in this mode alone contribute to the public treasury in a ratio to their abilities. To make them do this it is necessary that recourse be had to *excises,* the proper objects of which are particular kinds of manufactures. New York is more deeply interested in these considerations than such of her citizens as contend for limiting the power of the Union to external taxation may be aware of. New York is an importing State, and is not likely speedily to be, to any great extent, and from a greater disproportion between her population and territory is less likely, than some other states, speedily to become in any considerable degree a manufacturing State. She would, of course, suffer in a double light from restraining the jurisdiction of the Union to commercial imposts. [Fed. 254–55]

Alexander Hamilton, *The Federalist*, No. 36, January 8, 1788:

[1] The taxes intended to be comprised under the general denomination of internal taxes may be subdivided into those of the direct and those of the indirect kind. Though the objection be made to both, yet the reasoning upon it seems to be confined to the former branch. And indeed, as to the latter, by which must be understood duties and *excises* on articles of consumption, one is at a loss to conceive what can be the nature of the difficulties apprehended. The knowledge relating to them must evidently be of a kind that will either be suggested by the nature of the article itself, or can easily be procured from any well-informed man, especially of the mercantile class. The circumstances that may distinguish its situation in one State from its situation in another must be few, simple, and easy to be comprehended. . . . [Fed. 260–61]

[2] Let it be recollected that the proportion of these taxes is not to be left to the discretion of the national legislature, but is to be determined by the numbers of each State, as described in the second section of the first article. An actual census or enumeration of the people must furnish the rule, a circumstance which effectually shuts the door to partiality or oppression. The abuse of this power of taxation seems to have been provided against with guarded circumspection. In addition to the precaution just mentioned, there is a provision that "all duties, imposts, and *excises* shall be UNIFORM throughout the United States. [Fed. 261–62]

James Madison, *The Federalist*, No. 41, January 19, 1788:

Some, who have not denied the necessity of the power of taxation, have grounded a very fierce attack against the Constitution, on the language in which it is defined. It has been urged and echoed, that the power "to lay and collect taxes, duties, imposts, and *excises*, to pay the debts, and provide for the common defence and general welfare of the United States," amounts to an unlimited commission to exercise every power which may be alleged to be necessary for the common defence or general welfare. No stronger proof could be given of the distress under which these writers labor for objections, than their stooping to such a misconstruction. [Fed. 300]

Luther Martin, "Genuine Information," No. 10, February 1, 1788:

Thus, Sir, in consequence of this appellate jurisdiction and its extension to facts as well as to law, every arbitrary act of the general government, and every oppression of all those variety of officers appointed under its authority for the collection of taxes, duties, impost, *excise*, and other purposes, must be submitted to by the individual, or must be opposed with little prospect of success and almost a certain prospect of ruin, at least in those cases where the middle and common class of citizens are interested—Since to avoid that oppression, or to obtain redress, the application must be made to one of the courts of the United States . . . [DHRC16 10]

David Ramsay, "Civis," February 4, 1788:

. . . If then we are to be an united people, and the obvious ground of union must be, that all continental concerns should be managed by Congress—let us by those principles examine the new constitution. Look over the 8th section, which enumerates the powers of Congress, and point out one that is not essential on the before recited principles of union. The first is a power to lay and collect taxes, duties, imposts, and *excises*, to pay the debts, and provide for the common defence and general welfare of the United States. [DHRC16 22]

Samuel Bryan, "Centinel," No. 14, February 5, 1788:

[1] [Quoting Luther Martin:] By the eighth section of this article, Congress is to have power to lay and collect taxes, duties, imposts, and *excises*. . . . By the power to lay *excises*, a power very odious in its nature, since it authorises officers to go into your houses, your kitchens, your cellars, and to examine into your private concerns; the Congress may impose duties on every article of use or consumption, on the food that we eat—on the liquors we drink—on the cloaths we wear—on the glass which enlighten our houses—or the hearths necessary for our warmth and comfort. . . . [DHRC16 32–33]

[2] [Quoting Luther Martin:] . . . And though there is a provision that all duties, imposts and *excises* shall be uniform, that is, to be laid to the same amount on the same articles in each state, yet this will not prevent Congress from having it in their power to cause them to fall very unequal and much heavier on some states than on others, because these duties may be laid on articles but little or not at all used in some states, and of absolute necessity for the use and consumption of others, in which case the first would pay little or no part of the revenue arising therefrom, while the whole or nearly the whole of it would be paid by the last, to wit, the states which use and consume the articles on which the imposts and *excises* are laid. [DHRC16 34]

Massachusetts Convention, Proposed Amendents to the Constitution, February 6, 1788:

Fourthly, That Congress do not lay direct taxes, but when the monies arising from the impost and *excise* are insufficient for the publick exigencies; nor then, until Congress shall have first made a requisition upon the states, to assess, levy and pay their respective proportions of such requisition, agreeably to the census fixed in the said constitution, in such way and manner as the legislature of the state shall think best . . . [DHRC16 68]

Tench Coxe, "A Freeman," No. 3, February 6, 1788:

An observation of the honorable Mr. [James] Wilson's has been adduced, among other arguments, to prove, that despotism would follow such a general government. I believe with him and with you that such would be the consequence of a single national constitution, in which all the objects of society and government were so compleatly provided for, as to place the several states in the union on the footing of counties of the empire.—But permit me to ask you, gentlemen, will such be the condition of the states? Where is the county that can independently train its own militia, appoint its civil and militia officers, establish a peculiar system of penal laws, issue criminal process in its own name, erect corporations, impose direct taxes, *excises* and duties, hold lands in its own right, commence war on any emergency, regulate descents, prescribe the qualifications of electors, alter its constitution or the principles of its government, divide itself into separate and independent parts, join itself to another state, issue writs for elections, and regulate the same, enact inspection laws, erect courts, appoint judges, commission all its officers, create new offices, sell and give away its lands, erect fortifications, and, in short where is the county in the union, or in the world, that can exercise in any instance independent legislative, executive or judicial powers? [DHRC16 49–50]

John Williams to ———, January 29, 1788, published in *Albany Federal Herald*, February 25, 1788:

. . . The direct taxation, and to be collected by officers of Congress, are powers which cannot be granted agreeable to our present constitution, nor will it be very convenient for Congress officers, and our state collectors, to be collecting both at one time, and as Congress may lay a poll tax, how will that agree with us. I need not tell you the injustices of it. If the new constitution is adopted, Congress hath all the impost and *excise;* this latter may be laid heavy on taverns and spirits, so that the emoluments from taverns, which are now converted to the use of the poor, must go to Congress; and what is yet worse, all the duties arising from any duties or *excise,* are to be appropriated to the use of Congress.
[DHRC16 200]

"The Impartial Examiner," No. 1, February 27-March 5, 1788:

[1] I believe, it is acknowledged that the establishment of *excises* has been one of the greatest grievances, under which the English nation has labored for almost a century and an half. Although this may seem an oeconomical tax, as arising out of manufactures, from which the industrious may derive advantages; and whereof the wealthy by consuming the greatest share, will of course contribute the largest proportion of the tax: yet the nature of it being such, as requires severe laws for its execution, it has justly become an object of general detestation. This has induced Judge Blackstone to declare that "the rigour and arbitrary proceedings of *excise* laws seem hardly compatible with the temper of a free nation." While, therefore, you are freemen—while you are unused to feel any other power, but such as can be exercised within the bounds of moderation and decency, it, doubtless, behoves you to consider whether it is an eligible step to subject yourselves to a new species of authority, which may warrant the most flagrant violations of the sacred rights of habitation. If this branch of revenue takes place, all the consequent rigour of *excise* laws will necessarily be introduced in order to enforce a due collection. . . . [DHRC8 421–22]

[2] You will, doubtless, consider whether the inconveniencies may not be very disagreeable, and perhaps injurious, to which this country may be subjected by *excise* laws,—by direct taxation of every kind,—by the establishment of foederal courts. You will advert to the dangerous and oppressive consequences, that may ensue from the introduction of standing armies in times of peace . . .
[DHRC8 462–63]

Melancton Smith, *An Address to the People of the State of New York,* c. April 1788:

[1] The constitution has been opposed, because it gives to the legislature an unlimited power of taxation both with respect to direct and indirect taxes, a right

to lay and collect taxes, duties, imposts and *excises* of every kind and description, and to any amount. In this there has been as general a concurrence of opinion as in the former. [Ford 102]

[2] . . . If then, the capital embarrassment in our present government arises from the want of money, and this constitution effectually authorises the raising of it, how are the taxes to be lessened by it? Certainly money can only be raised by taxes of some kind or other; it must be got either by additional impositions on trade, by *excise,* or by direct taxes, or what is more probable, by all together. In either way, it amounts to the same thing, and the position is clear, that as the necessities of the nation require more money than is now raised, the taxes must be enhanced. This you ought to know, and prepare yourselves to submit to. . . . [Ford 108]

John Dickinson, "Fabius," No. 6, 1788:

[Quoting Lord Belhaven in Parliament]: "When I consider this treaty as it hath been explained, and spoke to, before us these three weeks by past; I see the English constitution remaining firm, the same two houses of Parliament, the same taxes, the same customs, the same *excises,* the same trading companies, the same municipal laws and courts of judicature; and all ours either subject to regulations or annihilations, only we are to have the honor to pay their old debts, and to have some few persons present for witnesses, to the validity of the deed, when they are pleased to contract more." [Ford 198]

EX POST FACTO LAW

United States Constitution, September 17, 1787:

[Article I, Section 9:] No Bill of Attainder or *ex post facto Law* shall be passed.

[Article I, Section 10:] No State shall enter into any Treaty, Alliance, or Confederation; grant Letters of Marque and Reprisal; coin Money; emit Bills of Credit; make any Thing but gold and silver Coin a Tender in Payment of Debts; pass any Bill of Attainder, *ex post facto Law,* or Law impairing the Obligation of Contracts, or grant any Title of Nobility.

* * * * *

Maryland Constitution, November 11, 1776:

[Declaration of Rights, Article 15:] That retrospective laws, punishing facts committed before the existence of such laws, and by them only declared criminal, are oppressive, unjust, and incompatible with liberty; wherefore no *ex post facto law* ought to be made. [Thorpe 1688]

North Carolina Constitution, December 18, 1776:

[Declaration of Rights, Article 24:] That retrospective laws, punishing facts committed before the existence of such laws, and by them only declared criminal, are oppressive, unjust, and incompatible with liberty; wherefore no *ex post facto law* ought to be made. [Thorpe 2788]

George Mason, Objections to the Constitution, October 7, 1787:

Both the general Legislature & the State Legislatures are expressly prohibited making *ex post facto Laws;* tho' there never was or can be a Legislature but must & will make such Laws, when Necessity & the public Safety require them; which will hereafter be a Breach of all the Constitutions in the Union, and afford Precedents for other Innovations. . . . [DHRC8 45]

Richard Henry Lee [?], "The Federal Farmer," No. 4, October 12, 1787:

. . . If the federal constitution is to be construed so far in connection with the state constitution, as to leave the trial by jury in civil causes, for instance, secured; on the same principles it would have left the trial by jury in criminal causes, the benefits of the writ of habeas corpus, &c. secured; they all stand on the same footing; they are the common rights of Americans, and have been recognized by the state constitutions: But the convention found it necessary to recognize or re-establish the benefits of that writ, and the jury trial in criminal cases. As to *expost facto laws,* the convention has done the same in one case, and gone further in another. It is a part of the compact between the people of each state and their rulers, that no *expost facto laws* shall be made. But the convention, by Art. 1, Sect. 10, have put a sanction upon this part even of the state compacts. In fact, the 9th and 10th Sections in Art. 1, in the proposed constitution, are no more nor less, than a partial bill of rights; they establish certain principles as part of the compact upon which the federal legislators and officers can never infringe. It is here wisely stipulated, that the federal legislature shall never pass a bill of attainder, or *expost facto law;* that no tax shall be laid on articles exported, &c. The establishing of one right implies the necessity of establishing another and similar one. [Ford 314]

Tench Coxe, *An Examination of the Constitution for the United States of America*, No. 4, October 21, 1787:

Laws, made after the commission of the fact, have been a dreadful engine in the hands of tyrannical governors. Some of the most virtuous and shining characters in the world have been put to death, by laws formed to render them punishable, for parts of their conduct which innocence permitted, and to which patriotism impelled them. These have been called *ex post facto laws,* and are exploded by the new system. If a time of public contention shall hereafter arrive, the firm and ardent friends to liberty may know the length to which they can push their noble opposition, on the foundation of the laws. Should their country's cause impel them further, they will be acquainted with the hazard, and using those arms which Providence has put into their hands, will make a solemn appeal to "the power above." [Ford 147–48]

Oliver Ellsworth, "The Landholder," No. 6, December 10, 1787:

The publication of Col. [George] Mason's reasons for not signing the new Constitution, has extorted some truths that would otherwise in all probability have remained unknown to us all. His reasons, like Mr. [Elbridge] Gerrys, are most of them *ex post facto*—have been revised in New-Y—k by R.H.L. [Richard Henry Lee] and by him brought into their present artful and insidious form. . . .
[DHRC8 229]

James Madison, *The Federalist*, No. 44, January 25, 1788:

Bills of attainder, *ex post facto laws,* and laws impairing the obligation of contracts, are contrary to the first principles of the social compact, and to every principle of sound legislation. The two former are expressly prohibited by the declarations prefixed to some of the State constitutions, and all of them are prohibited by the spirit and scope of these fundamental charters. Our own experience has taught us, nevertheless, that additional fences against these dangers ought not to be omitted. Very properly, therefore, have the convention added this constitutional bulwark in favor of personal security and private rights; and I am much deceived if they have not, in so doing, as faithfully consulted the genuine sentiments as the undoubted interests of their constituents. . . .

[Ford 319]

Alexander White [?], "An Independent Freeholder," January 25, 1788:

That the exclusion of *ex post facto laws* should be made an objection is to me astonishing. I do an action to day which is in itself innocent and prohibited by no law, at a future day you pass a law to punish me for it. Let every man's own mind answer whether this is just, and whether the existance of such a power is not inconsistent with the principles of liberty? Colonel M——n [Mason] says every legislature will make such laws, which in other words is saying every legislature will do wrong. . . . [DHRC8 327]

"Civis Rusticus," January 30, 1788:

Ex post facto laws have ever been considered as abhorrent from liberty: necessity and public safety never can require them—"If laws do not punish an offender, let him go unpunished; let the legislature, admonished of the defect of the laws, provide against the commission of future crimes of the same sort—The escape of one delinquent can never produce so much harm to the community, as may arise from the infraction of a rule, upon which the purity of public justice, and the existence of civil liberty essentially depend"—Paeley's Principles of Moral Philosophy, vol. 2. p. 234. Octavo Ed. [DHRC8 338]

Alexander C. Hanson, *Remarks on the Proposed Plan of a Federal Government*, c. January 31, 1788:

[1] The restraints laid on the state legislatures will tend to secure domestic tranquility, more than all the bills, or declarations, of rights, which human policy could devise. It is very justly asserted, that the plan contains an avowal of many rights. It provides that no man, shall suffer by *ex post facto laws* or bills of attainder. It declares, that gold and silver only shall be a tender for specie debts; and that no law shall impair the obligation of a contract. [Ford 243]

[2] . . . What then are the powers an individual state will lose? She will no longer be able to deny congress that, which congress, at this moment, has a right to demand. She will have no power to enter into a treaty, alliance, or confederation. She shall, in time of war, grant no letters of marque and reprisal. She shall coin no money, emit no bills of credit, nor make any thing but gold and silver a tender in payment of debts. She shall pass no bill of attainder, or *ex post facto law,* or law impairing the obligation of a contract. She shall grant no title of nobility. . . . [Ford 251]

David Ramsay, "Civis," February 4, 1788:

. . . be on your guard against the misrepresentations of men who are involved in debt; such may wish to see the constitution rejected, because of the following clause, "no state shall emit bills of credit, make any thing but gold and silver coin, a tender in payment of debts, pass any *ex post facto law,* or law impairing the obligation of contracts." This will doubtless bear hard on debtors who wish to defraud their creditors, but it will be real service to the honest part of the community. Examine well the characters and circumstances of men who are averse to the new constitution. Perhaps you will find that the above recited clause is the real ground of the opposition of some of them, though they may artfully cover it with a splendid profession of zeal for state privileges and general liberty. [DHRC16 26]

James Iredell, "Marcus," No. 1, February 20, 1788:

As to the common law, it is difficult to know what is meant by that part of the objection. So far as the people are now entitled to the benefit of the common law, they certainly will have a right to enjoy it under the new constitution, till altered by the general Legislature, which even in this point has some cardinal limits assigned to it. What are most acts of Assembly but a deviation in some degree from the principles of the common law? The people are expressly secured (contrary to Mr. Mason's wishes) against *ex post facto laws,* so that the tenure of any property at any time held under the principles of the common law, cannot be altered by any act of the future general legislature. . . . [DHRC16 164]

"The New Litany," February 21, 1788:

Spare us, good Lord.

From all evil and mischievous members of the state legislature, from the sin of ingratitude, from the power of *ex post facto laws,* and from everlasting damnation. [DHRC16 178]

Samuel Bryan, "Centinel," No. 16, February 26, 1788:

[1] Fellow-Citizens, The new constitution instead of being the panecea or cure of every grievance so delusively represented by its advocates will be found upon

examination like Pandora's box, replete with every evil. The most specious clauses of this system of ambition and iniquity contain latent mischief, and premedated villainy. By section 9th of the 1st article, "No *ex post facto law* shall be passed." This sounds very well upon a superficial consideration, and I dare say has been read by most people with approbation. Government undoubtedly ought to avoid retrospective laws as far as may be, as they are generally injurious and fraudulent: Yet there are occasions when such laws are not only just but highly requisite. An *ex post facto law* is a law made after the fact, so that the Congress under the new constitution are precluded from all controul over transactions prior to its establishment. This prohibition would skreen the numerous public defaulters, as no measure could be constitutionally taken to compel them to render an account and restore the public money; the unaccounted millions lying in their hands would become their private property. . . .

[DHRC16 218]

[2] . . . If equal provision had been made for the debts due to the United States, as against the United States, the ex post facto clause would not have so pernicious an operation. [DHRC16 219]

George Nicholas [?], "The State Soldier," No. 3, March 12, 1788:

To a man thus zealous, the want of authority to pass *ex post facto laws* may be a great objection to the new constitution indeed, as they might be rendered highly useful to, and a great improvement on, the art of speculation. But in all other cases they have ever been considered a great curse, since they can only be productive of a halter to the innocent and ignorant. [DHRC8 488]

"An Impartial Citizen," No. 6, March 13, 1788:

[1] . . . Even Mr. Mason, a man of great reputed abilities, has seriously objected, that the general and state Legislatures are restrained from making *ex post facto laws:* Though there never was nor will be a Legislature, but what must and will make such laws, when necessity and the public safety will require it: That the making such laws will hereafter be a breach of all the Constitutions in the Union, and afford precedents for further innovations. . . . [DHRC8 492]

[2] . . . *Ex post facto laws* are universally allowed to be the most dangerous ingredients of any government. Neither lives nor property can be secure, where such laws are expressly or impliedly admitted or countenanced by the Constitution. Such a law is in effect an inversion of the right order of things, by giving future energy to antecedent facts. Does not a law that declares a legal pre-existent fact to be illegal, amount to a deprivation of men's rights? Does it not wantonly subject men to evils which the most consummate wisdom, joined with the most intuitive foresight, can neither foresee or advert. If such a law be admitted by the Constitution, can any immunity or declaration of rights counterveil its pernicious operation? Is there a planter in Virginia that would not detest a law, that

would punish a man for having done what was lawful at the time of doing it? The learned Judge Blackstone, in the first volume of his excellent Commentaries, page 43, speaking of the impropriety of enforcing laws, without a previous promulgation, says, that "there is still a more unreasonable method than this, which is called, making of *laws ex post facto;* when, after an action (indifferent in itself) is committed, the Legislature then, for the first time, declares it to have been a crime, and inflicts a punishment on the person who has committed it. Here it is impossible that the party could foresee that an action, innocent when it was done, should be afterwards converted to guilt by a subsequent law; he had therefore no cause to abstain from it, and all punishment for not abstaining, must of consequence be cruel and unjust. All laws should therefore be made to commence in future." . . . [DHRC8 493]

[3] . . . What necessity can warrant or justify so flagrant and outrageous an attack on the rights of mankind? I aver and can maintain, that if, in any age or country, the public safety depended on an *ex post facto law,* it was owing to some capital defect in the form of government, and that the passing such a law did not in reality meliorate the situation of public affairs. Weak and bad governments require violent means to support them; but a well regulated system, a government whereof the direct end and basis are political liberty, need not recur to such flagitious and detestable means as this kind of law to support it. In this assertion I am warranted by the opinion of the great Montesquieu. It being therefore a maxim of natural and universal jurisprudence, that no law should be made to punish a man for the commission of an act, which was not unlawful at the time of doing it, the Convention most wisely inserted a clause in the Constitution, that no such law should be passed. When, therefore, a man of Mr. Mason's supposed political knowledge, objects to so admirable a clause, a clause whereon depends, in a great measure, the existence of our liberties, we need not be in the least surprised at the "flimsy sophistry," indecent virulence, and fallacious accusations, against the new Constitution . . . [DHRC8 493–94]

George Nicholas [?], "The State Soldier," No. 4, March 19, 1788:

[1] Under this government neither the Congress nor state legislature could, by direct laws, deprive us of any property we might hold under the general law of the land, or punish us for any offence committed previous to the passage of such laws, since they are prohibited from passing *ex post facto laws*. . . .

[DHRC8 510–11]

[2] That there will go no more power out of the peoples' hands by the adoption of this constitution than what is already given up, is obvious, because the state legislature and Congress together have in their hands, at this time, every authority which is proposed to be given to the new head, and that too without any restraints on those of the state. The right of passing *ex post facto laws,* the power of administering partial taxation, and a right to procrastinate justice, or interfere, in their legislative capacity, in private affairs, make up the only compound

necessary to give a dismal hue to the finest features of any government. Yet such are the powers already given into the hands of government as to justify and produce all those acts. [DHRC8 511]

James Iredell, "Marcus," No. 5, March 19, 1788:

My ideas of liberty are so different from those of Mr. Mason, that in my opinion this very prohibition is one of the most valuable parts of the new Constitution. *Ex post facto laws* may some times be convenient, but that they are ever absolutely necessary I shall take the liberty to doubt, till that necessity can be made apparent. Sure I am, they have been the instrument of some of the grossest acts of tyranny that were ever exercised, and have this never failing consequence, to put the minority in the power of a passionate and unprincipled majority, as to the most sacred things; and the plea of necessity is never wanting where it can be of any avail. This very clause, I think, is worth ten thousand Declarations of Rights, if this the most essential right of all was omitted in them. A man may feel some pride in his security, when he knows that what he does innocently and safely to-day, according to the laws of his country, cannot be tortured into guilt and danger to-morrow. But if it should happen, that a great and over-ruling necessity, acknowledged and felt by all, should make a deviation from this prohibition excusable, shall we not be more safe in leaving the excuse for an extraordinary exercise of power to rest upon the apparent equity of it alone, than to leave the door open to a tyranny it would be intolerable to bear? [DHRC16 428]

Alexander Hamilton, *The Federalist*, No. 78, May 28, 1788:

The complete independence of the courts of justice is peculiarly essential in a limited Constitution. By a limited Constitution, I understand one which contains certain specified exceptions to the legislative authority; such, for instance, as that it shall pass no bills of attainder, no *ex post facto laws,* and the like. Limitations of this kind can be preserved in practice no other way than through the medium of courts of justice, whose duty it must be to declare all acts contrary to the manifest tenor of the Constitution void. . . . [Fed. 491]

Alexander Hamilton, *The Federalist*, No. 84, May 28, 1788:

It may well be a question, whether these are not, upon the whole, of equal importance with any which are to be found in the constitution of this State. The establishment of the writ of habeas corpus, the prohibition of *ex post facto laws,* and of TITLES OF NOBILITY, to which we have no corresponding provision in our Constitution, are perhaps greater securities to liberty and republicanism than any it contains. The creation of crimes after the commission of the fact, or, in other words, the subjecting of men to punishment for things which, when they were done, were breaches of no law, and the practice of arbitrary imprisonments, have been, in all ages, the favorite and most formidable instruments of tyranny. [Fed. 533]

South Carolina Constitution, June 3, 1790:

[Article IX, Section 2:] No freemen of this State shall be taken, or imprisoned, or disseized of his freehold, liberties, or privileges, or outlawed or exiled, or in any manner destroyed, or deprived of his life, liberty or property, but by the judgment of his peers, or by the law of the land; nor shall any bill of attainder, *ex post facto law,* or law impairing the obligation of contracts, ever be passed by the legislature of this State. [Thorpe 3264]

Pennsylvania Constitution, September 2, 1790:

[Article IX, Section 17:] That no *ex post facto law,* nor any law impairing contracts, shall be made. [Thorpe 3101]

EXTRAORDINARY OCCASIONS

United States Constitution, September 17, 1787:

[Article II, Section 3:] He [the President] shall from time to time give to the Congress Information of the State of the Union, and recommend to their Consideration such Measures as he shall judge necessary and expedient; he may, on *extraordinary Occasions,* convene both Houses, or either of them, and in Case of Disagreement between them, with Respect to the Time of Adjournment, he may adjourn them to such Time as he shall think proper; he shall receive Ambassadors and other public Ministers; he shall take Care that the Laws be faithfully executed, and shall Commission all the Officers of the United States.

* * * * *

Virginia Company, Ordinances for the Colony, July 24, 1621:

[Article 4:] The other Council, more generally to be called by the Governor, once yearly, and no oftener, but for very *extraordinary and important occasions,* shall consist, for the present, of the said Council of State, and of two Burgesses out of every Town, Hundred, or other particular Plantation, to be respectively chosen by the Inhabitants: Which Council shall be called The General Assembly, wherein (as also in the said Council of State) all Matters shall be decided, determined, and ordered, by the greater Part of the Voices then present; reserving to the Governor always a Negative Voice. And this General Assembly shall have free Power to treat, consult, and conclude, as well of all *emergent Occasions* concerning the Publick Weal of the said Colony and every Part thereof, as also to make, ordain, and enact such general Laws and Orders, for the Behoof of the said Colony, and the good Government thereof, as shall, from time to time, appear necessary or requisite . . . [Thorpe 3811]

The New England Confederation, May 19, 1643:

[Article 10:] That in *extraordinary occasions,* when meetings are summoned by three magistrates of any Jurisdiction, or two as in the fifth article, if any of the

Commissioners come not, due warning being given or sent, it is agreed that four of the Commissioners shall have power to direct a war which cannot be delayed, and to send for due proportions of men out of each Jurisdiction, as well as six might do if all met; but not less than six shall determine the justice of the war, or allow the demands or bills of charges, or cause any levies to be made for the same. [Thorpe 81]

Government of New Haven Colony, October 27, 1643:

This Generall Court shall always sitt att Newhaven, (unless upon *weighty occasions* the Generall Court see cause for a time to sitt elsewhere,) and shall assemble twice every yeare, namely, the first Wednesday in Aprill, & the last Wednesday in October, in the later of which courts the Governor, the Deputy Governor and all the magistrates for the whole jurisdiction with a Treasurer, a Secretary and Marshall, shall yearly be chosen by all the free burgesses before mentioned, besides which two fixed courts, the Governor, or in his absence, the Deputy Governor, shall have power to summon a Generall Court att any other time, as the urgent and *extraordinary occasions* of the jurisdiction may require, and att all Generall Courts, whether ordinary or extraordinary, the Governor and Deputy Governor, and all the rest of the magistrates for the jurisdiction, with the Deputyes for the severall plantations, shall sitt together, till the affayres of the jurisdiction be dispatched or may safely be respited . . . [Thorpe 528]

James II, Commission to Sir Edmund Andros for the Dominion of New England, April 7, 1688:

And Wee do hereby give and graunt unto you full power where you shall see cause and shall judge any offender or offenders in capitall and criminall matters, or for any fines or forfeitures due unto us, fit objects of our mercy, to pardon such offenders and to remit such fines & forfeitures, treason and wilfull murder only excepted, in which case you shall likewise have power upon *extraordinary occasions* to grant reprieves to the offenders therein untill and to the intent our pleasure may be further known. [Thorpe 1866]

New York Constitution, April 20, 1777:

[Article 18:] That the governor shall continue in office three years, and shall, by virtue of his office, be general and commander-in-chief of all the militia, and admiral of the navy of this State; that he shall have power to convene the assembly and senate on *extraordinary occasions;* to prorogue them from time to time, provided such prorogations shall not exceed sixty days in the space of any one year . . . [Thorpe 2632–33]

Noah Webster, *An Examination into the Leading Principles of the Federal Constitution*, October 17, 1787:

On *extraordinary occasions,* when the vacancies of the [Roman] senate were numerous, the consuls used to nominate some of the most respectable of the equestrian order to be chosen by the people. [Ford 38n]

James Madison, *The Federalist*, No. 49, February 2, 1788:

There is certainly great force in this reasoning, and it must be allowed to prove that a constitutional road to the decision of the people ought to be marked out and kept open, for certain great and *extraordinary occasions*. But there appear to be insuperable objections against the proposed recurrence to the people, as a provision in all cases for keeping the several departments of power within their constitutional limits. [Fed. 348]

James Madison, *The Federalist*, No. 51, February 6, 1788:

. . . An absolute negative on the legislature appears, at first view, to be the natural defence with which the executive magistrate should be armed. But perhaps it would be neither altogether safe nor alone sufficient. On ordinary *occasions* it might not be exerted with the requisite firmness, and on *extraordinary occasions* it might be perfidiously abused. May not this defect of an absolute negative be supplied by some qualified connection between this weaker department and the weaker branch of the stronger department, by which the latter may be led to support the constitutional rights of the former, without being too much detached from the rights of its own department? [Fed. 357]

Alexander Hamilton, *The Federalist*, No. 69, March 14, 1788:

The President is to be the "commander-in-chief of the army and navy of the United States, and of the militia of the several States, when called into the actual service of the United States. He is to have power to grant reprieves and pardons for offences against the United States, except in cases of impeachment; to recommend to the consideration of Congress such measures as he shall judge necessary and expedient; to convene, on *extraordinary occasions,* both houses of the legislature, or either of them, and, in case of disagreement between them with respect to the time of adjournment, to adjourn them to such time as he shall think proper; to take care that the laws be faithfully executed; and to commission all officers of the United States." In most of these particulars, the power of the President will resemble equally that of the king of Great Britain and of the governor of New York. [Fed. 445–46]

Georgia Constitution, May 6, 1789:

[Article II, Section 8:] He [the Governor] shall issue writs of election to fill up all vacancies that happen in the senate or house of representatives, and shall have power to convene the general assembly on *extraordinary occasions,* and shall give them, from time to time, information of the state of the republic, and recommend to their consideration such measures as he may deem necessary and expedient. [Thorpe 788]

South Carolina Constitution, June 3, 1790:

[Article II, Section 13:] He [the Governor] may, on *extraordinary occasions,* convene the general assembly; and in case of disagreement between the two houses with respect to the time of adjournment adjourn them to such time as he shall think proper, not beyond the fourth Monday in the month of November then ensuing. [Thorpe 3262–63]

Pennsylvania Constitution, September 2, 1790:

[Article II, Section 12:] He [the Governor] may, on *extraordinary occasions,* convene the general assembly; and in case of disagreement between the two houses with respect to the time of adjournment, adjourn them to such time as he shall think proper, not exceeding four months. [Thorpe 3096]

FAITH AND CREDIT

United States Constitution, September 17, 1787:

[Article IV, Section 1:] Full *Faith and Credit* shall be given in each State to the Public Acts, Records, and judicial Proceedings of every other State. And the Congress may by general Laws prescribe the Manner in which such Acts, Records and Proceedings shall be proved, and the Effect thereof.

* * * * *

United States Articles of Confederation, November 15, 1777:

[Article IV:] Full *faith and credit* shall be given in each of these states to the records, acts and judicial proceedings of the courts and magistrates of every other state.

Noah Webster, *An Examination into the Leading Principles of the Federal Constitution*, October 17, 1787:

But it will be conceded that the supreme head of the states must have power, competent to the purposes of our union, or it will be, as it now is, a useless body, a mere expense, without any advantage. To pay our public debt, to support foreign ministers and our own civil government, money must be raised; and if the duties and imposts are not adequate to these purposes, where shall the money be obtained? It will be answered, let Congress apportion the sum to be raised, and leave the legislatures to collect the money. Well this is all that is intended by the clause under consideration; with the addition of a federal power that shall be sufficient to oblige a delinquent state to comply with the requisition. Such power must exist somewhere, or the debts of the United States can never be paid. For want of such power, our *credit* is lost and our national *faith* is a bye-word. [Ford 49]

"A True Friend," November 14, 1787:

At the time that Great Britain withdrew her assistance and her *credit,* and demanded reimbursements, some states drove away the lenders and destroyed the general confidence, by opposing the uniform tax, which congress wanted to establish, to pay the arrears of the money borrowed during the war, and for the extinction of capitals since that time, the European nations have seen nothing in us but divided states, legislative powers jealous, contradictory and *faithless*. Even the owners of large capitals among us, have sent their pecuniary fortunes to foreign countries; the scarcity of specie is become extraordinary by these causes united together; the distrust is become general, and from thence all our evils have originated. The interest on money has risen to an enormous rate; all transactions upon trust have been ruinous for the person who asked for *credit;* what would have been looked upon as usury and punishable, is become legal and authorised by the circumstances. Our public funds have fallen into contempt . . . [DHRC8 162]

Alexander C. Hanson, *Remarks on the Proposed Plan of a Federal Government*, c. January 31, 1788:

I have here perhaps touched a string, which secretly draws together many of the foes to the plan. Too long have we sustained evils, resulting from injudicious emissions of paper, and from the operation of tender laws. To bills of *credit* as they are now falsely called, may we impute the entire loss of confidence between men. Hence it is, that specie has, in a great degree, ceased its proper office, and been confined to speculations, baneful to the public, and enriching a few enterprising sharp-sighted men, at the expence not only of the ignorant, slothful, and needy, but of their country's best benefactors. Hence chiefly are the bankruptcies throughout America, and the disreputable ruinous state of our commerce. Hence is it principally, that America hath lost its *credit* abroad, and American *faith* become a proverb. The convention plainly saw, that nothing short of a renunciation of the right to emit bills of *credit* could produce that grand consummation of policy, the RESTORATION OF PUBLIC AND PRIVATE *FAITH*. [Ford 243]

"Brutus," No. 13, February 21, 1788:

The states are now subject to no such actions. All contracts entered into by individuals with states, were made upon the *faith and credit* of the states, and the individuals never had in contemplation any compulsory mode of obliging the government to fulfil its engagements. [DHRC16 173]

"James Bowdoin," February 27, 1788:

I have lately received a letter from Mr. J—— A—— [John Adams], our A—— d-r [Ambassador] at London, he is pleased with my compliment on his volume, it was, I told him of much service to us. He has endeavoured through Bobby's [Robert Morris's] *credit,* to contract for the necessaries we wrote for; but he found it would not do: He then pledged the *faith* of the United States to fulfil the contracts he has made. He has also entered into other treaties for the other articles, which I shall be more particular about, by a safer opportunity. [DHRC16 239]

"A.B.C.," March 5, 1788:

The friends of *public credit and national faith* are all federal. [DHRC16 321]

Benjamin Workman [?], "Philadelphiensis," No. 11, March 8, 1788:

But what is the result of their unshaken loyalty to the cause of liberty, and the honor of their country? What recompence will the honest and industrious Pennsylvanians receive for their patriotism, if the new government be established? Such a return as perhaps history does not afford a single instance similar to. So base a violation of public justice and plighted *faith,* is certainly a novelty in politics, and begins a new epoch in history. Pennsylvania, instead of receiving *credit* for the immense sums she has paid into the general treasury, will be placed on a footing with the most delinquent state in the union; and which is highly probable she and all the other states will be taxed hereafter in an exact ratio of the sums they have hitherto raised. Consequently our former acts of generosity, in support of public *faith,* is to terminate in a two-fold loss to our citizens. . . . [DHRC16 363–64]

Oliver Ellsworth, "The Landholder," No. 12, March 17, 1788:

. . . At the commencement of peace, America was placed in a singular situation. Fear of a common danger could no longer bind us together—patriotism had done its best and was wearied with exertions rewarded only by ingratitude—our federal system was inadequate for national government and justice, and from inexperience the great body of the people were ignorant what consequences should flow from the want of them. Experiments in public *credit,* though ruinous to thousands, and a disregard to the promises of government had been pardoned in the moment of extreme necessity, and many honest men did not realize that a repetition of them in an hour less critical would shake the existence of society. Men full of evil and of desperate fortune were ready to propose every method of public fraud that can be effected by a violation of public *faith* and depreciating promises. This poison of the community, was their only preservative from deserved poverty, and from prisons appointed to be the reward of indolence and knavery. . . . [DHRC16 405–06]

Melancton Smith, *An Address to the People of the State of New York*, c. April 1788:

On this head, all the powers of rhetoric, and arts of description, are employed to paint the condition of this country, in the most hideous and frightful colors. We are told, that agriculture is without encouragement; trade is languishing; private *faith and credit* are disregarded, and public *credit* is prostrate; that the laws and magistrates are contemned and set at naught; that a spirit of licentiousness is rampant, and ready to break over every bound set to it by the government; that private embarrassments and distresses invade the house of every man of middling property, and insecurity threatens every man in affluent circumstances: in short, that we are in a state of the most grievous calamity at home, and that we are contemptible abroad, the scorn of foreign nations, and the ridicule of the world. From this high-wrought picture, one would suppose that we were in a condition the most deplorable of any people upon earth. . . . [Ford 94]

FINE, FINES

United States Constitution, Bill of Rights, December 15, 1791:

[Article VIII:] Excessive bail shall not be required, nor *excessive fines* imposed, nor cruel and unusual punishments inflicted.

* * * * *

Magna Carta, June 15, 1215:

[Article 3:] If moreover the heir of any one of wuch shall be under age and shall be in wardship, when he comes of age he shall have his inheritance without relief and without a *fine*. [SDECH 43]

[Article 20:] A free man shall not be *fined* for a small offence, except in proportion to the measure of the offence; and for a great offence he shall be *fined* in proportion to the magnitude of the offence, saving his freehold; and a merchant in the same way, saving his merchadise; and the villain shall be *fined* in the same way, saving his wainage, if he shall be at our mercy; and none of the above *fines* shall be imposed except by oaths of honest men of the neighborhood. [SDECH 45]

[Article 21:] Earls and barons shall only be *fined* by their peers, and only in proportion to their offence. [SDECH 45]

[Article 22:] A clergyman shall be *fined,* like those before mentioned, only in proportion to his lay holding, and not according to the extent of his ecclesiastial office. [SDECH 45]

[Article 55:] All *fines* which have been imposed unjustly and against the law of the land, and all penalties imposed unjustly and against the law of the land are altogether excused, or will be on the judgment of the twenty-five barons of whom mention is made below in connection with the security of the peace, or on the judgment of the majority of them . . . [SDECH 49]

Charter of the Dutch West India Company, June 3, 1621:

[Article 1:] . . . And whoever shall presume without the consent of this Company, to sail or to traffic in any of the Places within the aforesaid Limits granted to this Company, he shall forfeit the ships and the goods which shall be found for sale upon the aforesaid coasts and lands; the which being actually seized by the aforesaid Company, shall be by them kept for their own Benefit and Behoof. And in case such ships or goods shall be sold either in other countries or havens they may touch at, the owners and partners must be *fined* for the value of those ships and goods: Except only, that they who before the date of this charter, shall have sailed or been sent out of these or any other countries, to any of the aforesaid coasts, shall be able to continue their trade for the sale of their goods, and come back again, or otherwise, until the expiration of this charter, if they have had any before, and not longer . . . [Thorpe 60]

Charles I, Patent to Sir Robert Heath, October 30, 1629:

. . . Furthermore know yee that we for ourselves our heires & successors doe give power to the said Sr. Robert (of whose faith prudence industry & provident circumspection we have great confidence) & to his heires & assignes for the good & happy Government of the said Province to forme make & enact & publish under the seale of the said Sr. Robert his heires & assignes what lawes soever may concerne the publicke state of the said province or the private profitt of all according to the wholesome directions of & with the counsell assent & approbation of the Freeholders of the same Province or the Major part of them who when & as often as need shall require shall by the aforesaid Sr. Robert Heath his Heires & Assignes & in that forme which to him or them shall seem best, be called together to make lawes & those to be for all men within the said province & the bounds of it for the time being or under his or their Government or power either sayling towards Carolana or returning from thence either outward to England or outward to any other dominion of ours whatsoever constituted by imposition of *fines* imprisonment or any other constraint whatsoever . . .

[Thorpe 71]

Charles I, Charter of Maryland, June 20, 1632:

[Article 7:] [We grant the Proprietors of the colony] . . . free, full, and absolute Power, by the Tenor of these Presents, to Ordain, Make, and Enact Laws, of what Kind soever, according to their sound Discretions, whether relating to the Public State of the said Province, or the private Utility of Individuals, of and with the Advice, Assent, and Approbation of the Free-Men of the same Province, or the greater Part of them, or of their Delegates or Deputies, whom We will shall be called together for the framing of Laws, when, and as often as Need shall require, by the aforesaid now Baron of Baltimore, and his Heirs, and in the Form which shall seem best to him or them and the same to publish under the Seal of the aforesaid now Baron of Baltimore, and his Heirs, and duly to execute the same upon all Persons, for the time being, within the aforesaid Province, and the Limits thereof, or under his or their Government and Power, in Sailing towards Maryland, or thence Returning, Outward-bound, either to England, or elsewhere, whether to any other Part of Our, or of and foreign Dominions, wheresoever established, by the Imposition of *Fines*, Imprisonment, and other Punishment whatsoever; even if it be necessary, and the Quality of the Offence require it, by Privation of Member, or Life, by him the aforesaid now Baron of Baltimore, and his Heirs, or by his or their Deputy, Lieutenant, Judges, Justices, Magistrates, Officers, and Ministers, to be constituted and appointed according to the Tenor and true Intent of these Presents . . .

[Thorpe 1679–80]

Fundamental Orders of Connecticut, 1638–39:

It is ordered, sentenced, and decreed, that the deputies thus chosen, shall have power and liberty to appoint a time and a place of meeting together, before any general court, to advise and consult of all such things as may concern the good of the public; as also to examine their own elections, whether according to the order; and if they or the greatest part of them find any election to lie illegal, they may seclude such for the present from their meeting, and return the same and their reasons to the court; and if it prove true, the court may *fine* the party or parties so intruding upon the town, if they see cause, and give out a warrant to go to a new election in a legal way, either in part or in whole; also the said deputies shall have power to *fine* any that shall be disorderly at their meeting, or for not coming in due time or place, according to appointment; and they may return said *fine* into the court, if it be refused to be paid, and the treasurer to take notice of it, and to estreat or levy the same as he doth other *fines*.

[Thorpe 521–22]

Government of New Haven Colony, October 27, 1643:

[1] All such free burgesses shall have power in each towne or plantation within this jurisdiction to chuse fitt and able men, from amongst themselves, being church members as before, to be the ordinary judges, to heare and determine all inferior causes, whether civill or criminall, provided that no civill cause to be tryed in any of these plantation Courts in value exceed 20L., and thatt the punishment in such criminals, according to the minde of God, revealed in his word, touching such offences, doe nott exceed stocking and whipping, or if the *fine* be pecuniary, thatt itt exceed nott five pounds. . . . [Thorpe 527]

[2] . . . in which meetings of magistrates, less then fower shall nott be accounted a Court, nor shall they carry on any busines as a Court, butt itt is expected and required, thatt all the magistrates in this jurisdiction doe constantly attend the publique service att the times before mentioned, & if any of them be absent att

one of the clock in the afternoone on Munday aforesaid, when the court shall sitt, or if any of them depart the towne without leave, while the court sitts, he or they shall pay for any such default, twenty shillings *fine,* unless some providence of God occasion the same, which the Court of Magistrates shall judge off from time to time . . . [Thorpe 527]

[3] . . . jurisdiction be dispatched or may safely be respited, and if any of the said magistrates or Deputyes shall either be absent att the first sitting of the said Generall Court, (unless some providence of God hinder, which the said Court shall judge of,) or depart, or absent themselves disorderly before the Court be finished he or they shall each of them pay twenty shillings *fine,* with due considerations of further aggravations if there shall be cause . . . [Thorpe 528]

[4] These generalls being thus layd and settled, though with purpose thatt the scircumstantialls, such as the vallue of the causes to be tryed in the Plantation Courts, the ordinary and fixed times of meetings, both for the Generall Courts, and courts of magistrates, how oft and when they shall sitt, with the *fines* for absence or default, be hereafter considered off, continued or altered, as may best and most advance the course of justice, and best sute the occasions of the plantations, the Court proceed to present perticular busines of the jurisdiction. [Thorpe 529]

Charles II, Charter of Connecticut, April 23, 1662:

[The General Court shall have authority] . . . from Time to Time to Make, Ordain, and Establish all manner of wholesome, and reasonable Laws, Statutes, Ordinances, Directions, and Instructions, not Contrary to the Laws of this Realm of England, as well for settling the Forms, and Ceremonies of Goverument, and Magistracy, fit and necessary for the said Plantation, and the Inhabitants there, as for Naming, and Stiling all Sorts of Officers, both Superior and Inferior, which they shall find Needful for the Government, and Plantation of the said Colony, and the distingishing and setting forth of the several Duties, Powers, and Limits of every such Office and Place, and the Forms of such Oaths not being contrary to the Laws and Statutes of this Our Realm of England, to be administered for the Execution of the said several Offices and Places as also for the disposing and ordering of the Election of such of the said Officers as are to be annually chosen, and of such others as shall succeed in case of Death or Removal, and administring the said Oath to the newly-elected Officers, and granting necessary Commissions, and for Imposition of lawful *Fines,* Mulcts, Imprisonment or other Punishment upon Offenders and Delinquents according to the Course of other Corporations within this our Kingdom of England, and the same Laws, *Fines,* Mulcts and Executions, to alter, change, revoke, annul, release, or pardon under their Common Seal, as by the said General Assembly, or the major Part of them shall be thought fit . . . [Thorpe 533–34]

New Jersey Proprietors, Concession and Agreement, February 10, 1664:

According to the constitution of the General Assembly, to appoint courts and officers in cases criminal; and to impower them to inflict penalties upon offenders against any of the laws in force in the said Province, as the said laws shall ordain; whether by *fine,* imprisonment, banishment, corporal punishment, or to the taking away of member or life itself if there be cause for it. [Thorpe 2540]

Carolina Proprietors, Concessions and Agreements, 1665:

Item according to the constitutions of the Genll Assembly to appoint Courts and officers in Cases Cryminall and to impower them to inflict penaltyes upon offenders against any of ye said Lawes in force in ye said Countyes as ye said Lawes shall ordaine wheither by *fine* Imprisonment Banishmt corporall punishmt or to ye taking away of member of or Life itselfe if there be cause for it.
[Thorpe 2760]

Fundamental Constitutions of Carolina, March 1, 1669:

Forty-seven. The proprietors' courts have a power to mitigate all *fines* and suspend all execution in criminal causes, either before or after sentence, in any of the other inferior courts respectively. [Thorpe 2778]

Fundamental Constitutions of West New Jersey, 1676:

[Chapter 20:] That in all matters and causes, civil and criminal, proof is to be made by the solemn and plain averment, of at least two honest and reputable persons; and in case that any person or persons shall bear false witness, and bring in his or their evidence, contrary to the truth of the matter as shall be made plainly to appear, that then every such person or persons, shall in civil causes, suffer the penalty which would be due to the person or persons he or they bear witness against. And in case any witness or witnesses, on the behalf of any person or persons, indicted in a criminal cause, shall be found to have borne false witness for fear, gain, malice or favour and thereby hinder the due execution of the law, and deprive the suffering person or persons of their due satisfaction, that then and in all other cases of false evidence, such person or persons, shall be first severely *fined,* and next that he or they shall forever be disabled from being admitted in evidence, or into any public office, employment, or service within this province. [Thorpe 2550–51]

[Chapter 21:] That all and every person and persons whatsoever, who shall prosecute or prefer any indictment or information against others for any personal injuries, or matter criminal, or shall prosecute for any other criminal cause, (treason, murther, and felony, only excepted) shall and and may be master of his own process, and have full power to forgive and remit the person or persons offending against him or herself only, as well before as after judgment, and condemnation, and pardon and remit the sentence, *fine* and punishment of the person or persons offending, be it personal or other whatsoever. [Thorpe 2551]

Pennsylvania Frame of Government, Laws Agreed Upon in England, May 5, 1682:

[Article 18:] That all *fines* shall be moderate, and saving men's contenements, merchandize, or wainage. [Thorpe 3061]

James II, Commission to Sir Edmund Andros for the Dominion of New England, April 7, 1688:

And Wee do hereby give and graunt unto you full power where you shall see cause and shall judge any offender or offenders in capitall and criminall matters, or for any *fines* or forfeitures due unto us, fit objects of our mercy, to pardon such offenders and to remit such *fines* & forfeitures, treason and wilfull murder only excepted, in which case you shall likewise have power upon extraordinary occasions to grant reprieves to the offenders therein untill and to the intent our pleasure may be further known. [Thorpe 1866]

English Bill of Rights, October 23, 1689:

[1] And *excessive fines* have been imposed. [SDECH 413]

[2] And several grants and promises made of *fines* and forfeitures before any conviction or judgment against the persons upon whom the same were to be levied. [SDECH 463]

[3] That excessive bail ought not to be required nor *excessive fines* imposed nor cruel and unusual punishment inflicted. [SDECH 465]

[4] That all grants and promises of *fines* and forfeitures of particular persons before conviction are illegal and void. [SDECH 465]

William and Mary, Charter of Massachusetts Bay, October 7, 1691:

[We authorize the General Court] . . . to impose *Fines* mulcts Imprisonments and other Punishments And to impose and leavy proportionable and reasonable Assessments Rates and Taxes upon the Estates and Persons of all and every the Proprietors and Inhabitants of our said Province or Territory to be Issued and disposed of by Warrant under the hand of the Governor of our said Province for the time being with the advice and Consent of the Councill for Our service in the necessary defence and support of our Government of our said Province or Territory and the Protection and Preservation of the Inhabitants there . . .
[Thorpe 1882]

George II, Charter of Georgia, June 9, 1732:

[The Trustees of the colony are authorized] . . . to give, grant, let and demise the said manors, messuages, lands, tenements, hereditaments, goods, chattels and things whatsoever aforesaid, by lease or leases, for term of years, in possession at the time of granting thereof, and not in reversion, not exceeding the term of thirty-one years, from the time of granting thereof; on which in case no *fine* be taken, shall be reserved the full value, and in case a *fine* be taken, shall be reserved at least a moiety of the full value that the same shall reasonably and bona fide be worth at the time of such demise . . . [Thorpe 766]

Virginia Bill of Rights, June 12, 1776:

[Section 9:] That excessive bail ought not to be required, nor excessive *fines* imposed, nor cruel and unusual punishments inflicted. [Thorpe 3813]

Pennsylvania Constitution, September 28, 1776:

[Frame of Government, Section 20:] The president, and in his absence the vice-president, with the council, five of whom shall be a quorum, shall have power . . . to grant pardons, and remit *fines,* in all cases whatsoever, except in cases of impeachment; and in cases of treason and murder, shall have power to grant reprieves, but not to pardon, until the end of the next sessions of assembly but there shall be no remission or mitigation of punishments on impeachments, except by act of the legislature . . . [Thorpe 3087–88]

[*Ibid.,* Section 29:] Excessive bail shall not be exacted for bailable offences: And all *fines* shall be moderate. [Thorpe 3089]

Maryland Constitution, November 11, 1776:

[Declaration of Rights, Article 13:] That the levying taxes by the poll is grievous and oppressive, and ought to be abolished; that paupers ought not to be assessed for the support of government; but every other person in the State ought to contribute his proportion of public taxes, for the support of government, according to his actual worth, in real or personal property, within the State; yet *fines,* duties, or taxes, may properly and justly be imposed or laid, with a political view, for the good government and benefit of the community. [Thorpe 1687]

[*Ibid.,* Article 22:] That excessive bail ought not to be required, nor *excessive fines* imposed, nor cruel or unusual punishments inflicted, by the courts of law. [Thorpe 1688]

[Form of Government, Article 11:] . . . and to prevent altercation about such bills, it is declared, that no bill imposing duties or customs for the mere regulation of commerce, or inflicting *fines* for the reformation of morals, or to enforce the execution of the laws, by which an incidental revenue may arise, shall be accounted a money bill; but every bill assessing, levying, or applying taxes or supplies for the support of government or the current expenses of the state, or appropriating money in the treasury, shall be deemed a money bill.

[Thorpe 1693]

North Carolina Constitution, December 18, 1776:

[Declaration of Rights, Article 10:] That excessive bail should not be required, nor *excessive fines* imposed, nor cruel or unusual punishments inflicted.

[Thorpe 2788]

Georgia Constitution, February 5, 1777:

[Article 19:] The governor shall, with the advice of the executive council, exercise the executive powers of government, according to the laws of this State and the constitution thereof, save only in the case of pardons and remission of *fines,* which he shall in no instance grant; but he may reprieve a criminal, or suspend a *fine,* until the meeting of the assembly, who may determine therein as they shall judge fit. [Thorpe 781]

[Article 59:] *Excessive fines* shall not be levied, nor excessive bail demanded.

[Thorpe 785]

Vermont Constitution, July 8, 1777:

[Preamble:] They [the New York legislature] have passed an act, annexing a penalty thereto, of thirty pounds *fine* and six months imprisonment, on any person who should refuse assisting the sheriff, after being requested, for the purpose of executing writs of possession. [Thorpe 3738]

[Declaration of Rights, Article 1:] That all men are born equally free and independent, and have certain natural, inherent and unalienable rights, amongst which are the enjoying and defending life and liberty; acquiring, possessing and protecting property, and pursuing and obtaining happiness and safety. Therefore, no male person, born in this country, or brought from over sea ought to be holden by law, to serve any person, as a servant, slave or apprentice, after he arrives to the age of twenty-one years, nor female, in like manner, after she arrives to the age of eighteen years, unless they are bound by their own consent, after they arrive to such age, or bound by law, for the payment of debts, damages, *fines,* costs, or the like. [Thorpe 3739–40]

[Frame of Government, Section 18:] The Governor, and in his absence, the Lieutenant or Deputy Governor, with the Council—seven of whom shall be a quorum—shall have power . . . to grant pardons, and remit *fines,* in all cases whatsoever, except cases of impeachment, and in cases of treason and murder—shall have power to grant reprieves, but not to pardon, until the end of the next session of the Assembly: but there shall be no remission or mitigation of punishment, on impeachments, except by act of legislation. . . . [Thorpe 3745]

[*Ibid.*, Section 26:] Excessive bail shall not be exacted for bailable offences: and all *fines* shall be moderate. [Thorpe 3746]

[*Ibid.*, Section 30:] All *fines*, license money, fees and forfeitures, shall according to the direction hereafter to be made by the General Assembly. [Thorpe 3746]

Massachusetts Constitution, March 2, 1780:

[Declaration of Rights, Article 26:] No magistrate or court of law shall demand excessive bail or sureties, impose *excessive fines*, or inflict cruel or unusual punishments. [Thorpe 1892]

[Frame of Government, Chapter I:3:2:] And the house of representatives shall have power from time to time to impose *fines* upon such towns as shall neglect to choose and return members to the same, agreeably to this constitution. [Thorpe 1898]

New Hampshire Constitution, June 2, 1784:

[Bill of Rights, Article 33:] No magistrate or court of law shall demand excessive bail or sureties, impose *excessive fines*, or inflict cruel or unusual punishments. [Thorpe 2457]

[Form of Government:] [Authority is given the the General Court] . . . to impose *fines*, mulcts, imprisonments, and other punishments; and to impose and levy proportional and reasonable assessments, rates and taxes, upon all the inhabitants of, and residents within the said state . . . [Thorpe 2458]

Vermont Constitution, July 4, 1786:

[Preamble:] They [the New York legislature] have passed an act, annexing a penalty thereto, of thirty pounds' *fine*, and six months' imprisonment, on any person who should refuse assisting the Sheriff, after being requested, for the purpose of executing writs of possession. [Thorpe 3750]

[Declaration of Rights, Article 1:] That all men are born equally free and independent, and have certain natural, inherent and unalienable rights; amongst which are, the enjoying and defending life and liberty—acquiring, possessing and protecting property—and pursuing and obtaining happiness and safety. Therefore, no male person, born in this country, or brought from over sea, ought to be holden by law to serve any person, as a servant, slave, or apprentice, after he arrives to the age of twenty-one years; nor female, in like manner, after she arrives to the age of eighteen years; unless they are bound by their own consent after they arrive to such age; or bound by law for the payment of debts, damages, *fines*, costs, or the like. [Thorpe 3751–52]

[Frame of Government, Section 11:] The Governor, and in his absence, the Lieutenant-Governor, with the Council, (a major part of whom, including the Governor or Lieutenant-Governor, shall be a quorum to transact business) shall have power . . . to grant pardons, and remit *fines* in all cases whatsoever, except in treason and murder, in which they shall have power to grant reprieves but not to pardon, until after the end of the next session of Assembly, and except in cases of impeachment, in which there shall be no remission or mitigation of punishment, but by act of legislation . . . [Thorpe 3756]

[*Ibid.*, Section 29:] All prosecutions shall commence by the authority of the State of Vermont—all indictments shall conclude with these words, Against the peace and dignity of the State. And all *fines* shall be proportionate to the offences. [Thorpe 3759]

The New Jersey Plan of Union, June 15, 1787:

[Article 3:] Res[olve]d that in addition to the powers vested in the U. States in Congress, by the present existing articles of Confederation, they be authorized to pass acts for raising a revenue, by levying a duty or duties on all goods or merchandizes of foreign growth or manufacture imported into any part of the U. States, by Stamps on paper, vellum or parchment, and by a postage on all letters or packages passing through the general post office, to be applied to such federal purposes as they shall deem proper & expedient, to make rules and regulations for the collection thereof, and the same from time to time, to alter & amend in such manner as they shall think proper: to pass Acts for the regulation of trade & commerce as well with foreign nations as with each other: provided that all punishments, *fines,* forfeitures & penalties to be incurred for contravening such acts rules and regulations shall be adjudged by the Common law Judiciarys of the State in which any offence contrary to the true intent & meaning of such Acts rules & regulations shall have been committed or perpetrated . . .

[DHRC1 251]

United States Confederation Congress, The Northwest Ordinance, July 13, 1787:

[Article 2:] The inhabitants of the said territory shall always be entitled to the benefits of the writs of habeas corpus, and of the trial by jury; of a proportionate representation of the people in the legislature, and of judicial proceedings according to the course of the common law. All persons shall be bailable, unless for capital offences, where the proof shall be evident, or the presumption great. All *fines* shall be moderate; and no cruel or unusual punishments shall be inflicted. No man shall be deprived of his liberty or property, but by the judgment of his peers, or the law of the land, and should the public exigencies make it necessary, for the common preservation, to take any persons property, or to demand his particular services, full compensation shall be made for the same. . . .

[Thorpe 960–61]

Richard Henry Lee, Proposed Amendments to the Constitution, October 16, 1787:

. . . That the elections should be free and frequent; That the right administration of justice should be secured by the independency of the judges; That excessive bail, excessive *fines,* or cruel and unusual punishments, should not be demanded or inflicted; That the right of the people to assemble peaceably, for the purpose of petitioning the legislature, shall not be prevented . . . [DHRC 65]

Tench Coxe, *An Examination of the Constitution for the United States of America*, No. 4, October 21, 1787:

. . . The trial by jury is not excluded in these foederal courts. In all criminal cases, where the property, liberty or life of the citizen is at stake, he has the benefit of a jury. If convicted on impeachment, which is never done by a jury in any country, he cannot be *fined,* imprisoned or punished, but only may be disqualified from doing public mischief by losing his office, and his capacity to hold another. . . . [Ford 149]

James Madison, *The Federalist*, No. 18, December 7, 1787:

[1] The members [of the Greek Amphictyonic Confederation] retained the character of independent and sovereign states, and had equal votes in the federal council. This council had a general authority to propose and resolve whatever it judged necessary for the common welfare of Greece; to declare and carry on war; to decide, in the last resort, all controversies between the members; to *fine* the aggressing party; to employ the whole force of the confederacy against the disobedient; to admit new members. . . . [Fed. 171]

[2] . . . The Phocians having ploughed up some consecrated ground belonging to the temple of Apollo, the Amphictyonic council, according to the superstition of the age, imposed a *fine* on the sacrilegious offenders. The Phocians, being abetted by Athens and Sparta, refused to submit to the decree. . . . [Fed. 173]

Dissent of the Pennsylvania Convention's Minority, December 18, 1787:

[1] That excessive bail ought not to be required, nor *excessive fines* imposed, nor cruel nor unusual punishments inflicted. [DHRC2 623]

[2] First, the personal liberty of every man, probably from sixteen to sixty years of age may be destroyed by the power Congress have in organizing and governing of the militia. As militia they may be subjected to *fines* to any amount, levied in a military manner; they may be subjected to corporal punishments of the most disgraceful and humiliating kind, and to death itself, by the sentence of a court

martial. To this our young men will be more immediately subjected, as a select militia, composed of them, will best answer the purposes of government.
[DHRC2 638]

Tench Coxe, "A Freeman," No. 3, February 6, 1788:

Impeachments within the several states will afford them opportunities of exerting the most dignified and aweful powers of sovereignty. The people of every state, by their constitutional representatives, may impeach the public officer, however great or daring, that shall presume to violate their exclusive rights, or offend against the peace and dignity of their commonwealth, and may punish him, on conviction, by *fine,* imprisonment or death, without any possible interference of Congress. [DHRC16 51–52]

"A Virginian," February 13, 1788:

. . . 2dly. I think by the plan in its present form, the governors which are thereby to be set up at Philadelphia, will have it in their power to make war on any terms they please: If so, no doubt but they may point out the part every man shall take therein, or be liable to such *fines* and penalties as they may think proper to impose; therefore gentlemen [the Virginia Quakers] as you are principled against war, in case we should be so unhappy as to be again involved therein, to whom will you apply for indulgence on account of your religious scruples? . . . [DHRC8 36]

"The Impartial Examiner," No. 1, March 4, 1788:

. . . can it be said that they have exceeded the limits of their jurisdiction, when that has no limits; when no provision has been made for such a right?—When no responsibility on the part of Congress has been required by the constitution? The same observation may be made on any arbitrary or capricious imprisonments contrary to the law of the land. The same may be made, if excessive bail should be required; if *excessive fines* should be imposed; if cruel and unusual punishments should be inflicted; if the liberty of the press should be restrained . . .
[DHRC8 462]

United States Congress, Judiciary Act of September 24, 1789:

[Section 9:] . . . That the district courts shall have, exclusively of the courts of the several States, cognizance of all crimes and offences that shall be cognizable under the authority of the United States, committed within their respective districts, or upon the high seas; where no other punishment than whipping, not exceeding thirty stripes, a *fine* not exceeding one hundred dollars, or a term of imprisonment not exceeding six months, is to be inflicted . . . [USSL1 76–77]

South Carolina Constitution, June 3, 1790

[Article II, Section 7:] He shall have power to grant reprieves and pardons, after conviction, (except in cases of impeachment,) in such manner, on such terms, and under such restrictions as he shall think proper; and he shall have power to remit *fines* and forfeitures unless otherwise directed by law. [Thorpe 3262]

[Article IX, Section 4:] Excessive bail shall not be required, nor excessive *fines* imposed, nor cruel punishments inflicted. [Thorpe 3264]

Pennsylvania Constitution, September 2, 1790:

[Article II, Section 9:] He [the Governor] shall have power to remit *fines* and forfeitures, and grant reprieves and pardons, except in cases of impeachment. [Thorpe 3096]

[Article IX, Section 13:] That excessive bail shall not be required, nor *excessive fines* imposed, nor cruel punishments inflicted. [Thorpe 3101]

GRIEVANCES, REDRESS OF

United States Constitution, Bill of Rights, December 15, 1791:

[Article I:] Congress shall make no law respecting an establishment of religion, or prohibiting the free exercise thereof; or abridging the freedom of speech, or of the press; or the right of the people peaceably to assemble, and to petition the government for a *redress of grievances*.

* * * * *

English Bill of Rights, December 16, 1689:

And that for *redress of all grievances* and for the amending, strengthening and preserving of the laws parliaments ought to be held frequently. [SDECH 465]

Pennsylvania Frame of Government, November 7, 1696:

And be it further enacted by the authority aforesaid, That the Assembly, shall sit upon their own adjournments, and committees, and continue, in order to prepare and propose bills, *redress grievances,* and impeach criminals, or such persons as they shall think fit to be there impeached, until the Governor and Council, for the time being, shall dismiss them . . . [Thorpe 3075]

William Penn, Charter of Priveleges for Pennsylvania, October 28, 1701:

[Article 2:] . . . Which Assembly shall have Power to chuse a Speaker and other their Officers; and shall be Judges of the Qualifications and Elections of their own Members; sit upon their own Adjournments; appoint Committees; prepare Bills in order to pass into Laws; impeach Criminals, and *redress Grievances;* and shall have all other Powers and Privileges of an Assembly, according to the Rights of the free-born Subjects of England, and as is usual in any of the King's Plantations in America. [Thorpe 3078]

William Penn, Charter of Delaware, October 28, 1701:

[Article 2:] . . . Which Assembly shall have Power to chuse a Speaker and other their Officers; and shall be Judges of the Qualifications and Elections of their own Members; sit upon their own Adjournments; appoint Committees; prepare Bills in order to pass into Laws; impeach Criminals, and *redress Grievances;* and shall have all other powers and Privileges of an Assembly, according to the Rights of the free-born Subjects of England, and as is usual in any of the King's Plantations in America. [Thorpe 559]

First Continental Congress, Declaration and Resolves, October 14, 1774:

And whereas, Assemblies have been frequently dissolved, contrary to the rights of the people, when they attempted to deliberate on *grievances;* and their dutiful, humble, loyal, & reasonable petitions to the crown for *redress,* have been repeatedly treated with contempt, by his majesty's ministers of state . . .
[JCC1 66]

Thomas Paine, *Common Sense*, January 9, 1776:

In short, independence is the only bond that can tie and keep us together. We shall then see our object, and our ears will be legally shut against the schemes of an intriguing, as well as a cruel enemy. We shall then, too, be on a proper footing to treat with Britain; for there is reason to conclude, that the pride of that court will be less hurt by treating with the American States for terms of peace, than with those, whom she denominates, ''rebellious subjects,'' for terms of accommodation. It is our delaying it that, encourages her to hope for conquest, and our backwardness tends only to prolong the war. As we have, without any good effect therefrom, withheld our trade to Obtain a *redress of our grievances,* let us now try the alternative, by independently *redressing* them ourselves, and then offering to open the trade. The mercantile and reasonable part of England will be still with us; because, peace, with trade, is preferable to war without it. And if this offer be not accepted, other courts may be applied to. [CWTP1 46]

South Carolina Constitution, March 26, 1776:

[Preamble:] . . . And whereas the delegates of all the colonies on this continent from Nova Scotia to Georgia, assembled in a general Congress at Philadelphia, in the most dutiful manner laid their complaints at the foot of the throne, and humbly implored their sovereign that his royal authority and interposition might be used for their relief from the *grievances* occasioned by those statutes, and assured His Majesty that harmony between Great Britain and America, ardently desired by the latter, would be thereby immediately restored, and that the colonists confided in the magnanimity and justice of the King and Parliament for *redress of the many other grievances* under which they labored. And whereas these complaints being wholly disregarded, statutes still more cruel than those above mentioned have been enacted, prohibiting the intercourse of the colonies with each other, restricting their trade, and depriving many thousands of people of the means of subsistence, by restraining them from fishing on the American coast. . . . [Thorpe 3242]

Pennsylvania Constitution, September 28, 1776:

[Declaration of Rights, Article 16:] That the people have a right to assemble together, to consult for their common good, to instruct their representatives, and to apply to the legislature for *redress of grievances,* by address, petition, or remonstrance. [Thorpe 3084]

[Frame of Government, Section 9:] The members of the house of representatives shall be chosen annually by ballot, by the freemen of the commonwealth, on the second Tuesday in October forever, (except this present year,) and shall meet on the fourth Monday of the same month, and shall be stiled, The general assembly of the representatives of the freemen of Pennsylvania, and shall have power to choose their speaker, the treasurer of the state, and their other officers; sit on their own adjournments; prepare bills and enact them into laws; judge of the elections and qualifications of their own members; they may expel a member, but not a second time for the same cause; they may administer oaths or affirmations on examination of witnesses; *redress grievances;* impeach state criminals; grant charters of incorporation; constitute towns, boroughs, cities, and counties; and shall have all other powers necessary for the legislature of a free state or commonwealth: But they shall have no power to add to, alter, abolish, or infringe any part of this constitution. [Thorpe 3084–85]

Maryland Constitution, November 11, 1776:

[Declaration of Rights, Article 10:] That, for *redress of grievances,* and for amending, strengthening and preserving the laws, the Legislature ought to be frequently convened. [Thorpe 1687]

[Article 11:] That every, man hath a right to petition the Legislature, for the *redress of grievances,* in a peaceable and orderly manner. [Thorpe 1687]

North Carolina Constitution, December 18, 1776:

[Declaration of Rights, Article 18:] That the people have a right to assemble together, to consult for their common good, to instruct their Representatives, and to apply to the Legislature, for *redress of grievances.* [Thorpe 2788]

[*Ibid.,* Article 20:] That, for *redress of grievances,* and for amending and strengthening the laws, elections ought to be often held. [Thorpe 2788]

New York Constitution, April 20, 1777:

[Preamble:] Whereas the many tyrannical and oppressive usurpations of the King and Parliament of Great Britain on the rights and liberties of the people of the American colonies had reduced them to the necessity of introducing a government by congresses and committees, as temporary expedients, and to exist no longer than the *grievances* of the people should remain without *redress* . . .
[Thorpe 2623]

Vermont Constitution, July 8, 1777:

[Declaration of Rights, Article 18:] That the people have a right to assemble together, to consult for their common good—to instruct their representatives, and to apply to the legislature for *redress of grievances,* by address, petition or remonstrance. [Thorpe 3741–42]

[Frame of Government, Section 8:] The members of the House of Representatives . . . shall have power to choose their Speaker, Secretary of the State, their Clerk, and other necessary officers of the house—sit on their own adjournments—prepare bills and enact them into laws—judge of the elections and qualifications of their own members—they may expel a member, but not a second time for the same cause—They may administer oaths (or affirmations) on examination of witnesses—*redress grievances*—impeach State criminals—grant charters of incorporation—constitute towns, boroughs, cities and counties, and shall have all other powers necessary for the legislature of a free State . . .
[Thorpe 3742–43]

Massachusetts Constitution, March 2, 1780:

[Bill of Rights, Article 19:] The people have a right, in an orderly and peaceable manner, to assemble to consult upon the common good; give instructions to their representatives, and to request of the legislative body, by the way of addresses, petitions, or remonstrances, *redress* of the wrongs done them, and of the *grievances* they suffer. [Thorpe 1892]

[*Ibid.,* Article 22:] The legislature ought frequently to assemble for the *redress of grievances,* for correcting, strengthening, and confirming the laws, and for making new laws, as the common good may require. [Thorpe 1892]

New Hampshire Constitution, June 2, 1784:

[Bill of Rights, Article 31:] The legislature ought frequently to assemble for the *redress of grievances,* for correcting, strengthening and confirming the laws, and for making new ones, as the common good may require. [Thorpe 2457]

[*Ibid.,* Article 32:] The people have a right in an orderly and peaceable manner, to assemble and consult upon the common good, give instructions to their rep-

resentatives; and to request of the legislative body, by way of petition or remonstrance, *redress* ofthe wrongs done them, and of the *grievances* they suffer.
[Thorpe 2457]

Vermont Constitution, July 4, 1786:

[Declaration of Rights, Article 22:] That the people have a right to assemble together, to consult for their common good—to instruct their representatives, and to apply to the Legislature for *redress of grievances,* by address, petition or remonstrance.
[Thorpe 3754]

[Frame of Governmen, Section 9:] The representatives . . . shall have power to choose their Speaker, Secretary of the State, their Clerk and other necessary officers of the house—sit on their own adjournments—prepare, bills, and enact them into laws—judge of the elections and qualifications of their own members: they may expel members, but not for causes known to their constituents antecedent to their election; they may administer oaths, or affirmations, in matters depending before them—*redress grievances*—impeach State criminals—grant charters of incorporation—constitute towns, boroughs, cities and counties . . .
[Thorpe 3755]

Dissent of the Pennsylvania Convention's Minority, December 18, 1787:

For the moderate exercise of this power, there is no control left in the state governments, whose intervention is destroyed. No relief, or *redress of grievances* can be extended, as heretofore, by them. There is not even a declaration of RIGHTS to which the people may appeal for the vindication of their wrongs in the court of justice. They must therefore, implicitly, obey the most arbitrary laws, as the worst of them will be pursuant to the principles and form of the constitution, and that strongest of all checks upon the conduct of administration, responsibility to the people, will not exist in this government. . . .
[DHRC2 636]

Luther Martin, "Genuine Information," No. 10, February 1, 1788:

Thus, Sir, in consequence of this appellate jurisdiction and its extension to facts as well as to law, every arbitrary act of the general government, and every oppression of all those variety of officers appointed under its authority for the collection of taxes, duties, impost, excise, and other purposes, must be submitted to by the individual, or must be opposed with little prospect of success and almost a certain prospect of ruin, at least in those cases where the middle and common class of citizens are interested—Since to avoid that oppression, or to obtain *redress,* the application must be made to one of the courts of the United States—by good fortune should this application be in the first instance attended with success, and should damages be recovered equivalent to the injury sustained, an appeal lies to the supreme court, in which case the citizen must at once give up his cause, or he must attend to it at the distance of perhaps more than a thousand miles from the place of his residence, and must take measures to procure before that court on the appeal all the evidence necessary to support his action, which even if ultimately prosperous must be attended with a loss of time, a neglect of business, and an expence which will be greater than the original *grievance,* and to which men in moderate circumstances would be utterly unequal. [DHRC16 10]

James Madison, *The Federalist*, No. 58, February 20, 1788:

. . . This power over the purse may, in fact, be regarded as the most complete and effectual weapon with which any constitution can arm the immediate representatives of the people, for obtaining a *redress of every grievance,* and for carrying into effect every just and salutary measure. [Fed. 391]

Mercy Otis Warren, Observations on the New Constitution, February 1788:

We were then told by him [former Royal Governor Thomas Hutchinson], in all the soft language of insinuation, that no form of government of human construction can be perfect—that we had nothing to fear—that we had no reason to complain—that we had only to acquiesce in their illegal claims, and to submit to the requisitions of parliament, and doubtless the lenient hand of government would *redress all grievances,* and remove the oppressions of the people:—Yet we soon saw armies of mercenaries encamped on our plains—our commerce ruined—our harbours blockaded—and our cities burnt. . . .
[DHRC16 283–84]

Pennsylvania Constitution, September 2, 1790:

[Article IX, Section 20:] That the citizens have a right, in a peaceable manner, to assemble together for their common good, and to apply to those invested with the powers of government for *redress of grievances,* or other proper purposes, by petition, address, or remonstrance. [Thorpe 3101]

IMMUNITIES

United States Constitution, September 17, 1787:

[Article IV, Section 2:] The Citizens of each State shall be entitled to all Privileges and *Immunities* of Citizens in the several States.

* * * * *

Ferdinand and Isabella of Spain, Privileges and *Immunities* Granted to Christopher Columbus, April 30, 1492:

. . . and that they treat you and your Lieutenants, by you appointed, for executing the employments of Admiral, Vice-Roy, and Governour, as such in all respects, and give you all the perquisites and other things belonging and appertaining to the said offices; and allow, and cause to be allowed you, all the honours, graces, concessions, prehaminences, prerogatives, *immunities,* and other things, or any of them which are due to you, by virtue of your commands of Admiral, Vice-roy, and Governour, and to be observed completely, so that nothing be diminished . . . [Thorpe 40]

James I, First Charter of Virginia, April 10, 1606:

Also we do, for Us, our Heirs, and Successors, Declare, by these Presents, that all and every the Persons being our Subjects, which shall dwell and inhabit within every or any of the said several Colonies and Plantations, and every of their children, which shall happen to be born within any of the Limits and Precincts of the said several Colonies and Plantations, shall Have and enjoy all Liberties, Franchises, and *Immunities,* within any of our other Dominions, to all Intents and Purposes, as if they had been abiding and born, within this our Realm of England, or any other of our said Dominions. [Thorpe 3788]

James I, Second Charter of Virginia, May 23, 1609:

[1] Also we do for Us, our Heirs and Successors, Declare by these Presents, that all and every the Persons being our Subjects, which shall go and inhabit within the said Colony and Plantation, and every their Children and Posterity, which shall happen to be born within any of the Limits thereof, shall Have and Enjoy all Liberties, Franchizes, and *Immunities* of Free Denizens and natural Subjects within any of our other Dominions to all Intents and Purposes, as if they had been abiding and born within this our Realm of England, or in any other of our Dominions. [Thorpe 3800]

[2] And further, we do, by these Presents Ratify and Confirm unto the said Treasurer and Company, and their Successors, all the Privileges, Franchises, Liberties, and *Immunities* granted in our said former Letters-patents, and not in these our Letters-patents, revoked, altered, changed, or abridged. [Thorpe 3801]

[3] And finally our Will and Pleasure is, and we do further hereby for Us, our Heirs, and Successors, Grant and Agree, to and with the said Treasurer and Company, and their Successors, that all and singular Person and Persons, which shall at any Time or Times hereafter adventure any Sum or Sums of Money, in and towards the said Plantation of the said Colony in Virginia, and shall be admitted by the said Council and Company, as Adventurers of the said Colony in Form aforesaid, and shall be enrolled in the Book or Records of the Adventurers of the said Company, shall and may be accounted, accepted, taken, held, and reputed Adventurers of the said Colony, and shall, and may enjoy all and singular Grants, Privileges, Liberties, Benefits, Profits, Commodities and *Immunities,* Advantages and Emoluments whatsoever, as fully, largely, amply, and absolutely, as if they and every of them, had been precisely, plainly, singularly, and distinctly named and inserted in these our Letters-patents. [Thorpe 3801–02]

James I, Third Charter of Virginia, 1611–1612:

[1] And further, Our Will and Pleasure is, and We do by these Presents, Grant and Confirm . . . [that designated individuals] who since Our said last Letters-Patents are become Adventurers, and have joined themselves with the former Adventurers and Planters of the said Company and Society, shall from henceforth be reputed, deemed, and taken to be, and shall be Brethren and free Members of the Company; and shall and may respectively, and according to the Proportion and Value of their several Adventures, Have, Hold, and Enjoy, all such Interest, Right, Title, Privileges, Preheminences, Liberties, Franchises, *Immunities,* Profits, and Commodities, whatsoever, in as large and ample and beneficial Manner to all Intents, Constructions, and Purposes, as any other Adventures nominated and expressed in any our former Letters-Patents, or any of them have or may have by Force and Virtue of these Presents, or any our former Letters-Patents whatsoever. [Thorpe 3804–85]

[2] . . . And that all such Persons so elected, chosen, and admitted to be of the said Company as aforesaid, shall thereupon be taken, reputed, and held, and shall be free Members of the said Company, and shall have, hold, and enjoy all and singular Freedoms, Liberties, Franchises, Privileges, *Immunities,* Benefits, Profits and Commodities whatsoever, to the said Company in any Sort belonging or appertaining, as fully, freely and amply as any other Adventurers now being, or which hereafter at any Time shall be of the said Company, hath, have, shall, may, might, or ought to have and enjoy the same to all Intents and Purposes whatsoever. . . . [Thorpe 3806]

[3] And lastly, we do, by these Presents Ratify and Confirm unto the said Treasurer and Company, and their Successors, for ever, all and all Manner of Privileges, Franchises, Liberties, *Immunities,* Preheminences, Profits, and Commodities, whatsoever, granted unto them in any our former Letters-patent, and not in these Presents revoked altered, changed, or abridged. . . . [Thorpe 3810]

James I, The Charter of New England, November 3, 1620:

[1] . . . And whereas, since that Time, upon the humble Petition of the said Adventurers and Planters of the said first Collonye, We have been graciously pleased to make them one distinct and entire Body by themselves, giving unto them their distinct Lymitts and Bounds, and have upon their like humble Request, granted unto them divers Liberties, Priveliges, Enlargements, and *Immunityes,* as in and by Our severall Letters-Patents it doth and may more at large appeare. . . . [Thorpe 1828]

[2] . . . and to that Purpose and Intent have desired of Us, for their better Encouragement and Satisfaction herein, and that they may avoide all Confusion, Questions, or Differences between themselves, and those of the said first Collonye, We would likewise be graciously leased to make certaine Adventurers, intending to erect and establish fishery, Trade, and Plantacion, within the Territoryes, Precincts, and Lymitts of the said second Colony, and their Successors, one several distinct and entire Body, and to grant unto them, such Estate, Liberties, Priveliges, Enlargements, and *Immunityes* there, as in these our Letters-Pattents hereafter particularly expressed and declared.

[Thorpe 1828]

[3] . . . And further, Wee do hereby for Us, our Heires and Successors, grant unto the said Councill established at Plymouth, that they and their Successors, by the same Name, be and shall be, and shall continue Persons able and capable in the Law, from time to time, and shall by that Name, of Councill aforesaid, have full Power and Authority, and lawful Capacity and Hability, as well to purchase, take, hold, receive, enjoy, and to have, and their Successors for ever, any Manors, Lands, Tenements, Rents, Royalties, Privileges, *Immunities,* Reversions, Annuities, Hereditaments, Goods, and Chattles whatsoever, of or from Us, our Heirs, and Successors, and of or from any other Person or Persons

whatsoever, as well in and within this our Realme, of England, as in and within any other Place or Places whatsoever or wheresoever . . . [Thorpe 1831]

[4] . . . Also, Wee do for Us, our Heires, and Successors, declare by these Presents, that all and every the Persons, beinge our Subjects, which shall goe and inhabitt within the said Collony and Plantation, and every of their Children and Posterity, which shall happen to be born within the Limitts thereof, shall have and enjoy all Liberties, and franchizes, and *Immunities* of free Denizens and naturall Subjects within any of our other Dominions, to all Intents and Purposes, as if they had been abidinge and born within this our Kingdome of England, or any other our Dominions. [Thorpe 1839]

[5] . . . And Wee also do by these Presents, ratifye and confirm unto the said Councill and their Successors, all Priveliges, franchises, Liberties, *Immunities* granted in our said former Letters-patents, and not in these our Letters-patents revoked, altered, changed or abridged, altho' Expressed, Mentioned, &c. [Thorpe 1840]

Council of New England, Grant of the Province of Maine, August 10, 1622:

As also all the lands, soyle, grounds, harbors, ports, rivers, mines, mineralls, pearls, pretious stones, woods, quarries, marshes, waters, fishings, hunting, hawking, fowling, and other commodities and hereditaments whatsoever; with all and singular their appurtenances, together with all prerogatives, rights, royalties, jurisdictions, privileges, franchises, liberties, preheminences, marine power, in and upon ye said seas and rivers; as also all escheats and casualties thereof, as flotson, jetson, lagon, with anchorage, and other such duties, *immunities,* sects, isletts and appurtenances whatsoever, with all the estate, right title, interest, and claim and demands whatsoever wch ye said President and councill, and their successors, of right ought to have or claim in or to the said porcons of lands, rivers, and other ye said premises . . . [Thorpe 1623]

Charles I, Charter of Massachusetts Bay, March 4, 1629:

[1] [We grant] . . . all the saide Parte of Newe England in America, lyeing and extending betweene the Boundes and Lymytts in the said recited Indenture expressed, and all Landes and Groundes, Place and Places, Soyles, Woods and Wood Groundes, Havens, Portes, Rivers, Waters, Mynes, Mineralls, Jurisdiccons, Rightes, Royalties, Liberties, Freedomes, *Immunities,* Priviledges, Franchises, Preheminences, Hereditaments, and Comodities whatsoever, to them the saide Sir Henry Rosewell, [etc.] . . . [Thorpe 1848]

[2] And, further our Will and Pleasure is, and Wee doe hereby for Us, our Heires and Successors, ordeyne and declare, and graunte to the saide Governor and Company, and their Successors, That all and every the Subjects of Us, our Heires or Successors, which shall goe to and inhabite within the saide Landes

and Premisses hereby menconed to be graunted, and every of their Children which shall happen to be borne there, or on the Seas in goeing thither, or retorning from thence, shall have and enjoy all liberties and *Immunities* of free and naturall Subjects within any of the Domynions of Us, our Heires or Successors, to all Intents, Construccons, and Purposes whatsoever, as yf they and everie of them were borne within the Realme of England. . . . [Thorpe 1856–57]

Charles I, Patent to Sir Robert Heath, October 30, 1629:

[1] . . . And furthermore the patronages and advowsons of all churches which shall happen to be built hereafter in the said Region Territory & Isles and limitts by the increase of the religion & worship of Christ Together with all & singular these & these soe amply, Rights Jurisdictions, priviledges prerogatives Royaltyes libertyes *immunityes* with Royall rights & franchises whatsoever as well by sea as by land, within that Region Territory Isles & limitts aforesaid To have exercise use & enjoy in like manner as any Bishop of Durham within the B[isho]pricke or County palatine of Durham in our kingdome of England ever heretofore had held used or enjoyed or of right ought or could have hold use or enjoy. . . . [Thorpe 70]

[2] . . . [we] doe for ourselves our heires & successors give full & free power to the foresayd Sr. Robert Heath Knight his heires & assignes to confere favours graces & honours upon those well deserveing citizens that inhabit within the foresayd province & the same with whatever Titles & dignityes (provided they be not the same as are now used in England) to adorne at his pleasure alsoe to erect villages into Borowes & Borowes into Cittyes for the meritts of the inhabitants and conveniency of the places with priviledges & befitting *immunityes* to be erected & incorporated, & to doe all other & singular upon the premises which shall seem most convenient to him or them, although they be such which of their owne natures doe require mandates or warrant more especiall then is expressed in these presents . . . [Thorpe 74]

Charles I, Charter of Maryland, June 20, 1632:

[Section 4:] And furthermore the Patronages, and Advowsons of all Churches which (with the increasing Worship and Religion of Christ) within the said Region, Islands, Islets, and Limits aforesaid, hereafter shall happen to be built, together with License and Faculty of erecting and founding Churches, Chapels, and Places of Worship, in convenient and suitable places, within the Premises, and of causing the same to be dedicated and consecrated according to the Ecclesiastical Laws of our Kingdom of England, with all, and singular such, and as ample Rights, Jurisdictions, Privileges, Prerogatives, Royalties, Liberties, *Immunities,* and royal Rights, and temporal Franchises whatsoever, as well by Sea as by Land, within the Region, Islands, Islets, and Limits aforesaid, to he had, exercised, used, and enjoyed, as any Bishop of Durham, within the Bishoprick or County Palatine of Durham, in our Kingdom of England, ever heretofore hath had, held, used, or enjoyed, or of right could, or ought to have, hold, use, or enjoy. [Thorpe 1678–79]

[Section 14:] . . . also to erect and incorporate Towns into Boroughs, and Boroughs into Cities, with suitable Privileges and *Immunities,* according to the Merits of the Inhabitants, and Convenience of the Places; and to do all and singular other Things in the Premises, which to him or them shall seem fitting and convenient . . . [Thorpe 1683]

Surrender of the Charter of New England, June 7, 1635:

. . . And then the said then Duke of Lenox, Marquess of Buckingham, Marquess of Hamilton, Earl of Pembroke, and Earl of Arundel, and the said others of the Nobility and Gentry therein named, and the survivors of them and their successors, to be elected as in the said Letters Patents is expressed, did by the said Letters Patents incorporate, erect, ordain, name, constitute, and establish to be one body politick and corporate, in Deed and Name, by the Name of the Council of Plymouth aforesaid, in the said County of Devon, for the planting, ruling, and governing of New England in America aforesaid, To have perpetual succession, with divers other powers, priviledges, *immunities,* provisions, and restrictions, for the propagation and establishing of true Religion in those parts, and for the better regulating of the same plantations, as in and by the said Letters Patents . . . [Thorpe 1860–61]

Charles I, Grant of the Province of Maine, April 3, 1639:

[1] . . . and alsoe All Patronages and Advowsons Free Disposicons and Donacons of all and every such Churches and Chappells as shalbee made and erected within the said Province and Premisses or any of them with full power lycense and authority to builde and erecte or cause to be builte and erected soe many Churches and Chappells there as to the said Sir Ferdinando Gorges his heires and assignes shall seeme meete and convenient and to dedicate and consecrate the same or cause the same to bee dedicated and consecrated according to the Ecclesiastical Lawes of this our Realme of England togeather with all and singuler and as large and ample Rights Jurisdiccons Priviledges Prerogatives Royalties Liberties *Immunityes* Franchises Preheminences and Hereditaments as well by Sea as by Lande within the said Province and Premisses and the Precincts and Coasts of the same or any of them and within the Seas belonging or adjacent to them or any of them as the Bishopp of Durham within the Bishopricke or Countie Palatine of Duresme in our Kingdome of England now hath useth or enjoyeth or of right hee ought to have use or enjoie within the said Countie Palatine as if the same were herein particulerly menconed and expressed. [Thorpe 1627]

[2] . . . and shall have and injoy all Liberties Francheses and *Immunityes* of or belonging to any the naturall borne subjects of this our Kingdome of England

within this our Kingdome and within all other of our Domynions to all intents and purposes as if they had beene abydeing and borne within this our Kingdome or any other of our Dominions . . . [Thorpe 1635]

Surrender of the Patent of Plymouth Colony to the Freemen, March 2, 1640:

. . . the said William Bradford doth by the free and full consent approbacon and agreement of the said Old Planters or Purchasers together with the likeing approbacon and acceptacon of the other part of the said Corporacon surrender into the hands of the whole court consisting of the Freemen of this Corporacon of New Plymouth all that the right and title power authorytie priviledges *immunities* and freedomes graunted in the said Letters Patents by the said Right Honorable Councell for New England reserveing his and their personall Right of Freemen together with the said Old Planters aforesaid except the said Lands before excepted, declaring the Freemen of this Corporacon together with all such as shall be legally admitted into the same his associates . . . [Thorpe 1862]

Charles II, Charter of Connecticut, April 23, 1662:

And further, Our Will and Pleasure is, and We do for Us, Our Heirs and Successors, ordain, declare, and grant unto the said Governor and Company, and their Successors, That all, and every the Subjects of Us, Our Heirs, or Successors, which shall go to inhabit within the said Colony, and every of their Children, which shall happen to be born there, or on the Seas in going thither, or returning from thence, shall have and enjoy all Liberties and *Immunities* of free and natural Subjects within any the Dominions of Us, Our Heirs or Successors, to all Intents, Constructions and Purposes whatsoever, as if they and every of them were born within the realm of England . . . [Thorpe 533]

Charles II, Charter of Carolina, March 24, 1663:

And furthermore, the patronage and advowsons of all the churches and chappels, which as Christian religion shall increase within the country, isles, islets and limits aforesaid, shall happen hereafter to be erected, together with license and power to build and found churches, chappels and oratories, in convenient and fit places, within the said bounds and limits, and to cause them to be Dedicated and consecrated according to the ecclesiastical laws of our Kingdom of England, together with all and singular the like, and as ample rights, jurisdictions, priviledges, prerogatives, royalties, liberties, *immunities* and franchises of what kind soever, within the countries, isles, islets and limits aforesaid.

[Thorpe 2744]

Charles II, Charter of Rhode Island, July 8, 1663:

And further, our will and pleasure is, and wee doe, for us, our heires and successours, ordeyn, declare and graunt, unto the sayd Governour and Company, and their successours, that all and every the subjects of us, our heires and successours, which are already planted and settled within our sayd Collony of Providence Plantations, or which shall hereafter goe to inhabit within the sayd Collony, and all and every of theire children by which have byn borne there, or which shall happen hereafter to bee borne there, or on the sea, goeing thither, or retourneing from thence, shall have and enjoye all libertyes and *immunityes* of free and naturall subjects within any the dominions of us, our heires or successours, to all intents, constructions and purposes, whatsoever, as if they, and every of them, were borne within the realme of England. . . .

[Thorpe 3220]

Carolina Proprietors, Declaration and Proposals, August 25, 1663:

We will grant the full benefit of these *immunities* to the undertakers and settlers which, by the charter, is granted to us (for our services to his majesty) in relation to freedom of customs, of tools of all sorts useful there, to be exported from England for the planters' use; and of certain growths of the plantations, as wine, oil, raisins of all sorts, olives, capers, wax, currants, almonds, and silks, to be imported into any of his majesty's dominions for seven years for each commodity, after four tons of every respective species is imported as aforesaid in one bottom. [Thorpe 2755]

New Jersey Proprietors, Concession and Agreement, February 10, 1664:

That all persons that are or shall become subjects of the King of England, and swear, or subscribe allegiance to the King, and faithfulness to the lords, shall be admitted to plant and become freemen of the said Province, and enjoy the freedoms and *immunities* hereafter express'd, until some stop or contradiction be made by us the Lords, or else the Governor, Council and Assembly, which shall be in force until the Lords see cause to the contrary: provided that such stop shall not any ways prejudice the right or continuance of any person that have been receiv'd before such stop or orders come from the General Assembly. [Thorpe 2536]

Carolina Proprietors, Concessions and Agreements, 1665:

[1] That all persons that are or shalbecome subjects to the King of England and sware or subscribe allegiance to the King and faithfulness to the Lords as above shalbe admitted to plant and become freemen of the Province and enjoy the freedomes and *Immunities* hereafter exprest until some stop or Contradiccon be

made by us the Lords or else by the Governor Councill and Assembly wch shalbe in force untill the Lords see Cause to the Contrary provided yt such stop shall not anywayes prejudice ye right or Continewance of any person that hath beene recd before such stop or order come from the Lords or Genll Assembly.

[Thorpe 2757]

[2] It is our will and desire that ye Inhabitants of the said Countyes and adventurers theither shall enjoye all the same *Immunityes* from Customes for exporting certine goods from these Realmes of England &c theither as ye Kinge hath been graciously pleased to graunt to us as alsoe for ye Incorragement of the Manufactrs of wine silke oyle ollives fruite almonds &c. menconed in the pattent have priveledge for bringing them Custome free into any of his Majties dominions for ye same time and upon ye same tearmes as we ourselves may by our Pattent. [Thorpe 2761]

Charles II, Charter of Carolina, June 30, 1665:

. . . And furthermore, the patronage and advowsons of all the churches and chapels, which, as Christian religion shall increase within the province, territory, isles, and limits aforesaid, shall happen hereafter to be erected; together with licence and power to build and found churches, chapels and oratories, in convenient and fit places within the said bounds and limits; and to cause them to be dedicated and consecrated, according to the ecclesiastical laws of our kingdom of England; together with all and singular the like and as ample rights, jurisdictions, privileges, prerogatives, royalties, liberties, *immunities,* and franchises of what kind soever, within the territory, isles, islets and limits aforesaid: To have, hold, use, exercise, and enjoy the same, as amply, fully and in as ample manner, as any Bishop of Durham, in our kingdom of England, ever heretofore had, held, used, or enjoyed, or of right ought or could have, use, or enjoy . . .

[Thorpe 2762–63]

New Jersey Propietors, Deed of Revision, July 1, 1676:

. . . And also all that his moiety or half part of all rivers, rivelets, mines, minerals, quarries, woods, fishings, hawkings, huntings, fowlings, and all other royalties, profits, forts franchises, liberties, governments, powers, priviledges, commodities, hereditaments and *immunities* whatsoever, to the said land and premises belonging . . . [Thorpe 2554]

Charles II, Charter of Pennsylvania, 1681:

And Wee doe furher, for us, our heires and Successors, Give and grant unto the said William Penn, his heires and assignes, free and absolute power, to Divide the said Countrey and Islands into Townes, Hundreds and Counties, and to erect and incorporate Townes into Borroughs, and Borroughs into Citties, and to make and constitute faires and Marketts therein, with all other convenient priviledges and *immunities,* according to the meritt of the inhabitants, and the fitnes of the places, and to doe all and every other thing and things touching the premisses, which to him or them shall seeme meet and requisite, albeit they be such as of their owne nature might otherwise require a more especiall comandment and Warrant then in these presents is expressed. [Thorpe 3040]

William and Mary, Charter of Massachusetts Bay, October 7, 1691:

And further Our Will and Pleasure is and Wee doe hereby for Us Our Heires and Successors Grant Establish and Ordaine That all and every of the Subjects of Us Our Heires and Successors which shall goe to and Inhabit within Our said Province and Territory and every of their Children which shall happen to be born there or on the Seas in goeing thither or returning from thence shall have and enjoy all Libertyes and *Immunities* of Free and naturall Subjects within any of the Dominions of Us Our Heires and Successors to all Intents Construccons and purposes whatsoever as if they and every of them were borne within this Our Realme of England . . . [Thorpe 1880–81]

Pennsylvania Frame of Government, November 7, 1696:

Provided always, and it is hereby enacted, That neither this act, nor any other act, or acts whatsoever, shall preclude, or debar the inhabitants of this province and territories, from claiming, having and enjoying any of the rights, privileges and *immunities,* which the said Proprietary, for himself, his heirs, and assigns, did formerly grant, or which of right belong unto them, the said inhabitants, by virtue of any law, charter or grants whatsoever, any thing herein contained to the contrary notwithstanding. [Thorpe 3076]

George II, Charter of Georgia, June 9, 1732:

. . . Also we do, for ourselves and successors, declare, by these presents, that all and every the persons which shall happen to be born within the said province, and every of their children and posterity, shall have and enjoy all liberties, franchises and *immunities* of free denizens and natural born subjects, within any of our dominions, to all intents and purposes, as if abiding and born within this our kingdom of Great-Britain, or any other of our dominions . . . [Thorpe 773]

First Continental Congress, Declaration and Resolves, October 14, 1774:

[1] That our ancestors, who first settled these colonies, were at the time of their emigration from the mother country, entitled to all the rights, liberties, and *immunities* of free and natural-born subjects within the realm of England. [JCC1 68]

[2] That these, his majesty's colonies, are likewise entitled to all the *immunities* and privileges granted & confirmed to them by royal charters, or secured by their several codes of provincial laws. [JCC1 69]

New Jersey Constitution, July 2, 1776:

[Article 19:] That there shall be no establishment of any one religious sect in this Province, in preference to another; and that no Protestant inhabitant of this Colony shall be denied the enjoyment of any civil right, merely on account of his religious principles; but that all persons, professing a belief in the faith of any Protestant sect, who shall demean themselves peaceably under the government, as hereby established, shall be capable of being elected into any office of profit or trust, or being a member of either branch of the Legislature, and shall fully and freely enjoy every privilege and *immunity,* enjoyed by others their fellow subjects. [Thorpe 2597–98]

United States Continental Congress, Draft Articles of Confederation, July 12, 1776:

[Article 6:] The Inhabitants of each Colony shall henceforth always have the same Rights, Liberties, Privileges, *Immunities* and Advantages, in the other Colonies, which the said Inhabitants now have, in all Cases whatever, except in those provided for by the next following Article. [DHRC1 80]

[Article 7:] The Inhabitants of each Colony shall enjoy all the Rights, Liberties, Privileges, *Immunities,* and Advantages, in Trade, Navigation, and Commerce, in any other Colony, and in going to and from the same from and to any Part of the World, which the Natives of such Colony . . . [DHRC1 80]

Pennsylvania Constitution, September 28, 1776:

[Frame of Government, Section 45:] Laws for the encouragement of virtue, and prevention of vice and immorality, shall be made and constantly kept in force, and provision shall be made for their due execution: And all religious societies or bodies of men heretofore united or incorporated for the advancement of religion or learning, or for other pious and charitable purposes, shall be encouraged and protected in the enjoyment of the privileges, *immunities* and estates which they were accustomed to enjoy, or could of right have enjoyed, under the laws and former constitution of this state. [Thorpe 3091]

Vermont Constitution, July 8, 1777:

[Frame of Government, Section 41:] Laws for the encouragement of virtue and prevention of vice and immorality, shall be made and constantly kept in force; and provision shall be made for their due execution; and all religious societies or bodies of men, that have or may be hereafter united and incorporated, for the advancement of religion and learning, or for other pious and charitable purposes, shall be encouraged and protected in the enjoyment of the privileges, *immunities* and estates which they, in justice, ought to enjoy, under such regulations, as the General Assembly of this State shall direct. [Thorpe 3748]

United States Articles of Confederation, November 15, 1777:

[Article IV:] The better to secure and perpetuate mutual friendship and intercourse among the people of the different states in this union, the free inhabitants of each of these states, paupers, vagabonds and fugitives from Justice excepted, shall be entitled to all privileges and *immunities* of free citizens in the several states; and the people of each state shall have free ingress and regress to and from any other state, and shall enjoy therein all the privileges of trade and commerce, subject to the same duties, impositions and restrictions as the inhabitants thereof respectively . . .

Massachusetts Constitution, March 2, 1780:

[Declaration of Rights, Article 12:] No subject shall be held to answer for any crimes or offence, until the same is fully and plainly, substantially, and formally, described to him; or be compelled to accuse, or furnish evidence against himself. And every subject shall have a right to produce all proofs that may be favorable to him; to meet the witnesses against him face to face, and to be fully heard in his defence by himself, or his counsel, at his election. And no subject shall be arrested, imprisoned, despoiled, or deprived of his property, *immunities,* or privileges, but out of the protection of the law, exiled, or deprived of his life, liberty, or estate, but by the judgment of his peers, or the law of the land. [Thorpe 1891]

[Frame of Government, Chapter V:1:1:] . . . it is declared, that the PRESIDENT AND FELLOWS OF HARVARD COLLEGE, in their corporate capacity, and their successors in that capacity, their officers and servants, shall have, hold, use, exercise, and enjoy, all the powers, authorities, rights, liberties, privileges, *immunities,* and franchises, which they now have, or are entitled to have, hold, use, exercise, and enjoy; and the same are hereby ratified and confirmed unto them, the said president and fellows of Harvard College, and to their successors, and to their officers and servants, respectively, forever. [Thorpe 1906–07]

[*Ibid.,* Chapter V:2:] . . . it shall be the duty of legislatures and magistrates, in all future periods of this common-wealth, to cherish the interests of literature and the sciences, and all seminaries of them; especially the university at Cambridge, public schools and grammar schools in the towns; to encourage private societies and public institutions, rewards and *immunities,* for the promotion of agriculture, arts, sciences, commerce, trades, manufactures, and a natural history of the country . . . [Thorpe 1907]

New Hampshire Constitution, June 7, 1784:

[Bill of Rights, Article 15:] No subject shall be held to answer for any crime, or offence, until the same is fully and plainly, substantially and formally, described to him; or be compelled to accuse or furnish evidence against himself. And every subject shall have a right to produce all proofs that may be favorable to himself; to meet the witnesses against him face to face, and to be fully heard in his defence by himself, and counsel. And no subject shall be arrested, imprisoned, despoiled, or deprived of his property, *immunities*, or privileges, put out of the protection of the law, exiled or deprived of his life, liberty, or estate, but by the judgment of his peers or the law of the land. [Thorpe 2455]

[Form of Government:] . . . it shall be the duty of the legislators and the magistrates, in all future periods of this government to cherish the interest of literature and the sciences and all seminaries and public schools, to encourage private and public institutions, rewards and *immunities* for the promotion or agriculture, arts, sciences, commerce, trades, manufactures and natural history of the country . . . [Thorpe 2467]

Vermont Constitution, July 4, 1786:

[Frame of Government, Article 38:] . . . And all religious societies, or bodies of men, that may be hereafter united or incorporated, for the advancement of religion and learning, or for other pious and charitable purposes, shall be encouraged and protected in the enjoyment of the privileges, *immunities*, and estates, which they in justice ought to enjoy, under such regulations as the General Assembly of this State shall direct. [Thorpe 3760]

Alexander Hamilton, *The Federalist*, No. 11, November 24, 1787:

A mature consideration of the objects suggested by these questions will justify a belief that the real disadvantages to Britain from such a state of things, conspiring with the prepossessions of a great part of the nation in favor of the America trade, and with the importunities of the West India islands, would produce a relaxation in her present system, and would let us into the enjoyment of privileges in the markets of those islands and elsewhere, from which our trade would derive the most substantial benefits. Such a point gained from the British government, and which could not be expected without an equivalent in exemptions and *immunities* in our markets, would be likely to have a correspondent effect on the conduct of other nations, who would not be inclined to see themselves altogether supplanted in our trade. [Fed. 138]

James Madison, *The Federalist*, No. 19, December 8, 1787:

We may form some judgment of this scheme of military coercion from a sample given by Thuanus. In Donawerth, a free and imperial city of the circle of Suabia, the Abbe de St. Croix enjoyed certain *immunities* which had been reserved to him. In the exercise of these, on some public occasions, outrages were committed on him by the people of the city. The consequence was that the city was put under the ban of the empire . . . [Fed. 179]

James Madison, *The Federalist*, No. 42, January 22, 1788:

The dissimilarity in the rules of naturalization has long been remarked as a fault in our system, and as laying a foundation for intricate and delicate questions. In the fourth article of the Confederation, it is declared "that the free inhabitants of each of these States, paupers, vagabonds, and fugitives from justice excepted, shall be entitled to all privileges and *immunities* of free citizens in the several States; and the people of each State shall, in every other, enjoy all the privileges of trade and commerce," etc. There is a confusion of language here, which is remarkable. Why the terms free inhabitants are used in one part of the article, free citizens in another, and people in another; or what was meant by superadding to "all privileges and *immunities* of free citizens," "all the privileges of trade and commerce," cannot easily be determined. . . . [Fed. 307]

"Brutus," No. 12, February 14, 1788:

. . . there is certainly as good reason why individuals, living in the same state, should have justice, as those who live in different states. Moreover, the constitution expressly declares, that "the citizens of each state shall be entitled to all the privileges and *immunities* of citizens in the several states." It will therefore be no fiction, for a citizen of one state to set forth, in a suit, that he is a citizen of another; for he that is entitled to all the privileges and *immunities* of a country, is a citizen of that country. And in truth, the citizen of one state will, under this constitution, be a citizen of every state. [DHRC16 121]

James Iredell, "Marcus," No. 4, March 12, 1788:

The first mentioned is, "That the Congress may grant monopolies in trade and commerce." Upon examining the Constitution, I find it expressly provided, "That no preference shall be given to the ports of one State over those of another;" and that "Citizens of each State shall be entitled to all privileges and *immunities* of citizens in the several States." These provisions appear to me to be calculated for the very purpose Mr. [George] Mason wishes to secure. . . . [DHRC16 380]

"An Impartial Citizen," No. 6, March 13, 1788:

. . . Does not a law that declares a legal pre-existent fact to be illegal, amount to a deprivation of men's rights? Does it not wantonly subject men to evils which the most consummate wisdom, joined with the most intuitive foresight, can neither foresee or advert. If such a law be admitted by the Constitution, can any *immunity* or declaration of rights counterveil its pernicious operation? Is there a planter in Virginia that would not detest a law, that would punish a man for having done what was lawful at the time of doing it? . . . [DHRC8 493]

Alexander Hamilton, *The Federalist*, No. 80, May 28, 1788:

It may be esteemed the basis of the Union, that "the citizens of each State shall be entitled to all the privileges and *immunities* of citizens of the several States." And if it be a just principle that every government ought to possess the means of executing its own provisions by its own authority, it will follow, that in order to the inviolable maintenance of that equality of privileges and *immunities* to which the citizens of the Union will be entitled, the national judiciary ought to preside in all cases in which one State or its citizens are opposed to another State or its citizens. . . . [Fed. 502]

Alexander Hamilton, *The Federalist*, No. 81, May 28, 1788:

It is inherent in the nature of sovereignty not to be amenable to the suit of an individual without its consent. This is the general sense, and the general practice of mankind; and the exemption, as one of the attributes of sovereignty, is now enjoyed by the government of every State in the Union. Unless, therefore, there is a surrender of this *immunity* in the plan of the convention, it will remain with the States, and the danger intimated must be merely ideal. . . . [Fed. 511]

Alexander Hamilton, *The Federalist*, No. 84, May 28, 1788:

. . . Is it one object of a bill of rights to declare and specify the political privileges of the citizens in the structure and administration of the government? This is done in the most ample and precise manner in the plan of the convention; comprehending various precautions for the public security, which are not to be found in any of the State constitutions. Is another object of a bill of rights to define certain *immunities* and modes of proceeding, which are relative to personal and private concerns? This we have seen has also been attended to, in a variety of cases, in the same plan. Adverting therefore to the substantial meaning of a bill of rights, it is absurd to allege that it is not to be found in the work of the convention. . . . [Fed. 536]

South Carolina Constitution, June 3, 1790:

[Article VIII, Section 2:] The rights, privileges, *immunities,* and estates of both civil and religious societies, and of corporate bodies, shall remain as if the constitution of this State had not been altered or amended. [Thorpe 3264]

Pennsylvania Constitution, September 2, 1790:

[Article VII, Section 3:] The rights, privileges *immunities,* and estates of religious societies and corporate bodies shall remain as if the constitution of this State had not been altered or amended. [Thorpe 3099]

INFERIOR COURTS

United States Constitution, September 17, 1787:

[Article I, Section 8:] [Congress shall have power] To constitute Tribunals *inferior* to the supreme *Court* . . .

[Article III, Section 1:] The judicial Power of the United States, shall be vested in one supreme *Court,* and in such *inferior Courts* as the Congress may from time to time ordain and establish. The Judges, both of the supreme and *inferior Courts,* shall hold their Offices during good Behaviour, and shall, at stated Times, receive for their Services, a Compensation, which shall not be diminished during their Continuance in Office.

* * * * *

Government of Rhode Island, March, 1641:

[Article 19:] It is ordered, that the major part of the *Courts,* being lawfully assembled at the place and houre appointed, shall have full Powre to transact the business that shall be Presented: Provided, it be the Major part of the Body entire, if it be the Generall *Court* (present) or the Major part of the Magistrates, with the Jury in the *inferior Courts;* and that such acts concluded and issued be of as full authority as if there were all present. Provided, there be due and seasonable notice given of every such *Court.* [Thorpe 3209]

Charles II, Charter of Rhode Island, July 8, 1663:

[Governor and company shall have power] . . . to apoynt, order and direct, erect and settle, such places and *courts* of jurisdiction, for the heareinge and determininge of all actions, cases, matters and things, happening within the sayd collonie and plantatione, and which shall be in dispute, and depending there, as they shall thinke fit; and alsoe to distinguish and sett forth the severall names and titles, duties, powers and limitts, of each *court,* office and officer, superior and *inferior* . . . [Thorpe 3215]

Fundamental Constitutions of Carolina, March 1, 1669:

[Article 47:] The proprietors' *courts* have a power to mitigate all fines and suspend all execution in criminal causes, either before or after sentence, in any of the other *inferior courts* respectively. [Thorpe 2778]

New Jersey Constitution, July 2, 1776:

[Article 12:] That the Judges of the Supreme *Court* shall continue in office for seven years: the Judges of the *Inferior Court* of Common Pleas in the several counties, Justices of the Peace, Clerks of the Supreme *Court,* Clerks of the *Inferior Court* of Common Pleas and Quarter Sessions, the Attorney-General, and Provincial Secretary, shall continue in office for five years: and the Provincial Treasurer shall continue in office for one year, and that they shall be severally appointed by the Council and Assembly, in manner aforesaid, and commissioned by the Governor, or, in his absence, the Vice-President of the Council. Provided always, that the said officers, severally, shall be capable of being re-appointed, at the end of the terms severally before limited; and that any of the said officers shall be liable to be dismissed, when adjudged guilty of misbehaviour, by the Council, on an impeachment of the Assembly. [Thorpe 2596]

Delaware Constitution, September 10, 1776:

[Article 13:] The justices of the *courts* of common pleas and orphans' *courts* shall have the power of holding *inferior courts* of chancery, as heretofore, unless the legislature shall otherwise direct. [Thorpe 565]

Vermont Constitution, July 8, 1777:

[Frame of Government, Section 27:] That the General Assembly, when legally formed, shall appoint times and places for county elections, and at such times and places, the freemen in each county respectively, shall have the liberty of choosing the judges of *inferior court* of common pleas, sheriff, justices of the peace, and judges of probates, commissioned by the Governor and Council, during good behavior, removable by the General Assembly upon proof of mal-administration. [Thorpe 3746]

Massachusetts Constitution, March 2, 1780:

[Frame of Government, Chapter VI:2:] No person holding the office of judge of the supreme judicial *court*—secretary—attorney-general—solicitor-general—treasurer or receiver-general—judge of probate—commissary-general—sheriff—clerk of the house of representatives—register of probate—register of deeds—clerk of the supreme judicial *court*—clerk of the *inferior court* of common pleas—

or officer of the customs, including in this description naval officers—shall at the same time have a seat in the senate or house of representatives . . .

[Thorpe 1909]

New Hampshire Constitution, June 2, 1784:

[Form of Government:] The clerks of the superior *court* of judicature, *inferior courts* of common pleas and general sessions of the peace, shall be appointed by the respective *courts* during pleasure. . . . [Thorpe 2467]

[*Ibid.*:] No person shall be capable of exercising at the same time, more than one of the following offices within this state, viz. Judge of probate, sheriff, register of deeds; and never more than two offices of profit, which may be held by appointment of the president, or president and council, or senate and house of representatives, or superior or *inferior courts;* military offices, and offices of justices of the peace, excepted. [Thorpe 2469]

[*Ibid.*:] No person holding the office of judge of the superior *court,* secretary, treasurer of the state, judge of probate, attorney-general, commissary-general, judge of the maritime *court,* or judge of the *court* of admiralty, military officers receiving pay from the continent or this state, excepting officers of the militia occasionally called forth on an emergency; judge of the *inferior court* of common pleas, register of deeds, president, professor or instructor of any college, sheriff, or officer of the customs, including naval-officers, shall at the same time have a seat in the senate or house of representatives, or council . . . [Thorpe 2469]

The Virginia Plan of Union, May 29, 1787:

[Article 9:] Res[olve]d that a National Judiciary be established to consist of one or more supreme tribunals, and of *inferior* tribunals to be chosen by the National Legislature, to hold their *offices* during good behaviour; and to receive punctually at stated times fixed compensation for their services, in which no increase or diminution shall be made so as to affect the persons actually in *office,* at the time of such increase or diminution. That the jurisdiction of the *inferior* tribunals shall be to hear and determine in the first instance, and of the supreme tribunal to hear & determine in the dernier resort, all piracies & felonies on the high seas, captures from an enemy; cases in which foreigners or citizens of other States applying to such jurisdictions may be interested, or which respect the collection of the National revenue; impeachments of any National *officers,* and questions which may involve the national peace and harmony.

[DHRC1 244–45]

Richard Henry Lee [?], "The Federal Farmer," No. 2, October 9, 1787:

Under one general government alone, there could be but one judiciary, one supreme and a proper number of *inferior courts*. I think it would be totally impracticable in this case to preserve a due administration of justice, and the real benefits of the jury trial of the vicinage—there are now supreme *courts* in each state in the union, and a great number of county and other *courts subordinate* to each supreme *court*—most of these supreme and *inferior courts* are itinerant, and hold their sessions in different parts every year of their respective states, counties and districts—with all these moving *courts,* our citizens, from the vast extent of the country, must travel very considerable distances from home to find the place where justice is administered. I am not for bringing justice so near to individuals as to afford them any temptation to engage in law suits; though I think it one of the greatest benefits in a good government, that each citizen should find a *court* of justice within a reasonable distance, perhaps, within a day's travel of his home; so that, without great inconveniences and enormous expense, he may have the advantages of his witnesses and jury—it would be impracticable to derive these advantages from one judiciary—the one supreme *court* at most could only set in the center of the union, and move once a year into the center of the eastern and southern extremes of it—and, in this case, each citizen, on an average, would travel 150 or 200 miles to find this *court*—that, however, *inferior courts* might be properly placed in the different counties, and districts of the union, the appellate jurisdiction would be intolerable and expensive. [Ford 289–90]

Richard Henry Lee [?], "The Federal Farmer," No. 3, October 10, 1787:

There are some powers proposed to be lodged in the general government in the judicial department, I think very unnecessarily, I mean powers respecting questions arising upon the internal laws of the respective states. It is proper the federal judiciary should have powers coextensive with the federal legislature—that is, the power of deciding finally on the laws of the union. By Art. 3, Sec. 2. the powers of the federal judiciary are extended (among other things) to all cases between a state and citizens of another state—between citizens of different states—between a state or the citizens thereof, and foreign states, citizens or subjects. Actions in all these cases, except against a state government, are now brought and finally determined in the law *courts* of the states respectively and as there are no words to exclude these *courts* of their jurisdiction in these cases, they will have concurrent jurisdiction with the *inferior federal courts* in them; and, therefore, if the new constitution be adopted without any amendment in this respect, all those numerous actions, now brought in the state *courts* between our citizens and foreigners, between citizens of different states, by state governments against foreigners, and by state governments against citizens of other states, may also be brought in the federal *courts;* and an appeal will lay in them from the state *courts* or federal *inferior courts* to the supreme judicial *court* of the union. In almost all these cases, either party may have the trial by jury in the state *courts;* except paper money and tender laws, which are wisely guarded against in the proposed constitution; justice may be obtained in these *courts* on reasonable terms; they must be more competent to proper decisions on the laws of their respective states, than the federal states can possibly be. I do not, in any point of view, see the need of opening a new jurisdiction in these causes... [Ford 306–7]

Noah Webster, *An Examination into the Leading Principles of the Federal Constitution*, October 17, 1787:

[1] With respect to other civil and criminal actions,the powers and jurisdiction of the several judiciaries of each state, remain unimpaired. Nor is there anything novel in allowing appeals to the supreme *court*. Actions are mostly to be tried in the state where the crimes are committed—But appeals are allowed under our present confederation, and no person complains; nay, were there no appeal, every man would have reason to complain, especially when a final judgement, in an *inferior court,* should affect property to a large amount. But why is an objection raised against an appellate jurisdiction in the supreme *court,* respecting fact as well as law? Is it less safe to have the opinions of two juries than of one? I suspect many people will think this is no defect in the constitution.... [Ford 53]

[2] But the truth is, the creation of all *inferior courts* is in the power of Congress; and the constitution provides that Congress may make such exceptions from the right of appeals as they shall judge proper. When these *courts* are erected, their jurisdictions will be ascertained, and in small actions, Congress will doubtless direct that a sentence in a *subordinate court* shall, to a certain amount, be definite and final. All objections therefore to the judicial powers of the federal *courts* appear to me as trifling as any of the preceding. [Ford 53–54]

Hugh Williamson, Address at Edenton, North Carolina, November 8, 1787:

[1] ... The powers that are now to be committed to the national Legislature, as they are detailed in the 8th section of the first article, have already been chiefly delegated to the Congress under one form or another, except those which are contained in the first paragraph of that section. And the objects that are now to be submitted to the Supreme Judiciary, or to the *Inferior Courts,* are those which naturally arise from the constitutional laws of Congress.... [DHRC16 203]

[2] ... The authors of this remark have not fully considered the question, else they must have recollected that the poor of this country have little to do with foreigners, or with the citizens of distant States. They do not consider that there may be an *Inferior Court* in every State; nor have they recollected that the appeals being with such exceptions, and under such regulations as Congress shall make, will never be permitted for trifling sums, or under trivial pretences, unless we

can suppose that the national Legislature shall be composed of knaves and fools. . . . [DHRC16 204]

Alexander White [?], "An Independent Freeholder," January 18, 1788:

. . . All men agree that a general Government for the union is absolutely necessary. How nugatory and vain would the acts of that government be were there no *courts* to enforce their execution? It is objected that the judges will not be independent, the words of the Constitution are, "The judges both of the supreme and *inferior courts* shall hold their offices during good behaviour, and shall at stated times receive for their services a compensation, which shall not be diminished during their continuance in office." Let the objector pen a more effectual clause. . . . [DHRC8 312]

James Madison, *The Federalist*, No. 47, January 30, 1788:

The language of Virginia is still more pointed on this subject. Her constitution declares, "that the legislative, executive, and judiciary departments shall be separate and distinct; so that neither exercise the powers properly belonging to the other; nor shall any person exercise the powers of more than one of them at the same time, except that the justices of county *courts* shall be eligible to either House of Assembly." Yet we find not only this express exception, with respect to the members of the *inferior courts*, but that the chief magistrate, with his executive council, are appointable by the legislature; that two members of the latter are triennially displaced at the pleasure of the legislature; and that all the principal offices, both executive and judiciary, are filled by the same department. . . . [Fed. 341–42]

Alexander C. Hanson. *Remarks on the Proposed Plan of a Federal Government*, c. January 31, 1788:

[1] The judiciary power is to be vested in one supreme *court*, fixed at the seat of government, with the ease and convenience of the people, the congress may hereafter appoint *inferior courts* in each of the states. The jurisdiction of this supreme *court* is to be partly original, and partly appellate. With respect to the extent of either, there can be no possible doubt, as there is neither ambiguity nor uncertainty in the relative expressions. [Ford 236]

[2] One doubt arising on the judiciary article is, whether in these cases of appellate jurisdiction, the appeal lies both from the state *courts*, and the *inferior federal courts*, or only from the former, or only from the latter. [Ford 237]

[3] Another doubt is, whether the *inferior courts* are to be branches of the supreme *court*, constituted for convenience, and having equal jurisdiction, both original and appellate, with the supreme *court*, or whether the *inferior courts* are to be

confined to an original jurisdiction in those cases, wherein the supreme *court* has appellate jurisdiction. [Ford 237]

[4] I shall not presume to decide absolutely on the genuine construction of an article, which is said to have caused much private debate and perplexity. I am however fully persuaded, that, as the article speaks of an original and appellate jurisdiction, of a supreme *court,* and *inferior courts;* and, as there is no intimation of appeals from the several state tribunals, the *inferior federal courts* are intended to have original jurisdiction in all cases, wherein the supreme *court* has appellate jurisdiction; and the appeal lies only from them. I can, almost, with confidence, maintain, that, as there is no express clause, or necessary implication, to oust the jurisdiction of state *courts,* an action, after the adoption of the plan, may be instituted in any *court,* having, at this time, a jurisdiction. And if an action be brought in a state *court,* I do not, at present, perceive, that it can, in any manner, be transferred to the supreme or *inferior federal court.* [Ford 237]

[5] According then to the best of my judgment the affair stands thus. The supreme federal *court* will have an exclusive original jurisdiction in all cases relative to the rights of ambassadors, other ministers, and consuls; because, as I humbly conceive, the several state governments have at this time nothing to do with these cases. With respect to the cases, in which a state may be party, the supreme federal *court,* and the several state *courts,* will have, I conceive, concurrent original jurisdiction, provided a state may, at this time, institute an action in its own name, in the *courts* of another state. The *inferior federal courts,* and the state *courts,* will, I conceive, have concurrent original jurisdiction in all the enumerated cases wherein an appeal lies to the supreme *court,* except only the cases created by or under the proposed constitution, in which, as they do not now exist, the *inferior federal courts* will have exclusive jurisdiction. From the state *inferior courts,* I further apprehend, that an appeal will lie, in all cases, to their own high *courts* of appeal, as heretofore. [Ford 237–38]

Luther Martin, "Genuine Information," No. 10, February 1, 1788:

[1] By the third article, the judicial power of the United States is vested in one supreme *court,* and in such *inferior courts,* as the Congress may from time to time ordain and establish.—These *courts,* and these only, will have a right to decide upon the laws of the United States, and all questions arising upon their construction, and in a judicial manner to carry those laws into execution; to which the *courts* both superior and *inferior* of the respective States and their judges and other magistrates are rendered incompetent. . . . [DHRC16 8]

[2] . . . Should a citizen of Virginia, Pennsylvania, or any other of the United States be indebted to, or have debts due from, a citizen of this State, or any other claim be subsisting on one side or the other, in consequence of commercial or other transactions, it is only in the *courts* of Congress that either can apply for redress. The case is the same should any claims subsist between citizens of

this State and foreigners, merchants, mariners and others, whether of a commercial or of any other nature, they must be prosecuted in the same *courts;* and though in the first instance they may be brought in the *inferior,* yet an appeal may be made to the supreme judiciary, even from the remotest State in the union. [DHRC16 8–9]

[3] And in all those cases where the general government has jurisdiction in civil questions, the proposed constitution not only makes no provision for the trial by jury in the first instance, but by its appellate jurisdiction absolutely takes away that inestimable priviledge, since it expressly declares the supreme *court* shall have appellate jurisdiction both as to law and fact.—Should, therefore, a jury be adopted in the *inferior court,* it would only be a needless expence, since on an appeal the determination of that jury even on questions of fact, however honest and upright, is to be of no possible effect—the supreme *court* is to take up all questions of fact—to examine the evidence relative thereto—to decide upon them in the same manner as if they had never been tried by a jury—Nor is trial by jury secured in criminal cases; it is true, that in the first instance, in the *inferior court* the trial is to be by jury, in this and in this only, is the difference between criminal and civil cases; but, Sir, the appellate jurisdiction extends, as I have observed, to cases criminal as well as to civil, and on the appeal the *court* is to decide not only on the law but on the fact, if, therefore, even in criminal cases the general government is not satisfied with the verdict of the jury, its officer may remove the prosecution to the supreme *court,* and there the verdict of the jury is to be of no effect, but the judges of this *court* are to decide upon the fact as well as the law, the same as in civil cases. [DHRC16 9]

[4] . . . Nor was this the effect of inattention, nor did it arise from any real difficulty in establishing and securing jury trials by the proposed constitution, if the convention had wished so to do—But the same reason influenced here as in the case of the establishment of *inferior courts;*—as they could not trust State judges, so would they not confide in State juries. . . . [DHRC16 10]

Samuel Bryan, "Centinel," No. 14, February 5, 1788:

. . . They may likewise oblige all proceedings of a judicial nature to be stamped to give them effect—those stamp duties may be imposed to any amount they please, and under the pretence of securing the collection of these duties, and to prevent the laws which imposed them from being evaded, the Congress may bring the decision of all questions relating to the conveyance, disposition and rights of property and every question relating to contracts between man and man into the *courts* of the general government.—Their *inferior courts* in the first instance and the superior *court* by appeal. . . . [DHRC16 33]

Alexander White, "To the Citizens of Virginia," February 22, 1788:

They assert, that in appeals from *courts* proceeding according to the rules of the civil law, the facts as well as the law will be re-examined, and even new facts brought forward in the *court* of appeals. These gentlemen, perhaps it may be said, are not civilians, and may have been mistaken, but they seem to have read Blackstone, and from him they must have learned "that it is a practice unknown to our law, when a superior *court* is reviewing the sentence of an *inferior,* to examine the justice of the former decree, by evidence that was never produced below," that these misrepresentations were not made through inattention, but designedly to deceive, is evident, because in the course of their discussion, they have drawn inferrences from each fact so mistated. [DHRC8 403]

"The Impartial Examiner," No. 1, February 27, 1788:

The supreme *court* is another branch of foederal authority, which wears the aspect of imperial jurisdiction, clad in dread array, and spreading its wide domain into all parts of the continent. This is to be co-extensive with the legislature, and, like that, is to swallow up all other *courts* of judicature.—For what is that judicial power which "shall extend to all cases in law and equity" in some having "original," in all others "appellate jurisdiction," but an establishment universal in its operation? And what is that "appellate jurisdiction both as to law and fact," but an establishment, which may in effect operate as original jurisdiction?—Or what is an appeal to enquire into facts after a solemn adjudication in any *court* below, but a trial de novo? And do not such trials clearly imply an incompetency in the *inferior courts* to exercise any kind of judicial authority with rectitude? Hence, will not this eventually annihilate their whole jurisdiction?... [DHRC8 423]

"Brutus," No. 14, February 28, 1788:

[1] The appellate jurisdiction granted to the supreme *court,* in this paragraph, has justly been considered as one of the most objectionable parts of the constitution: under this power, appeals may be had from the *inferior courts* to the supreme, in every case to which the judicial power extends, except in the few instances in which the supreme *court* will have original jurisdiction. [DHRC16 256]

[2] . . . I have not been fortunate enough to see in any publication this clause taken up and considered. It is certain however, they do not admit the explanation which those who oppose the constitution give it, or otherwise they would not so frequently charge them with want of candor, for alledging that it takes away the trial by jury, appeals from an *inferior* to a superior *court,* as practised in the civil law *courts,* are well understood. In these *courts,* the judges determine both on the law and the fact; and appeals are allowed from the *inferior* to the superior *courts,* on the whole merits: the superior tribunal will re-examine all the facts as well as the law, and frequently new facts will be introduced, so as many times to render the cause in the *court* of appeals very different from what it was in the *court* below. [DHRC16 257]

[3] If we understand the appellate jurisdiction in any other way, we shall be left utterly at a loss to give it a meaning; the common law is a stranger to any such jurisdiction: no appeals can lie from any of our common law *courts,* upon the merits of the case; the only way in which they can go up from an *inferior* to a superior tribunal is by habeas corpus before a hearing, or by certiorari, or writ of error, after they are determined in the *subordinate courts;* but in no case, when they are carried up, are the facts re-examined, but they are always taken as established in the *inferior court.* [DHRC16 258]

"Brutus," No. 14, March 6, 1788:

[1] . . . An appeal from one *court* and jury, to another *court* and jury, is a thing altogether unknown in the laws of our state, and in most of the states in the union. A practice of this kind prevails in the eastern states; actions are there commenced in the *inferior courts,* and an appeal lies from them on the whole merits to the superior *courts:* the consequence is well known, very few actions are determined in the *lower courts;* it is rare that a case of any importance is not carried by appeal to the supreme *court,* and the jurisdiction of the *inferior courts* is merely nominal; this has proved so burthensome to the people in Massachusetts, that it was one of the principal causes which excited the insurrection in that state, in the year past; very few sensible and moderate men in that state but what will admit, that the *inferior courts* are almost entirely useless, and answer very little purpose, save only to accumulate costs against the poor debtors who are already unable to pay their just debts. [DHRC16 258]

[2] But as this system now stands, there is to be as many *inferior courts* as Congress may see fit to appoint, who are to be authorised to originate and in the first instance to try all the cases falling under the description of this article; there is no security that a trial by jury shall be had in these *courts,* but the trial here will soon become, as it is in Massachusetts' *inferior courts,* mere matter of form; for an appeal may be had to the supreme *court* on the whole merits. This *court* is to have power to determine in law and in equity, on the law and the fact, and this *court* is exalted above all other power in the government, subject to no controul, and so fixed as not to be removeable, but upon impeachment, which I shall hereafter shew, is much the same thing as not to be removeable at all. [DHRC16 331]

Luther Martin, "To the Citizens of Maryland," No. 2, March 21, 1788:

[1] When this clause was introduced, it was not established that *inferior continental courts* should be appointed for trial of all questions arising on treaties and on the laws of the general government, and it was my wish and hope that

every question of that kind would have been determined, in the first instance, in the *courts* of the respective states . . . [DHRC16 452–53]

[2] . . . It was afterwards altered and amended (if it can be called an amendment) to the form in which it stands in the system now published, and, as *inferior* continental, and not state, *courts* are originally to decide on those questions, it is now worse than useless; for being so altered as to render the treaties and laws made under the general government superior to our constitution, if the system is adopted, it will amount to a total and unconditional surrender to that government, by the citizens of this state, of every right and privilege secured to them by our citizens of this state, of every right and privilege secured to them by our constitution, and an express compact and stipulation with the general government, that it may, at its discretion, make laws in direct violation of those rights . . . [DHRC16 453]

[3] That I ''voted an appeal should lay to the supreme judiciary of the United States, for the correction of all errors both in law and fact,'' in rendering judgment, is most true; and it is equally true that if it had been so ordained by the Constitution, the supreme judiciary would only have had an appellate jurisdiction, of the same nature with that possessed by our high *court* of appeals, and could not in any respect intermeddle with any fact decided by a jury; but as the clause now stands, an appeal being given in general terms from the *inferior courts,* both as to law and fact, it not only doth, but was avowedly intended to give a power very different from what our *court* of appeals, or any *court* of appeals in the United States or in England enjoys—a power of the most dangerous and alarming nature, that of setting at nought the verdict of a jury, and having the same facts which they had determined, without any regard or respect to their determination, examined and ultimately decided by the judges themselves; and that by judges immediately appointed by the government. [DHRC16 453]

Melancton Smith, *An Address to the People of the State of New York*, c. April 1788:

. . . As a higher authority than these, I appeal to the amendments proposed by the Massachusetts; these are to be considered as the sense of that body upon the defects of the system. And it is a fact, which I will venture to assert, that a large majority of the convention were of opinion, that a number of additional alterations ought to be made. Upon reading the articles which they propose as amendments, it will appear that they object to indefinite powers in the legislature—to the power of laying direct taxes—to the authority of regulating elections—to the extent of the judicial powers, both as it respects the *inferior court* and the appellate jurisdiction—to the smallness of the representation, &c. . . .

[Ford 103–04]

Alexander Hamilton, *The Federalist*, No. 81, May 28, 1788:

[1] Having now examined, and, I trust, removed the objections to the distinct and independent organization of the Supreme *Court,* I proceed to consider the propriety of the power of constituting *inferior courts,* and the relations which will subsist between these and the former. [Fed. 509]

[2] This power has been absurdly represented as intended to abolish all the county *courts* in the several States, which are commonly called *inferior courts.* But the expressions of the Constitution are, to constitute "tribunals *INFERIOR* TO THE SUPREME *COURT.;* and the evident design of the provision is to enable the institution of local *courts, subordinate* to the Supreme, either in States or larger districts. It is ridiculous to imagine that county *courts* were in contemplation. [Fed. 509n]

[3] The power of constituting *inferior courts* is evidently calculated to obviate the necessity of having recourse to the Supreme *Court* in every case of federal cognizance. It is intended to enable the national government to institute or authorize, in each State or district of the United States, a tribunal competent to the determination of matters of national jurisdiction within its limits. [Fed. 509]

[4] I am not sure, but that it will be found highly expedient and useful, to divide the United States into four or five or half a dozen districts; and to institute a federal *court* in each district, in lieu of one in every State. The judges of these *courts,* with the aid of the State judges, may hold circuits for the trial of causes in the several parts of the respective districts. Justice through them may be administered with ease and despatch; and appeals may be safely circumscribed within a narrow compass. This plan appears to me at present the most eligible of any that could be adopted; and in order to it, it is necessary that the power of constituting *inferior courts* should exist in the full extent in which it is to be found in the proosed Constitution. [Fed. 510]

[5] . . . In cases in which a State might happen to be a party, it would ill suit its dignity to be turned over to an *inferior tribunal.* [Fed. 511]

[6] Let us resume the train of our observations. We have seen that the original jurisdiction of the Supreme *Court* would be confined to two classes of causes, and those of a nature rarely to occur. In all other cases of federal cognizance, the original jurisdiction would appertain to the *inferior tribunals;* and the Supreme *Court* would have nothing more than an appellate jurisdiction, "with such exceptions and under such regulations as the Congress shall make." [Fed. 512]

[7] But it does not follow that the re-examination of a fact once ascertained by a jury, will be permitted in the Supreme *Court.* Why may not it be said, with the strictest propriety, when a writ of error is brought from an *inferior* to a superior *court* of law in this State, that the latter has jurisdiction of the fact as well as the law? It is true it cannot institute a new inquiry concerning the fact, but it takes cognizance of it as it appears upon the record, and pronounces the

law arising upon it. This is jurisdiction of both fact and law; nor is it even possible to separate them. Though the common-law *courts* of this State ascertain disputed facts by a jury, yet they unquestionably have jurisdiction of both fact and law; and accordingly when the former is agreed in the pleadings, they have no recourse to a jury, but proceed at once to judgment. I contend, therefore, on this ground, that the expressions, "appellate jurisdiction, both as to law and fact," do not necessarily imply a re-examination in the Supreme *Court* of facts decided by juries in the *inferior courts*. [Ford 512–13]

Alexander Hamilton, *The Federalist*, No. 82, May 28, 1788:

[1] The only thing in the proposed Constitution, which wears the appearance of confining the causes of federal cognizance to the federal *courts,* is contained in this passage:—"The JUDICIAL POWER of the United States shall be vested in one Supreme *Court,* and in such *inferior courts* as the Congress shall from time to time ordain and establish." This might either be construed to signify, that the supreme and *subordinate courts* of the Union should alone have the power of deciding those causes to which their authority is to extend; or simply to denote, that the organs of the national judiciary should be one Supreme *Courts,* and as many *subordinate courts* as Congress should think proper to appoint; or in other words, that the United States should exercise the judicial power with which they are to be invested, through one supreme tribunal, and a certain number of *inferior* ones, to be instituted by them. The first excludes, the last admits, the concurrent jurisdiction of the State tribunals; and as the first would amount to an alienation of State power by implication, the last appears to me the most natural and the most defensible construction. [Fed. 515–16]

[2] Here another question occurs: What relation would subsist between the national and State *courts* in these instances of concurrent jurisdiction? I answer, that an appeal would certainly lie from the latter, to the Supreme *Court* of the United States. The Constitution in direct terms gives an appellate jurisdiction to the Supreme *Court* in all the enumerated cases of federal cognizance in which it is not to have an original one, without a single expression to confine its operation to the *inferior federal courts*. The objects of appeal, not the tribunals from which it is to be made, are alone contemplated. From this circumstance, and from the reason of the thing, it ought to be construed to extend to the State tribunals. Either this must be the case, or the local *courts* must be excluded from a concurrent jurisdiction in matters of national concern, else the judiciary authority of the Union may be eluded at the pleasure of every plaintiff or prosecutor. . . . [Fed. 516–17]

[3] But could an appeal be made to lie from the State *courts* to the *subordinate federal judicatories?* This is another of the questions which have been raised, and of greater difficulty than the former. The following considerations countenance the affirmative. The plan of the convention, in the first place, authorizes the national legislature "to constitute tribunals *inferior to the Supreme Court.*"

It declares, in the next place, that "the JUDICIAL POWER of the United States shall be vested in one Supreme *Court,* and in such *inferior courts* as Congress shall ordain and establish"; and it then proceeds to enumerate the cases to which this judicial power shall extend. It afterwards divides the jurisdiction of the Supreme *Court* into original and appellate, but gives no definition of that of the *subordinate courts.* The only outlines described for them, are that they shall be "*inferior* to the Supreme *Court,*" and that they shall not exceed the specified limits of the federal judiciary. Whether their authority shall be original or appellate, or both, is not declared. All this seems to be left to the discretion of the legislature. And this being the case, I perceive at present no impediment to the establishment of an appeal from the State *courts* to the *subordinate national tribunals;* and many advantages attending the power of doing it maybe imagined. It would diminish the motives to the multiplication of federal *courts,* and would admit of arrangements calculated to contract the appellate jurisdiction of the Supreme *Court.* The State tribunals may then be left with a more entire charge of federal causes; and appeals, in most cases in which they may be deemed proper, instead of being carried to the Supreme *Court,* may be made to lie from the State *courts* to district courts of the Union. [Fed. 517–18]

Georgia Constitution, May 6, 1789:

[Article III, Section 1:] A superior *court* shall be held in each county twice in every year; in which shall be tried, and brought to final decision, all causes, civil and criminal, except such as may be subject to a Federal *court,* and such as may, by law, be referred to *inferior* jurisdiction. [Thorpe 788]

South Carolina Constitution, June 3, 1790:

[Article III, Section 1:] The Judicial power shall be vested in such superior and *inferior courts* of law and equity as the legislature shall, from time to time, direct and establish. [Thorpe 3263]

INFERIOR OFFICERS

United States Constitution, September 17, 1787:

[Article II, Section 2:] He [the President] shall have Power, by and with the Advice and Consent of the Senate, to make Treaties, provided two thirds of the Senators present concur; and he shall nominate, and by and with the Advice and Consent of the Senate, shall appoint Ambassadors, other public Ministers and Consuls, Judges of the supreme Court, and all other *Officers* of the United States, whose Appointments are not herein otherwise provided for, and which shall be established by Law: but the Congress may by Law vest the Appointment of such *inferior Officers,* as they think proper, in the President alone, in the Courts of Law, or in the Heads of Departments.

* * * * *

Charles I, Charter of Massachusetts Bay, March 4, 1629:

[1] [The Governor and Company shall have power] . . . to make, ordeine, and establishe all Manner of wholesome and reasonable Orders, Lawes, Statutes, and Ordinces, Direccons, and Instruccons, not contrairie to the Lawes of this our Realme of England, as well for setling of the Formes and Ceremonies of Governmt and Magistracy fitt and necessary for the said Plantacon, and the Inhabitants there, and for nameing and setting of all sorts of *Officers,* both superior and *inferior,* which they shall finde needefull for that Government and Plantacon, and the distinguishing and setting forth of the severall duties, Powers, and Lymytts of every such *Office* and Place, and the Formes of such Oathes warrantable by the Lawes and Statutes of this our Realme of England, as shalbe respectivelie ministred unto them for the Execucon of the said severall *Offices* and Places; as also for the disposing and ordering of the Eleccons of such of the said *Officers* as shalbe annuall, and of such others as shalbe to succeede in Case of Death or Removeall, and ministring the said Oathes to the newe elected *Officers* . . . [Thorpe 1857]

[2] . . . and by theis Presents for Us, our Heires, and Successors, ordeyning and appointing, that all such Orders, Lawes, Statuts and Ordinances, Instruccons and Direccons, as shalbe soe made by the Governor, or Deputie Governor of the said Company, and such of the Assistants and Freemen as aforesaide, and published in Writing, under their comon Seale, shalbe carefullie and dulie observed, kept, performed, and putt in Execucon, according to the true Intent and Meaning of the same; and theis our Letters-patents, or the Duplicate or exemplificacon thereof, shalbe to all and everie such *Officers,* superior and *inferior,* from Tyme to Tyme, for the putting of the same Orders, Lawes, Statutes, and Ordinances, Instruccons, and Direccons, in due Execucon against Us, our Heires and Successors, a sufficient Warrant and Discharge. [Thorpe 1857–58]

Charles II, Charter of Connecticut, April 23, 1662:

[1] [The Governor and Company shall have power] . . . from Time to Time to Make, Ordain, and Establish all manner of wholesome, and reasonable Laws, Statutes, Ordinances, Directions, and Instructions, not Contrary to the Laws of this Realm of England, as well for settling the Forms, and Ceremonies of Government, and Magistracy, fit and necessary for the said Plantation, and the Inhabitants there, as for Naming, and Stiling all Sorts of *Officers,* both Superior and *Inferior,* which they shall find Needful for the Government, and Plantation of the said Colony, and the distingishing and setting forth of the several Duties, Powers, and Limits of every such *Office* and Place, and the Forms of such Oaths not being contrary to the Laws and Statutes of this Our Realm of England, to be administered for the Execution of the said several *Offices* and Places as also for the disposing and ordering of the Election of such of the said *Officers* as are to be annually chosen, and of such others as shall succeed in case of Death or Removal, and administring the said Oath to the newly-elected *Officers,* and granting necessary Commissions . . . [Thorpe 533–34]

[2] . . . and by these Presents for Us, Our Heirs and Successors, ordaining and appointing, that all such Laws, Statutes and Ordinances, Instructions, Impositions and Directions as shall be so made by the Governor, Deputy-Governor, and Assistants as aforesaid, and published in Writing under their Common Seal, shall carefully and duly be observed, kept, performed, and put in Execution, according to the true Intent and Meaning of the same, and these Our Letters Patents, or the Duplicate, or Exemplification thereof, shall be to all and such *Officers,* Superiors and *Inferiors* from Time to Time, for the putting of the same Orders, Laws, Statutes, Ordinances, Instructions, and Directions in due Execution, against Us, Our Heirs and Successors, a sufficient Warrant and Discharge. [Thorpe 534]

Charles II, Charter of Rhode Island, July 8, 1663:

[1] [The Governor and Company shall have power] . . . to apoynt, order and direct, erect and settle, such places and courts of jurisdiction, for the heareinge

and determininge of all actions, cases, matters and things, happening within the sayd collonie and plantatione, and which shall be in dispute, and depending there, as they shall thinke fit; and alsoe to distinguish and sett forth the severall names and titles, duties, powers and limitts, of each court, *office* and *officer,* superior and *inferior;* and alsoe to contrive and apoynt such formes of oaths and attestations, not repugnant, but, as neare as may bee, agreeable, as aforesayd, to the lawes and statutes of this oure realme, as are conveniente and requisite, with respect to the due administration of justice, and due execution and discharge of all *offices* and places of trust by the persons that shall bee therein concerned; and alsoe to regulate and order the waye and manner of all elections to *offices* and places of trust . . . [Thorpe 3215]

[2] And these our letters patent, or the duplicate or exemplification thereof, shall bee to all and everie such *officer,* superiour or *inferiour,* from tyme to tyme, for the putting of the same orders, lawes, statutes, ordinances, instructions and directions, in due execution, against us, oure heires and successours, a sufficient warrant and discharge. [Thorpe 3216]

New Hampshire Constitution, January 5, 1776:

That general and field *officers* of the militia, on any vacancy, be appointed by the two houses, and all *inferior officers* be chosen by the respective companies. [Thorpe 2453]

New Jersey Constitution, July 2, 1776:

[Article 10:] That captains, and all other *inferior officers* of the militia, shall be chosen by the companies, in the respective counties; but field and general officers, by the Council and Assembly. [Thorpe 2596]

Vermont Constitution, July 4, 1786:

[Frame of Government, Article 19:] The inhabitants of this Commonwealth shall be trained and armed for its defence, under such regulations, restrictions, and exceptions, as the General Assembly shall by law direct. The several companies of militia shall, as often as vacancies happen, elect their captains and other *inferior officers;* and the captains and subalterns shall nominate and recommend the field *officers* of their respective regiments, who shall appoint their staff-*officers.* [Thorpe 3758]

The Virginia Plan of Union, May 29, 1787:

[Article 9:] Res[olve]d that a National Judiciary be established to consist of one or more supreme tribunals, and of *inferior* tribunals to be chosen by the National Legislature, to hold their *offices* during good behaviour; and to receive punctually at stated times fixed compensation for their services, in which no increase or diminution shall be made so as to affect the persons actually in *office*, at the time of such increase or diminution. That the jurisdiction of the *inferior* tribunals shall be to hear & determine in the first instance, and of the supreme tribunal to hear and determine in the dernier resort, all piracies & felonies on the high seas, captures from an enemy; cases in which foreigners or citizens of other States applying to such jurisdictions may be interested, or which respect the collection of the National revenue; impeachments of any National *officers*, and questions which may involve the national peace and harmony. [DHRC1 244]

Tench Coxe, *An Examination of the Constitution for the United States of America*, September 26, 1787:

. . . He [the President] will have no authority to make a treaty, without two-thirds of the senate, nor can he appoint ambassadors or other great *officers* without their approbation, which will remove the idea of patronage and influence, and of personal obligation and dependence. The appointment of even the *inferior officers* may be taken out of his hands by an act of congress at any time; he can create no nobility or titles of honor, nor take away *offices* during good behaviour. His person is not so much protected as that of a member of the house of representatives; for he may be proceeded against like any other man in the ordinary course of law. He appoints no *officer* of the separate states. . . .
[Ford 139]

Richard Henry Lee, "The Federal Farmer," No. 4, October 12, 1787:

It is doubtful whether the vice-president is to have any qualifications; none are mentioned; but he may serve as president, and it may be inferred, he ought to be qualified therefore as the president; but the qualifications of the president are required only of the person to be elected president. By art. 2, sect. 2, "But the congress may by law vest the appointment of such *inferior officers* as they think proper in the president alone, in the courts of law, or in the heads of the departments:" Who are *inferior officers?* May not a congress disposed to vest the appointment of all *officers* in the president, under this clause, vest the appointment of almost every *officer* in the president alone, and destroy the check mentioned in the first part of the clause, and lodged in the senate. It is true, this check is badly lodged, but then some check upon the first magistrate in appointing *officers*, ought it appears by the opinion of the convention, and by the general opinion, to be established in the constitution. . . . [Ford 310–11]

Georgia Constitution, May 6, 1789:

[Article IV, Section 2:] All elections shall be by ballot, and the house of representatives, in all appointments of State *officers*, shall vote for three persons; and a list of the three persons having the highest number of votes shall be signed by the speaker, and sent to the senate, which shall from such list determine, by a majority of their votes, the *officer* elected, except militia *officers* and the secretaries of the governor, who shall be appointed by the governor alone, under such regulations and restrictions as the general assembly may prescribe. The general assembly may vest the appointment of *inferior officers* in the governor, the courts of justice, or in such other manner as they may by law establish.

[Thorpe 789]

INHABITANT, INHABITANTS

[Note: This list is selective. It represents a complete search only of constitutional documents dealing with the colonies and states as a whole; the rest of the list contains a sample of one out of twenty-five occurrences in the remaining documents in the database.]

United States Constitution, September 17, 1787:

[Article I, Section 2:] No Person shall be a Representative who shall not have attained to the Age of twenty five Years, and been seven Years a Citizen of the United States, and who shall not, when elected, be an *Inhabitant* of that State in which he shall be chosen.

[Article I, Section 3:] No Person shall be a Senator who shall not have attained to the Age of thirty Years, and been nine Years a Citizen of the United States, and who shall not, when elected, be an *Inhabitant* of that State for which he shall be chosen.

[Article II, Section 1:] The Electors shall meet in their respective States, and vote by Ballot for two Persons, of whom one at least shall not be an *Inhabitant* of the same State with themselves. And they shall make a List of all the Persons voted for, and of the Number of Votes for each; which List they shall sign and certify, and transmit sealed to the Seat of the Government of the United States, directed to the President of the Senate. . . .

* * * * *

Elizabeth I, Letters Patent to Sir Humphrey Gilbert, June 11, 1578:

. . . And if the saide Sir Humfrey, his heires and assignes, shall not make or cause to bee made satisfaction accordingly, within such time so to be limited; that then it shall be lawfull to us, our heires and successours, to put the said Sir Humfrey, his heires and assignes, and adherents, and all the *inhabitants* of the said places to be discovered as is aforesaide, or any of them out of our allegiance and protection, and that from and after such time of putting out of protection the saide Sir Humfrey, and his heires, assignes, adherents and others so to be put out, and the said places within their habitation, possession and rule, shall lie out of our protection and allegiance, and free for all princes and others to pursue with hostilitie as being not our Subjects . . . [Thorpe 52]

Council of New England, Grant of the Province of Maine, August 10, 1622:

And the said Sr. Ferdinando Gorges and Capt. John Mason doe further covenant for them, their heyres and assignes, that they will establish such government in the said porcons of lands and islands granted unto them, and the same will from time to time continue, as shall be agreeable, as neere as may be to the laws and customs of the realme of England; and if they shall be charged at any time to have neglected their duty therein, that thus they well conforme the same according to the directions of the President and councill; or in default thereof it shall be lawful for any of the aggrieved *inhabitants* and planters, being tennts upon ye said lands, to appeal to ye chief courts of justices of the President and councill. . . . [Thorpe 1624]

English Petition of Right, June 7, 1628:

And whereas of late great companies of soldiers and mariners have been dispersed into divers counties of the realm, and the *inhabitants* against their wills have been compelled to receive them into their houses, and there to suffer them to sojourn, against the laws and customs of this realm, and to the great grievance and vexation of the people. [SDECH 340–41]

Charles I, Charter of Maryland, June 20, 1632:

[Article 21:] And furthermore We will, and by these Presents, for Us, our Heirs and Successors, do grant unto the aforesaid now Baron of Baltimore, his Heirs and Assigns, and to the Freeholders and *Inhabitants* of the said Province, both Present and to come, and to every of them, that the said Province, and the Freeholders or *Inhabitants* of the said Colony or Country, shall not henceforth be held or reputed a Member or Part of the Land of Virginia, or of any other Colony already transported, or hereafter to be transported, or be dependent on the same, or subordinate in any kind of Government, from which We do separate both the said Province, and *Inhabitants* thereof, and by these Presents do will to be distinct, and that they may be immediately subject to our Crown of England, and dependent on the same forever. [Thorpe 1685]

Fundamental Orders of Connecticut, 1638–39:

It is Ordered, sentenced and decreed, that there shall be yerely two generall Assemblies or Courts, the one the second thursday in Aprill, the other the second thursday in September, following; the first shall be called the Courte of Election, wherein shall be yerely Chosen from tyme to tyme soe many Magestrats and other publike Officers as shall be found requisitte: Whereof one to be chosen Governour for the yeare ensueing and untill another be chosen, and noe other Magestrate to be chosen for more then one yeare; prvided allwayes there be sixe chosen besids the Governour; wch being chosen and sworne according to an Oath recorded for that purpose shall have power to administer justice according to the Lawes here established, and for want thereof according to the rule of the word of God; wch choise shall be made by all that are admitted freemen and have taken the Oath of Fidellity, and doe cohabitte wthn this Jurisdiction, (having beene admitted *Inhabitants* by the major prt of the Towne wherein they live, or the mayor prte of such as shall be then prsent. [Thorpe 519–20]

The New England Confederation, May 19, 1643:

[Article 4:] It is by these Confederates agreed that the charge of all just wars, whether offensive or defensive, upon what part or member of this Confederation soever they fall, shall both in men, provisions, and all other disbursements be borne by all the parts of this Confederation in different proportions according to their different ability in manner following, namely, that the Commissioners for each Jurisdiction from time to time, as there shall be occasion, bring a true account and number of all their males in every Plantation, or any way belonging to or under their several Jurisdictions, of what quality or condition soever they be, from sixteen years old to three-score, being *inhabitants* there. And that according to the different numbers which from time to time shall be found in each Jurisdiction upon a true and just account, the service of men and all charges of the war be borne by the poll: each Jurisdiction or Plantation being left to their own just course and custom of rating themselves and people according to their different estates with due respects to their qualities and exemptions amongst themselves though the Confederation take no notice of any such privilege . . . [Thorpe 78]

Carolina Proprietors, Concessions and Agreements, 1665

It is our will and desire that ye *Inhabitants* of the said Countyes and adventurers theither shall enjoye all the same Immunityes from Customes for exporting certine goods from these Realmes of England &c theither as ye Kinge hath been graciously pleased to graunt to us as alsoe for ye Incorragement of the Manufactrs of wine silke oyle ollives fruite almonds &c. menconed in the pattent have priveledge for bringing them Custome free into any of his Majties dominions for ye same time and upon ye same tearmes as we ourselves may by our Pattent. [Thorpe 2761]

Charles II, Commission Constituting a President and Council for New Hampshire, September 18, 1680:

. . . And whereas ye Government of yt part of the said Province of New-Hampshire, so limited & bounded as aforesaid hath not yet bin granted unto any person or persons whatsoever but ye same still remains & is under Our im'ediate care & protection; To the end therefore, yt Our loving Subjects, ye Planters and *Inhabitants* within ye limits aforesaid, may be protected and Defended in their respective rights, liberties & properties, & yt due & impartiall Justice may be duly administred in all cases civill & criminall; & yt all possible care may be taken for ye quiet & orderly Government of ye same: Now know ye, that We by & with ye advice of Our Privy Councell, have thought fit to erect, & constitute, & by these prsents for us our hrs & successrs do erect constitute & appoint a President & Councell, to take care of ye said Tract of land called The Province of New-Hampshire, & of the Planters & *Inhabitants* thereof; & to Order, rule & Govern ye same according to such methods & regulations, as are herein after specified and declared. . . . [Thorpe 2446]

Charles II, Charter of Pennsylvania, February 28, 1681:

Provided alwayes, and our will and pleasure is, that neither the said William Penn, nor his heires, or any other the *inhabitants* of the said Province, shall at any time hereafter have or maintain any Correspondence with any other king, prince, or State, or with any of theire subjects, who shall then be in Warr against us, our heires or Successors; Nor shall the said William Penn, or his heires, or any other the *Inhabitants* of the said Province, make Warre or doe any act of Hostility against any other king, prince, or State, or any of theire Subjects, who shall then be in league or amity with us, our heires or successors.

[Thorpe 3041–42]

William and Mary, Charter of Massachusetts Bay, October 7, 1691:

. . . To Have and to hold the said Territories Tracts Countreys Lands Hereditaments and all and singular other the premisses with their and every of their Appurtences to Our said Subjects the *Inhabitants* of Our said Province of the Massachusetts Bay in New England and their Successors to their only proper use and behoofe for evermore . . . [Thorpe 1877]

William Penn, Charter of Privileges for Pennsylvania, October 28, 1701:

And Whereas I was then pleased to promise, That I would restore the said Charter to them again, with necessary Alterations, or in lieu thereof, give them another, better adapted to answer the present Circumstances and Conditions of the said

Inhabitants; which they have now, by their Representatives in General Assembly met at Philadelphia, requested me to grant. [Thorpe 3077]

George II, Charter of Georgia, June 9, 1732:

. . . And we do, by these presents, for us, our heirs and successors, will and declare, that from and after the termination of the said term or twenty-one years, such form of government and method of making laws, statutes and ordinances, for the better governing and ordering the said province of Georgia, and the *inhabitants* thereof, shall be established and observed within the same, as we, our heirs and successors, shall hereafter ordain and appoint, and shall be agreeably to law . . . [Thorpe 776–77]

The Albany Plan of Union, July 10, 1754:

POWER TO MAKE LAWS, LAY DUTIES, &C

That for these purposes they [the President General and Grand Council] have power to make laws, and lay and levy such general duties, imposts, or taxes as to them shall appear most equal and just (considering the ability and other circumstances of the *inhabitants* in the several colonies), and such as may be collected with the least inconvenience to the people; rather discouraging luxury than loading industry with unnecessary burthens. [Thorpe 85]

First Continental Congress, Declaration and Resolves, October 14, 1774:

[1] That the *inhabitants* of the English Colonies in North America, by the immutable laws of nature, the principles of the English constitution, and the several charters or compacts, have the following Rights. [JCC1 67]

[2] To these grievous acts and measures Americans cannot submit, but in hopes that their fellow subjects in Great- Britain will, on a revision of them, restore us to that state in which both countries found happiness and prosperity, we have for the present only resolved to pursue the following peaceable measures: . . . 1st. To enter into a non-importation, non-consumption, and non-exportation agreement or association. 2. To prepare an address to the people of Great-Britain, and a memorial to the *inhabitants* of British America, & 3. To prepare a loyal address to his Majesty, agreeable to resolutions already entered into. [JCC1 73]

Thomas Paine, *Common Sense,* January 9, 1776:

Secondly. That as even the best terms which we can expect to obtain can amount to no more than a temporary expedient, or a kind of government by guardianship, which can last no longer than till the colonies come of age, so the general face and state of things, in the interim will be unsettled and unpromising. Emigrants of property will not choose to come to a country whose form of government hangs but by a thread, and who is every day tottering on the brink of commotion and disturbance; and numbers of the present *inhabitants* would lay hold of the interval to dispose of their effects, and quit the continent. [CWTP1 26]

South Carolina Constitution, March 26, 1776:

[Preamble:] . . . the English laws and a free government, to which the *inhabitants* of Quebec were entitled by the King's royal proclamation, are abolished and French laws are restored; the Roman Catholic religion (although before tolerated and freely exercised there) and an absolute government are established in that province, and its limits extended through a vast tract of country so as to border on the free Protestant English settlements, with design of using a whole people differing in religious principles from the neighboring colonies, and subject to arbitrary Power, as fit instruments to overawe and subdue the colonies. . . . [Thorpe 3241–42]

United States Continental Congress, Draft Articles of Confederation, July 12, 1776:

[Article 6:] The *Inhabitants* of each Colony shall henceforth always have the same Rights, Liberties, Privileges, Immunities, and Advantages, in the other Colonies, which the said *Inhabitants* now have, in all Cases whatever, except in those provided for by the next following Article. [DHRC1 80]

[Article 7:] The *Inhabitants* of each Colony shall enjoy all the Rights, Liberties, Privileges, Immunities, and Advantages, in Trade, Navigation, and Commerce, in any other Colony, and in going to and from the same from and to any Part of the World, which the Natives of such Colony enjoy. [DHRC1 80]

[Article 11:] All Charges of Wars and all other Expences that shall be incurred for the common Defence, or general Welfare, and allowed by the United States assembled, shall be defrayed out of a common Treasury, which shall be supplied by the several Colonies in Proportion to the Number of *Inhabitants* of every Age, Sex and Quality, except Indians not paying Taxes, in each Colony, a true Account of which, distinguishing the white *Inhabitants,* shall be triennially taken and transmitted to the Assembly of the United States. The Taxes for paying that Proportion shall be laid and levied by the Authority and Direction of the Legislatures of the several Colonies, within the Time agreed upon by United States assembled. [DHRC1 80]

[Article 18:] The United States assembled shall have Authority for the Defence and Welfare of the United Colonies and every of them, to agree upon and fix the necessary Sums and Expences—To emit Bills, or to borrow Money on the Credit of the United Colonies—To raise Naval Forces—To agree upon the Number of Land Forces to be raised, and to make Requisitions from the Legislature of each Colony, or the Persons therein authorized by the Legislature to execute such Requisitions, for the Quota of each Colony, which is to be in Proportion to the Number of white *Inhabitants* in that Colony, which Requisitions shall be binding, and thereupon the Legislature of each Colony of the Persons authorized as aforesaid, shall appoint the Regimental Officers, raise the Men, and arm and equip them in a soldier-like Manner . . . [DHRC1 83]

New York Constitution, April 20, 1777:

[Article 5:] That as soon after the expiration of seven years (subsequent to the termination of the present war) as may be a census of the electors and *inhabitants* in this State be taken, under the direction of the legislature. And if, on such census, it shall appear that the number of representatives in assembly from the said counties is not justly proportioned to the number of electors in the said counties respectively, that the legislature do adjust and apportion the same by that rule. . . . [Thorpe 2629–30]

United States Articles of Confederation, November 15, 1777:

[Article IV:] The better to secure and perpetuate mutual friendship and intercourse among the people of the different states in this union, the free *inhabitants* of each of these states, paupers, vagabonds and fugitives from Justice excepted, shall be entitled to all privileges and immunities of free citizens in the several states; and the people of each state shall have free ingress and regress to and from any other state, and shall enjoy therein all the privileges of trade and commerce, subject to the same duties, impositions and restrictions as the *inhabitants* thereof respectively, provided that such restriction shall not extend so far as to prevent the removal of property imported into any state, to any other state of which the Owner is an *inhabitant;* provided also that no imposition, duties or restriction shall be laid by any state, on the property of the united states, or either of them.

[Article IX:] The united states in congress assembled shall have authority . . . to agree upon the number of land forces, and to make requisitions from each state for its quota, in proportion to the number of white *inhabitants* in such state; which requisition shall be binding, and thereupon the legislature of each state shall appoint the regimental officers, raise the men and cloath, arm and equip them in a soldier like manner, at the expence of the united states, and the officers and men so cloathed, armed and equipped shall march to the place appointed, and within the time agreed on by the united states in congress assembled. . . .

Massachusetts Constitution, March 2, 1780:

[Chapter I:2:2:] The senate shall be the first branch of the legislature; and the senators shall be chosen in the following manner, viz.: there shall be a meeting on the first Monday in April, annually, forever, of the *inhabitants* of each town in the several counties of this commonwealth; to be called by the selectmen, and warned in due course of law, at least seven days before the first Monday in April, for the purpose of electing persons to be senators and councillors; and at such meetings every male *inhabitant* of twenty-one years of age and upwards, having a freehold estate within the commonwealth, of the annual income of three pounds, or any estate of the value of sixty pounds, shall have a right to give in his vote for the senators for the district of which he is an *inhabitant*. And to remove all doubts concerning the meaning of the word "*inhabitant*" in this constitution, every person shall be considered as an *inhabitant,* for the purpose of electing and being elected into any office, or place within this state, in that town, district, or plantation where he dwelleth, or hath his home.

[Thorpe 1895–96]

New Hampshire Constitution, June 2, 1784:

[Form of Government:] Provided nevertheless, That no person shall be capable of being elected a senator, who is not of the protestant religion, and seized of a freehold estate in his own right of the value of two hundred pounds, lying within this state, who is not of the age of thirty years, and who shall not have been an *inhabitant* of this state for seven years immediately preceding his election; and at the time thereof he shall be an *inhabitant* of the district for which he shall be chosen. [Thorpe 2460]

Vermont Constitution, July 4, 1786:

. . . And whereas the Territory, which now comprehends the State of Vermont, did antecedently of right belong to the government of New-Hampshire and the former Governor thereof, viz. his excellency Benning Wentworth Esq. granted many charters of lands and corporations within this State to the present *inhabitants* and others. And whereas the late Lieutenant-Governor Colden, of New York, with others, did, in violation, of the tenth command, covet those very lands: and by a false representation, made to the Court of Great-Britain, (in the year 1764, that for the convenience of trade and administration of justice, the *inhabitants* were desirous of being annexed to that government) obtained jurisdiction of those very identical lands, ex parte, which ever was and is disagreeable to the *inhabitants*. And whereas the Legislature of New-York ever have, and still continue, to disown the good people of this State, in their landed property, which will appear in the complaints hereafter inserted, and in the 36th section of their present Constitution, in which is established the Grants of Land made by that government. [Thorpe 3750]

The Virginia Plan of Union, May 29, 1787:

[Article 2:] Res[olve]d therefore that the rights of suffrage in the National Legislature ought to be proportioned to the Quotas of contribution, or to the number of free *inhabitants,* as the one or the other rule may seem best in different cases. [DHRC1 243]

Charles Pinckney's Plan of Union, May 29, 1787:

[Article 4:] [House of Delegates] to consist of ———Member for every ——— thousand *Inhabitants* 3/5 of Blacks included Senate to be elected from four Districts—to serve by Rotation of four Years . . . [DHRC1 246]

The New Jersey Plan of Union, June 15, 1787:

[Article 3:] Res[olve]d that whenever requisitions shall be necessary, instead of the rule for making requisitions mentioned in the articles of Confederation, the United States in Cong[res]s be authorized to make such requisitions in proportion to the whole number of white & other free citizens & *inhabitants* of every age sex and condition including those bound to servitude for a term of years & three fifths of all other persons not comprehended in the foregoing description, except Indians not paying taxes . . . [DHRC1 251]

United States Confederation Congress, The Northwest Ordinance, July 13, 1787:

[1] . . . and real estates may be conveyed by lease and release, or bargain and sale, signed, sealed, and delivered by the person, being of full age, in whom the estate may be, and attested by two witnesses, provided such wills be duly proved, and such conveyances be acknowledged, or the execution thereof duly proved, and be recorded within one year after proper magistrates, courts, and registers, shall be appointed for that purpose; and personal property may be transferred by delivery, saving, however, to the French and Canadian *inhabitants,* and other settlers of the Kaskaskies, Saint Vincents, and the neighboring villages, who have heretofore professed themselves citizens of Virginia, their laws and customs now in force among them, relative to the descent and conveyance of property. [Thorpe 958]

[2] So soon as there shall be five thousand free male *inhabitants,* of full age, in the district, upon giving proof thereof to the governor, they shall receive authority, with time and place, to elect representatives from their counties or townships, to represent them in the general assembly: Provided, That for every five hundred free male *inhabitants* there shall be one representative, and so on, progressively, with the number of free male *inhabitants,* shall the right of representation increase, until the number of representatives shall amount to twenty-

five; after which the number and proportion of representatives shall be regulated by the legislature . . . [Thorpe 959]

[Article 2:] The *inhabitants* of the said territory shall always be entitled to the benefits of the writs of habeas corpus, and of the trial by jury; of a proportionate representation of the people in the legislature, and of judicial proceedings according to the course of the common law. . . . [Thorpe 960–61]

[Article 4:] The said territory, and the States which may be formed therein, shall forever remain a part of this confederacy of the United States of America, subject to the Articles of Confederation, and to such alterations therein as shall be constitutionally made; and to all the acts and ordinances of the United States in Congress assembled, conformable thereto. The *inhabitants* and settlers in the said territory shall be subject to pay a part of the Federal debts, contracted, or to be contracted, and a proportional part of the expenses of government to be apportioned on them by Congress, according to the same common rule and measure by which apportionments thereof shall be made on the other States . . . [Thorpe 961]

[*Ibid.*:] . . . The navigable waters leading into the Mississippi and Saint Lawrence, and the carrying places between the same, shall be common highways, and forever free, as well to the *inhabitants* of the said territory as to the citizens of the United States, and those of any other States that may be admitted into the confederacy, without any tax, impost, or duty therefor. [Thorpe 961–62]

[Article 5:] . . . And it is further understood and declared, that the boundaries of these three States shall be subject so far to be altered, that, if Congress shall hereafter find it expedient, they shall have authority to form one or two States in that part of the said territory which lies north of an east and west line drawn through the southerly bend or extreme of Lake Michigan. And whenever any of the said States shall have sixty thousand free *inhabitants* therein, such State shall be admitted by its delegates, into the Congress of the United States, on an equal footing with the original States, in all respects whatever; and shall be at liberty to form a permanent constitution and State government: Provided, The constitution and government, so to be formed, shall be republican, and in conformity to the principles contained in these articles, and, so far as it can be consistent with the general interest of the confederacy, such admission shall be allowed at an earlier period, and when there may be a less number of free *inhabitants* in the State than sixty thousand. [Thorpe 962]

Richard Henry Lee [?], "The Federal Farmer," No. 3, October 10, 1787:

First. As to the organization—the house of representatives, the democrative branch, as it is called, is to consist of 65 members: that is, about one representative for fifty thousand *inhabitants,* to be chosen biennially—the federal legislature may increase this number to one for each thirty thousand *inhabitants,* abating fractional numbers in each state.—Thirty-three representatives will make a quorum for doing business, and a majority of those present determine the sense of the house.—I have no idea that the interests, feelings, and opinions of three or four millions of people, especially touching internal taxation, can be collected in such a house. . . . [Ford 295]

Noah Webster, *An Examination of the Leading Principles of the Federal Constitution*, October 17, 1787:

The house of representatives is the more immediate voice of the separate states—here the states are represented in proportion to their number of *inhabitants*—here the separate interests will operate with their full force, and the violence of parties and the jealousies produced by interfering interests, can be restrained and quieted only by a body of men, less local and dependent. [Ford 41]

"Cato Uticensis," October 17, 1787:

In the hour of distress, in the moment of confusion and perilous danger, after separately declaring themselves sovereign and independent, the Thirteen States of America associated together in a Foederal league, for their common defence, an affair of such magnitude, formed under the influence of such unfavorable circumstances, could not fail of receiving a tinge from them; consequently, when the war, that link, which supplied each defect was over, the yawnings and the chasms of the building began to give evident marks of the hastiness of the workmen: America saw, that without the help of a better cement, the different members were likely to fall asunder, and that, though we may find a lodging in some of the separated pavilions, we must bid adieu to the grandeur and dignity of being *inhabitants* of a stately palace. [DHRC8 71]

Tobias Lear, "Brutus," December 6, 1787:

. . . Under the present confederation the smaller States enjoy an equal voice, in the national council, with the larger. The impropriety of this cannot but strike every person in the most forcible manner, for it is a violation of the rights of the people to suffer a State, which, perhaps, contains but thirty thousand *inhabitants,* to have an equal weight in matters of general concern, with one which contains four hundred thousand. And, on the other hand, it could not be expected that the smaller States would willingly and wholly relinquish a privilege which was the basis of their national importance. This, I think, will readily account for the equal representation which is given in the Senate, and the proportionate representation which we find in the House of Representatives . . .

[DHRC8 214]

Dissent of the Pennsylvania Assembly's Minority, December 18, 1787:

The *inhabitants* of the several States shall have liberty to fowl and hunt in seasonable times on the lands they hold, and on all other lands in the United States not enclosed, and in like manner to fish in all navigable waters, and others not private property, without being restrained therein by any laws to be passed by the legislature of the United States. [DHRC2 624]

Alexander Hamilton, *The Federalist*, No. 26, December 22, 1787:

It may not be amiss in this place concisely to remark the origin and progress of this idea, which aims at the exclusion of military establishments in time of peace. Though in speculative minds it may arise from a contemplation of the nature and tendency of such institutions, fortified by the events that have happened in other ages and countries, yet as a national sentiment, it must be traced to those habits of thinking which we derive from the nation from whom the *inhabitants* of these States have in general sprung. [Fed. 214]

David Ramsay, "Civis," February 4, 1788:

. . . On the other hand, they have agreed to change the federal rule of paying the continental debt, according to the value of land as laid down in the confederation, for a new principle of apportionment, to be founded on the numbers of *inhabitants* in the several states respectively. This is an immense concession in our favor. . . . [DHRC16 25]

"A Citizen of the United States," February 13, 1788:

. . . Mr. R. H. Lee and other gentlemen of the southern states object that commercial regulations will be under the undue controul of the eastern states—the *inhabitants* of the latter complain of the unequal burthen of an impost, of which the southern states must pay but very little from the nature of their population—In the middle states the clamor of opposition has been from the want of a bill of rights . . . [DHRC16 115]

James Madison, *The Federalist*, No. 56, February 16, 1788:

As this objection evidently proceeds from a comparison of the proposed number of representatives with the great extent of the United States, the number of their *inhabitants,* and the diversity of their interests, without taking into view at the same time the circumstances which will distinguish the Congress from other legislative bodies, the best answer that can be given to it will be a brief explanation of these peculiarities. [Fed. 379]

Circular Letter to the Fayette, Kentucky, County Court, February 29, 1788:

In all general questions which affect a community at large it is Usual for them in some Manner to Signify their dislike, or approbation to it, and wherever it hath proved inconvenient for the whole Society to convene together, it hath heretofore been Judged expedient for them to elect representatives to declare their sentiments upon the Occasion. There Never was and we may Venture to declare there Never will be a greater call to the *inhabitants* of the Western Country than at the present Moment to consider coolly and dispassionately the effects which will insue to them and their posterity by the Adoption or rejection of the proposed Foedral Constitution. [DHRC8 434]

Mercy Otis Warren, *Observations on the New Constitution*, February 1788:

Mankind may amuse themselves with theoretick systems of liberty, and trace its social and moral effects on sciences, virtue, industry, and every improvement of which the human mind is capable; but we can only discern its true value by the practical and wretched effects of slavery; and thus dreadfully will they be realized, when the *inhabitants* of the Eastern States are dragging out a miserable existence, only on the gleanings of their fields; and the Southern, blessed with a softer and more fertile climate, are languishing in hopeless poverty . . . [DHRC16 274]

Oliver Ellsworth, "The Landholder," No.11, March 10, 1788:

It has been said that you object to the number of *inhabitants* being a ratio to determine your proportion of the national expence—that your lands are poor but the climate favourable to population, which will draw a share of expence beyond your ability to pay. I do not think this objection well founded. Long experience hath taught that the number of industrious *inhabitants* in any climate is not only the strength, but the wealth of a state, and very justly measures their ability for defraying public expences, without encroaching on the necessary support of life. . . . [DHRC16 368]

John Dickinson, "Fabius," No. 2, 1788:

Can this limited, fluctuating senate, placed amidst such powers, if it should become willing, ever become able, to make America pass under its yoke? The senators will generally be *inhabitants* of places very distant one from another. They can scarcely be acquainted till they meet. Few of them can ever act together for any length of time, unless their good conduct recommends them to a re-election; and then there will be frequent changes in a body dependant upon the acts of other bodies, the legislatures of the several states, that are altering every year. Machiavel and Caesar Borgia together could not form a conspiracy in such a senate, destructive to any but themselves and their accomplices.

[Ford 172–73]

United States Congress, Judiciary Act of September 24, 1789:

[Section 11:] . . . But no person shall be arrested in one district for trial in another, in any civil action before a circuit or district court. And no civil suit shall be brought before either of said courts against an *inhabitant* of the United States, by any original process in any other district than that whereof he is an *inhabitant,* or in which he shall be found at the time of serving the writ, nor shall any district or circuit court have cognizance of any suit to recover the contents of any promissory note or other chose in action in favor of an assignee, unless a suit might have been prosecuted in such court to recover the said contents if no assignment had been made, except in cases of foreign bills of exchange. . . .

[USSL1 79]

Pennsylvania Constitution, September 2, 1790:

[Article I, Section 8:] No person shall be a senator, who shall not have attained the age of twenty-five years, and have been a citizen and *inhabitant* of the State four years next before his election, and the last year thereof an *inhabitant* of the district for which he shall be chosen, unless be shall have been absent on the public business of the United States, or of this State. [Thorpe 3093]

INSURRECTION, INSURRECTIONS

United States Constitution, September 17, 1787:

[Article I, Section 8:] [Congress shall have power] To provide for calling forth the Militia to execute the Laws of the Union, suppress *Insurrections* and repel Invasions.

* * * * *

James I, The Charter of New England, November 3, 1620:

And Wee do further of our especiall Grace, certaine Knowledge, and mere Motion, grant, declare, and ordain, that such principall Governor, as from time to time shall be authorized and appointed in Manner and Forme in these Presents heretofore expressed, shall have full Power and Authority to use and exercise marshall Laws in Cases of Rebellion, *Insurrection* and Mutiny, in as large and ample Manner as our Lieutenants in our Counties within our Realme of England have or ought to have by Force of their Commission of Lieutenancy.

[Thorpe 1833]

Charles II, Grant of the Province of Maine to the Duke of York, March 12, 1664:

. . . And wee do further of our speciall grace certaine knowledge and meere mocon grant ordaine and declare that such governors officers and ministers as from time to time shall be authorized and appointed in manner and forme aforesaid shall and may have full power and authority to use and exercise martiall law in cases of rebellion *insurreccon* and mutinie in as large and ample manner as our Lieutenants in our countyes within our Realme of England have or ought to have by force of their commission of Lieutenancy or any law or statute of this our Realme. [Thorpe 1639]

Charles II, Grant of the Province of Maine to the Duke of York, June 29, 1674:

And wee do further of our Especiall Grace certaine knowledge and meer motion graunt ordaine and declare that such Governors Deputyes Officers and Ministers as from time to time shall bee authorized and appointed in manner and forme aforesaid shall and may have full power and authority within the Territoryes aforesaid to use and exercise Marshall Lawe in cases of rebellion *insurrection* and Mutiny in as large and ample manner as our Lieutenants in our Countyes within Our realme of England have or ought to have by force of their Commission of Lieutenancy or any law or Statute of this our realme . . . [Thorpe 1642]

James II, Commission to Sir Edmund Andros for the Dominion of New England, April 7, 1688:

. . . And also to execute martiall law in time of invasion *insurrection* or warr, and during the continuance of the same, and upon soldiers in pay, and to do and execute all and every other thing which to a Captain Generall doth or ought of right to belong, as fully and amply as any our Captain Generall doth or hath usually don. [Thorpe 1866]

New Jersey Proprietors, Surrender of Rights, April 15, 1702:

. . . And the late King did thereby grant, ordain and declare, that such Governors, officers, ministers as from time to time should be authorized and appointed in manner and form aforesaid, should and might have full power and authority to use and exercise martial law in cases of rebellion, *insurrection* and mutiny, in as large and ample manner as the lieutenants of his said Majesty in his counties of the realm of England had, or ought to have, by their commissions of lieutenancy, or any law or statute of the said realm of England . . . [Thorpe 2586]

Thomas Paine, *Common Sense*, January 9, 1776:

. . . From Britain we can expect nothing but ruin. If she is once admitted to the government of America again, this Continent will not be worth living in. Jealousies will be always arising; *insurrections* will be constantly happening; and who will go forth to quell them? Who will venture his life to reduce his own countrymen to a foreign obedience? The difference between Pennsylvania and Connecticut, respecting some unlocated lands, shows the insignificance of a British government, and fully proves, that nothing but Continental authority can regulate Continental matters. [CWTP1 35–36]

South Carolina Constitution, March 26, 1776:

[Preamble:] . . . And whereas, instead of obtaining that justice, to which the colonists were and are of right entitled, the unnatural civil war into which they were thus precipitated and are involved, hath been prosecuted with unremitted violence, and the governors and others bearing the royal commission in the colonies having broken the most solemn promises and engagements, and violated every obligation of honor, justice, and humanity, have caused the persons of divers good people to be seized and imprisoned, and their properties to be forcibly taken and detained, or destroyed, without any crime or forfeiture; excited domestic *insurrections;* proclaimed freedom to servants and slaves, enticed or stolen them from, and armed them against their masters . . . [Thorpe 3242]

Virginia Constitution, June 29, 1776:

[The King has tyrannized] . . . By inciting *insurrections* of our fellow subjects, with the allurements of forfeiture and confiscation . . . [Thorpe 3815]

United States Declaration of Independence, July 4, 1776:

. . . He [the King] has excited domestic *insurrections* amongst us, and has endeavoured to bring on the inhabitants of our frontiers, the merciless Indian Savages, whose known rule of warfare, is an undistinguished destruction of all ages, sexes and conditions. . . .

New Hampshire Constitution, June 2, 1784:

[Bill of Rights, Article 17:] In criminal prosecutions, the trial of facts in the vicinity where they happen, is so essential to the security of the life, liberty and estate of the citizen, that no crime or offence ought to be tried in any other county than that in which it is committed; except in cases of general *insurrection* in any particular county, when it shall appear to the Judges of the Superior Court, that an impartial trial cannot be had in the county where the offence may be committed, and upon their report, the assembly shall think proper to direct the trial in the nearest county in which an impartial trial can be obtained.
[Thorpe 2455–56]

***Virginia Herald*, October 11, 1787:**

A correspondent observes, that there cannot be a greater proof of the virtue of our countrymen in the late Federal Convention, than the constitution which they have exhibited to the states, as the result of their deliberations. The expediency of the plan of government which they have proposed arises from the provisions which they have so judiciously made for preventing *insurrections* against the laws, and for procuring obedience to the federal constitution. We have seen with how much contempt the resolutions of our Congress have been treated, when they have laid before the states, in the most expressive terms, the necessity of adopting certain measures which they have proposed . . . [DHRC8 52]

Noah Webster, *An Examination of the Leading Principles of the Federal Constitution*, October 17, 1787:

[1] . . . But I see no occasion for any power in Congress to interfere with the choice of their own body—They will have power to suppress *insurrections*, as they ought to have . . . [Ford 44]

[2] Congress likewise are to have power to provide for organizing, arming and disciplining the militia, but have no other command of them, except when in actual service. Nor are they at liberty to call out the militia at pleasure—but only, to execute the laws of the union, suppress *insurrections*, and repel invasions. For these purposes, government must always be armed with a military force, if the occasion should require it: otherwise laws are nugatory, and life and property insecure. [Ford 52]

[3] Excepting that clause the constitution is good—it guarantees the fundamental principles of our several constitutions—it guards our rights—and while it vests extensive powers in Congress, it vests no more than are necessary for our union. Without powers lodged somewhere in a single body, fully competent to lay and collect equal taxes and duties—to adjust controversies between different states—to silence contending interests—to suppress *insurrections*—to regulate commerce—to treat with foreign nations, our confederation is a cobweb—liable to be blown asunder by every blast of faction that is raised in the remotest corner of the United States. [Ford 61–62]

Pelatiah Webster, *The Weakness of Brutus Exposed*, November 4, 1787:

There can be no doubt that each State will receive from the union great support and protection against the invasions and inroads of foreign enemies, as well as against riots and *insurrections* of their own citizens; and of consequence, the course of their internal administration will be secured by this means against any interruption or embarrassment from either of these causes. [Ford 128]

Alexander Hamilton, *The Federalist*, No. 6, November 14, 1787:

Let the point of extreme depression to which our national dignity and credit have sunk, let the inconveniences felt everywhere from a lax and ill administration of government, let the revolt of a part of the State of North Carolina, the late menacing disturbances in Pennsylvania, and the actual *insurrections* and rebellions in Massachusetts, declare———! [Fed. 113]

Alexander Hamilton, *The Federalist*, No. 8, November 20, 1787:

. . . The smallness of the army renders the natural strength of the community an overmatch for it; and the citizens, not habituated to look up to the military power for protection, or to submit to its oppressions, neither love nor fear the soldiery; they view them with a spirit of jealous acquiescence in a necessary evil, and stand ready to resist a power which they suppose may be exerted to the prejudice of their rights. The army under such circumstances may usefully aid the magistrate to suppress a small faction, or an occasional mob, or *insurrection;* but it will be unable to enforce encroachments against the united efforts of the great body of the people. [Fed. 122]

Alexander Hamilton, *The Federalist*, No. 9, November 21, 1787:

[1-Title:] Union as a Barrier to Faction and *Insurrection*. [Fed. 124]

[2] A Firm Union will be of the utmost moment to the peace and liberty of the States, as a barrier against domestic faction and *insurrection*. It is impossible to read the history of the petty republics of Greece and Italy without feeling sensations of horror and disgust at the distractions with which they were continually agitated, and at the rapid succession of revolutions by which they were kept in a state of perpetual vibration between the extremes of tyranny and anarchy. . . . [Fed. 124]

[3] [Quoting Montesquieu:] "Should a popular *insurrection* happen in one of the confederate states, the others are able to quell it. Should abuses creep into one part, they are reformed by those that remain sound. The state may be destroyed on one side, and not on the other; the confederacy may be dissolved, and the confederates preserve their sovereignty." [Fed. 127]

[4] . . . They have, at the same time, an intimate connection with the more immediate design of this paper; which is, to illustrate the tendency of the Union to repress domestic faction and *insurrection*. [127–28]

Alexander Hamilton, *The Federalist*, No. 16, December 4, 1787:

. . . As to those partial commotions and *insurrections,* which sometimes disquiet society, from the intrigues of an inconsiderable faction, or from sudden or occasional ill-humors that do not infect the great body of the community, the general government could command more extensive resources for the suppression of disturbances of that kind than would be in the power of any single member. . . . [Fed. 166–67]

"Americanus," No. 1, December 5, 1787:

. . . To complete the full measure of our calamities, it was found, that civil *insurrections* had disturbed the tranquility of some of the states, and that all were, in a peculiar manner, liable to be invaded . . . [DHRC8 201]

James Madison, *The Federalist*, No. 19, December 8, 1787:

They [the Swiss cantons] are kept together by the peculiarity of their topographical position; by their individual weakness and insignificancy; by the fear of powerful neighbors, to one of which they were formerly subject; by the few sources of contention among a people of such simple and homogeneous manners; by their joint interest in their dependent possessions; by the mutual aid they stand in need of, for suppressing *insurrections* and rebellions, an aid expressly stipulated, and often required and afforded; and by the necessity of some regular and permanent provision for accommodating disputes among the cantons. . . .
[Fed. 181]

Dissent of the Pennsylvania Convention's Minority, December 18, 1787:

Thirdly, the absolute command of Congress over the militia may be destructive of public liberty; for under the guidance of an arbitrary government, they may be made the unwilling instruments of tyranny. The militia of Pennsylvania may be marched to New England or Virginia to quell an *insurrection* occasioned by the most galling oppression, and aided by the standing army, they will no doubt be successful in subduing their liberty and independency; but in so doing, although the magnanimity of their minds will be extinguished, yet the meaner passions of resentment and revenge will be increased, and these in turn will be the ready and obedient instruments of despotism to enslave the others . . .
[DHRC2 638]

Alexander Hamilton, *The Federalist*, No. 25, December 21, 1787:

. . . The conduct of Massachusetts affords a lesson on the same subject, though on different ground. That State (without waiting for the sanction of Congress, as the articles of the Confederation require) was compelled to raise troops to quell a domestic *insurrection,* and still keeps a corps in pay to prevent a revival of the spirit of revolt. The particular constitution of Massachusetts opposed no obstacle to the measure; but the instance is still of use to instruct us that cases are likely to occur under our government, as well as under those of other nations, which will sometimes render a military force in time of peace essential to the security of the society, and that it is therefore improper in this respect to control the legislative discretion. . . . [Fed. 212]

Alexander Hamilton, *The Federalist*, No. 26, December 22, 1787:

. . . But the question again recurs, upon what pretence could he be put in possession of a force of that magnitude in time of peace? If we suppose it to have been created in consequence of some domestic *insurrection* or foreign war, then it becomes a case not within the principles of the objection; for this is levelled against the power of keeping up troops in time of peace. Few persons will be so visionary as seriously to contend that military forces ought not to be raised to quell a rebellion or resist an invasion; and if the defence of the community under such circumstances should make it necessary to have an army so numerous as to hazard its liberty, this is one of those calamities for which there is neither preventative nor cure. . . . [Fed. 218]

Alexander Hamilton, *The Federalist*, No. 28, December 26, 1787:

[1] That there may happen cases in which the national government may be necessitated to resort to force, cannot be denied. Our own experience has corroborated the lessons taught by the examples of others nations; that emergencies of this sort will sometimes arise in all societies, however constituted; that seditions and *insurrections* are, unhappily, maladies as inseparable from the body politic as tumors and eruptions from the natural body; that the idea of governing at all times by the simple force of law (which we have been told is the only admissible principle of republican government), has no place but in the reveries of those political doctors whose sagacity disdains the admonitions of experimental instruction. [Fed. 222]

[2] . . . An *insurrection,* whatever may be its immediate cause, eventually endangers all government. Regard to the public peace,if not to the rights of the Union, would engage the citizens to whom the contagion had not communicated itself to oppose the insurgents; and if the general government should be found in practice conducive to the prosperity and felicity of the people, it were irrational to believe that they would be disinclined to its support. [Fed. 223]

[3] If, on the contrary, the *insurrection* should pervade a whole State, or principal part of it, the employment of a different kind of force might become unavoidable. It appears that Massachusetts found it necessary to raise troops for repressing the disorders within that State; that Pennsylvania, from the mere apprehension of commotions among a part of her citizens, has thought proper to have recourse to the same measure. . . . [Fed. 223]

[4] . . . All candid and intelligent men must, upon due consideration, acknowledge that the principle of the objection is equally applicable to either of the two cases; and that whether they have one government for all the States, or different governments for different parcels of them, or even if there should be an entire separation of the States, there might sometimes be a necessity to make use of a force constituted differently from the militia, to preserve the peace of the community and to maintain the just authority of the laws against those violent invasions of them which amount to *insurrections* and rebellions. [Fed. 224]

Alexander Hamilton, *The Federalist*, No. 29, January 9, 1788:

[1] The power of regulating the militia, and of commanding its services in times of *insurrection* and invasion are natural incidents to the duties of superintending

the common defence, and of watching over the internal peace of the Confederacy. [Fed. 226]

[2] In times of *insurrection,* or invasion, it would be natural and proper that the militia of a neighboring State should be marched into another, to resist a common enemy, or to guard the republic against the violence of faction or sedition. This was frequently the case, in respect to the first object, in the course of the late war; and this mutual succor is, indeed, a principal end of our political association. . . . [Fed. 231]

James Madison, *The Federalist*, No. 43, January 23, 1788:

[1] . . . *Insurrections* in a State will rarely induce a federal interposition, unless the number concerned in them bear some proportion to the friends of government. It will be much better that the violence in such cases should be repressed by the superintending power, than that the majority should be left to maintain their cause by a bloody and obstinate contest. The existence of a right to interpose, will generally prevent the necessity of exerting it. [Fed. 313]

[2] Should it be asked, what is to be the redress for an *insurrection* pervading all the States, and comprising a superiority of the entire force, though not a constitutional right? the answer must be, that such a case, as it would be without the compass of human remedies, so it is fortunately not within the compass of human probability; and that is a sufficient recommendation of the federal Constitution, that it diminishes the risk of a calamity for which no possible constitution can provide a cure. [Fed. 314]

Luther Martin, "Genuine Information," No. 11, February 5, 1788:

. . . It was further said that if the general government was not by its constitution to interfere, the inconvenience would soon remedy itself, for that as the population increased in those States, their legislatures would be obliged to consent to the erection of new States to avoid the evils of a civil war, but as by the proposed constitution the general government is obliged to protect each State against domestic violence, and consequently will be obliged to assist in suppressing such commotions and *insurrections* as may take place from the struggle to have new States erected, the general government ought to have a power to decide upon the propriety and necessity of establishing or erecting a new State even without the approbation of the legislature of such States, within whose jurisdiction the new State should be erected, and for this purpose I submitted to the convention the following proposition—"That on the application of the inhabitants of any district of territory within the limits of any of the States, it shall be lawful for the legislature of the United States, if they shall under all circumstances think it reasonable, to erect the same into a new State, and admit it into the union without the consent of the State of which the said district may be a part." And it was said that we surely might trust the general government with this power with consent of the State of which the said district may be a part." And it was said that we surely might trust the general government with this power with more propriety than with many others with which they were proposed to be entrusted—and that as the general government was bound to suppress all *insurrections* and commotions which might arise on this subject, it ought to be in the power of the general government to decide upon it, and not in the power of the legislature of a single State by obstinately and unreasonably opposing the erection of a new State to prevent its taking effect, and thereby extremely to oppress that part of its citizens which live remote from, and inconvenient to, the seat of its government, and even to involve the union in war to support its injustice and oppression. . . . [DHRC16 40–41]

"Brutus," No. 12, February 7, 1788:

. . . Another end declared is "to insure domestic tranquility." This comprehends a provision against all private breaches of the peace, as well as against all public commotions or general *insurrections;* and to attain the object of this clause fully, the government must exercise the power of passing laws on these subjects, as well as of appointing magistrates with authority to execute them. And the courts will adopt these ideas in their expositions. [DHRC16 75]

"The Arraignment of Centinel," February 28, 1788:

. . . contriving, and with all his strength, soul, body, and goose quill (even to an unprecedented degree of flaming zeal and enthusiasm) to disturb the peace and common tranquillity of the aforesaid most illustrious United States, by dogmatical, proditorious publications, (lies and other hellish devices) to stir up and move opposition, faction, riot, sedition, *insurrection,* civil wars, rebellion and murder, against the aforesaid most illustrious United States, the Honorable the Congress, His Excellency General Washington, and divers others members of the honorable the continental and state conventions, and against their new proposed glorious frame of government, for promoting the peace, liberty and safety of the aforesaid most illustrious United States . . . [DHRC16 259]

Alexander White, "To the Citizens of Virginia," February 29, 1788:

They propose "that the power of organizing, arming and disciplining the militia, remain with the individual States, and that Congress ought not to have authority to call or march any of them out of their own States." The militia being under the general government, will in a great degree render a standing army unnecessary. *Insurrections,* such as that of Shays in Massachusetts, may generally be suppressed by them and hostile attacks from Indians repelled. . . .

[DHRC8 441]

Mercy Otis Warren, *Observations on the New Constitution*, February 1788:

. . . But the character of this people is not averse to a degree of subordination: the truth of this appears from the easy restoration of tranquility, after a dangerous *insurrection* in one of the states; this also evinces the little necessity of a complete revolution of government throughout the union. . . . [DHRC16 288]

"A Federal Republican," March 5, 1788:

Thus will you be necessarily compelled either to make a bold effort to extricate yourselves from these grievous and oppressive extortions, or you will be fatigued by fruitless attempts into the quiet and peaceable surrender of those rights, for which, the blood of your fellow citizens has been shed in vain. But the latter will, no doubt, be the melancholy fate of a people once inspired with the love of liberty, as the power vested in Congress of sending troops for suppressing *insurrections,* will always enable them to stifle the first struggles of freedom. [DHRC8 459]

"Brutus," No. 14, March 6, 1788:

. . . it is rare that a case of any importance is not carried by appeal to the supreme court, and the jurisdiction of the inferior courts is merely nominal; this has proved so burthensome to the people in Massachusetts, that it was one of the principal causes which excited the *insurrection* in that state, in the year past; very few sensible and moderate men in that state but what will admit, that the inferior courts are almost entirely useless, and answer very little purpose, save only to accumulate costs against the poor debtors who are already unable to pay their just debts. [DHRC16 328]

James Iredell, "Marcus," No. 4, March 12, 1788:

. . . It is in the power of the Parliament if they dare to exercise it, to abolish the trial by jury altogether—but woe be to the man who should dare to attempt it—it would undoubtedly produce an *insurrection* that would hurl every tyrant to the ground who attempted to destroy that great and just favorite of the English nation. We certainly shall be always sure of this guard at least, upon any such act of folly or insanity in our Representatives: They soon would be taught the consequence of sporting with the feelings of a free people . . . [DHRC16 383]

"An Impartial Citizen," No. 6, March 13, 1788:

[1] . . . The Congress can provide for calling forth the militia only in three cases, viz. to execute the laws of the Union, suppress *insurrections,* and repel invasions: Ought not these three things to be done? . . . [DHRC8 499]

[2] If the Congress were to call forth the militia of this State to quel an *insurrection* in Connecticut, when with infinitely more ease and convenience the Militia of Massachusetts, or some adjacent State, could effect it, the consequence would be an universal, just and irresistable alarm and struggle throughout the Continent . . . [DHRC8 499]

Political Club of Danville, Kentucky, Debates on the Constitution, March 22, 1788:

. . . Mr Innes: The Militia of Kentucky to suppress *insurrections* in Massachusetts.

Mr Muter: That Militia may be called to enforce the execution of a Writ &c. . . . [DHRC8 414]

Alexander Hamilton, *The Federalist*, No. 74, March 25, 1788:

. . . . But the principal argument for reposing the power of pardoning in this case to the Chief Magistrate is this; in seasons of *insurrection* or rebellion, there are often critical moments, when a well-timed offer of pardon to the insurgents or rebels may restore the tranquillity of the common wealth; and which, if suffered to pass unimproved, it may never be possible afterwards to recall. The dilatory process of convening the legislature, or one of its branches, for the purpose of obtaining its sanction to the measure, would frequently be the occasion of letting slip the golden opportunity. The loss of a week, a day, an hour, may sometimes be fatal. . . . [Fed. 475]

"George Bryan," March 26, 1788:

. . . Shays *insurrection* has been made a great engine of terror to dispose people of that country to receive chains, if the western counties can be kept down. Shays and his adherents were roused to what they did by excessive taxes; perhaps contrived to dispose the New-England states to receive the new system, to which they would otherwise be averse. [DHRC16 489]

Alexander Hamilton, *The Federalist*, No. 85, May 28, 1788:

The additional securities to republican government, to liberty, and to property, to be derived from the adoption of the plan under consideration, consist chiefly in the restraints which the preservation of the Union will impose on local factions and *insurrections,* and on the ambition of powerful individuals in single States, who may acquire credit and influence enough, from leaders and favorites, to become the despots of the people . . . [Fed. 542]

INVASION, INVASIONS

United States Constitution, September 17, 1787:

[Article I, Section 8:] [Congress shall have power] To provide for calling forth the Militia to execute the Laws of the Union, suppress Insurrections and repel *Invasions*.

[Article I, Section 9:] The Privilege of the Writ of Habeas Corpus shall not be suspended, unless when in Cases of Rebellion or *Invasion* the public Safety may require it.

[Article IV, Section 4:] The United States shall guarantee to every State in this Union a Republican Form of Government, and shall protect each of them against *Invasion;* and on Application of the Legislature, or of the Executive (when the Legislature cannot be convened) against domestic Violence.

* * * * *

James I, Second Charter of Virginia, May 23, 1609:

And we do also Grant and confirm to the said Treasurer and Company, and their Successors, as also to all and every such Governor, or other Officers, and Ministers, as by our said Council shall be appointed to have Power and Authority of Government and Command in and over the said Colony and Plantation; That they, and every of them, shall and lawfully may from Time to Time and at all Times for ever hereafter, for their several Defence and Safety, encounter, expulse, repel, and resist by Force and Arms, as well by Sea as by Land, and all Ways and Means whatsoever, all and every such Person and Persons whatsoever as (without the special Licence of the said Treasurer and Company and their Successors) shall attempt to inhabit within the said several Precincts and Limits of the said Colony and Plantation; And also all and every such Person and Persons whatsoever, as shall enterprize or attempt at any Time hereafter, Destruction, *Invasion,* Hurt, Detriment, or Annoyance, to the said Colony and Plantation, as is likewise specified in the said former Grant . . .

[Thorpe 3799–3800]

James I, The Charter of New England, November 3, 1620:

. . . and wee do also, for Us, our Heires, and Successors, grant to the said Councell and their Successors and to all and every such Governours, other Officers, or Ministers, as by the said Councill shall be appointed to have Power and Authority of Government and Command in and over the said Collony and Plantation, that they and every of them, shall, and lawfulll may, from time to time, and att all Times hereafter for ever, for their severall Defence and Safety, encounter, expulse, repel, and resist by Force of Arms, as well by Sea as by Land, and all Ways and Meanes whatsoever, all such Person and Persons, as without the speciall Licence of the said Councell and their Successors, or the greater Part of them, shall attempt to inhabitt within the said severall Precincts and Limitts of the said Collony and Plantation. And also all, and every such person or Persons whatsoever, as shall enterprize or attempt att any time hereafter Destruction, *Invasion,* Detriment, or Annoyance to the said Collony and Plantation . . . [Thorpe 1835–36]

Council of New England, Charter of Plymouth Colony, January 13, 1629:

. . . And by virtue of the authority to us derived by his said late Majesty's letters pattents to take apprehend seize and make prize of all such persons their shipps and goods as shall attempte to inhabite or trade with the savage people of that cuntry within the severall precincts and limitts of his and their severall plantacon, or shall enterprise or attempt att any tyme destruccon *invasion* detriment or annoyance to his and their said plantacon . . . [Thorpe 1845]

Charles I, Charter of Massachusetts Bay, March 4, 1629:

. . . at all Tymes hereafter for their speciall Defence and Safety, to incounter, expulse, repell, and resist by Force of Armes, aswell by Sea as by Lande, and by, all fitting Waies and Meanes whatsoever, all such Person and Persons, as shall at any Tyme hereafter, attempt or enterprise the Destruccon, *Invasion,* Detriment, or Annoyaunce to the said Plantation or Inhabitants, and to take and surprise by all Waies and Meanes whatsoever, all and every such Person and Persons, with their Shippes, Armour, Municon, and other Goodes, as shall in hostile manner *invade* or attempt the defesting of the said Plantacon, or the Hurt of the said Company and Inhabitants . . . [Thorpe 1858]

Charles I, Grant of the Province of Maine, April 3, 1639:

And because in a Country soe farr distant and seated amongst soe many barbarous nations the Intrusions or *Invasions* aswell of the barbarous people as of Pirates and other enemies maye be justly feared Wee Doe therefore for as our heires and successors give and graunte unto the said Sir Fardinando Gorges his heires and assignes full power and authoritie that hee the said Sir Fardinando Gorges his heires and assignes aswell by him and themselves as by his and theire Deputyes Captaynes or other Officers for the tyme being shall or lawfullye maye muster leavie rayse armes and ymploye all person and persons whatsoever inhabiteing or resideing within the said Province or Premisses for the resisting or withstanding of such Enymies or Pyrates both att Lande and att Sea . . .

[Thorpe 1630]

The New England Confederation, May 19, 1643:

[Article 5:] . . . But in any such case of sending men for present aid, whether before or after such order or alteration, it is agreed that at the meeting of the Commissioners for this Confederation, the cause of such war or *invasion* be duly considered: and if it appear that the fault lay in the parties so *invaded* then that Jurisdiction or Plantation make just satisfaction, both to the *invaders* whom they have injured, and bear all the charges of the war themselves, without requiring any allowance from the rest of the Confederates towards the same. And further that if any Jurisdiction see any danger of *invasion* approaching, and there be time for a meeting, that in such a case three magistrates of the Jurisdiction may summon a meeting at such convenient place as themselves shall think meet, to consider and provide against the threatened danger . . . [Thorpe 79]

Charles II, Charter of Connecticut, April 23, 1662:

. . . and at all Times hereafter, for their special Defence and Safety, to Assemble, Martial-Array, and put in warlike Posture the Inhabitants of the said Colony, and to Commissionate, Impower, and Authorize such Person or Persons as they shall think fit, to lead and conduct the said Inhabitants, and to encounter, expulse, repel and resist by Force of Arms, as well by Sea as by Land, and also to kill, slay, and destroy by all fitting Ways, Enterprises, and Means whatsoever, all and every such Person or Persons as shall at any Time hereafter attempt or enterprize the Destruction, *Invasion,* Detriment, or Annoyance of the said Inhabitants or Plantation, and to use and exercise the Law Martial in such Cases only as Occasion shall require, and to take or surprize by all Ways and Means whatsoever, all and every such Person and Persons, with their Ships, Armour, Ammunition and other Goods of such as shall in such hostile Manner *invade* or attempt the defeating of the said Plantation, or the hurt of the said Company and Inhabitants, and upon just Causes to *invade* and destroy the Natives, or other Enemies of the said Colony. [Thorpe 534–35]

Charles II, Charter of Carolina, March 24, 1663:

[Article 15:] And because that in so remote a country, and scituate among so many barbarous nations, and the *invasions* as well of salvages as of other enemies, pirates and robbers, may probably be feared . . . [Thorpe 2751]

Charles II, Charter of Rhode Island, July 8, 1663:

. . . to assemble, exercise in arms, martiall array, and putt in warlyke posture, the inhabitants of the sayd collonie, for theire speciall defence and safety; and to lead and conduct the sayd inhabitants, and to encounter, expulse, expell and resist, by force of armes, as well by sea as by lande; and alsoe to kill, slay and destroy, by all fitting wayes, enterprizes and meanes, whatsoever, all and every such person or persons as shall, att any tyme hereafter, attempt or enterprize the destruction, *invasion,* detriment or annoyance of the sayd inhabitants or Plantations; and to use and exercise the lawe martiall in such cases only as occasion shall necessarily require . . . [Thorpe 3218]

Charles II, Grant of the Province of Maine to the Duke of York, March 12, 1664:

. . . all times hereafter forever for theire severall defence and safety encounter expulse repell and resist by force of arms as well by sea as by land and all wayes and means whatsoever all such person and persons as without the speciall licence of our said deare brother his heires or assignes shall attempt to inhabit within the severall precincts and limitts of our said territoryes and islands and also all and every such person and persons whatsoever as shall enterprize or attempt at any time hereafter the destruccon *invasion* detriment or annoyance to ye parts places or islands aforesaid or any parte thereof . . . [Thorpe 1640]

Charles II, Charter of Carolina, June 30, 1665:

And because that in so remote a country, and situate among so many barbarous nations, the *invasions* of savages and other enemies, pirates and robbers, may probably be feared . . . [Thorpe 2769]

Fundamental Constitutions of Carolina, March 1, 1669:

[Article 35:] The councillor's court, consisting of one of the proprietors, and his six councillors, who shall be called vice-chancellors, shall have the custody of the seal of the palatine, under which charters of lands, or otherwise, commissions and grants of the palatine's court shall pass. And it shall not be lawful to put the seal of the palatinate to any writing which is not signed by the palatine or his deputy and three other proprietors or their deputies. To this court also belong all state matters, despatches and treaties with the neighbor Indians. To this court also belong all *invasions* of the law, of liberty of conscience, and all *invasions* of the public peace, upon pretence of religion, as also the license of printing. . . . [Thorpe 2777]

New Jersey Proprietors, Declaration of Intent and Meaning, December 6, 1672:

As to the fourth article, in case of foreign *invasion* or intestine mutiny or rebellion; it shall be lawful for the Governor and his Council to call in to their aid, any persons whatsoever whether freeholder or not. [Thorpe 2545]

Charles II, Commission Constituting a President and Council for New Hampshire, September 18, 1680:

. . . if any *invasions* shall at any time be made, or other destruction, detriment, or an'oyance made or done by Indians, or others upon or unto Our good subjects inhabiting within ye said Prov: of New H: We do by these prsents, for Us Our heirs & successors, declare, Ordaine & grant, that it shall & may be lawfull to & for Our said subjects, so com'issionated by Our said Councell from time to time, & at all times for their speciall defence & safety, to encounter, expell, repell, & resist by force of arms, & all other fitting ways & means whatsoever, all & every such person & persons, as shall at any time hereafter attempt or enterprze ye destruction *invasion* detriment or an'oyance of any of Our said loving subjects, or their plantations or estates. . . . [Thorpe 2448]

James II, Commission to Sir Edmund Andros for the Dominion of New England, April 7, 1688:

And Wee do hereby give and grant unto you the said Sr Edm Andros by your self your Captains and Commanders, by you to be authorized, full power and authority to levy arme muster command or employ, all persons whatsoever residing within our said Territory and Dominion of New England, and, as occasion shall serve, them to transferr from one place to another for the resisting and withstanding all enemies pyrats and rebells, both at land and sea, and to transferr such forces to any of our Plantations in America or the Territories thereunto belonging, as occasion shall require for the defence of the same against the *invasion* or attempt of any of our enemies, and then, if occasion shall require to pursue and prosecute in or out of the limits of our said Territories and Plantations or any of them, And if it shall so please God, them to vanquish; and, being taken, according to the law of arms to put to death or keep and preserve alive, at your discretion. And also to execute martiall law in time of *invasion* insurrection or warr, and during the continuance of the same, and upon soldiers in pay . . . [Thorpe 1866]

William and Mary, Charter of Massachusetts Bay, October 7, 1691:

. . . to lead and Conduct them and with them to Encounter Expulse Repell Resist and pursue by force of Armes aswell by Sea as by Land within or without the limitts of Our said Province or Territory and alsoe to kill slay destroy and Conquer by all fitting wayes Enterprises and meanes whatsoever all and every such Person and Persons as shall at any time hereafter Attempt or Enterprize the destruccon *Invasion* Detriment or Annoyance of Our said Province or Territory and to use and exercise the Law Martiall in time of actuall Warr *Invasion* or Rebellion as occasion shall necessarily require . . . [Thorpe 1884]

New Jersey Proprietors, Surrender of Rights, April 15, 1702:

. . . and at all times then after or for ever, for their several defence and safety, encounter expulse, repel and resist by force of arms, as well by sea as by land, and all ways and means whatsoever, all such person or persons as without the especial licence of the said James Duke of York, his heirs and assigns, should attempt to inabit within the several precincts and limits of the said territories and islands; and also all and every such person and persons whatsoever as should enterprize, or attempt at any time then after, the destruction or *invasion,* detriment or annoyance to the parts, places or islands aforesaid, or any part thereof . . . [Thorpe 2587]

George II, Charter of Georgia, June 9, 1732:

. . . and also to kill, slay and destroy, and conquer by all fitting ways, enterprizes and means whatsoever, all and every such person or persons as shall at any time hereafter, in any hostile manner, attempt or enterprize the destruction, *invasion,* detriment or annoyance of our said colony; and to use and exercise the martial law in time of actual war and *invasion* or rebellion, in such cases, where by law the same may be used or exercised . . . [Thorpe 776]

The Mecklenburgh County, North Carolina, Resolutions, May 31, 1775:

[Article 1:] That whosoever directly or indirectly abets, or in any way, form, or manner countenances the unchartered and dangerous *invasion* of our rights, as claimed by Great Britain, is an enemy to this country—to America—and to the inherent and inalienable rights of man. [Thorpe 2786]

Thomas Paine, *Common Sense*, January 9, 1776:

Besides, the taking up arms, merely to enforce the repeal of a pecuniary law, seems as unwarrantable by the divine law, and as repugnant to human feelings, as the taking up arms to enforce obedience thereto. The object, on either side, doth not justify the ways and means; for the lives of men are too valuable to be cast away on such trifles. It is the violence which is done and threatened to our persons; the destruction of our property by an armed force; the *invasion* of our country by fire and sword, which conscientiously qualifies the use of arms: and the instant in which such a mode of defence became necessary, all subjection to Britain ought to have ceased; and the independency of America should have been considered, as dating its era from, and published by, the first musket that was fired against her. . . . [CWTP1 45]

South Carolina Constitution, March 26, 1776:

[Preamble:] . . . And whereas large fleets and armies having been sent to America in order to enforce the execution of those laws, and to compel an absolute and implicit submission to the will of a corrupt and despotic administration, and in consequence thereof, hostilities having been commenced in the Massachusetts Bay, by the troops under command of General Gage, whereby a number of peaceable, helpless, and unarmed people were wantonly robbed and murdered, and there being just reason to apprehend that like hostilities would be committed in all the other colonies. The colonists were therefore driven to the necessity of taking up arms, to repel force by force, and to defend themselves and their properties against lawless *invasions* and depredations. [Thorpe 3242]

John Adams, *Thoughts on Government*, April 1776:

A militia law requiring all men, or with very few exceptions besides cases of conscience, to be provided with arms and ammunition, to be trained at certain seasons, and requiring counties, towns, or other small districts to be provided with public stocks of ammunition and entrenching utensils, and with some settled plans for transporting provisions after the militia, when marched to defend their country against sudden *invasions,* and requiring certain districts to be provided with field-pieces, companies of matrosses and perhaps some regiments of light horse, is always a wise institution, and in the present circumstances of our country indispensible. [PJA4 91]

Virginia Constitution, June 29, 1776:

[Preamble:] By dissolving legislative Assemblies repeatedly and continually, for opposing with manly firmness his *invasions* of the rights of the people . . . [Thorpe 3814]

United States Declaration of Independence, July 4, 1776:

[1] . . . He [the King] has dissolved Representative Houses repeatedly, for opposing with manly firmness his *invasions* on the rights of the people. . . .

[2] . . . He has refused for a long time, after such dissolutions, to cause others to be elected; whereby the Legislative powers, incapable of Annihilation, have returned to the People at large for their exercise; the State remaining in the mean time exposed to all the dangers of *invasion* from without, and convulsions within. . . .

Massachusetts Constitution, March 2, 1780:

[Frame of Government, Chapter II:1:7:] [The governor as commander-in-chief shall have power] . . . for the special defence and safety of the commonwealth, to assemble in martial array, and put in warlike posture, the inhabitants thereof, and to lead and conduct them, and with them to encounter, repel, resist, expel, and pursue, by force of arms, as well by sea as by land, within or without the limits of this commonwealth, and also to kill, slay, and destroy, if necessary, and conquer, by all fitting ways, enterprises, and means whatsoever, all and every such person and persons as shall, at any time hereafter, in a hostile manner, attempt or enterprise the destruction, *invasion,* detriment, or annoyance of this commonwealth; and to use and exercise, over the army and navy, and over the militia in actual service, the law-martial, in time of war or *invasion,* and also in time of rebellion, declared by the legislature to exist, as occasion shall necessarily require; and to take and surprise, by all ways and means whatsoever, all and every such person or persons, with their ships, arms, ammunition, and other goods, as shall, in a hostile manner, *invade,* or attempt the *invading,* conquering, or annoying this commonwealth . . . [Thorpe 1901]

New Hampshire Constitution, June 2, 1784:

[Form of Government:] . . . and also to kill slay, destroy, if necessary, and conquer by all fitting ways, enterprize and means, all and every such person and persons as shall, at any time hereafter, in a hostile manner, attempt or enterprize the destruction, *invasion,* detriment, or annoyance of this state; and to use and exercise over the army and navy, and over the militia in actual service, the law-martial in time of war, invasion, and also in rebellion, declared by the legislature to exist, as occasion shall necessarily require . . . [Thorpe 2464]

William Pierce to St. George Tucker, September 28, 1787, published in *Gazette of the State of Georgia*, March 20, 1788:

[1] In my judgment, when there are restraints on power to prevent its *invading* the positive rights of a people, there is no necessity for any such thing as a Bill of Rights. I conceive civil liberty is sufficiently guarded when personal security, personal liberty, and private property, are made the peculiar care of government. Now the defined powers of each department of the government, and the restraints

that naturally follow, will be sufficient to prevent the *invasion* of either of those rights. Where then can be the necessity for a Bill of Rights? . . .

[DHRC16 443]

[2] I set this down as a truth founded in nature, that a nation habituated to freedom will never remain quiet under an *invasion* of its liberties. The English history presents us with a proof of this. . . . [DHRC16 444]

Richard Henry Lee [?], "The Federal Farmer," No. 1, October 8, 1787:

The first principal question that occurs, is, Whether, considering our situation, we ought to precipitate the adoption of the proposed constitution? If we remain cool and temperate, we are in no immediate danger of any commotions; we are in a state of perfect peace, and in no danger of *invasions;* the state governments are in the full exercise of their powers; and our governments answer all present exigencies, except the regulation of trade, securing credit, in some cases, and providing for the interest, in some instances, of the public debts . . .

[Ford 280–81]

Richard Henry Lee [?], "The Federal Farmer," No. 3, October 10, 1787:

. . . The power in the general government to lay and collect internal taxes, will render its powers respecting armies, navies and the militia, the more exceptionable. By the constitution it is proposed that congress shall have power "to raise and support armies, but no appropriation of money to that use shall be for a longer term than two years; to provide and maintain a navy; to provide for calling forth the militia to execute the laws of the union; suppress insurrections, and repel *invasions:* to provide for organizing, arming, and disciplining the militia;" reserving to the states the right to appoint the officers, and to train the militia according to the discipline prescribed by congress; congress will have unlimited power to raise armies, and to engage officers and men for any number of years; but a legislative act applying money for their support can have operation for no longer term than two years, and if a subsequent congress do not within the two years renew the appropriation, or further appropriate monies for the use of the army, the army will be left to take care of itself. . . . [Ford 304]

Noah Webster, *An Examination into the Leading Principles of the Federal Constitution*, October 17, 1787:

[1] The powers lodged in Congress are extensive; but it is presumed that they are not too extensive. The first object of the constitution is to unite the states into one compact society, for the purpose of government, if such union must exist, or the states be exposed to foreign *invasions,* internal discord, reciprocal

encroachments upon each others property—to weakness and infamy, which no person will dispute; what powers must be collected and lodged in the supreme head or legislature of these states. The answer is easy: This legislature must have exclusive jurisdiction in all matters in which the states have a mutual interest. . . . [Ford 45]

[2] Congress likewise are to have power to provide for organizing, arming and disciplining the militia, but have no other command of them, except when in actual service. Nor are they at liberty to call out the militia at pleasure—but only, to execute the laws of the union, suppress insurrections, and repel *invasions*. For these purposes, government must always be armed with a military force, if the occasion should require it: otherwise laws are nugatory, and life and property insecure. [Ford 52]

[3] . . . But reverse the case; suppose every man to act without control or fear of punishment—every man would be free, but no man would be sure of his freedom one moment. Each would have the power of taking his neighbor's life, liberty, or property; and no man would command more than his own strength to repel the *invasion*. The case is the same with states. If the states should not unite into one compact society, every state may trespass upon its neighbor, and the injured state has no means of redress but its own military force. [Ford 55]

[4] The present situation of our American states is very little better than a state of nature—Our boasted state sovereignties are so far from securing our liberty and property, that they, every moment, expose us to the loss of both. That state which commands the heaviest purse and longest sword, may at any moment, lay its weaker neighbor under tribute; and there is no superior power now existing, that can regularly oppose the *invasion* or redress the injury. From such liberty, 0 Lord, deliver us! [Ford 55]

[5] . . . The liberties of America, therefore, and her forms of government, stand on the broadest basis. Removed from the fears of a foreign *invasion* and conquest, they are not exposed to the convulsions that shake other governments; and the principles of freedom are so general and energetic, as to exclude the possibility of a change in our republican constitutions. [Ford 60]

Pelatiah Webster, *The Weakness of Brutus Exposed*, November 4, 1787:

There can be no doubt that each State will receive from the union great support and protection against the *invasions* and inroads of foreign enemies, as well as against riots and insurrections of their own citizens; and of consequence, the course of their internal administration will be secured by this means against any interruption or embarrassment from either of these causes. [Ford 128]

John Jay, *The Federalist*, No. 4, November 7, 1787:

What would the militia of Britain be if the English militia obeyed the government of England, if the Scotch militia obeyed the government of Scotland, and if the Welsh militia obeyed the government of Wales? Suppose an *invasion;* would those three governments (if they agreed at all) be able, with all their respective forces, to operate against the enemy so effectually as the single government of Great Britain would? [Fed. 103]

Hugh Williamson, Speech at Edenton, North Carolina, November 8, 1787:

But it is a Government, unless I am greatly mistaken, that gives the fairest promise of being firm and honorable; safe from Foreign *Invasion* or Domestic Sedition. A Government by which our commerce must be protected and enlarged; the value of our produce and of our lands must be encreased; the labourer and the mechanic must be encouraged and supported. It is a form of Government that is perfectly fitted for protecting Liberty and Property, and for cherishing the good Citizen and the Honest Man. [DHRC16 208]

Alexander Hamilton, *The Federalist*, No. 7, November 17, 1787:

. . . There are even dissimilar views among the States as to the general principle of discharging the public debt. Some of them, either less impressed with the importance of national credit, or because their citizens have little, if any, immediate interest in the question, feel an indifference, if not a repugnance, to the payment of the domestic debt at any rate. These would be inclined to magnify the difficulties of a distribution. Others of them, a numerous body of whose citizens are creditors to the public beyond the proportion of the State in the total amount of the national debt, would be strenuous for some equitable and effective provision. The procrastinations of the former would excite the resentments of the latter. The settlement of a rule would, in the meantime, be postponed by real differences of opinion and affected delays. The citizens of the States interested would clamor; foreign powers would urge for the satisfaction of their just demands, and the peace of the States would be hazarded to the double contingency of external *invasion* and internal contention. [Ford 117]

Alexander Hamilton, *The Federalist*, No. 8, November 20, 1787:

[1] . . . The nations of Europe are encircled with chains of fortified places, which mutually obstruct *invasion*. Campaigns are wasted in reducing two or three frontier garrisons, to gain admittance into an enemy's country. Similar impediments occur at every step, to exhaust the strength and delay the progress of an *invader*. Formerly, an *invading* army would penetrate into the heart of a neighboring country almost as soon as intelligence of its approach could be

received; but now a comparatively small force of disciplined troops, acting on the defensive, with the aid of posts, is able to impede, and finally to frustrate, the enterprises of one much more considerable. . . . [Fed. 119–20]

[2] There is a wide difference, also, between military establishments in a country seldom exposed by its situation to internal *invasions,* and in one which is often subject to them, and always apprehensive of them. The rulers of the former can have no good pretext, if they are even so inclined, to keep on foot armies so numerous as must of necessity be maintained in the latter. . . . [Fed. 122]

[3] The kingdom of Great Britain falls within the first description. An insular situation, and a powerful marine, guarding it in a great measure against the possibility of foreign *invasion,* supersede the necessity of a numerous army within the kingdom. A sufficient force to make head against a sudden descent, till the militia could have time to rally and embody, is all that has been deemed requisite. . . . [Ford 123]

Alexander Hamilton, *The Federalist*, No. 16, December 4, 1787:

The plausibility of this objection will vanish the moment we advert to the essential difference between a mere NON-COMPLIANCE and a DIRECT and ACTIVE RESISTANCE. If the interposition of the State legislatures be necessary to give effect to a measure of the Union, they have only NOT TO ACT, or to ACT EVASIVELY, and the measure is defeated. This neglect of duty may be disguised under affected but unsubstantial provisions, so as not to appear, and of course not to excite any alarm in the people for the safety of the Constitution. The State leaders may even make a merit of their surreptitious *invasions* of it on the ground of some temporary convenience, exemption, or advantage. [Ford 165–66]

James Madison, *The Federalist*, No. 20, December 11, 1787:

This unhappy people [the Dutch] seem to be now suffering from popular convulsions, from dissensions among the states, and from the actual *invasion* of foreign arms, the crisis of their destiny. All nations have their eyes fixed on the awful spectacle. The first wish prompted by humanity is, that this severe trial may issue in such a revolution of their government as will establish their union, and render it the parent of tranquillity, freedom, and happiness . . . [Ford 185]

Dissent of the Pennsylvania Convention's Minority, December 18, 1787:

As Congress have the control over the time of the appointment of the president general, of the senators and of the representatives of the United States, they may prolong their existence in office, for life, by postponing the time of their election and appointment, from period to period, under various pretenses, such as an apprehension of *invasion,* the factious disposition of the people, or any other plausible pretence that the occasion may suggest . . . [DHRC2 628–29]

Alexander Hamilton, *The Federalist*, No. 24, December 19, 1787:

. . . we should find it expedient to increase our frontier garrisons in some ratio to the force by which our Western settlements might be annoyed. There are, and will be, particular posts, the possession of which will include the command of large districts of territory, and facilitate future *invasions* of the remainder. It may be added that some of those posts will be keys to the trade with the Indian nations. Can any man think it would be wise to leave such posts in a situation to be at any instant seized by one or the other of two neighboring and formidable powers? . . . [Fed. 207–208]

Alexander Hamilton, *The Federalist*, No. 26, December 22, 1787:

. . . Few persons will be so visionary as seriously to contend that military forces ought not to be raised to quell a rebellion or resist an *invasion;* and if the defence of the community under such circumstances should make it necessary to have an army so numerous as to hazard its liberty, this is one of those calamities for which there is neither preventative nor cure. . . . [Fed. 218]

Alexander Hamilton, *The Federalist*, No. 28, December 26, 1787:

[1] . . . All candid and intelligent men must, upon due consideration, acknowledge that the principle of the objection is equally applicable to either of the two cases; and that whether they have one government for all the States, or different governments for different parcels of them, or even if there should be an entire separation of the States, there might sometimes be a necessity to make use of a force constituted differently from the militia, to preserve the peace of the community and to maintain the just authority of the laws against those violent *invasions* of them which amount to insurrections and rebellions. [Fed. 224]

[2] It may safely be received as an axiom in our political system, that the State governments will, in all possible contingencies, afford complete security against *invasions* of the public liberty by the national authority. Projects of usurpation cannot be masked under pretences so likely to escape the penetration of select bodies of men, as of the people at large. . . . [Fed. 225]

Alexander Hamilton, *The Federalist*, No. 33, January 2, 1788:

[1] . . . Suppose, by some forced constructions of its authority (which, indeed, cannot easily be imagined), the Federal legislature should attempt to vary the law of descent in any State, would it not be evident that, in making such an attempt, it had exceeded its jurisdiction, and infringed upon that of the State? Suppose, again, that upon the pretence of an interference with its revenues, it

should undertake to abrogate a land-tax imposed by the authority of a State; would it not be equally evident that this was an *invasion* of that concurrent jurisdiction in respect to this species of tax, which its Constitution plainly supposes to exist in the State governments?... [Fed. 246]

[2]... But it will not follow from this doctrine that acts of the larger society which are not pursuant to its constitutional powers, but which are *invasions* of the residuary authorities of the smaller societies, will become the supreme law of the land. These will be merely acts of usurpation, and will deserve to be treated as such.... [Fed. 247]

Alexander Hamilton, *The Federalist*, No. 34, January 4, 1788:

... But would it be wise, or would it not rather be the extreme of folly to stop at this point, and to leave the government intrusted with the care of the national defence in a state of absolute incapacity to provide for the protection of the community against future *invasions* of the public peace, by foreign war or domestic convulsions? If, on the contrary, we ought to exceed this point, where can we stop, short of an indefinite power of providing for emergencies as they may arise?... [Fed. 250]

Alexander Hamilton, *The Federalist*, No. 29, January 9, 1788:

[1] The power of regulating the militia, and of commanding its services in times of insurrection and *invasion* are natural incidents to the duties of superintending the common defence, and of watching over the internal peace of the Confederacy. [Fed. 226]

[2] In times of insurrection, or *invasion*, it would be natural and proper that the militia of a neighboring State should be marched into another, to resist a common enemy, or to guard the republic against the violence of faction or sedition. This was frequently the case, in respect to the first object, in the course of the late war; and this mutual succor is, indeed, a principal end of our political association.... [Fed. 231]

George Nicholas [?], "The State Soldier," No. 1, January 16, 1788:

... It is not at all surprising however that you should be brought to believe your liberties are now in danger, when you are thus shewn how that bravery you have once felt in your favor, is likely to take residence in the breasts of those thus capable of any thing. By thus assuming our names [i.e., as former soldiers] and holding to view their own genuine characters, designing men do us more real injury, and their own cause more essential service, than those who insinuate that we shall be preferred from our former services to share the spoils when our country shall fall a prey to aristocratical *invasion*. These last only add insult to misfortune: For there is but little in our influence to rouse your jealousy, and

much less in our situations to excite your envy, unless the nobleness of your gratitude should make you wish to share in our poverty and fears. . . .
[DHRC8 307–308]

James Madison, *The Federalist*, No. 43, January 23, 1788:

A protection against *invasion* is due from every society to the parts composing it. The latitude of the expression here used seems to secure each State, not only against foreign hostility, but against ambitious or vindictive enterprises of its more powerful neighbors. . . . [Fed. 312]

James Madison, *The Federalist*, No. 44, January 25, 1788:

. . . The truth is, that this ultimate redress may be more confided in against unconstitutional acts of the federal than of the State legislatures, for this plain reason, that as every such act of the former will be an *invasion* of the rights of the latter, these will be ever ready to mark the innovation, to sound the alarm to the people, and to exert their local influence in effecting a change of federal representatives. There being no such intermediate body between the State legislatures and the people interested in watching the conduct of the former, violations of the State constitutions are more likely to remain unnoticed and unredressed. [Fed. 322]

Alexander C. Hanson, *Remarks on the Proposed Plan of a Federal Government*, c. January 31, 1788:

[1] Can this writer imagine, that congress will presume to use this power, without the occurrence of some one or more of the cases, the contemplation whereof induced the convention to create it. These are the cases of *invasion* by a foreign power; of neglect, or obstinate refusal, in a state legislature; of the prevalance of a party, prescribing so as to suit a sinister purpose, or injure the general government. . . . [Ford 227]

[2] . . . But, notwithstanding the universal contagion of the alarm, did the states, on that occasion, comply with the requisition? Suppose even an *invasion* by a foreign power,—in what manner could congress provide for its own defence? In the contemptible light in which America has lately stood, is it reasonable to expect she will be suffered to remain long in peace? The distance between the two continents is the only circumstance on which we can rely. All Europe is now in suspence; and the result of your deliberations will instruct her in the part she shall act. [Ford 244–45]

[3] . . . Are not the regulations of property, the regulations of the penal law, the protection of the weak, the promotion of useful arts, the whole internal government of their respective republics; are not these the main objects of every wise and honest legislature? Are not these things still in their power; and, whilst free

from *invasion* or injuries abroad, are not these almost the only things, in which sovereignty is exercised? [Ford 252]

James Madison, *The Federalist*, No. 48, February 1, 1788:

. . . After discriminating, therefore, in theory, the several classes of power, as they may in their nature be legislative, executive, or judiciary, the next and most difficult task is to provide some practical security for each, against the *invasion* of the others. What this security ought to be, is the great problem to be solved. [Fed. 343]

James Madison, *The Federalist*, No. 49, February 2, 1788:

. . . One of the precautions which he [Thomas Jefferson in *Notes on the State of Virginia*] proposes, and on which he appears ultimately to rely as a palladium to the weaker departments of power against the *invasions* of the stronger, is perhaps altogether his own, and as it immediately relates to the subject of our present inquiry, ought not to be overlooked. [Fed. 348]

David Ramsay, "Civis," February 4, 1788:

By the new constitution, you will be protected with the force of the union, against domestic violence and foreign *invasion*. You will have a navy to defend your coast.—The respectable figure you will make among the nations, will so far command the attention of foreign powers, that it is probable you will soon obtain such commercial treaties, as will open to your vessels the West-India islands, and give life to your expiring commerce. [DHRC16 26]

"An Old Whig," No. 8, February 6, 1788:

. . . It would not by any means be extravagant to say, that a new continental convention ought to be called, if it were only for the sake of preserving that sacred palladium—the inestimable right of trial by jury.—But even if we were to delude ourselves so far as to believe that it would be entirely in the power of the future legislature to set every thing right, to build up our liberties against all *invasions,* and to protect us from every political calamity, still we ought not to repose all our liberty and all our happiness in the virtue of our future rulers. . . . [DHRC16 53]

Oliver Ellsworth, "The Landholder," No. 11, March 10, 1788:

. . . With the present generation of men, national interest is the measure by which war or peace are determined; and when we see the British nation, by a late treaty paying an enormous annual subsidy to the little principality of Hesse Cassel for the purpose of retaining her in military alliance, it should teach us the necessity of those parts in the Constitution, which enable the efficient force of the whole to be opposed to an *invasion* of any part. [DHRC16 367]

James Iredell, "Marcus," No. 4, March 12, 1788:

. . . The absurdity of our being prohibited from preparing to resist an *invasion* till after it had actually taken place, is so glaring that no man can consider it for a moment without being struck with astonishment, to see how rashly, and with how little consideration gentlemen, whose characters are certainly respectable, have suffered themselves to be led away by so delusive an idea. The example of other countries, so far from warranting any such limitation of power, is directly against it. . . . [DHRC16 385]

"An Impartial Citizen," No. 6, March 13, 1788:

. . . The congress cannot make an instrument of tyranny of the militia: The Congress can only provide for arming and disciplining them. The propriety of this results from that of an uniformity of discipline and armour throughout the States, which must be self-evident. The Congress can provide for calling forth the militia only in three cases, viz. to execute the laws of the Union, suppress insurrections, and repel *invasions:* Ought not these three things to be done? Still the respective States have the authority of training the militia according to the congressional discipline; still they have the appointment of the officers: This renders the States perfectly secure. . . . [DHRC8 499]

Alexander Hamilton, *The Federalist*, No. 70, March 15, 1788:

. . . Every man the least conversant in Roman history, knows how often that republic was obliged to take refuge in the absolute power of a single man, under the formidable title of Dictator, as well against the intrigues of ambitious individuals who aspired to the tyranny, and the seditions of whole classes of the community whose conduct threatened the existence of all government, as against the *invasions* of external enemies who menaced the conquest and destruction of Rome. [Fed. 451]

Alexander Hamilton, *The Federalist*, No. 78, May 28, 1788:

. . . But it is easy to see, that it would require an uncommon portion of fortitude in the judges to do their duty as faithful guardians of the Constitution, where legislative *invasions* of it had been instigated by the major voice of the community. [Fed. 494]

Alexander Hamilton, *The Federalist*, No. 84, May 28, 1788:

. . . We know that newspapers are taxed in Great Britain, and yet it is notorious that the press nowhere enjoys greater liberty than in that country. And if duties of any kind may be laid without a violation of that liberty, it is evident that the extent must depend on legislative discretion, regulated by public opinion; so that, after all, general declarations respecting the liberty of the press, will give it no greater security than it will have without them. The same *invasions* of it may be effected under the State constitutions which contain those declarations through the means of taxation, as under the proposed Constitution, which has nothing of the kind. It would be quite as significant to declare that government ought to be free, that taxes ought not to be excessive, etc., as that the liberty of the press ought not to be restrained. [Fed. 536n]

Pennsylvania Constitution, September 2, 1790:

[Article IX, Section 14:] That all prisoners shall be bailable by sufficient sureties, unless for capital offences, when the proof is evident or presumption great; and the privilege of the writ of habeas corpus shall not be suspended, unless when, in cases of rebellion or *invasion,* the public safety may require it.

[Thorpe 3101]

JEOPARDY

United States Constitution, Bill of Rights, December 15, 1791:

[Article V:] No person shall be held to answer for a capital, or otherwise infamous crime, unless on a presentment or indictment of a Grand Jury, except in cases arising in the land or naval forces, or in the Militia, when in actual service in time of War or public danger; nor shall any person be subject *for the same offense* to be *twice put in jeopardy* of life or limb; nor shall be compelled in any criminal case to be a witness against himself, nor be deprived of life, liberty, or property, without due process of law; nor shall private property be taken for public use, without just compensation.

* * * * *

Edmund Randolph, Letter on the Federal Constitution, October 10, 1787:

. . . But how shall we speak of the intrusion of troops? Shall we arm citizens against citizens, and habituate them to shed kindred blood? Shall we risk the inflicting of wounds which will generate a rancour never to be subdued? Would there be no room to fear, that an army accustomed to fight for the establishment of authority, would salute an emperor of their own? Let us not bring these things into *jeopardy*. Let us rather substitute the same process by which individuals are compelled to contribute to the government of their own States. . . .

[DHRC8 266]

John Jay, *The Federalist*, No. 2, October 31, 1787:

. . . They who promote the idea of substituting a number of distinct confederacies in the room of the plan of the convention, seem clearly to foresee that the rejection of it would put the continuance of the Union in the utmost *jeopardy*. That certainly would be the case, and I sincerely wish that it may be as clearly foreseen by every good citizen, that whenever the dissolution of the Union arrives, America will have reason to exclaim, in the words of the poet: "FAREWELL! A LONG FAREWELL TO ALL MY GREATNESS." [Fed. 96–97]

Alexander Hamilton, *The Federalist*, No. 25, December 21, 1787:

. . . . Who shall judge of the continuance of the danger? This must undoubtedly be submitted to the national government, and the matter would then be brought to this issue, that the national government, to provide against apprehended danger, might in the first instance raise troops, and might afterwards keep them on foot as long as they supposed the peace or safety of the community was in any degree of *jeopardy*. It is easy to perceive that a discretion so latitudinary as this would afford ample room for eluding the force of the provision. [Fed. 210]

Alexander Hamilton, *The Federalist*, No. 26, December 22, 1787:

But it is an evil infinitely less likely to attend us in a united than in a disunited state; nay, it may be safely asserted that it is an evil altogether unlikely to attend us in the latter situation. It is not easy to conceive a possibility that dangers so formidable can assail the whole Union, as to demand a force considerable enough to place our liberties in the least *jeopardy,* especially if we take into our view the aid to be derived from the militia, which ought always to be counted upon as a valuable and powerful auxiliary. But in a state of disunion (as has been fully shown in another place), the contrary of this supposition would become not only probable, but almost unavoidable. [Fed. 218]

Alexander Hamilton, *The Federalist*, No. 78, May 28, 1788:

. . . And it proves, in the last place, that as liberty can have nothing to fear from the judiciary alone, but would have every thing to fear from its union with either of the other departments; that as all the effects of such a union must ensue from a dependence of the former on the latter, notwithstanding a nominal and apparent separation; that as, from the natural feebleness of the judiciary, it is in continual *jeopardy* of being overpowered, awed, or influenced by its coordinate branches; and that as nothing can contribute so much to its firmness and independence as permanency in office, this quality may therefore be justly regarded as an indispensable ingredient in it constitution, and, in a great measure, as the citadel of the public justice and the public security. [Fed. 491]

Alexander Hamilton, *The Federalist*, No. 85, May 28, 1788:

I answer in the next place, that I should esteem it the extreme of imprudence to prolong the precarious state of our national affairs, and to expose the Union to the *jeopardy* of successive experiments, in the chimerical pursuit of a perfect plan. I never expect to see a perfect work from imperfect man. . . . [Fed. 544]

Pennsylvania Constitution, September 2, 1790:

[Article IX, Section 10:] That no person shall, for any indictable *offence,* be proceeded against criminally by information, except in cases arising in the land or naval forces, or in the militia, when in actual service in time of war or public danger, or, by leave of the court, for oppression and misdemeanor in office. No person shall, for the *same offence, be twice put in jeopardy* of life or limb; nor shall any man's property be taken or applied to public use without the consent of his representatives, and without just compensation being made.

[3100–3101]

LAW OF NATIONS

United States Constitution, September 17, 1987:

[Article I, Section 8:] [Congress shall haver power] To define and punish Piracies and Felonies committed on the high Seas, and Offenses against the *Law of Nations* . . .

* * * * *

Thomas Paine, *Common Sense*, January 9, 1776:

. . . Where is our redress? No going to *law with nations;* cannon are the barristers of crowns; and the sword, not of justice, but of war, decides the suit. . . .
[CWTP1 44]

Charles Pinckney's Plan of Union, May 29, 1787:

[The United States legislature shall have power] of instituting a federal judicial Court, to which an Appeal shall be allowed from the judicial Courts of the several States in all Causes wherein Questions shall arise on the Construction of Treaties made by U.S. or on the Law of Nations . . . [DHRC1 247]

Edmund Randolph, Letter on the Federal Constitution, October 10, 1787:

If we examine the constitutions and laws of the several states, it is immediately discovered, that the *law of nations* is unprovided with sanctions in many cases, which deeply affect public dignity and public justice. The letter, however of the confederation does not permit Congress to remedy these defects, and such an authority, although evidently deducible from its spirit, cannot without violation of the second article, be assumed. Is it not a political phenomenon, that the head of the confederacy should be doomed to be plunged into war, from its wretched impotency to check offences against this law? And sentenced to witness in unavailing anguish the infraction of their engagements to foreign sovereigns? [DHRC8 263]

Richard Henry Lee [?], "The Federal Farmer," No. 3, October 10, 1787:

. . . The trial by jury is secured only in those few criminal cases, to which the federal laws will extend—as crimes committed on the seas, against the *laws of nations,* treason and counterfeiting the federal securities and coin: But even in these cases, the jury trial of the vicinage is not secured—particularly in the large states, a citizen may be tried for a crime committed in the state, and yet tried in some states 500 miles from the place where it was committed; but the jury trial is not secured at all in civil causes. . . . [Ford 307–308]

John Jay, *The Federalist,* No. 3, November 3, 1787:

[1] It is of high importance to the peace of America that she observe the *laws of nations* towards all these powers, and to me it appears evident that this will be more perfectly and punctually done by one national government than it could be either by thirteen separate States or by three or four distinct confederacies. [Fed. 98]

[2] Because, under the national government, treaties and articles of treaties, as well as the *laws of nations,* will always be expounded in one sense and executed in the same manner,—whereas adjudications on the same points and questions, in thirteen States, or in three or four confederacies, will not always accord or be consistent . . . [Fed. 98]

[3] So far, therefore, as either designed or accidental violations of treaties and the *laws of nations* afford just causes of war, they are less to be apprehended under one general government than under several lesser ones, and in that respect the former most favors the safety of the people. [Fed. 99]

Dissent of the Pennsylvania Convention's Minority, December 18, 1787:

. . . That the courts to be established would decide on all cases of law and equity, which is a well-known characteristic of the civil law, and these courts would have conusance not only of the laws of the United States, and of treaties, and of cases affecting ambassadors, but of all cases of admiralty and maritime jurisdiction, which last are matters belonging exclusively to the *civil law, in every nation* in Christendom. . . . [DHRC2 633]

John Adams to William S. Smith, December 26, 1787 (From Adams' *Defence of the Constitutions;* published in *New York Journal*, February 23, 1788):

. . . All nations, from the beginning, have been agitated by the same passions. The principles developed in these letters, will go a great way, in explaining every phenomenon that occurs in the history of government. The vegetable and animal kingdoms, and those heavenly bodies whose existence and movements we are, as yet, only permitted faintly to perceive, do not appear to be governed by *laws* more uniform or certain than those that regulate the moral and political world. *Nations* move by unalterable rules; and education, discipline, and *laws*, make the greatest difference in their accomplishments, happiness and perfection. . . . [DHRC16 193]

James Madison, *The Federalist*, No. 42, January 22, 1788:

[1] The second class of powers, lodged in the general government, consist of those which regulate the intercourse with foreign nations, to wit: to make treaties; to send and receive ambassadors, other public ministers, and consuls; to define and punish piracies and felonies committed on the high seas, and offences against the *law of nations;* to regulate foreign commerce, including a power to prohibit, after the year 1808, the importation of slaves, and to lay an intermediate duty of ten dollars per head, as a discouragement to such importations. [Fed. 302]

[2] The power to define and punish piracies and felonies committed on the high seas, and offences against the *law of nations,* belongs with equal propriety to the general government, and is a still greater improvement on the articles of Confederation. These articles contain no provision for the case of offences against the *law of nations;* and consequently leave it in the power of any indiscreet member to embroil the Confederacy with foreign nations. The provision of the federal articles on the subject of piracies and felonies extends no further than to the establishment of courts for the trial of these offences. The definition of piracies might, perhaps, without inconveniency, be left to the *law of nations;* though a legislative definition of them is found in most municipal codes. A definition of felonies on the high seas is evidently requisite. Felony is a term of loose signification, even in the common law of England; and of various import in the statute law of that kingdom. But neither the common nor the statute law of that, or of any other nation, ought to be a standard for the proceedings of this, unless previously made its own by legislative adoption. . . .
[Fed. 303–304]

Luther Martin, "Genuine Information," No. 10, February 1, 1788:

To save the citizens of the respective States from this disagreeable dilemma, and to secure them from being punishable as traitors to the United States when acting expressly in obedience to the authority of their own State, I wished to have obtained as an amendment to the third section of this article the following clause: "Provided that no act or acts done by one or more of the States against the United States, or by any citizen of any one of the United States under the authority of one or more of the said States, shall be deemed treason or punished as such; but in case of war being levied by one or more of the States against the United States the conduct of each party towards the other, and their adherents respectively, shall be regulated by the *laws of war and of nations.*"

[DHRC16 11]

James Madison, *The Federalist*, No. 53, February 9, 1788:

A branch of knowledge which belongs to the acquirements of a federal representative, and which has not been mentioned, is that of foreign affairs. In regulating our own commerce, he ought to be not only acquainted with the treaties between the United States and other nations, but also with the commercial policy and *laws of other nations*. He ought not to be altogether ignorant of the *law of nations;* for that, as far as it is a proper object of municipal legislation, is submitted to the federal government. . . . [Fed. 368]

"An Impartial Citizen," No. 5, February 28, 1788:

[1] . . . The Executive in each State on the Continent, is vested with the power of pardoning offences, under different restrictions and modifications. In Virginia, the Governor, with the advice of the Council of State, hath this power, except in cases of impeachment—Thus do they at once enjoy the advantages of Democracy and Monarchy.—Montesquieu and all other writers on the *law of nations* and government, urge, that the delegation of this power to one man, is highly expedient. Common sense tells us so without going further—for, if a popular Assembly were to posses this power, it would be impossible that they would not abuse it. . . . [DHRC8 429]

[2] Before I proceed further, I mean to obviate any unfair conclusions that may be made from my frequent mention of Montesquieu, Grotius, and other writers on government and the *law of nations*. My frequent recurrence to these authors may savour to some illiberal persons, of pedantry, and perhaps of arrogance; yet every person of any acquired knowledge must know, that on speculative subjects, the best theories as well as experience must be recurred to. . . .

[DHRC8 430]

"Brutus," No. 14, February 28, 1788:

[1] Ambassadors, and other public ministers, claim, and are entitled by the *law of nations,* to certain privileges, and exemptions, both for their persons and their servants. [DHRC16 256]

[2] The meanest servant of an ambassador is exempted by the *law of nations* from being sued for debt. Should a suit be brought against such an one by a citizen, through inadvertency or want of information, he will be subject to an action in the supreme court. All the officers concerned in issuing or executing the process will be liable to like actions. Thus may a citizen of a state be compelled, at great expence and inconveniency, to defend himself against a suit, brought against him in the supreme court, for inadvertently commencing an action against the most menial servant of an ambassador for a just debt.

[DHRC16 256]

Alexander White, "To the Citizens of Virginia," February 29, 1788:

. . . The provision that treaties shall be the supreme law of the land, is no more than declaring that the *law of nations* shall take place in America—for if you mean to support an intercourse with the other nations of the earth, you must appoint some men or body of men to conduct that intercourse, and if you do not provide the means to carry their treaties into effect, you subject yourselves to all the horrors of war, whenever any one State shall fail in compliance. To support this doctrine, I could produce many authorities, but it seems too evident to require proof. . . . [DHRC8 442]

Mercy Otis Warren, *Observations on the New Constitution*, February 1788:

. . . This mode of trial [trial by jury in civil cases] the learned Judge Blackstone observes, "has been coeval with the first rudiments of civil government, that property, liberty and life, depend on maintaining in its legal force the constitutional trial by jury." He bids his readers pauze, and with Sir Matthew Hale observes, how admirably this mode is adapted to the investigation of truth beyond any other the world can produce. Even the party who have been disposed to swallow, without examination, the proposals of the secret conclave [the constitutional convention], have started on a discovery that this essential right was curtailed; and shall a privilege, the origin of which may be traced to our Saxon ancestors—that has been a part of the *law of nations*, even in the feudatory systems of France, Germany and Italy—and from the earliest records has been held so sacred, both in ancient and modern Britain, that it could never be shaken by the introduction of Norman customs, or any other conquests or change of government . . . [DHRC16 279]

John Jay, *The Federalist*, No. 64, March 5, 1788:

As to corruption, the case is not supposable. He must either have been very unfortunate in his intercourse with the world, or possess a heart very susceptible of such impressions, who can think it probable that the President and two thirds of the Senate will ever be capable of such unworthy conduct. The idea is too gross and too invidious to be entertained. But in such a case, if it should ever happen, the treaty so obtained from us would, like all other fraudulent contracts, be null and void by the *law of nations*. [Fed. 425]

James Iredell, "Marcus," No. 4, March 12, 1788:

As to the constituting new crimes, and inflicting unusual and severe punishment, certainly the cases enumerated wherein the Congress are empowered either to define offences, or prescribe punishments, are such as are proper for the exercise of such authority in the general Legislature of the union. They only relate to "counterfeiting the securities and current coin of the United States; to piracies and felonies committed on the high seas, and offences against the *law of nations*, and to treason against the United States." These are offences immediately affecting the security, the honor or the interest of the United States at large, and of course must come within the sphere of the Legislative authority which is entrusted with their protection. . . . [DHRC16 381]

Oliver Ellsworth, "The Landholder," No. 12, March 17, 1788:

. . . The Creator of nature and its *laws*, made justice as necessary for *nations* as for individuals and this necessity hath been sealed by the fate of all obstinate offenders. If you will not hear your own groans, nor feel the pangs of your own torture it must continue until removed by a political anihilation. Such as do not pity themselves cannot be long pitied. [DHRC16 407]

Alexander Hamilton, *The Federalist*, No. 80, May 28, 1788:

[1] . . . A distinction may perhaps be imagined between cases arising upon treaties and the *laws of nations* and those which may stand merely on the footing of the municipal law. The former kind may be supposed proper for the federal jurisdiction, the latter for that of the States. But it is at least problematical, whether an unjust sentence against a foreigner, where the subject of controversy was wholly relative to the lex loci, would not, if unredressed, be an aggression upon his sovereign, as well as one which violated the stipulations of a treaty or the general *law of nations*. And a still greater objection to the distinction would result from the immense difficulty, if not impossibility, of a practical discrimination between the cases of one complexion and those of the other. So great a proportion of the cases in which foreigners are parties, involve national questions, that it is by far most safe and most expedient to refer all those in which they are concerned to the national tribunals. [Fed. 501]

[2] The fifth point will demand little animadversion. The most bigoted idolizers of State authority have not thus far shown a disposition to deny the national judiciary the cognizances of maritime causes. These so generally depend on the

laws of nations, and so commonly affect the rights of foreigners, that they fall within the considerations which are relative to the public peace. The most important part of them are, by the present Confederation, submitted to federal jurisdiction. [Fed. 502]

Alexander Hamilton, *The Federalist*, No. 83, May 28, 1788:

But this is not, in my estimation, the greatest objection. I feel a deep and deliberate conviction that there are many cases in which the trial by jury is an ineligible one. I think it so particularly in cases which concern the public peace with foreign nations—that is, in most cases where the question turns wholly on the *laws of nations*. Of this nature, among others, are all prize causes. Juries cannot be supposed competent to investigations that require a thorough knowledge of the *laws and usages of nations;* and they will sometimes be under the influence of impressions which will not suffer them to pay sufficient regard to those considerations of public policy which ought to guide their inquiries. . . .

[Fed. 526]

United States Congress, Judiciary Act of September 24, 1789:

[Section 9:] That the district courts shall have, exclusively of the courts of the several States, cognizance of all crimes and offenses that shall be cognizable under the authority of the United States, committed within their respective districts, or upon the high seas; where no other punishment than whipping, not exceeding thirty stripes, a fine not exceeding one hundred dollars, or a term of imprisonment not exceeding six months, is to be inflicted . . . And shall also have cognizance, concurrent with the courts of the several States, or the circuit courts, as the case may be, of all causes where an alien sues for a tort only in violation of the *law of nations* or a treaty of the United States. . . .

[USSL1 76–77]

[Section 13:] That the Supreme Court shall have exclusive jurisdiction of all controversies of a civil nature, where a state is a party, except between a state and its citizens; and except also between a state and citizens of other states, or aliens, in which latter case it shall have original but not exclusive jurisdiction. And shall have exclusively all such jurisdiction of suits or proceedings against ambassadors or other public ministers, or their domestics, or domestic servants, as a court of law can have or exercise consistently with the *law of nations;* and original, but not exclusive jurisdiction of all suits brought by ambassadors or other public ministers, or in which a consul or vice-consul shall be a party. . . .

[USSL1 80–81]

LAWS, EXECUTION OF

United States Constitution, September 17, 1787:

[Article I, Section 8:] [Congress shall have power] To provide for calling forth the Militia to *execute the Laws of the Union,* suppress Insurrections and repel Invasions . . .

[*Ibid.*:] To make all *Laws* which shall be necessary and proper for carrying into *Execution* the foregoing Powers, and all other Powers vested by this Constitution in the Government of the United States, or in any Department or Officer thereof.

[Article I, Section 10:] No State shall, without the Consent of the Congress, lay any Imposts or Duties on Imports or Exports, except what may be absolutely necessary for *executing its inspection laws;* and the net Produce of all Duties and Imposts, laid by any State on Imports or Exports, shall be for the Use of the Treasury of the United States; and all such *Laws* shall be subject to the Revision and Control of the Congress.

[Article II, Section 3:] He [the President] shall from time to time give to the Congress Information of the State of the Union, and recommend to their Consideration such Measures as he shall judge necessary and expedient; he may, on extraordinary Occasions, convene both Houses, or either of them, and in Case of Disagreement between them, with Respect to the Time of Adjournment, he may adjourn them to such Time as he shall think proper; he shall receive Ambassadors and other public Ministers; he shall take Care that the *Laws be faithfully executed,* and shall Commission all the Officers of the United States.

* * * * *

Charles I, Charter of Maryland, June 20, 1632:

[Article 7:] . . . We, for Us, our Heirs and Successors, do grant unto the said now Baron, (in whose Fidelity, Prudence, Justice, and provident Circumspection of Mind, We repose the greatest Confidence) and to his Heirs, for the good and happy Government of the said Province, free, full, and absolute Power, by the

Tenor of these Presents, to Ordain, Make, and Enact *Laws,* of what Kind soever, according to their sound Discretions, whether relating to the Public State of the said Province, or the private Utility of Individuals, of and with the Advice, Assent, and Approbation of the Free-Men of the same Province, or the greater Part of them, or of their Delegates or Deputies, whom We will shall be called together for the framing of *Laws,* when, and as often as Need shall require, by the aforesaid now Baron of Baltimore, and his Heirs, and in the Form which shall seem best to him or them and the same to publish under the Seal of the aforesaid now Baron of Baltimore, and his Heirs, and duly to *execute* the same upon all Persons, for the time being, within the aforesaid Province, and the Limits thereof . . . [Thorpe 1679–80]

Fundamental Orders of Connecticut, 1638–1639:

[1] The Oath of the Govrnr, for the Prsent

I N. W. being now chosen to be Govrnor wthin this Jurisdiction, for the yeare ensueing, and until a new be chosen, doe sweare by the greate and dreadfull name of the everliveing God, to prmote the publicke good and peace of the same, according to the best of my skill; as also will mayntayne all lawfull priviledges of this Commonwealth; as also that all wholsome *lawes* that are or shall be made by lawfull authority here established, be duly *executed;* and will further the *execution* of Justice according to the rule of Gods word; so helpe me God, in the name of the Lo: Jesus Christ. [Thorpe 522]

[2] The Oath of a Magestrate, for the Prsent

I, N. W. being chosen a Magestrate wthin this Jurisdiction for the yeare ensueing, doe sweare by the great and dreadful name of the everliveing God, to prmote the publike good and peace of the same, according to the best of my skill, and that I will mayntayne all the lawfull priviledges thereof according to my understanding, as also assist in the *execution of all such wholesome lawes* as are made or shall be made by lawfull authority heare established, and will further the *execution* of Justice for the tyme aforesaid according to the righteous rule of Gods word; so helpe me God, etc. [Thorpe 523]

Charles I, Grant of the Province of Maine, April 3, 1639:

. . . itt shall and may be lawefull to and for the said Sir Fardinando Gorges his heires and assignes as well by him and themselves as by his and theire deputies Captaynes or other Officers under his or theire seale in that behalfe to bee authorised (to whome wee alsoe for us our heires and successors doe give and graunte full power and authoritye to doe and *execute* the same) to use and *execute martial lawe* against such Rebells Traytors Mutyners and Seditious Persons in as ample manner and forme as anie Captayne Generall in the Warrs or as any Lieuetennante or Lieuetennants of any Countie within this our Realme of England by vertue of his or there Office or Place maie or have beene accustomed in tyme of Warre Rebellion or Mutynie to doe and performe. [Thorpe 1630–31]

Government of Rhode Island, March 1641:

[Article 3:] It is ordered and unanimously agreed upon, that the Government which this Bodie Politick doth attend unto in this Island, and the Jurisdiction thereof, in favour of our Prince is a DEMOCRACIE, or Popular Government; that is to say, It is in the Powre of the Body of Freemen orderly assembled, or the major part of them, to make or constitute Just *Lawes,* by which they will be related, and to depute from among themselves such Ministers as shall see them faithfully *executed* between Man and Man. [Thorpe 3207–208]

Patent for Providence Plantations, March 14, 1643:

. . . Together with full Power and Authority to rule themselves, and such others as shall hereafter inhabit within any Part of the said Tract of land, by such a Form of Civil Government, as by voluntary consent of all, or the greater Part of them, they shall find most suitable to their Estate and Condition; and, for that End, to make and ordain such Civil *Laws* and Constitutions, and to inflict such punishments upon Transgressors, and for *Execution* thereof, so to place, and displace Officers of Justice, as they, or the greater Part of them, shall by free Consent agree unto. . . . [Thorpe 3210]

Government of New Haven Colony, October 27, 1643:

Secondly they [the General Court] shall have power to mak and repeale *lawes,* and, while they are in force, to require *execution* of them in all the severall plantations. [Thorpe 528]

Charles II, Charter of Connecticut, April 23, 1662:

. . . willing, commanding and requiring, and by these Presents for Us, Our Heirs and Successors, ordaining and appointing, that all such *Laws,* Statutes and Ordinances, Instructions, Impositions and Directions as shall be so made by the Governor, Deputy-Governor, and Assistants as aforesaid, and published in Writing under their Common Seal, shall carefully and duly be observed, kept, performed, and put in *Execution,* according to the true Intent and Meaning of the same, and these Our Letters Patents, or the Duplicate, or Exemplification thereof, shall be to all and such Officers, Superiors and Inferiors from Time to Time, for the putting of the same Orders, *Laws,* Statutes, Ordinances, Instructions, and Directions in due *Execution,* against Us, Our Heirs and Successors, a sufficient Warrant and Discharge. [Thorpe 534]

Charles II, Charter of Carolina, March 24, 1663:

. . . when and as often as need shall require, we will that the said Edward Earl of Clarendon, George Duke of Albemarle, William Lord Craven, John Lord Berkley, Anthony Lord Ashley, Sir George Carteret, Sir William Berkley, and Sir John Colleton, and their heirs, shall from time to time assemble in such manner and form as to them shall seem best, and the same *laws duly to execute* upon all people within the said province and limits thereof, for the time being, or which shall be constituted under the power and government of them or any of them, either sailing towards the said province of Carolina, or returning from thence towards England, or any other of our, or foreign dominions, by imposition of penalties, imprisonment or any other punishment . . . [Thorpe 2745]

Charles II, Charter of Rhode Island, July 8, 1663:

[1] . . . willing, commanding and requireing, and by these presents, for us, oure heires and successours, ordeyneing and apoynting, that all such *lawes* statutes, orders and ordinances, instructions, impositions and directiones, as shall bee soe made by the Governour, deputye-Governour, Assistants and freemen, or such number of them as aforesayd, and published in writinge, under theire common seale, shall bee carefully and duely observed, kept, performed and putt in *execution,* accordinge to the true intent and meaning of the same. [Thorpe 3216]

[2] And these our letters patent, or the duplicate or exempliffication thereof, shall bee to all and everie such officer, superiour or inferiour, from tyme to tyme, for the putting of the same orders, *lawes,* statutes, ordinances, instructions and directions, in due *execution,* against us, oure heires and successours, a sufficient warrant and discharge. [Thorpe 3216]

Charles II, Charter of Carolina, June 30, 1665:

. . . and the same *laws duly to execute,* upon all people within the said province or territory, county, baronny, or colony, or the limits thereof, for the time being, which shall be constituted, under the power, and government of them or any of them, either sailing towards the said province, or territory of Carolina, or returning from thence towards England, or any other of our, or foreign dominions, by imposition of penalties, imprisonment, or any other punishment . . .
[Thorpe 2764]

Fundamental Constitutions of Carolina, March 1, 1669:

[Article 66:] The grand jury at the several assizes shall, upon their oaths, and under their hands and seals, deliver in to their itinerant judges a presentment of such grievances, misdemeanors, exigencies, or defects, which they think necessary for the public good of the country; which presentments shall, by the itinerant judges, at the end of their circuit, be delivered in to the grand council at their next sitting. And whatsoever therein concerns the *execution of laws* already made, the several proprietors' courts, in the matters belonging to each of them, respectively, shall take cognizance of it, and give such order about it as shall be effectual for the due *execution of the laws*. But whatever concerns the making of any new *law*, shall be referred to the several respective courts to which that matter belongs, and be by them prepared and brought to the grand council. [Thorpe 2780]

Charles II, Grant of the Province of Maine to the Duke of York, June 29, 1674:

. . . And also to make ordaine and establish all manner of *lawes* orders direccons instructions formes and ceremonyes of Government and Magistracy fit and necessary for and concerning the Government of the Territoryes and Islands aforesaid so always as the same bee not contrary to the *Lawes* and Statutes of this our realme of England, but as neare as may bee agreeable thereunto and the same at all times hereafter to put in *execution* abrogate revoke or change not onely within the precincts of the said Territoryes or Islands but also upon the seas in going and coming to and from the same as hee or they in their good discretions shall think fittest for the good of the adventurers and inhabitants.

[Thorpe 1642]

Fundamental Constitutions of West New Jersey, 1676:

[Article 20:] . . . And in case any witness or witnesses, on the behalf of any person or persons, indicted in a criminal cause, shall be found to have borne false witness for fear, gain, malice or favour and thereby hinder the due *execution of the law*, and deprive the suffering person or persons of their due satisfaction, that then and in all other cases of false evidence, such person or persons, shall be first severely fined, and next that he or they shall forever be disabled from being admitted in evidence, or into any public office, employment, or service within this province. [Thorpe 2550–51]

New Jersey Proprietiors, Deed of Revision, July 1, 1676:

[1] . . . And by other good and sufficient conveyances and assurances in the *law duly executed*, reciting the said Letters Patents herein before recited, and the several and respective premises thereby granted; his Royal Highness he the said James Duke of York, for the considerations therein mentioned, did grant, convey and assure to John Lord Berkley and Sir George Carteret their heirs and assigns forever, all that tract of land adjacent to New England, and lying and being to the westward of Long Island and Manhatan Island . . . [Thorpe 2553]

[2] . . . and by several other good and sufficient conveyances and assurances in the *law duly executed*, the said moiety or half part of the said tract of land, and

the said moiety or half part of all and every other the said several and respective premises so convey'd unto the said John Fenwick as aforesaid, with all and every the right, members and appurtenances of the same, were convey'd unto . . . [Thorpe 2554]

Duke of York, Grant of West New Jersey, August 6, 1680:

. . . as for the defending, guarding and keeping of the same; as also for the well governing of the same, and of all such as are or shall be inhabitting in the same, and for the making, ordaining, and *executing of necessary and convenient laws* and constitutions, in order to such government, and the punishing and pardoning offences, and offenders, as occasion shall require . . . [Thorpe 2563]

Charles II, Charter of Pennsylvania, February 28, 1681:

. . . and under his and their Seales to publish any *Lawes* whatsoever, for the raising of money for the publick use of the said Province, or for any other End, apperteyning either unto the publick state, peace, or safety of the said Countrey, or unto the private utility of perticular persons, according unto their best discretions, by and with the advice, assent, and approbation of the Freemen of the said Countrey, or the greater parte of them, or of their Delegates or Deputies, whom for the Enacting of the said *Lawes,* when, and as often as need shall require, Wee will that the said William Penn and his heires, shall assemble in such sort and forme, as to him and them shall seeme best, and the same *Lawes duly to execute,* unto and upon all People within the said Countrey and the Limitts thereof. [Thorpe 3037]

Duke of York, Confirmation of Deed to the New Jersey Proprietors, March 14, 1682:

. . . as for the defending, guarding and keeping of the same; as also for the well governing of the same, and of all such as shall be inhabiting the same, and for the making, ordaining and *executing of necessary and convenient laws* and constitutions, in order to such government; and the punishing and pardoning offences and offenders, as occasion shall require . . . [Thorpe 2571]

Pennsylvania Frame of Government, April 25, 1682:

[Preface:] I know some say, let us have good *laws,* and no matter for the men that *execute* them: but let them consider, that though good *laws* do well, good men do better: for good *laws* may want good men, and be abolished or evaded [invaded] by ill men; but good men will never want good *laws,* nor suffer ill ones. . . . [Thorpe 3054]

[Article 8:] That the Governor and provincial Council shall take care, that all *laws,* statutes and ordinances, which shall at any time be made within the said province, be duly and diligently *executed.* [Thorpe 3056]

Pennsylvania Frame of Government, April 2, 1683:

[Article 6:] That the Governor and provincial Council shall take care that all *laws,* statutes and ordinances, which shall, at any time, be made within the said province and territories, be duly and diligently *executed.* [Thorpe 3065]

Fundamental Constitutions of East New Jersey, 1683:

. . . for restraining such and preserving of the people in deligence and in good order, the great Council is to make more particular *laws,* which are punctually to be put in *execution.* [Thorpe 2580]

James II, Commission to Sir Edmund Andros for the Dominion of New England, April 7, 1688:

[1] And Wee do hereby give and grant unto you full power and authority to constitute and appoint Judges and in cases requisite Commissioners of Oyer and Terminer, Justices of the Peace, Sheriffs, & all other necessary Officers and Ministers within our said Territory, for the better administration of Justice and putting the *lawes in execution,* & to administer such oath and oaths as are usually given for the due *execution* and performance of offices and places and for the cleering of truth in judiciall causes. [Thorpe 1865]

[2] . . . And also to *execute martiall law* in time of invasion insurrection or warr, and during the continuance of the same, and upon soldiers in pay, and to do and *execute* all and every other thing which to a Captain Generall doth or ought of right to belong, as fully and amply as any our Captain Generall doth or hath usually don. [Thorpe 1866]

[3] And forasmuch as divers mutinies & disorders do happen by persons shipped and imployed at Sea, and to the end that such as shall be shipped or imployed at Sea may be better governed and ordered; Wee do hereby give and grant unto you the said Sr Edmund Andros our Captain Generall and Governor in Cheif, full power and authority to constitute and appoint Captains, Masters of Ships, and other Commanders, commissions to *execute the law martial,* and to use such proceedings authorities, punishment, correction and *execution* upon any offender or offenders who shall be mutinous seditious, disorderly or any way unruly either at sea or during the time of their abode or residence in any of the ports harbors or bays of our said Territory and Dominion, as the Cause shall be found to require, according to *martial law.* . . . [Thorpe 1867]

English Bill of Rights, December 16, 1689:

[1] [The King attempted to subvert the laws] By assuming and exercising a power of dispensing with and suspending of laws, and the *execution of laws,* without consent of parliament. [SDECH 463]

[2] That the pretended power of suspending of laws or the *execution of laws* by regal authority without consent of parliament is illegal. [SDECH 464]

[3] That the pretended power of dispensing with laws or the *execution of laws* by regal authority as it hath been assumed and exercised of late is illegal. [SDECH 464]

William and Mary, Charter of Massachusetts Bay, October 7, 1691:

. . . Willing Comanding and Requireing and by these presents for us Our heires and Successors Ordaining and appointing that all such Orders *Lawes* Statutes and Ordinances Instructions and Directions as shall be soe made and published under our Seale of our said Province or Territory shall be Carefully and duely observed kept and performed and put in *Execution* according to the true intent and meaning of these presents . . . [Thorpe 1883]

Pennsylvania Frame of Goverment, November 7, 1696:

Be it further enacted by the authority aforesaid, That the Governor and Council shall take care that all the *laws,* statutes and ordinances, which shall at and time be made within the said province and territories, be duly and diligently *executed.* [Thorpe 3074]

New Jersey Proprietors, Surrender of Rights, April 15, 1702:

[1] . . . and also to make, ordain and establish, all manner of orders, *laws,* directions, instructions, forms and ceremonies of government and magistracy, fit and necessary for and concerning the government of the Territories and islands aforesaid, so always as the same were not contrary to the *laws* and statutes of the realm of England, but as near as might be agreeable thereunto; and the same at all times then after to put in *execution* or abrogate, revoke or change, not only within the precinct of the said Territories or islands, but also upon the seas in going and coming to and from the same, as he and they in their good direction should think to be fittest for the good of the adventurers and inhabitants there. . . . [Thorpe 2586]

[2] . . . and to make, ordain and establish any orders, *laws,* directions, instruments, forms or ceremonies of government and magistracy, for or concerning the government of the Provinces aforesaid or either of them, or on the sea in going and coming to or from thence, or to put in *execution,* or abrogate, revoke

or change such as are already made for or concerning such government, or any of them . . . [Thorpe 2588]

First Continental Congress, Declaration and Resolves, October 14, 1774:

And whereas, in the last session of Parliament, three statutes were made . . . and another, intituled "An act for the impartial administration of justice, in the cases of persons questioned for any act done by them in the *execution of the law*, or for the suppression of riots and tumults, in the province of the Massachusetts-bay, in New England." And another statute was then made, "for making more effectual provision for the government of the province of Quebec, &c. All which statutes are impolitic, unjust, and cruel, as well as unconstitutional, and most dangerous and destructive of American rights. [JCC1 55–56]

Thomas Paine, *Common Sense*, January 9, 1776:

The present time, likewise, is that peculiar time which never happens to a nation but once, viz. the time of forming itself into a government. Most nations have let slip the opportunity, and by that means have been compelled to receive *laws* from their conquerors, instead of making *laws* for themselves. First, they had a king, and then a form of government; whereas, the articles or charter of government, should be formed first, and men delegated to *execute* them afterwards: but from the errors of other nations let us learn wisdom, and lay hold of the present opportunity—to begin government at the right end. [CWTP1 36–37]

John Adams, *Thoughts on Government*, April, 1776:

[1] . . . That, as a Republic is the best of governments, so that particular arrangement of the powers of society, or in other words, that form of government which is best contrived to secure an impartial and exact *execution of the laws,* is the best of Republics. [PJA4 87]

[2] Because a single Assembly, possessed of all the powers of government, would make arbitrary laws for their own interest, *execute all laws* arbitrarily for their own interest, and adjudge all controversies in their own favour. [PJA4 88]

South Carolina Constitution, March 26, 1776:

[Preamble:] . . . And whereas large fleets and armies having been sent to America in order to enforce the *execution of those laws,* and to compel an absolute and implicit submission to the will of a corrupt and despotic administration, and in consequence thereof, hostilities having been commenced in the Massachusetts Bay, by the troops under command of General Gage, whereby a number of peaceable, helpless, and unarmed people were wantonly robbed and murdered, and there being just reason to apprehend that like hostilities would be committed in all the other colonies. . . . [Thorpe 3242]

Virginia Bill of Rights, June 12, 1776:

[Section 7:] That all power of suspending *laws,* or the *execution of laws,* by any authority, without consent of the representatives of the people, is injurious to their rights, and ought not to be exercised. [Thorpe 3813]

Pennsylvania Constitution, September 28, 1776:

[Declaration of Rights, Article 14:] That a frequent recurrence to fundamental principles, and a firm adherence to justice, moderation, temperance, industry, and frugality are absolutely necessary to preserve the blessings of liberty, and keep a government free: The people ought therefore to pay particular attention to these points in the choice of officers and representatives, and have a right to exact a due and constant regard to them, from their legislatures and magistrates, in the making and *executing such laws* as are necessary for the good government of the state. [Thorpe 3083–84]

[Frame of Government, Section 20:] . . . they [the President and Executive Council] are also to take care that the *laws be faithfully executed;* they are to expedite the *execution* of such measures as may be resolved upon by the general assembly; and they may draw upon the treasury for such sums as shall be appropriated by the house . . . [Thorpe 3088]

[*Ibid.,* Section 40:] THE OATH OR AFFIRMATION OF OFFICE

I — do swear (or affirm) that I will faithfully *execute* the office of — for the — of — and will do equal right and justice to all men, to the best of my judgment and abilities, according to *law.* [Thorpe 3090]

[Section 45:] *Laws* for the encouragement of virtue, and prevention of vice and immorality, shall be made and constantly kept in force, and provision shall be made for their due *execution* . . . [Thorpe 3091]

[Section 47:] . . . They [the Council of Censors] are also to enquire whether the public taxes have been justly laid and collected in all parts of this commonwealth, in what manner the public monies have been disposed of, and whether the *laws have been duly executed.* For these purposes they shall have power to send for persons, papers, and records; they shall have authority to pass public censures, to order impeachments, and to recommend to the legislature the repealing such *laws* as appear to them to have been enacted contrary to the principles of the constitution. . . . [Thorpe 3091–92]

Maryland Constitution, November 11, 1776:

[Declaration of Rights, Article 7:] That no power of suspending *laws,* or the *execution of laws,* unless by or derived from the Legislature, ought to be exercised or allowed. [Thorpe 1687]

[Form of Government, Article 11:] . . . and to prevent altercation about such bills, it is declared, that no bill imposing duties or customs for the mere regulation of commerce, or inflicting fines for the reformation of morals, or to enforce the *execution of the laws,* by which an incidental revenue may arise, shall be accounted a money bill; but every bill assessing, levying, or applying taxes or supplies for the support of government or the current expenses of the state, or appropriating money in the treasury, shall be deemed a money bill.

[Thorpe 1693]

North Carolina Constitution, December 18, 1776:

[Declaration of Rights, Article 5:] That all powers of suspending *laws,* or the *execution of laws,* by any authority, without consent of the Representatives of the people, is injurious to their rights, and ought not to be exercised.

[Thorpe 2787]

Georgia Constitution, February 5, 1777:

[Article 24:] The governor's oath:

". . . and use my utmost endeavors to protect the people thereof in the secure enjoyment of all their rights, franchises, and privileges; and that the *laws* and ordinances of the State be duly observed, and that *law* and justice in mercy be *executed* in all judgments. . . ." [Thorpe 781]

New York Constitution, April 20, 1777:

[Article 19:] That it shall be the duty of the governor to inform the legislature, at every session, of the condition of the State, so far as may respect his department; to recommend such matters to their consideration as shall appear to him to concern its good government, welfare, and prosperity; to correspond with the Continental Congress, and other States; to transact all necessary business with the officers of government, civil and military; to take care that the *laws are faithfully executed* to the best of his ability; and to expedite all such measures as may be resolved upon by the legislature. [Thorpe 2633]

Vermont Constitution, July 8, 1777:

[Declaration of Rights, Article 16:] That frequent recurrence to fundamental principles, and a firm adherence to justice, moderation, temperance, industry and frugality, are absolutely necessary to preserve the blessings of liberty, and keep government free. The people ought, therefore, to pay particular attention to these points, in the choice of officers and representatives, and have a right to exact a due and constant regard to them, from their legislators and magistrates, in the making and *executing such laws* as are necessary for the good government of the State. [Thorpe 3741]

[Frame of Government, Section 18:] . . . They [the Governor and Executive Council] are also, to take care that the *laws be faithfully executed.* They are to expedite the *execution* of such measures as may be resolved upon by General Assembly; and they may draw upon the Treasurer for such sums as may be appropriated by the House . . . [Thorpe 3745]

[*Ibid.*, Section 41:] *Laws* for the encouragement of virtue and prevention of vice and immorality, shall be made and constantly kept in force; and provision shall be made for their due *execution* . . . [Thorpe 3748]

[*Ibid.*, Section 44:] . . . They [the Council of Censors] are also to enquire whether the public taxes have been justly laid and collected, in all parts of this Commonwealth—in what manner the public monies have been disposed of, and whether the *laws have been duly executed.* . . . [Thorpe 3748]

Massachusetts Constitution, March 2, 1780:

[Preamble:] The body politic is formed by a voluntary association of individuals: it is a social compact, by which the whole people covenants with each citizen, and each citizen with the whole people, that all shall be governed by certain *laws* for the common good. It is the duty of the people, therefore in framing a constitution of government, to provide for an equitable mode of making *laws,* as well as for an impartial interpretation and a faithful *execution* of them; that every man may, at all times, find his security in them. [Thorpe 1889]

[Declaration of Rights, Article 18]: A frequent recurrence to the fundamental principles of the constitution, and a constant adherence to those of piety, justice, moderation, temperance, industry, and frugality, are absolutely necessary to preserve the advantages of liberty, and to maintain a free government. The people ought, consequently, to have a particular attention to all those principles, in the choice of their officers and representatives: and they have a right to require of their lawgivers and magistrates an exact and constant observance of them, in the formation and *execution of the laws* necessary for the good administration of the commonwealth. [Thorpe 1892]

[*Ibid.*, Article 20:] The power of suspending the *laws,* or the *execution of the laws,* ought never to be exercised but by the legislature, or by authority derived from it, to be exercised in such particular cases only as the legislature shall expressly provide for. [Thorpe 1892]

New Hampshire Constitution, June 2, 1784:

[Bill of Rights, Article 29:] The power of suspending the *laws or the execution of them,* ought never to be exercised but by the legislature, or by authority derived therefrom, to be exercised in such particular cases only as the legislature shall expressly provide for. [Thorpe 2457]

[*Ibid.*, Article 38:] A frequent recurrence to the fundamental principles of the Constitution, and a constant adherence to justice, moderation temperance, industry, frugality, and all the social virtues, are indispensably necessary to preserve the blessing of liberty and good government; the people ought, therefore, to have a particular regard to all those principles in the choice of their officers and representatives: and they have a right to require of their law-givers and magistrates, an exact and constant observance of them in the formation and *execution of the laws* necessary for the good administration of government. [Thorpe 2457]

Vermont Constitution, July 4, 1786:

[Declaration of Rights, Article 17:] The power of suspending *laws,* or the *execution of laws,* ought never to be exercised, but by the Legislature, or by authority derived from it, to be exercised in such particular cases only as the Legislature shall expressly provide for. [Thorpe 3753]

[*Ibid.,* Article 20:] That frequent recurrence to fundamental principles, and a firm adherence to justice, moderation, temperance, industry, and frugality, are absolutely necessary to preserve the blessings of liberty, and keep government free; the people ought therefore to pay particular attention to these points, in the choice of officers and representatives; and have a right, in a legal way, to exact a due and constant regard to them, from their legislators and magistrates, in the making and *executing such laws* as are necessary for the good government of the State. [Thorpe 3754]

[Frame of Government, Section 11:] . . . They [the Governor and Council] are also to take care that the *laws be faithfully executed.* They are to expedite the *execution* of such measures as may be resolved upon by the General Assembly: and they may draw upon the Treasurer for such sums as may be appropriated by the House of Representatives. . . . [Thorpe 3756]

[*Ibid.,* Section 38:] *Laws* for the encouragement of virtue, and prevention of vice and immorality, ought to be constantly kept in force, and duly *executed;* and a competent number of schools ought to be maintained in each town for the convenient instruction of youth . . . [Thorpe 3760]

[*Ibid.,* Section 40:] . . . they [the Council of Censors] are also to inquire whether the public taxes have been justly laid and collected in all parts of this Commonwealth—in what manner the public monies have been disposed of—and whether the *laws have been duly executed.* . . . [Thorpe 3761]

The Virginia Plan of Union, May 29, 1787:

[Article 7:] Res[olve]d that a National Executive be instituted, to be chosen by the National Legislature for the term of ——— years, to receive punctually, at stated times, a fixed compensation for the services rendered, in which no increase or diminution shall be made so as to affect the Magistracy, existing at the time of the increase or diminution, and to be ineligible a second time; and that besides a general authority to *execute the National laws*,it ought to enjoy the Executive rights vested in Congress by the Confederation. [DHRC1 244]

Alexander Hamilton's Plan of Union, June 18, 1787:

The Supreme Executive authority of the United States to be vested in a governor to be elected to serve during good behaviour. His election to be made by Electors chosen by the people in the Election Districts aforesaid, or by electors chosen for that purpose by the respective legislatures—provided that if an election be not made within a limited time the President of the Senate shall be the Governor.—The Governor to have a negative upon all laws about to be passed—and to have the *execution of all laws* passed—to be the Commander in Chief of the land and naval forces and of the Militia of the United States . . .
[DHRC1 254]

Richard Henry Lee [?], "The Federal Farmer," No. 1, October 1, 1787:

. . . My uniform federal attachments, and the interest I have in the protection of property, and a steady *execution of the laws,* will convince you, that, if I am under any bias at all, it is in favor of any general system which shall promise those advantages. The instability of our *laws* increases my wishes for firm and steady government; but then, I can consent to no government, which, in my opinion, is not calculated equally to preserve the rights of all orders of men in the community . . . [Ford 279]

Richard Henry Lee [?], "The Federal Farmer," No. 2, October 9, 1787:

[1] There are other considerations which tend to prove that the idea of one consolidated whole, on free principles, is ill-founded—the *laws* of a free government rest on the confidence of the people, and operate gently—and never can extend the influence very far—if they are *executed* on free principles, about the centre, where the benefits of the government induce the people to support it voluntarily; yet they must be *executed* on the principles of fear and force in the extremes—This has been the case with every extensive republic of which we have any accurate account. [Ford 290]

[2] . . . The general government, organized as it is, may be adequate to many valuable objects, and be able to carry its *laws* into *execution* on proper principles in several cases; but I think its warmest friends will not contend, that it can carry all the powers proposed to be lodged in it into effect, without calling to its aid a military force, which must very soon destroy all elective governments in the country, produce anarchy, or establish despotism. . . . [Ford 292–93]

[3] . . . The powers lodged in the general government, if exercised by it, must intimately effect the internal police of the states, as well as external concerns; and there is no reason to expect the numerous state governments, and their connections, will be very friendly to the *execution of federal laws* in those internal affairs, which hitherto have been under their own immediate management. There is more reason to believe, that the general government, far removed from the people, and none of its members elected oftener than once in two years, will be forgot or neglected, and its *laws* in many cases disregarded, unless a multitude of officers and military force be continually kept in view, and employed to enforce the *execution of the laws,* and to make the government feared and respected. No position can be truer than this. That in this country either neglected *laws,* or a military *execution* of them, must lead to a revolution, and to the destruction of freedom. Neglected *laws* must first lead to anarchy and confusion; and a military *execution of laws* is only a shorter way to the same point—despotic government. [Ford 293]

Richard Henry Lee [?], "The Federal Farmer," No. 3, October 10, 1787:

[1] Should the general government think it politic, as some administration (if not all) probably will, to look for a support in a system of influence, the government will take every occasion to multiply *laws,* and officers to *execute* them, considering these as so many necessary props for its own support. . . .
[Ford 302]

[2] . . . I see no provision made for calling out the posse comitatus for *executing the laws* of the union, but provision is made for congress to call forth the militia for the *execution* of them—and the militia in general, or any select part of it, may be called out under military officers, instead of the sheriff to enforce an *execution of federal laws,* in the first instance, and thereby introduce an entire military *execution of the laws.* I know that powers to raise taxes, to regulate the military strength of the community on some uniform plan, to provide for its defence and internal order, and for duly *executing the laws,* must be lodged somewhere; but still we ought not so to lodge them, as evidently to give one order of men in the community, undue advantages over others; or commit the many to the mercy, prudence, and moderation of the few. . . . [Ford 306]

Richard Henry Lee [?], "The Federal Farmer," No. 4, October 12, 1787:

I confess I do not see in what cases the congress can, with any pretence of right, make a *law* to suppress the freedom of the press; though I am not clear, that congress is restrained from laying any duties whatever on printing, and from laying duties particularly heavy on certain pieces printed, and perhaps congress may require large bonds for the payment of these duties. Should the printer say, the freedom of the press was secured by the constitution of the state in which he lived, congress might, and perhaps, with great propriety, answer, that the federal constitution is the only compact existing between them and the people; in this compact the people have named no others, and therefore congress, in exercising the powers assigned them, and in making *laws to carry them into execution,* are restrained by nothing beside the federal constitution, any more than a state legislature is restrained by a compact between the magistrates and people of a county, city, or town of which the people, in forming the state constitution, have taken no notice. [Ford 316–17]

Noah Webster, *An Examination into the Leading Principles of the Federal Constitution*, October 17, 1787:

[1] . . . One half the evils in a state arise from a lax *execution of the laws;* and it is impossible that an executive officer can act with vigor and impartiality, when his office depends on the popular voice. An annual popular election of executive officers is the sure source of a negligent, partial and corrupt administration. . . . [Ford 36]

[2] . . . In this point therefore I conceive the plan proposed in America to be an improvement on the Roman constitution. In all free governments, that is, in all countries, where *laws* govern, and not men, the supreme magistrate should have it in his power to *execute any law,* however unpopular, without hazarding his person or office. The *laws* are the sole guardians of right, and when the magistrate dares not act, every person is insecure. [Ford 36–37]

[3] Congress likewise are to have power to provide for organizing, arming and disciplining the militia, but have no other command of them, except when in actual service. Nor are they at liberty to call out the militia at pleasure—but only, to *execute the laws* of the union, suppress insurrections, and repel invasions. For these purposes, government must always be armed with a military force, if the occasion should require it: otherwise *laws* are nugatory, and life and property insecure. [Ford 52]

[4] . . . It is also intimated as a probable event, that the federal courts will absorb the judiciaries of the federal states. This is a mere suspicion, without the least foundation. The jurisdiction of the federal states is very accurately defined and easily understood. It extends to the cases mentioned in the constitution, and to the *execution of the laws* of Congress, respecting commerce, revenue, and other general concerns. [Ford 52–53]

[5] . . . The supreme power in America cannot enforce unjust *laws* by the sword; because the whole body of the people are armed, and constitute a force superior to any band of regular troops that can be, on any pretence, raised in the United States. A military force, at the command of Congress, can *execute no laws,* but such as the people perceive to be just and constitutional; for they will possess

the Power, and jealousy will instantly inspire the inclination, to resist the *execution of a law* which appears to them unjust and oppressive. . . . [Ford 56]

[6] . . . The [Roman] Licinian *law* limited all possessions to five hundred acres of land; which, had it been fully *executed,* would have secured the commonwealth. [Ford 58]

John Jay, *The Federalist*, No. 3, November 3, 1787:

Because, under the national government, treaties and articles of treaties, as well as the *laws* of nations, will always be expounded in one sense and *executed* in the same manner,—whereas adjudications on the same points and questions, in thirteen States, or in three or four confederacies, will not always accord or be consistent . . . [Fed. 98]

***Virginia Independent Chronicle*, November 28, 1787:**

Great apprehensions are entertained from the general establishment of an excise *law*. It is considered as too dangerous an instrument to be put into the hands of Congress. But these apprehensions, Sir, are absurd. They originate from trifles, light as air: They exist only in idea. Excise *laws* are no more violations of the rights of the people than any other *laws, and they may be as safely executed.* In Pennsylvania excise *laws* have long prevailed. It was the original mode of taxation, practised by as virtuous a legislature as ever was delegated, to raise money for the support of government. To *execute* it, no standing army was thought necessary. No man's house was broke open. The rights and properties of the people were not outraged. On the contrary, it was submitted to without murmurring, *executed* without violence; and I challenge any man to mention a single instance in which any individual was injured in that state by the operation of an excise law for near one hundred years. Why, then, may we not intrust Congress with the power of establishing *excise laws* and regulating the operation of them? Why may not *excise laws be executed* with the same safety and same convenience by officers appointed by Congress, as it has been in the state of Pennsylvania by officers appointed by its legislature . . . [DHRC8 178]

Alexander Hamilton, *The Federalist*, No. 15, December 1, 1787:

. . . In an association where the general authority is confined to the collective bodies of the communities that compose it, every breach of the *laws* must involve a state of war; and military *execution* must become the only instrument of civil obedience. Such a state of things can certainly not deserve the name of government, nor would any prudent man choose to commit his happiness to it. [Fed. 159–60]

Alexander Hamilton, *The Federalist*, No. 16, December 4, 1787:

[1] . . . Whoever considers the populousness and strength of several of these States singly at the present juncture, and looks forward to what they will become, even at the distance of half a century, will at once dismiss as idle and visionary any scheme which aims at regulating their movements by *laws* to operate upon them in their collective capacities, and to be *executed* by a coercion applicable to them in the same capacities. A project of this kind is little less romantic than the monster-taming spirit which is attributed to the fabulous heroes and demigods of antiquity. [Fed. 164–65]

[2] To this reasoning it may perhaps be objected, that if any State should be disaffected to the authority of the Union, it could at any time obstruct the *execution of its laws,* and bring the matter to the same issue of force, with the necessity of which the opposite scheme is reproached. [Fed. 165]

[3] But if the *execution of the laws* of the national government should not require the intervention of the State legislatures, if they were to pass into immediate operation upon the citizens themselves, the particular governments could not interrupt their progress without an open and violent exertion of an unconstitutional power. . . . [Fed. 166]

"Americanus," No. 1, December 5, 1787:

. . . he shall take care, that the *laws be faithfully executed*, and shall commission all the officers of the United States. In every other instance, he can accomplish no object, effect no design, without the concurrence of the senate. Thus authorised and thus fettered, I do not see any act, that the president can, of himself, perform, which ought to render him an object of apprehension. . . .
[DHRC8 203–204]

James Madison, *The Federalist*, No. 19, December 8, 1787:

The impossibility of maintaining order and dispensing justice among these sovereign subjects, produced the experiment of dividing the [German] empire into nine or ten circles or districts; of giving them an interior organization, and of charging them with the military *execution of the laws* against delinquent and contumacious members. This experiment has only served to demonstrate more fully the radical vice of the constitution. Each circle is the miniature picture of the deformities of this political monster. They either fail to *execute* their commissions, or they do it with all the devastation and carnage of civil war. . . .
[Fed. 179]

Alexander Hamilton, *The Federalist*, No. 21, December 12, 1787:

. . . There is no express delegation of authority to them [the Confederation Congress] to use force against delinquent members . . . If we are unwilling to impair the force of this applauded provision, we shall be obliged to conclude, that the United States afford the extraordinary spectacle of a government destitute even of the shadow of constitutional power to enforce the *execution of its own laws*. It will appear, from the specimens which have been cited, that the American Confederacy, in this particular, stands discriminated from every other institution of a similar kind, and exhibits a new and unexampled phenomenon in the political world. [Fed. 186–87]

"Nov. Anglus," December 12, 1787:

That there are a set of men now resident in this country, who are enemies to its political happiness, and who anticipate with horror a permanent national government, is a fact known to every man of observation. A want of energy in the *laws* of some States, and a want of their *execution* in others, has unfortunately cultivated this evil, until its reformation has become a business of both difficulty and danger; and it may now perhaps be questioned whether, the liberal spirit of Americans since the conclusion of the late war, has not proved unfortunately superior to a suspicion of characters. [DHRC8 255]

Dissent of the Pennsylvania Convention's Minority, December 18, 1787:

[1] Such various, extensive, and important powers combined in one body of men are inconsistent with all freedom; the celebrated Montesquieu tells us, that "when the legislative and executive powers are united in the same person, or in the same body of magistrates, there can be no liberty, because apprehensions may arise, lest the same monarch or senate should enact tyrannical *laws,* to *execute* them in a tyrannical manner." [DHRC2 635]

[2] From the foregoing investigation, it appears that the Congress under this constitution will not possess the confidence of the people, which is an essential requisite in a good government; for unless the *laws* command the confidence and respect of the great body of the people, so as to induce them to support them, when called on by the civil magistrate, they must be *executed* by the aid of a numerous standing army, which would be inconsistent with every idea of liberty. . . . [DHRC2 637]

Alexander Hamilton, *The Federalist*, No. 27, December 25, 1787:

[1] It has been urged, in different shapes, that a Constitution of the kind proposed by the convention cannot operate without the aid of a military force to *execute its laws*. This, however, like most other things have been alleged on that side, rests on mere general assertion, unsupported by any precise or intelligible designation of the reasons upon which it is founded. . . . [Fed. 219]

[2] . . . It will be sufficient here to remark, that until satisfactory reasons can be assigned to justify an opinion, that the federal government is likely to be administered in such a manner as to render it odious or contemptible to the people, there can be no reasonable foundation for the supposition that the *laws* of the Union will meet with any greater obstruction from them, or will stand in need of any other methods to enforce their *execution,* than the *laws* of the particular members. [Fed. 220]

[3] The plan reported by the convention, by extending the authority of the federal head to the individual citizens of the several States, will enable the government to employ the ordinary magistracy of each, in the *execution of its laws*. It is easy to perceive that this will tend to destroy, in the common apprehension, all distinction between the sources from which they might proceed; and will give the federal government the same advantage for securing a due obedience to its authority which is enjoyed by the government of each State . . . [Fed. 221]

[4] . . . Thus the legislatures, courts, and magistrates, of the respective members, will be incorporated into the operations of the national government as far as its just and constitutional authority extends; and will be rendered auxiliary to the enforcement of its laws. Any man who will pursue, by his own reflections, the consequences of this situation, will perceive that there is good ground to calculate upon a regular and peaceable *execution of the laws* of the Union, if its powers are administered with a common share of prudence. . . . [Fed. 221–22]

Alexander Hamilton, *The Federalist*, No. 32, January 2, 1788:

. . . The first clause of the same section empowers Congress "to lay and collect taxes, duties, imposts and excises"; and the second clause of the tenth section of the same article declares that "no State shall, without the consent of Congress, lay any imposts or duties on imports or exports, except for the purpose of *executing its inspection laws*." Hence would result an exclusive power in the Union to lay duties on imports and exports, with the particular exception mentioned; but this power is abridged by another clause, which declares that no tax or duty shall be laid on articles exported from any State; in consequence of which qualification, it now only extends to the duties on imports. . . .
[Fed. 242]

Alexander Hamilton, *The Federalist*, No. 29, January 9, 1788:

[1] In order to cast an odium upon the power of calling forth the militia to *execute the laws* of the Union, it has been remarked that there is nowhere any provision in the proposed Constitution for calling out the POSSE COMITATUS, to assist the magistrate in the *execution* of his duty, whence it has been inferred that military force was intended to be his only auxiliary. . . . [Fed. 227]

[2] . . . It would be as absurd to doubt that a right to pass all *laws* necessary and proper to *execute* its declared powers would include that of requiring the assis-

tance of the citizens to the officers, who may be intrusted with the *execution of those laws,* as it would be to believe that a right to enact *laws* necessary and proper for the imposition and collection of taxes would involve that of varying the rules of descent and of the alienation of landed property, or of abolishing the trial by jury in cases relating to it. . . . [Fed. 227–28]

James Madison, *The Federalist*, No. 37, January 11, 1788:

. . . Energy in government is essential to that security against external and internal danger, and to that prompt and salutary *execution of the laws* which enter into the very definition of good government. Stability in government is essential to national character and to the advantages annexed to it, as well as to that repose and confidence in the minds of the people, which are among the chief blessings of civil society. . . . [Fed. 267]

James Madison, *The Federalist*, No. 47, January 30, 1788:

The reasons on which Montesquieu grounds his maxim are a further demonstration of his meaning. "When the legislative and executive powers are united in the same person or body," says he, "there can be no liberty, because apprehensions may arise lest the same monarch or senate should enact tyrannical *laws* to *execute* them in a tyrannical manner." . . . [Fed. 338]

Alexander C. Hanson, *Remarks on the Proposed Plan of a Federal Government*, c. January 31, 1788:

[1] . . . But the members of this convention perceiving, from the experience of these states, from the history of ancient and modern states, and, I may add, from the principles of human nature, that the same body of men ought not to make and *execute laws;* and that one body alone ought not to do the first, have separated the executive, so far as was proper, from the legislative; and this last they have divided into two branches, composed of different materials, distinct from, and totally independent of, each other. [Ford 225]

[2] That the people should either make *laws* to bind themselves, or elect persons, without whose consent, no *laws* shall be made, is essential to their freedom. But universal experience forbids, that they should immediately choose persons for the *execution of the laws*. Shall the legislature then, or the senate, or the house of representatives, have this appointment? A council thus chosen would be dependent on its electors; and it would be the same thing in many respects, as if the legislature should *execute its own laws*. Can you believe, that a council, chosen annually, or once in two or three years, would dare to pursue, in all cases, the dictates of its own judgment, contrary to the known will of those, who will soon have an opportunity of removing them? . . . [Ford 230]

[3] A choice of jurisdictions has been ever esteemed a valuable right, even where they are both of the same kind. The purpose of extending so far the jurisdiction of the federal judiciary, is to give every assurance to the general government, of a faithful *execution of its laws,* and to give citizens, states, and foreigners, an assurance of the impartial administration of justice. Without the salutary institution, the federal government might frequently be obstructed, and its servants want protection. . . . [Ford 238]

[4] . . . She [*i.e.,* Maryland under the Constitution] shall coin no money, emit no bills of credit, nor make any thing but gold and silver a tender in payment of debts. She shall pass no bill of attainder, or ex post facto *law,* or *law* impairing the obligation of a contract. She shall grant no title of nobility. She shall not, without consent of congress, lay any duty on imports or exports, except what may be necessary for *executing her inspection laws.* She shall not, without consent of congress, lay any duty on tonnage, keep troops or ships of war, in time of peace . . . [Ford 251]

Luther Martin, "Genuine Information," No. 10, February 1, 1788:

[1] By the third article, the judicial power of the United States is vested in one supreme court, and in such inferior courts, as the Congress may from time to time ordain and establish.—These courts, and these only, will have a right to decide upon the *laws* of the United States, and all questions arising upon their construction, and in a judicial manner to carry those *laws into execution;* to which the courts both superior and inferior of the respective States and their judges and other magistrates are rendered incompetent. . . . [DHRC16 8]

[2] Thus, Sir, jury trials, which have ever been the boast of the English constitution, which have been by our several State constitutions so cautiously secured to us,—jury trials which have so long been considered the surest barrier against arbitrary power, and the palladium of liberty,—with the loss of which the loss of our freedom may be dated, are taken away by the proposed form of government, not only in a great variety of questions between individual and individual, but in every case whether civil or criminal arising under the *laws* of the United States or the *execution of those laws.* [DHRC16 9]

Samuel Bryan, "Centinel," No. 14, February 5, 1788:

. . . at the same time the construction of every *law* imposing any and all these taxes and duties, and directing the collection of them, and every question arising thereon, and on the conduct of the officers appointed to *execute these laws,* and to collect these taxes and duties so various in their kinds, are taken away from the courts of justice of the different states, and confined to the courts of the general government, there to be heard and determined by judges holding their offices under the appointment, not of the states, but of the general government. [DHRC16 33–34]

"Brutus," No. 12, February 7, 1788:

[1] . . . And the courts are vested with the supreme and uncontroulable power, to determine, in all cases that come before them, what the constitution means; they cannot, therefore, *execute a law,* which, in their judgment, opposes the constitution, unless we can suppose they can make a superior law give way to an inferior. The legislature, therefore, will not go over the limits by which the courts may adjudge they are confined. And there is little room to doubt but that they will come up to those bounds, as often as occasion and opportunity may offer, and they may judge it proper to do it. For as on the one hand, they will not readily pass *laws* which they know the courts will not *execute,* so on the other, we may be sure they will not scruple to pass such as they know they will give effect, as often as they may judge it proper. [DHRC16 73]

[2] . . . Now to make a union of this kind perfect, it is necessary to abolish all inferior governments, and to give the general one compleat legislative, executive and judicial powers to every purpose. The courts therefore will establish it as a rule in explaining the constitution. To give it such a construction as will best tend to perfect the union or take from the state governments every power of either making or *executing laws*. The second object is "to establish justice." This must include not only the idea of instituting the rule of justice, or of making *laws* which shall be the measure or rule of right, but also of providing for the application of this rule or of administering justice under it. And under this the courts will in their decisions extend the power of the government to all cases they possibly can, or otherwise they will be restricted in doing what appears to be the intent of the constitution they should do, to wit, pass *laws* and provide for *the execution of them,* for the general distribution of justice between man and man. Another end declared is "to insure domestic tranquility." This comprehends a provision against all private breaches of the peace, as well as against all public commotions or general insurrections; and to attain the object of this clause fully, the government must exercise the power of passing *laws* on these subjects, as well as of appointing magistrates with authority to *execute them*. And the courts will adopt these ideas in their expositions. I might proceed to the other clause, in the preamble, and it would appear by a consideration of all of them separately, as it does by taking them together, that if the spirit of this system is to be known from its declared end and design in the preamble, its spirit is to subvert and abolish all the powers of the state government, and to embrace every object to which any government extends. [DHRC16 74–75]

William Ward [?], "Republicus," February 16, 1788:

. . . The inconsistencies that attend the idea of two houses are innumerable. Take one, supposing them both our representatives (tho' it will be hard to prove them so) it makes their constituents to say in many instances by their representatives in one house, "this shall be a *law,*" by their representatives in the other with respect to the same bill; "This shall not be a *law*". It impowers one body of men to enact statutes; and another to forbid their being carried into *execution*. It resembles a man putting forth his right hand to do some important business and then stretching forth his left hand to prevent it . . . [DHRC8 380]

"The New Litany," February 21, 1788:

That it may please thee to incline the hearts of thy people to adopt the new Foederal Constitution; to endow the president thereof, the vice-president, senators and house of representatives, with grace, wisdom and understanding, to make and *execute such laws* as will best tend to secure to thy people the blessings of liberty, peace and concord, in those states, and that they may so far retrieve their lost credit, that they no longer be a reproach and hissing amongst the nations of the earth. [DHRC8 400]

"The Impartial Examiner," No. 1, February 27, 1788:

I believe, it is acknowledged that the establishment of excises has been one of the greatest grievances, under which the English nation has labored for almost a century and an half. Although this may seem an oeconomical tax, as arising out of manufactures, from which the industrious may derive advantages; and whereof the wealthy by consuming the greatest share, will of course contribute the largest proportion of the tax: yet the nature of it being such, as requires severe *laws for its execution,* it has justly become an object of general detestation. . . . [DHRC8 421–22]

"An Impartial Citizen," No. 5, February 28, 1788:

It is also objected by Mr. [George] Mason, that under their own construction of the general clause, at the end of the enumerated powers, the Congress may grant monopolies in trade, constitute new crimes, inflict unusual punishments, and in short, do whatever they please. Nothing can be more groundless and ridiculous than this. The words of this clause so much dreaded by Mr. Mason, are, "To make all laws which shall be necessary and proper for carrying into *execution* the foregoing powers, and all other powers vested by this Constitution in the government of the United States, or in any department or officer thereof." Now, I insist that Mr. Mason's construction on this clause is absolutely puerile, and by no means warranted by the words, which are chosen with peculiar propriety. When a power is vested any where, from the nature of things it must be understood to be attended by such other incidental powers as are necessary to give it efficacy; for to say, that a power is given, without the power of enforcing it, is a solecism in language. In this case, the *laws* which Congress can make, for carrying into *execution* the conceded powers, must not only be necessary, but proper—So that if those powers cannot be *executed* without the aid of a *law*, granting commercial monopolies, inflicting unusual punishments, creating new crimes, or commanding any unconstitutional act; yet, as such a *law* would be manifestly not proper, it would not be warranted by this clause, without absolutely departing from the usual acceptation of words. . . . [DHRC8 431]

William Ward [?], "Republicus," March 1, 1788:

To conclude, I can think of but one source of right to government, or any branch of it; and that is the people. They, and only they, have a right to determine whether they will make *laws, or execute them,* or do both in a collective body, or by a delegated authority. . . . [DHRC8 451]

***Winchester Virginia Gazette*, March 7, 1788:**

Similar to this will be the fate of America, if the Federal Constitution should be adopted and ratified in its present form. The powers granted to Congress are boundless in some instances of the utmost consequence to the people, particularly their interferance with the internal police of the States; their power of embarrassing the freedom of their own election; their taxing the people without immediate representation; their power of raising an army for two years, which may be lengthened to any term for pretended reasons, which never failed to be done, as a principal step to tyranny; their power of legislation blended with that of the *execution of their own laws,* without controul. . . . [DHRC8 470–71]

"An Impartial Citizen," No. 6, March 13, 1788:

. . . The congress cannot make an instrument of tyranny of the militia: The Congress can only provide for arming and disciplining them. The propriety of this results from that of an uniformity of discipline and armour throughout the States, which must be self-evident. The Congress can provide for calling forth the militia only in three cases, viz. to *execute the laws* of the Union, suppress insurrections, and repel invasions: Ought not these three things to be done? . . . [DHRC8 499]

Alexander Hamilton, *The Federalist*, No. 69, March 14, 1788:

The President is ". . . . to take care that the *laws be faithfully executed;* and to commission all officers of the United States." In most of these particulars, the power of the President will resemble equally that of the king of Great Britain and of the governor of New York. [Fed. 445–46]

Political Club of Danville, Kentucky, Debates on the Constitution, March 22, 1788:

Mr Muter: That Militia may be called to enforce the *execution* of a Writ &c. and therefore wanted the sentence "*executed the Laws* &c." be struck out. [DHRC8 414]

Alexander Hamilton, *The Federalist*, No. 75, March 26, 1788:

. . . The essence of the legislative authority is to enact *laws*, or, in other words, to prescribe rules for the regulation of the society; while the *execution of the laws*, and the employment of the common strength, either for this purpose or for the common defence, seem to comprise all the functions of the executive magistrate. The power of making treaties is, plainly, neither the one nor the other. It relates neither to the *execution of the subsisting laws*, nor to the enaction of new ones; and still less to an exertion of the common strength. Its objects are CONTRACTS with foreign nations, which have the force of *law*, but derive it from the obligations of good faith. . . . [Fed. 476]

Melancton Smith, *An Address to the People of the State of New York*, c. April 1788:

. . . The merchant drives his commerce, and none can deprive him of the gain he honestly acquires; all classes and callings of men amongst us are protected in their various pursuits, and secured by the *laws* in the possession and enjoyment of the property obtained in those pursuits. The *laws are as well executed* as they ever were, in this or any other country. Neither the hand of private violence, nor the more to be dreaded hand of legal oppression, are reached out to distress us. [Ford 94]

Alexander Hamilton, *The Federalist*, No. 81, May 28, 1788:

. . . the most discerning cannot foresee how far the prevalency of a local spirit may be found to disqualify the local tribunals for the jurisdiction of national causes; whilst every man may discover, that courts constituted like those of some of the States would be improper channels of the judicial authority of the Union. State judges, holding their offices during pleasure, or from year to year, will be too little independent to be relied upon for an inflexible *execution of the national laws*. And if there was a necessity for confiding the original cognizance of causes arising under those *laws* to them, there would be a correspondent necessity for leaving the door of appeal as wide as possible. . . . [Fed. 510]

Alexander Hamilton, *The Federalist*, No. 82, May 28, 1788:

. . . Agreeably to the remark already made, the national and State systems are to be regarded as ONE WHOLE. The courts of the latter will of course be natural auxiliaries to the *execution of the laws* of the Union, and an appeal from them will as naturally lie to that tribunal which is destined to unite and assimilate the principles of national justice and the rules of national decisions. . . .

[Fed. 517]

Alexander Hamilton, *The Federalist*, No. 83, May 28, 1788:

It is evident that it can have no influence upon the legislature, in regard to the amount of taxes to be laid, to the objects upon which they are to be imposed, or to the rule by which they are to be apportioned. If it can have any influence, therefore, it must be upon the mode of collection, and the conduct of the officers intrusted with the *execution of the revenue laws*. [Fed. 522]

John Dickinson, "Fabius," No. 4, 1788:

Our government under the proposed confederation, will be guarded by a repetition of the strongest cautions against excesses. In the senate the sovereignties of the several states will be equally represented; in the house of representatives, the people of the whole union will be equally represented; and, in the president, and the federal independent judges, so much concerned in the *execution of the laws,* and in the determination of their constitutionality, the sovereignties of the several states and the people of the whole union, may be considered as conjointly represented. [Ford 184]

South Carolina Constitution, June 3, 1790:

[Article II, Section 8:] He [the Governor] shall take care that the *laws be faithfully executed* in mercy.

Pennsylvania Constitution, September 2, 1790:

[Article II, Section 13:] He [the Governor] shall take care that the *laws be faithfully executed.* [Thorpe 3096]

LAWS, GENERAL

United States Constitution, September 17, 1787:

[Article IV, Section 1:] Full Faith and Credit shall be given in each State to the Public Acts, Records, and judicial Proceedings of every other State. And the Congress may by *general Laws* prescribe the Manner in which such Acts, Records and Proceedings shall be proved, and the Effect thereof.

* * * * *

The Mayflower Compact, November 11, 1620:

. . . Do by these Presents, solemnly and mutually, in the Presence of God and one another, covenant and combine ourselves together into a civil Body Politick, for our better Ordering and Preservation, and Furtherance of the Ends aforesaid: And by Virtue hereof do enact, constitute, and frame, such just and equal *Laws,* Ordinances, Acts, Constitutions, and Officers, from time to time, as shall be thought most meet and convenient for the *general* Good of the Colony; unto which we promise all due Submission and Obedience. . . . [Thorpe 1841]

Virginia Company, Ordinances for the Colony, July 24, 1621:

. . . And this General Assembly shall have free Power to treat, consult, and conclude, as well of all emergent Occasions concerning the Publick Weal of the said Colony and every Part thereof, as also to make, ordain, and enact such *general Laws* and Orders, for the Behoof of the said Colony, and the good Government thereof, as shall, from time to time, appear necessary or requisite . . . [Thorpe 3811]

Charles II, Charter of Pennsylvania, February 28, 1681:

. . . And our further will and pleasure is, that the *Lawes* for regulateing and governing of Propertie within the said Province, as well for the descent and enjoyment of lands, as likewise for the enjoyment and succession of goods and Chattles, and likewise as to Felonies, shall bee and continue the same, as they shall bee for the time being by the *generall course of the Law* in our Kingdome of England, untill the said *Lawes* shall bee altered by the said William Penn, his heires or assignes, and by the Freemen of the said Province, their Delegates or Deputies, or the greater Part of them. [Thorpe 3038–39]

The Albany Plan of Union, July 10, 1754:

POWER TO MAKE LAWS, LAY DUTIES, &c

That for these purposes they have power to make *laws,* and lay and levy such *general* duties, imposts, or taxes as to them shall appear most equal and just (considering the ability and other circumstances of the inhabitants in the several colonies), and such as may be collected with the least inconvenience to the people; rather discouraging luxury than loading industry with unnecessary burthens. [Thorpe 85]

Maryland Constitution, November 11, 1776:

[Declaration of Rights, Article 33:] That, as it is the duty of every man to worship God in such manner as he thinks most acceptable to him; all persons, professing the Christian religion, are equally entitled to protection in their religious liberty; wherefore no person ought by any *law* to be molested in his person or estate on account of his religious persuasion or profession, or for his religious practice; unless, under colour of religion, any man shall disturb the good order, peace or safety of the State, or shall infringe the *laws* of morality, or injure others, in their natural, civil, or religious rights; nor ought any person to be compelled to frequent or maintain, or contribute, unless on contract, to maintain any particular place of worship, or any particular ministry; yet the Legislature may, in their discretion, lay a *general* and equal tax, for the support of the Christian religion; leaving to each individual the power of appointing the payment over of the money, collected from him, to the support of any particular place of worship or minister, or for the benefit of the poor of his own denomination, or the poor in general of any particular county . . . [Thorpe 1689]

George Mason, Objections to the Constitution, October 7, 1787:

There is no Declaration of Rights; and the *Laws of the general Government* being paramount to the Laws & Constitutions of the several States, the Declarations of Rights in the separate States are no Security. Nor are the People secured even in the Enjoyment of the Benefits of the common-Law; which stands here upon no other Foundation than it's having been adopted by the respective Acts forming the Constitutions of the several States. [DHRC8 43]

Richard Henry Lee [?], "The Federal Farmer," No. 3, October 10, 1787:

I am not sufficiently acquainted with the laws and internal police of all the states to discern fully, how *general bankrupt laws,* made by the union, would effect them, or promote the public good. I believe the property of debtors, in the several states, is held responsible for their debts in modes and forms very different. If uniform bankrupt laws can be made without producing real and substantial inconveniences, I wish them to be made by congress. [Ford 306]

Richard Henry Lee [?], "The Federal Farmer," No. 4, October 12, 1787:

. . . The trials by jury in civil causes, it is said, varies so much in the several states, that no words could be found for the uniform establishment of it. If so, the federal legislation will not be able to establish it by any *general laws.* . . . [Ford 315]

Noah Webster, *An Examination into the Leading Principles of the Federal Constitution*, October 17, 1787:

It is also intimated as a probable event, that the federal courts will absorb the judiciaries of the federal states. This is a mere suspicion, without the least foundation. The jurisdiction of the federal states is very accurately defined and easily understood. It extends to the cases mentioned in the constitution, and to the execution of the *laws* of Congress, respecting commerce, revenue, and other *general* concerns. [Ford 52–53]

Hugh Williamson, Address at Edenton, North Carolina, November 8, 1787:

[1] When Gentlemen are pleased to complain, that little power is left in the hands of the separate States; they should be advised to cast an eye upon the large code of *laws,* which have passed in this State since the peace. Let them consider how few of those *laws* have been framed, for the *general* benefit of the Nation. Nine out of ten of them, are domestic; calculated for the sole use of this State, or of particular citizens. There must still be use for such *laws,* though you should enable the Congress to collect a revenue for National purposes, and the collection of that revenue includes the chief of the new powers, which are now to be committed to the Congress. [DHRC16 203]

[2] . . . The several States reserve every power that can be exercised for the particular use and comfort of the State. They do not yield a single power which is not purely of a national concern; nor do they yield a single power which is not absolutely necessary to the safety and prosperity of the nation, nor one that

could be employed to any effect in the hands of particular States. The powers of Judiciary naturally arise from those of the Legislature. Questions that are of a national concern, and those cases which are determinable by the *general laws* of the nation, are to be referred to the national Judiciary, but they have not any thing to do with a single case either civil or criminal, which respects the private and particular concerns of a State or its citizens. [DHRC16 204]

Virginia Independent Chronicle, November 28, 1787:

. . . I feel an attachment to my country approaching nearly to enthusiasm, and as long as I have a heart or a hand I will vigorously oppose every measure, that might tend to injure it. You know, Sir, the warmth of my disposition and the ardent love, which I have from the first dawn of reason invariably possessed for my country. You, then, Sir, will acquit me of every sinister design, when I solemnly declare to you with my hand upon my heart, that, in my humble opinion no danger ought to be apprehended or will issue from the establishment and operation of a *general excise law*. [DHRC8 179]

Alexander Hamilton, _The Federalist_, No. 22, December 14, 1787:

This is the more necessary where the frame of the government is so compounded that the laws of the whole are in danger of being contravened by the laws of the parts. In this case, if the particular tribunals are invested with a right of ultimate jurisdiction, besides the contradictions to be expected from differences of opinion there will be much to fear from the bias of local views and prejudices, and from the interference of local regulations. As often as such an interference was to happen, there would be reason to apprehend that the provisions of the particular laws might be preferred to those of the *general laws;* for nothing is more natural to men in office than to look with peculiar deference towards that authority to which they owe their official existence. . . . [Fed. 197]

James Madison, _The Federalist_, No. 42, January 22, 1788:

The power of prescribing the *general laws,* the manner in which the public acts, records, and judicial proceedings of each State shall be proved, and the effect they shall have in other States, is an evident and valuable improvement on the clause relating to this subject in the articles of Confederation. The meaning of the latter is extremely indeterminate, and can be of little importance under any interpretation which it will bear. The power here established may be rendered a very convenient instrument of justice, and be particularly beneficial on the borders of contiguous States, where the effects liable to justice may be suddenly and secretly translated, in any stage of the process, within a foreign jurisdiction. [Fed. 308]

"Civis Rusticus," January 30, 1788:

. . . The people of England have no other security for the liberty of the press, than we have—Their own spirit, and an act of parliament—their act of parliament may be repealed—our Bill of Rights may be repealed. Of that no man has any fear, of this no man need have, while this spirit is in the people—"This peculiar privilege must last (says a learned writer) as long as our government remains, in any degree, free and independent—it is seldom that liberty of any kind is lost at once—slavery has so frightful an aspect to men accustomed to freedom, that it must steal upon them by degrees, and disguise itself in a thousand shapes in order to be received—But, if the liberty of the press ever be lost, it will be lost at once.—The *general laws* against sedition and libelling are at present as strong as they can possibly be made, nothing can impose a further restraint, but, either clapping an imprimatur on the press, or giving to the court very large discretionary powers, to punish whatever displeases them—but these concessions would be such a bare faced violation of liberty, that they will probably be the last efforts of a despotic government—Hume's essay vol. 1. p. 17." [DHRC8 337–38]

James Madison, *The Federalist*, No. 56, February 16, 1788:

. . . In every State there have been made, and must continue to be made, regulations on this subject which will, in many cases, leave little more to be done by the federal legislature, than to review the different *laws,* and reduce them in *one general act.* A skillful individual in his closet, with all the local codes before him, might compile a law on some subjects of taxation for the whole Union, without any aid from oral information . . . [Fed. 380]

"An Impartial Citizen," No. 5, February 28, 1788:

. . . Mr. [George] Mason, as in his other objections, reasons in the most unfair, and least scientific way imaginable, viz. Arguing against a measure from a remote possibility of its being abused. Human sagacity cannot devise any law, but what, in its operations, may in some instances bear hard. It is impossible by any *general law,* to prevent punishments from being in some unforeseen cases, inadequate to offences—To obviate this inconvenience, a power of pardoning ought to be vested some where in a State. All civilized nations have accordingly adopted this measure; and there is hardly a respectable writer who has not inculcated the expediency of pardons. . . . [DHRC8 428]

"Brutus," No. 14, March 6, 1788:

But these evils have not happened from any defect in the judicial departments of the states; the courts indeed are bound to take notice of these laws, and so will the courts of the *general* government be under obligation to observe the *laws made by the general legislature;* not repugnant to the constitution; but so

far have the judicial been from giving undue latitude of construction to *laws* of this kind, that they have invariably strongly inclined to the other side. . . .
[DHRC16 330]

George Nicholas [?], "The State Soldier," No. 4, March 19, 1788:

Under this government neither the Congress nor state legislature could, by direct laws, deprive us of any property we might hold under the *general law* of the land, or punish us for any offence committed previous to the passage of such laws, since they are prohibited from passing ex post facto laws. Nor could they injure the value of any species of property by partial taxes . . .
[DHRC8 510–11]

"Brutus," No. 15, March 20, 1788:

. . . In this situation, the *general* legislature, might pass one *law* after another, extending the general and abridging the state jurisdictions, and to sanction their proceedings would have a course of decisions of the judicial to whom the constitution has committed the power of explaining the constitution.—If the states remonstrated, the constitutional mode of deciding upon the validity of the *law,* is with the supreme court, and neither people, nor state legislatures, nor the *general* legislature can remove them or reverse their decrees.
[DHRC16 434–35]

Luther Martin, "To the Citizens of Maryland," No. 2, March 21, 1788:

When this clause was introduced, it was not established that inferior continental courts should be appointed for trial of all questions arising on treaties and on the *laws of the general government,* and it was my wish and hope that every question of that kind would have been determined, in the first instance, in the courts of the respective states; had this been the case, the propriety and the necessity that treaties duly made and ratified, and the *laws of the general government* should be binding on the state judiciaries, which were to decide upon them, must be evident to every capacity, while, at the same time, if such treaties or *laws* were inconsistent with our [Maryland's] constitution and bill of rights, the judiciaries of this state would be bound to reject the first and abide by the last; since in the form I introduced the clause, notwithstanding treaties and the *laws of the general government* were intended to be superior to the *laws* of our state government, where they should be opposed to each other, yet that they were not proposed, nor meant to be superior to our constitution and bill of rights. It was afterwards altered and amended (if it can be called an amendment) to the form in which it stands in the system now published, and, as inferior continental, and not state, courts are originally to decide on those questions, it is now worse than useless; for being so altered as to render the treaties and *laws made under the general government* superior to our constitution, if the system is adopted, it will amount to a total and unconditional surrender to that government, by the citizens of this state, of every right and privilege secured to them by our constitution, and an express compact and stipulation with the general government, that it may, at its discretion, make *laws* in direct violation of those rights . . .

[DHRC16 452–53]

Alexander Hamilton, *The Federalist*, No. 80, May 28, 1788:

. . . But it is at least problematical, whether an unjust sentence against a foreigner, where the subject of controversy was wholly relative to the lex loci, would not, if unredressed, be an aggression upon his sovereign, as well as one which violated the stipulations of a treaty or the *general law* of nations. . . . [Fed. 501]

Alexander Hamilton, *The Federalist*, No. 85, May 28, 1788:

The zeal for attempts to amend, prior to the establishment of the Constitution, must abate in every man who is ready to accede to the truth of the following observations of a writer [David Hume] equally solid and ingenious: "To balance a large state or society (says he), whether monarchical or republican, on *general laws,* is a work of so great difficulty, that no human genius, however comprehensive, is able, by the mere dint of reason and reflection, to effect it. The judgments of many must unite in the work; experience must guide their labor; time must bring it to perfection, and the feeling of inconveniences must correct the mistakes which they inevitably fall into in their first trials and experiments." [Fed. 546–47]

LIFE OR LIMB

United States Constitution, Bill of Rights, December 15, 1791:

[Article V:] No person shall be held to answer for a capital, or otherwise infamous crime, unless on a presentment or indictment of a Grand Jury, except in cases arising in the land or naval forces, or in the Militia, when in actual service in time of War or public danger; nor shall any person be subject for the same offense to be twice put in jeopardy of *life or limb;* nor shall be compelled in any criminal case to be a witness against himself, nor be deprived of life, liberty, or property, without due process of law; nor shall private property be taken for public use, without just compensation.

* * * * *

Magna Carta, June 15, 1215:

Nothing shall henceforth be given or taken for a writ of inquisition concerning *life or limbs;* but it shall be given freely and not denied. [SDECH 47]

English Petition of Right, June 7, 1628:

And whereas also by authority of Parliament, in the 25th year of the reign of King Edward the Third, it is declared and enacted, that no man shall be forejudged of *life or limb* against the form of the Great Charter, and the law of the land; and by the said Great Charter and other the laws and statutes of this your realm, no man ought to be adjudged to death but by the laws established in this your realm, either by the customs of the same realm, or by Acts of Parliament: and whereas no offender of what kind soever is exempted from the proceedings to be used, and punishments to be inflicted by the laws and statutes of this your realm . . . [SDECH 341]

Charles I, Patent to Sir Robert Heath, October 30, 1629:

. . . & we grant to the said Sr. Robert his heires & assignes free full & all kind of power by the Tenour of these presents if the qualitye of the offence requires it to punish by the losse of *life or limbe* by himself his heires or assignes, or by their Deputyes Lieutenants Judges Justices Magestrates Officers & ministers to be constituted & made according to the tenour & true intent of these presents duely to be executed . . . [Thorpe 71]

Fundamental Constitutions of West New Jersey, 1676:

[Chapter 17:] That no Proprietor, freeholder or inhabitant of the said Province of West New Jersey, shall be deprived or condemned of *life, limb,* liberty, estate, property or any ways hurt in his or their privilegs, freedoms or franchises, upon any account whatsoever, without a due tryal, and judgment passed by twelve good and lawful men of his neighborhood first had . . . [Thorpe 2549]

Charles II, Commission Constituting a President and Council for New Hampshire, September 18, 1680:

. . . And Our further will & pleasure is & so we do hereby declare; That in all criminall cases, where punishmt to be inflicted upon ye offenders, shall extend to loss of *life or limb* (ye case of willfull murder only excepted) ye party convicted shall either be sent over into this Our Kingdom of Engd, with a true state of his case & conviction; or execuc'on shall be respited untill ye case shall be here represented unto Us, Our heirs & successors, in Our & their Privie Councell, and Orders sent & returned therein. . . . [Thorpe 2448]

James Madison, *The Federalist*, No. 54, February 12, 1788:

. . . In being protected, on the other hand, *in his life and in his limbs,* against the violence of all others, even the master of his labor and his liberty; and in being punishable himself for all violence committed against others,—the slave is no less evidently regarded by the law as a member of the society, not as a part of the irrational creation; as a moral person, not as a mere article of property. The federal Constitution, therefore, decides with great propriety on the case of our slaves, when it views them in the mixed character of persons and of property. This is in fact their true character. [Fed. 370–71]

Pennsylvania Constitution, September 2, 1790:

[Article IX, Section 10:] That no person shall, for any indictable offence, be proceeded against criminally by information, except in cases arising in the land or naval forces, or in the militia, when in actual service in time of war or public danger, or, by leave of the court, for oppression and misdemeanor in office. No person shall, for the same offence, be twice put in jeopardy of *life or limb;* nor shall any man's property be taken or applied to public use without the consent of his representatives, and without just compensation being made.

[Thorpe 3100–3101]

MIGRATION

(Emigration, Immigration)

United States Constitution, September 17, 1787:

[Article I, Section 9:] The *Migration* or Importation of such Persons as any of the States now existing shall think proper to admit, shall not be prohibited by the Congress prior to the Year one thousand eight hundred and eight, but a Tax or duty may be imposed on such Importation, not exceeding ten dollars for each Person.

* * * * *

First Continental Congress, Declaration and Resolves, October 14, 1774:

[1] That our ancestors, who first settled these colonies, were at the time of their *emigration* from the mother country, entitled to all the rights, liberties, and immunities of free and natural born subjects, within the realm of England. [JCC1 68]

[2] That by such *emigration* they by no means forfeited, surrendered, or lost any of those rights, but that they were, and their descendants now are, entitled to the exercise and enjoyment of all such of them, as their local and other circumstances enable them to exercise and enjoy. [JCC1 68]

Thomas Paine, *Common Sense,* January 9, 1776:

[1] Thus necessity, like a gravitating power, would soon form our newly arrived *emigrants* into society, the reciprocal blessings of which would supersede, and render the obligations of law and government unnecessary while they remained perfectly just to each other; but as nothing but Heaven is impregnable to vice, it will unavoidably happen, that in proportion as they surmount the first difficulties of *emigration,* which bound them together in a common cause, they will begin

to relax in their duty and attachment to each other; and this remissness will point out the necessity, of establishing some form of government to supply the defect of moral virtue. [CWTP1 5]

[2] . . . This new world hath been the asylum for the persecuted lovers of civil and religious liberty from every Part of Europe. Hither have they fled, not from the tender embraces of the mother, but from the cruelty of the monster; and it is so far true of England, that the same tyranny which drove the first *emigrants* from home pursues their descendants still. [CWTP1 19]

[3] Secondly. That as even the best terms which we can expect to obtain can amount to no more than a temporary expedient, or a kind of government by guardianship, which can last no longer than till the colonies come of age, so the general face and state of things in the interim will be unsettled and unpromising. *Emigrants* of property will not choose to come to a country whose form of government hangs but by a thread, and who is every day tottering on the brink of commotion and disturbance; and numbers of the present inhabitants would lay hold of the interval, to dispose of their effects, and quit the continent. [CWTP1 26]

United States Declaration of Independence, July 4, 1776:

[1] He [the King] has endeavoured to prevent the population of these States; for that purpose obstructing the Laws of Naturalization of Foreigners; refusing to pass others to encourage their *migrations* hither, and raising the conditions of new Appropriations of Lands. . . .

[2] . . . Nor have We been wanting in attentions to our British brethren. We have warned them from time to time of attempts by their legislature to extend an unwarrantable jurisdiction over us. We have reminded them of the circumstances of our *emigration* and settlement here. We have appealed to their native justice and magnanimity, and we have conjured them by the ties of our common kindred to disavow these usurpations, which, would inevitably interrupt our connections and correspondence. . . .

Pennsylvania Constitution, September 28, 1776:

[Declaration of Rights, Article 15:] That all men have a natural inherent right to *emigrate* from one state to another that will receive them, or to form a new state in vacant countries, or in such countries as they can purchase, whenever they think that thereby they may promote their own happiness. [Thorpe 3084]

Maryland Constitution, November 11, 1776:

[Declaration of Rights, Article 3:] That the inhabitants of Maryland are entitled to the common law of England, and the trial by jury, according to the course of that law, and to the benefit of such of the English statutes, as existed at the time of their first *emigration,* and which, by experience, have been found applicable to their local and other circumstances, and of such others as have been since made in England, or Great Britain, and have been introduced, used and practised by the courts of law or equity . . . [Thorpe 1686–87]

Vermont Constitution, July 8, 1777:

[Preamble:] They [the New York legislature] have, and still continue, an unjust claim to those lands, which greatly retards *emigration* into, and the settlement of, this State. [Thorpe 3738]

[*Ibid.*:] They have hired foreign troops, *emigrants* from Scotland, at two different times, and armed them, to drive us out of possession. [Thorpe 3738]

[Declaration of Rights, Article 17:] That all people have a natural and inherent right to *emigrate* from one State to another, that will receive them; or to form a new State in vacant countries, or in such countries as they can purchase, whenever they think that thereby they can promote their own happiness. [Thorpe 3741]

Vermont Constitution, July 4, 1786:

[Preamble:] They [the New York legislature] have and still continue an unjust claim to those lands, which greatly retards emigration into any settlement of this State. [Thorpe 3750]

[*Ibid.*:] They have hired foreign troops, *emigrants* from Scotland, at two different times, and armed them to drive us out of possession. [Thorpe 3750]

[Declaration of Rights, Article 21:] That all people have a natural and inherent right to *emigrate* from one State to another, that will receive them; or to form a new State in vacant countries, or in such countries as they can purchase whenever they think that thereby they can promote their own happiness. [Thorpe 3754]

Tench Coxe, *An Examination of the Constitution for the United States of America*, No. 1, September 26, 1787:

To take a proper view of the ground on which we stand, it may be necessary to recollect the manner in which the United States were originally settled and established. Want of charity in the religious systems of Europe, and of justice in their political governments, were the principal moving causes, which drove the *emigrants* of various countries to the American continent. . . . [Ford 135]

Noah Webster, *An Examination into the Leading Principles of the Federal Constitution*, October 17, 1787:

Representation would have, in some measure, prevented the consequences; but the admission of every man to a suffrage will ever open the door to corruption.

In such a state as Connecticut, where there is no conflux of foreigners, no introduction of seamen, servants, &c., and scarcely an hundred persons in the state who are not natives, and very few whose education and connexions do not attach them to the government; at the same time few men have property to furnish the means of corruption, very little danger could spring from admitting every man of age and discretion to the privilege of voting for rulers But in the large towns of America there is more danger. A master of a vessel may put votes in the hands of his crew, for the purpose of carrying an election for a party Such things have actually taken place in America. Besides, the middle states are receiving *emigrations* of poor people, who are not at once judges of the characters of men, and who cannot be safely trusted with the choice of legislators.

[Ford 43–44n]

Letter from New York, October 26, 1787, published in *Virginia Independent Chronicle*, November 14, 1787:

There is a most strange desire to give foreigners the advantage in legal pursuits over our fellow citizens. Where this Donquixotism in politics finds its equal I do not know. It has I am sure no foundation in practice; for can there be justice in allowing a foreigner, who resides at the foederal court, to drag a citizen with whom he has any money transaction, from Georgia to the foederal court to answer the foreigners suit? Is there a nation in the world in which an American has such a superiority over the natives? Is it not always held, that the utmost a foreigner can expect, is to be upon a par with the natives? what foreigner will disire to become a citizen, when by so doing he will lose that extraordinary pre-eminence? One would think it was calculated to make our country swarm with foreigners, instead of *emigrants*—and invite them to prey upon the American natives, who must either yield to every demand of a foreigner, or be utterly ruined in the litigation. [DHRC8 157–58]

James Madison, *The Federalist*, No. 42, January 22, 1788:

Attempts have been made to pervert this clause into an objection against the Constitution, by representing it on one side as a criminal toleration of an illicit practice, and on another as calculated to prevent voluntary and beneficial *emigrations* from Europe to America. I mention these misconstructions, not with a view to give them an answer, for they deserve none, but as specimens of the manner and spirit in which some have thought fit to conduct their opposition to the proposed government. [Fed. 304]

Letter from Wilmington, North Carolina, February 2, 1788, published in *Charleston City Gazette*, February 11, 1788:

I am just arrived at this place, on my return to the northward, having spent more than a year past in travelling through those parts of the United States bounding on the Ohio and Missisippi. The situation and soil of those territories, in general, are extremely flattering, but the immense population that has already taken place in these parts has really astonished me. The face of these countries is every day visibly improving; forests as old as the creation are hourly falling before the ax of the hardy *emigrant* from the old states; elegant farms in abundance are already settled along the banks of some of the deepest and most beautiful rivers that America can boast of; and, in short, every circumstance seems to point out that country as the future seat of a great and powerful empire of confederated republics. . . . [DHRC16 106]

David Ramsay, "Civis," February 4, 1788:

. . . It must be known to many of you, that the Southern states, from their vast extent of uncultivated country, are daily receiving new settlers; but in New-England their country is so small, and their land so poor, that their inhabitants are constantly *emigrating*. As the rule of representation in Congress is to vary with the number of inhabitants, our influence in the general government will be constantly increasing. In fifty years, it is probable that the Southern states will have a great ascendency over the Eastern. . . . [DHRC16 23]

William Ward [?], "Republicus," March 1, 1788:

This leads me to Art. 1 Sect. 9. "The *migration* or importation of such persons, as any of the States now existing, shall think proper to admit, shall not be prohibited by the Congress prior to the year 1808; (twenty years hence) but a tax, or duty may be imposed on such importation, not exceeding ten dollars for each person." An excellent clause this, in an Algerine constitution; but not so well calculated (I hope) for the latitude of America. It is not to be disguised that by "such persons," slaves are principally, if not wholly intended: and shall this be found among the principles of a free people, and making a radical part of the grand base, on which they would erect an edifice sacred to liberty. . . . [DHRC8 450]

Pennsylvania Constitution, September 2, 1790:

[Article IX, Section 25:] That *emigration* from the State shall not be prohibited. [Thorpe 3101]

MINISTERS, PUBLIC

United States Constitution, September 17, 1787:

[Article II, Section 2:] He [the President] shall have Power, by and with the Advice and Consent of the Senate, to make Treaties, provided two thirds of the Senators present concur; and he shall nominate, and by and with the Advice and Consent of the Senate, shall appoint Ambassadors, other *public Ministers* and Consuls, Judges of the supreme Court, and all other Officers of the United States, whose Appointments are not herein otherwise provided for, and which shall be established by Law: but the Congress may by Law vest the Appointment of such inferior Officers, as they think proper, in the President alone, in the Courts of Law, or in the Heads of Departments.

[Article II, Section 3:] He shall from time to time give to the Congress Information of the State of the Union, and recommend to their Consideration such Measures as he shall judge necessary and expedient; he may, on extraordinary Occasions, convene both Houses, or either of them, and in Case of Disagreement between them, with Respect to the Time of Adjournment, he may adjourn them to such Time as he shall think proper; he shall receive Ambassadors and other *public Ministers;* he shall take Care that the Laws be faithfully executed, and shall Commission all the Officers of the United States.

[Article III, Section 2:] The judicial Power shall extend to all Cases, in Law and Equity, arising under this Constitution, the Laws of the United States, and Treaties made, or which shall be made, under their Authority;—to all Cases affecting Ambassadors, other *public Ministers* and Consuls;—to all Cases of admiralty and maritime Jurisdiction;—to Controversies to which the United States shall be a Party;—to Controversies between two or more States;—between a State and Citizens of another State;—between Citizens of different States,—between Citizens of the same State claiming Lands under Grants of different States, and between a State, or the Citizens thereof, and foreign States, Citizens or Subjects.

[*Ibid.*:] In all Cases affecting Ambassadors, other *public Ministers* and Consuls, and those in which a State shall be Party, the supreme Court shall have original Jurisdiction. In all the other Cases before mentioned, the supreme Court shall have appellate Jurisdiction, both as to Law and Fact, with such Exceptions, and under such Regulations as the Congress shall make.

* * * * *

Richard Henry Lee [?], "The Federal Farmer," No. 3, October 10, 1787:

. . . Whether the jury trial is not excluded [from] the supreme judicial court is an important question. By Art. 3, Sec. 2, all cases affecting ambassadors, other *public ministers,* and consuls, and in those cases in which a state shall be party, the supreme court shall have jurisdiction. In all the other cases before mentioned, the supreme court shall have appellate jurisdiction, both as to law and fact, with such exception, and under such regulations as the congress shall make. By court is understood a court consisting of judges; and the idea of a jury is excluded. This court, or the judges, are to have jurisdiction on appeals, in all the cases enumerated, as to law and fact; the judges are to decide the law and try the fact, and the trial of the fact being assigned to the judges by the constitution, a jury for trying the fact is excluded; however, under the exceptions and powers to make regulations, congress may, perhaps, introduce the jury, to try the fact in most necessary cases. [Ford 308]

"Cato Uticensis," October 17, 1787:

In any dispute between you and the revenue officers and excisemen of Congress, it is true, that it is provided, the trial shall be, in the first instance, within the state, though before a Foederal tribunal: It is said in par. 3. sect. 2. art. 3, "The trial of all crimes except in cases of impeachments shall be by jury; and such trial shall be held in the state where the crimes shall be committed;" but what does this avail, when an appeal will lie against you to the Supreme Foederal Court—In the paragraph preceding the one just now quoted, it is said, "In all cases affecting ambassadors, other *public ministers* and consuls, and those in which a state shall be a party, the Supreme Court shall have original jurisdiction. In all the other cases before mentioned, the Supreme Court shall have appellate jurisdiction, both as to law and fact, with such exceptions and under such regulations as the Congress shall make." But, where is this Supreme Court to sit? Will it not be, where Congress shall fix its residence? Thither then you will be carried for trial. Who are to be your jury? Is there any provision made, that you shall have a Venire from your county, or even from your state, as they please to call it? No! you are to be tried within the territory of Congress, and Congress itself is to be a party; you are to be deprived of the benefit of a jury from your vicinage, that boast and birthright of a freeman. [DHRC8 74]

Dissent of the Pennsylvania Convention's Minority, December 18, 1787:

That the judiciary power of the United States shall be confined to cases affecting ambassadors, other *public ministers* and consuls; to cases of admiralty and maritime jurisdiction; to controversies to which the United States shall be a party; to controversies between two or more states—between a state and citizens of different states—between citizens claiming lands under grants of different states, and between a state or the citizens thereof and foreign states, and in criminal cases, to such only as are expressly enumerated in the constitution, and that the United States in Congress assembled shall not have power to enact laws, which shall alter the laws of descents and distribution of the effects of deceased persons, the titles of lands or goods, or the regulation of contracts in the individual states. [DHRC2 625]

James Madison, *The Federalist*, No. 42, January 22, 1788:

[1] The second class of powers, lodged in the general government, consist of those which regulate the intercourse with foreign nations, to wit: to make treaties; to send and receive ambassadors, other *public ministers,* and consuls; to define and punish piracies and felonies committed on the high seas, and offences against the law of nations; to regulate foreign commerce, including a power to prohibit, after the year 1808, the importation of slaves, and to lay an intermediate duty of ten dollars per head, as a discouragement to such importations. [Fed. 302]

[2] The powers to make treaties and to send and receive ambassadors, speak their own propriety. Both of them are comprised in the articles of Confederation, with this difference only, that the former is disembarrassed, by the plan of the convention, of an exception, under which treaties might be substantially frustrated by regulations of the States; and that a power of appointing and receiving "other *public ministers* and consuls," is expressly and very properly added to the former provision concerning ambassadors. The term ambassador, if taken strictly, as seems to be required by the second of the articles of Confederation, comprehends the highest grade only of *public ministers,* and excludes the grades which the United States will be most likely to prefer, where foreign embassies may be necessary. And under no latitude of construction will the term comprehend consuls. Yet it has been found expedient, and has been the practice of Congress, to employ the inferior grades of *public ministers,* and to send and receive consuls. [Fed. 302–303]

"Civis Rusticus," January 30, 1788:

The judiciary of the United States have original jurisdiction only, in all cases affecting ambassadors, other *public ministers* and consuls, and those in which a state shall be party—The convention has only crayoned the outlines, it is left to the Congress, to fill up and colour the canvas . . . [DHRC8 336]

Alexander C. Hanson, *Remarks on the Proposed Plan of a Federal Government*, c. January 31, 1788:

The original jurisdiction of the supreme court extends

I. To all cases, in which may be concerned an ambassador, any *public minister*, or a consul. [Ford 236]

Luther Martin, "Genuine Information," No. 10, February 1, 1788:

. . . To the courts of the general government are also confined all cases in law or equity, arising under the proposed constitution, and treaties made under the authority of the United States—all cases affecting ambassadors, other *public ministers* and consuls—all cases of admiralty and maritime jurisdiction—all controversies to which the United States are a party—all controversies between two or more States—between a State and citizens of another State—between citizens of the same State claiming lands under grants of different States, and between a State or the citizens thereof, and foreign States, citizens, or subjects.— Whether therefore, any laws or regulations of the Congress, or any acts of its president or other officers are contrary to, or not warranted by the constitution, rests only with the judges, who are appointed by Congress to determine; by whose determinations every State must be bound. . . . [DHRC16 8]

"Brutus," No. 13, February 21, 1788:

. . . The cases affecting ambassadors, *public ministers,* and consuls—of admiralty and maritime jurisdiction; controversies to which the United States are a party, and controversies between states, it is proper should be under the cognizance of the courts of the union, because none but the general government, can, or ought to pass laws on their subjects. But, I conceive the clause which extends the power of the judicial to controversies arising between a state and citizens of another state, improper in itself, and will, in its exercise, prove most pernicious and destructive. [DHRC16 172]

***New York Journal*, February 23, 1788:**

The *minister* of the United States, at the court of London [John Adams], has been constantly in the *public* employ, from the commencement of the American revolution. This gentleman was a delegate in Congress when the confederation was devised, and is said to have had no inconsiderable influence in its formation. . . . [DHRC16 192]

"Brutus," No. 14, February 28, 1788:

[1] Ambassadors, and other *public ministers,* claim, and are entitled by the law of nations, to certain privileges, and exemptions, both for their persons and their servants. [DHRC16 256]

[2] . . . But in all these cases it is declared, the supreme court shall have appellate jurisdiction, except in those which affect ambassadors, other *public ministers* and consuls, and those in which a state shall be a party. If then this section extends the power of the judicial, to criminal cases, it allows appeals in such cases. If the power of the judicial is not extended to criminal matters by this section, I ask, by what part of this system does it appear, that they have any cognizance of them? [DHRC16 256]

"Brutus," No. 14, March 6, 1788:

The courts of the respective states might therefore have been securely trusted, with deciding all cases between man and man, whether citizens of the same state or of different states, or between foreigners and citizens, and indeed for ought I see every case that can arise under the constitution or laws of the United States, ought in the first instance to be tried in the court of the state, except those which might arise between states, such as respect ambassadors, or other *public ministers,* and perhaps such as call in question the claim of lands under grants from different states. . . . [DHRC16 330–31]

Alexander Hamilton, *The Federalist*, No. 67, March 11, 1788:

The second clause of the second section of the second article empowers the President of the United States "to nominate, and by and with the advice and consent of the Senate, to appoint ambassadors, other *public ministers* and consuls, judges of the Supreme Court, and all other officers of United States whose appointments are not in the Constitution otherwise provided for, and which shall be established by law." Immediately after this clause follows another in these words: "The President shall have power to fill up all vacancies that may happen during the recess of the Senate, by granting commissions which shall expire at the end of their next session." It is from this last provision that the pretended power of the President to fill vacancies in the Senate has been deduced. A slight attention to the clauses, and to the obvious meaning of the terms, will satisfy us that the deduction is not even colorable. [Fed. 438]

Alexander Hamilton, *The Federalist*, No. 69, March 14, 1788:

[1] The President is also to be authorized to receive ambassadors and other *public ministers*. This, though it has been a rich theme of declamation, is more a matter of dignity than of authority. It is a circumstance which will be without consequence in the administration of the government; and it was far more convenient that it should be arranged in this manner, than that there should be a necessity of convening the legislature, or one of its branches, upon every arrival of a foreign *minister,* though it were merely to take the place of a departed predecessor. [Fed. 448]

[2] The President is to nominate, and, with the advice and consent of the Senate, to appoint ambassadors and other *public ministers,* judges of the Supreme Court, and in general all officers of the United States established by law, and whose appointments are not otherwise provided for by the Constitution. The king of Great Britain is emphatically and truly styled the fountain of honor. He not only appoints to all offices, but can create offices. He can confer titles of nobility at pleasure; and has the disposal of an immense number of church preferments. There is evidently a great inferiority in the power of the President, in this particular, to that of the British king . . . [Fed. 448–49]

Alexander Hamilton, *The Federalist*, No. 77, April 2, 1788:

The only remaining powers of the Executive are comprehended in giving information to Congress of the state of the Union; in recommending to their consideration such measures as he shall judge expedient; in convening them, or either branch, upon extraordinary occasions; in adjourning them when they cannot themselves agree upon the time of adjournment; in receiving ambassadors and other *public ministers;* in faithfully executing the laws; and in commissioning all the officers of the United States. [Fed. 448]

Alexander Hamilton, *The Federalist*, No. 80, May 28, 1788:

[1] Having thus laid down and discussed the principles which ought to regulate the constitution of the federal judiciary, we will proceed to test, by these principles, the particular powers of which, according to the plan of the convention, it is to be composed. It is to comprehend "all cases in law and equity arising under the Constitution, the laws of the United States, and treaties made, or which shall be made, under their authority; to all cases affecting ambassadors, other *public ministers,* and consuls; to all cases of admiralty and maritime jurisdiction; to controversies to which the United States shall be a party; to controversies between two or more States; between a State and citizens of another State; between citizens of different States; between citizens of the same State claiming lands under grants of different States; and between a State or the citizens thereof and foreign states, citizens, and subjects." This constitutes the entire mass of the judicial authority of the Union. . . . [Fed. 503]

[2] [The judicial authority of the United States will extend] To treaties made, or which shall be made, under the authority of the United States, and to all cases affecting ambassadors, other *public ministers,* and consuls. These belong to the fourth class of the enumerated cases, as they have an evident connection with the preservation of the national peace. [Fed. 504]

Alexander Hamilton, *The Federalist*, No. 81, May 28, 1788:

The Supreme Court is to be invested with original jurisdiction, only "in cases affecting ambassadors, other *public ministers,* and consuls, and those in which

A STATE shall be a party." *Public ministers* of every class are the immediate representatives of their sovereigns. All questions in which they are concerned are so directly connected with the public peace, that, as well for the preservation of this, as out of respect to the sovereignties they represent, it is both expedient and proper that such questions should be submitted in the first instance to the highest judicatory of the nation. . . . [Fed. 510–11]

United States Congress, Judiciary Act of September 24, 1789:

[Section 13:] That the Supreme Court shall have exclusive jurisdiction of all controversies of a civil nature, where a state is a party, except between a state and its citizens; and except also between a state and citizens of other states, or aliens, in which latter case it shall have original but not exclusive jurisdiction. And shall have exclusively all such jurisdiction of suits or proceedings against ambassadors or other *public ministers,* or their domestics, or domestic servants, as a court of law can have or exercise consistently with the law of nations; and original, but not exclusive jurisdiction of all suits brought by ambassadors, or other *public ministers,* or in which a consul, or vice-consul shall be a party. And the trial of issues in fact in the Supreme Court, in all actions at law against citizens of the United States, shall be by jury. The Supreme Court shall also have appellate jurisdiction from the circuit courts and courts of the several states in the cases herein after specially provided for; and shall have power to issue writs of prohibition to the district courts, when proceeding as courts of admiralty and maritime jurisdiction, and writs of mandamus, in cases warranted by the principle and usages of law, to any courts appointed, or persons holding office under the authority of the United States. [USSL1 80–81]

MONEY, PUBLIC

United States Constitution, September 17, 1787:

[Article I, Section 9:] No *Money* shall be drawn from the Treasury, but in Consequence of Appropriations made by Law; and a regular Statement and Account of the Receipts and Expenditures of all *public Money* shall be published from time to time.

* * * * *

Carolina Proprietors, Declaration and Proposals, August 25, 1663:

In consideration of the premises, we do expect by way of acknowledgment, and towards the charge we have been and shall be at, one half-penny for every acre that shall be granted as aforesaid, within the time before limited and exressed; and that the court-houses and houses for *public* meetings be erected by the *public moneys* of the colony on the lands taken up by us; but to be and continue to the country's use forever, they paying some small acknowledgement

[Thorpe 2755]

Fundamental Constitutions of Carolina, March 1, 1669:

[Article 33:] . . . This court [the ''palatine's court''] shall have power to call parliaments, to pardon all offences, to make elections of all officers in the proprietors dispose, and to nominate and appoint port towns; and also shall have power by their order to the treasurer to dispose of all *public* treasure, excepting *money* granted by the parliament, and by them directed to some particular *public* use . . . [Thorpe 2776]

Charles II, Charter of Pennsylvania, February 28, 1681:

. . . That We reposing speciall trust and Confidence in the fidelitie, wisedom, Justice, and provident circumspection of the said William Penn for us, our heires and Successors, Doe grant free, full, and absolute power by vertue of these presents to him and his heires, and to his and their Deputies, and Lieutenants, for the good and happy government of the said countrey to ordeyne, make, and enact, and under his and their Seales to publish any Lawes whatsoever, for the raising of *money* for the *publick* use of the said Province, or for any other End, apperteyning either unto the *publick* state, peace, or safety of the said Countrey, or unto the private utility of perticular persons, according unto their best discretions, by and with the advice, assent, and approbation of the Freemen of the said Countrey . . . [Thorpe 3037]

James II, Commission to Sir Edmund Andros for the Dominion of New England, April 7, 1688:

And our further will and pleasure is, that all *publick money* raised or to be raised or appointed for the support of the government within our said territory and dominion be issued out by warrant or order from you by & with the advise and consent of our Councill as aforesaid. [Thorpe 1865]

Pennsylvania Constitution, September 28, 1776:

[Frame of Government, Section 47:] . . . They [the Council of Censors] are also to enquire whether the *public* taxes have been justly laid and collected in all parts of this commonwealth, in what manner the *public monies* have been disposed of, and whether the laws have been duly executed. For these purposes they shall have power to send for persons, papers, and records; they shall have authority to pass *public* censures, to order impeachments, and to recommend to the legislature the repealing such laws as appear to them to have been enacted contrary to the principles of the constitution. . . . [Thorpe 3091–92]

North Carolina Constitution, December 18, 1776:

[Form of Government, Article 25:] That no persons, who heretofore have been, or hereafter may be, receivers of *public* the *monies,* shall have a seat in either House of General Assembly, or be eligible to any office in this State, until such person shall have fully accounted for and paid into the treasury all sums for which they may be accountable and liable. [Thorpe 2792]

[Form of Government, Article 26:] That no Treasurer shall have a seat, either in the Senate, House of Commons, or Council of State, during his continuance in that office, or before he shall have finally settled his accounts with the *public,* for all the *monies* which may be in his hands at the expiration of his office belonging to the State, and hath paid the same into the hands of the succeeding Treasurer. [Thorpe 2792]

Vermont Constitution, July 8, 1777:

[Frame of Government, Section 44:] . . . They [the Council of Censors] are also to enquire whether the *public* taxes have been justly laid and collected, in all parts of this Commonwealth—in what manner the *public monies* have been disposed of, and whether the laws have been duly executed. For these purposes they shall have power to send for persons, papers and records; they shall have authority to pass *public* censures—to order impeachments, and to recommend to the legislature the repealing such laws as appear to them to have been enacted contrary to the principles of the constitution. . . . [Thorpe 3748–49]

United States Articles of Confederation, November 15, 1777:

[Article IX:] [The Committee of the States shall have power] . . . to ascertain the necessary sums of *Money* to be raised for the service of the united states, and to appropriate and apply the same for defraying the *public* expenses—to borrow *money,* or emit bills on the credit of the united states, transmitting every half year to the respective states an account of the sums of *money* so borrowed or emitted . . . [DHRC2 91]

South Carolina Constitution, March 19, 1778:

[Article 16:] That all *money* bills for the support of government shall originate in the house of representatives, and shall not be altered or amended by the senate, but may be rejected by them, and that no *money* be drawn out of the *public* treasury but by the legislative authority of the State. . . . [Thorpe 3252]

Vermont Constitution, July 4, 1786:

[Frame of Government, Section 50:] . . . they [the Council of Censors] are also to inquire whether the *public* taxes have been justly laid and collected in all parts of this Commonwealth—in what manner the *public monies* have been disposed of—and whether the laws have been duly executed. For these purposes, they shall have power to send for persons, papers, and records; they shall have authority to pass *public* censures—to order impeachments—and to recommend to the Legislature the repealing such laws as appear to them to have been enacted contrary to the principles of the Constitution . . . [Thorpe 3761]

Tobias Lear, "Brutus," December 6, 1787:

"The Senate have the power of originating appropriations of *money*." If to this had been added a power to draw *money* from the treasury, without the concurrence of the other house, there would have been validity in the objection; but as it now stands it is rendered nugatory by a clause in the ninth section of the first article in the proposed constitution, which says, "No *money* shall be drawn from the treasury, but in consequence of appropriations made by law:'' As no law can have effect until it has passed both houses, the House of Representatives must concur in every appropriation of *money* before it can be drawn from the treasury, and they have an equal right with the Senate to originate appropriations of *money;* so that any evils which may arise from an improper application of the *public money* must either originate with, or have the assent of the immediate Representatives of the people; and as ''a regular statement and account of the receipts and expenditure of all *public money* shall be published from time to time,'' there will be a pretty effectual check to any misapplication or misappropriation of the *public* treasure. [DHRC8 215]

''An Impartial Citizen,'' January 10, 1788:

. . . The President in many important cases, must have the concurrence of the Senate, wherein his sole decision might be dangerous. The compensation for his services cannot be augmented, nor can he receive any other emolument from the United States, or any of them, during the period for which he shall have been elected: Nor can he appropriate the *public money* to any use, but what is expressly provided by law; which, together with the minutely complex mode of election (from which arises the strong improbability of his being re-elected) so cautiously guards and limits his quadrennial power, as to leave him dignity enough for the execution of his office, without the possibility of making a bad use of it,—and this security is still heightened by his responsibility to impeachment. No *money* is to be drawn from the Treasury but in consequence of appropriations made by law; and regular accounts of the *public* receipts and expenditures of *money,* are to be published: A provision highly wise, and productive of moderation in the government, and confidence therein by the people; an advantage this system has over all the governments of antiquity, and over most, if not over all, the governments at present in Europe. . . . [DHRC8 295]

James Madison, *The Federalist*, No. 43, January 23, 1788:

The necessity of a like authority over forts, magazines, etc., established by the general government, is not less evident. The *public money* expended on such places, and the *public* property deposited in them, require that they should be exempt from the authority of the particular State. Nor would it be proper for the places on which the security of the entire Union may depend, to be in any degree dependent on a particular member of it. . . . [Fed. 310]

Spurious ''Centinel,'' February 16, 1788:

. . . Think on that, my countrymen, we must not only be governed, be insulted by being governed, but we must pay these demagogues for coming from all parts of the continent, to lay their heads together how to govern us most effectually—for this, we must pay them mileage, pay them wages, fill their purses, supply their tables to keep them in idleness to riot on the fat of the land, to plot, contrive, and juggle us into good order and government. Now all this *money* might be saved to the *public*, by each man governing himself, and doing as he pleased, which by nature he has a right to do. [DHRC16 134]

Alexander White, "To the Citizens of Virginia," February 22, 1788:

[Quoting Tacitus:] "As to war and military expeditions, the [Roman] consuls had almost sovereign power; had the care of raising armies; of setling the number of troops which the allies were seperately to furnish, and of nominating the principal officers to serve under them. When they were in the field, they had the right of condemning and punishing without appeal. They disposed of the *public money* at their pleasure and applied it as they judged convenient, the questor constantly attending them, and supplying them with such sums as they required, out of the funds assigned them for the service. [DHRC8 407]

Samuel Bryan, "Centinel," No. 16, February 26, 1788:

[1] . . . An ex post facto law is a law made after the fact, so that the Congress under the new constitution are precluded from all controul over transactions prior to its establishment. This prohibition would skreen the numerous *public* defaulters, as no measure could be constitutionally taken to compel them to render an account and restore the *public money;* the unaccounted millions lying in their hands would become their private property. Hitherto these characters from their great weight and numbers have had the influence to prevent an investigation of their accounts, but if this constitution be established, they may set the *public* at defiance, as they would be completely exonerated of all demands of the United States against them. . . . [DHRC16 218–19]

[2] The immaculate convention, that is said to have possessed the fullness of patriotism, wisdom and virtue, contained a number of the principal *public* defaulters; and these were the most influential members, and chiefly instrumental in the framing of the new constitution: There were several of this description in the deputation from the state of Pennsylvania, who have long standing and immense accounts to settle, and MILLIONS perhaps to refund. The late Financier [U.S. Superintendent of Finance Robert Morris] alone, in the capacity of chairman of the commercial committee of Congress, early in the late war, was entrusted with millions of *public money,* which to this day remain unaccounted for, nor has he settled his accounts as Financier. . . . [DHRC16 219]

Mercy Otis Warren, *Observations on the New Constitution*, February 1788:

[1] . . . where then were the class who now come forth importunately urging that our political salvation depends on the adoption of a system at which freedom

spurns?—Were not some of them hidden in the corners of obscurity, and others wrapping themselves in the bosom of our enemies for safety? Some of them were in the arms of infancy; and others speculating for fortune, by sporting with *public money;* while a few, a very few of them were magnanimously defending their country, and raising a character, which I pray heaven may never be sullied by aiding measures derogatory to their former exertions. . . . [DHRC16 276]

[2] . . . and shall a privilege [trial by jury], the origin of which may be traced to our Saxon ancestors—that has been a part of the law of nations, even in the fewdatory systems of France, Germany and Italy—and from the earliest records has been held so sacred, both in ancient and modern Britain, that it could never be shaken by the introduction of Norman customs, or any other conquests or change of government—shall this inestimable privilege be relinquished in America—either thro' the fear of inquisition for unaccounted thousands of *public monies* in the hands of some who have been officious in the fabrication of the consolidated system, or from the apprehension that some future delinquent possessed of more power than integrity, may be called to a trial by his peers in the hour of investigation? [DHRC16 279]

[3] As the new Congress are empowered to determine their own salaries, the requisitions for this purpose may not be very moderate, and the drain for *public moneys* will probably rise past all calculation . . . [DHRC16 280]

"The Impartial Examiner," No. 1, March 5, 1788:

. . . Hence it follows, that in the midst of this general contageon a few men—or one—more powerful than all others, industriously endeavor to obtain all authority; and by means of great wealth—or embezzling the *public money,*—perhaps totally subvert the government, and erect a system of aristocratical or monarchic tyranny in its room. . . . [DHRC8 465]

Benjamin Workman [?], "Philadelphiensis," No. 11, March 8, 1788:

My Fellow Citizens, Every day opens a new scene of the baseness of the conspirators, their intentions of screening themselves from rendering an account of the *public money* so fraudulently detained, will rank them among the meanest traitors, that ever dishonoured the human character. How must their consciences condemn them, when avarice and lust of dominion are suffered for a moment to subside, and reason and reflection take their place? . . . [DHRC16 363]

"An Impartial Citizen," No. 6, March 13, 1788:

[1] . . . If there be a probability of an attack by foreign nations, or of an overthrow of the government by civil discord, we ought not to wait the enemies attack in either case. It is sophistry in the extreme to suppose, that standing armies will be kept in time of profound peace, when there is no necessity for it. As a regular

statement and account of the *public* receipts and expenditures of *money,* are to be published from time to time, for the inspection and examination of the *public;* and as this cannot, on any pretext, be kept secret from the people should armies be unnecessarily maintained the sums which their maintenance would cost would be universally known, and as universally would the measure be reprobated . . . [DHRC8 498]

[2] . . . The necessity of publishing regularly the amounts of monies received and expended, will most certainly prevent an improper application of the *public money;* it being provided also by the Constitution, that no appropriations of money shall be made, but in consequence of laws for that purpose enacted. . . . [DHRC8 499]

Alexander Hamilton, *The Federalist*, No. 72, March 19, 1788:

. . . The actual conduct of foreign negotiations, the preparatory plans of finance, the application and disbursement of the *public moneys* in conformity to the general appropriations of the legislature, the arrangement of the army and navy, the direction of the operations of war,—these, and other matters of a like nature, constitute what seems to be most properly understood by the administration of government. . . . [Fed. 462–63]

Samuel Bryan, "Centinel," No. 17, March 24, 1788:

. . . the conspirators have asserted, that his [former U.S. Superintendent of Finance Robert Morris's] accounts were finally settled in November, 1784, for which they pretend to have vouchers, and by a pompous display of certain resolutions of Congress, respecting a particular charge of fraud against him, as commercial agent to the United States, they vainly hope to divert the *public* attention from his great delinquency, in never accounting for the millions of *public money,* entrusted to him in that line. When we consider the immense sums of *money* taken up by Mr. M——s, as commercial agent, to import military supplies, and even to trade in behalf of the United States, at a time when the risque was so great, that individuals would not venture their property; that all these transactions were conducted under the private firm of W[illin]g and M[orris], which afforded unrestrained scope to peculation and embezzlement of the *public* property, by enabling Mr. M——s to throw the loss of all captures by the enemy, at that hazardous period, on the *public,* and converting most of the safe arrivals (which were consequently very valuable) into his private property . . . [DHRC16 475–76]

Melancton Smith, *An Address to the People of the State of New York*, c. April 1788:

[1] . . . *Money* is to pour into our country through every channel—Arts and manufactures are to rear their heads, and every mechanic find full employ—

Those who are in debt, are to find easy means to procure *money* to pay them—*Public* burdens and taxes are to be lightened, and yet all our *public* debts are soon to be discharged.—With such vain and delusive hopes are the minds of many honest and well meaning people fed, and by these means are they led inconsiderately to contend for a government, which is made to promise what it cannot perform . . . [Ford 107]

[2] . . . The powers of Congress under the confederation are completely competent either to declare war against them, or to form treaties. *Money,* it is true, is necessary to do both these. This only brings us to this conclusion, that the great defect in our present government, is the want of powers to provide *money* for the *public* exigencies. I am willing to grant reasonable powers, on this score, but not unlimited ones . . . [Ford 112–13]

Georgia Constitution, May 6, 1789:

[Article I, Section 17:] . . . And no *money* shall be drawn out of the treasury, or from the *public* funds of this State, except by appropriations made by law. [Thorpe 787]

South Carolina Constitution, June 3, 1790:

[Article I, Section 17:] No *money* shall be drawn out of the *public* treasury, but by the legislative authority of the State. [Thorpe 3261]

NATURALIZATION

United States Constitution, September 17, 1787:

[Article I, Section 8:] [Congress shall have power] . . . To establish an uniform Rule of *Naturalization,* and uniform Laws on the subject of Bankruptcies throughout the United States.

* * * * *

New Jersey Proprietors, Concession and Agreement, February 10, 1664:

[1] By act (as aforesaid) to give to all strangers, as to they shall seem meet, a *naturalization,* and all such freedoms, and privileges within the said Province as to his majesty's subjects do of right belong, they swearing or subscribing as aforesaid; which said strangers, so *naturalized* and privileged, shall be in all respects accounted in the said Province, as the King's *natural* subjects.
[Thorpe 2539]

[2] . . . Provided always, That no person arriving in the said Province, with purpose to settle (they being subjects or *naturalized* as aforesaid) be denied a grant of such proportions of land as at the time of their arrival that are due to themselves or servants, by concession from us as aforesaid; but have full licence to take up and settle the same, in such order and manner as is granted or prescrib'd. All lands (notwithstanding the powers in the Assembly aforesaid) shall be taken up by warrant from the Governor, and confirm'd by the Governor and Council, under a seal to be provided for that purpose, in such order and method as shall be set down in this declaration, and more at large in the instruction to the Governors, and Council. [Thorpe 2542]

Carolina Proprietors, Concessions and Agreements, 1665:

By act as aforesd to give unto all strangers as to them shall seeme meete a *Naturalizion* and all such freedomes and priveledges within the sd Countyes as to his Majes subjects doe of right belong they swearing or subscribing as aforesd wch said strangers soe *naturallized* and priveledged shall alsoe have the same Imunityes from Customes as is granted by the Kinge to us and by us to ye said Countyes and shall not be lyable to any other Customes then the rest of his Majties subjects in the sd Counties are but be in all respects accompted in the Province and Countyes aforesaid as the King's *naturall* subjects.

[Thorpe 2759]

Fundamental Constitutions of Carolina, March 1, 1669:

[Article 118:] Whatsoever alien shall, in this form, before any precinct register, subscribe these fundamental constitutions, shall be thereby *naturalized.*

[Thorpe 2786]

Pennsylvania Frame of Government, April 2, 1683:

[Article 21:] And, for the satisfaction and encouragement of all aliens, I do give and grant, that, if any alien, who is, or shall be a purchaser, or who doth, or shall, inhabit in this province or territories thereof, shall decease at any time before he can well be *naturalized,* his right and interest therein shall notwithstanding descend to his wife and children, or other his relations, be he testate, or intestate, according to the laws of this province or territories thereof, in such cases provided, in as free and ample manner, to all intents and purposes, as if the said alien had been *naturalized.* [Thorpe 3068]

Virginia Constitution, June 29, 1776:

[Preamble:] [The King has attempted to tyrannize] . . . By endeavouring to prevent the population of our country, and, for that purpose, obstructing, the laws for the *naturalization* of foreigners . . . [Thorpe 3815]

United States Declaration of Independence, July 4, 1776:

. . . He [the King] has endeavoured to prevent the population of these States; for that purpose obstructing the Laws of *Naturalization* of Foreigners; refusing to pass others to encourage their migrations hither, and raising the conditions of new Appropriations of Lands. . . .

New York Constitution, April 20, 1777:

[Article 42:] And this convention doth further, in the name and by the authority of the good people of this State, ordain, determine, and declare that it shall be in the discretion of the legislature to *naturalize* all such persons, and in such manner, as they shall think proper: Provided, All such of the persons so to be by them *naturalized,* as being born in parts beyond sea, and out of the United

States of America, shall come to settle in and become subjects of this State, shall take an oath of allegiance to this State, and abjure and renounce all allegiance and subjection to all and every foreign king, prince, potentate, and State in all matters, ecclesiastical as well as civil. [Thorpe 2637–38]

The New Jersey Plan of Union, June 15, 1787:

[Article 8:] Res[olve]d the rule for *naturalization* ought to be the same in every State. [DHRC1 253]

Richard Henry Lee [?], "The Federal Farmer," No. 1, October 8, 1787:

. . . We may consolidate the states as to certain national objects, and leave them severally distinct independent republics, as to internal police generally. Let the general government consist of an executive, a judiciary, and balanced legislature, and its powers extend exclusively to all foreign concerns, causes arising on the seas to commerce, imports, armies, navies, Indian affairs, peace and war, and to a few internal concerns of the community; to the coin, post offices, weights and measures, a general plan for the militia, to *naturalization,* and, perhaps to bankruptcies, leaving the internal police of the community, in other respects, exclusively to the state governments . . . [Ford 286–87]

Richard Henry Lee [?], "The Federal Farmer," No. 3, October 10, 1787:

In the second place it is necessary, therefore, to examine the extent, and the probable operations of some of those extensive powers proposed to be vested in this government. These powers, legislative, executive, and judicial, respect internal as well as external objects. Those respecting external objects, as all foreign concerns, commerce, imposts, all causes arising on the seas, peace and war, and Indian affairs, can be lodged no where else, with any propriety, but in this government. Many powers that respect internal objects ought clearly to be lodged in it; as those to regulate trade between the states, weights and measures, the coin or current monies, post-offices, *naturalization,* &c. These powers may be exercised without essentially effecting the internal police of the respective states . . . [Ford 300–301]

Alexander Hamilton, *The Federalist*, No. 32, January 2, 1788:

. . . The third will be found in that clause which declares that Congress shall have power "to establish an UNIFORM RULE of *naturalization* throughout the United States." This must necessarily be exclusive, because if each State had power to prescribe a DISTINCT RULE, there could not be a UNIFORM RULE. [Fed. 242]

James Madison, *The Federalist*, No. 42, January 22, 1788:

[1] . . . I shall confine myself to a cursory review of the remaining powers comprehended under this third description, to wit: to regulate commerce among the several States and the Indian tribes; to coin money, regulate the value thereof, and of foreign coin: to provide for the punishment of counterfeiting the current coin and securities of the United States; to fix the standard of weights and measures; to establish a uniform rule of *naturalization,* and uniform laws of bankruptcy; to prescribe the manner in which the public acts, records, and judicial proceedings of each State shall be proved, and the effect they shall have in other States; and to establish post-offices and post-roads. [Fed. 305]

[2] The dissimilarity in the rules of *naturalization* has long been remarked as a fault in our system, and as laying a foundation for intricate and delicate questions. In the fourth article of the Confederation, it is declared "that the free inhabitants of each of these States, paupers, vagabonds, and fugitives from justice excepted, shall be entitled to all privileges and immunities of free citizens in the several States; and the people of each State shall, in every other, enjoy all the privileges of trade and commerce," etc. There is a confusion of language here, which is remarkable. Why the terms free inhabitants are used in one part of the article, free citizens in another, and people in another; or what was meant by superadding to "all privileges and immunities of free citizens," "all the privileges of trade and commerce," cannot easily be determined. It seems to be a construction scarcely avoidable, however, that those who come under the denomination of free inhabitants of a State, although not citizens of such State, are entitled, in every other State, to all the privileges of free citizens of the latter; that is, to greater privileges than they may be entitled to in their own State: so that it may be in the power of a particular State, or rather every State is laid under a necessity, not only to confer the rights of citizenship in other States upon any whom it may admit to such rights within itself, but upon any whom it may allow to become inhabitants within its jurisdiction. But were an exposition of the term "inhabitants" to be admitted which would confine the stipulated privileges to citizens alone, the difficulty is diminished only, not removed. The very improper power would still be retained by each State, of *naturalizing* aliens in every other State. In one State, residence for a short term confirms all the rights of citizenship: in another, qualifications of greater importance are required. An alien, therefore legally incapacitated for certain rights in the latter, may, by previous residence only in the former, elude his incapacity; and thus the law of one State be preposterously rendered paramount to the law of another, within the jurisdiction of the other. We owe it to mere casualty, that very serious embarrassments on this subject have been hitherto escaped. By the laws of several States, certain descriptions of aliens, who had rendered themselves obnoxious, were laid under interdicts inconsistent not only with the rights of citizenship but with the privilege of residence. What would have been the consequence, if such persons, by residence or otherwise, had acquired the character of citizens under the laws of

another State, and then asserted their rights as such, both to residence and citizenship, within the State proscribing them? Whatever the legal consequences might have been other consequences would probably have resulted, of too serious a nature not to be provided against. The new Constitution has accordingly, with great propriety, made provision against them, and all others proceeding from the defect of the Confederation on this head, by authorizing the general government to establish a uniform rule of *naturalization* throughout the United States. [Fed. 307–308]

NECESSARY AND PROPER (LAWS)

[Note: This list contains occurrences of "necessary" and/or "proper" in conjunction with "law" or "laws".]

United States Constitution, September 17, 1787:

[Article I, Section 8:] [Congress shall have power] To make all *Laws which shall be necessary and proper* for carrying into Execution the foregoing Powers, and all other Powers vested by this Constitution in the Government of the United States, or in any Department or Officer thereof.

[Article I, Section 10:] No State shall, without the Consent of the Congress, lay any Imposts or Duties on Imports or Exports, except what may be absolutely *necessary* for executing it's inspection *Laws:* and the net Produce of all Duties and Imposts, laid by any State on Imports or Exports, shall be for the Use of the Treasury of the United States; and all such *Laws* shall be subject to the Revision and Control of the Congress.

* * * * *

James I, Second Charter of Virginia, May 23, 1609:

And also [the Council shall have power] to make, ordain, and establish all Manner of Orders, *Laws,* Directions, Instructions, Forms and Ceremonies of Government and Magistracy, fit and *necessary* for and concerning the Government of the said Colony and Plantation; And the same, at all Times hereafter, to abrogate, revoke, or change . . . [Thorpe 3798]

James I, The Charter of New England, November 3, 1620:

. . . And further, of our especiall Grace, certaine Knowlege, and mere Motion, for Us, our Heires and Successors, Wee do by these Presents give and grant full

Power and Authority to the said Councill and their Successors . . . to make, ordaine, and establish all Manner of Orders, *Laws,* Directions, Instructions, Forms, and Ceremonies of Government and Magistracy fitt and *necessary* for and concerning the Government of the said Collony and Plantation, so always as the same be not contrary to the *Laws* and Statutes of this our Realme of England . . . [Thorpe 1832]

Virginia Company, Ordinances for the Colony, July 24, 1621:

. . . And this General Assembly shall have free Power to treat, consult, and conclude, as well of all emergent Occasions concerning the Publick Weal of the said Colony and every Part thereof, as also to make, ordain, and enact such general *Laws* and Orders, for the Behoof of the said Colony, and the good Government thereof, as shall, from time to time, appear *necessary* or requisite . . . [Thorpe 3811]

Charles I, Charter of Massachusetts Bay, March 4, 1629:

. . . Wee doe of our further Grace, certen Knowledg and meere Mocon, give and graunte to the saide Governor and Company, and their Successors, That it shall And maie be *lawfull,* to and for the Governor or Deputie Governor, and such of the Assistants and Freemen of the said Company for the Tyme being as shalbe assembled in any of their generall Courts aforesaide, or in any other Courtes to be specially sumoned and assembled for that Purpose, or the greater Parte of them (whereof the Governor or Deputie Governor, and six of the Assistants to be alwaies seaven) from tyme to tyme, to make, ordeine, and establishe all Manner of wholesome and reasonable Orders, *Lawes,* Statutes, and Ordinces, Direccons, and Instruccons, not contrairie to the *Lawes* of this our Realme of England, aswell for setling of the Formes and Ceremonies of Governmt and Magistracy fitt and *necessary* for the said Plantacon . . . [Thorpe 1857]

Agreement of the Settlers of Exeter, New Hampshire, August 4, 1639:

Whereas it hath pleased the Lord to move the Heart of our dread Sovereign Charles by the Grace of God King &c. to grant Licence and Libertye to sundry of his subjects to plant themselves in the Westerne parts of America. We his loyal Subjects Brethern of the Church in Exeter situate and lying upon the River Pascataqua with other Inhabitants there, considering with ourselves the holy Will of God and our own *Necessity* that we should not live without wholesome *Lawes* and Civil Government among us of which we are altogether destitute . . . [Thorpe 2445]

Charles II, Charter of Connecticut, April 23, 1662:

. . . and also from Time to Time to Make, Ordain, and Establish all manner of wholesome, and reasonable *Laws,* Statutes, Ordinances, Directions, and Instructions, not Contrary to the *Laws* of this Realm of England, as well for settling the Forms, and Ceremonies of Government, and Magistracy, fit and *necessary* for the said Plantation, and the Inhabitants there . . . [Thorpe 533]

New Jersey Proprietors, Concession and Agreement, February 10, 1664:

[1] That the inhabitants being freemen, or chief agents to others of the Province aforesaid; do as soon as this our commission shall arrive, by virtue of a writ in our names by the Governor to be for the present (until our seal arrives) sealed and signed, make choice of twelve deputies or representatives from amongst themselves; who being chosen are to join with the said Governor and council for the making of such *laws,* ordinances and constitution as shall be *necessary* for the present good and welfare of the said Province. . . . [Thorpe 2537]

[2] [The General Assembly shall have power] To enact and make all such *laws,* acts and constitutions as shall be *necessary* for the well government of the said Province, and them to repeal: provided, that the same be consonant to reason, and as near as may be conveniently agreeable to the *laws* and customs of his majesty's kingdom of England . . . [Thorpe 2537–38]

[3] [The General Assembly shall have power] . . . to enact, constitute and ordain all such other *laws* and constitutions as shall or may be *necessary* for the good, prosperity and settlement of the said Province, excepting what by these presents is excepted, and conforming to the limitations herein expressed. [Thorpe 2539]

Charles II, Grant of the Province of Maine to the Duke of York, March 12, 1664:

And further that it shall and may be *lawfull* to and for our said dearest brother his heires and assignes by these presents . . . to make ordaine and establish all manner of orders *lawes* directions instruccons formes and ceremonyes of government and magistracy fitt and *necessary* for and concerning the government of the territoryes and islands aforesaid so alwayes as the same be not contrary to the *lawes* and statutes of this our Realme of England . . . [Thorpe 1639]

Carolina Proprietors, Concessions and Agreements, 1665:

[1] That the inhabitants being freemen or chiefe agents to others of ye Countyes aforesd doe as soone as this our Comission shall arrive by virtue of a writt in our names by the Governor to be for ye present (untill our seale comes) sealed and syned make choice of twelve Deputyes or representatives from amongst themselves whoe being chosen are to joyne with him the sd Governor and Councill for the makeing of such *Lawes* Ordinances and Constitutions as shalbe *necessary* for the present good and welfare of the severall Countyes aforesd . . . [Thorpe 2757–58]

[2] [The General Assembly shall have power] To enact and make all such *Lawes* Acts and Constitutions as shalbe necessary for the well Government of ye County for wch they shalbe chosen and them to repeale provided that the same be consonant to reason and as near as they may be conveniently agreable to the Lawes and Customes of his Majties Kingdom of England . . . [Thorpe 2758]

[3] [The General Assembly shall have power] Lastly to enact constitute and ordaine all such other *Lawes* actes and constitutions as shall or may be necessary for the good prosperity and setlement of ye said Countyes excepting wt by these pesents are excepted and conformeing to Limtacons herein exprest. [Thorpe 2760]

Charles II, Grant of the Province of Maine to the the Duke of York, June 29, 1674:

And further that it shall and may bee *lawfull* to and for our said dearest brother his heirs and assigns by these presents . . . to make ordaine and establish all manner of *lawes* orders direccons instructions formes and ceremonyes of Government and Magistracy fit and *necessary* for and concerning the Government of the Territoryes and Islands aforesaid so always as the same bee not contrary to the *Lawes* and Statutes of this our realme of England . . . [Thorpe 1642]

Duke of York, Grant of West New Jersey, August 6, 1680:

And whereas by the said several grants so made by his said Majesty unto his said Royal Highness as aforesaid, several powers and authority are and were given and granted unto his said Royal Highness his heirs and assigns to be executed by his said Royal Highness, his heirs and assigns, or by the deputies, agents or commissioners of his said Royal Highness, his heirs or assigns, which, are *necessary* as well for the planting, peopling and improving of all and every the respective lands, places and territories thereby granted, and for the transporting thither from time to time, such of his Majesty's subjects as should be willing to go or be transported into those parts, or any of them; as for the defending, guarding and keeping of the same; as also for the well governing of the same, and of all such as are or shall he inhabitting in the same, and for the making, ordaining, and executing of *necessary and convenient laws* and constitutions, in order to such government . . . [Thorpe 2563]

Government of West New Jersey, November 25, 1681:

That there shall be a General Free Assembly for the Province aforesaid yearly and every year, at a day certain, chosen by the free people of the said Province, whereon all the representatives for the said Province, shall be summoned to appear, to consider of the affairs of the said Province, and to make and ordain such acts, and *laws,* as shall be requisite and *necessary* for the good government and prosperity of the free people of the said Province; and (if *necessity* shall require) the Governor for the time being, with the consent of his Council, may and shall issue out writts to convene the Assembly sooner, to consider and answer the *necessities* of the people of the said Province. [Thorpe 2565–66]

Duke of York, Confirmation to the New Jersey Proprietors, March 14, 1682:

. . . And whereas by the said several recited Letters Patents, made by his said Majesty unto his said Royal Highness as aforesaid, several powers and authorities are and were given and granted unto his said Royal Highness, his heirs or assigns, or by the deputies, agents or commissioners of his said Royal Highness, his heirs or assigns, which are *necessary* as well for the planting, peopleing and improving of all and every the respective lands, places and territories thereof granted; and for the transporting thither from time to time such of his Majesty's subjects as should be willing to go or be transported into those parts, or any of them, as for the defending, guarding and keeping of the same; as also for the well governing of the same, and of all such as shall be inhabiting the same, and for the making, ordaining and executing of *necessary and convenient laws* and constitutions, in order to such government . . . [Thorpe 2751]

William and Mary, Charter of Massachusetts Bay, October 7, 1691:

And we doe further for us our Heires and Successors Give and Grant to the said Governor and the great and Generall Court or Assembly of our said Province or Territory for the time being full Power and Authority from time to time to make ordaine and establish all manner of wholesome and reasonable Orders *Laws* Statutes and Ordinances Directions and Instructions either with penalties or without (soe as the same be not repugnant or contrary to the *Lawes* of this our Realme of England) as they shall Judge to be for the good and welfare of our said Province or Territory And for the Government and Ordering thereof and of the People Inhabiting or who shall Inhabit the same and for the *necessary* support and Defence of the Government thereof. [Thorpe 1882]

New Jersey Proprietors, Surrender of Rights, April 15, 1702:

. . . and further that it should and might be *lawful* to and for the said Duke of York, his heirs and assigns from time to time to nominate, constitute, ordain and confirm such *laws* as aforesaid, by such name or names or stiles as to him or them shall seem good; and likewise to revoke, discharge, change and alter as well all and singular Governors, officers and ministers, which then after should be by him or them thought fit or needful to be made or used within the aforesaid parts and islands; and also to make, ordain and establish, all manner of orders, *laws,* directions, instructions, forms and ceremonies of government and magistracy, fit and *necessary* for and concerning the government of the Territories and islands aforesaid, so always as the same were not contrary to the *laws* and statutes of the realm of England, but as near as might be agreeable thereunto . . . [Thorpe 2586]

George II, Charter of Georgia, June 9, 1732:

[1] . . . And we do hereby, for us, our heirs and successors, give and grant unto the said corporation, and their successors, full power and authority to constitute, or make, such and so many by-*laws,* constitutions, orders and ordinances, as to them, or the greater part of them, at their general meeting for that purpose, shall seem *necessary* and convenient for the well ordaining and governing of the said corporation; and the said by-*laws,* constitutions, orders and ordinances, or any of them, to alter and annul, as they or the major part of them then present shall see requisite . . . [Thorpe 770]

[2] And we do hereby, for our heirs and successors, ordain, will and establish, that for and during the term of twenty-one years, to commence from the date of these our letters patent, the said corporation assembled for that purpose, shall and may form and prepare, *laws,* statutes and ordinances, fit and *necessary* for and concerning the government of the said colony, and not repugnant to the *laws* and statutes of England . . . [Thorpe 772]

The Albany Plan of Union, July 10, 1754:

That they [the Grand Council] make such *laws* as they judge *necessary* for regulating all Indian trade. [Thorpe 84]

Benjamin Franklin, Proposed Articles of Confederation, July 21, 1775:

[Article 5:] That the Power and Duty of the Congress shall extend to the Determining on War and Peace, to sending and receiving Ambassadors, and entring into Alliances, the Reconciliation with Great Britain; the Settling all Disputes and Differences between Colony and Colony about limits or any other cause if such should arise; and the Planting of new Colonies when *proper*. The Congress shall also make such general Ordinances as tho' *necessary* to the General Welfare, particular Assemblies cannot be competent to, viz. those that may relate to our general Commerce or general Currency; to the Establishment of Posts; and the Regulation of our common Forces. . . . [PBF22 122–23]

South Carolina Constitution, March 26, 1776:

[Preamble:] Whereas the British Parliament, claiming of late years a right to bind the North American colonies by *law* in all cases whatsoever, have enacted statutes for raising a revenue in those colonies and disposing of such revenue

as they thought *proper,* without the consent and against the will of the colonists. . . .
[Thorpe 3241]

Virginia Constitution, June 29, 1776:

[Preamble:] Whereas George the third, King of Great Britain and Ireland, and elector of Hanover, heretofore intrusted with the exercise of the kingly office in this government, hath endeavoured to pervert the same into a detestable and insupportable tyranny, by putting his negative on *laws* the most wholesome and *necessary* for the public good . . . [Thorpe 3814]

United States Declaration of Independence, July 4, 1776:

He [the King] has refused his Assent to *Laws,* the most wholesome and *necessary* for the public good.

Pennsylvania Constitution, September 28, 1776:

[Declaration of Rights, Article 14:] That a frequent recurrence to fundamental principles, and a firm adherence to justice, moderation, temperance, industry, and frugality are absolutely necessary to preserve the blessings of liberty, and keep a government free: The people ought therefore to pay particular attention to these points in the choice of officers and representatives, and have a right to exact a due and constant regard to them, from their legislatures and magistrates, in the making and executing such *laws as are necessary* for the good government of the state. [Thorpe 3083–84]

[Frame of Government, Section 15:] To the end that laws before they are enacted may be more maturely considered, and the inconvenience of hasty determinations as much as possible prevented, all bills of public nature shall be printed for the consideration of the people, before they are read in general assembly the last time for debate and amendment; and, except on occasions of sudden *necessity,* shall not be passed into *laws* until the next session of assembly . . .
[Thorpe 3086]

Maryland Constitution, November 11, 1776:

[Form of Government, Article 11:] That the senate may be at full and perfect liberty to exercise their judgment in passing *laws;* and that they may not be compelled by the house of delegates, either to reject a money bill, which the emergency of affairs may require, or to assent to some other act of legislation, in their conscience and judgment injurious to the public welfare, the house of delegates shall not, on any occasion, or under any pretence, annex to, or blend with, a money bill, any matter, clause, or thing not immediately relating to, and *necessary* for the imposing, assessing, levying, or applying the taxes or supplies to be raised for the support of government, or the current expenses of the state . . . [Thorpe 1692–93]

Georgia Constitution, February 5, 1777:

[Article 8:] All *laws* and ordinances shall be three times read, and each reading shall be on different and separate days, except in cases of great *necessity* and danger; and all *laws* and ordinances shall be sent to the executive council after the second reading, for their perusal and advice. [Thorpe 779]

Vermont Constitution, July 8, 1777:

[Declaration of Rights, Article 16:] That frequent recurrence to fundamental principles, and a firm adherence to justice, moderation, temperance, industry and frugality, are absolutely *necessary* to preserve the blessings of liberty, and keep government free. The people ought, therefore, to pay particular attention to these points, in the choice of officers and representatives, and have a right to exact a due and constant regard to them, from their legislators and magistrates, in the making and executing such *laws* as are *necessary* for the good government of the State. [Thorpe 3741]

[Frame of Government, Section 14:] To the end that *laws,* before they are enacted, may be more maturely considered, and the inconveniency of hasty determination as much as possible prevented, all bills of public nature, shall be first laid before the Governor and Council, for their perusal and proposals of amendment, and shall be printed for the consideration of the people, before they are read in General Assembly, for the last time of debate and amendment; except temporary acts, which, after being laid before the Governor and Council, may (in case of sudden *necessity*) be passed into *laws;* and no other shall be passed into *laws,* until the next session of assembly. . . . [Thorpe 3744]

South Carolina Constitution, March 19, 1778:

[Article 39:] That the whole State shall as soon as *proper laws* can be passed for these purposes, be divided into districts and counties, and county courts established. [Thorpe 3257]

Massachusetts Constitution, March 2, 1780:

[Declaration of Rights, Article 18:] A frequent recurrence to the fundamental principles of the constitution, and a constant adherence to those of piety, justice, moderation, temperance, industry, and frugality, are absolutely *necessary* to preserve the advantages of liberty, and to maintain a free government. The people ought, consequently, to have a particular attention to all those principles, in the choice of their officers and representatives: and they have a right to require of their lawgivers and magistrates an exact and constant observance of them, in the formation and execution of the *laws necessary* for the good administration of the commonwealth. [Thorpe 1892]

[Frame of Government, Chapter I:1:4:] And further, full power and authority are hereby given and granted to the said general court, from time to time, to make, ordain, and establish, all manner of wholesome and reasonable orders, *laws,* statutes, and ordinances, directions and instructions, either with penalties or without; so as the same be not repugnant or contrary to this constitution, as they shall judge to be for the good and welfare of this commonwealth, and for the government and ordering thereof, and of the subjects of the same, and for the *necessary* support and defence of the government thereof . . .

[Thorpe 1894]

[Frame of Government, Chapter II:1:13:] As the public good requires that the governor should not be under the undue influence of any of the members of the general court by a dependence on them for his support, that he should in all cases act with freedom for the benefit of the public, that he should not have his attention *necessarily* diverted from that object to his private concerns, and that he should maintain the dignity of the commonwealth in the character of its chief magistrate, it is *necessary* that he should have an honorable stated salary, of a fixed and permanent value, amply sufficient for those purposes, and established by standing *laws;* and it shall be among the first acts of the general court, after the commencement of this constitution, to establish such salary by *law* accordingly. [Thorpe 1903]

New Hampshire Constitution, June 2, 1784:

[Bill of Rights, Article 38:] A frequent recurrence to the fundamental principles of the Constitution, and a constant adherence to justice, moderation temperance, industry, frugality, and all the social virtues, are indispensably *necessary* to preserve the blessing of liberty and good government; the people ought, therefore, to have a particular regard to all those principles in the choice of their officers and representatives: and they have a right to require of their law-givers and magistrates, an exact and constant observance of them in the formation and execution of the *laws necessary* for the good administration of government.

[Thorpe 2457]

[Frame of Government:] And farther, full power and authority are hereby given and granted to the said general court, from time to time, to make, ordain and establish, all manner of wholesome and reasonable orders, *laws,* statutes, ordinances, directions and instructions, either with penalties or without; so as the same be not repugnant, or contrary to this constitution, as they may judge for the benefit and welfare of this state, and for the governing and ordering thereof, and of the subjects of the same, for the *necessary* support and defence of the government thereof . . . [Thorpe 2458]

Vermont Constitution, July 4, 1786:

[Declaration of Rights, Article 20:] That frequent recurrence to fundamental principles, and a firm adherence to justice, moderation, temperance, industry, and frugality, are absolutely *necessary* to preserve the blessings of liberty, and keep government free; the people ought therefore to pay particular attention to these points, in the choice of officers and representatives; and have a right, in a legal way, to exact a due and constant regard to them, from their legislators and magistrates, in the making and executing such *laws* as are *necessary* for the good government of the State. [Thorpe 3754]

United States Confederation Congress, The Northwest Ordinance, July 13, 1787:

The governor and judges, or a majority of them, shall adopt and publish in the district such *laws* of the original States, criminal and civil, as may be *necessary,* and best suited to the circumstances of the district, and report them to Congress from time to time, which *laws* shall be in force in the district until the organization of the general assembly therein, unless disapproved of by Congress; but afterwards the legislature shall have authority to alter them as they shall think fit. [Thorpe 958]

George Mason, Objections to the Constitution, October 7, 1787:

Both the general Legislature & the State Legislatures are expressly prohibited making ex post facto *Laws;* tho' there never was or can be a Legislature but must & will make such *Laws,* when *Necessity* & the public Safety require them; which will hereafter be a Breach of all the Constitutions in the Union, and afford Precedents for other Innovations.— [DHRC8 45]

Richard Henry Lee [?], "The Federal Farmer," No. 2, October 9, 1787:

. . . The general government, organized as it is, may be adequate to many valuable objects, and be able to carry its *laws* into execution on *proper* principles in several cases; but I think its warmest friends will not contend, that it can carry all the powers proposed to be lodged in it into effect, without calling to its aid a military force, which must very soon destroy all elective governments in the country, produce anarchy, or establish despotism. . . . [Ford 292–93]

Richard Henry Lee [?], "The Federal Farmer," No. 3, October 10, 1787:

Should the general government think it politic, as some administration (if not all) probably will, to look for a support in a system of influence, the government will take every occasion to multiply *laws,* and officers to execute them, considering these as so many *necessary* props for its own support. Should this system of policy be adopted, taxes more productive than the impost duties will, probably, be wanted to support the government, and to discharge foreign demands, without leaving any thing for the domestic creditors. . . . [Ford 302]

Richard Henry Lee [?], "The Federal Farmer," No. 4, October 12, 1787:

The federal constitution, the *laws* of congress made in pursuance of the constitution, and all treaties must have full force and effect in all parts of the United States; and all other *laws,* rights and constitutions which stand in their way must yield: It is *proper* the national *laws* should be supreme, and superior to state or district *laws;* but then the national *laws* ought to yield to unalienable or fundamental rights—and national *laws,* made by a few men,should extend only to a few national objects. This will not be the case with the *laws* of congress: To have any *proper* idea of their extent, we must carefully examine the legislative, executive and judicial powers proposed to be lodged in the general government, and consider them in connection with a general clause in art. 1, sect. 8, in these words (after enumerating a number of powers) "To make all *laws which shall be necessary and proper* for carrying into execution the foregoing powers, and all other powers vested by this constitution in the government of the United States, or in any department or officer thereof."—The powers of this government as has been observed, extend to internal as well as external objects, and to those objects to which all others are subordinate; it is almost impossible to have a just conception of their powers, or of the extent and number of the *laws which may be deemed necessary and proper* to carry them into effect, till we shall come to exercise those powers and make the *laws*. In making *laws* to carry those powers into effect, it is to be expected, that a wise and prudent congress will pay respect to the opinions of a free people, and bottom their *laws* on those principles which have been considered as essential and fundamental in the British, and in our government: But a congress of a different character will not be bound by the constitution to pay respect to those principles. [Ford 312–313]

Noah Webster, *An Examination into the Leading Principles of the Federal Constitution*, October 17, 1787:

The states in their separate capacity, cannot provide for the common defence; nay in case of a civil war, a state cannot secure its own existence. The only question therefore is, whether it is *necessary* to unite, and provide for our common defence and general welfare. For this question being once decided in the affirmative, leaves no room to controvert the *propriety* of constituting a power over the whole United States, adequate to these general purposes.
[Ford 50–51]

"Cato Uticensis," October 17, 1787:

[1] . . . Did it ever enter the mind of any one of you, that you could live to see the day, that any other government, but the General Assembly of Virginia, should have power of direct taxation in this state? How few of you ever expected to see excise *laws,* the instruments of tyranny, in force in your country? But, who could imagine, that any man but a Virginian, were they found to be *necessary,* would ever have a voice towards enacting them? That any tribunal, but the Courts of Virginia, would be allowed to take cognizance of disputes between her citizens and their tax-gatherers and their excisemen? And that, if it should ever be found *necessary* to curse this land with these hateful excisemen, any one, but a fellow citizen, should be intrusted with that office? [DHRC8 73]

[2] For my part, I cannot discover the *necessity* there was of allowing Congress to subject us to excise *laws,* unless, that considering the extensiveness of the single republic into which this Constitution would collect all the others, and the well known difficulty of governing large republics with harmony and ease, it was thought expedient to bit our mouths with massive curbs, to break us, bridled with excise *laws,* and managed by excisemen, into an uniform, sober pace, and thus, gradually, tame the troublesome mettle of the freeman. This *necessity* could not, surely, arise from the desire of furnishing Congress with a sufficient revenue, to enable it to exercise the prerogatives, which every friend to America would wish to see vested in it; as it would, by unanimous consent, have the management of the impost, it could increase it to any amount, and this would fall sufficiently uniform on every one, according to his ability . . . [DHRC8 73]

Frederick, Virginia, County Meeting, October 22, 1787:

. . . During this period a confederation was formed adequate to the purposes of its institution, while disinterested patriotism universally prevailed: that this spirit should long continue, unabated, was not to be expected: history proves the *necessity* of a supreme power and efficacious *laws* in every state; and the best constituted confederacies, ancient and modern, have not been able to maintain internal peace, or to exert their natural force with effect against foreign enemies, where each member of the union retained its sovereignty . . . [DHRC8 92]

Alexander Hamilton, *The Federalist*, No. 23, December 18, 1787:

If the circumstances of our country are such as to demand a compound instead of a simple, a confederate instead of a sole, government, the essential point which will remain to be adjusted will be to discriminate the OBJECTS, as far as it can be done, which shall appertain to the different provinces or departments of power; allowing to each the most ample authority for fulfilling the objects committed to its charge. Shall the Union be constituted the guardian of the common safety? Are fleets and armies and revenues *necessary* to this purpose?

The government of the Union must be empowered to pass all *laws,* and to make all regulations which have relation to them. The same must be the case in respect to commerce, and to every other matter to which its jurisdiction is permitted to extend. . . . [Fed. 201]

Dissent of the Pennsylvania Convention's Minority, December 18, 1787:

. . . if the state governments should presume to impose taxes, duties or excises on the same articles with Congress, the latter may abrogate and repeal the *laws* whereby they are imposed, upon the allegation that they interfere with the due collection of their taxes, duties or excises, by virtue of the following clause, part of section 8th, article 1st, viz.: 1st, ''To make all *laws which shall be necessary and proper* for carrying into execution the foregoing powers, and all other powers vested by this constitution in the government of the United States, or in any department or officer thereof.''

The Congress might gloss over this conduct by construing every purpose for which the State legislatures now lay taxes, to be for the ''general welfare,'' and therefore as of their jurisdiction. [DHRC2 627]

Alexander Hamilton, *The Federalist*, No. 31, January 1, 1788:

Those of them which have been most labored with that view seem in substance to amount to this: ''It is not true, because the exigencies of the Union may not be susceptible of limitation, that its power of laying taxes ought to be unconfined. Revenue is as requisite to the purposes of the local administrations as to those of the Union; and the former are at least of equal importance with the latter to the happiness of the people. It is, therefore, as *necessary* that the State governments should be able to command the means of supplying their wants, as that the national government should possess the like faculty in respect to the wants of the Union. But an indefinite power of taxation in the latter might, and probably would in time, deprive the former of the means of providing for their own *necessities;* and would subject them entirely to the mercy of the national legislature. As the *laws* of the Union are to become the supreme *law* of the land, as it is to have power to pass all *laws* that may be *NECESSARY* for carrying into execution the authorities with which it is proposed to vest it, the national government might at any time abolish the taxes imposed for State objects upon the pretence of an interference with its own. It might allege a *necessity* of doing this in order to give efficacy to the national revenues. And thus all the resources of taxation might by degrees become the subjects of federal monopoly, to the entire exclusion and destruction of the State governments.'' [Fed. 238–39]

Alexander Hamilton, *The Federalist*, No. 33, January 2, 1788:

[1] The residue of the argument against the provisions of the Constitution in respect to taxation is ingrafted upon the following clause;—the last clause of the eighth section of the first article of the plan under consideration authorizes the national legislature "to make all *laws which shall be necessary and proper* for carrying into execution the powers by that Constitution vested in the government of the United States, or in any department or officer thereof"; and the second clause of the sixth article declares, "that the Constitution and the *laws* of the United States made in pursuance thereof, and the treaties made by their authority shall be the supreme *law* of the land, any thing in the constitution or *laws* of any State to the contrary notwithstanding." [Fed. 244]

[2] What is a power, but the ability or faculty of doing a thing? What is the ability to do a thing, but the power of employing the means *necessary* to its execution? What is a LEGISLATIVE power, but a power of making *LAWS?* What are the means to execute a LEGISLATIVE power, but *LAWS?* What is the power of laying and collecting taxes, but a legislative power, or a power of making *laws,* to lay and collect taxes? What are the *proper* means of executing such a power, but *necessary and proper laws?* [Fed. 245]

[3] . . . It conducts us to this palpable truth, that a power to lay and collect taxes must be a power to pass all *laws necessary and proper* for the execution of that power; and what does the unfortunate and calumniated provision in question do more than declare the same truth, to wit, that the national legislature, to whom the power of laying and collecting taxes had been previously given, might, in the execution of that power, pass all *laws necessary and proper* to carry it into effect? I have applied these observations thus particularly to the power of taxation, because it is the immediate subject under consideration, and because it is the most important of the authorities proposed to be conferred upon the Union. But the same process will lead to the same result, in relation to all other powers declared in the Constitution. And it is expressly to execute these powers that the sweeping clause, as it has been affectedly called, authorizes the national legislature to pass all *necessary and proper laws*. If there is any thing exceptionable, it must be sought for in the specific powers upon which this general declaration is predicated. The declaration itself, though it may be chargeable with tautology or redundancy, is at least perfectly harmless. [Fed. 245–46]

[4] But it may be again asked, Who is to judge of the *necessity and propriety of the laws* to be passed for executing the powers of the Union? I answer, first that this question arises as well and as fully upon the simple grant of those powers as upon the declaratory clause; and I answer, in the second place, that the national government, like every other, must judge, in the first instance, of the *proper* exercise of its powers, and its constituents in the last. If the federal government should overpass the just bounds of its authority and make a tyrannical use of its powers, the people, whose creature it is, must appeal to the standard

they have formed, and take such measures to redress the injury done to the Constitution as the exigency may suggest and prudence justify. The *propriety of a law,* in a constitutional light, must always be determined by the nature of the powers upon which it is founded. Suppose, by some forced constructions of its authority (which, indeed, cannot easily be imagined), the Federal legislature should attempt to vary the *law* of descent in any State, would it not be evident that, in making such an attempt, it had exceeded its jurisdiction, and infringed upon that of the State? Suppose, again, that upon the pretence of an interference with its revenues, it should undertake to abrogate a land-tax imposed by the authority of a State; would it not be equally evident that this was an invasion of that concurrent jurisdiction in respect to this species of tax, which its Constitution plainly supposes to exist in the State governments? . . . [Fed. 246]

[5] . . . If individuals enter into a state of society, the *laws* of that society must be the supreme regulator of their conduct. If a number of political societies enter into a larger political society, the *laws* which the latter may enact, pursuant to the powers intrusted to it by its constitution, must *necessarily* be supreme over those societies, and the individuals of whom they are composed. . . . [Fed. 247]

Alexander Hamilton, *The Federalist*, No. 34, January 4, 1788:

. . . Nothing, therefore, can be more fallacious than to infer the extent of any power, *proper* to be lodged in the national government, from an estimate of its immediate *necessities.* There ought to be a CAPACITY to provide for future contingencies as they may happen; and as these are illimitable in their nature, it is impossible safely to limit that capacity. . . . [Fed. 249]

Alexander Hamilton, *The Federalist*, No. 29, January 9, 1788:

. . . The same persons who tell us in one breath, that the powers of the federal government will be despotic and unlimited, inform us in the next, that it has not authority sufficient even to call out the POSSE COMITATUS. The latter, fortunately, is as much short of the truth as the former exceeds it. It would be as absurd to doubt that a right to pass all *laws necessary and proper* to execute its declared powers would include that of requiring the assistance of the citizens to the officers, who may be intrusted with the execution of those *laws,* as it would be to believe that a right to enact *laws necessary and proper* for the imposition and collection of taxes would involve that of varying the rules of descent and of the alienation of landed property, or of abolishing the trial by jury in cases relating to it. . . . [Fed. 227–228]

"An Impartial Citizen," January 10, 1788:

. . . [The President's limited veto is] An infinite advantage over the so much extolled constitution of England, where the Executive can put an absolute negative on the best *law,* and prevent the Legislative from proceeding on the most *necessary* and urgent occasion. The President in many important cases, must have the concurrence of the Senate, wherein his sole decision might be dangerous. . . . [DHRC8 295]

James Madison, *The Federalist*, No. 42, January 22, 1788:

[1] The power to define and punish piracies and felonies committed on the high seas, and offences against the *law* of nations, belongs with equal *propriety* to the general government, and is a still greater improvement on the articles of Confederation. . . . [Fed. 303]

[2] . . . For the sake of certainty and uniformity, therefore, the power of defining felonies in this case was in every respect *necessary and proper*. [Fed.304]

James Madison, *The Federalist*, No. 43, January 23, 1788:

"To dispose of and make all needful rules and regulations respecting the territory or other property belonging to the United States, with a proviso, that nothing in the Constitution shall be so construed as to prejudice any claims of the United States, or of any particular State."

This is a power of very great importance, and required by considerations similar to those which show the *propriety* of the former. The proviso annexed is *proper* in itself, and was probably rendered absolutely *necessary* by jealousies and questions concerning the Western territory sufficiently known to the public. [Fed. 311]

James Madison, *The Federalist*, No. 44, January 25, 1788:

[1] The sixth and last class consists of the several powers and provisions by which efficacy is given to all the rest.

Of these the first is, "the power to make all *laws which shall be necessary and proper* for carrying into execution the foregoing powers, and all other powers vested by this Constitution in the government of the United States, or in any department or office thereof."

Few parts of the Constitution have been assailed with more intemperance than this; yet on a fair investigation of it, no part can appear more completely invulnerable. Without the substance of this power, the whole Constitution would be a dead letter. Those who object to the article, therefore, as a part of the Constitution, can only mean that the form of the provision is *improper*. But have they considered whether a better form could have been substituted? [Fed.320]

[2] There are four other possible methods which the Constitution might have taken on this subject. They might have copied the second article of the existing Confederation, which would have prohibited the exercise of any power not

expressly delegated; they might have attempted a positive enumeration of the powers comprehended under the general terms "*necessary and proper*"; they might have attempted a negative enumeration of them, by specifying the powers excepted from the general definition; they might have been altogether silent on the subject, leaving these *necessary and proper* powers to construction and inference. [Fed. 320]

[3] . . . As the powers delegated under the new system are more extensive, the government which is to administer it would find itself still more distressed with the alternative of betraying the public interests by doing nothing, or of violating the Constitution by exercising powers by doing nothing, or of violating the Constitution by exercising powers indispensably *necessary and proper,* but, at the same time, not expressly granted. [Fed. 321]

[4] Had the convention attempted a positive enumeration of the powers *necessary and proper* for carrying their other powers into effect, the attempt would have involved a complete digest of *laws* on every subject to which the Constitution relates; accommodated too, not only to the existing state of things, but to all the possible changes which futurity may produce; for in every new application of a general power, the particular powers, which are the means of attaining the object of the general power, must always *necessarily* vary with that object, and be often *properly* varied whilst the object remains the same. [Fed. 321]

[5] Had they attempted to enumerate the particular powers or means not *necessary or proper* for carrying the general powers into execution, the task would have been no less chimerical; and would have been liable to this further objection, that every defect in the enumeration would have been equivalent to a positive grant of authority. If, to avoid this consequence, they had attempted a partial enumeration of the exceptions, and described the residue by the general terms, not *necessary or proper,* it must have happened that the enumeration would comprehend a few of the excepted powers only; that these would be such as would be least likely to be assumed or tolerated, because the enumeration would of course select such as would be least *necessary or proper;* and that the *unnecessary and improper* powers included in the residuum, would be less forcibly excepted, than if no partial enumeration had been made. [Fed. 321]

"Civis Rusticus," January 30, 1788:

[1] The infraction of the present treaty [with Great Britain] shews the *necessity* of treaties having the force of *laws*—When any publicity of them will not be injurious to America, they will be submitted to the representatives in Congress. . . . [DHRC8 337]

[2] Ex post facto *laws* have ever been considered as abhorrent from liberty: *necessity* and public safety never can require them . . . [DHRC8 338]

Alexander C. Hanson, *Remarks on the Proposed Plan of a Federal Government*, c. January 31, 1788:

[1] Art. I, sec. 8, par. the last. "To make all *laws, which shall be necessary and be proper* for carrying into execution the foregoing powers, and all other powers vested by this constitution, in the government of the United States, or in any department or officer thereof."

It is apprehended, that this sweeping clause will afford pretext, for freeing congress from all constitutional restraints. [Ford 33]

[2] I take the construction of these words to be precisely the same, as if the clause had preceded further and said, "No act of congress shall be valid, unless it have relation to the foregoing powers, and be *necessary and proper* for carrying them into execution." But say the objectors, "The congress, being itself to judge of the *necessity and propriety,* may pass any act, which it may deem expedient, for any other purpose." This objection applies with equal force to each particular power, defined by the constitution; and, if there were a bill of rights, congress might be said to be the judge of that also. They may reflect however, that every judge in the union, whether of federal or state appointment, (and some persons would say every jury) will have a right to reject any act, handed to him as a *law,* which he may conceive repugnant to the constitution.

It may nevertheless strike you at first view, that a provision, so obviously apt to excite distrust, might have well been omitted. So indeed it might, were there a possibility of providing every thing, *necessary and proper,* for carrying into effect the various powers, intended to be conferred. Without this general clause, it were easy to suppose cases, wherein a particular clause might be incompetent to its own purpose. [Ford 234]

[3] Should the compact authorize the sovereign, or head to do all things it may think *necessary and proper,* then there is no limitation to its authority; and the liberty of each citizen in the union has no other security, than the sound policy, good faith, virtue, and perhaps proper interests, of the head. [Ford 241]

[4] . . . She [Maryland] shall not, without consent of congress, lay any duty on imports or exports, except what may be *necessary* for executing her inspection *laws*. She shall not, without consent of congress, lay any duty on tonnage, keep troops or ships of war, in time of peace . . . [Ford 251]

Luther Martin, "Genuine Information," No. 11, February 5, 1788:

. . . It was further said [in the Philadelphia Convention] that if the general government was not by its constitution to interfere, the inconvenience would soon remedy itself, for that as the population increased in those States, their legislatures would be obliged to consent to the erection of new States to avoid the evils of a civil war, but as by the proposed constitution the general government is obliged to protect each State against domestic violence, and consequently will be obliged to assist in suppressing such commotions and insurrections as may take place from the struggle to have new States erected, the general government ought to have a power to decide upon the *propriety and necessity* of establishing or erecting a new State even without the approbation of the legislature of such States, within whose jurisdiction the new State should be erected, and for this purpose I submitted to the convention the following proposition—"That on the application of the inhabitants of any district of territory within the limits of any of the States, it shall be *lawful* for the legislature of the United States, if they shall under all circumstances think it reasonable, to erect the same into a new State, and admit it into the union without the consent of the State of which the said district may be a part." . . . [DHRC16 40]

Tench Coxe, "A Freeman," No. 3, February 6, 1788:

You apprehend the power of Congress to lay direct taxes will tend to produce consolidation. But the several states possess that power also, and by an early, wise and faithful exercise of it, can always supercede the use of it by Congress. For example; if ten thousand pounds were apportioned to Pennsylvania, to make up the interest on our foreign debts by the end of 1788, a tax for which would be laid in July, our legislature might proceed in the most easy and expeditious way to raise the money, against the time when the foederal government must *necessarily* proceed, and by paying our quota into the foederal treasury would fulfil the requisitions of the *law*. A foederal government, that shall possess the least degree of policy or virtue, would never attempt to interfere with such honest, wise and effectual arrangements of any state. . . . [DHRC16 50–51]

Benjamin Workman [?], "Philadelphiensis," No. 9, February 6, 1788:

Among the substantial objections to the great powers of the president, that of his negative upon the *laws,* is one of the most inconsiderable, indeed it is more a sound than any thing else; For, if he be a bold enterprising fellow, there is little fear of his ever having to exercise it. The two branches of the legislature, will be at his service; no *law* contrary to his sentiments, however salutary in its operation, dare be mentioned by them. As a body, and as individuals, they will be his sycophants and flatterers. But, if on the contrary he should not be a man of spirit, a thing very improbable, as none but an ambitious man, well versed in the ways of men, could have the address to be raised to that elevated station; if, however, I say, he should not be a man of an enterprising spirit, in that case he will be a minion of the aristocratics, doing according to their will and pleasure, and confirming every *law* they may think *proper* to make, without any regard to their public utility. [DHRC16 58–59]

"Brutus," No. 12, February 7, 1788:

. . . The legislature, therefore, will not go over the limits by which the courts may adjudge they are confined. And there is little room to doubt but that they will come up to those bounds, as often as occasion and opportunity may offer, and they may judge it *proper* to do it. For as on the one hand, they will not readily pass *laws* which they know the courts will not execute, so on the other, we may be sure they will not scruple to pass such as they know they will give effect, as often as they may judge it *proper*. [DHRC16 73]

James Madison, *The Federalist*, No. 53, February 9, 1788:

. . . Yet some knowledge of the affairs, and even of the *laws*, of all the States, ought to be possessed by the members [Congressmen] from each of the States. How can foreign trade be *properly* regulated by uniform *laws*, without some acquaintance with the commerce, the ports, the usages, and the regulations of the different States? . . . [Fed. 367]

"Brutus," No. 12, February 14, 1788:

This same manner of explaining the constitution, will fix a meaning, and a very important one too, to the 12th clause of the same section, which authorises the Congress to make all *laws which shall be proper and necessary* for carrying into effect the foregoing powers, &c. A voluminous writer in favor of this system, has taken great pains to convince the public, that this clause means nothing: for that the same powers expressed in this, are implied in other parts of the constitution. Perhaps it is so, but still this will undoubtedly be an excellent auxilliary to assist the courts to discover the spirit and reason of the constitution, and when applied to any and every of the other clauses granting power, will operate powerfully in extracting the spirit from them. [DHRC16 120]

James Madison, *The Federalist*, No. 56, February 16, 1788:

. . . In every State there have been made, and must continue to be made, regulations on this subject which will, in many cases, leave little more to be done by the federal legislature, than to review the different *laws*, and reduce them in one general act. A skillful individual in his closet, with all the local codes before him, might compile a law on some subjects of taxation for the whole Union, without any aid from oral information, and it may be expected that whenever internal taxes may be *necessary*, and particularly in cases requiring uniformity throughout the States, the more simple objects will be preferred. . . .

[Fed. 380]

"An Old Planter," February 20, 1788:

When we choose an assembly to make *laws* and regulate the government of this state, what would an assembly avail, if they had not power to inforce every act *necessary* for our government? [DHRC8 395]

James Iredell, "Marcus," No. 1, February 20, 1788:

[1] . . . For similar reasons, I dread not any power of originating appropriations of money as mentioned in the objection. While the concurrence of the other House must be had, and as that must *necessarily* be the most weighty in the government, I think no danger is to be apprehended. The Senate has no such authority as to awe or influence the House of Representatives, and it will be as *necessary* for one as for the other that *proper* active measures should be pursued. . . . [DHRC16 167]

[2] . . . As to the power of trying impeachments, let Mr. Mason shew where this power could more *properly* have been placed. It is a *necessary* power in every free government, since even the Judges of the Supreme Court of Judicature themselves may require a trial, and other public officers might have too much influence before an ordinary and common Court. . . . [DHRC16 168]

"Brutus," No. 13, February 21, 1788:

[1] The evil consequences that will flow from the exercise of this power, will best appear by tracing it in its operation. The constitution does not direct the mode in which an individual shall commence a suit against a state or the manner in which the judgement of the court shall be carried into execution, but it gives the legislature full power to pass *all laws which shall be proper and necessary* for the purpose. And they certainly must make provision for these purposes, or otherwise the power of the judicial will be nugatory. For, to what purpose will the power of a judicial be, if they have no mode, in which they can call the parties before them? Or of what use will it be, to call the parties to answer, if after they have given judgment, there is no authority to execute the judgment? We must, therefore, conclude, that the legislature will pass *laws* which will be effectual in this head. An individual of one state will then have a legal remedy against a state for any demand he may have against a state to which he does not belong. . . . [DHRC16 173]

[2] As to the idea that the legislature cannot provide for levying an execution on a state, I believe it is not well founded. I presume the last paragraph of the 8th section of article 1, gives the Congress express power to pass any *laws they may judge proper and necessary* for carrying into execution the power vested in the judicial department. And they must exercise this power, or otherwise the courts of justice will not be able to carry into effect the authorities with which they are invested. For the constitution does not direct the mode in which the courts are to proceed, to bring parties before them, to try causes, or to carry the judgment of the courts into execution. Unless they are pointed out by *law,* how are they to proceed, in any of the cases of which they have cognizance? . . . [DHRC16 174]

"The Impartial Examiner," No. 1, February 27, 1788:

. . . If this branch of revenue takes place, all the consequent rigour of excise *laws* will *necessarily* be introduced in order to enforce a due collection. On any charges of offence in this instance you will see yourselves deprived of your boasted trial by jury. The much admired common *law* process will give way to some quick and summary mode, by which the unhappy defendant will find himself reduced, perhaps to ruin, in less time than a charge could be exhibited against him in the usual course. [DHRC8 422]

"James Bowdoin," February 27, 1788:

[This is a pseudonymous, satirical article, supposedly addressed to James Wilson:] You are an admirable man, the most useful in the convention; but you was rather for taking too much at one time; the double powers of our little sexentially elected senate; the controul over the press; the abolition of trial by jury in civil cases, and the common *law* proceedings; internal taxation; the pecuniary dependency of the judges, and their great powers; the standing army; the smallness of the lower house; the exclusion of rotation; and the "powers to make all *laws which we may think necessary and proper*." And that these *laws* and the treaties of the little senate should be the supreme *law* of the land, over the constitutions and *laws* of the several states. These would have been quite sufficient for us; with them alone we could chain down all America . . . [DHRC16 240]

"An Impartial Citizen," No. 5, February 28, 1788:

It is also objected by Mr. [George] Mason, that under their own construction of the general clause, at the end of the enumerated powers, the Congress may grant monopolies in trade, constitute new crimes, inflict unusual punishments, and in short, do whatever they please. Nothing can be more groundless and ridiculous than this. The words of this clause so much dreaded by Mr. Mason, are, "To make all *laws which shall be necessary and proper* for carrying into execution the foregoing powers, and all other powers vested by this Constitution in the government of the United States, or in any department or officer thereof." Now, I insist that Mr. Mason's construction on this clause is absolutely puerile, and by no means warranted by the words, which are chosen with peculiar *propriety*. When a power is vested any where, from the nature of things it must be understood to be attended by such other incidental powers as are *necessary* to give it efficacy; for to say, that a power is given, without the power of enforcing it, is a solecism in language. In this case, the *laws* which Congress can make, for carrying into execution the conceded powers, must not only be *necessary, but proper*—So that if those powers cannot be executed without the aid of a *law,* granting commercial monopolies, inflicting unusual punishments, creating new crimes, or commanding any unconstitutional act; yet, as such a *law* would be manifestly not *proper,* it would not be warranted by this clause, without absolutely departing from the usual acceptation of words. . . . [DHRC8 431]

"A Federal Republican," March 5, 1788:

. . . Instead of a Congress whose members could serve but three years out of six, and then to return to a level with their fellow citizens, and who were liable at all times, whenever the States might deem it *necessary,* to be recalled; Congress, by this new Constitution, will be composed of a body whose members during the time they are appointed to serve, can receive no check from their constituents. Instead of the powers formerly granted to Congress of ascertaining each State's quota of men and money, to be raised by the Legislatures of the different States in such a mode as they might think *proper,* Congress, by this new government, will be invested with the formidable powers of raising armies, and levying money, totally independent of the different States. . . . [DHRC8 458]

James Iredell, "Marcus," No. 4, March 12, 1788:

"To make all *laws which shall be necessary and proper* for carrying into execution the foregoing powers, and all other powers vested by this Constitution in the United States, or in any department or office thereof."

Those powers would be useless, except acts of Legislation could be exercised upon them. It was not possible for the Convention, nor is it for any human body, to foresee and provide for all contingent cases that may arise. Such cases must therefore be left to be provided for by the general Legislature, as they shall happen to come into existence. If Congress, under pretence of exercising the power delegated to them, should, in fact, by the exercise of any other power, usurp upon the rights of the different Legislatures, or of any private citizens, the people will be exactly in the same situation as if there had been an express provision against such power in particular, and yet they had presumed to exercise it. It would be an act of tyranny, against which no parchment stipulations can guard; and the Convention surely can be only answerable for the *propriety* of the powers given, not for the future virtues of all with whom those powers may be entrusted. It does not therefore appear to me, that there is any weight in this objection more than in others . . . [DHRC16 379–80]

"An Impartial Citizen," No. 6, March 13, 1788:

[1] . . . Even Mr. [George] Mason, a man of great reputed abilities, has seriously objected, that the general and state Legislatures are restrained from making ex post facto *laws:* Though there never was nor will be a Legislature, but what must and will make such *laws,* when *necessity* and the public safety wil require it: That the making such *laws* will hereafter be a breach of all the Constitutions in the Union, and afford precedents for further innovations. I do not by any

means wish to detract from that gentleman any part of his merited reputation; yet can any thing be more expressive, and demonstrative of the imbecility of human nature, than that persons who are supposed; and actually affect to be connoisseurs in politics, should be so totally ignorant of the first principles of civil polity, as to mistake for a defect in a Constitution, that which it ought to be most highly extolled for; the very best part it ought to contain? . . . [DHRC8 492]

[2] . . . But let us suppose for a moment that the members of Congress will at some future period continue longer in their places than the Constitution provides, under the color of a *law* made by themselves for that purpose or of urgent *necessity*, or the like; what will be the consequence? Will not this be as open and flagrant a violation of the Constitution as any other measure they could possibly attempt? . . . [DHRC8 497]

George Nicholas [?], "The State Soldier," No. 4, March 19, 1788:

Under such restraints and useful regulations, it cannot be denied but that the authorities contained in a firm and efficient government are *necessary* to procure safety, and give to that machine a *proper* motion; unless there be those so chimerical and speculative as to expect government, like a wind-mill, to go on by airy efforts only. [DHRC8 511]

James Iredell, "Marcus," No. 5, March 19, 1788:

My ideas of liberty are so different from those of Mr. [George] Mason, that in my opinion this very prohibition is one of the most valuable parts of the new Constitution. Ex post facto *laws* may some times be convenient, but that they are ever absolutely *necessary* I shall take the liberty to doubt, till that *necessity* can be made apparent. Sure I am, they have been the instrument of some of the grossest acts of tyranny that were ever exercised, and have this never failing consequence, to put the minority in the power of a passionate and unprincipled majority, as to the most sacred things; and the plea of *necessity* is never wanting where it can be of any avail. This very clause, I think, is worth ten thousand Declarations of Rights, if this the most essential right of all was omitted in them. A man may feel some pride in his security, when he knows that what he does innocently and safely to-day, according to the *laws* of his country, cannot be tortured into guilt and danger tomorrow. But if it should happen, that a great and over-ruling *necessity*, acknowledged and felt by all, should make a deviation from this prohibition excusable, shall we not be more safe in leaving the excuse for an extraordinary exercise of power to rest upon the apparent equity of it alone, than to leave the door open to a tyranny it would be intolerable to bear? . . . [DHRC16 428]

Luther Martin, "To the Citizens of Maryland," No. 2, March 21, 1788:

[1] When this clause was introduced, it was not established that inferior continental courts should be appointed for trial of all questions arising on treaties and on the *laws* of the general government, and it was my wish and hope that every question of that kind would have been determined, in the first instance, in the courts of the respective states; had this been the case, *the propriety and the necessity* that treaties duly made and ratified, and the *laws* of the general government should be binding on the state judiciaries, which were to decide upon them, must be evident to every capacity, while, at the same time, if such treaties or *laws* were inconsistent with our constitution and bill of rights, the judiciaries of this state would be bound to reject the first and abide by the last . . . [DHRC16 452–53]

[2] . . . But the proposed constitution being intended and empowered to act not only on states, but also immediately on individuals, it renders a recognition and a stipulation in favour of the rights both of states and of men, not only *proper,* but in my opinion, absolutely *necessary.*—I endeavoured to obtain a restraint on the powers of the general government, as to standing armies, but it was rejected. . . . [DHRC16 455–56]

Georgia Constitution, May 6, 1789:

[Article I, Section 16:] The general assembly shall have power to make all *laws and ordinances which they shall deem necessary and proper* for the good of the State, which shall not be repugnant to this constitution. [Thorpe 787]

[Article IV, Section 7:] At the general election for members of assembly, in the year one thousand seven hundred and ninety-four, the electors in each county shall elect three persons to represent them in a convention, for the purpose of taking into consideration the alterations *necessary* to be made in this constitution, who shall meet at such time and place as the general assembly may appoint; and if two-thirds of the whole number shall meet and concur, they shall proceed to agree on such alterations and amendments as they may think *proper:* Provided, That after two-thirds shall have concurred to proceed to alterations and amendments, a majority shall determine on the particulars of such alterations and amendments. [Thorpe 789]

Pennsylvania Constitution, September 2, 1790:

[Article V, Section 6:] The supreme court and the several courts of common pleas shall, beside the powers heretofore usually exercised by them, have the power of a court of chancery, so far as relates to the perpetuating of testimony, the obtaining of evidence from places not within the State, and the care of the persons and estates of those who are non compotes mentis. And the legislature shall vest in the said courts such other powers to grant relief in equity as shall be found *necessary;* and may, from time to time, enlarge or diminish those powers, or vest them in such other courts as they shall judge *proper* for the due administration of justice. [Thorpe 3098]

NOBILITY, TITLE OF NOBILITY

United States Constitution, September 17, 1787:

[Article I, Section 9:] No *Title of Nobility* shall be granted by the United States: And no Person holding any Office of Profit or Trust under them, shall, without the Consent of the Congress, accept of any present, Emolument, Office, or *Title,* of any kind whatever, from any King, Prince or foreign State.

[Article I, Section 10:] No State shall enter into any Treaty, Alliance, or Confederation; grant Letters of Marque and Reprisal; coin Money; emit Bills of Credit; make any Thing but gold and silver Coin a Tender in Payment of Debts; pass any Bill of Attainder, ex post facto Law, or Law impairing the Obligation of Contracts, or grant any *Title of Nobility*.

* * * * *

Surrender of the Charter of New England, June 7, 1635:

. . . Thomas, now Earl of Arundell, and divers others of his *Nobility* and Gentry of this realme of England, therein named, to be the first and present Councill established at Plymouth aforesaid, for the planting, ruling, and governing of New England in America aforesaid . . . [Thorpe 1860]

Fundamental Constitutions of Carolina, March 1, 1669:

[Article 4:] Each signiory, barony, and colony shall consist of twelve thousand acres; the eight signiories being the share of the eight proprietors, and the eight baronies of the *nobility;* both which shares, being each of them one-fifth of the whole, are to be perpetually annexed the one to the proprietors, the other to the hereditary *nobility,* leaving the colonies, being three-fifths, amongst the people; so that in setting out and planting the lands, the balance of the government may be preserved. [Thorpe 2772]

[Article 9:] There shall be just as many landgraves as there are counties, and twice as many caziques, and no more. These shall be the hereditary *nobility* of the province, and by right of their dignity be members of parliament. Each landgrave shall have four baronies, and each cazique two baronies, hereditarily and unalterably annexed to and settled upon the said dignity. [Thorpe 2773]

[Article 60:] Each proprietor's deputy shall be always one of his six councillors, respectively; and in case any of the proprietors hath not, in his absence out of Carolina, a deputy, commissioned under his hand and seal, the eldest *nobleman* of his courtshall of course be his deputy. [Thorpe 2779]

[Article 63:] In every precinct there shall be a court, consisting of a steward and four justices of the precinct, being inhabitants and having three hundred acres of free hold within the said precinct who shall judge all criminal causes; except for treason, murder, and any other offences punishable with death, and except all criminal causes of the *nobility;* and shall judge also all civil causes whatsoever . . . [Thorpe 2780]

United States Continental Congress, Draft Articles of Confederation, July 12, 1776:

[Article 4:] No Colony or Colonies, without the Consent of the United States assembled, shall send any Embassy to or receive any Embassy from, or enter into any Treaty, Convention or Conference with the King or Kingdom of Great-Britain, or any foreign Prince or State; nor shall any Colony or Colonies, nor any Servant or Servants of the United States, or of any Colony or Colonies, accept of any Present, Emolument, Office, or *Title* of any Kind whatever, from the King or Kingdom of Great-Britain, or any foreign Prince or State; nor shall the United States assembled, or any Colony grant any *Title of Nobility*. [DHRC1 79]

Maryland Constitution, November 11, 1776:

[Declaration of Rights, Article 40:] That no *title of nobility*, or hereditary honours, ought to be granted in this State. [Thorpe 1690]

Georgia Constitution, February 5, 1777:

[Article 11:] No person shall be entitled to more than one vote, which shall be given in the county where such person resides, except as before excepted; nor shall any person who holds any *title of nobility* be entitled to a vote, or be capable of serving as a representative, or hold any post of honor, profit, or trust in this State, whilst such person claims his *title of nobility;* but if the person shall give up such distinction, in the manner as may be directed by any future legislation, then, and in such case, he shall be entitled to a vote, and represent, as before directed, and enjoy all the other benefits of a free citizen. [Thorpe 780]

United States Articles of Confederation, November 15, 1777:

[Article VI:] No state without the Consent of the united states in congress assembled, shall send any embassy to, or receive any embassy from, or enter into any conference, agreement, or alliance or treaty with any King prince or state; nor shall any person holding any office of profit or trust under the united states, or any of them, accept of any present, emolument, office or *title* of any kind whatever from any king, prince or foreign state; nor shall the united states in congress assembled, or any of them, grant any *title of nobility.*

Tench Coxe, *An Examination of the Constitution for the United States of America*, No. 1, September 26, 1787:

. . . The appointment of even the inferior officers may be taken out of his [the President's] hands by an act of congress at any time; he can create no *nobility or titles of honor,* nor take away offices during good behaviour. . . .

[Ford 139]

Tench Coxe, *An Examination of the Constitution for the United States of America*, No. 2, September 28, 1787:

We have seen that the late honorable convention, in designating the nature of the chief executive office of the United States, having deprived it of all the dangerous appendages of royalty, and provided for the frequent expiration of its limited powers—As our president bears no resemblance to a king, so we shall see the senate have no similitude to *nobles.* [Ford 140]

Noah Webster, *An Examination into the Leading Principles of the Federal Constitution*, October 17, 1787:

[1] People who have heard and read of the European governments, founded on the different ranks of monarch, *nobility* and people, seem to view the senate in America, where there is no difference of ranks and *titles,* as a useless branch—or as a servile imitation of foreign constitutions of government, without the same reasons. This is a capital mistake. Our senates, it is true, are not composed of a different order of men; but the same reasons, the same necessity for distinct branches of the legislature exists in all governments. But in most of our American constitutions, we have all the advantages of checks and balance, without the danger which may arise from a superior and independent order of men.

[Ford 34–35]

[2] The house of peers in England is a body originally and totally independent of the people—the senate in Rome was mostly composed of patrician or *noble* families, and after the first election of a senator, he was no longer dependent on the people—he held his seat for life. But the senate of the United States can

have no separate interests from the body of the people; for they live among them—they are chosen by them—they must be dismissed from their place once in six years and may at any time be impeached for malpractices—their property is situated among the people, and with their persons, subject to the same laws. No *title* can be granted, but the temporary *titles* of office, bestowed by the voluntary election of the people; and no preeminence can be acquired but by the same means. [Ford 42]

[3] . . . "Thus this weak constitution of government," says the ingenious Mr. Moyle, speaking of the aristocracy of Rome, "not founded on the true center of dominion,land, nor on any standing foundation of authority, nor rivetted in the esteem and affections of the people; and being attacked by strong passion, general interest and the joint forces of the people, mouldered away of course, and pined of a lingering consumption, till it was totally swallowed up by the prevailing faction, and the *nobility* were moulded into the mass of the people." The people, notwithstanding the nominal authority of the patricians, proceeded regularly in enlarging their own powers. . . . [Ford 57]

[4] The Romans proceeded thus step by step to triumph over the aristocracy, and to crown their privileges, they procured the right of being elected to the highest offices of the state. By acquiring the property of the plebians, the *nobility*, several times, held most of the power of the state; but the people, by reducing the interest of money, abolishing debts, or by forcing other advantages from the patricians, generally held the power of governing in their own hands.

[Ford 58]

[5] On reviewing the English history, we observe a progress similar to that in Rome—an incessant struggle for liberty from the date of Magna Charta, in John's reign, to the revolution. The struggle has been successful, by abridging the enormous power of the *nobility*. But we observe that the power of the people has increased in an exact proportion to their acquisitions of property. . . .

[Ford 58]

Tench Coxe, *An Examination of the Constitution for the United States of America*, No. 4, October 21, 1787:

. . . or should a foreign power seduce or over-awe the people of any state, so as to cause them to vest in the families of any ambitious citizens or foreigners the powers of hereditary governors, whether as Kings or *Nobles*, that such investment of powers would be void in itself, and every person attempting to execute them would also be guilty of treason. [Ford 145–46]

Alexander Hamilton, *The Federalist*, No. 17, December 5, 1787:

[1] . . . In those instances in which the monarch finally prevailed over his vassals, his success was chiefly owing to the tyranny of those vassals over their dependents. The barons, or *nobles*, equally the enemies of the sovereign and the

oppressors of the common people, were dreaded and detested by both; till mutual danger and mutual interest effected a union between them fatal to the power of the aristocracy. Had the *nobles*, by a conduct of clemency and justice, preserved the fidelity and devotion of their retainers and followers, the contests between them and the prince must almost always have ended in their favor, and in the abridgement or subversion of the royal authority. [Fed. 170]

[2] This is not an assertion founded merely in speculation or conjecture. Among other illustrations of its truth which might be cited, Scotland will furnish a cogent example. The spirit of clanship which was, at an early day, introduced into that kingdom, uniting the *nobles* and their dependents by ties equivalent to those of kindred, rendered the aristocracy a constant overmatch for the power of the monarch, till the incorporation with England subdued its fierce and ungovernable spirit, and reduced it within those rules of subordination which a more rational and more energetic system of civil polity had previously established in the latter kingdom. [Fed. 170]

Tobias Lear, "Brutus," December 6, 1787:

. . . So long as the national Legislature continues to be elective—so long as the members of it will, at the expiration of the time for which they were chosen, mix with, and become the people, where they must feel all the good or ill effects of their doings while legislators—and so long as *titles of nobility* and hereditary rank cannot be established, so long will it be impossible for the one or the few to destroy the liberties of American citizens. [DHRC8 216]

Dissent of the Pennsylvania Convention's Minority, December 18, 1787:

[Quoting Montesquieu:] Again, there is no liberty, if the power of judging be not separated from the legislative and executive powers. Were it joined with the legislative, the life and liberty of the subject would be exposed to arbitrary control; for the judge would then be legislator. Were it joined to the executive power, the judge might behave with all the violence of an oppressor. There would be an end of everything, were the same man, or the same body of the *nobles*, or of the people, to exercise those three powers; that of enacting laws, that of executing the public resolutions, and that of judging the crimes or differences of individuals. [DHRC2 635]

"Americanus," No. 2, December 19, 1787:

[1] . . . Could a senate, consisting of few members and modified like ours, erect itself into a perpetual body on the ruins of thirteen independent states, to whom it owes its political existence? Could it corrupt or annihilate the foederal house of representatives, a more numerous body than itself, chosen by the unbought,

unbiassed voices of an enlightened people, and without whose concurrence it could effect no design? Could they exercise an aristocratical power over the different states, so distant from each other, with the same impunity, that a numerous *nobility* might do over their respective vassals and dependents? To admit suppositions of this kind is to insult the sacred majesty of the people, sport with their undertakings, and by attempting to scare them with visionary dangers to treat them like children. [DHRC8 246]

[2] . . . I shall, Sir, mention but one more check, which the senate has to encounter. Perhaps it may be considered as trifling, but, in my humble opinion it is as strong, as it is extensive. Should an aristocracy be established in this body, it must be confined to particular families. As we have no *nobility,* and as no one family can claim a superiority over another, it is natural to suppose, that each would operate as a check to the other, and from a principle of jealousy, if not of patriotism, endeavor to counteract the ambitious hopes of all. If power thus restrained is not safe, I ask, by what human means can it be rendered more so? . . . [DHRC8 247]

"An Impartial Citizen," January 10, 1788:

. . . The Senate is composed of men, who are in a secondary degree chosen by the people, and who are, at fixed periods, reducible to the station from whence they were taken, where they will feel and participate [in] the burdens of the people, whose interest they cannot forget, without forgetting their own: An advantage over the government of Britain, whose Senate consists of hereditary *nobles,* who thinking themselves superior to, may totally forget the interests of, the people. . . . [DHRC8 295]

James Madison, *The Federalist*, No. 39, January 16, 1788:

[1] . . . The same title [that of a republic] has been bestowed on Venice, where absolute power over the great body of the people is exercised, in the most absolute manner, by a small body of hereditary *nobles*. Poland, which is a mixture of aristocracy and of monarchy in their worst forms, has been dignified with the same appellation. . . . [Fed. 280]

[2] . . . It is essential to such a government that it be derived from the great body of the society, not from an inconsiderable proportion, or a favored class of it; otherwise a handful of tyrannical *nobles,* exercising their oppressions by a delegation of their powers, might aspire to the rank of republicans, and claim for their government the honorable title of republic. . . . [Fed. 281]

[3] Could any further proof be required of the republican complexion of this system, the most decisive one might be found in its absolute prohibition of *titles of nobility,* both under the federal and the State governments; and in its express guaranty of the republican form to each of the latter. [Fed. 282]

James Madison, *The Federalist*, No. 44, January 25, 1788:

. . . The prohibition with respect to *titles of nobility* is copied from the articles of Confederation, and needs no comment. [Fed. 319]

Alexander C. Hanson, *Remarks on the Proposed Plan of a Federal Government*, c. January 31, 1788:

[1] . . . What then are the powers an individual state will lose [under the Constitution]? She will no longer be able to deny congress that, which congress, at this moment, has a right to demand. She will have no power to enter into a treaty, alliance, or confederation. She shall, in time of war, grant no letters of marque and reprisal. She shall coin no money, emit no bills of credit, nor make any thing but gold and silver a tender in payment of debts. She shall pass no bill of attainder, or ex post facto law, or law impairing the obligation of a contract. She shall grant no *title of nobility*. . . . [Ford 251]

[2] An aristocracy can perhaps subsist with only a moderate extent of territory and population. But it is a farce to talk of an aristocracy; when there are two branches, so differently formed; when the members of each are chosen for a reasonable term; and when their reappointment depends on the good opinion of their countrymen. It is not in nature,that a man with the least portion of common sense can believe the people of America will consent to such a deplorable change in their constitution, as shall confine all power to a few *noble* families, or that, without their consent, the change will be effected, by internal policy, or force. [Ford 256]

Massachusetts Convention, Proposed Amendments to the Constitution, February 6, 1788:

[Article 9:] Congress shall, at no time, consent, that any person, holding an office of trust or profit, under the United States, shall accept of a *title of nobility,* or any other *title* or office, from any king, prince, or foreign state. [DHRC16 69]

Alexander White, "To the Citizens of Virginia," February 22, 1788:

[1] . . . On the contrary, where the people have had the choice of their rulers, although that choice has been confined to a particular order of men, they have not only preserved their liberties, but improved them. I will illustrate this from the constitution and history of Rome. The Roman commonwealth consisted of two orders of men patricians or *nobles* and plebeians or commons . . . [DHRC8 406]

[2] The senate moreover, had the power of creating a dictator, before whom all other magistrates bowed their heads. From this sketch of the Roman government,

you may observe how much more effectually our liberties are secured than the liberties of the Roman people, yet the Roman people not only maintained their liberties, but encreased them by repeated concessions from the *nobles* for upwards of 400 years, and this without bloodshed. . . . [DHRC8 407]

Mercy Otis Warren, *Observations on the New Constitution*, February 1788:

But as a variety of objections to the heterogeneous phantom, have been repeatedly laid before the public, by men of the best abilities and intentions; I will not expatiate long on a Republican form of government, founded on the principles of monarchy—a democratick branch with the features of aristocracy—and the extravagance of *nobility* pervading the minds of many of the candidates for office, with the poverty of peasantry hanging heavily on them, and insurmountable, from their taste for expence, unless a generous provision should be made in the arrangement of the civil list . . . [DHRC16 277]

James Madison, *The Federalist*, No. 63, March 1, 1788:

But if any thing could silence the jealousies on this subject, it ought to be the British example. The Senate there, instead of being elected for a term of six years, and of being unconfined to particular families or fortunes, is an hereditary assembly of opulent *nobles*. . . . [Fed. 419]

"An Impartial Citizen," No. 6, March 13, 1788:

. . . They [the opponents of the Constitution] instance the aristocratic Senate in the petty kingdom of Sweden, as an anticipatory proof of the loss of our liberty. The *nobles* which composed the Senate in Sweden were hereditary, not elective: They were amenable to none; their mere will and pleasure was the constituent and criterion of their legislative or other public acts. As there is no similarity in our Federal Senate to them, no parallel can be drawn from thence . . .
[DHRC8 498]

Alexander Hamilton, *The Federalist*, No. 69, March 14, 1788:

[1] . . . The king of Great Britain is emphatically and truly styled the fountain of honor. He not only appoints to all offices, but can create offices. He can confer *titles of nobility* at pleasure; and has the disposal of an immense number of church preferments. There is evidently a great inferiority in the power of the President, in this particular, to that of the British king . . . [Fed. 449]

[2] . . . The one [the President] can confer no privileges whatever: the other [the King] can make denizens of aliens, *noblemen* of commoners: can erect corporations with all the rights incident to corporate bodies. . . . [Fed. 450]

Alexander Hamilton, *The Federalist*, No. 71, March 18, 1788:

. . . If a British House of Commons, from the most feeble beginnings, from the mere power of assenting or disagreeing to the imposition of a new tax, have, by rapid strides, reduced the prerogatives of the crown and the privileges of the *nobility* within the limits they conceived to be compatible with the principles of a free government, while they raised themselves to the rank and consequence of co-equal branch of the legislature . . . , what would be to be feared from an elective magistrate of four years' duration, with the confined authorities of a President of the United States? . . . [Fed. 462]

Samuel Bryan, "Centinel," No. 17, March 24, 1788:

The discovery of the intended fraud, which for magnitude and audacity, is unparalelled, must open the eyes of the deluded to the true character and principles of the men who had assumed the garb of patriotism, with an insidious design of enslaving and robbing their fellow-citizens—of establishing those odious distinctions between the well born and the great body of the people, of degrading the latter to the level of slaves, and elevating the former to the rank of *nobility*. [DHRC16 476]

Alexander Hamilton, *The Federalist*, No. 84, May 28, 1788:

[1] . . . The establishment of the writ of habeas corpus, the prohibition of ex post facto laws, and of *TITLES OF NOBILITY*, to which we have no corresponding provision in our Constitution, are perhaps greater securities to liberty and republicanism than any it contains. . . . [Fed. 533]

[2] Nothing need be said to illustrate the importance of the prohibition of *titles of nobility*. This may truly be denominated the corner-stone of republican government; for so long as they are excluded, there can never be serious danger that the government will be any other than that of the people. [Fed. 533]

Alexander Hamilton, *The Federalist*, No. 85, May 28, 1788:

The additional securities to republican government, to liberty, and to property, to be derived from the adoption of the plan under consideration, consist chiefly in the restraints which the preservation of the Union will impose on local factions and insurrections, and on the ambition of powerful individuals in single States, who may acquire credit and influence enough, from leaders and favorites, to become the despots of the people; in the diminution of the opportunities to foreign intrigue, which the dissolution of the Confederacy would invite and facilitate; in the prevention of extensive military establishments, which could not fail to grow out of wars between the States in a disunited situation; in the express guaranty of a republican form of government to each; in the absolute and universal exclusion of *titles of nobility;* and in the precautions against the repetition of those practices on the part of the State governments which have undermined the foundations of property and credit, have planted mutual distrust in the breasts of all classes of citizens, and have occasioned an almost universal prostration of morals. [Fed. 542]

John Dickinson, "Fabius," No. 8, 1788:

[Footnote:] Justice Blackstone argues in like manner, after admitting the "expediency" of *titles of nobility*. "It is also expedient that their owners should form an independent and separate branch of the legislature"—otherwise "their privileges would soon be borne down and overwhelmed." [Ford 207n]

John Dickinson, "Fabius," No. 9, 1788:

. . . Is there more danger to our liberty, from such a president as we are to have, than to that of Britons from an hereditary monarch with a vast revenue—absolute in the erection and disposal of offices, and in the exercise of the whole executive power—in the command of the militia, fleets, and armies, and the direction of their operations—in the establishments of fairs and markets, the regulation of weights and measures, and coining of money—who can call parliaments with a breath, and dissolve them with a nod—who can, at his will, make war, peace, and treaties irrevocably binding the nation—and who can grant pardons and *titles of nobility,* as it pleases him? . . . [Ford 212]

South Carolina Constitution, June 3, 1790:

[Article IX, Section 5] The legislature shall not grant any *title of nobility* or hereditary distinction, nor create any office the appointment to which shall be for any longer time than during good behavior. [Thorpe 3264]

Pennsylvania Constitution, September 2, 1790:

[Article IX, Section 24:] That the legislature shall not grant any *title of nobility* or hereditary distinction, nor create any office the appointment of which shall be for a longer term than during good behavior. [Thorpe 3101]

OFFICE OF HONOR

United States Constitution, September 17, 1787:

[Article I, Section 3:] Judgment in Cases of Impeachment shall not extend further than to removal from *Office,* and disqualification to hold and enjoy any *Office of honor,* Trust or Profit under the United States: but the Party convicted shall nevertheless be liable and subject to Indictment, Trial, Judgment and Punishment, according to Law.

* * * * *

Ferdinand and Isabella of Spain, Privileges and Prerogatives Granted to Christopher Columbus, April 30, 1492:

[1] And we being willing to *honour* and favour you for the reasons aforesaid: Our will is, That you, Christopher Columbus, after discovering and conquering the said Islands and Continent in the said ocean, or any of them, shall be our Admiral of the said Islands and Continent you shall so discover and conquer; and that you be our Admiral, Vice-Roy, and Governour in them, and that for the future, you may call and stile yourself, D. Christopher Columbus, and that your sons and successors in the said employment, may call themselves Dons, Admirals, Vice-Roys, and Governours of them; and that you may exercise the *office* of Admiral, with the charge of Vice-Roy and Governour of the said Islands and Continent, which you and your Lieutenants shall conquer, and freely decide all causes, civil and criminal, appertaining to the said employment of Admiral, Vice-Roy, and Governour, as you shall think fit in justice, and as the Admirals of our kingdoms use to do . . . [Thorpe 39]

[2] . . . and that they treat you and your Lieutenants, by you appointed, for executing the employments of Admiral, Vice-Roy, and Governour, as such in all respects, and give you all the perquisites and other things belonging and appertaining to the said *offices;* and allow, and cause to be allowed you, all the *honours,* graces, concessions, prehaminences, prerogatives, immunities, and

other things, or any of them which are due to you, by virtue of your commands of Admiral, Vice-roy, and Governour, and to be observed completely, so that nothing be diminished . . . [Thorpe 40]

English Petition of Right, June 7, 1628:

. . . and that your Majesty would be also graciously pleased, for the further comfort and safety of your people, to declare your royal will and pleasure, that in the things aforesaid all your *officers* and ministers shall serve you according to the laws and statutes of this realm, as they tender the *honour* of your Majesty, and the prosperity of this kingdom. [SDECH 342]

New York Constitution, April 20, 1777:

[Article 33:] That the power of impeaching all *officers* of the State, for mal and corrupt conduct in their respective *offices,* be vested in the representatives of the people in assembly; but that it shall always be necessary that two third parts of the members present shall consent to and agree in such impeachment. That previous to the trial of every impeachment, the members of the said court shall respectively be sworn truly and impartially to try and determine the charge in question, according to evidence; and that no judgment of the said court shall be valid unless it be assented to by two third parts of the members then present; nor shall it extend farther than to removal from *office,* and disqualification to hold or enjoy any place of *honor,* trust, or profit under this State. But the party so convicted shall be, nevertheless, liable and subject to indictment, trial, judgment, and punishment, according to the laws of the land. [Thorpe 2635]

South Carolina Constitution, March 19, 1778:

[Article 36:] " . . . And I do swear [or affirm, as the case may be] that I will, to the utmost of my power, support, maintain, and defend the said State against the said King George the Third, and his heirs and successors, and his or their abettors, assistants, and adherents, and will serve the said State, in the *office* of ———, with fidelity and *honor,* and according to the best of my skill and understanding: So help me God." [Thorpe 3255]

Massachusetts Constitution, March 2, 1780:

[Declaration of Rights, Article 29:] It is essential to the preservation of the rights of every individual, his life, liberty, property, and character, that there be an impartial interpretation of the laws, and administration of justice. It is the right of every citizen to be tried by judges as free, impartial, and independent as the lot of humanity will admit. It is, therefore, not only the best policy, but for the security of the rights of the people, and of every citizen, that the judges of the supreme judicial court should hold their *offices* as long as they behave themselves well; and that they should have *honorable* salaries ascertained and established by standing laws. [Thorpe 1893]

[Frame of Government, Chapter I:2:8:] The senate shall be a court with full authority to hear and determine all impeachments made by the house of representatives, against any *officer* or *officers* of the commonwealth, for misconduct and mal-administration in their *offices*. But previous to the trial of every impeachment the members of the senate shall respectively be sworn, truly and impartially to try and determine the charge in question, according to evidence. Their judgment, however, shall not extend further than to removal from *office* and disqualification to hold or enjoy any place of *honor,* trust, or profit, under this commonwealth; but the party so convicted shall be, nevertheless, liable to indictment, trial, judgment, and punishment, according to the laws of the land. [Thorpe 1897–98]

[*Ibid.*, Chapter II:2:1]: There shall be annually elected a lieutenant-governor of the commonwealth of Massachusetts, whose title shall be, His *Honor;* and who shall be qualified, in point of [religion,] property, and residence in the commonwealth, in the same manner with the governor; and the day and manner of his election, and the qualifications of the electors, shall be the same as are required in the election of a governor. The return of the votes for this *officer,* and the declaration of his election, shall be in the same manner . . .

[Thorpe 1903–04]

New Hampshire Constitution, June 2, 1784:

[Bill of Rights, Article 35:] It is essential to the preservation of the rights of every individual, his life, liberty, property and character, that there be an impartial interpretation of the laws, and administration of justice. It is the right of every citizen to be tried by judges as impartial as the lot of humanity will admit. It is therefore not only the best policy, but for the security of the rights of the people, that the judges of the supreme (or superior) judicial court should hold their *offices* so long as they behave well; and that they should have *honorable* salaries, ascertained and established by standing laws. [Thorpe 2457]

[Form of Government:] The senate shall be a court with full power and authority to hear and determine all impeachments made by the house of representatives, against any *officer* or *officers* of the state, for misconduct, or mal-administration in their *offices*. But previous to the trial of any such impeachment, the members of the senate shall respectively be sworn, truly and impartially to try and determine the charge in question according to evidence. Their judgment, however, shall not extend farther than removal from *office,* disqualification to hold or enjoy any place of *honor,* trust or profit under this state; but the party so convicted, shall nevertheless be liable to indictment, trial, judgment, and punishment, according to laws of the land. [Thorpe 2461]

Virginia Statute of Religious Liberty, January 16, 1786:

. . . that therefore the proscribing any citizen as unworthy the public confidence by laying upon him an incapacity of being called to *offices* of trust and emolument, unless he profess or renounce this or that religious opinion, is depriving him injuriously of those privileges and advantages to which in common with his fellow citizens, he has a natural right; that it tends only to corrupt the principles of that religion it is meant to encourage, by bribing with a monopoly of worldly *honors* and emoluments, those who will externally profess and conform to it . . . [CVA8 690]

Tench Coxe, *An Examination of the Constitution for the United States of America*, No. 1, September 26, 1787:

. . . He [the President] will have no authority to make a treaty, without two-thirds of the senate, nor can he appoint ambassadors or other great *officers* without their approbation, which will remove the idea of patronage and influence, and of personal obligation and dependence. The appointment of even the inferior *officers* may be taken out of his hands by an act of congress at any time; he can create no nobility or titles of *honor,* nor take away *offices* during good behaviour. His person is not so much protected as that of a member of the house of representatives; for he may be proceeded against like any other man in the ordinary course of law. He appoints no *officer* of the separate states. . . . [Ford 139]

Tench Coxe, *An Examination of the Constitution for the United States of America*, No. 2, September 28, 1787:

First, then, not being hereditary, their [the Senators'] collective knowledge, wisdom, and virtue are not precarious, for by these qualities alone they are to obtain their *offices;* and they will have none of the peculiar follies and vices of those men, who possess power merely because their fathers held it before them, for they will be educated (under equal advantages, and with equal prospects) among and on a footing with the other sons of a free people. If we recollect the characters, who have, at various periods, filled the seats of congress, we shall find this expectation perfectly reasonable. Many young men of genius, and many characters of more matured abilities without fortunes, have been *honored* with that trust. Wealth has had but few representatives there . . . [Ford 140]

Tench Coxe, *An Examination of the Constitution for the United States of America*, No. 4, October 21, 1787:

[1] The people will remain, under the proposed constitution, the fountain of power and public *honour*. The president, the Senate, and the House of Representatives, will be the channels through which the stream will flow—but it will

flow from the people, and from them only. Every *office,* religious, civil and military will be either their immediate gift, or it will come from them through the hands of their servants. And this, as observed before, will be guaranteed to them under the state constitution which they respectively approve; for they cannot be royal forms, cannot be aristocratical, but must be republican. [Ford 147]

[2] The influence which foreign powers may attempt to exercise in our affairs was foreseen, and a wholesome provision has been made against it; for no person holding an *office* under the United States is permitted to enjoy any foreign *honours,* powers or emoluments. [Ford 150]

Luther Martin, "Genuine Information," No. 12, February 8, 1788:

Indulge me, Sir, in a single observation further. There are persons who endeavour to hold up the idea that this system [the Constitution] is only opposed by the *officers* of government—I, Sir, am in that predicament.—I have the *honor* to hold an appointment in this State. Had it been considered any objection, I presume I should not have been appointed to the convention—If it could have any effect on my mind, it would only be that of warming my heart with gratitude, and rendering me more anxious to promote the true interest of that State which has conferred upon me the obligation, and to heighten my guilt had I joined in sacrificing its essential rights—But, Sir, it would be well to remember, that this system is not calculated to diminish the number or the value of *offices*—on the contrary, if adopted, it will be productive of an enormous increase in their number—many of them will be also of great *honour* and emolument. Whether, Sir, in this variety of appointments and in the scramble for them, I might not have as good a prospect to advantage myself as many others is not for me to say—but this, Sir, I can say with truth, that so far was I from being influenced in my conduct by interest, or the consideration of *office,* that I would cheerfully resign the appointment I now hold—I would bind myself never to accept another either under the general government or that of my own State . . .

[DHRC16 92–93]

"James Bowdoin," February 27, 1788:

. . . But if we succeed in this plan [the Constitution], we shall never again be troubled with the people, never dread the event of elections; we shall enjoy our places, *honors,* and preferments, and leave them to our children after us. We shall be able to keep the people at a proper distance, and establish our numerous friends and relations in lucrative and substantial *offices*. [DHRC16 240]

Alexander White, "To the Citizens of Virginia," February 29, 1788:

. . . It is said the representation is unsafe because it is so exposed to corruption and undue influence, by the gift of the numerous places of *honor* and emolument at the disposal of the executive, by the arts and address of the great and designing, and by direct bribery? The members of Congress can hold no *office* during the time they remain members, nor can they enjoy any *office* which shall be created, or the emoluments of which shall be increased during the time for which they were elected.—Name to me the country in which the members of the legislature or the executive council are so far removed from influence . . .

[DHRC8 439–440]

Alexander Hamilton, *The Federalist*, No. 68, March 12, 1788:

The process of election affords a moral certainty, that the *office* of President will never fall to the lot of any man who is not in an eminent degree endowed with the requisite qualifications. Talents for low intrigue, and the little arts of popularity, may alone suffice to elevate a man to the first *honors* in a single State; but it will require other talents, and a different kind of merit, to establish him in the esteem and confidence of the whole Union, or of so considerable a portion of it as would be necessary to make him a successful candidate for the distinguished *office* of President of the United States. . . . [Fed. 442–443]

Alexander Hamilton, *The Federalist*, No. 69, March 14, 1788:

The President is to nominate, and, with the advice and consent of the Senate, to appoint ambassadors and other public ministers, judges of the Supreme Court, and in general all *officers* of the United States established by law, and whose appointments are not otherwise provided for by the Constitution. The king of Great Britain is emphatically and truly styled the fountain of *honor*. He not only appoints to all *offices*, but can create *offices*. He can confer titles of nobility at pleasure; and has the disposal of an immense number of church preferments. There is evidently a great inferiority in the power of the President, in this particular, to that of the British king . . . [Fed. 448–449]

Alexander Hamilton, *The Federalist*, No. 71, March 18, 1788:

. . . It is a general principle of human nature, that a man will be interested in whatever he possesses, in proportion to the firmness or precariousness of the tenure by which he holds it; will be less attached to what he holds by a momentary or uncertain title, than to what he enjoys by a durable or certain title; and, of course, will be willing to risk more for the sake of the one, than for the sake of the other. This remark is not less applicable to a political privilege, or *honor*, or trust, than to any article of ordinary property. The inference from it is, that a man acting in the capacity of chief magistrate, under a consciousness that in a very short time he must lay down his *office*, will be apt to feel himself too little interested in it to hazard any material censure or perplexity, from the independent exertion of his powers, or from encountering the ill-humors, however transient, which may happen to prevail, either in a considerable part of the society itself, or even in a predominant faction in the legislative body. . . . [Fed. 458–459]

Alexander Hamilton, *The Federalist*, No. 72, March 19, 1788:

Another ill effect of the exclusion would be the temptation to sordid views, to peculation, and, in some instances, to usurpation. An avaricious man, who might happen to fill the *office,* looking forward to a time when he must at all events yield up the emoluments he enjoyed, would feel a propensity, not easy to be resisted by such a man, to make the best use of the opportunity he enjoyed while it lasted, and might not scruple to have recourse to the most corrupt expedients to make the harvest as abundant as it was transitory; though the same man, probably, with a different prospect before him, might content himself with the regular perquisites of his situation, and might even be unwilling to risk the consequences of an abuse of his opportunities. His avarice might be a guard upon his avarice. Add to this that the same man might be vain or ambitious, as well as avaricious. And if he could expect to prolong his *honors* by his good conduct, he might hesitate to sacrifice his appetite for them to his appetite for gain. But with the prospect before him of approaching an inevitable annihilation, his avarice would be likely to get the victory over his caution, his vanity, or his ambition. [Fed. 464]

Luther Martin, "To the Citizens of Maryland," No. 2, March 21, 1788:

. . . I most sacredly believe their object is the total abolition and destruction of all state governments, and the erection, on their ruins, of one great and extensive empire, calculated to aggrandize and elevate its rulers and chief *officers,* far above the common herd of mankind—to enrich them with wealth, and to encircle them with *honours* and glory—and which, according to my judgment, on the maturest reflection, must, inevitably, be attended with the most humiliating and abject slavery of their fellow-citizens, by the sweat of whose brows, and by the toil of whose bodies, it can only be effected . . . [DHRC16 457]

Alexander Hamilton, *The Federalist*, No. 77, April 2, 1788:

. . . If, to avoid an accumulation of *offices,* there was to be a frequent change in the persons who were to compose the council [of appointment], this would involve the mischiefs of a mutable administration in their full extent. Such a council would also be more liable to executive influence than the Senate, because they would be fewer in number, and would act less immediately under the public inspection. Such a council, in fine, as a substitute for the plan of the convention, would be productive of an increase of expense, a multiplication of the evils which spring from favoritism and intrigue in the distribution of public *honors,* a decrease of stability in the administration of the government, and a diminution of the security against an undue influence of the Executive. And yet such a council has been warmly contended for as an essential amendment in the proposed Constitution. [Fed. 487–488]

Melancthon Smith, *An Address to the People of the State of New York,* c. April 1788:

. . . When the government is once organized, and all the *offices* under it filled, the inducements which our great men will have to support it, will be much stronger than they are now to urge its reception. Many of them will then hold places of great *honour* and emolument, and others will then be candidates for such places. It is much harder to relinquish *honours* or emoluments, which we have in possession, than to abandon the pursuit of them, while the attainment is held in a state of uncertainty. . . . [Ford 91–92]

United States Senate, Address to George Washington, May 7, 1789:

Sir: We, the Senate of the United States, return you our sincere thanks for your excellent speech delivered to both houses of Congress, congratulate you on the complete organization of the Federal Government, and felicitate ourselves and our fellow-citizens on your elevation to the *office* of President, an *office* highly important by the powers constitutionally annexed to it and extremely *honorable* from the manner in which the appointment is made. . . . [Annals 32]

South Carolina Constitution, June 3, 1790:

[Article V, Section 3:] The governor, lieutenant-governor, and all the civil *officers* shall be liable to impeachment for any misdemeanor in *office;* but judgment in such cases shall not extend further than to a removal from *office,* and disqualification to hold any *office of honor,* trust, or profit under this State. The party convicted shall, nevertheless, be liable to indictment, trial, judgment, and punishment according to law. [Thorpe 3263]

Pennsylvania Constitution, September 2, 1790:

[Article IV, Section 3:] The governor, and all other civil *officers* under this commonwealth, shall be liable to impeachment for any misdemeanor in *office.* But judgment, in such cases, shall not extend further than to removal from *office,* and disqualification to hold any *office of honor,* trust, or profit under this commonwealth. The party, whether convicted or acquitted, shall nevertheless be liable to indictment, trial, judgment, and punishment according to law.

[Thorpe 3097]

ORDER, ORDERS

(Legislative)

[Note: this list compiles references to legislative orders; it does not include executive or court orders. Other uses of the word "order" and other forms of the word were not searched systematically. Only a few samples of the repetitious Virginia Assembly proceedings are presented.]

United States Constitution, September 17, 1787:

[Article I, Section 7:] Every *Order,* Resolution, or Vote to which the Concurrence of the Senate and House of Representatives may be necessary (except on a question of Adjournment) shall be presented to the President of the United States; and before the Same shall take Effect, shall be approved by him, or being disapproved by him, shall be repassed by two thirds of the Senate and House of Representatives, according to the Rules and Limitations prescribed in the Case of a Bill.

* * * * *

James I, First Charter of Virginia, April 10, 1606:

And moreover, we do Grant and agree, for Us, our Heirs and Successors; that the said several Councils of and for the said several Colonies, shall and lawfully may, by Virtue hereof, from time to time, without any Interruption of Us, our Heirs or Successors, give and take *Order,* to dig, mine, and search for all Manner of Mines of Gold, Silver, and Copper, as well within any Part of their said several Colonies, as of the said main Lands on the Backside of the same Colonies . . . [Thorpe 3786]

James I, Second Charter of Virginia, May 23, 1609:

[1] [Council shall have power] . . . also to make, ordain, and establish all Manner of *Orders,* Laws, Directions, Instructions, Forms and Ceremonies of Government and Magistracy, fit and necessary for and concerning the Government of the said

Colony and Plantation; And the same, at all Times hereafter, to abrogate, revoke, or change, not only within the Precincts of the said Colony, but also upon the Seas, in going and coming to and from the said Colony, as they in their good Discretion, shall think to be fittest for the Good of the Adventurers and inhabitants there. [Thorpe 3798]

[2] . . . Straightly charging and commanding the President and Council now resident in the said Colony upon their Allegiance, after Knowledge given unto them of our Will and Pleasure by these presents signified and declared that they forthwith be obedient to such Governor or Governors as by our said Council here resident shall be named and appointed as aforesaid, and to all Directions, *Orders* and Commandments which they shall receive from them, as well in the present resigning and giving up of their Authority, Offices, Charge and Places, as in all other Attendance as shall be by them from time to time required. [Thorpe 3798]

[3] . . . We for Us, our Heirs, and Successors are likewise pleased and contented, and by these Presents do Give and Grant unto the said Treasurer and Company, and their Successors, and to such Governors, Officers, and Ministers, as shall be by our said Council constituted and appointed according to the Natures and Limits of their Offices and Places respectively, that they shall and may from Time to Time, for ever hereafter, within the said Precincts of Virginia, or in the way by Seas thither and from thence, have full and absolute Power and Authority to correct, punish, pardon, govern, and rule all such the Subjects of Us, our Heires, and Successors as shall from Time to Time adventure themselves in any Voyage thither, or that shall at any Time hereafter, inhabit in the Precincts and Territories of the said Colony as aforesaid, according to such *Orders,* Ordinances, Constitutions, Directions, and Instructions, as by our said Council as aforesaid, shall be established; And in Defect thereof in case of Necessity, according to the good Discretions of the said Governor and Officers respectively, as well in Cases capital and criminal, as civil, both Marine and other; So always as the said Statutes, Ordinances and Proceedings as near as conveniently may be, be agreeable to the Laws, Statutes, Government, and Policy of this our Realm of England. [Thorpe 3801]

James I, The Charter of New England, November 3, 1620:

[1] . . . And our Will and Pleasure is, that the said fourty Persons, or the greater Number of them, shall and may, from time to time, and at any time hereafter, at their owne Will and Pleasure, according to the Laws, Ordinances, and *Orders* of or by them, or by the greater Part of them, hereafter in Manner and forme in these Presents mentioned, to be agreed upon, to elect and choose amongst themselves one of the said fourty Persons for the Time being, to be President of the said Councill, which President soe elected and chosen, Wee will, shall continue and be President of the said Councill for so long a Time as by the *Orders* of the said Councill, from time to time to be made, as hereafter is mentioned, shall be thought fitt, and no longer; unto which President, or in his

Absence, to any such Person as by the *Order* of the said Councill shall be thereunto appointed, Wee do give Authority to give *Order* for the warning of the said Council, and summoning the Company to their Meetings. . . .
[Thorpe 1831]

[2] And Wee do further by these Presents, for Us, our Heires and Successors, grant unto the said Councill and their Successors, that it shall and may be lawfull to and for the said Councill, and their Successors for the Time being, in their discretions, from time to time to admitt such and so many Person and Persons to be made free and enabled to trade traffick unto, within, and in New-England aforesaid, and unto every Part and Parcell thereof, or to have, possess, or enjoy, any Lands or Hereditaments in New-England aforesaid, as they shall think fitt, according to the Laws, *Orders,* Constitutions, and Ordinances, by the said Councill and their Successors from time to time to be made and established by Virtue of, and according to the true Intent of these Presents, and under such Conditions, Reservations, and agreements as the said Councill shall set downe, *order* and direct, and not otherwise. . . . [Thorpe 1832]

[3] . . . and also to make, ordaine, and establish all Manner of *Orders,* Laws, Directions, Instructions, Forms, and Ceremonies of Government and Magistracy fitt and necessary for and concerning the Government of the said Collony and Plantation, so always as the same be not contrary to the Laws and Statutes of this our Realme of England . . . [Thorpe 1832]

[4] . . . and from thence have full and absolute Power and Authority to correct, punish, pardon, governe, and rule all such the Subjects of Us, our Heires and Successors, as shall from time to time adventure themselves in any Voyage thither, or that shall att any Time heerafter inhabit in the Precincts or Territories of the said Collony as aforesaid, according to such Laws, *Orders,* Ordinances, Directions, and Instructions as by the said Councill aforesaid shall be established . . . [Thorpe 1833]

[5] . . . Wee, therefore, for preventing so great and enormous Abuses and Misdemeanors, Do, by these Presents for Us, our Heires, and Successors, give and grant unto the said President or his Deputy, or such other Person or Persons, as by the *Orders* of the said Councill shall be appointed by Warrant under his or their Hand or Hands, to send for, or cause to be apprehended, all and every such Person and Persons, who shall be noted, or accused, or found at any time or times hereafter to offend or misbehave themselves in any the Affaires before mentioned and expressed . . . [Thorpe 1838]

Charter of the Dutch West India Company, June 3, 1621:

[Article 13:] And the States of the respective United Provinces are authorized, to lay before their High Mightinesses' ordinary deputies, or before the magistrates of the cities of these Provinces, any *order* for registering the members, together with the election of managers, if they find they can do it according to the constitution of their Provinces. . . . [Thorpe 62]

Virginia Company, Ordinances for the Colony, July 24, 1621:

[Section 2:] We therefore, the said Treasurer, Council, and Company, by Authority directed to us from his Majesty under the Great Seal, upon mature Deliberation, do hereby *order* and declare that, from hence forward, there shall be Two Supreme Councils in Virginia for the better Government of the said Colony aforesaid. [Thorpe 3811]

[Section 4:] The other Council, more generally to be called by the Governor, once yearly, and no oftener, but for very extraordinary and important occasions, shall consist, for the present, of the said Council of State, and of two Burgesses out of every Town, Hundred, or other particular Plantation, to be respectively chosen by the Inhabitants: Which Council shall be called The General Assembly, wherein (as also in the said Council of State) all Matters shall be decided, determined, and *ordered,* by the greater Part of the Voices then present; reserving to the Governor always a Negative Voice. And this General Assembly shall have free Power to treat, consult, and conclude, as well of all emergent Occasions concerning the Publick Weal of the said Colony and every Part thereof, as also to make, ordain, and enact such general Laws and *Orders,* for the Behoof of the said Colony, and the good Government thereof, as shall, from time to time, appear necessary or requisite . . . [Thorpe 3811]

[Section 6:] . . . that after the Government of the said Colony shall once have been well framed, and settled accordingly, which is to be done by Us, as by Authority derived from his Majesty, and the same shall have been so by us declared, no *Orders* of Court afterwards shall bind the said Colony, unless they be ratified in like Manner in the General Assemblies. . . . [Thorpe 3812]

Council of New England, Charter of Plymouth Colony, January 13, 1629:

[1] . . . And the said councell doe further graunt and agree to and with the said William Bradford his heires associatts and assignes and every of them, his and their factors agents tenants and servants and all such as hee or they shall send and employ aboute his said particular plantacon, shall and may from tyme to tyme freely and lawfully goe and returne trade and traffique as well with the Englishe as any of the natives within the precints aforesaid, with liberty of fishinge upon any parte of the sea coaste and sea shoares of any the seas or islands adjacente and not beinge inhabited or otherwise disposed of by *order* of the said president and councell . . . [Thorpe 1844]

[2] . . . Alsoe it shall be lawfull and free for the said William Bradford his associatts his heires and assignes att all tymes hereafter to incorporate by some usual or fitt name and title, him or themselves or the people there inhabitinge

under him or them with liberty to them and their successors from tyme to time to frame, and make *orders* ordinances and constitucons as well for the better governmente of their affairs here and the receavinge or admittinge any to his or their society as alsoe for the better governmt of his or their people and affaires in New Englande or of his and their people att sea in goeinge thither, or returninge from thence, and the same to putt in execucon or cause to be putt in execucon by such officers and ministers as he and they shall authorize and depute: Provided that the said lawes and *orders* be not repugnante to the lawes of Englande, or the frame of governmente by the said presidente and councell hereafter to be established. [Thorpe 1844–1845]

Charles I, Charter of Massachusetts Bay, March 4, 1629:

[1] . . . it shall And maie be lawfull, to and for the Governor or Deputie Governor, and such of the Assistants and Freemen of the said Company for the Tyme being as shalbe assembled in any of their generall Courts aforesaide, or in any other Courtes to be specially sumoned and assembled for that Purpose, or the greater Parte of them (whereof the Governor or Deputie Governor, and six of the Assistants to be alwaies seaven) from tyme to tyme, to make, ordeine, and establishe all Manner of wholesome and reasonable *Orders,* Lawes, Statutes, and Ordinces, Direccons, and Instruccons, not contrairie to the Lawes of this our Realme of England . . . [Thorpe 1857]

[2] . . . Willing, comaunding, and requiring, and by theis Presents for Us, our Heires, and Successors, ordeyning and appointing, that all such *Orders,* Lawes, Statuts and Ordinances, Instruccons and Direccons, as shalbe soe made by the Governor, or Deputie Governor of the said Company, and such of the Assistants and Freemen as aforesaide, and published in Writing, under their comon Seale, shalbe carefullie and dulie observed, kept, performed, and putt in Execucon, according to the true Intent and Meaning of the same; and theis our Letters-patents, or the Duplicate or exemplificacon thereof, shalbe to all and everie such Officers, superior and inferior, from Tyme to Tyme, for the putting of the same *Orders,* Lawes, Statutes, and Ordinances, Instruccons, and Direccons, in due Execucon against Us, our Heires and Successors, a sufficient Warrant and Discharge. [Thorpe 1857–58]

[3] And Wee Doe further, for Us, our Heires and Successors, give and graunt to the said Governor and Company, and their Successors by theis Presents, that all and everie such Chiefe Comaunders, Captaines, Governors, and other Officers and Ministers, as by the said *Orders,* Lawes, Statuts, Ordinances, Instruccons, or Direccons of the said Governor and Company for the Tyme being, shalbe from Tyme to Tyme hereafter ymploied either in the Government of the saide Inhabitants and Plantacon, or in the Waye by Sea thither, or from thence, according to the Natures and Lymitts of their Offices and Places respectively, shall from Tyme to Tyme hereafter for ever, within the Precincts and Partes of Newe England hereby menconed to be graunted and confirmed,

or in the Waie by Sea thither, or from thence, have full and Absolute Power and Authoritie to correct, punishe, parrdon, governe, and rule all such the Subjects of Us, our Heires and Successors, as shall from Tyme to Tyme adventure themselves in any Voyage thither or from thence, or that shall at any Tyme hereafter, inhabite within the Precincts and Partes of Newe England aforasaid, according to the *Orders,* Lawes, Ordinances, Instruccons, and Direccons aforesaid, not being repugnant to the Lawes and Statutes of our Realme of England as aforesaid. . . . [Thorpe 1858]

Fundamental *Orders* of Connecticut, 1638–39:

[Preamble:] . . . and doe, for our selves and our Successors and such as shall be adjoyned to us att any tyme hereafter, enter into Combination and Confederation togather, to mayntayne and prsearve the liberty and purity of the gospell of our Lord Jesus wch we now prfesse, as also the disciplyne of the Churches, wch according to the truth of the said gospell is now practised amongst us; As also in our Civell Affaires to be guided and governed according to such Lawes, Rules, *Orders* and decrees as shall be made, *ordered* & decreed, as followeth:—— [Thorpe 519]

[Article 6:] It is *Ordered,* sentenced and decreed, that the Govrnor shall, ether by himselfe or by the secretary, send out summons to the Constables of every Towne for the cauleing of these two standing Courts, on[e] month at lest before their sevrall tymes: And also if the Govrnor and the gretest prte of the Magestrats see cause uppon any spetiall occation to call a generall Courte, they may give *order* to the secretary soe to doe wthin fowerteene dayes warneing; and if urgent necessity so require, uppon a shorter notice, giveing sufficient grownds for yt to the deputyes when they meete, or els be questioned for the same; And if the Govrnor and Mayor prte of Magestrats shall ether neglect or refuse to call the two Generall standing Courts or ether of them, as also at other tymes when the occations of the Commonwelth require, the Freemen thereof, or the Mayor prte of them, shall petition to them soe to doe: if then yt be ether denyed or neglected the said Freemen or the Mayor prte of them shall haue power to give *order* to the Constables of the seuerall Townes to doe the same, and so may meete togather, and chuse to themselves a Moderator, and may prceed to do any Acte of power, wch any other Generall Courte may. [Thorpe 520–21]

[Article 8:] It is *Ordered,* sentenced and decreed, that Wyndsor, Hartford and Wethersfield shall have power, ech Towne, to send fower of their freemen as deputyes to every Generall Courte; and whatsoeuer other Townes shall be hereafter added to this Jurisdiction, they shall send so many deputyes as the Courte shall judge meete, a resonable prportion to the number of Freemen that are in the said Townes being to be attended therein; wch deputyes shall have the power of the whole Towne to give their voats and alowance to all such lawes and *orders* as may be for the publike good, and unto wch the said Townes are to be bownd. [Thorpe 521]

[Article 9:] It is *ordered* and decreed, that the deputyes thus chosen shall have power and liberty to appoynt a tyme and a place of meeting togather before any Generall Courte to advise and consult of all such things as may concerne the good of the publike, as also to examine their owne Elections, whether according to the *order,* and if they or the gretest prte of them find any election to be illegall they may seclud such for prsent from their meeting, and returne the same and their resons to the Courte . . . [Thorpe 521]

Fundamental Agreement of New Haven Colony, June 4, 1639:

. . . All having spoken their apprehensions it was agreed upon, and Mr. Robert Newman was desired to write it as an *order* whereunto every one, that hereafter should be admitted here as planters, should submit, and testify the same by subscribing their names to the *order:* Namely, that church members only shall be free burgesses, and that they only shall choose magistrates and officers among themselves, to have power of transacting all the public civil affairs of this plantation; of making and repealing laws, dividing of inheritances, deciding of differences that may arise, and doing all things and businesses of like nature. [Thorpe 525]

The New England Confederation, May 19, 1643:

[Article 8:] It is also agreed that the Commissioners for this Confederation hereafter at their meetings, whether ordinary or extraordinary, as they may have commission or opportunity, do endeavor to frame and establish agreements and *orders* in general cases of a civil nature, wherein all the Plantations are interested, for preserving of peace among themselves, for preventing as much as may be all occasion of war or differences with others . . . [Thorpe 80]

Government of New Haven Colony, October 27, 1643:

It was agreed and concluded as a foundamentall *order* nott to be disputed or questioned hereafter, thatt none shall be admitted to be free burgesses in any of the plantations within this jurisdiction for the future, butt such planters as are members of some or other of the approved churches of New England, nor shall any butt such freemen burgesses have any vote in any election, (the six present freemen att Milforde enjoying the liberty with the cautions agreed,) nor shall any power or trust in the ordering of any civill affayres, be att any time putt into the hands of any other than such church members, though as free planters, all have right to their inheritance & to comerce, acccording to such grants, *orders* and lawes as shall be made concerning the same. [Thorpe 526–527]

Charles II, Charter of Connecticut, April 23, 1662:

. . . willing, commanding and requiring, and by these Presents for Us, Our Heirs and Successors, ordaining and appointing, that all such Laws, Statutes and

Ordinances, Instructions, Impositions and Directions as shall be so made by the Governor, Deputy-Governor, and Assistants as aforesaid, and published in Writing under their Common Seal, shall carefully and duly be observed, kept, performed, and put in Execution, according to the true Intent and Meaning of the same, and these Our Letters Patents, or the Duplicate, or Exemplification thereof, shall be to all and such Officers, Superiors and Inferiors from Time to Time, for the putting of the same *Orders,* Laws, Statutes, Ordinances, Instructions, and Directions in due Execution, against Us, Our Heirs and Successors, a sufficient Warrant and Discharge. [Thorpe 534]

Charles II, Charter of Rhode Island, July 8, 1663:

[1] [The Governor and Company shall have power] . . . from tyme to tyme, to make, ordeyne, constitute or repeal, such lawes, statutes, *orders* and ordinances, formes and ceremonies of government and magistracye as to them shall seeme meete for the good and wellfare of the sayd Company, and for the government and ordering of the landes and hereditaments, hereinafter mentioned to be graunted, and of the people that doe, or att any tyme hereafter shall, inhabitt or bee within the same; soe as such lawes, ordinances and constitutiones, soe made, bee not contrary and repugnant unto, butt, as neare as may bee, agreeable to the lawes of this our realme of England, considering the nature and constitutione of the place and people there; and alsoe to apoynt, *order* and direct, erect and settle, such places and courts of jurisdiction, for the heareinge and determininge of all actions, cases, matters and things, happening within the sayd collonie and plantatione, and which shall be in dispute, and depending there, as they shall thinke fit . . . [Thorpe 3215]

[2] . . . and alsoe to *order,* direct and authorize the imposing of lawfull and reasonable fynes, mulcts, imprisonments, and executing other punishments pecuniary and corporal, upon offenders and delinquents, according to the course of other corporations within this oure kingdom of England; and agayne to alter, revoke, annull or pardon, under their common seale or otherwyse, such fynes, mulcts, imprisonments, sentences, judgments and condemnations, as shall bee thought fitt; and to direct, rule, *order* and dispose of, all other matters and things, and particularly that which relates to the makinge of purchases of the native Indians, as to them shall seeme meete; whereby oure sayd people and inhabitants, in the sayd Plantationes, may be soe religiously, peaceably and civilly governed, as that, by theire good life and orderlie conversatione, they may win and invite the native Indians of the countrie to the knowledge and obedience of the onlie true God, and Saviour of mankinde; willing, commanding and requireing, and by these presents, for us, oure heires and successours, ordeyneing and apoynting, that all such lawes statutes, *orders* and ordinances, instructions, impositions and directiones, as shall bee soe made by the Governour, deputye-Governour, Assistants and freemen, or such number of them as aforesayd, and published in writinge, under theire common seale, shall bee carefully and duely observed,

kept, performed and putt in execution, accordinge to the true intent and meaning of the same. [Thorpe 3215–3216]

[3] And these our letters patent, or the duplicate or exempliffication thereof, shall bee to all and everie such officer, superiour or inferiour, from tyme to tyme, for the putting of the same *orders,* lawes, statutes, ordinances, instructions and directions, in due execution, against us, oure heires and successours, a sufficient warrant and discharge. . . . [Thorpe 3216]

New Jersey Proprietors, Concession and Agreement, February 10, 1664:

That all persons that are or shall become subjects of the King of England, and swear, or subscribe allegiance to the King, and faithfulness to the lords, shall be admitted to plant and become freemen of the said Province, and enjoy the freedoms and immunities hereafter express'd, until some stop or contradiction be made by us the Lords, or else the Governor, Council and Assembly, which shall be in force until the Lords see cause to the contrary: provided that such stop shall not any ways prejudice the right or continuance of any person that have been receiv'd before such stop or *orders* come from the General Assembly. [Thorpe 2536]

Carolina Proprietors, Concessions and Agreements, 1665:

[Article 7:] That all persons that are or shalbecome subjects to the King of England and sware or subscribe allegiance to the King and faithfulness to the Lords as above shalbe admitted to plant and become freemen of the Province and enjoy the freedomes and Immunities hereafter exprest until some stop or Contradiccon be made by us the Lords or else by the Governor Councill and Assembly wch shalbe in force untill the Lords see Cause to the Contrary provided yt such stop shall not anywayes prejudice ye right or Continewance of any person that hath beene recd before such stop or *order* come from the Lords or Genll Assembly. [Thorpe 2757]

Fundamental Constitutions of Carolina, March 1, 1669:

[Section 33:] . . . This court [the palatine's court] shall have power to call parliaments, to pardon all offences, to make elections of all officers in the proprietors dispose, and to nominate and appoint port towns; and also shall have power by their *order* to the treasurer to dispose of all public treasure, excepting money granted by the parliament, and by them directed to some particular public use; and also shall have a negative upon all acts, *orders,* votes, and judgments of the grand council and the parliament, except only as in sections six and twelve . . . [Thorpe 2776]

[Section 50:] The grand council shall consist of the palatine and seven proprietors, and the forty-two councillors of the several proprietors' courts, who shall have power to determine any controversy that may arise between any of the proprietors' courts, about their respective jurisdictions, or between the members of the same court, about their manner and methods of proceedings; to make peace and war, leagues, treaties, &c., with any of the neighbor Indians; to issue out their general *orders* to the constable's and admiral's courts, for the raising, disposing, or disbanding the forces, by land or by sea. [Thorpe 2778–79]

[Section 76:] No act or *order* of parliament shall be of any force, unless it be ratified in open parliament, during the same session, by the palatine or his deputy, and three more of the lords proprietors or their deputies; and then not to continue longer in force but until the next biennial parliament, unless in the mean time it be ratified under the hands and seals of the palatine himself, and three more of the lords proprietors themselves, and by their *order* published at the next biennial parliament. [Thorpe 2781–82]

Charles II, Commission Constituting a President and Council for New Hampshire, September 18, 1680:

. . . And Our Will & pleasure is, That Our said Councell shall from time to time have & use such Seal only, for ye sealing of their Acts, *Orders* & proceedings, as shall be sent unto them by Us, Our heirs & successors, for yt purpose. . . . [Thorpe 2447]

Government of West New Jersey, November 25, 1681:

In testimony whereof I have hereunto put my hand and seal, the day and year above written. SAMUEL JENNINGS, Deputy Governor.

Thomas Ollive, Speaker, to the General Free Assembly per *order* and in the name of the whole Assembly. [Thorpe 2567]

Pennsylvania Frame of Government, Laws Agreed Upon in England, May 5, 1682:

[Article 40:] That all other matters and things not herein provided for, which shall, and may, concern the public justice, peace or safety of the said province; and the raising and imposing taxes, customs, duties, or other charges whatsoever, shall be, and are, hereby referred to the *order,* prudence and determination of the Governor and freemen, in provincial Council and General Assembly, to be held, from time to time, in the said province. [Thorpe 3063]

Fundamental Constitutions of East New Jersey, 1683

It shall be the priviledge of every member of the great Council, to propose any bill in *order* to a law, which being admitted to be debated, shall be determined by the vote, wherein two parts of three shall only conclude; but of this twelve of the Proprietors, or their proxies, must be assenting; which shall also be requisite after the number of freemen are double . . . [Thorpe 2575]

William and Mary, Charter of Massachusetts Bay, October 7, 1691:

[1] . . . And we doe further for us our Heires and Successors Give and Grant to the said Governor and the great and Generall Court or Assembly of our said Province or Territory for the time being full Power and Authority from time to time to make ordaine and establish all manner of wholesome and reasonable *Orders* Laws Statutes and Ordinances Directions and Instructions either with penalties or without (soe as the same be not repugnant or contrary to the Lawes of this our Realme of England) as they shall Judge to be for the good and welfare of our said Province or Territory And for the Government and Ordering thereof and of the People Inhabiting or who shall Inhabit the same and for the necessary support and Defence of the Government thereof. [Thorpe 1882]

[2] . . . And for the better secureing and maintaining Liberty of Conscience hereby granted to all persons at any time being and resideing within our said Province or Territory as aforesaid Willing Comanding and Requireing and by these presents for us Our heires and Successors Ordaining and appointing that all such *Orders* Lawes Statutes and Ordinances Instructions and Directions as shall be soe made and published under our Seale of our said Province or Territory shall be Carefully and duely observed kept and performed and put in Execution according to the true intent and meaning of these presents Provided alwaies and Wee doe by these presents for us Our Heires and Successors Establish and Ordaine that in the frameing and passing of all such *Orders* Laws Statutes and Ordinances and in all Elections and Acts of Government whatsoever to be passed made or done by the said Generall Court or Assembly or in Councill the Governor of our said Province or Territory of the Massachusetts Bay in New England for the time being shall have the Negative voice and that without his consent or Approbation signified and declared in Writeing no such *Orders* Laws Statutes Ordinances Elections or other Acts of Government whatsoever soe to be made passed or done by the said Generall Assembly or in Councill shall be of any Force effect or validity anything herein contained to the contrary in anywise notwithstanding. [Thorpe 1883]

[3] And wee doe for us Our Heires and Successors Establish and Ordaine that the said *Orders* Laws Statutes and Ordinances be by the first opportunity after the makeing thereof sent or Transmitted unto us Our Heires and Successors under the Publique Seale to be appointed by us for Our or their approbation or Disallowance . . . [Thorpe 1883]

[4] . . . Provided alwais that incase Wee our Heires or Successors shall not within the Terme of Three Yeares after the presenting of such *Orders* Lawes Statutes or Ordinances as aforesaid signifie our or their Disallowance of the same Then

the said *orders* Lawes Statutes or Ordinances shall be and continue in full force and effect according to the true Intent and meaneing of the same untill the Expiracon thereof or that the same shall be Repealed by the Generall Assembly of our said Province for the time being . . . [Thorpe 1883]

William Penn, Charter of Privileges for Pennsylvania, October 28, 1701:

[Section 2:] . . . Which Assembly shall have Power to chuse a Speaker and other their Officers; and shall be Judges of the Qualifications and Elections of their own Members; sit upon their own Adjournments; appoint Committees; prepare Bills in *order* to pass into Laws; impeach Criminals, and redress Grievances; and shall have all other Powers and Privileges of an Assembly, according to the Rights of the free-born Subjects of England, and as is usual in any of the King's Plantations in America. [Thorpe 3078]

This Charter of Privileges being distinctly read in Assembly; and the whole and every Part thereof, being approved of and agreed to, by us, we do thankfully receive the same from our Proprietary and Governor at Philadelphia, this Twenty-Eighth Day of October, One Thousand Seven Hundred and One. Signed on Behalf, and by *Order* of the Assembly, per JOSEPH GROWDON, Speaker. [Thorpe 3081]

George I, Explanatory Charter of Massachusetts Bay, August 26, 1725:

. . . And did thereby also for themselves their Heires and Successors Provide Establish and Ordain that in the Framing and Passing of all *Orders* laws Statutes and Ordinances and in all Eleccons and Acts of Government whatsoever to be passed made or done by the said General Court or Assembly or in Council the Governor of the said Province or Territory of the Massachusetts Bay in New England for the time being should have the Negative Voice and that without his Consent or Approbacon Signified and Declared in writing no such *Orders* laws Statutes Ordinances Eleccons or other Acts of Government whatsoever so to be made passed or done by the said General Assembly or in Council should be of any force Effect or Validity any thing therein contained to the contrary in any wise notwithstanding . . . [Thorpe 1887]

George II, Charter of Georgia, June 9, 1732:

[1] . . . And we do hereby, for us, our heirs and successors, give and grant unto the said corporation, and their successors, full power and authority to constitute, or make, such and so many by-laws, constitutions, *orders* and ordinances, as to them, or the greater part of them, at their general meeting for that purpose, shall seem necessary and convenient for the well ordaining and governing of the

said corporation; and the said by-laws, constitutions, *orders* and ordinances, or any of them, to alter and annul, as they or the major part of them then present shall see requisite: and in and by such by-laws, rules, *orders* and ordinances, to sell, impose and inflict, reasonable pains and penalties upon offender or offenders, who shall transgress, break or violate the said by-laws, constitutions, *orders* and ordinances, so made as aforesaid, and to mitigate the same as they or the major part of them present shall find cause, which said gains and penalties, shall and may be levied, sued for, taken, retained and recovered, by the said corporation and their successors, by their officers and servants, from time to time, to be appointed for that purpose, by action of debt, or by any other lawful ways or means, to the use and behoof of the said corporation and their successors, all and singular: which by-laws, constitutions, *orders* and ordinances, so as aforesaid to be made, we will shall be duly observed and kept, under the pains and penalties therein to be contained, so always, as the said by-laws, constitutions, *orders,* and ordinances, pains and penalties, from time to time to be made and imposed, be reasonable and not contrary or repugnant to the laws or statutes of this our realm . . . [Thorpe 770]

[2] . . . And that all and every person or persons, who shall at any time hereafter inhabit or reside within our said province, shall be, and are hereby declared to be free, and shall not be subject to or be bound to obey any laws, *orders,* statutes or constitutions, which have been heretofore made, *ordered* or enacted by, for, or as, the laws, *orders,* statutes or constitutions of our said province of South-Carolina, (save and except only the commander in chief of the militia, of our said province of Georgia, to our governor for the time being of South-Carolina, in manner hereafter declared;) but shall be subject to, and bound to obey, such laws, *orders,* statutes and constitutions as shall from time to time be made, *ordered* and enacted, for the better government of the said province of Georgia, in the manner hereinafter declared. [Thorpe 771–72]

The Albany Plan of Union, July 10, 1754:

[1] That they [the Grand Council] may appoint a General Treasurer and Particular Treasurer in each government, when necessary; and from time to time may *order* the sums in the treasuries of each government into the general treasury, or draw on them for special payments, as they find most convenient. [Thorpe 85]

[2] Yet no money to issue but by joint *orders* of the President-General and Grand Council; except where sums have been appropriated to particular purposes, and the President-General is previously empowered by an act to draw such sums. [Thorpe 85]

[3] Each Colony May Defend Itself On Emergency, &c, That the particular military as well as civil establishments in each colony remain in their present state, the general constitution notwithstanding; and that on sudden emergencies any colony may defend itself, and lay the accounts of expense thence arising

before the President-General and General Council, who may allow and *order* payment of the same, as far as they judge such accounts just and reasonable.
[Thorpe 86]

New Hampshire Constitution, January 5, 1776:

And it is further resolved, That if the present unhappy dispute with Great Britain should continue longer than this present year, and the Continental Congress give no instruction or direction to the contrary, the Council be chosen by the people of each respective county in such manner as the Council and house of Representatives shall *order*. [Thorpe 2452]

South Carolina Constitution, March 26, 1776:

By *order* of the congress, March 26, 1776.
WILLIAM HENRY DRAYTON President. Attested: PETER TIMOTHY, Secretary. [Thorpe 3248]

New Jersey Constitution, July 2, 1776:

In Provincial Congress, New Jersey, Burlington. July 2, 1776. By *order* of Congress.
SAMUEL TUCKER, Pres. WILLIAM PATTERSON, Secretary.
[Thorpe 2598]

Pennsylvania Constitution, September 28, 1776:

[Frame of Government, Section 47, on the Council of Censors:] . . . And whose duty it shall be to enquire whether the constitution has been preserved inviolate in every part; and whether the legislative and executive branches of government have performed their duty as guardians of the people, or assumed to themselves, or exercised other or greater powers than they are intitled to by the constitution. They are also to enquire whether the public taxes have been justly laid and collected in all parts of this commonwealth, in what manner the public monies have been disposed of, and whether the laws have been duly executed. For these purposes they shall have power to send for persons, papers, and records; they shall have authority to pass public censures, to *order* impeachments, and to recommend to the legislature the repealing such laws as appear to them to have been enacted contrary to the principles of the constitution. . . .
[Thorpe 3091–92]

Passed in Convention the 28th day of September, 1776, and signed by their *order*. BENJ. FRANKLIN, Prest. [Thorpe 3092]

Maryland Constitution, November 11, 1776:

[Declaration of Rights:] This Declaration of Rights was assented to, and passed, in Convention of the Delegates of the freemen of Maryland, begun and held at Annapolis, the 14th day of August, A. D. 1776.

By *order* of the Convention. MAT. TILGHMAN, President. [Thorpe 1691]

[Form of Government, Article 12:] . . . They [the House of Delegates] may also punish, by imprisonment, any person who shall be guilty of a breach of privilege, by arresting on civil process, or by assaulting any of their members, during their sitting, or on their way to, or return from, the house of delegates, or by any assault of, or obstruction to their officers, in the execution of any *order* or process, or by assaulting or obstructing any witness, or any other person, attending on, or on their way to or from the house, or by rescuing any person committed by the house; and the senate may exercise the same power in similar cases. [Thorpe 1693]

This Form of Government was assented to, and passed in Convention of the Delegates of the freemen of Maryland, begun and held at the city of Annapolis, the fourteenth of August, A. D. one thousand seven hundred and seventy-six.

By *order* of the Convention. M. TILGHMAN, President. [Thorpe 1701]

North Carolina Constitution, December 18, 1776:

December the eighteenth, one thousand seven hundred and seventy-six, read the third time, and ratified in open Congress.

By *order,* JAMES GREEN, jun. secretary. [Thorpe 2794]

Georgia Constitution, February 5, 1777:

[Article 63:] No alteration shall be made in this constitution without petitions from a majority of the counties, and the petitions from each county to be signed by a majority of voters in each county within this State; at which time the assembly shall *order* a convention to be called for that purpose, specifying the alterations to be made, according to the petitions preferred to the assembly by the majority of the counties as aforesaid. [Thorpe 785]

New York Constitution, April 20, 1777:

[Article 42:] And this convention doth further, in the name and by the authority of the good people of this State, ordain, determine, and declare that it shall be in the discretion of the legislature to naturalize all such persons, and in such manner, as they shall think proper: Provided, All such of the persons so to be by them naturalized, as being born in parts beyond sea, and out of the United States of America, shall come to settle in and become subjects of this State, shall take an oath of allegiance to this State, and abjure and renounce all allegiance and subjection to all and every foreign king, prince, potentate, and State in all matters, ecclesiastical as well as civil.

By *order*. LEONARD GANSEVOORT, President pro tempore.

[Thorpe 2637–38]

Vermont Constitution, July 8, 1777:

[Frame of Government, Section 44:] . . . For these purposes they [the Council of Censors] shall have power to send for persons, papers and records; they shall have authority to pass public censures—to *order* impeachments, and to recommend to the legislature the repealing such laws as appear to them to have been enacted contrary to the principles of the constitution. . . .

[Thorpe 3748–49]

United States Articles of Confederation, November 15, 1777:

[Article IX:] . . . The united states in congress assembled shall also be the last resort on appeal in all disputes and differences now subsisting or that hereafter may arise between two or more states concerning boundary, jurisdiction or any other cause whatever; which authority shall always be exercised in the manner following. Whenever the legislative or executive authority or lawful agent of any state in controversy with another shall present a petition to congress, stating the matter in question and praying for a hearing, notice thereof shall be given by *order* of congress to the legislative or executive authority of the other state in controversy, and a day assigned for the appearance of the parties by their lawful agents, who shall then be directed to appoint by joint consent, commissioners or judges to constitute a court for hearing and determining the matter in question . . .

Massachusetts Constitution, March 2, 1780:

[Frame of Government, Chapter I:1:4:] And further, full power and authority are hereby given and granted to the said general court, from time to time, to make, ordain, and establish, all manner of wholesome and reasonable *orders*, laws, statutes, and ordinances, directions and instructions, either with penalties or without; so as the same be not repugnant or contrary to this constitution, as they shall judge to be for the good and welfare of this commonwealth, and for the government and ordering thereof, and of the subjects of the same, and for the necessary support and defence of the government thereof . . .

[Thorpe 1894]

[*Ibid.*:] . . . And while the public charges of government, or any part thereof, shall be assessed on polls and estates, in the manner that has hitherto been practised, in order that such assessments may be made with equality, there shall be a valuation of estates within the commonwealth, taken anew once in every ten years at least, and as much oftener as the general court shall *order*. [Thorpe 1895]

[Chapter I:3:10:] The house of representatives shall be the judge of the returns, elections, and qualifications of its own members, as pointed out in the constitution; shall choose their own speaker; appoint their own officers, and settle the rules and *orders* of proceeding in their own house. They shall have authority to punish by imprisonment every person, not a member, who shall be guilty of disrespect to the house, by any disorderly or contemptuous behavior in its presence; or who, in the town where the general court is sitting, and during the time of its sitting, shall threaten harm to the body or estate of any of its members, for any thing said or done in the house; or who shall assault any of them therefor; or who shall assault, or arrest, any witness, or other person, *ordered* to attend the house, in his way in going or returning; or who shall rescue any person arrested by the order of the house. [Thorpe 1899]

United States Confederation Congress, Ordinance for the Government of the West, April 23, 1784:

That the settlers on any territory so purchased and offered for sale, shall, either on their own petition, or on the *order* of Congress, receive authority from them, with appointments of time and place for their free males of full age, within the limits of their state, to meet together, for the purpose of establishing a temporary government, to adopt the constitution and laws of any one of the original states; so that such laws nevertheless shall be subject to alteration by their ordinary legislature . . . [DHRC1 151]

New Hampshire Constitution, June 2, 1784:

[Form of Government:] And farther, full power and authority are hereby given and granted to the said general court, from time to time, to make, ordain and establish, all manner of wholesome and reasonable *orders*, laws, statutes, ordinances, directions and instructions, either with penalties or without; so as the same be not repugnant, or contrary to this constitution, as they may judge for the benefit and welfare of this state, and for the governing and ordering thereof, and of the subjects of the same, for the necessary support and defence of the government thereof . . . [Thorpe 2458]

[*Ibid.*:] And while the public charges of government or any part thereof, shall be assessed on polls and estates in the manner that has heretofore been practiced; in order that such assessments may be made with equality, there shall be a valuation of the estates within the state taken anew once in every five years at least, and as much oftener as the general court shall *order*. [Thorpe 2459]

[*Ibid.*:] And the several counties in this state, shall, until the general court shall *order* otherwise, be districts for the election of senators, and shall elect the following number . . . [Thorpe 2459]

[*Ibid.*:] . . . They [the House of Representatives] shall have authority to punish by imprisonment, every person who shall be guilty of disrespect to the house in its presence, by any disorderly or contemptuous behaviour, or by threatening, or ill treating any of its members; or by obstructing its deliberations; every person guilty of a breach of its privileges in making arrests for debt, or by assaulting any member during his attendance at any session; in assaulting or disturbing any one of its offices in the execution of any *order* or procedure of the house, in assaulting any witness, or other person; *ordered* to attend by and during his attendance of the house, or in rescuing any person arrested by *order* of the house, knowing them to be such. . . . [Thorpe 2462]

Vermont Constitution, July 4, 1786:

[Frame of Government, Section 40 on Council of Censors:] . . . For these purposes, they shall have power to send for persons, papers, and records; they shall have authority to pass public censures—to *order* impeachments—and to recommend to the Legislature the repealing such laws as appear to them to have been enacted contrary to the principles of the Constitution . . . [Thorpe 3761]

Virginia Assembly Proceedings, October 25, 1787:

The House according to the *order* of the day resolved itself into a committee of the whole House on the report of the Foederal Convention lately held at Philadelphia, and after some time spent therein, Mr. Speaker resumed the chair, and Mr. Mathews reported that the committee had, according to *order,* had the said report under their consideration, and gone through the same, and come to several resolutions thereupon, which he read in his place, and afterwards delivered in at the clerk's table, where the same were again read . . . [DHRC8 112]

Pelatiah Webster, *The Weakness of Brutus Exposed*, November 14, 1787:

The most despotic monarch that can exist, must have his councils, and officers of state; and I can't see any one circumstance of their being appointed under a monarchy, that can afford any chance of their being any wiser or better, than ours may be. 'Tis true indeed, the despot may, if he pleases, act without any advice at all; but when he does so, I conceive it will be very rare that the nation will receive greater advantages from his unadvised edicts, than may be drawed from the deliberate acts and *orders* of our supreme powers. . . . [Ford 130]

Virginia Assembly Proceedings, December 4, 1787:

Mr. Henry presented according to *order,* a bill Concerning the convention to be held in June next, and the same was received and read the first time, and *ordered* to [be] read a second time. [DHRC8 186]

Virginia Assembly Proceedings, December 8, 1787:

Be it therefor enacted that a sum of money not exceeding———pounds shall be preserved in the Treasury subject to the *order* and disposal of the Convention appointed to meet in the City of Richmond on the first Munday in June next for defraying the expences of the Members thereof or any other expences as beforementioned and that Such money shall be made good from the funds now appropriated or which may hereafter be appropriated to the support of Civil Government and provided the said fund should by any means prove deficient then such deficiency shall be made good from any unappropriated money in the Treasury. [DHRC8 189]

Virginia Assembly, Act Concerning the State Convention, December 12, 1787:

[Section 4:] Be it therefore enacted, That a sum of money not exceeding eight thousand pounds shall be reserved in the treasury subject to the *order* and disposal of the Convention appointed to meet in the city of Richmond on the first Monday in June next, for defraying the expences of the members thereof, or any other expences as before mentioned, and that such money shall be made good from the funds now appropriated, or which may hereafter be appropriated, to the support of civil government; and provided the said fund should by any means prove deficient, then such deficiency shall be made good from any unappropriated money in the treasury. [DHRC8 191]

George Washington, First Inaugural Address, April 30, 1789:

Among the vicissitudes incident to life no event could have filled me with greater anxieties than that of which the notification was transmitted by your [Congress's] *order,* and received on the 14th day of the present month. On the one hand, I was summoned by my country, whose voice I can never hear but with veneration and love, from a retreat which I had chosen with the fondest predilection, and, in my flattering hopes, with an immutable decision, as the asylum of my declining years . . . [Annals 27]

Georgia Constitution, May 6, 1789:

[Article II, Section 11:] The great seal of the State shall be deposited in the office of the secretary, and it shall not be affixed to any instrument of writing without it be by *order* of the governor or general assembly; and the general assembly may direct the great seal to be altered. [Thorpe 788]

South Carolina Constitution, June 3, 1790:

[Article I, Section 13:] Each house may punish, by imprisonment, during sitting, any person not a member, who shall be guilty of disrespect to the house, by any disorderly or contemptuous behavior in its presence, or who, during the time of its sitting, shall threaten harm to the body or estate of any member, for anything said or done in either house, or who shall assault any of them therefor, or who shall assault or arrest any witness, or other person, *ordered* to attend the house, in his going to or returning there from, or who shall rescue any person arrested by the order of the House. [Thorpe 3260]

Done in convention at Columbia, in the State of South Carolina, the third day of June, in the year of our Lord 1790, and in the fourteenth year of the Independence of the United States of America.

By the unanimous *order* of the convention. CHARLES PINCKNEY, President. [Thorpe 3265]

Pennsylvania Constitution, September 2, 1790:

[Article I, Section 23:] Every *order,* resolution, or vote to which the concurrence of both houses may be necessary (except on a question of adjournment) shall be presented to the governor, and, before it shall take effect, be approved by him, or, being disapproved, shall be repassed by two-thirds of both houses, according to the rules and limitations prescribed in case of a bill.

[Thorpe 3095]

PARDON, PARDONS

United States Constitution, September 17, 1787:

[Article II, Section 2:] The President shall be Commander in Chief of the Army and Navy of the United States, and of the Militia of the several States, when called into the actual Service of the United States; he may require the Opinion, in writing, of the principal Officer in each of the executive Departments, upon any Subject relating to the Duties of their respective Offices, and he shall have Power to grant Reprieves and *Pardons* for Offenses against the United States, except in Cases of Impeachment.

* * * * *

Magna Carta, June 15, 1215:

And all ill-will, grudges, and anger sprung up betweeen us [*i.e.*, King John] and our men, clergy and laymen, from the time of the dispute, we have fully renounced and *pardoned* to all. . . . [SDECH 52]

Elizabeth I, Letters Patent to Sir Humphrey Gilbert, June 11, 1578:

. . . wee for us, our heires and successours are likewise pleased and contented, and by these presents doe give and graunt to the sayd sir Humfrey and his heires and assignes for ever, that he and they, and every or any of them, shall and may, from time to time, for ever hereafter within the sayd mentioned remote lands and countreys, and in the way by the Seas thither, and from thence, have full and meere power and authoritie to correct, punish, *pardon,* governe and rule by their, and every or any of their good discretions and policies, as well in causes capitall or criminall, as civill, both marine and other, all such our subjects and others, as shall from time to time hereafter adventure themselves in the sayd journeys or voyages habitative or possessive, or that shall at any time hereafter inhabite any such lands, countreys or territories as aforesayd . . . [Thorpe 51]

Elizabeth I, Charter to Sir Walter Raleigh, March 25, 1584:

. . . we for us, our heires and successors, are likewise pleased and contented, and by these presents do give and graunt to the said Walter Ralegh, his heires and assignes for ever, that hee and they, and every or any of them, shall and may from time to time for ever hereafter, within the said mentioned remote landes and Countreis in the way by the seas thither, and from thence, have full and meere power and authoritie to correct, punish, *pardon,* governe, and rule by their and every or any of their good discretions and pollicies, as well in causes capital, or criminall, as civil, both marine and other, all such our subjects as shall from time to time adventure themselves in the said journies or voyages, or that shall at any time hereafter inhabite any such landes, countreis, or territories as aforesaide . . . [Thorpe 55]

James I, Second Charter of Virginia, May 23, 1609:

. . . We for Us, our Heirs, and Successors are likewise pleased and contented, and by these Presents do Give and Grant unto the said Treasurer and Company, and their Successors, and to such Governors, Officers, and Ministers, as shall be by our said Council constituted and appointed according to the Natures and Limits of their Offices and Places respectively, that they shall and may from Time to Time, for ever hereafter, within the said Precincts of Virginia, or in the way by Seas thither and from thence, have full and absolute Power and Authority to correct, punish, *pardon,* govern, and rule all such the Subjects of Us, our Heires, and Successors as shall from Time to Time adventure themselves in any Voyage thither, or that shall at any Time hereafter, inhabit in the Precincts and Territories of the said Colony as aforesaid . . . [Thorpe 3801]

James I, The Charter of New England, November 3, 1620:

. . . Wee, for Us, our Heires and Successors, are likewise pleased and contented, and by these Presents do give and grant unto the said Council and their Successors, and to such Governors, Officers, and Ministers, as shall be by the said Councill constituted and appointed according to the natures and Limitts of their Offices and Places respectively, that they shall and may, from time to time for ever heerafter, within the said Precincts of New-England, or in the Way by the Seas thither, and from thence have full and absolute Power and Authority to correct, punish, *pardon,* governe, and rule all such the Subjects of Us, our Heires and Successors, as shall from time to time adventure themselves in any Voyage thither . . . [Thorpe 1833]

Charles I, Patent to Sir Robert Heath, October 30, 1629:

. . . And also to the said Sr. Robert Heath his heires & assignes as to them shall seem most meet power of constituting & ordaining Judges & Justices Magestrates

& officers whatsoever for whatsoever causes and with what power soever & in what forme by sea or by land. Alsoe crimes & all excesses whatsoever against such lawes either before judgement received or after, power of remitting releasing *pardoning* & abolishing . . . [Thorpe 71]

Charles I, Charter of Maryland, June 20, 1632:

[Article 7:] [We grant the Proprietor power] to constitute and ordain Judges, Justices, Magistrates and Officers of what kind, for what Cause and with what Power soever, within that Land, and the Sea of those Parts, and in such form as to the said now Baron of Baltimore, or his Heirs, shall seem most fitting; And also to Remit, Release, *Pardon,* and Abolish, all Crimes and Offences whatsoever against such Laws, whether before, or after Judgment passed . . . [Thorpe 1680]

Charles I, Grant of the Province of Maine, April 3, 1639:

. . . And Wee Doe further for us our heires and successors give and graunte unto the said Sir Fardinando Gorges his heires and assignes full power and authoritie to *pardon* remitt and release all offences and offendors within the said province and Premisses against all every or any the said Lawes Ordynances or Constitucons . . . [Thorpe 1629]

Charles II, Charter of Connecticut, April 23, 1662:

[Governor and Company shall have power] for Imposition of lawful Fines, Mulcts, Imprisonment or other Punishment upon Offenders and Delinquents according to the Course of other Corporations within this our Kingdom of England, and the same Laws, Fines, Mulcts and Executions, to alter, change, revoke, annul, release, or *pardon* under their Common Seal, as by the said General Assembly, or the major Part of them shall be thought fit . . . [Thorpe 534]

Charles II, Charter of Carolina, March 24, 1663:

[The Proprietors shall have power] . . . also, to remit, release, *pardon* and abolish (whether before judgment or after) all crimes and offences whatsoever, against the said laws, and to do all and every other thing and things, which unto the compleat establishment of justice unto courts, sessions, and forms of judicature and manners of proceedings therein do belong, although in these presents express mention be not made thereof . . . [Thorpe 2746]

Charles II, Charter of Rhode Island, July 8, 1663:

[1] . . . but that all and everye person and persons may, from tyme to tyme, and at all tymes hereafter, freelye and fullye have and enjoye his and theire owne

judgments and consciences, in matters of religious concernments, throughout the tract of lande hereafter mentioned; they behaving themselves peaceablie and quietlie, and not useing this libertie to lycentiousnesse and profanenesse, nor to the civill injurye or outward disturbeance of others; any lawe, statute, or clause, therein contayned, or to bee contayned, usage or custome of this realme, to the contrary hereof, in any wise, notwithstanding. And that they may bee in the better capacity to defend themselves, in theire just rights and libertyes against all the enemies of the Christian faith, and others, in all respects, wee have further thought fit, and at the humble petition of the persons aforesayd are gratiously pleased to declare, That they shall have and enjoye the benefitt of our late act of indempnity and free *pardon,* as the rest of our subjects in other our dominions and territoryes have; and to create and makc them a bodye politique or corporate, with the powers and priviledges hereinafter mentioned. [Thorpe 3213]

[2] . . . [The Governor and Company shall have power] alsoe to order, direct and authorize the imposing of lawfull and reasonable fynes, mulcts, imprisonments, and executing other punishments pecuniary and corporal, upon offenders and delinquents, according to the course of other corporations within this oure kingdom of England; and agayne to alter, revoke, annull or *pardon,* under their common seale or otherwyse, such fynes, mulcts, imprisonments, sentences, judgments and condemnations, as shall bee thought fitt . . . [Thorpe 3215]

New Jersey Proprietors, Concession and Agreement, February 10, 1664:

[Article 5:] [The Governor and Council shall have power] Where they see cause, after condemnation, to repreive until the case be presented, with a copy of the whole tryal, proceeding and proofs to the Lords, who will accordingly *pardon* or command execution of the sentence of the offender; who is in mean time to be kept in safe custody till the pleasure of the Lords be known. [Thorpe 2540]

Charles II, Grant of the Province of Maine to the Duke of York, March 12, 1664:

. . . and wee do further of our speciall grace certaine knowledge and meere mocon for us our heires and successors give and grant unto our said dearest brother James Duke of Yorke his heires deputyes agents commissioners and assignes by these presents full and absolute power and authority to correct punish *pardon* governe and rule all such the subjects of us our heires and successors who may from time to time adventure themselves into any of the parts or places aforesaid . . . [Thorpe 1638]

Carolina Proprietors, Concessions and Agreements, 1665:

Item where they see cause after condemnacon [the Governor and Council shall have power] to reprieve untill the Case may be presented with a Copy of ye

whole tryall proceedings and proofes to ye Lords who will accordingly eather *pardon* or comand execution of ye sentence on the offender who is in ye meane time to be kept in safe custody till the pleasure of ye Lords be knowne.
[Thorpe 2760–61]

Charles II, Charter of Carolina, June 30, 1665:

. . . And also, [the Proprietors shall have power] to remit, release, *pardon,* and abolish, whether before judgment or after, all crimes and offences whatsoever against the said laws . . . [Thorpe 2764]

Fundamental Constitutions of Carolina, March 1, 1669:

[Article 33:] The palatine's court shall consist of the palatine and seven proprietors, wherein nothing shall be acted without the presence and consent of the palatine or his deputy, and three other of the proprietors, or their deputies. This court shall have power to call parliaments, to *pardon* all offences, to make elections of all officers in the proprietors dispose, and to nominate and appoint port towns . . . [Thorpe 2776]

Charles II, Grant of the Province of Maine to the Duke of York, June 29, 1674:

. . . and wee do further, of our speciall grace certaine knowledge and meer motion for Us Our heirs and successors give and graunt unto our said Dearest brother James Duke of Yorke his heirs Deputyes Agents commissioners and assignes by these presents full and absolute power and authority to correct punish *pardon* govern and rule all such the subjects of us our heirs and successors or any other person or persons as shall from time to time adventure themselves into any of the parts or places aforesaid . . . [Thorpe 1641–42]

Fundamental Constitutions of West New Jersey, 1676:

[Chapter 21:] That all and every prson and persons whatsoever, who shall prosecute or prefer any indictment or information against others for any personal injuries, or matter criminal, or shall prosecute for any other criminal cause, (treason, murther, and felony, only excepted) shall and and may be master of his own process, and have full power to forgive and remit the person or persons offending against him or herself only, as well before as after judgment, and condemnation, and *pardon* and remit the sentence, fine and punishment of the person or persons offending, be it personal or other whatsoever. [Thorpe 2551]

New Jersey Proprietors, Deed of Revision, July 1, 1676:

. . . in and by which said Letters Patent his said Majesty did likewise give and grant unto his said dearest brother James Duke of York, his heirs, deputies, agents commissioners and assigns, full and absolute power and authority for the correcting, punishing, *pardoning,* governing and ruling such of the subjects of his said Majesty, of his heirs and successors, as shall at any time adventure themselves into the said port and places, or inhabit there, according to such laws, orders, ordinances, directions and instructions, as by his said Majesty's said dearest brother, or his assigns, shall be established . . . [Thorpe 2552–53]

Duke of York, Grant of West New Jersey, August 6, 1680:

. . . and for the making, ordaining, and executing of necessary and convenient laws and constitutions, in order to such government, and the punishing and *pardoning* offences, and offenders, as occasion shall require . . . [Thorpe 2563]

Charles II, Charter of Pennsylvania, February 28, 1681:

And wee doe likewise give and grant unto the said William Penn, and his heires, and to his and their Deputies and Lieutenants, full power and authoritie . . . Also to remitt, release, *pardon,* and abolish whether before Judgement or after all Crimes and Offences whatsoever comitted within the said Countrey against the said Lawes, Treason and wilful and malitious Murder onely excepted, and in those Cases to grant Reprieves, until Our pleasure may bee known therein . . . [Thorpe 3037–38]

Duke of York, Confirmation to the New Jersey Proprietors, March 14, 1682:

. . . and for the making, ordaining and executing of necessary and convenient laws and constitutions, in order to such government; and the punishing and *pardoning* offences and offenders, as occasion shall require . . . [Thorpe 2571]

Fundamental Constitutions of East New Jersey, 1683:

[Article 10:] Forasmuch as by the Patent, the power of *pardoning* in capital offences, is vested in the four and twenty Proprietors; it is hereby declared, that the said power of *pardoning* shall never be made use of but by the consent of eighteen of the Proprietors, or their proxies: Nevertheless, it shall be in the power of the Governor, in conjunction with four Proprietors, who for the time are judges of the Court of Appeals, to reprieve any person after the day of execution appointed, for some time, not exceeding a month. [Thorpe 2578]

James II, Commission to Sir Edmund Andros for the Dominion of New England, April 7, 1688:

And Wee do hereby give and graunt unto you full power where you shall see cause and shall judge an offender or offenders in capitall and criminall matters, or for any fines or forfeitures due unto us, fit objects of our mercy, to *pardon* such offenders and to remit such fines & forfeitures, treason and wilfull murder only excepted, in which case you shall likewise have power upon extraordinary occasions to grant reprieves to the offenders therein untill and to the intent our pleasure may be further known. [Thorpe 1866]

English Bill of Rights, December 16, 1689:

Provided that no charter or grant or *pardon,* granted before the three and twentieth day of October in the year of our Lord one thousand six hundred eighty-nine, shall be any ways impeached or invalidated by this act, but that the same shall be and remain of the same force and effect in law and no other than as if this Act had never been made. [SDECH 469]

New Jersey Proprietors, Surrender of Rights, April 15, 1702:

[1] . . . And by the same Letters Patents the late King Charles the Second, for himself, his heirs and successors, did give and grant to the said James Duke of York, his heirs, deputies, agents, commissioners and assigns, full and absolute power and authority to correct, punish, *pardon,* govern and rule all such subjects of the said King his heirs and successors, as should from time to time adventure themselves into the parts and places aforesaid, or that should at any time then after inhabit within the same, according to such laws, orders, ordinances, directions and instructions as by the said Duke of York, or his assigns, should be established . . . [Thorpe 2586]

[2] ..these the said powers and authorities to correct, punish, *pardon,* govern and rule all or any of her Majesty's subjects or others, who now inhabit or hereafter shall adventure into or inhabit within the said Provinces of East Jersey, and West Jersey, or either of them . . . [Thorpe 2588]

John Adams, *Thoughts on Government*, April 1776:

The Governor should have the command of the militia, and of all your armies. The power of *pardons* should be with the Governor and Council. [PJA4 90]

Virginia Constitution, June 29, 1776:

. . . But he [the Governor] shall, with the advice of the Council of State, have the power of granting reprieves or *pardons,* except where the prosecution shall have been carried on by the House of Delegates, or the law shall otherwise particularly direct; in which cases, no reprieve or *pardon* shall be granted, but by resolve of the House of Delegates. [Thorpe 3817]

New Jersey Constitution, July 2, 1776:

[Article 9:] That the Governor and Council, (seven whereof shall be a quorum) be the Court of Appeals, in the last resort, in all clauses of law, as heretofore; and that they possess the power of granting *pardons* to criminals, after condemnation, in all cases of treason, felony, or other offences. [Thorpe 2596]

Delaware Constitution, September 10, 1776:

[Article 7:] . . . he [the Governor] shall have the power of granting *pardons* or reprieves, except where the prosecution shall be carried on by the house of assembly, or the law shall otherwise direct, in which cases no *pardon* or reprieve shall be granted, but by a resolve of the house of assembly, and may exercise all the other executive powers of government, limited and restrained as by this constitution is mentioned, and according to the laws of the State. . . .
[Thorpe 563]

Pennsylvania Constitution, September 28, 1776:

[Frame of Government, Section 20:] The president, and in his absence the vice-president, with the council, five of whom shall be a quorum, shall have power . . . to grant *pardons,* and remit fines, in all cases whatsoever, except in cases of impeachment; and in cases of treason and murder, shall have power to grant reprieves, but not to *pardon,* until the end of the next sessions of assembly but there shall be no remission or mitigation of punishments on impeachments, except by act of the legislature . . . [Thorpe 3087–88]

Maryland Constitution, November 11, 1776:

[Article 33:] That the governor . . . may alone exercise all other the executive powers of government, where the concurrence of the council is not required, according to the laws of this state, and grant reprieves or *pardons,* for any crime, except in such cases where the law shall otherwise direct . . . [Thorpe 1696]

North Carolina Constitution, December 18, 1776:

[Form of Government, Article 19:] That the Governor, for the time being . . . shall have the power of granting *pardons* and reprieves, except where the prosecution shall be carried on by the General Assembly, or the law shall otherwise direct; in which case he may, in the recess, grant a reprieve until the next sitting of the General Assembly . . . [Thorpe 2791]

Georgia Constitution, February 5, 1777:

[Article 19:] The governor shall, with the advice of the executive council, exercise the executive powers of government, according to the laws of this State and the constitution thereof, save only in the case of *pardons* and remission of fines, which he shall in no instance grant; but he may reprieve a criminal, or suspend a fine, until the meeting of the assembly, who may determine therein as they shall judge fit. [Thorpe 781]

New York Constitution, April 20, 1777:

[Article 18:] That the governor shall continue in office three years, and shall, by virtue of his office, be general and commander-in-chief of all the militia, and admiral of the navy of this State; that he shall have power to convene the assembly and senate on extraordinary occasions; to prorogue them from time to time, provided such prorogations shall not exceed sixty days in the space of any one year; and, at his discretion, to grant reprieves and *pardons* to persons convicted of crimes, other than treason or murder, in which he may suspend the execution of the sentence, until it shall be reported to the legislature at their subsequent meeting; and they shall either *pardon* or direct the execution of the criminal, or grant a further reprieve. [Thorpe 2632–33]

Vermont Constitution, July 8, 1777:

[Frame of Government, Section 18: The Governor, and in his absence, the Lieutenant or Deputy Governor, with the Council . . . shall have power to grant *pardons,* and remit fines, in all cases whatsoever, except cases of impeachment, and in cases of treason and murder—shall have power to grant reprieves, but not to *pardon,* until the end of the next session of the Assembly: but there shall be no remission or mitigation of punishment, on impeachments, except by act of legislation. . . . [Thorpe 3745]

Massachusetts Constitution, March 2, 1780:

[Chapter II:I:8:] The power of *pardoning* offences, except such as persons may be convicted of before the senate by an impeachment of the house, shall be in the governor, by and with the advice of council; but no charter of *pardon,* granted by the governor, with advice of the council before conviction, shall avail the party pleading the same, notwithstanding any general or particular expressions contained therein, destructive of the offence or offences intended to be *pardoned.* [Thorpe 1901–02]

New Hampshire Constitution, June 2, 1784:

[Form of Government:] The power of *pardoning* offences, except such as persons may be convicted of [treason] before the senate by impeachment of the house, shall be in the president by and with the advice of the council: but no charter of *pardon* granted by the president with advice of council, before conviction, shall avail the party pleading the same, notwithstanding any general particular expressions contained therein, descriptive of the offence or offences intended to be *pardoned*. [Thorpe 2464]

Vermont Constitution, July 4, 1786:

[Frame of Government, Section 11:] The Governor, and in his absence, the Lieutenant-Governor, with the Council . . . shall have power to grant *pardons,* and remit fines in all cases whatsoever, except in treason and murder, in which they shall have power to grant reprieves but not to *pardon,* until after the end of the next session of Assembly, and except in cases of impeachment, in which there shall be no remission or mitigation of punishment, but by act of legislation. . . . [Thorpe 3756]

Alexander Hamilton's Plan of Union, June 18, 1787:

[The supreme executive of the United States shall] . . . have the power of *pardoning* all offences but treason, which he shall not *pardon* without the approbation of the Senate. [DHRC1 254]

George Mason, Objections to the Constitution, October 7, 1787:

The President of the United States has the unrestrained Power of granting *Pardons* for Treason; which may be sometimes excercised to screen from Punishment those whom he had secretly instigated to commit the Crime, & thereby prevent a Discovery of his own Guilt. [DHRC8 44]

Edmund Randolph, Letter on the Federal Constitution, October 10, 1787:

But I am sanguine in hoping that in every other justly obnoxious clause, Virginia will be seconded by a majority of the States. I hope that she will be seconded. . . . 4. In taking from him [the President] the power of *pardoning* for treason at least before conviction. . . . [DHRC8 273]

John Jay, *The Federalist*, No. 3, November 3, 1787:

In the year 1685, the state of Genoa having offended Louis XIV., endeavored to appease him. He demanded that they should send their Doge, or chief magistrate, accompanied by four of their senators, to France, to ask his *pardon* and receive his terms. They were obliged to submit to it for the sake of peace. Would he on any occasion either have demanded or have received the like humiliation from Spain, or Britain, or any other powerful nation? [Fed. 100]

"Americanus," No. 1, December 5, 1787:

What are then the mighty powers which he [the President] possesses distinct and separate from the senate? He shall have a negative upon all bills. But, if two thirds of each house, upon reconsideration, should agree to the bill, it shall become a law, and the president's negative will be no impediment; he shall have power to grant reprieves and *pardons* for offences against the United States, except in cases of impeachment; he shall take care, that the laws be faithfully executed, and shall commission all the officers of the United States. In every other instance, he can accomplish no object, effect no design, without the concurrence of the senate. . . . [DHRC8 203–204]

James Madison, *The Federalist*, No. 20, December 11, 1787:

The executive magistrate of the union [of the Netherlands] is the stadtholder, who is now an hereditary prince. His principal weight and influence in the republic are derived from this independent title; from his great patrimonial estates; from his family connections with some of the chief potentates of Europe; and, more than all, perhaps, from his being stadtholder in the several provinces, as well as for the union; in which provincial quality he has the appointment of town magistrates under certain regulations, executes provincial decrees, presides when he pleases in the provincial tribunals, and has throughout the power of *pardon*. [Fed. 182–83]

Dissent of the Pennsylvania Convention's Minority, December 18, 1787:

The president general is dangerously connected with the senate; his coincidence with the views of the ruling junto in that body is made essential to his weight and importance in the government, which will destroy all independency and purity in the executive department, and having the power of *pardoning* without the concurrence of a council, he may screen from punishment the most treasonable attempts that may be made on the liberities of the people, when instigated by his coadjutors in the senate. . . . [DHRC2 635]

Alexander White [?], "An Independent Freeholder," January 25, 1788:

. . . Indeed his [George Mason's] Observations with regard to the power of *pardoning* have no weight, but on a supposition that rulers are generally inclined to do wrong. I agree that the vices as well as the frailties of men ought to be guarded against, but cannot agree that they will intentionally do wrong without strong inducements, that they will injure the public without fair prospects of great advantage to themselves. . . . [DHRC8 327]

James Madison, *The Federalist*, No. 47, January 30, 1788:

[1] According to the constitution of Pennsylvania, the president, who is the head of the executive department, is annually elected by a vote in which the legislative

department predominates. In conjunction with an executive council, he appoints the members of the judiciary department, and forms a court of impeachment for trial of all officers, judiciary as well as executive. The judges of the Supreme Court and justices of the peace seem also to be removable by the legislature; and the executive power of *pardoning* in certain cases, to be referred to the same department. . . . [Fed. 340–41]

[2] . . . [In Virginia] The executive prerogative of *pardon,* also, is in one case vested in the legislative department. [Fed. 342]

[3] In the constitution of Georgia, where it is declared "that the legislative, executive, and judiciary departments shall be separate and distinct, so that neither exercise the powers properly belonging to the other," we find that the executive department is to be filled by appointments of the legislature; and the executive prerogative of *pardon* to be finally exercised by the same authority. Even justices of the peace are to be appointed by the legislature. [Fed. 342]

"Civis Rusticus," January 30, 1788:

. . . The president's having the unrestrained power of *pardoning* for treasons is another objection; and why? "it may be sometimes exercised to screen from punishment those whom he, (the president) had secretly instigated to commit the crime, and thereby prevent a discovery of his own guilt"—I appeal to this worthy gentleman [George Mason] himself, I appeal to the public, whether there be in this objection, more of validity and force, or chimera and imagination.
[DHRC8 336–37]

"James Bowdoin," February 27, 1788:

. . . we might have given up the rest to the winds: the controul over the elections; the command of the militia; the power of the senate to alter money bills; the powers of president to *pardon* criminals, to command in person the armies, navies, and militia, &c. and his long appointment, his right of being re-elected; omission of declarations in favor of liberty of conscience, and twenty others, which have been of great hurt to us, might have been left out. . . .
[DHRC16 240]

"An Impartial Citizen," No. 5, February 28, 1788:

[1] It is objected, that the President has the power of *pardoning* offences against the United States, and Mr. [George] Mason discovers that the President may prevent a discovery and punishment of his own crimes by this power; by forgiving those whom he had secretly instigated to the commission of crimes—The most of the other antifederalists enumerate this as one of the defects they pretend to discover in this system. Governor [Edmund] Randolph seems only to extend this objection to the President's power of *pardoning*

before conviction. Mr. Mason, as in his other objections, reasons in the most unfair, and least scientific way imaginable, viz. Arguing against a measure from a remote possibility of its being abused. Human sagacity cannot devise any law, but what, in its operations, may in some instances bear hard. It is impossible by any general law, to prevent punishments from being in some unforeseen cases, inadequate to offences—To obviate this inconvenience, a power of *pardoning* ought to be vested some where in a State. All civilized nations have accordingly adopted this measure; and there is hardly a respectable writer who has not inculcated the expediency of *pardons*. Demosthenes, Seneca, Cicero, Diodorus Siculus, and a vast multiplicity of other ancient and modern authors are quoted by Grotius on this subject, in the 20th chap. of his second book de jure belli ac pacis, who are all as well as he himself, advocates for the remission of punishments in some cases. The Marquis de Beccaria, 'tis true, thinks that *pardons* ought to be excluded in a perfect Legislation, where punishments are mild but certain—But indeed, to make this maxim maintainable, punishments ought to be very mild—And the learned Blackstone, in his admirable Commentaries, has clearly shewn the propriety of *pardoning*. It has been reckoned one of the principal defects of Democracy, that this power could not subsist in it, as from the nature of things, such a power could not with propriety be vested in many, and it can be delegated to one Supreme Executive Head with infinitely more propriety than to a multitude, or even in a few. In the American States it has been found, contrary to the opinion of theorists, that this power could exist in a Democracy, without impairing its republican spirit. The Executive in each State on the Continent, is vested with the power of *pardoning* offences, under different restrictions and modifications. . . . [DHRC8 428–29]

[2] . . . The President of the United States (when the Supreme Court, or other inferior Federal Courts, have judged according to the letter of the law, which may be rigorous) mitigates the sentence according to the true spirit of all laws, which teaches "never to sacrifice a man but in evident necessity"—But lest he should abuse this trust, he is not empowered to *pardon* in cases of impeachments. Where the conduct of an officer entrusted with the administration of some public affairs is such, that the Representatives, in order to ensure justice to the public, accuse him before the Senate, the President cannot interpose his *pardon*. The history of mankind, from the most remote antiquity, will inform us, that Officers of State or those entrusted with public administration of affairs, have ever been the most forward in plots and conspiracies against their country. In case such officers in the United States should conspire against their country, they cannot flatter themselves with the hopes of extorting from the President a remission of their punishment. The certainty of this will render conspiracies less certain and less frequent. And should the President *pardon* in common cases before conviction, or afterwards forgive notorious villains, or persons who should be unfit objects of mercy, this would be such a misfeasance of his office, as would subject himself to be personally impeached. . . . [DHRC8 429–30]

[3] . . . His personal responsibility clearly demonstrates Mr. Mason's assertion to be a most puerile insinuation. The power of the Governor of Virginia in *pardoning*, is not reprobated;—yet his power is very similar to that of the President:—the difference is, that the Governor cannot *pardon* without the advice of the Council of State . . . [DHRC8 430]

[4] . . . In England, the constitutional concession of absolute perfection to the Chief Magistrate, may render a Constitution with Counsellors concerning the propriety of exerting the power of *pardoning*, necessary; but with us this necessity is excluded, because the President will be liable to be punished in person . . . [DHRC8 430]

William Ward [?], "Republicus," March 1, 1788:

. . . An extraordinary refinement this [the Electoral College], on the plain simple business of election; and of which the grand convention have certainly the honour of being the first inventors; and that for an officer too, of so much importance as a president; invested with legislative and executive powers—who is to be commander in chief of the army, navy, militia, &c. grant reprieves and *pardons*, have a temporary negative on all bills and resolves, convene and adjourn both houses of congress, be supreme conservator of laws, commission all officers, make treaties, &c. &c. and who is to continue four years, and is only removable on conviction of treason or bribery and triable only by the senate, who are to be his own council whose interest in every instance runs paralel with his own: and who are neither the officers of the people nor accountable to them . . . [DHRC8 448]

James Iredell, "Marcus," No. 3, March 5, 1788:

[1] Nobody can contend upon any rational principles, that a power of *pardoning* should not exist somewhere in every government, because it will often happen in every country, that men are obnoxious to a legal conviction, who yet are entitled, from some favorable circumstances in their case, to a merciful interposition in their favor. The advocates of monarchy have accordingly boasted of this, as one of the advantages of that form of government, in preference to a Republican; nevertheless this authority is vested in the Stadtholder in Holland, and I believe is vested in every Executive power in America. . . . [DHRC16 322]

[2] . . . The probability of the President of the United States committing an act of treason against his country is very slight; he is so well guarded by the other powers of government, and the natural strength of the people at large must be so weighty, that in my opinion it is the most chimerical apprehension that can be entertained. Such a thing is however possible, and accordingly he is not exempt from a trial, if he should be guilty, or supposed guilty, of that or any other offence. I entirely lay out of the consideration, the improbability of a man

honored in such a manner by his country, risquing, like General Arnold, the damnation of his fame to all future ages, though it is a circumstance of some weight in considering, whether, for the sake of such a remote and improbable danger as this, it would be prudent to abridge this power of *pardoning* in a manner altogether unexampled, and which might produce mischiefs, the extent of which, it is not perhaps easy at present to foresee. In estimating the value of any power it is possible to bestow, we have to chuse between inconveniences of some sort or other, since no institution of man can be entirely free from all. . . . [DHRC16 322–23]

[3] . . . Now suppose, in the very midst of a war of extreme consequence to our safety or prosperity, the President could prevail upon a gentleman of abilities to go into the enemy's country, to serve in the useful, but dishonorable character of a spy: Such are certainly maintained by all vigilant governments, and in proportion to the ignominy of the character, and the danger sustained in the enemy's country, ought to be his protection and security in his own. This man renders very useful services; perhaps, by timely information prevents the destruction of his country. Nobody knows of these secret services but the President himself; his adherence however to the enemy is notorious: He is afterwards intercepted in endeavouring to return to his own country, and having been perhaps a man of distinction before, he is proportionably obnoxious to his country at large for his supposed treason. Would it not be monstrous, that the President should not have it in his power to *pardon* this man? or that it should depend upon mere solicitation and favor, and perhaps, though the President should state the fact as it really was, some zealous partizan, with his jealousy constantly fixed upon the President, might insinuate that in fact the President and he were secret traitors together, and thus obtain a rejection of the President's application. . . . [DHRC16 323]

[4] . . . But, says Mr. [George] Mason, "The President may sometimes exercise this power to screen from punishment those whom he had secretly instigated to commit the crime, and thereby prevent a discovery of his own guilt." This is possible, but the probability of it is surely too slight to endanger the consequences of abridging a power which seems so generally to have been deemed necessary in every well regulated government. It may also be questioned, whether, supposing such a participation of guilt, the President would not expose himself to greater danger by *pardoning,* than by suffering the law to have its course. Was it not supposed, by a great number of intelligent men, that Admiral Byng's execution was urged on to satisfy a discontented populace, when the Administration, by the weakness of the force he was entrusted with, were, perhaps the real cause of the miscarriage before Minorca? Had he been acquitted, or *pardoned* he could perhaps have exposed the real fault: As a prisoner under so heavy a charge, his recrimination would have been discredited as merely the effort of a man in despair to save himself from an ignominious punishment. If a President

should *pardon* an accomplice, that accomplice then would be an unexceptionable witness. . . . [DHRC16 324]

[5] . . . But when we consider how necessary it is in many cases to make use of accomplices to convict their associates, and what little regard ought in general to be paid to a guilty man swearing to save his own life, we shall probably think that the jealousies which (by prohibiting *pardons* before conviction) ever disabled the Executive authority from procuring unexceptionable testimony of this sort, may more fairly be ascribed to the natural irritation of the public mind at the time when the Constitutions were formed, than to an enlarged and full consideration of the whole subject. Indeed, it could scarcely be avoided, that when arms were first taken up in the cause of liberty, to save us from the immediate crush of arbitrary power, we should lean too much rather to the extreme, of weakening than of strengthening the Executive power in our own government. In England, the only restriction upon this power in the King, in case of Crown prosecutions (one or two slight cases excepted) is, that his *pardon* is not pleadable in bar of an impeachment; but he may *pardon* after conviction, even on an impeachment; which is an authority not given to our President, who in cases of impeachment has no power either of *pardoning* or reprieving.

[DHRC16 325–26]

Alexander Hamilton, *The Federalist*, No. 69, March 14, 1788:

[1] The President is to be the "commander-in-chief of the army and navy of the United States, and of the militia of the several States, when called into the actual service of the United States. He is to have power to grant reprieves and *pardons* for offences against the United States, except in cases of impeachment; to recommend to the consideration of Congress such measures as he shall judge necessary and expedient; to convene, on extraordinary occasions, both houses of the legislature, or either of them, and, in case of disagreement between them with respect to the time of adjournment, to adjourn them to such time as he shall think proper; to take care that the laws be faithfully executed; and to commission all officers of the United States." In most of these particulars, the power of the President will resemble equally that of the king of Great Britain and of the governor of New York. . . . [Fed. 445–46]

[2] . . . The power of the President, in respect to *pardons,* would extend to all cases, except those of impeachment. The governor of New York may *pardon* in all cases, even in those of impeachment, except for treason and murder. Is not the power of the governor, in this article, on a calculation of political consequences, greater than that of the President? All conspiracies and plots against the government, which have not been matured into actual treason, may be screened from punishment of every kind, by the interposition of the prerogative of *pardoning*. If a governor of New York, therefore, should be at the head of any such conspiracy, until the design had been ripened into actual hostility he could insure his accomplices and adherents an entire impunity. A President of

the Union, on the other hand, though he may even *pardon* treason, when prosecuted in the ordinary course of law, could shelter no offender, in any degree, from the effects of impeachment and conviction. Would not the prospect of a total indemnity for all the preliminary steps be a greater temptation to undertake and persevere in an enterprise against the public liberty, than the mere prospect of an exemption from death and confiscation, if the final execution of the design, upon an actual appeal to arms, should miscarry? . . . [Fed. 446–47]

Alexander Hamilton, *The Federalist*, No. 74, March 25, 1788:

[1-Title:] The Military and *Pardoning* Powers of the President. [Fed. 473]

[2] He [the President] is also to be authorized to grant "reprieves and *pardons* for offences against the United States, except in cases of impeachment." Humanity and good policy conspire to dictate, that the benign prerogative of *pardoning* should be as little as possible fettered or embarrassed. The criminal code of every country partakes so much of necessary severity, that without an easy access to exceptions in favor of unfortunate guilt, justice would wear a countenance too sanguinary and cruel. . . . [Fed. 473]

[3] The expediency of vesting the power of *pardoning* in the President has, if I mistake not, been only contested in relation to the crime of treason. This, it has been urged, ought to have depended upon the assent of one, or both, of the branches of the legislative body. I shall not deny that there are strong reasons to be assigned for requiring in this particular the concurrence of that body, or of a part of it. . . . [Fed. 474]

[4] . . . But the principal argument for reposing the power of *pardoning* in this case to the Chief Magistrate is this; in seasons of insurrection or rebellion, there are often critical moments, when a well-timed offer of *pardon* to the insurgents or rebels may restore the tranquillity of the commonwealth; and which, if suffered to pass unimproved, it may never be possible afterwards to recall. The dilatory process of convening the legislature, or one of its branches, for the purpose of obtaining its sanction to the measure, would frequently be the occasion of letting slip the golden opportunity. . . . [Fed. 475]

"George Bryan," March 26, 1788:

. . . The business being irksome, Mr. [Thomas] M'Kean, alledging it was indelicate for him to act where he was ill-used, persuaded Mr. [William Augustus] Atlee, and laboured me to send up our warrant. I represented the danger of risquing insult to our precept, advising delay, and the rather, as no hasty steps had been taken to bring the city rioters to justice. Mr. A. and Mr. [Jacob] Rush sent up their warrant. It lay some time in Carlisle, unexecuted, to bring the accused to submit and ask *pardon*. Nothing being done however, in this way, about 26th of February the sheriff was set to work. . . . [DHRC16 489]

John Dickinson, "Fabius," No. 9, 1788:

. . . Is there more danger to our liberty, from such a president as we are to have, than to that of Britons from an hereditary monarch with a vast revenue—absolute in the erection and disposal of offices, and in the exercise of the whole executive power—in the command of the militia, fleets, and armies, and the direction of their operations—in the establishments of fairs and markets, the regulation of weights and measures, and coining of money—who can call parliaments with a breath, and dissolve them with a nod—who can, at his will, make war, peace, and treaties irrevocably binding the nation—and who can grant *pardons* and titles of nobility, as it pleases him? . . . [Ford 212]

Georgia Constitution, May 6, 1789:

[Article II, Section 7:] He [the Governor] shall have power to grant reprieves for offences against the State, except in cases of impeachment, and to grant *pardons,* in all cases after conviction, except for treason or murder, in which cases he may respite the execution, and make a report thereof to the next general assembly, by whom a *pardon* may be granted. [Thorpe 788]

South Carolina Constitution, June 3, 1790:

[Article II, Section 7:] He [the Governor] shall have power to grant reprieves and *pardons,* after conviction, (except in cases of impeachment,) in such manner, on such terms, and under such restrictions as he shall think proper; and he shall have power to remit fines and forfeitures unless otherwise directed by law. [Thorpe 3262]

Pennsylvania Constitution, September 2, 1790:

[Article II, Section 9:] He [the Governor] shall have power to remit fines and forfeitures, and grant reprieves and *pardons,* except in cases of impeachment. [Thorpe 3096]

PEOPLE

[Note: This list is selective; it represents a complete search only of constitutional documents dealing with the colonies and states as a whole; the rest of the list represents a sample of one out of fifty occurrences in the remaining documents in the database.]

United States Constitution, September 17, 1787:

[Preamble:] We the *People* of the United States, in Order to form a more perfect Union, establish Justice, insure domestic Tranquility, provide for the common defence, promote the general Welfare, and secure the Blessings of Liberty to ourselves and our Posterity, do ordain and establish this Constitution for the United States of America.

[Article I, Section 2:] The House of Representatives shall be composed of Members chosen every second Year by the *People* of the several States, and the Electors in each State shall have the Qualifications requisite for Electors of the most numerous Branch of the State Legislature.

United States Constitution, Bill of Rights, December 15, 1787:

[Article I:] Congress shall make no law respecting an establishment of religion, or prohibiting the free exercise thereof; or abridging the freedom of speech, or of the press; or the right of the *people* peaceably to assemble, and to petition the Government for a redress of grievances.

[Article II:] A well regulated Militia, being necessary to the security of a free State, the right of the *people* to keep and bear Arms, shall not be infringed.

[Article IV:] The right of the *people* to be secure in their persons, houses, papers, and effects, against unreasonable searches and seizures, shall not be violated, and no Warrants shall issue, but upon probable cause, supported by Oath or affirmation, and particularly describing the place to be searched, and the persons or things to be seized.

[Article IX:] The enumeration in the Constitution, of certain rights, shall not be construed to deny or disparage others retained by the *people*.

[Article X:] The powers not delegated to the United States by the Constitution, nor prohibited by it to the States, are reserved to the States respectively, or to the *people*.

* * * * *

Magna Carta, June 15, 1215:

[Article 42:] It is allowed henceforth to any one to go out from our kingdom, and to return, safely and securely, by land and by water, saving their fidelity to us [*i.e.*, King John], except in time of war for some short time, for the common good of the kingdom; excepting persons imprisoned and outlawed according to the law of the realm, and *people* of a land at war with us, and merchants, of whom it shall be done as is before said. [SDECH 47–48]

Ferdinand and Isabella of Spain, Privileges and Prerogatives Granted to Christopher Columbus, April 30, 1492:

. . . We command Prince John, our most dearly beloved Son, the Infants, Dukes, Prelates, Marquesses, Great Masters and Military Orders, Priors, Commendaries, our Counsellors, Judges, and other Officers of Justice whatsoever, belonging to our Household, Courts, and Chancery, and Constables of Castles, Strong Houses, and others; and all Corporations, Bayliffs, Governours, Judges, Commanders, Sea Officers; and the Aldermen, Common Council, Officers, and Good *People* of all Cities, Lands, and Places in our Kingdoms and Dominions, and in those you shall conquer and subdue . . . [Thorpe 39–40]

English Petition of Right, June 7, 1628:

[Article 2:] Yet nevertheless, of late divers commissions directed to sundry Commissioners in several counties, with instructions, have issued; by means whereof your *people* have been in divers places assembled, and required to lend certain sums of money unto your Majesty, and many of them upon their refusal so to do, have had an oath administered unto them, not warrantable by the laws or statutes of this realm, and have been constrained to become bound and make appearance and give attendance before your Privy Council, and in other places, and others of them have been therefore imprisoned, confined, and sundry other ways molested and disquieted; and divers other charges have been laid and levied upon your *people* in several counties, by Lord Lieutenants, Deputy Lieutenants, Commissioners for Musters, Justices of Peace and others, by command or direction from your Majesty or your Privy Council, against the laws and free custom of this realm. [SDECH 340]

[Article 6:] And whereas of late great companies of soldiers and mariners have been dispersed into divers counties of the realm, and the inhabitants against their wills have been compelled to receive them into their houses, and there to suffer them to sojourn, against the laws and customs of this realm, and to the great grievance and vexation of the *people*. [SDECH 340–41]

[Article 10:] . . . and that your Majesty would be pleased to remove the said soldiers and mariners, and that your *people* may not be so burdened in time to come; and that the aforesaid commissions for proceeding by martial law, may be revoked and annulled . . . [SDECH 342]

[Article 11:] . . . and that your Majesty would also vouchsafe to declare, that the awards, doings, and proceedings, to the prejudice of your *people,* in any of the premises, shall not be drawn hereafter into consequence or example; and that your Majesty would be also graciously pleased, for the further comfort and safety of your *people,* to declare your royal will and pleasure, that in the things aforesaid all your officers and ministers shall serve you according to the laws and statutes of this realm, as they tender the honor of your Majesty, and the prosperity of this kingdom. [SDECH 342]

Charles I, Grant of the Province of Maine, April 3, 1639:

To all to whom these Presents shall come Greeting Whereas Sir Ferdinando Gorges Knight hath been an humble suitor unto us to graunte and confirme unto him and his heires a parte and porcon of the Countrie of America now commonly called or knowne by the name of New England in America in theise Presents hereafter described by the meets and boundes thereof with divers and sundrie priviledges and jurisdiccons for the welfare and good of the state of those Colonies that shalbee drawne thither and for the better governement of the *people* that shall live and inhabite within the lymits and precints thereof whiche parte or porcon of the said Countrie wee have heretofore (amongst other things) for us our heires and successors taken into actuall and reall possession or in defaulte of such actuall and reall possession formerly taken . . . [Thorpe 1625–26]

Fundamental Orders of Connecticut, 1638–39:

Forasmuch as it hath pleased the Allmighty God by the wise disposition of his divyne prvidence so to Order and dispose of things that we the Inhabitants and Residents of Windsor, Harteford and Wethersfield are now cohabiting and dwelling in and uppon the River of Conectecotte and the Lands thereunto adjoyneing; And well knowing where a *people* are gathered togather the word of God requires that to mayntayne the peace and union of such a *people* there should be an orderly and decent Government established according to God, to order and dispose of the affayres of the *people* at all seasons as occation shall require; doe therefore assotiate and conjoyne our selves to be as one Publike State or Commonwelth . . . [Thorpe 519]

The New England Confederation, May 19, 1643:

. . . and whereas we live encompassed with *people* of several nations and strange languages which hereafter may prove injurious to us or our posterity. And forasmuch as the natives have formerly committed sundry insolence and outrages upon several Plantations of the English and have of late combined themselves against us . . . [Thorpe 77]

Government of West New Jersey, November 25, 1681:

[Article 4:] . . . and if the Governor for the time being, his heirs or successors and Council, or any of them, shall attempt to make or enact any such law or laws of him or themselves without the consent, act and concurrence of the General Asserably; that from thenceforth, he, they, or so many of them as shall be guilty thereof, shall, upon legal conviction, be deemed and taken for enemies to the free *people* of the said Province; and such act so attempted to be made, to be of no force. [Thorpe 2566]

English Bill of Rights, December 16, 1689:

[1] And they do claim, demand and insist upon all and singular the premises as their undoubted rights and liberties and that no declarations, judgments, doings or proceedings to the prejudice of the *people* in any of the said premises ought in any wise to be drawn hereafter into consequence or example. [SDECH 465]

[2] . . . do pray that it may be declared and enacted, that all and singular the rights and liberties asserted and claimed in the said declaration are the true, ancient and indubitable rights and liberties of the *people* of this kingdom, and so shall be esteemed, allowed, adjudged, deemed and taken to be, and that all and every the particulars aforesaid shall be firmly and strictly holden and observed, as they are expressed in the said declaration . . . [SDECH 466]

[3] . . . and thereunto the said Lords spiritual and temporal and commons do in the names of all the *people* aforesaid most humbly and faithfully submit themselves, their heirs and posterities for ever: and do faithfully promise that they will stand to, maintain and defend Their said Majesties, and also the limitation and succession of the crown herein specified and contained to the utmost of their powers with their lives and estates against all persons whatsoever that shall attempt anything to the contrary. . . . [SDECH 467–68]

[4] . . . that all and every person and persons that is, are or shall be reconciled to or shall hold communion with the See or Church of Rome, or shall profess the popish religion, or shall marry a papist, shall be excluded and be forever incapable to inherit, possess or enjoy the crown and government of this realm and Ireland, and the dominions thereunto belonging, or any part of the same, or to have, use or exercise any regal power authority or jurisdiction within the same; and in all and every such case or cases the *people* of these realms shall

be and are hereby absolved of their allegiance; and the said crown and government shall from time to time descend to and be enjoyed by such person or persons, being Protestants, as should have inherited and enjoyed the same, in case the said person or persons so reconciled, holding communion, or professing, or marrying, as aforesaid were naturally dead . . . [SDECH 468]

The Albany Plan of Union, July 10, 1754:

[1] PRESIDENT-GENERAL AND GRAND COUNCIL

That the said general government be administered by a President-General, to be appointed and supported by the crown; and a Grand Council, to be chosen by the representatives of the *people* of the several colonies met in their respective Assemblies. [Thorpe 83]

[2] POWER TO MAKE LAWS, LAY DUTIES, &C

That for these purposes they have power to make laws, and lay and levy such general duties, imposts, or taxes as to them shall appear most equal and just (considering the ability and other circumstances of the inhabitants in the several colonies), and such as may be collected with the least inconvenience to the *people;* rather discouraging luxury than loading industry with unnecessary burthens. [Thorpe 85]

First Continental Congress, Declaration and Resolves, October 14, 1774:

[1] Whereas, since the close of the last war, the British parliament, claiming a power of right to bind the *people* of America, by statute in all cases whatsoever, hath in some acts expressly imposed taxes on them, and in others, under various pretences, but in fact for the purpose of raising a revenue, hath imposed rates and duties payable in these colonies . . . [JCC1 63–64]

[2] And whereas, Assemblies have been frequently dissolved, contrary to the rights of the *people,* when they attempted to deliberate on grievances; and their dutiful, humble, loyal, & reasonable petitions to the crown for redress, have been repeatedly treated with contempt, by His Majesty's ministers of state. [JCC1 66]

[3] The good *people* of the several Colonies of New- hampshire, Massachusetts-bay, Rhode-Island and Providence plantations, Connecticut, New-York, New-Jersey, Pennsylvania, Newcastle, Kent and Sussex on Delaware, Maryland, Virginia, North Carolina, and South Carolina, justly alarmed at these arbitrary proceedings of parliament and administration, have severally elected, constituted, and appointed deputies to meet and sit in general congress, in the city of Philadelphia, in order to obtain such establishment, as that their religion, laws, and liberties, may not be subverted. [JCC1 66–67]

[4] That the foundation of English liberty, and of all free government, is a right in the *people* to participate in their legislative council: and as the English colonists are not represented, and from their local and other circumstances, cannot properly be represented in the British parliament, they are entitled to a free and exclusive power of legislation in their several provincial legislatures, where their right of representation can alone be preserved, in all cases of taxation and internal polity, subject only to the negative of their sovereign, in such manner as has been heretofore used and accustomed. . . . [JCC1 68]

[5] . . . we have for the present only resolved to pursue the following peaceable measures: . . . 1st. To enter into a non-importation, non-consumption, and non-exportation agreement or association. 2. To prepare an address to the *people* of Great-Britain, and a memorial to the inhabitants of British America, & 3. To prepare a loyal address to his Majesty, agreeable to resolutions already entered into. [JCC1 73]

Thomas Paine, *Common Sense*, January 9, 1776:

But the king, you will say, has a negative in England; the *people* there can make no laws without his consent. In point of right and good order, there is something very ridiculous, that a youth of twenty-one (which hath often happened) shall say to several millions of *people*, older and wiser than himself, "I forbid this or that act of yours to be law." . . . [CWTP1 25–26]

South Carolina Constitution, March 26, 1776:

[Preamble:] . . . persons are liable to be sent to and tried in Great Britain for an offence created and made capital by one of those statutes, though committed in the colonies; the harbor of Boston was blocked up; *people* indicted for murder in the Massachusetts Bay may, at the will of a governor, be sent for trial to any other colony, or even to Great Britain . . . [Thorpe 3241]

John Adams, *Thoughts on Government*, April 1776:

The foundation of every government is some principle or passion in the minds of the *people*. The noblest principles and most generous affections in our nature, then, have the fairest chance to support the noblest and most generous models of government. [PJA4 87]

Virginia Bill of Rights, June 12, 1776:

[Title:] A declaration of rights made by the representatives of the good *people* of Virginia, assembled in full and free convention; which rights do pertain to them and their posterity, as the basis and foundation of government.

[Thorpe 3812]

United States Declaration of Independence, July 4, 1776:

[1] When in the Course of human events, it becomes necessary for one *people* to dissolve the political bands which have connected them with another, and to assume among the powers of the earth, the separate and equal station to which the Laws of Nature and of Nature's God entitle them, a decent respect to the opinions of mankind requires that they should declare the causes which impel them to the separation.

[2] We hold these truths to be self-evident, that all men are created equal, that they are endowed by their Creator with certain unalienable Rights, that among these are Life, Liberty and the pursuit of Happiness. That to secure these rights, Governments are instituted among Men, deriving their just powers from the consent of the governed. That whenever any Form of Government becomes destructive of these ends, it is the Right of the *People* to alter or to abolish it, and to institute new Government, laying its foundation on such principles and organizing its powers in such form, as to them shall seem most likely to effect their Safety and Happiness. . . .

[3] He [the King] has refused to pass other Laws for the accommodation of large districts of *people,* unless those *people* would relinquish the right of Representation in the Legislature, a right inestimable to them and formidable to tyrants only.

[4] . . . He has dissolved Representative Houses repeatedly, for opposing with manly firmness his invasions on the rights of the *people*. . . .

[5] . . . He has refused for a long time, after such dissolutions, to cause others to be elected; whereby the Legislative powers, incapable of Annihilation, have returned to the *People* at large for their exercise; the State remaining in the mean time exposed to all the dangers of invasion from without, and convulsions within. . . .

[6] . . . He has erected a multitude of New Offices, and sent hither swarms of Officers to harass our *People,* and eat out their substance. . . .

[7] . . . He has plundered our seas, ravaged our Coasts, burnt our towns, and destroyed the lives of our *people*. . . .

[8] In every stage of these Oppressions We have Petitioned for Redress in the most humble terms: Our repeated Petitions have been answered only by repeated injury. A Prince, whose character is thus marked by every act which may define a Tyrant, is unfit to be the ruler of a free *people*.

[9] We, therefore, the Representatives of the united States of America, in General Congress Assembled, appealing to the Supreme Judge of the world for the rectitude of our intentions, do, in the Name, and by Authority of the good *People* of these Colonies, solemnly publish and declare, That these United Colonies are, and of Right ought to be Free and Independent States . . .

Pennsylvania Constitution, September 28, 1776:

[Declaration of Rights, Article 5:] That government is, or ought to be, instituted for the common benefit, protection and security of the *people,* nation or community; and not for the particular emolument or advantage of any single man, family or set of men, who are a part only of that community; And that the community hath an indubitable, unalienable and indefeasible right to reform, alter, or abolish government in such manner as shall be by that community judged most conducive to the public weal. [Thorpe 3082–83]

North Carolina Constitution, December 18, 1776:

[Declaration of Rights, Article 1:] That all political power is vested in and derived from the *people* only. [Thorpe 2787]

New York Constitution, April 20, 1777:

[Article 33:] That the power of impeaching all officers of the State, for mal and corrupt conduct in their respective offices, be vested in the representatives of the *people* in assembly; but that it shall always be necessary that two third parts of the members present shall consent to and agree in such impeachment. . . . [Thorpe 2635]

United States Articles of Confederation, November 15, 1777:

[Article IV:] The better to secure and perpetuate mutual friendship and intercourse among the *people* of the different states in this union, the free inhabitants of each of these states, paupers, vagabonds and fugitives from Justice excepted, shall be entitled to all privileges and immunities of free citizens in the several states; and the *people* of each state shall have free ingress and regress to and from any other state, and shall enjoy therein all the privileges of trade and commerce, subject to the same duties, impositions and restrictions as the inhabitants thereof respectively, provided that such restriction shall not extend so far as to prevent the removal of property imported into any state, to any other state of which the Owner is an inhabitant . . .

[Article IX:] The united states in congress assembled, shall have the sole and exclusive right and power of determining on peace and war, except in the cases mentioned in the sixth article—of sending and receiving ambassadors—entering into treaties and alliances, provided that no treaty of commerce shall be made whereby the legislative power of the respective states shall be restrained from imposing such imposts and duties on foreigners, as their own *people* are subjected to, or from prohibiting the exportation or importation of any species of goods or commodities whatsoever . . .

Massachusetts Constitution, March 2, 1780:

[Bill of Rights, Article 17:] The *people* have a right to keep and to bear arms for the common defence. And as, in time of peace, armies are dangerous to liberty, they ought not to be maintained without the consent of the legislature; and the military power shall always be held in an exact subordination to the civil authority, and be governed by it. [Thorpe 1892]

Virginia Statute of Religious Liberty, January 16, 1786:

And though we well know that this Assembly, elected by the *people* for the ordinary purposes of legislation only, have no power to restrain the acts of succeeding assemblies, constituted with powers equal to our own, and that therefore to declare this act to be irrevocable would be of no effect in law; yet as we are free to declare, and do declare, that the rights hereby asserted are of the natural rights of mankind, and that if any act shall hereafter be passed to repeal the present, or to narrow its operation, such act will be an infringement of natural right. [CVA8 691]

Vermont Constitution, July 4, 1786:

[Declaration of Rights, Article 6:] That all power being originally inherent in, and consequently derived from the *people;* therefore, all officers of government, whether legislative or executive, are their trustees and servants, and at all times, in a legal way, accountable to them. [Thorpe 3752]

The Virginia Plan of Union, May 29, 1787:

[Article 4:] Resolved, that the members of the first branch of the National Legislature ought to be elected by the *people* of the several States every ——— for the terms of ——— . . . [DHRC1 243]

[Article 15:] Resolved that the amendments which shall be offered to the Confederation, by the Convention ought at a proper time, or times, after the approbation of Congress to be submitted to an assembly or assemblies of Representatives, recommended by the several Legislatures to be expressly chosen by the *people,* to consider and decide thereon. [DHRC1 245]

Charles Pinckney's Plan of Union, May 29, 1787:

[Article 4:] [House of Delegates] to consist of one Member for every ——— thousand Inhabitants 3/5 of Blacks included Senate to be elected from four Districts—to serve by Rotation of four Years—to be elected by the H.D. either from among themselves or the *People* at large. [DHRC1 246]

[Article 5:] The Senate and H.D. shall by joint Ballot annually chuse the Presidt. U.S. from among themselves or the *People* at large. . . . [DHRC1 246]

Alexander Hamilton's Plan of Union, June 18, 1787:

[1] The Assembly to consist of persons elected by the *People* to serve for three years. [DHRC1 253]

[2] The Senate to consist of persons elected to serve during good behaviour. Their election to be made by Electors chosen for that purpose by the *People*. In order to this, the States to be divided into election districts. . . .
[DHRC1 253–54]

[3] The Supreme Executive authority of the United States to be vested in a governor, to be elected to serve during good behaviour. His election to be made by Electors chosen by electors chosen by the *people* in the election districts aforesaid; or by electors chosen for that purpose by the respective legislatures . . . [DHRC1 254]

United States Confederation Congress, The Northwest Ordinance, July 13, 1787:

[Preamble:] It is hereby ordained and declared, by the authority aforesaid, that the following articles shall be considered as articles of compact, between the original States and the *people* and States in the said territory, and forever remain unalterable, unless by common consent . . . [Thorpe 960]

[Article II:] The inhabitants of the said territory shall always be entitled to the benefits of the writs of habeas corpus, and of the trial by jury; of a proportionate representation of the *people* in the legislature, and of judicial proceedings according to the course of the common law. . . . [Thorpe 960–61]

Debates in the Constitutional Convention, September 15, 1787:

Col: [George] Mason 2ded. & followed Mr. [Edmund] Randolph in animadversions on the dangerous power and structure of the Government, concluding that it would end either in monarchy, or a tyrannical aristocracy; which, he was in doubt, but one or other, he was sure. This Constitution had been formed without the knowledge or idea of the *people*. A second Convention will know more of the sense of the *people,* and be able to provide a system more consonant to it. It was improper to say to the *people*, take this or nothing. . . .
[DHRC8 11]

Tench Coxe, *An Examination of the Constitution for the United States of America*, No. 1, September 26, 1787:

It is evident, from this short detail, and the reflections which arise from it, that the quarrel between the United States and the parliament of Great Britain did not arise so much from objections to the form of government, though undoubtedly a better one by far is now within our reach, as from a difference concerning certain important rights, resulting from the essential principles of liberty, which their constitution actually preserved to all the subjects residing within the realm. It was not asserted by America, that the *people* of the island of Great Britain were slaves, but that we, though possessed absolutely of the same rights, were not admitted to enjoy an equal degree of freedom. [Ford 136]

William Pierce to St. George Tucker, September 28, 1787, published in *Gazette of the State of Georgia*, March 20, 1788:

. . . Was this question proposed to each of the states separately, "What kind of government is best calculated for the *people* of the United States?" there would be as many different opinions as there are different Interests. . . .

[DHRC16 443]

Richard Henry Lee [?], "The Federal Farmer," No. 2, October 9, 1787:

In examining the proposed constitution carefully, we must clearly perceive an unnatural separation of these powers from the substantial representation of the *people*. The state governments will exist, with all their governors, senators, representatives, officers and expences; in these will be nineteen twentieths of the representatives of the *people;* they will have a near connection, and their members an immediate intercourse with the *people;* and the probability is, that the state governments will possess the confidence of the *people,* and be considered generally as their immediate guardians. [Ford 292]

Richard Henry Lee [?], "The Federal Farmer," No. 5, October 15, 1787:

Thus I have examined the federal constitution as far as a few days leisure would permit. It opens to my mind a new scene; instead of seeing powers cautiously lodged in the hands of numerous legislators, and many magistrates, we see all important powers collecting in one centre, where a few men will possess them almost at discretion. And instead of checks in the formation of the government, to secure the rights of the *people* against the usurpations of those they appoint to govern, we are to understand the equal division of lands among our *people,* and the strong arm furnished them by nature and situation, are to secure them against those usurpations. If there are advantages in the equal division of our lands, and the strong and manly habits of our *people,* we ought to establish governments calculated to give duration to them, and not governments which never can work naturally, till that equality of property, and those free and manly habits shall be destroyed; these evidently are not the natural basis of the proposed constitution. . . . [Ford 318–19]

Noah Webster, *An Examination of the Leading Principles of the Federal Constitution*, October 17, 1787:

[1] I cannot help remarking the singular jealousy of the constitution of Pennsylvania, which requires that a bill shall be published for the consideration of the *people,* before it is enacted into a law, except in extraordinary cases. This annihilates the legislature, and reduces it to an advisory body. . . . [Ford 34n]

[2] Rome exhibited a demonstrative proof of the inseparable connexion between property and dominion. The first form of its government was an elective monarchy—its second, an aristocracy; but these forms could not be permanent, because they were not supported by property. The kings at first and afterwards the patricians had nominally most of the power; but the *people,* possessing most of the lands, never ceased to assert their privileges, till they established a commonwealth. And the kings and senate could not have held the reigns of government in their hands so long as they did, had they not artfully contrived to manage the established religion, and play off the superstitious credulity of the *people* against their own power. "Thus this weak constitution of government," says the ingenious Mr. Moyle, speaking of the aristocracy of Rome, "not founded on the true center of dominion, land, nor on any standing foundation of authority, nor rivetted in the esteem and affections of the *people;* and being attacked by strong passion, general interest and the joint forces of the *people,* mouldered away of course, and pined of a lingering consumption, till it was totally swallowed up by the prevailing faction, and the nobility were moulded into the mass of the *people.*" The *people,* notwithstanding the nominal authority of the patricians, proceeded regularly in enlarging their own powers. . . . [Ford 57]

"Cato Uticensis," October 17, 1787:

The ingenious Lord Shaftsbury has said, that a wheel within a wheel was an absurdity in politics; but, where was this ever so manifest, as in this Foederal Constitution. The phantom of sovereignty, which is left the state, enables it to legislate in many instances, and lay taxes; to have its tax-gatherers and excisemen too. Unhappy situation where the natural jealousy and the pride inherent in two separate governments, presiding over the same *people,* will induce them to vie in the race of taxation to snatch the prize, the spoils of the citizen, that is to glut the vanity of their respective consequence! . . . [DHRC8 75]

Virginia Assembly, October 25, 1787:

Resolved unanimously, that the proceedings of the Foederal Convention transmitted to the General Assembly through the medium of Congress, be submitted to a Convention of the *people* for their full and free investigation, discussion, and decision. [DHRC8 115–116]

John Jay, *The Federalist*, No. 4, November 7, 1787:

My last paper assigned several reasons why the safety of the *people* would be best secured by union against the danger it may be exposed to by just causes of war given to other nations; and those reasons show that such causes would not only be more rarely given, but would also be more easily accommodated, by a national government than either by the State governments or the proposed little confederacies. [Fed. 100–101]

"Americanus," No. 1, December 5, 1787:

. . . From the manner in which the president is elected, it must be acknowledged, that he is amenable to the *people,* and that they may have him removed from office, when he misapplies the powers, with which he is entrusted. It is a maxim universally true, that the power, which creates, can also annihilate.

[DHRC8 203]

James Madison, *The Federalist*, No. 19, December 8, 1787:

We may form some judgment of this scheme of military coercion from a sample given by Thuanus. In Donawerth, a free and imperial city of the circle of Suabia, the Abbe de St. Croix enjoyed certain immunities which had been reserved to him. In the exercise of these, on some public occasions, outrages were committed on him by the *people* of the city. . . . [Fed. 179]

Oliver Ellsworth, "The Landholder," No. 6, December 10, 1787:

. . . But do not believe that the *people* of Virginia are all thus selfish: No, there is a Washington, a Blair, a Maddison and a Lee, (not R.H.L.) and I am persuaded there is a majority of liberal, just and foederal men in Virginia . . .

[DHRC8 230]

Dissent of the Pennsylvania Convention's Minority, December 18, 1787:

For the moderate exercise of this power, there is no control left in the state governments, whose intervention is destroyed. No relief, or redress of grievances, can be extended as heretofore, by them. There is not even a declaration of RIGHTS to which the *people* may appeal for the vindication of their wrongs in the court of justice. They must therefore, implicitly, obey the most arbitrary laws, as the worst of them will be pursuant to the principles and form of the constitution, and that strongest of all checks upon the conduct of administration, responsibility to the *people,* will not exist in this government. The permanency of the appointments of senators and representatives, and the control the Congress have over their election, will place them independent of the sentiments and resentment of the *people,* and the administration having a greater interest in the government than in the community, there will be no consideration to restrain them from oppression and tyranny. In the government of this state [Pennsylvania], under the old confederation, the members of the legislature are taken from among the *people,* and their interests and welfare are so inseparably connected with those of their constituents, that they can derive no advantage from oppressive laws and taxes . . . [DHRC2 636]

Alexander Hamilton, *The Federalist*, No. 28, December 26, 1787:

It may safely be received as an axiom in our political system, that the State governments will, in all possible contingencies, afford complete security against invasions of the public liberty by the national authority. Projects of usurpation cannot be masked under pretences so likely to escape the penetration of select bodies of men, as of the *people* at large. The legislatures will have better means of information. They can discover the danger at a distance; and possessing all the organs of the civil power, and the confidence of the *people,* they can at once adopt a regular plan of opposition, in which they can combine all the resources of the community. . . . [Fed. 225]

"An Impartial Citizen," No. 1, January 10, 1788:

. . . . No money is to be drawn from the Treasury but in consequence of appropriations made by law; and regular accounts of the public receipts and expenditures of money, are to be published: A provision highly wise, and productive of moderation in the government, and confidence therein by the *people;* an advantage this system has over all the governments of antiquity, and over most, if not over all, the governments at present in Europe. . . . [DHRC8 295]

James Madison, *The Federalist*, No. 39, January 16, 1788:

On examining the first relation, it appears, on one hand, that the Constitution is to be founded on the assent and ratification of the *people* of America, given by deputies elected for the special purpose; but, on the other, that this assent and ratification is to be given by the *people,* not as individuals composing one entire nation, but as composing the distinct and independent States to which they respectively belong. It is to be the assent and ratification of the several States, derived from the supreme authority in each State,—the authority of the *people* themselves. The act, therefore, establishing the Constitution, will not be a national, but a federal act. [Fed. 283]

James Madison, *The Federalist*, No. 45, January 26, 1788:

. . . The Senate will be elected absolutely and exclusively by the State legislatures. Even the House of Representatives, though drawn immediately from the *people,* will be chosen very much under the influence of that class of men, whose influence over the *people* obtains for themselves an election into the State legislatures. Thus, each of the principal branches of the federal government will owe its existence more or less to the favor of the State governments, and must consequently feel a dependence, which is much more likely to beget a disposition too obsequious than too overbearing towards them. . . . [Fed. 327]

"Civis Rusticus," January 30, 1788:

A standing army without the consent of the representatives of the *people* in Congress there never can be: to their wisdom and their discretion we submit—Necessity may oblige America to raise an army—and who can judge of this necessity so well as Congress? Where can this power be more safely reposed? Dr. [Adam] Smith (in his "Wealth of Nations," book 5. ch. 1.) is of opinion in some cases, that a standing army is not dangerous to liberty—of this the *people* of America will judge, and a *people* jealous of their liberty, vigiliant over executory magistracy, will oppose with their united voice this institution, when they discover its end to be usurpation and tyranny. [DHRC8 338]

Alexander C. Hanson, *Remarks on the Proposed Plan of a Federal Government*, c. January 31, 1788:

By their scheme, however, thus deeply concerted, the house of representatives is to be chosen by the *people* once in two years; and if they have acted so as to warrant any reasonable apprehension of their designs, it will be easy at any time, to prevent their election. The truth is, that very few of them either wish to be elected, or would consent to serve, either in that house, or in the senate. I have exercised my imagination to devise in what manner they or any other men, supposing them to bear full sway in both houses, could erect this imaginary fabric of power. I request any person to point out any law, or system of laws, that could be possibly contrived for that purpose, obtain the final assent of each branch, and be carried into effect, contrary to the interests and wishes of a free, intelligent, prying *people,* accustomed to the most unbounded freedom of inquiry. . . . [Ford 221–22]

James Madison, *The Federalist*, No. 49, February 2, 1788:

We found in the last paper, that mere declarations in the written constitution are not sufficient to restrain the several departments within their legal rights. It appears in this, that occasional appeals to the *people* would be neither a proper nor an effectual provision for that purpose. . . . [Fed. 351]

David Ramsay, "Civis," February 4, 1788:

... If then we are to be an united *people,* and the obvious ground of union must be, that all continental concerns should be managed by Congress—let us by these principles examine the new constitution.... [DHRC16 22]

Massachusetts Convention, Ratification of the Constitution, February 6, 1788:

The convention having impartially discussed, and fully considered, the constitution for thc United States of America, reported to Congress, by the convention of delegates from the United States, of America, and submitted to us, by a resolution of the General Court of the said commonwealth, passed the twenty fifth day of October last past; and acknowledging with grateful hearts the goodness of the Supreme Ruler of the universe, in affording the *people* of the United States, in the course of his Providence, an opportunity, deliberately and peaceably, without fraud or surprise, of entering into an explicit and solemn compact with each other, by assenting to and ratifying a new constitution, in order to form a more perfect union, establish justice, insure domestick tranquillity, provide for the common defence, promote the general welfare, and secure the blessings of liberty to themselves, and their posterity—DO, in the name and in behalf of the *people* of the commonwealth of Massachusetts, ASSENT to and RATIFY the said constitution, for the United States of America.

[DHRC16 67–68]

Spurious "Centinel," February 16, 1788:

... Now, of what use can our reason be to us, if after we have come (or ought to have come) to years of discretion, we are still to be led, guided, and bandied about by those who pretend to know better than we?—And, who pray are those who are to be thus led, guided, and bandied about? Why, the *people!*—Strange! that three millions of *people* should be led, guided, and bandied about by ninety or an hundred aristocratical, demagogical, tyrannical conspirators!—Would it not be more according to order, propriety, and the nature of things, that the ninety or an hundred conspirators should be led, guided, and bandied about by the three millions of *people.* [DHRC16 134]

James Madison, *The Federalist*, No. 57, February 19, 1788:

If this spirit shall ever be so far debased as to tolerate a law not obligatory on the legislature, as well as on the *people,* the *people* will be prepared to tolerate any thing but liberty. [Fed. 385]

"An Old Planter," February 20, 1788:

Our lands are now taxed by their value, but by the constitution they can only be taxed by the poll, or number of our *people,* so that an acre of land in Virginia will not pay a sixth of what an acre of equal land will pay in Pennsylvania or Massachusetts. . . . [DHRC8 396]

Samuel Bryan, "Centinel," No. 15, February 22, 1788:

. . . this reluctance to change, has been found to be the greatest security of free governments, and the principal bulwark of liberty; for the aspiring and ever-restless spirit of ambition would otherwise, by her deceptive wiles and ensnaring glosses, triumph over the freest and most enlightened *people*. It is the peculiar misfortune of the *people* of these United States, at this awful crisis of public affairs, to have lost this useful, this absolutely necessary jealousy of innovation in government, and thereby to lie at the mercy and be exposed to all the artifices of ambition, without this usual shield to protect them from imposition. . . . [DHRC 189–90]

Circular Letter to the Fayette, Kentucky, County Court, February 28, 1788:

That the *people* may have an Opportunity of Making a Judicious Choice of representatives upon this Occasion, we recommend that the Election be kept Open each day during the sitting of the Court, & that this letter be read each day preceeding the Opning of the poles. [DHRC16 263]

Alexander White, "To the Citizens of Virginia," February 29, 1788:

. . . The dissentients attempt to prove that the new government will not be a confederacy of states, but one consolidated government from the power of Congress over the purse and sword. I conceive that without those powers we should not deserve the name of a seperate *people*. Should it remain with the several states to raise or not to raise men and money, our confederation would be no more than a treaty of friendship and alliance between independent nations. . . . [DHRC8 438]

James Madison, *The Federalist*, No. 63, March 1, 1788:

. . . Many of the defects, as we have seen, which can only be supplied by a senatorial institution, are common to a numerous assembly frequently elected by the *people,* and to the *people* themselves. There are others peculiar to the former, which require the control of such an institution. . . . [Fed. 416]

Letter from a New York Quaker, March 3, 1788, published in *Poughkeepsie County Journal*, March 18, 1788:

How differently *people* in dissimilar situations view the same object! here, a very decided majority think (and with them thy friend) that a union of the American States, as exemplified in the new constitution, is friendly to property; consistent with freedom; and favorable to morality and religion. Whereas in thy county I am told many think exactly the reverse. [DHRC16 409]

***Pennsylvania Gazette*, March 5, 1788:**

The American character, says a correspondent, has been traduced as turbulent and disorderly by some foreign nations. The treatment which the great question of the foederal constitution has received from all the *people* of America fully contradicts that opinion. Though there are individuals in every part of the union, who wish alterations and though there is a majority of that sentiment in a few districts, and although great pains have been taken (probably from a sense of duty in some) to exhibit the constitution in an unfavorable light, yet we have heard of no popular body that has risen against it. While this proves the great majority, who are desirous to obtain or disposed to accept the proposed constitution, it shews the orderly and good dispositions that prevail among that part of the *people,* who have not yet seen reason to think favorably of the new foederal government. The Americans seem to be duly impressed with the propriety and duty of making the voice of the majority the law of the land. Could a minority of 49 govern a majority of 51, there would be no possibility of saying at what number it would end. The ambitious and designing, by lessening the minority by degrees, might bring us under the government even of one. How dangerous, then, must it appear to every jealous and sincere friend of liberty, to dispense, upon any occasion, with the great rule of republics, that the voice of the majority of the *people* is the unalterable law. [DHRC16 320–21]

"A Virginian," March 12, 1788:

Again, when I contemplate the worthy characters who composed the late Convention, my breast is filled with indignation to find their labour for the common good requited by suspicion of designs equally iniquitous and improbable, and this chiefly by *people* in office, whose narrow souls are alarmed at the idea of having their imaginary importance diminished. . . . [DHRC8 481]

Alexander Hamilton, *The Federalist*, No. 70, March 15, 1788:

In the single instance in which the governor of this State [New York] is coupled with a council—that is, in the appointment to offices, we have seen the mischiefs of it in the view now under consideration. Scandalous appointments to important offices have been made. Some cases, indeed, have been so flagrant that ALL

PARTIES have agreed in the impropriety of the thing. When inquiry has been made, the blame has been laid by the governor on the members of the council, who, on their part, have charged it upon his nomination; while the *people* remain altogether at a loss to determine, by whose influence their interests have been committed to hands so unqualified and so manifestly improper. . . . [Fed. 456]

George Nicholas [?], "The State Soldier," No. 4, March 19, 1788:

There were three things in the first place which made it necessary to establish this court [*i.e.*, the Supreme Court]—the first is, the disputes that might arise between the different states, which could not otherwise [have] been determined but by a recourse to arms—the second is, in disputes between foreigners and citizens, without which general and impartial mode of trial under a foederal government, an end would soon be put to foreign credit, and of course to that extensive commerce which alone can ensure a lasting value to our property—and the third is, in disputes between citizens of different states, which alone could prevent that jealousy that must have been accited by trials in the state where only one of the parties resided; and which would have been destructive of that confidence and harmony which will ever be requisite to preserve that union and agreement, without which, this new government itself would cease to exist. And the two last are the only cases in which the *people* can be much affected; and that in most instances only by appeal. [DHRC8 512]

John Jay, *An Address to the People of the State of New York*,, c. April 15, 1788:

. . . Such other foreign nations, if any such there be, who, jealous of our growing importance, and fearful that our commerce and navigation should impair their own—who behold our rapid population with regret, and apprehend that the enterprising spirit of our *people,* when seconded by power and probability of success, may be directed to objects not consistent with their policy or interests, cannot fail to wish that we may continue a weak and a divided *people*.

[Ford 82]

Alexander Hamilton, *The Federalist*, No. 84, May 28, 1788:

. . . The two branches of the legislature are, in the first instance, to consist of only sixty-five persons, which is the same number of which Congress, under the existing Confederation, may be composed. It is true that this number is intended to be increased; but this is to keep pace with the progress of the population and resources of the country. It is evident that a less number would, even in the first instance, have been unsafe, and that a continuance of the present number would, in a more advanced stage of population, be a very inadequate representation of the *people*. [Fed. 539]

John Dickinson, "Fabius," No. 3, 1788:

This president is to be chosen, not by the *people* at large, because it may not be possible, that all the freemen of the empire should always have the necessary information, for directing their choice of such an officer; nor by Congress, lest it should disturb the national councils; nor by any one standing body whatever, for fear of undue influence. [Ford 171–72]

John Dickinson, "Fabius," No. 9, 1788:

. . . What an infatuated, depraved *people* must Americans become, if, with such unequalled advantages, committed to their trust in a manner almost miraculous, they lose their liberty? Through a single organ of representation, in the legislature only, of the kingdom just mentioned [Great Britain], though that organ is diseased, such portions of popular sense and integrity have been conveyed into the national councils, as have purified other parts, and preserved the whole in its present state of healthfulness. To their own vigour and attention, therefore, is that *people,* under providence, indebted for the blessings they enjoy. . . .

[Ford 213]

PERSON, PERSONS

[Note: This list is selective. It represents a complete search only of constitutional documents dealing with the colonies and states as a whole; the rest of the list contains a sample of one out of seventy occurrences in the remaining documents in the database.]

United States Constitution, September 17, 1787:

[Article I, Section 2:] No *Person* shall be a Representative who shall not have attained to the Age of twenty five Years, and been seven Years a Citizen of the United States, and who shall not, when elected, be an Inhabitant of that State in which he shall be chosen.

[*Ibid.*:] Representatives and direct Taxes shall be apportioned among the several States which may be included within this Union, according to their respective Numbers, which shall be determined by adding to the whole Number of free *Persons,* including those bound to Service for a Term of Years, and excluding Indians not taxed, three fifths of all other *Persons*. The actual Enumeration shall be made within three Years after the first Meeting of the Congress of the United States, and within every subsequent Term of ten Years, in such Manner as they shall by Law direct. . . .

[Article I, Section 3:] No *Person* shall be a Senator who shall not have attained to the Age of thirty Years, and been nine Years a Citizens of the United States, and who shall not, when elected, be an Inhabitant of that State for which he shall be chosen.

[*Ibid.*:] The Senate shall have the sole Power to try all Impeachments. When sitting for that Purpose, they shall be on Oath or Affirmation. When the President of the United States is tried, the Chief Justice shall preside: And no *Person* shall be convicted without the Concurrence of two thirds of the Members present.

[Article I, Section 6:] No Senator or Representative shall, during the Time for which he was elected, be appointed to any civil Office under the Authority of the United States which shall have been created, or the Emoluments whereof shall have been encreased during such time; and no *Person* holding any Office under the United States, shall be a Member of either house during his Continuance in Office.

[Article I, Section 7:] . . . But in all such Cases the Votes of both Houses shall be determined by yeas and Nays, and the Names of the *Persons* voting for and against the Bill shall be entered on the Journal of each House respectively. . . .

[Article I, Section 9:] The Migration or Importation of such *Persons* as any of the States now existing shall think proper to admit, shall not be prohibited by the Congress prior to the Year one thousand eight hundred and eight, but a Tax or duty may be imposed on such Importation, not exceeding ten dollars for each *Person*.

[*Ibid.*:] No Title of Nobility shall be granted by the United States: And no *Person* holding any Office of Profit or Trust under them, shall, without the Consent of the Congress, accept of any present, Emolument, Office, or Title, of any kind whatever, from any King, Prince or foreign State.

[Article II, Section 1:] Each State shall appoint, in such Manner as the Legislature thereof may direct, a Number of Electors, equal to the whole Number of Senators and Representatives to which the State may be entitled in the Congress: but no Senator or Representative, or *Person* holding an Office of Trust or Profit under the United States, shall be appointed an Elector.

[*Ibid.*:] The Electors shall meet in their respective States, and vote by Ballot for two *Persons*, of whom one at least shall not be an Inhabitant of the same State with themselves. And they shall make a List of all the *Persons* voted for, and of the Number of Votes for each; which List they shall sign and certify, and transmit sealed to the Seat of the Government of the United States, directed to the President of the Senate. The President of the Senate shall, in the Presence of the Senate and House of Representatives, open all the Certificates, and the Votes shall then be counted. The *Person* having the greatest Number of Votes shall be the President, if such Number be a Majority of the whole Number of Electors appointed; and if there be more than one who have such Majority, and have an equal Number of Votes, then the House of Representatives shall immediately chuse by Ballot one of them for President; and if no *person* have a Majority, then from the five highest on the List the said House shall in like Manner choose the President. But in chusing the President, the Votes shall be taken by States, the Representation from each State having one Vote; A quorum for this Purpose shall consist of a Member or Members from two thirds of the States, and a Majority of all the States shall be necessary to a Choice. In every Case, after the Choice of the President, the *Person* having the greatest Number of Votes of the Electors shall be the Vice President. But if there should remain two or more who have equal Votes, the Senate shall choose from them by Ballot the Vice President.

[*Ibid.*:] No *Persons* except a natural born Citizen, or a Citizen of the United States, at the time of the Adoption of this Constitution, shall be eligible to the Office of President; neither shall any *Person* be eligible to that Office who shall not have attained to the Age of thirty five Years, and been fourteen Years a Resident within the United States.

[Article III, Section 3:] Treason against the United States, shall consist only in levying War against them, or in adhering to their Enemies, giving them Aid and Comfort. No *Person* shall be convicted of Treason unless on the Testimony of two Witnesses to the same overt Act, or on Confession in open Court.

[*Ibid.*:] The Congress shall have Power to declare the Punishment of Treason, but no Attainder of Treason shall work Corruption of Blood, or Forfeiture except during the Life of the *Person* attainted.

[Article IV, Section 2:] A *Person* charged in any State with Treason, Felony, or other Crime, who shall flee from Justice, and be found in another State, shall on Demand of the executive Authority of the State from which he fled, be delivered up, to be removed to the State having Jurisdiction of the Crime.

[*Ibid.*:] No *Person* held to Service or Labour in one State, under the Laws thereof, escaping into another, shall, in Consequence of any Law or Regulation therein, be discharged from such Service or Labor, But shall be delivered up on Claim of the Party to whom such Service or Labor may be due.

United States Constitution, Bill of Rights, December 15, 1791:

[Article IV:] The right of the people to be secure in their *persons,* houses, papers, and effects, against unreasonable searches and seizures, shall not be violated, and no Warrants shall issue, but upon probable cause, supported by Oath or affirmation, and particularly describing the place to be searched, and the *persons* or things to be seized.

[Article V:] No *person* shall be held to answer for a capital, or otherwise infamous crime, unless on a presentment or indictment of a Grand Jury, except in cases arising in the land or naval forces, or in the Militia, when in actual service in time of War or public danger; nor shall any *person* be subject for the same offence to be twice put in jeopardy of life or limb . . .

* * * * *

Magna Carta, June 15, 1215:

[1] No constable shall require any knight to give money in place of his ward of a castle if he is willing to furnish that ward in his own *person* or through another honest man, if he himself is not able to do it for a reasonable cause . . .

[SDECH 46]

[2] Men who dwell outside the forest shall not henceforth come before our justiciars of the forest, on common summons, unless they are in a pleas of, or pledges for any person or persons who are arrested on account of the forest.

[SDECH 48]

Elizabeth I, Letters Patent to Sir Humphrey Gilbert, June 11, 1578:

And moreover, we doe by these presents for us, our heires and successours, give and graunt licence to the sayde Sir Humfrey Gilbert, his heires or assignes, and to every of them, that hee and they, and every or any of them shall, and may from time to time, and all times for ever hereafter, for his and their defence, encounter, expulse, repell and resist, as well by Sea as by land, and by all other wayes whatsoever, all and every such *person* and *persons* whatsoever, as without the special licence and liking of the sayd Sir Humfrey, and of his heires and assignes, shall attempt to inhabite within the sayd countreys . . . [Thorpe 50]

James I, Third Charter of Virginia, 1611–12:

. . . In all and every of which said Great and General Courts, so assembled, our Will and Pleasure is, and we do, for Us, our Heirs and Successors, for ever, Give and Grant to the said Treasurer and Company, and their Successors for ever, by these Presents, that they, the said Treasurer and Company, or the greater Number of them, so assembled, shall and may have full Power and Authority, from Time to Time, and at all Times hereafter, to elect and chuse discreet *Persons,* to be of our said Council for the said first Colony in Virginia, and to nominate and appoint such Officers as they shall think fit and requisite, for the Government, managing, ordering, and dispatching of the Affairs of the said Company . . . [Thorpe 3805–3806]

James I, The Charter of New England, November 3, 1620:

. . . And our Will and Pleasure is, that the said fourty *Persons,* or the greater Number of them, shall and may, from time to time, and at any time hereafter, at their owne Will and Pleasure, according to the Laws, Ordinances, and Orders of or by them, or by the greater Part of them, hereafter in Manner and forme in these Presents mentioned, to be agreed upon, to elect and choose amongst themselves one of the said fourty *Persons* for the Time being, to be President of the said Councill, which President soe elected and chosen, Wee will, shall continue and be President of the said Councill for so long a Time as by the Orders of the said Councill, from time to time to be made, as hereafter is mentioned, shall be thought fitt, and no longer; unto which President, or in his Absence, to any such *Person* as by the Order of the said Councill shall be thereunto appointed, Wee do give Authority to give Order for the warning of the said Council, and summoning the Company to their Meetings. . . .

[Thorpe 1831]

English Petition of Right, June 7, 1628:

[1] . . . and by authority of Parliament holden in the five and twentieth year of the reign of King Edward the Third, it is declared and enacted, that from thenceforth no *person* should be compelled to make any loans to the King against his will, because such loans were against reason and the franchise of the land . . . [SDECH 339]

[2] . . . nevertheless of late time divers commissions under your Majesty's great seal have issued forth, by which certain *persons* have been assigned and appointed Commissioners with power and authority to proceed within the Land, according to the justice of martial law against such soldiers or mariners, or other dissolute *persons* joining with them, as should commit any murder, robbery, felony, mutiny, or other outrage or misdemeanour whatsoever . . . [SDECH 341]

[3] . . . and that the aforesaid commissions, for proceeding by martial law, may be revoked and annulled; and that hereafter no commissions of like nature may issue forth to any *person* or *persons* whatsoever to be executed as aforesaid, lest by color of them any of your Majesty's subjects be destroyed or put to death contrary to the laws and franchise of the land. [SDECH 342]

Charles I, Charter of Massachusetts Bay, March 4, 1629:

. . . And Wee doe further, for Us, our Heires and Successors, give and graunte to the said Governor and Company, and their Successors, by theis Presents, that it shall and maie be lawfull, to and for the Chiefe Comaunders, Governors, and officers of the said Company for the Time being, who shalbe resident in the said Parte of newe England in America, by theis Presents graunted, and others there inhabiting by their Appointment and Direccon, from Tyme to Tyme, and at all Tymes hereafter for their speciall Defence and Safety, to incounter, expulse repell, and resist by Force of Armes, aswell by Sea as by Lande, and by, all fitting Waies and Meanes whatsoever, all such *Person* and *Persons,* as shall at any Tyme hereafter, attempt or enterprise the Destruccon, Invasion, Detriment, or Annoyaunce to the said Plantation or Inhabitants, and to take and surprise by all Waies and Meanes whatsoever, all and every such *Person* and *Persons,* with their Shippes, Armour, Municon, and other Goodes, as shall in hostile manner invade or attempt the defeating of the said Plantacon, or the Hurt of the said Company and Inhabitants . . . [Thorpe 1858]

Charles I, Grant of the Province of Maine, April 3, 1639:

. . . and the said *person* and *persons* according to the said Estate and Estates soe assigned and graunted to have and enjoye the same and to make erect and ordeyne in and uppon the said Province and Premisses or in and uppon any of them or any parte or parcell of them soe many severall and distincte Mannors as to the said Sir Fardinando Gorges his heires and assignes from tyme to tyme shall seeme meete . . . [Thorpe 1632]

The New England Confederation, May 19, 1643:

[Article 4:] . . . and that according to their different charge of each Jurisdiction and Plantation the whole advantage of the war (if it pleased God so to bless their endeavors) whether it be in lands, goods, or *persons,* shall be proportionably divided among the said Confederates. [Thorpe 78]

[Article 8:] . . . And that upon the escape of any prisoner whatsoever, or fugitive for any criminal cause, whether breaking prison, or getting from the officer, or otherwise escaping, upon the certificate of two magistrates of the Jurisdiction out of which the escape is made, that he was a prisoner, or such an offender at the time of the escape, the magistrates, or some of them of that Jurisdiction where for the present the said prisoner or fugitive abideth, shall forthwith grant such a warrant as the case will bear, for the apprehending of any such *person,* and the delivery of him into the hands of the officer or other *person* who pursues him. And if there be help required, for the safe returning of any, such offender, then it shall be granted to him that craves the same, he paying the charges thereof. [Thorpe 80]

Charles II, Charter of Connecticut, April 23, 1662:

Provided also, And Our Will and Pleasure is, That as well such as are by these Presents appointed to be the present Governor, Deputy-Governor, and Assistants of the said Company, as those that shall succeed them, and all other Officers to be appointed and chosen, as aforesaid, shall before they undertake the Execution of their said Offices and Places respectively, take their several and respective corporal Oaths for the due and faithful Performance of their Duties, in their several Offices and Places, before such *Person* or *Persons* as are by these Presents hereafter appointed to take and receive the same . . . [Thorpe 532]

Charles II, Charter of Carolina, March 24, 1663:

[Article 16:] . . . we do give and grant by these presents, full power and authority, to exercise martial law against mutinous and seditious *persons* of those parts, such as shall refuse to submit themselves to their government, or shall refuse to serve in the wars, or shall fly to the enemy . . . [Thorpe 2752]

Charles II, Charter of Rhode Island, July 8, 1663:

Alsoe our will and pleasure is, and wee doe hereby declare unto all Christian Kings, Princes and States, that if any *person,* which shall hereafter bee of the sayd Company or Plantations, or any other, by apoyntment of the sayd Governour and Company for the tyme beinge, shall at any tyme or tymes hereafter, rob or spoyle, by sea or land, or do any hurt, unlawfull hostillity to any of the subjects of us, oure heires or successours, or any of the subjects of any Prince or State, beinge then in league with us, oure heires, or successours, upon complaint of such injury done to any such Prince or State, or theire subjects, wee, our heires and successours, will make open proclamation within any parts of oure realme of England, fitt for that purpose, that the *person* or *persons* committing any such robbery or spoyle shall, within the tyme lymtted by such proclamation, make full restitution or satisfaction of all such injuries, done or committed, soe as the sayd Prince, or others soe complaineinge, may bee fully satisfyed and contented . . . [Thorpe 3218–19]

New Jersey Proprietors, Concession and Agreement, February 10, 1664:

. . . Provided always, that the before mentioned land and all other whatsoever, that shall be taken up and so settled in the said Province, shall afterward from time to time for the space of thirteen years from the date hereof, be held upon the conditions aforesaid, continuing one able man servant or two such weaker servants as aforesaid, on every hundred acres a master or mistress shall possess, besides what was granted for his or her own *person:* In failure of which upon other disposure to the present occupant, or his assigns, there shall be three years given to such for their compleating the said number of *persons,* or for their sale or dispositions of such part of their lands as are not so people'd within such time of three years. . . . [Thorpe 2542]

Fundamental Constitutions of West New Jersey, 1676:

[Chapter 23:] That in all publick courts of justice for tryals of causes, civil or criminal any *person* or *persons,* inhabitants of the said Province may freely come into, and attend the said courts, and hear and be present, at all or any such tryals as shall be there had or passed, that justice may not be done in a corner nor in any covert manner, being intended and resolved, by the help of the Lord, and by these our Concessions and Fundamentals, that all and every *person* and *persons* inhabiting the said Province, shall, as far as in us lies, be free from oppression and slavery. [Thorpe 2551]

Charles II, Commission Constituting a President and Council for New Hampshire, September 18, 1680:

. . . And if any of ye members of ye said Councell shall happen to die, Our Will and pleasure is, & We do hereby direct & appoint ye remainder of ye Councell to elect some other *person* to be a member of ye said Councell for ye time being; & to send over the name of such *person* so chosen, & the names of two more, whom they shall judg fitly qualified for that imployment . . . [Thorpe 2450]

Pennsylvania Frame of Government, Laws Agreed Upon in England, May 5, 1682:

[Article 26:] . . . And in case any *person* so called to evidence, shall be convicted of wilful falsehood, such *person* shall suffer and undergo such damage or penalty, as the *person,* or *persons,* against whom he or she bore false witness, did, or should, undergo; and shall also make satisfaction to the party wronged, and be publicly exposed as a false witness, never to be credited in any court, or before any Magistrate, in the said province. [Thorpe 3062]

English Bill of Rights, December 16, 1689:

[1] Whereas the Lords Spiritual and Temporal and Commons, assembled at Westminster lawfully, fully, and freely representing all the Estates of the people of this realm, did upon the thirteenth day of February in the year of our Lord one thousand six hundred eighty-eight, present unto their Majesties, then called and known by the names and stile of William and Mary, prince and princess of Orange, being present in their proper *persons,* a certain Declaration in writing, made by the said Lords and Commons, in the words following . . .
[SDECH 462–63]

[2] And whereas of late years partial, corrupt and unqualified *persons* have been returned and served on juries in trials and particularly diverse jurors in trials for high treason, which were not freeholders. [SDECH 463]

[3] And excessive bail hath been required of *persons* committed in criminal cases, to elude the benefit of the laws made for the liberty of the subjects.
[SDECH 463]

[4] And several grants and promises made of fines and forfeitures before any conviction or judgment against the *persons* upon whom the same were to be levied. [SDECH 463]

[5] And whereas the said late king James the Second having abdicated the government and the throne being thereby vacant, His Highness the prince of Orange (whom it hath pleased Almighty God to make the glorious instrument of delivering this kingdom from popery and arbitrary power) did (by the advice of the Lords Spiritual and Temporal, and diverse principal *persons* of the commons) cause letters to be written to the lords spiritual and temporal, being Protestants; and other letters to the several counties, cities, universities, buroughs and Cinque ports for the choosing of such *persons* to represent them, as were of right to be sent to parliament to meet and sit at Westminster upon the two and twentieth day of January in this year one thousand six hundred eighty and eight in order to such an establishment as that their religion, laws and liberties might not again be in danger of being subverted; upon which letters elections having been accordingly made. [SDECH 464]

[6] That all grants and promises of fines and forfeitures of particular *persons* before conviction are illegal and void. [SDECH 465]

[7] . . . And that the oaths hereafter mentioned to be taken by all *persons* of whom the oaths of allegiance and supremacy might be required by law instead of them; and that the said oaths of allegiance and supremacy be abrogated. [SDECH 466]

[8] I, A. B., do swear, that I do from my heart abhor, detest and abjure as impious and heretical this damnable doctrine and position that princes excommunicated or deprived by the pope or any authority of the see of Rome may be deposed or murdered by their subjects or any other whatsoever. And I do declare That no foreign prince, *person,* prelate, state or potentate hath or ought to have any jurisdiction, power, superiority, preeminence or authority, ecclesiastical or spiritual, within this realm: So help me God. [SDECH 466]

[9] And the said lords spiritual and temporal and commons, seriously considering how it hath pleased Almighty God, in his marvelous providence and merciful goodness to this nation to provide and preserve their said Majesties' royal *persons* most happily to reign over us upon the throne of their ancestors for which they render unto Him from the bottom of their hearts their humblest thanks and praises, do truly, firmly, assuredly and in the sincerity of their hearts think, and do hereby recognize, acknowledge and declare that King James the Second having abdicated the government and Their Majesties having accepted the crown and royal dignity aforesaid Their said Majesties did become, were, are, and of right ought to be by the laws of this realm our sovereign liege lord and lady king and queen of England, France and Ireland and the dominions thereunto belonging, in and to whose princely *persons* the royal state, crown and dignity of the said realms with all honors, stiles, titles, regalities, prerogatives, powers, jurisdictions and authorities to the same belonging and appertaining are most fully, rightfully and entirely invested and incorporated, united and annexed. [SDECH 467]

[10] . . . That they will stand to maintain and defend Their said Majesties, and also the limitation and succession of the crown herein specified and contained to the utmost of their powers with their lives and estates against all *persons* whatsoever that shall attempt anything to the contrary. And whereas it hath been found by experience, that it is inconsistent with the safety and welfare of this Protestant kingdom to be governed by a popish prince or by any king or queen marrying a papist the said lords spiritual and temporal and commons do further pray, that it may be enacted, that all and every *person* and *persons* that is, are or shall be reconciled to or shall hold communion with the See or Church of Rome, or shall profess the popish religion, or shall marry a papist, shall be excluded and be forever incapable to inherit, possess or enjoy the crown and government of this realm and Ireland and the dominions thereunto belonging, or any part of the same, or to have, use or exercise any regal power, authority or jurisdiction within the same; and in all and every such case or cases the people of these realms shall be and are hereby absolved of their allegiance; and the said crown and government shall from time to time descend to and be enjoyed by such *person* or *persons,* being Protestants, as should have inherited and enjoyed

the same, in case the said *person* or *persons* so reconciled, holding communion or professing, or marrying, as aforesaid, were naturally dead; and that every king and queen of this realm, who at any time hereafter shall come to and succeed in the imperial crown of this kingdom, shall on the first day of the meeting of the first parliament, next after his or her coming to the crown, sitting in his or her throne in the house of peers in the presence of the lords and commons therein assembled, or at his or her coronation, before such *person* or *persons* who shall administer the coronation oath to him or her at the time of his or her taking the said oath (which shall first happen), make, subscribe and audibly repeat the declaration mentioned in the statute made in the thirtieth year of the reign of King Charles the Second entitled An Act for the more effectual preserving the King's *Person* and Government, by disabling Papists from sitting in either House of Parliament. . . . [SDECH 467–68]

William Penn, Plan of Colonial Union, c. February 8, 1697:

[Article 2:] That in Order to it two *persons,* well Qualified for Sense Sobriety and Substance, be appointed by each Province, as their Representatives or Deputies; which in the whole make the Congress to Consist of Twenty *persons*. [PWP3 482]

[Article 6:] That their business shall be [to] hear and Adjust all matters of complaint or difference Betweene Province and Province; as 1st where *Persons* quit their own Province and go to another, that they may avoid their Just debts, tho' able to Pay them . . . [PWP3 482]

George II, Charter of Georgia, June 9, 1732:

. . . and that they [*i.e.,* the corporation and its successors], or two thirds of such of them, that shall be present at such yearly meeting, and at no other meeting of the said corporation, between the hours of ten in the morning and four in the afternoon of the same day, choose and elect such *person* or *persons* to be members of the said corporation, as they shall think beneficial to the good designs of the said corporation. And our further will and pleasure is, that if it shall happen that any *person* hereinafter by us appointed, as the common council of the said corporation, or any *persons* to be elected or admitted members of the said common council in the manner hereafter directed, shall die, or shall by writing under his and their hands respectively resign his or their office or offices of common council man or common council men; the said corporation, or the part of such of them as shall be present, shall and may at such meeting, on the said third Thursday in March yearly, in manner as aforesaid, next after such death or resignation, and at no other meeting of the said corporation, into the room or place of such *person* or *persons* so dead or so resigning, elect and choose one or more such *person* or *persons,* being members of the said corporation, as to them shall seem meet; and our will is, that all and every the *person* or *persons* which shall from time to time hereafter be elected common council men of the said corporation as aforesaid, do and shall, before he or they act as common men of the said corporation, take an oath for the faithful and due execution of their office . . . [Thorpe 767–68]

First Continental Congress, Declaration and Resolves, October 14, 1774:

[1] And whereas, in the last session of Parliament, three statutes were made . . . and another, intituled "An act for the impartial administration of justice, in the cases of *persons* questioned for any act done by them in the execution of the law, or for the suppression of riots and tumults, in the province of the Massachusetts-bay, in New England." . . . [JCC1 65–66]

[2] Also the 12 Geo. 3, ch. 24, entitled "An act for the better preserving his Majesty's dockyards, magazines, ships, ammunition, and stores," which declares a new offence in America, and deprives the American subject of a constitutional trial by jury of the vicinage, by authorizing the trial of any *person* charged with the committing any offence described in the said act, out of the realm, to be indicted and tried for the same in any shire or county within the realm. [JCC1 72]

Benjamin Franklin, Proposed Articles of Confederation, c. July 21, 1775:

[Article 2:] The said United Colonies hereby severally enter into a firm League of Friendship with each other binding on themselves and their Posterity, for their common Defence against their Enemies, for the Security of their Liberties and Propertys, the Safety of their *Persons* and Families, and their mutual and general welfare. [PBF22 122]

[Article 9:] An Executive Council shall be appointed by the Congress out of their own Body, consisting of 12 *Persons;* of whom the first Appointment one Third, viz. 4, shall be for one Year, 4 for two Years, and 4 for three Years; and as the said Terms expire, the vacancies shall be filled by Appointments for three Years, whereby one Third of the Members will be changed annually. And each *Person* who has served the said Term of three Years as Counsellor, shall have a Respite of three Years, before he can be elected again. . . .
[PBF22 124]

[Article 11:] . . . The Boundaries and Lands of all the other Indians shall also be ascertain'd and secur'd to them in the same manner; and *Persons* appointed to reside among them in proper Districts, who shall take care to prevent Injustice in the Trade with them, and be enabled at our General Expence by occasional small Supplies, to relieve their personal Wants and Distresses. . . .
[PBF22 124–25]

Thomas Paine, *Common Sense*, January 9, 1776:

In order to gain a clear and just idea of the design and end of government, let us suppose a small number of *persons* settled in some sequestered part of the earth, unconnected with the rest; they will then represent the first peopling of any country, or of the world. In this state of natural liberty, society will be their first thought. . . . [CWTP1 5]

United States Continental Congress, Draft Articles of Confederation, July 12, 1776:

[Article 14:] . . . All Purchases of Lands not included within those Limits, where ascertained, to be made by Contracts between the United States assembled, or by *Persons* for that Purpose authorized by them, and the great Councils of the Indians, for the general Benefit of all the United Colonies. [DHRC1 81]

[Article 18:] [Congress shall appoint] one of their number to preside, and a suitable *Person* for Secretary . . . [DHRC1 83]

[*Ibid.*:] The United States assembled shall have Authority for the Defence and Welfare of the United Colonies and every of them . . . To agree upon the Number of Land Forces to be raised, and to make Requisitions from the Legislature of each Colony, or the *Persons* therein authorized by the Legislature to execute such Requisitions, for the Quota of each Colony, which is to be in Proportion to the Number of white Inhabitants in that Colony, which Requisitions shall be binding, and thereupon the Legislature of each Colony of the *Persons* authorized as aforesaid, shall appoint the Regimental Officers, raise the Men, and arm and equip them in a soldier-like Manner . . . [DHRC1 83]

[*Ibid.*:] No *Person* shall be capable of being a Delegate for more than three Years in any Term of six Years. [DHRC1 84]

[*Ibid.*:] No *Person* holding any Office under the United States, for which he, or another for his Benefit, receives any Salary, Fees, or Emolument of any Kind, shall be capable of being a Delegate. [DHRC1 84]

[Article 19:] This Council [of the States] shall have Power to receive and open all Letters directed to the United States, and to return proper Answers; but not to make any Engagements that shall be binding on the United States—To correspond with the Legislature of each Colony, and all *Persons* acting under the Authority of the United States, or of the said Legislatures . . . —In Case of the Death or Removal of any Officer within the Appointment of the United States assembled, to employ a *Person* to fulfill the Duties of such Office until the Assembly of the States meet . . . —To appoint a proper *Person* for their Clerk, who shall take an Oath of Secrecy, and Fidelity, before he enters on the Exercise of his Office . . . [DHRC1 84–85]

Pennsylvania Constitution, September 28, 1776:

[Frame of Government, Section 19:] For the present the supreme executive council of this state shall consist of twelve *persons* chosen in the following manner : The freemen of the city of Philadelphia, and of the counties of Philadelphia, Chester, and Bucks, respectively, shall choose by ballot one *person* for the city, and one for each county aforesaid, to serve for three years and no longer, at the time and place for electing representatives in general assembly. . . . [Thorpe 3086–87]

Maryland Constitution, November 11, 1776:

[Declaration of Rights, Article 33:] That, as it is the duty of every man to worship God in such manner as he thinks most acceptable to him; all *persons,* professing the Christian religion, are equally entitled to protection in their religious liberty; wherefore no *person* ought by any law to be molested in his *person* or estate on account of his religious persuasion or profession, or for his religious practice; unless, under colour of religion, any man shall disturb the good order, peace or safety of the State, or shall infringe the laws of morality, or injure others, in their natural, civil, or religious rights; nor ought any *person* to be compelled to frequent or maintain, or contribute, unless on contract, to maintain any particular place of worship, or any particular ministry . . . [Thorpe 1689]

North Carolina Constitution, December 18, 1776:

[Form of Government, Article 12:] That every *person,* who shall be chosen a member of the Senate or House of Commons, or appointed to any office or place of trust, before taking his seat, or entering upon the execution of his office, shall take an oath to the State; and all officers shall also take an oath of office. [Thorpe 2791]

New York Constitution, April 20, 1777:

[Article 15:] That whenever the assembly and senate disagree, a conference shall be held, in the preference of both, and be managed by committees, to be by them respectively chosen by ballot. That the doors, both of the senate and assembly, shall at all times be kept open to all *persons,* except when the welfare of the State shall require their debates to be kept secret. . . . [Thorpe 2632]

United States Articles of Confederation, November 15, 1777:

[Article IV:] If any *Person* guilty of, or charged with treason, felony, or other high misdemeanor in any state, shall flee from Justice, and be found in any of the united states, he shall upon demand of the Governor or executive power, of the state from which he fled, be delivered up and removed to the state having jurisdiction of his offence.

[Article V:] No state shall be represented in Congress by less than two, nor by more than seven Members; and no *person* shall be capable of being a delegate for more than three years in any term of six years; nor shall any *person,* being a delegate, be capable of holding any office under the united states, for which he, or another for his benefit receives any salary, fees or emolument of any kind.

[*Ibid.*:] Freedom of speech and debate in Congress shall not be impeached or questioned in any Court, or place out of Congress, and the members of congress shall be protected in their *persons* from arrests and imprisonments, during the time of their going to and from, and attendance on congress, except for treason, felony, or breach of the peace.

[Article VI:] . . . nor shall any *person* holding any office of profit or trust under the united states, or any of them, accept of any present, emolument, office or title of any kind whatever from any king, prince or foreign state; nor shall the united states in congress assembled, or any of them, grant any title of nobility.

[Article VIII:] All charges of war, and all other expences that shall be incurred for the common defence or general welfare, and allowed by the united states in congress assembled, shall be defrayed out of a common treasury, which shall be supplied by the several states, in proportion to the value of all land within each state, granted to or surveyed for any *Person,* as such land and the buildings and improvements thereon shall be estimated according to such mode as the united states in congress assembled, shall from time to time direct and appoint. . . .

[Article IX:] . . . but if they [*i.e.*, state agents] cannot agree, congress shall name three *persons* out of each of the united states, and from the list of such *persons* each party shall alternately strike out one, the petitioners beginning, until the number shall be reduced to thirteen; and from that number not less than seven, nor more than nine names as congress shall direct, shall in the presence of congress be drawn out by lot, and the *persons* whose names shall be so drawn or any five of them, shall be commissioners or judges, to hear and finally determine the controversy, so always as a major part of the judges who shall hear the cause shall agree in the determination: and if either party shall neglect to attend at the day appointed, without showing reasons, which congress shall judge sufficient, or being present shall refuse to strike, the congress shall proceed to nominate three *persons* out of each state, and the secretary of congress shall strike in behalf of such party absent or refusing; and the judgment and sentence of the court to be appointed, in the manner before prescribed, shall be final and conclusive . . .

[*Ibid.*:] The united states in congress assembled shall have authority . . . to appoint one of their number to preside, provided that no *person* be allowed to serve in the office of president more than one year in any term of three years . . .

South Carolina Constitution, March 19, 1778:

[Article 28:] . . . nor shall any *person* be eligible as sheriff in any district unless he shall have resided therein for two years previous to the election.
[Thorpe 3254]

Massachusetts Constitution, March 2, 1780:

[Frame of Government, Chatper I;1:2:] . . . but in all such cases, the votes of both houses shall be determined by yeas and nays; and the names of the *persons* voting for, or against, the said bill or resolve, shall be entered upon the public records of the commonwealth. . . . [Thorpe 1894]

Vermont Constitution, July 4, 1786:

[Declaration of Rights, Article 13:] That no warrant or writ to attach the *person* or estate of any freeholder within this State, shall be issued in civil action, without the *person* or *persons,* who may request such warrant or attachment, first make oath, or affirm before the authority who may be requested to issue the same, that he or they are in danger of losing his, her, or their debts.
[Thorpe 3753]

The Virginia Plan of Union, May 29, 1787:

[Article 5:] Res[olve]d that the members of the second branch of the National Legislature ought to be elected by those of the first, out of a proper number of *persons* nominated by the individual Legislatures, to be of the age of ——— years at least . . . [DHRC1 243–44]

[Article 9:] Res[olve]d that a National Judiciary be established to consist of one or more supreme tribunals, and of inferior tribunals to be chosen by the National Legislature, to hold their offices during good behavior; and to receive punctually at stated times fixed compensation for their services, in which no increase or diminution shall be made so as to affect the *persons* actually in office at the time of such increase or diminution. . . . [DHRC1 244]

The New Jersey Plan of Union, June 15, 1787:

[Article 3:] Res[olve]d that whenever requisitions shall be necessary, instead of the rule for making requisitions mentioned in the articles of Confederation, the United States in Cong[res]s be authorized to make such requisitions in proportion to the whole number of white & other free citizens & inhabitants of every age sex and condition including those bound to servitude for a term of years & three fifths of all other *persons* not comprehended in the foregoing description, except Indians not paying taxes . . . [DHRC1 251]

[Article 4:] Res[olve]d that the United States in Cong[res]s be authorized to elect a federal Executive to consist of ——— *persons,* to continue in office for the term of ——— years, to receive punctually at stated times a fixed compensation for their services, in which no increase or diminution shall be made so as to affect the *persons* composing the Executive at the time of such increase or diminution, to be paid out of the federal treasury; . . . provided that none of the *persons* composing the federal Executive shall on any occasion take command of any troops, so as personally to conduct any enterprise as General or in other capacity. [DHRC1 252]

[Article 5:] Res[olve]d that a federal Judiciary be established to consist of a supreme Tribunal the Judges of which to be appointed by the Executive, & to hold their offices during good behaviour, to receive punctually at stated times a fixed compensation for their services in which no increase or diminution shall be made so as to affect *persons* actually in office at the time of such increase or diminution . . . [DHRC1 252]

Alexander Hamilton's Plan of Union, June 18, 1787:

[1] The Assembly to consist of *persons* elected by the people to serve for three years. [DHRC1 253]

[2] The Senate to consist of *persons* elected to serve during good behaviour. Their election to be made by Electors chosen for that purpose by the People. . . . [DHRC1 253–54]

United States Confederation Congress, The Northwest Ordinance, July 13, 1787:

[1] . . . Provided, That no *person* be eligible or qualified to act as a representative, unless he shall have been a citizen of one of the United States three years, and be a resident in the district, or unless he shall have resided in the district three years . . . [Thorpe 959]

[2] . . . As soon as representatives shall be elected the governor shall appoint a time and place for them to meet together, and when met they shall nominate ten *persons,* residents in the district, and each possessed of a freehold in five hundred acres of land, and return their names to Congress, five of whom Congress shall appoint and commission to serve as aforesaid; and whenever a vacancy shall happen in the council, by death or removal from office, the house of representatives shall nominate two *persons,* qualified as aforesaid, for each vacancy, and return their names to Congress, one of whom Congress shall appoint and commission for the residue of the term; and every five years, four months at least before the expiration of the time of service of the members of the council, the

said house shall nominate ten *persons*, qualified as aforesaid, and return their names to Congress, five of whom Congress shall appoint and commission to serve as members of the council five years, unless sooner removed. . . . [Thorpe 959–960]

[Article I:] No *person*, demeaning himself in a peaceable and orderly manner, shall ever be molested on account of his mode of worship, or religious sentiments, in the said territory. [Thorpe 960]

[Article II:] The inhabitants of the said territory shall always be entitled to the benefits of the writs of habeas corpus, and of the trial by jury; of a proportionate representation of the people in the legislature, and of judicial proceedings according to the course of the common law. All *persons* shall be bailable, unless for capital offences, where the proof shall be evident, or the presumption great. All fines shall be moderate; and no cruel or unusual punishments shall be inflicted. No man shall be deprived of his liberty or property, but by the judgment of his peers, or the law of the land, and should the public exigencies make it necessary, for the common preservation, to take any *persons* property, or to demand his particular services, full compensation shall be made for the same. . . . [Thorpe 960–61]

[Article VI:] There shall be neither slavery nor involuntary servitude in the said territory, otherwise than in punishment of crimes, whereof the party shall have been duly convicted: Provided always, That any *person* escaping into the same, from whom labor or service is lawfully claimed in any one of the original States, such fugitive may be lawfully reclaimed, and conveyed to the *person* claiming his or her labor or service as aforesaid. [Thorpe 962]

Richard Henry Lee, Proposed Amendments to the Constitution, October 16, 1787:

. . . that the citizens shall not be exposed to unreasonable searches, seizure of their *persons,* houses, papers or property; and it is necessary for the good of society, that the administration of government be conducted with all possible maturity of judgment, for which reason it hath been the practice of civilized nations, and so determined by every state in the Union . . . [DHRC8 65]

Noah Webster, *An Examination of the Leading Principles of the Federal Constitution*, October 17, 1787:

The powers lodged in Congress are extensive; but it is presumed that they are not too extensive. The first object of the constitution is to unite the states into one compact society, for the purpose of government, if such union must exist, or the states be exposed to foreign invasions, internal discord, reciprocal encroachments upon each others property—to weakness and infamy, which no *person* will dispute; what powers must be collected and lodged in the supreme head or legislature of these states. . . . [Ford 45]

David Ramsay, "Civis," February 4, 1788:

. . . In a state of nature, each man is free and may do what he pleases; but in society, every individual must sacrifice a part of his natural rights; the minority must yield to the majority, and the collective interest must controul particular interests. When thirteen *persons* constitute a family, each should forego every thing that is injurious to the other twelve. When several families constitute a parish, or county, each may adopt any regulations it pleases with regard to its domestic affairs, but must be abridged of that liberty in other cases, where the good of the whole is concerned. [DHRC16 22]

James Madison, *The Federalist*, No. 54, February 12, 1788:

. . . In being protected, on the other hand, in his life and in his limbs, against the violence of all others, even the master of his labor and his liberty; and in being punishable himself for all violence committed against others,—the slave is no less evidently regarded by the law as a member of the society, not as a part of the irrational creation; as a moral *person,* not as a mere article of property. The federal Constitution, therefore, decides with great propriety on the case of our slaves, when it views them in the mixed character of *persons* and of property. This is in fact their true character. . . . [Fed. 370–71]

"An Old Planter," February 20, 1788:

. . . But when I look at the objections of these three dissenters, as judiciously collected in a late paper—I find they hardly agree amongst themselves in any one of them, so that if they had been the sole *persons* employed to frame a constitution, some two of them, would have rejected almost every objection, stated by the third—this forms another strong presumption that the government now proposed to us is good. [DHRC8 395]

Archibald Maclaine, "Publicola," March 27, 1788:

. . . The great number of respectable *persons* who are in favour of the new government, and the impossibility that the greatest part of them can derive any partial benefit from it, are irrefragable proofs that they act from conviction.
[DHRC16 496]

Alexander Hamilton, *The Federalist*, No. 84, May 28, 1788:

. . . The two branches of the legislature are, in the first instance, to consist of only sixty-five *persons,* which is the same number of which Congress, under the existing Confederation, may be composed. It is true that this number is intended to be increased; but this is to keep pace with the progress of the population and resources of the country. . . . [Fed. 539]

John Dickinson, "Fabius," No. 3, 1788:

When any *persons* speak of a consideration, do they, or do they not acknowledge, that the whole is interested in the safety of every part—in the agreement of parts—in the relation of parts to one another—to the whole—or, to other societies? If they do—then,the authority of the whole, must be co-extensive with its interests . . . [Ford 178]

PETITION (RIGHT TO)

United States Constitution, Bill of Rights, December 15, 1791:

[Article I:] Congress shall make no law respecting an establishment of religion, or prohibiting the free exercise thereof; or abridging the freedom of speech, or of the press; or the *right* of the people peaceably to assemble, and to *petition the government* for a redress of grievances.

* * * * *

English Bill of Rights, December 16, 1689:

That it is the *right of the subjects to petition the king* and all commitments and prosecutions for such petitioning are illegal. [SDECH 464]

First Continental Congress, Declaration and Resolves, October 14, 1774:

That they [the colonies] have a *right* peaceably to assemble, consider of their grievances, and *petition the King;* and that all prosecutions, prohibitory proclamations, and commitments for the same, are illegal. [JCC1 70]

Pennsylvania Constitution, September 28, 1776:

[Declaration of Rights, Article 16:] That the people have a *right* to assemble together, to consult for their common good, to instruct their representatives, and to apply to the legislature for redress of grievances, by address, *petition,* or remonstrance. [Thorpe 3084]

Maryland Constitution, November 11, 1776:

[Declaration of Rights, Article 11:] That every man hath a *right to petition* the Legislature, for the redress of grievances, in a peaceable and orderly manner. [Thorpe 1687]

Vermont Constitution, July 8, 1777:

[Declaration of Rights, Article 18:] That the people have a *right* to assemble together, to consult for their common good—to instruct their representatives, and to apply to the legislature for redress of grievances, by address, *petition* or remonstrance. [Thorpe 3741–42]

Massachusetts Constitution, March 2, 1780:

[Declaration of Rights, Article 19:] The people have a *right,* in an orderly and peaceable manner, to assemble to consult upon the common good; give instructions to their representatives, and to request of the legislative body, by the way of addresses, *petitions,* or remonstrances, redress of the wrongs done them, and of the grievances they suffer. [Thorpe 1892]

New Hampshire Constitution, June 2, 1784:

[Bill of Rights, Article 32:] The people have a *right* in an orderly and peaceable manner, to assemble and consult upon the common good, give instructions to their representatives; and to request of the legislative body, by way of *petition* or remonstrance, redress of the wrongs done them, and of the grievances they suffer. [Thorpe 2457]

Vermont Constitution, July 4, 1786:

[Declaration of Rights, Article 22:] That the people have a *right* to assemble together, to consult for their common good—to instruct their representatives, and to apply to the Legislature for redress of grievances, by address, *petition* or remonstrance. [Thorpe 3754]

Richard Henry Lee, Proposed Amendments to the Constitution, October 16, 1787:

. . . That the elections should be free and frequent; That the right administration of justice should be secured by the independency of the judges; That excessive bail, excessive fines, or cruel and unusual punishments, should not be demanded or inflicted; That the *right* of the people to assemble peaceably, for the purpose of *petitioning* the legislature, shall not be prevented; that the citizens shall not be exposed to unreasonable searches, seizure of their persons, houses, papers or property . . . [DHRC8 65]

Alexander White [?], "An Independent Freeholder," January 18, 1788:

. . . But is America in the situation Great Britain was in at the time of the revolution in that country, or in which she herself was at the time of the revolution in this? Nothing can be more remote; here is neither a total nor partial dissolution of Government; our social compacts and all our ancient *rights* remain entire, except such as are expressly granted to Congress. And this affords an answer to many objections, such as that religious liberty, the Freedom of the Press, the *right of Petitioning* the Legislature, &c. &c. &c. are not secured; no power over these matters being granted to Congress, she never can interpose to destroy them. Much more safely may we rest the Constitution on this ground than on a bill of *rights* . . . [DHRC8 311]

Pennsylvania Constitution, September 2, 1790:

[Article IX, Section 20:] That the citizens have a *right,* in a peaceable manner, to assemble together for their common good, and to apply to those invested with the powers of government for redress of grievances, or other proper purposes, by *petition,* address, or remonstrance. [Thorpe 3101]

POWER, POWERS

[Note: This list is selective. It represents a complete search only of constitutional documents dealing with the colonies and states as a whole; the rest of the list contains a sample of one out of seventy occurrences in the remaining documents in the database.]

United States Constitution, September 17, 1787:

[Article I, Section 1:] All legislative *Powers* herein granted shall be vested in a Congress of the United States, which shall consist of a Senate and House of Representatives.

[Article I, Section 2:] The House of Representatives shall choose their Speaker and other Officers; and shall have the sole *Power* of Impeachment.

[Article I, Section 3:] The Senate shall have the sole *Power* to try all Impeachments. When sitting for that Purpose, they shall be on Oath or Affirmation. When the President of the United States is tried, the Chief Justice shall preside: and no Person shall be convicted without the Concurrence of two thirds of the Members present.

[Article I, Section 8:] The Congress shall have *Power* To lay and collect Taxes, Duties, Imposts and Excises, to pay the Debts and provide for the common Defence and general Welfare of the United States; but all Duties, Imposts and Excises shall be uniform throughout the United States. . . . [here follows a list of the other powers of Congress]

[*Ibid.*:] To make all Laws which shall be necessary and proper for carrying into Execution the foregoing *Powers,* and all other *Powers* vested by this Constitution in the Government of the United States, or in any Department or Officer thereof.

[Article I, Section 10:] No State shall, without the Consent of Congress, lay any Duty of Tonnage, keep Troops, or Ships of War in time of Peace, enter into any Agreement or Compact with another State, or with a foreign *Power,* or engage in War, unless actually invaded, or in such imminent Danger as will not admit of delay.

[Article II, Section 1:] The executive *Power* shall be vested in a President of the United States of America. He shall hold his Office during the Term of four Years, and, together with the Vice President chosen for the same Term, be elected, as follows

[*Ibid.*:] In Case of the Removal of the President from Office, or of his Death, Resignation, or Inability to discharge the *Powers* and Duties of the said Office, the Same shall devolve on the Vice President . . .

[Article II, Section 2:] . . . he [the President] may require the Opinion, in writing, of the principal Officer in each of the executive Departments, upon any Subject relating to the Duties of their respective Offices, and he Shall have *Power* to grant Reprieves and Pardons for Offenses against the United States, except in Cases of Impeachment.

[*Ibid.*:] He shall have *Power,* by and with the Advice and Consent of the Senate, to make Treaties, provided two thirds of the Senators present concur; and he shall nominate, and by and with the Advice and Consent of the Senate, shall appoint Ambassadors, other public Ministers and Consuls, Judges of the supreme Court, and all other Officers of the United States, whose Appointments are not herein otherwise provided for, and which shall be established by Law . . .

[*Ibid.*:] The President shall have *Power* to fill up all Vacancies that may happen during the Recess of the Senate, by granting Commissions which shall expire at the End of their next Session.

[Article III, Section 1:] The judicial *Power* of the United States, shall be vested in one supreme Court, and in such inferior Courts as the Congress may from time to time ordain and establish. The Judges, both of the supreme and inferior Courts, shall hold their Offices during good Behaviour, and shall, at stated Times, receive for their Services, a Compensation, which shall not be diminished during their Continuance in Office.

[Article III, Section 2:] The judicial *Power* shall extend to all Cases, in Law and Equity, arising under this Constitution, the Laws of the United States, and Treaties made, or which shall be made, under their Authority;—to all Cases affecting Ambassadors, other public Ministers and Consuls;—to all Cases of admiralty and maritime Jurisdiction;—to Controversies to which the United States shall be a Party;—to Controversies between two or more States;—between a State and Citizens of another State;—between Citizens of different States,—between Citizens of the same State claiming Lands under Grants of different States, and between a State, or the Citizens thereof, and foreign States, Citizens or Subjects.

[Article III, Section 3:] The Congress shall have *Power* to declare the Punishment of Treason, but no Attainder of Treason shall work Corruption of Blood, or Forfeiture except during the Life of the Person attainted.

[Article IV, Section III:] The Congress shall have *Power* to dispose of and make all needful Rules and Regulations respecting the Territory or other Property belonging to the United States; and nothing in this Constitution shall be so construed as to Prejudice any Claims of the United States, or of any particular State.

United States Constitution, Bill of Rights, December 15, 1791:

[Article X:] The *powers* not delegated to the United States by the Constitution, nor prohibited by it to the States, are reserved to the States respectively, or to the people.

* * * * *

Magna Carta, June 15, 1215:

Since, moreover, for the sake of God, and for the improvement of our kingdom, and for the better quieting of the hostility sprung up lately between us and our barons, we have made all these concessions; wishing them to enjoy these in a complete and firm stability forever, we make and concede to them the security described below; that is to say, that they shall elected twenty-five barons of the kingdom, whom they will, who ought with all their *power* to observe, hold, and cause to be observed, the peace and liberties which we have conceded to them . . . [SDECH 50–51]

English Petition of Right, June 7, 1628:

. . . nevertheless of late time divers commissions under your Majesty's great seal have issued forth, by which certain persons have been assigned and appointed Commissioners with *power* and authority to proceed within the land, according to the justice of martial law, against such soldiers or mariners, or other dissolute persons joining with them, as should commit any murder, robbery, felony, mutiny, or other outrage or misdemeanour whatsoever, and by such summary course and order, as is agreeable to martial law, and is used in armies in time of war, to proceed to the trial and condemnation of such offenders, and them to cause to be executed and put to death, according to the law martial.

[SDECH 341]

Charles I, Patent to Sir Robert Heath, October 30, 1629:

Know that we of our free grace certain knowledge & meere motion doe thinke fit to erect the sayd Region Territory & Isles into a Province & by the fulness of our *power* & Kingly Authority for us our heires & successors, we doe erect & incorporate them into a province & name the same Carolina or the province of Carolina, & the foresaid Isles the Carolarns Islands & soe we will that in all times hereafter they shall be named. And because we herebefore have ordained

& made the foresd. Sr. Robert Heath Knight true lord & proprietor of all the aforenamed Province. Furthermore know yee that we for ourselves our heires & successors doe give *power* to the said Sr. Robert (of whose faith prudence industry & provident circumspection we have great confidence) & to his heires & assignes for the good & happy Government of the said Province to forme make & enact & publish under the seale of the said Sr. Robert his heires & assignes what lawes soever may concerne the publicke state of the said province or the private profitt of all according to the wholesome directions of & with the counsell assent & approbation of the Freeholders of the same Province or the Major part of them . . . [Thorpe 71]

Fundamental Agreement of New Haven Colony, June 4, 1639:

Query V. Whether free burgesses shall be chosen out of the church members, they that are in the foundation work of the church being actually free burgesses, and to choose to themselves out of the like estate of church fellowship, and the *power* of choosing magistrates and officers from among themselves, and the *power* of making and repealing laws, according to the word, and the dividing of inheritances, and deciding of differences that may arise, and all the businesses of like nature are to be transacted by those free burgesses? This was put to vote and agreed unto by lifting up of hands twice, as in the former it was done. . . . [Thorpe 525]

The New England Confederation, May 19, 1643:

[Article 6:] It is also agreed, that for the managing and concluding of all affairs proper, and concerning the whole Confederation two Commissioners shall be chosen by and out of each of these four Jurisdictions: namely, two for the Massachusetts, two for Plymouth, two for Connecticut, and two for New Haven, being all in Church-fellowship with us, which shall bring full *power* from their several General Courts respectively to hear, examine, weigh, and determine all affairs of our war, or peace, leagues, aids, charges, and numbers of men for war, division of spoils and whatsoever is gotten by conquest, receiving of more Confederates for Plantations into combination with any of the Confederates, and all things of like nature, which are the proper concomitants or consequents of such a Confederation for amity, offence, and defence: not intermeddling with the government of any of the Jurisdictions, which by the third article is preserved entirely to themselves. But if these eight Commissioners when they meet shall not all agree yet it [is] concluded that any six of the eight agreeing shall have *power* to settle and determine the business in question. . . . [Thorpe 79]

[Article 7:] It is further agreed that at each meeting of these eight Commissioners, whether ordinary or extraordinary, they or six of them agreeing as before, may choose their President out of themselves whose office and work shall be to take care and direct for order and a comely carrying on of all proceedings in the present meeting: but he shall be invested with no such *power* or respect, as by which he shall hinder the propounding or progress of any business, or any way cast the scales otherwise than in the precedent article is agreed. [Thorpe 80]

[Article 10:] That in extraordinary occasions, when meetings are summoned by three magistrates of any Jurisdiction, or two as in the fifth article, if any of the Commissioners come not, due warning being given or sent, it is agreed that four of the Commissioners shall have *power* to direct a war which cannot be delayed, and to send for due proportions of men out of each Jurisdiction, as well as six might do if all met . . . [Thorpe 81]

Charles II, Charter of Carolina, June 30, 1665:

We will also, and by these presents, for us, our heirs and successors, do give and grant licence by this our charter, unto the said Edward Earl of Clarendon, George Duke of Albemarle, William Earl of Craven, John Lord Berkeley, Anthony Lord Ashley, Sir George Carteret, Sir John Colleton, and Sir William Berkeley, and their heirs and assigns, and to all the inhabitants and dwellers in the province or territory aforesaid, both present and to come, full *power* and absolute authority, to import or unlade, by themselves or their servants, factors, or assigns, all merchandises and goods whatsoever that shall arise of the fruits and commodities of the said province or territory . . . [Thorpe 2766]

English Bill of Rights, December 16, 1689:

[1] [The King endeavoured to subvert the liberties of the kingdom] . . . By assuming and exercising a *power* of dispensing with and suspending of laws, and the execution of laws, without consent of parliament. [SDECH 463]

[2] By committing and prosecuting diverse worthy prelates for humbly petitioning to be excused from concurring to the said assumed *power*. [SDECH 463]

[3] And whereas the said late King James the Second having abdicated the government and the throne being thereby vacant, His Highness the Prince of Orange (whom it hath pleased Almighty God to make the glorious instrument of delivering this kingdom from popery and arbitrary *power*) did (by the advice of the lords spiritual and temporal, and diverse principal persons of the commons) cause letters to be written to the Lords Spiritual and Temporal, being Protestants; and other letters to the several counties, cities, universities, buroughs and Cinque ports for the choosing of such persons to represent them . . . [SDECH 464]

[4] That the pretended *power* of suspending of laws or the execution of laws by regal authority without consent of parliament is illegal. [SDECH 464]

[5] That the pretended *power* of dispensing with laws or the execution of laws by regal authority as it hath been assumed and exercised of late is illegal. [SDECH 464]

[6] The said lords spiritual and temporal and commons assembled at Westminster do resolve, that William and Mary, prince and princess of Orange, be and be declared king and queen of England, France and Ireland and the dominions thereunto belonging to hold the crown and royal dignity of the said kingdoms and dominions to them the said prince and princess during their lives and the life of the survivor of them; and that the sole and full exercise of the regal *power* be only in and executed by the said prince of Orange in the names of the said prince and princess during their joint lives . . . [SDECH 465–66]

[7] I, A. B., do swear that I do from my heart abhor, detest and abjure as impious and heretical this damnable doctrine and position that princes excommunicated or deprived by the pope or any authority of the see of Rome may be deposed or murdered by their subjects or any other whatsoever. And I do declare that no foreign prince, person, prelate, state or potentate hath or ought to have any jurisdiction, *power,* superiority, preeminence or authority ecclesiastical or spiritual, within this realm . . . [SDECH 466]

[8] . . . [Parliament does] hereby recognize, acknowledge and declare that King James the Second having abdicated the government and Their Majesties having accepted the crown and royal dignity [as] aforesaid, their said Majesties did become, were, are and of right ought to be by the laws of this realm our sovereign liege lord and lady, king and queen of England, France and Ireland and the dominions thereunto belonging, in and to whose princely persons the royal state, crown and dignity of the said realms, with all honors, stiles, titles, regalities, prerogatives, *powers,* jurisdictions and authorities to the same belonging and appertaining, are most fully, rightfully and entirely invested and incorporated, united and annexed. . . . [SDECH 467]

[9] . . . and that the entire, perfect and full exercise of the regal *power* and government be only in and executed by His Majesty, in the names of both their Majesties, during their joint lives; and after their deceases the said crown and premises shall be and remain to the heirs of the body of Her Majesty; and for default of such issue to her Royal Highness the princess Anne of Denmark and the heirs of her body; and for default of such issue to the heirs of the body of His said Majesty: and thereunto the said lords spiritual and temporal and commons do in the names of all the people aforesaid most humbly and faithfully submit themselves, their heirs and posterities forever; and do faithfully promise that they will stand to, maintain and defend Their said Majesties, and also the limitation and succession of the crown herein specified and contained to the utmost of their *powers* with their lives and estates against all persons whatsoever that shall attempt anything to the contrary. . . . [SDECH 467–68]

[10] . . . that all and every person and persons, that is, are or shall be reconciled to or shall hold communion with the See or Church of Rome, or shall profess the popish religion or shall marry a papist shall be excluded and be forever incapable to inherit, possess or enjoy the crown and government of this realm and Ireland and the dominions thereunto belonging, or any part of the same, or

to have, use or exercise any regal *power,* authority or jurisdiction within the same; and in all and every such case or cases the people of these realms shall be and are hereby absolved of their allegiance . . . [SDECH 468]

William and Mary, Charter of Massachusetts Bay, October 7, 1691:

. . . And wee doe for us our Heires and Successors Give and grant that the said Generall Court or Assembly shall have full *power* and Authority to name and settle annually all Civill Officers within the said Province such Officers Excepted the Election and Constitution of whome wee have by these presents reserved to us Our Heires and Successors or to the Governor of our said Province for the time being and to Sett forth the severall Duties *Powers* and Lymitts of every such Officer to be appointed by the said Generall Court or Assembly and the formes of such Oathes not repugnant to the Lawes and Statutes of this our Realme of England . . . [Thorpe 1882]

The Albany Plan of Union, July 10, 1754:

[1] CONTINUANCE

That the Grand Council have *power* to choose their speaker and shall neither be dissolved, prorogued, nor continued sitting longer than six weeks at one time, without their own consent or the special command of the crown. [Thorpe 84]

[2] *POWER* OF PRESIDENT-GENERAL AND GRAND COUNCIL; TREATIES OF PEACE AND WAR

That the President-General, with the advice of the Grand Council, hold or direct all Indian treaties in which the general interest of the colonies may be concerned; and make peace or declare war with Indian nations. [Thorpe 84]

[3] *POWER* TO MAKE LAWS, LAY DUTIES, &C

That for these purposes they have *power* to make laws, and lay and levy such general duties, imposts, or taxes as to them shall appear most equal and just (considering the ability and other circumstances of the inhabitants in the several colonies), and such as may be collected with the least inconvenience to the people; rather discouraging luxury than loading industry with unnecessary burthens. [Thorpe 85]

[4] DEATH OF THE PRESIDENT-GENERAL

That in case of the death of the President-General, the Speaker of the Grand Council for the time being shall succeed, and be vested with the same *powers* and authorities, to continue till the King's pleasure be known. [Thorpe 86]

First Continental Congress, Declaration and Resolves, October 14, 1774:

[1] Whereas, since the close of the last war, the British parliament, claiming a *power* of right to bind the people of America, by statute in all cases whatsoever,

hath in some acts expressly imposed taxes on them, and in others, under various pretences, but in fact for the purpose of raising a revenue, hath imposed rates and duties payable in these colonies, established a board of commissioners, with unconstitutional *powers,* and extended the jurisdiction of courts of Admiralty, not only for collecting the said duties, but for the trial of causes merely arising within the body of a county. [JCC1 63–64]

[2] That they [the colonists] are entitled to life, liberty, & property, and they have never ceded to any sovereign *power* whatever, a right to dispose of either without their consent. [JCC1 67]

[3] That the foundation of English liberty, and of all free government, is a right in the people to participate in their legislative council: and as the English colonists are not represented, and from their local and other circumstances, cannot properly be represented in the British parliament, they are entitled to a free and exclusive *power* of legislation in their several provincial legislatures, where their right of representation can alone be preserved, in all cases of taxation and internal polity, subject only to the negative of their sovereign, in such manner as has been heretofore used and accustomed.... [JCC1 68]

[4] It is indispensably necessary to good government, and rendered essential by the English constitution, that the constituent branches of the legislature be independent of each other; that, therefore, the exercise of legislative *power* in several colonies, by a council appointed, during pleasure, by the crown, is unconstitutional, dangerous, and destructive to the freedom of American legislation. [JCC1 70]

[5] All and each of which the aforesaid deputies, in behalf of themselves, and their constituents, do claim, demand, and insist on, as their indubitable rights and liberties; which cannot be legally taken from them, altered or abridged by any *power* whatever, without their own consent, by their representatives in their several provincial legislatures. [JCC1 70–71]

[6] The several Acts of 4 Geo. 3, ch. 15 & ch. 34–5 Geo. 3, ch. 25–6 Geo. 3, ch. 52–7 Geo. 3, ch. 41 & 46–8 Geo. 3, ch. 22, which impose duties for the purpose of raising a revenue in America, extend the *powers* of the admiralty courts beyond their ancient limits, deprive the American subject of trial by jury . . . [JCC1 71]

Benjamin Franklin, Proposed Articles of Confederation, c. July 21, 1775:

[Article 5:] That the *Power* and Duty of the Congress shall extend to the Determining on War and Peace, to sending and receiving Ambassadors, and entring into Alliances, the Reconciliation with Great Britain; the Settling all Disputes and Differences between Colony and Colony about limits or any other cause if such should arise; and the Planting of new Colonies when proper. The Congress shall also make such general Ordinances as tho' necessary to the General Welfare, particular Assemblies cannot be competent to, viz. those that may relate to our general Commerce or general Currency; to the Establishment of Posts; and the Regulation of our common Forces. The Congress shall also have the Appointment of all Officers civil and military, appertaining to the general Confederacy, such as General Treasurer Secretary, &c. [PBF22 122–23]

Thomas Paine, *Common Sense*, January 9, 1776:

A government of our own is our natural right: and when a man seriously reflects on the precariousness of human affairs, he will become convinced, that it is infinitely wiser and safer, to form a Constitution of our own in a cool deliberate manner, while we have it in our *power,* than to trust such an interesting event to time and chance. If we omit it now, some Massenello may hereafter arise, who laying hold of popular disquietudes, may collect together the desperate and the discontented, and by assuming to themselves the *powers* of government, may sweep away the liberties of the continent like a deluge. . . .

[CWTP1 29–30]

John Adams, *Thoughts on Government*, April 1776:

. . . That it may be the interest of this Assembly to do strict justice at all times, it should be an equal representation, or in other words equal interests among the people should have equal interests in it. Great care should be taken to effect this, and to prevent unfair, partial, and corrupt elections. Such regulations, however, may be better made in times of greater tranquility than the present, and they will spring up themselves naturally, when all the *powers* of government come to be in the hands of the people's friends. At present it will be safest to proceed in all established modes to which the people have been familiarized by habit. [PJA4 87–88]

Virginia Constitution, June 29, 1776:

. . . and he [the Governor] shall, with the advice of a Council of State, exercise the executive *powers* of government, according to the laws of this Commonwealth; and shall not, under any pretence, exercise any *power* or prerogative, by virtue of any law, statute or custom of England. But he shall, with the advice of the Council of State, have the *power* of granting reprieves or pardons, except where the prosecution shall have been carried on by the House of Delegates, or the law shall otherwise particularly direct; in which cases, no reprieve or pardon shall be granted, but by resolve of the House of Delegates. [Thorpe 3816–17]

New Jersey Constitution, July 2, 1776:

[Article 6:] That the Council shall also have *power* to prepare bills to pass into laws, and have other like *powers* as the Assembly, and in all respects be a free and independent branch of the Legislature of this Colony; save only, that they shall not prepare or alter any money bill—which shall lie the privilege of the Assembly; that the Council shall, from time to time, be convened by the Governor or Vice-President, but must be convened, at all times, when the Assembly sits; for which purpose the Speaker of the House of Assembly shall always, immediately after an adjournment, give notice to the Governor, or Vice-President, of the time and place to which the House is adjourned. [Thorpe 2596]

United States Declaration of Independence, July 4, 1776:

[1] When in the Course of human events, it becomes necessary for one people to dissolve the political bands which have connected them with another, and to assume among the *powers* of the earth, the separate and equal station to which the Laws of Nature and of Nature's God entitle them, a decent respect to the opinions of mankind requires that they should declare the causes which impel them to the separation.—We hold these truths to be self-evident, that all men are created equal, that they are endowed by their Creator with certain unalienable Rights, that among these are Life, Liberty and the pursuit of Happiness.—That to secure these rights, Governments are instituted among Men, deriving their just *powers* from the consent of the governed,—That whenever any Form of Government becomes destructive of these ends, it is the Right of the People to alter or to abolish it, and to institute new Government, laying its foundation on such principles and organizing its *powers* in such form, as to them shall seem most likely to effect their Safety and Happiness . . .

[2] . . . He [the King] has obstructed the Administration of Justice, by refusing his Assent to Laws for establishing Judiciary *Powers*. . . .

[4] . . . He has affected to render the Military independent of and superior to the Civil *Power*. . . .

[5] . . . For suspending our own Legislature, and declaring themselves invested with *Power* to legislate for us in all cases whatsoever. . . .

[6] . . . That these United Colonies are, and of Right ought to be Free and Independent States; that they are Absolved from all Allegiance to the British Crown, and that all political connection between them and the State of Great Britain, is and ought to be totally dissolved; and that as Free and Independent States, they have full *Power* to levy War, conclude Peace, contract Alliances, establish Commerce, and to do all other Acts and Things which Independent States may of right do. . . .

United States Continental Congress, Draft Articles of Confederation, July 12, 1776:

[Article 16:] For the more convenient Management of the general Interests of the United States, Delegates should be annually appointed in such Manner as the Legislature of each Colony shall direct, to meet at the City of Philadelphia, in the Colony of Pennsylvania, until otherwise ordered by the United States assembled; which Meeting shall be on the first Monday of November in every Year, with a *Power* reserved to those who appointed the said Delegates, respectively to recall them at any Time within the Year, and to send new Delegates in their stead for the remainder of the Year. . . . [DHRC1 81–82]

[Article 18:] The United States assembled shall have the sole and exclusive Right and *Power* of determining on Peace and War, except in the Cases mentioned in the thirteenth Article—Of establishing Rules for deciding in all Cases, what Captures on Land or Water shall be legal—In what Manner Prizes taken by land or naval Forces in the Service of the United States shall be divided or appropriated—Granting Letters of Marque and Reprisal in Times of Peace—Appointing Courts for the Trial of all Crimes, Frauds and Piracies committed on the High Seas, or any navigable River, not within the Body of a County or Parish—Establishing Courts for receiving and determining finally Appeals in all Cases of Captures—Sending and receiving Ambassadors under any Character—Entering into Treaties and Alliances—Settling all Disputes and Differences now subsisting, or that hereafter may arise between two or more Colonies concerning Boundaries, Jurisdictions, or any other Cause whatever—Coining Money and regulating the Value thereof—Regulating the Trade, and managing all Affairs with the Indians—Limiting the Bounds of those Colonies, which by Charter or Proclamation, or under any Pretence, are said to extend to the South Sea, and ascertaining those Bounds of any other Colony that appear to be indeterminate—Assigning Territories for new Colonies, either in Lands to be thus separated from Colonies and heretofore purchased or obtained by the Crown of Great-Britain from the Indians, or hereafter to be purchased or obtained from them—Disposing of all such Lands for the general Benefit of all the United Colonies—Ascertaining Boundaries to such new Colonies, within which Forms of Government are to be established on the Principles of Liberty—Establishing and regulating Post-Offices throughout all the United Colonies, on the Lines of Communication from one Colony to another—Appointing General Officers of the Land Forces in the Service of the United States—Commissioning such other Officers of the said Forces as shall be appointed by Virtue of the tenth Article—Appointing all the Officers of the Naval Forces in the Service of the United States—Making Rules for the Government and Regulation of the Said Land and Naval Forces, and directing the operations—Appointing a Council of State, and such Committees and civil Officers as may be necessary for managing the general Affairs of the United States, under their Direction while assembled, and in their Recess, of the Council of State—Appointing one of their number to preside, and a suitable Person for Secretary—And adjourning to any time within the Year. [DHRC1 82–83]

[Article 19:] This Council [of the States] shall have *Power* to receive and open all Letters directed to the United States, and to return proper Answers; but not to make any Engagements that shall be binding on the United States—To correspond with the Legislature of each Colony, and all Persons acting under the Authority of the United States, or of the said Legislatures—To apply to such Legislatures, or to the Officers in the several Colonies who are entrusted with the executive *Powers* of Government, for occasional Aid whenever and wherever necessary—To give Counsel to the Commanding Officers, and direct military Operations by Sea and Land, not changing any Objects or Expeditions determined on by the United States assembled, unless an Alteration of Circumstances which shall come to the Knowledge of the Council after the Recess of the States, shall make such Change absolutely necessary—To attend to the Defence and Preservation of Forts and strong Posts, and to prevent the Enemy from acquiring new Holds—To procure Intelligence of the Condition and Designs of the Enemy—To expedite the Execution of such Measures as may be resolved on by the United States assembled, in Pursuance of the *Powers* hereby given to them—To draw upon the Treasurers for such Sums as may be appropriated by the United States assembled, and for the Payment of such Contracts as said Council may make in Pursuance of the *Powers* hereby given to them—To superintend and controul or suspend all Officers civil and military, acting under the Authority of the United States—In Case of the Death or Removal of any Officer within the Appointment of the United States assembled, to employ a Person to fulfill the Duties of such Office until the Assembly of the States meet—To fulfill the Duties of such Office until the Assembly of the States meet—To publish and disperse authentic Accounts of military Operations—To summon an Assembly of the States at any earlier Day than that appointed for their next Meeting, if any great and unexpected Emergency should render it necessary for the Safety or Welfare of the United Colonies or any of them—To prepare Matters for the Consideration of the United States, and to lay before them at their next Meeting all Letters and Advices received by the Council, with a Report of their Proceedings—To appoint a proper Person for their Clerk, who shall take an Oath of Secrecy, and Fidelity, before he enters on the Exercise of his Office—Seven Members shall have *Power* to act—In Case of the Death of any Member, the Council shall immediately apply to his surviving Colleagues to appoint some one of themselves to be a Member thereof till the Meeting of the States, and if only one survives, they shall give him immediate Notice, that he may take his Seat as a Councilor till such Meeting. [DHRC1 84–85]

Pennsylvania Constitution, September 28, 1776:

[Declaration of Rights, Article 4:] That all *power* being originally inherent in, and consequently derived from, the people; therefore all officers of government, whether legislative or executive, are their trustees and servants, and at all times accountable to them. [Thorpe 3082]

Vermont Constitution, July 8, 1777:

[Frame of Government, Section 18:] The Governor, and in his absence, the Lieutenant or Deputy Governor, with the Council—seven of whom shall be a quorum—shall have *power* to appoint and commissionate all officers, (except those who are appointed by the General Assembly,) agreeable to this frame of government, and the laws that may be made hereafter . . . [Thorpe 3745]

United States Articles of Confederation, November 15, 1777:

[Article II:] Each state retains its sovereignty, freedom and independence, and every *Power,* Jurisdiction and right, which is not by this confederation expressly delegated to the United States, in Congress assembled.

[Article IV:] If any Person guilty of, or charged with treason, felony, or other high misdemeanor in any state, shall flee from Justice, and be found in any of the united states, he shall upon demand of the Governor or executive *power,* of the state from which he fled, be delivered up and removed to the state having jurisdiction of his offence.

[Article V:] For the more convenient management of the general interests of the united states, delegates shall be annually appointed in such manner as the legislature of each state shall direct, to meet in Congress on the first Monday in November, in every year, with a *power* reserved to each state, to recall its delegates, or any of them, at any time within the year, and to send others in their stead, for the remainder of the Year.

[Article IX:] The united states in congress assembled, shall have the sole and exclusive right and *power* of determining on peace and war, except in the cases mentioned in the sixth article—of sending and receiving ambassadors—entering into treaties and alliances, provided that no treaty of commerce shall be made whereby the legislative *power* of the respective states shall be restrained from imposing such imposts and duties on foreigners, as their own people are subjected to, or from prohibiting the exportation or importation of any species of goods or commodities whatsoever—of establishing rules for deciding in all cases, what captures on land or water shall be legal, and in what manner prizes taken by land or naval forces in the service of the united states shall be divided or appropriated—of granting letters of marque and reprisal in times of peace—appointing courts for the trial of piracies and felonies committed on the high seas and establishing courts for receiving and determining finally appeals in all cases of captures, provided that no member of congress shall be appointed a judge of any of the said courts.

[*Ibid.:*] The united states in congress assembled shall also have the sole and exclusive right and *power* of regulating the alloy and value of coin struck by their own authority, or by that of the respective states—fixing the standard of weights and measures throughout the united states—regulating the trade and managing all affairs with the Indians, not members of any of the states, provided that the legislative right of any state within its own limits be not infringed or violated—establishing and regulating post offices from one state to another, throughout all the united states, and exacting such postage on the papers passing through the same as may be requisite to defray the expenses of the said office—appointing all officers of the land forces, in the service of the united states, excepting regimental officers—appointing all the officers of the naval forces, and commissioning all officers whatever in the service of the united states—making rules for the government and regulation of the said land and naval forces, and directing their operations.

[*Ibid.*:] The congress of the united states shall have *power* to adjourn to any time within the year, and to any place within the united states, so that no period of adjournment be for a longer duration than the space of six Months . . .

[Article X:] The committee of the states, or any nine of them, shall be authorized to execute, in the recess of congress, such of the *powers* of congress as the united states in congress assembled, by the consent of nine states, shall from time to time think expedient to vest them with; provided that no *power* be delegated to the said committee, for the exercise of which, by the articles of confederation, the voice of nine states in the congress of the united states assembled is requisite.

[Article XIII:] And wheras it hath pleased the Great Governor of the World to incline the hearts of the legislatures we respectively represent in congress, to approve of, and to authorize us to ratify the said articles of confederation and perpetual union. Know ye that we the undersigned delegates, by virtue of the *power* and authority to us given for that purpose, do by these presents, in the name and in behalf of our respective constituents, fully and entirely ratify and confirm each and every of the said articles of confederation and perpetual union . . .

Massachusetts Constitution, March 2, 1780:

[Chapter II:2:3:] Whenever the chair of the governor shall be vacant, by reason of his death, or absence from the commonwealth, or otherwise, the lieutenant governor, for the time being, shall, during such vacancy, perform all the duties incumbent upon the governor, and shall have and exercise all the *powers* and authorities, which by this constitution the governor is vested with, when personally present. [Thorpe 1904]

New Hampshire Constitution, June 2, 1784:

[Form of Government:] The *power* of pardoning offences, except such as persons may be convicted of before the senate by impeachment of the house, shall be in the president by and with the advice of the council . . . [Thorpe 2464]

Virginia Statute of Religious Liberty, January 16, 1786:

[1] Whereas Almighty God hath created the mind free; that all attempts to influence it by temporal punishments, or burdens, or by civil incapacitations, tend only to beget habits of hypocrisy and meanness, and are a departure from the plan of the Holy Author of our religion, who, being Lord both of body and mind, yet chose not to propagate it by coercions on either, as was in his Almighty *power* to do . . . [CVA8 690]

[2] . . . that to suffer the civil magistrate to intrude his *powers* into the field of opinion, and to restrain the profession or propagation of principles on supposition of their ill tendency, is a dangerous fallacy, which at once destroys all religious liberty, because he being of course judge of that tendency will make his opinions the rule of judgment, and approve or condemn the sentiments of others only as they shall square with or differ from his own . . . [CVA8 690–91]

[3] And though we well know that this Assembly, elected by the people for the ordinary purposes of legislation only, have no *power* to restrain the acts of succeeding assemblies, constituted with *powers* equal to our own, and that therefore to declare this act to be irrevocable would be of no effect in law; yet as we are free to declare, and do declare, that the rights hereby asserted are of the natural rights of mankind, and that if any act shall hereafter be passed to repeal the present, or to narrow its operation, such act will be an infringement of natural right. [CVA8 691]

Report of the Annapolis Convention, September 14, 1786:

[1] That, pursuant to their several appointments, they met, at Annapolis in the State of Maryland, on the eleventh day of September Instant, and having proceeded to a Communication of their *powers;* they found, that the States of New York, Pennsylvania and Virginia had, in substance, and nearly in the same terms, authorised their respective Commissioners . . . [DHRC1 182]

[2] That the State of Delaware, had given similar *powers* to their Commissioners, with this difference only that the Act to be framed by virtue of those *powers,* is required to be reported "to the United States in Congress Assembled, to be agreed to by them, and confirmed by the Legislatures of every State." [DHRC1 183]

[3] That the express terms of the *powers* to your Commissioners supposing a deputation from all the States, and having for object the Trade and Commerce of the United States, Your Commissioners did not conceive it advisable to proceed on the business of their mission, under the Circumstance of so partial and defective a representation. [DHRC1 183]

[4] In this persuasion, Your Commissioners submit an opinion, that the Idea of extending the *powers* of their Deputies, to other objects than those of Commerce which has been adopted by the State of New Jersey, was an improvement on

the original plan, and will deserve to be incorporated into that of a future Convention, they are the more naturally led to this conclusion, as in the course of their reflections on the subject, they have been induced to think, that the *power* of regulating trade is of such comprehensive extent, and will enter so far into the general System of the foederal government, that to give it efficacy, and to obviate questions and doubts concerning its precise nature and limits may require a correspondent adjustment of other parts of the Foederal System.
[DHRC1 183–84]

[5] Your Commissioners decline an enumeration of those national circumstances on which their opinion respecting the propriety of a future Convention with more enlarged *powers,* is founded; as it would be useless intrusion of facts and observations, most of which have been frequently the subject of public discussion, and none of which can have escaped the penetration of those to whom they would in this instance be addressed. . . . [DHRC1 184]

The Virginia Plan of Union, May 29, 1787:

[Article 14:] Res[olve]d that the Legislative Executive & Judiciary *powers* within the several States ought to be bound by oath to support the articles of Union.
[DHRC1 245]

Charles Pinckney's Plan of Union, May 29, 1787:

[Article 5:] The Senate and [House of Delegates] shall by joint Ballot annually chuse the Presidt. U.S. from among themselves or the People at large.—In the Presidt. the executive Authority of the U.S. shall be vested.—His *Powers* and Duties. He shall have a Right to advise with the Heads of the different Departments as his Council. [DHRC1 246]

[Article 11:] The exclusive *Powers* of S. & H.D. in [Congress] assembled.
[DHRC1 246]

[Article 12:] The S. & H.D. in C. ass. shall have the exclusive *Power* of regulating Trade and levying Imposts—Each State may lay Embargoes in Time of Scarcity. [DHRC1 246]

[Article 13:] ——— of establishing Post Offices. [DHRC1 246]

[Article 15:] They [Congress] shall have the exclusive *Power* of declaring what shall be Treason and Misp[rision] of Treason agt. U.S.—and of instituting a federal judicial Court, to which an Appeal shall be allowed from the judicial Courts of the several States in all Causes wherein Questions shall arise on the Construction of Treaties made by U.S. or on the Law of Nations . . .
[DHRC1 247]

[Article 22:] *Power* of dividing annexing and consolidating States on the Consent and Petition of such States. [DHRC1 247]

[Article 25:] The said States of [New Hampshire] &c. guarrantee muturally each other and their Rights against all other *Powers* and against all Rebellions, &c. [DHRC1 247]

The New Jersey Plan of Union, June 15, 1787:

[Article 2:] Res[olve]d that in addition to the *powers* vested in the U. States in Congress, by the present existing articles of Confederation, they be authorized to pass acts for raising a revenue, by levying a duty or duties on all goods or merchandizes of foreign growth or manufacture imported into any part of the U. States, by Stamps on paper, vellum or parchment, and by a postage on all letters or packages passing through the general post-office, to be applied to such federal purposes as they shall deem proper & expedient . . . [DHRC1 251]

[Article 3:] . . . provided that none of the *powers* hereby vested in the U. States in Cong[res]s shall be exercised without the consent of at least ——— States, and in that proportion if the number of Confederated States should hereafter be increased or diminished. [DHRC1 251]

[Article 6:] Res[olve]d that all Acts of the U. States in Cong[res]s made by virtue and in pursuance of the *powers* hereby & by the articles of Confederation vested in them, and all Treaties made & ratified under the authority of the U. States, shall be the supreme law of the respective States, so far forth as those Acts or Treaties shall relate to the said States or their Citizens, and that the Judiciary of the several States shall be bound thereby in their decisions, any thing in the respective laws of the Individual States to the contrary notwithstanding; and that if any State, or any body of men in any State shall oppose or prevent the carrying into execution such acts or treaties, the federal Executive shall be authorized to call forth the *power* of the Confederated States, or so much thereof as may be necessary to enforce and compel an obedience to such Acts, or an observance of such Treaties. [DHRC1 252–53]

Alexander Hamilton's Plan of Union, June 18, 1787:

[1] The Supreme Legislative *Power* of the United States of America to be vested in two distinct bodies of men—the one to be called the Assembly the other the Senate; who together shall form the Legislature of the United States, with *power* to pass all laws whatsoever, subject to the negative hereafter mentioned. [DHRC1 253]

[2] . . . The Governor to have a negative upon all laws about to be passed—and to have the execution of all laws passed—to be the Commander in Chief of the land and naval forces and of the Militia of the United States—to have the direction of war, when authorized or began—to have, with the advice and approbation of the Senate the *power* of making all treaties—to have the appointment of the heads or chief officers of the departments of finance war and foreign affairs—to have the nomination of all other officers (ambassadors to foreign nations

included) subject to the approbation or rejection of the Senate—to have the *power* of pardoning all offenses but treason, which he shall not pardon without the approbation of the Senate. [DHRC1 254]

[3] The Senate to have the sole *power* of declaring war—the *power* of advising and approving all treaties—the *power* of approving or rejecting all appointments of officers except the heads or chiefs of the departments of finance war and foreign affairs. [DHRC1 254]

[4] The Legislature of the United States to have *power* to institute Courts in each state for the determination of all causes of capture and of all matters relating to their revenues, or in which the Citizens of foreign nations are concerned. [DHRC1 254]

United Confederation States Congress, The Northwest Ordinance, July 13, 1787:

[1] Previous to the organization of the general assembly the governor shall appoint such magistrates, and other civil officers, in each county or township, as he shall find necessary for the preservation of the peace and good order in the same. After the general assembly shall be organized the *powers* and duties of magistrates and other civil officers shall be regulated and defined by the said assembly . . . [Thorpe 959]

[2] . . . The governor shall have *power* to convene, prorogue, and dissolve the general assembly when, in his opinion, it shall be expedient. [Thorpe 960]

Tench Coxe, *An Examination of the Constitution for the United States of America*, No. 1, September 26, 1787:

[1] Our President will fall very much short indeed of any prince in his annual income, which will not be hereditary, but the absolute allowance of the people, passing through the hands of their other servants from year to year, as it becomes necessary. There will be no burdens on the nation, to provide for his heir, or other branches of his family. It is probable, from the state of property in America, and other circumstances, that many citizens will exceed him in show and expense,—those dazzling trappings of kingly rank and *power*. . . . [Ford 139]

[2] . . . He will have no influence from placemen in the legislature, nor can he prorogue or dissolve it. He will have no *power* over the treasures of the state; and, lastly, as he is created through the electors, by the people at large, he must ever look up to the support of his creators. From such a servant, with *powers* so limited and transitory, there can be no danger, especially when we consider the solid foundations on which our national liberties are immoveably fixed, by the other provisions of this excellent constitution. Whatever of dignity or authority he possesses, is a delegated part of their majesty and their political omnipotence, transiently vested in him by the people themselves, for their own happiness. [Ford 139]

Alexandria, Virginia, Town Meeting, September 28, 1787:

The proposed foederal constitution was read, and unanimously approved of—and it was resolved, that William Hunter, jun. Robert T. Hooe, William Hartshorne, James Keith, William Brown, William Herbert, Charles Simms, David Arell, and John Fitzgerald, Esquires, be appointed a committee to meet the freeholders of Fairfax county, at Price's Old Fields, on Tuesday, the second day of October next, for the purpose of instructing the delegates of this county, to use their utmost *power* and abilities to obtain in the next General Assembly a recommendation from that honourable body, to the freeholders of the state at large, for the holding a convention as speedily as possible, for the purpose of adopting the aforesaid constitution. [DHRC8 23]

Richard Henry Lee [?], "The Federal Farmer," No. 1, October 8, 1787:

The confederation was formed when great confidence was placed in the voluntary exertions of individuals, and of the respective states; and the framers of it, to guard against usurpation, so limited, and checked the *powers,* that, in many respects, they are inadequate to the exigencies of the union. We find, therefore, members of congress urging alterations in the federal system almost as soon as it was adopted. It was early proposed to vest congress with *powers* to levy an impost, to regulate trade, &c. but such was known to be the caution of the states in parting with *power,* that the vestment even of these, was proposed to be under several checks and limitations. . . . [Ford 283]

Richard Henry Lee [?], "The Federal Farmer," No. 3, October 10, 1787:

. . . All these circumstances considered, is it wise, prudent, or safe, to vest the *powers* of laying and collecting internal taxes in the general government, while imperfectly organized and inadequate; and to trust to amending it hereafter, and making it adequate to this purpose? It is not only unsafe but absurd to lodge *power* in a government before it is fitted to receive it? It is confessed that this *power* and representation ought to go together. Why give the *power* first? Why give the *power* to the few, who, when possessed of it, may have address enough to prevent the increase of representation? Why not keep the *power,* and, when necessary, amend the constitution, and add to its other parts this *power,* and a proper increase of representation at the same time? Then men who may want the *power* will be under strong inducements to let in the people, by their representatives, into the government, to hold their due proportion of this *power.* . . . [Ford 302–303]

Richard Henry Lee [?], "The Federal Farmer," No. 5, October 15, 1787:

. . . One party is composed of little insurgents, men in debt, who want no law, and who want a share of the property of others; these are called levellers, Shayites, &c. The other party is composed of a few, but more dangerous men, with their servile dependents; these avariciously grasp at all *power* and property; you may discover in all the actions of these men, an evident dislike to free and equal government, and they will go systematically to work to change, essentially, the forms of government in this country; these are called aristocrats, m——ites, &c. &c. Between these two parties is the weight of the community; the men of middling property, men not in debt on the one hand, and men, on the other, content with republican governments, and not aiming at immense fortunes, offices, and *power*. . . . [Ford 321]

Noah Webster, *An Examination of the Leading Principles of the Federal Constitution*, October 17, 1787:

[1] The views of the convention I believe to be perfectly upright—They might mean to place the election of representatives and senators beyond the reach of faction—They doubtless had good reasons, in their minds, for the clause—But I see no occasion for any *power* in Congress to interfere with the choice of their own body—They will have *power* to suppress insurrections, as they ought to have; but the clause in Italics gives needless and dangerous *powers*—I hope the states will reject it with decency, and adopt the whole system, without altering another syllable. [Ford 44]

[2] But the truth is, the creation of all inferior courts is in the *power* of Congress; and the constitution provides that Congress may make such exceptions from the right of appeals as they shall judge proper. When these courts are erected, their jurisdictions will be ascertained, and in small actions, Congress will doubtless direct that a sentence in a subordinate court shall, to a certain amount, be definite and final. All objections therefore to the judicial *powers* of the federal courts appear to me as trifling as any of the preceding. [Ford 53–54]

Tench Coxe, *An Examination of the Constitution for the United States of America*, No. 4, October 21, 1787:

The apprehensions of the people have bee excited, perhaps by persons with good intentions, about the *powers* of the new government to raise an army. Let us consider this point with moderation and candour. As enemies will sometimes insult us, invade our country and capture our property, it is clear a *power* in our government to oppose, restrain or destroy them, is necessary to our honor, safety and existence. The military should, however, be regarded with a watchful eye; for it is a profession that is liable to dangerous perversion. But the *powers* vested in the foederal government do not go the length which has been said. A standing army is not granted or intended, for there can be no provision for its continuing three years, much less for its permanent establishment. Two years are the utmost time for which the money can be given. It will be under all the restrictions which wisdom and jealousy can suggest, and the original grant of the supplies must be made by the House of representatives, the immediate delegates of the people. The Senate and President, who also derive their *power* from the people, appoint the officers; and the heads of the departments, who must submit their accounts to the whole legislature, are to pay and provide them, as shall be directed by the laws that shall contain the conditions of the grant. . . . [Ford 150–51]

Virginia Assembly, October 25, 1787:

Mr. [Patrick] Henry rose to oppose the resolution as it then stood. He did not question the propriety or necessity of calling a Convention. No man, he said, was more truly federal than himself: But he conceived that if this resolution was adopted, the Convention would only have it in their *power* to say, that the new plan should be adopted, or rejected; and that, however defective it might appear to them, they would not be authorized to propose amendments. . . .

[DHRC8 113]

Hugh Williamson, Address at Edenton, North Carolina, November 8, 1787:

We have been told that the Liberty of the Press is not secured by the New Constitution. Be pleased to examine the plan, and you will find that the Liberty of the Press and the laws of Mahomet are equally affected by it. The New Government is to have the *power* of protecting literary property; the very *power* which you have by a special act delegated to the present Congress. There was a time in England, when neither book, pamphlet, nor paper could be published without a licence from Government. That restraint was finally removed in the year 1694 and by such removal, their press became perfectly free, for it is not under the restraint of any licence. Certainly the new Government can have no *power* to impose restraints. . . . [DHRC16 202]

Oliver Ellsworth, "The Landholder," No. 6, December 10, 1787:

. . . Mr. [George] Mason would have it in the *power* of the southern states to prevent any navigation-act. This clause, as unequal and partial in the extreme to the southern states, was rejected; because it ought to be left on the same footing with other national concerns, and because no state would have a right to complain of a navigation-act which should leave the carrying business equally open to them all. Those who preferred cultivating their lands would do so; those who chose to navigate and become carriers would do that. The loss of this question determined Mr. Mason against the signing the doings of the convention, and is undoubtedly among his reasons as drawn for the southern states; but for the eastern states this reason would not do. It would convince us that Mr. Mason preferred the subjects of every foreign *power* to the subjects of the United States who live in New-England . . . [DHRC8 230]

Alexander Hamilton, *The Federalist*, No. 21, December 12, 1787:

The next most palpable defect of the subsisting Confederation is the total want of a SANCTION to its laws. The United States,as now composed, have no *powers* to exact obedience, or punish disobedience to the resolutions, either by pecuniary mulcts, by a suspension of divestiture of privileges, or by any other constitutional mode. There is no express delegation of authority to them to use force against delinquent members; and if such a right should be ascribed to the federal head, as resulting from the nature of the social compact between the States, it must be by inference and construction, in the face of that part of the second article, by which it is declared, "that each State shall retain every *power,* jurisdiction, and right, not expressly delegated to the United States in Congress assembled." . . . [Fed. 186]

Dissent of the Pennsylvania Convention's Minority, December 18, 1787:

. . . It has been alleged that the words "pursuant to the constitution" are a restriction upon the authority of Congress; but when it is considered that by other sections they are invested with every efficient *power* of government, and which may be exercised to the absolute destruction of the state governments, without any violation of even the forms of the constitution, this seeming restriction, as well as every other restriction in it, appears to us to be nugatory and delusive; and only introduced as a blind upon the real nature of the government. In our opinion, "pursuant to the constitution" will be co-extensive with the will and pleasure of Congress, which, indeed, will be the only limitation of their *powers*. [DHRC2 628]

Alexander Hamilton, *The Federalist*, No. 27, December 25, 1787:

. . . As far as I have been able to divine the latent meaning of the objectors, it seems to originate in a presupposition that the people will be disinclined to the exercise of federal authority in any matter of an internal nature. Waiving any exception that might be taken to the inaccuracy or inexplicitness of the distinction between internal and external, let us inquire what ground there is to presuppose that disinclination in the people. Unless we presume at the same time that the *powers* of the general government will be worse administered than those of the State government, there seems to be no room for the presumption of ill-will, disaffection, or opposition in the people. . . . [Fed. 219]

Alexander Hamilton, *The Federalist*, No. 32, January 2, 1788:

A case which may perhaps be thought to resemble the latter, but which is in fact widely different, affects the question immediately under consideration. I mean the *power* of imposing taxes on all articles other than exports and imports. This, I contend, is manifestly a concurrent and coequal authority in the United States and in the individual States. There is plainly no expression in the granting clause which makes that *power* exclusive in the Union. . . . [Fed. 242]

Alexander Hamilton, *The Federalist*, No. 36, January 8, 1788:

It has been very properly observed by different speakers and writers on the side of the Constitution, that if the exercise of the *power* of internal taxation by the Union should be discovered on experiment to be really inconvenient, the federal government may then forbear the use of it, and have recourse to requisitions in its stead. By way of answer to this, it has been triumphantly asked, Why not in the first instance omit that ambiguous *power,* and rely upon the latter source? Two solid answers may be given. The first is, that the exercise of that *power,* if convenient, will be preferable, because it will be more effectual; and it is impossible to prove in theory, or otherwise than by the experiment, that it cannot be advantageously exercised. The contrary, indeed, appears most probable. The second answer is, that the existence of such a *power* in the Constitution will have a strong influence in giving efficacy to requisitions. When the States know that the Union can apply itself without their agency, it will be a powerful motive for exertion on their part. [Fed. 262]

James Madison, *The Federalist*, No. 40, January 18, 1788:

. . . In some instances, as has been shown, the *powers* of the new government will act on the States in their collective characters. In some instances, also, those of the existing government act immediately on individuals. In cases of capture; of piracy; of the post office; of coins, weights, and measures; of trade with the Indians; of claims under grants of land by different States; and, above all, in the case of trials by courts-martial in the army and navy, by which death may be inflicted without the intervention of a jury, or even of a civil magistrate;—in all these cases the *powers* of the Confederation operate immediately on the persons and interests of individual citizens. . . . [Fed. 289]

"Valerius," January 23, 1788:

. . . Is not the president responsible to the people, who, indirectly, elect him, and to the house of representatives, who can impeach him? Is not the senate amenable to the different state legislatures; by whose breath they exist and can be in a moment annihilated, and to the house of representatives also, which has the sole *power* of impeachment? . . . [DHRC8 316]

James Madison, *The Federalist*, No. 44, January 25, 1788:

Had the Constitution been silent on this head, there can be no doubt that all the particular *powers* requisite as means of executing the general *powers* would have resulted to the government, by unavoidable implication. No axiom is more clearly established in law, or in reason, than that wherever the end is required, the means are authorized; wherever a general *power* to do a thing is given, every particular *power* necessary for doing it is included. . . . [Fed. 321–22]

Letter from Maryland, January 29, 1788, published in Philadelphia *Independent Gazetteer*, February 8, 1788:

The federal hacks assert, that whoever dares to utter a syllable in disapprobation of their cause, is from that instant, to be publicly charged as inimical to his country; and as they have the advantage of every press, from New Hampshire, to Georgia, to circulate their calumnies, the unfortunate objects of their rancour, in that extent of country, can only resort to two or three, at most, who have spirit and independence enough to publish in vindication of these devoted victims to *power* and tyranny. This circumstance accounts fully for the unanimity that prevails throughout the whole continent, in adopting the new federal government, for wherever there is a printing press, there you will find some federal hacks, or company of hacks, who claim an absolute dominion over Mr. Type, as if unlimited monarchy had already been established in this wretched country. The Post-Offices are also under the influence of these sons of *power,* so much so that a paper printed at New-York cannot find its way to Philadelphia, Baltimore, or any of the other states . . . [DHRC16 88]

James Madison, *The Federalist*, No. 47, January 30, 1788:

If we look into the constitutions of the several States, we find that, notwithstanding the emphatical and, in some instances, the unqualified terms in which this axiom has been laid down, there is not a single instance in which the several departments of *power* have been kept absolutely separate and distinct. New Hampshire, whose constitution was the last formed, seems to have been fully aware of the impossibility and inexpediency of avoiding any mixture whatever of these departments, and has qualified the doctrine by declaring "that the legislative, executive, and judiciary *powers* ought to be kept as separate from, and independent of, each other as the nature of a free government will admit; or as is consistent with that chain of connection that binds the whole fabric of the constitution in one indissoluble bond of unity and amity." Her constitution accordingly mixes these departments in several respects. . . . [Fed. 339]

Tench Coxe, "A Freeman," No. 3, February 6, 1788:

. . . Where is the county that can independently train its own militia, appoint its civil and militia officers, establish a peculiar system of penal laws, issue criminal process in its own name, erect corporations, impose direct taxes, excises and duties, hold lands in its own right, commence war on any emergency, regulate descents, prescribe the qualifications of electors, alter its constitution or the principles of its government, divide itself into separate and independent parts, join itself to another state, issue writs for elections, and regulate the same, enact inspection laws, erect courts, appoint judges, commission all its officers, create new offices, sell and give away its lands, erect fortifications, and, in short where is the county in the union, or in the world, that can exercise in any instance independent legislative, executive or judicial *powers?* [DHRC16 49–50]

William Ward [?], "Republicus," February 16, 1788:

. . . In this I shall confine myself to civil liberty, and that natural liberty or freedom of mankind, in an unconnected state, (or as some say, in a state of nature) from whence it arises: and shall first enquire what this natural freedom is, it is obvious at first sight, that this is neither more nor less than a *power* of self government, a performance of all our actions agreable to our own will; or in plainer terms, it is a doing as we please; under the direction of reason, the great, primary, and never-ceasing law of nature. As long as any man does so he has a right to enjoy his person, life, and property, free from all molestation whatsoever; and were he able, even to repel the combined *power* of the world, in any attempt to deprive him of either . . . [DHRC8 375–76]

James Iredell, "Marcus," No. 1, February 20, 1788:

As to the want of a Declaration of Rights.

The introduction of these in England, from which the idea was originally taken, was in consequence of usurpations of the Crown, contrary, as was conceived, to the principles of their government. But there, no original constitution is to be found, and the only meaning of a declaration of rights in that country is, that in certain particulars specified, the Crown had no authority to act. Could this have been necessary, had there been a Constitution in being, by which it could have been clearly discerned whether the Crown had such authority or not? Had the people by a solemn instrument delegated particular *powers* to the Crown at the formation of their government, surely the Crown which in that case could claim under that instrument only, could not have contended for more *power* than was conveyed by it. So it is in regard to the new Constitution here: The future government which may be formed under that authority, certainly cannot act beyond the warrant of that authority. As well might they attempt to impose a King upon America, as go one step in any other respect beyond the terms of their institution. The question then only is, whether more *power* will be vested in the future government than is necessary for the general purposes of the Union. . . .

[DHRC16 163–64]

Alexander Hamilton, *The Federalist*, No. 59, February 22, 1788:

. . . If we are in a humor to presume abuses of *power*, it is as fair to presume them on the part of the State governments as on the part of the general government. And as it is more consonant to the rules of a just theory, to trust the Union with the care of its own existence, than to transfer that care to any other hands, if abuses of *power* are to be hazarded on the one side or on the other, it is more rational to hazard them where the *power* would naturally be placed, than where the *power* would unnaturally be placed. [Fed. 395]

"An Impartial Citizen," No. 5, February 28, 1788:

It is objected, that the President has the *power* of pardoning offences against the United States, and Mr. [George] Mason discovers that the President may prevent a discovery and punishment of his own crimes by this *power;* by forgiving those whom he had secretly instigated to the commission of crimes—The most of the other antifederalists enumerate this as one of the defects they pretend to discover in this system. Governor [Edmund] Randolph seems only to extend this objection to the President's *power* of pardoning before conviction. . . . [DHRC8 428]

Circular Letter to the Fayette, Kentucky, County Court, February 28, 1788:

By the *power* to regulate commerce, we loose the Navigation of the Mississippi; population will cease, and Our lands become of little Value. By Uniform duties and imposts, and the prohibition of a tax or duty on Articles exported from any State, we Never shall be able to encourage Manufactaries and our wealth be carried to the Eastern & Southern States. The *power* Over the Militia, may leave us in a defenceless State and subject us to the ravages of the Merciless Savages; And Upon Our Separation being established, a Number of our Citizens will be draged by the *power* of the Foedral Court Six or eight hundred Miles to contest their Legal Claims. [DHRC16 262–63]

"Brutus," No. 14, March 6, 1788:

The just way of investigating any *power* given to a government, is to examine its operation supposing it to be put in exercise. If upon enquiry, it appears that the *power*, if exercised, would be prejudicial, it ought not to be given. For to answer objections made to a *power* given to a government, by saying it will never be exercised, is really admitting that the *power* ought not to be exercised, and therefore ought not to be granted. [DHRC16 331]

Alexander Hamilton, *The Federalist*, No. 66, March 8, 1788:

A fourth objection to the Senate, in the capacity of a court of impeachments, is derived from its union with the Executive in the *power* of making treaties. This, it has been said, would constitute the senators their own judges, in every case of a corrupt or perfidious execution of that trust. . . . [Fed. 434]

George Nicholas [?], "The State Soldier," No. 3, March 12, 1788:

In respect to the tyranny those gentlemen paint in such horrid colours, it appears to me, but little need be said; for it is not only true, that those who are the loudest about liberty, have always been the greatest tyrants themselves when they have had it in their *power;* but it is also clear that while in the very act of the one, they are even then exercising the very worst kind of the other. For it being a fixed point that human nature cannot exist without the assistance of government, and there being no *power* to which mankind are incident, more terrible than fear, it follows, that to keep men under a perpetual alarm about what they cannot, agreeable to their own natures, get rid of, is to worry them out with one oppression and thereby fit them for every other. . . .

[DHRC8 487]

James Iredell, "Marcus," No. 5, March 19, 1788:

My ideas of liberty are so different from those of Mr. [George] Mason, that in my opinion this very prohibition is one of the most valuable parts of the new Constitution. Ex post facto laws may some times be convenient, but that they are ever absolutely necessary I shall take the liberty to doubt, till that necessity can be made apparent. Sure I am, they have been the instrument of some of the grossest acts of tyranny that were ever exercised, and have this never failing consequence, to put the minority in the *power* of a passionate and unprincipled majority, as to the most sacred things; and the plea of necessity is never wanting where it can be of any avail. . . . [DHRC16 428]

Alexander Hamilton, *The Federalist*, No. 73, March 21, 1788:

The first thing that offers itself to our observation, is the qualified negative of the President upon the acts or resolutions of the two houses of the legislature; or, in other words, his *power* of returning all bills with objections, to have the effect of preventing their becoming laws, unless they should afterwards be ratified by two thirds of each of the component members of the legislative body.

[Fed. 468]

Luther Martin, "To the Citizens of Maryland," No. 3, March 28, 1788:

If it is easy to obtain proper amendments, do not let us sacrifice every thing that ought to be dear to freemen, for want of insisting upon its being done, while we have the *power*. [DHRC16 500]

Alexander Hamilton, *The Federalist*, No. 77, April 2, 1788:

I could not with propriety conclude my observations on the subject of appointments without taking notice of a scheme for which there have appeared some, though but few advocates; I mean that of uniting the House of Representatives in the *Power* of making them. I shall, however, do little more than mention it, as I cannot imagine that it is likely to gain the countenance of any considerable part of the community. A body so fluctuating and at the same time so numerous, can never be deemed proper for the exercise of that *power*. . . . [Fed. 488]

John Jay, *An Address to the People of the State of New York*, c. April 15, 1788:

By the Confederation as it now stands, the direction of general and national affairs is committed to a single body of men, viz. the Congress. They may make war, but are not empowered to raise men or money to carry it on. They may make peace, but without *power* to see the terms of it observed.—They may form alliances, but without ability to comply with the stipulations on their part—They may enter into treaties of commerce, but without *power* to enforce them at home or abroad—They may borrow money, but without having the means of repayment—They may partly regulate commerce, but without authority to execute their ordinances—They may appoint ministers and other officers of trust, but without *power* to try or punish them for misdemeanors . . . [Ford 72]

John Dickinson, "Fabius," No. 5, 1788:

In more modern times, the Florentines exhibited a memorable example. They were divided into violent parties; and the prevailing one vested exorbitant *powers* in the house of Medici, then possessed, as it was judged, of more money than any crowned head in Europe. Though that house engaged and persevered in the attempt, yet the people were never despoiled of their liberty, until they were overwhelmed by the armies of foreign princes, to whose enterprizes their situation exposed them. [Ford 190]

Georgia Constitution, May 6, 1789:

[Article II, Section 1:] The executive *power* shall be vested in a governor, who shall hold his office during the term of two years, and shall be elected in the following manner: [Thorpe 787]

United States Congress, Judiciary Act of September 24, 1789:

[Section 13:] . . . The Supreme Court shall also have appellate jurisdiction from the circuit courts and courts of the several states in the cases hereinafter specially provided for; and shall have *power* to issue writs of prohibition to the district courts, when proceeding as courts of admiralty and maritime jurisdiction, and writs of mandamus, in cases warranted by the principle and usages of law, to any courts appointed, or persons holding office under the authority of the United States. [USSL1 81]

PRESS, FREEDOM OF THE

(Liberty of the Press)

United States Constitution, Bill of Rights, December 15, 1791:

[Article I:] Congress shall make no law respecting an establishment of religion, or prohibiting the free exercise thereof; or abridging the *freedom* of speech, or *of the press;* or the right of the people peaceably to assemble, and to petition the government for a redress of grievances.

* * * * *

Virginia Bill of Rights, June 12, 1776:

[Section 12:] That the *freedom of the press* is one of the great bulwarks of *liberty,* and can never be restrained but by despotic governments. [Thorpe 3814]

Pennsylvania Constitution, September 28, 1776:

[Declaration of Rights, Article 12:] That the people have a right to freedom of speech, and of writing, and publishing their sentiments; therefore the *freedom of the press* ought not to be restrained. [Thorpe 3083]

[Frame of Government, Section 35:] The *printing presses shall be free* to every person who undertakes to examine the proceedings of the legislature, or any part of government. [Thorpe 3090]

Maryland Constitution, November 11, 1776:

[Declaration of Rights, Section 38:] That the *liberty of the press* ought to be inviolably preserved. [Thorpe 1690]

North Carolina Constitution, December 18, 1776:

[Declaration of Rights, Article 15:] That the *freedom of the press* is one of the great bulwarks of *liberty*, and therefore ought never to be restrained.
[Thorpe 2788]

Georgia Constitution, February 5, 1777:

[Article 61:] *Freedom of the press* and trial by jury to remain inviolate forever. [Thorpe 785]

Vermont Constitution, July 8, 1777:

[Declaration of Rights, Article 14:] That the people have a right to freedom of speech, and of writing and publishing their sentiments; therefore, the *freedom of the press* ought not be restrained. [Thorpe 3741]

[Frame of Government, Section 32:] The *printing presses shall be free* to every person who undertakes to examine the proceedings of the legislature or any part of government. [Thorpe 3746–47]

South Carolina Constitution, March 19, 1778:

[Article 43:] That the *liberty of the press* be inviolably preserved.
[Thorpe 3257]

Massachusetts Constitution, March 2, 1780:

[Declaration of Rights, Article 16:] The *liberty of the press* is essential to the security of *freedom* in a state, it ought not, therefore, to be restricted in this commonwealth. [Thorpe 1892]

New Hampshire Constitution, June 2, 1784:

[Bill of Rights, Article 22:] The *Liberty of the Press* is essential to the security of *freedom* in a state; it ought, therefore, to be inviolably preserved.
[Thorpe 2456]

Vermont Constitution, July 4, 1786:

[Declaration of Rights, Article 15:] That the people have a right of freedom of speech and of writing and publishing their sentiments, concerning the transactions of government—and therefore the *freedom of the press* ought not to be restrained. [Thorpe 3753]

James Wilson, Speech on the Federal Constitution, October 6, 1787:

[1] . . . it would have been superfluous and absurd, to have stipulated with a foederal body of our own creation, that we should enjoy those privileges, of which we are not divested either by the intention or the act that has brought that body into existence. For instance, the *liberty of the press,* which has been a copious subject of declamation and opposition: what controul can proceed from the foederal government, to shackle or destroy that sacred palladium of national *freedom?* If, indeed, a power similar to that which has been granted for the regulation of commerce, had been granted to regulate literary publications, it would have been as necessary to stipulate that the *liberty of the press* should be preserved inviolate, as that the impost should be general in its operation. . . .
[Ford 156]

[2] . . . In truth, then, the proposed system possesses no influence whatever upon the *press;* and it would have been merely nugatory, to have introduced a formal declaration upon the subject; nay, that very declaration might have been construed to imply that some degree of power was given, since we undertook to define its extent. [Ford 156–57]

George Mason, Objections to the Constitution, October 7, 1787:

There is no Declaration of any kind for preserving the *Liberty of the Press,* the Tryal by jury in civil Causes; nor against the Danger of standing Armys in time of Peace. [DHRC8 45]

Richard Henry Lee [?], "The Federal Farmer," No. 4, October 12, 1787:

I confess I do not see in what cases the congress can, with any pretence of right, make a law to suppress the *freedom of the press;* though I am not clear, that congress is restrained from laying any duties whatever on printing, and from laying duties particularly heavy on certain pieces printed, and perhaps congress may require large bonds for the payment of these duties. Should the printer say, the *freedom of the press* was secured by the constitution of the state in which he lived, congress might, and perhaps, with great propriety, answer, that the federal constitution is the only compact existing between them and the people; in this compact the people have named no others, and therefore congress, in exercising the powers assigned them, and in making laws to carry them into execution, are restrained by nothing beside the federal constitution . . .
[Ford 316]

Richard Henry Lee [?], "The Federal Farmer," No. 5, October 15, 1787:

What can be the views of those gentlemen in Pennsylvania, who precipitated decisions on this subject? What can be the views of those gentlemen in Boston, who countenanced the Printers in shutting up the *press* against a fair and *free* investigation of this important system [the Constitution] in the usual way. The members of the convention have done their duty—why should some of them fly to their states—almost forget a propriety of behavior, and precipitate measures for the adoption of a system of their own making? . . . [Ford 322–23]

Richard Henry Lee to Edmund Randolph, October 16, 1787:

. . . Yet there is no restraint in form of a bill of rights, to secure (what Doctor Blackstone calls) that residuum of human rights, which is not intended to be given up to society, and which indeed is not necessary to be given for any good social purpose. The rights of conscience, the *freedom of the press,* and the trial by jury are at mercy. [DHRC8 62]

Richard Henry Lee, Proposed Amendments to the Constitution, October 16, 1787:

. . . it is submitted,—That the new constitution proposed for the government of the United States be bottomed upon a declaration or bill of rights, clearly and precisely stating the principles upon which this social compact is founded, to wit: That the rights of conscience in matters of religion ought not to be violated—That the *freedom of the press* shall be secured—That the trial by jury in criminal and civil cases, and the modes prescribed by the common law for the safety of life in criminal prosecutions, shall be held sacred . . . [DHRC8 65]

Noah Webster, *An Examination into the Leading Principles of the Federal Constitution*, October 17, 1787:

[1] It is alledged that the *liberty of the press* is not guaranteed by the new constitution. But this objection is wholly unfounded. The *liberty of the press* does not come within the jurisdiction of federal government. It is firmly established in all the states either by law, or positive declarations in bills of right; and not being mentioned in the federal constitution, is not—and cannot be abridged by Congress, it stands on the basis of the respective state-constitutions. Should any state resign to Congress the exclusive jurisdiction of a certain district, which should include any town where *presses* are already established, it is in the power of the state to reserve the *liberty of the press,* or any other fundamental privilege, and make it an immutable condition of the grant, that such rights shall never be violated. All objections therefore on this score are "baseless visions." [Ford 48]

[2] The *liberty of the press,* trial by jury, the Habeas Corpus writ, even Magna Charta itself, although justly deemed the palladia of *freedom,* are all inferior considerations, when compared with a general distribution of real property among every class of people. The power of entailing estates is more dangerous to *liberty*

and republican government, than all the constitutions that can be written on paper, or even than a standing army. Let the people have property, and they will have power—a power that will for ever be exerted to prevent a restriction of the *press,* and abolition of trial by jury, or the abridgement of any other privilege. The *liberties* of America, therefore, and her forms of government, stand on the broadest basis. Removed from the fears of a foreign invasion and conquest, they are not exposed to the convulsions that shake other governments; and the principles of *freedom* are so general and energetic, as to exclude the possibility of a change in our republican constitutions. [Ford 59–60]

[3] The English writers on law and government consider Magna Charta, trial by juries, the Habeas Corpus act, and the *liberty of the press,* as the bulwarks of *freedom.* All this is well. But in no government of consequence in Europe, is *freedom* established on its true and immoveable foundation. The property is too much accumulated, and the accumulations too well guarded, to admit the true principle of republics. . . . [Ford 60n]

[4] . . . But in America, and here alone, we have gone at once to the fountain of *liberty,* and raised the people to their true dignity. Let the lands be possessed by the people in fee-simple, let the fountain be kept pure, and the streams will be pure of course. Our jealousy of trial by jury, the *liberty of the press,* &c., is totally groundless. Such rights are inseparably connected with the power and dignity of the people, which rest on their property. They cannot be abridged. . . . [Ford 61n]

Tench Coxe, *An Examination of the Constitution for the United States of America*, No. 4, October 21, 1787:

The old foederal constitution [the Articles of Confederation] contained many of the same things, which from error or disingenousness are urged against the new ones. Neither of them have a bill of rights, nor does either notice the *liberty of the press,* because they are already provided for by the state constitutions; and relating only to personal rights, they could not be mentioned in a contract among foreign states. [Ford 148]

Virginia Independent Chronicle, October 31, 1787:

Mr. [James Wilson's] speech to the meeting at Philadelphia, says a correspondent, is really a laughable performance. When the people, said the orator, established the powers of legislation under their separate governments, they vested their representatives with every right and authority, which they did not in explicit terms reserve; but the congressional authority is to be collected from the positive grant alone, expressed in the instrument. This, it seems, is so self-evident a principle, as to be never in danger of being questioned in future, and it will no doubt be sufficient security for posterity to know, that a Pennsylvania attorney established it; and from thence thought himself sufficiently authorised to draw the following conclusion. "Hence it is evident that in the former case every thing which is not reserved is given, but, in the latter the reverse prevails, and every thing which is not given is reserved." Bravo J——y! this is rare security for the *liberty of the press,* "that sacred palladium of national *freedom.*" [DHRC8 138]

Hugh Williamson, Address at Edenton, North Carolina, November 8, 1787:

[1] . . . We are told that there should have been a section for securing the Trial by Jury in Civil cases, and the *Liberty of the Press:* that there should also have been a Declaration of Rights. . . . [DHRC16 202]

[2] We have been told that the *Liberty of the Press* is not secured by the New Constitution. Be pleased to examine the plan, and you will find that the *Liberty of the Press* and the laws of Mahomet are equally affected by it. The New Government is to have the power of protecting literary property; the very power which you have by a special act delegated to the present Congress. There was a time in England, when neither book, pamphlet, nor paper could be published without a licence from Government. That restraint was finally removed in the year 1694 and by such removal, their *press became perfectly free,* for it is not under the restraint of any licence. Certainly the new Government can have no power to impose restraints. The citizens of the United States have no more occasion for a second Declaration of Rights, than they have for a section in favor of the *press.* . . . [DHRC16 202]

Dissent of the Pennsylvania Convention's Minority, December 18, 1787:

[1] That the people have a right to the freedom of speech, of writing and publishing their sentiments, therefore, the *freedom of the press* shall not be restrained by any law of the United States. [DHRC2 623]

[2] The first consideration that this review suggests, is the omission of a BILL OF RIGHTS ascertaining and fundamentally establishing those unalienable and personal rights of men, without the full, free, and secure enjoyment of which there can be no *liberty,* and over which it is not necessary for a good government to have the control. The principal of which are the rights of conscience, personal *liberty* by the clear and unequivocal establishment of the writ of habeas corpus, jury trial in criminal and civil cases, by an impartial jury of the vicinage or country; with the common law proceedings, for the safety of the accused in criminal prosecutions; and the *liberty of the press,* that scourge of tyrants, and the grand bulwark of every other *liberty* and privilege; the stipulations heretofore made in favor of them in the state constitutions are entirely superseded by this Constitution. [DHRC2 630–31]

George Nicholas [?], "The State Soldier," No. 1, January 16, 1788:

. . . And thus too respecting a bill of rights, and the *liberty of the press,* it may also be said, the objection has been diminished by the new plan: For what security had we on this head before but that which was in our state constitutions? And of what is the republican form of government which Congress is now to guarantee to each state to consist? Certainly of any thing each state shall think proper that does not take from Congress what this constitution absolutely claims. . . . [DHRC8 306]

Alexander White [?], "An Independent Freeholder," January 18, 1788:

. . . But is America in the situation Great Britain was in at the time of the revolution in that country, or in which she herself was at the time of the revolution in this? Nothing can be more remote; here is neither a total nor partial dissolution of Government; our social compacts and all our ancient rights remain entire, except such as are expressly granted to Congress. And this affords an answer to many objections, such as that religious liberty, the *Freedom of the Press,* the right of Petitioning the Legislature, &c. &c. &c. are not secured; no power over these matters being granted to Congress, she never can interpose to destroy them. . . . [DHRC8 311]

James Madison, *The Federalist*, No. 41, January 19, 1788:

Had no other enumeration or definition of the powers of the Congress been found in the Constitution, than the general expressions just cited, the authors of the objection might have had some color for it; though it would have been difficult to find a reason for so awkward a form of describing an authority to legislate in all possible cases. A power to destroy the *freedom of the press,* the trial by jury; or even to regulate the course of descents, or the forms of conveyances, must be very singularly expressed by the terms "to raise money for the general welfare." [Fed. 300–01]

"Civis Rusticus," January 30, 1788:

"No declaration of the *liberty of the press.*" Our [Virginia's] Bill of Rights declares, and it is not repealed, that the *freedom of the press* is one of the great bulwarks of the *liberty* of the people, and never can be restrained, but by despotic power. The people of England have no other security for the *liberty of the press,* than we have—Their own spirit, and an act of parliament—their act of parliament may be repealed—our Bill of Rights may be repealed. Of that no man has any fear, of this no man need have, while this spirit is in the people—"This peculiar privilege must last (says a learned writer) as long as our government remains, in any degree, *free* and independent—it is seldom that *liberty* of any kind is lost at once—slavery has so frightful an aspect to men accustomed to *freedom,* that it must steal upon them by degrees, and disguise itself in a thousand shapes in order to be received—But, if the *liberty of the press* ever be lost, it will be lost at once.—The general laws against sedition and libelling are at present as strong as they can possibly be made, nothing can impose a further restraint, but, either clapping an imprimatur on the *press,* or giving to the court very large discretionary powers, to punish whatever displeases them—but these concessions would be such a bare faced violation of *liberty,* that they will probably be the last efforts of a despotic government—Hume's essay vol. 1. p. 17."

[DHRC8 337–38]

Alexander C. Hanson, *Remarks on the Proposed Plan of a Federal Government*, c. January 31, 1788:

[1] . . . I have exercised my imagination to devise in what manner they [the members of the Federal Convention] or any other men, supposing them to bear full sway in both houses, could erect this imaginary fabric of power. I request any person to point out any law, or system of laws, that could be possibly contrived for that purpose, obtain the final assent of each branch, and be carried into effect, contrary to the interests and wishes of a *free,* intelligent, prying people, accustomed to the most unbounded *freedom* of inquiry. To begin by an attempt to restrain the *press,* instead of promoting their designs would be the most effectual thing to prevent them. [Ford 221–22]

[2] Whilst mankind shall believe *freedom* to be better than slavery; whilst our lands shall be generally distributed, and not held by a few insolent barons, on the debasing terms of vassalage; whilst we shall teach our children to read and write; whilst the *liberty of the press,* that grand palladium, which tyrants are compelled to respect, shall remain; whilst a spark of public love shall animate even a small part of the people; whilst even self-love shall be the general ruling principle; so long will it be impossible for an aristocracy to arise from the proposed plan. . . . [Ford 256]

Spencer Roane, "A Plain Dealer," February 13, 1788:

Mr. DAVIS, As you have the character of being a very independent printer, and as the time is yet at hand when the *liberty of the press,* and the *free* discussion of public measures, are considered as the first data of *free* government, I doubt not you will publish the following observation in your useful paper.—To know the head which dictated them can be of no use to the public, and will add no weight to the publication; being written by an obscure citizen, but anxiously wishing for the prosperity of this country. The author judges, that when the majesty of office is laid aside, and its possessor enters the lists as a writer, a signal is thereby given for *free* animadversion; yet such as is decent and respectful, and with which the *freedom of the press* should ever be dignified. [DHRC8 363]

Benjamin Workman [?], "Philadelphiensis," No. 10, February 20, 1788:

[1] One of the members of the virtuous minority of the convention of Massachusetts openly declared in that assembly, that pushing on this accursed system would produce a civil war: the freemen of New-England, the best soldiers on the continent, have had their eyes opened, and begin to see through the conspiracy; that sacred palladium of *liberty*, the *freedom of the press*, has dispelled the cloud, and cleared their understandings. In that state, through the influence of the tyrants of Boston, very little information has reached the people; the *press*, generally speaking, was devoted to the well-born and their tools . . . [DHRC16 159]

[2] The amendments proposed by the president [John Hancock, president of the Massachusetts Convention] will be another source of mischief; the people cannot be so ignorant as to be deceived by so pitiful a manoeuvre. Here is a positive acknowledgement made by one of its advocates, who hopes to be appointed the little king if not the big one, that it is objectionable; and his amendments are introduced as a blind; the weighty ones are untouched: not a whimper of the extraordinary powers of the President-general, the standing army, the *liberty of the press*, &c. No, no! if these glorious parts be lopped off, what would become of the monarchy-men? . . . [DHRC16 160]

Alexander White, "To the Citizens of Virginia," February 22, 1788:

The *freedom* of speech and of the *press*, are likewise out of the jurisdiction of Congress.—But, if by an abuse of that *freedom* I attempt to excite sedition in the Commonwealth, I may be punished—should I be unjustly accused of such an offence, the trial by a jury of my countrymen is my security—if what I have said or wrote corresponds with their general sense of the subject, I shall be acquitted. . . . [DHRC8 404–05]

David Ramsay, "Civis," February 24, 1788:

In a country like our's, abounding with *free* men all of one rank, where property is equally diffused, where estates are held in fee simple, the *press free*, and the means of information common; tyranny cannot readily find admission under any form of government; but its admission is next to impossible, under one where the people are the source of all power, and elect either mediately by their representatives, or immediately by themselves the whole of their rulers. [DHRC16 26]

John Leland, Objections to the Constitution, c. February 1788:

We have no assurance that the *liberty of the press* will be allowed under this Constitution— [DHRC8 426]

Mercy Otis Warren, *Observations on the New Constitution*, February 1788:

There is no security in the profered system, either for the rights of conscience, or the *liberty of the Press:* Despotism usually while it is gaining ground, will suffer men to think, say, or write what they please; but when once established, if it is thought necessary to subserve the purposes of arbitrary power, the most unjust restrictions may take place in the first instance, and an imprimator on the *Press* in the next, may silence the complaints, and forbid the most decent remonstrances of an injured and oppressed people. [DHRC16 279]

"The Impartial Examiner," No. 1, March 5, 1788:

. . . can it be said that they have exceeded the limits of their jurisdiction, when that has no limits; when no provision has been made for such a right?—When no responsibility on the part of Congress has been required by the constitution? The same observation may be made on any arbitrary or capricious imprisonments contrary to the law of the land. The same may be made, if excessive bail should be required; if excessive fines should be imposed; if cruel and unusual punishments should be inflicted; if the *liberty of the press* should be restrained; in a word—if laws should be made totally derogatory to the whole catalogue of rights, which are now secure under your present form of government.
[DHRC8 462]

Matthias Bartgis, Editorial Announcement, *Virginia Gazette,* March 7, 1788:

[1] Although the secret views of an ungrateful party, may aim an undeserved destruction at the first attempt to establish that safe-guard to the *liberties* of an independent people, a *free Press,* in the Borough of Winchester, yet, he is unalterably determined to persevere in his professional character, an unbiassed, impartial Printer, and depend on the rectitude of his intentions, and future productions, for the issue. [DHRC8 468]

[2] Being ever desirous of obtaining Public Patronage, he asks the aid of the learned, by affording their assistance in political and other essays. The present being a most important Crisis of the national affairs of this country, it must be evident to the least thoughtful, that the body of the people should be well informed of the nature of any Government that may be proposed for their adoption; therefore, *free* discussions on that momentous subject, as well as interesting

intelligence from the several quarters of the world, will be thankfully received, and impartially published; and while a just record is made of every occurrence which may come to the knowledge of the Conductor, tending to promote the interest of society, it is determined, that in future private characters shall be secure from the poisoned shafts of envy and malice, cast through the medium of his *Press;* yet, discussions of a private nature, wrote with decency, will find *free* access. [DHRC8 468–69]

Virginia Gazette, March 7, 1788:

Messieurs BARTGIS and Co. The *Freedom of the PRESS* is the unalienable Right of a *free* Government particularly when matters of the greatest moment demand the serious attention, and *free* discussion of the citizens.

[DHRC8 469]

James Iredell, "Marcus," No. 4, March 12, 1788:

[1] . . . I now proceed to the three great cases:—The *Liberty of the Press*—The Trial by Jury in civil cases, and a Standing Army in time of peace.

[DHRC16 382]

[2] The *Liberty of the Press* is always a grand topic for declamation; but the future Congress will have no other authority over this than to secure to authors for a limited time the exclusive privilege of publishing their works. This authority has long been exercised in England, where the *press is as free* as among ourselves, or in any country in the world, and surely such an encouragement to genius is no restraint on the *liberty of the press,* since men are allowed to publish what they please of their own; and so far as this may be deemed a restraint upon others it is certainly a reasonable one, and can be attended with no danger of copies not being sufficiently multiplied, because the interest of the proprietor will always induce him to publish a quantity fully equal to the demand—besides, that such encouragement may give birth to many excellent writings which would otherwise have never appeared. If the Congress should exercise any other power over the *press* than this, they will do it without any warrant from this Constitution, and must answer for it as for any other act of tyranny. [DHRC16 382]

George Nicholas [?], "The State Soldier," No. 3, March 12, 1788:

[1] But notwithstanding all that has been said about the *liberty of the press* being destroyed by the new constitution, I scarcely expect to find a sufficient remnant of that great blessing even in our present system to bring this paper to our view. [DHRC8 483–84]

[2] For to those very causes which some attribute the destruction of the *liberty of the press,* I look up for its becoming more unbounded—since clear it is, there

are great restraints of that sort already, nor can any thing else be expected in a government as popular as this is. [DHRC8 484]

[3] The *liberty of the press* is not always one of the most lovely traits of the *freest* governments:—for as the most popular kinds have generally been thought the most *free*, it follows that the most *free* will not be the most favorable to that spirit which is necessary to constitute the *liberty of the press*. [DHRC8 484]

[4] When on the other hand, in those governments whose heads are the establishment of birth, and the detestation of the majority, the assistance of the *press* is to be found on the side of the people. And this it is that is called the *liberty of the press*. [DHRC8 484–85]

[5] In England where government has always had some of the ablest men for its opponents, with the popular voice of the people on their side, the *liberty of the press* is such that even the dignity of the crown does not protect men from ridicule and abuse. [DHRC8 485]

[6] Thus having remarked on the designs of some of the principal enemies to the constitution with that *freedom* which becomes the spirit of an independent man, to which none of those gentlemen themselves can with propriety object, since they are all such great friends to the *Liberty of the press,* I shall return again to the more pleasing subject of the constitution, and endeavor in my next to answer, in as plain a manner as I can, such objections to it as I think worthy of notice. [DHRC8 489]

Virginia Gazette, March 14, 1788:

To succeed disaffection or disgust, in any state or business, is not only unpleasing, but often attended with many disadvantages. Should any unfavourable prejudices, previous to this, have taken place against the original *Press* in this place, through any cause whatever, the Subscriber hopes, from the kindness of the respectable public, that it will not operate obliquely to the injury of the successor in the business. On his part, he will ever endeavour to avoid intestine broils; but, if he is professionally led into any party, he hopes it will be justly applied to the nature of his business, and not as a voluntary act. As a preparatory, anonimous pieces, tending to injure the reputation, will ever be secluded. Through him, the amiable characters of the virtuous Fair, and honest man, shall never be wounded; yet, this Gazette will ever be *free* and open for a full discussion of all momentous subjects unbiassed by party, he will aim to be just. . . .
[DHRC8 469]

"Senex," March 19, 1788:

[1] I must now give the State Soldier that applause he merits, and candidly admit his arguments about the *liberty of the press,* cannot be suspected of—one—Plagiarism, for no antient or modern sage ever before attempted to prove the

press cannot flourish in a *free* country, and that the soil of despotism affords it more nourishment, than pure earth cultivated in a popular style . . .
[DHRC8 506]

[2] . . . A *free press* is their faithful guardian, by bringing to light the silent advances of ambition—by informing the community at large of the good or evil that may flow from any proposition. The present crisis confirms it beyond the reach of scepticism, and had printers betrayed the public, by refusing to insert those strictures patriotism, vanity, or selfishness have brought forth, the new constitution would have been eagerly adopted, without reflecting on those vices and virtues that seem to contend in the womb, and alternately create admiration and indignation in the contemplating mind of every citizen. [DHRC8 506]

[3] Such are the consequences of *free* discussion,—may its source, the *liberty of the press,* remain a perpetual blessing to America, and her sons who fought and bled like the Old Soldier, for *free* constitutions, perfect the great work, not adopt a creed recently execrated, become cynically sullen, or stigmatize old friends for retaining republican sentiments. [DHRC8 507]

"A Ploughman," March 19, 1788:

These sentiments are stubborn truths which none upon earth but an American dare hold up to the publick; but if the Federal Constitution be ratified, the *Liberty of the PRESS,* that palladium of *Freedom,* will be lost also. [DHRC8 509]

George Nicholas [?], "The State Soldier," No. 4, March 19, 1788:

And in doing this, I have been unavoidably led to answer some of the individual objections to the constitution themselves—among these are the want of a bill of rights, the equality in the senate, and the *liberty of the press*—all of which I shall avoid recapitulating at this time, with an intention of confining myself wholly to those objections which I have not heretofore entered fully into.
[DHRC8 509–10]

Luther Martin, "To the Citizens of Maryland," No. 2, March 21, 1788:

An honourable member from South-Carolina, most anxiously sought to have a clause inserted, securing the *Liberty of the Press,* and repeatedly brought this subject before the Convention, but could not obtain it.—I am almost positive he made the same attempt to have a stipulation in favour of Liberty of Conscience, but in vain.—The more the system advanced, the more was I impressed with the nccessity of not merely attempting to secure a few rights, but of digesting and forming a complete bill of rights . . . [DHRC16 456]

Samuel Bryan, "Centinel," No. 17, March 24, 1788:

The citizens of this state, which is in advance in its payments to the federal treasury, whilst some of the others have not paid a farthing since war, ought in a peculiar manner to resent the intended imposition, and make its authors experience their just resentment; it is incumbent upon them in particular manner, to exert themselves to frustrate the measures of the conspirators, and set an example to those parts of the union, who have not enjoyed the blessing of a *free press* on this occasion, but are still enveloped in the darkness of delusion, and enthralled by the fascination of names. [DHRC16 476]

***Virginia Gazette*, April 2, 1788:**

The Editors sincerely wish that the new Constitution had been so framed, that every paragraph published on that important subject, could have been truly federal, but when opinions vary, and it is submitted to the People for *free* discussion, to see men in public office taking undue measures to establish it, without a thorough investigation, and by means which not only grossly infringes on the *liberties* of the people, but strikes a fatal blow at their very political existence, the Editors think it a duty incumbent on them as Printers of a public paper, to give the alarm. It ever has been, (even under the tyrannical government of Britain) an invariable privilege to suffer, for the public good, a *free* passage for news-papers in the mails, but of late, for reasons which the Editors wish not to suggest, they are prohibited. Whatever may be the views of public men at the present day, if they should be continued in office (which it is more than probable they will, unless from their present conduct they are well guarded against) may we not expect the same measures? which, if practised, we may bid adieu to that scourge to tyrants, an unrestrained *Press*. [DHRC8 519]

John Jay, *An Address to the People of the State of New York*, c. April 15, 1788:

We are told, among other strange things, that the *liberty of the press* is left insecure by the proposed Constitution, and yet that Constitution says neither more nor less about it, than the Constitution of the State of New York does. . . .
[Ford 76]

Melancton Smith, *An Address to the People of the State of New York*, April 1788:

[1] . . . The suggestion, that the *liberty of the press* is secure, because it is not in express words spoken of in the constitution, and that the trial by jury is not taken away, because it is not said in so many words and letters it is so, is puerile and unworthy of a man who pretends to reason. We contend,that by the indefinite powers granted to the general government, the *liberty of the press* may be restricted by duties, &c. and therefore the constitution ought to have stipulated for its *freedom*. . . . [Ford 113–14]

[2] The author [John Jay] manifests levity in referring to the constitution of this state, to shew that it was useless to stipulate for the *liberty of the press*, or to

insert a bill of rights in the constitution. With regard to the first, it is perhaps an imperfection in our constitution that the *liberty of the press* is not expressly reserved; but still there was not equal necessity of making this reservation in our State as in the general Constitution, for the common and statute law of England, and the laws of the colony are established, in which this privilege is fully defined and secured. . . . [Ford 114]

Alexander Hamilton, *The Federalist*, No. 84, May 28, 1788:

[1] . . . For why declare that things shall not be done which there is no power to do? Why, for instance, should it be said that the *liberty of the press* shall not be restrained, when no power is given by which restrictions may be imposed? I will not contend that such a provision would confer a regulating power; but it is evident that it would furnish, to men disposed to usurp, a plausible pretence for claiming that power. They might urge with a semblance of reason, that the Constitution ought not to be charged with the absurdity of providing against the abuse of an authority which was not given, and that the provision against restraining the *liberty of the press* afforded a clear implication, that a power to prescribe proper regulations concerning it was intended to be vested in the national government. This may serve as a specimen of the numerous handles which would be given to the doctrine of constructive powers, by the indulgence of an injudicious zeal for bills of rights. [Fed. 535]

[2] On the subject of the *liberty of the press,* as much as has been said, I cannot forbear adding a remark or two: in the first place, I observe, that there is not a syllable concerning it in the constitution of this State [New York]; in the next, I contend, that whatever has been said about it in that of any other State, amounts to nothing. What signifies a declaration, that "the *liberty of the press* shall be inviolably preserved"? What is the *liberty of the press?* Who can give it any definition which would not leave the utmost latitude for evasion? I hold it to be impracticable; and from this I infer, that its security, whatever fine declarations may be inserted in any constitution respecting it, must altogether depend on public opinion, and on the general spirit of the people and of the government. . . . [Fed. 535]

[3] To show that there is a power in the Constitution by which the *liberty of the press* may be affected, recourse has been had to the power of taxation. It is said that duties may be laid upon the publications so high as to amount to a prohibition. I know not by what logic it could be maintained, that the declarations in the State constitutions, in favor of the *freedom of the press,* would be a constitutional impediment to the imposition of duties upon publications by the State legislatures. It cannot certainly be pretended that any degree of duties, however low, would be an abridgement of the *liberty of the press.* We know that newspapers are taxed in Great Britain, and yet it is notorious that the *press* nowhere enjoys greater *liberty* than in that country. And if duties of any kind may be laid without a violation of that *liberty,* it is evident that the extent must depend on legislative

discretion, regulated by public opinion; so that, after all, general declarations respecting the *liberty of the press,* will give it no greater security than it will have without them. The same invasions of it may be effected under the State constitutions which contain those declarations through the means of taxation, as under the proposed Constitution, which has nothing of the kind. It would be quite as significant to declare that government ought to be free, that taxes ought not to be excessive, etc., as that the *liberty of the press* ought not to be restrained. [Fed. 535–36n]

Alexander Hamilton, *The Federalist*, No. 85, May 28, 1788:

It is remarkable, that the resemblance of the plan of the convention to the act which organizes the government of this State holds, not less with regard to many of the supposed defects, than to the real excellences of the former. Among the pretended defects are the re-eligibility of the Executive, the want of a council, the omission of a formal bill of rights, the omission of a provision respecting the *liberty of the press*. These and several others which have been noted in the course of our inquiries are as much chargeable on the existing constitution of this State, as on the one proposed for the Union . . . [Fed. 541]

John Dickinson, "Fabius," No. 2, 1788:

The course of regular inquiry demands, that these objections should be considered in the first place. If they are removed, then all the rest of the objections, concerning unnecessary taxations, standing armies, the abolishment of trial by jury, the *liberty of the press,* the freedom of commerce, the judicial, executive, and legislative authorities of the several states, and the rights of citizens, and the other abuses of federal government, must, of consequence, be rejected, if the principle contains the salutary, purifying, and preserving qualities attributed to it. . . . [Ford 168–69]

Georgia Constitution, May 6, 1789:

[Article IV, Section 3:] *Freedom of the press* and trial by jury shall remain inviolate. [Thorpe 789]

South Carolina Constitution, June 3, 1790:

[Article IX, Section 6:] The trial by jury as heretofore used in this State, and the *liberty of the press,* shall be forever inviolably preserved. [Thorpe 3264]

Pennsylvania Constitution, September 2, 1790:

[Article IX, Section 7:] That the *printing-presses shall be free* to every person who undertakes to examine the proceeding of the legislature, or any branch of government, and no law shall ever be made to restrain the right thereof. The free communication of thoughts and opinions is one of the invaluable rights of man; and every citizen may freely speak, write, and print on any subject, being responsible for the abuse of that liberty. . . . [Thorpe 3100]

PRIVILEGES AND IMMUNITIES

United States Constitution, September 17, 1787:

[Article IV, Section 2:] The Citizens of each State shall be entitled to all *Privileges and Immunities* of Citizens in the several States.

* * * * *

Ferdinand and Isabella of Spain, Privileges and Prerogatives Granted to Christopher Columbus, April 30, 1492:

. . . and allow, and cause to be allowed you, all the honours, graces, concessions, prehaminences, prerogatives, *immunities,* and other things, or any of them which are due to you, by virtue of your commands of Admiral, Viceroy, and Governour, and to be observed completely, so that nothing be diminished; and that they make no objection to this, or any part of it, nor suffer it to be made; forasmuch as we from this time forward, by this our letter, bestow on you the employments of Admiral, Vice-Roy, and perpetual Governour forever: and we put you into possession of the said offices, and of every of them, and full power to use and exercise them, and to receive the perquisites and salaries belonging to them, or any of them, as was said above. Concerning all which things, if it be requisite, and you shall desire it, We command our Chancellour, Notaries, and other Officers, to pass, seal, and deliver to you, our Letter of *Privilege,* in such form and legal manner, as you shall require or stand in need of. . . . [Thorpe 40]

James I, Second Charter of Virginia, May 23, 1609:

[1] And further, we do, by these Presents Ratify and Confirm unto the said Treasurer and Company, and their Successors, all the *Privileges,* Franchises, Liberties, and *Immunities* granted in our said former Letters-patents, and not in these our Letters-patents, revoked, altered, changed, or abridged.

[Thorpe 3801]

[2] . . . that all and singular Person and Persons, which shall at any Time or Times hereafter adventure any Sum or Sums of Money, in and towards the said Plantation of the said Colony in Virginia, and shall be admitted by the said Council and Company, as Adventurers of the said Colony in Form aforesaid, and shall be enrolled in the Book or Records of the Adventurers of the said Company, shall and may be accounted, accepted, taken, held, and reputed Adventurers of the said Colony, and shall, and may enjoy all and singular Grants, *Privileges,* Liberties, Benefits, Profits, Commodities and *Immunities,* Advantages and Emoluments whatsoever, as fully, largely, amply, and absolutely, as if they and every of them, had been precisely, plainly, singularly, and distinctly named and inserted in these our Letters-patents. [Thorpe 3802]

James I, Third Charter of Virginia, 1611–12:

[1] [The members of the company] . . . shall and may respectively, and according to the Proportion and Value of their several Adventures, Have, Hold, and Enjoy, all such Interest, Right, Title, *Privileges,* Preheminences, Liberties, Franchises, *Immunities,* Profits, and Commodities, whatsoever, in as large and ample and beneficial Manner to all Intents, Constructions, and Purposes, as any other Adventures nominated and expressed in any our former Letters-Patents, or any of them have or may have by Force and Virtue of these Presents, or any our former Letters-Patents whatsoever. [Thorpe 3805]

[2] . . . And that all such Persons so elected, chosen, and admitted to be of the said Company as aforesaid, shall thereupon be taken, reputed, and held, and shall be free Members of the said Company, and shall have, hold, and enjoy all and singular Freedoms, Liberties, Franchises, *Privileges, Immunities,* Benefits, Profits and Commodities whatsoever, to the said Company in any Sort belonging or appertaining, as fully, freely and amply as any other Adventurers now being, or which hereafter at any Time shall be of the said Company, hath, have, shall, may, might, or ought to have and enjoy the same to all Intents and Purposes whatsoever. . . . [Thorpe 3806]

[3] And lastly, we do, by these Presents Ratify and Confirm unto the said Treasurer and Company, and their Successors, for ever, all and all Manner of *Privileges,* Franchises, Liberties, *Immunities,* Preheminences, Profits, and Commodities, whatsoever, granted unto them in any our former Letters-patent, and not in these Presents revoked altered, changed, or abridged. . . . [Thorpe 3810]

James I, The Charter of New England, November 3, 1620:

[1] . . . And whereas, since that Time, upon the humble Petition of the said Adventurers and Planters of the said first Collonye, We have been graciously pleased to make them one distinct and entire Body by themselves, giving unto them their distinct Lymitts and Bounds, and have upon their like humble Request, granted unto them divers Liberties, *Priveliges,* Enlargements, and *Immunityes,*

as in and by Our severall Letters-Patents it doth and may more at large appeare. . . . [Thorpe 1828]

[2] . . . We would likewise be graciously pleased to make certaine Adventurers, intending to erect and establish fishery, Trade, and Plantacion, within the Territoryes, Precincts, and Lymitts of the said second Colony, and their Successors, one several distinct and entire Body, and to grant unto them, such Estate, Liberties, *Priveliges,* Enlargements, and *Immunityes* there, as in these our Letters-Pattents hereafter particularly expressed and declared. . . . [Thorpe 1828]

[3] . . . And further, Wee do hereby for Us, our Heires and Successors, grant unto the said Councill established at Plymouth, that they and their Successors, by the same Name, be and shall be, and shall continue Persons able and capable in the Law, from time to time, and shall by that Name, of Councill aforesaid, have full Power and Authority, and lawful Capacity and Hability, as well to purchase, take, hold, receive, enjoy, and to have, and their Successors for ever, any Manors, Lands, Tenements, Rents, Royalties, *Privileges, Immunities,* Reversions, Annuities, Hereditaments, Goods, and Chattles whatsoever, of or from Us, our Heirs, and Successors, and of or from any other Person or Persons whatsoever, as well in and within this our Realme, of England, as in and within any other Place or Places whatsoever or wheresoever . . . [Thorpe 1831]

[4] . . . And Wee also do by these Presents, ratifye and confirm unto the said Councill and their Successors, all *Priveliges,* franchises, Liberties, *Immunities* granted in our said former Letters-patents, and not in these our Letters-patents revoked, altered, changed or abridged, altho' Expressed, Mentioned, &c. [Thorpe 1840]

Council of New England, Grant of the Province of Maine, August 10, 1622:

As also all the lands, soyle, grounds, harbors, ports, rivers, mines, mineralls, pearls, pretious stones, woods, quarries, marshes, waters, fishings, hunting, hawking, fowling, and other commodities and hereditaments whatsoever; with all and singular their appurtenances, together with all prerogatives, rights, royalties, jurisdictions, *privileges,* franchises, liberties, preheminences, marine power, in and upon ye said seas and rivers; as also all escheats and casualties thereof, as flotson, jetson, lagon, with anchorage, and other such duties, *immunities,* sects, isletts and appurtenances whatsoever, with all the estate, right title, interest, and claim and demands whatsoever wch ye said President and councill, and their successors, of right ought to have or claim in or to the said porcons of lands, rivers, and other ye said premises, as is aforesaid by reason or force of his highness' said Letters Patents, in as free, large, ample and beneficial manner, to all intents, constructions and purposes whatsoever, as in and by the said Letters Patents ye same are among other things granted to the said President and councill aforesaid . . . [Thorpe 1623]

Charles I, Charter of Massachusetts Bay, March 4, 1629:

[We grant] . . . all the saide Parte of Newe England in America, lyeing and extending betweene the Boundes and Lymytts in the said recited Indenture expressed, and all Landes and Groundes, Place and Places, Soyles, Woods and Wood Groundes, Havens, Portes, Rivers, Waters, Mynes, Mineralls, Jurisdiccons, Rightes, Royalties, Liberties, Freedomes, *Immunities, Priviledges,* Franchises, Preheminences, Hereditaments, and Comodities whatsoever, to them the saide Sir Henry Rosewell, Sir John Younge, Thomas Southcott, John Humfrey, John Endecott, and Simon Whetcombe, theire Heires and Assignes . . .

[Thorpe 1848–49]

Charles I, Patent to Sir Robert Heath, October 30, 1629:

[1] . . . And furthermore [we grant] the patronages and advowsons of all churches which shall happen to be built hereafter in the said Region Territory & Isles and limitts by the increase of the religion & worship of Christ Together with all & singular these & these soe amply, Rights Jurisdictions, *priviledges* prerogatives Royaltyes libertyes *immunityes* with Royall rights & franchises whatsoever as well by sea as by land, within that Region Territory Isles & limitts aforesaid To have exercise use & enjoy in like manner as any Bishop of Durham within the B[isho]pricke or County palatine of Durham in our kingdome of England ever heretofore had held used or enjoyed or of right ought or could have hold use or enjoy. . . . [Thorpe 70]

[2] . . . doe for ourselves our heires & successors give full & free power to the foresayd Sr. Robert Heath Knight his heires & assignes to confere favours graces & honours upon those well deserveing citizens that inhabit within the foresayd province & the same with whatever Titles & dignityes (provided they be not the same as are now used in England) to adorne at his pleasure alsoe to erect villages into Borowes & Borowes into Cittyes for the meritts of the inhabitants and conveniency of the places with *priviledges* & befitting *immunityes* to be erected & incorporated, & to doe all other & singular upon the premises which shall seem most convenient to him or them, although they be such which of their owne natures doe require mandates or warrant more especiall than is expressed in these presents . . . [Thorpe 74]

Charles I, Charter of Maryland, June 20, 1632:

[Article 4:] . . . with all, and singular such, and as ample Rights, Jurisdictions, *Privileges,* Prerogatives, Royalties, Liberties, *Immunities,* and royal Rights, and temporal Franchises whatsoever, as well by Sea as by Land, within the Region, Islands, Islets, and Limits aforesaid, to be had, exercised, used, and enjoyed, as any Bishop of Durham, within the Bishoprick or County Palatine of Durham, in our Kingdom of England, ever heretofore hath had, held, used, or enjoyed, or of right could, or ought to have, hold, use, or enjoy. [Thorpe 1679]

[Article 14:] . . . also to erect and incorporate Towns into Boroughs, and Boroughs into Cities, with suitable *Privileges and Immunities,* according to the Merits of the Inhabitants, and Convenience of the Places; and to do all and singular other Things in the Premises, which to him or them shall seem fitting and convenient; even although they shall be such as, in their own Nature, require a more special Commandment and Warrant than in these Presents may be expressed. [Thorpe 1683]

Surrender of the Charter of New England, June 7, 1635:

. . . [the King] did by the said Letters Patents incorporate, erect, ordain, name, constitute, and establish to be one body politick and corporate, in Deed and Name, by the Name of the Council of Plymouth aforesaid, in the said County of Devon, for the planting, ruling, and governing of New England in America aforesaid, To have perpetual succession, with divers other powers, *priviledges, immunities,* provisions, and restrictions, for the propagation and establishing of true Religion in those parts, and for the better regulating of the same plantations, as in and by the said Letters Patents, do Reference Thereunto had more plainly and at large appeareth. . . . [Thorpe 1861]

Charles I, Grant of the Province of Maine, April 3, 1639:

. . . togeather with all and singuler and as large and ample Rights Jurisdiccons *Priviledges* Prerogatives Royalties Liberties *Immunityes* Franchises Preheminences and Hereditaments as well by Sea as by Lande within the said Province and Premisses and the Precincts and Coasts of the same or any of them and within the Seas belonging or adjacent to them or any of them as the Bishopp of Durham within the Bishopricke or Countie Palatine of Duresme in our Kingdome of England now hath useth or enjoyeth or of right hee ought to have use or enjoie within the said Countie Palatine as if the same were herein particulerly menconed and expressed. [Thorpe 1627]

Surender of the Patent of Plymouth Colony to the Freemen, March 2, 1640:

. . . and the said William Bradford doth by the free and full consent approbacon and agreement of the said Old Planters or Purchasers together with the likeing approbacon and acceptacon of the other part of the said Corporacon surrender into the hands of the whole court consisting of the Freemen of this Corporacon of New Plymouth all that the right and title power authorytie *priviledges immunities* and freedomes graunted in the said Letters Patents by the said Right Honorable Councell for New England reserveing his and their personall Right of Freemen together with the said Old Planters aforesaid except the said Lands before excepted, declaring the Freemen of this Corporacon together with all such as shall be legally admitted into the same his associates . . . [Thorpe 1862]

Charles II, Charter of Carolina, March 24, 1663:

[Article 3:] And furthermore, the patronage and advowsons of all the churches and chappels, which as Christian religion shall increase within the country, isles, islets and limits aforesaid, shall happen hereafter to be erected, together with license and power to build and found churches, chappels and oratories, in convenient and fit places, within the said bounds and limits, and to cause them to be Dedicated and consecrated according to the ecclesiastical laws of our Kingdom of England, together with all and singular the like, and as ample rights, jurisdictions, *priviledges,* prerogatives, royalties, liberties, *immunities* and franchises of what kind soever, within the countries, isles, islets and limits aforesaid.

[Thorpe 2744]

Carolina Proprietors, Concessions and Agreements, 1665:

It is our will and desire that ye Inhabitants of the said Countyes and adventurers thither shall enjoye all the same *Immunityes* from Customes for exporting certine goods from these Realmes of England &c theither as ye Kinge hath been graciously pleased to graunt to us as alsoe for ye Incorragement of the Manufactrs of wine silke oyle ollives fruite almonds &c. menconed in the pattent have *priveledge* for bringing them Custome free into any of his Majties dominions for ye same time and upon ye same tearmes as we ourselves may by our Pattent. [Thorpe 2761]

Charles II, Charter of Carolina, June 30, 1665:

. . . together with all and singular the like and as ample rights, jurisdictions, *privileges,* prerogatives, royalties, liberties, *immunities,* and franchises of what kind soever, within the territory, isles, islets and limits aforesaid: To have, hold, use, exercise, and enjoy the same, as amply, fully and in as ample manner, as any Bishop of Durham, in our kingdom of England, ever heretofore had, held, used, or enjoyed, or of right ought or could have, use, or enjoy . . .

[Thorpe 2763]

New Jersey Proprietors, Deed of Revision, July 1, 1676:

. . . And also all that his moiety or half part of all rivers, rivelets, mines, all other royalties, profits, forts franchises, liberties, governments, powers, *priviledges,* commodities, hereditaments and *immunities* whatsoever, to the said land and premises belonging; with their and every of their appurtenances, in as full, ample and beneficial manner to all intents and purposes as the same was granted to the said John Lord Berkley and the said Sir George Carteret, their heirs and assigns, by him his said Royal Highness the said James Duke of York . . .

[Thorpe 2544]

Charles II, Charter of Pennsylvania, February 28, 1681:

And Wee doe further, for us, our heires and Successors, Give and grant unto the said William Penn, his heires and assignes, free and absolute power, to Divide the said Countrey and Islands into Townes, Hundreds and Counties, and to erect and incorporate Townes into Borroughs, and Borroughs into Citties, and to make and constitute faires and Marketts therein, with all other convenient *priviledges and immunities,* according to the meritt of the inhabitants, and the fitnes of the places . . . [Thorpe 3040]

Pennsylvania Frame of Government, November 7, 1696:

Provided always, and it is hereby enacted, That neither this act, nor any other act, or acts whatsoever, shall preclude, or debar the inhabitants of this province and territories, from claiming, having and enjoying any of the rights, *privileges and immunities,* which the said Proprietary, for himself, his heirs, and assigns, did formerly grant, or which of right belong unto them, the said inhabitants, by virtue of any law, charter or grants whatsoever, any thing herein contained to the contrary notwithstanding. [Thorpe 3076]

United States Continental Congress, Declaration and Resolves, October 14, 1774:

That these, his majesty's colonies, are likewise entitled to all the *immunities and privileges* granted & confirmed to them by royal charters, or secured by their several codes of provincial laws. [JCC1 69]

New Jersey Constitution, July 2, 1776:

[Article 19:] That there shall be no establishment of any one religious sect in this Province, in preference to another; and that no Protestant inhabitant of this Colony shall be denied the enjoyment of any civil right, merely on account of his religious principles; but that all persons, professing a belief in the faith of any Protestant sect, who shall demean themselves peaceably under the government, as hereby established, shall be capable of being elected into any office of profit or trust, or being a member of either branch of the Legislature, and shall fully and freely enjoy every *privilege and immunity,* enjoyed by others their fellow subjects. [Thorpe 2597–98]

Vermont Constitution, July 8, 1777:

[Frame of Government, Article 41:] . . . and all religious societies or bodies of men, that have or may be hereafter united and incorporated, for the advancement of religion and learning, or for other pious and charitable purposes, shall be encouraged and protected in the enjoyment of the *privileges, immunities* and estates which they, in justice, ought to enjoy, under such regulations, as the General Assembly of this State shall direct. [Thorpe 3748]

United States Continental Congress, Draft Articles of Confederation, July 12, 1776:

[Article 6:] The Inhabitants of each Colony shall henceforth always have the same Rights, Liberties, *Privileges, Immunities,* and Advantages, in the other Colonies, which the said Inhabitants now have, in all Cases whatever, except in those provided for by the next following Article. [DHRC1 80]

[Article 7:] The Inhabitants of each Colony shall enjoy all the Rights, Liberties, *Privileges, Immunities,* and Advantages, in Trade, Navigation, and Commerce, in any other Colony, and in going to and from the same from and to any Part of the World, which the Natives of such Colony enjoy. [DHRC1 80]

Pennsylvania Constitution, September 28, 1776:

[Frame of Government, Section 45:] . . . And all religious societies or bodies of men heretofore united or incorporated for the advancement of religion or learning, or for other pious and charitable purposes, shall be encouraged and protected in the enjoyment of the *privileges, immunities* and estates which they were accustomed to enjoy, or could of right have enjoyed, under the laws and former constitution of this state. [Thorpe 3091]

United States Articles of Confederation, November 15, 1777:

[Article IV:] The better to secure and perpetuate mutual friendship and intercourse among the people of the different states in this union, the free inhabitants of each of these states, paupers, vagabonds and fugitives from Justice excepted, shall be entitled to all *privileges and immunities* of free citizens in the several states; and the people of each state shall have free ingress and regress to and from any other state, and shall enjoy therein all the *privileges* of trade and commerce, subject to the same duties, impositions and restrictions as the inhabitants thereof respectively, provided that such restriction shall not extend so far as to prevent the removal of property imported into any state, to any other state of which the Owner is an inhabitant; provided also that no imposition, duties or restriction shall be laid by any state, on the property of the united states, or either of them.

Massachusetts Constitution, March 2, 1780:

[Declaration of Rights, Article 12:] . . . And no subject shall be arrested, imprisoned, despoiled, or deprived of his property, *immunities, or privileges,* but out of the protection of the law, exiled, or deprived of his life, liberty, or estate, but by the judgment of his peers, or the law of the land. [Thorpe 1891]

[Chapter V:1:1:] . . . it is declared, that the PRESIDENT AND FELLOWS OF HARVARD COLLEGE, in their corporate capacity, and their successors in that capacity, their officers and servants, shall have, hold, use, exercise, and enjoy, all the powers, authorities, rights, liberties, *privileges, immunities,* and franchises, which they now have, or are entitled to have, hold, use, exercise, and enjoy; and the same are hereby ratified and confirmed unto them, the said president and fellows of Harvard College, and to their successors, and to their officers and servants, respectively, forever. [Thorpe 1906–07]

New Hampshire Constitution, June 2, 1784:

[Bill of Rights, Article 15:] . . . And no subject shall be arrested, imprisoned, despoiled, or deprived of his property, *immunities, or privileges,* put out of the protection of the law, exiled or deprived of his life, liberty, or estate, but by the judgment of his peers or the law of the land. [Thorpe 2455]

Vermont Constitution, July 4, 1786:

[Frame of Government, Section 38:] . . . And all religious societies, or bodies of men, that may be hereafter united or incorporated, for the advancement of religion and learning, or for other pious and charitable purposes, shall be encouraged and protected in the enjoyment of the *privileges, immunities,* and estates, which they in justice ought to enjoy, under such regulations as the General Assembly of this State shall direct. [Thorpe 3760]

Alexander Hamilton, *The Federalist*, No. 11, November 24, 1787:

A mature consideration of the objects suggested by these questions will justify a belief that the real disadvantages to Britain from such a state of things, conspiring with the prepossessions of a great part of the nation in favor of the America trade, and with the importunities of the West India islands, would produce a relaxation in her present system, and would let us into the enjoyment of *privileges* in the markets of those islands and elsewhere, from which our trade would derive the most substantial benefits. Such a point gained from the British government, and which could not be expected without an equivalent in exemptions and *immunities* in our markets, would be likely to have a correspondent effect on the conduct of other nations, who would not be inclined to see themselves altogether supplanted in our trade. [Fed. 138]

James Madison, *The Federalist*, No. 42, January 22, 1788:

The dissimilarity in the rules of naturalization has long been remarked as a fault in our system, and as laying a foundation for intricate and delicate questions. In the fourth article of the Confederation, it is declared "that the free inhabitants of each of these States, paupers, vagabonds, and fugitives from justice excepted, shall be entitled to all *privileges and immunities* of free citizens in the several States; and the people of each State shall, in every other, enjoy all the *privileges* of trade and commerce,'' etc. There is a confusion of language here, which is remarkable. Why the terms free inhabitants are used in one part of the article, free citizens in another, and people in another; or what was meant by superadding to ''all *privileges and immunities* of free citizens'' ''all the *privileges* of trade and commerce,'' cannot easily be determined. It seems to be a construction scarcely avoidable, however, that those who come under the denomination of free inhabitants of a State, although not citizens of such State, are entitled, in every other State, to all the *privileges* of free citizens of the latter; that is, to greater *privileges* than they may be entitled to in their own State: so that it may be in the power of a particular State, or rather every State is laid under a necessity, not only to confer the rights of citizenship in other States upon any whom it may admit to such rights within itself, but upon any whom it may allow to become inhabitants within its jurisdiction. But were an exposition of the term ''inhabitants'' to be admitted which would confine the stipulated *privileges* to citizens alone, the difficulty is diminished only, not removed. . . . [Fed. 307]

''Brutus,'' No. 12, February 14, 1788:

. . . Moreover, the constitution expressly declares, that ''the citizens of each state shall be entitled to all the *privileges and immunities* of citizens in the several states.'' It will therefore be no fiction, for a citizen of one state to set forth, in a suit, that he is a citizen of another; for he that is entitled to all the *privileges and immunities* of a country, is a citizen of that country. And in truth, the citizen of one state will, under this constitution, be a citizen of every state.

[DHRC16 121]

James Iredell, ''Marcus,'' No. 4, March 12, 1788:

The first mentioned is, ''That the Congress may grant monopolies in trade and commerce.'' Upon examining the Constitution, I find it expressly provided, ''That no preference shall be given to the ports of one State over those of another;'' and that ''Citizens of each State shall be entitled to all *privileges and immunities* of citizens in the several States.'' These provisions appear to me to be calculated for the very purpose Mr. [George] Mason wishes to secure. Can they be consistent with any monopoly in trade and commerce? . . .

[DHRC16 380]

Alexander Hamilton, *The Federalist*, No. 80, May 28, 1788:

It may be esteemed the basis of the Union, that ''the citizens of each State shall be entitled to all the *privileges and immunities* of citizens of the several States.'' And if it be a just principle that every government ought to possess the means of executing its own provisions by its own authority, it will follow, that in order to the inviolable maintenance of that equality of *privileges and immunities* to which the citizens of the Union will be entitled, the national judiciary ought to preside in all cases in which one State or its citizens are opposed to another State or its citizens . . . [Fed. 502]

Alexander Hamilton, *The Federalist*, No. 81, May 28, 1788:

It is inherent in the nature of sovereignty not to be amenable to the suit of an individual without its consent. This is the general sense, and the general practice of mankind; and the exemption, as one of the attributes of sovereignty, is now enjoyed by the government of every State in the Union. Unless, therefore, there is a surrender of this *immunity* in the plan of the convention, it will remain with the States, and the danger intimated must be merely ideal. The circumstances which are necessary to produce an alienation of State sovereignty were discussed in considering the article of taxation, and need not be repeated here. A recurrence to the principles there established will satisfy us, that there is no color to pretend that the State governments would, by the adoption of that plan, be divested of the *privilege* of paying their own debts in their own way, free from every constraint but that which flows from the obligations of good faith. . . .

[Fed. 511]

Alexander Hamilton, *The Federalist*, No. 84, May 28, 1788:

. . . And the proposed Constitution, if adopted, will be the bill of rights of the Union. Is it one object of a bill of rights to declare and specify the political *privileges* of the citizens in the structure and administration of the government? This is done in the most ample and precise manner in the plan of the convention; comprehending various precautions for the public security, which are not to be found in any of the State constitutions. Is another object of a bill of rights to define certain *immunities* and modes of proceeding, which are relative to personal and private concerns? This we have seen has also been attended to, in a variety of cases, in the same plan. . . . [Fed. 536]

South Carolina Constitution, June 3, 1790:

[Article VIII, Section 2:] The rights, *privileges, immunities,* and estates of both civil and religious societies, and of corporate bodies, shall remain as if the constitution of this State had not been altered or amended. [Thorpe 3264]

Pennsylvania Constitution, September 2, 1790:

[Article VII, Section 3:] The rights, *privileges immunities,* and estates of religious societies and corporate bodies shall remain as if the constitution of this State had not been altered or amended. [Thorpe 3099]

PROPERTY, PRIVATE

United States Constitution Bill of Rights, December 15, 1791:

[Article V:] No person shall be held to answer for a capital, or otherwise infamous crime, unless on a presentment or indictment of a Grand Jury, except in cases arising in the land or naval forces, or in the Militia, when in actual service in time of War or public danger; nor shall any person be subject for the same offence to be twice put in jeopardy of life or limb; nor shall be compelled in any criminal case to be a witness against himself, nor be deprived of life, liberty, or property, without due process of law; nor shall *private property* be taken for public use, without just compensation.

* * * * *

Pennsylvania Constitution, September 28, 1776:

[Frame of Government, Section 43:] The inhabitants of this state shall have liberty to fowl and hunt in seasonable times on the lands they hold, and on all other lands therein not inclosed; and in like manner to fish in all boatable waters, and others not *private property*. [Thorpe 3091]

Vermont Constitution, July 8, 1777:

[Declaration of Rights, Article 2:] That *private property* ought to be subservient to public uses, when necessity requires it; nevertheless, whenever any particular man's property is taken for the use of the public, the owner ought to receive an equivalent in money. [Thorpe 3740]

[Frame of Government, Section 39:] That the inhabitants of this State, shall have liberty to hunt and fowl, in seasonable times, on the lands they hold, and on other lands (not enclosed;) and, in like manner, to fish in all boatable and other waters, not *private property*, under proper regulations, to be hereafter made and provided by the General Assembly. [Thorpe 3748]

Vermont Constitution, July 4, 1786:

[Declaration of Rights, Article 2:] That *private property* ought to be subservient to public uses, when necessity requires it; nevertheless, whenever any particular man's *property* is taken for the use of the public, the owner ought to receive an equivalent in money. [Thorpe 3752]

[Frame of Government, Article 37:] The inhabitants of this State shall have liberty, in seasonable times, to hunt and fowl on the lands they hold, and on other lands not inclosed; and in like manner to fish in all boatable and other waters, not *private property,* under proper regulations, to be hereafter made and provided by the General Assembly. [Thorpe 3760]

United States Confederation Congress, The Northwest Ordinance, July 13, 1787:

[Article 2:] . . . No man shall be deprived of his liberty or *property,* but by the judgment of his peers, or the law of the land, and should the public exigencies make it necessary, for the common preservation, to take any persons *property,* or to demand his particular services, full compensation shall be made for the same. And, in the just preservation of rights and *property,* it is understood and declared, that no law ought ever to be made or have force in the said territory, that shall, in any manner whatever, interfere with or affect *private* contracts, or engagements, bona fide, and without fraud previously formed. [Thorpe 961]

William Pierce to St. George Tucker, September 28, 1787, published in *Gazette of the State of Georgia*, March 20, 1788:

In my judgment, when there are restraints on power to prevent its invading the positive rights of a people, there is no necessity for any such thing as a Bill of Rights. I conceive civil liberty is sufficiently guarded when personal security, personal liberty, and *private property,* are made the peculiar care of government. Now the defined powers of each department of the government, and the restraints that naturally follow, will be sufficient to prevent the invasion of either of those rights. Where then can be the necessity for a Bill of Rights? . . .

[DHRC16 443]

Tench Coxe, *An Examination of the Constitution for the United States of America*, No. 4, October 21, 1787:

. . . The known principles of justice, the attachment to trial by jury whenever it can be used, the instructions of the state legislatures, the instructions of the people at large, the operation of the foederal regulations on the *property* of a president, a senator, a representative, a judge, as well as on that of a *private*

citizen, will certainly render those regulations as favorable as possible to property; for life and liberty are put more than ever into the hands of the juries. . . .
[Ford 150]

Dissent of the Pennsylvania Convention's Minority, December 18, 1787:

The inhabitants of the several states shall have liberty to fowl and hunt in seasonable times, on the lands they hold, and on all other lands in the United States not enclosed, and in like manner to fish in all navigable waters, and others not *private property,* without being restrained therein by any laws to be passed by the legislature of the United States. [DHRC2 624]

Samuel Bryan, "Centinel," No. 16, February 26, 1788:

. . . An ex post facto law is a law made after the fact, so that the Congress under the new constitution are precluded from all controul over transactions prior to its establishment. This prohibition would skreen the numerous public defaulters, as no measure could be constitutionally taken to compel them to render an account and restore the public money; the unaccounted millions lying in their hands would become their *private property*. Hitherto these characters from their great weight and numbers have had the influence to prevent an investigation of their accounts, but if this constitution be established, they may set the public at defiance, as they would be completely exonerated of all demands of the United States against them. . . . [DHRC16 218–19]

Samuel Bryan, "Centinel," No. 17, March 24, 1788:

. . . When we consider the immense sums of money taken up by Mr. [Robert Morris], as commercial agent, to import military supplies, and even to trade in behalf of the United States, at a time when the risque was so great, that individuals would not venture their *property;* that all these transactions were conducted under the private firm of [Willing] and M——, which afforded unrestrained scope to peculation and embezzlement of the public property, by enabling Mr. M——s to throw the loss of all captures by the enemy, at that hazardous period, on the public, and converting most of the safe arrivals (which were consequently very valuable) into his *private property* . . . [DHRC16 475–76]

Melancton Smith, *An Address to the People of the State of New York*, c. April 1788:

. . . We are told, that agriculture is without encouragement; trade is languishing; *private* faith and credit are disregarded, and public credit is prostrate; that the laws and magistrates are contemned and set at naught; that a spirit of licentiousness is rampant, and ready to break over every bound set to it by the government;

that *private* embarrassments and distresses invade the house of every man of middling property, and insecurity threatens every man in affluent circumstances . . . [Ford 94]

John Dickinson, "Fabius," No. 9, 1788:

These gentlemen will acknowledge, that Britain has sustained many internal convulsions, and many foreign wars, with a gradual advancement in freedom, power, and prosperity. They will acknowledge, that no nation has existed that ever so perfectly united those distant extremes, *private security of life, liberty, and property,* with exertion of public force—so advantageously combined the various powers of militia, troops, and fleets—or so happily blended together arms, arts, science, commerce, and agriculture. . . . [Ford 211]

PUNISHMENT, PUNISHMENTS

(Punish, Punishing, etc.)

United States Constitution, September 17, 1787:

[Article I, Section 3:] Judgment in Cases of Impeachment shall not extend further than to removal from Office, and disqualification to hold and enjoy any Office of honor, Trust or Profit under the United States: but the Party convicted shall nevertheless be liable and subject to Indictment, Trial, Judgment and *Punishment,* according to Law.

[Article I, Section 5:] Each House may determine the Rules of its Proceedings, *punish* its Members for disorderly Behaviour, and, with the Concurrence of two thirds, expel a Member.

[Article I, Section 8:] [Congress shall have power] To provide for the *Punishment* of counterfeiting the Securities and current Coin of the United States.

[*Ibid.*:] [Congress shall have power] . . . To define and *punish* Piracies and Felonies committed on the high Seas, and Offenses against the Law of Nations.

[Article III, Section 3:] The Congress shall have Power to declare the *Punishment* of Treason, but no Attainder of Treason shall work Corruption of Blood, or Forfeiture except during the Life of the Person attainted.

United States Contitution, Bill of Rights, December 15, 1791:

[Article VIII:] Excessive bail shall not be required, nor excessive fines imposed, nor *cruel and unusual punishments* inflicted.

* * * * *

Ferdinand and Isabella of Spain, Privileges and Prerogatives Granted to Christopher Columbus, April 30, 1492:

. . . and that you may exercise the office of Admiral, with the charge of Vice-Roy and Governour of the said Islands and Continent, which you and your

Lieutenants shall conquer, and freely decide all causes, civil and criminal, appertaining to the said employment of Admiral, Vice-Roy, and Governour, as you shall think fit in justice, and as the Admirals of our kingdoms use to do; and that you have power to *punish* offenders . . . [Thorpe 39]

Elizabeth I, Letters Patent to Sir Humphrey Gilbert, June 11, 1578:

. . . wee for us, our heires and successours are likewise pleased and contented, and by these presents doe give and graunt to the sayd sir Humfrey and his heires and assignes for ever, that he and they, and every or any of them, shall and may, from time to time, for ever hereafter within the sayd mentioned remote lands and countreys, and in the way by the Seas thither, and from thence, have full and meere power and authoritie to correct, *punish,* pardon, governe and rule by their, and every or any of their good discretions and policies, as well in causes capitall or criminall, as civill, both marine and other, all such our subjects and others, as shall from time to time hereafter adventure themselves in the sayd journeys or voyages habitative or possessive, or that shall at any time hereafter inhabite any such lands, countreys or territories as aforesayd, [Thorpe 51]

Elizabeth I, Charter to Sir Walter Raleigh, March 25, 1584:

. . . we for us, our heires and successors, are likewise pleased and contented, and by these presents do give and graunt to the said Walter Ralegh, his heires and assignes for ever, that hee and they, and every or any of them, shall and may from time to time for ever hereafter, within the said mentioned remote landes and Countreis in the way by the seas thither, and from thence, have full and meere power and authoritie to correct, *punish,* pardon, governe, and rule by their and every or any of their good discretions and pollicies, as well in causes capital, or criminall, as civil, both marine and other, all such our subjects as shall from time to time adventure themselves in the said journies or voyages, or that shall at any time hereafter inhabite any such landes, countreis, or territories as aforesaide . . . [Thorpe 55]

James I, Second Charter of Virginia, May 23, 1609:

. . . We for Us, our Heirs, and Successors are likewise pleased and contented, and by these Presents do Give and Grant unto the said Treasurer and Company, and their Successors, and to such Governors, Officers, and Ministers, as shall be by our said Council constituted and appointed according to the Natures and Limits of their Offices and Places respectively, that they shall and may from Time to Time, for ever hereafter, within the said Precincts of Virginia, or in the way by Seas thither and from thence, have full and absolute Power and Authority to correct, *punish,* pardon, govern, and rule all such the Subjects of Us, our Heires, and Successors as shall from Time to Time adventure themselves in any

Voyage thither, or that shall at any Time hereafter, inhabit in the Precincts and Territories of the said Colony as aforesaid . . . [Thorpe 3800–3801]

James I, Third Charter of Virginia, 1611–1612:

. . . Or else, at their [the Council's] Discretions, to remand and send back the said Offenders, or any of them, unto the said Colony in Virginia, there to be proceeded against and *punished,* as the Governor, Deputy or Council there, for the Time being, shall think meet . . . [Thorpe 3809]

James I, The Charter of New England, November 3, 1620:

[1] . . . and by these Presents do give and grant unto the said Council and their Successors, and to such Governors, Officers, and Ministers, as shall be by the said Councill constituted and appointed according to the natures and Limitts of their Offices and Places respectively, that they shall and may, from time to time for ever heerafter, within the said Precincts of New-England, or in the Way by the Seas thither, and from thence have full and absolute Power and Authority to correct, *punish,* pardon, governe, and rule all such the Subjects of Us, our Heires and Successors, as shall from time to time adventure themselves in any Voyage thither, or that shall att any Time heerafter inhabit in the Precincts or Territories of the said Collony as aforesaid, according to such Laws, Orders, Ordinances, Directions, and Instructions as by the said Councill aforesaid shall be established . . . [Thorpe 1833]

[2] . . . and also upon any insolent, contemptuous, or irreverent Carriage or Misbehaviour, to or against the said Councill, to be shewed or used by any such Person or Persons so called, convened, and appearing before them as aforesaid, that in all such Cases, our said Councill, or any two or more of them for the Time being, shall and may have full Power and Authority, either heere to bind them over with good Sureties for their good Behaviour, and further therein to proceed, to all Intents and Purposes as it is used in other like Cases within our Realme of England, or else at their Discretions to remand and send back the said offenders, or any of them, to the said Collony of New-England, there to be proceeded against and *punished* as the Governour's Deputy or Councill there for the Time being, shall think meete, or otherwise according to such Laws and Ordinances as are, and shall be, in Use there, for the well ordering and good Government of the said Collony. [Thorpe 1838–39]

Charter of the Dutch West India Company, June 3, 1621:

[Article 45:] All which privileges, freedoms and exemptions, together with the assistance herein before mentioned, in all their particulars and articles, we have, with full knowledge of the business, given, granted, promised and agreed to the aforesaid Company; giving granting, agreeing and promising moreover that they shall enjoy them peaceably and freely; ordaining that the same shall be observed and kept by all the magistrates, officers and subjects of the United Netherlands, without doing anything contrary thereto directly or indirectly, either within or out of these Netherlands, on penalty of being *punished* both in life and goods as obstacles to the common welfare of this country, and transgressors of our ordinance . . . [Thorpe 67]

English Petition of Right, June 7, 1628:

[1] . . . and whereas no offender of what kind soever is exempted from the proceedings to be used, and *punishments* to be inflicted by the laws and statutes of this your realm; nevertheless of late time divers commissions under your Majesty's Great Seal have issued forth, by which certain persons have been assigned and appointed Commissioners with power and authority to proceed within the land, according to the justice of martial law . . . [SDECH 341]

[2] And also sundry grievous offenders, by colour thereof claiming an exemption, have escaped the *punishments* due to them by the laws and statutes of this your realm, by reason that divers of your officers and ministers of justice have unjustly refused, or forborne to proceed against such offenders according to the same laws and statutes, upon pretence that the said offenders were *punishable* only by martial law, and by authority of such commissions as aforesaid; which commissions, and all other of like nature, are wholly and directly contrary to the said laws and statutes of this your realm. [SDECH 341]

Charles I, Patent to Sir Robert Heath, October 30, 1629:

[1] . . . & we grant to the said Sr. Robert his heires & assignes free full & all kind of power by the Tenour of these presents if the qualitye of the offence requires it to *punish* by the losse of life or limbe by himself his heires or assignes, or by their Deputyes Lieutenants Judges Justices Magestrates Officers & ministers to be constituted & made according to the tenour & true intent of these presents duely to be executed . . . [Thorpe 71]

[2] . . . we by these presents for us our heires & successors doe give & grant power and authoritye most ample to himself or by Captaines Deputyes or other their officers authorised to this purpose under their seales, against all authors of innovations, seditions against the Government of him or them, withdrawing themselves speakers evill of the militia, renegadors, deserters—or any others whatsoever offending against the matter manner & discipline military shall by them be *punished* by law militarye soe freely and in such ample manner & forme as any Captaine Generall by the vertue of his office may or could doe. [Thorpe 74]

Charles I, Charter of Massachusetts Bay, March 4, 1629:

And Wee Doe further, for Us, our Heires and Successors, give and graunt to the said Governor and Company, and their Successors by theis Presents, that all and everie such Chiefe Comaunders, Captaines, Governors, and other Officers and Ministers, as by the said Orders, Lawes, Statuts, Ordinances, Instruccons, or Direccons of the said Governor and Company for the Tyme being, shalbe from Tyme to Tyme hereafter ymploied either in the Government of the saide Inhabitants and Plantacon, or in the Waye by Sea thither, or from thence, according to the Natures and Lymitts of their Offices and Places respectively, shall from Tyme to Tyme hereafter for ever, within the Precincts and Partes of Newe England hereby menconed to be graunted and confirmed, or in the Waie by Sea thither, or from thence, have full and Absolute Power and Authoritie to correct, *punishe,* parrdon, governe, and rule all such the Subjects of Us, our Heires and Successors, as shall from Tyme to Tyme adventure themselves in any Voyage thither or from thence . . . [Thorpe 1858]

Charles I, Charter of Maryland, June 20, 1632:

[Article 7:] [Lord Baltimore, his deputies, heirs and successors shall have power] . . . duly to execute the same [laws] upon all Persons, for the time being, within the aforesaid Province, and the Limits thereof, or under his or their Government and Power, in Sailing towards Maryland, or thence Returning, Outward-bound, either to England, or elsewhere, whether to any other Part of Our, or of any foreign Dominions, wheresoever established, by the Imposition of Fines, Imprisonment, and other *Punishment* whatsoever; even if it be necessary, and the Quality of the Offence require it, by Privation of Member, or Life . . .

[Thorpe 1680]

Charles I, Grant of the Province of Maine, April 3, 1639:

. . . And therefore Wee Doe hereby for us our heires and successors charge and command prohibite and forbidd all the subjects of us our heires and successors of what degree qualitie or condicon soever they bee that none of them directlie or indirectlie presume to trade or adventure to traffique into or from nor to inhabite or abide in the said Province of Mayne Island Dominion and Places hereby menconed or intended to bee graunted or any of them other then the said Sir Fardinando Gorges his heires and asssignes and his and theire deputies and factors unless itt bee with the license and consent of the said Fardinando Gorges his heires and assignes first had and obteyned in that behalf in writeinge under his or theire hands and seales under payne of our idignacon and alsoe of suche penaltyes *punishments* as by the Lawes and Ordinances of the said Sir Fardinand Gorges his heires and assignes to bee made in that behalfe shalbee appoynted.

[Thorpe 1635]

Patent for Providence Plantations, March 14, 1643:

. . . Together with full Power and Authority to rule themselves, and such others as shall hereafter inhabit within any Part of the said Tract of land, by such a Form of Civil Government, as by voluntary consent of all, or the greater Part of them, they shall find most suitable to their Estate and Condition; and, for that End, to make and ordain such Civil Laws and Constitutions, and to inflict such *punishments* upon Transgressors, and for Execution thereof, so to place, and displace Officers of Justice, as they, or the greater Part of them, shall by free Consent agree unto. Provided nevertheless, that the said Laws, Constitutions, and *Punishments,* for the Civil Government of the said Plantations, be conformable to the Laws of England, so far as the Nature and Constitution of the place will admit. . . . [Thorpe 3210–11]

Government of New Haven Colony, October 27, 1643:

All such free burgesses shall have power in each towne or plantation within this jurisdiction to chuse fitt and able men, from amongst themselves, being church members as before, to be the ordinary judges, to heare and determine all inferior causes, whether civill or criminall, provided that no civill cause to be tryed in any of these plantation Courts in value exceed 20 Pounds, and thatt the *punishment* in such criminals, according to the minde of God, revealed in his word, touching such offences, doe nott exceed stocking and whipping, or if the fine be pecuniary, thatt itt exceed nott five pounds. . . . [Thorpe 527]

Charles II, Charter of Connecticut, April 23, 1662:

[The Governor and Company shall have power for] . . . granting necessary Commissions, and for Imposition of lawful Fines, Mulcts, Imprisonment or other *Punishment* upon Offenders and Delinquents according to the Course of other Corporations within this our Kingdom of England, and the same Laws, Fines, Mulcts and Executions, to alter, change, revoke, annul, release, or pardon under their Common Seal, as by the said General Assembly, or the major Part of them shall be thought fit . . . [Thorpe 534]

Charles II, Charter of Carolina, March 24, 1663:

[The proprietors] shall from time to time assemble in such manner and form as to them shall seem best, and the same laws duly to execute upon all people within the said province and limits thereof, for the time being, or which shall be constituted under the power and government of them or any of them, either sailing towards the said province of Carolina, or returning from thence towards England, or any other of our, or foreign dominions, by imposition of penalties, imprisonment or any other *punishment;* yea, if it shall be needfull, and the quality of the offence requires it, by taking away member and life . . .
[Thorpe 2745]

Charles II, Charter of Rhode Island, July 8, 1663:

[1] That our royall will and pleasure is, that noe person within the sayd colonye, at any tyme hereafter, shall bee any wise molested, *punished,* disquieted, or called in question, for any differences in opinione in matters of religion, and doe not actually disturb the civill peace of our sayd colony . . . [Thorpe 3213]

[2] . . . [Governor and Company shall have power] . . . alsoe to order, direct and authorize the imposing of lawfull and reasonable fynes, mulcts, imprisonments, and executing other *punishments* pecuniary and corporal, upon offenders and delinquents, according to the course of other corporations within this oure kingdom of England . . . [Thorpe 3215]

New Jersey Proprietors, Concession and Agreement, February 10, 1664:

[1] . . . And whosoever shall subscribe and not swear, and shall violate his promise in that subscription, shall be liable to the same *punishment* that the persons are or may be that have sworn and broken their oaths. [Thorpe 2536]

[2] That no person qualified as aforesaid within the said Province, at any time shall be any ways molested, *punished,* disquieted or called in question for any difference in opinion or practice in matter of religious concernments, who do not actually disturb the civil peace of the said Province . . . [Thorpe 2537]

[3] [The Governor and Council are] . . . To see that all courts establish'd by the laws of the General Assembly, and all ministers and officers, civil and military, do and execute their several duties and offices respectively, according to the laws in force; and to *punish* them for swerving from the laws, or acting contrary to their trust, as the nature of their offences shall require. [Thorpe 2539]

[4] According to the constitution of the General Assembly, to appoint courts and officers in cases criminal; and to impower them to inflict penalties upon offenders against any of the laws in force in the said Province, as the said laws shall ordain; whether by fine, imprisonment, banishment, corporal *punishment,* or to the taking away of member or life itself if there be cause for it. [Thorpe 2540]

Charles II, Grant of the Province of Maine to the Duke of York, March 12, 1664:

. . . and wee do further of our speciall grace certaine knowledge and meere mocon for us our heires and successors give and grant unto our said dearest brother James Duke of Yorke his heires deputyes agents commissioners and assignes by these presents full and absolute power and authority to correct *punish* pardon governe and rule all such the subjects of us our heires and successors who may from time to time adventure themselves into any of the parts or places aforesaid . . . [Thorpe 1638]

Carolina Proprietors, Concessions and Agreements, 1665:

[1] . . . And whosoever shall subscribe and not sware, and shall vyolate his promis in that Subscription shalbe lyable to the same *punishmt* that the persons are or may be that have sworne and broken their oathes . . . [Thorpe 2757]

[2] That noe person or persons quallifyed as aforesaid within the Province or all or any of the Countyes before exprest at any time shalbe anywayes molested *punished* disquieted or called in question for any differences in opinion or practice in matters of religious concernment whoe doe not actually disturbe the civill peace of the said Province or Countyes . . . [Thorpe 2757]

[3] The Governors are with the Councill before exprest:

1. Item to see that all Courts established by the Lawes of ye Genll Assembly and all Ministers and offices Civill or Military doe and execute their severall dutyes and offices respectively according to the Lawes in force and to *punish* them from swerveing from the Lawes or acting contrary to their trust as the nature of their offence shall require. [Thorpe 2760]

[4] According to the constitutions of the Genll Assembly to appoint Courts and officers in Cases Cryminall and to impower them to inflict penaltyes upon offenders against any of ye said Lawes in force in ye said Countyes as ye said Lawes shall ordaine wheither by fine Imprisonment Banishmt corporall *punishmt* or to ye taking away of member of or Life itselfe if there be cause for it. [Thorpe 2760]

Charles II, Charter of Carolina, June 30, 1665:

[1] . . . and the same laws duly to execute, upon all people within the said province or territory, county, baronny, or colony, or the limits thereof, for the time being, which shall be constituted, under the power, and government of them or any of them, either sailing towards the said province, or territory of Carolina, or returning from thence towards England, or any other of our, or foreign dominions, by imposition of penalties, imprisonment, or any other *punishment;* yea, if it shall be needful, and the quality of the offence require it, by taking away member and life . . . [Thorpe 2764]

[2] . . . And that no person or persons unto whom such liberty shall be given, shall be any way molested, *punished,* disquieted, or called in question, for any differences in opinion, or practice in matters of religious concernments, who do not actually disturb the civil peace of the province, county or colony, that they shall make their abode in . . . [Thorpe 2771]

Fundamental Constitutions of Carolina, March 1, 1669:

[Section 63:] In every precinct there shall be a court, consisting of a steward and four justices of the precinct, being inhabitants and having three hundred acres of free hold within the said precinct who shall judge all criminal causes; except for treason, murder, and any other offences *punishable* with death, and except all criminal causes of the nobility . . . [Thorpe 2780]

[Section 65:] For treason, murder, and all other offences *punishable* with death, there shall be a commission, twice a year at least, granted unto one or more members of the grand council or colleges; who shall come as itinerant judges to the several counties and with the sheriff and four justices shall hold assizes to judge all such causes . . . [Thorpe 2780]

[Section 108:] Assemblies, upon what pretence soever of religion, not observing and performing the above said rules, shall not be esteemed as churches, but unlawful meetings, and be *punished* as other riots. [Thorpe 2785]

Charles II, Grant of the Province of Maine to the Duke of York, June 29, 1674:

. . . and wee do further, of our speciall grace certaine knowledge and meer motion for Us Our heirs and successors give and graunt unto our said Dearest brother James Duke of Yorke his heirs Deputyes Agents commissioners and assignes by these presents full and absolute power and authority to correct *punish* pardon govern and rule all such the subjects of us our heirs and successors or any other person or persons as shall from time to time adventure themselves into any of the parts or places aforesaid . . . [Thorpe 1641–42]

Fundamental Constitutions of West New Jersey, 1676:

[Chapter 16:] That no men, nor number of men upon earth, hath power or authority to rule over men's consciences in religious matters, therefore it is consented, agreed and ordained, that no person or persons whatsoever within the said Province, at any time or times hereafter, shall be any ways upon any pretence whatsoever, called in question, or the least *punished* or hurt, either in person, estate, or priviledge, for the sake of his opinion, judgment, faith or worship towards God in matters of religion. But that all and every such person, and persons, may from time to time, and at all times, freely and fully have, and enjoy his and their judgments, and the exercises of their consciences in matters of religious worship throughout all the said Province. [Thorpe 2549]

[Chapter 21:] That all and every person and persons whatsoever, who shall prosecute or prefer any indictment or information against others for any personal injuries, or matter criminal, or shall prosecute for any other criminal cause, (treason, murther, and felony, only excepted) shall and and may be master of his own process, and have full power to forgive and remit the person or persons offending against him or herself only, as well before as after judgment, and condemnation, and pardon and remit the sentence, fine and *punishment* of the person or persons offending, be it personal or other whatsoever.
[Thorpe 2551]

New Jersey Proprietors, Deed of Revision, July 1, 1676:

. . . in and by which said Letters Patent his said Majesty did likewise give and grant unto his said dearest brother James Duke of York, his heirs, deputies, agents commissioners and assigns, full and absolute power and authority for the correcting, *punishing*, pardoning, governing and ruling such of the subjects of his said Majesty, of his heirs and successors, as shall at any time adventure themselves into the said port and places, or inhabit there, according to such laws, orders, ordinances, directions and instructions, as by his said Majesty's said dearest brother, or his assigns, shall be established . . . [Thorpe 2552–53]

Duke of York, Grant of West Jersey, August 6, 1680:

. . . as also for the well governing of the same, and of all such as are or shall be inhabitting in the same, and for the making, ordaining, and executing of necessary and convenient laws and constitutions, in order to such government, and the *punishing* and pardoning offences, and offenders, as occasion shall require . . . [Thorpe 2563]

Charles II, Commission Constituting a President and Council for New Hampshire, September 18, 1680:

[1] . . . & any 5 of the Councell for ye time being shall have full power & authority, to hold plea in all causes from time to time, as well in pleas of ye Crown, as in matters relating to ye conservation of ye peace, & *punishment* of offenders, as in civill suits & actions between partie & partie; or between Us & any of Our subjects there . . . [Thorpe 2447]

[2] . . . And Our further will & pleasure is & so we do hereby declare; That in all criminall cases, where *punishmt* to be inflicted upon ye offenders, shall extend to loss of life or limb (ye case of willfull murder only excepted) ye party convicted shall either be sent over into this Our Kingdom of Engd, with a true state of his case & conviction; or execuc'on shall be respited untill ye case shall be here represented unto Us, Our heirs & successors, in Our & their Privie Councell, and Orders sent & returned therein. . . . [Thorpe 2448]

[3] . . . & also to sum'on & convene any person or persons before them & *punish* contempts; & to cause ye Oath of Allegeance to be administered to all & every person & persons, who shall be admitted to any Office, freedom, or preferments . . . [Thorpe 2449]

Duke of York, Confirmation to New Jersey Proprietors, March 14, 1682:

. . . and the *punishing* and pardoning offences and offenders, as occasion shall require . . . [Thorpe 2571]

Pennsylvania Frame of Government, April 25, 1682:

[Article 11:] That the Governor and provincial Council shall, at all times, have power to inspect the management of the public treasury, and *punish* those who shall convert any part thereof to any other use, than what hath been agreed upon by the Governor, provincial Council, and General Assembly. [Thorpe 3056]

[Article 13:] . . . Secondly, a committee of justice and safety, to secure the peace of the Province, and *punish* the mal-administration of those who subvert justice to the prejudice of the public, or private, interest. . . . [Thorpe 3057]

[Laws Agreed Upon in England, May 5, 1682: Article 17:] That all briberies and extortion whatsoever shall be severely *punished*. [Thorpe 3061]

[*Ibid.*, Article 30:] That all scandalous and malicious reporters, backbiters, defamers and spreaders of false news, whether against Magistrates, or private persons, shall be accordingly severely *punished*, as enemies to the peace and concord of this province. [Thorpe 3062]

[*Ibid.*, Article 37:] . . . all prizes, stage-plays, cards, dice, May-games, gamesters, masques, revels, bull-baitings, cock-fightings, bear-baitings, and the like, which excite the people to rudeness, cruelty, looseness, and irreligion, shall be respectively discouraged, and severely *punished*, according to the appointment of the Governor and freemen in provincial Council and General Assembly . . . [Thorpe 3063]

Pennsylvania Frame of Government, April 2, 1683:

[Article 9:] That the Governor and provincial Council shall, at all times, have power to inspect the management of the public treasury, and *punish* those who shall convert any part thereof to any other use, than what hath been agreed upon by the Governor, provincial Council and Assembly. [Thorpe 3965]

Fundamental Constitutions of East New Jersey, 1683:

[Article 21:] That all witnesses coming or called to testify their knowledge in or to any matter or thing in any court or before any lawful authority within the Province, shall there have and deliver in their evidence by solemnly promissing to speak the truth, the whole truth and nothing but the truth to the matter in question. And in case any person so doing shall be afterwards convicted of willful falsehood, both such persons as also those who have proved to have suborn, shall undergo the damage and *punishment* both in criminal and in civil; the person against whom they did or should have incurred, which if it reach not his life, he shall be publickly exposed as a false witness, never afterwards to be credited before any court; the like *punishment* in cases of forgery, and both criminals to be stigmatized. [Thorpe 2581]

James II, Commission to Sir Edmund Andros for the Dominion of New England, April 7, 1688:

[1] And wee do by these presents ordain constitute and appoint you or the Commander in Cheif for the time being, and the Councill of our said territory & dominion for the time being, to be a constant and setled Court of Record for ye administration of justice to all our subjects inhabiting within our said Territory and Dominion, in all causes as well civill as Criminall with full power and authority to hold pleas in all cases, from time to time, as well in Pleas of the Crown and in all matters relateing to the conservation of the peace and *punishment* of offenders, as in Civill causes and actions between party and party, or between us and any of our subjects there, whether the same do concerne the realty and relate to any right of freehold & inheritance or whether the same do concerne the personality and relate to matter of debt contract damage or other personall injury . . . [Thorpe 1865]

[2] And forasmuch as divers mutinies & disorders do happen by persons shipped and imployed at Sea, and to the end that such as shall be shipped or imployed at Sea may be better governed and ordered; Wee do hereby give and grant unto you the said Sr Edmund Andros our Captain Generall and Governor in Cheif, full power and authority to constitute and appoint Captains, Masters of Ships, and other Commanders, commissions to execute the law martial, and to use such proceedings authorities, *punishment,* correction and execution upon any offender or offenders who shall be mutinous seditious, disorderly or any way unruly either at sea or during the time of their abode or residence in any of the ports harbors or bays of our said Territory and Dominion, as the Cause shall be found to require, according to martial law. . . . [Thorpe 1867]

[3] . . . Provided also that all disorders and misdemeanors committed on shore by and Captain Commander, Lieutent, Master, or other officer seaman soldier or person whatsoever belonging to any of our ships of warr or other vessel acting by immediate commission or warrent from our self under the Great Seal of our Admiralty or from our High Admll from England for the time being may be tryed & *punished* according to the lawes of the place where any such disorders offences and misdemeanors shall be so committed on shore, notwithstanding such offender be in our actuall service and borne in our pay on board any such our shipps of warr or other vessels acting by immediate Commission or warrant from our self or our High Admirall as aforesaid . . . [Thorpe 1868]

English Bill of Rights, December 16, 1689:

[1] And excessive fines have been imposed. And *illegal and cruel punishments* inflicted. [SDECH 463]

[2] That excessive bail ought not to be required nor excessive fines imposed nor *cruel and unusual punishment* inflicted. [SDECH 465]

William and Mary, Charter of Massachusetts Bay, October 7, 1691:

. . . And alsoe to impose Fines mulcts Imprisonments and other *Punishments* And to impose and leavy proportionable and reasonable Assessments Rates and Taxes upon the Estates and Persons of all and every the Proprietors and Inhabitants of our said Province or Territory to be Issued and disposed of by Warrant under the hand of the Governor of our said Province for the time being with the advice and Consent of the Councill for Our service in the necessary defence and support of our Government of our said Province or Territory and the Protection and Preservation of the Inhabitants there . . . [Thorpe 1882]

Pennsylvania Frame of Government, November 7, 1696:

[1] . . . and in case any Sheriff shall misbehave himself, in the management of any of the said elections, he shall be *punished* accordingly, at the discretion of the Governor and Council, for the time being. [Thorpe 3073]

[2] Be it further enacted by the authority aforesaid, That the Governor and Council shall, at all times, have power to inspect the management of the public treasury, and *punish* those who shall convert any part thereof to any other use, than what hath been agreed upon by the Governor, Council and Assembly. [Thorpe 3074]

New Jersey Proprietors, Surrender of Rights, April 15, 1702:

[1] . . . And by the same Letters Patents the late King Charles the Second, for himself, his heirs and successors, did give and grant to the said James Duke of York, his heirs, deputies, agents, commissioners and assigns, full and absolute power and authority to correct, *punish,* pardon, govern and rule all such subjects of the said King his heirs and successors, as should from time to time adventure themselves into the parts and places aforesaid, or that should at any time then after inhabit within the same, according to such laws, orders, ordinances, directions and instructions as by the said Duke of York, or his assigns, should be established . . . [Thorpe 2586]

[2] . . . . the present Proprietors of the said Provinces of East Jersey, and West Jersey, for the consideration and to the intent aforesaid, have surrendered and yielded up, and by these presents for us and our heirs, do surrender and yield up unto our Sovereign Lady Anne by the grace of God Queen of England, Scotland, France, and Ireland, Defender of the Faith, &c. her heirs and successors, all these the said powers and authorities to correct, *punish,* pardon, govern and rule all or any of her Majesty's subjects or others, who now are or inhabit or hereafter shall adventure into or inhabit within the said Provinces of East Jersey, and West Jersey, or either of them . . . [Thorpe 2588]

New Hampshire Constitution, January 5, 1776:

[Preamble:] The sudden and abrupt departure of his Excellency John Wentworth, Esq., our late Governor, and several of the Council, leaving us destitute of legislation, and no executive courts being open to *punish* criminal offenders . . . [Thorpe 2542]

Thomas Paine, *Common Sense*, January 9, 1776:

[1] . . . Samuel continued to reason with them but to no purpose; he set before them their ingratitude, but all would not avail; and seeing them fully bent on their folly, he cried out, I will call unto the Lord, and he shall sent thunder and rain (which then was a *punishment,* being the time of wheat harvest) that ye may perceive and see that your wickedness is great which ye have done in the sight of the Lord, IN ASKING YOU A KING . . . [CWTP1 12]

[2] . . . 'Tis is not in the power of Britain or of Europe to conquer America, if she doth not conquer herself by delay and timidity. The present winter is worth an age if rightly employed, but if lost or neglected, the whole continent will partake of the misfortune; and there is no *punishment* which that man doth not deserve, be he who, or what, or where he will, that may be the means of sacrificing a season so precious and useful. [CWTP1 23]

John Adams, *Thoughts on Government*, April 1776:

. . . For misbehaviour the grand inquest of the Colony, the House of Representatives, should impeach them [the judges] before the Governor and Council, where they should have time and opportunity to make their defence; but if convicted, should be removed from their offices, and subjected to such other *punishment* as shall be thought proper. [PJA4 91]

Virginia Bill of Rights, June 12, 1776:

[Section 9:] That excessive bail ought not to be required, nor excessive fines imposed, nor *cruel and unusual punishments* inflicted. [Thorpe 3813]

Virginia Constitution, June 29, 1776:

If all or any of the Judges of the General Court should on good grounds (to be judged of by the House of Delegates) be accused of any of the crimes or offences above mentioned, such House of Delegates may, in like manner, impeach the Judge or Judges so accused, to be prosecuted in the Court of Appeals; and he or they, if found guilty, shall be *punished* in the same manner as is prescribed in the preceding clause. [Thorpe 3818]

United States Declaration of Independence, July 4, 1776:

. . . For protecting them, by a mock Trial, from *punishment* for any Murders which they should commit on the Inhabitants of these States . . .

Pennsylvania Constitution, September 28, 1776:

[Frame of Goverment, Section 20:] [The President and Council] . . . shall have power to grant pardons, and remit fines, in all cases whatsoever, except in cases of impeachment; and in cases of treason and murder, shall have power to grant reprieves, but not to pardon, until the end of the next sessions of assembly but there shall be no remission or mitigation of *punishments* on impeachments, except by act of the legislature . . . [Thorpe 3087–88]

[*Ibid.,* Section 38:] The penal laws as heretofore used shall be reformed by the legislature of this state, as soon as may be, and *punishments* made in some cases less sanguinary, and in general more proportionate to the crimes. [Thorpe 3090]

[*Ibid.,* Section 39:] To deter more effectually from the commission of crimes, by continued visible *punishments* of long duration, and to make sanguinary *punishments* less necessary; houses ought to be provided for *punishing* by hard labour, those who shall be convicted of crimes not capital . . . [Thorpe 3090]

Maryland Constitution, November 11, 1776:

[Declaration of Rights, Article 15:] That retrospective laws, *punishing* facts committed before the existence of such laws, and by them only declared criminal, are oppressive, unjust, and incompatible with liberty; wherefore no ex post facto law ought to be made. [Thorpe 1688]

[*Ibid.,* Article 22:] That excessive bail ought not to be required, nor excessive fines imposed, nor *cruel or unusual punishments* inflicted, by the courts of law. [Thorpe 1688]

[*Ibid.,* Article 29:] That no person, except regular soldiers, mariners, and marines in the service of this State, or militia when in actual service, ought in and case to be subject to or *punishable* by martial law. [Thorpe 1689]

[Form of Government, Article 12:] That the House of delegates may *punish,* by imprisonment, any person who shall be guilty of a contempt, in their view, by any disorderly or riotous behavior, or by threats to, or abuse of their members, or by any obstruction to their proceedings. They may also *punish,* by imprisonment, any person who shall be guilty of a breach of privilege, by arresting on civil process, or by assaulting any of their members, during their sitting, or on their way to, or return from, the House of Delegates, or by any assault of, or obstruction to their officers, in the execution of any order or process, or by assaulting or obstructing any witness, or any other person, attending on, or on their way to or from the House, or by rescuing any person committed by the House; and the Senate may exercise the same power in similar cases.

[Thorpe 1693]

[*Ibid.*, Article 39:] That, if any Senator, Delegate to Congress or Assembly, or member of the Council, shall hold or execute any office of profit, or receive, directly or indirectly, at any time, the profits, or any part of the profits, of any office exercised by any other person, during his acting as Senator, Delegate to Congress or Assembly, or member of the Council—his seat (on conviction in a court of law, by the oath of two credible witnesses) shall be void; and he shall suffer the *punishment* for wilful and corrupt perjury, or be banished this State for ever, or disqualified for ever from holding any office or place of trust or profit, as the Court may adjudge. [Thorpe 1697]

[*Ibid.*, Article 53:] That if any Governor, Chancellor, Judge, Register of Wills, Attorney-General, Register of the Land Office, Register of the Chancery Court, or any Clerk of the common law courts, Treasurer, Naval Officer, Sheriff, Surveyor or Auditor of public accounts, shall receive, directly or indirectly, at any time, the profits, or any part of the profits of any office, held by any other person, during his acting in the office to which he is appointed; his election, appointment and commission (on conviction in a court of law by oath of two credible witnesses) shall be void; and he shall suffer the *punishment* for wilful and corrupt perjury, or be banished this State forever, or disqualified forever from holding any office or place of trust or profit, as the court may adjudge.

[Thorpe 1700]

North Carolina Constitution, December 18, 1776:

[Declaration of Rights, Article 10:] That excessive bail should not be required, nor excessive fines imposed, nor *cruel or unusual punishments* inflicted.

[Thorpe 2788]

[*Ibid.*, Article 24:] That retrospective laws, *punishing* facts committed before the existence of such laws, and by them only declared criminal, are oppressive, unjust, and incompatible with liberty; wherefore no ex post facto law ought to be made. [Thorpe 2788]

[Form of Government, Article 34:] . . . Provided, That nothing herein contained shall be construed to exempt preachers of treasonable or seditious discourses, from legal trial and *punishment*. [Thorpe 2793]

New York Constitution, April 20, 1777:

[Article 33:] . . . That previous to the trial of every impeachment, the members of the said court shall respectively be sworn truly and impartially to try and determine the charge in question, according to evidence; and that no judgment of the said court shall be valid unless it be assented to by two third parts of the members then present; nor shall it extend farther than to removal from office, and disqualification to hold or enjoy any place of honor, trust, or profit under this State. But the party so convicted shall be, nevertheless, liable and subject to indictment, trial, judgment, and *punishment,* according to the laws of the land. [Thorpe 2635]

Vermont Constitution, July 8, 1777:

[Frame of Government, Section 18:] [The Governor and Council] . . . shall have power to grant reprieves, but not to pardon, until the end of the next session of the Assembly: but there shall be no remission or mitigation of *punishment,* on impeachments, except by act of legislation. They are also, to take care that the laws be faithfully executed. . . . [Thorpe 3745]

[*Ibid.,* Section 35:] To deter more effectually from the commission of crimes, by continued visible *punishment* of long duration, and to make sanguinary *punishments* less necessary; houses ought to be provided for *punishing,* by hard labor, those who shall be convicted of crimes not capital . . .

[Thorpe 3747]

South Carolina Constitution, March 19, 1778:

[Article 13:] . . . The qualification of electors shall be that every free white man, and no other person, who acknowledges the being of a God, and believes in a future state of rewards and *punishments,* and who has attained to the age of one and twenty years, and hath been a resident and an inhabitant in this State for the space of one whole year before the day appointed for the election he offers to give his vote at, and hath a freehold at least of fifty acres of land, or a town lot, and hath been legally seized and possessed of the same at least six months previous to such election, or hath paid a tax the preceding year, or was taxable the present year, at least six months previous to the said election, in a sum equal to the tax on fifty acres of land, to the support of this government, shall be deemed a person qualified to vote for, and shall be capable of electing, a representative or representatives to serve as a member or members in the senate and house of representatives . . . [Thorpe 3251–52]

[Article 38:] That all persons and religious societies who acknowledge that there is one God, and a future state of rewards and *punishments,* and that God is publicly to be worshipped, shall be freely tolerated. . . . [Thorpe 3255]

[Article 38:] That there is one eternal God, and a future state of rewards and *punishments.* [Thorpe 3256]

[Article 40:] That the penal laws, as heretofore used, shall be reformed, and *punishments* made in some cases less sanguinary, and in general more proportionate to the crime. [Thorpe 3257]

Massachusetts Constitution, March 2, 1780:

[Declaration of Rights, Article 12:] And the legislature shall not make any law that shall subject any person to a capital or infamous *punishment,* excepting for the government of the army and navy, without trial by jury. [Thorpe 1891]

[*Ibid.,* Article 24:] Laws made to *punish* for actions done before the existence of such laws, and which have not been declared crimes by preceding laws, are unjust, oppressive, and inconsistent with the fundamental principles of a free government. [Thorpe 1892]

[*Ibid.,* Article 26:] No magistrate or court of law shall demand excessive bail or sureties, impose excessive fines, or inflict *cruel or unusual punishments.* [Thorpe 1892]

[Frame of Government, Chapter I:2:8:] The senate shall be a court with full authority to hear and determine all impeachments made by the house of representatives, against any officer or officers of the commonwealth, for misconduct and mal-administration in their offices. But previous to the trial of every impeachment the members of the senate shall respectively be sworn, truly and impartially to try and determine the charge in question, according to evidence. Their judgment, however, shall not extend further than to removal from office and disqualification to hold or enjoy any place of honor, trust, or profit, under this commonwealth; but the party so convicted shall be, nevertheless, liable to indictment, trial, judgment, and *punishment,* according to the laws of the land. [Thorpe 1897–98]

[*Ibid.,* Chapter I:3:10:] The house of representatives shall be the judge of the returns, elections, and qualifications of its own members, as pointed out in the constitution; shall choose their own speaker; appoint their own officers, and settle the rules and orders of proceeding in their own house. They shall have authority to *punish* by imprisonment every person, not a member, who shall be guilty of disrespect to the house, by any disorderly or contemptuous behavior in its presence; or who, in the town where the general court is sitting, and during the time of its sitting, shall threaten harm to the body or estate of any of its members, for any thing said or done in the house; or who shall assault any of them therefor; or who shall assault, or arrest, any witness, or other person, ordered to attend the house, in his way in going or returning; or who shall rescue any person arrested by the order of the house. [Thorpe 1899]

[*Ibid.,* Chapter I:3:11:] The senate shall have the same powers in the like cases; and the governor and council shall have the same authority to *punish* in like cases: provided, that no imprisonment on the warrant or order of the governor, council, senate, or house of representatives, for either of the above described offences, be for a term exceeding thirty days. [Thorpe 1899]

New Hampshire Constitution, June 2, 1784:

[Declaration of Rights, Article 16:] . . . Nor shall the legislature make any law that shall subject any person to a capital *punishment,* excepting for the government of the army and navy, and the militia in actual service, without trial by jury. [Thorpe 2455]

[*Ibid.,* Article 18:] All penalties ought to be proportioned to the nature of the offence. No wise legislature will affix the same *punishment* to the crimes of theft, forgery and the like, which they do to those of murder and treason; where the same undistinguishing severity is exerted against all offences; the people are led to forget the real distinction in the crimes themselves, and to commit the most flagrant with as little compunction as they do those of the lightest dye: For the same reason a multitude of sanguinary laws is both impolitic and unjust. The true design of all *punishments* being to reform, not to exterminate, mankind. [Thorpe 2456]

[*Ibid.,* Article 23:] Retrospective laws are highly injurious, oppressive and unjust. No such laws, therefore, should be made, either for the decision of civil causes, or the *punishment* of offences. [Thorpe 2456]

[*Ibid.,* Article 33:] No magistrate or court of law shall demand excessive bail or sureties, impose excessive fines, or inflict *cruel or unusual punishments.* [Thorpe 2457]

[Form of Government:] And farther, full power and authority are hereby given and granted to the said general court . . . also to impose fines, mulcts, imprisonments, and other *punishments;* and to impose and levy proportional and reasonable assessments, rates and taxes, upon all the inhabitants of, and residents within the said state; and upon all estates within the same. . . . [Thorpe 2458]

[*Ibid.:*] . . . Their [the senate's] judgment [in cases of impeachment], however, shall not extend farther than removal from office, disqualification to hold or enjoy any place of honor, trust or profit under this state; but the party so convicted, shall nevertheless be liable to indictment, trial, judgment, and *punishment,* according to laws of the land. [Thorpe 2461]

[*Ibid.:*] The house of representatives shall choose their own speaker, appoint their own officers, and settle the rules of proceedings in their own house. They shall have authority to *punish* by imprisonment, every person who shall be guilty of disrespect to the house in its presence, by any disorderly or contemptuous behaviour, or by threatening, or ill treating any of its members . . . [Thorpe 2462]

Virginia Statute of Religious Liberty, January 16, 1786:

Whereas Almighty God hath created the mind free; that all attempts to influence it by temporal *punishments,* or burthens, or by civil incapacitations, tend only to beget habits of hypocrisy and meanness, and are a departure from the plan of the Holy Author of our religion, who, being Lord both of body and mind, yet chose not to propagate it by coercions on either, as was in his Almighty power to do . . . [CVA8 690]

Vermont Constitution, July 4, 1786:

[Frame of Government, Section 11:] [The Governor and Council] . . . shall have power to grant pardons, and remit fines in all cases whatsoever, except in treason and murder, in which they shall have power to grant reprieves but not to pardon, until after the end of the next session of Assembly, and except in cases of impeachment, in which there shall be no remission or mitigation of *punishment,* but by act of legislation. . . . [Thorpe 3756]

[*Ibid.,* Section 31:] . . . and any elector, who shall receive any gift or reward for his vote, in meat, drink, monies or otherwise, shall forfeit his right to elect at that time, and suffer such other penalty as the laws shall direct: and any person who shall, directly or indirectly, give, promise or bestow any such rewards to be elected, shall thereby be rendered incapable to serve for the ensuing year, and be subject to such further *punishment* as a future Legislature shall direct. [Thorpe 3759]

[*Ibid.,* Section 34:] To deter more effectually from the commission of crimes, by continued visible *punishment,* of long duration, and to make sanguinary *punishment* less necessary, means ought to be provided for *punishing* by hard labour, those who shall be convicted of crimes not capital, whereby the criminal shall be employed for the benefit of the public, or for reparation of injuries done to private persons . . . [Thorpe 3760]

The New Jersey Plan of Union, June 15, 1787:

[Article 2:] [Congress is authorized] . . . to pass Acts for the regulation of trade & commerce as well with foreign nations as with each other: provided that all *punishments,* fines, forfeitures & penalties to be incurred for contravening such acts rules and regulations shall be adjudged by the Common law Judiciarys of the State in which any offence contrary to the true intent & meaning of such Acts rules & regulations shall have been committed or perpetrated . . . [DHRC1 251]

United States Confederation Congress, The Northwest Ordinance, July 13, 1787:

[Article 2:] The inhabitants of the said territory shall always be entitled to the benefits of the writs of habeas corpus, and of the trial by jury; of a proportionate representation of the people in the legislature, and of judicial proceedings according to the course of the common law. All persons shall be bailable, unless for capital offences, where the proof shall be evident, or the presumption great.

All fines shall be moderate; and no *cruel or unusual punishments* shall be inflicted. No man shall be deprived of his liberty or property, but by the judgment of his peers, or the law of the land . . . [Thorpe 960–61]

[Article 6:] There shall be neither slavery nor involuntary servitude in the said territory, otherwise than in *punishment* of crimes, whereof the party shall have been duly convicted: Provided always, That any person escaping into the same, from whom labor or service is lawfully claimed in any one of the original States, such fugitive may be lawfully reclaimed, and conveyed to the person claiming his or her labor or service as aforesaid. [Thorpe 962]

Tench Coxe, *An Examination of the Constitution for the United States of America*, No. 2, September 28, 1787:

They [the Senators] can only, by conviction or impeachment, remove and incapacitate a dangerous officer, but the *punishment* of him as a criminal remains within the province of the courts of law, to be conducted under all the ordinary forms and precautions, which exceedingly diminishes the importance of their judicial powers. . . . [Ford 142]

George Mason, Objections to the Constitution, October 7, 1787:

[1] The President of the United States has the unrestrained Power of granting Pardons for Treason; which may be sometimes excercised to screen from *Punishment* those whom he had secretly instigated to commit the Crime, & thereby prevent a Discovery of his own Guilt. [DHRC8 44]

[2] Under their own Construction of the general Clause at the End of the enumerated Powers, the Congress may grant Monopolies in Trade & Commerce, constitute new Crimes, inflict *unusual & severe Punishments,* and extend their Power as far as they shall think proper; so that the State Legislatures have no Security for the Powers now presumed to remain to them; or the People for their Rights. [DHRC8 45]

Richard Henry Lee, Proposed Amendments to the Constitution, October 16, 1787:

. . . That the new constitution proposed for the government of the United States be bottomed upon a declaration or bill of rights, clearly and precisely stating the principles upon which this social compact is founded, to wit . . . That excessive bail, excessive fines, or *cruel and unusual punishments,* should not be demanded or inflicted . . . [DHRC8 65]

Noah Webster, *An Examination into the Leading Principles of the Federal Constitution*, October 17, 1787:

. . . But reverse the case; suppose every man to act without control or fear of *punishment*—every man would be free, but no man would be sure of his freedom one moment. Each would have the power of taking his neighbor's life, liberty, or property; and no man would command more than his own strength to repel the invasion. . . . [Ford 55]

"Cato Uticensis," October 17, 1787:

. . . Consider that if you pass the Foederal Constitution in toto, you subject yourselves to see the doors of your houses, the impenetrable castles of freemen, fly open before the magic wand of an exciseman, and, that, if you should resent and *punish* the insolence of office, the daring brutality of the publican, perhaps offered to the wife of thy bosom, you will be dragged for trial before a distant tribunal, and there, perhaps, condemned without enjoying the benefit of a jury from your vicinage, your unalienable birthright as a freeman. [DHRC8 75]

Tench Coxe, *An Examination of the Constitution for the United States of America*, No. 4, October 21, 1787:

[1] Laws, made after the commission of the fact, have been a dreadful engine in the hands of tyrannical governors. Some of the most virtuous and shining characters in the world have been put to death, by laws formed to render them *punishable,* for parts of their conduct which innocence permitted, and to which patriotism impelled them. . . . [Ford 147]

[2] . . . The trial by jury is not excluded in these foederal courts. In all criminal cases, where the property, liberty or life of the citizen is at stake, he has the benefit of a jury. If convicted on impeachment, which is never done by a jury in any country, he cannot be fined, imprisoned or *punished,* but only may be disqualified from doing public mischief by losing his office, and his capacity to hold another. . . . [Ford 149]

John Jay, *The Federalist*, No. 3, November 3, 1787:

[1] Because, even if the governing party in a State should be disposed to resist such temptations, yet, as such temptations may, and commonly do, result from circumstances peculiar to the State, and may affect a great number of the inhabitants, the governing party may not always be able, if willing, to prevent the injustice meditated, or to *punish* the aggressors. But the national government, not being affected by those local circumstances, will neither be induced to commit the wrong themselves, nor want power or inclination to prevent or *punish* its commission by others. [Fed. 99]

[2] . . . Not a single Indian war has yet been occasioned by aggressions of the present federal government, feeble as it is; but there are several instances of Indian hostilities having been provoked by the improper conduct of individual States, who, either unable or unwilling to restrain or *punish* offenses, have given occasion to the slaughter of many innocent inhabitants. [Fed. 99]

Pelatiah Webster, *The Weakness of Brutus Exposed*, November 4, 1787:

[1] I suppose that neither Brutus nor any of his friends would wish to see our government embroiled abroad; and therefore will admit it necessary to institute some federal authority, sufficient to *punish* any individual or State, who shall violate our treaties with foreign nations, insult their dignity, or abuse their citizens, and compel due reparation in all such cases. [Ford 120–21]

[2] The greatest wisdom, care, and caution, has been used in the mode of their appointment; in the restraints and checks under which they must act; in the numerous discussions and deliberations which all their acts must pass through, before they can receive the stamp of authority; in the terrors of *punishment* if they misbehave. I say, in all these ways the greatest care has been used to procure and form a good Congress. [Ford 124]

[3] . . . For 'tis a truth worthy of great attention, that laws are not made so much for the righteous as for the wicked; who never fail to shelter themselves from *punishment,* whenever they can, under the defects of the law, and the weakness of government. [Ford 127]

"A True Friend," November 14, 1787:

. . . The interest on money has risen to an enormous rate; all transactions upon trust have been ruinous for the person who asked for credit; what would have been looked upon as usury and *punishable,* is become legal and authorised by the circumstances. . . . [DHRC8 162]

Alexander Hamilton, *The Federalist*, No. 15, December 1, 1787:

Government implies the power of making laws. It is essential to the idea of a law, that it be attended with a sanction; or, in other words, a penalty or *punishment* for disobedience. If there be no penalty annexed to disobedience, the resolutions or commands which pretend to be laws will, in fact, amount to nothing more than advice or recommendation. . . . [Fed. 159]

"Americanus," No. 1, December 5, 1787:

. . . Should he [the President], however, at any time be impelled by ambition, or blinded by passion, and boldly attempt to pass the bounds prescribed to his power, he is liable to be impeached and removed from office; and afterwards he is subject to indictment, trial, judgment, and *punishment* according to law. Are not these sufficient checks upon his conduct? . . . [DHRC8 203]

James Madison, *The Federalist*, No. 18, December 7, 1787:

. . . As a further provision for the efficacy of the federal powers, they [the members of the Greek Amphictyonic Council] took an oath mutually to defend and protect the united cities, to *punish* the violators of this oath, and to inflict vengeance on sacrilegious despoilers of the temple. [Fed. 171]

James Madison, *The Federalist*, No. 19, December 8, 1787:

. . . [The Duke of Bavaria] soon appeared before the city with a corps of ten thousand troops, and finding it a fit occasion, as he had secretly intended from the beginning, to revive an antiquated claim, on the pretext that his ancestors had suffered the place to be dismembered from his territory, he took possession of it in his own name, disarmed, and *punished* the inhabitants, and reannexed the city to his domains. [Fed. 180]

Alexander Hamilton, *The Federalist*, No. 21, December 12, 1787:

The next most palpable defect of the subsisting Confederation is the total want of a SANCTION to its laws. The United States, as now composed, have no powers to exact obedience, or *punish* disobedience to the resolutions, either by pecuniary mulcts, by a suspension or divestiture of privileges, or by any other constitutional mode. . . . [Fed. 186]

Dissent of the Pennsylvania Convention's Minority, December 18, 1787:

[1] That excessive bail ought not to be required, nor excessive fines imposed, nor *cruel nor unusual punishments* inflicted. [DHRC2 623]

[2] . . . The senate is a constituent branch of the legislature, it has judicial power in judging on impeachments, and in this case unites in some measure the characters of judge and party, as all the principal officers are appointed by the president general, with the concurrence of the senate, and therefore they derive their offices in part from the senate. This may bias the judgments of the senators, and tend to screen great delinquents from *punishment*. . . . [DHRC2 634]

[3] The president general is dangerously connected with the senate; his coincidence with the views of the ruling junto in that body is made essential to his weight and importance in the government, which will destroy all independency and purity in the executive department; and having the power of pardoning without the concurrence of a council, he may screen from *punishment* the most treasonable attempts that may be made on the liberties of the people, when instigated by his coadjutors in the senate . . . [DHRC2 635]

[4] First, the personal liberty of every man, probably from sixteen to sixty years of age may be destroyed by the power Congress have in organizing and governing of the militia. As militia they may be subjected to fines to any amount, levied in a military manner; they may be subjected to corporal *punishments of the most disgraceful and humiliating kind,* and to death itself, by the sentence of a court martial. To this our young men will be more immediately subjected, as a select

militia, composed of them, will best answer the purposes of government. [DHRC2 638]

Alexander Hamilton, *The Federalist*, No. 27, December 25, 1787:

The hope of impunity is a strong incitement to sedition; the dread of *punishment,* a proportionably strong discouragement to it. Will not the government of the Union, which, if possessed of a due degree of power can call to its aid the collective resources of the whole Confederacy, be more likely to repress the former sentiment and to inspire the latter, than that of a single State, which can only command the resources within itself? . . . [Fed. 220]

James Madison, *The Federalist*, No. 42, January 22, 1788:

[1] The second class of powers, lodged in the general government, consist of those which regulate the intercourse with foreign nations, to wit: to make treaties; to send and receive ambassadors, other public ministers, and consuls; to define and *punish* piracies and felonies committed on the high seas, and offences against the law of nations . . . [Fed. 302]

[2] The power to define and *punish* piracies and felonies committed on the high seas, and offences against the law of nations, belongs with equal propriety to the general government, and is a still greater improvement on the articles of Confederation. These articles contain no provision for the case of offences against the law of nations; and consequently leave it in the power of any indiscreet member to embroil the Confederacy with foreign nations. . . . [Fed. 303]

[3] . . . I shall confine myself to a cursory review of the remaining powers comprehended under this third description, to wit: to regulate commerce among the several States and the Indian tribes; to coin money, regulate the value thereof, and of foreign coin; to provide for the *punishment* of counterfeiting the current coin and securities of the United States. . . . [Fed. 305]

[4] The *punishment* of counterfeiting the public securities, as well as the current coin, is submitted of course to that authority which is to secure the value of both. [Fed. 307]

James Madison, *The Federalist*, No. 43, January 23, 1788:

As treason may be committed against the United States, the authority of the United States ought to be enabled to *punish* it. But as new-fangled and artificial treasons have been the great engines by which violent factions, the natural offspring of free government, have usually wreaked their alternate malignity on each other, the convention have, with great judgment, opposed a barrier to this peculiar danger, by inserting a constitutional definition of the crime, fixing the proof necessary for conviction of it, and restraining the Congress, even in *pun-*

ishing it, from extending the consequences of guilt beyond the person of its author. [Fed. 310]

Alexander White [?], "An Independent Freeholder," January 25, 1788:

That the exclusion of ex post facto laws should be made an objection is to me astonishing. I do an action to day which is in itself innocent and prohibited by no law, at a future day you pass a law to *punish* me for it. Let every man's own mind answer whether this is just, and whether the existance of such a power is not inconsistent with the principles of liberty? . . . [DHRC8 327]

"Civis Rusticus," January 30, 1788:

[1] . . . The president's having the unrestrained power of pardoning for treasons is another objection [by George Mason]; and why? "it may be sometimes exercised to screen from *punishment* those whom he, (the president) had secretly instigated to commit the crime, and thereby prevent a discovery of his own guilt"—I appeal to this worthy gentleman himself, I appeal to the public, whether there be in this objection, more of validity and force, or chimera and imagination. [DHRC8 336–37]

[2] " . . . The general laws against sedition and libelling are at present as strong as they can possibly be made, nothing can impose a further restraint, but, either clapping an imprimatur on the press, or giving to the court very large discretionary powers, to *punish* whatever displeases them—but these concessions would be such a bare faced violation of liberty, that they will probably be the last efforts of a despotic government—Hume's essay vol. 1. p. 17." [DHRC8 338]

[3] Ex post facto laws have ever been considered as abhorrent from liberty: necessity and public safety never can require them—[quoting Paley:] "If laws do not *punish* an offender,let him go *unpunished;* let the legislature, admonished of the defect of the laws, provide against the commission of future crimes of the same sort. . . . " [DHRC8 338]

Alexander C. Hanson, *Remarks on the Proposed Plan of a Federal Government*, c. January 31, 1788:

. . . After gaining the assent of the senate, the bill must be submitted to the objections of the president. He is not in any manner dependent on the legislature, which can, in no manner, *punish* him, except for some crime known to the laws. He is elected by persons chosen for that special purpose. He receives a compensation, which cannot be diminished or increased, during his continuance in office. The term of his commission is limited to four years, unless he shall have acted so as to merit the people's favour. From the mode of his election, it is impossible he can intrigue to advantage; and, from the nature of other things, he will never succeed by bribery and corruption. Like any other individual, he is liable to *punishment*. Finally, at the expiration of his office, he returns into the mass of the people. [Ford 225–26]

Luther Martin, "Genuine Information," No. 10, February 1, 1788:

[1] By the principles of the American revolution, arbitrary power may and ought to be resisted even by arms if necessary—The time may come when it shall be the duty of a State, in order to preserve itself from the oppression of the general government, to have recourse to the sword—In which case the proposed form of government declares that the State and every of its citizens who act under its authority are guilty of a direct act of treason—reducing by this provision the different States to this alternative that they must tamely and passively yield to despotism or their citizens must oppose it at the hazard of the halter if unsuccessful—and reducing the citizens of the State which shall take arms to a situation in which they must be exposed to *punishment,* let them act as they will, since if they obey the authority of their State government, they will be guilty of treason against the United States . . . [DHRC16 11]

[2] To save the citizens of the respective States from this disagreeable dilemma, and to secure them from being *punishable* as traitors to the United States when acting expressly in obedience to the authority of their own State, I wished to have obtained as an amendment to the third section of this article the following clause: "Provided that no act or acts done by one or more of the States against the United States, or by any citizen of any one of the United States under the authority of one or more of the said States, shall be deemed treason or *punished* as such; but in case of war being levied by one or more of the States against the United States the conduct of each party towards the other, and their adherents respectively, shall be regulated by the laws of war and of nations."
[DHRC16 11]

Samuel Bryan, "Centinel," No. 14, February 5, 1788:

[Quoting Luther Martin:] " . . . Had this proposition been acceded to, the dangerous and oppressive power in the general government of imposing direct taxes on the inhabitants, which it now enjoys in all cases, would have been only vested in it in case of the non-compliance of a state, as a *punishment* for its delinquency, and would have ceased that moment that the state complied with the requisition. . . . " [DHRC16 34]

Tench Coxe, "A Freeman," No. 3, February 6, 1788:

. . . The people of every state, by their constitutional representatives, may impeach the public officer, however great or daring, that shall presume to violate their exclusive rights, or offend against the peace and dignity of their commonwealth, and may *punish* him, on conviction, by fine, imprisonment or death, without any possible interference of Congress. [DHRC16 51–52]

Benjamin Workman [?], "Philadelphiensis," No. 9, February 6, 1788:

[1] . . . Every freeman of America ought to hold up this idea to himself, that he has no superior but God and the laws. But this tyrant [the President] will be so much his superior, that he can at any time he thinks proper, order him out in the militia to exercise, and to march when and where he pleases. His officers can wantonly inflict the most disgraceful *punishment* on a peaceable citizen, under pretence of disobedience, or the smallest neglect of militia duty. [DHRC16 58]

[2] . . . When government [under the Constitution] thinks proper, under the pretence of writing a libel, &c. it may imprison, inflict the most *cruel and unusual punishment,* seize property, carry on prosecutions, &c. and the unfortunate citizen has no magna charta, no bill of rights, to protect him; nay, the prosecution may be carried on in such a manner that even a jury will not be allowed him. . . . [DHRC16 59]

Massachusetts Convention, Proposed Amendments to the Constitution, February 6, 1788:

[Article 6:] That no person shall be tried for any crime by which he may incur an *infamous punishment,* or loss of life, until he be first indicted by a grand jury, except in such cases as may arise in the government and regulation of the land and naval forces. [DHRC16 68]

Luther Martin, "Genuine Information," No. 12, February 8, 1788:

The part of the system, which provides that no religious test shall ever be required as a qualification to any office or public trust under the United States, was adopted by a very great majority of the convention, and without much debate,—however, there were some members so unfashionable as to think that a belief of the existence of a Deity, and of a state of future rewards and *punishments* would be some security for the good conduct of our rulers, and that in a Christian country it would be at least decent to hold out some distinction between the professors of Christianity and downright infidelity or paganism. [DHRC16 89]

James Madison, *The Federalist*, No. 54, February 12, 1788:

. . . In being protected, on the other hand, in his [i.e., the slave's] life and in his limbs, against the violence of all others, even the master of his labor and his liberty; and in being *punishable* himself for all violence committed against others,—the slave is no less evidently regarded by the law as a member of the society, not as a part of the irrational creation; as a moral person, not as a mere article of property. . . . [Fed. 370]

Alexander White, "To the Citizens of Virginia," February 22, 1788:

[1] The freedom of speech and of the press, are likewise out of the jurisdiction of Congress.—But, if by an abuse of that freedom I attempt to excite sedition in the Commonwealth, I may be *punished*—should I be unjustly accused of such an offence, the trial by a jury of my countrymen is my security—if what I have said or wrote corresponds with their general sense of the subject, I shall be acquitted. . . . [DHRC8 404–405]

[2] [Quoting Polybius:] . . . As to war and military expeditions, the [Roman] consuls had almost sovereign power; had the care of raising armies; of setling the number of troops which the allies were seperately to furnish, and of nominating the principal officers to serve under them. When they were in the field, they had the right of condemning and *punishing* without appeal. . . . [DHRC8 407]

John Hancock, Speech to Massachusetts Legislature, February 27, 1788:

. . . I hope and pray, that the gratitude of their Hearts may be expressed by a proper use of those inestimable blessings,—by the greatest exertions of Patriotism,—by forming and supporting Institutions for cultivating the human Understanding, and for the greatest Progress of the Arts and Sciences,—by establishing Laws for the support of Piety, Religion and Morality, as well as for *punishing* Vice and Wickedness . . . [DHRC16 226]

James Iredell, "Marcus," No. 2, February 27, 1788:

. . . I am persuaded it will in general be thought infinitely more safe, as well as more just, that the President who acts should be responsible for his conduct, following advice at his peril, than that there should be a danger of *punishing* any man for an erroneous opinion which might possibly be sincere. Besides the morality of this scheme, which may well be questioned, its inexpediency is glaring, since it would be so plausible an excuse, and the insincerity of it so difficult to detect; the hopes of impunity this avenue to escape, would afford, would nearly take away all dread of *punishment*. . . . [DHRC16 246]

"An Impartial Citizen," No. 5, February 28, 1788:

[1] . . . It is objected, that the President has the power of pardoning offences against the United States, and Mr. [George] Mason discovers that the President may prevent a discovery and *punishment* of his own crimes by this power . . . [DHRC8 428]

[2] . . . Human sagacity cannot devise any law, but what, in its operations, may in some instances bear hard. It is impossible by any general law, to prevent *punishments* from being in some unforeseen cases, inadequate to offences—To obviate this inconvenience, a power of pardoning ought to be vested some where in a State. All civilized nations have accordingly adopted this measure; and there is hardly a respectable writer who has not inculcated the expediency of pardons. Demosthenes, Seneca, Cicero, Diodorus Siculus, and a vast multiplicity of other ancient and modern authors are quoted by Grotius on this subject, in the 20th chap. of his second book de jure belli ac pacis, who are all as well as he himself, advocates for the remission of *punishments* in some cases. The Marquis de Beccaria, 'tis true, thinks that pardons ought to be excluded in a perfect Legislation, where *punishments* are mild but certain—But indeed, to make this maxim maintainable, *punishments* ought to be very mild—And the learned Blackstone, in his admirable Commentaries, has clearly shewn the propriety of pardoning. . . . [DHRC8 428–29]

[3] . . . In case such officers in the United States should conspire against their country, they cannot flatter themselves with the hopes of extorting form the President a remission of their *punishment*. The certainty of this will render conspiracies less certain and less frequent. . . . [DHRC8 429]

[4] It is also objected by Mr. Mason, that under their own construction of the general clause, at the end of the enumerated powers, the Congress may grant monopolies in trade, constitute new crimes, inflict *unusual punishments,* and in short, do whatever they please. Nothing can be more groundless and ridiculous than this. . . . [DHRC8 431]

[5] . . . So that if those powers cannot be executed without the aid of a law, granting commercial monopolies, inflicting *unusual punishments,* creating new crimes, or commanding any unconstitutional act; yet, as such a law would be manifestly not proper, it would not be warranted by this clause, without absolutely departing from the usual acceptation of words. . . . [DHRC8 431]

Mercy Otis Warren, *Observations on the New Constitution*, February 1788:

[1] . . . If such is the influence of government on the character and manners, and undoubtedly the observation is just, must we not subscribe to the opinion of the celebrated Abbe Mable? "That there are disagreeable seasons in the unhappy situation of human affairs, when policy requires both the intention and the power of doing mischief to be *punished;* and that when the [Roman] senate proscribed the memory of Caesar they ought to have put Anthony to death, and extinguished the hopes of Octavius." . . . [DHRC16 275]

[2] . . . The education of the advocates for monarchy should have taught them, and their memory should have suggested that [quoting Luther Martin] "monarchy is a species of government fit only for a people too much corrupted by luxury,

avarice, and a passion for pleasure, to have any love for their country, and whose vices the fear of *punishment* alone is able to restrain . . . " [DHRC16 286]

John Jay, *The Federalist*, No. 64, March 5, 1788:

[1] . . . From this cause, probably, proceed the fears and apprehensions of some, that the President and Senate may make treaties without an equal eye to the interests of all the States. Others suspect that two thirds will oppress the remaining third, and ask whether those gentlemen are made sufficiently responsible for their conduct; whether, if they act corruptly, they can be *punished;* and if they make disadvantageous treaties, how are we to get rid of those treaties? [Fed. 424]

[2] . . . In short, as the Constitution has taken the utmost care that they [the Senators] shall be men of talents, and integrity, we have reason to be persuaded that the treaties they make will be as advantageous as, all circumstances considered, could be made; and so far as the fear of *punishment* and disgrace can operate, that motive to good behavior is amply afforded by the article on the subject of impeachments. [Fed. 425]

"The Impartial Examiner," No. 1, March 5, 1788:

. . . The same observation may be made on any arbitrary or capricious imprisonments contrary to the law of the land. The same may be made, if excessive bail should be required; if excessive fines should be imposed; if *cruel and unusual punishments* should be inflicted; if the liberty of the press should be restrained; in a word—if laws should be made totally derogatory to the whole catalogue of rights, which are now secure under your present form of government. [DHRC8 462]

James Iredell, "Marcus," No. 3, March 5, 1788:

[1] . . . But, says Mr.[George] Mason, "The President may sometimes exercise this power to screen from *punishment* those whom he had secretly instigated to commit the crime, and thereby prevent a discovery of his own guilt." This is possible, but the probability of it is surely too slight to endanger the consequences of abridging a power which seems so generally to have been deemed necessary in every well regulated government. . . . [DHRC16 324]

[2] . . . Was it not supposed, by a great number of intelligent men, that Admiral Byng's execution was urged on to satisfy a discontented populace [in England], when the Administration, by the weakness of the force he was entrusted with, were, perhaps the real cause of the miscarriage before Minorca? Had he been acquitted, or pardoned he could perhaps have exposed the real fault: As a prisoner under so heavy a charge, his recrimination would have been discredited as merely

the effort of a man in despair to save himself from an ignominious *punishment*. . . . [DHRC16 324]

Alexander Hamilton, *The Federalist*, No. 65, March 7, 1788:

. . . The *punishment* which may be the consequence of conviction upon impeachment, is not to terminate the chastisement of the offender. After having been sentenced to a perpetual ostracism from the esteem and confidence, and honors and emoluments of his country, he will still be liable to prosecution and *punishment* in the ordinary course of law. . . . [Fed. 428]

Luther Martin, Reply to a Newspaper Writer, March 7, 1788:

. . . I confess I should have been both disappointed and mortified—It would have had at least the appearance, that the Landholder had discovered something in my principles, which he considered congenial with his own—However great may be my political sins, to be cursed with his approbation and applause, would be a *punishment* much beyond their demerit. . . . [DHRC16 343]

Alexander Hamilton, *The Federalist*, No. 66, March 8, 1788:

[1] . . . After having combined with the Executive in betraying the interests of the nation in a ruinous treaty, what prospect, it is asked, would there be of their [the Senators] being made to suffer the *punishment* they would deserve, when they were themselves to decide upon the accusation brought against them for the treachery of which they have been guilty? [Fed. 434–35]

[2] . . . The convention might with propriety have meditated the *punishment* of the Executive, for a deviation from the instructions of the Senate, or a want of integrity in the conduct of the negotiations committed to him; they might also have had in view the *punishment* of a few leading individuals in the Senate, who should have prostituted their influence in that body as the mercenary instruments of foreign corruption: but they could not, with more or with equal propriety, have contemplated the impeachment and *punishment* of two thirds of the Senate, consenting to an improper treaty, than of a majority of that or of the other branch of the national legislature, consenting to a pernicious or unconstitutional law,—a principle which, I believe, has never been admitted into any government. . . . [Fed. 435]

[3] . . . The truth is, that in all such cases it is essential to the freedom and to the necessary independence of the deliberations of the body, that the members of it should be exempt from *punishment* for acts done in a collective capacity; and the security to the society must depend on the care which is taken to confide the trust to proper hands, to make it their interest to execute it with fidelity, and to make it as difficult as possible for them to combine in any interest opposite to that of the public good. [Fed. 435]

[4] So far as might concern the misbehavior of the Executive in perverting the instructions or contravening the views of the Senate, we need not be apprehensive of the want of a disposition in that body to *punish* the abuse of their confidence, or to vindicate their own authority. . . . [Fed. 436]

Jonathan Williams, Jr., "The Fabrick of Freedom," March 8, 1788:

Here Justice holds her even scales,
And grasps her rightful sword;
As Truth directs she never fails,
To *punish* or reward:
Her equal law is Virtue's guide,
And Virtue's sons therein confide. [DHRC16 360]

Benjamin Workman [?], "Philadelphiensis," No. 11, March 8, 1788:

If on the broad basis of equity and justice, crimes and *punishments* have their proper proportion: What *punishment* then, on the scale of moderation, could counterpoise, or atone, for a crime so aggravated as that charged to the majority of the members of the late federal convention? . . . [DHRC16 363]

James Iredell, "Marcus," No. 4, March 12, 1788:

[1] As to the constituting new crimes, and inflicting *unusual and severe punishment,* certainly the cases enumerated wherein the Congress are empowered either to define offences, or prescribe *punishments,* are such as are proper for the exercise of such authority in the general Legislature of the union. . . .
[DHRC16 381]

[2] . . . The Congress having, for these reasons, a just right to authority in the above particulars, the question is, whether it is practicable and proper to prescribe the limits to its exercise, for fear that they should inflict *punishments unusual and severe?* It may be observed in the first place, that a declaration against "*cruel and unusual punishments,*" formed part of an article in the Bill of Rights at the Revolution in England, in 1688. The prerogative of the Crown having been grossly abused in some preceding reigns, it was thought proper to notice every grievance they had endured, and those declarations went to an abuse of power in the crown only, but were never intended to limit the authority of Parliament. . . . [DHRC16 381]

[3] . . . From these articles in the State Constitutions, many things were attempted to be transplanted into our new Constitution, which would either have been nugatory or improper: This is one of them. The expressions "*unusual and severe,*" or "*cruel and unusual,*" surely would have been too vague to have been of any consequence, since they admit of no clear and precise signification. If to guard against *punishments* being too severe, the Convention had enumerated

a vast variety of *cruel punishments,* and prohibited the use of any of them, let the number have been ever so great, an inexhaustible fund must have been unmentioned, and if our government had been disposed to be *cruel,* their invention would only have been put to a little more trouble. If to avoid this difficulty, they had determined, not negatively, what *punishments* should not be exercised, but positively what *punishments* should, this must have led them into a labyrinth of detail which in the original constitution of a government would have appeared perfectly ridiculous, and not left a room for such changes according to circumstances, as must be in the power of every Legislature that is rationally formed. . . . [DHRC16 381–82]

"An Impartial Citizen," No. 6, March 13, 1788:

[1] . . . If such a law [an ex post facto law] be admitted by the Constitution, can any immunity or declaration of rights counterveil its pernicious operation? Is there a planter in Virginia that would not detest a law, that would *punish* a man for having done what was lawful at the time of doing it? The learned Judge Blackstone, in the first volume of his excellent Commentaries, page 43, speaking of the impropriety of enforcing laws, without a previous promulgation, says, that "there is still a more unreasonable method than this, which is called, making of laws ex post facto; when, after an action (indifferent in itself) is committed, the Legislature then, for the first time, declares it to have been a crime, and inflicts a *punishment* on the person who has committed it. Here it is impossible that the party could foresee that an action, innocent when it was done, should be afterwards converted to guilt by a subsequent law; he had therefore no cause to abstain from it, and all *punishment* for not abstaining, must of consequence be *cruel and unjust.* All laws should therefore be made to commence in future." The learned Judge, in the same page, quotes Cicero, the most learned, and perhaps the wisest of the ancient Romans, who expresses his detestation of such laws in the most nervous and energetic language. Another celebrated author declares, that "If laws do not *punish* an offender, let him go *unpunished;* let the Legislature, admonished of the defect of the laws, provide against the commission of future crimes of the same sort: The escape of one delinquent can never produce so much harm to the community, as may arise from the infraction of a rule, upon which the purity of public justice, and the existence of civil liberty essentially depend." Every other writer of reputation, who writes on this subject, breathes the same sentiments . . . [DHRC8 493]

[2] . . . It being therefore a maxim of natural and universal jurisprudence, that no law should be made to *punish* a man for the commission of an act, which was not unlawful at the time of doing it, the Convention most wisely inserted a clause in the Constitution, that no such law should be passed. . . .
[DHRC8 494]

[3] . . . Every Legislature, and the people in every State, would certainly direct their Representative members and Senators, to vote the dismission of the [stand-

ing] army. This would be as certainly done; or a neglect of such directions would be severely censured and *punished*. When a standing army will be unnecessarily maintained in the United States, there will not be a particle of virtue in the people; they will be ripe for the most corrupt government. [DHRC8 498]

[4] If the Congress were to call forth the militia of this State [Virginia] to quel an insurrection in Connecticut, when with infinitely more ease and convenience the Militia of Massachusetts, or some adjacent State, could effect it, the consequence would be an universal, just and irresistable alarm and struggle throughout the Continent: Every State would be deeply interested in opposing so very oppressive an act. It cannot be supposed that the Congress will ever hazard so dangerous a measure. Its members must be idiots or madmen to attempt so wanton a depression of liberty. The members of a Congress who would enact such a measure, would be amenable to their constituents, and every degree of *punishment* that constituents can any way inflict, would most surely be inflicted on them. . . . DHRC8 499–500]

Alexander Hamilton, *The Federalist*, No. 69, March 14, 1788:

[1] The President of the United States would be liable to be impeached, tried, and, upon conviction of treason, bribery, or other high crimes or misdemeanors, removed from office; and would afterwards be liable to prosecution and *punishment* in the ordinary course of law. The person of the king of Great Britain is sacred and inviolable; there is no constitutional tribunal to which he is amenable; no *punishment* to which he can be subjected without involving the crisis of a national revolution. In this delicate and important circumstance of personal responsibility, the President of confederated America would stand upon no better ground than a governor of New York, and upon worse ground than the governors of Maryland and Delaware. [Fed. 444–45]

[2] . . . The governor of New York may pardon in all cases, even in those of impeachment, except for treason and murder. Is not the power of the governor, in this article, on a calculation of political consequences, greater than that of the President? All conspiracies and plots against the government, which have not been matured into actual treason, may be screened from *punishment* of every kind, by the interposition of the prerogative of pardoning. . . . [Fed. 447]

[3] The President of the United States would be an officer elected by the people for four years; the king of Great Britain is a perpetual and hereditary prince. The one would be amenable to personal *punishment* and disgrace; the person of the other is sacred and inviolable. . . . [Fed. 450]

Alexander Hamilton, *The Federalist*, No. 70, March 15, 1788:

[1] . . . In the legislature, promptitude of decision is oftener an evil than a benefit. The differences of opinion, and the jarrings of parties in that department of the government, though they may sometimes obstruct salutary plans, yet often pro-

mote deliberation and circumspection, and serve to check excesses in the majority. When a resolution too is once taken, the opposition must be at an end. That resolution is a law, and resistance to it *punishable*. . . . [Fed. 454]

[2] But one of the weightiest objections to a plurality in the Executive, and which lies as much against the last as the first plan, is, that it tends to conceal faults and destroy responsibility. Responsibility is of two kinds—to censure and to *punishment*. The first is the more important of the two, especially in an elective office. Man, in public trust, will much oftener act in such a manner as to render him unworthy of being any longer trusted, than in such a manner as to make him obnoxious to legal *punishment*. But the multiplication of the Executive adds to the difficulty of detection in either case. It often becomes impossible, amidst mutual accusations, to determine on whom the blame or the *punishment* of a pernicious measure, or series of pernicious measures, ought really to fall. . . .
[Fed. 455]

[3] It is evident from these considerations, that the plurality of the Executive tends to deprive the people of the two greatest securities they can have for the faithful exercise of any delegated power, first, the restraints of public opinion, which lose their efficacy, as well on account of the division of the censure attendant on bad measures among a number, as on account of the uncertainty on whom it ought to fall; and, secondly, the opportunity of discovering with facility and clearness the misconduct of the persons they trust, in order, either to their removal from office, or to their actual *punishment* in cases which admit of it. [Fed. 456]

George Nicholas [?], "The State Soldier," No. 4, March 19, 1788:

Under this government neither the Congress nor state legislature could, by direct laws, deprive us of any property we might hold under the general law of the land, or *punish* us for any offence committed previous to the passage of such laws, since they are prohibited from passing ex post facto laws. . . .
[DHRC8 510–11]

Alexander Hamilton, *The Federalist*, No. 74, March 25, 1788:

. . . It is not to be doubted, that a single man of prudence and good sense is better fitted, in delicate conjunctures, to balance the motives which may plead for and against the remission of the *punishment*, than any numerous body whatever. . . . [Fed. 474]

Archibald Maclaine, "Publicola," March 27, 1788:

. . . It is a maxim in the British government that the King can do no wrong; that is, he is not amenable to the courts of justice, as the law has not provided any *punishment* for his misconduct; but the President of the United States will be liable to be impeached by the representatives of the people, and to be tried for his crimes. . . . [DHRC16 496]

John Jay, *An Address to the People of the State of New York*, c. April 15, 1788:

. . . They [the Confederation Congress] may appoint ministers and other officers of trust, but without power to try or *punish* them for misdemeanors—They may resolve, but cannot execute either with dispatch or with secrecy—In short, they may consult, and deliberate, and recommend, and make requisitions, and they who please, may regard them. [Ford 72]

Alexander Hamilton, *The Federalist*, No. 81, May 28, 1788:

. . . There never can be danger that judges, by a series of deliberate usurpations on the authority of the legislature, would hazard the united resentment of the body intrusted with it, while this body was possessed of the means of *punishing* their presumption, by degrading them from their stations. While this ought to remove all apprehensions on the subject, it affords, at the same time, a cogent argument for constituting the Senate a court for the trial of impeachments. [Fed. 509]

Alexander Hamilton, *The Federalist*, No. 83, May 28, 1788:

[1] . . . But I must acknowledge that I cannot readily discern the inseparable connection between the existence of liberty, and the trial by jury in civil cases. Arbitrary impeachments, arbitrary methods of prosecuting pretended offences, and arbitrary *punishments* upon arbitrary convictions, have ever appeared to me to be the great engines of judicial despotism; and these have all relation to criminal proceedings. . . . [Fed. 522]

[2] . . . Wilful abuses of a public authority to the oppression of the subject, and every species of official extortion, are offences against the government, for which the persons who commit them may be indicted and *punished* according to the circumstances of the case. [Fed. 523]

Alexander Hamilton, *The Federalist*, No. 84, May 28, 1788:

. . . The creation of crimes after the commission of the fact, or, in other words, the subjecting of men to *punishment* for things which, when they were done, were breaches of no law, and the practice of arbitrary imprisonments, have been, in all ages, the favorite and most formidable instruments of tyranny. . . . [Fed. 533]

John Dickinson, "Fabius," No. 2, 1788:

This president will be no dictator. Two thirds of the representatives and the senate may pass any law, notwithstanding his dissent; and he is removable and *punishable* for misbehaviour. [Ford 172]

John Dickinson, "Fabius," No. 5, 1788:

. . . [On the Greek Achaean League:] Their chief officer called Strategos, was chosen in the Congress by a majority of votes. He presided in the Congress, commanded the forces, and was vested with great powers, especially in time of war: but was liable to be called to an account by the Congress, and *punished,* if convicted of misbehaviour. [Ford 192]

John Dickinson, "Fabius," No. 7, 1788:

. . . But, we ought not to pass such a sentence against our country, and the interests of freedom: Though, no sentence whatever can be equal to the atrocity of our guilt, if through enormity of obstinacy or baseness, we betray the cause of our posterity and of mankind, by providence committed to our parental and fraternal care. There is reason to believe, that the calamities of nations are the *punishments* of their sins. [Ford 200–201]

Georgia Constitution, May 6, 1789:

[Article I, Section 13:] Each house shall be judges of the elections, returns, and qualifications of its own members, with powers to expel or *punish* for disorderly behavior. [Thorpe 786]

United States Congress, Judiciary Act of September 24, 1789:

[Section 9:] That the district courts shall have, exclusively of the courts of the several States, cognizance of all crimes and offences that shall be cognizable under the authority of the United States, committed within their respective districts, or upon the high seas; where no other *punishment* than whipping, not exceeding thirty stripes, a fine not exceeding one hundred dollars, or a term of imprisonment not exceeding six months, is to be inflicted. . . . [USSL1 76–77]

[Section 33:] . . . And if a person committed by a justice of the supreme or a judge of a district court for an offence not punishable with death, shall afterwards procure *bail,* and there be no judge of the United States in the district to take the same, if may be taken by any judge of the supreme or superior court of law of such state. [USSL1 91–92]

South Carolina Constitution, June 3, 1790:

[Article I, Section 12:] Each house shall choose by ballot its own officers, determine its rules of proceeding, *punish* its members for disorderly behavior, and (with the concurrence of two-thirds) expel a member, but not a second time for the same cause. [Thorpe 3260]

[Article I, Section 13:] Each house may *punish,* by imprisonment, during sitting, any person not a member, who shall be guilty of disrespect to the house, by any disorderly or contemptuous behavior in its presence, or who, during the time of its sitting, shall threaten harm to the body or estate of any member, for anything said or done in either house . . . [Thorpe 3260]

[Article V, Section 3:] The governor, lieutenant-governor, and all the civil officers shall be liable to impeachment for any misdemeanor in office; but judgment in such cases shall not extend further than to a removal from office, and disqualification to hold any office of honor, trust, or profit under this State. The party convicted shall, nevertheless, be liable to indictment, trial, judgment, and *punishment* according to law. [Thorpe 3263]

[Article IX, Section 4:] Excessive bail shall not be required, nor excessive fines imposed, nor *cruel punishments* inflicted. [Thorpe 3264]

Pennsylvania Constitution, September 2, 1790:

[Article I, Section 13:] Each house may determine the rules of its proceedings, *punish* its members for disorderly behavior, and, with the concurrence of two-thirds, expel a member, but not a second time for the same cause; and shall have all other powers necessary for a branch of the legislature of a free State. [Thorpe 3094]

[Article IV, Section 3:] The governor, and all other civil officers under this commonwealth, shall be liable to impeachment for any misdemeanor in office. But judgment, in such cases, shall not extend further than to removal from office, and disqualification to hold any office of honor, trust, or profit under this commonwealth. The party, whether convicted or acquitted, shall nevertheless be liable to indictment, trial, judgment, and *punishment* according to law. [Thorpe 3097]

[Article IX, Section 4:] That no person, who acknowledges the being of a God and a future state of rewards and *punishments,* shall, on account of his religious sentiments, be disqualified to hold any office or place of trust or profit under this commonwealth. [Thorpe 3100]

[Article IX, Section 13:] That excessive bail shall not be required, nor excessive fines imposed, nor *cruel punishments* inflicted. [Thorpe 3101]

REBELLION, REBELLIONS

United States Constitution, September 17, 1789:

[Article I, Section 9:] The Privilege of the Writ of Habeas Corpus shall not be suspended, unless when in Cases of *Rebellion* or Invasion the public Safety may require it.

* * * * *

James I, Second Charter of Virginia, May 23, 1609:

And we do further of our special Grace, certain Knowledge, and mere Motion, Grant, Declare, and Ordain, that such principal Governor, as from Time to Time shall duly and lawfully be authorized and appointed in Manner and Form in these Presents heretofore expressed, shall have full Power and Authority, to use and exercise Martial Law in Cases of *Rebellion* or Mutiny, in as large and ample Manner as our Lieutenants in our Counties within this our Realm of England have or Ought to have, by Force of their Commissions of Lieutenancy.

[Thorpe 3801]

James I, The Charter of New England, November 3, 1620:

And Wee do further of our especiall Grace, certaine Knowledge, and mere Motion, grant, declare, and ordain, that such principall Governor, as from time to time shall be authorized and appointed in Manner and Forme in these Presents heretofore expressed, shall have full Power and Authority to use and exercise marshall Laws in Cases of *Rebellion,* Insurrection and Mutiny, in as large and ample Manner as our Lieutenants in our Counties within our Realme of England have or ought to have by Force of their Commission of Lieutenancy.

[Thorpe 1833]

Charles I, Patent to Sir Robert Heath, October 30, 1629:

We will also & by this our charter doe give power, liberty and Authority to the foresayd Sr. Robert Heath Knight his heires & assignes that in case of *Rebellion* sudden tumult or sedition, if any such shall chance to be which (God forbid) either upon the land within this Province aforesayd, or upon the wide Ocean, either makeing a journey towards Carolana aforesayd or returning from thence, we by these presents for us our heires & successors doe give & grant power and authoritye most ample to himself or by Captaines Deputyes or other their officers authorised to this purpose under their seales, against all authors of innovations, seditions against the Government of him or them . . . [Thorpe 73–74]

Charles I, Charter of Maryland, June 20, 1632:

[Section 13:] We also will, and by this our Charter, do give unto the aforesaid now Baron of Baltimore, and to his Heirs and Assigns, Power, Liberty, and Authority, that, in Case of *Rebellion,* sudden Tumult, or Sedition, if any (which God forbid) should happen to arise, whether upon Land within the Province aforesaid, or upon the High Sea in making a Voyage to the said Province of Maryland, or in returning thence, they may, by themselves, or by their Captains, or other Officers, thereunto deputed under their Seals (to whom We, for Us, our Heirs and Successors, by, these Presents, do Give and Grant the fullest Power and Authority) exercise Martial Law as freely, and in as ample Manner and Form, as any Captain-General of an Army . . . [Thorpe 1682]

Charles I, Grant of the Province of Maine, April 3, 1639:

. . . And We Doe further for us our heires and successors give and graunte unto the said Sir Fardinando Gorges his heires and assignes in case any *Rebellion* sudden tumult or mutynie shall happen to arise either uppon the said Lande within the said Province and Premisses or any of them or Coastes of the same or uppon the mayne Sea in passing thither or returning from thence or in any such expedicon or service as aforesaid itt shall and may be lawefull to and for the said Sir Fardinando Gorges his heires and assignes as well by him and themselves as by his and theire deputies Captaynes or other Officers under his or theire seale in that behalfe to bee authorised (to whome wee alsoe for us our heires and successors doe give and graunte full power and authoritye to doe and execute the same) to use and execute martial lawe against such *Rebells* Traytors Mutyners and Seditious Persons in as ample manner and forme as anie Captayne Generall in the Warrs or as any Lieuetennante or Lieuetennants of any Countie within this our Realme of England by vertue of his or their Office or Place maie or have beene accustomed in tyme of Warre *Rebellion* or Mutynie to doe and performe. [Thorpe 1630–31]

Charles II, Charter of Carolina, March 24, 1663:

[Article 16:] Also our will and pleasure is, and by this our charter we give unto the said Edward Earl of Clarendon, George Duke of Albemarle, William Lord Craven, John Lord Berkley, Anthony Lord Ashley, Sir George Carteret, Sir William Berkley, and Sir John Colleton, their heirs and assigns, full power, liberty and authority, in case of *rebellion,* tumult or sedition, (if any should happen,) which God forbid, either upon the land within the province aforesaid, or upon the main sea, in making a voyage thither, or returning from thence, by him or themselves their captains, deputies and officers, to be authorized under his or their seals for that purpose, to whom also, for us, our heirs and successors, we do give and grant by these presents, full power and authority, to exercise martial law against mutinous and seditious persons of those parts, such as shall refuse to submit themselves to their government, or shall refuse to serve in the wars, or shall fly to the enemy . . . [Thorpe 2751–52]

New Jersey Proprietors, Concession and Agreement, February 10, 1664:

[1] By act (as aforesaid) to constitute train'd bands and companies, with the number of soldiers, for the safety, strength and defence of the said Province; and of the forts, castles, cities, &c. To suppress all mutinies and *rebellions;* to make war offensive and defensive with all Indians, strangers and foreigners, as they shall see cause . . . [Thorpe 2539]

[2] . . . The Governor with the advice of his Council, unless some present danger will not permit him, to advise to muster and train all forces within the said Province, to prosecute war, pursue an enemy, suppress all *rebellions,* and mutinies, as well by sea as land; and to exercise the whole militia, as fully as we by the grant from his Royal Highness can impower them to do . . .
[Thorpe 2540]

Charles II, Grant of the Province of Maine to the Duke of York, March 12, 1664:

. . . And wee do further of our speciall grace certaine knowledge and meere mocon grant ordaine and declare that such governors officers and ministers as from time to time shall be authorized and appointed in manner and forme aforesaid shall and may have full power and authority to use and exercise martiall law in cases of *rebellion* insurreccon and mutinie in as large and ample manner as our Lieutenants in our countyes within our Realme of England have or ought to have by force of their commission of Lieutenancy or any law or statute of this our Realme. [Thorpe 1639]

Carolina Proprietors, Concessions and Agreements, 1665:

[1] [Assembly shall have power] by act as aforesd to constitute trayne bands and Companys with the number of souldiers for the safety strength and defence of the said Countyes and Province and of the Forts Castles Cityes &c to suppress all meutinyes and *Rebellions*. To make warr offensive and defensive with all Indians Strangers and Foraigners as they shall see cause and to persue any Enemy by sea as well as by land if need be out of ye Lymitts and Jurisdiccons of ye sd County with the perticculer consent of the Governor and under the Conduct of our Leut: Gen: or Commander in Cheife or whome he shall appoint.
[Thorpe 2759]

[2] [Governor shall have power] . . . with the advise of his Councill unless some present danger will soe permit him to advize to muster and trayne all ye soldiers wthin the said County or Countyes to prosecute warr persue an Enemy suppress *rebelions* and mewtinies as well by sea as Land and to exercise the whole Millitia as fully as by our Letters pattents from the kinge wee can impower him or them to doe . . . [Thorpe 2760]

Charles II, Charter of Carolina, June 30, 1665:

Also, our will and pleasure is, and by this our charter, we do give and grant unto the said Edward Earl of Clarendon, George Duke of Albemarle, William Earl of Craven, John Lord Berkeley, Anthony Lord Ashley, Sir George Carteret, Sir John Colleton, and Sir William Berkeley, their heirs and assigns, full power, liberty and authority, in case of *rebellion,* tumult, or sedition, (if any should happen, which God forbid) either upon the land within the province aforesaid, or upon the main sea in making a voyage thither, or returning from thence, by him and themselves, their Captains, Deputies, or officers, to be authorised under his or their seal for what purpose . . . [Thorpe 2770]

New Jersey Proprietors, Declaration of Intent and Meaning, December 6, 1672:

. . . in case of foreign invasion or intestine mutiny or *rebellion;* it shall be lawful for the Governor and his Council to call in to their aid, any persons whatsoever whether freeholder or not. [Thorpe 2545]

Charles II, Grant of the Province of Maine to the Duke of York, June 29, 1674:

And wee do further of our Especiall Grace certaine knowledge and meer motion graunt ordaine and declare that such Governors Deputyes Officers and Ministers as from time to time shall bee authorized and appointed in manner and forme aforesaid shall and may have full power and authority within the Territoryes aforesaid to use and exercise Marshall Lawe in cases of *rebellion* insurrection and Mutiny in as large and ample manner as our Lieutenants in our Countyes within Our realme of England have or ought to have by force of their Commission of Lieutenancy or any law or Statute of this our realme . . . [Thorpe 1642]

Fundamental Constitutions of East New Jersey, 1683:

[Article 7:] [It has been agreed that the assembly shall have power] . . . to suppress all mutinies and *rebellions;* to make war offensive and defensive, against all and every one that shall infest the said Province, not only to keep the enemy out of their limits, but also, in case of necessity, the enemy by sea and land to pursue out of the limits and jurisdiction of the said Province. . . . [Thorpe 2576]

William and Mary, Charter of Massachusetts Bay, October 7, 1691:

And Wee doe by these presents for us Our Heires and Successors Grant Establish and Ordaine that the Governor of our said Province or Territory for the time being shall have full Power by himselfe or by any Cheif Comander or other Officer or Officers to be appointed by him . . . to kill slay destroy and Conquer by all fitting wayes Enterprises and meanes whatsoever all and every such Person and Persons as shall at any time hereafter Attempt or Enterprize the destruccon Invasion Detriment or Annoyance of Our said Province or Territory and to use and exercise the Law Martiall in time of actuall Warr Invasion or *Rebellion* as occasion shall necessarily require and alsoe from time to time to Erect Forts . . . [Thorpe 1884]

New Jersey Proprietors, Surrender of Rights, April 15, 1702:

. . . And the late King [Charles II] did thereby grant, ordain and declare, that such Governors, officers, ministers as from time to time should be authorized and appointed in manner and form aforesaid, should and might have full power and authority to use and exercise martial law in cases of *rebellion,* insurrection and mutiny, in as large and ample manner as the lieutenants of his said Majesty in his counties of the realm of England had, or ought to have, by their commissions of lieutenancy, or any law or statute of the said realm of England. . . . [Thorpe 2586]

George II, Charter of Georgia, June 9, 1732:

. . . And we do by these presents for us, our heirs and successors, will, grant and ordain, that the said corporation and their successors, shall have full power . . . to use and exercise the martial law in time of actual war and invasion or *rebellion,* in such cases, where by law the same may be used or exercised . . . [Thorpe 776]

Thomas Paine, *Common Sense*, January 9, 1776:

The most plausible plea which hath ever been offered in favor of hereditary succession is, that it preserves a nation from civil wars; and were this true, it would be weighty; whereas, it is the most barefaced falsity ever imposed upon mankind. The whole history of England disowns the fact. Thirty kings and two minors have reigned in that distracted kingdom since the conquest, in which time there have been (including the revolution) no less than eight civil wars and nineteen *rebellions*. Wherefore instead of making for peace, it makes against it, and destroys the very foundation it seems to stand upon. [CWTP1 15]

South Carolina Constitution, March 26, 1776:

. . . and whereas a statute hath been lately passed [by Parliament], whereby, under pretence that the said colonies are in open *rebellion,* all trade and commerce whatsoever with them is prohibited; vessels belonging to their inhabitants trading in, to, or from the said colonies, with the cargoes and effects on board such vessels, are made lawful prize, and the masters and crews of such vessels are subjected by force to act on board the King's ships against their country and dearest friends; and all seizures and detention or destruction of the persons and properties of the colonists which have at any time been made or committed for withstanding or suppressing the said pretended *rebellion,* and which shall be made in the said act, or for the service of the public, are justified, and persons suing for damages in such cases are, on failing their suits, subjected to payment of very heavy expenses. . . . [Thorpe 3242–43]

Massachusetts Constitution, March 2, 1780:

[Frame of Government, Chapter II:1:7:] [The governor shall have power] . . . to use and exercise, over the army and navy, and over the militia in actual service, the law-martial, in time of war or invasion, and also in time of *rebellion,* declared by the legislature to exist, as occasion shall necessarily require . . .
[Thorpe 1901]

New Hampshire Constitution, June 2, 1784:

[Form of Government:] The president of this state for the time being, shall be commander in chief of the army and navy, and all the military forces of the state, by sea and land; and shall have full power . . . to use and exercise over the army and navy, and over the militia in actual service, the law-martial in time of war, invasion, and also in *rebellion,* declared by the legislature to exist, as occasion shall necessarily require . . . [Thorpe 2463–64]

Charles Pinckney's Plan of Union, May 29, 1787:

[Article 25:] The said States . . . guarrantee mutually each other and their Rights against all other Powers and against all Rebellions &c. [DHRC1 247]

Edmund Randolph, Letter on the Federal Constitution, October 10, 1787:

Amidst these disappointments, it would afford some consolation, if when *rebellion* shall threaten any state, an ultimate asylum could be found under the wing of Congress. But it is at least equivocal, whether they can intrude forces into a state, rent asunder by civil discord, even with the purest solicitude for our foederal welfare, and on the most urgent intreaties of the state itself. . . . [DHRC8 264]

Alexander Hamilton, *The Federalist*, No. 6, November 14, 1787:

Let the point of extreme depression to which our national dignity and credit have sunk, let the inconveniences felt everywhere from a lax and ill administration of government, let the revolt of a part of the State of North Carolina, the late menacing disturbances in Pennsylvania, and the actual insurrections and *rebellions* in Massachusetts, declare———! [Fed. 113]

James Madison, *The Federalist*, No. 19, December 8, 1787:

They [the Swiss cantons] are kept together . . . by the mutual aid they stand in need of, for suppressing insurrections and *rebellions,* an aid expressly stipulated, and often required and afforded; and by the necessity of some regular and permanent provision for accommodating disputes among the cantons. . . . [Fed. 181]

Alexander Hamilton, *The Federalist*, No. 26, December 22, 1787:

. . . Few persons will be so visionary as seriously to contend that military forces ought not to be raised to quell a *rebellion* or resist an invasion; and if the defence of the community under such circumstances should make it necessary to have an army so numerous as to hazard its liberty, this is one of those calamities for which there is neither preventative nor cure. . . . [Fed. 218]

Alexander Hamilton, *The Federalist*, No. 28, December 26, 1787:

. . . and that whether we have one government for all the States, or different governments for different parcels of them, or even if there should be an entire separation of the States, there might sometimes be a necessity to make use of a force constituted differently from the militia, to preserve the peace of the community and to maintain the just authority of the laws against those violent invasions of them which amount to insurrections and *rebellions*. [Fed. 224]

Alexander Hamilton, *The Federalist*, No. 34, January 4, 1788:

What are the chief sources of expense in every government? What has occasioned that enormous accumulation of debts with which several of the European nations are oppressed? The answer plainly is, wars and *rebellions,* the support of those institutions which are necessary to guard the body politic against these two most mortal diseases of society. . . . [Fed. 251]

***Pennsylvania Mercury*, February 28, 1788:**

[1] . . . [the writer "Centinel" is accused of] contriving, and with all his strength, soul, body, and goose quill (even to an unprecedented degree of flaming zeal and enthusiasm) to disturb the peace and common tranquillity of the aforesaid most illustrious United States, by dogmatical, proditorious publications, (lies and other hellish devices) to stir up and move opposition, faction, riot, sedition, insurrection, civil wars, *rebellion* and murder, against the aforesaid most illustrious United States, the Honorable the Congress, His Excellency General Washington, and divers others members of the honorable the continental and state conventions, and against their new proposed glorious frame of government . . . [DHRC16 259]

[2] . . . and which libellous papers, together with hand-bills, in both German and English, the aforesaid Centinel, as a false traitor, &c. did clandestinely convey by private hands, into some of the back counties, particularly Cumberland, Franklin and Fayette, to raise and stir up riot, opposition, civil wars, and *rebellion,* and which actually took effect in the town of Carlisle. [DHRC16 259]

[3] And also this same Centinel, as a false traitor, &c. did hold a treasonable correspondence with certain other well known traitors of the minority, by the names of W——, F—— and S——, a detestable triumviri, disturbers of the peace of society, insignificant babblers, noisy, ignorant, impertinent politicasters, assiduous seekers of their own interest, office hunters, makers of paper money and test laws, seceders, protestors, promoters of riot, faction, sedition, discord, civil wars and *rebellion;* and at the same time impudently, ungraciously, burlesquically and ironically, together (with a very small number of other low, trifling slubberdegullions of an inferior class) calling themselves Patriots! [DHRC16 260]

Alexander Hamilton, *The Federalist*, No. 74, March 25, 1788:

. . . But the principal argument for reposing the power of pardoning in this case to the Chief Magistrate is this; in seasons of insurrection or *rebellion,* there are often critical moments, when a well-timed offer of pardon to the insurgents or *rebels* may restore the tranquillity of the commonwealth; and which, if suffered to pass unimproved, it may never be possible afterwards to recall. . . .

[Fed. 475]

John Dickinson, "Fabius," No. 6, 1788:

. . . other persons of distinction and large numbers of the people of Scotland were filled with the utmost aversion to the union [with England]; and if the greatest diligence and prudence had not been employed by its friends in removing misapprehensions and refuting misrepresentations, and by the then subsisting government for preserving the public peace, there would certainly have been a *rebellion*. [Ford 198]

John Dickinson, "Fabius," No. 7, 1788:

[Article 16:] . . . The other fault, of which, as yet, there are no symptoms among us, is the thirst of empire. This is a vice, that ever has been, and from the nature of things, ever must be, fatal to republican forms of government. Our wants, are sources of happiness: our irregular desires, of misery. The abuse of prosperity, is *rebellion* against Heaven; and succeeds accordingly. [Ford 202]

Pennsylvania Constitution, September 2, 1790:

[Article IX, Section 14:] That all prisoners shall be bailable by sufficient sureties, unless for capital offences, when the proof is evident or presumption great; and the privilege of the writ of habeas corpus shall not be suspended, unless when, in cases of *rebellion* or invasion, the public safety may require it.

[Thorpe 3101]

RELIGION, ESTABLISHMENT OF

(Established Church)

United States Constitution, Bill of Rights, December 15, 1791:

[Article I:] Congress shall make no law respecting an *establishment of religion,* or prohibiting the free exercise thereof; or abridging the freedom of speech, or of the press; or the right of the people peaceably to assemble, and to petition the Government for a redress of grievances.

* * * * *

Surrender of the Charter of New England, June 7, 1635:

. . . did by the said Letters Patents incorporate, erect, ordain, name, constitute, and establish to be one body politick and corporate, in Deed and Name, by the Name of the Council of Plymouth aforesaid, in the said County of Devon, for the planting, ruling, and governing of New England in America aforesaid, To have perpetual succession, with divers other powers, priviledges, immunities, provisions, and restrictions, for the propagation and *establishing of true Religion* in those parts, and for the better regulating of the same plantations, as in and by the said Letters Patents, do Reference Thereunto had more plainly and at large appeareth. . . . [Thorpe 1861]

Charles I, Grant of the Province of Maine, April 3, 1639:

And for the better governement of such our Subjects and others as att any tyme shall happen to dwell or reside within the said Province and Premisses or passe to or from the same our will and pleasure is that the *Religion nowe professed in the Church of England* and Ecclesiasticall Governement nowe used in the same shalbee forever hereafter professed and with asmuch convenient speede as may bee setled and *established* in and throughout the said Province and premisses and every of them . . . [Thorpe 1628]

Charles II, Charter of Carolina, March 24, 1663:

[Article 18:] And because it may happen that some of the people and inhabitants of the said province, cannot in their private opinions, conform to the publick exercise of *religion,* according to the liturgy, form and ceremonies of the *church* of England, or take and subscribe the oaths and articles, made and *established* in that behalf, and for that the same, by reason of the remote distances of these places, will, we hope be no breach of the unity and uniformity *established* in this nation; our will and pleasure therefore is, and we do by these presents, for us, our heirs and successors, give and grant unto the [proprietors] . . . full and free license, liberty and authority, by such legal ways and means as they shall think fit, to give and grant unto such person or persons, inhabiting and being within the said province, or any part thereof, who really in their judgments, and for conscience sake cannot or shall not conform to the said liturgy and ceremonies, and take and subscribe the oaths and articles aforesaid, or any of them, such indulgencies and dispensations in that behalf, for and during such time and times, and with such limitations and restrictions as they, the said [proprietors] . . . shall in their discretion think fit and reasonable, and with this express proviso, and limitation also, that such person and persons, to whom such indulgencies and dispensations shall be granted as aforesaid, do and shall from time to time declare and continue, all fidelity, loyalty and obedience to us, our heirs and successors, and be subject and obedient to all other the laws, ordinances, and constitutions of the said province, in all matters whatsoever, as well ecclesiastical as civil, and do not in any wise disturb the peace and safety thereof, or scandalize or reproach the said liturgy, forms and ceremonies, or anything relating thereunto, or any person or persons whatsoever, for or in respect of his or their use or exercise thereof, or his or their obedience and conformity, thereunto.

[Thorpe 2752–53]

Charles II, Charter of Rhode Island, July 8, 1663:

. . . and because some of the people and inhabitants of the same colonie cannot, in theire private opinions, conforme to the publique exercise of *religion,* according to the litturgy, formes and ceremonyes of the *Church* of England, or take or subscribe the oathe and articles made and *established* in that behalfe; and for that the same, by reason of the remote distances of those places, will (as wee hope) bee noe breach of the unitie and uniformitie *established* in this nation: Have therefore thought fit, and doe hereby publish, graunt, ordeyne and declare, That our royall will and pleasure is, that noe person within the sayd colonye, at any tyme hereafter, shall bee any wise molested, punished, disquieted, or called in question, for any differences in opinione in matters of *religion,* and doe not actually disturb the civill peace of our sayd colony; but that all and everye person and persons may, from tyme to tyme, and at all tymes hereafter, freelye and fullye have and enjoye his and theire owne judgments and consciences, in matters of *religious* concernments, throughout the tract of lande hereafter mentioned . . . [Thorpe 3212–13]

Charles II, Charter of Carolina, June 30, 1665:

And because it may happen that some of the people and inhabitants of the said province cannot, in their private opinions, conform to the public exercise of *religion* according to the liturgy, forms, and ceremonies of the *Church* of England, or take and subscribe the oaths and articles made and *established* in that behalf; and for that the same, by reason of the remote distances of those places, will, as we hope, be no breach of the unity and conformity *established* in this nation; our will and pleasure therefore is, and we do, by these presents, for us, our heirs and successors, give and grant unto the said [proprietors] . . . full and free licence, liberty, and authority, by such ways and means as they shall think fit, to give and grant unto such person and persons, inhabiting and being within the said province or territory, hereby or by the said recited Letters Patents mentioned to be granted as aforesaid, or any part thereof, such indulgences and dispensations, in that behalf, for and during such time and times, and with such limitations and restrictions, as they the said [proprietors] . . . shall, in their discretion, think fit and reasonable: And that no person or persons unto whom such liberty shall be given, shall be any way molested, punished, disquieted, or called in question, for any differences in opinion, or practice in matters of *religious* concernments, who do not actually disturb the civil peace of the province, county or colony, that they shall make their abode in: But all and every such person and persons may, from time to time, and at all times, freely and quietly have and enjoy his and their judgments and consciences, in matters of *religion,* throughout all the said province or colony they behaving themselves peaceably, and not using this liberty to licentiousness, nor to the civil injury, or outward disturbance of others: Any law, statute, or clause, contained or to be contained, usage or custom of our realm of England, to the contrary hereof, in any-wise, notwithstanding. [Thorpe 2771]

First Continental Congress, Declaration and Resolves, November 14, 1774:

Also [we protest] the act passed the same session [of Parliament] for *establishing the Roman Catholick Religion* in the province of Quebec, abolishing the equitable system of English laws, and erecting a tyranny there, to the great danger, from so great a dissimilarity of *Religion,* law, and government of the neighbouring British colonies, by the assistance of whose blood and treasure the said country was conquered from France. [JCC1 72]

South Carolina Constitution, March 26, 1776:

[Preamble:] . . . the English laws and a free government, to which the inhabitants of Quebec were entitled by the King's royal proclamation, are abolished and French laws are restored; the Roman Catholic *religion* (although before tolerated and freely exercised there) and an absolute government are *established* in that province, and its limits extended through a vast tract of country so as to border on the free Protestant English settlements, with design of using a whole people differing in *religious* principles from the neighboring colonies, and subject to arbitrary Power, as fit instruments to overawe and subdue the colonies.

[Thorpe 3241–42]

New Jersey Constitution, July 2, 1776:

[Article 19:] That there shall be no *establishment of any one religious sect* in this Province, in preference to another; and that no Protestant inhabitant of this Colony shall be denied the enjoyment of any civil right, merely on account of his *religious* principles; but that all persons, professing a belief in the faith of any Protestant sect, who shall demean themselves peaceably under the government, as hereby *established,* shall be capable of being elected into any office of profit or trust, or being a member of either branch of the Legislature, and shall fully and freely enjoy every privilege and immunity, enjoyed by others their fellow subjects. [Thorpe 2597–98]

Delaware Constitution, September 10, 1776:

[Article 29:] There shall be no *establishment of any one religious sect* in this State in preference to another; and no clergyman or preacher of the gospel, of any denomination, shall be capable of holding any civil office in this State, or of being a member of either of the branches of the legislature, while they continue in the exercise of the pastoral function. [Thorpe 567–68]

Maryland Constitution, November 11, 1776:

[Declaration of Rights, Article 32:] . . . and every incumbent of the *church of England,* who hath remained in his parish, and performed his duty, shall be entitled to receive the provision and support *established* by the act, entitled "An act for the support of the clergy of the *church of England,* in this Province," till the November court of this present year . . . [Thorpe 1689]

North Carolina Constitution, December 18, 1776:

[Form of Government, Article 34:] That there shall be no *establishment of any one religious church or denomination* in this State, in preference to any other;

neither shall any person, on any pretence whatsoever, be compelled to attend any place of worship contrary to his own faith or judgment... [Thorpe 2793]

South Carolina Constitution, March 19, 1778:

[Article 38:] That all persons and *religious* societies who acknowledge that there is one God, and a future state of rewards and punishments, and that God is publicly to be worshipped, shall be freely tolerated. The Christian Protestant *religion* shall be deemed, and is hereby constituted and declared to be, the *established religion* of this State. That all denominations of Christian Protestants in this State, demeaning themselves peaceably and faithfully, shall enjoy equal *religious* and civil privileges. To accomplish this desirable purpose without injury to the *religious* property of those societies of Christians which are by law already incorporated for the purpose of *religious* worship, and to put it fully into the power of every other society of Christian Protestants, either already formed or hereafter to be formed, to obtain the like incorporation, it is hereby constituted, appointed, and declared that the respective societies of the *Church* of England that are already formed in this State for the purpose of *religious* worship shall still continue in corporate and hold the *religious* property now in their possession. And that whenever fifteen or more male persons, not under twenty-one years of age, professing the Christian protestant *religion,* and agreeing to unite themselves in a society for the purposes of *religious* worship, they shall, (on complying with the terms hereinafter mentioned,) be, and be constituted a *church,* and be esteemed and regarded in law as of the *established religion* of the State, and on a petition to the legislature shall be entitled to be incorporated and to enjoy equal privileges. That every society of Christians so formed shall give themselves a name or denomination by which they shall be called and known in law, and all that associate with them for the purposes of worship shall be esteemed as belonging to the society so called. But that previous to the *establishment* and incorporation of the respective societies of every denomination as aforesaid, and in order to entitle them thereto, each society so petitioning shall have agreed to and subscribed in a book the following five articles, without which no agreement or union of men upon pretence of *religion* shall entitle them to be incorporated and esteemed as a *church of the established religion* of this State.

[Thorpe 3255–56]

[*Ibid.*:] ... And that the people of this State may forever enjoy the right of electing their own pastors or clergy, and at the same time that the State may have sufficient security for the due discharge of the pastoral office, by those who shall be admitted to be clergymen, no person shall officiate as minister of any *established church* who shall not have been chosen by a majority of the society to which he shall minister, or by persons appointed by the said majority, to choose and procure a minister for them ... [Thorpe 3256]

Virginia Statute of Religious Liberty, January 16, 1786:

I. that the impious presumption of legislators and rulers, civil as well as ecclesiastical, who being themselves but fallible and uninspired men, have assumed dominion over the faith of others, setting up their own opinions and modes of thinking as the only true and infallible, and as such endeavoring to impose them on others, have *established and maintained false religions* over the greatest part of the world, and through all time; that to compel a man to furnish contributions of money for the propagation of opinions which he disbelieves, is sinful and tyrannical . . . [CVA8 690]

Tench Coxe, *An Examination of the Constitution for the United States of America*, No. 1, September 26, 1787:

The British king is the great bishop or supreme head of an *established church,* with an immense patronage annexed. In this capacity he commands a number of votes in the house of lords, by creating bishops, who, besides their great incomes, have votes in that assembly, and are judges in the last resort. These prelates have also many honorable and lucrative places to bestow, and thus from their wealth, learning, dignities, powers, and patronage, give a great lustre and an enormous influence to the crown. [Ford 137]

Richard Henry Lee [?], "The Federal Farmer," [?], No. 4, October 12, 1787:

It is true, we are not disposed to differ much, at present, about *religion;* but when we are making a constitution, it is to be hoped, for ages and millions yet unborn, why not *establish the free exercise of religion,* as a part of the national compact. . . . [Ford 315]

Noah Webster, *An Examination of the Leading Principles of the Federal Constitution*, October 17, 1787:

[1] . . . In the same manner, the principles and habits, as well as the power of the Americans are directly opposed to standing armies: and there is as little necessity to guard against them by positive constitutions, as to prohibit the *establishment of the Mahometan religion. . . .* [Ford 52]

[2] . . . And the kings and senate [in Rome] could not have held the reigns of government in their hands so long as they did, had they not artfully contrived to manage the *established religion,* and play off the superstitious credulity of the people against their own power. . . . [Ford 57]

Tench Coxe, *An Examination of the Constitution for the United States of America*, No. 4, October 21, 1787:

. . . In Italy, Spain, and Portugal, no protestant can hold a public trust. In England every Presbyterian, and other person not of their *established church,* is incapable of holding an office. No such impious deprivation of the rights of men can take place under the new foederal constitution. The convention has the honour of proposing the first public act, by which any nation has ever divested itself of a power, every exercise of which is a trespass on the Majesty of Heaven.

[Ford 146]

John Hancock, Speech to the Massachusetts Legislature, February 27, 1788:

. . . I hope and pray, that the gratitude of their [the people's] Hearts may be expressed by a proper use of those inestimable blessings,—by the greatest exertions of Patriotism,—by forming and supporting Institutions for cultivating the human Understanding, and for the greatest Progress of the Arts and Sciences,—by *establishing* Laws for the support of Piety, *Religion* and Morality, as well as for punishing Vice and Wickedness,—and by exibiting in the great Theatre of the World, those social, public and private Virtues, which give more Dignity to a People, possessing their own Sovereignty, than Crowns and Diadems afford to Sovereign Princes. . . . [DHRC16 226]

Alexander Hamilton, *The Federalist*, No. 71, March 18, 1788:

. . . If a British House of Commons, from the most feeble beginnings, from the mere power of assenting or disagreeing to the imposition of a new tax, have, by rapid strides, reduced the prerogatives of the crown and the privileges of the nobility within the limits they conceived to be compatible with the principles of a free government, while they raised themselves to the rank and consequence of co-equal branch of the legislature; if they have been able, in one instance, to abolish both the royalty and the aristocracy, and to overturn all the ancient *establishments,* as well in the *Church* as State; if they have been able, on a recent occasion, to make the monarch tremble at the prospect of an innovation attempted by them, what would be to be feared from an elective magistrate of four years' duration, with the confined authorities of a President of the United States? . . . [Fed. 462]

Pennsylvania Constitution, September 2, 1790:

[Article IX, Section 3:] That all men have a natural and indefeasible right to worship Almighty God according to the dictates of their own consciences; that no man can of right be compelled to attend, erect, or support any place of worship, or to maintain any ministry, against his consent; that no human authority can, in any case whatever, control or interfere with the rights of conscience; and that no preference shall ever be given, by law, to any *religious establishments* or modes of worship. [Thorpe 3100]

RELIGION, FREE EXERCISE OF

(Religious Freedom, Religious Liberty)

United States Constitution, Bill of Rights, December 15, 1791:

[Article I:] Congress shall make no law respecting an establishment of *religion,* or prohibiting the *free exercise thereof;* or abridging the freedom of speech, or of the press; or the right of the people peaceably to assemble, and to petition the Government for a redress of grievances.

* * * * *

Charles I, Charter of Massachusetts Bay, March 4, 1629:

. . . and for the directing, ruling, and disposeing of all other Matters and Thinges, whereby our said People, Inhabitants there, may be soe *religiously,* peaceablie, and civilly governed, as their good Life and orderlie Conversacon, maie wynn and incite the Natives of Country, to the Knowledge and Obedience of the onlie true God and Savior of Mankinde, and the Christian Fayth, which in our Royall Intencon, and the Adventurers *free* Profession, is the principall Ende of this Plantacion. . . . [Thorpe 1857]

Charles I, Patent to Sir Robert Heath, October 30, 1629:

. . . And furthermore the patronages and advowsons of all churches which shall happen to be built hereafter in the said Region Territory & Isles and limitts by the increase of the *religion* & worship of Christ Together with all & singular these & these soe amply, Rights Jurisdictions, priviledges prerogatives Royaltyes *libertyes* immunityes with Royall rights & franchises whatsoever as well by sea as by land, within that Region Territory Isles & limitts aforesaid To have *exercise* use & enjoy in like manner as any Bishop of Durham within the B[isho]pricke or County palatine of Durham in our kingdome of England ever heretofore had held used or enjoyed or of right ought or could have hold use or enjoy. . . .

[Thorpe 70]

Charles II, Charter of Carolina, March 24, 1663:

And furthermore, the patronage and advowsons of all the churches and chappels, which as Christian *religion* shall increase within the country, isles, islets and limits aforesaid, shall happen hereafter to be erected, together with license and power to build and found churches, chappels and oratories, in convenient and fit places, within the said bounds and limits, and to cause them to be Dedicated and consecrated according to the ecclesiastical laws of our Kingdom of England, together with all and singular the like, and as ample rights, jurisdictions, priviledges, prerogatives, royalties, *liberties,* immunities and franchises of what kind soever, within the countries, isles, islets and limits aforesaid.

[Thorpe 2744]

Charles II, Charter of Rhode Island, July 8, 1663:

And whereas, in theire humble addresse, they have *freely* declared, that it is much on their hearts (if they may be permitted), to hold forth a livlie experiment, that a most flourishing civill state may stand and best bee maintained, and that among our English subjects, with a full *libertie in religious concernements;* and that true pietye rightly grounded upon gospell principles, will give the best and greatest security to sovereignetye, and will lay in the hearts of men the strongest obligations to true loyaltye: Now know yee, that wee beinge willinge to encourage the hopefull undertakeinge of oure sayd loyall and loveinge subjects, and to secure them in the *free exercise and enjoyment of all theire civill and religious rights,* appertaining to them, as our loveing subjects; and to preserve unto them that *libertye,* in the true Christian faith and worshipp of God, which they have sought with soe much travaill, and with peaceable myndes, and loyall subjection to our royall progenitors and ourselves, to enjoye; and because some of the people and inhabitants of the same colonie cannot, in theire private opinions, conforms to the publique *exercise of religion,* according to the litturgy, formes and ceremonyes of the Church of England, or take or subscribe the oathe and articles made and established in that behalfe; and for that the same, by reason of the remote distances of those places, will (as wee hope) bee noe breach of the unitie and uniffornitie established in this nation: Have therefore thought fit, and doe hereby publish, graunt, ordeyne and declare, That our royall will and pleasure is, that noe person within the sayd colonye, at any tyme hereafter, shall bee any wise molested, punished, disquieted, or called in question, for any differences in opinione in matters of *religion,* and doe not actually disturb the civill peace of our sayd colony; but that all and everye person and persons may, from tyme to tyme, and at all tymes hereafter, *freelye* and fullye have and enjoye his and theire owne judgments and consciences, in matters of *religious* concernments, throughout the tract of lande hereafter mentioned; they behaving themselves peaceablie and quietlie, and not useing this *libertie* to lycentiousnesse and profanenesse, nor to the civill injurye or outward disturbeance of others; any lawe, statute, or clause, therein contayned, or to bee contayned, usage or custome of this realme, to the contrary hereof, in any wise, notwithstanding. . . . [Thorpe 3212–13]

Carolina Proprietors, Declaration and Proposals, August 25, 1663:

[Article 5:] We will grant, in as ample manner as the undertakers shall desire, *freedom and liberty of conscience in all religious or spiritual things,* and to be kept inviolably with them, we having power in our charter so to do.

[Thorpe 2755]

New Jersey Proprietors, Concession and Agreement, February 10, 1664:

That no person qualified as aforesaid within the said Province, at any time shall be any ways molested, punished, disquieted or called in question for any difference in opinion or practice in matter of *religious* concernments, who do not actually disturb the civil peace of the said Province; but that all and every such person and persons may from time to time, and at all times, *freely* and fully have and enjoy his and their judgments and consciences in matters of *religion* throughout the said province they behaving themselves peaceably and quietly, and not using this *liberty* to licentiousness, nor to the civil injury or outward disturbance of others . . . [Thorpe 2537]

Carolina Proprietors, Concessions and Agreements, 1665:

That noe person or persons quallifyed as aforesaid within the Province or all or any of the Countyes before exprest at any time shalbe anywayes molested punished disquieted or called in question for any differences in opinion or practice in matters of *religious* concernment whoe doe not actually disturbe the civill peace of the said Province or Countyes but that all and every such person and persons from to time and at all times *freely* and fully have and enjoye his and their judgements and contiences in mattrs of *religion* throughout all the sd Province they behaving themselves peaceably and quietly and not using this *Liberty* to Lycentiousness nor to the Civill Injury or outward disturbance of others, any Law statute or clause conteyned or to be conteyned usuage or custom of this realme of England to the contrary hereof in anywise notwithstanding.

[Thorpe 2757]

Charles II, Charter of Carolina, June 30, 1665:

[1] . . . And furthermore, the patronage and advowsons of all the churches and chapels, which, as Christian *religion* shall increase within the province, territory, isles, and limits aforesaid, shall happen hereafter to be erected; together with

licence and power to build and found churches, chapels and oratories, in convenient and fit places within the said bounds and limits; and to cause them to be dedicated and consecrated, according to the ecclesiastical laws of our kingdom of England; together with all and singular the like and as ample rights, jurisdictions, privileges, prerogatives, royalties, *liberties,* immunities, and franchises of what kind soever, within the territory, isles, islets and limits aforesaid . . .
[Thorpe 2762–63]

[2] And because it may happen that some of the people and inhabitants of the said province cannot, in their private opinions, conform to the public *exercise of religion* according to the liturgy, forms, and ceremonies of the Church of England, or take and subscribe the oaths and articles made and established in that behalf; and for that the same, by reason of the remote distances of those places, will, as we hope, be no breach of the unity and conformity established in this nation; our will and pleasure therefore is, and we do, by these presents, for us, our heirs and successors, give and grant unto the said [proprietors] . . . full and *free* licence, *liberty,* and authority, by such ways and means as they shall think fit, to give and grant unto such person and persons, inhabiting and being within the said province or territory, hereby or by the said recited Letters Patents mentioned to be granted as aforesaid, or any part thereof, such indulgences and dispensations, in that behalf, for and during such time and times, and with such limitations and restrictions, as they the said [proprietors] . . . shall, in their discretion, think fit and reasonable: And that no person or persons unto whom such *liberty* shall be given, shall be any way molested, punished, disquieted, or called in question, for any differences in opinion, or practice in matters of *religious* concernments, who do not actually disturb the civil peace of the province, county or colony, that they shall make their abode in: But all and every such person and persons may, from time to time, and at all times, *freely* and quietly have and enjoy his and their judgments and consciences, in matters of *religion,* throughout all the said province or colony they behaving themselves peaceably, and not using this *liberty* to licentiousness, nor to the civil injury, or outward disturbance of others . . . [Thorpe 2771]

Fundamental Constitutions of Carolina, March 1, 1669:

[Article 35:] . . . To this [councillors'] court also belong all invasions of the law, of *liberty* of conscience, and all invasions of the public peace, upon pretence of *religion,* as also the license of printing. The twelve assistants belonging to this court shall be called recorders. [Thorpe 2777]

[Article 97:] But since the natives of that place, who will be concerned in our plantation, are utterly strangers to Christianity, whose idolatry, ignorance, or mistake gives us no right to expel or use them ill; and those who remove from other parts to plant there will unavoidably be of different opinions concerning matters of *religion, the liberty whereof* they will expect to have allowed them, and it will not be reasonable for us, on this account, to keep them out, that civil peace may be maintained amidst diversity of opinions, and our agreement and compact with all men may be duly and faithfully observed; the violation whereof, upon what pretence soever, cannot be without great offence to Almighty God, and great scandal to the true *religion* which we profess; and also that Jews, heathens, and other dissenters from the purity of Christian *religion* may not be scared and kept at a distance from it, but, by having an opportunity of acquainting themselves with the truth and reasonableness of its doctrines, and the peaceableness and inoffensiveness of its professors, may, by good usage and persuasion, and all those convincing methods of gentleness and meekness, suitable to the rules and design of the gospel, be won ever to embrace and unfeignedly receive the truth; therefore, any seven or more persons agreeing in any *religion,* shall constitute a church or profession, to which they shall give some name, to distinguish it from others. [Thorpe 2783–84]

Fundamental Constitutions of West New Jersey, 1676:

[Chapter 16:] That no men, nor number of men upon earth, hath power or authority to rule over men's consciences in *religious* matters, therefore it is consented, agreed and ordained, that no person or persons whatsoever within the said Province, at any time or times hereafter, shall be any ways upon any pretence whatsoever, called in question, or the least punished or hurt, either in person, estate, or priviledge, for the sake of his opinion, judgment, faith or worship towards God in matters of *religion*. But that all and every such person, and persons, may from time to time, and at all times, *freely* and fully have, and enjoy his and their judgments, and the *exercises* of their consciences in matters of *religious* worship throughout all the said Province. [Thorpe 2549]

Charles II, Commission Constituting a President and Council for New Hampshire, September 18, 1680:

. . . And above all things we do by these prsents will, require & comand Our said Councell to take all possible care for ye discountenancing of vice, & incouraging of vertue & good living; that by such examples ye infidel may be invited & desire to partake of ye Christian *Religion,* & for ye greater ease & satisfacc'on of our sd loving subjects in matters of *Religion* We do hereby will, require & com'and yt *liberty* of conscience shall be allowed unto all protestants; & yt such especially as shall be conformable to ye rites of ye Church of Engld shall be particularly countenanced & incouraged. . . . [Thorpe 2448]

Fundamental Constitutions of East New Jersey, 1683:

[Article 16:] All persons living in the Province who confess and acknowledge the one Almighty and Eternal God, and hold themselves obliged in conscience to live peaceably and quietly in a civil society, shall in no way be molested or prejudged for their *religious* persuasions and *exercise* in matters of faith and worship; nor shall they be compelled to frequent and maintain any *religious* worship, place or ministry whatsoever: Yet it is also hereby provided, that no man shall be admitted a member of the great or common Council, or any other place of publick trust, who shall not profaith in Christ Jesus, and solemnly declare that he doth no ways hold himself obliged in conscience to endeavour alteration in the government, or seeks the turning out of any in it or their ruin or prejudice, either in person or estate, because they are in his opinion hereticks, or differ in their judgment from him: Nor by this article is it intended, that any under the notion of this *liberty* shall allow themselves to avow atheism, irreligiousness, or to practice cursing, swearing, drunkenness, prophaness, whoring, adultery, murdering or any kind of violence, or indulging themselves in stage plays, masks, revells or such like abuses . . . [Thorpe 2579–80]

William and Mary, Charter of Massachusetts Bay, October 7, 1691:

. . . and to dispose of matters and things whereby our Subjects inhabitants of our said Province may be *Religiously* peaceably and Civilly Governed Protected and Defended soe as their good life and orderly Conversation may win the Indians Natives of the Country to the knowledge and obedience of the onely true God and Saviour of Mankinde and the Christian Faith which his Royall Majestie our Royall Grandfather king Charles the first in his said Letters Patents declared was his Royall Intentions And the Adventurers *free* Possession to be the Princepall end of the said Plantation And for the better secureing and maintaining *Liberty* of Conscience hereby granted to all persons at any time being and resideing within our said Province or Territory as aforesaid . . . [Thorpe 1882–83]

William Penn, Charter of Privileges for Pennsylvania, October 28, 1701:

[Article 1:] Because no People can be truly happy, though under the greatest Enjoyment of Civil *Liberties,* if abridged of the *Freedom of their Consciences, as to their Religious Profession and Worship:* And Almighty God being the only Lord of Conscience, Father of Lights and Spirits; and the Author as well as Object of all divine Knowledge, Faith and Worship, who only doth enlighten the Minds, and persuade and convince the Understandings of People, I do hereby grant and declare, That no Person or Persons, inhabiting in this province or Territories, who shall confess and acknowledge One almighty God, the Creator, Upholder and Ruler of the World; and profess him or themselves obliged to live quietly under the Civil Government, shall be in any Case molested or prejudiced, in his or their Person or Estate, because of his or their conscientious Persuasion or Practice, nor be compelled to frequent or maintain any *religious* Worship, Place or Ministry, contrary to his or their Mind, or to do or suffer any other Act or Thing, contrary to their *religious* Persuasion. [Thorpe 3077]

William Penn, Charter of Delaware, October 28, 1701:

[Article 1:] Because no People can be truly happy, though under the greatest Enjoyment of Civil *Liberties,* if abridged of the *Freedom of their Consciences, as to their Religious Profession and Worship:* And Almighty God being the only Lord of Conscience, Father of Lights and Spirits; and the Author as well as Object of all divine Knowledge, Faith and Worship, who only doth enlighten the Minds, and persuade and convince the Understandings of People, I do hereby grant and declare, That no Person or Persons, inhabiting in this Province or Territories, who shall confess and acknowledge One almighty God, the Creator, Upholder and Ruler of the World; and professes him or themselves obliged to live quietly under the Civil Government, shall be in any Case molested or prejudiced, in his or their Person or Estate, because of his or their consciencious Persuasion or Practice, nor be compelled to frequent or maintain any *religious* Worship, Place or Ministry, contrary to his or their Mind, or to do or suffer any other Act or Thing, contrary to their *religious* Persuasion. [Thorpe 558]

George II, Charter of Georgia, June 9, 1732:

. . . And for the greater ease and encouragement of our loving subjects and such others as shall come to inhabit in our said colony, we do by these presents, for us, our heirs and successors, grant, establish and ordain, that forever hereafter, there shall be a *liberty* of conscience allowed in the worship of God, to all persons inhabiting, or which shall inhabit or be resident within our said province, and that all such persons, except papists, shall have a *free exercise of their religion,* so they be contented with the quiet and peaceable enjoyment of the same, not giving offence or scandal to the government. . . . [Thorpe 773]

Thomas Paine, *Common Sense*, January 9, 1776:

[1] . . . This new world hath been the asylum for the persecuted lovers of civil and *religious liberty* from every part of Europe. Hither have they fled, not from the tender embraces of the mother, but from the cruelty of the monster; and it is so far true of England, that the same tyranny which drove the first emigrants from home pursues their descendants still. [CWTP1 19]

[2] The conferring members being met, let their business be to frame a Continental Charter, or Charter of the United Colonies; (answering to what is called the Magna Charta of England) fixing the number and manner of choosing Members of Congress, Members of Assembly, with their date of sitting, and drawing the line of business and jurisdiction between them: Always remembering, that our strength is continental, not provincial. Securing *freedom* and property to all men, and above all things the *free exercise of religion,* according to the dictates of conscience; with such other matter as is necessary for a charter to contain. . . . [CWTP1 29]

South Carolina Constitution, March 26, 1776:

[Preamble:] . . . the English laws and a *free* government, to which the inhabitants of Quebec were entitled by the King's royal proclamation, are abolished and French laws are restored; the Roman Catholic *religion* (although before *tolerated and freely exercised* there) and an absolute government are established in that province, and its limits extended through a vast tract of country so as to border on the *free* Protestant English settlements, with design of using a whole people differing in *religious* principles from the neighboring colonies, and subject to arbitrary Power, as fit instruments to overawe and subdue the colonies . . .

[Thorpe 3241–42]

Virginia Bill of Rights, June 12, 1776:

[Section 16:] That *religion,* or the duty which we owe to our Creator, and the manner of discharging it can be directed only by reason and conviction, not by force or violence; and therefore all men are equally entitled to the *free exercise of religion,* according to the dictates of conscience; and that it is the mutual duty of all to practise Christian forbearance, love, and charity towards each other.

[Thorpe 3814]

New Jersey Constitution, July 2, 1776:

[Article 19:] That there shall be no establishment of any one *religious* sect in this Province, in preference to another; and that no Protestant inhabitant of this Colony shall be denied the enjoyment of any civil right, merely on account of his *religious* principles; but that all persons, professing a belief in the faith of any Protestant sect, who shall demean themselves peaceably under the government, as hereby established, shall be capable of being elected into any office of profit or trust, or being a member of either branch of the Legislature, and shall fully and *freely* enjoy every privilege and immunity, enjoyed by others their fellow subjects. [Thorpe 2597–98]

United States Continental Congress, Draft Articles of Confederation, July 12, 1776:

[Article 2:] The said Colonies unite themselves so as never to be divided by an Act whatever, and hereby severally enter into a firm League of Friendship with each other, for their common Defence, the Security of their *Liberties,* and their mutual and general Welfare, binding the said Colonies to assist one another against all Force offered to or attacks made upon them or any of them, on Account of *Religion,* Sovereignty, Trade, or any other Pretence whatever.

[DHRC1 79]

Pennsylvania Constitution, September 28, 1776:

[Declaration of Rights, Article 2:] That all men have a natural and unalienable right to worship Almighty God according to the dictates of their own consciences and understanding: And that no man ought or of right can be compelled to attend any *religious* worship, or erect or support any place of worship, or maintain any ministry, contrary to, or against, his own *free* will and consent: Nor can any man, who acknowledges the being of a God, be justly deprived or abridged of any civil right as a citizen, on account of his *religious* sentiments or peculiar mode of *religious* worship: And that no authority can or ought to be vested in, or assumed by any power whatever, that shall in any case interfere with, or in any manner controul, *the right of conscience in the free exercise of religious worship.* [Thorpe 3082]

Maryland Constitution, November 11, 1776:

[Declaration of Rights, Article 33:] That, as it is the duty of every man to worship God in such manner as he thinks most acceptable to him; all persons, professing the Christian *religion,* are equally entitled to protection in their *religious liberty;* wherefore no person ought by any law to be molested in his person or estate on account of his *religious* persuasion or profession, or for his *religious* practice; unless, under colour of *religion,* any man shall disturb the good order, peace or safety of the State, or shall infringe the laws of morality, or injure others, in their natural, civil, or *religious rights;* nor ought any person to be compelled to frequent or maintain, or contribute, unless on contract, to maintain any particular place of worship, or any particular ministry; yet the Legislature may, in their discretion, lay a general and equal tax, for the support of the Christian *religion;* leaving to each individual the power of appointing the payment over of the money, collected from him, to the support of any particular place of worship or minister, or for the benefit of the poor of his own denomination, or the poor in general of any particular county . . . [Thorpe 1689]

North Carolina Constitution, December 18, 1776:

[Form of Government, Article 34:] That there shall be no establishment of any one *religious* church or denomination in this State, in preference to any other; neither shall any person, on any pretence whatsoever, be compelled to attend any place of worship contrary to his own faith or judgment, nor be obliged to pay, for the purchase of any glebe, or the building of any house of worship, or for the maintenance of any minister or ministry, contrary to what he believes right, or has voluntarily and personally engaged to perform; but all persons shall be at *liberty to exercise* their own mode of worship:—Provided, That nothing herein contained shall be construed to exempt preachers of treasonable or seditious discourses, from legal trial and punishment. [Thorpe 2793]

Georgia Constitution, February 5, 1777:

[Article 56:] All persons whatever shall have the *free exercise of their religion;* provided it be not repugnant to the peace and safety of the State; and shall not, unless by consent, support any teacher or teachers except those of their own profession. [Thorpe 784]

New York Constitution, April 20, 1777:

[Article 38:] And whereas we are required, by the benevolent principles of rational *liberty,* not only to expel civil tyranny, but also to guard against that spiritual oppression and intolerance wherewith the bigotry and ambition of weak and wicked priests and princes have scourged mankind, this convention doth further, in the name and by the authority of the good people of this State, ordain, determine, and declare, that the *free exercise and enjoyment of religious profession and worship,* without discrimination or preference, shall forever hereafter be allowed, within this State, to all mankind: Provided, That the *liberty* of conscience, hereby granted, shall not be so construed as to excuse acts of licentiousness or justify practices inconsistent with the peace or safety of this State. [Thorpe 2636–37]

Vermont Constitution, July 8, 1777:

[Declaration of Rights, Article 3:] That all men have a natural and unalienable right to worship Almighty God, according to the dictates of their own consciences and understanding, regulated by the word of God; and that no man ought, or of right can be compelled to attend any *religious* worship, or erect, or support any place of worship, or maintain any minister, contrary to the dictates of his conscience; nor can any man who professes the protestant *religion,* be justly deprived or abridged of any civil right, as a citizen, on account of his *religious* sentiment, or peculiar mode of *religious* worship, and that no authority can, or ought to be vested in, or assumed by, any power whatsoever, that shall, in any case, interfere with, or in any manner controul, the rights of conscience, in the *free exercise of religious worship:* nevertheless, every sect or denomination of people ought to observe the Sabbath, or the Lord's day, and keep up, and support, some sort of *religious* worship, which to them shall seem most agreeable to the revealed will of God. [Thorpe 3740]

South Carolina Constitution, March 19, 1778:

[Article 38:] That all persons and *religious* societies who acknowledge that there is one God, and a future state of rewards and punishments, and that God is publicly to be worshipped, shall be *freely tolerated.* The Christian Protestant *religion* shall be deemed, and is hereby constituted and declared to be, the established *religion* of this State. That all denominations of Christian Protestants in this State, demeaning themselves peaceably and faithfully, shall enjoy equal *religious* and civil privileges. . . . [Thorpe 3255–56]

[*Ibid.*:] No person shall, by law, be obliged to pay towards the maintenance and support of a *religious* worship that he does not *freely* join in, or has not voluntarily engaged to support. But the churches, chapels, parsonages, glebes, and all other property now belonging to any societies of the Church of England, or any other *religious* societies, shall remain and be secured to them forever. . . .
[Thorpe 3257]

Massachusetts Constitution, March 2, 1780:

[Declaration of Rights, Article 2:] It is the right as well as the duty of all men in society, publicly, and at stated seasons, to worship the Supreme Being, the great Creator and Preserver of the universe. And no subject shall be hurt, molested or restrained, in his person, *liberty,* or estate, for worshipping God in the manner and season most agreeable to the dictates of his own conscience; or for his *religious* profession of sentiments; provided he doth not disturb the public peace, or obstruct others in their *religious* worship. [Thorpe 1889]

New Hampshire Constitution, June 2, 1784:

[Bill of Rights, Article 5:] Every individual has a natural and unalienable right to worship God according to the dictates of his own conscience, and reason; and no subject shall be hurt, molested, or restrained in his person, *liberty* or estate for worshipping God, in the manner and season most agreeable to the dictates of his own conscience, or for his *religious* profession, sentiments or persuasion; provided he doth not disturb the public peace, or disturb others, in their *religious* worship. [Thorpe 2454]

Virginia Statute of Religious Liberty, January 16, 1786:

[1] Whereas Almighty God hath created the mind *free;* that all attempts to influence it by temporal punishments or burthens, or by civil incapacitations, tend only to beget habits of hypocrisy and meanness, and are a departure from the plan of the Holy Author of our *religion,* who being Lord both of body and mind, yet chose not to propagate it by coercions on either, as was in his Almighty power to do; that the impious presumption of legislators and rulers, civil as well as ecclesiastical, who, being themselves but fallible and uninspired men, have assumed dominion over the faith of others, setting up their own opinions and modes of thinking as the only true and infallible, and as such endeavoring to impose them on others, hath established and maintained false *religions* over the greatest part of the world, and through all time; that to compel a man to furnish contributions of money for the propagation of opinions which he disbelieves, is sinful and tyrannical; that even the forcing him to support this or that teacher

of his own *religious* persuasion, is depriving him of the comfortable *liberty* of giving his contributions to the particular pastor whose morals he would make his pattern, and whose powers he feels most persuasive to righteousness, and is withdrawing from the ministry those temporary rewards, which proceeding from an approbation of their personal conduct, are an additional incitement to earnest and unremitting labors for the instruction of mankind; that our civil rights have no dependence on our *religious* opinions, any more than our opinions in physics or geometry; that therefore the proscribing any citizen as unworthy the public confidence by laying upon him an incapacity of being called to offices of trust and emolument, unless he profess or renounce this or that *religious* opinion, is depriving him injuriously of those privileges and advantages to which in common with his fellow-citizens he has a natural right, that it tends only to corrupt the principles of that *religion* it is meant to encourage, by bribing with a monopoly of worldly honors and emoluments, those who will externally profess and conform to it; that though, indeed, these are criminal who do not withstand such temptation, yet neither are those innocent who lay the bait in their way; that to suffer the civil magistrate to intrude his powers into the field of opinion, and to restrain the profession or propagation of principles on supposition of their ill tendency, is a dangerous fallacy, which at once destroys all *religious liberty,* because he being of course judge of that tendency, will make his opinions the rule of judgment, and approve or condemn the sentiments of others only as they shall square with or differ from his own; that it is time enough for the rightful purposes of civil government, for its officers to interfere, when principles break out into overt acts against peace and good order; and finally, that truth is great and will prevail if left to herself, that she is the proper and sufficient antagonist to error, and has nothing to fear from the conflict, unless by human interposition disarmed of her natural weapons, *free* argument and debate, errors ceasing to be dangerous when it is permitted *freely* to contradict them. [CVA8 690–91]

[2:] Be it enacted by the General Assembly, that no man shall be compelled to frequent or support any *religious* worship, place or ministry whatsoever, nor shall be enforced, restrained, molested, or burdened in his body or goods, nor shall otherwise suffer on account of his *religious* opinions or belief; but that all men shall be *free* to profess, and by argument to maintain, their opinion in matters of *religion,* and that the same shall in no wise diminish, enlarge or affect their civil capacities. [CVA 691]

Vermont Constitution, July 4, 1786:

[Declaration of Rights, Article 3:] That all men have a natural and unalienable right to worship Almighty God according to the dictates of their own consciences and understanding, as in their opinion shall be regulated by the word of God; and that no man ought, or of right can be compelled to attend any *religious* worship, or erect or support any place of worship, or maintain any minister, contrary to the dictates of his conscience; nor can any man be justly deprived or abridged of any civil right as a citizen, on account of his *religious* sentiments, or peculiar mode of *religious* worship; and that no authority can, or ought to be vested in, or assumed by any power whatsoever, that shall in any case interfere with, or in any manner control the rights of conscience, in the *free exercise of religious worship:* Nevertheless, every sect or denomination of Christians ought to observe the Sabbath or Lord's day, and keep up some sort of *religious* worship, which to them shall seem most agreeable to the revealed will of God.

[Thorpe 3752]

Tench Coxe, *An Examination of the Constitution for the United States of America*, No. 1, September 26, 1787:

To take a proper view of the ground on which we stand, it may be necessary to recollect the manner in which the United States were originally settled and established. Want of charity in the *religious* systems of Europe, and of justice in their political governments, were the principal moving causes, which drove the emigrants of various countries to the American continent. The Congregationalists, Quakers, Presbyterians and other British dissenters, the Catholics of England and Ireland, the Hugonots of France, the German Lutherans, Calvinists and Moravians, with several other societies, established themselves in the different colonies, thereby laying the ground of that liberality in ecclesiastical affairs, which has been observable since the late revolution. *Religious liberty* naturally promotes corresponding dispositions in matters of government. . . .

[Ford 135]

Richard Henry Lee [?], "The Federal Farmer," No. 4, October 12, 1787:

It is true, we are not disposed to differ much, at present, about *religion;* but when we are making a constitution, it is to be hoped, for ages and millions yet unborn, why not establish the *free exercise of religion,* as a part of the national compact. There are other essential rights, which we have justly understood to be the rights of freemen; as *freedom* from hasty and unreasonable search warrants, warrants not founded on oath, and not issued with due caution, for searching and seizing men's papers, property, and persons. . . . [Ford 315]

Richard Henry Lee, Proposed Amendments to the Constitution, October 16, 1787:

. . . from respect for the public sentiment on this subject, it is submitted,—That the new constitution proposed for the government of the United States be bottomed upon a declaration or bill of rights, clearly and precisely stating the principles upon which this social compact is founded, to wit: That the *rights of conscience in matters of religion* ought not to be violated—That the *freedom* of the press shall be secured . . . [DHRC8 65]

Dissent of the Pennsylvania Convention's Minority, December 18, 1787:

[1] The right of conscience shall be held inviolable; and neither the legislative, executive nor judicial powers of the United States shall have authority to alter, abrogate or infringe any part of the constitution of the several states, which provide for the preservation of *liberty in matters of religion*. [DHRC2 623]

[2] The absolute unqualified command that Congress have over the militia may be made instrumental to the destruction of all *liberty,* both public and private; whether of a personal, civil or *religious* nature. [DHRC2 638]

Alexander White [?], "An Independent Freeholder," January 18, 1788:

. . . here is neither a total nor partial dissolution of Government; our social compacts and all our ancient rights remain entire, except such as are expressly granted to Congress. And this affords an answer to many objections, such as that *religious liberty,* the *Freedom* of the Press, the right of Petitioning the Legislature, &c. &c. &c. are not secured; no power over these matters being granted to Congress, she never can interpose to destroy them. . . .

[DHRC8 311]

James Madison, *The Federalist*, No. 51, February 6, 1788:

. . . In a *free* government the security for civil rights must be the same as that for *religious* rights. It consists in the one case in the multiplicity of interests, and in the other in the multiplicity of sects. The degree of security in both cases will depend on the number of interests and sects; and this may be presumed to depend on the extent of country and number of people comprehended under the same government. . . . [Fed. 358]

Alexander White, "To the Citizens of Virginia," February 22, 1788:

. . . There are other things so clearly out of the power of Congress, that the bare recital of them is sufficient, I mean the [quoting the dissent of the Pennsylvania minority] "rights of conscience, or *religious liberty*—the rights of bearing arms for defence, or for killing game—the *liberty* of fowling, hunting and fishing—the right of altering the laws of descents and distribution of the effects of deceased persons and titles of lands and goods, and the regulation of contracts in the individual States." These things seem to have been inserted among their objections, merely to induce the ignorant to believe that Congress would have a power over such objects and to infer from their being refused a place in the Constitution, their intention to exercise that power to the oppression of the people. . . .

[DHRC8 404]

John Leland, Objections to the Constitution, c. February 1788:

What is dearest of all—*Religious Liberty,* is not Sufficiently Secured, No *religious* test is required as a Qualification to fill any office under the United States, but if a Majority of Congress with the presedent favour one System more then another, they may oblige all others to pay to the Support of their System as Much as they please, & if Oppression does not ensue, it will be owing to the Mildness of Administration & not to any Constitutional defense, & if the Manners of People are so far Corrupted, that they cannot live by republican principles, it is Very Dangerous leaving *religious Liberty* at their Marcy. [DHRC8 426]

Georgia Constitution, May 6, 1789:

[Article IV, Section 5:] All persons shall have the *free exercise of religion* without being obliged to contribute to the support of any *religious* profession but their own. [DHRC16 789]

South Carolina Constitution, June 3, 1790:

[Article VIII, Section 1:] The *free exercise and enjoyment of religious profession and worship,* without discrimination or preference, shall forever hereafter be allowed within this State to all mankind: Provided, That the *liberty* of conscience thereby declared shall not be so construed as to excuse acts of licentiousness, or justify practices inconsistent with the peace or safety of this State.

[Thorpe 3264]

RELIGIOUS TEST

United States Constitution, September 17, 1787:

[Article VI:] The Senators and Representatives before mentioned, and the Members of the several State Legislatures, and all executive and judicial Officers, both of the United States and of the several States, shall be bound by Oath or Affirmation, to support this Constitution; but no *religious Test* shall ever be required as a Qualification to any Office or public Trust under the United States.

* * * * *

Pennsylvania Constitution, September 28, 1776:

[Frame of Government, Section 10:] And each member [of the legislature], before he takes his seat, shall make and subscribe the following declaration, viz:.

I do believe in one God, the creator and governor of the universe, the rewarder of the good and the punisher of the wicked. And I do acknowledge the Scriptures of the Old and New Testament to be given by Divine inspiration.

And no further or other *religious test* shall ever hereafter be required of any civil officer or magistrate in this State. [Thorpe 3085]

Maryland Constitution, November 11, 1776:

[Declaration of Rights, Article 35:] That no other *test* or qualification ought to be required, on admission to any office of trust or profit, than such oath of support and fidelity to this State, and such oath of office, as shall be directed by this Convention, or the Legislature of this State, and a declaration of a belief in the Christian *religion*. [Thorpe 1690]

Vermont Constitution, July 8, 1777:

[Frame of Government, Section 9:] And each member [of the legislature], before he takes his seat, shall make and subscribe the following declaration, viz.

"I do believe in one God, the Creator and Governor of the universe, the rewarder of the good and punisher of the wicked. And I do acknowledge the scriptures of the old and new testament to be given by divine inspiration, and own and profess the protestant *religion*."

And no further or other *religious test* shall ever, hereafter, be required of any civil officer or magistrate in this State. [Thorpe 3743]

Vermont Constitution, July 4, 1786:

[Frame of Government, Section 12:] And each member [of the legislature], before he takes his seat, shall make and subscribe the following declaration viz.

You do believe in one God, the Creator and Governor of the Universe the rewarder of the good, and punisher of the wicked. And you do acknowledge the scriptures of the Old and New Testament to be given by divine inspiration; and own and profess the Protestant *religion*.

And no further or other *religious test* shall ever hereafter be required of any civil officer or magistrate, in this State. [Thorpe 3757]

Tench Coxe, *An Examination of the Constitution for the United States of America*, No. 4, October 21, 1787:

No *religious test* is ever to be required of any officer or servant of the United States. The people may employ any wise or good citizen in the execution of the various duties of the government. In Italy, Spain, and Portugal, no protestant can hold a public trust. In England every Presbyterian, and other person not of their established church, is incapable of holding an office. No such impious deprivation of the rights of men can take place under the new foederal constitution. The convention has the honour of proposing the first public act, by which any nation has ever divested itself of a power, every exercise of which is a trespass on the Majesty of Heaven. [Ford 146]

Luther Martin, "Genuine Information," No. 12, February 8, 1788:

The part of the system, which provides that no *religious test* shall ever be required as a qualification to any office or public trust under the United States, was adopted by a very great majority of the convention, and without much debate,—however, there were some members so unfashionable as to think that a belief of the existence of a Deity, and of a state of future rewards and punishments would be some security for the good conduct of our rulers, and that in a Christian country it would be at least decent to hold out some distinction between the professors of Christianity and downright infidelity or paganism. [DHRC16 89]

John Leland, Objections to the Constitution, c. February 1788:

What is dearest of all—Religious Liberty, is not Sufficiently Secured, No *religious test* is required as a Qualification to fill any office under the United States, but if a Majority of Congress with the presedent favour one Systom more then another, they may oblige all others to pay to the Support of their System as Much as they please, & if Oppression does not ensue, it will be owing to the Mildness of Administration & not to any Constitutional defense, & if the Manners of People are so far Corrupted, that they cannot live by republican principles, it is Very Dangerous leaving religious Liberty at their Marcy— [DHRC8 426]

REPUBLICAN FORM OF GOVERNMENT

[Note: This list is composed of all occurrences in the database of ''Republican'' and its variants in close conjunction with ''Government'' and its variants.]

United States Constititution, September 17, 1787:

[Article IV, Section 4:] The United States shall guarantee to every State in this Union a *Republican Form of Government,* and shall protect each of them against Invasion; and on Application of the Legislature, or of the Executive (when the Legislature cannot be convened) against domestic Violence.

* * * * *

Thomas Paine, *Common Sense*, January 9, 1776:

[1] Near three thousand years passed away, from the Mosaic account of the creation, till the Jews under a national delusion requested a king. Till then their *form of government* (except in extraordinary cases, where the Almighty interposed) was a kind of *Republic,* administered by a judge and the elders of the tribe. Kings they had none, and it was held sinful to acknowledge any being under that title but the Lords of Hosts. And when a man seriously reflects on the idolatrous homage which is paid to the persons of kings, he need not wonder that the Almighty, ever jealous of his honor, should disapprove of a *form of government* which so impiously invades the prerogative of heaven.

[CWTP1 10]

[2] The nearer any *government approaches to a Republic*, the less business there is for a king. It is somewhat difficult to find a proper name for the *government* of England. Sir William Meredith calls it a *Republic;* but in its present state it is unworthy of the name, because the corrupt influence of the crown, by having all the places in its disposal, hath so effectually swallowed up the power, and eaten out the virtue of the House of Commons (the *republican* part in the

Constitution) that the G*overnment* of England is nearly as monarchical as that of France or Spain. . . . [CWTP1 16]

[3] Where there are no distinctions there can be no superiority; perfect equality affords no temptation. The *Republics* of Europe are all (and we may say always) in peace. Holland and Switzerland are without wars, foreign or domestic: Monarchical *governments,* it is true, are never long at rest; the crown itself is a temptation to enterprising ruffians at home; and that degree of pride and insolence ever attendant on regal authority, swells into a rupture with foreign powers in instances where a *republican government,* by being formed on more natural principles, would negotiate the mistake. [CWTP1 27]

John Adams, *Thoughts on Government*, April 1776:

A man must be indifferent to the sneers of modern Englishmen to mention in their company the names of Sidney, Harrington, Locke, Milton, Nedham, Neville, Burnet, and Hoadly. No small fortitude is necessary to confess that one has read them. The wretched condition of this country, however, for ten or fifteen years past, has frequently reminded me of their principles and reasonings. They will convince any candid mind, that there is no good *government but what is Republican*. That the only valuable part of the British constitution is so; because the very definition of a *republic* is "an Empire of Laws, and not of men." That, as a *Republic is the best of governments,* so that particular arrangement of the powers of society, or, in other words that *form of government,* which is best contrived to secure an impartial and exact execution of the laws, is the best of *Republics*. [PJA4 87]

United States Confederation Congress, Ordinance for the Government of the West, April 23, 1784:

That their [*i.e.*, new states in the Northwest Territory] respective *governments shall be republican*. [DHRC1 152]

The Virginia Plan of Union, May 29, 1787:

Res[olve]d that a *Republican Government* & the territory of each State, except in the instance of a voluntary junction of *Government* and territory, ought to be guaranteed by the United States to each State. [DHRC1 245]

United States Confederation Congress, The Northwest Ordinance, July 13, 1787:

[1] And for extending the fundamental principles of civil and religious liberty, which form the basis whereon these *republics,* their laws and constitutions, are erected; to fix and establish those principles as the basis of all laws, constitutions, and *governments,* which forever hereafter shall be formed in the said territory;

to provide, also, for the establishment of States, and permanent *government* therein, and for their admission to a share in the Federal councils on an equal footing with the original States, at as early periods as may be consistent with the general interest: [Thorpe 960]

[2] [Article V:] . . . And whenever any of the said States shall have sixty thousand free inhabitants therein, such State shall be admitted by its delegates, into the Congress of the United States, on an equal footing with the original States, in all respects whatever; and shall be at liberty to form a permanent constitution and State *government:* Provided, The constitution and *government, so to be formed, shall be republican,* and in conformity to the principles contained in these articles, and, so far as it can be consistent with the general interest of the confederacy, such admission shall be allowed at an earlier period, and when there may be a less number of free inhabitants in the State than sixty thousand. [Thorpe 962]

Tench Coxe, *An Examination of the Constitution for the United States of America*, No. 1, September 26, 1787:

When the declaration of independence compleated the separation between the two countries, new *governments* were necessarily established. Many circumstances led to the adoption of the *republican form,* among which was the predilection of the people. In devising the frames of *government,* it may have been difficult to avoid extremes opposite to the vices of that we had just rejected; nevertheless, many of the state constitutions we have chosen are truly excellent. . . . [Ford 136]

Richard Henry Lee [?], "The Federal Farmer," No. 1, October 8, 1787:

[1] The present moment discovers a new face in our affairs. Our object has been all along, to reform our federal system and to strengthen our *governments*—to establish peace, order and justice in the community—but a new object now presents. The plan of *government* now proposed is evidently calculated totally to change, in time, our condition as a people. Instead of being thirteen *republics,* under a federal head, it is clearly designed to make us one consolidated *government.* . . . [Ford 282]

[2] There are three different *forms of free government* under which the United States may exist as one nation; and now is, perhaps, the time to determine to which we will direct our views. 1. Distinct *republics* connected under a federal head. In this case the respective state *governments* must be the principal guardians of the peoples rights, and exclusively regulate their internal police; in them must rest the balance of *government.* . . . [Ford 286]

Richard Henry Lee [?], "The Federal Farmer," No. 2, October 9, 1787:

There are other considerations which tend to prove that the idea of one consolidated whole, on free principles, is ill-founded—the laws of a free *government* rest on the confidence of the people, and operate gently—and never can extend the influence very far—if they are executed on free principles, about the centre, where the benefits of the *government* induce the people to support it voluntarily; yet they must be executed on the principles of fear and force in the extremes—This has been the case with every extensive *republic* of which we have any accurate account. [Ford 290]

Richard Henry Lee [?], "The Federal Farmer," No. 5, October 15, 1787:

[1] . . . This subject of consolidating the states is new: and because forty or fifty men have agreed in a system, to suppose the good sense of this country, an enlightened nation, must adopt it without examination, and though in a state of profound peace, without endeavouring to amend those parts they perceive are defective, dangerous to freedom, and destructive of the valuable principles of *republican government*—is truly humiliating. It is true there may be danger in delay; but there is danger in adopting the system in its present *form* . . . [Ford 320]

[2] . . . Between these two parties is the weight of the community; the men of middling property, men not in debt on the one hand, and men, on the other, content with *republican governments,* and not aiming at immense fortunes, offices, and power. . . . [Ford 321]

Noah Webster, *An Examination of the Leading Principles of the Federal Constitution*, October 17, 1787:

[1] Virtue, patriotism, or love of country, never was and never will be, till mens' natures are changed, a fixed, permanent principle and support of *government*. But in an agricultural country, a general possession of land in fee simple, may be rendered perpetual, and the inequalities introduced by commerce, are too fluctuating to endanger *government*. An equality of property, with a necessity of alienation, constantly operating to destroy combinations of powerful families, is the very soul of a *republic*—While this continues, the people will inevitably possess both power and freedom; when this is lost, power departs, liberty expires, and a commonwealth will inevitably assume some other *form*. [Ford 59]

[2] The liberty of the press, trial by jury, the Habeas Corpus writ, even Magna Charta itself, although justly deemed the palladia of freedom, are all inferior considerations, when compared with a general distribution of real property among every class of people. The power of entailing estates is more dangerous to liberty

and *republican government,* than all the constitutions that can be written on paper, or even than a standing army. Let the people have property, and they will have power—a power that will for ever be exerted to prevent a restriction of the press, and abolition of trial by jury, or the abridgement of any other privilege. The liberties of America, therefore, and her *forms of government,* stand on the broadest basis. Removed from the fears of a foreign invasion and conquest, they are not exposed to the convulsions that shake other *governments;* and the principles of freedom are so general and energetic, as to exclude the possibility of a change in our *republican* constitutions. [Ford 59–60]

[3] Montesquieu supposed virtue to be the principle of a *republic*. He derived his notions of this *form of government* from the astonishing firmness, courage and patriotism which distinguished the *republics* of Greece and Rome. But this virtue consisted in pride, contempt of strangers and a martial enthusiasm which sometimes displayed itself in defence of their country. These principles are never permanent—they decay with refinement, intercourse with other nations and increase of wealth. No wonder then that these *republics* declined, for they were not founded on fixed principles; and hence authors imagine that *republics* cannot be durable. None of the celebrated writers on *government* seems to have laid sufficient stress on a general possession of real property in fee-simple. Even the authors of the Political Sketches, in the Museum for the month of September, seems to have passed it over in silence; although he combats Montesquieu's system, and to prove it false, enumerates some of the principles which distinguish our *governments* from others, and which he supposes constitutes the support of *republics*. [Ford 60n]

[4] The English writers on law and *government* consider Magna Charta, trial by juries, the Habeas Corpus act, and the liberty of the press, as the bulwarks of freedom. All this is well. But in no *government* of consequence in Europe, is freedom established on its true and immoveable foundation. The property is too much accumulated, and the accumulations too well guarded, to admit the true principle of *republics*. . . . [Ford 60n]

[5] The constitution defines the powers of Congress; and every power not expressly delegated to that body, remains in the several state-legislatures. The sovereignty and the *republican form of government* of each state is guaranteed by the constitution; and the bounds of jurisdiction between the federal and respective state *governments,* are marked with precision. In theory, it has all the energy and freedom of the British and Roman *governments,* without their defects, In short, the privileges of freemen are interwoven into the feelings and habits of the Americans . . . [Ford 65]

"Cato Uticensis," October 17, 1787:

[1] For my part, I cannot discover the necessity there was of allowing Congress to subject us to excise laws, unless, that considering the extensiveness of the

single *republic* into which this Constitution would collect all the others, and the well known difficulty of *governing large republics* with harmony and ease, it was thought expedient to bit our mouths with massive curbs, to break us, bridled with excise laws, and managed by excisemen, into an uniform, sober pace, and thus, gradually, tame the troublesome mettle of the freeman. . . . [DHRC8 73]

[2] . . . Consider, whether you are willing to see the state of Virginia dwindle into the insignificance of a town corporate: and as the Mayor Court of Alderman and Common Council in this make by-laws for its own *government,* you are satisfied with a Governor, Senate, and Assembly, which will have the same authority as "the United States shall guarantee to every state in this Union a *Republican FORM of government.*" Consider that if you pass the Foederal Constitution in toto, you subject yourselves to see the doors of your houses, the impenetrable castles of freemen, fly open before the magic wand of an exciseman . . . [DHRC8 75]

Tench Coxe, *An Examination of the Constitution for the United States of America*, No. 4, October 21, 1787:

The United States guarantee to every state in the union a separate *republican form of government.* From thence it follows that any man or body of men, however rich or powerful, who shall make an alteration in the *form of government* of any state, whereby the powers thereof shall be attempted to be taken out of the hands of the people at large, will stand guilty of high treason . . .

[Ford 145]

Alexander Hamilton, *The Federalist*, No. 1, October 27, 1787:

[1] I propose, in a series of papers, to discuss the following interesting particulars:—The utility of the UNION to your political prosperity—The insufficiency of the present Confederation to preserve that Union—The necessity of a *government* at least equally energetic with the one proposed, to the attainment of this object—The conformity of the proposed Constitution to the true principles of *republican government*—Its analogy to your own State constitution—and lastly, The additional security which its adoption will afford to the preservation of that species of government to liberty, and to property. [Fed. 92]

Pelatiah Webster, *The Weakness of Brutus Exposed*, November 4, 1787:

[1] And when he has run himself out of breath with this dreary declamation, he comes to the conclusion he set out with, viz. That the Thirteen States are too big for a *republican government,* which requires small territory, and can't be supported in more extensive nations; that in large states liberty will soon be swallowed up,and lost in the magnitude of power requisite in the *government,* &c. [Ford 122]

[2] I now come to consider the grand proposition which Brutus sets out with, concludes with, and interlards all along, and which seems to be the great gift of his performance, viz. That a confederation of the Thirteen States into one great *republic* is not best for them: and goes on to prove by a variety of arguments, that a *republican form of government* is not compatible, and cannot be convenient to so extensive a territory as the said States possess. He begins by taking one assumption for granted (for I can't see that his arguments prove it at all) viz. That the Constitution proposed will melt down and destroy the jurisdiction of the particular States, and consolidate them all into one great *republic*. [Ford 127]

[3] But after all, supposing this event should take place, and by some strange fatality, the several states should be melted down, and merged in the great commonwealth, in the form of counties, or districts; I don't see why a commonwealth mode of *government,* would not be as suitable and convenient for the great State, as any other *form* whatever; I cannot see any sufficient ground or reason, for the position pretty often and boldly advanced, that a *republican form of government* can never be suitable for any nation of extensive territory, and numerous population: for if Congress can be chosen by the several States, though under the form and name of counties, or election districts, and be in every respect, instituted as directed by the new constitution, I don't see but we shall have as suitable a national council, as wise a legislative and as strong and safe an executive power,as can be obtained under any *form of government* whatever; let our territory be ever so extensive or populous. [Ford 129–30]

[4] The Romans rose, from small beginnings, to a very great extent of territory, population, and wisdom; I don't think their constitution of *government,* was near so good as the one proposed to us, yet we find their power, strength, and establishment, were raised to their utmost height, under a *republican form of government*. Their State received very little acquisition of territory, strength, or wealth, after their *government* became imperial; but soon began to weaken and decay. [Ford 130]

[5] The Carthagenians acquired an amazing degree of strength, wealth, and extent of dominion, under a *republican form of government*. Neither they or the Romans, owed their dissolution to any causes arising from that kind of *government:* 'twas the party rage, animosity, and violence of their citizens, which destroyed them both; it weakened them, 'till the one fell under the power of their enemy, and was thereby reduced to ruin; the other changed their *form of government,* to a monarchy which proved in the end, equally fatal to them. [Ford 130]

"A True Friend," November 14, 1787:

. . . Read, and reflect on the new constitution; it secures us inviolably our rights and prerogatives as a *republican* nation, preciously preserving the nature of a *government* purely democratical. By the nomination of our representatives, without distinction or inheritance, it will procure us the order, strength and unanimity indispensible for a nation. . . . [DHRC8 164]

Alexander Hamilton, *The Federalist*, No. 9, November 21, 1787:

[1] From the disorders that disfigure the annals of those *republics* the advocates of despotism have drawn arguments, not only against the *forms of republican government,* but against the very principles of civil liberty. They have decried all free *government* as inconsistent with the order of society, and have indulged themselves in malicious exultation over its friends and partisans. . . . [Fed. 125]

[2] But it is not to be denied that the portraits they have sketched of *republican government* were too just copies of the originals from which they were taken. If it had been found impracticable to have devised models of a more perfect structure, the enlightened friends to liberty would have been obliged to abandon the cause of that species of *government* as indefensible. The science of politics, however, like most other sciences, has received great improvement. The efficacy of various principles is now well understood, which were either not known at all, or imperfectly known to the ancients. The regular distribution of power into distinct departments; the introduction of legislative balances and checks; the institution of courts composed of judges holding their offices during good behavior; the representation of the people in the legislature by deputies of their own election: these are wholly new discoveries, or have made their principal progress towards perfection in modern times. They are means, and powerful means, by which the excellences of *republican government* may be retained and its imperfections lessened or avoided. To this catalogue of circumstances that tend to the amelioration of popular systems of civil *government,* I shall venture, however novel it may appear to some, to add one more, on a principle which has been made the foundation of an objection to the new Constitution; I mean the ENLARGEMENT of the ORBIT within which such systems are to revolve, either in respect to the dimensions of a single State, or to the consolidation of several smaller States into one great Confederacy. . . . [Fed. 125]

[3] The utility of a Confederacy, as well to suppress faction and to guard the internal tranquillity of States, as to increase their external force and security, is in reality not a new idea. It has been practiced upon in different countries and ages, and has received the sanction of the most approved writers on the subjects of politics. The opponents of the plan proposed have, with great assiduity, cited and circulated the observations of Montesquieu on the necessity of a contracted territory for a *republican government*. But they seem not to have been apprised of the sentiments of that great man expressed in another part of his work, not to have adverted to the consequences of the principle to which they subscribe with such ready acquiescence. [Fed. 125–26]

[4] So far are the suggestions of Montesquieu from standing in opposition to a general Union of the States, that he explicitly treats of a CONFEDERATE

REPUBLIC as the expedient for extending the sphere of popular *government,* and reconciling the advantages of monarchy with those of *republicanism.* [Fed. 126–27]

[5] "It is very probable" (says [Montequieu]) "that mankind would have been obliged at length to live constantly under the *government* of a single person, had they not contrived a kind of constitution that has all the internal advantages of a *republican,* together with the external force of a monarchical, *government.* I mean a CONFEDERATE *REPUBLIC.* [Fed. 127]

[6] [Quoting Montesquieu:] "As this *government* is composed of small *republics,* it enjoys the internal happiness of each; and with respect to its external situation, it is possessed, by means of the association, of all the advantages of large monarchies." [Fed. 127]

James Madison, *The Federalist*, No. 10, November 22, 1787:

[1] A *republic,* by which I mean a *government* in which the scheme of representation takes place, opens a different prospect, and promises the cure for which we are seeking. Let us examine the points in which it varies from pure democracy, and we shall comprehend both the nature of the cure and the efficacy which it must derive from the Union. [Fed. 133]

[2] The two great points of difference between a democracy and a *republic* are: first, the delegation of the *government,* in the latter, to a small number of citizens elected by the rest; secondly, the greater number of citizens, and greater sphere of country, over which the latter may be extended. [Fed. 133–34]

[3] The other point of difference is, the greater number of citizens and extent of territory which may be brought within the compass of *republican than of democratic government;* and it is this circumstance principally which renders factious combinations less to be dreaded in the former than in the latter. The smaller the society, the fewer probably will be the distinct parties and interests composing it; the fewer the distinct parties and interests, the more frequently will a majority be found of the same party; and the smaller the number of individuals composing a majority, and the smaller the compass within which they are placed, the more easily will they concert and execute their plans of oppression. Extend the sphere and you take in a greater variety of parties and interests; you make it less probable that a majority of the whole will have a common motive to invade the rights of other citizens; or if such a common motive exists, it will be more difficult for all who feel it to discover their own strength, and to act in unison with each other. . . . [Fed. 135]

[4] In the extent and proper structure of the Union, therefore, we behold a *republican* remedy for the diseases most incident to *republican government.* And according to the degree of pleasure and pride we feel in being *republicans,* ought to be our zeal in cherishing the spirit and supporting the character of Federalists. [Fed. 136]

James Madison, *The Federalist*, No. 14, November 30, 1787:

The error which limits *republican government* to a narrow district has been unfolded and refuted in preceding papers. I remark here only that it seems to owe its rise and prevalence chiefly to the confounding of a *republic* with a democracy, applying to the former reasonings drawn from the nature of the latter. The true distinction between these *forms* was also adverted to on a former occasion. It is, that in a democracy, the people meet and exercise the *government* in person; in a *republic,* they assemble and administer it by their representatives and agents. A democracy, consequently, will be confined to a small spot. A *republic* may be extended over a large region. [Fed. 150]

James Madison, *The Federalist*, No. 18, December 7, 1787:

. . . The Abbe Mably, in his observations on Greece, says that the popular *government,* which was so tempestuous elsewhere, caused no disorders in the members of the Achaean *republic,* because it was there tempered by the general authority and laws of the confederacy. [Fed. 174]

Alexander Hamilton, *The Federalist*, No. 22, December 14, 1787:

[1] The right of equal suffrage among the States is another exceptionable part of the Confederation. Every idea of proportion and every rule of fair representation conspire to condemn a principle, which gives to Rhode Island an equal weight in the scale of power with Massachusetts, or Connecticut, or New York; and to Delaware an equal voice in the national deliberations with Pennsylvania, or Virginia, or North Carolina. Its operation contradicts the fundamental maxim of *republican government,* which requires that the sense of the majority should prevail. . . . [Fed. 193]

[2] In *republics,* persons elevated from the mass of the community, by the suffrages of their fellow-citizens, to stations of great preeminence and power, may find compensations for betraying their trust, which, to any but minds animated and guided by superior virtue, may appear to exceed the proportion of interest they have in the common stock, and to overbalance the obligations of duty. Hence it is that history furnishes us with so many mortifying examples of the prevalency of foreign corruption in *republican governments.* . . .
[Fed. 196]

Dissent of the Pennsylvania Assembly's Minority, December 18, 1787:

[1] We dissent, first, because it is the opinion of the most celebrated writers on *government,* and confirmed by uniform experience, that a very extensive territory cannot be governed on the principles of freedom, otherwise than by a confederation of *republics,* possessing all the powers of internal *government;* but united in the management of their general, and foreign concerns. [DHRC2 625]

[2] The celebrated Montesquieu, in his Spirit of Laws, vol. i., page 12, says, "That in a democracy there can be no exercise of sovereignty, but by the suffages of the people, which are their will; now the sovereign's will is the sovereign himself; the laws, therefore, which establish the right of suffrage, are fundamental to this *government*. In fact, it is as important to regulate in a *republic* in what manner, by whom, and concerning what suffrages are to be given, as it is in a monarchy to know who is the prince, and after what manner he ought to govern." The time, mode and place of the election of representatives, senators and president-general of the United States ought not to be under the control of Congress, but fundamentally ascertained and established. [DHRC2 629]

Alexander Hamilton, *The Federalist*, No. 28, December 26, 1787:

That there may happen cases in which the national *government* may be necessitated to resort to force, cannot be denied. Our own experience has corroborated the lessons taught by the examples of others nations; that emergencies of this sort will sometimes arise in all societies, however constituted; that seditions and insurrections are, unhappily, maladies as inseparable from the body politic as tumors and eruptions from the natural body; that the idea of governing at all times by the simple force of law (which we have been told is the only admissible principle of *republican government*), has no place but in the reveries of those political doctors whose sagacity disdains the admonitions of experimental instruction. [Fed. 222]

Alexander Hamilton, *The Federalist*, No. 31, January 1, 1788:

It should not be forgotten that a disposition in the State *governments* to encroach upon the rights of the Union is quite as probable as a disposition in the Union to encroach upon the rights of the State *governments*. What side would be likely to prevail in such a conflict, must depend on the means which the contending parties could employ towards insuring success. As in *republics* strength is always on the side of the people, and as there are weighty reasons to induce a belief that the State *governments* will commonly possess most influence over them, the natural conclusion is that such contests will be most apt to end to the disadvantage of the Union . . . [Fed. 240]

Alexander Hamilton, *The Federalist*, No. 34, January 4, 1788:

. . . If, on the one hand, it should be observed that the expenses incurred in the prosecution of the ambitious enterprises and vainglorious pursuits of a monarchy are not a proper standard by which to judge of those which might be necessary in a *republic*, it ought, on the other hand, to be remarked that there should be as great a disproportion between the profusion and extravagance of a wealthy kingdom in its domestic administration, and the frugality and economy which in that particular become the modest simplicity of *republican government*. If we balance a proper deduction from one side against that which it is supposed ought to be made from the other, the proportion may still be considered as holding good. [Fed. 251]

James Madison, *The Federalist*, No. 37, January 11, 1788:

Among the difficulties encountered by the convention, a very important one must have lain in combining the requisite stability and energy in *government*, with the inviolable attention due to liberty and to the *republican form*. Without substantially accomplishing this part of their undertaking, they would have very imperfectly fulfilled the object of their appointment, or the expectation of the public; yet that it could not be easily accomplished, will be denied by no one who is unwilling to betray his ignorance of the subject. . . . [Fed. 267]

James Madison, *The Federalist*, No. 39, January 16, 1788:

[1] The first question that offers itself is, whether the general *form and aspect of the government* be strictly *republican*. It is evident that no other *form* would be reconcilable with the genius of the people of America; with the fundamental principles of the Revolution; or with that honorable determination which animates every votary of freedom, to rest all our political experiments on the capacity of mankind for self-*government*. If the plan of the convention, therefore, be found to depart from the *republican* character, its advocates must abandon it as no longer defensible. [Fed. 280]

[2] What, then, are the distinctive characters of the *republican form?* Were an answer to this question to be sought, not by recurring to principles, but in the application of the term by political writers, to the constitutions of different States, no satisfactory one would ever be found. Holland, in which no particle of the supreme authority is derived from the people, has passed almost universally under the denomination of a *republic*. The same title has been bestowed on Venice, where absolute power over the great body of the people is exercised, in the most absolute manner, by a small body of hereditary nobles. Poland, which is a mixture of aristocracy and of monarchy in their worst *forms,* has been dignified with the same appellation. The *government* of England, which has one *republican* branch only, combined with an hereditary aristocracy and monarchy, has, with equal impropriety, been frequently placed on the list of *republics*. These examples, which are nearly as dissimilar to each other as to a genuine *republic,* show the extreme inaccuracy with which the term has been used in political disquisitions. [Fed. 280]

[3] If we resort for a criterion to the different principles on which different *forms of government* are established, we may define a *republic* to be, or at least may bestow that name on, a *government* which derives all its powers directly or

indirectly from the great body of the people, and is administered by persons holding their offices during pleasure, for a limited period, or during good behavior. It is essential to such a *government* that it be derived from the great body of the society, not from an inconsiderable proportion, or a favored class of it; otherwise a handful of tyrannical nobles, exercising their oppressions by a delegation of their powers, might aspire to the rank of *republicans*, and claim for their *government* the honorable title of *republic*. It is sufficient for such a *government* that the persons administering it be appointed, either directly or indirectly, by the people; and that they hold their appointments by either of the tenures just specified; otherwise every *government* in the United States, as well as every other popular *government* that has been or can be well organized or well executed, would be degraded from the *republican* character. . . .

[Fed. 280–81]

[4] Could any further proof be required of the *republican* complexion of this system, the most decisive one might be found in its absolute prohibition of titles of nobility, both under the federal and the State *governments;* and in its express guaranty of the *republican form* to each of the latter. [Fed. 282]

[5] "But it was not sufficient," say the adversaries of the proposed Constitution, "for the convention to adhere to the *republican form*. They ought, with equal care, to have preserved the federal *form*, which regards the Union as a Confederacy of sovereign states; instead of which, they have framed a national *government*, which regards the Union as a consolidation of the States." And it is asked by what authority this bold and radical innovation was undertaken? . . .

[Fed. 282]

George Nicholas [?], "The State Soldier," No. 1, January 16, 1788:

. . . And thus too respecting a bill of rights, and the liberty of the press, it may also be said, the objection has been diminished by the new plan: For what security had we on this head before but that which was in our state constitutions? And of what is the *republican form of government* which Congress is now to guarantee to each state to consist? Certainly of any thing each state shall think proper that does not take from Congress what this constitution absolutely claims. Even the very one we now have, or such parts of it as do not extend that far, may be that *form of government* which this new plan obliges Congress to guarantee. . . . [DHRC8 306]

Alexander White [?], "The Independent Freeholder," January 18, 1788:

. . . I shall not attempt to discuss the question, whether vesting the executive powers of *government* in a President and Council appointed by him, as proposed by R. H. L. [Richard Henry Lee] Esquire, or in the President and Senate, as proposed by the Federal Convention would be preferable? I shall only observe, that the Convention seem to have had in view the *government* of Rome, the greatest and wisest *republic,* of which we read in history, confering however, much less power on the President, Vice-President and Senate than the Roman Consuls and Senate enjoyed in the purest times of the *republic* . . .

[DHRC8 311–12]

James Madison, *The Federalist*, No. 43, January 23, 1788:

[1] In a confederacy founded on *republican* principles, and composed of *republican* members, the superintending *government* ought clearly to possess authority to defend the system against aristocratic or monarchical innovations. The more intimate the nature of such a union may be, the greater interest have the members in the political institutions of each other; and the greater right to insist that the *forms of government* under which the compact was entered into should be substantially maintained. But a right implies a remedy; and where else could the remedy be deposited, than where it is deposited by the Constitution? *Governments* of dissimilar principles and *forms* have been found less adapted to a federal coalition of any sort, than those of a kindred nature. . . . [Fed. 311–12]

[2] . . . To the second question it may be answered, that if the general *government* should interpose by virtue of this constitutional authority, it will be, of course, bound to pursue the authority. But the authority extends no further than to a guaranty of a *republican form of government,* which supposes a preexisting *government* of the *form* which is to be guaranteed. As long, therefore, as the existing *republican forms* are continued by the States, they are guaranteed by the federal Constitution. Whenever, the States may choose to substitute other *republican forms,* they have a right to do so, and to claim the federal guaranty for the latter. The only restriction imposed on them is, that they shall not exchange *republican* for anti-*republican* Constitutions: a restriction which, it is presumed, will hardly be considered as a grievance. [Fed. 312]

[3] At first view, it might seem not square with the *republican* theory, to suppose, either a majority have not the right, or that a minority will have the force, to subvert a *government,* and consequently, that the federal interposition can never be required, but when it would be improper. But theoretic reasoning, in this as in most other cases, must be qualified by the lessons of practice. . . .

[Fed. 313]

[4] Is it true that force and right are necessarily on the same side in *republican governments?* May not the minor party possess such a superiority of pecuniary resources, of military talents and experience, or of secret succors from foreign powers, as will render it superior also in an appeal to the sword? . . .

[Fed. 313]

James Madison, *The Federalist*, No. 44, January 25, 1788:

. . . The loss which America has sustained since the peace, from the pestilent effects of paper money on the necessary confidence between man and man, on the necessary confidence in public councils, on the industry and morals of people, and on the character of *republican government,* constitutes an enormous debt against the State chargeable with this unadvised measure, which must long remain unsatisfied . . . [Fed. 318]

"Civis Rusticus," January 30, 1788:

The last efforts of a despotic *government!* Can we then a popular *government,* a guaranteed *republic,* fear this more under the proposed, than the present constitution? [DHRC8 338]

Alexander C. Hanson, *Remarks on the Proposed Plan of a Federal Government*, c. January 31, 1788:

[Title Page:] Remarks on the Proposed Plan of a Federal *Government,* Addressed to the Citizens of the United States of America, And Particularly to the People of Maryland, By Aristides. "As a confederated *government* is composed of petty *republics,* it enjoys the internal happiness of each; and with regard to its external situation, by means of the association, it possesses all the advantages of extensive monarchies." Mont[esquieu]. Sp. of Laws, B. 9, Ch. I. [Ford 219]

[1] To consolidate the whole thirteen states into a single organization, was out of the convention's contemplation,—for two unanswerable reasons. In the first place, they were satisfied, that not one of the states would renounce its sovereignty. In the next place, they considered, that, in a single *government,* with a great extent of territory, the advantages are most unequally diffused. As the extreme parts are scarcely sensible of its protection, so are they scarcely under its domination. It is generally agreed, that a great extended nation can long continue under no single *form of government,* except a despotism into which, either a *republic,* or a limited monarchy, will be certain to degenerate. And hence, if I understand the man who styles himself a Centinel, he insinuates, that, if these states will persist in remaining under one head, they must soon fall under the dominion of a despot. But, my fellow-citizens, in a confederate *republic,* consisting of distinct states, completely organized within themselves, and each of no greater extent than is proper for a *republican form,* almost all the blessings of *government* are equally diffused. Its protection extends to the remotest corner, and there every man is under restraint of laws. [Ford 247–48]

[2] A true federal *republic* is always capable of accession by the peaceable and friendly admission of new single states. Its true size is neither greater nor less than that, which may comprehend all the states, which, by their contiguity, may become enemies, unless united under one common head, capable of reconciling all their differences. Such a *government* as this, excels any single *government,* extending over the same territory, as a band of brothers is superior to a band of slaves, or as thirteen common men, for the purposes of agriculture, would be superior to a giant, enjoying strength of body equal to them all. [Ford 248]

[3] Shall America then form one grand federal *republic?* Or shall she, after experiencing the benefits of even an imperfect union, and when a union the most perfect is requisite for her permanent safety;—shall she, in this situation, divide into thirteen contemptible single *governments,* exposed to every insult and wrong from abroad, and watching each other's motions, with all the captiousness of jealous rivals? Or shall she divide into two or more federal *republics,* actuated by the same malignant dispositions? In either of these cases, after struggling through infinite toils, difficulty, and danger, should the thirteen single states be, at last, delivered from foreign foes, they will fall upon each other; and no man can predict, what *forms of government,* or division of territory, shall finally obtain. Two or three federal *republics* might possibly retain their independence. But they would be in the same situation, with respect to each other, as France, England, and Spain, scarcely ever free from war . . . [Ford 248–49]

[4] . . . Are not the regulations of property, the regulations of the penal law, the protection of the weak, the promotion of useful arts, the whole internal *government* of their respective *republics;* are not these the main objects of every wise and honest legislature? Are not these things still in their power; and, whilst free from invasion or injuries abroad, are not these almost the only things, in which sovereignty is exercised? [Ford 252]

James Madison, *The Federalist*, No. 49, February 2, 1788:

[1] The author of the "Notes on the State of Virginia," [Thomas Jefferson] quoted in the last paper, has subjoined to that valuable work the draught of a constitution, which had been prepared in order to be laid before a convention expected to be called in 1783, by the legislature, for the establishment of a constitution for that commonwealth. The plan, like every thing from the same pen, marks a turn of thinking, original, comprehensive, and accurate; and is the more worthy of attention as it equally displays fervent attachment to *republican government* and an enlightened view of the dangerous propensities against which it ought to be guarded. . . . [Fed. 347–48]

[2] As the people are the only legitimate fountain of power, and it is from them that the constitutional charter, under which the several branches of *government* hold their power, is derived, it seems strictly consonant to the *republican* theory, to recur to the same original authority, not only whenever it may be necessary to enlarge, diminish, or new-model the powers of the *government,* but also whenever any one of the departments may commit encroachments on the chartered authorities of the others. . . . [Fed. 348]

[3] But the greatest objection of all is, that the decisions which would probably result from such appeals would not answer the purpose of maintaining the constitutional equilibrium of the *government*. We have seen that the tendency of *republican governments* is to an aggrandizement of the legislative at the expense of the other departments. . . . [Fed. 350]

Samuel Bryan, "Centinel," No. 14, February 5, 1788:

[1] . . . It was insisted that *governments of a republican nature,* are those best calculated to preserve the freedom and happiness of the citizen—That *governments* of this kind, are only calculated for a territory but small in its extent—That the only method by which an extensive continent like America could be connected and united together consistent with the principles of freedom, must be by having a number of strong and energetic state *governments* for securing and protecting the rights of the individuals forming those *governments,* and for regulating all their concerns . . . [DHRC16 36]

[2] . . . the testimony of experience, the opinions of the most celebrated writers, and the nature of the case demonstrated in the clearest manner, that so extensive a territory as these United States includes, could not be *governed* by any other mode than a confederacy of *republics* consistent with the principles of freedom, and that their own conviction was, that nothing short of the supremacy of despotism could connect and bind together this country under ONE *GOVERNMENT?* Has any one a doubt now remaining of the guilt of the conspirators!

[DHRC16 37]

Luther Martin, "Genuine Information," No. 11, February 5, 1788:

This representation was made in convention, and it was further urged that the territory of these States were too large, and that the inhabitants thereof would be too much disconnected for a *republican government* to extend to them its benefits, which is only suited to a small and compact territory . . .

[DHRC16 40]

James Madison, *The Federalist*, No. 51, February 6, 1788:

[1] First. In a single *republic,* all the power surrendered by the people is submitted to the administration of a single *government;* and the usurpations are guarded against by a division of the *government* into distinct and separate departments. In the compound *republic* of America, the power surrendered by the people is first divided between two distinct *governments,* and then the portion allotted to each subdivided among distinct and separate departments. Hence a double security arises to the rights of the people. The different *governments* will control each other, at the same time that each will be controlled by itself. [Fed. 357]

[2] . . . This view of the subject must particularly recommend a proper federal system to all the sincere and considerate friends of *republican government,* since it shows that in exact proportion as the territory of the Union may be formed into more circumscribed Confederacies, or States, oppressive combinations of a majority will be facilitated; the best security, under the *republican forms,* for the rights of every class of citizens, will be diminished; and consequently the

stability and independence of some member of the *government,* the only other security, must be proportionally increased. . . . [Fed. 358]

Letter from Wilmington, North Carolina, February 6, 1788, published in *Charleston Gazette,* February 11, 1788:

. . . It must give pain to a reflective mind when it considers that such oceans of blood have been repeatedly spilt in Europe, often for the sake of some miserable and insignificant spot of territory, when such a noble and extensive region as that of which I am speaking, has been so long neglected, as if hardly worth the attention of a civilized race of men.—God grant that we may speedily establish a free and energetic *government* upon the broad basis of *republican* equality, which may take the western territories under its wing, and assist them in repelling any insults that may be offered by the jealous and avaricious devotees on the other side of the Missisippi [*i.e.,* the Spanish] or those insolent intruders [*i.e.,* the British], who, contrary to the faith of treaties, still possess our posts to the northward. [DHRC16 106–107]

James Madison, *The Federalist,* No. 52, February 8, 1788:

Those of the former are to be the same with those of the electors of the most numerous branch of the State legislature. The definition of the right of suffrage is very justly regarded as a fundamental article of *republican government.* It was incumbent on the convention, therefore, to define and establish this right in the Constitution. . . . [Fed. 360]

James Madison, *The Federalist,* No. 55, February 13, 1788:

[1] . . . The improbability of such a mercenary and perfidious combination of the several members of *government,* standing on as different foundations as *republican* principles will well admit, and at the same time accountable to the society over which they are placed, ought alone to quiet this apprehension. . . . [Fed. 378]

[2] . . . As there is a degree of depravity in mankind which requires a certain degree of circumspection and distrust, so there are other qualities in human nature which justify a certain portion of esteem and confidence. *Republican government* presupposes the existence of these qualities in a higher degree than any other *form.* . . . [Fed. 378–79]

Spencer Roane, "A Plain Dealer," February 13, 1788:

. . . But, how shall I express my dislike of the ultimatum of his Excellency's [*i.e.,* Edmund Randolph's] letter, wherein he declares "that if after our best efforts for amendments, they cannot be obtained, he will adopt the Constitution as it is." How is this declaration reconcileable to a former opinion of his Excellency's, expressed to the Hon. Richard H. Lee, and repeated by the latter gentleman in his letter, as printed in the public papers—"that either a monarchy or an aristocracy will be generated from the proposed Constitution." Good God! how can the first Magistrate and Father of a free *republican government,* after a feeble parade of opposition, and before his desired plan of amendments has been determined upon, declare that he will accept a Constitution which is to beget a monarchy or an aristocracy? How can such a determination be reconciled to the feelings of Virginia, and to the principles which prevailed in almost every legislature in the union, who looked no farther than the amendment of our present *republican* confederation? I have charity to believe that the respectable characters who signed this Constitution, did so, thinking that neither a monarchy nor an aristocracy would ensue, but that they should thereby preserve and meliorate the *republic* of America: but never until now, that his Excellency has let the cat out of the bag, did I suppose, that any member of the Convention, at least any from the *republican* state of Virginia, member of the Convention, at least any from the *republican* state of Virginia, would accept a Constitution, whereby the *republic* of his Constituents is to be sacrificed in its infancy, and before it has had a fair trial. . . . [DHRC8 364–65]

James Madison, *The Federalist*, No. 57, February 19, 1788:

[1] Of all the objections which have been framed against the federal Constitution, this [that the House of Representatives "favours the elevation of the few on the ruins of the many."] is perhaps the most extraordinary. Whilst the objection itself is levelled against a pretended oligarchy, the principle of it strikes at the very root of *republican government.* [Fed. 383]

[2] The aim of every political constitution is, or ought to be, first to obtain for rulers men who possess most wisdom to discern, and most virtue to pursue, the common good of the society; and in the next place, to take the most effectual precautions for keeping them virtuous whilst they continue to hold their public trust. The elective mode of obtaining rulers is the characteristic policy of *republican government*. . . . [Fed. 383]

[3] Let me now ask what circumstance there is in the constitution of the House of Representatives that violates the principles of *republican government,* or favors the elevation of the few on the ruins of the many? Let me ask whether every circumstance is not, on the contrary, strictly conformable to these principles, and scrupulously impartial to the rights and pretensions of every class and description of citizens? [Fed. 383]

[4] Such will be the relation between the House of Representatives and their constituents. Duty, gratitude, interest, ambition itself, are the chords by which they will be bound to fidelity and sympathy with the great mass of the people. It is possible that these may all be insufficient to control the caprice and wickedness of man. But are they not all that *government* will admit, and that human

prudence can devise? Are they not the genuine and the characteristic means by which *republican government* provides for the liberty and happiness of the people? Are they not the identical means on which every State *government* in the Union relies for the attainment of these important ends? What then are we to understand by the objection which this paper has combated? What are we to say to the men who profess the most flaming zeal for *republican government,* yet boldly impeach the fundamental principle of it; who pretend to be champions for the right and the capacity of the people to choose their own rulers, yet maintain that they will prefer those only who will immediately and infallibly betray the trust committed to them? [Fed. 385–86]

"The Impartial Examiner," No. 1, February 20, 1788:

. . . It is true, "the United States shall guarantee to every state in this union a *republican form of government:"* yet they do not guarantee to the different states their present *forms of government,* or the bill of rights thereto annexed, or any of them; and the expressions are too vague, too indefinite to create such a compact by implication. It is possible that a *"republican form" of government* may be built upon as absolute principles of despotism as any oriental monarchy ever yet possessed. I presume that the liberty of a nation depends, not on planning the frame of *government,* which consists merely in fixing and delineating the powers thereof; but on prescribing due limits to those powers, and establishing them upon just principles. [DHRC8 393]

James Madison, *The Federalist*, No. 62, February 27, 1788:

[1] The equality of representation in the Senate is another point, which, being evidently the result of compromise between the opposite pretensions of the large and the small States, does not call for much discussion. If indeed it be right, that among a people thoroughly incorporated into one nation, every district ought to have a proportional share in the *government,* and that among independent and sovereign States, bound together by a simple league, the parties, however unequal in size, ought to have an equal share in the common councils, it does not appear to be without some reason that in a compound *republic,* partaking both of the national and federal character, the *government* ought to be founded on a mixture of the principles of proportional and equal representation. . . . [Fed. 408]

[2] First. It is a misfortune incident to *republican government,* though in a less degree than to other *governments,* that those who administer it may forget their obligations to their constituents, and prove unfaithful to their important trust. In this point of view, a senate, as a second branch of the legislative assembly, distinct from, and dividing the power with, a first, must be in all cases a salutary check on the *government*. It doubles the security to the people, by requiring the concurrence of two distinct bodies in schemes of usurpation of perfidy, where the ambition or corruption of one would otherwise be sufficient. This is a pre-

caution founded on such clear principles, and now so well understood in the United States, that it would be more than superfluous to enlarge on it. I will barely remark, that as the improbability of sinister combinations will be in proportion to the dissimilarity in the genius of the two bodies, it must be politic to distinguish them from each other by every circumstance which will consist with a due harmony in all proper measures, and with the genuine principles of *republican government.* [Fed. 409]

Alexander White, "To the Citizens of Virginia," February 29, 1788:

It is said, "that an extensive territory cannot be *governed* on the principles of freedom otherwise than by a confederation of *republics,* possessing all the powers of internal *government,* but united in the management of their general and foreign concerns." This is the very *government* we propose to establish. The separate states retain all the powers of internal *government.* . . . [DHRC8 438]

Mercy Otis Warren, *Observations on the New Constitution*, February 1788:

[1] But as a variety of objections to the heterogeneous phantom, have been repeatedly laid before the public, by men of the best abilities and intentions; I will not expatiate long on a *Republican form of government,* founded on the principles of monarchy—a democratick branch with the features of aristocracy—and the extravagance of nobility pervading the minds of many of the candidates for office . . . [DHRC16 277]

[2] Notwithstanding the delusory promise to guarantee a *Republican form of government* to every State in the Union—If the most discerning eye could discover any meaning at all in the engagement, there are no resources left for the support of internal *government,* or the liquidation of the debts of the State. . . . [DHRC16 280]

[3] . . . The causes which have inspired a few men assembled for very different purposes with such a degree of temerity as to break with a single stroke the union of America, and disseminate the seeds of discord through the land may be easily investigated, when we survey the partizans of monarchy in the state conventions, urging the adoption of a mode of *government* that militates with the former professions and exertions of this country, and with all ideas of *republicanism,* and the equal rights of men. [DHRC16 284]

[4] It is true this country lately armed in opposition to regal despotism—impoverished by the expences of a long war, and unable immediately to fulfil their public or private engagements, have appeared in some instances, with a boldness of spirit that seemed to set at defiance all authority, *government,* or order, on the one hand; while on the other, there has been, not only a secret wish, but an open avowal of the necessity of drawing the reins of *government* much too taught, not only for *republicanism* but for a wise and limited monarchy.—But

the character of this people is not averse to a degree of subordination: the truth of this appears from the easy restoration of tranquility, after a dangerous insurrection in one of the states; this also evinces the little necessity of a complete revolution of *government* throughout the union. But it is a *republican* principle that the majority should rule; and if a spirit of moderation could be cultivated on both sides, till the voice of the people at large could be fairly heard it should be held sacred. . . . [DHRC16 288]

"The Impartial Examiner," No. 1, March 5, 1788:

It is next to impossible to enslave a people immediately after a firm struggle against oppression, while the sense of past injury is recent and strong. But after some time this impression naturally wears off;—the ardent glow of freedom gradually evaporates;—the charms of popular equality, which arose from the *republican* plan, insensibly decline;—the pleasures, the advantages derived from the new kind of *government* grow stale through use. Such declension in all these vigorous springs of action necessarily produces a supineness. . . .

[DHRC8 464–65]

***Pennsylvania Gazette*, March 5, 1788:**

. . . The ambitious and designing, by lessening the minority by degrees, might bring us under the *government* even of one. How dangerous, then, must it appear to every jealous and sincere friend of liberty, to dispense, upon any occasion, with the great rule of *republics,* that the voice of the majority of the people is the unalterable law. [DHRC16 321]

James Iredell, "Marcus," No. 3, March 5, 1788:

[1] Nobody can contend upon any rational principles, that a power of pardoning should not exist somewhere in every *government,* because it will often happen in every country, that men are obnoxious to a legal conviction, who yet are entitled, from some favorable circumstances in their case, to a merciful interposition in their favor. The advocates of monarchy have accordingly boasted of this, as one of the advantages of that *form of government,* in preference to a *Republican;* nevertheless this authority is vested in the Stadtholder in Holland, and I believe is vested in every Executive power in America. It seems to have been wisely the aim of the late Convention in forming a general *government* for America, to combine the acknowledged advantages of the British Constitution with proper *Republican* checks, to guard as much as possible against abuses; and it would have been very strange if they had omitted this which has the sanction of such great antiquity in that country, and if I am not mistaken, an universal adoption in America. . . . [DHRC16 322]

[2] . . . There is little danger of an abuse of such a power [*i.e.,* the power of pardoning] when we know how apt most men are in a *Republican government,*

to court popularity at too great an expence, rather than to do a just and beneficent action, in opposition to strong prevailing prejudices, among the people. . . . [DHRC16 324]

Alexander Hamilton, *The Federalist*, No. 66, March 8, 1788:

But this hypothesis, such as it is, has already been refuted in the remarks applied to the duration in office prescribed for the senators. It was by them shown, as well on the credit of historical examples, as from the reason of the thing, that the most popular branch of every *government*, partaking of the *republican* genius, by being generally the favorite of the people, will be as generally a full match, if not an overmatch, for every other member of the *Government*. [Fed. 433]

Alexander Hamilton, *The Federalist*, No. 68, March 12, 1788:

Nothing was more to be desired than that every practicable obstacle should be opposed to cabal, intrigue, and corruption. These most deadly adversaries of *republican government* might naturally have been expected to make their approaches from more than one quarter, but chiefly from the desire in foreign powers to gain an improper ascendant in our councils. . . . [Fed. 441]

Alexander Hamilton, *The Federalist*, No. 70, March 15, 1788:

[1] There is an idea, which is not without its advocates, that a vigorous Executive is inconsistent with the genius of *republican government*. The enlightened well-wishers to this species of *government* must at least hope that the supposition is destitute of foundation; since they can never admit its truth, without at the same time admitting the condemnation of their own principles. Energy in the Executive is a leading character in the definition of good *government*. . . . [Fed. 451]

[2] . . . The Roman history records many instances of mischiefs to the *republic* from the dissensions between the Consuls, and between the military Tribunes, who were at times substituted for the Consuls. But it gives us no specimens of any peculiar advantages derived to the state from the circumstance of the plurality of those magistrates. That the dissensions between them were not more frequent or more fatal, is matter of astonishment, until we advert to the singular position in which the *republic* was almost continually placed, and to the prudent policy pointed out by the circumstances of the state, and pursued by the Consuls, of making a division of the *government* between them. . . . [Fed. 452–53]

Alexander Hamilton, *The Federalist*, No. 71, March 18, 1788:

[1] There are some who would be inclined to regard the servile pliancy of the Executive to a prevailing current, either in the community or in the legislature, as its best recommendation. But such men entertain very crude notions, as well of the purposes for which *government* was instituted, as of the true means by

which the public happiness may be promoted. The *republican* principle demands that the deliberate sense of the community should *govern* the conduct of those to whom they intrust the management of their affairs; but it does not require an unqualified complaisance to every sudden breeze of passion, or to every transient impulse which the people may receive from the arts of men, who flatter their prejudices to betray their interests. . . . [Fed. 459]

[2] . . . The tendency of the legislative authority to absorb every other, has been fully displayed and illustrated by examples in some preceding numbers. In *governments purely republican,* this tendency is almost irresistible. The representatives of the people, in a popular assembly, seem sometimes to fancy that they are the people themselves, and betray strong symptoms of impatience and disgust at the least sign of opposition from any other quarter; as if the exercise of its rights, by either the executive or judiciary, were a breach of their privilege and an outrage to their dignity. . . . [Fed. 460]

Alexander Hamilton, *The Federalist*, No. 73, March 21, 1788:

If a magistrate so powerful and so well fortified as a British monarch, would have scruples about the exercise of the power under consideration, how much greater caution may be reasonably expected in a President of the United States, clothed for the short period of four years with the executive authority of a *government wholly and purely republican?* [Fed. 471]

John Jay, *An Address to the People of the State of New York*, c. April 15, 1788:

[1] . . . You find that not only those men, but others of similar characters, and of whom you have also had very ample experience, advise you to adopt it [the Constitution]. You find that whole States concur in the sentiment, and among them are your next neighbors; both whom have shed much blood in the cause o liberty, and have manifested as strong and constant a predilection for a free *Republican Government* as any State in the Union, and perhaps in the world. They perceive not those latent mischiefs in it, with which some double-sighted politicians endeavor to alarm you. . . . [Ford 85]

[2] . . . If the people of our nation, instead of consenting to be governed by laws of their own making, and rulers of their own choosing, should let licentiousness, disorder, and confusion reign over them, the minds of men every where, will insensibly become alienated from *republican forms,* and prepared to prefer and acquiesce in *Governments,* which, though less friendly to liberty, afford more peace and security. [Ford 86]

Melancton Smith, *An Address to the People of the State of New York*, c. April 1788:

The advocates for the proposed new constitution, having been beaten off the field of argument, on its merits, have now taken new ground. They admit it is liable to well-founded objections—that a number of its articles ought to be amended; that if alterations do not take place, a door will be left open for an undue administration, and encroachments on the liberties of the people; and many of them go so far as to say, if it should continue for any considerable period, in its present *form,* it will lead to a subversion of our equal *republican forms of government*. . . . [Ford 91]

Alexander Hamilton, *The Federalist*, No. 78, May 28, 1788:

[1] . . . The standard of good behavior for the continuance in office of the judicial magistracy, is certainly one of the most valuable of the modern improvements in the practice of *government*. In a monarchy it is an excellent barrier to the despotism of the prince; in a *republic* it is a no less excellent barrier to the encroachments and oppressions of the representative body. And it is the best expedient which can be devised in any *government,* to secure a steady, upright, and impartial administration of the laws. [Fed. 490]

[2] . . . Though I trust the friends of the proposed Constitution will never concur with its enemies in questioning that fundamental principle of *republican government,* which admits the right of the people to alter or abolish the established Constitution, whenever they find it inconsistent with their happiness, yet it is not to be inferred from this principle, that the representatives of the people, whenever a momentary inclination happens to lay hold of a majority of their constituents, incompatible with the provisions in the existing Constitution, would, on that account, be justifiable in a violation of those provisions . . . [Fed. 494]

Alexander Hamilton, *The Federalist*, No. 83, May 28, 1788:

The friends and adversaries of the plan of the convention, if they agree in nothing else, concur at least in the value they set upon the trial by jury; or if there is any difference between them it consists in this: the former regard it as a valuable safeguard to liberty; the latter represent it as the very palladium of free *government*. For my own part, the more the operation of the institution has fallen under my observation, the more reason I have discovered for holding it in high estimation; and it would be altogether superfluous to examine to what extent it deserves to be esteemed useful or essential in a representative *republic,* or how much more merit it may be entitled to, as a defence against the oppressions of an hereditary monarch, than as a barrier to the tyranny of popular magistrates in a popular *government*. . . . [Fed. 521–22]

Alexander Hamilton, *The Federalist*, No. 84, May 28, 1788:

Nothing need be said to illustrate the importance of the prohibition of titles of nobility. This may truly be denominated the corner-stone of *republican government;* for so long as they are excluded, there can never be serious danger that the *government* will be any other than that of the people. [Fed. 533]

Alexander Hamilton, *The Federalist*, No. 85, May 28, 1788:

The additional securities to *republican government,* to liberty, and to property, to be derived from the adoption of the plan under consideration, consist chiefly in the restraints which the preservation of the Union will impose on local factions and insurrections, and on the ambition of powerful individuals in single States, who may acquire credit and influence enough, from leaders and favorites, to become the despots of the people; in the diminution of the opportunities to foreign intrigue, which the dissolution of the Confederacy would invite and facilitate; in the prevention of extensive military establishments, which could not fail to grow out of wars between the States in a disunited situation; in the express guaranty of a *republican form of government* to each; in the absolute and universal exclusion of titles of nobility; and in the precautions against the repetition of those practices on the part of the State *governments* which have undermined the foundations of property and credit, have planted mutual distrust in the breasts of all classes of citizens, and have occasioned an almost universal prostration of morals. [Fed. 542]

John Dickinson, "Fabius," No. 5, 1788:

[1] It has been considered,what are the rights to be contributed, and how they are to be managed; and it has been said, that *republican* tranquility and prosperity have commonly been promoted, in proportion to the strength of *government* for protecting the worthy against the licentious. [Ford 188]

[2] Here the reader, is respectfully requested, to assist the intentions of the writer, by keeping in mind, the ideas of a single *republic* with one democratic branch in its *government,* and of a confederation of *republics* with one or several democratic branches in the *government* of the confederation, or in the government of its parts, so that as he proceeds, a comparison may easily run along, between any of these and the proposed plan. [Ford 189]

John Dickinson, "Fabius," No. 7, 1788:

. . . The other fault, of which, as yet, there are no symptoms among us, is the thirst of empire. This is a vice, that ever has been, and from the nature of things, ever must be, fatal to *republican forms of government*. Our wants, are sources of happiness: our irregular desires, of misery. The abuse of prosperity, is rebellion against Heaven; and succeeds accordingly. [Ford 202]

John Dickinson, "Fabius," No. 8, 1788:

[1] The proposed confederation offers to us a system of diversified representation in the legislative, executive, and judicial departments, as essentially necessary to the good *government* of an extensive *republican* empire. . . . [Ford 204]

[2] It has been asserted, that a very extensive territory cannot be ruled by a *government of republican form*. What is meant by this proposition? Is it intended to abolish all ideas of connection, and to precipitate us into the miseries of division, either as single states, or partial confederacies? . . . [Ford 204]

[3] . . . It is true, that extensive territory has in general been arbitrarily *governed;* and it is as true, that a number of *republics,* in such territory, loosely connected, must inevitably rot into despotism. [Ford 205]

[4] It is said—Such territory has never been *governed* by a confederacy of *republics*. Granted. But, where was there ever a confederacy of *republics,* in such territory, united, as these states are to be by the proposed constitution? . . . [Ford 205]

[5] . . . So far is the assertion from being true, that "a very extensive territory cannot be ruled by a *government of a republican form,*" that such a territory cannot be well-ruled by a *government of any other form*. [Ford 206]

[6] The proposition was expressly made upon this principle, that a territory of such extent as that of United America, could not be safely and advantageously *governed,* but by a combination of *republics,* each retaining all the rights of supreme sovereignty, excepting such as ought to be contributed to the union . . . [Ford 207]

[7] The principle appears to be well founded in reason, Why cannot a very extensive territory be ruled by a *government of republican form?* They answered, because its power must languish through distance of parts. . . . [Ford 207]

George Washington, First Inaugural Address, April 30, 1789:

. . . and since the preservation of the sacred fire of liberty and the destiny of the *republican model of Government* are justly considered, as deeply, perhaps as finally, staked on the experiment intrusted to the hands of the American people. [Annals 28]

RESIDENT, RESIDENTS

United States Constitution, September 17, 1787:

[Article II, Section 1:] No Person except a natural born Citizen, or a Citizen of the United States, at the time of the Adoption of this Constitution, shall be eligible to the Office of President; neither shall any Person be eligible to that Office who shall not have attained to the Age of thirty five Years, and been fourteen Years a *Resident* within the United States.

* * * * *

Elizabeth I, Charter to Sir Walter Raleigh, March 25, 1584:

. . . that they, and every or any of them, being either borne within our saide Realmes of Englande, or Irelande, or in any other place within our allegiance, and which hereafter shall be inhabiting within any the lands, Countreis, and territories, with such licence (as aforesaide) shall and may have all the priviledges of free Denizens, and persons native of England, and within our allegiance in such like ample maner and fourme, as if they were borne and personally *resident* within our saide Realme of England, any lawe, custome, or usage to the contrary notwithstanding. [Thorpe 55]

James I, Second Charter of Virginia, May 23, 1609:

[1] . . . Therefore we Do Ordain, establish and confirm that there shall be perpetually one Council here *resident,* according to the Tenour of our former Letters-Patents; Which Council shall have a Seal for the better Government and Administration of the said Plantation, besides the legal Seal of the Company or Corporation, as in our former Letters-Patents is also expressed. [Thorpe 3796]

[2] And further, of our special Grace, certain Knowledge, and mere Motion, for Us, our Heirs and Successors, we do, by these Presents, Give and Grant full Power and Authority to our said Council here *resident,* as well at this present

time, as hereafter from time to time, to nominate, make, constitute, ordain and confirm, by such Name or Names, Stile or Stiles, as to them shall seem good . . . [Thorpe 3797–98]

[3] And we do also declare that for divers Reasons and Considerations, Us thereunto especially moving, our Will and Pleasure is, and We do hereby ordain, that immediately from and after such Time as any such Governor or principal Officer, so to be nominated and appointed by our said Council, for the Government of the said Colony as aforesaid, shall arrive in Virginia, and give Notice unto the Colony there *resident,* of our Pleasure in this Behalf, the Government Power and Authority of the President and Council heretofore by our former Letters-patents there established, and all Laws and Constitutions by them formerly made shall utterly cease and be determined; And all Officers, Governors, and Ministers formerly constituted and appointed, shall be discharged, anything in our former Letters-patents concerning the said Plantation contained in any wise to the contrary notwithstanding; Straightly charging and commanding the President and Council now *resident* in the said Colony upon their Allegiance, after Knowledge given unto them of our Will and Pleasure by these presents signified and declared that they forthwith be obedient to such Governor or Governors as by our said Council here *resident* shall be named and appointed as aforesaid, and to all Directions, Orders and Commandments which they shall receive from them, as well in the present resigning and giving up of their Authority, Offices, Charge and Places, as in all other Attendance as shall be by them from time to time required. [Thorpe 3798]

[4] And we do further by these presents Ordain and establish, that the said Treasurer and Council here *resident,* and their successors or any four of them being assembled (the Treasurer being one) shall from time to time have full Power and Authority to admit and receive any other Person into their Company, Corporation, and Freedom . . . [Thorpe 3798]

Council of New England, Grant of the Province of Maine, August 10, 1622:

. . . And ye sd Sr. Ferdinando Gorges and Capt. John Mason doe covenant and grant, to and with ye said President and councill, their successors and assigns, by these presents, that they, the said Sr. Ferdinando Gorges and Capt. John Mason, shall and will, before the expiracon of three years, to be accompted from the day of the date hereof, have in or upon the said porcons of lands, or some part thereof; one parte with a competent guard, and ten families at least of his Majestie's subjects *resident* and being in and upon ye same premises; or in default thereof shall and will forfeit and loose to the said President and councill the sum of one hundred pounds sterling money . . . [Thorpe 1624–25]

Charles I, Charter of Massachusetts Bay, March 4, 1629:

. . . And Wee doe further, for Us, our Heires and Successors, give and graunte to the said Governor and Company, and their Successors, by theis Presents, that it shall and maie be lawfull, to and for the Chiefe Comaunders, Governors, and officers of the said Company for the Time being, who shalbe *resident* in the said Parte of newe England in America, by theis Presents graunted, and others there inhabiting by their Appointment and Direccon, from Tyme to Tyme, and at all Tymes hereafter for their speciall Defence and Safety, to incounter, expulse repell, and resist by Force of Armes, aswell by Sea as by Lande, and by, all fitting Waies and Meanes whatsoever, all such Person and Persons, as shall at any Tyme hereafter, attempt or enterprise the Destruccon, Invasion, Detriment, or Annoyaunce to the said Plantation or Inhabitants . . . [Thorpe 1858]

Charles I, Charter of Maryland, June 20, 1632:

[Article 15:] We will also, and by these Presents do, for Us, our Heirs and Successors, give and grant License by this our Charter, unto the aforesaid now Baron of Baltimore, his Heirs and Assigns, and to all Persons whatsoever, who are, or shall be *Residents* and Inhabitants of the Province aforesaid, freely to import and unlade, by themselves, their Servants, Factors or Assigns, all Wares and Merchandizes whatsoever, which shall be collected out of the Fruits and Commodities of the said Province . . . [Thorpe 1683]

[Article 16:] . . . Which Liberties and Privileges, the said Subjects of Us, our Heirs and Successors, shall enjoy, without notable Damage or Injury in any wise to be done to the aforesaid now Baron of Baltimore, his Heirs or Assigns, or to the *Residents* and Inhabitants of the same Province in the Ports, Creeks, and Shores aforesaid, and especially in the Woods and Trees there growing. . . . [Thorpe 1684]

[Article 20:] . . . that We, our Heirs, and Successors, at no Time hereafter, will impose, or make or cause to be imposed, any Impositions, Customs, or other Taxations, Quotas, or Contributions whatsoever, in or upon the *Residents* or Inhabitants of the Province aforesaid for their Goods, Lands, or Tenements within the same Province, or upon any Tenements, Lands, Goods or Chattels within the Province aforesaid, or in or upon any Goods or Merchandizes within the Province aforesaid, or within the Ports or Harbors of the said Province, to be laden or unladen . . . [Thorpe 1685]

Fundamental Orders of Connecticut, 1638–39:

Forasmuch as it hath pleased the Allmighty God by the wise disposition of his divyne prvidence so to Order and dispose of things that we the Inhabitants and *Residents* of Windsor, Harteford and Wethersfield are now cohabiting and dwelling in and uppon the River of Conectecotte and the Lands thereunto adjoyneing . . . [Thorpe 519]

Charles I, Grant of the Province of Maine, April 3, 1639:

[1] . . . the said Lawes and Constitucons to extend as well to such as shalbee passing unto or returning from the said Province and Premisses as unto the Inhabitants and *Residents* of or within the same and the same to bee put in execucon by the said Sir Fardinando Gorges his heires or assignes or by his or theire Deputies Lieuetenants Judges Officers or Ministers in that behalfe lawfully authorized . . . [Thorpe 1628]

[2] . . . and to appoynt and constitute from tyme to tyme Judges Justices Magistrates and Officers as well of the said Courte and Courtes of Justice as otherwise aswell by Sea as by Lande for the hearing and determining of all manner of Causes whatsoever within and concerning the said Province and Premisses or any of them or the Inhabitants or *Residents* there and Passengers to or from the same aswell by Lande as by Sea . . . [Thorpe 1628–29]

[3] . . . And that the Inhabitants and *Residents* within the said Province and Premisses and Passengers to and from the same may within fortie days after sentence given in the said Courtes (where appeales in like Courtes within this Kingdome are admitted) appeale to the said Sir Fardinando Gorges his heires or assignes or his or theire generall Governour or Chiefe Deputie of the said Province or Premisses for the tyme being . . . [Thorpe 1629]

[4] . . . And likewise by force of armes to recover from any person or persons all such Territories Domynions Landes Places Goods Chattels and Wares which hereafter shalbee taken from the said Sir Fardinando Gorges his heires or assignes or from his or theire Deputyes Officers or Servants or from any the Plantors Inhabitants or *Residents* of or within the said Province or Premisses or from any, other Members Aydors or Assistors of the said Sir Fardinando Gorges his heires or assignes . . . [Thorpe 1630]

[5] . . . to minister and give Oaths of allegiance and supremacie according to the formes now established in this our Realme of England to all and every such person and persons as they shall thinke fitt that shall att any tyme or tymes goe or passe into the said Province and Premises or any of them or shalbee *resident* or abideing there . . . [Thorpe 1636]

Government of Rhode Island, March 1641:

[Article 14:] It is ordered, that a Booke shall be provided, wherein the Secretary shall write all such Lawes and Acts, as are made and constituted by the Body, to be left alway in that Towne where the said Secretary is not *resident* . . . [Thorpe 3208]

Charles II, Charter of Connecticut, April 23, 1662:

And We do further for Us, Our Heirs and Successors, give and grant unto the said Governor and Company, and their Successors, by these Presents, That it shall and may be lawful to, and for the Chief Commanders, Governors and Officers of the said Companv for the Time being, who shall be *resident* in the Parts of New-England hereafter mentioned, and others inhabiting there, by their Leave, Admittance, Appointment, or Direction, from Time to Time, and at all Times hereafter, for their special Defence and Safety, to Assemble, Martial-Array, and put in warlike Posture the Inhabitants of the said Colony . . .

[Thorpe 534]

Pennsylvania Frame of Government, Laws Agreed Upon in England, May 5, 1682:

[Article 2:] That every inhabitant in the said province, that is or shall be, a purchaser of one hundred acres of land, or upwards, his heirs and assigns, and every person who shall have paid his passage, and taken up one hundred acres of land, at one penny an acre, and have cultivated ten acres thereof, and every person, that hath been a servant, or bonds-man, and is free by his service, that shall have taken up his fifty acres of land, and cultivated twenty thereof, and every inhabitant, artificer, or other *resident* in the said province, that pays scot and lot to the government; shall be deemed and accounted a freeman of the said province . . . [Thorpe 3060]

William and Mary, Charter of Massachusetts Bay, October 7, 1691:

. . . Wee doe by these presents for us Our heires and Successors Grant Establish and Ordaine that for ever hereafter there shall be a liberty of Conscience allowed in the Worshipp of God to all Christians (Except Papists) Inhabiting or which shall Inhabit or be *Resident* within our said Province or Territory . . .

[Thorpe 1881]

Pennsylvania Frame of Government, November 7, 1696:

And, to the end it may be known who those are, in this province and territories, who ought to have right of, or to be deemed freemen, to chuse, or be chosen, to serve in Council and Assembly, as aforesaid, Be it enacted by the authority aforesaid, That no inhabitant of this province or territories, shall have right of electing, or being elected as aforesaid, unless they be free denizens of this government, and are of the age of twenty-one years, or upwards, and have fifty acres of land, ten acres whereof being seated and cleared, or be otherwise worth fifty pounds lawful money of this government, clear estate, and have been *resident* within this government for the space of two years next before such election. [Thorpe 3071]

George II, Charter of Georgia, June 9, 1732:

. . . And for the greater ease and encouragement of our loving subjects and such others as shall come to inhabit in our said colony, we do by these presents, for us, our heirs and successors, grant, establish and ordain, that forever hereafter, there shall be a liberty of conscience allowed in the worship of God, to all persons inhabiting, or which shall inhabit or be *resident* within our said province, and that all such persons, except papists, shall have a free exercise of their religion . . . [Thorpe 773]

Virginia Constitution, June 29, 1776:

The other shall be called The Senate, and consist of twenty-four members, of whom thirteen shall constitute a House to proceed on business; for whose election, the different counties shall be divided into twenty-four districts; and each county of the respective district, at the time of the election of its Delegates, shall vote for one Senator, who is actually a *resident* and freeholder within the district, or duly qualified according to law, and is upwards of twenty-five years of age . . . [Thorpe 3816]

Maryland Constitution, November 11, 1776:

[Form of Government, Article 2:] . . . and, when assembled, they shall proceed to elect, viva voce, four Delegates, for their respective counties, of the most wise, sensible, and discreet of the people, *residents* in the county where they are to be chosen, one whole year next preceding the election, above twenty-one years of age, and having in the State, real or personal property above the value of five hundred pounds current money . . . [Thorpe 1691]

[*Ibid.*, Article 15:] . . . and they [the electors], or any twenty-four of them, so met, shall proceed to elect, by ballot, either out of their own body, or the people at large, fifteen senators, (nine of whom to be *residents* on the western, and six to be *residents* on the eastern shore,) men of the most wisdom, experience, and virtue, above twenty-five years of age, *residents* of the state above three whole years next preceding the election, land having therein real and personal property, above the value of one thousand pounds, current money. [Thorpe 1694]

[*Ibid.*, Article 16:] That the senators shall be balloted for at one and the same time; and out of the gentlemen, *residents* of the western shore, who shall be proposed as senators, the nine who shall, on striking the ballots, appear to have greatest numbers in their favor, shall be accordingly declared and returned duly elected; and out of the gentlemen, *residents* on the eastern shore, who shall be proposed as senators, the six who shall, on striking the ballots, appear to have the greatest numbers in their favor, shall be accordingly declared and returned duly elected . . . [Thorpe 1694]

[*Ibid.,* Article 26:] That the senators and delegates, (on the second Tuesday of November, seventeen hundred and seventy-seven, and annually on the second Tuesday of November, for ever thereafter, elect by joint ballot (in the same manner as senators are directed to be chosen) five of the most sensible, discreet, and experienced men, above twenty-five years of age, *residents* in the state above three years next preceding the election . . . [Thorpe 1695]

[*Ibid.,* Article 27:] . . . That no person, unless above twenty-one years of age, and a *resident* in the state more than five years next preceding the election, and having real and personal estate in this state above the value of one thousand pounds current money, shall be eligible to sit in congress. [Thorpe 1695]

[*Ibid.,* Article 30:] That no person, unless above twenty-five years of age, a *resident* in this state above five years next preceding the election, and having in the state real and personal property above the value of five thousand pounds current money (one thousand pounds whereof, at least, to be of freehold estate) shall be eligible as governor. [Thorpe 1696]

[*Ibid.,* Article 46:] That all civil officers, hereafter to be appointed for the several counties of this State, shall have been *residents* of the county, respectively, for which they shall be appointed, six months next before their appointment; and shall continue *residents* of their county, respectively, during their continuance in office. [Thorpe 1699]

North Carolina Constitution, December 18, 1776:

[Form of Government, Article 15:] . . . That no person, under thirty years of age, and who has not been a *resident* in this State above five years, and having, in the State, a freehold in lands and tenements above the value of one thousand pounds, shall be eligible as a Governor. [Thorpe 2791]

Georgia Constitution, February 5, 1777:

[Article 6:] The representatives shall be chosen out of the *residents* in each county, who shall have resided at least twelve months in this State, and three months in the county where they shall be elected; except the freeholders of the counties of Glynn and Camden, who are in a state of alarm, and who shall have the liberty of choosing one member each, as specified in the articles of this constitution, in any other county, until they have *residents* sufficient to qualify them for more; and they shall be of the Protestant religion, and of the age of twenty-one years, and shall be possessed in their own right of two hundred and fifty acres of land, or some property to the amount of two hundred and fifty pounds. [Thorpe 779]

[Article 9:] All male white inhabitants, of the age of twenty-one years, and possessed in his own right of ten pounds value, and liable to pay tax in this State, or being of any mechanic trade, and shall have been *resident* six months in this State, shall have a right to vote at all elections for representatives, or any other officers, herein agreed to be chosen by the people at large; and every person having a right to vote at any election shall vote by ballot personally.

[Thorpe 779]

New York Constitution, April 20, 1777:

[Article 5:] . . . And further, that once in every seven years, after the taking of the said first census, a just account of the electors *resident* in each county shall be taken, and if it shall thereupon appear that the number of electors in any county shall have increased or diminished one or more seventieth parts of the whole number of electors, which, on the said first census, shall be found in this State, the number of representatives for such county shall be increased or diminished accordingly, that is to say, one representative for every seventieth part as aforesaid. [Thorpe 2630]

[Article 7:] . . . Provided always, That every person who now is a freeman of the city of Albany, or who was made a freeman of the city of New York on or before the fourteenth day of October, in the year of our Lord one thousand seven hundred and seventy-five, and shall be actually and usually *resident* in the said cities, respectively, shall be entitled to vote for representatives in assembly within his said place of residence. [Thorpe 2630–31]

South Carolina Constitution, March 19, 1778:

[Article 5:] That every person who shall be elected governor and commander-in-chief of the State, or lieutenant-governor, or a member of the privy council, shall be qualified as forthwith; that is to say, the governor and lieutenant-governor shall have been *residents* in this State for ten years and the members of the privy council five years, preceding their said election, and shall have in this State a settled plantation or freehold in their and each of their own right of the value of at least ten thousand pounds currency, clear of debt, and on being elected they shall respectively take an oath of qualification in the house of representatives. [Thorpe 3249]

[Article 12:] . . . and that no person shall be eligible to a seat in the said senate unless he be of the Protestant religion, and hath attained the age of thirty years, and hath been a *resident* in this State at least five years. Not less than thirteen members shall be a quorum to do business, but the president or any three members may adjourn from day to day. No person who resides in the parish or district for which he is elected shall take his seat in the senate, unless he possess a settled estate and freehold in his own right in the said parish or district of the value of two thousand pounds currency at least, clear of debt; and no non-*resident* shall be eligible to a seat in the said senate unless he is owner of a settled estate and freehold in his own right, in the parish or district where he is elected, of the value of seven thousand pounds currency at least, also clear of debt. [Thorpe 3250–51]

[Article 13:] . . . The qualification of electors shall be that every free white man, and no other person, who acknowledges the being of a God, and believes in a future state of rewards and punishments, and who has attained to the age of one and twenty years, and hath been a *resident* and an inhabitant in this State for the space of one whole year before the day appointed for the election he offers to give his vote at, and hath a freehold at least of fifty acres of land, or a town lot, and hath been legally seized and possessed of the same at least six months previous to such election, or hath paid a tax the preceding year, or was taxable the present year, at least six months previous to the said election, in a sum equal to the tax on fifty acres of land, to the support of this government, shall be deemed a person qualified to vote for, and shall be capable of electing, a representative or representatives to serve as a member or members in the senate and house of representatives, for the parish or district where he actually is a *resident,* or in any other parish or district in this State where he hath the like freehold. Electors shall take an oath or affirmation of qualification, if required by the returning officer. No person shall be eligible to sit in the house of representatives unless he be of the Protestant religion, and hath been a *resident* in this State for three years previous to his election. The qualification of the elected, if *residents* in the parish or district for which they shall be returned, shall be the same as mentioned in the election act, and construed to mean clear of debt. But no non-*resident* shall be eligible to a seat in the house of representatives unless he is owner of a settled estate and freehold in his own right of the value of three thousand and five hundred pounds currency at least, clear of debt, in the parish or district for which he is elected. [Thorpe 3251–52]

Massachusetts Constitution, March 2, 1780:

[Frame of Government, Chapter I:1:4:] . . . [The General Court has power] to impose and levy proportional and reasonable assessments, rates, and taxes, upon all the inhabitants of, and persons *resident,* and estates lying, within the said commonwealth; and also to impose and levy reasonable duties and excises upon any produce goods, wares, merchandise, and commodities, whatsoever . . . [Thorpe 1894]

[*Ibid.,* Chapter I:3:4:] Every male person, being twenty-one years of age, and *resident* in any particular town in this commonwealth for the space of one year next preceding, having a freehold estate within the said town of the annual income of three pounds, or any estate of the value of sixty pounds, shall have a right to vote in the choice of a representative or representatives for the said town. [Thorpe 1898]

United States Confederation Congress, Ordinance for the Government of the West, April 23, 1784:

That the lands of non-*resident* proprietors shall, in no case be taxed higher than those of *residents* within any new state, before the admission thereof to a vote by its delegates in Congress. [DHRC1 152]

New Hampshire Constitution, June 2, 1784:

[Form of Government:] . . . [The General Court has power] to impose and levy proportional and reasonable assessments, rates and taxes, upon all the inhabitants of, and *residents* within the said state; and upon all estates within the same . . . [Thorpe 2458]

United States Confederation Congress, The Northwest Ordinance, July 13, 1787:

[1] Be it ordained by the authority aforesaid, That the estates both of *resident* and non-*resident* proprietors in the said territory, dying intestate, shall descend to, and be distributed among, their children and the descendants of a deceased child in equal parts, the descendants of a deceased child or grandchild to take the share of their deceased parent in equal parts among them; and where there shall be no children or descendants, then in equal parts to the next of kin, in equal degree . . . [Thorpe 957–58]

[2] . . . Provided, That no person be eligible or qualified to act as a representative, unless he shall have been a citizen of one of the United States three years, and be a *resident* in the district, or unless he shall have resided in the district three years; and, in either case, shall likewise hold in his own right, in fee-simple, two hundred acres of land within the same: Provided also, That a freehold in fifty acres of land in the district, having been a citizen of one of the States, and being *resident* in the district, or the like freehold and two years' residence in the district, shall be necessary to qualify a man as an elector of a representative. [Thorpe 959]

[3] . . . As soon as representatives shall be elected the governor shall appoint a time and place for them to meet together, and when met they shall nominate ten persons, *residents* in the district, and each possessed of a freehold in five hundred acres of land, and return their names to Congress, five of whom Congress shall appoint and commission to serve as aforesaid . . . [Thorpe 959–60]

[4] [Article 4:] . . . No tax shall be imposed on land the property of the United States; and in no case shall non-*resident* proprietors be taxed higher than *residents*. The navigable waters leading into the Mississippi and Saint Lawrence, and the carrying places between the same, shall be common highways, and forever free, as well to the inhabitants of the said territory as to the citizens of the United States . . . [Thorpe 961]

"Nov. Anglus," December 12, 1787:

That there are a set of men now *resident* in this country, who are enemies to its political happiness, and who anticipate with horror a permanent national government, is a fact known to every man of observation. . . . [DHRC8 235]

James Madison, *The Federalist*, No. 43, January 23, 1788:

. . . Nothing can be more chimerical than to imagine that in a trial of actual force, victory may be calculated by the rules which prevail in a census of the inhabitants, or which determine the event of an election! May it not happen, in fine, that the minority of CITIZENS may become a majority of PERSONS, by the accession of alien *residents,* of a casual concourse of adventurers, or of those whom the constitution of the State has not admitted to the rights of suffrage? . . .

[Fed. 313–14]

Alexander C. Hanson, *Remarks on the Proposed Plan of a Federal Government*, c. January 31, 1788:

The house of representatives is to be the immediate choice of the people, and one man is to represent 30,000 souls. In an affair of so much importance, and in districts containing so many suffrages, it is not to be supposed, that a worthless character will succeed by those arts, which have, sometimes, prevailed in county elections. It is to be expected, that, in general, the people will choose men of talents and character. Were they even so inclined, they can choose none but of ripe age, who have been, at least, seven years citizens of the United States, and, at the time of election, *residents* of the respective state. Whatever laws shall be proposed, or assented to by these men, are to bind themselves, their children, and their connections. . . . [Ford 225]

South Carolina Constitution, June 3, 1790:

[Article I, Section 4:] Every free white man, of the age of twenty-one years, being a citizen of this State, and having resided therein two years previous to the day of election, and who hath a freehold of fifty acres of land or a town lot, of which he hath been legally seized and possessed at least six months before such election, or, not having such freehold or town lot, hath been a *resident* in the election district in which he offers to give his vote six months before the said election, and hath paid a tax the preceding year of three shillings sterling towards the support of this government, shall have a right to vote for a member or members to serve in either branch of the legislature for the election district in which he holds such property or is so *resident.* [Thorpe 3258–59]

[Article I, Section 6:] No person shall be eligible to a seat in the house of representatives unless he is a free white man, of the age of twenty-one years, and hath been a citizen and *resident* in this State three years previous to his election. If a *resident* in the election district, he shall not be eligible to a seat in the house of representatives unless he be legally seized and possessed in his own right of a settled freehold estate of five hundred acres of land and ten negroes, or of a real estate of the value of one hundred and fifty pounds sterling, clear of debt. If a non-*resident,* he shall be legally seized and possessed of a settled freehold estate therein of the value of five hundred pounds sterling, clear of debt. [Thorpe 3259]

[Article I, Section 8:] No person shall be eligible to a seat in the senate unless he is a free white man, of the age of thirty years, and hath been a citizen and *resident* in this State give years previous to his election. If a *resident* in the election district, he shall not be eligible unless he be legally seized and possessed, in his own right, of a settled freehold estate of the value of three hundred pounds sterling, clear of debt. If a non-*resident* in the election district, he shall not be eligible unless he be legally seized and possessed in his own right of a settled freehold estate in the said district of the value of one thousand pounds sterling, clear of debt. [Thorpe 3259–60]

RESOLUTION

(Legislative)

[Note: This list concentrates on general discussions of legislative resolutions; only a small sample of the large number of references to specific legislation is included.]

United States Constitution, September 17, 1787:

[Article I, Section 7:] Every Order, *Resolution,* or Vote to which the Concurrence of the Senate and House of Representatives may be necessary (except on a question of Adjournment) shall be presented to the President of the United States; and before the Same shall take Effect, shall be approved by him, or being disapproved by him, shall be repassed by two thirds of the Senate and House of Representatives, according to the Rules and Limitations prescribed in the Case of a Bill.

* * * * *

Charter of the Dutch West India Company, June 3, 1621:

[Article 11:] And that this company may be strengthened by a good government, to the greatest profit and satisfaction of all concerned, we have ordained, that the said government shall be vested in five chambers of managers; one at Amsterdam,—this shall have the management of four-ninths parts; one chamber in Zealand, for two-ninth parts; one chamber at the Maeze, for one-ninth part; one chamber in North Holland, for one-ninth-part; and the fifth chamber in Friesland, with the city and country, for one-ninth part; upon the condition entered in the record of our *resolutions,* and the Act past respecting it. . . . [Thorpe 61–62]

[Article 20:] The aforesaid general meeting being summoned, it shall meet to resolve when they shall fit out, and how many vessels they will send to each place, the company in general observing that no particular chamber shall undertake any, thing in opposition to the foregoing *resolution,* but shall be held to carry the same effectually into execution. And if any chamber shall be found not following the common *resolution,* or contravening it, we have authorized, and by these presents do authorize, the said meeting, immediately to cause reparation to be made of every defect or contravention, wherein we, being desired, will assist them. [Thorpe 63]

[Article 40:] . . . Provided that all the ships of war and merchant-men (that shall be with those provided and manned as aforesaid) shall be under an admiral appointed by us according to the previous advise of the aforesaid General Company, and shall obey our commands, together with the *resolutions* of the Company, if it shall be necessary, in the same manner as in time of war; so notwithstanding that the merchantmen shall not unnecessarily hazard their lading. [Thorpe 66]

[Article 42:] . . . in case of a war, all the prizes which shall be taken from enemies and pirates within the aforesaid limits, by the Company or their assistants; also the goods which shall be seized by virtue of our proclamation, after deducting all expenses and the damage which the Company shall suffer in taking each prize, together with the just part of his excellency the admiral, agreeable to our *resolution* of the first of April sixteen hundred and two . . . [Thorpe 66]

Surrender of the Patent of Plymouth Colony to the Freemen, March 2, 1640:

. . . Be it Knowne unto all men therefore by these presents That the said William Bradford for himself his heires together with the said purchasers do onely reserve unto themselves their heires and assignes those three tracts of land menconed in the said *resolucon* order and agreement . . . [Thorpe 1862]

Fundamental Constitutions of East New Jersey, 1683:

. . . And that all things may proceed in good order, the said committee shall propound to the great Council what they judge convenient and necessary for the keeping the peace within the said Province, and for publick defence without, by the said great Council to be approved and corrected, as they, according to exigence of affairs, shall judge fit; the execution of which *resolutions* of the great Council shall be committed to the care of the said committee. But because through the scruples of such of the Proprietors, or their proxies, as have no freedom to use arms, the *resolutions* of the great Council may be in this point obstructed, it is resolved and agreed, and it is by these presents resolved and agreed, that in things of this nature, the votes of these Proprietors shall only be of weight at such time or times as one of these two points are under deliberation, which shall not be concluded where twelve of the Proprietors and two thirds of the whole Council, as in other cases, are not consenting . . . [Thorpe 2577]

English Bill of Rights, December 16, 1689:

Upon which Their said Majesties did accept the crown and royal dignity of the kingdoms of England, France and Ireland and the dominions thereunto belonging, according to the *resolution* and desire of the said Lords and commons, contained in the said declaration. [SDECH 466]

First Continental Congress, Declaration and Resolves, October 14, 1774:

To these grievous acts and measures, Americans cannot submit, but in hopes that their fellow subjects in Great- Britain will, on a revision of them, restore us to that state in which both countries found happiness and prosperity, we have for the present only *resolved* to pursue the following peaceable measures: . . . 3. To prepare a loyal address to his Majesty, agreeable to *Resolutions* already entered into. [JCC1 73]

South Carolina Constitution, March 26, 1776:

[Article 25:] That the president and commander-in-chief, with the advice and consent of the privy council, may appoint during pleasure, until otherwise directed by *resolution* of the general assembly and legislative council, all other necessary officers, except such as are by law directed to be otherwise chosen. [Thorpe 3247]

[Article 28:] That the *resolutions* of the Continental Congress, now of force in this colony, shall so continue until altered or revoked by them. [Thorpe 3247]

[Article 29:] That the *resolutions* of this or any former congress of this colony, and all laws now of force here, (and not hereby altered,) shall so continue until altered or repealed by the legislature of this colony, unless where they are temporary, in which case they shall expire at the times respectively limited for their duration. [Thorpe 3247]

Delaware Constitution, September 10, 1776:

[Article 24:] All acts of assembly in force in this State on the 15th day of May last (and not hereby altered, or contrary to the *resolutions* of Congress or of the late house of assembly of this State) shall so continue, until altered or repealed by the legislature of this State, unless where they are temporary in which case they shall expire at the times respectively limited for their duration. [Thorpe 566]

Pennsylvania Constitution, September 28, 1776:

[Frame of Government, Section 10:] . . . I ——— do swear (or affirm) that as a member of this assembly, I will not propose or assent to any bill, vote, or *resolution,* which shall appear to me injurious to the people . . . [Thorpe 3085]

[*Ibid.*, Section 14:] The votes and proceedings of the general assembly shall be printed weekly during their sitting, with the yeas and nays, on any question, vote or *resolution*, where any two members require it, except when the vote is taken by ballot; and when the yeas and nays are so taken every member shall have a right to insert the reasons of his vote upon the minutes, if he desires it. [Thorpe 3085–86]

New York Constitution, April 20, 1777:

[Preamble, quoting the New York Provincial Congress, May 31, 1776:] "Resolved, That it be recommended to the electors in the several counties in this colony, by election, in the manner and form prescribed for the election of the present congress, either to authorize (in addition to the powers vested in this congress) their present deputies, or others in the stead of their present deputies, or either of them, to take in to consideration the necessity and propriety of instituting such new government as in and by the said *resolution* of the Continental Congress is described and recommended . . ." [Thorpe 2625]

[*Ibid.*:] "And whereas the object of the aforegoing *resolutions* is of the utmost importance to the good people of this colony . . ." [Thorpe 2625]

[Body of constitution:] And whereas the good people of the said colony, in pursuance of the said *resolution*, and reposing special trust and confidence in the members of this convention, have appointed, authorized, and empowered them for the purposes, and in the manner, and with the powers in and by the said resolve specified, declared, and mentioned. [Thorpe 2625]

[*Ibid.*:] By virtue of which several acts, declarations, and proceedings mentioned and contained in the afore-cited resolves or *resolutions* of the general Congress of the United American States, and of the congresses or conventions of this State, all power whatever therein hath reverted to the people thereof . . . [Thorpe 2628]

[Article 35:] . . . And this convention doth further ordain that the resolves or *resolutions* of the congresses of the colony of New York, and of the convention of the State of New York, now in force, and not repugnant to the government established by this constitution, shall be considered as making part of the laws of this State . . . [Thorpe 2636]

Vermont Constitution, July 8, 1777:

[Frame of Government, Section 9:] I ——— do solemnly swear, by the ever living God, (or, I do solemnly affirm in the presence of Almighty God) that as a member of this assembly, I will not propose or assent to any bill, vote, or *resolution*, which shall appear to me injurious to the people . . . [Thorpe 3743]

[*Ibid.*, Section 13:] The votes and proceedings of the General Assembly shall be printed, weekly, during their sitting, with the yeas and nays, on any question, vote or *resolution,* where one-third of the members require it; (except when the votes are taken by ballot) and when the yeas and nays are so taken, every member shall have a right to insert the reasons of his votes upon the minutes, if he desire it. [Thorpe 3744]

South Carolina Constitution, March 19, 1778:

[Article 34:] That the *resolutions* of the late congress of this State, and all laws now of force here, (and not hereby altered,) shall so continue until altered or repealed by the legislature of this State, unless where they are temporary, in which case they shall expire at the times respectively limited for their duration. [Thorpe 3255]

Massachusetts Constitution, March 2, 1780:

[Chapter II:3:5:] The *resolutions* and advice of the council shall be recorded in a register, and signed by the members present; and this record may be called for at any time by either house of the legislature; and any member of the council may insert his opinion, contrary to the *resolution* of the majority. [Thorpe 1904]

New Hampshire Constitution, June 2, 1784:

[Form of Government:] The *resolutions* and advice of the council shall be recorded in a register, and signed by the members present, and this record may be called for at any time, by either house of the legislature, and any member of the council may enter his opinion contrary to the *resolution* of the majority. [Thorpe 2466]

United States Confederation Congress, Ordinance on the Western Territory, May 20, 1785:

[1] And whereas Congress by their *resolution* of September 16th and 18th, in the year 1776, and the 12th of August 1780, stipulated grants of land to certain officers and soldiers of the late continental army, and by the *resolution* of 22d September 1780, stipulated grants of land to certain officers in the hospital department of the late continental army; for complying therefore with such engagements, Be it ordained, That the secretary at war, from the returns in his office, or such other sufficient evidence as the nature of the case may admit, determine who are the objects of the above *resolutions* and engagements, and the quantity of land to which such persons or their representatives are respectively entitled, and cause the townships, or fractional parts of townships, hereinbefore reserved for the use of the late continental army, to be drawn for in such manner as he shall deem expedient, to answer the purpose of an impartial distribution. . . . [DHRC1 161]

[2] And be it further ordained, That three townships adjacent to lake Erie be reserved to be hereafter disposed of by Congress, for the use of the officers, men, and others, refugees from Canada, and the refugees from Nova-Scotia, who are or may be entitled to grants of land under *resolutions* of Congress now existing, or which may hereafter be made respecting them, and for such other purposes as Congress may hereafter direct. [DHRC1 162]

Vermont Constitution, July 4, 1786:

[Frame of Government, Section 12:] You ——— do solemnly swear, (or affirm) that, as a member of this Assembly, you will not propose or assent to any bill, vote or *resolution,* which shall appear to you injurious to the people . . . [Thorpe 3757]

United States Confederation Congress, the Northwest Ordinance, July 13, 1787:

[Article VI:] Be it ordained by the authority aforesaid, That the *resolutions* of the 23d of April, 1784, relative to the subject of this ordinance, be, and the same are hereby, repealed, and declared null and void. [Thorpe 1962]

Edmund Randolph, Letter on the Federal Constitution, October 10, 1787:

[1] Should the people of America surrender these powers, they can be paramount to the constitutions and ordinary acts of legislation, only by being delegated by them. I do not pretend to affirm, but I venture to believe, that if the confederation had been solemnly questioned in opposition to our constitution or even to one of our laws, posterior to it, it must have given way. For never did it obtain with us a higher ratification, than a *resolution* of Assembly in the daily form. [DHRC8 267]

[2] It is said in the *resolutions,* which accompany the constitution, that it is to be submitted to a convention of delegates chosen in each State by the people thereof, for their assent and ratification. . . . [DHRC8 271]

***Virginia Herald*, October 11, 1787:**

. . . The expediency of the plan of government which they have proposed arises from the provisions which they have so judiciously made for preventing insurrections against the laws, and for procuring obedience to the federal constitution. We have seen with how much contempt the *resolutions* of our Congress have been treated, when they have laid before the states, in the most expressive terms, the necessity of adopting certain measures which they have proposed. . . . [DHRC8 52]

Noah Webster, *An Examination of the Leading Principles of the Federal Constitution*, October 17, 1787:

[1] . . . I will instance only their *resolution* to build a Federal Town. When we were involved in a debt, of which we could hardly pay the interest, and when Congress could not command a shilling, the very proposition was extremely absurd. Congress themselves became ashamed of the *resolution,* and rescinded it with as much silence as possible. Many other acts of that body are equally reprehensible—but respect forbids me to mention them. [Ford 32–33]

[2] . . . This foolish *resolution* [in Connecticut] would have disgraced school boys—the senate saved the honor of the state, by rejecting it with disdain—and within two months, every representative was ashamed of the conduct of the house. All public bodies have these fits of passion, when their conduct seems to be perfectly boyish; and in these paroxisms, a check is highly necessary. [Ford 33]

[3] Pennsylvania exhibits many instances of this hasty conduct. At one session of the legislature, an armed force is ordered, by a precipitate *resolution,* to expel the settlers at Wioming from their possessions—at a succeeding session, the same people are confirmed in their possessions. . . . [Ford 33–34]

Petersburg, Virginia, Town Meeting, October 24, 1787:

That these *resolutions* be forwarded to the delegates of Dinwiddie and Prince George, who are requested to use their influence for immediately calling a convention to be held at as early a day as circumstances will possibly admit. [DHRC8 97]

Virginia General Assembly Proceedings, October 25, 1787:

[1] . . . Mr. Mathews reported that the committee had, according to order, had the said report under their consideration, and gone through the same, and come to several *resolutions* thereupon, which he read in his place, and afterwards delivered in at the clerk's table, where the same were again read . . . [DHRC8 112]

[2] The second, third, fourth, fifth, sixth and last *resolutions* were severally read a second time, and, on the question put thereupon, agreed to by the House. [DHRC8 112]

John Dawson and James Monroe to the Freeholders of Fredericksburg, Virginia, October 26, 1787:

On yesterday we went into a committee of the whole, and now take the liberty of forwarding to you several *resolutions* which were unanimously agreed to. . . . [DHRC8 121]

Pelatiah Webster, *The Weakness of Brutus Exposed*, November 4, 1787:

The particular interest which every member of Congress has in every public order and *resolution,* is another strong motive to right action. For every act to which any member gives his sanction, if it be raising an army, levying a tax, instituting a court, or any other act to bind the States,—such act will equally bind himself, his nearest connections, and his posterity. [Ford 124]

"A True Friend," November 14, 1787:

France has offered us some advantages in her free ports. She allows us a trade with her islands limited to certain articles. What have we done, and what can we do to requite it, and obtain more prerogatives? And what can we do to guard against the prohibitions of other nations? As long as we shall only be able to pass partial *resolutions,* crossed, and rendered useless by the other legislative powers. [DHRC8 160]

Letter on the Virginia Convention, November 17, 1787, published in *Virginia Independent Chronicle*, December 5, 1787:

The *resolution* of the Assembly for calling a convention, have just come to hand. They are in the highest degree excellent. There is not an expression omitted, which I could wish to have in. . . . [DHRC8 200]

Alexander Hamilton, *The Federalist*, No. 15, December 1, 1787:

[1] . . . Except as to the rule of apportionment, the United States has an indefinite discretion [under the Confederation] to make requisitions for men and money; but they have no authority to raise either, by regulations extending to the individual citizens of America. The consequence of this is, that though in theory their *resolutions* concerning those objects are laws, constitutionally binding on the members of the Union, yet in practice they are mere recommendations which the States observe or disregard at their option. [Fed. 158]

[2] Government implies the power of making laws. It is essential to the idea of a law, that it be attended with a sanction; or, in other words, a penalty or punishment for disobedience. If there be no penalty annexed to disobedience, the *resolutions* or commands which pretend to be laws will, in fact, amount to nothing more than advice or recommendation. . . . [Fed. 159]

[3] . . . This simple proposition will teach us, how little reason there is to expect, that the persons intrusted with the administration of the affairs of the particular members of a confederacy will at all times be ready, with perfect good-humor, and an unbiased regard to the public weal, to execute the *resolutions* or decrees of the general authority. . . . [Fed. 161]

[4] . . . Those who have been conversant in the proceedings of popular assemblies; who have seen how difficult it often is, where there is no exterior pressure of circumstances, to bring them to harmonious *resolutions* on important points, will readily conceive how impossible it must be to induce a number of such assemblies, deliberating at a distance from each other, at different times, and under different impressions, long to cooperate in the same views and pursuits. [Fed. 161]

Alexander Hamilton, *The Federalist*, No. 16, December 4, 1787:

[1] The result of these observations to an intelligent mind must be clearly this, that if it be possible at any rate to construct a federal government capable of regulating the common concerns and preserving the general tranquillity, it must be founded, as to the objects committed to its care, upon the reverse of the principle contended for by the opponents of the proposed Constitution. It must carry its agency to the persons of the citizens. It must stand in need of no intermediate legislation; but must itself be empowered to employ the arm of the ordinary magistrate to execute its own *resolutions*. The majesty of the national authority must be manifested through the medium of the courts of justice. . . . [Fed. 165]

[2] . . . If the judges were not embarked in a conspiracy with the legislature, they would pronounce the *resolutions* of such a majority to be contrary to the supreme law of the land, unconstitutional, and void. . . . [Fed. 166]

James Madison, *The Federalist*, No. 19, December 8, 1787:

The prerogatives of the [Holy Roman] emperor are numerous. The most important of them are: his exclusive right to make propositions to the diet; to negative its *resolutions;* to name ambassadors; to confer dignities and titles; to fill vacant electorates . . . [Fed. 178]

Alexander Hamilton, *The Federalist*, No. 21, December 12, 1787:

The next most palpable defect of the subsisting Confederation is the total want of a SANCTION to its laws. The United States,as now composed, have no powers to exact obedience, or punish disobedience to the *resolutions,* either by pecuniary mulcts, by a suspension of divestiture of privileges, or by any other constitutional mode. . . . [Fed. 186]

Alexander Hamilton, *The Federalist*, No. 22, December 14, 1787:

It may be objected to this, that not seven but nine States, or two thirds of the whole number, must consent to the most important *resolutions;* and it may be thence inferred that nine States would always comprehend a majority of the

Union. But this does not obviate the impropriety of an equal vote between States of the most unequal dimensions and populousness . . . [Fed. 194]

Dissent of the Pennsylvania Convention's Minority, December 18, 1787:

[1] Affairs were in this situation when on the 28th of September last, a *resolution* was proposed to the assembly by a member of the house who had been also a member of the federal convention, for calling a state convention to be elected within ten days for the purpose of examining and adopting the proposed constitution of the United States, though at this time the house had not received it from Congress. . . . [DHRC2 620–21]

[2] . . . That violence and outrage which had been so often threatened was now practiced; some of the members were seized the next day by a mob collected for the purpose, and forcibly dragged to the house, and there detained by force whilst the quorum of the legislature, so formed, completed their *resolution*. . . . [DHRC2 621]

[3] [Quoting Montesquieu:] . . . "There would be an end of everything, were the same man, or the same body of the nobles, or of the people, to exercise those three powers; that of enacting laws; that of executing the public *resolutions;* and that of judging the crimes or differences of individuals." [DHRC2 635]

Alexander Hamilton, *The Federalist*, No. 26, December 22, 1787:

The legislature of the United States will be obliged, by this provision, once at least in every two years, to deliberate upon the propriety of keeping a military force on foot; to come to a new *resolution* on the point; and to declare their sense of the matter, by a formal vote in the face of their constituents. . . . [Fed. 216]

James Madison, *The Federalist*, No. 40, January 18, 1788:

The recommendatory act of Congress is in the words following: "Whereas, there is provision in the articles of Confederation and perpetual Union, for making alterations therein, by the assent of a Congress of the United States, and of the legislatures of the several States; and whereas experience hath evinced that there are defects in the present Confederation; as a mean to remedy which, several of the States, and particularly the State of New York, by express instructions to their delegates in Congress, have suggested a convention for the purposes expressed in the following *resolution;* and such convention appearing to be the most probable mean of establishing in these States a firm national government." [Fed. 286–87]

Massachusetts Convention, Ratification of the Constitution, February 6, 1788:

The convention having impartially discussed, and fully considered, the constitution for the United States of America, reported to Congress, by the convention of delegates from the United States, of America, and submitted to us, by a *resolution* of the General Court of the said commonwealth, passed the twenty fifth day of October last past . . . [DHRC16 67–68]

[2] RESOLVED, That the assent and ratification aforesaid be engrossed on parchment, together with the recommendation and injunction aforesaid, and with this *resolution* . . . [DHRC16 69]

James Madison, *The Federalist*, No. 52, February 8, 1788:

. . . Virginia was the colony which stood first in resisting the parliamentary usurpations of Great Britain; it was the first also in espousing, by public act, the *resolution* of independence. . . . [Fed. 363]

Luther Martin, "Genuine Information," No. 12, February 8, 1788:

. . . Accordingly as the *resolutions* were originally adopted by the convention, and as they were reported by the committee of detail, it was proposed that this system should be laid before Congress for their approbation . . . [DHRC16 90]

James Madison, *The Federalist*, No. 54, February 12, 1788:

. . . The new Constitution is, in this respect, materially different from the existing Confederation, as well as from that of the United Netherlands, and other similar confederacies. In each of the latter, the efficacy of the federal *resolutions* depends on the subsequent and voluntary *resolutions* of the states composing the union. Hence the states, though possessing an equal vote in the public councils, have an unequal influence, corresponding with the unequal importance of these subsequent and voluntary *resolutions*. Under the proposed Constitution, the federal acts will take effect without the necessary intervention of the individual States. . . . [Fed. 373]

Alexander White, "To the Citizens of Virginia," February 22, 1788:

[1] . . . They set out with asserting that the present confederation carried us successfully through the war, when it is notorious that it did not receive the sanction of the states till after the decisive blow was struck in the field, and the treaty of alliance concluded with France; before this time Congress exercised unlimited powers, and their *resolutions* were carried into effect by the spirit of the people. [DHRC8 403]

[2] . . . They state that on the 28th day of September last a *resolution* passed the house of assembly for calling a convention to be elected within ten days.—This was not the fact, the election was appointed on the 1st Tuesday in November, 39 days after passing the *resolution*. Is it possible they can be ignorant of this? . . . [DHRC8 403]

[3] [Quoting Polybius:] " . . . Upon them [the consuls] turned whatever related to the deliberations of the senate. They admitted ambassadors into it; proposed the public affairs, and reduced its *resolutions* to form, in writing—They carried them to the people . . . " [DHRC8 406]

James Madison, *The Federalist*, No. 62, February 27, 1788:

[1] Another advantage accruing from this ingredient in the Constitution of the Senate is, the additional impediment it must prove against improper acts of legislation. No law or *resolution* can now be passed without the concurrence, first, of a majority of the people, and then, of a majority of the States. . . . [Fed. 409]

[2] The necessity of a senate is not less indicated by the propensity of all single and numerous assemblies to yield to the impulse of sudden and violent passions, and to be seduced by factious leaders into intemperate and pernicious *resolutions*. Examples on this subject might be cited without number . . . [Fed. 410]

John Hancock, Speech to the Massachusetts Assembly, February 27, 1788:

. . . The Convention which you appointed to deliberate upon that important subject, have concluded their Session, after having adopted & ratified the proposed plan, according to their *resolution*, a copy whereof, I have directed the Secretary to lay before you. [DHRC16 224–25]

"An Impartial Citizen," No. 5, February 28, 1788:

. . . As in the nature of things unanimity cannot be obtained in the decisions of popular assemblies, almost all nations among whom *resolutions* are formed by suffrages, have fixed upon a majority of voices as the most obvious, easy, and natural criterion of determination. . . . [DHRC8 432–33]

Mercy Otis Warren, *Observations on the New Constitution*, February 1788:

. . . This circumstance is regretted in strong terms by Mr. [Luther] Martin, a member from Maryland, who acknowledges "He had no idea that all the wisdom, integrity, and virtue of the States was contained in that Convention, and that he wished to have corresponded with gentlemen of eminent political characters abroad, and to give their sentiments due weight''—he adds, ''so extremely solicitous were they, that their proceedings should not transpire, that the members were prohibited from taking copies of their *resolutions,* or extracts from the Journals, without express permission, by vote.'' . . . [DHRC16 285]

Alexander Hamilton, *The Federalist*, No. 68, March 12, 1788:

The appointment of an extraordinary person, as Vice-President, has been objected to as superfluous, if not mischievous. It has been alleged, that it would have been preferable to have authorized the Senate to elect out of their own body an officer answering that description. But two considerations seem to justify the ideas of the convention in this respect. One is, that to secure at all times the possibility of a definite *resolution* of the body, it is necessary that the President should have only a casting vote. And to take the senator of any State from his seat as senator, to place him in that of President of the Senate, would be to exchange, in regard to the State from which he came, a constant for a contingent vote. . . . [Fed. 443]

George Nicholas [?], ''The State Soldier,'' No. 3, March 12, 1788:

[Footnote:] See Journals of Assembly of Virginia 1784, *resolution* proposing to give Congress a right to compel the states to comply with their requisitions by force of arms—Who by?— [DHRC8 489]

Alexander Hamilton, *The Federalist*, No. 70, March 15, 1788:

[1] New York has no council except for the single purpose of appointing to offices; New Jersey has a council whom the governor may consult. But I think, from the terms of the constitution, their *resolutions* do not bind him. [Fed. 452n]

[2] . . . In the legislature, promptitude of decision is oftener an evil than a benefit. The differences of opinion, and the jarrings of parties in that department of the government, though they may sometimes obstruct salutary plans, yet often promote deliberation and circumspection, and serve to check excesses in the majority. When a *resolution* too is once taken, the opposition must be at an end. That *resolution* is a law, and resistance to it punishable. . . . [Fed. 454]

[3] ''I was overruled by my council. The council were so divided in their opinions that it was impossible to obtain any better *resolution* on the point.'' These and similar pretexts are constantly at hand, whether true or false. . . . [Fed. 455]

[4] . . . But even there [in England] the king is not bound by the *resolutions* of his council, though they are answerable for the advice they give. He is the absolute master of his own conduct in the exercise of his office, and may observe or disregard the counsel given to him at his sole discretion. [Fed. 456]

Alexander Hamilton, *The Federalist*, No. 73, March 21, 1788:

[1] The first thing that offers itself to our observation, is the qualified negative of the President upon the acts or *resolutions* of the two houses of the legislature; or, in other words, his power of returning all bills with objections, to have the effect of preventing their becoming laws, unless they should afterwards be ratified by two thirds of each of the component members of the legislative body. [Fed. 468]

[2] . . . From these clear and indubitable principles results the propriety of a negative, either absolute or qualified, in the Executive, upon the acts of the legislative branches. Without the one or the other, the former would be absolutely unable to defend himself against the depredations of the latter. He might gradually be stripped of his authorities by successive *resolutions,* or annihilated by a single vote. And in the one mode or the other, the legislative and executive powers might speedily come to be blended in the same hands. . . . [Fed. 469]

[3] . . . A king of Great Britain, with all his train of sovereign attributes, and with all the influence he draws from a thousand sources, would, at this day, hesitate to put a negative upon the joint *resolutions* of the two houses of Parliament. . . . [Fed. 470]

[4] . . . It is to be hoped that it will not often happen that improper views will govern so large a proportion as two thirds of both branches of the legislature at the same time; and this, too, in spite of the counterposing weight of the Executive. It is at any rate far less probable that this should be the case, than that such views should taint the *resolutions* and conduct of a bare majority. . . . [Fed. 472]

Samuel Bryan, "Centinel," No. 17, March 24, 1788:

. . . In the face of a *resolution* of Congress of the 20th June, 1785, declaring their intention of appointing 3 commissioners, to settle and adjust the receipts and expenditures of the late financier [Robert Morris]; the conspirators have asserted, that his accounts were finally settled in November, 1784, for which they pretend to have vouchers, and by a pompous display of certain *resolutions* of Congress, respecting a particular charge of fraud against him, as commercial agent to the United States, they vainly hope to divert the public attention from his great delinquency, in never accounting for the millions of public money, entrusted to him in that line. . . . [DHRC16 475]

Alexander Hamilton, *The Federalist*, No. 75, March 26, 1788:

[1] . . . It has been shown, under the second head of our inquiries, that all provisions which require more than the majority of any body to its *resolutions,* have a direct tendency to embarrass the operations of the government, and an indirect one to subject the sense of the majority to that of the minority. . . . [Fed. 478]

[2] To require a fixed proportion of the whole body would not, in all probability, contribute to the advantages of a numerous agency, better than merely to require a proportion of the attending members. The former, by making a determinate number at all times requisite to a *resolution,* diminishes the motives to punctual attendance. The latter, by making the capacity of the body to depend on a proportion which may be varied by the absence or presence of a single member, has the contrary effect. And as, by promoting punctuality, it tends to keep the body complete, that is great likelihood that its *resolutions* would generally be dictated by as great a number in this case as in the other; while there would be much fewer occasions of delay. [Fed. 479]

Alexander Hamilton, *The Federalist*, No. 76, April 1, 1788:

. . . A single well-directed man, by a single understanding, cannot be distracted and warped by that diversity of views, feelings, and interests, which frequently distract and warp the *resolutions* of a collective body. There is nothing so apt to agitate the passions of mankind as personal considerations, whether they relate to ourselves or to others, who are to be the objects of our choice or preference . . . [Fed. 481]

John Dickinson, "Fabius," No. 1, April 10, 1788:

Every person appears to be affected. Those who wish the adoption of the plan [i.e., the Constitution], consider its rejection as the source of endless contests, confusions, and misfortunes; and they also consider a *resolution* to alter, without previously adopting it, as a rejection. [Ford 165]

Alexander Hamilton, *The Federalist*, No. 78, May 28, 1788:

. . . The judiciary, on the contrary, has no influence over either the sword or the purse; no direction either of the strength or of the wealth of the society; and can take no active *resolution* whatever. It may truly be said to have neither FORCE nor WILL, but merely judgment; and must ultimately depend upon the aid of the executive arm even for the efficacy of its judgments. [Fed. 490]

John Dickinson, "Fabius," No. 4, 1788:

Another question remains. How are the contributed rights to be managed? The *resolution* has been in great measure anticipated, by what has been said concerning the system proposed. Some few reflections may perhaps finish it. [Ford 181]

John Dickinson, "Fabius," No. 5, 1788:

While the danger was at some distance, the states of Greece looked to remote friends for assistance. Disappointed in these speculations, tho' the vast arma-ments of their enemies were constantly rolling towards them, still there was no firmness in their union, no vigor in their *resolutions*. [Ford 191n]

John Dickinson, "Fabius," No. 7, 1788:

. . . For history informs us, that so true were they [the Greek Achaen League] to their noble and benevolent principles, that, in their diet, "no *resolutions* were taken, but what were equally advantageous to the whole confederacy, and the interest of each part so consulted, as to leave no room for complaints."

[Ford 201–202]

Pennsylvania Constitution, September 2, 1790:

[Article I, Section 23:] Every order, *resolution,* or vote to which the concurrence of both houses may be necessary (except on a question of adjournment) shall be presented to the governor, and, before it shall take effect, be approved by him, or, being disapproved, shall be repassed by two-thirds of both houses, according to the rules and limitations prescribed in case of a bill.

[Thorpe 3095]

REVENUE

[Note: This is a sample list, consisting of all references in constitutions and fundamental laws and one out of three of the remaining occurrences in the database.]

United States Constitution, September 17, 1787:

[Article I, Section 7:] All Bills for raising *Revenue* shall originate in the House of Representatives; but the Senate may propose or concur with Amendments as on other Bills.

[Article I, Section 9:] No Preference shall be given by any Regulation of Commerce or *Revenue* to the Ports of one State over those of another: nor shall Vessels bound to, or from, one State, be obliged to enter, clear, or pay Duties in another.

* * * * *

Charles I, Charter of Maryland, June 20, 1632:

[Article 10:] We will also, and of our more abundant Grace, for Us, our Heirs and Successors, do firmly charge, constitute, ordain, and command, that the said Province be of our Allegiance; and that all and singular the Subjects and Liege-Men of Us, our Heirs and Successors, transplanted, or hereafter to be transplanted into the Province aforesaid, and the Children of them, and of others their Descendants, whether already born there, or hereafter to be born, be and shall be Natives and Liege-Men of Us, our Heirs and Successors, of our Kingdom of England and Ireland; and in all Things shall be held, treated, reputed, and esteemed as the faithful Liege-Men of Us, and our Heirs and Successors, born within our Kingdom of England; also Lands, Tenements, *Revenues,* Services, and other Hereditaments whatsoever, within our Kingdom of England, and other our Dominions, to inherit, or otherwise purchase, receive, take, have, hold, buy, and possess, and the same to use and enjoy, and the same to give, sell, alien and bequeath . . . [Thorpe 1681]

Charles II, Grant of the Province of Maine to the Duke of York, March 12, 1664:

. . . appertaining with theire and every of theire appurtenances and all our estate right title interest benefitt advantage claime and demand of in or to the said lands and premises or any part or parcell thereof and the revercon and revercons remainder and remainders together with the yearly and other ye rents *revenues* and proffitts of all and singular the said premisses and of every part and parcell thereof to have and to hold all and singular the said lands islands hereditaments and premisses with their and every of their appurtenances hereby given and granted or hereinbefore menconed to be given and granted unto our dearest brother James Duke of Yorke . . . [Thorpe 1638]

Fundamental Constitutions of Carolina, March 1, 1669:

[Article 43:] The treasurer's court, consisting of a proprietor and his six councillors, called under-treasurers, shall take care of all matters that concern the public *revenue* and treasury. The twelve assistants shall be called auditors. [Thorpe 2777]

[Article 115:] All *revenues* and profits belonging to the lords proprietors in common shall be divided into ten parts, whereof the palatine shall have three, and each proprietor one; but if the palatine shall govern by a deputy, the deputy shall have one of those three-tenths, and the palatine the other two-tenths. [Thorpe 2785]

Charles II, Grant of the Province of Maine to the Duke of York, June 29, 1674:

. . . And all our Estate right title and interest benefit and advantage claime and demand of in or to the said lands or premisses or any part or parcell thereof and the revercon and revercons remainder and remainders together with the yearly and other rents *revenues* and proffits of the premises and of every part and parcell thereof [Thorpe 1641]

New Jersey Proprietors, Deed of Revision, July 1, 1676:

. . . and the reversion and reversions, remainder and remainders; together with the yearly and other rents, *revenues,* and profits of all and singular the said premisses, and every part and parcel thereof; to have and to hold unto his said Majesty's said dear brother, the said James Duke of York, his heirs and assigns for ever . . . [Thorpe 2552]

Duke of York, Grant of West New Jersey, August 6, 1680:

. . . with their and every of their appurtenances, and all his said Majesty's estate, right, titles, interest, benefit, advantage, claim and demand of, in and to the same premises, or any part or parcel thereof, and the reversion and reversions, remainder, and remainders, together with the yearly and other rents, *revenues* and profits of the same, and of every part and parcel thereof, to hold unto his said Royal Highness, the said James Duke of York, his heirs and assigns for ever . . . [Thorpe 2561]

Duke of York, Confirmation to New Jersey Proprietors, March 14, 1682:

. . . and all his said Majesty's estate, right, title, interest, benefit, advantage, claim and demand of, in and to the same premises, or any part or parcel thereof, and the reversion and reversions, remainder and remainders, together with the yearly and other rents, *revenues* and profits of the same, and of every part and parcel thereof, to hold unto his said Royal Highness the said James, Duke of York, his heirs and assigns forever . . . [Thorpe 2568]

George II, Charter of Georgia, June 9, 1732:

. . . And our will and pleasure is, that the common council of the said corporation for the time being, or the major part of them who shall be present, being assembled for that purpose, shall from time to time, for, and during, and unto the full end and expiration of twenty-one years, to commence from the date of these our letters patent, have full power and authority to nominate, make, constitute and commission, ordain and appoint, by such name or names, style or styles, as to them shall seem meet and fitting, all and singular such governors, judges, magistrates, ministers and officers, civil and military, both by sea and land, within the said districts, as shall by them be thought fit and needful to be made or used for the said government of the said colony; save always, and except such offices only as shall by us, our heirs and successors, be from time to time constituted and appointed, for the managing collecting and receiving such *revenues,* as shall from time to time arise within the said province of Georgia, and become due to us, our heirs and successors. [Thorpe 775]

First Continental Congress, Declaration and Resolves, October 14, 1774:

[1] Whereas, since the close of the last war, the British parliament, claiming a power of right to bind the people of America, by statute in all cases whatsoever, hath, in some acts expressly imposed taxes on them, and in others, under various pretenses, but in fact for the purpose of raising a *revenue,* hath imposed rates and duties payable in these colonies, established a board of commissioners, with unconstitutional powers, and extended the jurisdiction of courts of Admiralty, not only for collecting the said duties, but for the trial of causes merely arising within the body of a county. [JCC1 63–64]

[2] . . . But, from the necessity of the case, and a regard to the mutual interest of both countries, we cheerfully consent to the operation of such acts of the British parliament, as are bona fide, restrained to the regulation of our external commerce, for the purpose of securing the commercial advantages of the whole empire to the mother country, and the commercial benefits of its respective members, excluding every idea of taxation, internal or external, for raising a *revenue* on the subjects in America, without their consent. [JCC1 68–69]

[3] The several Acts of 4 Geo. 3 ch. 15 & ch. 34. 5 Geo. 3 ch. 25. 6 Geo. 3 ch. 52. 7 Geo. 3 ch. 41 & 46. 8 Geo. 3 ch. 22. which impose duties for the purpose of raising a *revenue* in America, extend the powers of the admiralty courts beyond their ancient limits, deprive the American subject of trial by jury, authorize the judges' certificate to indemnify the prosecutor from damages that he might otherwise be liable to, requiring oppressive security from a claimant of ships and goods seized, before he shall be allowed to defend his property, and are subversive of American rights. [JCC1 71–72]

South Carolina Constitution, March 26, 1776:

[Preamble:] Whereas the British Parliament, claiming of late years a right to bind the North American colonies by law in all cases whatsoever, have enacted statutes for raising a *revenue* in those colonies and disposing of such *revenue* as they thought proper, without the consent and against the will of the colonists. And whereas it appearing to them that (they not being represented in Parliament) such claim was altogether unconstitutional, and, if admitted, would at once reduce them from the rank of freemen to a state of the most abject slavery . . . [Thorpe 3241]

John Adams, *Thoughts on Government*, April 1776:

The very mention of sumptuary laws will excite a smile. Whether our countrymen have wisdom and virtue enough to submit to them I know not; but the happiness of the people might be greatly promoted by them, and a *revenue* saved sufficient to carry on this war forever. Frugality is a great *revenue,* besides curing us of vanities, levities, and fopperies which are real antidotes to all great, manly and warlike virtues. [PJA4 91]

Maryland Constitution, November 11, 1776:

[Form of Government, Article 10:] That the house of Delegates may originate all money bills, propose bills to the senate, or receive those offered by that body, and assent, dissent, or propose amendments; that they may inquire, on the oath of witnesses, into all complaints, grievances, and offenses, as the grand inquest of this state, and may commit any person, for any crime, to the public jail, there to remain till he be discharged by due course of law. They may expel any member for a great misdemeanor, but not a second time for the same cause. They may examine and pass all accounts of the state, relating either to the collection or expenditure of the *revenue,* or appoint auditors to state and adjust the same . . . [Thorpe 1692]

[*Ibid.,* Article 11:] . . . and to prevent altercation about such bills, it is declared, that no bill imposing duties or customs for the mere regulation of commerce, or inflicting fines for the reformation of morals, or to enforce the execution of the laws, by which an incidental *revenue* may arise, shall be accounted a money bill; but every bill assessing, levying, or applying taxes or supplies for the support of government or the current expenses of the state, or appropriating money in the treasury, shall be deemed a money bill. [Thorpe 1693]

The Virginia Plan of Union, May 29, 1787:

[Article 9:] Res[olve]d that a National Judiciary be established to consist of one or more supreme tribunals, and of inferior tribunals to be chosen by the National Legislature, to hold their offices during good behaviour; and to receive punctually at stated times fixed compensation for their services, in which no increase or diminution shall be made so as to affect the persons actually in office, at the time of such increase or diminution. That the jurisdiction of the inferior tribunals shall be to hear & determine in the first instance, and of the supreme tribunal to hear and determine in the dernier resort, all piracies & felonies on the high seas, captures from an enemy; cases in which foreigners or citizens of other States applying to such jurisdictions may be interested, or which respect the collection of the National *revenue;* impeachments of any National officers, and questions which may involve the national peace and harmony.

[DHRC1 244–45]

The New Jersey Plan of Union, June 15, 1787:

[Article 2:] Res[olve]d that in addition to the powers vested in the U. States in Congress, by the present existing articles of Confederation, they be authorized to pass acts for raising a *revenue,* by levying a duty or duties on all goods or merchandises of foreign growth or manufacture imported into any part of the U. States, by Stamps on paper, vellum or parchment, and by a postage on all letters or packages passing through the general post-office, to be applied to such federal purposes as they shall deem proper & expedient . . . [DHRC1 251]

[Article 5:] . . . that the Judiciary so established shall have authority to hear & determine in the first instance on all impeachments of federal officers, & by way of appeal in the dernier resort in all cases touching the rights of Ambassadors, in all cases of captures from an enemy, in all cases of piracies & felonies on the high seas, in all cases in which foreigners may be interested, in the construction of any treaty or treaties, or which may arise on any of the Acts for regulation of trade, or the collection of the federal *Revenue:* that none of the

Judiciary shall during the time they remain in office be capable of receiving or holding any other office or appointment during the time of service, or for ——— thereafter. [DHRC1 252]

Alexander Hamilton's Plan of Union, June 18, 1787:

[1] The Supreme Judicial authority of the United States to be vested in twelve Judges, to hold their offices during good behaviour with adequate and permanent salaries. This Court to have original jurisdiction in all causes of capture and an appellative jurisdiction (from the Courts of the several states) in all causes in which the *revenues* of the general government or the citizens of foreign nations are concerned. [DHRC1 254]

[2] The Legislature of the United States to have power to institute Courts in each state for the determination of all causes of capture and of all matters relating to their *revenues,* or in which the citizens of foreign nations are concerned. [DHRC1 254]

James Wilson, Speech on the Federal Constitution, October 6, 1787:

The power of direct taxation has likewise been treated as an improper delegation to the foederal government; but when we consider it as the duty of that body to provide for the national safety, to support the dignity of the union, and to discharge the debts contracted upon the collective faith of the states, for their common benefit, it must be acknowledged that those, upon whom such important obligations are imposed, ought, in justice and in policy, to possess every means requisite for a faithful performance of their trust. But why should we be alarmed with visionary evils? I will venture to predict, that the great *revenue* of the United States must, and always will, be raised by impost; for, being at once less obnoxious, and more productive, the interest of the government will be best promoted by the accommodation of the people. Still, however, the object of direct taxation should be within reach in all cases of emergency; and there is no more reason to apprehend oppression in the mode of collecting a *revenue* from this resource, than in the form of impost, which, by universal assent, is left to the authority of the foederal government. . . . [Ford 160]

Richard Henry Lee [?], "The Federal Farmer," No. 1, October 8, 1787:

My letters to you last winter, on the subject of a well balanced national government for the United States, were the result of a free enquiry; when I passed from that subject to enquiries relative to our commerce, *revenues,* past administration, &c. I anticipated the anxieties I feel, on carefully examining the plan of government proposed by the convention. It appears to be a plan retaining some federal features; but to be the first important step, and to aim strongly at one consolidated government of the United States. . . . [Ford 279]

Edmund Randolph, Letter on the Federal Constitution, October 10, 1787:

As strongly too am I persuaded, that requisitions for money will not be more cordially received. For besides the distrust, which would prevail with respect to them also; besides the opinion, entertained by each state of its own liberality and unsatisfied demands against the United States, there is another consideration, not less worthy of attention. The first rule for determining each quota was the value of all land granted or surveyed, and of the buildings and improvements thereon. It is no longer doubted, that an equitable, uniform mode of estimating that value, is impracticable; and therefore twelve states have substituted the number of inhabitants under certain limitations, as the standard according to which money is to be furnished. But under the subsisting articles of the union, the assent of the thirteenth state is necessary, and has not yet been given. This does of itself lessen the hope of procuring a *revenue* for foederal uses; and the miscarriage of the impost almost rivets our despondency. [DHRC8 264]

Noah Webster, *An Examination of the Leading Principles of the Federal Constitution*, October 17, 1787:

The boundaries of the several states were not drawn with a view to independence; and while this country was subject to Great Britain, they produced no commercial or political inconveniences. But the revolution has placed things on a different footing. The advantages of some states, and the disadvantages of others are so great—and so materially affect the business and interest of each, that nothing but an equalizing system of *revenue,* that shall reduce the advantages to some equitable proportion, can prevent a civil war and save the national debt. Such a system of *revenue* is the sine qua non of public justice and tranquillity. [Ford 62–63]

"Cato Uticensis," October 17, 1787:

Should it not, at least, have been provided, that those *revenue* officers and excisemen, against whom free governments have, always, justly entertained a jealousy, should be citizens of the state? Was it inadmissible, that, they should be endued with the bowels of fellow-citizens? Are we not to expect, that New England will now send us *revenue* officers, instead of their onions and their apples? When you observe, that the few places, already, under Congress in this state [Virginia] are in the hands of strangers, you will own, that my suspicion is not without some foundation . . . [DHRC8 74]

Hugh Williamson, Address at Edenton, North Carolina, November 8, 1787:

[1] When Gentlemen are pleased to complain, that little power is left in the hands of the separate States; they should be advised to cast an eye upon the

large code of laws, which have passed in this State since the peace. Let them consider how few of those laws have been framed, for the general benefit of the Nation. Nine out of ten of them, are domestic; calculated for the sole use of this State, or of particular citizens. There must still be use for such laws, though you should enable the Congress to collect a *revenue* for National purposes, and the collection of that *revenue* includes the chief of the new powers, which are now to be committed to the Congress. [DHRC16 203]

[2] . . . Does one of the States attempt to raise a little money by imposts or other commercial regulations.—A neighboring State immediately alters her laws and defeats the *revenue,* by throwing the trade into a different channel. Instead of supporting or assisting, we are uniformly taking the advantage of one another. Such an assemblage of people are not a nation. . . . [DHRC16 206]

Alexander Hamilton, *The Federalist*, No. 7, November 17, 1787:

The opportunities which some States would have of rendering others tributary to them by commercial regulations would be impatiently submitted to by the tributary States. The relative situation of New York, Connecticut, and New Jersey, would afford an example of this kind. New York, from the necessities of *revenue,* must lay duties on her importations. A great part of these duties must be paid by the inhabitants of the two other States in the capacity of consumers of what we import. . . . [Fed. 116–17]

Alexander Hamilton, *The Federalist*, No. 12, November 27, 1787:

[1] [Title:] Union and the National *Revenue.* [Fed. 142]

[2] No person acquainted with what happens in other countries will be surprised at this circumstance. In so opulent a nation as that of Britain, where direct taxes from superior wealth must be much more tolerable, and, from the vigor of the government, much more practicable, than in America, far the greatest part of the national *revenue* is derived from taxes of the indirect kind, from imposts, and from excises. Duties on imported articles form a large branch of this latter description. [Fed. 144]

[3] If these remarks have any foundation, that state of things which will best enable us to improve and extend so valuable a resource must be best adapted to our political welfare. And it cannot admit of a serious doubt, that this state of things, must rest on the basis of a general Union. As far as this would be conducive to the interests of commerce, so far it must tend to the extension of the *revenue* to be drawn from that source. . . . [Fed. 144]

[4] What will be the consequence, if we are not able to avail ourselves of the resource in question in its full extent? A nation cannot long exist without *revenues.* Destitute of this essential support, it must resign its independence, and sink into the degraded condition of a province. This is an extremity to which

no government will of choice accede. *Revenue,* therefore, must be had at all events. In this country, if the principal part be not drawn from commerce, it must fall with oppressive weight upon land. It has been already intimated that excises, in their true signification, are too little in unison with the feelings of the people, to admit of great use being made of that mode of taxation; nor, indeed, in the States where almost the sole employment is agriculture, are the objects proper for excise sufficiently numerous to permit very ample collections in that way. [Fed. 146–47]

Alexander Hamilton, *The Federalist*, No. 13, November 28, 1787:

As connected with the subject of *revenue,* we may with propriety consider that of economy. The money saved from one object may be usefully applied to another, and there will be so much the less to be drawn from the pockets of the people. If the States are united under one government, there will be but one national civil list to support; if they are divided into several confederacies, there will be as many different national civil lists to be provided for—and each of them, as to the principal departments, coextensive with that which would be necessary for a government of the whole. The entire separation of the States into thirteen unconnected sovereignties is a project too extravagant and too replete with danger to have many advocates. . . . [Fed. 147–48]

Tobias Lear, "Brutus," December 6, 1787:

The 7th section of the first article in the proposed constitution says, "All bills for raising *revenue* shall originate in the House of Representatives; but the Senate may propose or concur with amendments as on other bills." This is putting a power into the hands of the Senate with more safety than can generally be done—it is giving them the power of doing good, almost without the possibility of doing harm; for it would be folly to suppose that the House of Representatives, or any other body of men, could form a bill so completely perfect in all its parts as to admit of no amendment. A *revenue* bill will now have a double chance of attaining to perfection. The House of Representatives will discuss, form and send it up—the Senate will have it in their power to deliberate, debate upon it, and propose amendments, if necessary; but they can go no further, the House of Representatives must concur with their amendments or they have no effect; and this will for ever prevent any pernicious consequences which might result from this part of their power. . . . [DHRC8 214]

James Madison, *The Federalist*, No. 19, December 8, 1787:

The prerogatives of the [German] emperor are numerous. The most important of them are: his exclusive right to make propositions to the diet; to negative its resolutions; to name ambassadors; to confer dignities and titles; to fill vacant electorates; to found universities; to grant privileges not injurious to the states of the empire; to receive and apply the public *revenues;* and generally to watch over the public safety. In certain cases, the electors form a council to him. In quality of emperor, he possesses no territory within the empire, nor receives any *revenue* for his support. But his *revenue* and dominions, in other qualities, constitute him one of the most powerful princes in Europe. [Fed. 178]

Alexander Hamilton, *The Federalist*, No. 21, December 12, 1787:

. . . Let Virginia be contrasted with North Carolina, Pennsylvania with Connecticut, or Maryland with New Jersey, and we shall be convinced that the respective abilities of those States, in relation to *revenue,* bear little or no analogy to their comparative stock in lands or to their comparative population. The position may be equally illustrated by a similar process between the counties of the same State. . . . [Fed. 188]

Dissent of the Pennsylvania Convention's Minority, December 18, 1787:

[1] As there is no one article of taxation reserved to the State governments, the Congress may monopolize every source of *revenue,* and thus indirectly demolish the State governments, for without funds they could not exist; the taxes, duties and excises imposed by Congress may be so high as to render it impracticable to levy farther sums on the same articles; but whether this should be the case or not, if the state governments should presume to impose taxes, duties, or excises, on the same articles with Congress, the latter may abrogate and repeal the laws whereby they are imposed, upon the allegation that they interfere with the due collection of their taxes, duties or excises . . . [DHRC2 627]

[2] As this government will not enjoy the confidence of the people, but be executed by force, it will be a very expensive and burthensome government. The standing army must be numerous, and as a further support, it will be the policy of this government to multiply officers in every department: judges, collectors, tax-gatherers, excisemen and the whole host of *revenue* officers, will swarm over the land, devouring the hard earnings of the industrious, like the locusts of old, impoverishing and desolating all before them. [DHRC2 639]

Alexander Hamilton, *The Federalist*, No. 23, December 18, 1787:

. . . that if we are in earnest about giving the Union energy and duration, we must abandon the vain project of legislating upon the States in their collective capacities; we must extend the laws of the federal government to the individual citizens of America; we must discard the fallacious scheme of quotas and requisitions, as equally impracticable and unjust. The result from all this is that the Union ought to be invested with full power to levy troops; to build and equip fleets; and to raise the *revenues* which will be required for the formation and support of an army and navy, in the customary and ordinary modes practiced in other governments. [Fed. 201]

Robert Yates and John Lansing, Objections to the Constitution, December 21, 1787:

Reasoning in this manner, we were of opinion, that the leading feature of every amendment, ought to be the preservation of the individual states in their uncontrolled constitutional rights, and that in reserving these, a mode might have been devised of granting to the confederacy, the monies arising from a general system of *revenue;* the power of regulating commerce and enforcing the observance of foreign treaties, and other necessary matters of less moment. [Farrand3 246]

Alexander Hamilton, *The Federalist*, No. 30, December 28, 1787:

[1] It has been already observed that the federal government ought to possess the power of providing for the support of the national forces; in which proposition was intended to be included the expense of raising troops, of building and equipping fleets, and all other expenses in any wise connected with military arrangements and operations. But these are not the only objects to which the jurisdiction of the Union, in respect to *revenue,* must necessarily be empowered to extend. It must embrace a provision for the support of the national civil list; for the payment of the national debts contracted, or that may be contracted; and, in general, for all those matters which will call for disbursements out of the national treasury. The conclusion is that there must be interwoven, in the frame of the government, a general power of taxation, in one shape or another. [Fed. 231–32]

[2] Let us attend to what would be the effects of this situation in the very first war in which we should happen to be engaged. We will presume, for argument's sake, that the *revenue* arising from the impost duties answers the purposes of a provision for the public debt and of a peace establishment for the Union. Thus circumstanced, a war breaks out. What would be the probable conduct of the government in such an emergency? Taught by experience that proper dependence could not be placed on the success of requisitions, unable by its own authority to lay hold of fresh resources, and urged by considerations of national danger, would it not be driven to the expedient of diverting the funds already appropriated from their proper objects to the defence of the State? . . . [Fed. 235]

Alexander Hamilton, *The Federalist*, No. 31, January 1, 1788:

As theory and practice conspire to prove that the power of procuring *revenue* is unavailing when exercised over the States in their collective capacities, the federal government must of necessity be invested with an unqualified power of taxation in the ordinary modes. [Fed. 238]

Alexander Hamilton, *The Federalist*, No. 33, January 2, 1788:

. . . The propriety of a law, in a constitutional light, must always be determined by the nature of the powers upon which it is founded. Suppose, by some forced constructions of its authority (which, indeed, cannot easily be imagined), the Federal legislature should attempt to vary the law of descent in any State, would it not be evident that, in making such an attempt, it had exceeded its jurisdiction, and infringed upon that of the State? Suppose, again, that upon the pretence of an interference with its *revenues,* it should undertake to abrogate a land-tax imposed by the authority of a State; would it not be equally evident that this was an invasion of that concurrent jurisdiction in respect to this species of tax, which its Constitution plainly supposes to exist in the State governments? . . .

[Fed. 246]

Alexander Hamilton, *The Federalist*, No. 34, January 4, 1788:

[1] I flatter myself it has been clearly shown in my last number that the particular States, under the proposed Constitution, would have COEQUAL authority with the Union in the article of *revenue,* except as to duties on imports. As this leaves open to the States far the greatest part of the resources of the community, there can be no color for the assertion that they would not possess means as abundant as could be desired for the supply of their own wants, independent of all external control. That the field is sufficiently wide will more fully appear when we come to advert to the inconsiderable share of the public expenses for which it will fall to the lot of the State governments to provide. [Fed. 248]

[2] In framing a government for posterity as well as ourselves, we ought, in those provisions which are designed to be permanent, to calculate, not on temporary, but on permanent causes of expense. If this principle be a just one, our attention would be directed to a provision in favor of the State governments for an annual sum of about two hundred thousand pounds; while the exigencies of the Union could be susceptible of no limits, even in imagination. In this view of the subject, by what logic can it be maintained that the local governments ought to command, in perpetuity, an EXCLUSIVE source of *revenue* for any sum beyond the extent of two hundred thousand pounds? To extend its power further, in exclusion of the authority of the Union, would be to take the resources of the community out of those hands which stood in need of them for the public welfare, in order to put them into other hands which could have no just or proper occasion for them. [Fed. 252]

[3] The preceding train of observation will justify the position which has been elsewhere laid down, that "A CONCURRENT JURISDICTION in the article of taxation was the only admissible substitute for an entire subordination, in respect to this branch of power, of State authority to that of the Union." Any separation of the objects of *revenue* that could have been fallen upon, would have amounted to a sacrifice of the great INTERESTS of the Union to the POWER

of the individual States. The convention thought the concurrent jurisdiction preferable to that subordination; and it is evident that it has at least the merit of reconciling an indefinite constitutional power of taxation in the Federal government with an adequate and independent power in the States to provide for their own necessities. . . . [Fed. 253]

Alexander Hamilton, *The Federalist*, No. 35, January 5, 1788:

So far as these observations tend to inculcate a danger of the import duties being extended to an injurious extreme it may be observed, conformably to a remark made in another part of these papers, that the interest of the *revenue* itself would be a sufficient guard against such an extreme. I readily admit that this would be the case, as long as other resources were open; but if the avenues to them were closed, HOPE, stimulated by necessity, would beget experiments, fortified by rigorous precautions and additional penalties, which, for a time, would have the intended effect, till there had been leisure to contrive expedients to elude these new precautions. . . . [Fed. 255]

Alexander Hamilton, *The Federalist*, No. 36, January 8, 1788:

[1] There is another objection of a somewhat more precise nature that claims our attention. It has been asserted that a power of internal taxation in the national legislature could never be exercised with advantages, as well from the want of a sufficient knowledge of local circumstances, as from an interference between the *revenue* laws of the Union and of the particular States. The supposition of a want of proper knowledge seems to be entirely destitute of foundation. If any question is depending in a State legislature respecting one of the counties, which demands a knowledge of local details, how is it acquired? No doubt from the information of the members of the county. Cannot the like knowledge be obtained in the national legislature from the representatives of each State? . . .

[Fed. 260]

[2] . . . In other cases, the probability is that the United States will either wholly abstain from the objects preoccupied for local purposes, or will make use of the State officers and State regulations for collecting the additional imposition. This will best answer the views of *revenue,* because it will save expense in the collection, and will best avoid any occasion of disgust to the State governments and to the people. At all events, here is a practicable expedient for avoiding such an inconvenience; and nothing more can be required than to show that evils predicted do not necessarily result from the plan. [Fed. 263]

James Madison, *The Federalist*, No. 38, January 12, 1788:

. . . We may calculate, therefore, that a rich and fertile country [the West], of an area equal to the inhabited extent of the United States, will soon become a national stock. Congress have assumed the administration of this stock. They have begun to render it productive. Congress have undertaken to do more: they have proceeded to form new States, to erect temporary governments to appoint officers for them, and to prescribe the conditions on which such States shall be admitted into the Confederacy. All this has been done; and done without the least color of constitutional authority. Yet no blame has been whispered; no alarm has been sounded. A GREAT AND INDEPENDENT fund of *revenue* is passing into the hands of a SINGLE BODY of men, who can RAISE TROOPS to an INDEFINITE NUMBER, and appropriate money to their support for an INDEFINITE PERIOD OF TIME. And yet there are men, who have not only been silent spectators of this prospect, but who are advocates for the system which exhibits it; and, at the same time, urge against the new system the objections which we have heard. . . . [Fed.279]

James Madison, *The Federalist*, No. 45, January 26, 1788:

If the federal government is to have collectors of *revenue*, the State governments will have theirs also. And as those of the former will be principally on the seacoast, and not very numerous, whilst those of the latter will be spread over the face of the country, and will be very numerous, the advantage in this view also lies on the same side. It is true, that the Confederacy is to possess, and may exercise, the power of collecting internal as well as external taxes throughout the States; but it is probable that this power will not be resorted to, except for supplemental purposes of *revenue;* than an option will then be given to the States to supply their quotas by previous collections of their own; and that the eventual collection, under the immediate authority of the Union, will generally be made by the officers, and according to the rules, appointed by the several States. . . . [Fed. 327–28]

Tench Coxe, "A Freeman," February 6, 1788:

The lordship of the soil is one of the most valuable and powerful appendages of sovereignty—This remains in full perfection with every state. From them must grants flow, to them must be paid the annual acknowledgment, whether it be a mere compliance with form in the rendering of a pepper corn, or a solid *revenue* in the payment of a quit-rent. To them also, as original and rightful proprietaries and lords of the soil, will the estates of extinct families revert. [DHRC15 51]

"A Citizen of the United States," February 13, 1788:

. . . In the middle states the clamor of opposition has been from the want of a bill of rights—Besides these, the commercial states object to parting with their commercial *revenues;* while the non-importing states complain of being tributary to the others.—Notwithstanding these various objections, all who urge them acknowledge the merit of the new system in other points, and frequently in those parts opposed by others. . . . [DHRC16 115]

Alexander Hamilton, *The Federalist*, No. 60, February 23, 1788:

. . . And thirdly, that men accustomed to investigate the sources of public prosperity upon a large scale, must be too well convinced of the utility of commerce, to be inclined to inflict upon it so deep a wound as would result from the entire exclusion of those who would best understand its interest from a share in the management of them. The importance of commerce, in the view of *revenue* alone, must effectually guard it against the enmity of a body which would be continually importuned in its favor, by the urgent calls of public necessity. [Fed. 401]

Alexander White, "To the Citizens of Virginia," February 22, 1788:

. . . They attempt to alarm you by a direful train of evils which Congress MAY do. They MAY command the whole or any part of your property by taxes and imposts; they MAY monopolize every source of *revenue,* and thus demolish the State Governments; they MAY prolong their existance in office for life, by postponing the times of elections and appointments, and having gained that point, may fill up vacancies themselves, and MAY depute some body in the respective States to fill up vacancies of Senators, until they can venture to assume it themselves, and finally complete the system of despotism by continuing themselves and their children in the government. . . . [DHRC8 405]

"The Impartial Examiner," No. 1, February 27, 1788:

. . . So different are many species of property, so various the productions, so unequal the profits arising, even from the same species of property, in different states, that no general mode of contribution can well be adopted in such a manner as at once to affect all in an equitable degree. Hence may arise disagreeable objects of contention. A diversity of interests will produce a diversity of schemes. Thus each state, as it is natural will endeavor to raise a *revenue* by such means, as may appear least injurious to its own interest: a source of dissention manifestly detrimental to that harmony, which is necessary to support the confederation. I cannot conceive it impracticable to reform the foederal system in such a manner as to ensure a compliance with the necessary requisitions of Congress from the different state legislatures. Then all the several states being left to raise their own share of the *revenue,* and being the only proper judges of the mode most convenient to themselves, it is highly probable that this important branch of government would be carried on more generally to the satisfaction of each state; and would tend to promote a spirit of concord between all the parts of this great community. . . . [DHRC8 421]

Mercy Otis Warren, *Observations on the New Constitution*, February 1788:

Mankind may amuse themselves with theoretick systems of liberty, and trace its social and moral effects on sciences, virtue, industry, and every improvement of which the human mind is capable; but we can only discern its true value by the practical and wretched effects of slavery; and thus dreadfully will they be realized, when the inhabitants of the Eastern States are dragging out a miserable existence, only on the gleanings of their fields; and the Southern, blessed with a softer and more fertile climate, are languishing in hopeless poverty; and when asked, what is become of the flower of their crop, and the rich produce of their farms—they may answer in the hapless stile of the Man of La Mancha,—"The steward of my Lord has seized and sent it to Madrid."—Or, in the more literal language of truth, The exigencies of government require that the collectors of the *revenue* should transmit it to the Federal City. [DHRC16 274]

Benjamin Workman [?], "Philadelphiensis," No. 11, March 8, 1788:

. . . Pennsylvania, instead of receiving credit for the immense sums she has paid into the general treasury, will be placed on a footing with the most delinquent state in the union; and which is highly probable she and all the other states will be taxed hereafter in an exact ratio of the sums they have hitherto raised. Consequently our former acts of generosity, in support of public faith, is to terminate in a two-fold loss to our citizens. In the first place we have nearly ruined ourselves already, through our punctuality in paying our quota of the public debt; and secondly, to complete the scene, our future quotas of continental *revenue* will be apportioned to the exertions we have heretofore made: That is in plain terms, Pennsylvania will be much worse under this cruel system of tyranny [*i.e.*, the Constitution] in consequence of her fidelity and honor, than she would have been had she never attempted to pay a shilling of public debt . . . [DHRC16 364]

Oliver Ellsworth, "The Landholder," No. 11, March 10, 1788:

A national *revenue* and the manner of collecting it is another very interesting matter, and here the citizens of New-Hampshire have better terms offered them, than their local situation can ever enable them to demand or enforce. Impost and duties on trade which must be collected in the great importing towns, are the means by which an American *revenue* will be principally, and perhaps, wholly raised. But a point of your state comes near the sea, and that point so situated that it never can collect commerce, and become an emporium for the whole state—Nineteen parts in twenty of New-Hampshire are greatly inland, so that local situation necessitates you to be an agricultural people; and this is not a hard necessity if you now form such a political connection with the other states, as will entitle you to a just share in that *revenue* they raise on commerce. . . . [DHRC16 368]

Melancton Smith, *An Address to the People of the State of New York*, c. April 1788:

The amount of the *revenue* from impost for two years past, has not exceeded fifty thousands pounds currency, per annum, and a drawback of duties is allowed by law, upon all goods exported to the beforementioned states, in casks or packages unbroken. [Ford 105]

Alexander Hamilton, *The Federalist*, No. 84, May 28, 1788:

. . . As to persons to be employed in the collection of the *revenues,* it is unquestionably true that these will form a very considerable addition to the number of federal officers [under the Constitution]; but it will not follow that this will occasion an increase of public expense. It will be in most cases nothing more than an exchange of State for national officers. In the collection of all duties, for instance, the persons employed will be wholly of the latter description. The States individually will stand in no need of any for this purpose. What difference can it make in point of expense to pay officers of the customs appointed by the State or by the United States? [Fed. 539]

John Dickinson, "Fabius," No. 8, 1788:

It is said—Such territory has never been governed by a confederacy of republics. Granted. But, where was there ever a confederacy of republics, in such territory, united, as these states are to be by the proposed constitution? . . . Or, in which, a provision was made for the federal *revenue,* without recurring to coercion against states, the miserable expedient, of every other confederacy that has existed, an expedient always attended with odium, and often with a delay productive of irreparable damage? . . . [Ford 205]

South Carolina Constitution, June 3, 1790:

[Article I, Section 15:] Bills for raising a *revenue* shall originate in the house of representatives, but may be altered, amended, or rejected by the senate. All other bills may originate in either house, and may be amended, altered, or rejected by the other. [Thorpe 3260]

Pennsylvania Constitution, September 2, 1790:

[Article I, Section 20:] All bills for raising *revenue* shall originate in the house of representatives; but the senate may propose amendments, as in other bills. [Thorpe 3094]

SAFETY, PUBLIC

United States Constitution, September 17, 1787:

[Article I, Section 9:] The Privilege of the Writ of Habeas Corpus shall not be suspended, unless when in Cases of Rebellion or Invasion the *public Safety* may require it.

* * * * *

Charles I, Patent to Sir Robert Heath, October 30, 1629:

Moreover that New Carolana may happily increase by the multitude of people thronging thither & alsoe that they be firmely defended from the incursions of the Barbarous & of others practicall or plundering enemyes. Therefore we for ourselves our Heires & Successors at the will & pleasure of the sayd Sr. Robert Heath his heires and assignes, doe give & grant by these presents to all men & our subjects, leiges of our heires and successors both those in present & to come (unless it shall be in an especiall manner forbidden) power, licence & libertye to build & fortifye themselves & their familyes in the sayd Province of Carolana for the *publicke safety* of their seats there planted, tilled & inhabited with forts castles & other fortifications, with fitting shipes alsoe & convenient furniture for transportation the statute of fugitives or any other whatsoever contrary to these premises in any wise notwithstanding. . . . [Thorpe 72]

Charles II, Charter of Pennsylvania, February 28, 1681:

. . . Know ye therefore, That We reposing speciall trust and Confidence in the fidelitie, wisedom, Justice, and provident circumspection of the said William Penn for us, our heires and Successors, Doe grant free, full, and absolute power by vertue of these presents to him and his heires, and to his and their Deputies, and Lieutenants, for the good and happy government of the said countrey to ordeyne, make, and enact, and under his and their Seales to publish any Lawes whatsoever, for the raising of money for the publick use of the said Province, or for any other End, apperteyning either unto the *publick* state, peace, or *safety* of the said Countrey, or unto the private utility of perticular persons, according unto their best discretions, by and with the advice, assent, and approbation of the Freemen of the said Countrey, or the greater parte of them, or of their Delegates or Deputies . . . [Thorpe 3037]

Pennsylvania Frame of Government, Laws Agreed Upon in England, May 5, 1682:

[Article 40:] That all other matters and things not herein provided for, which shall, and may, concern the *public* justice, peace or *safety* of the said province; and the raising and imposing taxes, customs, duties, or other charges whatsoever, shall be, and are, hereby referred to the order, prudence and determination of the Governor and freemen, in provincial Council and General Assembly, to be held, from time to time, in the said province. [Thorpe 3063]

Pennsylvania Frame of Government, November 7, 1696:

And be it further enacted by the authority aforesaid, That the Governor and Council shall, from time to time have the care of the management of all *public* affairs, relating to the peace, *safety,* justice, treasury, trade, and improvement of the province and territories, and to the good education of youth, and sobriety of the manners of the inhabitants therein, as aforesaid. [Thorpe 3074]

William Penn, Plan of Colonial Union, c. February 8, 1697:

[Article 1:] That the severall Collonies before mentioned do meet once a year, and oftner if need be dureing the Warr, and at least once in two yeares in times of Peace, by their Stated and Appointed Deputies, to Debate and Resolve of such Measures, as are most adviseable for their better understanding, and the *Publick* Tranquility and *Safety*. [PWP3 482]

North Carolina Constitution, December 18, 1776:

[Form of Government, Article 18:] The Governor, for the time being, shall be captain-general and commander in chief of the militia; and, in the recess of the General Assembly, shall have power, by and with the advice of the Council of State, to embody the militia for the *public safety*. [Thorpe 2791]

George Mason, Objections to the Constitution, October 7, 1787:

Both the general Legislature & the State Legislatures are expressly prohibited making ex post facto Laws; tho' there never was or can be a Legislature but must & will make such Laws, when Necessity & the *public Safety* require them;

which will hereafter be a Breach of all the Constitutions in the Union, and afford Precedents for other Innovations. [DHRC8 45]

Noah Webster, *An Examination of the Leading Principles of the Federal Constitution*, October 17, 1787:

But what is tyranny? Or how can a free people be deprived of their liberties? Tyranny is the exercise of some Power over a man, which is not warranted by law, or necessary for the *public safety*. A people can never be deprived of their liberties, while they retain in their own hands, a power sufficient to any other power in the state. This position leads me directly to enquire, in what consists the power of a nation or of an order of men? [Ford 55]

Tench Coxe, *An Examination of the Constitution for the United States of America*, No. 4, October 21, 1787:

Observations have been made on the power given to the foederal Government in regard to the elections of Representatives and Senators. The regulations of these elections are, by the first part of the clause, to be prescribed by the state legislatures, who are certainly the proper bodies, if they will always execute the duty. But in case the union or the *public safety* should be endangered by an omission of this duty, as in the case of Rhode-island, then the legislature of the United States can name for the people a convenient time, and do other matters necessary to insure the free exercise of their right of election. . . . [Ford 151]

James Madison, *The Federalist*, No. 19, December 8, 1787:

The prerogatives of the [German] emperor are numerous. The most important of them are: his exclusive right to make propositions to the diet; to negative its resolutions; to name ambassadors; to confer dignities and titles; to fill vacant electorates; to found universities; to grant privileges not injurious to the states of the empire; to receive and apply the public revenues; and generally to watch over the *public safety*. . . . [Fed. 178]

James Madison, *The Federalist*, No. 20, December 11, 1787:

. . . A weak constitution must necessarily terminate in dissolution, for want of proper powers, or the usurpation of powers requisite for the *public safety*. Whether the usurpation, when once begun, will stop at the salutary point, or go forward to the dangerous extreme, must depend on the contingencies of the moment. . . . [Fed. 184]

Alexander Hamilton, *The Federalist*, No. 22, December 14, 1787:

. . . Hence, slow and scanty levies of men, in the most critical emergencies of our affairs; short enlistments at an unparalleled expense; continual fluctuations in the troops, ruinous to their discipline and subjecting the *public safety* frequently to the perilous crisis of a disbanded army. . . . [Fed. 192]

Alexander Hamilton, *The Federalist*, No. 23, December 18, 1787:

[1] Whether there ought to be a federal government intrusted with the care of the common defence is a question in the first instance, open for discussion; but the moment it is decided in the affirmative, it will follow that that government ought to be clothed with all the powers requisite to complete execution of its trust. And unless it can be shown that the circumstances which may affect the *public safety* are reducible within certain determinate limits; unless the contrary of this position can be fairly and rationally disputed, it must be admitted, as a necessary consequence, that there can be no limitation of that authority which is to provide for the defence and protection of the community, in any matter essential to its efficacy—that is, in any matter essential to the formation, direction, or support of the NATIONAL FORCES. [Fed. 200]

[2] Who [is] so likely to make suitable provisions for the public defence as that body to which the guardianship of the *public safety* is confided; which, as the center of information, will best understand the extent and urgency of the dangers that threaten; as the representative of the WHOLE, will feel itself most deeply interested in the preservation of every part; which, from the responsibility implied in the duty assigned to it, will be most sensibly impressed with the necessity of proper exertions; and which, by the extension of its authority throughout the States, can alone establish uniformity and concert in the plans and measures by which the *common safety* is to be secured? Is there not a manifest inconsistency in devolving upon the federal government the care of the general defence, and leaving in the State governments the effective powers by which it is to be provided for? . . . [Fed. 202]

Alexander Hamilton, *The Federalist*, No. 26, December 22, 1787:

The idea of restraining the legislative authority, in the means of providing for the national defence, is one of those refinements which owe their origin to a zeal for liberty more ardent than enlightened. We have seen, however, that it has not had thus far an extensive prevalency; that even in this country, where it made its first appearance, Pennsylvania and North Carolina are the only two States by which it has been in any degree patronized; and that all the others have refused to give it the least countenance; wisely judging that confidence must be placed somewhere; that the necessity of doing it, is implied in the very act of delegating power; and that it is better to hazard the abuse of that confidence than to embarrass the government and endanger the *public safety* by impolitic restrictions on the legislative authority. . . . [Fed. 213–14]

Alexander Hamilton, *The Federalist*, No. 30, December 28, 1787:

. . . We will presume, for argument's sake, that the revenue arising from the impost duties answers the purposes of a provision for the public debt and of a peace establishment for the Union. Thus circumstanced, a war breaks out. What would be the probable conduct of the government in such an emergency? Taught by experience that proper dependence could not be placed on the success of requisitions, unable by its own authority to lay hold of fresh resources, and urged by considerations of national danger, would it not be driven to the expedient of diverting the funds already appropriated from their proper objects to the defence of the State? It is not easy to see how a step of this kind could be avoided; and if it should be taken, it is evident that it would prove the destruction of public credit at the very moment that it was becoming essential to the *public safety*. To imagine that at such a crisis credit might be dispensed with, would be the extreme of infatuation. . . . [Ford 235]

"Civis Rusticus," January 30, 1788:

Ex post facto laws have ever been considered as abhorrent from liberty: necessity and *public safety* never can require them . . . [DHRC8 338]

James Madison, *The Federalist*, No. 50, February 5, 1788:

This conclusion cannot be invalidated by alleging that the State in which the experiment was made was at that crisis, and had been for a long time before, violently heated and distracted by the rage of party. Is it to be presumed, that at any future septennial epoch the same State will be free from parties? Is it to be presumed that any other State, at the same or any other given period, will be exempt from them? Such an event ought to be neither presumed nor desired; because an extinction of parties necessarily implies either a universal alarm for the *public safety,* or an absolute extinction of liberty. [Fed. 354]

James Madison, *The Federalist*, No. 55, February 13, 1788:

It is necessary also to recollect here the observations which were applied to the case of biennial elections. For the same reason that the limited powers of the Congress, and the control of the State legislatures, justify less frequent election than the *public safety* might otherwise require, the members of Congress need be less numerous than if they possessed the whole power of legislation, and were under no other than the ordinary restraints of other legislative bodies. [Fed. 376]

James Iredell, "Marcus," No. 4, March 12, 1788:

The subject of a standing army has been exhausted in so masterly a manner in two or three numbers of the Foederalist (a work which I hope will soon be in every body's hands) that, but for the sake of regularity in answering Mr. Mason's objections, I should not venture upon the same topic; and shall only presume to do so, with a reference for fuller satisfaction to that able performance. It is certainly one of the most delicate and proper cases for the consideration of a free people, and so far as a jealousy of this kind leads to any degree of caution not incompatible with the *public safety,* it is undoubtedly to be commended. Our jealousy of this danger has descended to us from our British ancestors . . . [DHRC16 383–84]

"An Impartial Citizen," No. 6, March 13, 1788:

[1] . . . Even Mr. Mason, a man of great reputed abilities, has seriously objected, that the general and state Legislatures are restrained from making ex post facto laws: Though there never was nor will be a Legislature, but what must and will make such laws, when necessity and the *public safety* will require it: That the making such laws will hereafter be a breach of all the Constitutions in the Union, and afford precedents for further innovations. . . . [DHRC8 492]

[2] . . . What necessity can warrant or justify so flagrant and outrageous an attack on the rights of mankind? I aver and can maintain, that if, in any age or country, the *public safety* depended on an ex post facto law, it was owing to some capital defect in the form of government, and that the passing such a law did not in reality meliorate the situation of public affairs. . . . [DHRC8 493–94]

Alexander Hamilton, *The Federalist*, No. 72, March 19, 1788:

A fourth ill effect of the exclusion [of the President from re-election] would be the banishing men from stations in which, in certain emergencies of the state, their presence might be of the greatest moment to the *public* interest or *safety*. There is no nation which has not, at one period or another, experienced an absolute necessity of the services of particular men in particular situations; perhaps it would not be too strong to say, to the preservation of its political existence. How unwise, therefore, must be every such self-denying ordinance as serves to prohibit a nation from making use its own citizens in the manner best suited to its exigencies and circumstances! . . . [Fed. 465]

Alexander Hamilton, *The Federalist*, No. 85, May 28, 1788:

Let us now pause and ask ourselves whether, in the course of these papers, the proposed Constitution has not been satisfactorily vindicated from the aspersions thrown upon it; and whether it has not been shown to be worthy of the public approbation, and necessary to the *public safety* and prosperity. Every man is bound to answer these questions to himself, according to the best of his conscience and understanding, and to act agreeably to the genuine and sober dictates of his judgment. . . . [Fed. 543]

Pennsylvania Constitution, September 2, 1790:

[Article IX, Section 14:] That all prisoners shall be bailable by sufficient sureties, unless for capital offences, when the proof is evident or presumption great; and the privilege of the writ of habeas corpus shall not be suspended, unless when, in cases of rebellion or invasion, the *public safety* may require it.

[Thorpe 3101]

SAME OFFENCE

[Note: This list does not include all close occurrences of the words ''same'' and ''offence''; it includes only those in which ''same'' directly modifies ''offence.'']

United States Constitution, Bill of Rights, December 15, 1787:

[Article V:] No person shall be held to answer for a capital, or otherwise infamous crime, unless on a presentment or indictment of a Grand Jury, except in cases arising in the land or naval forces, or in the Militia, when in actual service in time of War or public danger; nor shall any person be subject for the *same offence* to be twice put in jeopardy of life or limb; nor shall be compelled in any criminal case to be a witness against himself, nor be deprived of life, liberty, or property, without due process of law; nor shall private property be taken for public use, without just compensation.

* * * * *

First Continental Congress, Declaration and Resolves, October 14, 1774:

Also the 12 Geo. 3, ch. 24, entitled ''An act for the better securing his Majesty's dock-yards, magazines, ships, ammunition, and stores,'' which declares a new *offence* in America, and deprives the American subject of a constitutional trial by jury of the vicinage, by authorizing the trial of any person charged with the committing any *offence* described in the said act, out of the realm, to be indicted and tried for the *same* in any shire or county within the realm. [JCC1 72]

Delaware Constitution, September 10, 1776:

[Article 5:] The right of suffrage in the election of members for both houses shall remain as exercised by law at present; and each house shall choose its own speaker, appoint its own officers, judge of the qualifications and elections of its own members, settle its own rules of proceedings, and direct writs of election for supplying intermediate vacancies. They may also severally expel any of their own members for misbehavior, but not a second time in the same sessions for the *same offence,* if reelected; and they shall have all other powers necessary for the legislature of a free and independent State. [Thorpe 563]

New Hampshire Constitution, June 2, 1784:

[Bill of Rights, Article 16:] No subject shall be liable to be tried, after an acquittal, for the *same crime or offence*.—Nor shall the legislature make any law that shall subject any person to a capital punishment, excepting for the government of the army and navy, and the militia in actual service, without trial by jury.
[Thorpe 2455]

The New Jersey Plan of Union, June 15, 1787:

[Article 9:] Res[olve]d that a Citizen of one State committing an *offence* in another State of the Union, shall be deemed guilty of the *same offence* as if it had been committed by a Citizen of the State in which the *offence* was committed. [DHRC1 253]

Alexander Hamilton, *The Federalist*, No. 65, March 7, 1788:

These considerations seem alone sufficient to authorize a conclusion, that the Supreme Court would have been an improper substitute for the Senate, as a court of impeachments. There remains a further consideration, which will not a little strengthen this conclusion. It is this: The punishment which may be the consequence of conviction upon impeachment, is not to terminate the chastisement of the offender. After having been sentenced to a perpetual ostracism from the esteem and confidence, and honors and emoluments of his country, he will still be liable to prosecution and punishment in the ordinary course of law. Would it be proper that the persons who had disposed of his fame, and his most valuable rights as a citizen, in one trial, should, in another trial, for the *same offence,* be also the disposers of his life and his fortune? Would there not be the greatest reasons to apprehend, that error, in the first sentence, would be the parent of error in the second sentence? . . . [Fed. 428]

Pennsylvania Constitution, September 2, 1790:

[Article IX, Section 10:] That no person shall, for any indictable offence, be proceeded against criminally by information, except in cases arising in the land or naval forces, or in the militia, when in actual service in time of war or public danger, or, by leave of the court, for oppression and misdemeanor in office. No person shall, for the *same offence,* be twice put in jeopardy of life or limb; nor shall any man's property be taken or applied to public use without the consent of his representatives, and without just compensation being made.
[Thorpe 3100–3101]

SCIENCE, SCIENCES

United States Constitution, September 17, 1787:

[Article I, Section 8:] [Congress shall have power] . . . To promote the Progress of *Science* and useful Arts, by securing for limited Times to Authors and Inventors the exclusive Right to their respective Writings and Discoveries.

* * * * *

Elizabeth I, Letters Patent to Sir Humphrey Gilbert, June 11, 1578:

Know ye that of our especiall grace, certaine *science* and meere motion, we have given and granted, and by these presents for us, our heires and successours, doe give and graunt to our trustie and wel-beloved servaunt Sir Humphrey Gilbert . . . free libertie and licence from time to time, and at all times for ever hereafter, to discover, finde, search out, and view such remote, heathen and barbarous lands, countreys and territories not actually possessed of any Christian prince or people, as to him, his heirs & assignes, and to every or any of them, shall seeme good . . . [Thorpe 49]

Elizabeth I, Charter to Sir Walter Raleigh, March 24, 1584:

Knowe yee that of our especial grace, certaine *science,* and meere motion, we have given and graunted, and by these presents for us, our heires and successors, we give and graunt to our trustie and welbeloved servant Walter Ralegh . . . free libertie and licence from time to time, and at all times for ever hereafter, to discover, search, finde out, and view such remote, heathen and barbarous lands, countries, and territories, not actually possessed of any Christian Prince, nor inhabited by Christian People, as to him, his heires and assignes, and to every or any of them shall seeme good . . . [Thorpe 53]

Pennsylvania Frame of Government, April 15, 1682:

[Article 12:] That the Governour and provincial Council shall erect and order all publick schools and encourage and reward the authors of useful *Sciences* and laudable inventions in the said province. [Thorpe 3056]

Pennsylvania Frame of Government, April 2, 1683:

[Article 10:] That the Governor and provincial Council shall erect and order all public schools, and encourage and reward the authors of useful *sciences* and laudable inventions in the said province and territories thereof. [Thorpe 3066]

Pennsylvania Frame of Government, November 7, 1696:

Be it further enacted by the authority aforesaid, That the Governor and Council shall erect and order all public houses, and encourage and reward the authors of useful *sciences* and laudable inventions in the said province, and territories thereof. [Thorpe 3074]

Thomas Paine, *Common Sense*, January 9, 1776:

Should any body of men be hereafter delegated for this or some similar purpose, I offer them the following extracts from that wise observer on governments, Dragonetti. ''The *science*'' says he, ''of the politician consists in fixing the true point of happiness and freedom. Those men would deserve the gratitude of ages, who should discover a mode of government that contained the greatest sum of individual happiness, with the least national expense.'' Dragonetti on ''Virtues and Rewards.'' [CWTP1 29]

John Adams, *Thoughts on Government*, April 1776:

[1] If I was equal to the task of forming a plan for the government of a colony, I should be flattered with your request, and very happy to comply with it; because, as the divine *science* of politics is the *science* of social happiness, and the blessings of society depend entirely on the constitutions of government, which are generally institutions that last for many generations, there can be no employment more agreeable to a benevolent mind than a research after the best. [PJA4 86]

[2] . . . And these and all other elections, especially of Representatives, and Councillors, should be annual, there not being in the whole circle of the *sciences* a maxim more infallible than this, ''Where annual elections end, there slavery begins.'' [PJA4 89–90]

Massachusetts Constitution, March 2, 1780:

[Chapter V:1:1:] Whereas our wise and pious ancestors, so early as the year one thousand six hundred and thirty-six, laid the foundation of Harvard College, in which university many persons of great eminence have, by the blessing of God, been initiated in those arts and *sciences* which qualified them for public employments, both in church and state; and whereas the encouragement of arts and *sciences,* and all good literature, tends to the honor of God, the advantage of the Christian religion, and the great benefit of this and the other United States of America,—it is declared, that the PRESIDENT AND FELLOWS OF HARVARD COLLEGE, in their corporate capacity, and their successors in that capacity, their officers and servants, shall have, hold, use, exercise, and enjoy, all the powers, authorities, rights, liberties, privileges, immunities, and franchises, which they now have, or are entitled to have, hold, use, exercise, and enjoy . . . [Thorpe 1906]

[Chapter V:2:] Wisdom and knowledge, as well as virtue, diffused generally among the body of the people, being necessary for the preservation of their rights and liberties; and as these depend on spreading the opportunities and advantages of education in the various parts of the country, and among the different orders of the people, it shall be the duty of legislatures and magistrates, in all future periods of this common-wealth, to cherish the interests of literature and the *sciences,* and all seminaries of them; especially the university at Cambridge, public schools and grammar schools in the towns; to encourage private societies and public institutions, rewards and immunities, for the promotion of agriculture, arts, *sciences,* commerce, trades, manufactures, and a natural history of the country . . . [Thorpe 1907]

New Hampshire Constitution, June 2, 1784:

ENCOURAGEMENT OF LITERATURE, &C.

Knowledge, and learning, generally diffused through a community, being essential to the preservation of a free government; and spreading the opportunities and advantages of education through the various parts of the country, being highly conducive to promote this end; it shall be the duty of the legislators and the magistrates, in all future periods of this government to cherish the interest of literature and the *sciences* and all seminaries and public schools, to encourage private and public institutions, rewards and immunities for the promotion or agriculture, arts, *sciences,* commerce, trades, manufactures and natural history of the country . . . [Thorpe 2467]

Richard Henry Lee [?], "The Federal Farmer," No. 5, October 15, 1787:

[1] . . . If there are advantages in the equal division of our lands, and the strong and manly habits of our people, we ought to establish governments calculated to give duration to them, and not governments which never can work naturally, till that equality of property, and those free and manly habits shall be destroyed; these evidently are not the natural basis of the proposed constitution. No man

of reflection, and skilled in the *science* of government, can suppose these will move on harmoniously together for ages, or even for fifty years. . . .

[Ford 318–19]

[2] . . . Though each individual in the state conventions will not, probably, be so respectable as each individual in the federal convention, yet as the state conventions will probably consist of fifteen hundred or two thousand men of abilities, and versed in the *science* of government, collected from all parts of the community and from all orders of men, it must be acknowledged that the weight of respectability will be in them . . . [Ford 322]

Noah Webster, *An Examination of the Leading Principles of the Federal Constitution*, October 17, 1787:

[1] Besides, the design of a senate is not merely to check the legislative assembly, but to collect wisdom and experience. In most of our constitutions, and particularly in the proposed federal system, greater age and longer residence are required to qualify for the senate, than for the house of representatives. This is a wise provision. The house of representatives may be composed of new and unexperienced members—strangers to the forms of proceeding, and the *science* of legislation. But either positive institutions, or customs, which may supply their place, fill the senate with men venerable for age and respectability, experienced in the ways of men, and in the art of governing, and who are not liable to the bias of passions that govern the young. . . . [Ford 31–32]

[2] The age requisite to qualify for this office [the presidency] is thirty-five years. The age requisite for admittance to the Roman consulship was forty-three years. For this difference, good reasons may be assigned—the improvements in *science,* and particularly in government, render it practicable for a man to qualify himself for an important office, much earlier in life, than he could among the Romans; especially in the early part of their commonwealth, when the office was instituted. . . . [Ford 36]

Alexander Hamilton, *The Federalist*, No. 8, November 20, 1787:

. . . The means of revenue, which have been so greatly multiplied by the increase of gold and silver and of the arts of industry, and the *science* of finance, which is the offspring of modern times, concurring with the habits of nations, have produced an entire revolution in the system of war, and have rendered disciplined armies, distinct from the body of the citizens, the inseparable companions of frequent hostility. [Fed. 122]

Alexander Hamilton, *The Federalist*, No. 9, November 21, 1787:

. . . The *science* of politics, however, like most other *sciences,* has received great improvement. The efficacy of various principles is now well understood, which were either not known at all, or imperfectly known to the ancients. . . .

[Fed. 125]

"A True Friend," December 6, 1787:

[1] . . . It is a general principle in legislation, which, if well understood, would abridge very much the study of that *science* for the body of the people, that the greater the power is with which it invests its governors, the shorter should be the limits of its duration; and on the contrary, that the smaller the power is, the longer it may be permitted to continue. . . . [DHRC8 219]

[2] . . . Under these two grand guides, time and experience, we shall become expert in the intricate and complicated *science* of legislation; we shall be looked up to as models by other nations, instead of our servilely copying their institutions . . . [DHRC8 220]

James Madison, *The Federalist*, No. 18, December 7, 1787:

It is much to be regretted that such imperfect monuments remain of this curious political fabric [the Greek Achaen League]. Could its interior structure and regular operation be ascertained, it is probable that more light would be thrown by it on the *science* of federal government, than by any of the like experiments with which we are acquainted. [Fed. 174]

Alexander Hamilton, *The Federalist*, No. 25, December 21, 1787:

. . . The American militia, in the course of the late war, have, by their valor on numerous occasions, erected eternal monuments to their fame; but the bravest of them feel and know the liberty of their country could not have been established by their efforts alone, however great and valuable they were. War, like most other things, is a *science* to be acquired and perfected by diligence, by perseverance, by time, and by practice. [Fed. 211–12]

Alexander Hamilton, *The Federalist*, No. 31, January 1, 1788:

[1] . . . Of the same nature are these other maxims in ethics and politics, that there cannot be an effect without a cause; that the means ought to be proportioned to the end; that every power ought to be commensurate with its object; that there ought to be no limitation of a power destined to effect a purpose which is itself incapable of limitation. And there are other truths in the two latter *sciences* which, if they cannot pretend to rank in the class of axioms, are yet such direct inferences from them, and so obvious in themselves, and so agreeable to the nature and unsophisticated dictates of common-sense, that they challenge the assent of a sound and unbiased mind, with a degree of force and conviction almost equally irresistible. [Fed. 236–37]

[2] The objects of geometrical inquiry are so entirely abstracted from those pursuits which stir up and put in motion the unruly passions of the human heart, that mankind, without difficulty, adopt not only the more simple theorems of

the *science,* but even those abstruse paradoxes which, however they may appear susceptible of demonstration, are at variance with the natural conceptions which the mind, without the aid of philosophy, would be led to entertain upon the subject. . . . [Fed. 237]

[3] But in the *sciences* of morals and politics, men are found far less tractable. To a certain degree, it is right and useful that this should be the case. Caution and investigation are a necessary armor against error and imposition. But this untractableness may be carried too far, and may degenerate into obstinacy, perverseness, or disingenuity. . . . [Fed. 237]

Letter from Virginia, *Freeman's Journal*, January 2, 1788:

"Here I expected to be happily removed from the din of politics, but even in these remote wilds the people are deeply engaged in that *science*. The new Constitution is the subject of universal discussion. . . ." [DHRC8 283]

Alexander Hamilton, *The Federalist*, No. 29, January 9, 1788:

It requires no skill in the *science* of war to discern that uniformity in the organization and discipline of the militia would be attended with the most beneficial effects, whenever they were called into service for the public defence. . . . [Fed. 226]

James Madison, *The Federalist*, No. 37, January 11, 1788:

. . . Experience has instructed us that no skill in the *science* of government has yet been able to discriminate and define, with sufficient certainty, its three great provinces—the legislative, executive, and judiciary; or even the privileges and powers of the different legislative branches. Questions daily occur in the course of practice, which prove the obscurity which reigns in these subjects, and which puzzle the greatest adepts in political *science*. [Fed. 269]

"Valerius," January 23, 1788:

I am, sir, a plain, unlettered man; I pretend not to an extensive knowledge in the many *sciences* of government. I have, scarcely, the reading of an obscure individual. But, the little knowledge, which I do possess, and I sincerely thank the good being for that little—effectually secures me from being carried away by the haughty overbearance of great names . . . [DHRC8 314–15]

James Madison, *The Federalist*, No. 47, January 30, 1788:

The oracle who is always consulted and cited on this subject [the separation of governmental powers] is the celebrated Montesquieu. If he be not the author of this invaluable precept in the *science* of politics, he has the merit at least of displaying and recommending it most effectually to the attention of mankind. . . . [Fed. 337]

Alexander C. Hanson, *Remarks on the Proposed Plan of a Federal Government*, c. January 31, 1788:

[1] . . . The perfection of political *science* consists chiefly in providing mutual checks amongst the several departments of power, preserving at the same time, the dependance of the greatest on the people. . . . [Ford 222]

[2] . . . Could the immortal spirit of Montesquieu revisit the earth, and behold the model now offered to America, how quickly would his favorite republic sink in his estimation. In a new quarter of the globe scarcely heard of by the greater part of Europeans in his day, and since the commencement of the present century, he would see men who have attained a perfection in the *science* most conducive to human happiness, in that study which was the principal occupation of his life, in which his predecessors had acquired only a few glimmering lights, and of which it was reserved for him to develop most of the true first principles. [Ford 222–23n]

George Washington to the Marquis de Lafayette, February 7, 1788:

. . . We are not to expect perfection in this world: but mankind, in modern times, have apparently made some progress in the *science* of Government.—Should that which is now offered to the People of America, be found on experiment less perfect than it can be made—a Constitutional door is left open for its amelioration. . . . [DHRC8 356]

Spencer Roane, "A Plain Dealer," February 13, 1788:

[1] . . . The *science* of government is in itself simple and plain; and if in the history of mankind, no perfect government be found, let it be attributed to the chicane perfidy and ambition of those who fabricate them; and who are more or less in common with all mankind infected with a lust of power. . . . [DHRC8 365–66]

[2] . . . For if, as the celebrated Dr. Blackstone observes, "in every art, occupation, or *science*, commercial or mechanical, some method of instruction or apprenticeship is held necessary, how much more requisite will such apprenticeship be found to be, in the *science* of government, the noblest and most difficult of any!" [DHRC8 366]

Samuel Bryan, "Centinel," No. 15, February 22, 1788:

There are few of the maxims or opinions we hold, that are the result of our own investigation or observation, and even those we adopt from others are seldom on a conviction of their truth or propriety, but from the facination of example and the influence of what is or appears to be the general sentiment. The *science* of government being the most abstruse and unobvious of all others, mankind are more liable to be imposed upon by the artful and designing in systems and regulations of government, than on any other subject . . . [DHRC16 189]

John Hancock, Speech to the Massachusetts Legislature, February 27, 1788:

..I hope and pray, that the gratitude of their [the people's] Hearts may be expressed by a proper use of those inestimable blessings,—by the greatest exertions of Patriotism,—by forming and supporting Institutions for cultivating the human Understanding, and for the greatest Progress of the Arts and *Sciences,*—by establishing Laws for the support of Piety, Religion and Morality, as well as for punishing Vice and Wickedness . . . [DHRC16 226]

"An Impartial Citizen," No. 5, February 28, 1788:

. . . Mr. [George] Mason, as in his other objections, reasons in the most unfair, and least *scientific* way imaginable, viz. Arguing against a measure from a remote possibility of its being abused. . . . [DHRC8 428]

"The Landholder," No. 10, February 29, 1788:

You [Luther Martin] entered the Convention without a sufficient knowledge in the *science* of government, where you committed a succession of memorable blunders . . . [DHRC16 269]

Mercy Otis Warren, *Observations on the New Constitution*, February 1788:

[1] Mankind may amuse themselves with theoretick systems of liberty, and trace its social and moral effects on *sciences,* virtue, industry, and every improvement of which the human mind is capable; but we can only discern its true value by the practical and wretched effects of slavery . . . [DHRC16 274]

[2] . . . And when patriotism is discountenanced and publick virtue becomes the ridicule of the sycophant—when every man of liberality, firmness, and penetration, who cannot lick the hand stretched out to oppress, is deemed an enemy to the State—then is the gulph of despotism set open, and the grades to slavery, though rapid, are scarce perceptible—then genius drags heavily its iron chain—*science* is neglected, and real merit flies to the shades for security from reproach—the mind becomes enervated, and the national character sinks to a kind of apathy with only energy sufficient to curse the breast that gave it milk . . .
[DHRC16 275]

Alexander Hamilton, *The Federalist*, No. 66, March 8, 1788:

. . . An absolute or qualified negative in the executive upon the acts of the legislative body, is admitted, by the ablest adepts in political *science,* to be an indispensable barrier against the encroachments of the latter upon the former. And it may, perhaps, with no less reason be contended, that the powers relating to impeachments are, as before intimated, an essential check in the hands of that body upon the encroachments of the executive. . . . [Fed. 431]

Jonathan Williams, Jr., "The Fabrick of Freedom," March 8, 1788:

May *Science* and her handmaid Art,
To this new world belong!
And infant muses joy impart
In strains of sportive song!—
Apollo see! with glory drest,
Appears refulgent in the west.

America is thus become.
A seat to freedom dear,
Where virtuous strangers find a home,
And no oppression fear.
These rising States shall be renown'd,
By Plenty, Art, and *Science* crown'd. [DHRC16 361]

James Iredell, "Marcus," No. 4, March 12, 1788:

One of the powers given to Congress is, "To promote the progress of *science* and useful arts, by securing for limited times to authors and inventors, the exclusive right to their respective writings and discoveries." I am convinced Mr. [George] Mason did not mean to refer to this clause. He is a gentleman of too much taste and knowledge himself to wish to have our government established upon such principles of barbarism as to be able to afford no encouragement to genius. [DHRC16 386]

Archibald Maclaine, "Publicola," March 20, 1788:

. . . But were it [the Constitution] completely adapted to our present situation, so as to be unexceptionable to all, time would render it defective—Improvements in commerce and manufactures, in arts and *sciences;* an increase in population, and an alteration in manners, would render amendments to the new constitution necessary—nothing in this world can be permanent . . . [DHRC16 438]

Luther Martin, "To the Citizens of Maryland," March 21, 1788:

[1] . . . as we are apt to run into extremes, having at length become convinced of my comparative nothingness, in so august an assembly [the Philadelphia

Convention], and one in which the *science* of government was so perfectly understood, I might sink into such a state of modesty and diffidence, as not to be able to muster up resolution enough to break the seal of silence and open my lips, even after the rays of light had begun to penetrate my understanding, and in some measure to chase away those clouds of error and ignorance, in which it was enveloped on my first arrival—Perhaps, had I been treated with a more forbearing indulgence while committing those memorable blunders, for want of a sufficient knowledge in the *science* of Government, I might, after the rays of light had illuminated my mind, have rendered my country much more important services . . . [DHRC16 455]

[2] . . . at the same time, I must frankly acknowledge, however it may operate as a proof of my dullness and stupidity, that the [quoting "The Landholder":] "ignorance in the *science* of government" under which I laboured at first, was not removed by more than two months close application, under those august and enlightened masters of the *science,* with which the Convention abounded, nor was I able to discover during that time, either by my own researches, or by any light borrowed from those luminaries, any thing in the history of mankind, or in the sentiments of those who have favoured the world with their ideas on government, to warrant or countenance the motley mixture of a system proposed . . . [DHRC16 457]

[3] . . . And if the framing and approving the constitution now offered to our acceptance, is a proof of knowledge in the *science* of government, I not only admit, but I glory in my ignorance . . . [DHRC16 458]

[4] . . . My object was, in truth, the very reverse, as I had uniformly opposed the system in its progress, I wished to have been present at the conclusion, to have then given it my solemn negative, which I certainly should have done, even had I stood single and alone, being perfectly willing to leave it to the cool and impartial investigation both of the present and of future ages to decide who best understood the *science* of government—who best knew the rights of men and of states—who best consulted the true interest of America, and who most faithfully discharged the trust reposed in them, those who agreed to, or those who opposed, the new Constitution . . . [DHRC16 460]

Luther Martin, "To the Citizens of Maryland," No. 3, March 28, 1788:

. . . And if one of our judges, possessed of no common share of understanding, and of extensive acquired knowledge, who, as he informs us, has long made the *science* of government his peculiar study, so little understands the true import and construction of this constitution, and that too in a part more particularly within his own province, can it be wondered at that the people in general, whose knowledge in subjects of this nature is much more limited and circumscribed, should but imperfectly comprehend the extent, operation and consequences of so complex and intricate a system? . . . [DHRC16 499]

John Dickinson, "Fabius," No. 6, 1788:

Yet, what were the consequences to Scotland of that dreaded union with England? The cultivation of her virtues and the correction of her errors—The emancipation of one class of her citizens from the yoke of her superiors—A relief of other classes from the injuries and insults of the great—Improvements in agriculture, *science,* arts, trade, and manufactures—The profits of industry and ingenuity enjoyed under the protection of laws—peace and security at home, and encrease of respectability abroad. . . . [Ford 198–99]

John Dickinson, "Fabius," No. 9, 1788:

These gentlemen will acknowledge, that Britain has sustained many internal convulsions, and many foreign wars, with a gradual advancement in freedom, power, and prosperity. They will acknowledge, that no nation has existed that ever so perfectly united those distant extremes, private security of life, liberty, and property, with exertion of public force—so advantageously combined the various powers of militia, troops, and fleets—or so happily blended together arms, arts, *science,* commerce, and agriculture. . . . [Ford 211]

Pennsylvania Constitution, September 2, 1790:

[Article VII, Section 2:] The arts and *sciences* shall be promoted in one or more seminaries of learning. [Thorpe 3099]

SEARCHES AND SEIZURES

United States Constitution, Bill of Rights, December 15, 1791:

[Article IV:] The right of the people to be secure in their persons, houses, papers, and effects, against unreasonable *searches and seizures,* shall not be violated, and no Warrants shall issue, but upon probable cause, supported by Oath or affirmation, and particularly describing the place to be *searched,* and the persons or things to be *seized.*

* * * * *

Virginia Bill of Rights, June 12, 1776:

[Article 10:] That general warrants, whereby an officer or messenger may be commanded to *search* suspected places without evidence of a fact committed, or to *seize* any person or persons not named, or whose offence is not particularly described and supported by evidence, are grievous and oppressive, and ought not to be granted. [Thorpe 3814]

Pennsylvania Constitution, September 28, 1776:

[Declaration of Rights, Article 10:] That the people have a right to hold themselves, their houses, papers, and possessions free from *search and seizure,* and therefore warrants without oaths or affirmations first made, affording a sufficient foundation for them, and whereby any officer or messenger may be commanded or required to *search* suspected places, or to *seize* any person or persons, his or their property, not particularly described, are contrary to that right, and ought not to be granted. [Thorpe 3083]

Maryland Constitution, November 11, 1776:

[Declaration of Rights, Article 23:] That all warrants, without oath or affirmation, to *search* suspected places, or to *seize* any person or property, are grievous and oppressive; and all general warrants—to *search* suspected places, or to apprehend suspected persons, without naming or describing the place, or the person in special—are illegal and ought not to be granted. [Thorpe 1688]

North Carolina Constitution, December 18, 1776:

[Declaration of Rights, Article 11:] That general warrants

—whereby an officer or messenger may be commanded to *search* suspected places, without evidence of the fact committed, or to *seize* any person or persons, not named, whose offences are not particularly described, and supported by evidence—are dangerous to liberty, and ought not to be granted.

[Thorpe 2788]

Vermont Constitution, July 8, 1777:

[Declaration of Rights, Article 11:] That the people have a right to hold themselves, their houses, papers and possessions free from *search or seizure;* and therefore warrants, without oaths or affirmations first made, affording a sufficient foundation for them, and whereby any officer or messenger may be commanded or required to *search* suspected places, or to *seize* any person or persons, his, her or their property, not particularly described, are contrary to that right, and ought not to be granted. [Thorpe 3741]

Massachusetts Constitution, March 2, 1780:

[Declaration of Rights, Article 14:] Every subject has a right to be secure from all unreasonable *searches and seizures,* of his person, his houses, his papers, and all his possessions. All warrants, therefore, are contrary to this right, if the cause or foundation of them be not previously supported by oath or affirmation, and if the order in the warrant to a civil officer, to make *search* in suspected places, or to arrest one or more subjected persons, or to *seize* their property, be not accompanied with a special designation of the persons or objects of *search, arrest, or seizure;* and no warrant ought to be issued but in cases, and with the formalities prescribed by the laws. [Thorpe 1891]

New Hampshire Constitution, June 2, 1784:

[Bill of Rights, Article 19:] Every subject hath a right to be secure from all unreasonable *searches and seizures* of his person, his houses, his papers, and all his possessions. All warrants, therefore, are contrary to this right, if the cause or foundation of them be not previously supported by oath, or affirmation; and if the order in the warrant to a civil officer, to make *search* in suspected places, or to arrest one or more suspected persons, or to *seize* their property be not accompanied with a special designation of the persons or objects of *search, arrest, or seizure;* and no warrant ought to be issued but in cases, and with the formalities prescribed by the laws. [Thorpe 2456]

Vermont Constitution, July 4, 1786:

[Declaration of Rights, Article 12:] That the people have a right to hold themselves, their houses, papers and possessions, free from *search or seizure:* and therefore warrants, without oaths or affirmations first made, affording sufficient foundation for them, and whereby any officer or messenger may be commanded or required to *search* suspected places, or to *seize* any person or persons, his, her or their property not particularly described, are contrary to that right, and ought not to be granted. [Thorpe 3753]

Richard Henry Lee, Proposed Amendments to the Constitution, October 16, 1787:

. . . that the citizens shall not be exposed to unreasonable *searches, seizure* of their persons, houses, papers or property . . . [DHRC8 65]

Mercy Otis Warren, *Observations on the New Constitution*, February 1788:

. . . nor can we be so ungrateful to the memory of the patriots who counteracted their operation, as so soon after their manly exertions to save us from such a detestable instrument of arbitrary power, to subject ourselves to the insolence of any petty revenue officer to enter our houses, *search, insult, and seize* at pleasure. We are told by a gentleman of too much virtue and real probity to suspect he has a design to deceive—"that the whole constitution is a declaration of rights"—but mankind must think for themselves, and to many very judicious and discerning characters, the whole constitution with very few exceptions appears a perversion of the rights of particular states, and of private citizens . . .
[DHRC16 281]

Pennsylvania Constitution, September 2, 1790:

[Article IX, Section 8:] That the people shall be secure in their persons, houses, papers, and possessions from unreasonable *searches and seizures;* and that no warrant to *search* any place, or to *seize* any person or things, shall issue, without describing them as nearly as may be, nor without probable cause, supported by oath or affirmation. [Thorpe 3100]

SECRECY

(Governmental)

[Note: Occurrences of "Secrecy" and its variants were selected in all cases which involve the activities of governments and governmental agencies; when an occurrence involves only private citizens or groups of persons it was excluded from the list.]

United States Constitution, September 17, 1787:

[Article I, Section 5:] Each House shall keep a Journal of its Proceedings, and from time to time publish the same, excepting such Parts as may in their Judgment require *Secrecy;* and the Yeas and Nays of the Members of either House on any question shall, at the Desire of one fifth of those Present, be entered on the Journal. . . .

* * * * *

John Adams, *Thoughts on Government*, April 1776:

A Representative Assembly, altho' extremely well qualified, and absolutely necessary as a branch of the legislature, is unfit to exercise the executive power, for want of two essential properties, *secrecy* and despatch. [PJA4 88]

Virginia Constitution, June 29, 1776:

. . . This [privy] Council may appoint their own Clerk, who shall have a salary settled by law, and take an oath of *secrecy,* in such matters as he shall be directed by the board to conceal. . . . [Thorpe 3817]

United States Continental Congress, Draft Articles of Confederation, July 12, 1776:

[Article 18:] The Assembly of the United States to publish the Journal of their Proceedings monthly, except such Parts thereof relating to Treaties, Alliances, or military Operations, as in their Judgment require *Secrecy*—The Yeas and Nays of the Delegates of each Colony on any Question to be entered on the Journal, where it is desired by any other Delegate . . . [DHRC1 84]

[Article 19:] [The Council of State shall have power] . . . To appoint a proper Person for their Clerk, who shall take an Oath of *Secrecy,* and Fidelity before he enters on the Exercise of his Office . . . [DHRC1 85]

Maryland Constitution, November 11, 1776:

[Form of Government, Article 26:] . . . The council may appoint their own clerk, who shall take such oath of support and fidelity to this state, as this convention, or the legislature, shall direct; and of *secrecy,* in such matters as he shall be directed by the board to keep *secret.* [Thorpe 1695]

Georgia Constitution, February 5, 1777:

[Article 30:] When any affair that requires *secrecy* shall be laid before the governor and the executive council, it shall be the duty of the governor, and he is hereby obliged, to administer the following oath, viz:.

"I, A B, do solemnly swear that any business that shall be at this time communicated to the council I will not, in any manner whatever, either by speaking, writing, or otherwise, reveal the same to any person whatever, until leave given by the council, or when called upon by the house of assembly; and all this I swear without any reservation whatever; so help me God." [Thorpe 782]

New York Constitution, April 20, 1777:

[Article 15:] That whenever the assembly and senate disagree, a conference shall be held, in the preference of both, and be managed by committees, to be by them respectively chosen by ballot. That the doors, both of the senate and assembly, shall at all times be kept open to all persons, except when the welfare of the State shall require their debates to be kept *secret.* And the journals of all their proceedings shall be kept in the manner heretofore accustomed by the general assembly of the colony of New York; and except such parts as they shall, as aforesaid, respectively determine not to make public be from day to day (if the business of the legislature will permit) published. [Thorpe 2632]

United States Articles of Confederation, November 15, 1777:

[Article IX:] The congress of the united states shall have power to adjourn to any time within the year, and to any place within the united states, so that no period of adjournment be for a longer duration than the space of six Months, and shall publish the Journal of their proceedings monthly, except such parts thereof relating to treaties, alliances or military operations, as in their judgment require *secresy;* and the yeas and nays of the delegates of each state on any question shall be entered on the Journal, when it is desired by any delegate . . .

William Pierce to St. George Tucker, September 28, 1787, published in *Gazette of the State of Georgia*, March 20, 1788:

You ask me for such information as I can, with propriety, give you, respecting the proceedings of the Convention. In my letter from Philadelphia, in July last, I informed you that every thing was covered with the veil of *secresy*. It is now taken off, and the great work is presented to the public for their consideration. I enclose you a copy of it, with the letter which accompanies the Constitution. [DHRC16 442]

James Wilson, Speech on the Federal Constitution, October 6, 1787:

. . . But what would be our national situation, were it otherwise? [*i.e.*, if the national government were not allowed to maintain a standing army.] Every principle of policy must be subverted, and the government must declare war before they are prepared to carry it on. Whatever may be the provocation, however important the object in view, and however necessary dispatch and *secrecy* may be, still the declaration must precede the preparation, and the enemy will be informed of your intention, not only before you are equipped for an attack, but even before you are fortified for a defence. . . . [Ford 158]

George Mason, Objections to the Constitution, October 7, 1787:

The President of the United States has the unrestrained Power of granting Pardons for Treason; which may be sometimes excercised to screen from Punishment those whom he had *secretly* instigated to commit the Crime, & thereby prevent a Discovery of his own Guilt. [DHRC8 44]

Edmund Randolph, Letter on the Federal Constitution, October 10, 1787:

. . . To crown the whole, it is scarcely within the verge of possibility, that so numerous an assembly [as Congress under the Confederation] should acquire that *secrecy,* dispatch, and vigour, which are the test of excellence in the executive department. [DHRC8 268]

Alexander Hamilton, *The Federalist*, No. 6, November 14, 1787:

. . . An intelligent writer [the Abbé Mably] expresses himself on this subject to this effect: "NEIGHBORING NATIONS (says he) are naturally enemies of each other, unless their common weakness forces them to league in a CONFEDER-

ATIVE REPUBLIC, and their constitution prevents the differences that neighborhood occasions, extinguishing that *secret* jealousy which disposes all states to aggrandize themselves at the expense of their neighbors." . . . [Fed. 113]

Pelatiah Webster, *The Weakness of Brutus Exposed*, November 14, 1787:

The most despotic monarch that can exist, must have his councils, and officers of state; and I can't see any one circumstance of their being appointed under a monarchy, that can afford any chance of their being any wiser or better, than ours may be. 'Tis true indeed, the despot may, if he pleases, act without any advice at all; but when he does so, I conceive it will be very rare that the nation will receive greater advantages from his unadvised edicts, than may be drawed from the deliberate acts and orders of our supreme powers. All that can be said in favour of those, is, that they will have less chance of delay, and more of *secrecy,* than these; but I think it probable, that the latter will be grounded on better information, and greater wisdom; will carry more weights and be better supported. [Ford 130]

Dissent of the Pennsylvania Convention's Minority, December 18, 1787:

[1] . . . The [constitutional] convention sat upwards of four months. The doors were kept shut, and the members brought under the most solemn engagements of *secrecy*. Some of those who opposed their going so far beyond their powers retired, hopeless, from the convention, others had the firmness to refuse signing the plan altogether; and many who did sign it, did it not as a system they wholly approved, but as the best that could be then obtained, and notwithstanding the time spent on this subject, it is agreed on all hands to be a work of haste and accommodation. [DHRC2 620]

[2] Whilst the gilded chains were forging in the *secret* conclave [*i.e.*, the constitutional convention], the meaner instruments of the despotism without were busily employed in alarming the fears of the people with dangers which did not exist, and exciting their hopes of greater advantages from the expected plan than even the best government on earth could produce. [DHRC2 620]

[3] The proposed plan had not many hours issued forth from the womb of suspicious *secrecy,* until such as were prepared for the purpose were carrying about petitions for people to sign, signifying their approbation of the system, and requesting the legislature to call a convention. . . . [DHRC2 620]

"Americanus," No. 2, December 19, 1787:

. . . This unity of the executive authority constitutes, in my humble opinion, our greatest safety, and affords the most effectual means of restraining it within proper bounds. Was the president surrounded with counsellors, or was the executive power lodged in the hands of many persons, it would be difficult to discover the one, who might recommend an obnoxious measure. *Secrecy* and dispatch could not be expected. The unavoidable imbecility of measures would be retarded by the difficulty of procuring an unanimous consent, and the most important proceedings would be liable to interruption by a contrariety of opinions. . . . [DHRC8 245]

James Madison, *The Federalist*, No. 43, January 23, 1788:

Is it true that force and right are necessarily on the same side in republican governments? May not the minor party possess such a superiority of pecuniary resources, of military talents and experience, or of *secret* succors from foreign powers, as will render it superior also in an appeal to the sword? . . .

[Fed. 313]

"Civis Rusticus," January 30, 1788:

. . . The president's having the unrestrained power of pardoning for treasons is another objection; and why? [quoting George Mason:] "it may be sometimes exercised to screen from punishment those whom he, (the president) had *secretly* instigated to commit the crime, and thereby prevent a discovery of his own guilt"—I appeal to this worthy gentleman himself, I appeal to the public, whether there be in this objection, more of validity and force, or chimera and imagination. [DHRC8 336–37]

Alexander C. Hanson, *Remarks on the Proposed Plan of a Federal Government*, c. January 31, 1788:

For the honour of my countrymen, I hope this extreme reluctance to surrender power is confined to those, whose ambition, or private interest, would have all things subservient to the omnipotence of assembly. In the few years that the state constitutions have endured, has not every one seen pregnant proofs of the vain love of domination? Has he not also seen decisive marks of overbearing *secret* influence? Where are the instances of exalted patriotism? . . . [Ford 252]

David Ramsay, "Civis," February 4, 1788:

It has been objected, that the president, and two-thirds of the senate, though not of your election, may make treaties binding on this state [South Carolina]. Ask these objectors—do you wish to have any treaties? They will say yes.—Ask then who can be more properly trusted with the power of making them, than they to whom the convention have referred it? Can the state legislatures? They would consult their local interests—Can the Continental House of Representatives? When sixty-five men can keep a *secret,* they may. Observe the cautious guards which are placed around your interests. . . . [DHRC16 24]

Samuel Bryan, "Centinel," No. 14, February 5, 1788:

..I am happy to find the comment that I have made upon the nature and tendency of the new constitution, and my suspicions of the principles and designs of its authors, are fully confirmed by the evidence of the Honorable LUTHER MARTIN, Esquire, late deputy in the general convention. He has laid open the conclave, exposed the dark scene within, developed the mystery of the proceedings, and illustrated the machinations of ambition. His public spirit has drawn upon him the rage of the conspirators, for daring to remove the veil of *secrecy,* and announcing to the public the meditated, gilded mischief . . .

[DHRRC16 31–32]

James Madison, *The Federalist*, No. 55, February 13, 1788:

. . . The congress which conducted us through the Revolution was a less numerous body than their successors will be; they were not chosen by, nor responsible to, their fellow-citizens at large; though appointed from year to year, and recallable at pleasure, they were generally continued for three years, and, prior to the ratification of the federal articles, for a still longer term. They held their consultations always under the veil of *secrecy;* they had the sole transaction of our affairs with foreign nations; through the whole course of the war they had the fate of their country more in their hands than it is to be hoped will ever be the case with our future representatives . . . [Fed. 377–78]

Spencer Roane, "A Plain Dealer," February 13, 1788:

. . . but when it is considered, that the present is not the golden age—the epoch of virtue, candor and integrity—that the views of ambitious and designing men are continually working to their own aggrandisement and to the overthrow of liberty, and that the discordant interests of thirteen different commonwealths are to be reconciled and promoted by one general government; common reason will teach us, that the utmost caution, *secrecy,* and political sagacity is requisite to secure to each the important blessings of good government. [DHRC8 366]

James Madison, *The Federalist*, No. 58, February 20, 1788:

. . . The people can never err more than in supposing that by multiplying their representatives beyond a certain limit, they strengthen the barrier against the government of a few. Experience will forever admonish them that, on the contrary, after securing a sufficient number for the purposes of safety, of local information, and of diffusive sympathy with the whole society, they will counteract their own views by every addition to their representatives. The countenance of the government may become more democratic, but the soul that animates it will be more oligarchic. The machine will be enlarged, but the fewer, and often the more *secret,* will be the springs by which its motions are directed.

[Fed. 392]

Alexander White, "To the Citizens of Virginia," February 22, 1788:

. . . I shall now leave with you to judge what degree of respect is to be paid to the assertions and opinions of the minority of the convention of the State of Pennsylvania and return to their performance; expunge from it the opprobrious epithets so liberally bestowed on all who differ from them, such as [referring to the constitutional convention as a] *secret* conclave womb of suspicious *secrecy*—instruments and tools of despotism—supremacy of despotism, &c. &c. &c.—Substitute the proper names of men and measures.—Read it over again and you will find it a simple tale indeed. . . . [DHRC8 404]

"An Impartial Citizen," No. 5, February 28, 1788:

It is objected, that the President has the power of pardoning offences against the United States, and Mr. [George] Mason discovers that the President may prevent a discovery and punishment of his own crimes by this power; by forgiving those whom he had *secretly* instigated to the commission of crimes—The most of the other antifederalists enumerate this as one of the defects they pretend to discover in this system. . . . [DHRC8 428]

Alexander White, "To the Citizens of Virginia," February 29, 1788:

. . . Examine the plan of government. Do you observe the seeds of despotism sown there? On the contrary, do you not see more effectual precautions against the open or *secret* abuse of power, than in the Constitution of any government which has had the experience of ages, or in any plan which has been composed by philosophers or statesmen? . . . [DHRC8 443]

Mercy Otis Warren, *Observations on the New Constitution*, February 1788:

[1] . . . But I leave the field of general censure on the *secrecy* of its [*i.e.*, the Constitution's] birth, the rapidity of its growth, and the fatal consequences of suffering it to live to the age of maturity, and will particularize some of the most weighty objections to its passing through this continent in a gigantic size. . . .

[DHRC16 278]

[2] . . . Even the party who have been disposed to swallow, without examination, the proposals of the *secret* conclave [the constitutional convention], have started on a discovery that this essential right [trial by jury] was curtailed . . .

[DHRC16 279]

John Jay, *The Federalist*, No. 64, March 5, 1788:

[1] It seldom happens in the negotiation of treaties, of whatever nature, but that perfect *secrecy* and immediate despatch are sometimes requisite. There are cases where the most useful intelligence may be obtained, if the persons possessing it can be relieved from apprehensions of discovery. Those apprehensions will operate on those persons whether they are actuated by mercenary or friendly motives; and there doubtless are many of both descriptions, who would rely on the *secrecy* of the President, but who would not confide in that of the Senate, and still less in that of a large popular Assembly. . . . [Fed. 422]

[2] . . . So often and so essentially have we heretofore suffered from the want of *secrecy* and despatch, that the Constitution would have been inexcusably defective, if no attention had been paid to those objects. Those matters which in negotiations usually require the most *secrecy* and the most despatch, are those preparatory and auxiliary measures which are not otherwise important in a national view, than as they tend to facilitate the attainment of the objects of the negotiation. For these, the President will find no difficulty to provide; and should any circumstance occur which requires the advice and consent of the Senate, he may at any time convene them. Thus we see that the Constitution provides that our negotiations for treaties shall have every advantage which can be derived from talents, information, integrity, and deliberate investigations, on the one hand, and from *secrecy* and despatch on the other. [Fed. 423]

James Iredell, "Marcus," No. 3, March 5, 1788:

[1] . . . Let us now therefore consider some of the actual inconveniencies which would attend an abridgement of the power of the President in this respect. One of the great advantages attending a single Executive power is, the degree of *secrecy* and dispatch with which, on critical occasions, such a power can act. In war this advantage will often counterballance the want of many others. Now suppose, in the very midst of a war of extreme consequence to our safety or prosperity, the President could prevail upon a gentleman of abilities to go into the enemy's country, to serve in the useful, but dishonorable character of a spy: Such are certainly maintained by all vigilant governments, and in proportion to the ignominy of the character, and the danger sustained in the enemy's country, ought to be his protection and security in his own. This man renders very useful services; perhaps, by timely information prevents the destruction of his country. Nobody knows of these *secret* services but the President himself; his adherence however to the enemy is notorious: He is afterwards intercepted in endeavouring to return to his own country, and having been perhaps a man of distinction before, he is proportionably obnoxious to his country at large for his supposed treason. Would it not be monstrous, that the President should not have it in his power to pardon this man? or that it should depend upon mere solicitation and favor, and perhaps, though the President should state the fact as it really was,

some zealous partizan, with his jealousy constantly fixed upon the President, might insinuate that in fact the President and he were *secret* traitors together, and thus obtain a rejection of the President's application. . . . [DHRC16 323]

[2] . . . But, says Mr. Mason, "The President may sometimes exercise this power to screen from punishment those whom he had *secretly* instigated to commit the crime, and thereby prevent a discovery of his own guilt." This is possible, but the probability of it is surely too slight to endanger the consequences of abridging a power which seems so generally to have been deemed necessary in every well regulated government. . . . [DHRC16 324]

Luther Martin, Reply to a Newspaper Writer, March 7, 1788:

The business of the committees were not of a *secret* nature, nor were they conducted in a *secret* manner; I mean as to the members of the Convention. . . . [DHRC16 346]

Benjamin Workman [?], "Philadelphiensis," No. 11, March 8, 1788:

. . . Let these men [the members of the constitutional convention] but cooly consider the misery that must inevitably befal millions of their countrymen, in consequence of their treachery in framing this system of fraud and oppression; and remorse and deep anguish of soul must await them! Humanity brings a tear of sympathetic pity from the eye of their fellow men, whose ruin they had *secretly* projected. . . . [DHRC16 363]

George Nicholas [?], "The State Soldier," No. 3, March 12, 1788:

For he who was willing but a few years ago to vest Congress with the power of raising taxes by the absolute assistance of armies, could have little objection to a plan at this time, which only proposes to raise them by moderate means, was there not something of *secret* consequence involved in it. [DHRC8 489]

"An Impartial Citizen," No. 6, March 13, 1788:

. . . It is sophistry in the extreme to suppose, that standing armies will be kept in time of profound peace, when there is no necessity for it. As a regular statement and account of the public receipts and expenditures of money, are to be published from time to time, for the inspection and examination of the public; and as this cannot, on any pretext, be kept *secret* from the people should armies be unnecessarily maintained the sums which their maintenance would cost would be universally known, and as universally would the measure be reprobated. . . . [DHRC8 498]

Alexander Hamilton, *The Federalist*, No. 69, March 14, 1788:

. . . If we compare the publicity which must necessarily attend the mode of appointment by the President and an entire branch of the national legislature, with the privacy in the mode of appointment by the governor of New York, closeted in a *secret* apartment with at most four, and frequently with only two persons; and if we at the same time consider how much more easy it must be to influence the small number of which a council of appointment consist, than the considerable number of which the national Senate would consist, we cannot hesitate to pronounce that the power of the chief magistrate of this State, in the disposition of offices, must, in practice, be greatly superior to that of the Chief Magistrate of the Union. [Fed. 449]

Alexander Hamilton, *The Federalist*, No. 70, March 15, 1788:

[1] That unity is conducive to energy will not be disputed. Decision, activity, *secrecy,* and despatch will generally characterize the proceedings of one man in a much more eminent degree than the proceedings of any great number; and in proportion as the number is increased, these qualities will be diminished. [Fed. 452]

[2] "I was overruled by my council. The council were so divided in their opinions that it was impossible to obtain any better resolution on the point." These and similar pretexts are constantly at hand, whether true or false. And who is there that will either take the trouble or incur the odium of a strict scrutiny into the *secret* springs of the transaction? . . . [Fed. 455]

Luther Martin, "To the Citizens of Maryland," No. 2, March 21, 1788:

That I expressed great regret at being obliged to leave Philadelphia, and a fixed determination to return, if possible, before the Convention rose, is certain—That I might declare that I had rather lose an hundred guineas than not to be there at the close of the business is very probable—and it is possible that some who heard me say this, not knowing my reasons, which could not be expressed without a breach of that *secrecy* to which we were enjoined, might erroneously have concluded that my motive was the gratification of vanity, in having my name enrolled with those of a Franklin and a Washington. . . . [DHRC16 459]

Alexander Hamilton, *The Federalist*, No. 75, March 26, 1788:

The remarks made in a former number, which have been alluded to in another part of this paper, will apply with conclusive force against the admission of the House of Representatives to share in the formation of treaties. The fluctuating and, taking its future increase into the account, the multitudinous composition of that body, forbid us to expect in it those qualities which are essential to the proper execution of such a trust. Accurate and comprehensive knowledge of foreign politics; a steady and systematic adherence to the same views; a nice and uniform sensibility to national character; decision, *secrecy,* and despatch, are incompatible with the genius of a body so variable and so numerous. . . .

[Fed. 478]

John Jay, *An Address to the People of the State of New York*, c. April 15, 1788:

. . . They [Congress under the Confederation] may appoint ministers and other officers of trust, but without power to try or punish them for misdemeanors—They may resolve, but cannot execute either with dispatch or with *secrecy*—In short, they may consult, and deliberate, and recommend, and make requisitions, and they who please, may regard them. [Ford 72]

Melancton Smith, *An Address to the People of the State of New York*, April 1788:

. . . I will venture to say, that the idea of a government similar to the one proposed [i.e., the Constitution], never entered the minds of the legislatures who appointed the convention, and of but very few of the members who composed it, until they had assembled and heard it proposed in that body: much less had the people any conception of such a plan until after it was promulgated. While it was agitated, the debates of the convention were kept an impenetrable *secret,* and no opportunity was given for well informed men to offer their sentiments upon the subject. . . . [Ford 101]

John Dickinson, "Fabius," No. 2, 1788:

. . . If assaults upon liberty are to be guarded against, and surely they ought to be with sleepless vigilance, why should we depend more on the commander in chief of the army and navy of The United States, and of the militia of the several states, and on his counsellors, whom he may *secretly* influence, than of the senate to be appointed by the persons exercising the sovereign authority of the several states? . . . [Ford 173]

Pennsylvania Constitution, September 2, 1790:

[Article I, Section 14:] Each house shall keep a journal of its proceedings, and publish them weekly, except such parts as may require *secrecy:* And the yeas and nays of the members on any question shall, at the desire of any two of them, be entered on the journals. [Thorpe 3094]

[Article I, Section 15:] The doors of each house, and of committees of the whole, shall be open unless when the business shall be such as ought to be kept *secret*. [Thorpe 3094]

SERVICE, BOUND TO, HELD TO

[Note: This list is narrowly limited to variants of the word "service" combined with variants of the words "bind" and "hold." Other related words, including "slavery," are not included because they do not occur in the Constitution. The list also excludes the concepts of "held *by* service" and "bound *by* service," which reflect feudal arrangements of landholding and personal allegiance; rather, it concentrates rather on *persons held or bound to service* under various arrangements.]

United States Constitution, September 17, 1787:

[Article I, Section 2:] Representatives and direct Taxes shall be apportioned among the several States which may be included within this Union, according to their respective Numbers, which shall be determined by adding to the whole Number of free Persons, including those *bound to Service* for a Term of Years, and excluding Indians not taxed, three fifths of all other Persons. . . .

[Article IV, Section 2:] No Person *held to Service* or Labour in one State, under the Laws thereof, escaping into another, shall, in Consequence of any Law or Regulation therein, be discharged from such Service or Labor, but shall be delivered up on Claim of the Party to whom such Service or Labour may be due.

* * * * *

Fundamental Constitutions of Carolina, March 1, 1669:

[Article 116:] All inhabitants and freemen of Carolina above seventeen years of age, and under sixty, shall be *bound* to bear arms and *serve* as soldiers, whenever the grand council shall find it necessary. [Thorpe 2786]

Pennsylvania Constitution, September 28, 1776:

[Declaration of Rights, Article 8:] That every member of society hath a right to be protected in the enjoyment of life, liberty and property, and therefore is *bound* to contribute his proportion towards the expence of that protection, and yield his personal *service* when necessary, or an equivalent thereto . . .

[Thorpe 3083]

Vermont Constitution, July 8, 1777:

[Declaration of Rights, Article 1:] That all men are born equally free and independent, and have certain natural, inherent and unalienable rights, amongst which are the enjoying and defending life and liberty; acquiring, possessing and protecting property, and pursuing and obtaining happiness and safety. Therefore, no male person, born in this country, or brought from over sea ought to be *holden* by law, to *serve* any person, as a *servant,* slave or apprentice, after he arrives to the age of twenty-one years, nor female, in like manner, after she arrives to the age of eighteen years, unless they are *bound* by their own consent, after they arrive to such age, or *bound* by law, for the payment of debts, damages, fines, costs, or the like. [Thorpe 3739–40]

[*Ibid.,* Article 9:] That every member of society hath a right to be protected in the enjoyment of life, liberty and property, and therefore, is *bound* to contribute his proportion towards the expense of that protection, and yield his personal *service,* when necessary, or an equivalent thereto . . . [Thorpe 3740]

New Hampshire Constitution, June 2, 1784:

[Bill of Rights, Article 12:] Every member of the community has a right to be protected by it in the enjoyment of his life, liberty and property; he is therefore *bound* to contribute his share in the expence of such protection, and to yield his personal *service* when necessary, or an equivalent. . . . [Thorpe 2455]

Vermont Constitution, July 4, 1786:

[Declaration of Rights, Article 1:] That all men are born equally free and independent, and have certain natural, inherent and unalienable rights; amongst which are, the enjoying and defending life and liberty—acquiring, possessing and protecting property—and pursuing and obtaining happiness and safety. Therefore, no male person, born in this country, or brought from over sea, ought to be *holden* by law to *serve* any person, as a *servant,* slave, or apprentice, after he arrives to the age of twenty-one years; nor female, in like manner, after she arrives to the age of eighteen years; unless they are *bound* by their own consent after they arrive to such age; or *bound* by law for the payment of debts, damages, fines, costs, or the like. [Thorpe 3751–52]

[*Ibid.*, Article 10:] That every member of society hath a right to be protected in the enjoyment of life, liberty and property; and therefore is *bound* to contribute his proportion towards the expense of that protection, and yield his personal *service*, when necessary, or an equivalent thereto . . . [Thorpe 3753]

The New Jersey Plan of Union, June 15, 1787:

[Article 3:] Res[olve]d that whenever requisitions shall be necessary, instead of the rule for making requisitions mentioned in the articles of Confederation, the United States in Cong[res]s be authorized to make such requisitions in proportion to the whole number of white & other free citizens & inhabitants of every age sex and condition including those *bound to servitude* for a term of years & three fifths of all other persons not comprehended in the foregoing description, except Indians not paying taxes . . . [DHRC1 251]

SPEECH, FREEDOM OF

(Liberty of Speech)

United States Constitution, Bill of Rights, December 15, 1791:

[Article I:] Congress shall make no law respecting an establishment of religion, or prohibiting the free exercise thereof; or abridging the *freedom of speech,* or of the press; or the right of the people peaceably to assemble, and to petition the Government for a redress of grievances.

* * * * *

Fundamental Orders of Connecticut, 1638–39:

[Article 10:] . . . In wch [General] Courte the Governour or Moderator shall haue power to order the Courte to give *liberty of spech,* and silence unceasonable and disorderly *speakeing,* to put all things to voate, and in case the vote be equall to have the casting voice. . . . [Thorpe 522]

English Bill of Rights, December 16, 1689:

That the *freedom of speech* and debates or proceedings in parliament ought not to be impeached or questioned in any court or place out of parliament. [SDECH 465]

Pennsylvania Constitution, September 28, 1776:

[Declaration of Rights, Article 12:] That the people have a right to *freedom of speech,* and of writing, and publishing their sentiments; therefore the freedom of the press ought not to be restrained. [Thorpe 3083]

Maryland Constitution, November 11, 1776:

[Declaration of Rights, Article 8:] That *freedom of speech* and debates, or proceedings in the Legislature, ought not to be impeached in any other court or judicature. [Thorpe 1687]

Vermont Constitution, July 8, 1777:

[Declaration of Rights, Article 14:] That the people have a right to *freedom of speech,* and of writing and publishing their sentiments; therefore, the freedom of the press ought not be restrained. [Thorpe 3741]

United States Articles of Confederation, November 15, 1777:

[Article V:] *Freedom of speech* and debate in Congress shall not be impeached or questioned in any Court, or place out of Congress, and the members of congress shall be protected in their persons from arrests and imprisonments, during the time of their going to and from, and attendance on congress, except for treason, felony, or breach of the peace.

Massachusetts Constitution, March 2, 1780:

[Declartion of Rights, Article 21:] The *freedom* of deliberation, *speech,* and debate, in either house of the legislature, is so essential to the rights of the people, that it cannot be the foundation of any accusation or prosecution, action or complaint, in any other court or place whatsoever. [Thorpe 1892]

New Hampshire Constitution, June 2, 1784:

[Bill of Rights, Article 30:] The *freedom* of deliberation, *speech,* and debate, in either house of the legislature, is so essential to the rights of the people, that it cannot be the foundation of any action, complaint, or prosecution, in any other court or place whatsoever. [Thorpe 2457]

Vermont Constitution, July 4, 1786:

[Declaration of Rights, Article 15:] That the people have a right of *freedom of speech* and of writing and publishing their sentiments, concerning the transactions of government—and therefore the freedom of the press ought not to be restrained. [Thorpe 3753]

[*Ibid.,* Article 16:] The *freedom* of deliberation, *speech,* and debate, in the legislature, is so essential to the rights of the people, that it can not be the foundation of any accusation or prosecution, action or complaint, in any other court or place whatsoever. [Thorpe 3753]

Tench Coxe, *An Examination of the Constitution for the United States of America*, No. 3, September 29, 1787:

. . . [United States Representatives] are not to be restrained from the firm and plain language, which becomes the independent representatives of *freedom,* for there is to be a perfect *liberty of speech*. Without their consent, no monies can be obtained, no armies raised, no navies provided. . . . [Ford 144]

Dissent of the Pennsylvania Assembly's Minority, December 18, 1787:

That the people have a right to the *freedom of speech,* of writing and publishing their sentiments, therefore the freedom of the press shall not be restrained by any law of the United States. [DHRC2 623]

"A Virginia Planter," March 7, 1788:

Several personages in Congress will commend the *freedom* I take, to recapitulate the evils that may and will result from the present form of the Federal Constitution; to *speak* the truth, without just cause of offence, is the right of every *free* citizen. . . . [DHRC8 472]

John Dickinson, "Fabius," No. 1, April 10, 1788:

Before this tribunal of the people, let every one *freely speak,* what he really thinks, but with so sincere a reverence for the cause he ventures to discuss, as to use the utmost caution, lest he should lead any into errors, upon a point of such sacred concern as the public happiness. [Ford 166]

Pennsylvania Constitution, September 2, 1790:

[Article 9, Section 7:] . . . The *free* communication of thoughts and opinions is one of the invaluable rights of man; and every citizen may *freely speak,* write, and print on any subject, being responsible for the abuse of that *liberty*. In prosecutions for the publication of papers investigating the official conduct of officers or men in a public capacity, or where the matter published is proper for public information, the truth thereof may be given in evidence; and in all indictments for libels the jury shall have a right to determine the law and the facts, under the direction of the court, as in other cases. [Thorpe 3100]

SUFFRAGE

United States Constitution, September 17, 1787:

[Article V:] The Congress, whenever two thirds of both Houses shall deem it necessary, shall propose Amendments to this Constitution, or, on the Application of the Legislatures of two thirds of the several States, shall call a Convention for proposing Amendments, which, in either Case, shall be valid to all Intents and Purposes, as Part of this Constitution, when ratified by the Legislatures of three fourths of the several States, or by Conventions in three fourths thereof, as the one or the other Mode of Ratification may be proposed by the Congress; Provided that no Amendment which may be made prior to the Year One thousand eight hundred and eight shall in any Manner affect the first and fourth Clauses in the Ninth Section of the first Article; and that no State, without its Consent, shall be deprived of its equal *Suffrage* in the Senate.

* * * * *

New Hampshire Constitution, January 5, 1776:

We, the members of the Congress of New Hampshire, chosen and appointed by the free *suffrages* of the people of said colony, and authorized and empowered by them to meet together, and use such means and pursue such measures as we should judge best for the public good . . . [Thorpe 2451]

Virginia Bill of Rights, June 12, 1776:

[Section 6:] That elections of members to serve as representatives of the people, in assembly, ought to be free; and that all men, having sufficient evidence of permanent common interest with, and attachment to, the community, have the right of *suffrage,* and cannot be taxed or deprived of their property for public uses, without their own consent, or that of their representatives so elected, nor bound by any law to which they have not, in like manner, assented for the public good. [Thorpe 3813]

Virginia Constitution, June 29, 1776:

[1] . . . but when any city or borough shall so decrease, as that the number of persons, having right of *suffrage* therein, shall have been for the space of seven years successively less than half the number of voters in some one county in Virginia, such city or borough thenceforward shall cease to send a Delegate or Representative to the Assembly. [Thorpe 3816]

[2] The right of *suffrage* in the election of members for both Houses shall remain as exercised at present; and each House shall choose its own Speaker, appoint its own officers, settle its own rules of proceeding, and direct writs of election, for the supplying intermediate vacancies. [Thorpe 3816]

Delaware Constitution, September 10, 1776:

[Article 5:] The right of *suffrage* in the election of members for both houses shall remain as exercised by law at present; and each house shall choose its own speaker, appoint its own officers, judge of the qualifications and elections of its own members, settle its own rules of proceedings, and direct writs of election for supplying intermediate vacancies. . . . [Thorpe 563]

Maryland Constitution, November 11, 1776:

[Declaration of Rights, Article 5:] That the right in the people to participate in the Legislature is the best security of liberty, and the foundation of all free government; for this purpose, elections ought to be free and frequent, and every man, having property in, a common interest with, and an attachment to the community, ought to have a right of *suffrage.* [Thorpe 1687]

[Form of Government, Article 2:] That the House of Delegates shall be chosen in the following manner: All freemen, above twenty-one years of age, having a freehold of fifty acres of land, in the county in which they offer to vote, and residing therein—and all freemen, having property in this State above the value of thirty pounds current money, and having resided in the county, in which they offer to vote, one whole year next preceding the election, shall have a right of *suffrage,* in the election of Delegates for such county . . . [Thorpe 1691]

[*Ibid.,* Article 5:] That all persons, inhabitants of Baltimore town, and having the same qualifications as electors in the county, shall, on the same first Monday of October, seventeen hundred and seventy-seven, and on the same day in every year for ever thereafter, at such place in the said town as the judges shall appoint, elect, viva voce, by a majority of votes, two delegates, qualified as aforesaid; but, if the said inhabitants of the town shall so decrease, as that the number of persons having a right of *suffrage* therein shall have been, for the space of seven years successively, less than one-half the number of voters in some one county in this state, such town shall thenceforward cease to send two Delegates or Representatives to the House of Delegates, until the said town shall have one-half of the number of voters in some one county in this state. [Thorpe 1692]

[*Ibid.*, Article 42:] . . . All freemen above the age of twenty-one years, having a freehold of fifty acres of land in the county in which they offer to ballot, and residing therein—and all freemen above the age of twenty-one years, and having property in the State above the value of thirty pounds current money, and having resided in the county in which they offer to ballot one whole year next preceding the election—shall have a right of *suffrage*. . . . [Thorpe 1698]

New York Constitution, April 20, 1777:

[Preamble:] By virtue of which several acts, declarations, and proceedings mentioned and contained in the afore-cited resolves or resolutions of the general Congress of the United American States, and of the congresses or conventions of this State, all power whatever therein hath reverted to the people thereof, and this convention hath by their *suffrages* and free choice been appointed and among other thing authorized to institute and establish such a government as they shall deem best calculated to secure the rights and liberties of the good people of this State, most conducive of the happiness and safety of their constituents in particular, and of America in general. [Thorpe 2628]

[Article 21:] . . . And if, during such vacancy of the office of governor, the lieutenant-governor shall be impeached, displaced, resign, die, or be absent from the State, the president of the senate shall, in like manner as the lieutenant-governor, administer the government, until others shall be elected by the *suffrage* of the people, at the succeeding election. [Thorpe 2633]

Vermont Constitution, July 8, 1777:

[Frame of Government, Section 6:] I ——— solemnly swear, by the ever living God, (or affirm, in the presence of Almighty God,) that whenever I am called to give my vote or *suffrage*, touching any matter that concerns the State of Vermont, I will do it so, as in my conscience, I shall judge will most conduce to the best good of the same, as established by the constitution, without fear or favor of any man. [Thorpe 3742]

Vermont Constitution, July 4, 1786:

[Frame of Government, Section 18:] You solemnly swear, (or affirm) that whenever you give your vote or *suffrage*, touching any matter that concerns the State of Vermont, you will do it so as in your conscience you shall judge will most conduce to the best good of the same, as established by the Constitution, without fear or favour of any man. [Thorpe 3757–58]

The Virginia Plan of Union, May 29, 1787:

[Article 2:] Re[solve]d therefore that the rights of *suffrage* in the National Legislature ought to be proportioned to the Quotas of contribution, or to the number of free inhabitants, as the one or the other rule may seem best in different cases. [DHRC1 243]

William Pierce to St. George Tucker, September 28, 1787, published in *Gazette of the State of Georgia*, March 20, 1788:

[1] . . . The solemnity of the trial by jury is suited to the nature of criminal cases, because, before a man is brought to answer the indictment, the fact or truth of every accusation is inquired into by the Grand Jury, composed of his fellow citizens, and the same truth or fact afterwards (should the Grand Jury find the accusation well founded) is to be confirmed by the unanimous *suffrage* of twelve good men, "superior to all suspicion." I do not think there can be a greater guard to the liberties of a people than such a mode of trial on the affairs of life and death. . . . [DHRC16 445]

[2] It requires very little wisdom or foresight to see into the consequences of the government when put compleatly in motion. You will observe that one branch of the Legislature is to come from the People, the other from the several State Legislatures; one is to sympathize with the people at large, the other with the sovereignty of the states, but the *suffrages* of the two are unequal; the House of Commons will have sixty-five votes, whilst the Senate has only twenty-six. Some of the states will have eight and ten Members in the Lower House, some only two or three, but all will have an equal number in the Senate. . . .
[DHRC16 445]

Tench Coxe, *An Examination of the Constitution for the United States of America*, No. 3, September 29, 1787:

Each member of this truly popular assembly [the House of Representatives] will be chosen by about six thousand electors, by the poor as well as the rich. No decayed or venal borough will have an unjust share in their determinations—no old Sarum will send thither a representative by the voice of a single elector. As we shall have no royal ministers to purchase votes, so we shall have no votes for sale; for the *suffrages* of six thousand enlightened and independent freemen are above all price. . . . [Ford 143]

Edmund Randolph, Letter on the Federal Constitution, October 10, 1787:

[1] But now, sir, permit me to declare, that in my humble judgment the powers by which alone the blessings of a general government can be accomplished,

cannot be interwoven in the confederation without a change of its very essence; or in other words, that the confederation must be thrown aside. This is almost demonstrable from the inefficacy of requisitions and from the necessity of converting them into acts of authority. My *suffrage,* as a citizen, is also for additional powers. But to whom shall we commit these acts of authority, these additional powers? . . . [DHRC8 267]

[2] The two first points are the equality of *suffrage* in the Senate, and the submission of commerce to a mere majority in the legislature, with no other check than the revision of the President. I conjecture that neither of these things can be corrected; and particularly the former; without which we must have risen perhaps in disorder. [DHRC8 273]

Noah Webster, *An Examination of the Leading Principles of the Federal Constitution*, October 17, 1787:

[1] Another idea that naturally presents itself to our minds, on a slight consideration of the subject, is, that in a perfect government, all the members of a society should be present, and each give his *suffrage* in acts of legislation, by which he is to be bound. This is impracticable in large states; and even were it not, it is very questionable whether it would be the best mode of legislation. It was however practised in the free states of antiquity; and was the cause of innumerable evils. To avoid these evils, the moderns have invented the doctrine of representation, which seems to be the perfection of human government. [Ford 30]

[2] . . . Some partiality therefore for constituents is always expectable. To destroy it as much as possible, a political constitution should remove the grounds of local attachment. Connecticut and Maryland have wisely destroyed this attachment in their senates, by ordaining that the members shall be chosen in the state at large. The senators hold their seats by the *suffrages* of the state, not of a district; hence they have no particular number of men to fear or to oblige.— They represent the state; hence that union and firmness which the senates of those states have manifested on the most trying occasions, and by which they have prevented the most rash and iniquitous measures. [Ford 41n]

[3] In ancient Rome none but the free citizens had the right of a *suffrage* in the comitia or legislative assemblies. But in Sylla's time the Italian cities demanded the rights of the Roman citizens; alledging that they furnished two-thirds of the armies, in all their wars, and yet were despised as foreigners. Vell Paterc. lib. 2. cap. 15. This produced the Marsic or social war, which lasted two years, and carried off 300,000 men. Ibm. It was conducted and concluded by Pompey, father of Pompey the Great, with his lieutenants Sylla and Marius. But most of the cities eventually obtained the freedom of Rome; and were of course entitled to the rights of *suffrage* in the comitia. "Paulatim deinde recipiendo in civitatem, qui arma aut non ceperant aut deposuerant maturius, vires refectae sunt." Vell. Paterc. 2. 16. [Ford 43n]

[4] Representation would have, in some measure, prevented the consequences; but the admission of every man to a *suffrage* will ever open the door to corruption. In such a state as Connecticut, where there is no conflux of foreigners, no introduction of seamen, servants, &c., and scarcely an hundred persons in the state who are not natives, and very few whose education and connexions do not attach them to the government; at the same time few men have property to furnish the means of corruption, very little danger could spring from admitting every man of age and discretion to the privilege of voting for rulers But in the large towns of America there is more danger. A master of a vessel may put votes in the hands of his crew, for the purpose of carrying an election for a party Such things have actually taken place in America. Besides, the middle states are receiving emigrations of poor people, who are not at once judges of the characters of men, and who cannot be safely trusted with the choice of legislators.

[Ford 43–44n]

[5] Let us then consider the New Federal Constitution, as it really is, an improvement on the best constitutions that the world ever saw, in the house of representatives, the people of America have an equal voice and *suffrage,* The choice of men is placed in the freemen or electors at large; and the frequency of elections, and the responsibility of the members, will render them sufficiently dependent on their constituents. . . . [Ford 64]

John Dawson and James Monroe to the Freeholders of Fredericksburg, Richmond, Virginia, October 26, 1787:

While, gentlemen, we assure you, our exertions shall not be wanting to promote and forward the interest of you, and our country at large, we beg leave to observe, that as it is our duty, so it will afford us pleasure to render you any personal services: And should our conduct meet with your approbation, we doubt not but we shall be honoured with your *suffrages,* as we shall offer you our services in the approaching convention. . . . [DHRC8 121]

Alexander Hamilton, *The Federalist*, No. 9, November 21, 1787:

A distinction, more subtle than accurate, has been raised between a confederacy and a consolidation of the States. The essential characteristic of the first is said to be, the restriction of its authority to the members in their collective capacities, without reaching to the individuals of whom they are composed. It is contended that the national council ought to have no concern with any object of internal administration. An exact equality of *suffrage* between the members has also been insisted upon as a leading feature of a confederate government. These positions are, in the main, arbitrary; they are supported neither by principle nor precedent. . . . [Fed. 128]

James Madison, *The Federalist*, No. 10, November 22, 1787:

[1] On the other hand, the effect may be inverted. Men of factious tempers, of local prejudices, or of sinister designs, may, by intrigue, by corruption, or by other means, first obtain the *suffrages,* and then betray the interests, of the people. . . . [Fed. 134]

[2] In the next place, as each representative will be chosen by a greater number of citizens in the large than in the small republic, it will be more difficult for unworthy candidates to practice with success the vicious arts by which elections are too often carried; and the *suffrages* of the people being more free, will be more likely to center in men who possess the most attractive merit and the most diffusive and established characters. [Fed. 134]

Alexander Hamilton, *The Federalist*, No. 22, December 14, 1787:

[1] The right of equal *suffrage* among the States is another exceptionable part of the Confederation. Every idea of proportion and every rule of fair representation conspire to condemn a principle, which gives to Rhode Island an equal weight in the scale of power with Massachusetts, or Connecticut, or New York; and to Delaware an equal voice in the national deliberations with Pennsylvania, or Virginia, or North Carolina. Its operation contradicts the fundamental maxim of republican government, which requires that the sense of the majority should prevail. . . . [Fed. 193]

[2] In republics, persons elevated from the mass of the community, by the *suffrages* of their fellow-citizens, to stations of great preeminence and power, may find compensations for betraying their trust, which, to any but minds animated and guided by superior virtue, may appear to exceed the proportion of interest they have in the common stock, and to overbalance the obligations of duty. Hence it is that history furnishes us with so many mortifying examples of the prevalency of foreign corruption in republican governments. . . .

[Fed. 196]

Dissent of the Pennsylvania Assembly's Minority, December 18, 1787:

The celebrated Montesquieu, in his Spirit of Laws, vol. i., page 12th, says, "That in a democracy there can be no exercise of sovereignty, but by the suffages of the people, which are their will; now the sovereign's will is the sovereign himself; the laws, therefore, which establish the right of *suffrage,* are fundamental to this government. In fact, it is as important to regulate in a republic in what manner, by whom, and concerning what *suffrages* are to be given, as it is in a monarchy to know who is the prince, and after what manner he ought to govern." The time, mode and place of the election of representatives, senators and president general of the United States ought not to be under the control of Congress, but fundamentally ascertained and established. [DHRC2 629]

Alexander Hamilton, *The Federalist*, No. 35, January 5, 1788:

If we take into the account the momentary humors or dispositions which may happen to prevail in particular parts of the society, and to which a wise administration will never be inattentive, is the man whose situation leads to extensive inquiry and information less likely to be a competent judge of their nature, extent, and foundation than one of whose observation does not travel beyond the circle of his neighbors and acquaintances? Is it not natural that a man who is a candidate for the favor of the people, and who is dependent on the *suffrages* of his fellow-citizens for the continuance of his public honors, should take care to inform himself of their dispositions and inclinations, and should be willing to allow them their proper degree of influence upon his conduct? This dependence, and the necessity of being bound himself, and his posterity, by the laws to which he gives his assent, are the true, and they are the strong chords of sympathy between the representative and the constituent. [Fed. 258]

"An Impartial Citizen," January 10, 1788:

. . . The Legislative consists of two bodies, each of which is a check on the other: The Legislative, Executive, and Judiciary, are separate and distinct. The representation in the House of Representatives, is in proportion to the number of inhabitants in the respective constituent States: An advantage over the Federal Government of Holland, where each Province has an equal voice, although the Provinces are all different in extent, population, &c. Each state has an equal *suffrage* in the Senate, which precludes the possibility of a successful combination against the smaller by the greater States, which might otherwise be easily effected. . . . [DHRC8 294]

James Madison, *The Federalist*, No. 38, January 12, 1788:

What degree of agency these reputed lawgivers might have in their respective establishments, or how far they might be clothed with the legitimate authority of the people, cannot in every instance be ascertained. In some, however, the proceeding was strictly regular. Draco appears to have been intrusted by the people of Athens with indefinite powers to reform its government and laws. And Solon, according to Plutarch, was in a manner compelled, by the universal *suffrage* of his fellow-citizens, to take upon him the sole and absolute power of new-modelling the constitution. . . . [Fed. 272–73]

James Madison, *The Federalist*, No. 43, January 23, 1788:

[1] . . . The extent of this federal district is sufficiently circumscribed to satisfy every jealousy of an opposite nature. And as it to be appropriated to this use with the consent of the State ceding it; as the State will no doubt provide in the compact for the rights and the consent of the citizens inhabiting it; as the in-

habitants will find sufficient inducements of interest to become willing parties to the cession; as they will have had their voice in the election of the government which is to exercise authority over them; as a municipal legislature for local purposes, derived from their own *suffrages,* will of course be allowed them; and as the authority of the legislature of the State and of the inhabitants of the ceded part of it, to concur in the cession, will be derived from the whole people of the State, in their adoption of the Constitution, every imaginable objection seems to be obviated. [Fed. 310]

[2] Is it true that force and right are necessarily on the same side in republican governments? May not the minor party possess such a superiority of pecuniary resources, of military talents and experience, or of secret succors from foreign powers, as will render it superior also in an appeal to the sword? May not a more compact and advantageous position turn the scale on the same side, against a superior number so situated as to be less capable of a prompt and collected exertion of its strength? Nothing can be more chimerical than to imagine that in a trial of actual force, victory may be calculated by the rules which prevail in a census of the inhabitants, or which determine the event of an election! May it not happen, in fine, that the minority of CITIZENS may become a majority of PERSONS, by the accession of alien residents, of a casual concourse of adventurers, or of those whom the constitution of the State has not admitted to the rights of *suffrage?* I take no notice of an unhappy species of population [*i.e.*, the slaves] abounding in some of the States, who, during the calm of regular government, are sunk below the level of men; but who, in the tempestuous scenes of civil violence, may emerge into the human character, and give a superiority of strength to any party with which they may associate themselves. [Fed. 313–14]

[3] That useful alterations [in the Constitution] will be suggested by experience, could not but be foreseen. It will requisite, therefore, that a mode for introducing them should be provided. The mode preferred by the convention seems to be stamped with every mark of propriety. It guards equally against that extreme facility, which would render the Constitution too mutable; and that extreme difficulty, which might perpetuate its discovered faults. It, moreover, equally enables the general and the State governments to originate the amendment of errors, as they may be pointed out by the experience on one side, or on the other. The exception in favor of the equality of *suffrage* in the Senate, was probably meant as a palladium to the residuary sovereignty of the States, implied and secured by that principle of representation in one branch of the legislature; and was probably insisted on by the States particularly attached to that equality. The other exception must have been admitted on the same considerations which produced the privilege defended by it. [Fed. 315]

Alexander C. Hanson, *Remarks on the Proposed Plan of a Federal Government*, c. January 31, 1788:

[1] How then was I, some months after, disgusted at the repetition, of the arguments respecting the inequality of representatives in the first branch. We

were told, that the minority in convention reasoned on first principles, that, as all men, in a state of nature, are equal with respect to rights, so also are equal all separate and distinct states;—that, when individuals form a free government, they must all have equal *suffrage,* either in framing laws by themselves, or in choosing representatives, although one man be ten times stronger, richer, or wiser than another; so also, when several states unite, for common convenience, they must meet on terms of perfect equality, although one be ten times more wealthy, expensive and populous than another . . . [Ford 223]

[2] Against what is called equality in representation, the great Montesquieu seems to have declared by the strongest implication. In his Spirit of Laws, b. ch. 2, he says that the confederate republic of Lycia contained twenty-three associated towns: that, in the common council, the larger towns had three votes, the middling towns two, and the lesser only one; that they contributed to the common expence according to the proportion of *suffrages;* and, that were he to give the model of an excellent confederate republic, it should be that of Lycia. . . . [Ford 223n]

[3] The house of representatives is to be the immediate choice of the people, and one man is to represent 30,000 souls. In an affair of so much importance, and in districts containing so many *suffrages,* it is not to be supposed, that a worthless character will succeed by those arts, which have, sometimes, prevailed in county elections. It is to be expected, that, in general, the people will choose men of talents and character. . . . [Ford 225]

[4] Whether the state of Maryland shall be divided into six districts, for each to choose one man, or the people at large give their *suffrage* for the whole six, is hereafter to be settled by the assembly. The latter mode, on a variety of occasions, would be preferable. [Ford 225n]

[5] You have been told that the proposed plan was calculated peculiarly for the rich. In all governments, not merely despotic, the wealthy must, in most things, find an advantage, from the possession of that, which is too much the end and aim of mankind. In the proposed plan, there is nothing like a discrimination in their favour. How this amazing objection is to be supported, I am at a loss to conjecture. Is it a just cause of reproach, that the constitution effectually secures property? Or would the objectors introduce a general scramble? In eligibility to office, in *suffrage,* and in every other civil right, men are all on terms of perfect equality. And yet, notwithstanding this just equality, each man is to pay taxes in proportion to his ability, or his expences. [Ford 254]

Luther Martin, "Genuine Information," No. 11, February 5, 1788:

That it was inconsistent with the rights of free and independent States, to have their territory dismembered without their consent, was the principal argument used by the opponents of this proposition.—The truth of the objection we readily admitted, but at the same time, insisted that it was not more inconsistent with the rights of free and independent States than that inequality of *suffrage* and power which the large States had extorted from the others . . . [DHRC16 41]

James Madison, *The Federalist*, No. 52, February 8, 1788:

. . . The definition of the right of *suffrage* is very justly regarded as a fundamental article of republican government. It was incumbent on the convention, therefore, to define and establish this right in the Constitution. To have left it open for the occasional regulation of the Congress, would have been improper for the reason just mentioned. To have submitted it to the legislative discretion of the States, would have been improper for the same reason; and for the additional reason that it would have rendered too dependent on the State governments that branch of the federal government which ought to be dependent on the people alone. . . . [Fed. 360]

James Madison, *The Federalist*, No. 54, February 12, 1788:

. . . It is a fundamental principle of the proposed Constitution, that as the aggregate number of representatives allotted to the several States is to be determined by a federal rule, founded on the aggregate number of inhabitants, so the right of choosing this allotted number in each State is to be exercised by such part of the inhabitants as the State itself may designate. The qualifications on which the right of *suffrage* depend are not, perhaps, the same in any two States. In some of the States the difference is very material. In every State, a certain proportion of inhabitants are deprived of this right by the constitution of the State, who will be included in the census by which the federal Constitution apportions the representatives. . . . [Fed. 371–72]

"A Citizen of the United States," February 13, 1788:

It is curious to observe the difference and the contrariety of the objections made against the new constitution. His Excellency Governor [Edmund] Randolph urges the equality of *suffrage* in the senate as his principal objection—Mr. [Luther] Martin of Maryland inveighs with great bitterness against the inequality of *suffrage* in the house of representatives . . . [DHRC16 115]

William Ward [?], "Republicus," February 16, 1788:

And first the constitution should provide for a fair and equal representation. That is that every member of the union have a freedom of *suffrage* and that every equal number of people have an equal number of representatives; for if the preceding sentiments are just, no man deprived of *suffrage,* ought (unless he voluntarily adopt it at least implicitly) to be under the controul or direction of such constitution, or any law made in consequence of it . . . [DHRC8 377–78]

James Madison, *The Federalist*, No. 57, February 19, 1788:

[1] If we consider the situation of the men on whom the free *suffrages* of their fellow-citizens may confer the representative trust, we shall find it involving

every security which can be devised or desired for their fidelity to their constituents. [Fed. 384]

[2] Were the objection to be read by one who had not seen the mode prescribed by the Constitution for the choice of representatives, he could suppose nothing less than that some unreasonable qualification of property was annexed to the right of *suffrage;* or that the right of eligibility was limited to persons of particular families or fortunes; or at least that the mode prescribed by the State constitutions was, in some respect or other, very grossly departed from. We have seen how far such a supposition would err, as to the two first points. Nor would it, in fact, be less erroneous as to the last. . . . [Fed. 386]

[3] Is the consequence from this doctrine admissible? If we say that five or six hundred citizens are as many as can jointly exercise their right of *suffrage,* must we not deprive the people of the immediate choice of their public servants, in every instance where the administration of the government does not require as many of them as will amount to one for that number of citizens? [Fed. 386]

[4] Is the doctrine warranted by facts? It was shown in the last paper, that the real representation in the British House of Commons very little exceeds the proportion of one for every thirty thousand inhabitants. Besides a variety of powerful causes not existing here, and which favor in that country the pretensions of rank and wealth, no person is eligible as a representative of a county, unless he possess real estate of the clear value of six hundred pounds sterling per year; nor of a city or borough, unless he possess a like estate of half that annual value. To this qualification on the part of the county representatives is added another on the part of the county electors, which restrains the right of *suffrage* to persons having a freehold estate of the annual value of more than twenty pounds sterling, according to the present rate of money. Notwithstanding these unfavorable circumstances, and notwithstanding some very unequal laws in the British code, it cannot be said that the representatives of the nation have elevated the few on the ruins of the many. [Fed. 386–87]

Alexander Hamilton, *The Federalist*, No. 60, February 23, 1788:

I rather consult brevity in discussing the probability of a preference founded upon a discrimination between the different kinds of industry and property, because, as far as I understand the meaning of the objectors, they contemplate a discrimination of another kind. They appear to have in view, as the objects of the preference with which they endeavor to alarm us, those whom they designate by the description of "the wealthy and the well-born." These, it seems, are to be exalted to an odious preeminence over the rest of their fellow-citizens. At one time, however, their elevation is to be a necessary consequence of the smallness of the representative body; at another time it is to be effected by depriving the people at large of the opportunity of exercising their right of *suffrage* in the choice of that body. [Fed. 401–402]

Alexander Hamilton, *The Federalist*, No. 61, February 26, 1788:

. . . It may readily be perceived that it would not be more difficult to the legislature of New York to defeat the *suffrages* of the citizens of New York, by confining elections to particular places, than for the legislature of the United States to defeat the *suffrages* of the citizens of the Union, by the like expedient. . . .
[Fed. 404]

"An Impartial Citizen," No. 5, February 28, 1788:

. . . As in the nature of things unanimity cannot be obtained in the decisions of popular assemblies, almost all nations among whom resolutions are formed by *suffrages,* have fixed upon a majority of voices as the most obvious, easy, and natural criterion of determination. The causes urged by the antifederalists, for a departure from this rule, do not exist: The very idea of it tends to consider the northern States as a totally distinct people from us; whose interest militates against ours; and who would naturally combine against us. This idea is not founded in truth—It tends to dissolve that union that ought to be indissoluble—It ought therefore to be detested by every true American. [DHRC8 432–33]

Alexander White, "To the Citizens of Virginia," February 29, 1788:

. . . Montesquieu, says, (and the dissentients themselves make the quotation) "It is as important to regulate in a republic in what manner, by whom, and concerning what, *suffrages* are to be given, as it is in a monarchy to know who is the Prince, or how he is to govern." Can this certainly be obtained when these important points are to be determined in 13 seperate assemblies? . . . [DHRC8 440–41]

Mercy Otis Warren, *Observations on the New Constitution*, February 1788:

. . . But if the authors of the present visionary project [the Constitution], can by the arts of deception, precipitation and address, obtain a majority of *suffrages* in the conventions of the states to try the hazardous experiment, they may then make the same inglorious boast with this insidious politician, who may perhaps be their model, that "the union of the colonies was pretty well broken, and that he hoped never to see it renewed." [DHRC16 282]

James Madison, *The Federalist*, No. 63, March 1, 1788:

[1] . . . The senate of Carthage, also, whatever might be its power, or the duration of its appointment, appears to have been elective by the *suffrages* of the people. Similar instances might be traced in most, if not all the popular governments of antiquity.
[Fed. 417]

[2] Lastly, in Sparta we meet with the Ephori, and in Rome with the Tribunes; two bodies, small indeed in numbers, but annually elected by the whole body of the people, and considered as the representatives of the people, almost in their plenipotentiary capacity. The Cosmi of Crete were also annually elected by the people, and have been considered by some authors as an institution analogous to those of Sparta and Rome, with this difference only, that in the election of that representative body the right of *suffrage* was communicated to a part only of the people. [Fed. 417]

William Ward [?], "Republicus," March 1, 1788:

. . . Is it then become necessary, that a free people, should first resign their right of *suffrage* into other hands besides their own, and then, secondly, that those to whom they resign it should be compelled to choose men, whose persons, charracters manners or principles they know nothing of . . . [DHRC8 448]

Philadelphia *Independent Gazetteer*, March 7, 1788:

In the state of Pennsylvania it was adopted by an illegal mob convention, under the direction of the city junto: the majority in this convention were only elected by about 1–12th of the *suffrages* of the freemen of the state: And so entirely against the real sense of the state that it will be all undone. [DHRC16 341]

Alexander Hamilton, *The Federalist*, No. 66, March 8, 1788:

But independent of this most active and operative principle, to secure the equilibrium of the national House of Representatives, the plan of the convention has provided in its favor several important counterpoises to the additional authorities to be conferred upon the Senate. The exclusive privilege of originating money bills will belong to the House of Representatives. The same house will possess the sole right of instituting impeachments: is not this a complete counterbalance to that of determining them? The same house will be the umpire in all elections of the President, which do not unite the *suffrages* of a majority of the whole number of electors; a case which it cannot be doubted will sometimes, if not frequently, happen. The constant possibility of the thing must be a fruitful source of influence to that body. . . . [Fed. 433]

Letter from a New York Quaker, *Poughkeepsie Country Journal*, March 18, 1788:

[1] . . . Thus in the present case, however ill it would become friends to enlist under the banners of heated party, and thereby add fuel to that fire which already blazeth too high; yet I think as a body, they might exhibit their united weight in the legal line of *suffrage*, and perhaps be a means of giving tranquility to their country. [DHRC16 409]

[2] In order to avoid these monstrous evils and to procure those solid benefits which I think a firmer union of the States bids fair to introduce, I would seriously recommend to Friends in every part of the State to make it a matter of real concern to give their *suffrages* in such a manner as to make their importance as a body felt, and felt for the general good. . . . [DHRC16 410]

Alexander Hamilton, *The Federalist*, No. 72, March 19, 1788:

. . . If the exclusion [of the President from re-election] were to be perpetual, a man of irregular ambition, of whom alone there could be reason in any case to entertain apprehension, would, with infinite reluctance, yield to the necessity of taking his leave forever of a post in which his passion for power and preeminence had acquired the force of habit. And if he had been fortunate or adroit enough to conciliate the good-will of the people, he might induce them to consider as a very odious and unjustifiable restraint upon themselves, a provision which was calculated to debar them of the right of giving a fresh proof of their attachment to a favorite. There may be conceived circumstances in which this disgust of the people, seconding the thwarted ambition of such a favorite, might occasion greater danger to liberty, than could ever reasonably be dreaded from the possibility of perpetuation in office, by the voluntary *suffrages* of the community, exercising a constitutional privilege. [Fed. 466–67]

Alexander Hamilton, *The Federalist*, No. 76, April 1, 1788:

. . . Hence, in every exercise of the power of appointing to offices by an assembly of men, we must expect to see a full display of all the private and party likings and dislikes, partialities and antipathies, attachments and animosities, which are felt by those who compose the assembly. The choice which may at any time happen to be made under such circumstances, will of course be the result either of a victory gained by one party over the other, or of a compromise between the parties. In either case, the intrinsic merit of the candidate will be too often out of sight. In the first, the qualifications best adapted to uniting the *suffrages* of the party, will be more considered than those which fit the person for the station. In the last, the coalition will commonly turn upon some interested equivalent: "Give us the man we wish for this office, and you shall have the one you wish for that." This will be the usual condition of the bargain. And it will rarely happen that the advancement of the public service will be the primary object either of party victories or of party negotiations. [Fed. 481–82]

John Dickinson, "Fabius," No. 8, 1788:

The proposition was expressly made upon this principle, that a territory of such extent as that of United America, could not be safely and advantageously governed, but by a combination of republics, each retaining all the rights of supreme sovereignty, excepting such as ought to be contributed to the union; that for the securer preservation of these sovereignties, they ought to be represented in a body by themselves, and with equal *suffrage;* and that they would be annihilated, if both branches of the legislature were to be formed of representatives of the people, in proportion to the number of inhabitants in each state. [Ford 207]

United States Senate, Address to George Washington, May 7, 1789:

Sir: We, the Senate of the United States, return you our sincere thanks for your excellent speech delivered to both houses of Congress; congratulate you on the complete organization of the Federal Government; and felicitate ourselves and our fellow-citizens on your elevation to the office of President, an office highly important by the powers constitutionally annexed to it and extremely honorable from the manner in which the appointment is made. The unanimous *suffrage* of the elective body in your favor, is peculiarly expressive of the gratitude, confidence, and affection of the citizens of America, and is the highest testimonial at once of your merit and their esteem. . . . [Annals 32]

TAXES, DIRECT

United States Constitution, September 17, 1787:

[Article I, Section 2:] Representatives and *direct Taxes* shall be apportioned among the several States which may be included within this Union, according to their respective Numbers, which shall be determined by adding to the whole Number of free Persons, including those bound to Service for a Term of Years, and excluding Indians not taxed, three fifths of all other Persons. . . .

[Article I, Section 9:] No Capitation, or other *direct, Tax* shall be laid, unless in Proportion to the Census or Enumeration herein before directed to be taken.

* * * * *

James Wilson, Speech on the Federal Constitution, October 6, 1787:

The power of *direct taxation* has likewise been treated as an improper delegation to the foederal government; but when we consider it as the duty of that body to provide for the national safety, to support the dignity of the union, and to discharge the debts contracted upon the collective faith of the states, for their common benefit, it must be acknowledged that those, upon whom such important obligations are imposed, ought, in justice and in policy, to possess every means requisite for a faithful performance of their trust. But why should we be alarmed with visionary evils? I will venture to predict, that the great revenue of the United States must, and always will, be raised by impost; for, being at once less obnoxious, and more productive, the interest of the government will be best promoted by the accommodation of the people. Still, however, the object of *direct taxation* should be within reach in all cases of emergency; and there is no more reason to apprehend oppression in the mode of collecting a revenue from this resource, than in the form of impost, which, by universal assent, is left to the authority of the foederal government. . . . [Ford 160]

Richard Henry Lee [?], "The Federal Farmer," No. 3, October 10, 1787:

[1] . . . I am sensible also, that it is said that congress will not attempt to lay and collect internal *taxes;* that it is necessary for them to have the power, though it cannot probably be exercised.—I admit that it is not probable that any prudent congress will attempt to lay and collect internal *taxes,* especially *direct taxes:* but this only proves, that the power would be improperly lodged in congress, and that it might be abused by imprudent and designing men. [Ford 303]

[2] I have heard several gentlemen, to get rid of objections to this part of the constitution, attempt to construe the powers relative to *direct taxes,* as those who object to it would have them; as to these, it is said, that congress will only have power to make requisitions, leaving it to the states to lay and collect them. I see but very little colour for this construction, and the attempt only proves that this part of the plan cannot be defended. By this plan there can be no doubt, but that the powers of congress will be complete as to all kinds of *taxes* whatever . . . [Ford 303–304]

Richard Henry Lee [?], "The Federal Farmer," No. 4, October 12, 1787:

Third, there appears to me to be not only a premature deposit of some important powers in the general government—but many of those deposited there are undefined, and may be used to good or bad purposes as honest or designing men shall prevail. By Art.1, Sec. 2, representatives and *direct taxes* shall be apportioned among the several states, &c.—same art. sect. 8, the congress shall have powers to lay and collect *taxes,* duties, &c. for the common defence and general welfare, but all duties, imposts and excises, shall be uniform throughout the United States: By the first recited clause, *direct taxes* shall be apportioned on the states. This seems to favour the idea suggested by some sensible men and writers that congress, as to *direct taxes,* will only have power to make requisitions; but the latter clause, power to lay and collect *taxes,* &c. seems clearly to favor the contrary opinion, and, in my mind, the true one, the congress shall have power to *tax* immediately individuals, without the intervention of the state legislatures, in fact the first clause appears to me only to provide that each state shall pay a certain portion of the *tax,* and the latter to provide that congress shall have power to lay and collect *taxes,* that is to assess upon, and to collect of the individuals in the state, the states quota; but these still I consider as undefined powers, because judicious men understand them differently. [Ford 310]

"Cato Uticensis," October 17, 1787:

In Art. 1, Sect. 8. of the proposed Foederal Constitution; it is said, "Congress shall have power to lay and collect *taxes,* duties, imposts and excises."—Are you then, Virginians, about to abandon your country to the depredations of excisemen, and the pressure of excise laws? Did it ever enter the mind of any one of you, that you could live to see the day, that any other government, but the General Assembly of Virginia, should have power of *direct taxation* in this state? How few of you ever expected to see excise laws, the instruments of tyranny, in force in your country? But, who could imagine, that any man but a Virginian, were they found to be necessary, would ever have a voice towards enacting them?... [DHRC8 73]

Alexander Hamilton, *The Federalist*, No. 12, November 27, 1787:

[1] . . . It is evident from the state of the country, from the habits of the people, from the experience we have had on the point itself, that it is impracticable to raise any very considerable sums by *direct taxation*. *Tax* laws have in vain been multiplied; new methods to enforce the collection have in vain been tried; the public expectation has been uniformly disappointed, and the treasuries of the States have remained empty. The popular system of administration inherent in the nature of popular government, coinciding with the real scarcity of money incident to a languid and mutilated state of trade, has hitherto defeated every experiment for extensive collections, and has at length taught the different legislatures the folly of attempting them. [Fed. 143–44]

[2] No person acquainted with what happens in other countries will be surprised at this circumstance. In so opulent a nation as that of Britain, where *direct taxes* from superior wealth must be much more tolerable, and, from the vigor of the government, much more practicable, than in America, far the greatest part of the national revenue is derived from *taxes* of the indirect kind, from imposts, and from excises. . . . [Fed. 144]

Alexander Hamilton, *The Federalist*, No. 21, December 12, 1787:

Impositions of this kind usually fall under the denomination of indirect *taxes*, and must for a long time constitute the chief part of the revenue raised in this country. Those of the *direct* kind, which principally relate to land and buildings, may admit of a rule of apportionment. Either the value of land, or the number of the people, may serve as a standard. The state of agriculture and the populousness of a country have been considered as nearly connected with each other. And, as a rule, for the purpose intended, numbers, in the view of simplicity and certainty, are entitled to a preference. . . . [Fed. 190]

Dissent of the Pennsylvania Convention's Minority, December 18, 1787:

[1] The power of *direct taxation* applies to every individual, as Congress, under this government, is expressly vested with the authority of laying a capitation or

poll *tax* upon every person to any amount. This is a *tax* that, however oppressive in its nature, and unequal in its operation, is certain as to its produce and simple in its collection; it cannot be evaded like the objects of imposts or excise, and will be paid, because all that a man hath will he give for his head. . . .
[DHRC2 635–36]

[2] The power of *direct taxation* will further apply to every individual, as Congress may *tax* land, cattle, trades, occupations, etc. to any amount, and every object of internal *taxation* is of that nature, that however oppressive, the people will have but this alternative, either to pay the *tax,* or let their property be taken, for all resistance will be vain. The standing army and select militia would enforce the collection. [DHRC2 636]

Alexander Hamilton, *The Federalist*, No. 36, January 8, 1788:

The *taxes* intended to be comprised under the general denomination of internal *taxes* may be subdivided into those of the *direct* and those of the indirect kind. Though the objection be made to both, yet the reasoning upon it seems to be confined to the former branch. And indeed, as to the latter, by which must be understood duties and excises on articles of consumption, one is at a loss to conceive what can be the nature of the difficulties apprehended. . . .
[Fed. 260–61]

James Madison, *The Federalist*, No. 38, January 12, 1788:

. . . A patriot in a State that does not import or export, discerns insuperable objections against the power of *direct taxation*. The patriotic adversary in a State of great exports and imports, is not less dissatisfied that the whole burden of *taxes* may be thrown on consumption. . . . [Fed. 276]

James Madison, *The Federalist*, No. 40, January 18, 1788:

. . . In some instances, as has been shown, the powers of the new government [the Constitution] will act on the States in their collective characters. In some instances, also, those of the existing government [the Confederation] act immediately on individuals. In cases of capture; of piracy; of the post office; of coins, weights, and measures; of trade with the Indians; of claims under grants of land by different States; and, above all, in the case of trials by courts-martial in the army and navy, by which death may be inflicted without the intervention of a jury, or even of a civil magistrate;—in all these cases the powers of the Confederation operate immediately on the persons and interests of individual citizens. Do these fundamental principles require, particularly, that no *tax* should be levied without the intermediate agency of the States? The Confederation itself authorizes a *direct tax,* to a certain extent, on the post office. The power of coinage has been so construed by Congress as to levy a tribute immediately from that source also. . . . [Fed. 289]

Alexander C. Hanson, *Remarks on the Proposed Plan of a Federal Government*, c. January 31, 1788:

To the five per cent impost most of the states have more than once given their assent. This is the only *tax* which congress wishes immediately to impose. Of the imposition of assessment, capitation, or *direct taxes* of any kind, the congress entertains no idea at present; and although it be proper for the federal head to possess this power in reserve, nothing but some unforeseen disaster will ever drive them to such ineligible expedients. Setting aside the immediate advantages of revived credit and trade, and the increased value of your property and labour, you will be delivered, in a great measure, from that load of *direct taxation*, which has been so unequally borne, and produced so little substantial good.

[Ford 253]

Samuel Bryan, "Centinel," No. 14, February 5, 1788:

[1] [Quoting Luther Martin:] " . . . By the power to lay and collect *taxes*, they may proceed to *direct taxation* on every individual either by a capitation *tax* on their heads, or an assessment on their property. By this part of the section, therefore, the government has a power to lay what duties they please on goods imported—to lay what duties they please afterwards on whatever we use or consume—to impose stamp duties to what amount they please, and in whatever cases they please—afterwards to impose on the people *direct taxes*, by capitation *tax*, or by assessment, to what amount they choose, and thus to sluice them at every vein as long as they have a drop of blood, without any controul, limitation or restraint—while all the officers for collecting these *taxes*, stamp duties, imposts and excises, are to be appointed by the general government, under its direction, not accountable to the states . . . " [DHRC16 33]

[2] "Many of the members, and myself in the number, thought that the states were much better judges of the circumstances of their citizens, and what sum of money could be collected from them by *direct taxation*, and of the manner in which it could be raised, with the greatest ease and convenience to their citizens, than the general government could be; and that the general government ought not in any case to have the power of laying *direct taxes*, but in that of the delinquency of a state. Agreeable to this sentiment, I brought in a proposition on which a vote of the convention was taken. The proposition was as follows: 'And wherever the legislature of the United States shall find it necessary that revenue should be raised by *direct taxation*, having apportioned the same by the above rule, requisitions shall be made of the respective states to pay into the continental treasury their respective quotas within a time in the said requisition to be specified, and in case of any of the states failing to comply with such requisition, then and then only, to have power to devise and pass acts directing the mode and authorising the collection of the same.' Had this proposition been acceded to, the dangerous and oppressive power in the general government of

imposing *direct taxes* on the inhabitants, which it now enjoys in all cases, would have been only vested in it in case of the non-compliance of a state, as a punishment for its delinquency, and would have ceased that moment that the state complied with the requisition . . . " [DHRC16 34]

Massachusetts Convention, Proposed Amendments to the Constitution, February 6, 1788:

Fourthly, That Congress do not lay *direct taxes,* but when the monies arising from the impost and excise are insufficient for the publick exigencies; nor then, until Congress shall have first made a requisition upon the states, to assess, levy and pay their respective proportions of such requisition, agreeably to the census fixed in the said constitution, in such way and manner as the legislature of the state shall think best . . . [DHRC16 68]

Tench Coxe, "A Freeman," No. 3, February 6, 1788:

[1] . . . Where is the county that can independently train its own militia, appoint its civil and militia officers, establish a peculiar system of penal laws, issue criminal process in its own name, erect corporations, impose *direct taxes,* excises and duties, hold lands in its own right, commence war on any emergency, regulate descents, prescribe the qualifications of electors, alter its constitution or the principles of its government, divide itself into separate and independent parts, join itself to another state, issue writs for elections, and regulate the same, enact inspection laws, erect courts, appoint judges, commission all its officers, create new offices, sell and give away its lands, erect fortifications, and, in short where is the county in the union, or in the world, that can exercise in any instance independent legislative, executive or judicial powers? [DHRC16 49–50]

[2] You apprehend the power of Congress to lay *direct taxes* will tend to produce consolidation. But the several states possess that power also, and by an early, wise and faithful exercise of it, can always supercede the use of it by Congress. For example; if ten thousand pounds were apportioned to Pennsylvania, to make up the interest on our foreign debts by the end of 1788, a *tax* for which would be laid in July, our legislature might proceed in the most easy and expeditious way to raise the money, against the time when the foederal government must necessarily proceed, and by paying our quota into the foederal treasury would fulfil the requisitions of the law. . . . [DHRC16 50–51]

James Madison, *The Federalist*, No. 54, February 12, 1788:

The next view which I shall take of the House of Representatives relates to the appointment of its members to the several States, which is to be determined by the same rule with that of *direct taxes*. [Fed. 369]

John Williams to ———, January 29, 1788, published in *Albany Federal Herald*, February 25, 1788:

. . . The *direct taxation,* and to be collected by officers of Congress, are powers which cannot be granted agreeable to our present constitution, nor will it be very convenient for Congress officers, and our state collectors, to be collecting both at one time, and as Congress may lay a poll *tax,* how will that agree with us. I need not tell you the injustices of it. If the new constitution is adopted, Congress hath all the impost and excise; this latter may be laid heavy on taverns and spirits, so that the emoluments from taverns, which are now converted to the use of the poor, must go to Congress; and what is yet worse, all the duties arising from any duties or excise, are to be appropriated to the use of Congress.

[DHRC16 200]

"The Impartial Examiner," No. 1, February 27-March 5, 1787:

[February 27:] . . . Yet, I apprehend that these evils may result in a great measure from an exercise of that branch of legislative authority, which respects internal *direct taxation*. For in this, it is scarcely probable that the interest, ease or convenience of the several states can be so well consulted in the foederal assembly, as in their own respective legislatures. . . . [DHRC8 421]

[March 5:] You will, doubtless, consider whether the inconveniencies may not be very disagreeable, and perhaps injurious, to which this country may be subjected by excise laws,—by *direct taxation* of every kind,—by the establishment of foederal courts. . . . [DHRC8 462–63]

Luther Martin, "To the Citizens of Maryland," No. 1, March 18, 1788:

[Footnote:] According to this idea, I endeavoured to obtain as an amendment to the system, the following clause: "And whenever the legislature of the United States shall find it necessary that revenue shall be raised by *direct taxation,* having apportioned the same by the above rule, requisitions shall be made of the respective states to pay into the continental treasury their respective quotas, within a time in the said requisition to be specified; and in case of any of the states failing to comply with such requisition, then, and then only, to have power to devise and pass acts directing the mode, and authorizing the same in the state failing therein."—This was rejected, and that power, which I wished to have given the government only in this particular instance, is given to it, without any restraint or limitation, in every case. [DHRC16 420]

George Nicholas [?], "The State Soldier," No. 4, March 19, 1788:

The right of laying *direct taxes* is also objected to, though this is among the powers already given up by the people, and necessary for the existence of every government. Whether it extends itself over the whole continent or only a single state therefore, the effects will be the same to the people; and all the difference there will be, is, that less will be collected by the states individually, and more by the continent than now is. . . . [DHRC8 513]

Archibald Maclaine, "Publicola," March 20, 1788:

. . . *Taxes* are necessary for the support of every government, and though we shall always have a state establishment to support, the *taxes* for the union will be applied for our protection and defence from foreign enemies—Besides they will be rated by our own immediate representatives, and they and their families will be equally liable with ourselves. But it is not probable, in our present situation, that the federal government will want any *direct taxes* from the states, for a considerable time to come—I am persuaded that nothing but a rupture with some foreign power will make *taxation* necessary; and if we are enabled to make good our past engagements, there will be little or no danger of a war on our parts—But if it should be unavoidable, it is certainly better for us to pay a moderate *tax,* in order to be prepared to repel an enemy, than to suffer the country to be invaded and plundered. . . . [DHRC16 441]

Melancton Smith, *An Address to the People of the State of New York*, c. April 1788:

[1] The constitution has been opposed, because it gives to the legislature an unlimited power of *taxation* both with respect to direct and indirect *taxes,* a right to lay and collect *taxes,* duties, imposts and excises of every kind and description, and to any amount. In this there has been as general a concurrence of opinion as in the former. [Ford 102]

[2] . . . Upon reading the articles which they [the minority of the Pennsylvania convention] propose as amendments, it will appear that they object to indefinite powers in the legislature—to the power of laying *direct taxes*—to the authority of regulating elections—to the extent of the judicial powers, both as it respects the inferior court and the appellate jurisdiction—to the smallness of the representation, &c. . . . [Ford 103–104]

[3] . . . If then, the capital embarrassment in our present government arises from the want of money, and this constitution effectually authorises the raising of it, how are the *taxes* to be lessened by it? Certainly money can only be raised by *taxes* of some kind or other; it must be got either by additional impositions on trade, by excise, or by *direct taxes,* or what is more probable, by all together. In either way, it amounts to the same thing, and the position is clear, that as the necessities of the nation require more money than is now raised, the *taxes* must be enhanced. . . . [Ford 108]

TENDER IN PAYMENT OF DEBTS

United States Constitution, September 17, 1787:

[Article I, Section 10:] No State shall enter into any Treaty, Alliance, or Confederation; grant Letters of Marque and Reprisal; coin Money; emit Bills of Credit; make any Thing but gold and silver Coin a *Tender in Payment of Debts;* pass any Bill of Attainder, ex post facto Law, or Law impairing the Obligation of Contracts, or grant any Title of Nobility.

* * * * *

Richard Henry Lee [?], "The Federal Farmer," No. 1, October 8, 1787:

[1] . . . . During the war, the general confusion, and the introduction of paper money, infused in the minds of people vague ideas respecting government and credit. We expected too much from the return of peace, and of course we have been disappointed. Our governments have been new and unsettled; and several legislatures, by making *tender,* suspension, and paper money laws, have given just cause of uneasiness to creditors. By these and other causes, several orders of men in the community have been prepared, by degrees, for a change of government; and this very abuse of power in the legislatures, which in some cases has been charged upon the democratic part of the community, has furnished aristocratical men with those very weapons, and those very means, with which, in great measure, they are rapidly effecting their favorite object. . . .

[Ford 283]

[2] The conduct of several legislatures, touching paper money, and *tender* laws, has prepared many honest men for changes in government, which otherwise they would not have thought of—when by the evils, on the one hand, and by the secret instigations of artful men, on the other, the minds of men were become sufficiently uneasy, a bold step was taken, which is usually followed by a revolution, or a civil war. . . . [Ford 284]

Richard Henry Lee [?], "The Federal Farmer," No. 3, October 10, 1787:

. . . In almost all these cases, either party may have the trial by jury in the state courts; except paper money and *tender* laws, which are wisely guarded against in the proposed constitution; justice may be obtained in these courts on reasonable terms; they must be more competent to proper decisions on the laws of their respective states, than the federal states can possibly be. . . . [Ford 307]

Hugh Williamson, Speech at Edenton, North Carolina, November 8, 1787:

. . . It is provided in this system that there shall be no fraudulent *tender in the payments of debts*. Foreigners, with whom we have treaties, will trust our citizens on the faith of this engagement. And the citizens of different States will do the same. If the Congress had a negative on the laws of the several States, they would certainly prevent all such laws as might endanger the honor or peace of the nation, by making a *tender of base money;* but they have no such power, and it is at least possible that some State may be found in this Union, disposed to break the Constitution, and abolish private *debts* by such *tenders*. In these cases the Courts of the offending States would probably decide according to its own laws. The foreigner would complain; and the nation might be involved in war for the support of such dishonest measures. Is it not better to have a Court of Appeals in which the Judges can only be determined by the laws of the nation? . . . [DHRC16 203–204]

James Madison, *The Federalist*, No. 44, January 25, 1788:

. . . In addition to these persuasive considerations, it may be observed, that the same reasons which show the necessity of denying to the States the power of regulating coin, prove with equal force that they ought not to be at liberty to substitute a paper medium in the place of coin. Had every State a right to regulate the value of its coin, there might be as many different currencies as States, and thus the intercourse among them would be impeded; retrospective alterations in its value might be made, and thus the citizens of other States be injured, and animosities be kindled among the States themselves. The subjects of foreign powers might suffer from the same cause, and hence the Union be discredited and embroiled by the indiscretion of a single member. No one of these mischiefs is less incident to a power in the States to emit paper money, than to coin gold or silver. The power to make any thing but gold and silver a *tender in payment of debts*, is withdrawn from the States, on the same principle with that of issuing a paper currency. [Fed. 318–19]

Alexander C. Hanson, *Remarks on the Proposed Plan of a Federal Government*, c. January 31, 1788:

[1] The restraints laid on the state legislatures will tend to secure domestic tranquility, more than all the bills, or declarations, of rights, which human policy could devise. It is very justly asserted, that the plan contains an avowal of many rights. It provides that no man, shall suffer by ex post facto laws or bills of attainder. It declares, that gold and silver only shall be a *tender for specie debts;* and that no law shall impair the obligation of a contract. [Ford 243]

[2] I have here perhaps touched a string, which secretly draws together many of the foes to the plan. Too long have we sustained evils, resulting from injudicious emissions of paper, and from the operation of *tender laws*. To bills of *credit* as they are now falsely called, may we impute the entire loss of confidence between men. Hence it is, that specie has, in a great degree, ceased its proper office, and been confined to speculations, baneful to the public, and enriching a few enterprising sharp-sighted men, at the expence not only of the ignorant, slothful, and needy, but of their country's best benefactors. . . . [Ford 243]

[3] . . . What then are the powers an individual state will lose? She will no longer be able to deny congress that, which congress, at this moment, has a right to demand. She will have no power to enter into a treaty, alliance, or confederation. She shall, in time of war, grant no letters of marque and reprisal. She shall coin no money, emit no bills of credit, nor make any thing but gold and silver a *tender in payment of debts*. She shall pass no bill of attainder, or ex post facto law, or law impairing the obligation of a contract. . . . [Ford 251]

David Ramsay, "Civis," February 4, 1788:

. . . be on your guard against the misrepresentations of men who are involved in *debt;* such may wish to see the constitution rejected, because of the following clause "no state shall emit bills of credit, make any thing but gold and silver coin, a *tender in payment of debts,* pass any expost facto law, or law impairing the obligation of contracts." This will doubtless bear hard on *debtors* who wish to defraud their creditors, but it will be of real service to the honest part of the community. Examine well the characters & circumstances of men who are averse to the new constitution. Perhaps you will find that the above recited clause is the real ground of the opposition of some of them, though they may artfully cover it with a splendid profession of zeal for state privileges and general liberty. [DHRC16 26]

"An Old Planter," February 20, 1788:

Let us look around amongst the other states, would any wise or virtuous representation ever have proposed, far less issued (in a time of full peace and tranquility) paper money as a *legal tender?* Would there have been in any of the states opposition to laws for the furtherance of justice, the sole end and object of all government? Would there ever have been such an insult offered to the probity and understanding of men; as to suggest with impunity, the breach of public contracts, and the defrauding of the public creditors? Where such things are heard without censure, we may safely pronounce the governments defective . . . [DHRC8 396]

"Brutus," No. 14, March 6, 1788:

[1] . . . so far as I have been informed, the courts of justice in all the states, have ever been found ready, to administer justice with promptitude and impartiality according to the laws of the land; It is true in some of the states, paper money has been made, and the *debtor* authorised to discharge his debts with it, at a depreciated value, in others, *tender laws* have been passed, obliging the creditor to receive on execution other property than money in discharge of his demand, and in several of the states laws have been made unfavorable to the creditor and tending to render property insecure. [DHRC16 330]

[2] No pretext therefore, can be formed, from the conduct of the judicial courts which will justify giving such powers to the supreme general court, for their decisions have been such as to give just ground of confidence in them, that they will firmly adhere to the principles of rectitude, and there is no necessity of lodging these powers in the courts, in order to guard against the evils justly complained of, on the subject of security of property under this constitution. For it has provided, "that no state shall emit bills of credit, or make any thing but gold and silver coin a *tender in payment of debts*." It has also declared, that "no state shall pass any law impairing the obligation of contracts."—These prohibitions give the most perfect security against those attacks upon property which I am sorry to say some of the states have but too wantonly made, by passing laws sanctioning fraud in the *debtor* against his creditor. . . .
[DHRC16 330]

Oliver Ellsworth, "The Landholder," No. 12, March 17, 1788:

[1] To the Rhode-Island Friends of Paper-Money, *Tender-Acts* and Antifederalism. [DHRC16 405]

[2] . . . By your [i.e., Rhode Island's] system we see unrighteousness in the essence, in its effects, and in its native miseries. The rogues of every other state blush at the exhibition, and say you have betrayed them by carrying the matter too far. The very naming of your measures is a complete refutation of antifederalism, paper money and *tender acts,* for no man chooses such company in argument. [DHRC16 406]

Archibald Maclaine, "Publicola," March 20, 1788:

. . . The United States are, and for some years have been, without any national character—Foreigners say, and they say truly, that we have no government—Even in this state, our policy is so wretched, that we have lost all credit, the very soul of commerce. No foreigner, no not an individual of any of our sister states, will trust us with a shilling. Our paper money, and our judicial decisions, banish all confidence; and the former has banished all gold and silver—Let paper money be no longer a *tender,* and justice be done to those who have transactions with us, and I will venture to assert that we shall soon have among us, a pound value in gold and silver, for every shilling in paper which we now possess. Wherever depreciated money is a lawful *tender,* that which is good vanishes, as if by inchantment. [DHRC16 439]

TRANQUILITY

(Domestic, Public)

United States Constitution, September 17, 1787:

[Preamble:] WE THE PEOPLE of the United States, in Order to form a more perfect Union, establish Justice, insure *domestic Tranquility,* provide for the common defence, promote the general Welfare, and secure the Blessings of Liberty to ourselves and our Posterity, do ordain and establish this Constitution for the United States of America.

* * * * *

Government of West New Jersey, November 25, 1681:

Forasmuch as it hath pleased God, to bring us into this Province of West New Jersey, and settle us here in safety, that we may be a people to the praise and honour of his name, who hath so dealt with us, and for the good and welfare of our posterity to come, we the Governor and Proprietors, freeholders and inhabitants of West New Jersey, by mutual consent and agreement, for the prevention of innovasion and oppression, either upon us or our posterity, and for the preservation of the peace and *tranquility* of the same; and that all may be encouraged to go on chearfully in their several places: We do make and constitute these our agreements to be as fundamentals to us and our posterity, to be held inviolable, and that no person or persons whatsoever, shall or may make void or disanul the same upon any pretence whatsoever. [Thorpe 2565]

English Bill of Rights, December 16, 1689:

. . . and for preventing all questions and divisions in this realm by reason of any pretended titles to the crown and for preserving a certainty in the succession thereof, in and upon which the unity, peace, *tranquility* and safety of this nation doth under God wholly consist and depend, the said lords spiritual and temporal and commons do beseech Their Majesties, that it may be enacted, established and declared, that the crown and regal government of the said kingdoms and dominions, with all and singular the premises thereunto belonging and appertaining, shall be and continue to Their said Majesties and the survivor of them during their lives and the life of the survivor of them. . . . [SDECH 467]

William Penn, Plan of Colonial Union, c. February 8, 1697:

That the several colonies before mentioned, do meet once a year, and oftner if need be during the Warr, and at least once in two years in times of Peace, by their Stated and Appointed Deputies, to Debate and Resolve of such Measures, as are most adviseable for their better understanding, and their *publick Tranquility* and Safety. [PWP3 482]

Thomas Paine, *Common Sense,* January 9, 1776:

. . . it naturally follows, that the king's speech, as being a piece of finished villainy, deserved and still deserves, a general execration both by the Congress and the people. Yet as the *domestic tranquility* of a nation, depends greatly on the chastity of what may properly be called NATIONAL MATTERS, it is often better to pass some things over in silent disdain, than to make use of such new methods of dislike, as might introduce the least innovation on that guardian of our peace and safety. And, perhaps, it is chiefly owing to this prudent delicacy, that the king's speech hath not before now, suffered a public execution. . . .
[CWTP1 40]

John Adams, *Thoughts on Government*, April 1776:

. . . Great care should be taken to effect this, and to prevent unfair, partial, and corrupt elections. Such regulations, however, may be better made in times of greater *tranquillity* than the present; and they will spring up themselves naturally, when all the powers of government come to be in the hands of the people's friends. At present it will be safest to proceed in all established modes to which the people have been familiarised by habit. [PJA4 88]

Massachusetts Constitution, March 2, 1780:

[Preamble:] The end of the institution, maintenance, and administration of government, is to secure the existence of the body politic, to protect it, and to furnish the individuals who compose it with the power of enjoying in safety and *tranquillity* their natural rights, and the blessings of life: and whenever these great objects are not obtained, the people have a right to alter the government, and to take measures necessary for their safety, prosperity, and happiness.
[Thorpe 1888–89]

James Wilson, Address on the Constitution, October 6, 1787:

This constitution, it has been further urged, is of a pernicious tendency, because it tolerates a standing army in the time of peace. This has always been a popular topic of declamation: and yet I do not know a nation in the world, which has not found it necessary and useful to maintain the appearance of strength in a season of the most profound *tranquility*. Nor is it a novelty with us; for under the present articles of confederation, congress certainly possesses this reprobated power . . . [Ford 157–58]

Edmund Randolph, Letter on the Federal Constitution, October 10, 1787:

I saw however that the confederation was tottering from its own weakness, and that the sitting of the convention was a signal of its total insufficiency. I was therefore ready to assent to a scheme of government, which was proposed, and which went beyond the limits of the confederation, believing, that without being too extensive it would have preserved our *tranquility,* until that temper and that genius should be collected. [DHRC8 271]

Noah Webster, *An Examination of the Leading Principles of the Federal Constitution*, October 17, 1787:

[1] But the idea that Congress can levy taxes at pleasure is false, and the suggestion wholly unsupported. The preamble to the constitution is declaratory of the purposes of our union, and the assumption of any powers not necessary to establish justice, insure *domestic tranquility,* provide for the common defence, promote the general welfare, and to secure the blessings of liberty to ourselves and our Posterity, will be unconstitutional, and endanger the existence of Congress. . . . [Ford 50]

[2] . . . The advantages of some states, and the disadvantages of others are so great—and so materially affect the business and interest of each, that nothing but an equalizing system of revenue, that shall reduce the advantages to some equitable proportion, can prevent a civil war and save the national debt. Such a system of revenue is the sine qua non of *public justice and tranquillity*.
[Ford 62–63]

John Jay, *The Federalist*, No. 3, November 3, 1787:

At present I mean only to consider it as it respects security for the preservation of peace and *tranquillity,* as well as against dangers from foreign arms and influence, as from dangers of the like kind arising from domestic causes. . . . [Fed. 97]

John Jay, *The Federalist*, No. 4, November 7, 1787:

Apply these facts to our own case. Leave America divided into thirteen or, if you please, into three or four independent governments—what armies could they raise and pay—what fleets could they ever hope to have? If one was attacked, would the others fly to its succor, and spend their blood and money in its defence? Would there be no danger of their being flattered into neutrality by its specious promises, or seduced by a too great fondness for peace to decline hazarding their *tranquillity* and present safety for the sake of neighbors, of whom perhaps they have been jealous, and whose importance they are content to see diminished. Although such conduct would not be wise, it would, nevertheless, be natural. . . . [Fed. 103]

Alexander Hamilton, *The Federalist*, No. 6, November 14, 1787:

. . . And there are others [i.e., causes of hostility], not less numerous than either of the former, which take their origin entirely in private passions; in the attachments, enmities, interests, hopes, and fears of leading individuals in the communities of which they are members. Men of this class, whether the favorites of a king or of a people, have in too many instances abused the confidence they possessed; and assuming the pretext of some public motive, have not scrupled to sacrifice the *national tranquillity* to personal advantage or personal gratification. [Fed. 109]

"A True Friend," November 14, 1787:

Far from seeing our agriculture improve, our commerce flourish, our happiness and our inward *tranquility* increase, our reputation and our credit enlarge and extend itself abroad, (as we had reason to flatter ourselves) we have constantly seen the contrary since the epoch of our independence; our evils have accumulated and are become of a very alarming nature; our enemies abroad, and in our very bosom exult in putting our present situation in parallel with what it was before the revolution, and deceiving us on the causes, will not fail to attribute the source of our misfortunes to our scission with Great-Britain. [DHRC8 159]

Alexander Hamilton, *The Federalist*, No. 7, November 17, 1787:

. . . There is, perhaps, nothing more likely to disturb the *tranquillity* of nations than their being bound to mutual contributions for any common object that does not yield an equal and coincident benefit. For it is an observation, as true as it is trite, that there is nothing men differ so readily about as the payment of money. [Fed. 118]

Alexander Hamilton, *The Federalist*, No. 9, November 21, 1787:

The utility of a Confederacy, as well to suppress faction and to guard the *internal tranquillity* of States, as to increase their external force and security, is in reality not a new idea. It has been practiced upon in different countries and ages, and has received the sanction of the most approved writers on the subjects of politics. . . . [Fed. 125–126]

Alexander Hamilton, *The Federalist*, No. 13, November 28, 1787:

. . . and if we also take into view the military establishments which it has been shown would unavoidably result from the jealousies and conflicts of the several nations into which the States would be divided, we shall clearly discover that a separation would be not less injurious to the economy, than to the *tranquillity*, commerce, revenue, and liberty of every part. [Fed. 149–50]

Alexander Hamilton, *The Federalist*, No. 15, December 1, 1787:

This is the melancholy situation to which we have been brought by those very maxims and councils which would now deter us from adopting the proposed Constitution; and which, not content with having conducted us to the brink of a precipice, seem resolved to plunge us into the abyss that awaits us below. Here, my countrymen, impelled by every motive that ought to influence an enlightened people, let us make a firm stand for our safety, our *tranquillity*, our dignity, our reputation. Let us at last break the fatal charm which has too long seduced us from the paths of felicity and prosperity. [Fed. 157]

Alexander Hamilton, *The Federalist*, No. 16, December 4, 1787:

The result of these observations to an intelligent mind must be clearly this, that if it be possible at any rate to construct a federal government capable of regulating the common concerns and preserving the *general tranquillity*, it must be founded, as to the objects committed to its care, upon the reverse of the principle contended for by the opponents of the proposed Constitution. It must carry its agency to the persons of the citizens. It must stand in need of no intermediate legislation; but must itself be empowered to employ the arm of the ordinary magistrate to execute its own resolutions. The majesty of the national authority must be manifested through the medium of the courts of justice. The government of the Union, like that of each State, must be able to address itself immediately to the hopes and fears of individuals; and to attract to its support those passions which have the strongest influence upon the human heart. It must, in short, possess all the means, and have a right to resort to all the methods, of executing the powers with which it is intrusted, that are possessed and exercised by the governments of the particular States. [Fed. 165]

"Americanus," No. 1, December 5, 1787:

. . . To complete the full measure of our calamities, it was found, that civil insurrections had disturbed the *tranquility* of some of the states, and that all were, in a peculiar manner, liable to be invaded. To obviate these grievances by enlarging, in the amplest manner, the powers of the Foederal Government, and to advance the United States to that station of importance and respectability which they ought to possess among the nations of the world, it was proposed to call a General Convention. . . . [DHRC8 201]

James Madison, *The Federalist*, No. 19, December 8, 1787:

. . . The force of imperial sovereignty was insufficient to restrain such powerful dependents; or to preserve the unity and *tranquillity* of the [Frankish] empire. The most furious private wars, accompanied with every species of calamity, were carried on between the different princes and states. . . . [Fed. 177]

James Madison, *The Federalist*, No. 20, December 11, 1787:

. . . The first wish prompted by humanity is, that this severe trial may issue in such a revolution of their government as will establish their union [the Netherlands], and render it the parent of *tranquillity*, freedom, and happiness: The next, that the asylum under which, we trust, the enjoyment of these blessings will speedily be secured in this country, may receive and console them for the catastrophe of their own. [Fed. 185]

Alexander Hamilton, *The Federalist*, No. 25, December 21, 1787:

. . . The design of the objection, which has been mentioned, is to preclude standing armies in time of peace, though we have never been informed how far it is designed the prohibition should extend: whether to raising armies as well as to keeping them up in a season of *tranquillity* or not. If it be confined to the latter it will have no precise signification, and it will be ineffectual for the purpose intended. . . . [Fed. 210]

Alexander Hamilton, *The Federalist*, No. 34, January 4, 1788:

[1] . . . A cloud has been for some time hanging over the European world. If it should break forth into a storm, who can insure us that in its progress a part of its fury would not be spent upon us? No reasonable man would hastily pronounce that we are entirely out of its reach. Or if the combustible materials that now seem to be collecting should be dissipated without coming to maturity, or if a flame should be kindled without extending to us, what security can we have that our *tranquillity* will long remain undisturbed from some other course or from some other quarter? . . . [Fed. 250]

[2] . . . To judge from the history of mankind, we shall be compelled to conclude that the fiery and destructive passions of war reign in the human breast with much more powerful sway than the mild and beneficent sentiments of peace; and that to model our political systems upon speculations of lasting *tranquillity*, is to calculate on the weaker springs of the human character. [Fed. 251]

James Madison, *The Federalist*, No. 42, January 22, 1788:

. . . A very material object of this power [to regulate commerce] was the relief of the States which import and export through other States, from the improper contributions levied on them by the latter. Were these at liberty to regulate the trade between State and State, it must be foreseen that ways would be found out to load the articles of import and export, during the passage through their jurisdiction, with duties which would fall on the makers of the latter and the consumers of the former. We may be assured by past experience, that such a practice would be introduced by future contrivances; and both by that and a common knowledge of human affairs, that it would nourish unceasing animosities, and not improbably terminate in serious interruptions of the *public tranquillity*. To those who do not view the question through the medium of passion or of interest, the desire of the commercial States to collect, in any form, an indirect revenue from their uncommercial neighbors, must appear not less impolitic than it is unfair . . . [Fed. 305]

Alexander C. Hanson, *Remarks on the Proposed Plan of a Federal Government*, c. January 31, 1788:

The restraints laid on the state legislatures will tend to secure *domestic tranquility*, more than all the bills, or declarations, of rights, which human policy could devise. It is very justly asserted, that the plan contains an avowal of many rights. . . . [Ford 243]

James Madison, *The Federalist*, No. 49, February 2, 1788:

The danger of disturbing the *public tranquillity* by interesting too strongly the public passions, is a still more serious objection against a frequent reference of constitutional questions to the decision of the whole society. Notwithstanding the success which has attended the revisions of our established forms of government, and which does so much honor to the virtue and intelligence of the people of America, it must be confessed that the experiments are of too ticklish a nature to be unnecessarily multiplied. . . . [Fed. 349]

Massachuetts Convention, Ratification of the Constitution, February 6, 1788:

. . . and acknowledging with grateful hearts the goodness of the Supreme Ruler of the universe, in affording the people of the United States, in the course of his Providence, an opportunity, deliberately and peaceably, without fraud or surprise, of entering into an explicit and solemn compact with each other, by assenting to and ratifying a new constitution, in order to form a more perfect union, establish justice, insure *domestick tranquillity,* provide for the common defence, promote the general welfare, and secure the blessings of liberty to themselves, and their posterity—DO, in the name and in behalf of the people of the commonwealth of Massachusetts, ASSENT to and RATIFY the said constitution, for the United States of America. [DHRC16 68]

"Brutus," No. 12, February 7, 1788:

. . . Another end declared is "to insure *domestic tranquility.*" This comprehends a provision against all private breaches of the peace, as well as against all public commotions or general insurrections; and to attain the object of this clause fully, the government must exercise the power of passing laws on these subjects, as well as of appointing magistrates with authority to execute them. And the courts will adopt these ideas in their expositions. I might proceed to the other clause, in the preamble, and it would appear by a consideration of all of them separately, as it does by taking them together, that if the spirit of this system is to be known from its declared end and design in the preamble, its spirit is to subvert and abolish all the powers of the state government, and to embrace every object to which any government extends. [DHRC16 75]

"An Old Planter," February 20, 1788:

Let us look around amongst the other states, would any wise or virtuous representation ever have proposed, far less issued (in a time of full peace and *tranquility*) paper money as a legal tender? Would there have been in any of the states opposition to laws for the furtherance of justice, the sole end and object of all government? . . . [DHRC8 396]

John Hancock, Speech to the Massachusetts Legislature, February 27, 1788:

[1] . . . The objects of the proposed Constitution, are defence against external enemies, and the promotion of *tranquility* and happiness amongst the States. Whether it is well calculated for those important purposes, has been the subject of extensive and learned discussion in the Convention which you appointed. . . . [DHRC16 225]

[2] Gentlemen, As that BEING, in whose hands is the government of all the Nations of the Earth, and who putteth down one, and raiseth up another according to His Sovereign Pleasure, has given to the People of these States, a rich and an extensive Country; has in a marvellous manner, given them a name and a standing among the Nations of the World—has blessed them with external Peace,

and *internal Tranquility;*—I hope and pray, that the gratitude of their Hearts may be expressed by a proper use of those inestimable blessings . . .
[DHRC16 225–26]

"The Arraignment of Centinel," February 28, 1788:

The jurors for the most illustrious United States of America, upon their oaths do present, that —— Centinel, late of the Northern Liberties, in the county of Philadelphia, Esq. and within the jurisdiction of the aforesaid most illustrious United States, as a false traitor, not having the fear of God in his heart, neither in his eyes, nor weighing the duties of citizenship and allegiance, but moved and seduced by the instigation of Satan, Belzebub, Lucifer, Belial, and the whole herd of Devils, withdrawing the due obedience, which a true and faithful subject ought, should, and of right is bound to bear, towards the aforesaid most illustrious United States; contriving, and with all his strength, soul, body, and goose quill (even to an unprecedented degree of flaming zeal and enthusiasm) to disturb the peace and *common tranquillity* of the aforesaid most illustrious United States, by dogmatical, proditorious publications, (lies and other hellish devices) to stir up and move opposition, faction, riot, sedition, insurrection, civil wars, rebellion and murder, against the aforesaid most illustrious United States . . .
[DHRC16 258–59]

Mercy Otis Warren, *Observations on the New Constitution*, February 1788:

[1] . . . may the people be calm, and wait a legal redress; may the mad transport of some of our infatuated capitals subside; and every influential character through the States, make the most prudent exertions for a new general Convention, who may vest adequate powers in Congress, for all national purposes, without annihilating the individual governments, and drawing blood from every pore by taxes, impositions and illegal restrictions.—This step might again re-establish the Union, restore *tranquility* to the ruffled mind of the inhabitants, and save America from distresses, dreadful even in contemplation. . . . [DHRC16 286]

[2] . . . But the character of this people is not averse to a degree of subordination: the truth of this appears from the easy restoration of *tranquility,* after a dangerous insurrection in one of the states; this also evinces the little necessity of a complete revolution of government throughout the union. . . . [DHRC16 288]

Alexander Hamilton, *The Federalist*, No. 65, March 7, 1788:

Could the Supreme Court have been relied upon as answering this description? It is much to be doubted, whether the members of that tribunal would at all times be endowed with so eminent a portion of fortitude, as would be called for in the execution of so difficult a task [i.e., to serve as a court of impeachments] and it is still more to be doubted, whether they would possess the degree of credit and authority, which might, on certain occasions, be indispensable towards reconciling the people to a decision that should happen to clash with an accusation brought by their immediate representatives. A deficiency in the first, would be fatal to the accused∞ the last, dangerous to the *public tranquillity*. . . .

[Fed. 427]

***Poughkeepsie Country Journal*, March 18, 1788:**

. . . Thus in the present case, however ill it would become friends to enlist under the banners of heated party, and thereby add fuel to that fire which already blazeth too high; yet I think as a body, they might exhibit their united weight in the legal line of suffrage, and perhaps be a means of giving *tranquility* to their country. [DHRC16 409]

Letter from Massachusetts, March 19, 1788, published in *New York Journal*, March 24, 1788:

[1] [Reporting an unsuccessful amendment in the Massachusetts legislature:] . . . We have long been sensible of the imbecility of the confederation of the United States, and of the consequences of that imbecility, and therefore appointed delegates to the late general convention, for the sole and express purpose of revising the articles of confederation, and reporting to Congress and the several legislatures such alterations and provisions therein, as shall, when agreed to in Congress, and confirmed by the states, render the federal constitution adequate to the exigencies of government and the preservation of the union! If they had observed, and acted agreeably to their commission, no difficulty perhaps would have arisen from the numbers of a people spread over a vast extent of territory, containing such a great variety of soils, and under such extremes of climate, and with such different views and habits while they were so well united in that one object, we are fully persuaded that our national existence might in that way have been preserved with unanimity, *tranquility* and peace. We do not wish to be known to the world under any other appellation than that of the United States.

[DHRC16 227–28]

[4] . . . Every good government should have for its objects defence against external enemies, and the promotion of *internal tranquility* and happiness. While we suspend our opinion of the purity of intention, and of the great zeal for the interest and welfare with which the late convention assembled, we are in justice to our constituents constrained to say that the result of their deliberations does not seem well calculated for those valuable purposes. . . . [DHRC16 228]

Alexander Hamilton, *The Federalist*, No. 74, March 25, 1788:

. . . But the principal argument for reposing the power of pardoning in this case to the Chief Magistrate is this; in seasons of insurrection or rebellion, there are

often critical moments, when a well-timed offer of pardon to the insurgents or rebels may restore the *tranquillity of the commonwealth;* and which, if suffered to pass unimproved, it may never be possible afterwards to recall. . . .
[Fed. 475]

Archibald Maclaine, "Publicola," March 27, 1788:

. . . Those among us who are the most industrious to prevent a reform, have been some of the warmest opposers of the British government—Their zeal has been little short of persecution; but if we look around us, we shall discover, that a considerable number of them are such as were unknown or as persons of no consequence, previous to the war—They have arisen by accident into power, and influence, and now dread the loss of it. They make a merit of their uniform attachment to the American cause, though in fact many of them had nothing to lose, and consequently ran no risk in the contest; and since the peace has taken place, most of them have been equally uniform in opposing such measures as were best adapted to allay the animosities of parties, and restore the community to order and *tranquillity*—To this opposition, throughout all the states, it is owing, that a reform in government becomes necessary. [DHRC16 495]

John Jay, *An Address to the People of the State of New York*, c. April 15, 1788:

[1] That glorious war was succeeded by an advantageous peace. When danger disappeared, ease, *tranquility,* and a sense of security loosened the bands of union; and Congress and soldiers and good faith depreciated with their apparent importance. . . . [Ford 70]

[2] . . . It would little become us to verify the predictions of those who ventured to prophecy, that peace: instead of blessing us with happiness and *tranquility,* would serve only as the signal for factions, discords and civil contentions to rage in our land, and overwhelm it with misery and distress. [Ford 86]

Alexander Hamilton, *The Federalist*, No. 80, May 28, 1788:

[1] . . . As the denial or perversion of justice by the sentences of courts, as well as in any other manner, is with reason classed among the just causes of war, it will follow that the federal judiciary ought to have cognizance of all causes in which the citizens of other countries are concerned. This is not less essential to the preservation of the public faith, than to the security of the *public tranquillity*. . . . [Fed. 501]

[2] . . . History gives us a horrid picture of the dissensions and private wars which distracted and desolated Germany prior to the institution of the Imperial Chamber by Maximilian, towards the close of the fifteenth century; and informs us, at the same time, of the vast influence of that institution in appeasing the disorders

and establishing the *tranquillity of the empire*. This was a court invested with authority to decide finally all differences among the members of the Germanic body. [Fed. 501]

John Dickinson, "Fabius," No. 3, 1788:

[1] It is more pleasing, and may be more profitable to reflect, that, their [i.e., republics'] *tranquility* and prosperity have commonly been promoted, in proportion to the strength of their government for protecting the worthy against the licentious. [Ford 174]

[2] Each individual then must contribute such a share of his rights, as is necessary for attaining that security that is essential to freedom . . . What does he gain by it? The aid of those associated with him, for his relief from the incommodities of mental or bodily weakness—the pleasure for which his heart is formed—of doing good—protection against injuries—a capacity of enjoying his undelegated rights to the best advantage—a repeal of his fears—and *tranquility* of mind—or, in other words, that perfect liberty better described in the Holy Scriptures, than any where else, in these expressions—"When every man shall sit under his vine, and under his fig-tree, and none shall make him afraid." [Ford 176]

John Dickinson, "Fabius," No. 5, 1788:

It has been considered,what are the rights to be contributed, and how they are to be managed; and it has been said, that *republican tranquility* and prosperity have commonly been promoted, in proportion to the strength of government for protecting the worthy against the licentious. [Ford 188]

John Dickinson, "Fabius," No. 7, 1788:

If folly or wickedness prevailed in any parts friendly offices and salutary measures restored *tranquility*. Thus the public good was maintained. In its very formation, tyrannies and aristocracies submitted, by consent or compulsion. . . .

[Ford 201]

John Dickinson, Fabius," No. 9, 1788:

If to the union of England and Scotland, a just connection with Ireland be added, ecclesiastical establishments duly amended; additions to the peerage regulated, and representation of the commons properly improved, it is to be expected, that the *tranquility,* strength, reputation, and prosperity of the empire will be greatly promoted . . . [Ford 213n]

George Washington, First Inaugural Address, April 30, 1789:

Having thus imparted to you my sentiments, as they have been awakened by the occasion which brings us together, I shall take my present leave; but not without resorting once more to the benign Parent of the human race in humble supplication, that, since He has been pleased to favor the American people with opportunities for deliberating in perfect *tranquillity,* and dispositions for deciding with unparalleled unanimity on a form of government for the security of their union and the advancement of their happiness, so his divine blessing may be equally conspicuous in the enlarged views, the temperate consultations, and the wise measures on which the success of this Government must depend.

[Annals 29]

TREASON

United States Constitution, September 17, 1787:

[Article I, Section 6:] The Senators and Representatives shall receive a Compensation for their Services, to be ascertained by Law, and paid out of the Treasury of the United States. They shall in all Cases, except *Treason,* Felony and Breach of the Peace, be privileged from Arrest during their Attendance at the Session of their respective Houses, and in going to and returning from the same; and for any Speech or Debate in either House, they shall not be questioned in any other Place.

[Article II, Section 4:] The President, Vice President and all civil Officers of the United States, shall be removed from Office on Impeachment for, and Conviction of, *Treason,* Bribery, or other high Crimes and Misdemeanors.

[Article III, Section 3:] *Treason* against the United States, shall consist only in levying War against them, or in adhering to their Enemies, giving them Aid and Comfort. No Person shall be convicted of *Treason* unless on the Testimony of two Witnesses to the same overt Act, or on Confession in open Court.

[*Ibid.*:] The Congress shall have Power to declare the Punishment of *Treason,* but no Attainder of *Treason* shall work Corruption of Blood, or Forfeiture except during the Life of the Person attainted.

[Article IV, Section 2:] A Person charged in any State with *Treason,* Felony, or other Crime, who shall flee from Justice, and be found in another State, shall on Demand of the executive Authority of the State from which he fled, be delivered up, to be removed to the State having Jurisdiction of the Crime.

* * * * *

Fundamental Constitutions of Carolina, March 1, 1669:

[Article 63:] In every precinct there shall be a court, consisting of a steward and four justices of the precinct, being inhabitants and having three hundred acres of free hold within the said precinct who shall judge all criminal causes; except for *treason,* murder, and any other offences punishable with death, and except all criminal causes of the nobility; and shall judge also all civil causes whatsoever . . . [Thorpe 2780]

[Article 65:] For *treason,* murder, and all other offences punishable with death, there shall be a commission, twice a year at least, granted unto one or more members of the grand council or colleges . . . [Thorpe 2780]

Fundamental Constitutions of West New Jersey, 1676:

[Chapter 18:] And that no Proprietor, freeholder, freedenison, or inhabitant in the said Province, shall be attached, arrested, or imprisoned, for or by reason of any debt, duty, or thing whatsoever (cases felonious, criminal and *treasonable* excepted) before he have personal summon or summons . . . [Thorpe 2549]

[Chapter 21:] That all and every prson and persons whatsoever, who shall prosecute or prefer any indictment or information against others for any personal injuries, or matter criminal, or shall prosecute for any other criminal cause, (*treason,* murther, and felony, only excepted) shall and may be master of his own process . . . [Thorpe 2551]

Charles II, Charter of Pennsylvania, February 28, 1681:

. . . Also to remitt, release, pardon, and abolish whether before Judgement or after all Crimes and Offences whatsoever comitted within the said Countrey against the said Lawes, *Treason* and wilful and malitious Murder onely excepted, and in those Cases to grant Reprieves, until Our pleasure may bee known therein and to doe all and every other thing and things, which unto the compleate Establishment of Justice, unto Courts and Tribunalls, formes of Judicature, and manner of Proceedings doe belong, altho in these presents express mention bee not made thereof . . . [Thorpe 3038]

Pennsylvania Frame of Government, Laws Agreed Upon in England, May 5, 1682:

[Article 37:] That as a careless and corrupt administration of justice draws the wrath of God upon magistrates, so the wildness and looseness of the people provoke the indignation of God against a country: therefore, that all such offences against God, as swearing, cursing, lying, prophane talking, drunkenness, drinking of healths, obscene words, incest, sodomy, rapes, whoredom, fornication, and other uncleanness (not to be repeated) all *treasons,* misprisions, murders, duels, felony, seditions, maims, forcible entries, and other violences, to the persons and estates of the inhabitants within this province; all prizes, stage-plays, cards, dice, May-games, gamesters, masques, revels, bull-baitings, cock-fightings, bear-baitings, and the like, which excite the people to rudeness, cruelty, looseness, and irreligion, shall be respectively discouraged, and severely punished, according to the appointment of the Governor and freemen in provincial Council and General Assembly; as also all proceedings contrary to these laws, that are not here made expressly penal. [Thorpe 3063]

Fundamental Constitutions of East New Jersey, 1683:

[Article 22:] Fourteen years quiet possession shall give an unquestionable right, except in cases of infants, lunaticks or married women, or persons beyond sea or in prison. And whoever forfeits his estate to the government by commtting *treason* against the Crown of England, or in this Province, or by any other capital crime, the nearest of kin may redeem it within two months after the criminals death, by paying to the public treasury not above one hundred pounds, and not under five pounds sterling which proportion the common Council shall determine, according to the value of the criminals estate, and to the nature of the offence . . . [Thorpe 2581]

James II, Commission to Sir Edmund Andros for the Dominion of New England, April 7, 1688:

And Wee do hereby give and graunt unto you full power where you shall see cause and shall judge any offender or offenders in capitall and criminall matters, or for any fines or forfeitures due unto us, fit objects of our mercy, to pardon such offenders and to remit such fines & forfeitures, *treason* and wilfull murder only excepted, in which case you shall likewise have power upon extraordinary occasions to grant reprieves to the offenders therein untill and to the intent our pleasure may be further known. [Thorpe 1866]

English Bill of Rights, December 16, 1689:

[1] And whereas of late years partial, corrupt, and unqualified persons have been returned and served on juries in trials, and particularly diverse jurors in trials for high *treason,* which were not freeholders. [SDECH 463]

[2] That jurors ought to be duly impanelled and returned and jurors which pass upon men in trials for high *treason* ought to be freeholders. [SDECH 465]

First Continental Congress, Declaration and Resolves, October 14, 1774:

And it has lately been resolved in Parliament, that by force of a statute made in the thirty-fifth year of the reign of king Henry the eighth, colonists may be transported to England, and tried there upon accusations for *treasons* and misprisions, or concealments of *treasons,* committed in the colonies; and by a late statute, such trials have been directed in cases therein mentioned. [JCC1 65]

Thomas Paine, *Common Sense*, January 9, 1776:

. . . The property of no man is secure in the present unbraced system of things. The mind of the multitude is left at random, and seeing no fixed object before them, they pursue such as fancy or opinion presents. Nothing is criminal; there is no such thing as *treason;* wherefore, every one thinks himself at liberty to act as he pleases. . . . [CWTP1 43]

New Jersey Constitution, July 2, 1776:

[Article 9:] That the Governor and Council, (seven whereof shall be a quorum) be the Court of Appeals, in the last resort, in all clauses of law, as heretofore; and that they possess the power of granting pardons to criminals, after condemnation, in all cases of *treason,* felony, or other offences. [Thorpe 2596]

Pennsylvania Constitution, September 28, 1776:

[Frame of Government, Section 20:] . . . And [the president and executive council] shall have power to grant pardons, and remit fines, in all cases whatsoever, except in cases of impeachment; and in cases of *treason* and murder, shall have power to grant reprieves, but not to pardon, until the end of the next sessions of assembly but there shall be no remission or mitigation of punishments on impeachments, except by act of the legislature . . . [Thorpe 3087–88]

Maryland Constitution, November 11, 1776:

[Declaration of Rights, Article 16:] That no law, to attaint particular persons of *treason* or felony, ought to be made in any case, or at any time hereafter. [Thorpe 1688]

[Declaration of Rights, Article 24:] That there ought to be no forfeiture of any part of the estate of any person, for any crime except murder, or *treason* against the State, and then only on conviction and attainder. [Thorpe 1688]

North Carolina Constitution, December 18, 1776:

[Form of Government, Article 34:] . . . Provided, That nothing herein contained shall be construed to exempt preachers of *treasonable* or seditious discourses, from legal trial and punishment. [Thorpe 2793]

Georgia Constitution, February 5, 1777:

[Article 39:] All matters of breach of the peace, felony, murder, and *treason* against the State to be tried in the county where the same was committed. All matters of dispute, both civil and criminal, in any county where there is not a sufficient number of inhabitants to form a court, shall be tried in the next adjacent county where a court is held. [Thorpe 783]

New York Constitution, April 20, 1777:

[Article 18:] [The governor shall have power] . . . at his discretion, to grant reprieves and pardons to persons convicted of crimes, other than *treason* or murder, in which he may suspend the execution of the sentence, until it shall be reported to the legislature at their subsequent meeting; and they shall either pardon or direct the execution of the criminal, or grant a further reprieve. [Thorpe 2633]

Vermont Constitution, July 8, 1777:

[Frame of Government, Section 18:] . . . They [the governor and council] shall sit as judges to hear and determine on impeachments, taking to their assistance, for advice only, the justices of the supreme court; and shall have power to grant pardons, and remit fines, in all cases whatsoever, except cases of impeachment, and in cases of *treason* and murder—shall have power to grant reprieves, but not to pardon, until the end of the next session of the Assembly . . . [Thorpe 3745]

United States Articles of Confederation, November 15, 1777:

[Article IV:] If any Person guilty of, or charged with *treason,* felony, or other high misdemeanor in any state, shall flee from Justice, and be found in any of the united states, he shall upon demand of the Governor or executive power, of the state from which he fled, be delivered up and removed to the state having jurisdiction of his offence. [DHRC1 87]

[Article V:] Freedom of speech and debate in Congress shall not be impeached or questioned in any Court, or place out of Congress, and the members of congress shall be protected in their persons from arrests and imprisonments, during the time of their going to and from, and attendance on congress, except for *treason,* felony, or breach of the peace. [DHRC1 87–88]

Massachusetts Constitution, March 2, 1780:

[Article 25:] No subject ought, in any case, or in any time, to be declared guilty of *treason* or felony by the legislature. [Thorpe 1892]

New Hampshire Constitution, June 2, 1784:

[Bill of Rights, Article 18:] All penalties ought to be proportioned to the nature of the offence. No wise legislature will affix the same punishment to the crimes of theft, forgery and the like, which they do to those of murder and *treason;*

where the same undistinguishing severity is exerted against all offences; the people are led to forget the real distinction in the crimes themselves, and to commit the most flagrant with as little compunction as they do those of the lightest dye: For the same reason a multitude of sanguinary laws is both impolitic and unjust. . . . [Thorpe 2456]

Vermont Constitution, July 4, 1786:

[Frame of Government, Section 11:] . . . They [the governor and council] shall sit as Judges to hear and determine on impeachments, taking to their assistance, for advice only, the Judges of the Supreme Court; and shall have power to grant pardons, and remit fines in all cases whatsoever, except in *treason* and murder, in which they shall have power to grant reprieves but not to pardon, until after the end of the next session of Assembly, and except in cases of impeachment, in which there shall be no remission or mitigation of punishment, but by act of legislation. . . . [Thorpe 3756]

[*Ibid.*, Section 17:] No person ought, in any case, or in any time, to be declared guilty of *treason* or felony by the Legislature. [Thorpe 3757]

Charles Pinckney's Plan of Union, May 29, 1787:

[Article 15:] [Congress] shall have the exclusive Power of declaring what shall be Treason & Misp[rision] of Treason agt. U.S. . . . [DHRC1 247]

Alexander Hamilton's Plan of Union, June 18, 1787:

. . . The Governor to have a negative upon all laws about to be passed—and to have the execution of all laws passed—to be the Commander in Chief of the land and naval forces and of the Militia of the United States—to have the direction of war, when authorised or begun—to have with the advice and approbation of the Senate, the power of making all treaties—to have the appointment of the heads or chief officers of the departments of finance war and foreign affairs—to have the nomination of all other officers (ambassadors to foreign nations included) subject to the approbation or rejection of the Senate—to have the power of pardoning all offences but *treason,* which he shall not pardon without the approbation of the Senate. [DHRC1 254]

George Mason, Objections to the Constitution, October 7, 1787:

The President of the United States has the unrestrained Power of granting Pardons for *Treason;* which may be sometimes excercised to screen from Punishment those whom he had secretly instigated to commit the Crime, & thereby prevent a Discovery of his own Guilt. [DHRC8 44]

Richard Henry Lee [?], "The Federal Farmer," No. 3, October 10, 1787:

. . . The trial by jury is secured only in those few criminal cases, to which the federal laws will extend—as crimes committed on the seas, against the laws of nations, *treason* and counterfeiting the federal securities and coin: But even in these cases, the jury trial of the vicinage is not secured-particularly in the large states, a citizen may be tried for a crime committed in the state, and yet tried in some states 500 miles from the place where it was committed . . .

[Ford 307–308]

Edmund Randolph, Letter on the Federal Constitution, October 10, 1787:

But I am sanguine in hoping, that in every other, justly obnoxious clause, Virginia, will be seconded by a majority of the states. I hope, that she will be seconded . . . 4. in taking from him [the President] the power of pardoning for *treason,* at least before conviction . . . [DHRC8 273]

Tench Coxe, *An Examination of the Constitution for the United States of America*, No. 4, October 21, 1787:

[1] The United States guarantee to every state in the union a separate republican form of government. From thence it follows that any man or body of men, however rich or powerful, who shall make an alteration in the form of government of any state, whereby the powers thereof shall be attempted to be taken out of the hands of the people at large, will stand guilty of high *treason;* or should a foreign power seduce or over-awe the people of any state, so as to cause them to vest in the families of any ambitious citizens or foreigners the powers of hereditary governors, whether as Kings or Nobles, that such investment of powers would be void in itself, and every person attempting to execute them would also be guilty of *treason.* [Ford 145–46]

[2] . . . The trial by jury is not excluded in these foederal courts. In all criminal cases, where the property, liberty or life of the citizen is at stake, he has the benefit of a jury. If convicted on impeachment, which is never done by a jury in any country, he cannot be fined, imprisoned or punished, but only may be disqualified from doing public mischief by losing his office, and his capacity to hold another. If the nature of his offence, besides its danger to his country, should be criminal in itself—should involve a charge of fraud, murder or *treason*—he may be tried for such crime, but cannot be convicted without a jury. . . . [Ford 146]

Dissent of the Pennsylvania Convention's Minority, December 18, 1787:

The president-general is dangerously connected with the senate; his coincidence with the views of the ruling junto in that body is made essential to his weight and importance in the government, which will destroy all independency and purity in the executive department, and having the power of pardoning without the concurrence of a council, he may screen from punishment the most *treasonable* attempts that may be made on the liberties of the people, when instigated by his coadjutors in the senate. . . . [DHRC2 635]

"Tamony," January 9, 1788:

The extent thus opened for speculative enquiry, joined to real magnitude in the object, may be styled by enthusiasm or horizon, the eyes of few mens understanding can steadily behold the expression, though poetically just, reduced to common sense, means importance, and instead of superseding the duty incumbent on freeholders to judge for themselves, renders the neglect of doing so, *treason* against their country. . . . [DHRC8 287]

James Madison, *The Federalist*, No. 43, January 23, 1788:

As *treason* may be committed against the United States, the authority of the United States ought to be enabled to punish it. But as new-fangled and artificial *treasons* have been the great engines by which violent factions, the natural offspring of free government, have usually wreaked their alternate malignity on each other, the convention have, with great judgment, opposed a barrier to this peculiar danger, by inserting a constitutional definition of the crime, fixing the proof necessary for conviction of it, and restraining the Congress, even in punishing it, from extending the consequences of guilt beyond the person of its author. [Fed. 310]

"Civis Rusticus," January 30, 1788:

. . . The president's having the unrestrained power of pardoning for *treasons* is another objection; and why? "it may be sometimes exercised to screen from punishment those whom he, (the president) had secretly instigated to commit the crime, and thereby prevent a discovery of his own guilt"—I appeal to this worthy gentleman himself [George Mason], I appeal to the public, whether there be in this objection, more of validity and force, or chimera and imagination. [DHRC8 337]

Luther Martin, "Genuine Information," No. 10, February 1, 1788:

[1] By the third section of this article it is declared that *treason* against the United States, shall consist in levying war against them, or in adhering to their enemies giving them aid or comfort. [DHRC16 10]

[2] By the principles of the American revolution, arbitrary power may and ought to be resisted even by arms if necessary—The time may come when it shall be the duty of a State, in order to preserve itself from the oppression of the general

government, to have recourse to the sword—In which case the proposed form of government declares that the State and every of its citizens who act under its authority are guilty of a direct act of *treason*—reducing by this provision the different States to this alternative that they must tamely and passively yield to despotism or their citizens must oppose it at the hazard of the halter if unsuccessful—and reducing the citizens of the State which shall take arms to a situation in which they must be exposed to punishment, let them act as they will, since if they obey the authority of their State government, they will be guilty of *treason* against the United States—if they join the general government they will be guilty of *treason* against their own State. [DHRC16 10–11]

[3] . . . I wished to have obtained as an amendment to the third section of this article the following clause: "Provided that no act or acts done by one or more of the States against the United States, or by any citizen of any one of the United States under the authority of one or more of the said States, shall be deemed *treason* or punished as such; but in case of war being levied by one or more of the States against the United States the conduct of each party towards the other, and their adherents respectively, shall be regulated by the laws of war and of nations." [DHRC16 11]

Tench Coxe, "A Freeman," No. 3, February 6, 1788:

So independent will the state governments remain, that their laws may, and in some instances will, be severer than those of the union. *Treason* against the United States, for instance, cannot be attended with confiscation and corruption of blood; but by the existing laws of all the states, the unoffending families of attainted persons, stripped of all hereditary rights, and condemned to the bitter portion of extreme poverty, are left without their friend and parent, to meet the trials of the world alone . . . [DHRC16 50]

Alexander White, "To the Citizens of Virginia," February 22, 1788:

[Quoting Polybius:] "The senate nominated commissioners to take cognizance of all the extraordinary crimes which were committed at Rome and in Italy, and demanded the attention of the public authority, such as *treason*, conspiracy, poisoning and murder, and to pass sentence upon them. The affairs and causes of private men, or cities which had any relation to the State, were also judged by the senate. . . . " [DHRC8 407]

"The Arraignment of Centinel," February 28, 1788:

[1] And also this same Centinel, as a false traitor, &c. did hold a *treasonable* correspondence with certain other well known traitors of the minority . . .
[DHRC16 260]

[2] And moreover, the aforesaid Centinel, as a false traitor, &c. in order to fulfil those his most horrid and diabolical *treasons,* and traiterous compassings, imaginations and purposes aforesaid, and to leave nothing undone, which envy, hatred, malice, ambition and a diabolical heart could suggest, did collogue with certain wheel-barrow men, convicts and criminals, now in the new gaol of the city and county of Philadelphia, making use of all his interest and influence with divers others, sneakups, time-serving, pickthanks, sycophants, and traitors, &c. of his gang, to get him the aforesaid Centinel, chosen president of their society; and actually succeeded therein, as fully appears by the *treasonable* and traitorous resolves of the aforesaid society printed and published in the Pennsylvania Gazette, of which he the said Centinel, &c. is now president . . . [DHRC16 260]

[3] How say you, —— Centinel, are you guilty of this high *treason* and other matters, whereof you stand indicted, or not guilty? [DHRC16 260]

William Ward [?], "Republicus," March 1, 1788:

. . . An extraordinary refinement this [the electoral college], on the plain simple business of election; and of which the grand convention have certainly the honour of being the first inventors; and that for an officer too, of so much importance as a president; invested with legislative and executive powers—who is to be commander in chief of the army, navy, militia, &c. grant reprieves and pardons, have a temporary negative on all bills and resolves, convene and adjourn both houses of congress, be supreme conservator of laws, commission all officers, make treaties, &c. &c. and who is to continue four years, and is only removable on conviction of *treason* or bribery and triable only by the senate, who are to be his own council whose interest in every instance runs paralel with his own . . . [DHRC8 448]

James Iredell, "Marcus," No. 3, March 5, 1788:

[1] . . . The probability of the President of the United States committing an act of *treason* against his country is very slight; he is so well guarded by the other powers of government, and the natural strength of the people at large must be so weighty, that in my opinion it is the most chimerical apprehension that can be entertained. . . . [DHRC16 322]

[2] . . . Now suppose, in the very midst of a war of extreme consequence to our safety or prosperity, the President could prevail upon a gentleman of abilities to go into the enemy's country, to serve in the useful, but dishonorable character of a spy: Such are certainly maintained by all vigilant governments, and in proportion to the ignominy of the character, and the danger sustained in the enemy's country, ought to be his protection and security in his own. This man renders very useful services; perhaps, by timely information prevents the destruction of his country. Nobody knows of these secret services but the President himself; his adherence however to the enemy is notorious: He is afterwards

intercepted in endeavouring to return to his own country, and having been perhaps a man of distinction before, he is proportionably obnoxious to his country at large for his supposed *treason*. Would it not be monstrous, that the President should not have it in his power to pardon this man? or that it should depend upon mere solicitation and favor, and perhaps, though the President should state the fact as it really was, some zealous partizan, with his jealousy constantly fixed upon the President, might insinuate that in fact the President and he were secret traitors together, and thus obtain a rejection of the President's application. It is a consideration also of some moment, that there is scarcely any accusation more apt to excite popular prejudice than the charge of *treason*. There is perhaps no country in the world where justice is in general more impartially administered than in England; yet let any man read some of the trials for *treason* in that country even since the Revolution, he will see sometimes a fury influencing the Judges, as well as the Jury, that is extremely disgraceful. . . . [DHRC16 323]

George Nicholas [?], "The State Soldier," No. 3, March 12, 1788:

In those governments whose heads are the free choice of the people, it is ever to be found on the side of the state, as the same voice which promotes will protect its favorite; and where the success of an author depends on the breath of those who have thus promoted the man at whose character he aims, it would be deemed madness to make the attempt, and nothing less than *treason* to aid him in it. [DHRC8 484]

James Iredell, "Marcus," No. 4, March 12, 1788:

[1] As to the constituting new crimes, and inflicting unusual and severe punishment, certainly the cases enumerated wherein the Congress are empowered either to define offences, or prescribe punishments, are such as are proper for the exercise of such authority in the general Legislature of the union. They only relate to "counterfeiting the securities and current coin of the United States; to piracies and felonies committed on the high seas, and offences against the law of nations, and to *treason* against the United States." These are offences immediately affecting the security, the honor or the interest of the United States at large, and of course must come within the sphere of the Legislative authority which is entrusted with their protection. . . . [DHRC16 381]

[2] . . . Let us also remember, that as those who are to make those laws must, themselves be subject to them, their own interest and feelings will dictate to them not to make them unnecessarily severe; and that in the case of *treason*, which usually in every country exposes men most to the avarice and rapacity of government, care is taken that the innocent family of the offender shall not suffer for the *treason* of their relation. This is the crime with respect to which a jealousy is of the most importance, and accordingly it is defined with great plainness and

accuracy, and the temptations to abusive prosecutions guarded against as much as possible. . . . [DHRC16 382]

Alexander Hamilton, *The Federalist*, No. 69, March 14, 1788:

[1] The President of the United States would be liable to be impeached, tried, and, upon conviction of *treason,* bribery, or other high crimes or misdemeanors, removed from office; and would afterwards be liable to prosecution and punishment in the ordinary course of law. . . . [Fed. 444–45]

[2] . . . The power of the President, in respect to pardons, would extend to all cases, except those of impeachment. The governor of New York may pardon in all cases, even in those of impeachment, except for *treason* and murder. Is not the power of the governor, in this article, on a calculation of political consequences, greater than that of the President? All conspiracies and plots against the government, which have not been matured into actual *treason,* may be screened from punishment of every kind, by the interposition of the prerogative of pardoning. If a governor of New York, therefore, should be at the head of any such conspiracy, until the design had been ripened into actual hostility he could insure his accomplices and adherents an entire impunity. A President of the Union, on the other hand, though he may even pardon *treason,* when prosecuted in the ordinary course of law, could shelter no offender, in any degree, from the effects of impeachment and conviction. Would not the prospect of a total indemnity for all the preliminary steps be a greater temptation to undertake and persevere in an enterprise against the public liberty, than the mere prospect of an exemption from death and confiscation, if the final execution of the design, upon an actual appeal to arms, should miscarry? . . . [Fed. 446–47]

[3] . . . The better to judge of this matter, it will be necessary to recollect, that, by the proposed Constitution, the offence of *treason* is limited "to levying war upon the United States, and adhering to their enemies, giving them aid and comfort"; and that by the laws of New York it is confined within similar bounds. [Fed. 447]

"Brutus," No. 15, March 20, 1788:

The only clause in the constitution which provides for the removal of the judges from offices, is that which declares, that "the president, vice-president, and all civil officers of the United States, shall be removed from office, on impeachment for, and conviction of *treason,* bribery, or other high crimes and misdemeanors." By this paragraph, civil officers, in which the judges are included, are removable only for crimes. *Treason* and bribery are named, and the rest are included under the general terms of high crimes and misdemeanors. . . . [DHRC16 433]

Archibald Maclaine, "Publicola," March 20, 1788:

. . . All criminal matters must be tried, and finally determined, in the state where the offence may be committed, even if it should be *treason* against the United States; and though the federal courts must be confined to some particular cases specified in the new constitution, yet the rules of their conduct will have a powerful influence upon the courts of the state. . . . [DHRC16 440]

Alexander Hamilton, *The Federalist*, No. 74, March 25, 1788:

The expediency of vesting the power of pardoning in the President has, if I mistake not, been only contested in relation to the crime of *treason*. This, it has been urged, ought to have depended upon the assent of one, or both, of the branches of the legislative body. I shall not deny that there are strong reasons to be assigned for requiring in this particular the concurrence of that body, or of a part of it. As *treason* is a crime levelled at the immediate being of the society, when the laws have once ascertained the guilt of the offender, there seems a fitness in referring the expediency of an act of mercy towards him to the judgment of the legislature. And this ought the rather to be the case, as the supposition of the connivance of the Chief Magistrate ought not to be entirely excluded. But there are also strong objections to such a plan. It is not to be doubted, that a single man of prudence and good sense is better fitted, in delicate conjunctures, to balance the motives which may plead for and against the remission of the punishment, than any numerous body whatever. It deserves particular attention, that *treason* will often be connected with seditions which embrace a large proportion of the community; as lately happened in Massachusetts. In every such case, we might expect to see the representation of the people tainted with thc same spirit which had given birth to the offence. . . .

[Fed. 474]

John Dickinson, "Fabius," No. 3, 1788:

But, what is that share? and, how to be managed? Momentous questions! Here, flattery is *treason;* and error, destruction. [Ford 175]

Georgia Constitution, May 6, 1789:

[Article I, Section 14:] No senator or representative shall be liable to be arrested during his attendance on the general assembly, or for a reasonable time in going thereto or returning home, except it be for *treason,* felony, or breach of the peace; nor shall any member be liable to answer for anything spoken in debate in either house, in any court or place elsewhere. [Thorpe 786]

[Article II, Section 7:] He [the governor] shall have power to grant reprieves for offences against the State, except in cases of impeachment, and to grant pardons, in all cases after conviction, except for *treason* or murder, in which cases he may respite the execution, and make a report thereof to the next general assembly, by whom a pardon may be granted. [Thorpe 788]

South Carolina Constitution, June 3, 1790:

[Article I, Section 14:] The members of both houses shall be protected in their persons and estates, during their attendance on, going to, and returning from, the legislature, and ten days previous to their sitting, and ten days after the adjournment of the legislature. But these privileges shall not be extended so as to protect any member who shall be charged with *treason,* felony, or breach of the peace. [Thorpe 3260]

Pennsylvania Constitution, September 2, 1790:

[Article I, Section 17:] The senators and representatives shall receive a compensation for their services, to be ascertained by law, and paid out of the treasury of the commonwealth. They shall, in all cases, except *treason,* felony, and breach or surety of the peace, be privileged from arrest during their attendance at the session of the respective houses, and in going to and returning from the same: And for any speech or debate in either house they shall not be questioned in any other place. [Thorpe 3094]

[Article III, Section 3:] Electors shall, in all cases except *treason,* felony, and breach or surety of the peace, be privileged from arrest during their attendance on elections, and in going to and returning from them. [Thorpe 3096]

[Article IX, Section 18:] That no person shall be attainted of *treason* or felony by the legislature. [Thorpe 3101]

TRIAL, TRIALS

[Note: This list is not inclusive of the words ''trial'' and ''trials;'' it focuses on passages dealing with ''trial by jury'' and ''speedy and public trial.'']

United States Constitution, September 17, 1787:

[Article I, Section 3:] Judgment in Cases of Impeachment shall not extend further than to removal from Office, and disqualification to hold and enjoy any Office of honor, Trust or Profit under the United States: but the Party convicted shall nevertheless be liable and subject to Indictment, *Trial,* Judgment and Punishment, according to Law.

[Article III, Section 2:] The *Trial* of all Crimes, except in Cases of Impeachment, shall be by *Jury;* and such *Trial* shall be held in the State where the said Crimes shall have been committed; but when not committed within any State, the *Trial* shall be at such Place or Places as the Congress may by Law have directed.

United States Constitution, Bill of Rights, December 15, 1787:

[Article VI:] In all criminal prosecutions, the accused shall enjoy the right to a *speedy and public trial, by an impartial jury* of the State and district wherein the crime shall have been committed, which district shall have been previously ascertained by law, and to be informed of the nature and cause of the accusation; to be confronted with the witnesses against him; to have compulsory process for obtaining witnesses in his favor, and to have the Assistance of Counsel for his defence.

[Article VII:] In Suits at common law, where the value in controversy shall exceed twenty dollars, the right of *trial by jury* shall be preserved, and no fact *tried by a jury,* shall be otherwise re-examined in any Court of the United States, than according to the rules of the common law.

* * * * *

Plantation Agreement at Providence, Rhode Island, August 27, 1640:

[Article 6:] It may be, a man may be to depart the land, or to a farr parte of the land; or his estate may lye uppon a *speedy tryall* or the like case may fall out. [Thorpe 3207]

Fundamental Constitutions of Carolina, March 1, 1669:

[Article 27:] No landgrave or cazique shall be *tried* for any criminal cause in any but the chief justice's court, and that by a *jury* of his peers. [Thorpe 2775]

[Article 111:] No cause, whether civil or criminal, of any freeman, shall be *tried* in any court of judicature, without a *jury* of his peers. [Thorpe 2785]

Fundamental Laws of East New Jersey, 1676:

[Chapter 23:] That in all *publick* courts of justice for *tryals* of causes, civil or criminal any person or persons, inhabitants of the said Province may freely come into, and attend the said courts, and hear and be present, at all or any such *tryals* as shall be there had or passed, that justice may not be done in a corner nor in any covert manner . . . [Thorpe 2551]

Fundamental Constitutions of West New Jersey, 1683:

[Article 19:] That no person or persons within the said Province shall be taken and imprisoned, or be devised of his freehold, free custom or liberty, or be outlawed or exiled, or any other way destroyed; nor shall they be condemn'd or judgment pass'd upon them, but by lawful judgment of their peers: neither shall justice nor right be bought or sold, defered or delayed, to any person whatsoever: in order to which by the laws of the land, all *tryals* shall be by twelve men, and as near as it may be, peers and equals, and of the neighborhood, and men without just exception. . . . but the manner of returning *juries* shall be thus, the names of all the freemen above five and twenty years of age, within the district or boroughs out of which the *jury* is to be returned, shall be written on equal peices of parchment and put into a box, and then the number of the *jury* shall be drawn out by a child under ten years of age. . . .
[Thorpe 2580–81]

English Bill of Rights, December 16, 1689:

And whereas of late years partial, corrupt, and unqualified persons have been returned and served on *juries in trials,* and particularly diverse jurors in *trials* for high treason, which were not freeholders. [SDECH 463]

Pennsylvania Frame of Government, November 7, 1696:

The form of the attest to be given to the Traverse *Jury,* by four at a time, shall be thus, viz.: You solemnly promise that you will well and truly *try* the issue of traverse between the lord the King, and A. B. whom you have in charge, according to your evidence. [Thorpe 3073]

First Continental Congress, Declaration and Resolves, October 14, 1774:

[1] The several [Parliamentary] Acts of 4 Geo. 3, ch. 15 & ch. 34, 5 Geo. 3, ch. 25, 6 Geo. 3, ch. 52, 7 Geo. 3, ch. 41 & 46, 8 Geo. 3, ch. 22, which impose duties for the purpose of raising a revenue in America, extend the powers of the admiralty courts beyond their ancient limits, deprive the American subject of *trial by jury,* authorize the judges' certificate to indemnify the prosecutor from damages that he might otherwise be liable to, requiring oppressive security from a claimant of ships and goods seized, before he shall be allowed to defend his property, and are subversive of American rights. [JCC1 71–72]

[2] Also the 12 Geo. 3, ch. 24, entituled "An act for the better preserving his Majesty's dockyards, magazines, ships, ammunition, and stores," which declares a new offense in America, and deprives the American subject of a constitutional *trial by jury* of the vicinage, by authorizing the *trial* of any person charged with the committing any offense described in the said act, out of the realm, to be indicted and *tried* for the same in any shire or county within the realm. [JCC1 72]

South Carolina Constitution, March 26, 1776:

. . . and whereas the said claim being persisted in, other unconstitutional and oppressive statutes have been since enacted by which the powers of admiralty courts in the colonies are extended beyond their ancient limits, and jurisdiction is given to such courts in cases similar to those which in Great Britain are *triable by jury;* persons are liable to be sent to and *tried* in Great Britain for an offence created and made capital by one of those statutes, though committed in the colonies . . . [Thorpe 3241]

Virginia Bill of Rights, June 12, 1776:

[Section 8:] That in all capital or criminal prosecutions a man hath a right to demand the cause and nature of his accusation, to be confronted with the accusers and witnesses, to call for evidence in his favor, and to a *speedy trial by an impartial jury* of twelve men of his vicinage without whose unanimous consent he cannot be found guilty; nor can he be compelled to give evidence against himself; that no man be deprived of his liberty, except by the law of the land or the judgment of his peers. [Thorpe 3813]

[Section 11:] That in controversies respecting property, and in suits between man and man, the ancient *trial by jury* is preferable to any other, and ought to be held sacred. [Thorpe 3814]

Virginia Constitution, June 29, 1776:

[Whereas the King has acted tyrannically by] . . . depriving us of the benefits of *trial by jury:* [Thorpe 3815]

New Jersey Constitution, July 2, 1776:

[Article 22:] That the common law of England, as well as so much of the statute law, as have been heretofore practised in this Colony, shall still remain in force, until they shall be altered by a future law of the Legislature; such parts only excepted, as are repugnant to the rights and privileges contained in this Charter; and that the inestimable right of *trial by jury* shall remain confirmed as a part of the law of this Colony, without repeal, forever. [Thorpe 2598]

[Article 23:] I, A. B. do solemnly declare, that, as a member of the Legislative Council, I will not assent to any law, vote or proceeding, which shall appear to me injurious to the public welfare of said Colony, nor that shall annul or repeal that part of the third section in the Charter of this Colony, which establishes, that the elections of members of the Legislative Council and Assembly shall be annual; nor that part of the twenty-second section in said Charter, respecting the *trial by jury,* nor that shall annul, repeal, or alter any part or parts of the eighteenth or nineteenth sections of the same. [Thorpe 2598]

United States Declaration of Independence, July 4, 1776:

For depriving us in many cases, of the benefits of *Trial by jury* . . .

Pennsylvania Constitution, September 28, 1776:

[Declaration of Rights, Article 9:] That in all prosecutions for criminal offences, a man hath a right to be heard by himself and his council, to demand the cause and nature of his accusation, to be confronted with the witnesses, to call for evidence in his favour, and a *speedy public trial, by an impartial jury* of the country, without the unanimous consent of which *jury* he cannot be found guilty; nor can he be compelled to give evidence against himself; nor can any man be justly deprived of his liberty except by the laws of the land, or the judgment of his peers. [Thorpe 3083]

[*Ibid.,* Article 11:] That in controversies respecting property, and in suits between man and man, the parties have a right to *trial by jury,* which ought to be held sacred. [Thorpe 3083]

[Frame of Government, Section 25:] *Trials* shall be by *jury* as heretofore: And it is recommended to the legislature of this state, to provide by law against every corruption or partiality in the choice, return, or appointment of *juries*.

[Thorpe 3088]

Maryland Constitution, November 11, 1776:

[Declaration of Rights, Article 3:] That the inhabitants of Maryland are entitled to the common law of England, and the *trial by jury,* according to the course of that law, and to the benefit of such of the English statutes, as existed at the time of their first emigration, and which, by experience, have been found applicable to their local and other circumstances, and of such others as have been since made in England, or Great Britain, and have been introduced, used and practised by the courts of law or equity . . . [Thorpe 1686–87]

[*Ibid.,* Article 19:] That, in all criminal prosecutions, every man hath a right to be informed of the accusation against him; to have a copy of the indictment or charge in due time (if required) to prepare for his defence; to be allowed counsel; to be confronted with the witnesses against him; to have process for his witnesses; to examine the witnesses, for and against him, on oath; and to a *speedy trial by an impartial jury,* without whose unanimous consent he ought not be found guilty. [Thorpe 1688]

North Carolina Constitution, December 18, 1776:

[Declaration of Rights, Article 14:] That in all controversies at law, respecting property, the ancient mode of *trial, by jury,* is one of the best securities of the rights of the people, and ought to remain sacred and inviolable. [Thorpe 2788]

Georgia Constitution, February 5, 1777:

[Article 45:] All causes, of what nature soever, shall be *tried* in the supreme court, except as hereafter mentioned; which court shall consist of the chief-justice, and three or more of the justices residing in the county. In case of the absence of the chief-justice, the senior justice on the bench shall act as chief-justice, with the clerk of the county, attorney for the State, sheriff, coroner, constable, and the *jurors;* and in case of the absence of any of the aforementioned officers, the justices to appoint others in their room pro tempore. And if any plaintiff or defendant in civil causes shall be dissatisfied with the determination of the *jury,* then, and in that case, they shall be at liberty, within three days, to enter an appeal from that verdict, and demand a new *trial by a special jury,* to be nominated as follows, viz: each party, plaintiff and defendant, shall choose six, six more names shall be taken indifferently out of a box provided for that purpose, the whole eighteen to be summoned, and their names to be put together into the box, and the first twelve that are drawn out, being present, shall be the special *jury to try* the cause, and from which there shall be no appeal. [Thorpe 783]

[Article 61:] Freedom of the press and *trial by jury* to remain inviolate forever. [Thorpe 785]

New York Constitution, April 20, 1777:

[Article 41:] And this convention doth further ordain, determine, and declare, in the name and by the authority of the good people of this State, that *trial by jury,* in all cases in which it hath heretofore been used in the colony of New York, shall be established and remain inviolate forever . . . [Thorpe 26373]

Vermont Constitution, July 8, 1777:

[Declaration of Rights, Article 10:] That, in all prosecutions for criminal offences, a man hath a right to be heard, by himself and his counsel—to demand the cause and nature of his accusation—to be confronted with the witnesses—to call for evidence in his favor, and a *speedy public trial, by an impartial jury* of the country; without the unanimous consent of which *jury,* he cannot be found guilty; nor can he be compelled to give evidence against himself; nor can any man be justly deprived of his liberty, except by the laws of the land or the judgment of his peers. [Thorpe 3741]

[*Ibid.,* Article 13:] That, in controversies respecting property, and in suits between man and man, the parties have a right to a *trial by jury;* which ought to be held sacred. [Thorpe 3741]

[Frame of Government, Section 22:] *Trials shall be by jury;* and it is recommended to the legislature of this State to provide by law, against every corruption or partiality in the choice, and return, or appointment, of *juries.*[Thorpe 3746]

Massachusetts Constitution, March 2, 1780:

[Declaration of Rights, Article 12:] And the legislature shall not make any law that shall subject any person to a capital or infamous punishment, excepting for the government of the army and navy, without *trial by jury.* [Thorpe 1891]

[*Ibid.,* Article 15:] In all controversies concerning property, and in all suits between two or more persons, except in cases in which it has heretofore been otherways used and practised, the parties have a right to a *trial by jury;* and this method of procedure shall be held sacred, unless, in causes arising on the high seas, and such as relate to mariners' wages the legislature shall hereafter find it necessary to alter it. [Thorpe 1891–92]

New Hampshire Constitution, June 2, 1784:

[Bill of Rights, Article 16:] No subject shall be liable to be *tried,* after an acquittal, for the same crime or offence.—Nor shall the legislature make any law that shall subject any person to a capital punishment, excepting for the government of the army and navy, and the militia in actual service, without *trial by jury.*

[Thorpe 2455]

[*Ibid.,* Article 20:] In all controversies concerning property, and in all suits between two or more persons, except in cases in which it has been heretofore otherwise used and practiced, the parties have a right to a *trial by jury;* and this method of procedure shall be held sacred, unless in causes arising on the high seas, and such as relate to mariners wages, the legislature shall think it necessary hereafter to alter it. [Thorpe 2456]

[*Ibid.,* Article 21:] In order to reap the fullest advantage of the inestimable privilege of the *trial by jury,* great care ought to be taken that none but qualified persons should be appointed to serve; and such ought to be fully compensated for their travel, time and attendance. [Thorpe 2456]

Vermont Constitution, July 4, 1786:

[Declaration of Rights, Article 11:] That in all prosecutions for criminal offences, a man hath a right to be heard by himself and his counsel—to demand the cause and nature of his accusation—to be confronted with the witnesses—to call for evidence in his favour, and a *speedy public trial by an impartial jury* of the country, without the unanimous consent of which *jury* he cannot be found guilty—nor can he be compelled to give evidence against himself—nor can any man be justly deprived of his liberty, except by the laws of the land, or the judgment of his peers. [Thorpe 3753]

[*Ibid.,* Article 14:] That when an issue in fact, proper for the cognizance of a *jury,* is joined in a court of law, the parties have a right to a *trial by jury;* which ought to be held sacred. [Thorpe 3753]

[Frame of Government, Article 28:] *Trials* of issues, proper for the cognizance of a *jury,* in the Supreme and County Courts, shall be by *jury,* except where parties otherwise agree: and great care ought to be taken to prevent corruption or partiality in the choice and return, or appointment of *juries.* [Thorpe 3759]

United States Confederation Congress, The Northwest Ordinance, July 13, 1787:

[Article 2:] The inhabitants of the said territory shall always be entitled to the benefits of the writs of habeas corpus, and of the *trial by jury;* of a proportionate representation of the people in the legislature, and of judicial proceedings according to the course of the common law. . . . [Thorpe 960–61]

William Pierce to St. George Tucker, September 28, 1787, published in *Gazette of the State of Georgia*, March 20, 1788:

[1] A defect is found by some people in this new Constitution, because it has not provided, except in criminal cases, for *Trial by Jury*. I ask if the *trial by jury* in civil cases is really and substantially of any security to the liberties of a people. In my idea the opinion of its utility is founded more in prejudice than in reason. I cannot but think that an able Judge is better qualified to decide between man and man than any twelve men possibly can be. The *trial by jury* appears to me to have been introduced originally to soften some of the rigors of the feodal system . . . [DHRC16 444]

[2] As to *trial by jury* in criminal cases, it is right, it is just, perhaps it is indispensable,—the life of a citizen ought not to depend on the fiat of a single person. Prejudice, resentment, and partiality, are among the weaknesses of human nature, and are apt to pervert the judgment of the greatest and best of men. The solemnity of the *trial by jury* is suited to the nature of criminal cases, because, before a man is brought to answer the indictment, the fact or truth of every accusation is inquired into by the Grand *Jury*, composed of his fellow citizens, and the same truth or fact afterwards (should the Grand *Jury* find the accusation well founded) is to be confirmed by the unanimous suffrage of twelve good men, "superior to all suspicion." I do not think there can be a greater guard to the liberties of a people than such a mode of *trial* on the affairs of life and death. But here let it rest. [DHRC16 445]

James Wilson, Speech on the Federal Constitution, October 6, 1787:

Another objection that has been fabricated against the new constitution, is expressed in this disingenuous form—"the *trial by jury* is abolished in civil cases." I must be excused, my fellow citizens, if, upon this point, I take advantage of my professional experience, to detect the futility of the assertion. Let it be remembered, then, that the business of the foederal constitution was not local, but general—not limited to the views and establishments of a single state, but co-extensive with the continent, and comprehending the views and establishments of thirteen independent sovereignties. When, therefore, this subject was in discussion, we were involved in difficulties, which pressed on all sides, and no precedent could be discovered to direct our course. The cases open to a *jury*, differed in the different states; it was therefore impracticable, on that ground, to have made a general rule. The want of uniformity would have rendered any reference to the practice of the states idle and useless: and it could not, with any propriety, be said, that "the *trial by jury* shall be as heretofore:" since there has never existed any foederal system of jurisprudence, to which the declaration could relate. Besides, it is not in all cases that the *trial by jury* is adopted in civil questions: for causes depending in courts of admiralty, such as relate to maritime captures, and such as are agitated in the courts of equity, do not require the intervention of that tribunal. How, then, was the line of discrimination to be drawn? The convention found the task too difficult for them: and they left the business as it stands—in the fullest confidence, that no danger could possibly ensue, since the proceedings of the supreme court are to be regulated by the congress, which is a faithful representation of the people: and the oppression of government is effectually barred, by declaring that in all criminal cases, the *trial by jury* shall be preserved. [Ford 157]

George Mason, Objections to the Constitution, October 7, 1787:

There is no Declaration of any kind for preserving the Liberty of the Press, the *Tryal by jury* in civil Causes; nor against the Danger of standing Armys in time of Peace. [DHRC8 45]

Richard Henry Lee [?], "The Federal Farmer," No. 2, October 9, 1787:

[1] The essential parts of a free and good government are a full and equal representation of the people in the legislature, and the *jury trial* of the vicinage in the administration of justice . . . [Ford 288]

[2] Under one general government alone, there could be but one judiciary, one supreme and a proper number of inferior courts. I think it would be totally impracticable in this case to preserve a due administration of justice, and the real benefits of the *jury trial* of the vicinage . . . [Ford 289]

[3] . . . However, it is now said that the states differ so essentially in these respects, and even in the important article of the *trial by jury,* that when assembled in convention, they can agree to no words by which to establish that *trial,* or by which to ascertain and establish many other of these rights, as fundamental articles in the social compact. . . . [Ford 291]

Richard Henry Lee [?], "The Federal Farmer," No. 3, October 10, 1787:

[1] . . . therefore, if the new constitution be adopted without any amendment in this respect, all those numerous actions, now brought in the state courts between our citizens and foreigners, between citizens of different states, by state governments against foreigners, and by state governments against citizens of other states, may also be brought in the federal courts; and an appeal will lay in them from the state courts or federal inferior courts to the supreme judicial court of the union. In almost all these cases, either party may have the *trial by jury* in the state courts; except paper money and tender laws, which are wisely guarded against in the proposed constitution; justice may be obtained in these courts on reasonable terms; they must be more competent to proper decisions on the laws of their respective states, than the federal states can possibly be. . . .
[Ford 307]

[2] . . . The *trial by jury* is secured only in those few criminal cases, to which the federal laws will extend—as crimes committed on the seas, against the laws of nations, treason and counterfeiting the federal securities and coin: But even in these cases, the *jury trial* of the vicinage is not secured—particularly in the large states, a citizen may be *tried* for a crime committed in the state, and yet *tried* in some states 500 miles from the place where it was committed; but the *jury trial* is not secured at all in civil causes. Though the convention have not established this *trial,* it is to be hoped that congress, in putting the new system into execution, will do it by a legislative act, in all cases in which it can be done with propriety. Whether the *jury trial* is not excluded the supreme judicial court is an important question. By Art. 3, Sect. 2, all cases affecting ambassadors, other public ministers, and consuls,and in those cases in which a state shall be party, the supreme court shall have jurisdiction. In all the other cases before mentioned, the supreme court shall have appellate jurisdiction, both as to law and fact, with such exception, and under such regulations as the congress shall make. By court is understood a court consisting of judges; and the idea of a *jury* is excluded. This court, or the judges, are to have jurisdiction on appeals, in all the cases enumerated, as to law and fact; the judges are to decide the law and *try* the fact, and the *trial* of the fact being assigned to the judges by the constitution, a *jury for trying* the fact is excluded; however, under the exceptions and powers to make regulations, congress may, perhaps, introduce the *jury,* to *try* the fact in most necessary cases. [Ford 307–308]

[3] . . . and, therefore, the powers to determine on the law, in equity, and as to the fact, all will concentrate in the supreme court:—These powers, which by this constitution are blended in the same hands, the same judges, are in Great-Britain deposited in different hands—to wit, the decision of the law in the law judges, the decision in equity in the chancellor, and the *trial* of the fact in the *jury*. It is a very dangerous thing to vest in the same judge power to decide on the law, and also general powers in equity . . . [Ford 308]

Richard Henry Lee [?], "The Federal Farmer," No. 4, October 12, 1787:

[1] It will not be possible to establish in the federal courts the *jury trial* of the vicinage so well as in the state courts. [Ford 310]

[2] . . . If the federal constitution is to be construed so far in connection with the state constitution, as to leave the *trial by jury* in civil causes, for instance, secured; on the same principles it would have left the *trial by jury* in criminal causes, the benefits of the writ of habeas corpus, &c. secured; they all stand on the same footing; they are the common rights of Americans, and have been recognized by the state constitutions: But the convention found it necessary to recognize or re-establish the benefits of that writ, and the *jury trial* in criminal cases. . . . [Ford 314]

[3] . . . There are other essential rights, which we have justly understood to be the rights of freemen; as freedom from hasty and unreasonable search warrants, warrants not founded on oath, and not issued with due caution, for searching and seizing men's papers, property, and persons. The *trials by jury* in civil causes, it is said, varies so much in the several states, that no words could be found for the uniform establishment of it. If so, the federal legislation will not be able to establish it by any general laws. I confess I am of opinion it may be established, but not in that beneficial manner in which we may enjoy it, for the reasons before mentioned. When I speak of the *jury trial* of the vicinage, or the *trial* of the fact in the neighborhood, I do not lay so much stress upon the circumstance of our being *tried* by our neighbors: in this enlightened country men may be probably impartially *tried* by those who do not live very near them: but the *trial* of facts in the neighborhood is of great importance in other respects. . . . [Ford 315]

[4] The *trial by jury* is very important in another point of view. It is essential in every free country, that common people should have a part and share of influence, in the judicial as well as in the legislative department. To hold open to them the offices of senators, judges, and offices to fill which an expensive education is required, cannot answer any valuable purposes for them; they are not in a situation to be brought forward and to fill those offices; these, and most other offices of any considerable importance, will be occupied by the few. The few, the well born, &c. as Mr. [John] Adams calls them, in judicial decisions as well as in legislation, are generally disposed, and very naturally too, to favour those of their own description. [Ford 315–16]

[5] The *trial by jury* in the judicial department, and the collection of the people by their representatives in the legislature, are those fortunate inventions which have procured for them, in this country, their true proportion of influence, and the wisest and most fit means of protecting themselves in the community. Their situation, as *jurors* and representatives, enables them to acquire information end knowledge in the affairs and government of the society; and to come forward, in turn, as the centinels and guardians of each other. I am very sorry that even a few of our countrymen should consider *jurors* and representatives in a different point of view, as ignorant, troublesome bodies, which ought not to have any share in the concerns of government. [Ford 316]

Richard Henry Lee, Proposed Amendments to the Constitution, October 16, 1787:

[1] . . . That the rights of conscience in matters of religion ought not to be violated—That the freedom of the press shall be secured—That the *trial by jury* in criminal and civil cases, and the modes prescribed by the common law for the safety of life in criminal prosecutions, shall be held sacred . . .

[DHRC8 65]

[2] . . . That such parts of the new constitution be amended as provide imperfectly for the *trial* of criminals by a *jury* of the vicinage, and to supply the omission of a *jury trial* in civil causes or disputes about property between individuals, whereby the common law is directed, and as generally it is secured by the several state constitutions. That such parts of the new constitution be amended, as permit the vexatious and oppressive callings of citizens from their own country, and all controversies between citizens of different states and between citizens and foreigners, to be *tried* in a far distant court, and as it may be without a *jury,* whereby in a multitude of cases, the circumstances of distance and expence may compel numbers to submit to the most unjust and ill-founded demand . . .

[DHRC8 66]

Noah Webster, *An Examination of the Leading Principles of the Federal Constitution*, October 17, 1787:

[1] Some persons have ventured to publish an intimation, that by the proposed constitution, the *trial by jury* is abolished in all civil cases. Others very modestly insinuate, that it is in some cases only. The fact is, that *trial by jury* is not affected in any case, by the constitution; except in cases of impeachment, which are to be *tried* by the senate. None but persons in office in or under Congress can be impeached; and even after a judgment upon an impeachment, the offender is liable to a prosecution, before a common *jury,* in a regular course of law. The insinuation therefore that *trials by jury* are to be abolished, is groundless, and beyond conception, wicked. . . . [Ford 52]

[2] With respect to other civil and criminal actions,the powers and jurisdiction of the several judiciaries of each state, remain unimpaired. Nor is there anything novel in allowing appeals to the supreme court. Actions are mostly to be *tried* in the state where the crimes are committed—But appeals are allowed under our present confederation, and no person complains; nay, were there no appeal, every man would have reason to complain, especially when a final judgement, in an inferior court, should affect property to a large amount. But why is an objection raised against an appellate jurisdiction in the supreme court, respecting fact as well as law? Is it less safe to have the opinions of two *juries* than of one? I suspect many people will think this is no defect in the constitution. But perhaps it will destroy a material requisite of a good *jury,* viz. their vicinity to the cause of action. I have no doubt, that when causes were *tried,* in periods prior to the Christian aera, before twelve men, seated upon twelve stones, arranged in a circular form, under a huge oak, there was great propriety in submitting causes to men in the vicinity. The difficulty of collecting evidence, in those rude times, rendered it necessary that *juries* should judge mostly from their own knowledge of facts or from information obtained out of court. But in these polished ages, when *juries* depend almost wholly on the testimony of witnesses; and when a complication of interests, introduced by commerce and other causes, renders it almost impossible to collect men, in the vicinity of the parties, who

are wholly disinterested, it is no disadvantage to have a cause *tried by a jury* of strangers. Indeed the latter is generally the most eligible. [Ford 53]

[3] The liberty of the press, *trial by jury,* the Habeas Corpus writ, even Magna Charta itself, although justly deemed the palladia of freedom, are all inferior considerations, when compared with a general distribution of real property among every class of people. The power of entailing estates is more dangerous to liberty and republican government, than all the constitutions that can be written on paper, or even than a standing army. Let the people have property, and they will have power—a power that will for ever be exerted to prevent a restriction of the press, and abolition of *trial by jury,* or the abridgement of any other privilege. . . . [Ford 59–60]

[4] The English writers on law and government consider Magna Charta, *trial by juries,* the Habeas Corpus act, and the liberty of the press, as the bulwarks of freedom. All this is well. But in no government of consequence in Europe, is freedom established on its true and immoveable foundation. The property is too much accumulated, and the accumulations too well guarded, to admit the true principle of republics. But few centuries have elapsed, since the body of the people were vassals. To such men, the smallest extension of popular privileges, was deemed an invaluable blessing. Hence the encomiums upon *trial by juries,* and the articles just mentioned. But these people have never been able to mount to the source of liberty, estates in fee, or at least but partially; they are yet obliged to drink at the streams. Hence the English jealousy of certain rights, which are guaranteed by acts of parliament. But in America, and here alone, we have gone at once to the fountain of liberty, and raised the people to their true dignity. Let the lands be possessed by the people in fee-simple, let the fountain be kept pure, and the streams will be pure of course. Our jealousy of *trial by jury,* the liberty of the press, &c., is totally groundless. Such rights are inseparably connected with the power and dignity of the people, which rest on their property. . . . [Ford 60–61n]

"Cato Uticensis," October 17, 1787:

[1] In any dispute between you and the revenue officers and excisemen of Congress, it is true, that it is provided, the *trial* shall be, in the first instance, within the state, though before a Foederal tribunal: It is said in par. 3. sect. 2. art. 3, "The *trial* of all crimes except in cases of impeachments shall be by *jury;* and such *trial* shall be held in the state where the crimes shall be committed;" but what does this avail, when an appeal will lie against you to the Supreme Foederal Court—In the paragraph preceding the one just now quoted, it is said, "In all cases affecting ambassadors, other public ministers and consuls, and those in which a state shall be a party, the Supreme Court shall have original jurisdiction. In all the other cases before mentioned, the Supreme Court shall have appellate jurisdiction, both as to law and fact, with such exceptions and under such regulations as the Congress shall make." But, where is this Supreme

Court to sit? Will it not be, where Congress shall fix its residence? Thither then you will be carried for *trial*. Who are to be your *jury?* Is there any provision made, that you shall have a Venire from your county, or even from your state, as they please to call it? No! you are to be *tried* within the territory of Congress, and Congress itself is to be a party; you are to be deprived of the benefit of a *jury* from your vicinage, that boast and birthright of a freeman. [DHRC8 74]

[2] . . . Consider that if you pass the Foederal Constitution in toto, you subject yourselves to see the doors of your houses, the impenetrable castles of freemen, fly open before the magic wand of an exciseman, and, that, if you should resent and punish the insolence of office, the daring brutality of the publican, perhaps offered to the wife of thy bosom, you will be dragged for *trial* before a distant tribunal, and there, perhaps, condemned without enjoying the benefit of a *jury* from your vicinage, your unalienable birthright as a freeman. [DHRC8 75]

Tench Coxe, *An Examination of the Constitution for the United States of America*, No. 4, October 21, 1787:

Both the old and new foederal constitutions, and indeed the constitution of Pennsylvania, admit of courts in which no use is made of a *jury*. The board of property, the court of admiralty, and the high court of errors and appeals, in the state of Pennsylvania, as also the court of appeals under the old confederation, exclude *juries*. *Trial by jury* will therefore be in the express words of the Pennsylvania constitution, "as heretofore,"—almost always used, though sometimes omitted. *Trials* for lands lying in any state between persons residing in such state, for bonds, notes, book debts, contracts, trespasses, assumptions, and all other matters between two or more citizens of any state, will be held in the state courts by *juries,* as now. In these cases the foederal courts cannot interfere. But when a dispute arises between the citizens of any state about lands lying out of the bounds thereof, or when a *trial* is to be had between the citizens of any state and those of another, or the government of another, the private citizen will not be obliged to go into a court constituted by the state, with which, or with the citizens of which, his dispute is. He can appeal to a disinterested foederal court. This is surely a great advantage, and promises a fair *trial,* and an impartial judgment. The *trial by jury* is not excluded in these foederal courts. In all criminal cases, where the property, liberty or life of the citizen is at stake, he has the benefit of a *jury*. If convicted on impeachment, which is never done by a *jury* in any country, he cannot be fined, imprisoned or punished, but only may be disqualified from doing public mischief by losing his office, and his capacity to hold another. If the nature of his offence, besides its danger to his country, should be criminal in itself— should involve a charge of fraud, murder or treason—he may be *tried* for such crime, but cannot be convicted without a *jury*. In *trials* about property in the foederal courts, which can only be as above stated, there is nothing in the new constitution to prevent a *trial by jury*. No doubt it will be the mode in every case, wherein it is practicable. This will be adjusted by law, and it could not be done otherwise. In short, the sphere of jurisdiction for the foederal courts is limited, and that sphere only is subject to the regulations of our foederal government. The known principles of justice, the attachment to *trial by jury* whenever it can be used, the instructions of the state legislatures, the instructions of the people at large, the operation of the foederal regulations on the property of a president, a senator, a representative, a judge, as well as on that of a private citizen, will certainly render those regulations as favorable as possible to property; for life and liberty are put more than ever into the hands of the *juries*. Under the present constitution of all the states, a public officer may be condemned to imprisonment or death on impeachment, without a *jury;* but the new foederal constitution protects the accused, till he shall be convicted, from the hands of power, by rendering a *jury* the indispensible judges of all crimes. [Ford 148–50]

Virginia Independent Chronicle, October 31, 1787:

The futility of this assertion [by James Wilson], that, "the *trial by jury* is abolished in civil cases," is detected by him, "taking the advantage of his professional experience," and from this we learn, that it is not yet abolished, but that it may, if Congress think fit; but he undoubtedly knows, that *juries* are found inconvenient in excise business. . . . [DHRC8 138]

Hugh Williamson, Speech at Edenton, N.C., November 8, 1787:

. . . We are told that there should have been a section for securing tha *Trial by Jury* in Civil cases, and the Liberty of the Press: that there should also have been a Declaration of Rights. In the new system it is provided, that "Thc *Trial* of all crimes, except in cases of Impeachment," shall be by *Jury,* but this provision could not possibly be extended to all Civil cases. For it is well known that the *Trial by Jury* is not general and uniform throughout the United States, either in cases of Admiralty or of Chancery; hence it became necessary to submit the question to the General Legislature, who might accommodate their laws on this occasion to the desires and habits of the nation. Surely there is no prohibition in a case that is untouched. [DHRC16 202]

Letter from New York, _Virginia Independent Chronicle,_ November 14, 1787:

[1] . . . I have not only no objection to, but am extremely desirous of, a strong and general government, provided the fundamental principles of liberty be well secured. These I take to be, *trial by jury* as has been and is practised—the check of impeachment—the distinct organization and operation of the three great powers of government, the legislative, judicial, and executive. In all these great points the proposed constitution requires amendment, before it can be adopted even with safety. [DHRC8 156–57]

[2] In the constitution of the foederal court, where its jurisdiction is original, the securing *jury trial* in criminal, is, according to all legal reasoning, an exclusion of it in civil matters—and in its appellant function it is expressly said the court shall judge both of law and fact. This of course renders the finding of a *jury* below, totally nugatory. [DHRC8 157]

Virginia Independent Chronicle, November 28, 1787:

The judicial powers of the Foederal Courts have, also, been grossly misrepresented. It is said "that the *trial by jury* is to be abolished, and that the courts of the several states are to be annihilated." But these, Sir, are mistaken notions, scandalous perversions of truth. The courts of judicature in each state will still continue in their present situation. The *trial by jury* in all disputes between man and man in each state will still remain inviolate, and in all cases of this description, there can be no appeal to the Foederal Courts. It is only in particular specified cases, of which each state cannot properly take cognizance, that the judicial authority of the Foederal Courts can be exercised. Even in the congressional courts of judicature, the *trial* of all crimes except in cases of impeachment, shall be by *jury*. How then can any man say that the *trial by jury* will be abolished, and that the courts of the several states will be annihilated by the adoption of the Foederal Government? . . . [DHRC8 179]

Dissent of the Pennsylvania Convention's Minority, December 18, 1787:

[1] That in controversies respecting property, and in suits between man and man, *trial by jury* shall remain as heretofore, as well in the federal courts as in those of the several States. [DHRC2 623]

[2] That in all capital and criminal prosecutions, a man has a right to demand the cause and nature of his accusation, as well in the federal courts as in those of the several States; to be heard by himself and his counsel; to be confronted with the accusers and witnesses; to call for evidence in his favor, and a *speedy trial by an impartial jury* of his vicinage, without whose unanimous consent he cannot be found guilty, nor can he be compelled to give evidence against himself; and that no man be deprived of his liberty, except by the law of the land or the judgment of his peers. [DHRC2 623]

[3] The powers of a court of equity, vested by this constitution in the tribunals of Congress; powers which do not exist in Pennsylvania, unless so far as they can be incorporated with *jury trial*—would, in this State, greatly contribute to this event. The rich and wealthy suitors would eagerly lay hold of the infinite mazes, perplexities and delays, which a court of chancery, with the appellate powers of the Supreme Court in fact as well as law would furnish him with, and thus the poor man being plunged in the bottomless pit of legal discussion would drop his demand in despair. [DHRC2 630]

[4] The first consideration that this review suggests is the omission of a BILL OF RIGHTS ascertaining and fundamentally establishing those unalienable and personal rights of men, without the full, free and secure enjoyment of which there can be no liberty, and over which it is not necessary for a good government to have the control, the principal of which are the rights of conscience, personal liberty by the clear and unequivocal establishment of the writ of habeas corpus, *jury trial* in criminal and civil cases, by an impartial *jury* of the vicinage or county; with the common law proceedings, for the safety of the accused in criminal prosecutions . . . [DHRC2 630–31]

[5] . . . 1st. That the *trial by jury,* which is the grand characteristic of the common law, is secured by the constitution only in criminal cases. 2nd. That the appeal from both law and fact is expressly established, which is utterly inconsistent with the principles of the common law and *trials by jury*. The only mode in which an appeal from law and fact can be established is by adopting the principles and practice of the civil law, unless the United States should be drawn into the absurdity of calling and swearing *juries,* merely for the purpose of contradicting their verdicts, which would render *juries* contemptible and worse than useless. 3rd. That the courts to be established would decide on all cases of law and equity, which is a well-known characteristic of the civil law, and these courts would have cognizance not only of the laws of the United States and of treaties, and of cases affecting ambassadors, but of all cases of admiralty and maritime jurisdiction, which last are matters belonging exclusively to the civil law, in every nation in Christendom. [DHRC2 632–33]

[6] Not to enlarge upon the loss of the invaluable right of *trial by an unbiased jury,* so dear to every friend of liberty, the monstrous expense and inconveniences of the mode of proceeding to be adopted, are such as will prove intolerable to the people of this country. The lengthy proceedings of the civil law courts in the chancery of England, and in the courts of Scotland and France, are such that few men of moderate fortune can endure the expense of . . . [DHRC2 633]

[7] . . . Yet the costs in the courts of king's bench and common pleas in England, are infinitely greater than those which the people of this country have ever experienced. We abhor the idea of losing the transcendent privilege of *trial by jury,* with the loss of which, it is remarked by the same learned author [Blackstone], that in Sweden, the liberties of the commons were extinguished by an aristocratic senate; and that *trial by jury* and the liberty of the people went out together. At the same time we regret the intolerable delay, the enormous expense, and infinite vexation, to which the people of this country will be exposed from the voluminous proceedings of the courts of civil law, and especially from the appellate jurisdiction, by means of which a man may be drawn from the utmost boundaries of this extensive country to the seat of the supreme court of the nation to contend, perhaps, with a wealthy and powerful adversary. The consequence of this establishment will be an absolute confirmation of the power of aristo-

cratical influence in the courts of justice; for the common people will not be able to contend or struggle against it. [DHRC2 633–34]

[8] *Trial by jury* in criminal cases may also be excluded by declaring that the libeler, for instance shall be liable to an action of debt for a specified sum, thus evading the common law prosecution by indictment and *trial by jury*. And the common course of proceeding against a ship for breach of revenue laws by information (which will be classed among civil causes) will at the civil law be within the resort of a court, where no *jury* intervenes. Besides, the benefit of *jury trial,* in cases of a criminal nature, which cannot be evaded, will be rendered of little value, by calling the accused to answer far from home; there being no provision that the *trial be by a jury* of the neighborhood or country. . . . [DHRC2 634]

Alexander Hamilton, *The Federalist*, No. 29, January 9, 1788:

. . . It would be as absurd to doubt that a right to pass all laws necessary and proper to execute its declared powers would include that of requiring the assistance of the citizens to the officers, who may be intrusted with the execution of those laws, as it would be to believe that a right to enact laws necessary and proper for the imposition and collection of taxes would involve that of varying the rules of descent and of the alienation of landed property, or of abolishing the *trial by jury* in cases relating to it. . . . [Fed. 227–28]

James Madison, *The Federalist*, No. 40, January 18, 1788:

. . . In some instances, as has been shown, the powers of the new government will act on the States in their collective characters. In some instances, also, those of the existing government act immediately on individuals. In cases of capture; of piracy; of the post office; of coins, weights, and measures; of trade with the Indians; of claims under grants of land by different States; and, above all, in the case of *trials* by courts-martial in the army and navy, by which death may be inflicted without the intervention of a *jury,* or even of a civil magistrate;—in all these cases the powers of the Confederation operate immediately on the persons and interests of individual citizens. . . . [Fed. 289]

Alexander White [?], "An Independent Freeholder," January 18, 1788:

. . . jurisdiction of the federal courts will not extend to disputes relating to property, real or personal, to contracts or personal injuries between citizens, which in general are the subjects of litigation; the apprehension of oppression from those courts must appear groundless. *Trial by jury* in all criminal cases is expressly secured, and that the *trial* shall be in the state where the crime is committed. Can you expect that the number of courts and the times and places of holding them through all future ages should be ascertained? What would you have done in such an instrument of government with regard to civil causes? Would you say the *trial by jury* shall be in all cases? Is the court of chancery an institution to be abolished? Are you displeased with the mode of proceeding against sheriffs by motion, and in various other cases in which the legislature of this state has found it necessary to dispense with the *trial by jury?* And may not cases equally necessary happen under the continental government?

[DHRC8 313]

James Madison, *The Federalist*, No. 41, January 19, 1788:

. . . A power to destroy the freedom of the press, the *trial by jury;* or even to regulate the course of descents, or the forms of conveyances, must be very singularly expressed by the terms "to raise money for the general welfare."

[Fed. 301]

Alexander C. Hanson, *Remarks on the Proposed Plan of a Federal Government*, c. January 31, 1788:

The institution of the *trial by jury* has been sanctified by the experience of ages. It has been recognised by the constitution of every state in the union. It is deemed the birthright of Americans; and it is imagined, that liberty cannot subsist without it. The proposed plan expressly adopts it, for the decision of all criminal accusations, except impeachment; and is silent with respect to the determination of facts in civil causes. [Ford 240–41]

James Madison, *The Federalist*, No. 48, February 1, 1788:

The constitutional *trial by jury* had been violated, and powers assumed which had not been delegated by the constitution. [Fed. 346]

Luther Martin, "Genuine Information," No. 10, February 1, 1788:

[1] And in all those cases where the general government has jurisdiction in civil questions, the proposed constitution not only makes no provision for the *trial by jury* in the first instance, but by its appellate jurisdiction absolutely takes away that inestimable priviledge, since it expressly declares the supreme court shall have appellate jurisdiction both as to law and fact.—Should, therefore, a *jury* be adopted in the inferior court, it would only be a needless expence, since on an appeal the determination of that *jury* even on questions of fact, however honest and upright, is to be of no possible effect—the supreme court is to take up all questions of fact—to examine the evidence relative thereto—to decide upon them in the same manner as if they had never been *tried by a jury*—Nor is *trial by jury* secured in criminal cases; it is true, that in the first instance, in the inferior court the *trial is to be by jury,* in this and in this only, is the difference

between criminal and civil cases; but, Sir, the appellate jurisdiction extends, as I have observed, to cases criminal as well as to civil, and on the appeal the court is to decide not only on the law but on the fact, if, therefore, even in criminal cases the general government is not satisfied with the verdict of the *jury*, its officer may remove the prosecution to the supreme court, and there the verdict of the *jury* is to be of no effect, but the judges of this court are to decide upon the fact as well as the law, the same as in civil cases. [DHRC16 9]

[2] Thus, Sir, *jury trials*, which have ever been the boast of the English constitution, which have been by our several State constitutions so cautiously secured to us,—*jury trials* which have so long been considered the surest barrier against arbitrary power, and the palladium of liberty,—with the loss of which the loss of our freedom may be dated, are taken away by the proposed form of government . . . [DHRC16 9]

[3] . . . Nor was this the effect of inattention, nor did it arise from any real difficulty in establishing and securing *jury trials* by the proposed constitution, if the convention had wished so to do—But the same reason influenced here as in the case of the establishment of inferior courts;—as they could not trust State judges, so would they not confide in State *juries*. . . . [DHRC16 10]

"An Old Whig," No. 8, February 6, 1788:

[1] . . . For instance; the appellate jurisdiction both as to law and fact, which is given to the supreme court of the continent, and which annihilates the *trial by jury* in all civil causes, the Congress can only modify:—They cannot extinguish this power, so destructive to the principles of real liberty. It would not by any means be extravagant to say, that a new continental convention ought to be called, if it were only for the sake of preserving that sacred palladium—THE INESTIMABLE RIGHT OF TRIAL BY JURY. . . . [DHRC16 53]

[2] . . . Again; how could the stripping people of the right of *trial by jury* conduce to the strength of the state? Do we find the government in England at all weakened by the people retaining the right of *trial by jury?* Far from it. Yet these things which merely tend to oppress the people, without conducing at all to the strength of the state, are the last which aristocratic rulers would consent to restore to the people; because they encrease the personal power and importance of the rulers. Judges, unincumbered by *juries*, have been ever found much better friends to government than to the people. . . . [DHRC16 55]

Alexander White, "To the Citizens of Virginia," February 22, 1788:

The freedom of speech and of the press, are likewise out of the jurisdiction of Congress.—But, if by an abuse of that freedom I attempt to excite sedition in the Commonwealth, I may be punished—should I be unjustly accused of such an offence, the *trial by a jury* of my countrymen is my security . . . [DHRC8 404–405]

"The Impartial Examiner," No. 1, February 27, 1788:

[1] . . . If this branch of revenue takes place, all the consequent rigour of excise laws will necessarily be introduced in order to enforce a due collection. On any charges of offence in this instance you will see yourselves deprived of your boasted *trial by jury*. The much admired common law process will give way to some quick and summary mode, by which the unhappy defendant will find himself reduced, perhaps to ruin, in less time than a charge could be exhibited against him in the usual course. [DHRC8 422]

[2] . . . Or what is an appeal to enquire into facts after a solemn adjudication in any court below, but a *trial* de novo? And do not such *trials* clearly imply an incompetency in the inferior courts to exercise any kind of judicial authority with rectitude? Hence, will not this eventually annihilate their whole jurisdiction? Here is a system of jurisprudence to be erected, no less surprising than it is new and unusual. Here is an innovation, which bears no kind of analogy to any thing, that Englishmen, or Americans, the descendants of Englishmen, have ever yet experienced. Add to all, that this high prerogative court establishes no fundamental rule of proceeding, except that the *trial by jury* is allowed in some criminal cases. All other cases are left open—and subject "to such regulations as the Congress shall make."—Under these circumstances I beseech you all, as citizens of Virginia, to consider seriously whether you will not endanger the solemn *trial by jury*, which you have long revered, as a sacred barrier against injustice—which has been established by your ancestors many centuries ago, and transmitted to you, as one of the greatest bulwarks of civil liberty—which you have to this day maintained inviolate:—I beseech you, I say, as members of this commonwealth, to consider whether you will not be in danger of losing this inestimable mode of *trial* in all those cases, wherein the constitution does not provide for its security. Nay, does not that very provision, which is made, by being confined to a few particular cases, almost imply a total exclusion of the rest? . . .
[DHRC8 423]

"James Bowdoin," February 27, 1788:

You [James Wilson] are an admirable man, the most useful in the convention; but you was rather for taking too much at one time; the double powers of our little sexentially elected senate; the controul over the press; the abolition of *trial by jury* in civil cases, and the common law proceedings; internal taxation; the pecuniary dependency of the judges, and their great powers; the standing army; the smallness of the lower house; the exclusion of rotation; and the "powers to make all laws which we may think necessary and proper". . . . [DHRC16 240]

"Brutus," No. 14, February 28, 1788:

[1] I believe it is a new and unusual thing to allow appeals in criminal matters. It is contrary to the sense of our laws, and dangerous to the lives and liberties

of the citizen. As our law now stands, a person charged with a crime has a right to a fair and impartial *trial by a jury* of his country, and their verdict is final. If he is acquitted no other court can call upon him to answer for the same crime. But by this system, a man may have had ever so fair a *trial,* have been acquitted by ever so respectable a *jury* of his country; and still the officer of the government who prosecutes, may appeal to the supreme court. . . . [DHRC16 256–57]

[2] . . . I confess I do not know what the advocates of the system, would make it mean, for I have not been fortunate enough to see in any publication this clause taken up and considered. It is certain however, they do not admit the explanation which those who oppose the constitution give it, or otherwise they would not so frequently charge them with want of candor, for alledging that it takes away the *trial by jury,* appeals from an inferior to a superior court, as practised in the civil law courts, are well understood. . . . [DHRC16 257]

Alexander White, "To the Citizens of Virginia," February 29, 1788:

. . . But it is proposed [by the Pennsylvania convention's minority] "that in controversies respecting property, and in suits between man and man, *trial by jury* shall remain as heretofore; as well in the Federal Courts as in those of the several States." What does this mean? If "heretofore" refers as I suppose it was intended, to the ancient common law, you must give up the mode of recovering debts by attachments and petitions; your summary proceedings against sheriffs and collectors who have received taxes, or money on executions against lawyers who have received money for their clients; and in Pennsylvania the board of property must be done away, and the law authorising a single magistrate to give judgment to the amount of 10l. must be repealed. If it refers to the present times, you would prevent Congress and the legislatures of the other States from adopting measures which have been found so salutary in this state? Where the *trial by jury* shall or shall not be made in civil causes, may with safety be left to Congress as it is to all our State legislatures. It is in criminal cases only, that that mode of *trial* is essential to liberty. [DHRC8 442–43]

"The Landholder," No. 10, February 29, 1788:

Since the publication of the Constitution, every topic of vulgar declamation has been employed to persuade the people, that it will destroy the *trial by jury,* and is defective for being without a bill of rights. You, Sir [Luther Martin], had more candour in the Convention than we can allow to those declaimers out of it; there you never signified by any motion or expression whatever, that it stood in need of a bill of rights, or in anywise endangered the *trial by jury.* In these respects the Constitution met your entire approbation . . . [DHRC16 267–68]

Mercy Otis Warren, *Observations on the New Constitution*, February 1788:

The abolition of *trial by jury* in civil causes.—This mode of *trial* the learned Judge Blackstone observes, "has been coeval with the first rudiments of civil government, that property, liberty and life, depend on maintaining in its legal force the constitutional *trial by jury*." . . . [DHRC16 279]

James Iredell, "Marcus," No. 3, March 5, 1788:

. . . There is perhaps no country in the world where justice is in general more impartially administered than in England; yet let any man read some of the *trials* for treason in that country even since the Revolution, he will see sometimes a fury influencing the Judges, as well as the *Jury*, that is extremely disgraceful. . . . [DHRC16 323]

"Brutus," No. 14, March 6, 1788:

[1] It may still be insisted that this clause does not take away the *trial by jury* on appeals, but that this may be provided for by the legislature, under that paragraph which authorises them to form regulations and restrictions for the court in the exercise of this power. [DHRC16 328]

[2] . . . But supposing the Congress may under this clause establish the *trial by jury* on appeals. It does not seem to me that it will render this article much less exceptionable. An appeal from one court and *jury*, to another court and *jury*, is a thing altogether unknown in the laws of our state, and in most of the states in the union. . . . [DHRC16 328]

[3] From these remarks it appears, that the administration of justice under the powers of the judicial will be dilatory; that it will be attended with such an heavy expence as to amount to little short of a denial of justice to the poor and middling class of people who in every government stand most in need of the protection of the law; and that the *trial by jury*, which has so justly been the boast of our fore fathers as well as ourselves is taken away under them. [DHRC16 329]

[4] This method would preserve the good old way of administering justice, would bring justice to every man's door, and preserve the inestimable right of *trial by jury*. It would be following, as near as our circumstances will admit, the practice of the courts in England, which is almost the only thing I would wish to copy in their government. [DHRC16 331]

[5] But as this system now stands, there is to be as many inferior courts as Congress may see fit to appoint, who are to be authorised to originate and in the first instance to *try* all the cases falling under the description of this article; there is no security that a *trial by jury* shall be had in these courts, but the *trial* here will soon become, as it is in Massachusetts' inferior courts, mere matter of form . . . [DHRC16 331]

Alexander Hamilton, *The Federalist*, No. 65, March 7, 1788:

[1] . . . The necessity of a numerous court [*i.e.*, the Senate] for the *trial* of impeachments, is equally dictated by the nature of the proceeding. This can never be tied down by such strict rules, either in the delineation of the offence by the prosecutors, or in the construction of it by the judges, as in common cases serve to limit the discretion of courts in favor of personal security. There will be no *jury* to stand between the judges who are to pronounce the sentence of the law, and the party who is to receive or suffer it. The awful discretion which a court of impeachments must necessarily have, to doom to honor or to infamy the most confidential and the most distinguished characters of the community, forbids the commitment of the trust to a small number of persons.

[Fed. 428]

[2] These considerations seem alone sufficient to authorize a conclusion, that the Supreme Court would have been an improper substitute for the Senate, as a court of impeachments. There remains a further consideration, which will not a little strengthen this conclusion. It is this: The punishment which may be the consequence of conviction upon impeachment, is not to terminate the chastisement of the offender. After having been sentenced to a perpetual ostracism from the esteem and confidence, and honors and emoluments of his country, he will still be liable to prosecution and punishment in the ordinary course of law. Would it be proper that the persons who had disposed of his fame, and his most valuable rights as a citizen, in one *trial,* should, in another *trial,* for the same offence, be also the disposers of his life and his fortune? Would there not be the greatest reasons to apprehend, that error, in the first sentence, would be the parent of error in the second sentence? That the strong bias of one decision would be apt to overrule the influence of any new lights which might be brought to vary the complexion of another decision? Those who know any thing of human nature, will not hesitate to answer these questions in the affirmative; and will be at no loss to perceive, that by making the same persons judges in both cases, those who might happen to be the objects of prosecution would, in a great measure, be deprived of the double security intended them by a double *trial*. The loss of life and estate would often be virtually included in a sentence which, in its terms, imported nothing more than dismission from a present, and disqualification for a future, office. It may be said, that the intervention of a *jury,* in the second instance, would obviate the danger. But *juries* are frequently influenced by the opinions of judges. They are sometimes induced to find special verdicts, which refer the main question to the decision of the court. Who would be willing to stake his life and his estate upon the verdict of a *jury* acting under the auspices of judges; who had predetermined his guilt? [Fed. 428–29]

James Iredell, "Marcus," No. 4, March 12, 1788:

[1] . . . I now proceed to the three great cases:—The Liberty of the Press—The *Trial by Jury* in civil cases, and a Standing Army in time of peace.

[DHRC16 382]

[2] In respect to the *trial by jury* in civil cases, it must be observed, it is a mistake to suppose, that such a *trial* takes place in all civil cases now. Even in the common law Courts, such a *trial* is only had where facts are disputed between the parties, and there are even some facts *triable* by other methods. In the Chancery and Admiralty Courts, in many of the States, I am told, they have no *Juries* at all. The States in these particulars differ very much in their practice from each other: A general declaration therefore to preserve the *trial by Jury* in all civil cases, would only have produced confusion, so that the Courts afterwards in a thousand instances would not have known how to have proceeded. . . .

[DHRC16 382–83]

[3] . . . There is no danger of the *trial by Jury* being rejected, when so justly a favorite of the whole people. The Representatives of the people surely can have no interest in making themselves odious for the mere pleasure of being hated . . . [DHRC16 383]

[4] . . . We know the great influence of the monarchy in the British government, and upon what a different tenure the Commons there have their seats in Parliament, from that prescribed to our Representatives. We know also, they have a large standing army. It is in the power of the Parliament if they dare to exercise it, to abolish the *trial by jury* altogether—but woe be to the man who should dare to attempt it—it would undoubtedly produce an insurrection that would hurl every tyrant to the ground who attempted to destroy that great and just favorite of the English nation. . . . [DHRC16 383]

[5] . . . There is indeed little probability, that any degree of tyranny which can be figured to the most discoloured imagination, as likely to arise out of our government, could find an interest in attacking the *trial by Jury* in civil cases; and in criminal ones, where no such difficulties intervened as in the other, and where there might be supposed temptations to violate the personal security of a citizen, it is sacredly preserved. [DHRC16 383]

Archibald Maclaine, "Publicola," March 20, 1788:

. . . The constitution of the respective states, and the rights of the people, are to remain as under the confederation, excepting such parts as interfere with the express powers given to Congress by the new constitution. All the clamour therefore, which has been raised about the *trial by jury,* and the liberty of the press, might have been spared, as altogether unfounded. . . .

[DHRC16 436–37]

Luther Martin, "To the Citizens of Maryland," No. 2, March 21, 1788:

. . . These consist, as he ["The Landholder"] tells us, in giving my entire approbation to the system, as to those parts which are said to endanger a *trial by*

jury, and as to its want of a bill of rights, and in having too much candour there to signify that I thought it deficient in either of these respects . . .
[DHRC16 454]

Luther Martin, "To the Citizens of Maryland," No. 3, March 28, 1788:

. . . or what state is there that would have been averse to a bill of rights, or that would have wished for the destruction of *jury trial* in a great variety of cases, and in a particular manner in every case, without exception, where the government itself is interested? . . . [DHRC16 501]

John Jay, *An Address to the People of the State of New York*, c. April 15, 1788:

We are told, among other strange things, that the liberty of the press is left insecure by the proposed Constitution, and yet that Constitution says neither more nor less about it, than the Constitution of the State of New York does. We are told that it deprives us of *trial by jury,* whereas the fact is, that it expressly secures it in certain cases, and takes it away in none —it is absurd to construe the silence of this, or of our own constitution, relative to a great number of our rights, into a total extinction of them—silence and blank paper neither grant nor take away anything. [Ford 76]

Melancton Smith, *An Address to the People of the State of New York*, c. April 1788:

[1] The opposers to the constitution have said that it is dangerous, because the judicial power may extend to many cases which ought to be reserved to the decision of the State courts, and because the right of *trial by jury* is not secured in the judicial courts of the general government, in civil cases. All the opposers are agreed in this objection. [Ford 102–103]

[2] . . . The suggestion, that the liberty of the press is secure, because it is not in express words spoken of in the constitution, and that the *trial by jury* is not taken away, because it is not said in so many words and letters it is so, is puerile and unworthy of a man who pretends to reason. We contend,that by the indefinite powers granted to the general government, the liberty of the press may be restricted by duties, &c. and therefore the constitution ought to have stipulated for its freedom. The *trial by jury,* in all civil cases is left at the discretion of the general government, except in the supreme court on the appelate jurisdiction, and in this I affirm it is taken away, not by express words, but by fair and legitimate construction and inference; for the supreme court have expressly given them an appelate jurisdiction, in every case to which their powers extend (with two or three exceptions) both as to law and fact. The court are the judges; every

man in the country, who has served as a *juror,* knows, that there is a difference between the court and the *jury,* and that the lawyers in their pleading, make the distinction. If the court, upon appeals, are to determine both the law and the fact, there is no room for a *jury,* and the right of *trial* in this mode is taken away. [Ford 113–14]

Alexander Hamilton, *The Federalist*, No. 81, May 28, 1788:

[1] The propriety of this appellate jurisdiction [of the Supreme Court] has been scarcely called in question in regard to matters of law; but the clamors have been loud against it as applied to matters of fact. Some well-intentioned men in this State [New York], deriving their notions from the language and forms which obtain in our courts, have been induced to consider it as an implied supersedure of the *trial by jury,* in favor of the civil-law mode of *trial,* which prevails in our courts of admiralty, probate, and chancery. A technical sense has been affixed to the term "appellate," which, in our law parlance, is commonly used in reference to appeals in the course of the civil law. But if I am not misinformed, the same meaning would not be given to it in any part of New England. There an appeal from one *jury* to another, is familiar both in language and practice, is even a matter of course, until there have been two verdicts on one side. The word "appellate," therefore, will not be understood in the same sense in new England as in New York, which shows the impropriety of a technical interpretation derived from the jurisprudence of any particular State. The expression, taken in the abstract, denotes nothing more than the power of one tribunal to review the proceedings of another, either as to the law or fact, or both. The mode of doing it may depend on ancient custom or legislative provision (in a new government it must depend on the latter), and may be with or without the aid of a *jury,* as may be judged advisable. If, therefore, the re-examination of a fact once determined by a *jury,* should in any case be admitted under the proposed Constitution, it may be so regulated as to be done by a second *jury,* either by remanding the cause to the court below for a second *trial* of the fact, or by directing an issue immediately out of the Supreme Court. [Fed. 512]

[2] . . . It is therefore necessary that the appellate jurisdiction should, in certain cases, extend in the broadest sense to matters of fact. It will not answer to make an express exception of cases which shall have been originally *tried by a jury,* because in the courts of some of the States all causes are *tried* in this mode; and such an exception would preclude the revision of matters of fact, as well where it might be proper, as where it might be improper. To avoid all inconveniences, it will be safest to declare generally, that the Supreme Court shall possess appellate jurisdiction both as to law and fact, and that this jurisdiction shall be subject to such exceptions and regulations as the national legislature may prescribe. . . . [Fed. 513]

[3] This view of the matter, at any rate, puts it out of all doubt that the supposed abolition of the *trial by jury,* by the operation of this provision, is fallacious and

untrue. The legislature of the United States would certainly have full power to provide, that in appeals to the Supreme Court there should be no re-examination of facts where they had been *tried* in the original causes by *juries*. This would certainly be an authorized exception . . . [Fed. 514]

[4] . . . that the Supreme Court will possess an appellate jurisdiction, both as to law and fact, in all cases referred to them, both subject to any exceptions and regulations which may be thought advisable; that this appellate jurisdiction does, in no case, abolish the *trial by jury;* and that an ordinary degree of prudence and integrity in the national councils will insure us solid advantages from the establishment of the proposed judiciary, without exposing us to any of the inconveniences which have been predicted from that source. [Fed. 514]

Alexander Hamilton, *The Federalist*, No. 83, May 28, 1788:

[Title:] *Trial by Jury*; [Fed. 518]

[1] The objection to the plan of the convention, which has met with most success in this State [New York], and perhaps in several of the other States, is that relative to the want of a constitutional provision for the *trial by jury* in civil cases. The disingenuous form in which this objection is usually stated has been repeatedly adverted to and exposed, but continues to be pursued in all the conversations and writings of the opponents of the plan. The mere silence of the Constitution in regard to civil causes, is represented as an abolition of the *trial by jury,* and the declamations to which it has afforded a pretext are artfully calculated to induce a persuasion that this pretended abolition is complete and universal, extending not only to every species of civil, but even to criminal, causes. . . . [Fed. 518]

[2] . . . Hence, say they, as the Constitution has established the *trial by jury* in criminal cases, and is silent in respect to civil, this silence is an implied prohibition of *trial by jury* in regard to the latter. [Fed. 519]

[3] . . . This being the case, let me ask if it is consistent with common-sense to suppose that a provision obliging the legislative power to commit the *trial* of criminal causes to *juries,* is a privation of its right to authorize or permit that mode of *trial* in other cases? Is it natural to suppose, that a command to do one thing is a prohibition to the doing of another, which there was a previous power to do, and which is not incompatible with the thing commanded to be done? If such a supposition would be unnatural and unreasonable, it cannot be rational to maintain that an injunction of the *trial by jury* in certain cases is an interdiction of it in others. [Fed. 519]

[4] A power to constitute courts is a power to prescribe the mode of *trial;* and consequently, if nothing was said in the Constitution on the subject of *juries,* the legislature would be at liberty either to adopt that institution or to let it alone. This discretion, in regard to criminal causes, is abridged by the express injunction of *trial* by *jury* in all such cases; but it is, of course, left at large in relation to

civil causes, there being a total silence on this head. The specification of an obligation to *try* all criminal causes in a particular mode, excludes indeed the obligation or necessity of employing the same mode in civil causes, but does not abridge the power of the legislature to exercise that mode if it should be thought proper. The pretence, therefore, that the national legislature would not be at full liberty to submit all the civil causes of federal cognizance to the determination of *juries,* is a pretence destitute of all just foundation.

[Fed. 519–20]

[5] From these observations this conclusion results: that the *trial by jury* in civil cases would not be abolished; and that the use attempted to be made of the maxims which have been quoted, is contrary to reason and common-sense, and therefore not admissible. . . . [Fed. 520]

[6] . . . The position is too absurd to merit a refutation, and yet this is precisely the position which those must establish who contend that the *trial by juries* in civil cases is abolished, because it is expressly provided for in cases of a criminal nature. [Fed. 521]

[7] From these observations it must appear unquestionably true, that *trial by jury* is in no case abolished by the proposed Constitution, and it is equally true, that in those controversies between individuals in which the great body of the people are likely to be interested, that institution will remain precisely in the same situation in which it is placed by the State constitutions . . . [Fed. 521]

[8] The friends and adversaries of the plan of the convention, if they agree in nothing else, concur at least in the value they set upon the *trial by jury;* or if there is any difference between them it consists in this: the former regard it as a valuable safeguard to liberty; the latter represent it as the very palladium of free government. . . . [Fed. 521–22]

[9] . . . But I must acknowledge that I cannot readily discern the inseparable connection between the existence of liberty, and the *trial by jury* in civil cases. Arbitrary impeachments, arbitrary methods of prosecuting pretended offences, and arbitrary punishments upon arbitrary convictions, have ever appeared to me to be the great engines of judicial despotism; and these have all relation to criminal proceedings. The *trial by jury* in criminal cases, aided by the habeas corpus act, seems therefore to be alone concerned in the question. And both of these are provided for, in the most ample manner, in the plan of the convention. [Fed. 522]

[10] It has been observed, that *trial by jury* is a safeguard against an oppressive exercise of the power of taxation. This observation deserves to be canvassed.

[Fed. 522]

[11] As to the mode of collection in this State [New York], under our own Constitution, the *trial by jury* is in most cases out of use. The taxes are usually levied by the more summary proceeding of distress and sale, as in cases of rent. . . . [Fed. 522]

[12] And as to the conduct of the officers of the revenue, the provision in favor of *trial by jury* in criminal cases, will afford the security aimed at. Wilful abuses of a public authority to the oppression of the subject, and every species of official extortion, are offences against the government, for which the persons who commit them may be indicted and punished according to the circumstances of the case. [Fed. 522–23]

[13] The excellence of the *trial by jury* in civil cases appears to depend on circumstances foreign to the preservation of liberty. The strongest argument in its favor is, that it is a security against corruption. As there is always more time and better opportunity to tamper with a standing body of magistrates than with a *jury* summoned for the occasion, there is room to suppose that a corrupt influence would more easily find its way to the former than to the latter. The force of this consideration is, however, diminished by others. . . . [Fed. 523]

[14] . . . But making every deduction for these considerations, the *trial by jury* must still be a valuable check upon corruption. It greatly multiplies the impediments to its success. As matters now stand, it would be necessary to corrupt both court and *jury;* for where the *jury* have gone evidently wrong, the court will generally grant a new *trial,* and it would be in most cases of little use to practice upon the *jury,* unless the court could be likewise gained. Here then is a double security . . . [Fed. 523]

[15] Notwithstanding, therefore, the doubts I have expressed, as to the essentiality of *trial by jury* in civil cases to liberty, I admit that it is in most cases, under proper regulations, an excellent method of determining questions of property; and that on this account alone it would be entitled to a constitutional provision in its favor if it were possible to fix the limits within which it ought to be comprehended. There is, however, in all cases, great difficulty in this . . . [Fed. 523–24]

[16] The great difference between the limits of the *jury trial* in different States is not generally understood; and as it must have considerable influence on the sentence we ought to pass upon the omission complained of in regard to this point, an explanation of it is necessary. In this State [New York], our judicial establishments resemble, more nearly than in any other, those of Great Britain. We have courts of common law, courts of probates (analogous in certain matters to the spiritual courts in England), a court of admiralty, and a court of chancery. In the courts of common law only, the *trial by jury* prevails, and this with some exceptions. In all the others a single judge presides, and proceeds in general either according to the course of the canon or civil law, without the aid of a *jury*. In New Jersey, there is a court of chancery which proceeds like ours, but neither courts of admiralty nor of probates, in the sense in which these last are established with us. In that State the courts of common law have the cognizance of those causes which with us are determinable in the courts of admiralty and of probates, and of course the *jury trial* is more extensive in New Jersey than in New York. . . . [Fed. 524]

[17] It has been erroneously insinuated with regard to the court of chancery, that this court generally *tries* disputed facts by a *jury*. The truth is, that references to a *jury* in that court rarely happen, and are in no case necessary but where the validity of a devise of land comes into question. [Fed. 524n]

[18] . . . I believe, however, that in some of those States which have distinct courts of admiralty, the causes depending in them are *triable by juries*. In Georgia there are none but common-law courts, and an appeal of course lies from the verdict of one *jury* to another, which is called a special *jury,* and for which a particular mode of appointment is marked out. In Connecticut, they have no distinct courts either of chancery or of admiralty, and their courts of probates have no jurisdiction of causes. Their common-law courts have admiralty and, to a certain extent, equity jurisdiction. In cases of importance, their General Assembly is the only court of chancery. In Connecticut, therefore, the *trial by jury* extends in practice further than in any other State yet mentioned. Rhode Island is, I believe, in this particular, pretty much in the situation of Connecticut. Massachusetts and New Hampshire, in regard to the blending of law, equity, and admiralty jurisdictions, are in a similar predicament. In the four Eastern States, the *trial by jury* not only stands upon a broader foundation than in the other States, but it is attended with a peculiarity unknown, in its full extent, to any of them. There is an appeal of course from one *jury* to another, till there have been two verdicts out of three on one side. [Fed. 525]

[19] From this sketch it appears that there is a material diversity, as well in the modification as in the extent of the institution of *trial by jury* in civil cases, in the several States; and from this fact these obvious reflections flow: first, that no general rule could have been fixed upon by the convention which would have corresponded with the circumstances of all the States; and secondly, that more or at least as much might have been hazarded by taking the system of any one State for a standard, as by omitting a provision altogether and leaving the matter, as has been done, to legislative regulation. [Fed. 525]

[20] The propositions which have been made for supplying the omission have rather served to illustrate than to obviate the difficulty of the thing. The minority of Pennsylvania have proposed this mode of expression for the purpose—"*Trial by jury* shall be as heretofore"—and this I maintain would be senseless and nugatory. The United States, in their united or collective capacity, are the OBJECT to which all general provisions in the Constitution must necessarily be construed to refer. Now it is evident that though *trial by jury,* with various limitations, is known in each State individually, yet in the United States, as such, it is at this time altogether unknown, because the present federal government has no judiciary power whatever; and consequently there is no proper antecedent or previous establishment to which the term heretofore could relate. It would therefore be destitute of a precise meaning, and inoperative from its uncertainty. [Fed. 525–26]

[21] As, on the one hand, the form of the provision would not fulfil the intent of its proposers, so, on the other, if I apprehend that intent rightly, it would be in itself inexpedient. I presume it to be, that causes in the federal courts should be *tried by jury,* if, in the State where the courts sat, that mode of *trial* would obtain in a similar case in the State courts; that is to say, admiralty causes should be *tried* in Connecticut by a *jury,* in New York without one. The capricious operation of so dissimilar a method of *trial* in the same cases, under the same government, is of itself sufficient to indispose every well-regulated judgment towards it. Whether the cause should be *tried* with or without a *jury,* would depend, in a great number of cases, on the accidental situation of the court and parties. [Fed. 526]

[22] But this is not, in my estimation, the greatest objection. I feel a deep and deliberate conviction that there are many cases in which the *trial by jury* is an ineligible one. I think it so particularly in cases which concern the public peace with foreign nations—that is, in most cases where the question turns wholly on the laws of nations. Of this nature, among others, are all prize causes. *Juries* cannot be supposed competent to investigations that require a thorough knowledge of the laws and usages of nations . . . [Fed. 526]

[23] . . . Besides this, the circumstances that constitute cases proper for courts of equity are in many instances so nice and intricate, that they are incompatible with the genius of *trials by jury.* They require often such long, deliberate, and critical investigation as would be impracticable to men called from their occupations, and obliged to decide before they were permitted to return to them. . . . [Fed. 527]

[24] It is true that the separation of the equity from the legal jurisdiction is peculiar to the English system of jurisprudence: which is the model that has been followed in several of the States. But it is equally true that the *trial by jury* has been unknown in every case in which they have been united. And the separation is essential to the preservation of that institution in its pristine purity. The nature of a court of equity will readily permit the extension of its jurisdiction to matters of law; but it is not a little to be suspected, that the attempt to extend the jurisdiction of the courts of law to matters of equity will not only be unproductive of the advantages which may be derived from courts of chancery, on the plan upon which they are established in this State, but will tend gradually to change the nature of the courts of law, and to undermine the *trial by jury,* by introducing questions too complicated for a decision in that mode. [Fed. 527–28]

[25] It is in this form: "In civil actions between citizens of different States, every issue of fact, arising in actions at common law, may be *tried by a jury* if the parties, or either of them, request it." [Fed. 528]

[26] This, at best, is a proposition confined to one description of causes; and the inference is fair, either that the Massachusetts convention considered that as the only class of federal causes, in which the *trial by jury* would be proper; or

that if desirous of a more extensive provision, they found it impracticable to devise one which would properly answer the end. . . . [Fed. 528]

[27] . . . if we advert to the observations already made respecting the courts that subsist in the several States of the Union, and the different powers exercised by them, it will appear that there are no expressions more vague and indeterminate than those which have been employed to characterize that species of causes which it is intended shall be entitled to a *trial by jury*. In this State [New York], the boundaries between actions at common law and actions of equitable jurisdiction, are ascertained in conformity to the rules which prevail in England upon that subject. In many of the other States the boundaries are less precise. In some of them, every cause is to be *tried* in a court of common law, and upon that foundation every action may be considered as an action at common law, to be determined by a *jury*, if the parties, or either of them, choose it. Hence the same irregularity and confusion would be introduced by a compliance with this proposition, that I have already noticed as resulting from the regulation proposed by the Pennsylvania minority. . . . [Fed. 528–29]

[28] To avoid the embarrassments of a definition of the cases which the *trial by jury* ought to embrace, it is sometimes suggested by men of enthusiastic tempers, that a provision might have been inserted for establishing it in all cases whatsoever. For this, I believe, no precedent is to be found in any member of the Union; and the considerations which have been stated in discussing the proposition of the minority of Pennsylvania, must satisfy every sober mind that the establishment of the *trial by jury* in all cases would have been an unpardonable error in the plan. [Fed. 529–30]

[29] . . . [My observations] have tended to show that the security of liberty is materially concerned only in the *trial by jury* in criminal cases, which is provided for in the most ample manner in the plan of the convention; that even in far the greatest proportion of civil cases, and those in which the great body of the community is interested, that mode of *trial* will remain in its full force, as established in the State constitutions, untouched and unaffected by the plan of the convention; that it is in no case abolished by that plan; and that there are great if not insurmountable difficulties in the way of making any precise and proper provision for it in a Constitution for the United States. [Fed. 530]

[30] The best judges of the matter will be the least anxious for a constitutional establishment of the *trial by jury* in civil cases, and will be the most ready to admit that the changes which are continually happening in the affairs of society may render a different mode of determining questions of property preferable in many cases in which that mode of *trial* now prevails. . . . [Fed. 530]

[31] This is now clearly understood to be the case in Great Britain, and it is equally so in the State of Connecticut; and yet it may be safely affirmed that more numerous encroachments have been made upon the *trial by jury* in this State [New York] since the Revolution, though provided for by a positive article of our constitution, than has happened in the same time either in Connecticut

or Great Britain. It may be added that these encroachments have generally originated with the men who endeavor to persuade the people they are the warmest defenders of popular liberty, but who have rarely suffered constitutional obstacles to arrest them in a favorite career. . . . [Fed. 531]

[32] It certainly sounds not a little harsh and extraordinary to affirm that there is no security for liberty in a Constitution which expressly establishes the *trial by jury* in criminal cases, because it does not do it in civil also; while it is a notorious fact that Connecticut, which has been always regarded as the most popular State in the Union, can boast of no constitutional provision for either. [Fed. 531]

John Dickinson, "Fabius," No. 2, 1788:

The course of regular inquiry demands, that these objections should be considered in the first place. If they are removed, then all the rest of the objections, concerning unnecessary taxations, standing armies, the abolishment of *trial by jury,* the liberty of the press, the freedom of commerce, the judicial, executive, and legislative authorities of the several states, and the rights of citizens, and the other abuses of federal government, must, of consequence, be rejected . . . [Ford 168–69]

John Dickinson, "Fabius," No. 4, 1788:

[1] It seems highly probable, that those who would reject this labour of public love, would also have rejected the Heaven-taught institution of *trial by jury,* had they been consulted upon its establishment. . . . [Ford 184]

[2] *Trial by jury* and the dependence of taxation upon representation, those corner stones of liberty, were not obtained by a bill of rights, or any other records, and have not been and cannot be preserved by them. They and all other rights must be preserved, by soundness of sense and honesty of heart. . . . [Ford 186]

[3] . . . *Trial by jury* is our birth-right; and tempted to his own ruin, by some seducing spirit, must be the man, who in opposition to the genius of United America, shall dare to attempt its subversion. [Ford 186]

John Dickinson, "Fabius," No. 7, 1788:

Do the propositions of gentlemen who object, offer to our view, any of the great points upon which, the fate, fame, or freedom of nations has turned, excepting what some of them have said about *trial by jury;* and which has been frequently and fully answered? . . . [Ford 202]

Georgia Constitution, May 6, 1789:

[Article III, Section 2:] The general assembly shall point out the mode of correcting errors and appeals, which shall extend so far as to empower the judges to direct a new *trial by jury* within the county where the action originated, and which shall be final. [Thorpe 788]

[Article IV, Section 3:] Freedom of the press and *trial by jury* shall remain inviolate. [Thorpe 789]

United States Congress, Judiciary Act of September 24, 1789:

[Section 9:] . . . And the *trial* of issues in fact, in the district courts, in all causes except civil causes of admiralty and maritime jurisdiction, shall be by *jury*. [USSL1 77]

[Section 12:] . . . and the *trial* of issues in fact in the circuit courts shall, in all suits, except those in equity, and of admiralty, and maritime jurisdiction, be by *jury*. [USSL1 80]

[Section 13:] . . . And the *trial* of issues in fact in the Supreme Court, in all actions at law against citizens of the United States, shall be by *jury*. . . . [USSL1 81]

[Section 17:] . . . That all the said courts of the United States shall have power to grant new *trials,* in cases where there has been a trial by *jury* for reasons for which new *trails* have usually been granted in courts of law . . . [USSL1 83]

South Carolina Constitution, June 3, 1790:

[Article IX, Section 6:] The *trial by jury* as heretofore used in this State, and the liberty of the press, shall be forever inviolably preserved. [Thorpe 3264]

Pennsylvania Constitution, September 2, 1790:

[Article IX, Section 6:] That *trial by jury* shall be as heretofore, and the right thereof remain inviolate. [Thorpe 3100]

[Article IX, Section 9:] That in all criminal prosecutions the accused hath a right to be heard by himself and his counsel, to demand the nature and cause of the accusation against him, to meet the witnesses face to face, to have compulsory process for obtaining witnesses in his favor, and, in prosecutions by indictment or information, a *speedy public trial, by an impartial jury* of the vicinage . . . [Thorpe 3100]

TRUST, PUBLIC

United States Constitution, September 17, 1787:

[Article VI:] The Senators and Representatives before mentioned, and the Members of the several State Legislatures, and all executive and judicial Officers, both of the United States and of the several States, shall be bound by Oath or Affirmation, to support this Constitution; but no religious Test shall ever be required as a Qualification to any Office or *public Trust* under the United States.

* * * * *

Pennsylvania Frame of Government, Laws Agreed Upon in England, May 5, 1682:

[Article 27:] And, to the end that all officers chosen to serve within this province, may, with more care and diligence, answer the *trust* reposed in them, it is agreed, that no such person shall enjoy more than one *public* office, at one time.

[Thorpe 3062]

Fundamental Constitutions of East New Jersey, 1683:

[Article 12:] That whoever has any place of *publick trust* in another Province, tho' a Proprietor, shall not sit in the great or common Council, but by their proxies, unless thereunto particularly called by the one or other Council.

[Thorpe 2578]

[Article 16:] . . . Yet it is also hereby provided, that no man shall be admitted a member of the great or common Council, or any other place of *publick trust,* who shall not profaith in Christ Jesus, and solemnly declare that he doth no ways hold himself obliged in conscience to endeavour alteration in the government, or seeks the turning out of any in it or their ruin or prejudice, either in person or estate, because they are in his opinion hereticks, or differ in their judgment from him . . . [Thorpe 2580]

[Article 17:] To the end that all officers chosen to serve within the Province, may with the more care and deligence answer the *trust* reposed in them; it is agreed, that no such person shall enjoy more than one *public* office at one time . . . [Thorpe 2580]

Thomas Paine, *Common Sense*, January 9, 1776:

. . . The unwarrantable stretch likewise, which that house [the Pennsylvania Assembly] made in their last sitting, to gain an undue authority over the Delegates of that province, ought to warn the people at large, how they *trust* power out of their own hands. A set of instructions for the delegates were put together, which in point of sense and business would have dishonored a school-boy, and after being approved by a few, a very few, without doors, were carried into the house, and there passed in behalf of the whole colony; whereas, did the whole colony know, with what ill will that house hath entered on some necessary *public* measures, they would not hesitate a moment to think them unworthy of such a *trust*. [CWTP1 38]

Maryland Constitution, November 11, 1776:

[Declaration of Rights, Article 32:] That no person ought to hold, at the same time, more than one office of profit, nor ought any person, in *public trust,* to receive any present from any foreign prince or state, or from the United States, or any of them, without the approbation of this State. [Thorpe 1689]

Virginia Statute of Religious Liberty, January 16, 1786:

. . . that therefore the proscribing any citizen as unworthy the *public* confidence by laying upon him an incapacity of being called to offices of *trust* and emolument, unless he profess or renounce this or that religious opinion, is depriving him injuriously of those privileges and advantages to which in common with his fellow-citizens he has a natural right . . . [CVA8 690]

Tench Coxe, *An Examination of the Constitution for the United States*, No. 3, September 29, 1787:

. . . They [the United States House of Representatives] can compel the attendance of their members, that their *public* duty may not be evaded in times of difficulty or danger—The vote of each representative can be always known, as well as the proceedings of the house, that so the people may be acquainted with the conduct of those in whom they repose so important a *trust*. . . . [Ford 144]

Tench Coxe, *An Examination of the Constitution for the United States of America*, No. 4, October 21, 1787:

No religious test is ever to be required of any officer or servant of the United States. The people may employ any wise or good citizen in the execution of the various duties of the government. In Italy, Spain, and Portugal, no protestant can hold a *public trust*. In England every Presbyterian, and other person not of their established church, is incapable of holding an office. No such impious deprivation of the rights of men can take place under the new foederal constitution. . . . [Ford 146]

Pelatiah Webster, *The Weakness of Brutus Exposed*, November 4, 1787:

If all this will not produce a Congress fit to be *trusted,* and worthy of the *public* confidence, I think we may give the matter up as impracticable. . . .
[Ford 124]

Alexander Hamilton, *The Federalist*, No. 31, January 1, 1788:

A government ought to contain in itself every power requisite to the full accomplishment of the objects committed to its care, and to the complete execution of the *trusts* for which it is responsible, free from every other control but a regard to the *public* good and to the sense of the people. [Fed. 238]

James Madison, *The Federalist*, No. 49, February 2, 1788:

. . . The nature of their [*i.e.*, the legislators'] *public trust* implies a personal influence among the people, and that they are more immediately the confidential guardians of the rights and liberties of the people. With these advantages, it can hardly be supposed that the adverse party would have an equal chance for a favorable issue. [Fed. 350]

Luther Martin, "Genuine Information," No. 12, February 8, 1788:

The part of the system, which provides that no religious test shall ever be required as a qualification to any office or *public trust* under the United States, was adopted by a very great majority of the convention, and without much debate . . . [DHRC16 89]

James Madison, *The Federalist*, No. 55, February 13, 1788:

. . . through the whole course of the war they [*i.e.*, the Continental Congress] had the fate of their country more in their hands than it is to be hoped will ever be the case with our future representatives; and from the greatness of the prize at stake, and the eagerness of the party which lost it, it may well be supposed that the use of other means than force would not have been scrupled. Yet we know by happy experience that the *public trust* was not betrayed; nor has the purity of our *public* councils in this particular ever suffered, even from the whispers of calumny. [Fed. 378]

William Ward [?], "Republicus," February 16, 1788:

But again it should provide against their holding those *trusts* for long terms. This would call into *public* service a greater variety of estimable characters; would beget an emulation who should serve their country the most essentially; and make it perhaps as fashionable a virtue to serve the interest of the *public,* as it has been formerly a vice to serve the private interest of some favorite family or worthless dependent. . . . [DHRC8 378]

James Madison, *The Federalist*, No. 57, February 19, 1788:

The aim of every political constitution is, or ought to be, first to obtain for rulers men who possess most wisdom to discern, and most virtue to pursue, the common good of the society; and in the next place, to take the most effectual precautions for keeping them virtuous whilst they continue to hold their *public trust*. The elective mode of obtaining rulers is the characteristic policy of republican government . . . [Fed. 383]

Samuel Bryan, "Centinel," No. 16, February 26, 1788:

. . . The late Financier [Robert Morris] alone, in the capacity of chairman of the commercial committee of Congress, early in the late war, was *entrusted* with millions of *public* money, which to this day remain unaccounted for, nor has he settled his accounts as Financier. The others may also find it a convenient method to balance accounts with the *public;* they are sufficiently known and therefore need not be designated . . . [DHRC16 219]

"An Impartial Citizen," No. 5, February 28, 1788:

. . . The President of the United States (when the Supreme Court, or other inferior Federal Courts, have judged according to the letter of the law, which may be rigorous) mitigates the sentence according to the true spirit of all laws, which teaches "never to sacrifice a man but in evident necessity"—But lest he should abuse this *trust,* he is not empowered to pardon in cases of impeachments. Where the conduct of an officer *entrusted* with the administration of some *public* affairs is such, that the Representatives, in order to ensure justice to the *public,* accuse him before the Senate, the President cannot interpose his pardon. The history of mankind, from the most remote antiquity, will inform us, that Officers of State or those *entrusted* with *public* administration of affairs, have ever been the most forward in plots and conspiracies against their country. In case such officers in the United States should conspire against their country, they cannot flatter themselves with the hopes of extorting from the President a remission of their punishment. . . . [DHRC8 429]

James Madison, *The Federalist*, No. 63, March 1, 1788:

Yet however requisite a sense of national character may be, it is evident that it can never be sufficiently possessed by a numerous and changeable body. It can only be found in a number so small that a sensible degree of the praise and blame of *public* measures may be the portion of each individual; or in an assembly so durably invested with *public trust,* that the pride and consequence of its members may be sensibly incorporated with the reputation and prosperity of the community. . . . [Fed. 413]

Alexander Hamilton, *The Federalist*, No. 65, March 7, 1788:

[1] A well-constituted court for the trial of impeachments is an object not more to be desired than difficult to be obtained in a government wholly elective. The subjects of its jurisdiction are those offences which proceed from the misconduct of *public* men, or, in other words, from the abuse or violation of some *public trust*. They are of a nature which may with peculiar propriety be denominated POLITICAL, as they relate chiefly to injuries done immediately to the society itself. . . . [Fed. 426]

[2] The delicacy and magnitude of a *trust* which so deeply concerns the political reputation and existence of every man engaged in the administration of *public* affairs, speak for themselves. . . . [Fed. 426]

Alexander Hamilton, *The Federalist*, No. 70, March 15, 1788:

[1] Wherever two or more persons are engaged in any common enterprise or pursuit, there is always danger of difference of opinion. If it be a *public trust* or office, in which they are clothed with equal dignity and authority, there is peculiar danger of personal emulation and even animosity. From either, and especially from all these causes, the most bitter dissensions are apt to spring. . . . [Fed. 453]

[2] But one of the weightiest objections to a plurality in the Executive, and which lies as much against the last as the first plan, is, that it tends to conceal faults and destroy responsibility. Responsibility is of two kinds—to censure and to punishment. The first is the more important of the two, especially in an elective office. Man, in *public trust,* will much oftener act in such a manner as to render him unworthy of being any longer trusted, than in such a manner as to make him obnoxious to legal punishment. . . . [Fed. 455]

Luther Martin, "To the Citizens of Maryland," No. 1, March 18, 1788:

To you, my fellow-citizens, I hold myself in a particular manner accountable for every part of my conduct in the exercise of a *trust* reposed in me by you, and should consider myself highly culpable if I was to withhold from you any information in my possession, the knowledge of which may be material to enable you to form a right judgment on questions wherein the happiness of yourselves and your posterity are involved—Nor shall I ever consider it an act of condescension when impeached in my *public* conduct, or character, to vindicate myself at your bar, and to submit myself to your decision. . . . [DHRC16 415]

Luther Martin, "To the Citizens of Maryland," No. 2, March 21, 1788:

. . . It was my opinion, that to agree upon a ratification of the constitution by any less number than the whole thirteen states, is so directly repugnant to our present articles of confederation, and the mode therein prescribed for their alteration, and such a violation of the compact which the states, in the most solemn manner, have entered into with each other, that those who could advocate a contrary proposition, ought never to be confided in and *entrusted in public life*—I availed myself of this rule, and had the question taken on thirteen, which was rejected . . . [DHRC16 454]

Samuel Bryan, "Centinel," No. 17, March 24, 1788:

. . . the conspirators have asserted, that his accounts [i.e., Robert Morris's accounts as United States Superintendent of Finance] were finally settled in November, 1784, for which they pretend to have vouchers, and by a pompous display of certain resolutions of Congress, respecting a particular charge of fraud against him, as commercial agent to the United States, they vainly hope to divert the *public* attention from his great delinquency, in never accounting for the millions of *public* money, *entrusted* to him in that line. . . . [DHRC16 475]

USE, PUBLIC

United States Constitution, Bill of Rights, December 15, 1790:

[Article V:] No person shall be held to answer for a capital, or otherwise infamous crime, unless on a presentment or indictment of a Grand Jury, except in cases arising in the land or naval forces, or in the Militia, when in actual service in time of War or public danger; nor shall any person be subject for the same offence to be twice put in jeopardy of life or limb; nor shall be compelled in any criminal case to be a witness against himself, nor be deprived of life, liberty, or property, without due process of law; nor shall private property be taken for *public use,* without just compensation.

* * * * *

James I, The Charter of New England, November 3, 1620:

And further, Wee will and grant by these Presents, for Us, our Heires and Successors, unto the said Councill and their Successors, that they and their Successors shall have and enjoy for ever a Common Seale, to be engraven according to their Discretions; and that it shall be lawfull for them to appoint whatever Seale or Seales, they shall think most meete and necessary, either for their *Use,* as they are one united Body incorporate here, or for the *publick* of their Gouvernour and Ministers of New-England aforesaid . . . [Thorpe 1832]

Charles I, Grant of the Province of Maine, April 3, 1639:

And Wee doe further for us our heires and successors give and graunte unto the said Sir Fardinando Gorges his heires and assignes full power and authortie to divide all or anie parte of the Territories hereby granted or menconed to bee graunted as aforesaid into Provinces Counties Citties Townes Hundreds and Parishes or such other partes or porcons as hee or they shall thinke fitt and in them every or any of them to appoynt and allott out such porcons of Lande for *publique uses* Ecclesiasticall and Temporall of what kinde soever . . .

[Thorpe 1632]

Patent for Providence Plantations, March 14, 1643:

. . . And the said Earl and Commissioners, do further authorize, that the aforesaid Inhabitants, for the better transacting of their *public* Affairs to make and *use* a *public* Seal as the known Seal of Providence-Plantations, in the Narraganset-Bay, in New-England. . . . [Thorpe 3211]

Carolina Proprietors, Declaration and Proposals, August 25, 1663:

In consideration of the premises, we do expect by way of acknowledgment, and towards the charge we have been and shall be at, one half-penny for every acre that shall be granted as aforesaid, within the time before limited and expressed; and that the court-houses and houses for *public* meetings be erected by the *public* moneys of the colony on the lands taken up by us; but to be and continue to the country's *use* forever, they paying some small acknowledgement.

[Thorpe 2755]

Fundamental Constitutions of Carolina, March 1, 1669:

[Article 33:] The palatine's court . . . shall have power to call parliaments, to pardon all offences, to make elections of all officers in the proprietors dispose, and to nominate and appoint port towns; and also shall have power by their order to the treasurer to dispose of all *public* treasure, excepting money granted by the parliament, and by them directed to some particular *public use* . . .

[Thorpe 2776]

[Article 44:] The high steward's court . . . shall have power also to make any *public* building, or any new highway, or enlarge any old highway, upon any mans land whatsoever; as also to make cuts, channels, banks locks, and bridges, for making rivers navigable, or for draining fens, or any other *public use*. The damage the owner of such lands (on or through which any such *public* things shall be made) shall receive thereby shall be valued, and satisfaction made by such ways as the grand council shall appoint. . . . [Thorpe 2778]

Charles II, Charter of Pennsylvania, February 28, 1681:

. . . [We] Doe grant free, full, and absolute power by vertue of these presents to him [William Penn] and his heires, and to his and their Deputies, and Lieutenants, for the good and happy government of the said countrey to ordeyne, make, and enact, and under his and their Seales to publish any Lawes whatsoever, for the raising of money for the *publick use* of the said Province, or for any other End, apperteyning either unto the *publick* state, peace, or safety of the said Countrey, or unto the private utility of perticular persons, according unto their best discretions, by and with the advice, assent, and approbation of the Freemen of the said Countrey, or the greater parte of them, or of their Delegates or Deputies . . . [Thorpe 3037]

Pennsylvania Frame of Government, April 25, 1682:

[Article 11:] That the Governor and provincial Council shall, at all times, have power to inspect the management of the *public* treasury, and punish those who shall convert any part thereof to any other *use,* than what hath been agreed upon by the Governor, provincial Council, and General Assembly. [Thorpe 3056]

Pennsylvania Frame of Government, April 2, 1683:

[Article 9:] That the Governor and provincial Council shall, at all times, have power to inspect the management of the *public* treasury, and punish those who shall convert any part thereof to any other *use,* than what hath been agreed upon by the Governor, provincial Council and Assembly. [Thorpe 3065]

Fundamental Constitutions of East New Jersey, 1683:

[Article 7] . . . In pursuance thereof, there shall be a fourth committee erected, consisting of six proprietors, or their proxies, and three of the freemen, that are to set in the other three committees, which shall be such as to understand it their duty to *use* arms for the *publick* defence; which committee shall provide for the *publick* defence without and peace within, against all enemies whatsoever; and shall therefore be stiled the committee for the preservation of the *publick* peace . . . [Thorpe 2577]

[*Ibid.:*] . . . and that none of the Proprietors and other inhabitants may be forced to contribute any money for the *use* of arms, to which for conscience sake they have not freedom, that which is necessary for the *publick* defence, shall be borne by such as judge themselves in duty bound to *use* arms. . . . [Thorpe 2577–78]

Pennsylvania Frame of Government, November 7, 1696:

Be it further enacted by the authority aforesaid, That the Governor and Council shall, at all times, have power to inspect the management of the *public* treasury, and punish those who shall convert any part thereof to any other *use,* than what hath been agreed upon by the Governor, Council and Assembly.
[Thorpe 3074]

New Hampshire Constitution, January 5, 1776:

We, the members of the Congress of New Hampshire, chosen and appointed by the free suffrages of the people of said colony, and authorized and empowered by them to meet together, and *use* such means and pursue such measures as we should judge best for the *public* good; and in particular to establish some form of government, provided that measure should be recommended by the Continental Congress . . . [Thorpe 2451]

Virginia Bill of Rights, June 12, 1776:

[Section 6:] That elections of members to serve as representatives of the people, in assembly, ought to be free; and that all men, having sufficient evidence of permanent common interest with, and attachment to, the community, have the right of suffrage, and cannot be taxed or deprived of their property for *public uses,* without their own consent, or that of their representatives so elected, nor bound by any law to which they have not, in like manner, assented for the public good. [Thorpe 3813]

United States Continental Congress, Draft Articles of Confederation, July 12, 1776:

[Article 9:] . . . But every Colony shall always keep up a well regulated and disciplined MIlitia, sufficiently armed and accoutred; and shall provide and constantly have ready for *Use* in *public* Stores, a due Number of Field Pieces and Tents, and a proper Quantity of Ammunition, and Camp Equipage. [DHRC1 80]

Pennsylvania Constitution, September 28, 1776:

[Declaration of Rights, Article 8:] That every member of society hath a right to be protected in the enjoyment of life, liberty and property, and therefore is bound to contribute his proportion towards the expence of that protection, and yield his personal service when necessary, or an equivalent thereto: But no part of a man's property can be justly taken from him or applied to *public uses,* without his own consent, or that of his legal representatives . . . [Thorpe 3083]

Maryland Constitution, November 11, 1776:

[Declaration of Rights, Article 34:] That every gift, sale, or devise of lands, to any minister, *public* teacher, or preacher of the gospel, as such, or to any religious sect, order or denomination, or to or for the support, *use* or benefit of, or in trust for, any minister, *public* teacher, or preacher of the gospel, as such, or any religious sect, order or denomination—and every gift or sale of goods, or chattels, to go in succession, or to take place after the death of the seller or donor, or to or for such support, *use* or benefit—and also every devise of goods or chattels to or for the support, *use* or benefit of any minister, *public* teacher, or preacher of the gospel, as such, or any religious sect, order, or denomination, without the leave of the Legislature, shall be void; except always any sale, gift, lease or devise of any quantity of land, not exceeding two acres, for a church, meeting, or other house of worship, and for a burying-ground, which shall be improved, enjoyed or *used* only for such purpose—or such sale, gift, lease, or devise, shall be void. [Thorpe 1690]

Vermont Constitution, July 8, 1777:

[Declaration of Rights, Article 2:] That private property ought to be subservient to *public uses,* when necessity requires it; nevertheless, whenever any particular man's property is taken for the *use of the public,* the owner ought to receive an equivalent in money. [Thorpe 3740]

[*Ibid.,* Article 9:] That every member of society hath a right to be protected in the enjoyment of life, liberty and property, and therefore, is bound to contribute his proportion towards the expense of that protection, and yield his personal service, when necessary, or an equivalent thereto; but no part of a man's property can be justly taken from him, or applied to *public uses,* with out his own consent, or that of his legal representatives . . . [Thorpe 3740–41]

United States Articles of Confederation, November 15, 1777:

[Article VI:] . . . but every state shall always keep up a well regulated and disciplined militia, sufficiently armed and accoutered, and shall provide and constantly have ready for *use,* in *public* stores, a due number of field pieces and tents, and a proper quantity of arms, ammunition and camp equipage.

Massachusetts Constitution, March 2, 1780:

[Declaration of Rights, Article 10:] Each individual of the society has a right to be protected by it in the enjoyment of his life, liberty, and property, according to standing laws. He is obliged, consequently, to contribute his share to the expense of this protection; to give his personal service, or an equivalent, when necessary: but no part of the property of any individual can, with justice, be taken from him, or applied to *public uses,* without his own consent, or that of the representative body of the people. In fine, the people of this commonwealth are not controllable by any other laws than those to which their constitutional representative body have given their consent. And whenever the *public* exigencies require that the property of any individual should be appropriated to *public uses,* he shall receive a reasonable compensation therefor. [Thorpe 1891]

New Hampshire Constitution, June 2, 1784:

[Bill of Rights, Article 12:] Every member of the community has a right to be protected by it in the enjoyment of his life, liberty and property; he is therefore bound to contribute his share in the expence of such protection, and to yield his personal service when necessary, or an equivalent. But no part of a man's property shall be taken from him, or applied to *public uses,* without his own consent, or that of the representative body of the people. Nor are the inhabitants of this state controllable by any other laws than those to which they or their representative body have given their consent. [Thorpe 2455]

Vermont Constitution, July 4, 1786:

[Declaration of Rights, Article 2:] That private property ought to be subservient to *public uses,* when necessity requires it; nevertheless, whenever any particular man's property is taken for the *use of the public,* the owner ought to receive an equivalent in money. [Thorpe 3752]

[*Ibid.,* Article 10:] That every member of society hath a right to be protected in the enjoyment of life, liberty and property; and therefore is bound to contribute his proportion towards the expense of that protection, and yield his personal service, when necessary, or an equivalent thereto: but no part of a man's property can be justly taken from him, or applied to *public uses,* without his own consent, or that of the representative body of the freemen . . . [Thorpe 3753]

"An Impartial Citizen," January 10, 1788:

. . . The President in many important cases, must have the concurrence of the Senate, wherein his sole decision might be dangerous. The compensation for his services cannot be augmented, nor can he receive any other emolument from the United States, or any of them, during the period for which he shall have been elected: Nor can he appropriate the *public* money to any *use*, but what is expressly provided by law . . . [DHRC8 295]

Spencer Roane, "A Plain Dealer," February 13, 1788:

Mr. DAVIS, As you have the character of being a very independent printer, and as the time is yet at hand when the liberty of the press, and the free discussion of public measures, are considered as the first data of free government, I doubt not you will publish the following observation in your useful paper.—To know the head which dictated them can be of no *use* to the *public,* and will add no weight to the publication; being written by an obscure citizen, but anxiously wishing for the prosperity of this country. . . . [DHRC8 363]

Pennsylvania Constitution, September 2, 1790:

[Article IX, Section 10:] That no person shall, for any indictable offence, be proceeded against criminally by information, except in cases arising in the land or naval forces, or in the militia, when in actual service in time of war or *public* danger, or, by leave of the court, for oppression and misdemeanor in office. No person shall, for the same offence, be twice put in jeopardy of life or limb; nor shall any man's property be taken or applied to *public use* without the consent of his representatives, and without just compensation being made.

[Thorpe 3100–01]

VIOLENCE, DOMESTIC

United States Constitution, September 17, 1787:

[Article IV, Section 4:] The United States shall guarantee to every State in this Union a Republican Form of Government, and shall protect each of them against Invasion; and on Application of the Legislature, or of the Executive (when the Legislature cannot be convened) against *domestic Violence*.

* * * * *

Edmund Randolph, Letter on the Federal Constitution, October 10, 1787:

It follows too, that the general government ought to protect each state against *domestic as well as external violence*. [DHRC8 267]

Alexander Hamilton, *The Federalist*, No. 31, January 1, 1788:

As the duties of superintending the national defence and of securing the public peace against foreign or *domestic violence* involve a provision for casualties and dangers to which no possible limits can be assigned, the power of making that provision ought to know no other bounds than the exigencies of the nation and the resources of the community. [Fed. 238]

Alexander Hamilton, *The Federalist*, No. 43, January 23, 1788:

Protection against *domestic violence* is added with equal propriety. It has been remarked, that even among the Swiss cantons, which, properly speaking, are not under one government, provision is made for this object; and the history of that league informs us that mutual aid is frequently claimed and afforded; and as well by the most democratic, as the other cantons. A recent and well-known event among ourselves has warned us to be prepared for emergencies of a like nature. [Fed. 313]

David Ramsay, "Civis," February 4, 1788:

[1] . . . It is farther objected, that they have stipulated for a right to prohibit the importation of negroes after 21 years. On this subject observe, as they are bound to protect us from *domestic violence,* they think we ought not to increase our exposure to that evil, by an unlimited importation of slaves. Though Congress may forbid the importation of negroes after 21 years, it does not follow that they will. . . . [DHRC16 25]

[2] By the new constitution, you will be protected with the force of the union, against *domestic violence* and foreign invasion. You will have a navy to defend your coasts.—The respectable figure you will make among the nations, will so far command the attention of foreign powers, that it is probable you will soon obtain such commercial treaties, as will open to your vessels the West-India islands, and give life to your expiring commerce. [DHRC16 26]

Luther Martin, "Genuine Information," No. 11, February 5, 1788:

This representation was made in convention, and it was further urged that the territory of these States were too large, and that the inhabitants thereof would be too much disconnected for a republican government to extend to them its benefits, which is only suited to a small and compact territory—That a regard also for the peace and safety of the union, ought to excite a desire that those States should become in time divided into separate States, since when their population should become proportioned in any degree to their territory, they would from their strength and power become dangerous members of a federal government.—It was further said that if the general government was not by its constitution to interfere, the inconvenience would soon remedy itself, for that as the population increased in those States, their legislatures would be obliged to consent to the erection of new States to avoid the evils of a civil war, but as by the proposed constitution the general government is obliged to protect each State against *domestic violence,* and consequently will be obliged to assist in suppressing such commotions and insurrections as may take place from the struggle to have new States erected, the general government ought to have a power to decide upon the propriety and necessity of establishing or erecting a new State even without the approbation of the legislature of such States, within whose jurisdiction the new State should be erected . . . [DHRC16 40]

WAR, WARS

(Declare War; Engage in War; Levy War; Make War)

United States Constitution, September 17, 1787:

[Article I, Section 8:] [Congress shall have power] To *declare War,* grant Letters of Marque and Reprisal, and make Rules concerning Captures on Land and Water . . .

[Article I, Section 10:] No State shall, without the Consent of Congress, lay any Duty of Tonnage, keep Troops, or Ships of *War* in time of Peace, enter into any Agreement or Compact with another State, or with a foreign Power, or *engage in War,* unless actually invaded, or in such imminent Danger as will not admit of delay.

[Article III, Section 3:] Treason against the United States, shall consist only in *levying War* against them, or in adhering to their Enemies, giving them Aid and Comfort. No Person shall be convicted of Treason unless on the Testimony of two Witnesses to the same overt Act, or on Confession in open Court.

United States Constitution, Bill of Rights, December 15, 1791:

[Article III:] No Soldier shall, in time of peace be quartered in any house, without the consent of the Owner, nor in time of *war,* but in a manner to be prescribed by law.

[Article V:] No person shall be held to answer for a capital, or otherwise infamous crime, unless on a presentment or indictment of a Grand Jury, except in cases arising in the land or naval forces, or in the Militia, when in actual service in time of *War* or public danger; nor shall any person be subject for the same offence to be twice put in jeopardy of life or limb; nor shall be compelled in any criminal case to be a witness against himself, nor be deprived of life, liberty, or property, without due process of law; nor shall private property be taken for public use, without just compensation.

* * * * *

Charter of the Dutch West India Company, June 3, 1621:

[Article 10:] That all the goods of this company during the eight next ensuing years, be carried out of this country to the parts of the West-Indies and Africa, and other places comprehended within the aforesaid limits, and those which they shall bring into this country, shall be from outward and home convoys; provided, that if at the expiration of the aforesaid eight years, the state and situation of these Countries will not admit of this Freedom's continuing for a longer time, the said goods, and the merchandises coming from the places mentioned in this Charter, and exported again out of these countries, and the outward convoys and licenses, during the whole time of this Charter, shall not be rated higher by us than they have formerly been rated, unless we should be again *engaged in a war,* in which case, all the aforesaid goods and merchandises will not be rated higher by us than they were in the last list in time of *war*. [Thorpe 61]

Charles I, Patent to Sir Robert Heath, October 30, 1629:

. . . Therefore we for ourselves our Heires & successors have given to the foresayd Sr. Robert Heath Knight his heires & assignes by himself his Captains or other his officers, that all men of whatever condition, or wherever borne, being at that time in the Province of Carolana power to call to their colours, to cause Musters to *make warre,* to pursue enemyes & Robbers aforesaid by land & sea, even beyond the bounds of his province, and then (with Gods blessing) to overcome & to take, & being taken by right of warre to slay, or according to his pleasure to preserve, & all & every thing which doe appertaine to the right & office of a Captaine Generall or have been used to appertaine to be done & by these presents doe give full & free power as any Captaine Generall ever had.
[Thorpe 73]

The New England Confederation, May 19, 1643:

[Article 9:] And for that the justest wars may be of dangerous consequence, especially to the smaller Plantations in these United Colonies, it is agreed that neither the Massachusetts, Plymouth, Connecticut, nor New Haven, nor any of the members of them, shall at any time hereafter *begin, undertake, or engage themselves, or this Confederation, or any part thereof in any war whatsoever* (sudden exigencies, with the necessary consequents thereof excepted), which are also to be moderated as much as the case will permit, without the consent and agreement of the forementioned eight Commissioners, or at least six of them, as in the sixth article is provided . . . [Thorpe 80]

Charles II, Charter of Carolina, March 24, 1663:

And because that in so remote a country, and scituate among so many barbarous nations, and the invasions as well of salvages as of other enemies, pirates and robbers, may probably be feared; therefore we have given, and for us, our heirs and successors do give power [to the Carolina proprietors] . . . by themselves, or their captains, or other their officers, to levy, muster and train all sorts of men, of what condition or wheresoever born, in the said province for the time being, and to *make war* and pursue the enemies aforesaid, as well by sea as by land, yea, even without the limits of the said province, and by God's assistance to vanquish and take them, and being taken to put them to death by the law of war, or to save them at their pleasure; and to do all and every other thing, which unto the charge of a captain general of an army belongeth, or hath accustomed to belong, as fully and freely as any captain general of an army hath or ever had the same. [Thorpe 2751]

New Jersey Proprietors, Concession and Agreement, February 10, 1664:

[The Assembly shall have power] By act (as aforesaid) to constitute train'd bands and companies, with the number of soldiers, for the safety, strength and defence of the said Province; and of the forts, castles, cities, &c. To suppress all mutinies and rebellions; to *make war* offensive and defensive with all Indians, strangers and foreigners, as they shall see cause; and to pursue an enemy as well by sea as by land, if need be, out of the limits and jurisdictions of the said Province, with the particular consent of the Governor, and under his conduct, or of our commander in chief, or whom he shall appoint. [Thorpe 2539]

Charles II, Charter of Carolina, June 30, 1665:

And because that in so remote a country, and situate among so many barbarous nations, the invasions of savages and other enemies, pirates and robbers, may probably be feared; therefore, we have given, and for us, our heirs and successors, do give power by these presents [to the Carolina proprietors] . . . by themselves, or their Captains, or other officers, to levy, muster, and train up all sorts of men, of what condition soever, or wheresoever born, whether in the said province, or elsewhere, for the time being; and to *make war,* and pursue the enemies aforesaid, as well by sea, as by land; yea, even without the limits of the said province, and, by God's assistance, to vanquish and take them; and being taken, to put them to death, by the law of war, and to save them at their pleasure, and to do all and every other thing, which to the charge and office of a Captain-General of an army, hath had the same. [Thorpe 2769–70]

Fundamental Constitutions of Carolina, March 1, 1669:

[Article 50:] The grand council shall consist of the palatine and seven proprietors, and the forty-two councillors of the several proprietors' courts, who shall have power to determine any controversy that may arise between any of the proprietors' courts, about their respective jurisdictions, or between the members of the same court, about their manner and methods of proceedings; to *make peace and war*, leagues, treaties, &c., with any of the neighbor Indians; to issue out their general orders to the constable's and admiral's courts, for the raising, disposing, or disbanding the forces, by land or by sea. [Thorpe 2778–79]

Charles II, Charter of Pennsylvania, February 28, 1681:

[1] Provided alwayes, and our will and pleasure is, that neither the said William Penn, nor his heires, or any other the inhabitants of the said Province, shall at any time hereafter have or maintain any Correspondence with any other king, prince, or State, or with any of theire subjects, who shall then *be in Warr* against us, our heires or Successors; Nor shall the said William Penn, or his heires, or any other the Inhabitants of the said Province, *make Warre* or doe any act of Hostility against any other king, prince, or State, or any of theire Subjects, who shall then be in league or amity with us, our heires or successors. [Thorpe 3041–42]

[2] And, because in soe remote a Countrey, and scituate neare many Barbarous Nations, the incursions as well of the Savages themselves, as of other enemies, pirates and robbers, may probably be feared; Therefore Wee have gven, and for us, our heires and Successors, Doe give power by these presents unto the said William Penn, his heires and assignes, by themselves or theire Captaines or other their Officers, to levy, muster and traine all sorts of men, of what condition soever, or wheresoever borne, in the said Province of Pensilvania, for the time being, and to *make Warre,* and to pursue the enemies and Robbers aforesaid, as well by Sea as by Land, even without the Limitts of the said Province, and by God's assistance to vanquish and take them, and being taken to put them to death by the Law of Warre, or to save them, att theire pleasure, and to doe all and every other Thing which to the Charge and Office of a Captaine-Generall of an Army belongeth or hath accustomed to belong, as fully and freely as any Captaine-Generall of an Army hath ever had the same. [Thorpe 3042]

Government of West New Jersey, November 25, 1681:

That it shall not be lawful for the Governor of the said Province, his heirs or successors for the time being, and Council, or any of them, at any time or times hereafter, to *make or raise war* upon any accounts or pretence whatsoever, or to raise any military forces within the Province aforesaid, without the consent of the General Free Assembly for the time being. [Thorpe 2566]

Fundamental Constitutions of East New Jersey, 1683:

[Article 7:] [The Assembly shall have power] . . . to suppress all mutinies and rebellions; to *make war offensive and defensive,* against all and every one that shall infest the said Province, not only to keep the enemy out of their limits, but also, in case of necessity, the enemy by sea and land to pursue out of the limits and jurisdiction of the said Province. . . . [Thorpe 2576]

The Albany Plan of Union, July 10, 1754:

POWER OF PRESIDENT-GENERAL AND GRAND COUNCIL; TREATIES OF PEACE AND *WAR*

That the President-General, with the advice of the Grand Council, hold or direct all Indian treaties in which the general interest of the colonies may be concerned; and make peace or *declare war* with Indian nations. [Thorpe 84]

Benjamin Franklin, Proposed Articles of Confederation, July 21, 1775:

[Article 5:] That the Power and Duty of the Congress shall extend to the *Determining on War and Peace,* to sending and receiving Ambassadors, and entring into Alliances, the Reconciliation with Great Britain; the Settling all Disputes and Differences between Colony and Colony about limits or any other cause if such should arise; and the Planting of new Colonies when proper. . . . [PBF22 122–23]

[Article 10:] No Colony shall *engage in an offensive War* with any Nation of Indians without the Consent of the Congress, or great Council above-mentioned, who are first to consider the Justice and Necessity of such *War.* [PBF22 124]

Thomas Paine, *Common Sense*, January 9, 1776:

[1] . . . The laying of a country desolate with fire and sword, *declaring war* against the natural rights of all mankind, and extirpating the defenders thereof from the face of the earth, is the concern of every man to whom nature hath given the power of feeling . . . [CWTP1 3–4]

[2] In England a king hath little more to do than to *make war* and give away places; which in plain terms, is to empoverish the nation and set it together by the ears. . . . [CWTP1 16]

[3] But Britain is the parent country, say some. Then the more shame upon her conduct. Even brutes do not devour their young, nor savages *make war* upon their families . . . [CWTP1 19]

[4] Firstly—It is the custom of nations, when any two are *at war,* for some other powers, not *engaged in the quarrel,* to step in as mediators, and bring about the preliminaries of a peace: But while America calls herself the subject of

Great Britain, no power, however well disposed she may be, can offer her mediation. . . . [CWTP1 39]

South Carolina Constitution, March 26, 1776:

[Preamble:] . . . And whereas large reenforcements of troops and ships have been ordered and are daily expected in America for *carrying on war* against each of the united colonies by the most vigorous exertions. . . . [Thorpe 3243]

[Article 26:] That the president and commander-in-chief shall have no power to *make war* or peace, or enter into any final treaty, without the consent of the general assembly and legislative council. [Thorpe 3247]

New Jersey Constitution, July 2, 1776:

[Preamble:] Whereas all the constitutional authority ever possessed by the kings of Great Britain over these colonies, or their other dominions, was, by compact, derived from the people, and held of them, for the common interest of the whole society; allegiance and protection are, in the nature of things, reciprocal ties, each equally depending upon the other, and liable to be dissolved by the others being refused or withdrawn. And whereas George the Third, king of Great Britain, has refused protection to the good people of these colonies; and, by assenting to sundry acts of the British Parliament, attempted to subject them to the absolute dominion of that body; and has also *made war* upon them, in the most cruel and unnatural manner, for no other cause, than asserting their just rights—all civil authority under him is necessarily at an end, and a dissolution of government in each colony has consequently taken place. [Thorpe 2594]

United States Declaration of Independence, July 4, 1776:

[1] . . . He [the King] has abdicated Government here, by declaring us out of his Protection and *waging War* against us . . .

[2] . . . and that as Free and Independent States, they have full Power to *levy War,* conclude Peace, contract Alliances, establish Commerce, and to do all other Acts and Things which Independent States may of right do.—And for the support of this Declaration, with a firm reliance on the Protection of Divine Providence, we mutually pledge to each other our Lives, our Fortunes and our sacred Honor.

United States Continental Congress, Draft Articles of Confederation, July 12, 1776:

[Article 13:] No Colony or Colonies shall *engage in any War* without the previous Consent of the United States assembled, unless such Colony or Colonies be actually invaded by Enemies, or shall have received certain Advice of a Resolution being formed by some Nations of Indians to invade such Colony or Colonies, and the Danger is so imminent, as not to admit of a Delay, till the other Colonies can be consulted: Nor shall any Colony or Colonies grant Commissions to any Ships or Vessels of War, nor Letters of Marque or Reprisal, except it be after a *Declaration of War* by the United States assembled, and then only against the Kingdom or State and the Subjects thereof, against which *War has been so declared,* and under such Regulations as shall be established by the United States assembled. [DHRC1 81]

[Article 18:] The United States assembled shall have the sole and exclusive Right and Power of *determining on Peace and War,* except in the Cases mentioned in the thirteenth Article . . . [DHRC1 82]

[*Ibid.*:] But the United States assembled shall never impose or levy any Taxes or Duties, except in managing the Post-Office, nor interfere in the internal Police of any Colony, any further than such Police may be affected by the Articles of Confederation. The United States assembled shall never *engage the United Colonies in a War,* nor grant Letters of Marque and Reprisal in Time of Peace, nor enter into Treaties or Alliances, nor coin Money nor regulate the Value thereof, nor agree upon nor fix the Sums and Expences necessary for the Defence and Welfare of the United Colonies, or any of them, nor emit Bills, nor borrow Money on the Credit of the United Colonies, nor raise Naval Forces, nor agree upon the Number of Land Forces to be raised, unless the Delegates of nine Colonies freely assent to the same . . . [DHRC1 83–84]

Pennsylvania Constitution, September 28, 1776:

[Preamble:] . . . and the said king has not only withdrawn that protection, but commenced, and still continues to *carry on,* with unabated vengeance, *a most cruel and unjust war* against them, employing therein, not only the troops of Great Britain, but foreign mercenaries, savages and slaves, for the avowed purpose of reducing them to a total and abject submission to the despotic domination of the British parliament, with many other acts of tyranny, (more fully set forth in the declaration of Congress) whereby all allegiance and fealty to the said king and his successors, are dissolved and at an end, and all power and authority derived from him ceased in these colonies. [Thorpe 3081]

North Carolina Constitution, December 18, 1776:

[Frame of Government, Preamble:] Whereas allegiance and protection are, in their nature, reciprocal and the one should of right be refused when the other is withdrawn: And whereas George the Third, King of Great Britain, and late Sovereign of the British American Colonies, hath not only withdrawn from them his protection, but, by an act of the British Legislature, declared the inhabitants of these States out of the protection of the British crown, and all their property, found upon the high seas, liable to be seized and confiscated to the uses mentioned in the said act; and the said George the Third has also sent fleets and armies to *prosecute a cruel war* against them, for the purpose of reducing the inhabitants of the said Colonies to a state of abject slavery; in consequence whereof, all government under the said King, within the said Colonies, hath ceased, and a total dissolution of government in many of them hath taken place.

[Thorpe 2789]

Vermont Constitution, July 8, 1777:

[Preamble:] And whereas, the inhabitants of this State have (in consideration of protection only) heretofore acknowledged allegiance to the King of Great Britain, and the said King has not only withdrawn that protection, but commenced, and still continues to *carry on,* with unabated vengeance, a most *cruel and unjust war* against them; employing therein, not only the troops of Great Britain, but foreign mercenaries, savages and slaves, for the avowed purpose of reducing them to a total and abject submission to the despotic domination of the British parliament, with many other acts of tyranny, (more fully set forth in the declaration of Congress) whereby all allegiance and fealty to the said King and his successors, are dissolved and at an end . . . [Thorpe 3737]

United States Articles of Confederation, November 15, 1777:

[Article VI:] No state shall *engage in any war* without the consent of the united states in congress assembled, unless such state be actually invaded by enemies, or shall have received certain advice of a resolution being formed by some nation of Indians to invade such state, and the danger is so imminent as not to admit of a delay, till the united states in congress assembled can be consulted; nor shall any state grant commissions to any ships or vessels of war, nor letters of marque or reprisal, except it be after a *declaration of war* by the united states in congress assembled, and then only against the kingdom or state and the subjects thereof, against which *war has been so declared,* and under such regulations as shall be established by the united states in congress assembled . . .

[Article IX:] The united states in congress assembled, shall have the sole and exclusive right and power of *determining on peace and war,* except in the cases mentioned in the sixth article . . .

[*Ibid.*:] The united states in congress assembled shall never *engage in a war,* nor grant letters of marque and reprisal in time of peace, nor enter into any treaties or alliances . . .

Massachusetts Constitution, March 2, 1780:

[Frame of Government, Chapter II:1:7:] [The Governor as commander in chief shall have authority] to use and exercise, over the army and navy, and over the militia in actual service, the law-martial, in time of *war* or invasion, and also in time of rebellion, *declared by the legislature to exist,* as occasion shall necessarily require . . . [Thorpe 1901]

New Hampshire Constitution, June 2, 1784:

[Form of Government:] [The State President shall have power] to use and exercise, over the army and navy, and over the militia in actual service, the law-martial, in time of *war* or invasion, and also in time of rebellion, *declared by the legislature to exist,* as occasion shall necessarily require . . . [Thorpe 2464]

Vermont Constitution, July 4, 1786:

[Preamble:] And whereas the inhabitants of this State have (in consideration of protection only) heretofore acknowledged allegiance to the King of Great-Britain: and the said King has not only withdrawn that protection, but commenced and still continues to *carry on,* with unabated vengeance, a most *cruel and unjust war* against them; employing therein not only the troops of Great-Britain, but foreign mercenaries, savages, and slaves, for the avowed purpose of reducing them to a total and abject submission to the despotic domination of the British Parliament, with many more acts of tyranny, (more fully set forth in the Declaration of Congress) whereby all allegiance and fealty to the said King and his Successors are dissolved and at an end . . . [Thorpe 3749–50]

Alexander Hamilton's Plan of Union, June 18, 1787:

[1] . . . The Governor to have a negative upon all laws about to be passed—and to have the execution of all laws passed—to be the Commander in Chief of the land and naval forces and of the Militia of the United States—to have the direction of *war when authorized or begun* . . . [DHRC1 254]

[2] The Senate to have the sole power of *declaring war*—the power of advising and approving all treaties—the power of approving or rejecting all appointments of officers except the heads or chiefs of the departments of finance *war,* and foreign affairs. [DHRC1 254]

United States Confederation Congress, The Northwest Ordinance, July 13, 1787:

[Article 3:] Religion, morality, and knowledge being necessary to good government and the happiness of mankind, schools and the means of education shall forever be encouraged. The utmost good faith shall always be observed towards the Indians; their lands and property shall never be taken from them without their consent; and in their property, rights and liberty they never shall be invaded or disturbed, unless in *just and lawful wars authorized by Congress;* but laws founded in justice and humanity shall, from time to time, be made, for preventing wrongs being done to them, and for preserving peace and friendship with them. [Thorpe 961]

James Wilson, Speech on the Federal Constitution, October 6, 1787:

This constitution, it has been further urged, is of a pernicious tendency, because it tolerates a standing army in the time of peace. This has always been a popular topic of declamation: and yet I do not know a nation in the world, which has not found it necessary and useful to maintain the appearance of strength in a season of the most profound tranquility. Nor is it a novelty with us; for under the present articles of confederation, congress certainly possesses this reprobated power: and the exercise of it is proved at this moment by the cantonments along the banks of the Ohio. But what would be our national situation, were it otherwise? Every principle of policy must be subverted, and the government must *declare war* before they are prepared to carry it on. Whatever may be the provocation, however important the object in view, and however necessary dispatch and secrecy may be, still the *declaration* must precede the preparation, and the energy will be informed of your intention, not only before you are equipped for an attack, but even before you are fortified for a defence. . . .
[Ford 157–58]

Richard Henry Lee [?], "The Federal Farmer," No. 1, October 8, 1787:

There are three different forms of free government under which the United States may exist as one nation; and now is, perhaps, the time to determine to which we will direct our views. 1. Distinct republics connected under a federal head. In this case the respective state governments must be the principal guardians of the peoples rights, and exclusively regulate their internal police; in them must rest the balance of government. The congress of the states, or federal head, must consist of delegates amenable to, and removable by the respective states: This congress must have general directing powers; powers to require men and monies of the states; *to make treaties; peace and war;* to direct the operations of armies, &c. Under this federal modification of government, the powers of congress would be rather advisary or recommendatory than coercive. . . . [Ford 286]

Edmund Randolph, Letter on the Federal Constitution, October 10, 1787:

From thence it will follow, that the operations of peace and war will be clogged without regular advances of money, and that these will be slow indeed, if dependent on supplication alone. For what better name do requisitions deserve, which may be evaded or opposed, without the fear of coercion? But although coercion is an indispensable ingredient, it ought not to be directe against a state, as a state; it being impossible to attempt it except by blockading the trade of the delinquent, or *carrying war* into its bowels. [DHRC8 266]

John Jay, *The Federalist*, No. 2, October 31, 1787:

Similar sentiments have hitherto prevailed among all orders and denominations of men among us. To all general purposes we have uniformly been one people; each individual citizen everywhere enjoying the same national rights, privileges, and protection. As a nation we have *made peace and war;* as a nation we have vanquished our common enemies; as a nation we have formed alliances, and made treaties, and entered into various compacts and conventions with foreign states. [Fed. 94]

Pelatiah Webster, *The Weakness of Brutus Exposed*, November 4, 1787:

Another benefit they [the states] will receive from the controul of the supreme power of the union is this, viz. they will be restrained from making angry, oppressive, and destructive laws, from *declaring ruinous wars* with their neighbours, from fomenting quarrels and controversies, &c. all which ever weaken a state, tend to its fatal disorder, and often end in its dissolution. Righteousness exalts and strengthens a nation; but sin is a reproach and weakening of any people. [Ford 128]

John Jay, *The Federalist*, No. 4, November 7, 1787:

It is too true, however disgraceful it may be to human nature, that nations in general will *make war* whenever they have a prospect of getting any thing by it; nay, absolute monarchs will often *make war* when their nations are to get nothing by it, but for purposes and objects merely personal, such as a thirst for military glory, revenge for personal affronts, ambition, or private compacts to aggrandize or support their particular families or partisans. These and a variety of other motives, which affect only the mind of the sovereign, often lead him to *engage in wars* not sanctified by justice or the voice and interests of his people. But, independent of these *inducements to war,* which are more prevalent in absolute monarchies, but which well deserve our attention, there are others which affect nations as often as kings; and some of them will on examination be found to grow out of our relative situation and circumstances. [Fed. 101]

Alexander Hamilton, *The Federalist*, No. 6, November 14, 1787:

[1] Sparta, Athens, Rome, and Carthage were all republics; two of them, Athens and Carthage, of the commercial kind. Yet were they as often *engaged in wars,* offensive and defensive, as the neighboring monarchies of the same times. Sparta

was little better than a well-regulated camp; and Rome was never sated of carnage and conquest. [Fed. 111]

[2] In the government of Britain the representatives of the people compose one branch of the national legislature. Commerce has been for ages the predominant pursuit of that country. Few nations, nevertheless, have been more frequently *engaged in war;* and the wars in which that kingdom has been engaged have, in numerous instances, proceeded from the people. [Fed. 112]

Alexander Hamilton, *The Federalist*, No. 7, November 17, 1787:

It is sometimes asked, with an air of seeming triumph, what inducements could the States have, if disunited, to *make war* upon each other? It would be a full answer to this question to say—precisely the same inducements which have, at different times, deluged in blood all the nations in the world. But, unfortunately for us, the question admits of a more particular answer. There are causes of differences within our immediate contemplation, of the tendency of which, even under the restraints of a federal constitution, we have had sufficient experience to enable us to form a judgment of what might be expected if those restraints were removed. [Fed. 113–14]

Alexander Hamilton, *The Federalist*, No. 16, December 4, 1787:

. . . It is not probable, considering the genius of this country, that the complying States would often be inclined to support the authority of the Union by *engaging in a war* against the non-complying States. They would always be more ready to pursue the milder course of putting themselves upon an equal footing with the delinquent members by an imitation of their example. . . . [Fed. 164]

"Americanus," December 5, 1787:

When we were *engaged* in an obstinate and perilous *war,* nobly contending for the sacred rights of humanity, it was conceived essentially necessary to consolidate our strength by a foederal union. Under the auspices of this confederacy, defective as it was, and by the glorious exertions of as virtuous an army as ever shed blood in the cause of freedom, we secured our liberties and established our independence. But experience soon convinced us, that the powers of the confederation were inadequate to the purposes, for which it was instituted. . . .
[DHRC8 201]

James Madison, *The Federalist*, No. 18, December 7, 1787:

The members [of the Greek Amphictyonic League] retained the character of independent and sovereign states, and had equal votes in the federal council. This council had a general authority to propose and resolve whatever it judged necessary for the common welfare of Greece; *to declare and carry on war;* to decide, in the last resort, all controversies between the members; to fine the aggressing party; to employ the whole force of the confederacy against the disobedient; to admit new members. . . . [Fed. 171]

James Madison, *The Federalist*, No. 19, December 8, 1787:

The diet [of the German Empire] possesses the general power of legislating for the empire; of *making war and peace;* contracting alliances; assessing quotas of troops and money; constructing fortresses; regulating coin; admitting new members; and subjecting disobedient members to the ban of the empire, by which the party is degraded from his sovereign rights and his possessions for' feited. . . . [Fed. 177]

James Madison, *The Federalist*, No. 20, December 11, 1787:

The States-General [of the Netherlands] have authority to enter into treaties and alliances; to *make war and peace;* to raise armies and equip fleets; to ascertain quotas and demand contributions. In all these cases, however, unanimity and the sanction of their constituents are requisite. . . . [Fed. 182]

Alexander Hamilton, *The Federalist*, No. 22, December 14, 1787:

Suppose, for instance, we were *engaged in a war,* in conjunction with one foreign nation, against another. Suppose the necessity of our situation demanded peace, and the interest or ambition of our ally led him to seek the *prosecution of war,* with views that might justify us in making separate terms. In such a state of things, this ally of ours would evidently find it much easier, by his bribes and intrigues, to tie up the hands of government from making peacc, where two thirds of all the votes wcre requisite to that object, than where a simple majority would suffice. . . . [Fed. 195–96]

Alexander Hamilton, *The Federalist*, No. 26, December 22, 1787:

. . . As incident to the undefined power of *making war,* an acknowledged prerogative of the crown, Charles II. had, by his own authority, kept on foot in time of peace a body of 5,000 regular troops. And this number James II. increased to 30,000; who were paid out of his civil list. At the revolution, to abolish the exercise of so dangerous an authority, it became an article of the Bill of Rights then framed, that "the raising or keeping a standing army within the kingdom in time of peace, unless with the consent of Parliament, was against law."

[Fed. 214–15]

Alexander Hamilton, *The Federalist*, No. 30, December 28, 1787:

Let us attend to what would be the effects of this situation in the very first *war* in which we should happen to be *engaged.* We will presume, for argument's sake, that the revenue arising from the impost duties answers the purposes of a provision for the public debt and of a peace establishment for the Union. Thus circumstanced, a war breaks out. What would be the probable conduct of the government in such an emergency? . . . [Fed. 235]

Alexander Hamilton, *The Federalist*, No. 34, January 4, 1788:

In the kingdom of Great Britain, where all the ostentatious apparatus of monarchy is to be provided for, not above a fifteenth part of the annual income of the nation is appropriated to the class of expenses last mentioned [internal affairs]; the other fourteen fifteenths are absorbed in the payment of the interest of debts contracted for carrying on the *wars* in which that country has been *engaged,* and in the maintenance of fleets and armies. . . . [Fed. 251]

George Nicholas [?], "The State Soldier," No. 1, January 16, 1788:

Long had the friends to the late REVOLUTION observed how incomplete the business was when we contented ourselves under that form of government, after the return of peace, which was only designed to bind us together the more effectually to *carry on the war*—and which could not be expected to operate effectually in many cases, the expence of which no one at that time could foresee. . . . [DHRC8 304–305]

James Madison, *The Federalist*, No. 41, January 19, 1788:

[1] The powers falling within the first class are those of *declaring war* and granting letters of marque; of providing armies and fleets; of regulating and calling forth the militia; of levying and borrowing money. [Fed. 294–95]

[2] Is the power of *declaring war* necessary? No man will answer this question in the negative. It would be superfluous, therefore, to enter into a proof of the affirmative. The existing Confederation establishes this power in the most ample form. [Fed. 295]

James Madison, *The Federalist*, No. 44, January 25, 1788:

The prohibition against treaties, alliances, and confederations makes a part of the existing articles of Union; and for reasons which need no explanation, is copied into the new Constitution. The prohibition of letters of marque is another part of the old system, but is somewhat extended in the new. According to the former, letters of marque could be granted by the States after a *declaration of war;* according to the latter, these licenses must be obtained, as well during war as previous to its *declaration,* from the government of the United States. This alteration is fully justified by the advantage of uniformity in all points which relate to foreign powers; and of immediate responsibility to the nation in all those for whose conduct the nation itself is to be responsible. [Fed. 317–18]

"Civis Rusticus," January 30, 1788:

The infraction of the present treaty shews the necessity of treaties having the force of laws—When any publicity of them will not be injurious to America, they will be submitted to the representatives in Congress. The King of England can make peace or *declare war;* can make treaties, but, whenever the Commons disapprove of the measures by which these have been brought about, we know the consequences . . . [DHRC8 337]

"Nov. Anglus," January 30, 1788:

A people thus attacked, on all sides, by three powerful nations (through their own imprudence), and *engaged,* at the same time, *in a civil war* at three thousand miles distance, with a part of their own nation, and who have extricated themselves from such complicated difficulties, and who, notwithstanding their lots, have maintained with unabated splendour their active, national power, would have deserved the most honourable wreath of military laurels had their exertions been made in a better cause. [DHRC8 340–41]

Alexander C. Hanson, *Remarks on the Proposed Plan of a Federal Government*, c. January 31, 1788:

[1] Suppose a limitation in time of peace. What then is to be done on the prospect of a war? Should you make the distinction between profound peace and a threatened war, who is there, but congress, to determine on the exigency? If you make no distinction, then it will be expedient to *declare war,* at the instant in which the danger shall be conceived, in order that it may be lawful to prepare for only a just defence. . . . [Ford 235]

[2] . . . She [Maryland] shall not, without consent of congress, lay any duty on tonnage, keep troops or ships of war, in time of peace; enter into any agreement, or compact, with another state, or with a foreign power; or *engage in war,* unless actually invaded, or in such imminent danger, as will not admit of delay. [Ford 251]

Luther Martin, "Genuine Information," No. 10, February 1, 1788:

To save the citizens of the respective States from this disagreeable dilemma, and to secure them from being punishable as traitors to the United States when acting expressly in obedience to the authority of their own State, I wished to have obtained as an amendment to the third section of this article the following clause: "Provided that no act or acts done by one or more of the States against the United States, or by any citizen of any one of the United States under the authority of one or more of the said States, shall be deemed treason or punished as such; but in case of *war being levied* by one or more of the States against the United States the conduct of each party towards the other, and their adherents respectively, shall be regulated by the laws of war and of nations."

[DHRC16 11]

David Ramsay, "Civis," February 4, 1788:

When you authorised Congress to borrow money, and to contract debts for *carrying on the late war,* you could not intend to abridge them of the means of paying their engagements, made on your account. . . . [DHRC16 22]

"A Virginian," February 13, 1788:

. . . 2dly. I think by the plan in its present form, the governors which are thereby to be set up at Philadelphia, will have it in their power to *make war* on any terms they please: If so, no doubt but they may point out the part every man shall take therein, or be liable to such fines and penalties as they may think proper to impose . . . [DHRC8 367]

Alexander White, "To the Citizens of Virginia," February 22, 1788:

[Quoting Polybius]: " . . . It was the [Roman] senate which sent ambassadors, *declared war* against the enemies of the State, granted audience and gave answer to the deputies and ambassadors of foreign people and princes. It was the senate likewise which sent commissioners abroad to hear the complaints of the allies, to regulate the limits and the frontiers, to see good order observed in the provinces, and to decide the pretensions of States and Kingdoms." [DHRC8 407]

"The Impartial Examiner," No. 1, February 27, 1788:

. . . and whoever will take the trouble to examine, will find that by far the greater part of the different nations, who have fallen from the glorious state of liberty, owe their ruin to standing armies. It has been urged that they are necessary to provide against sudden attacks. Would not a well regulated militia, duly trained to discipline, afford ample security? Such, I conceive, to be the best, the surest means of protection, which a free people can have when not actually *engaged in war*. This kind of defence is attended with two advantages superior to any others . . . [DHRC8 422]

Alexander White, "To the Citizens of Virginia," February 29, 1788:

. . . Should it remain with the several states to raise or not to raise men and money, our confederation would be no more than a treaty of friendship and alliance between independent nations. The present Congress has the same power, and so I believe has the supreme council of every confederacy, the difference is, when the present Congress shall find it necessary to provide for our defence, and shall have *declared war,* and proportioned the men and money to be raised by each state, they have not the means to carry their acts into effect, and in case of failure of any of the states there is no constitutional remedy, the willing states must bear the whole burden, or have recourse to arms against the delinquents. . . . [DHRC8 438–39]

"A Federal Republican," March 5, 1788:

By the articles of Confederation, the Congress of the United States was vested with powers for conducting the common concerns of the continent. They had the sole and exclusive right and power of *determining on peace and war;* of sending and receiving ambassadors; of entering into treaties and alliances, and of pointing out the respective quotas of men and money which each State should furnish. But it was expressly provided that the money to be supplied by each State should be raised by the authority and direction of the Legislature thereof: Thus reserving to the States the important privilege of levying taxes upon their citizens in such manner as might be most conformable to their peculiar circumstances and form of government. With powers thus constituted, was Congress enabled to unite the general exertions of the continent in the cause of liberty, and *to carry us triumphantly through a long and bloody war.* It was not until some time after peace and a glorious independence had been established, that defects were discovered in that system of foederal government which had procured to us those blessings. . . . [DHRC8 457–58]

James Iredell, "Marcus," No. 4, March 12, 1788:

. . . What sort of a government must that be, which, upon the most certain intelligence that hostilities were meditated against it, could take no method for its defence, till after a formal *declaration of war,* or the enemy's standard was actually fixed upon the shore. The first has for some time been out of fashion; but if it had not, the restraint these gentlemen recommend, would certainly have brought it into disuse with every Power who meant to make war upon America. They would not be such fools as to give us the only warning we had informed them we would accept of, before we would take any steps to counteract their designs. . . . [DHRC16 385]

Alexander Hamilton, *The Federalist*, No. 69, March 14, 1788:

[1] . . . The President is to be commander-in-chief of the army and navy of the United States. In this respect his authority would be nominally the same with that of the king of Great Britain, but in substance much inferior to it. It would amount to nothing more than the supreme command and direction of the military and naval forces, as first General and admiral of the Confederacy; while that of

the British king extends to the *declaring of war* and to the raising and regulating of fleets and armies,—all which, by the Constitution under consideration, would appertain to the legislature. . . . [Fed. 446]

[2] . . . The better to judge of this matter, it will be necessary to recollect, that, by the proposed Constitution, the offence of treason is limited "to *levying war* upon the United States, and adhering to their enemies, giving them aid and comfort"; and that by the laws of New York it is confined within similar bounds. [Fed. 447]

[3] The President of the United States would be an officer elected by the people for four years; the king of Great Britain is a perpetual and hereditary prince. The one would be amenable to personal punishment and disgrace; the person of the other is sacred and inviolable. The one would have a qualified negative upon the acts of the legislative body; the other has an absolute negative. The one would have a right to command the military and naval forces of the nation; the other, in addition to this right, possesses that of *declaring war,* and of raising and regulating fleets and armies by his own authority. . . . [Fed. 450]

John Jay, *An Address to the People of the State of New York*, c. April 15, 1788:

By the Confederation as it now stands, the direction of general and national affairs is committed to a single body of men, viz. the Congress. They may *make war,* but are not empowered to raise men or money to carry it on. They may make peace, but without power to see the terms of it observed. . . . [Ford 72]

Melancton Smith, *An Address to the People of the State of New York*, c. April 1788:

[1] . . . There can be no reason to apprehend, that the other states will *make war* with us for not receiving the constitution proposed, until it is amended, but from one of the following causes: either that they will have just cause to do it, or that they have a disposition to do it. . . . [Ford 96]

[2] As to the inclination of the states to *make war* with us, for declining to accede, until it [the Constitution] is amended, this is highly improbable, not only because such a procedure would be most unjust and unreasonable in itself, but for various other reasons. . . . [Ford 97]

[3] . . . Can it then be presumed, that a country divided among themselves, upon a question where even the advocates for it, admit the system they contend for needs amendments, would *make war* upon a sister state, who only insist that that should be done before they receive it, which it is granted ought to be done after, and where it is confessed no obligation lies upon them by compact to do it. Can it, I say, be imagined, that in such a case, they would *make war* on a sister state? The idea is preposterous and chimerical. [Ford 98]

[4] . . . There are other governments also now existing, which are in a similar condition with our's, with regard to several particulars, on account of which this author denominates it "new and wonderful."—The king of Great Britain "*may make war,* but has not power to raise money to carry it on." He may borrow money, but it is without the means of repayment, &c. For these he is dependent on his parliament. But it is needless to add on this head, because it is admitted that the powers of the general government ought to be increased in several of the particulars this author instances. But these things are mentioned to shew, that the outcry made against the confederation, as being a system new, unheard of, and absurd, is really without foundation. [Ford 112]

[5] . . . With regard to the Algerines, there are but two ways in which their ravages can be prevented. The one is, by a successful *war* against them, and the other is by treaty. The powers of Congress under the confederation are completely competent either to *declare war* against them, or to form treaties. Money, it is true, is necessary to do both these. This only brings us to this conclusion, that the great defect in our present government, is the want of powers to provide money for the public exigencies. I am willing to grant reasonable powers, on this score, but not unlimited ones . . . [Ford 113]

John Dickinson, "Fabius," No. 5, 1788:

"The Achaean league" seems to be the next in dignity. It was at first, small, consisting of few states: afterwards, very extensive, constituting of many. In their diet or Congress, they enacted laws, disposed of vacant employments, *declared war,* made peace, entered into alliances, compelled every state of the union to obey its ordinances, and managed other affairs. Not only their laws, but their magistrates, council, judges, money, weights and measures, were the same. So uniform were they, that all seemed to be but one state. . . .

[Ford 191]

John Dickinson, "Fabius," No. 6, 1788:

[Quoted from Lord Belhaven's Speech in the House of Lords:] I think, I see a free and independent kingdom delivering up that, which all the world hath been fighting for since the days of Nimrod; yea, that, for which most of all the empires, kingdoms, states, principalities, and dukedoms of Europe, are at this very time *engaged in the most bloody and cruel wars* that ever were; to wit, a power to manage their own affairs by themselves, without the assistance and council of any other. [Ford 196]

John Dickinson, "Fabius," No. 9, 1788:

. . . Is there more danger to our liberty, from such a president as we are to have, than to that of Britons from an hereditary monarch with a vast revenue—absolute in the erection and disposal of offices, and in the exercise of the whole executive power—in the command of the militia, fleets, and armies, and the direction of their operations—in the establishments of fairs and markets, the regulation of weights and measures, and coining of money—who can call parliaments with a breath, and dissolve them with a nod—who can, at his will, *make war,* peace, and treaties irrevocably binding the nation—and who can grant pardons and titles of nobility, as it pleases him? . . . [Ford 212]

WELFARE

United States Constitution, September 17, 1787:

[Preamble:] WE THE PEOPLE of the United States, in Order to form a more perfect Union, establish Justice, insure domestic Tranquility, provide for the common defence, promote the *general Welfare,* and secure the Blessings of Liberty to ourselves and our Posterity, do ordain and establish this Constitution for the United States of America.

[Article I, Section 8:] The Congress shall have Power To lay and collect Taxes, Duties, Imposts and Excises, to pay the Debts and provide for the common Defence and *general Welfare* of the United States; but all Duties, Imposts and Excises shall be uniform throughout the United States.

* * * * *

James I, Third Charter of Virginia, 1611–1612:

[1] And further, Our Will and Pleasure is, and We do by these Presents, Grant and Confirm, for the Good and *Welfare* of the said Plantation, and that Posterity may hereafter know who have adventured and not been sparing of their Purses in such a noble and generous Action for the general Good of their Country, and at the Request and with the Consent of the Company aforesaid . . .

[Thorpe 3804]

[2] . . . [The General Court] shall likewise have full Power and Authority, to ordain and make such Laws and Ordinances, for the Good and *Welfare* of the said Plantation, as to them from Time to Time, shall be thought requisite and meet: So always, as the same be not contrary to the Laws and Statutes of this our Realm of England . . . [Thorpe 3806]

[3] . . . And yet nevertheless, we are contented and pleased, for the Good and *Welfare* of the said Plantation, that the said Treasurer and Company shall, for the Dispatch and Finishing of the said Lottery or Lotteries, have six Months Warning after the said Year ended, before our Will and Pleasure shall, for and

on that Behalf, be construed, deemed, and adjudged, to be in any wise altered and determined. [Thorpe 3809]

Charter of the Dutch West India Company, June 3, 1621:

[Article 1:] Be it known, that we knowing the prosperity of these countries, and the *welfare* of their inhabitants depends principally on navigation and trade, which in all former times by the said Countries were carried on happily, and with a great blessing to all countries and kingdoms . . . [Thorpe 59]

[*Ibid.*:] . . . and for that end there shall be erected one General Company, which we out of special regard to their common well-being, and to keep and preserve the inhabitants of those places in good, trade and *welfare,* will maintain and strengthen with our Help, Favour and assistance as far as the present state and condition of this Country will admit . . . [Thorpe 59]

[Article 45:] . . . ordaining that the same shall be observed and kept by all the magistrates, officers and subjects of the United Netherlands, without doing anything contrary thereto directly or indirectly, either within or out of these Netherlands, on penalty of being punished both in life and goods as obstacles to the *common welfare* of this country, and transgressors of our ordinance . . . [Thorpe 67]

Charles I, Charter of Massachusetts Bay, March 4, 1629:

[The Governor and Company shall have power] . . . to make Lawes and Ordinances for the Good and *Welfare* of the saide Company, and for the Government and ordering of the saide Landes and Plantacon, and the People inhabiting and to inhabite the same, as to them from tyme to tyme shalbe thought meete, soe as such Lawes and Ordinances be not contrarie or repugnant to the Lawes and Statuts of this our Realme of England. . . . [Thorpe 1853]

Charles I, Grant of the Province of Maine, April 3, 1639:

To all to whom these Presents shall come Greeting Whereas Sir Ferdinando Gorges Knight hath been an humble suitor unto us to graunte and confirme unto him and his heires a parte and porcon of the Countrie of America now commonly called or knowne by the name of New England in America in theise Presents hereafter described by the meets and boundes thereof with divers and sundrie priviledges and jurisdiccons for the *welfare* and good of the state of those Colonies that shalbee drawne thither and for the better governement of the people that shall live and inhabite within the lymits and precints thereof whiche parte or porcon of the said Countrie . . . [Thorpe 1625–26]

The New England Confederation, May 19, 1643:

[Article 2:] The said United Colonies for themselves and their posterities do jointly and severally hereby enter into a firm and perpetual league of friendship and amity for offence and defence, mutual advice and succor upon all just occasions both for preserving and propagating the truth and liberties of the Gospel and for their own *mutual safety and welfare.* [Thorpe 77]

Charles II, Charter of Carolina, March 24, 1663:

And further also, we do by these presents, for us, our heirs and successors, give and grant license to [the Proprietors] . . . full power, liberty and license to erect, raise and build within the said province and places aforesaid, or any part or parts thereof, such and so many forts, fortresses, castles, cities, buroughs, towns, villages and other fortifications whatsoever, and the same or any of them to fortify and furnish with ordinance, powder, shot, armory, and all other weapons, ammunition, habilements of war, both offensive and defensive, as shall be thought fit and convenient for the safety and *welfare* of the said province and places, or any part thereof . . . [Thorpe 2750]

New Jersey Proprietors, Concession and Agreement, February 10, 1664:

[1] . . . And the said register shall do all other thing or things that we by our instructions shall direct, and the Governor, Council and General Assembly shall ordain for the good and *welfare* of the said Province. [Thorpe 2536]

[2] That the Governor, Councellors, Assembly Men, Secretary, Surveyor, and all other officers of trust, shall swear or subscribe (in a book to be provided for that purpose) that they will bear true allegiance to the King of England, his heirs and successors; and that they will be faithful to the interests of the Lords Proprietors of the said Province and their heirs, executors and assigns; and endeavour the peace and *welfare* of the said Province . . . [Thorpe 2536]

[3] That the inhabitants being freemen, or chief agents to others of the Province aforesaid; do as soon as this our commission shall arrive, by virtue of a writ in our names by the Governor to be for the present (until our seal arrives) sealed and signed, make choice of twelve deputies or representatives from amongst themselves; who being chosen are to join with the said Governor and council for the making of such laws, ordinances and constitution as shall be necessary for the present good and *welfare* of the said Province. . . . [Thorpe 2537]

[4] By their enacting to be confirm'd as aforesaid, to erect, raise and build within the said Province or any part thereof, such and so many forts, fortresses, castles, cities, corporations, boroughs, towns, villages, and other places of strength and defence; and them or any of them, to incorporate with such charters and privileges, as to them shall seem good and the grant made unto us will permit; and

the same or any of them to fortify and furnish with such provisions and proportion of ordnance, powder, shot, armour, and all other weapons, ammunition and abiliments of war, both offensive and defensive, as shall be thought necessary and convenient for the safety and *welfare* of the said province. . . .

[Thorpe 2538–39]

Carolina Proprietors, Concessions and Agreements, 1665:

[1] That the inhabitants being freemen or chiefe agents to others of ye Countyes aforesd doe as soone as this our Comission shall arrive by virtue of a writt in our names by the Governor to be for ye present (untill our seale comes) sealed and syned make choice of twelve Deputyes or representatives from amongst themselves whoe being chosen are to joyne with him the sd Governor and Councill for the makeing of such Lawes Ordinances and Constitutions as shalbe necessary for the present good and *welfare* of the severall Countyes aforesd . . .

[Thorpe 2757–58]

[2] . . . to erect rayse and build within the sd Counties or any part thereof such and soe many Forts Fortresses Castles Cittyes Corporacons Borroughs Townes Villages and other places of strenkt and defence and them or any of them to incorporate with such Charters and priveledges as to them shall seeme good and our Charter will permit and the same or any of them to fortifie and furnish with such Proportions of ordinance powder shott Armor and all other Weapons Ammunition and Habillaments of warr both offensive and defensive as shalbe thought necessary and convenient for the safety and *welfare* of ye sd Countyes . . .

[Thorpe 2759]

Charles II, Charter of Carolina, June 30, 1665:

. . . to erect, raise and build, within the said province and places aforesaid, or any part or parts thereof, such and so many forts, fortresses, castles, cities, boroughs, towns villages, and other fortifications whatsoever; and the same, or any of them, to fortify and furnish with ordnance, powder, shot, armour, and all other weapons, ammunition, and habiliments of war, both defensive and offensive, as shall be thought fit and convenient, for the safety and *welfare* of the said province and places, or any part thereof . . . [Thorpe 2769]

Government of West New Jersey, November 25, 1681:

Forasmuch as it hath pleased God, to bring us into this Province of West New Jersey, and settle us here in safety, that we may be a people to the praise and honour of his name, who hath so dealt with us, and for the good and *welfare* of our posterity to come, we the Governor and Proprietors, freeholders and inhabitants of West New Jersey, by mutual consent and agreement, for the prevention of innovasion and oppression, either upon us or our posterity, and for the preservation of the peace and tranquility of the same . . . [Thorpe 2565]

Fundamental Constitutions of East New Jersey, 1683:

[Article 7:] . . . it is consented and agreed by the six and seven articles, that the great Assembly should have power, by act confirmed as there expressed, to erect, raise and build within the said Province, or anypart thereof, such and so many forts, castles, cities and other places of defence, and the same, or any of them, to fortify and furnish with such provisions and proportions of ordnance, powder, shot, armour and all other weapons, ammunition and abilments of war, both offensive and defensive, as shall be thought necessary and convenient for the safety and *welfare* of the said Province; as also to constitute train bands and companies, with the number of the soldiers, for the safety, strength and defence of the aforesaid Province . . . [Thorpe 2576]

James II, Commission to Sir Edmund Andros for the Dominion of New England, April 7, 1688:

And Wee do hereby give and grant unto you full power and authority, by and with the advise and consent of our said Councill or the major part of them, to make constitute and ordain lawes statutes and ordinances for the *public peace welfare* and good governmt of our said territory & dominion and of the people and inhabitants thereof, and such others as shall resort thereto, and for the benefit of us, our heires and successors. . . . [Thorpe 1864]

English Bill of Rights, December 16, 1689:

. . . And whereas it hath been found by experience, that it is inconsistent with the safety and *welfare* of this Protestant kingdom to be governed by a popish prince or by any king or queen marrying a papist the said lords spiritual and temporal and commons do further pray, that it may be enacted, that all and every person and persons that is, are or shall be reconciled to or shall hold communion with the See or Church of Rome, or shall profess the popish religion or shall marry a papist, shall be excluded and be forever incapable to inherit, possess or enjoy the crown and government of this realm and Ireland and the dominions thereunto belonging, or any part of the same, or to have, use or exercise any regal power, authority or jurisdiction within the same . . . [SDECH 468]

William and Mary, Charter of Massachusetts Bay, October 7, 1691:

[1] And whereas severall persons employed as Agents in behalfe of Our said Collony of the Massachusetts Bay in New England have made their humble application unto Us that Wee would be graciously pleased by Our Royall Charter to Incorporate Our Subjects in Our said Collony and to grant and confirme unto them such powers priviledges and Franchises as [in] Our Royall Wisdome should be thought most conduceing to Our Interest and Service and to the *Welfare* and

happy State of Our Subjects in New England and Wee being graciously pleased to gratifie Our said Subjects . . . [Thorpe 1875]

[2] . . . And we doe further for us our Heires and Successors Give and Grant to the said Governor and the great and Generall Court or Assembly of our said Province or Territory for the time being full Power and Authority from time to time to make ordaine and establish all manner of wholesome and reasonable Orders Laws Statutes and Ordinances Directions and Instructions either with penalties or without (soe as the same be not repugnant or contrary to the Lawes of this our Realme of England) as they shall Judge to be for the good and *welfare* of our said Province or Territory And for the Government and Ordering thereof and of the People Inhabiting or who shall Inhabit the same and for the necessary support and Defence of the Government thereof. [Thorpe 1882]

Benjamin Franklin, Proposed Articles of Confederation, c. July 21, 1775:

[Article 2:] The said United Colonies hereby severally enter into a firm League of Friendship with each other, binding on themselves and their Posterity, for their common Defence against their Enemies, for the Security of their Liberties and Propertys, the Safety of their Persons and Families, and their *mutual and general welfare*. [PBF22 122]

[Article 5:] That the Power and Duty of the Congress shall extend to the Determining on War and Peace, to sending and receiving Ambassadors, and entring into Alliances, the Reconciliation with Great Britain; the Settling all Disputes and Differences between Colony and Colony about limits or any other cause if such should arise; and the Planting of new Colonies when proper. The Congress shall also make such general Ordinances as tho' necessary to the *General Welfare*, particular Assemblies cannot be competent to, viz. those that may relate to our general Commerce or general Currency; to the Establishment of Posts; and the Regulation of our common Forces. The Congress shall also have the Appointment of all Officers civil and military, appertaining to the general Confederacy, such as General Treasurer Secretary, &c. [PBF22 122–23]

[Article 6:] All Charges of Wars, and all other general Expences to be incurr'd for the *common Welfare*, shall be defray'd out of a common Treasury, which is to be supply'd by each Colony in proportion to its Number of Male Polls between 16 and 60 Years of Age; the Taxes for paying that proportion are to be laid and levied by the Laws of each Colony. [PBF22 123]

New Jersey Constitution, July 2, 1776:

[Article 23:] "I, A. B. do solemnly declare, that, as a member of the Legislative Council, of the Colony of New-Jersey, I will not assent to any law, vote or proceeding, which shall appear to me injurious to the *public welfare* of said Colony, nor that shall annul or repeal that part of the third section in the Charter of this Colony, which establishes, that the elections of members of the Legislative Council and Assembly shall be annual . . . " [Thorpe 2598]

United States Continental Congress, Draft Articles of Confederation, July 12, 1776:

[Article 2:] The said Colonies unite themselves so as never to be divided by an Act whatever, and hereby severally enter into a firm League of Friendship with each other, for their common Defence, the Security of their Liberties, and their *mutual and general Welfare,* binding the said Colonies to assist one another against all Force offered to or attacks made upon them or any of them, on Account of Religion, Sovereignty, Trade, or any other Pretence whatever. [DHRC1 79]

[Article 11:] All Charges of Wars and all other Expences that shall be incurred for the common Defence, or *general Welfare,* and allowed by the United States assembled, shall be defrayed out of a common Treasury, which shall be supplied by the several Colonies in Proportion to the Number of Inhabitants of every Age, Sex and Quality, except Indians not paying Taxes, in each Colony . . . [DHRC1 80]

[Article 12:] Every Colony shall abide by the Determinations of the United States assembled, concerning the Services performed and Losses or Expences incurred by every Colony for the common Defence or *general Welfare,* and no Colony or Colonies shall in any Case whatever endeavor by force to procure Redress of any Injury or Injustice supposed to be done by the United States to such Colony or Colonies in not granting such Satisfactions, Indemnifications, Compensations, Retributions, Exemptions, or Benefits of any Kind, as such Colony or Colonies may think just or reasonable. [DHRC1 81]

[Article 18:] The United States assembled shall have Authority for the Defence and *Welfare* of the United Colonies and every of them, to agree upon and fix the necessary Sums and Expences—To emit Bills, or to borrow Money on the Credit of the United Colonies—To raise Naval Forces—To agree upon the Number of Land Forces to be raised, and to make Requisitions from the Legislature of each Colony . . . [DHRC1 83]

[*Ibid.:*] . . . The United States assembled shall never engage the United Colonies in a War, nor grant Letters of Marque and Reprisal in Time of Peace, nor enter into Treaties or Alliances, nor coin Money nor regulate the Value thereof, nor agree upon nor fix the Sums and Expences necessary for the Defence and *Welfare* of the United Colonies, or any of them, nor emit Bills, nor borrow Money on the Credit of the United Colonies, nor raise Naval Forces, nor agree upon the Number of Land Forces to be raised, unless the Delegates of nine Colonies freely assent to the same . . . [DHRC1 84]

[Article 19:] [The Council of the States shall have power] To summon an Assembly of the States at any earlier Day than that appointed for their next Meeting, if any great and unexpected Emergency should render it necessary for the Safety or *Welfare* of the United Colonies or any of them . . . [DHRC1 85]

Pennsylvania Constitution, September 28, 1776:

[Preamble:] . . . And whereas it is absolutely necessary for the *welfare* and safety of the inhabitants of said colonies, that they be henceforth free and independent States, and that just, permanent, and proper forms of government exist in every part of them, derived from and founded on the authority of the people only, agreeable to the directions of the honourable American Congress. . . .
[Thorpe 3081–82]

[Frame of Government, Section 13:] The doors of the house in which the representatives of the freemen of this state shall sit in general assembly, shall be and remain open for the admission of all persons who behave decently, except only when the *welfare* of this state may require the doors to be shut.
[Thorpe 3085]

Maryland Constitution, November 11, 1776:

[Form of Government, Article 11:] That the senate may be at full and perfect liberty to exercise their judgment in passing laws; and that they may not be compelled by the House of Delegates, either to reject a money bill, which the emergency of affairs may require, or to assent to some other act of legislation, in their conscience and judgment injurious to the *public welfare,* the House of Delegates shall not, on any occasion, or under any pretence, annex to, or blend with, a money bill, any matter, clause, or thing not immediately relating to, and necessary for the imposing, assessing, levying, or applying the taxes or supplies to be raised for the support of government, or the current expenses of the state . . . [Thorpe 1692–93]

New York Constitution, April 20, 1777:

[Article 15:] That whenever the assembly and senate disagree, a conference shall be held, in the preference of both, and be managed by committees, to be by them respectively chosen by ballot. That the doors, both of the senate and assembly, shall at all times be kept open to all persons, except when the *welfare* of the State shall require their debates to be kept secret. . . . [Thorpe 2632]

[Article 19:] That it shall be the duty of the governor to inform the legislature, at every session, of the condition of the State, so far as may respect his department; to recommend such matters to their consideration as shall appear to him to concern its good government, *welfare,* and prosperity . . .
[Thorpe 2633]

Vermont Constitution, July 8, 1777:

[Preamble:] Therefore, it is absolutely necessary, for the *welfare* and safety of the inhabitants of this State, that it should be, henceforth, a free and independent State; and that a just, permanent, and proper form of government, should exist in it, derived from, and founded on, the authority of the people only, agreeable to the direction of the honorable American Congress. [Thorpe 3739]

[Frame of Government, Section 12:] The doors of the house in which the representatives of the freemen of this State, shall sit, in General Assembly, shall be and remain open for the admission of all persons, who behave decently, except only, when the *welfare* of this State may require the doors to be shut. [Thorpe 3744]

United States Articles of Confederation, November 15, 1777:

[Article III:] The said states hereby severally enter into a firm league of friendship with each other, for their common defence, the security of their Liberties, and their mutual and *general welfare,* binding themselves to assist each other, against all force offered to, or attacks made upon them, or any of them, on account of religion, sovereignty, trade, or any other pretence whatever. [DHRC1 86]

[Article VIII:] All charges of war, and all other expenses that shall be incurred for the common defence or *general welfare,* and allowed by the united states in congress assembled, shall be defrayed out of a common treasury, which shall be supplied by the several states, in proportion to the value of all land within each state, granted to or surveyed for any Person, as such land and the buildings and improvements thereon shall be estimated according to such mode as the united states in congress assembled, shall from time to time direct and appoint. . . . [DHRC1 89]

[Article IX:] The united states in congress assembled shall never engage in a war, nor grant letters of marque and reprisal in time of peace, nor enter into any treaties or alliances, nor coin money, nor regulate the value thereof, nor ascertain the sums and expences necessary for the defence and *welfare* of the united states, or any of them, nor emit bills, nor borrow money on the credit of the united states, nor appropriate money, nor agree upon the number of vessels of war, to be built or purchased, or the number of land or sea forces to be raised, nor appoint a commander in chief of the army or navy, unless nine states assent to the same: nor shall a question on any other point, except for adjourning from day to day be determined, unless by the votes of a majority of the united states in congress assembled. . . . [DHRC1 92]

Massachusetts Constitution, March 2, 1780:

[Chapter I:1:4:] And further, full power and authority are hereby given and granted to the said general court, from time to time, to make, ordain, and establish, all manner of wholesome and reasonable orders, laws, statutes, and ordinances, directions and instructions, either with penalties or without; so as the same be not repugnant or contrary to this constitution, as they shall judge to be for the good and *welfare* of this commonwealth, and for the government and ordering thereof, and of the subjects of the same, and for the necessary support and defence of the government thereof . . . [Thorpe 1894]

[Chapter II:1:5:] The governor, with advice of council, shall have full power and authority, during the session of the general court, to adjourn or prorogue the same to any time the two houses shall desire . . . and to call it together sooner than the time to which it may be adjourned or prorogued, if the *welfare* of the commonwealth shall require the same . . . [Thorpe 1900–01]

New Hampshire Consitution, June 2, 1784:

[Form of Government:] And farther, full power and authority are hereby given and granted to the said general court, from time to time, to make, ordain and establish, all manner of wholesome and reasonable orders, laws, statutes, ordinances, directions and instructions, either with penalties or without; so as the same be not repugnant, or contrary to this constitution, as they may judge for the benefit and *welfare* of this state, and for the governing and ordering thereof, and of the subjects of the same, for the necessary support and defence of the government thereof . . . [Thorpe 2458]

[*Ibid.*:] The president with advice of Council, shall have full power and authority in the recess of the general court, to prorogue the same from time to time, not exceeding ninety days in any one recess of said court; and during the session of said court, to adjourn or prorogue it to any time the two houses may desire, and to call it together sooner than the time to which it may be adjourned, or prorogued, if the *welfare* of the state should require the same. [Thorpe 2463]

Vermont Constitution, July 4, 1786:

[Preamble:] Therefore it is absolutely necessary, for the *welfare* and safety of the inhabitants of this State, that it should be henceforth a free and independent State, and that a just, permanent, and proper form of government should exist in it, derived from and founded on the authority of the people only, agreeable to the direction of the honourable American Congress. [Thorpe 3751]

[Frame of Government, Section 13:] The doors of the House, in which the General Assembly of this Commonwealth shall sit, shall be open for the admission of all persons who behave decently, except only when the *welfare* of the State may require them to be shut. [Thorpe 3757]

Report of the Annapolis Convention, September 14, 1786:

If in expressing this wish, or in intimating any other sentiment, Your Commissioners should seem to exceed the strict bounds of their appointment, they

entertain a full confidence, that a conduct, dictated by an anxiety for the *welfare*, of the United States, will not fail to receive an indulgent construction.
[DHRC1 183]

The Virginia Plan of Union, May 29, 1787:

Resolved that the articles of Confederation ought to be so corrected and enlarged as to accomplish the objects proposed by their institution; namely "common defence, security of liberty and *general welfare*." [DHRC1 243]

Edmund Randolph, Letter on the Federal Constitution, October 10, 1787:

[1] Amidst these disappointments, it would afford some consolation, if when rebellion shall threaten any state, an ultimate asylum could be found under the wing of Congress. But it is at least equivocal, whether they can intrude forces into a state, rent asunder by civil discord, even with the purest solicitude for our *foederal welfare*, and on the most urgent intreaties of the state itself. Nay the very allowance of this power would be pageantry alone, from the want of money and of men. [DHRC8 264]

[2] My opinion always was, and still is, that every citizen of America, let the crisis be what it may, ought to have a full opportunity to propose through his representatives any amendment, which in his apprehension tends to the *public welfare*—By signing I should have contradicted this sentiment. [DHRC8 271]

Richard Henry Lee [?], "The Federal Farmer," No. 4, October 12, 1787:

Third, there appears to me to be not only a premature deposit of some important powers in the general government—but many of those deposited there are undefined, and may be used to good or bad purposes as honest or designing men shall prevail. By Art. 1, Sect. 2, representatives and direct taxes shall be apportioned among the several states, &c.—same art. sect. 8, the congress shall have powers to lay and collect taxes, duties, &c. for the common defence and *general welfare*, but all duties, imposts and excises, shall be uniform throughout the United States . . . [Ford 310]

Noah Webster, *An Examination of the Leading Principles of the Federal Constitution*, October 17, 1787:

[1] . . . The only question therefore is, whether the new constitution delegates to Congress any powers which do not respect the general interest and *welfare* of the United States, If these powers intrench upon the present sovereignty of any state, without having for an object the collective interest of the whole, the powers are too extensive. But if they do not extend to all concerns, in which the states

have a mutual interest, they are too limited. If in any instance the powers necessary for protecting the general interest, interfere with the constitutional rights of an individual state, such state has assumed powers that are inconsistent with the safety of the United States, and which ought instantly to be resigned. . . . [Ford 45–46]

[2] After examining the limits of the proposed congressional powers, I confess I do not think them too extensive—I firmly believe that the life, liberty and property of every man, and the peace and independence of each state, will be more fully secured under such a constitution of federal government, than they will under a constitution with more limited powers; and infinitely more safe than under our boasted distinct sovereignties. It appears to me that Congress will have no more power than will be necessary for our union and *general welfare;* and such power they must have or we are in a wretched state. . . . [Ford 46]

[3] It is insinuated that the constitution gives Congress the power of levying internal taxes at pleasure. This insinuation seems founded on the eighth section of the first article, which declares, that "Congress shall have power to lay and collect taxes, duties, imposts and excises, to pay the debts and provide for the common defence and *general welfare* of the United States." [Ford 48]

[4] But the idea that Congress can levy taxes at pleasure is false, and the suggestion wholly unsupported. The preamble to the constitution is declaratory of the purposes of our union, and the assumption of any powers not necessary to establish justice, insure domestic tranquility, provide for the common defence, promote the *general welfare,* and to secure the blessings of liberty to ourselves and our Posterity, will be unconstitutional, and endanger the existence of Congress. Besides,in the very clause which gives the power of levying duties and taxes,the purposes to which the money shall be appropriated are specified, viz. to pay the debts and provide for the common defence and *general welfare* of the United States. For these purposes money must be collected, and the power of collection must be lodged, sooner or later, in a federal head; or the common defence and *general welfare* must be neglected. [Ford 50]

[5] . . . for no powers are vested in Congress but what are included under the general expressions, of providing for the common defence and *general welfare* of the United States. Any powers not promotive of these purposes, will be unconstitutional;—consequently any appropriations of money to any other purpose will expose the Congress to the resentment of the states, and the members to impeachment and loss of their seats. [Ford 51n]

[6] The states in their separate capacity, cannot provide for the common defence; nay in case of a civil war, a state cannot secure its own existence. The only question therefore is, whether it is necessary to unite, and provide for our common defence and *general welfare*. For this question being once decided in the affirmative, leaves no room to controvert the propriety of constituting a power over the whole United States, adequate to these general purposes. [Ford 50–51]

Alexander Hamilton, *The Federalist*, No. 1, October 27, 1787:

[1] After an unequivocal experience of the inefficiency of the subsisting federal government, you are called upon to deliberate on a new Constitution for the United States of America. The subject speaks its own importance; comprehending in its consequences nothing less than the existence of the UNION, the safety and *welfare* of the parts of which it is composed, the fate of an empire in many respects the most interesting in the world. . . . [Fed. 89]

[2] In the course of the preceding observations, I have had an eye, my fellow-citizens, to putting you upon your guard against all attempts, from whatever quarter, to influence your decision in a matter of the utmost moment to your *welfare,* by any impressions other than those which may result from the evidence of truth. You will, no doubt, at the same time, have collected from the general scope of them, that they proceed from a source not unfriendly to the new Constitution. . . . [Fed. 91]

Pelatiah Webster, *The Weakness of Brutus Exposed*, November 4, 1787:

[1] I further apprehend, that Brutus is willing to have the *general interest and welfare* of the States well provided for and supported, and therefore will consent that there shall exist in the states, an authority to do all this effectually; but he seems grieved that Congress should be the judges of this *general welfare* of the states. If he will be kind enough to point out any other more suitable and proper judges, I will consent to have them admitted. [Ford 121]

[2] The constitution under Brutus's corrections would stand thus, viz. Congress would have power to raise money, but must not direct the quantity, or mode of levying it; they might raise armies, but must not judge to the number of soldiers necessary, or direct their destination; they ought to provide for the *general welfare,* but must not be judges of what that *welfare* consists in, or in what manner 'tis to be provided for; they might controul the several States, for defined national purposes, but must not be judges of what purposes would come within that definition, &c. [Ford 126]

[3] They [*i.e.,* the states] will indeed have the privilege of oppressing their own citizens by bad laws or bad administration; but the moment the mischief extends beyond their own State, and begins to affect the citizens of other States strangers, or the *national welfare,*—the salutary controul of the supreme power will check the evil, and restore strength and security, as well as honesty and right, to the offending state. [Ford 128–29]

***Virginia Gazette*, November 16, 1787:**

How much it redounds to the honor of a nation, says another correspondent, to see unanimity prevail in all proceedings where the *welfare* of the whole community is equally concerned. But how disgraceful does it appear, when, by the diabolical machinations of a few designing individuals, the minds of the people are suffered to be corrupted, and anarchy stalks triumphant through the land. . . . [DHRC8 166]

Alexander Hamilton, *The Federalist*, No. 12, November 27, 1787:

If these remarks have any foundation, that state of things which will best enable us to improve and extend so valuable a resource must be best adapted to our *political welfare*. And it cannot admit of a serious doubt, that this state of things, must rest on the basis of a general Union. As far as this would be conducive to the interests of commerce, so far it must tend to the extension of the revenue to be drawn from that source. . . . [Fed. 144]

James Madison, *The Federalist*, No. 18, December 7, 1787:

The members [of the Greek Amphictyonic Council] retained the character of independent and sovereign states, and had equal votes in the federal council. This council had a general authority to propose and resolve whatever it judged necessary for the *common welfare* of Greece; to declare and carry on war; to decide, in the last resort, all controversies between the members; to fine the aggressing party; to employ the whole force of the confederacy against the disobedient; to admit new members. . . . [Fed. 171]

Alexander Hamilton, *The Federalist*, No. 22, December 14, 1787:

. . . The larger States would after a while revolt from the idea of receiving the law from the smaller. To acquiesce in such a privation of their due importance in the political scale would be not merely to be insensible to the love of power, but even to sacrifice the desire of equality. It is neither rational to expect the first, nor just to require the last. The smaller States, considering how peculiarly their safety and *welfare* depend on union, ought readily to renounce a pretension which, if not relinquished, would prove fatal to its duration. [Fed. 193–94]

Alexander Hamilton, *The Federalist*, No. 23, December 18, 1787:

Defective as the present Confederation has been proved to be, this principle appears to have been fully recognized by the framers of it, though they have not made proper or adequate provision for its exercise. Congress have an unlimited discretion to make requisitions of men and money; to govern the army and navy; to direct their operations. As their requisitions are made constitutionally binding upon the States, who are in fact under the most solemn obligations to furnish the supplies required of them, the intention evidently was that the United States should command whatever resources were by them judged requisite to the "common defence and *general welfare*." It was presumed that a sense of their true interests, and a regard to the dictates of good faith, would be found sufficient pledges for the punctual performance of the duty of the members to the federal head. [Fed. 200–201]

Dissent of the Pennsylvania Convention's Minority, December 18, 1787:

[1] The Congress might gloss over this conduct by construing every purpose for which the state legislatures now lay taxes, to be for the "*general welfare,*" and therefore as of their jurisdiction. [DHRC2 627]

[2] We have before noticed the judicial power as it would affect a consolidation of the States into one government; we will now examine it, as it would affect the liberties and *welfare* of the people, supposing such a government were practicable and proper. [DHRC2 632]

[3] . . . In the government of this state, under the old confederation, the members of the legislature are taken from among the people, and their interests and *welfare* are so inseparably connected with those of their constituents, that they can derive no advantage from oppressive laws and taxes, for they would suffer in common with their fellow citizens; would participate in the burdens they impose on the community, as they must return to the common level, after a short period; and notwithstanding every exertion of influence, every means of corruption, a necessary rotation excludes them from permanency in the legislature.

[DHRC2 636]

[4] . . . But we will suppose, although in all probability it may never be realized in fact, that our deputies in Congress have the *welfare* of their constituents at heart, and will exert themselves in their behalf. What security could even this afford; what relief could they extend to their oppressed constitutents? To attain this, the majority of the deputies of the twelve other States in Congress must be alike well disposed . . . [DHRC2 637]

[5] In this investigation we have not confined our views to the interests or *welfare* of this state, in preference to the others. We have overlooked all local circumstances; we have considered this subject on the broad scale of the general good; we have asserted the cause of the present and future ages,—the cause of liberty and mankind. [DHRC2 639]

"Americanus," No. 2, December 19, 1787:

. . . The house of representatives, which has the exclusive right of originating bills of taxation, is composed of members elected directly by the people in the most exact proportion. The object of this representation is the common defence and *general welfare* of the United States. The concomitant right of taxation extends no farther. It is the express language of the constitution, that all monies, arising from the taxes imposed by Congress shall be appropriated to the support of the foederal government, the common defence of the United States, and the regular discharge of the national debts. . . . [DHRC8 248]

Robert Yates and John Lansing, Objections to the Constitution, December 21, 1787:

. . . we entertained an opinion, that a general government, however guarded by declarations of rights, or cautionary provisions, must unavoidably, in a short time, be productive of the destruction of the civil liberty of such citizens who could be effectually coerced by it: by reason of the extensive territory of the United States, the dispersed situation of its inhabitants, and the insuperable difficulty of controulling or counteracting the views of a set of men (however unconstitutional and oppressive their acts might be) possessed of all the powers of government; and who from their remoteness from their constituents and necessary permanency of office, could not be supposed to be uniformly actuated by an attention to their *welfare* and happiness . . . [Farrand3 246]

Alexander Hamilton, *The Federalist*, No. 26, December 22, 1787:

. . . The citizens of America have too much discernment to be argued into anarchy. And I am much mistaken, if experience has not wrought a deep and solemn conviction in the public mind, that greater energy of government is essential to the *welfare* and prosperity of the community. [Fed. 214]

Alexander Hamilton, *The Federalist*, No. 33, January 2, 1788:

. . . The Convention probably foresaw, what it has been a principal aim of these papers to inculcate, that the danger which most threatens our *political welfare* is that the State governments will finally sap the foundations of the Union; and might therefore think it necessary, in so cardinal a point, to leave nothing to construction. . . . [Fed. 246]

Alexander Hamilton, *The Federalist*, No. 34, January 4, 1788:

. . . In this view of the subject, by what logic can it be maintained that the local governments ought to command, in perpetuity, an EXCLUSIVE source of revenue for any sum beyond the extent of two hundred thousand pounds? To extend its power further, in exclusion of the authority of the Union, would be to take the resources of the community out of those hands which stood in need of them for the *public welfare,* in order to put them into other hands which could have no just or proper occasion for them. [Fed. 252]

"Tamony," January 9, 1788:

Those who contend for the new Constitution without amendment think differently, or must condemn their own assertions, for in place of ascertaining how natural rights are secured, or government prudently restrained, they continually exclaim in a tone that assumes authority, "rejection must precipitate into the gulphs of destruction,—adoption leads to national happiness and dignity—men whose fortunes are involved may dread an effective administration and join those who under a foederal system, would lose an importance dearer to them, than the *welfare* of their country." [DHRC8 286]

"An Impartial Citizen," January 10, 1788:

. . . Animated by the most sincere attachment to the *welfare* of the United States, and this State [Virginia] particularly, I thought it my duty as a citizen, to lay my sentiments before the public, with a view of promoting an examination of this Constitution . . . [DHRC8 294]

George Nicholas [?], "The State Soldier," No. 1, January 16, 1788:

[1] . . . But when confined to the likeness of situation itself, the same comparison is entirely unjust: For formerly we were governed by those who had no interest in our prosperity: But now it is our FRIENDS, our COUNTRYMEN, and our BRETHREN, on whom we are called to rely, whose very existence is so inseparable from our *welfare* as to render it impossible for them to injure us without giving a fatal stab to themselves and the happiness of their posterity. . . .
[DHRC8 307]

[2] . . . The period is not far distant however when it must be determined whether it be best to adopt it [the Constitution] as it now stands, or run the risk of losing it by attempting amendments. This last consideration, deeply impressed on the minds of those who are interested in the *welfare* of America, cannot fail to call forth your attention, when a fitter season shall demand it, and another paper give it circulation. [DHRC8 308]

James Madison, *The Federalist*, No. 41, January 19, 1788:

[1] Some, who have not denied the necessity of the power of taxation, have grounded a very fierce attack against the Constitution, on the language in which it is defined. It has been urged and echoed, that the power "to lay and collect taxes, duties, imposts, and excises, to pay the debts, and provide for the common defence and *general welfare* of the United States," amounts to an unlimited commission to exercise every power which may be alleged to be necessary for the common defence or *general welfare*. No stronger proof could be given of the distress under which these writers labor for objections, than their stooping to such a misconstruction. [Fed. 300]

[2] Had no other enumeration or definition of the powers of the Congress been found in the Constitution, than the general expressions just cited, the authors of the objection might have had some color for it; though it would have been

difficult to find a reason for so awkward a form of describing an authority to legislate in all possible cases. A power to destroy the freedom of the press, the trial by jury; or even to regulate the course of descents, or the forms of conveyances, must be very singularly expressed by the terms "to raise money for the *general welfare*." [Fed. 300–301]

[3] The objection here is the more extraordinary, as it appears that the language used by the convention is a copy from the articles of Confederation. The objects of the Union among the States, as described in article third, are, "their common defence, security of their liberties, and mutual and *general welfare*." The terms of article eighth are still more identical: "All charges of war and all other expenses that shall be incurred for the common defence or *general welfare,* and allowed by the United States in Congress, shall be defrayed out of a common treasury," etc. A similar language again occurs in article ninth. Construe either of these articles by the rules which would justify the construction put on the new Constitution, and they vest in the existing Congress a power to legislate in all cases whatsoever. But what would have been thought of that assembly, if, attaching themselves to these general expressions, and disregarding the specifications which ascertain and limit their import, they had exercised an unlimited power of providing for the common defence and *general welfare?* I appeal to the objectors themselves, whether they would in that case have employed the same reasoning in justification of Congress as they now make use of against the convention. How difficult it is for error to escape its own condemnation! [Fed. 301–302]

"Valerius," January 23, 1788:

The reflection you have thrown upon the house of representatives, savours strongly of an exasperated spirit; you stile it "a mere shred or rag of representation." But, the description is as false, as the language is vulgar. What! shall a body of the choicest sons of America, elected by the unbought, unbiassed voices of a whole nation, entrusted with sovereign powers, and whose important charge is the common defence and *general welfare* of thirteen confederated states, shall this body be stiled "the mere shred and rag of representation." For shame! sir, for shame! . . . [DHRC8 318]

James Madison, *The Federalist*, No. 45, January 26, 1788:

[1] . . . Is it too early for politicians to presume on our forgetting that the public good, the real *welfare* of the great body of the people, is the supreme object to be pursued; and that no form of government whatever has any other value than as it may be fitted for the attainment of this object. Were the plan of the convention adverse to the public happiness, my voice would be, Reject the plan. . . . [Fed. 325]

[2] . . . The change relating to taxation may be regarded as the most important; and yet the present Congress have as complete authority to REQUIRE of the States indefinite supplies of money for the common defence and *general welfare,* as the future Congress will have to require them of individual citizens; and the latter will be no more bound than the States themselves have been, to pay the quotas respectively taxed on them. . . . [Fed. 329]

James Madison, *The Federalist*, No. 46, January 29, 1788:

. . . Every one knows that a great proportion of the errors committed by the State legislatures proceeds from the disposition of the members to sacrifice the comprehensive and permanent interest of the State, to the particular and separate views of the counties or districts in which they reside. And if they do not sufficiently enlarge their policy to embrace the *collective welfare* of their particular State, how can it be imagined that they will make the aggregate prosperity of the Union, and the dignity and respectability of its government, the objects of their affections and consultations? . . . [Fed. 332]

Letter from Maryland, January 29, 1788, published in Philadelphia *Independent Gazetteer*, February 8, 1788:

. . . If Mr. [Luther] Martin refused the reiterated applications made to him on this occasion, they might naturally suppose that his objections were ill grounded and futile; or otherwise, that he sacrificed the *public welfare* to some private and interested considerations, highly incompatible with the dignity of a delegate to the honorable General Convention of the United States. . . . [DHRC16 87]

Alexander C. Hanson, *Remarks on the Proposed Plan of a Federal Government*, c. January 31, 1788:

Consider again the nature and intent of a federal republic. It consists of an assemblage of distinct states, each completely organized for the protection of its own citizens, and the whole consolidated, by express compact, under one head, for the *general welfare* and common defence. [Ford 241]

David Ramsay, "Civis," February 4, 1788:

[1] . . . Look over the 8th section, which enumerates the powers of Congress, and point out one that is not essential on the before recited principles of union. The first is a power to lay and collect taxes, duties, imposts and excises, to pay the debts, and provide for the common defence and *general welfare* of the United States. [HDRC16 22]

[2] When you authorised Congress to borrow money, and to contract debts for carrying on the late war, you could not intend to abridge them of the means of paying their engagements, made on your account. You may observe, that their

future power is confined to provide for the common defence and *general welfare* of the United States. If they apply money to any other purposes, they exceed their powers. . . . [DHRC16 22]

Massachusetts Convention, Ratification of the Constitution, February 6, 1788:

. . . by assenting to and ratifying a new constitution, in order to form a more perfect union, establish justice, insure domestick tranquillity, provide for the common defence, promote the *general welfare,* and secure the blessings of liberty to themselves, and their posterity—DO, in the name and in behalf of the people of the commonwealth of Massachusetts, ASSENT to and RATIFY the said constitution, for the United States of America. [DHRC16 68]

George Nicholas [?], "The State Soldier," No. 2, February 6, 1788:

[1] Through the feebleness of the UNION and popular turn of our system, the different interests of the states have heretofore been rendered somewhat discordant—Congress being entirely dependent on, and ever amenable to the state legislatures, that same fear of offending which has often operated on the state representative (in favor of a few to the prejudice of the many) extends itself to the continental delegate—which, when aided by the consideration of the dependence which most preferments have on the individual states, together with the insignificance of the present UNION, render the interest of a part more the object of foederal consideration than the *welfare* of the whole—whence arises that contention of interests in which some states may have suffered; and is at this time so much dreaded. [DHRC8 347]

[2] . . . When on the contrary if under the interference of a government whose existence will depend on the *welfare* of the whole, those necessary amendments may be made by sacrificing a small share of the interest of different parts, without endangering that last and deepest interest of the whole—the existence of the UNION. [DHRC8 351]

"Brutus," No. 12, February 7, 1788:

[1] To discover the spirit of the constitution, it is of the first importance to attend to the principal ends and designs it has in view. These are expressed in the preamble, in the following words, viz. "We, the people of the United States, in order to form a more perfect union, establish justice, insure domestic tranquility, provide for the common defence, promote the *general welfare,* and secure the blessings of liberty to ourselves and our posterity, do ordain and establish this constitution," &c. If the end of the government is to be learned from these words, which are clearly designed to declare it, it is obvious it has in view every object which is embraced by any government. The preservation of internal

peace—the due administration of justice—and to provide for the defence of the community, seems to include all the objects of government; but if they do not, they are certainly comprehended in the words, "to provide for the *general welfare*." . . . [DHRC16 74]

[2] This will certainly give the first clause in that article a construction which I confess I think the most natural and grammatical one, to authorise the Congress to do any thing which in their judgment will tend to provide for the *general welfare*, and this amounts to the same thing as general and unlimited powers of legislation in all cases. [DHRC16 75]

Luther Martin, "Genuine Information," No. 12, February 8, 1788:

. . . and you will easily perceive from this detail that a great portion of that time, which ought to have been devoted calmly and impartially to consider what alterations in our federal government would be most likely to procure and preserve the happiness of the union, was employed in a violent struggle on the one side to obtain all power and dominion in their own hands, and on the other to prevent it—and that the aggrandizement of particular States and particular individuals appears to have been much more the object sought after than the *welfare* of our country. [DHRC16 92]

James Iredell, "Marcus," No. 1, February 20, 1788:

[1] Because in their legislative capacity they [*i.e.*, the Senate] can do nothing without the concurrence of the House of Representatives, and we need look no further than England for a clear proof of the amazing consequence which Representatives of the people bear in a free government. There the King (who is hereditary, and therefore not so immediately interested, according to narrow views of interest which commonly govern Kings, to consult the *welfare* of his people) has the appointment to almost every office in the government, many of which are of high dignity and great pecuniary value . . . [DHRC16 165–66]

[2] . . . The institution of the Senate seems well calculated to answer this salutary purpose. Excluded as they are from places themselves, they appear to be as much above the danger of personal temptation as they can be. They have no permanent interest as a body to detach them from the *general welfare*, since six years is the utmost period of their existence, unless their respective legislatures are sufficiently pleased with their conduct to re-elect them. . . . [DHRC16 166]

"An Old Planter," February 20, 1788:

. . . and unhappily there are some amongst us deeply interested in deceiving us—these are zealous and active, whilst good men generally content themselves with regulating their own conduct, and are backward in exposing their tranquility for our benefit, because they see we are too indifferent, or too easily misled in what concerns our *welfare* as a people. [DHRC8 394]

Alexander Hamilton, *The Federalist*, No. 61, February 26, 1788:

. . . I allude to the circumstance of uniformity in the time of elections for the federal House of Representatives. It is more than possible that this uniformity may be found by experience to be of great importance to the *public welfare*, both as a security against the perpetuation of the same spirit in the body, and as a cure for the diseases of faction. . . . [Fed. 406]

Mercy Otis Warren, *Observations on the New Constitution*, February 1788:

. . . and as an elegant writer [Helvetius] observes, "To bewail every new birth as an encrease of misery, under a government where the mind is necessarily debased, and talents are seduced to become the panegyrists of usurpation and tyranny." He adds, "that even sedition is not the most indubitable enemy to the *publick welfare;* but that its most dreadful foe is despotism, which always changes the character of nations for the worse, and is productive of nothing but vice, that the tyrant no longer excites to the pursuits of glory or virtue . . . "

[DHRC16 275]

[2] Connecticut has pushed it [the Constitution] through with the precipitation of her neighbour, with few dissentient voices;—but more from irritation and resentment to a sister State, perhaps partiality to herself in her commercial regulations, than from a comprehensive view of the system, as a regard to the *welfare of all*. . . . [DHRC16 287]

James Madison, *The Federalist*, No. 63, March 1, 1788:

. . . The objects of government may be divided into two general classes: the one depending on measures which have singly an immediate and sensible operation; the other depending on a succession of well-chosen and well-connected measures, which have a gradual and perhaps unobserved operation. The importance of the latter description to the collective and permanent *welfare* of every country, needs no explanation. And yet it is evident that an assembly elected for so short a term as to be unable to provide more than one or two links in a chain of measures, on which the *general welfare* may essentially depend, ought not to be answerable for the final result, any more than a steward or tenant, engaged for one year, could be justly made to answer for plans or improvements which could not be accomplished in less than half dozen years. . . . [Fed. 414]

"The Impartial Examiner," No. 1, March 5, 1788:

. . . It is not to be feared that you need the force of persuasion, to exercise a proper freedom of enquiry into the merits of this proposed plan of government:

or that you will not pay a due attention to the *welfare* of that country, for which you have already so bravely exerted yourselves. Of this I am well assured . . . [DHRC8 461]

Benjamin Workman [?], "Philadelphiensis," No. 11, March 8, 1788:

The citizens of Pennsylvania have nobly shown their love for liberty, and attachment to the true interests of the union, by their generous exertions in favor of public credit. They have rigidly fulfilled their engagements in regard to the general debt; the requisitions of Congress have been strictly attended to, and fully answered. Add to this, that we have sunk a considerable part of the domestic debt, and in fact assumed a larger portion of it than in justice belonged to us. These spirited exertions, while they contributed to the *general welfare* of the union, and raised the reputation of the state, did not fail however to distress our farmers and every other class and description of citizens, very sensibly indeed. [DHRC16 363]

"An Impartial Citizen," No. 6, March 13, 1788:

. . . To compel any State by dint of arms to pay her quota, would be the utmost degree of political madness; it would generate the most implacable hatred of the citizens of some States to the rest: It seems also impracticable to effect it. Yet the public credit ought to be supported, and the common defence and *general welfare* provided for. How could this have been done, but by recurring to the same process whereby money is levied by the different State Governments? But even this will be seldom practised, or not to a great extent, as the impost will be very productive. . . . [DHRC8 499]

Letter from Massachusetts, March 19, 1788, published in *New York Journal*, March 24, 1788:

. . . Every good government should have for its objects defence against external enemies, and the promotion of internal tranquility and happiness. While we suspend our opinion of the purity of intention, and of the great zeal for the interest and *welfare* with which the late convention assembled, we are in justice to our constituents constrained to say that the result of their deliberations does not seem well calculated for those valuable purposes. . . . [DHRC8 228]

Luther Martin, "To the Citizens of Maryland," No. 2, March 21, 1788:

. . . Or even admitting I was not mortified, as I certainly ought to have been, from the Landholder's account of the matter, into a total loss of speech, was it in me, who considered the system, for a variety of reasons, absolutely inconsistent with your *political welfare* and happiness, a culpable neglect of duty in not endeavouring, and that against every chance of success, to remove one or two defects, when I had before ineffectually endeavoured to clear it of the others, which, therefore, I knew must remain. [DHRC16 455]

Samuel Bryan, "Centinel," No. 17, March 24, 1788:

Could it have been supposed seven years ago, that, before the wounds received in the late conflict for liberty were scarcely healed, a post master-general and his deputies would have had the daring presumption to convert an establishment intended to promote and secure the *public welfare* into an engine of despotism, by suppressing all those newspapers that contain the essays of patriotism and real intelligence, and propagating instead thereof falsehoods and delusion? . . . [DHRC16 476–77]

James Iredell, Address at Edenton, North Carolina, c. March 28–29, 1788:

. . . God forbid, indeed, that I should, by a blind admiration, imitate the conduct of those who indulge themselves in a blind rejection of it [the Constitution]. The one would be as unworthy of the dignity of a free people, as the other is derogatory of those sentiments of respect and deference which we owe the great characters who formed it; and owe certainly as much for our own sakes, whose *welfare* they took so much pains to consult, as from the sentiments of gratitude with which every mind of sensibility must remember their former eminent services to their country. . . . [DHRC16 498]

John Dickinson, "Fabius" No. 1, April 10, 1788:

. . . Thus, for instance, some inhabitants of large states may desire the system to be so altered, that they may possess more authority in the decisions of the government; or some inhabitants of commercial states may desire it to be so altered, that the advantages of trade may center almost wholly among themselves; and this predilection they may think compatible with the *common welfare*. Their judgment being thus warp'd, at the beginning of their deliberations, objections are accumulated as very important, that, without this prepossession, would never have obtained their approbation. . . . [Ford 166–67]

John Jay, *An Address to the People of the State of New York*, c. April 15, 1788:

As the importance of this question must be obvious to every man, whatever his private opinions respecting it may be, it becomes us all to treat it in that calm and temperate manner, which a subject so deeply interesting to the future *welfare* of our country and prosperity requires. Let us therefore as much as possible repress and compose that irritation in our minds, which to warm disputes about it may have excited. . . . [Ford 77–78]

John Dickinson, "Fabius," No. 3, 1788:

The dilemma is inevitable. There must either be one Will, or several wills. If but one will, all the people are concerned: if several wills, few comparatively are concerned. Surprizing! that this doctrine should be contended for by those, who declare, that the constitution is not founded on a bottom broad enough; and, though the whole people of the United States are to be trebly represented in it in three different modes of representation, and their servants will have the most advantageous situations and opportunities of acquiring all requisite information for the *welfare* of the whole union, yet insist for a privilege of opposing, obstructing, and confounding all their measures taken with common consent for the general weal, by the delays, negligences, rivalries, or other selfish views of parts of the union. [Ford 178]

John Dickinson, "Fabius," No. 5, 1788:

. . . As government is intended for the happiness of the people, the protection of the worthy against those of contrary characters, is calculated to promote the end of legitimate government, that is the general *welfare;* for the government will partake of the qualities of those whose authority is prevalent. . . .
[Ford 188]

John Dickinson, "Fabius," No. 7, 1788:

The reason is plain. As liberty and equality, or as well termed by Polybius, benignity, were the foundations of their institutions, and the energy of the government pervaded all the parts in things relating to the whole, it counteracted for the *common welfare,* the designs hatched by selfishness in separate councils. [Ford 201]

John Dickinson, "Fabius," No. 8, 1788:

[1] In the democracy of The United States, the people act by their representatives. This improvement collects the will of millions upon points concerning their *welfare,* with more advantage, than the will of hundreds could be collected under the ancient form. [Ford 206]

[2] It cannot be with reason apprehended, that Congress will refuse to act upon any articles calculated to promote the *common welfare,* though they may be unwilling to act upon such as are designed to advance partial interests . . .
[Ford 210]

John Dickinson, "Fabius," No. 9, 1788:

They ask not for compacts, of which the *national welfare,* and, in some cases, its existence, may demand violations. They despise such dangerous provisions against danger. [Ford 214]

United States Senate, Address to George Washington, May 7, 1789:

In the execution of the trust reposed in us, we shall endeavor to pursue that enlarged and liberal policy to which your speech so happily directs. We are conscious that the prosperity of each State is inseparably connected with the *welfare* of all, and that in promoting the latter, we shall effectually advance the former. . . . [Annals 32]

George Washington, Reply to the Senate, May 18, 1789:

. . . I now feel myself inexpressibly happy in a belief that Heaven, which has done so much for our infant nation, will not withdraw its providential influence before our political felicity shall have been completed, and in a conviction that the Senate will at all times co-operate in every measure which may tend to promote the *welfare* of this confederated Republic. . . . [Annals 38]

WITNESS, WITNESSES

[Note: This list includes occurrences of the noun ''witness'' in relationship to judicial and legislative proceedings.]

United States Constitution, September 17, 1787:

[Article III, Section 3:] Treason against the United States, shall consist only in levying War against them, or in adhering to their Enemies, giving them Aid and Comfort. No Person shall be convicted of Treason unless on the Testimony of two *Witnesses* to the same overt Act, or on Confession in open Court.

United States Constitution, Bill of Rights, December 15, 1791:

[Article V:] No person shall be held to answer for a capital, or otherwise infamous crime, unless on a presentment or indictment of a Grand Jury, except in cases arising in the land or naval forces, or in the Militia, when in actual service in time of War or public danger; nor shall any person be subject for the same offense to be twice put in jeopardy of life or limb; nor shall be compelled in any criminal case to be a *witness* against himself, nor be deprived of life, liberty, or property, without due process of law; nor shall private property be taken for public use, without just compensation.

[Article VI:] In all criminal prosecutions, the accused shall enjoy the right to a speedy and public trial, by an impartial jury of the State and district wherein the crime shall have been committed, which district shall have been previously ascertained by law, and to be informed of the nature and cause of the accusation; to be confronted with the *witnesses* against him; to have compulsory process for obtaining *witnesses* in his favor, and to have the Assistance of Counsel for his defence.

* * * * *

Magna Carta, June 15, 1215:

No Bailiff, for the future, shall put any one to his law on his simple affirmation, without credible *witnesses* brought for the purpose. [SDECH 47]

New Jersey Proprietors, Concession and Agreement, February 10, 1664:

That the chief Secretary or register which we have chosen, or shall choose, (we failing) that he shall choose, shall keep exact entries in fair books of all publick affairs: and to avoid deceits and lawsuits, shall record and enter all grants of land from the lords to the planters; and all conveyances of land, house or houses from man to man, as also all leases for land, house or houses, made or to be made by the landlord to any tenant for more than one year; which conveyance or lease shall be first acknowledged by the grantor or leasor, or proved by the oath of two *witnesses* to the lease or conveyance, before the Governor or some chief judge of a court for the time being, who shall under his hand on the backside of the said deed or lease, attest the acknowledgment or proof as aforesaid; which shall be a warrant for the register to record the same: which conveyance so recorded shall be good and effectual in law, notwithstanding any other conveyance, deed or lease for the said land, house or houses, or for any part thereof, altho' dated before the conveyance, deed or lease, recorded as aforesaid: And the said register shall do all other thing or things that we by our instructions shall direct, and the Governor, Council and General Assembly shall ordain for the good and welfare of the said Province. [Thorpe 2535–36]

Carolina Proprietors, Concessions and Agreements, 1665:

That the chiefe Registers or Secretarys which wee have chosen or shall chuse wee fayling that hee shall chuse shall keepe exact entereyes in faire bookes of all publicke affaires of the said Countyes and to avoide deceiptes and lawsuits shall record and enter all Graunts of Land from the Lords to the planter and all conveyances of Land howse or howses from man to man, As alsoe all leases for Land howse or howses made or to be made by the Landlord to any tenant for more than one yeare, which conveyance or Lease shalbe first acknowledged by the Grantr or Leasor or proved by the oath of two *witnesses* to the conveyance or Lease before the Governor or some Cheife Judge of a Court . . .

[Thorpe 2756]

Fundamental Constitutions of Carolina, March 1, 1669:

[Article 100:] In the terms of communion of every church or profession, these following shall be three; without which no agreement or assembly of men, upon pretence of religion, shall be accounted a church or profession within these rules: 1st. "That there is a God." II. "That God is publicly to be worshipped." III. "That it is lawful and the duty of every man, being thereunto called by those that govern, to bear *witness* to truth; and that every church or profession shall, in their terms of communion, set down the external way whereby they *witness* a truth as in the presence of God, whether it be by laying hands on or kissing the bible, as in the Church of England, or by holding up the hand, or any other sensible way." [Thorpe 2784]

Fundamental Constitutions of West New Jersey, 1676:

[Chapter 20:] That in all matters and causes, civil and criminal, proof is to be made by the solemn and plain averment, of at least two honest and reputable persons; and in case that any person or persons shall bear false *witness*, and bring in his or their evidence, contrary to the truth of the matter as shall be made plainly to appear, that then every such person or persons, shall in civil causes, suffer the penalty which would be due to the person or persons he or they bear *witness* against. And in case any *witness or witnesses,* on the behalf of any person or persons, indicted in a criminal cause, shall be found to have borne false *witness* for fear, gain, malice or favour and thereby hinder the due execution of the law, and deprive the suffering person or persons of their due satisfaction, that then and in all other cases of false evidence, such person or persons, shall be first severely fined, and next that he or they shall forever be disabled from being admitted in evidence, or into any public office, employment, or service within this province. [Thorpe 2550–51]

Duke of York, Grant of West New Jersey, August 6, 1680:

Thomas Heywood maketh oath, that the day and year within written, saw his Highness the Duke of York, sign, seal, and as his act, and deed, deliver this indenture to the use within mentioned, and afterwards subscribed his name as a *witness,* THOMAS HEYWOOD. Jur. 3d. die. September 1680. [Thorpe 2565]

Pennsylvania Frame of Government, April 25, 1682:

[Laws Agreed Upon in England, Article 1:] That the charter of liberties, declared, granted and confirmed the five and twentieth day of the second month, called April, 1682 before divers *witnesses,* by William Penn, Governor and chief Proprietor of Pensilvania, to all the freemen and planters of the said province, is hereby declared and approved, and shall be for ever held for fundamental in the government thereof, according to the limitations mentioned in the said charter. [Thorpe 3059–60]

[*Ibid.,* Article 15:] That all wills, in writing, attested by two *witnesses,* shall be of the same force as to lands, as other conveyances, being legally proved within forty days, either within or without the said province. [Thorpe 3061]

[*Ibid.*, Article 19:] That all marriages (not forbidden by the law of God, as to nearness of blood and affinity by marriage) shall be encouraged; but the parents, or guardians, shall be first consulted, and the marriage shall be published before it be solemnized; and it shall be solemnized by taking one another as husband and wife, before credible *witnesses;* and a certificate of the whole, under the hands of parties and *witnesses,* shall be brought to the proper register of that county, and shall be registered in his office. [Thorpe 3061]

[Article 26:] That all *witnesses,* coming, or called, to testify their knowledge in or to any matter or thing, in any court, or before any lawful authority within the said province, shall there give or deliver in their evidence, or testimony, by solemnly promising to speak the truth, the whole truth, and nothing but the truth, to the matter, or thing in question. And in case any person so called to evidence, shall be convicted of wilful falsehood, such person shall suffer and undergo such damage or penalty, as the person, or persons, against whom he or she bore false *witness,* did, or should, undergo; and shall also make satisfaction to the party wronged, and be publicly exposed as a false *witness,* never to be credited in any court, or before any Magistrate, in the said province. [Thorpe 3062]

Fundamental Constitutions of East New Jersey, 1683:

[Article 20:] That all marriages not forbidden in the law of God, shall be esteemed lawful, where the parents or gnardians being first acquainted, the marriage is publickly intimated in such places and manner as is agreeable to mens different perswasions in religion, being afterwards still solemnized before creditable *witnesses,* by taking one another as husband and wife, and a certificate of the whole, under the parties and *witnesses* hands, being brought to the proper register for that end, under a penalty if neglected. [Thorpe 2581]

[Article 21:] That all *witnesses* coming or called to testify their knowledge in or to any matter or thing in any court or before any lawful authority within the Province, shall there have and deliver in their evidence by solemnly promissing to speak the truth, the whole truth and nothing but the truth to the matter in question. And in case any person so doing shall be afterwards convict of willful falsehood, both such persons as also those who have proved to have suborn, shall undergo the damage and punishment both in criminal and in civil; the person against whom they did or should have incurred, which if it reach not his life, he shall be publickly exposed as a false *witness,* never afterwards to be credited before any court; the like punishment in cases of forgery, and both criminals to be stigmatized. [Thorpe 2581]

William Penn, Charter of Privileges for Pennsylvania, October 28, 1701:

[Article 5:] That all Criminals shall have the same Privileges of *Witnesses* and Council as their Prosecutors. [Thorpe 3079]

William Penn, Charter of Delaware, October 28, 1701:

[Article 5:] That all criminals shall have the same Privileges of *Witnesses* and Council as their Prosecutors. [Thorpe 560]

Virginia Bill of Rights, June 12, 1776:

[Section 8:] That in all capital or criminal prosecutions a man hath a right to demand the cause and nature of his accusation, to be confronted with the accusers and *witnesses,* to call for evidence in his favor, and to a speedy trial by an impartial jury of twelve men of his vicinage without whose unanimous consent he cannot be found guilty; nor can he be compelled to give evidence against himself; that no man be deprived of his liberty, except by the law of the land or the judgment of his peers. [Thorpe 3813]

New Jersey Constitution, July 2, 1776:

[Article 16:] That all criminals shall be admitted to the same privileges of *witnesses* and counsel, as their prosecutors are or shall be entitled to. [Thorpe 2597]

Pennsylvania Constitution, September 28, 1776:

[Declaration of Rights, Article 9:] That in all prosecutions for criminal offences, a man hath a right to be heard by himself and his council, to demand the cause and nature of his accusation, to be confronted with the *witnesses,* to call for evidence in his favour, and a speedy public trial, by an impartial jury of the country, without the unanimous consent of which jury he cannot be found guilty; nor can he be compelled to give evidence against himself; nor can any man be justly deprived of his liberty except by the laws of the land, or the judgment of his peers. [Thorpe 3083]

[Frame of Government, Section 9:] . . . they [the General Assembly] may expel a member, but not a second time for the same cause; they may administer oaths or affirmations on examination of *witnesses;* redress grievances; impeach state criminals . . . [Thorpe 3085]

Maryland Constitution, November 11, 1776:

[Declaration of Rights, Article 19:] That, in all criminal prosecutions, every man hath a right to be informed of the accusation against him; to have a copy of the indictment or charge in due time (if required) to prepare for his defence; to be allowed counsel; to be confronted with the *witnesses* against him; to have process for his *witnesses;* to examine the *witnesses,* for and against him, on oath; and to a speedy trial by an impartial jury, without whose unanimous consent he ought not be found guilty. [Thorpe 1688]

[*Ibid.,* Article 36:] . . . And that the people called Quakers, those called Dunkers, and those called Menonists, holding it unlawful to take an oath on any occasion, ought to be allowed to make their solemn affirmation, in the manner that Quakers have been heretofore allowed to affirm; and to be of the same avail as an oath, in all such cases, as the affirmation of Quakers hath been allowed and accepted within this State, instead of an oath. And further, on such affirmation, warrants to search for stolen goods, or for the apprehension or commitment of offenders, ought to be granted, or security for the peace awarded, and Quakers, Dunkers or Menonists ought also, on their solemn affirmation as aforesaid, to be admitted as *witnesses,* in all criminal cases not capital. Thorpe 1690]

[Form of Government, Article 10:] That the House of Delegates may originate all money bills, propose bills to the senate, or receive those offered by that body, and assent, dissent, or propose amendments; that they may inquire, on the oath of *witnesses,* into all complaints, grievances, and offenses, as the grand inquest of this state, and may commit any person, for any crime, to the public jail, there to remain till he be discharged by due course of law. . . . [Thorpe 1692]

[*Ibid.,* Article 12:] . . . They [the House of Delegates] may also punish, by imprisonment, any person who shall be guilty of a breach of privilege, by arresting on civil process, or by assaulting any of their members, during their sitting, or on their way to, or return from, the house of delegates, or by any assault of, or obstruction to their officers, in the execution of any order or process, or by assaulting or obstructing any *witness,* or any other person, attending on, or on their way to or from the house, or by rescuing any person committed by the house; and the senate may exercise the same power in similar cases. [Thorpe 1693]

[*Ibid.,* Article 53:] That if any Governor, Chancellor, Judge, Register of Wills, Attorney-General, Register of the Land Office, Register of the Chancery Court, or any Clerk of the common law courts, Treasurer, Naval Officer, Sheriff, Surveyor or Auditor of public accounts, shall receive, directly or indirectly, at any time, the profits, or any part of the profits of any office, held by any other person, during his acting in the office to which he is appointed; his election, appointment and commission (on conviction in a court of law by oath of two credible *witnesses*) shall be void . . . [Thorpe 1700]

North Carolina Constitution, December 18, 1776:

[Declaration of Rights, Article 7:] That, in all criminal prosecutions, every man has a right to be informed of the accusation against him, and to confront the accusers and *witnesses* with other testimony, and shall not be compelled to give evidence against himself. [Thorpe 2787]

Vermont Constitution, July 8, 1777:

[Declaration of Rights, Article 10:] That, in all prosecutions for criminal offences, a man hath a right to be heard, by himself and his counsel—to demand the cause and nature of his accusation—to be confronted with the *witnesses*—to call for evidence in his favor, and a speedy public trial, by an impartial jury of the country; without the unanimous consent of which jury, he cannot be found guilty; nor can he be compelled to give evidence against himself; nor can any man be justly deprived of his liberty, except by the laws of the land or the judgment of his peers. [Thorpe 3741]

[Frame of Government, Section 8:] . . . they [the General Assembly] may expel a member, but not a second time for the same cause—They may administer oaths (or affirmations) on examination of *witnesses*—redress grievances—impeach State criminals . . . [Thorpe 3742–43]

South Carolina Constitution, March 19, 1778:

[Article 38:] That it is lawful and the duty of every man being thereunto called by those that govern, to bear *witness* to the truth. [Thorpe 3256]

[*Ibid.*] And that every inhabitant of this State, when called to make an appeal to God as a *witness* to truth, shall be permitted to do it in that way which is most agreeable to the dictates of his own conscience. . . . [Thorpe 3256]

Massachusetts Constitution, March 2, 1780:

[Declaration of Rights, Article 12:] No subject shall be held to answer for any crimes or offence, until the same is fully and plainly, substantially, and formally, described to him; or be compelled to accuse, or furnish evidence against himself. And every subject shall have a right to produce all proofs that may be favorable to him; to meet the *witnesses* against him face to face, and to be fully heard in his defence by himself, or his counsel, at his election. . . . [Thorpe 1891]

[Form of Government, Chapter III:1:10:] . . . They [the House of Representatives] shall have authority to punish by imprisonment every person, not a member, who shall be guilty of disrespect to the house, by any disorderly or contemptuous behavior in its presence; or who, in the town where the general court is sitting, and during the time of its sitting, shall threaten harm to the body or estate of any of its members, for any thing said or done in the house; or who shall assault any of them therefor; or who shall assault, or arrest, any *witness*, or other person, ordered to attend the house, in his way in going or returning; or who shall rescue any person arrested by the order of the house. [Thorpe 1899]

New Hampshire Constitution, June 2, 1784:

[Bill of Rights, Article 15:] No subject shall be held to answer for any crime, or offence, until the same is fully and plainly, substantially and formally, described to him; or be compelled to accuse or furnish evidence against himself. And every subject shall have a right to produce all proofs that may be favorable to himself; to meet the *witnesses* against him face to face, and to be fully heard in his defence by himself, and counsel. . . . [Thorpe 2455]

[Form of Government:] . . . They [the House of Representatives] shall have authority to punish by imprisonment, every person who shall be guilty of disrespect to the house in its presence, by any disorderly or contemptuous behaviour, or by threatening, or ill treating any of its members; or by obstructing its deliberations; every person guilty of a breach of its privileges in making arrests for debt, or by assaulting any member during his attendance at any session; in assaulting or disturbing any one of its offices in the execution of any order or procedure of the house, in assaulting any *witness,* or other person; ordered to attend by and during his attendance of the house, or in rescuing any person arrested by order of the house, knowing them to be such. . . . [Thorpe 2462]

Vermont Constitution, July 4, 1786:

[Declaration of Rights, Article 11:] That in all prosecutions for criminal offences, a man hath a right to be heard by himself and his counsel—to demand the cause and nature of his accusation—to be confronted with the *witnesses*—to call for evidence in his favour, and a speedy public trial by an impartial jury of the country, without the unanimous consent of which jury he cannot be found guilty—nor can he be compelled to give evidence against himself—nor can any man be justly deprived of his liberty, except by the laws of the land, or the judgment of his peers. [Thorpe 3753]

United States Confederation Congress, The Northwest Ordinance, July 13, 1787:

. . . And until the governor and judges shall adopt laws as hereinafter mentioned, estates in the said territory may be devised or bequeathed by wills in writing, signed and sealed by him or her in whom the estate may be (being of full age) and attested by three *witnesses;*—and real estates may be conveyed by lease and release, or bargain and sale, signed, sealed, and delivered by the person, being of full age, in whom the estate may be, and attested by two *witnesses,* provided such wills be duly proved, and such conveyances be acknowledged, or the execution thereof duly proved, and be recorded within one year after proper magistrates, courts, and registers, shall be appointed for that purpose . . .
[Thorpe 958]

Richard Henry Lee [?], "The Federal Farmer," No. 2, October 9, 1787:

[1] . . . I am not for bringing justice so near to individuals as to afford them any temptation to engage in law suits; though I think it one of the greatest benefits in a good government, that each citizen should find a court of justice within a

reasonable distance, perhaps, within a day's travel of his home; so that, without great inconveniences and enormous expense, he may have the advantages of his *witnesses* and jury—it would be impracticable to derive these advantages from one judiciary—the one supreme court at most could only set in the center of the union, and move once a year into the center of the eastern and southern extremes of it—and, in this case, each citizen, on an average, would travel 150 or 200 miles to find this court . . . [Ford 289]

Richard Henry Lee [?], "The Federal Farmer," No. 4, October 12, 1787:

. . . When I speak of the jury trial of the vicinage, or the trial of the fact in the neighborhood, I do not lay so much stress upon the circumstance of our being tried by our neighbours: in this enlightened country men may be probably impartially tried by those who do not live very near them: but the trial of facts in the neighbourhood is of great importance in other respects. Nothing can be more essential than the cross examining *witnesses,* and generally before the triers of the facts in question. The common people can establish facts with much more ease with oral than written evidence; when trials of facts are removed to a distance from the homes of the parties and *witnesses,* oral evidence becomes intolerably expensive, and the parties must depend on written evidence, which to the common people is expensive and almost useless; it must be frequently taken ex porte, and but very seldom leads to the proper discovery of truth. [Ford 315]

Noah Webster, *An Examination of the Leading Principles of the Federal Constitution*, October 17, 1787:

. . . But in these polished ages, when juries depend almost wholly on the testimony of *witnesses;* and when a complication of interests,introduced by commerce and other causes, renders it almost impossible to collect men, in the vicinity of the parties, who are wholly disinterested, it is no disadvantage to have a cause tried by a jury of strangers. Indeed the latter is generally the most eligible. [Ford 53]

Dissent of the Pennsylvania Assembly's Minority, December 18, 1787:

That in all capital and criminal prosecutions, a man has a right to demand the cause and nature of his accusation, as well in the federal courts as in those of the several states; to be heard by himself and his counsel; to be confronted with the accusers and *witnesses;* to call for evidence in his favor, and a speedy trial by an impartial jury of his vicinage, without whose unanimous consent he cannot be found guilty, nor can he be compelled to give evidence against himself; and, that no man be deprived of his liberty, except by the law of the land or the judgment of his peers. [DHRC2 623]

Luther Martin, "Genuine Information," No. 12, February 8, 1788:

Agreeable to the articles of confederation entered into in the most solemn manner, and for the observance of which the States pledged themselves to each other, and called upon the Supreme Being as a *witness* and avenger between them, no alterations are to be made in those articles unless after they are approved by Congress, they are agreed to and ratified by the legislature of every State; but by the resolve of the convention this constitution is not to be ratified by the legislatures of the respective States, but is to be submitted to conventions chosen by the people, and if ratified by them is to be binding. [DHRC16 90]

"Brutus," No. 14, February 28, 1788:

. . . By this means, persons who may have disobliged those who execute the general government, may be subjected to intolerable oppression. They may be kept in long and ruinous confinement, and exposed to heavy and insupportable charges, to procure the attendence of *witnesses,* and provide the means of their defence, at a great distance from their places of residence. [DHRC16 257]

James Iredell, "Marcus," No. 3, March 5, 1788:

. . . If a President should pardon an accomplice, that accomplice then would be an unexceptionable *witness*. Before, he would be a *witness* with a rope about his own neck, struggling to get clear of it at all events. Would any men of understanding, or at least ought they to credit an accusation from a person under such circumstances? [DHRC16 324]

"The Impartial Examiner," No. 1, March 5, 1788:

. . . For instance, if Congress should pass a law that persons charged with capital crimes shall not have a right to demand the cause or nature of the accusation, shall not be confronted with the accusers or *witnesses,* or call for evidence in their own favor; and a question should arise respecting their authority therein,—can it be said that they have exceeded the limits of their jurisdiction, when that has no limits; when no provision has been made for such a right? . . .
[DHRC8 462]

"Brutus," No. 14, March 6, 1788:

The trouble and expence to the parties would be endless and intolerable. No man can say where the supreme court are to hold their sessions, the presumption is, however, that it must be at the seat of the general government: in this case parties must travel many hundred miles, with their *witnesses* and lawyers, to prosecute or defend a suit; no man of midling fortune, can sustain the expence of such a law suit, and therefore the poorer and midling class of citizens will be under the necessity of submitting to the demands of the rich and the lordly, in cases that will come under the cognizance of this court. If it be said, that to prevent this oppression, the supreme court will set in different parts of the union, it may be replied, that this would only make the oppression somewhat more tolerable, but by no means so much as to give a chance of justice to the poor and midling class. It is utterly impossible that the supreme court can move into so many different parts of the Union, as to make it convenient or even tolerable to attend before them with *witnesses* to try causes from every part of the United states; if to avoid the expence and inconvenience of calling *witnesses* from a great distance, to give evidence before the supreme court, the expedient of taking the deposition of *witnesses* in writing should be adopted, it would not help the matter. It is of great importance in the distribution of justice that *witnesses* should be examined face to face, that the parties should have the fairest opportunity of cross examining them in order to bring out the whole truth; there is something in the manner in which a *witness* delivers his testimony which cannot be committed to paper, and which yet very frequently gives a complexion to his evidence, very different from what it would bear if committed to writing, besides the expence of taking written testimony would be enormous; those who are acquainted with the costs that arise in the courts, where all the evidence is taken in writing, well know that they exceed beyond all comparison those of the common law courts, where *witnesses* are examined viva voce.

[DHRC16 328–29]

John Dickinson, "Fabius," No. 6, 1788:

[Quoting Lord Belhaven in Parliament:] When I consider this treaty as it hath been explained, and spoke to, before us these three weeks by past; I see the English constitution remaining firm, the same two houses of Parliament, the same taxes, the same customs, the same excises, the same trading companies, the same municipal laws and courts of judicature; and all ours either subject to regulations or annihilations, only we are to have the honor to pay their old debts, and to have some few persons present for *witnesses,* to the validity of the deed, when they are pleased to contract more. [Ford 198]

United States Congress, Judiciary Act of September 24, 1789:

[Section 30:] . . . That the mode of proof by oral testimony and examination of *witnesses* in open court shall be the same in all the courts of the United States, as well in the trial of causes in equity and of admiralty and maritime jurisdiction, as of actions at common law. . . . [USSL1 88]

[*Ibid.*:] . . . And in the trial of any cause of admiralty or maritime jurisdiction in a district court, the decree in which may be appealed from, if either party shall suggest to and satisfy the court that probably it will not be in his power to produce the *witnesses* there testifying before the circuit court should an appeal be had, and shall move that their testimony be taken down in writing, it shall be so done by the clerk of the court. [USSL1 89]

[*Ibid.*:] . . . and unless the same shall be made to appear on the trial of any cause, with respect to *witnesses* whose depositions may have been taken therein, such depositions shall not be admitted or used in the cause. [USSL1 90]

[Section 33:] . . . And copies of the process shall be returned as speedily as may be into the clerk's office of such court, together with the recognizances of the *witnesses* for their appearance to testify in the case; which recognizances the magistrate before whom the examination shall be, may require on pain of imprisonment. And if such commitment of the offender, or the *witnesses* shall be in a district other than that in which the offence is to be tried, it shall be the duty of the judge of that district where the delinquent is imprisoned, seasonably to issue, and of the marshal of the same district to execute, a warrant for the removal of the offender, and the *witnesses*, or either of them, as the case may be, to the district in which the trial is to be held. . . . [USSL1 91]

South Carolina Constitution, June 3, 1790:

[Article I, Section 13:] Each house may punish, by imprisonment, during sitting, any person not a member, who shall be guilty of disrespect to the house, by any disorderly or contemptuous behavior in its presence, or who, during the time of its sitting, shall threaten harm to the body or estate of any member, for anything said or done in either house, or who shall assault any of them therefor, or who shall assault or arrest any *witness*, or other person, ordered to attend the house, in his going to or returning there from, or who shall rescue any person arrested by order of the house. [Thorpe 3260]

Pennsylvania Constitution, September 2, 1790:

[Article IX, Section 9:] That in all criminal prosecutions the accused hath a right to be heard by himself and his counsel, to demand the nature and cause of the accusation against him, to meet the *witnesses* face to face, to have compulsory process for obtaining *witnesses* in his favor, and, in prosecutions by indictment or information, a speedy public trial, by an impartial jury of the vicinage; that he cannot be compelled to give evidence against himself, nor can he be deprived of his life, liberty, or property, unless by the judgment of his peers or the law of the land. [Thorpe 3100]

APPENDIX: CONCORDANCE TO THE CONSTITUTION

Charles W. Stearns

A.

B.

Choice—not choose a President, whenever the right of choice...... *Amend. XII.* 1.
of the whole number shall be necessary to a choice.......... *Amend. XII.* 2.
to vote at any election for the choice of Electors... .... *Amend. XIV.* 2.
Choose—New Hampshire shall be entitled to choose three......... *Art. I.* 2, 3.
House of Representatives shall choose their................. *Art. I.* 2, 5.
the Senate shall choose their other officers.................. *Art. I.* 3, 5.
choose, by ballot, one of them for President................ *Art. II.* 1, 3.
House shall, in like manner, choose the President .... *Art. II.* 1. 3.
shall choose from them by ballot, the Vice-President......... *Art. II.* 1, 3.
the House of Representatives shall choose immediately...... *Amend. XII.* 1.
if the House of Representatives shall not choose........... *Amend. XII.* 1.
the Senate shall choose the Vice-President.................. *Amend. XII.* 2.
Choosing—except as to the places of choosing Senators........... *Art. I.* 4, 1.
in choosing the President, the votes shall be taken.......... *Art. II.* 1, 3.
the Congress may determine the time of choosing........... *Art. II.* 1, 4.
in choosing the President, the votes shall be taken.......... *Amend. XII.* 1.
Chosen—chosen every second year by the people.................. *Art. I.* 2, 1.
inhabitant of that State in which he shall be chosen.......... *Art. I.* 2, 2.
Senators from each State, chosen by the legislature.......... *Art. I.* 3, 1.
that one-third may be chosen every second year............ *Art. I.* 3, 2.
inhabitant of that State for which he shall be chosen......... *Art. I.* 3, 3.
the Vice-President, chosen for the same term............... *Art. II.* 1, 1.
Citizen—seven years a citizen of the United States.............. *Art. I.* 2, 2.
been nine years a citizen of the United States............. *Art. I.* 3, 3.
no person, except a natural-born citizen, or a................ *Art. II.* 1, 5.
citizen of the United States at the time of.................. *Art. II.* 1, 5.
Citizens—between a State and citizens of another State........... *Art. III.* 2, 1.
between citizens of the same State claiming lands............ *Art. III.* 2, 1.
between a State or the citizens thereof, and foreign.......... *Art. III.* 2, 1.
and foreign States, citizens or subjects...................... *Art. III.* 2, 1.
the citizens of each State shall be entitled to all.............. *Art. IV.* 2, 1.
and immunities of citizens in the several States............... *Art. IV.* 2, 1.
against one of the United States, by citizens of another...... *Amend. XI.*
or by citizens or subjects of a foreign State.................. *Amend. XI.*
are citizens of the United States, and of the State wherein... *Amend. XIV.* 1.
abridge the privileges or immunities of citizens.............. *Amend. XIV.* 1.
twenty-one years of age, and citizens of the .... *Amend. XIV.* 2.
proportion which the number of such male citizens........... *Amend. XIV.* 2.
shall bear to the whole number of male citizens.............. *Amend. XIV.* 2.
the right of citizens of the United States, to vote............. *Amend. XV.* 1.
Civil—be appointed to any civil office under the authority......... *Art. I.* 6, 2.
the President, Vice-President, and all civil officers.......... *Art. II.* 4, 1.
any office, civil or military, under the United States........ *Amend. XIV.* 3.
Claim—of the party to whom such service, or labor............... *Art. IV.* 2, 3.
claim for the loss or emancipation of any slave.............. *Amend. XIV.* 4.
Claiming—between citizens of the same State, claiming lands...... *Art. III.* 2, 1.
Claims—of the United States or of any particular State........... *Art. IV.* 3, 2.
obligations and claims shall be held illegal and void.......... *Amend. XIV.* 4.
Class—of the Senators of the first class shall be vacated........... *Art. I.* 3, 2.
of the second class at the expiration of the fourth year....... *Art. I.* 3, 2.

D.

E.

F.

G.

H.

I.

Indian—among the several States, and with the Indian tribes......*Art. I.* 8, 3.
Indians—excluding Indians not taxed..........................*Art. I.* 2, 3.
excluding Indians not taxed..............................*Amend. XIV.* 2.
Indictment—subject to indictment, trial, judgment...............*Art. I.* 3, 7.
on a presentment or indictment of a grand jury.............*Amend. V.*
Ineligible—to the office of President, shall be eligible............*Amend. XII.* 3.
Infamous—crime, unless on a presentment or indictment..........*Amend. V.*
Inferior—constitute tribunals inferior to the Supreme Court.......*Art. I.* 8, 9.
by law vest the appointment of such inferior officers........*Art. II.* 2, 2.
in one Supreme Court, and in such inferior courts...........*Art. III.* 1, 1.
the judges, both of the Supreme and inferior courts..........*Art. III.* 1, 1.
Inflicted—nor cruel and unusual punishments inflicted............*Amend. VIII.*
Information—of the State of the Union, and recommend.........*Art. II.* 3, 1.
Informed—of the nature and cause of the accusation..............*Amend. VI.*
Infringed—to keep and bear arms shall not be infringed..........*Amend. II.*
Inhabitant—be an inhabitant of that State in which..............*Art. I.* 2, 2.
inhabitant of that State for which he shall be chosen.........*Art. I.* 3, 3.
shall not be an inhabitant of the same State................*Art. II.* 1, 3.
of the same State with themselves..........................*Amend. XII.* 1.
Inhabitants—of such State, being twenty-one years of age........*Amend. XIV.* 2.
Inspection—necessary for executing its inspection laws...........*Art. I.* 10, 2.
Insure—to establish justice, insure domestic tranquillity..........*Preamble.*
Insurrection—engaged in insurrection or rebellion................*Amend. XIV.* 3.
services for suppressing insurrection or rebellion............*Amend. XIV.* 4.
or obligation incurred in aid of insurrection.................*Amend. XIV.* 4.
Insurrections—suppress insurrections and repel invasions.........*Art. I.* 8, 15.
Intents—and purposes, as part of this Constitution................*Art. V.* 1, 1.
Invaded—unless actually invaded, or in such imminent............*Art. I.* 10, 2.
Invasion—in cases of rebellion or invasion, the public safety.......*Art. I.* 9, 2.
shall protect each of them against invasion...................*Art. IV.* 4, 1.
Invasions—suppress insurrections, and repel invasions... ....*Art. I.* 8, 15.
Inventors—securing, for limited times, to authors and inventors...*Art. I.* 8, 8.
Involuntary—servitude, except as a punishment for crime.........*Amend. XIII.* 1.
Issue—executive authority thereof shall issue writs................*Art. I.* 2, 4.
no warrants shall issue, but upon probable cause............*Amend. IV.*

J.

Jeopardy—to be twice put in jeopardy of life or limb..............*Amend. V.*
Journal—shall keep a journal of its proceedings..................*Art. I.* 5, 3.
one-fifth of those present, be entered on the journal..........*Art. I.* 5, 3.
shall enter the objections at large on their journal............*Art. I.* 7, 2.
entered on the journal of each House, respectively...........*Art. I.* 7, 2.
Judge—each House shall be the judge of the elections.............*Art. I.* 5, 1.
measures as he shall judge necessary and expedient. ....*Art. II.* 3, 1.
Judges—judges of the Supreme Court, and all other officers.......*Art. II.* 2, 2.
the judges, both of the Supreme and inferior courts.. ....*Art. III.* 1, 1.
the judges in every State shall be bound thereby............*Art. VI.* 1, 2.
Judgment—in cases of impeachment, shall not extend.............*Art. I.* 3, 7.
trial, judgment, and punishment, according to law...........*Art. I.* 3, 7.
parts, as may, in their judgment, require secrecy............*Art. I.* 5, 3.

K.

L.

O.

Q.

R.

Shall—they shall, in all cases, except treason, felony.............*Art. I.* 6, 1.
they shall not be questioned in any other place...............*Art. I.* 6, 1.
shall, during the time for which he was elected...............*Art. I.* 6, 2.
under the United States, shall be a member of either.........*Art. I.* 6, 2.
all bills for raising revenue shall originate in the...............*Art. I.* 7, 1.
shall, before it become a law, be presented to...............*Art. I.* 7, 2.
if he approve, he shall sign it; but if not, he shall...........*Art. I.* 7, 2.
he shall return it with his objections to that House...........*Art. I.* 7, 2.
shall enter the objections at large on their journal............*Art. I.* 7, 2.
shall be sent, together with the objections, to the other........*Art. I.* 7, 2.
House, by which it shall likewise be reconsidered............*Art. I.* 7, 2.
by two-thirds of that House, it shall become a law...........*Art. I.* 7, 2.
votes of both Houses shall be determined by yeas...........*Art. I.* 7, 2.
persons voting for and against the bill shall be entered.......*Art. I.* 7, 2.
shall be a law, in like manner as if he had signed it..........*Art. I.* 7, 2.
prevent its return, in which case it shall not be a law.........*Art. I.* 7, 2.
adjournment,) shall be presented to the President............*Art. I.* 7, 3.
before the same shall take effect, shall be approved..........*Art. I.* 7, 3.
Congress shall have power to lay and collect.................*Art. I.* 8, 1.
excises, shall be uniform throughout the United States.......*Art. I.* 8, 1.
to that use shall be for a longer term than two years..........*Art. I.* 8, 12.
shall not be prohibited by Congress prior to.................*Art. I.* 9, 1.
privilege of the writ of *habeas corpus*, shall not be...........*Art. I.* 9, 2.
attainder, or *ex post facto* law, shall be passed.............*Art. I.* 9, 3.
no capitation, or other direct tax shall be laid, unless........*Art. I.* 9, 4.
no tax or duty shall be laid on articles exported..............*Art. I.* 9, 5.
shall be given by any regulation of commerce...............*Art. I.* 9, 5.
nor shall vessels bound to or from one State.................*Art. I.* 9, 5.
no money shall be drawn from the treasury, but.............*Art. I.* 9, 6.
expenditures of all public money shall be published..........*Art. I.* 9, 6.
no title of nobility shall be granted by the .. ..*Art. I.* 9, 7.
shall, without the consent of Congress, accept of............*Art. I.* 9, 7.
no State shall enter into any treaty, alliance, or..............*Art. I.* 10, 1.
no State shall, without the consent of the Congress..........*Art. I.* 10, 2.
shall be for the use of the treasury of the United States......*Art. I.* 10, 2.
and all such laws shall be subject to the revision.............*Art. I.* 10, 2.
shall, without the consent of Congress, lay any duty.........*Art. I.* 10, 2.
executive power shall be vested in a President...............*Art. II.* 1, 1.
shall hold his office during the term of four years............*Art. II.* 1, 1.
each State shall appoint, in such manner as.................*Art. II.* 1, 2.
under the United States, shall be appointed an elector.......*Art. II.* 1, 2.
the electors shall meet in their respective States..............*Art. II.* 1, 3.
shall not be an inhabitant of the same State.................*Art. II.* 1, 3.
shall make a list of all the persons voted for................*Art. II.* 1, 3.
which list they shall sign, and certify, and transmit..........*Art. II.* 1, 3.
the President of the Senate, shall, in the presence of.........*Art. II.* 1, 3.
the certificates; and the votes shall then be counted.........*Art. II.* 1, 3.
shall be the President, if such number be a majority.........*Art. II.* 1, 3.
House of Representatives shall immediately choose..........*Art. II.* 1, 3.
House shall, in like manner, choose the President............*Art. II.* 1, 3.

State—whatever, from any king, prince, or foreign state............*Art. I.* 9, 7.
no State shall enter into any treaty, alliance, or..............*Art. I.* 10, 1.
no State shall, without the consent of the Congress...........*Art. I.* 10, 2.
duties and imposts laid by any State on imports.............*Art. I.* 10, 2.
no State shall, without the consent of Congress, lay..........*Art. I.* 10, 2.
compact with another State, or with a foreign power..........*Art. I.* 10, 2.
each State shall appoint, in such manner as..................*Art. II.* 1, 2.
to which the State may be entitled in the Congress...........*Art. II.* 1, 2.
shall not be an inhabitant of the same State..................*Art. II.* 1, 3.
the representation from each State having one vote...........*Art. II.* 1, 3.
information of the state of the Union, and recommend........*Art. II.* 3, 1.
between a State and citizens of another State................*Art. III.* 2, 1.
between citizens of the same State, claiming lands...........*Art. III.* 2, 1.
and between a State, or the citizens thereof, and foreign......*Art. III.* 2, 1.
and those in which a State shall be a party..................*Art. III.* 2, 2.
shall be held in the State where the said crimes..............*Art. III.* 2, 3.
when not committed within any State, the trial...............*Art. III.* 2, 3.
full faith and credit shall be given in each State..............*Art. IV.* 1, 1.
records, and judicial proceedings of every other State........*Art. IV.* 1, 1.
the citizens of each State shall be entitled to all..............*Art. IV.* 2, 1.
person charged in any State with treason, felony... ....*Art. VI.* 2, 2.
flee from justice, and be found in another State..............*Art. IV.* 2, 2.
on demand of the executive authority of the State............*Art. IV.* 2, 2.
removed to the State having jurisdiction of the crime.........*Art. IV.* 2, 2.
no person, held to service or labor in one State...............*Art. IV.* 2, 3.
but no new State shall be formed or erected..................*Art. IV.* 3, 1.
within the jurisdiction of any other State.....................*Art. IV.* 3, 1.
nor any State be formed by the junction of two...............*Art. IV.* 3, 1.
claims of the United States, or of any particular State.........*Art. IV.* 3, 2.
to every State in this Union a republican form of.............*Art. IV.* 4, 1.
that no State, without its consent, shall be deprived..........*Art. V.* 1, 1.
the judges in every State shall be bound thereby.............*Art. VI.* 1, 2.
or laws of any State to the contrary notwithstanding.........*Art. VI.* 1, 2.
and the members of the several State Legislatures...........*Art. VI.* 1, 3.
militia being necessary to the security of a free State.........*Amend. II.*
trial by an impartial jury of the State and district............*Amend. VI.*
one of the United States, by citizens of another State ....*Amend. XI.*
or by citizens, or subjects of any foreign State...............*Amend. XI.*
not be an inhabitant of the same State with themselves.......*Amend. XII.* 1.
the representation from each State having one vote...........*Amend. XII.* 1.
citizens of the United States, and of the State wherein......*Amend. XIV.* 1.
no State shall make or enforce any law, which shall..........*Amend. XIV.* 1.
nor shall any State deprive any person of life................*Amend. XIV.* 1.
counting the whole number of persons in each State..........*Amend. XIV.* 2.
the executive and judicial officers of a State.................*Amend. XIV.* 2.
inhabitants of such State, being twenty-one years of age.....*Amend. XIV.* 2.
male citizens, twenty-one years of age in such State..........*Amend. XIV.* 2.
under the United States, or under any State................*Amend. XIV.* 3.
or as a member of any State Legislature.....................*Amend. XIV.* 3.
as an executive or judicial officer of any State..............*Amend. XIV.* 3.

U.

V.

W.

Y.

INDEX

About the Author and Editors

THURSTON GREENE is a practicing attorney in Connecticut with a life-long concern for vital issues affecting the constitutional order of the United States.

STUART B. FLEXNER is a former editor-in-chief of the reference department at Random House.

DOUGLAS M. ARNOLD is a professional historian, author, and documentary editor.

CHRISTOPHER COLLIER is the Connecticut State Historian.

DOMINICK EGAN is a professional legal researcher and freelance writer.